Asylia

HELLENISTIC CULTURE AND SOCIETY

General Editors: Anthony W. Bulloch, Erich S. Gruen, A. A. Long, and *Andrew F. Stewart*

I. Alexander to Actium: The Historical Evolution of the Hellenistic Age, by *Peter Green*

II. Hellenism in the East: The Interaction of Greek and Non-Greek Civilizations from Syria to Central Asia after Alexander, edited by *Amélie Kuhrt* and *Susan Sherwin-White*

III. The Question of "Eclecticism": Studies in Later Greek Philosophy, edited by *J. M. Dillon* and *A. A. Long*

IV. Antigonus the One-Eyed and the Creation of the Hellenistic State, by *Richard A. Billows*

V. A History of Macedonia, by *R. Malcolm Errington*, translated by *Catherine Errington*

VI. Attic Letter-Cutters of 229 to 86 B.C., by *Stephen V. Tracy*

VII. The Vanished Library: A Wonder of the Ancient World, by *Luciano Canfora*

VIII. Hellenistic Philosophy of Mind, by *Julia Annas*

IX. Hellenistic Culture and History, by *Peter Green* et al.

X. The Best of the Argonauts: The Redefinition of the Epic Hero in Book 1 of Apollonius's Argonautica, by *James J. Clauss*

XI. Faces of Power: Alexander's Image and Hellenistic Politics, by *Andrew Stewart*

XII. Images and Ideologies: Self-Definition in the Hellenistic World, by *A. W. Bulloch* et al.

XIII. From Samarkand to Sardis: A New Approach to the Seleucid Empire, by *Susan Sherwin-White* and *Amélie Kuhrt*

XIV. Regionalism and Change in the Economy of Independent Delos, by *Gary Reger*

XV. Hegemony to Empire: The Development of the Roman Imperium in the East from 148 to 62 B.C., by *Robert Kallet-Marx*

XVI. Moral Vision in the Histories of Polybius, by *Arthur M. Eckstein*

XVII. The Hellenistic Settlements in Europe, the Islands, and Asia Minor, by *Getzel M. Cohen*

XVIII. Interstate Arbitrations in the Greek World, 337–90 B.C., by *Sheila L. Ager*

XIX. Theocritus's Urban Mimes: Mobility, Gender, and Patronage, by *Joan B. Burton*

XX. Athenian Democracy in Transition: Attic Letter-Cutters of 340 to 290 B.C., by *Stephen V. Tracy*

XXI. Pseudo-Hecataeus, On the Jews: Legitimizing the Jewish Diaspora, by *Bezalel Bar-Kochva*

XXII. Asylia: Territorial Inviolability in the Hellenistic World, by *Kent J. Rigsby*

XXIII. The Cynics: The Cynic Movement in Antiquity and Its Legacy, edited by *R. Bracht Branham* and *Marie-Odile Goulet-Cazé*

XXIV. The Politics of Plunder: Aitolians and their *Koinon* in the Early Hellenistic Era, 279–217 B.C., by *Joseph B. Scholten*

XXV. The Argonautika, by *Apollonios Rhodios*, translated, with introduction, commentary, and glossary by *Peter Green*

XXVI. Hellenistic Constructs: Culture, History, and Historiography, edited by *Paul Cartledge*

Asylia

Territorial Inviolability in the Hellenistic World

Kent J. Rigsby

UNIVERSITY OF CALIFORNIA PRESS
Berkeley Los Angeles London

This publication has been supported
by a subvention from Duke University

University of California Press
Berkeley and Los Angeles, California

University of California Press, Ltd.
Oxford, England

Library of Congress Cataloging-in-Publication Data

Rigsby, Kent J., 1945–
Asylia : territorial inviolability in the Hellenistic world / Kent J. Rigsby.
p. cm. — (Hellenistic culture and society ; 22)
Includes bibliographical references and index.
ISBN 0-520-20098-5 (alk. paper)
1. Asylum, Right of (Greek law) 2. Asylum, Right of (Greek law)—
Religious aspects. 3. Sacred space—Greece—History. I. Title.
II. Series.
KL4363.R54 1996
342.495′083–dc20
[344.950283] 95-22410
CIP

Printed in the United States of America
9 8 7 6 5 4 3 2 1

The paper used in this publication meets the minimum requirements of American National Standard for Information Sciences—Permanence of Paper for Printed Library Materials, ANSI Z39.48-1984.

To Carol

CONTENTS

LIST OF PLATES

PREFACE

This volume seeks to present the evidence for places being declared "sacred and inviolable" in the Hellenistic world. The material has long been known to historians. The modern interpretation of it, that the declarations established military neutrality, derives from Ezekiel Spanheim (1706). The locus classicus is Tacitus' account of the petitions by various cities in A.D. 22 and 23 for Roman confirmation of their status as inviolable. Every student of Greek coins is familiar with the title ΙΕΡΑΣ ΚΑΙ ΑΣΥΛΟΥ used by cities of the Greek East, and students of inscriptions of the Hellenistic period know the highly visible place of declarations of territorial inviolability in our documentation on interstate relations. Although this rich evidence has never been collected, such a corpus scarcely needs justification.[1] In no other way can we see the range of this gesture in space and time, its terminology and characteristics, and the historical circumstances of its development.

I first became interested in these texts at the urging of C. Bradford Welles of Yale University. Welles felt that the anomalies were not sufficiently appreciated ("They weren't supposed to do that anyway"). The project has grown and changed over the many intervening years, as it became clear that a corpus of the evidence would be of more use to scholars than another essay of historical interpretation. But in all the work that has led to this book, the challenge of Welles's originality, verve, and astuteness has been in my mind. His students cherish the memory of his extraordinary ability to ask penetrating and unexpected questions of ancient documents.

1. Wilhelm called for such a work in 1897 (*AEM* 20 [1897] 66, criticizing Barth's dissertation); Robert in 1934 (*Op. min. sel.* III 1605); and Préaux in 1954 (*Rec. Soc. Jean Bodin* VI *La Ville* [Brussels 1954] 118: "A complete chronological and topographical classification of the asylias, which so far as I know has not been done, would let us appreciate the variety and diversity of intentions and results of this institution")

Many have contributed to the completion of this work, in ways general and specific. Among institutions, I am grateful for the support of the Harvard Society of Fellows, the American School of Classical Studies in Athens, the Institute for Advanced Study in Princeton, the Institut für Altertumskunde in Cologne, the Kleinasiatische Kommission in Vienna, the National Endowment for the Humanities, the American Council of Learned Societies, and Duke University. Of the many individuals who have helped me over the years, I would thank in particular W. Blümel, G. W. Bowersock, B. F. Cook, Georges Daux, Thomas Drew-Bear, E. Erxleben, Erich Gruen, Christian Habicht, Klaus Hallof, Peter Herrmann, Arthur Houghton, Ludwig Koenen, Georges Le Rider, L. S. B. MacCoull, R. Merkelbach, H. Müller, John F. Oates, Georg Petzl, Louis Robert, W. Schindler, Hans Taeuber, and William H. Willis, who have variously shared their knowledge with me, saved me from errors, opened up new avenues of thought, and offered encouragement and practical assistance. I owe most to the patience of my wife and children.

LIST OF ABBREVIATIONS

In referring to ancient authors I follow the abbreviations of the *Oxford Classical Dictionary*^{2}; for journals, the *American Journal of Archaeology* where possible, otherwise *L'année philologique*; for epigraphical material, *Supplementum Epigraphicum Graecum*; for numismatic, *ANS Museum Notes* 23 (1978) 218–220; for papyrological, J. F. Oates et al., *Checklist of Editions of Greek and Latin Papyri*. The following are cited in abbreviated form.

Bellinger, "End"	A. R. Bellinger. "The End of the Seleucids." *Transact.Conn.Acad.Arts&Sci.* 38 (1949) 51–102.
Bickerman, *Institutions*	E. J. Bikerman. *Institutions des Séleucides.* Paris 1938.
Bickerman, *Religions*	———. *Religions and Politics in the Hellenistic and Roman Periods.* Como 1985.
Bickerman, *Studies*	———. *Studies in Jewish and Christian History* I–III. Leiden 1976–85.
Boesch	P. Boesch. Θεωρός. *Untersuchung zur Epangelie griechischer Feste.* Berlin 1908.
Burrell, "Neokoroi"	Barbara Burrell. "Neokoroi: Greek Cities of the Roman East." Ph.D. diss., Harvard University 1980.
De Saulcy, *Numismatique*	F. De Saulcy, *Numismatique de la Terre Sainte.* Paris 1874.
Feyel, *Contribution*	M. Feyel. *Contribution à l'épigraphie béotienne.* Paris 1943.
Flacelière, *Aitoliens*	R. Flacelière. *Les Aitoliens à Delphes.* Paris 1937.
Gauthier, *Symbola*	P. Gauthier. *Symbola: Les étrangers et la justice dans les cités grecques.* Nancy 1972.

Herrmann, "Antiochos"	P. Herrmann. "Antiochos der Grosse und Teos." *Anadolu* 9 (1965) 29–160.
Holleaux, *Etudes* I–VI	M. Holleaux. *Etudes d'épigraphie et d'histoire grecques* I–VI. Edited by L. Robert. Paris 1938–68.
Kahrstedt, *Syrische Territorien*	U. Kahrstedt. *Syrische Territorien in hellenistischer Zeit.* AbhGött n.F. 19.2. Göttingen 1926.
Nachtergael, *Les Galates*	G. Nachtergael. *Les Galates en Grèce et les Sôtéria de Delphes.* Brussels 1977.
Nock, *Essays* I–II	A. D. Nock. *Essays on Religion and the Ancient World* I–II. Cambridge, Mass. 1972.
Parke/Wormell I–II	H. W. Parke and D. E. W. Wormell, *The Delphic Oracle* I–II. Oxford 1956.
Robert, *DAM*	L. Robert. *Documents d'Asie mineure.* Paris 1987.
Robert, *Etudes anat.*	———. *Etudes anatoliennes.* Paris 1937.
Robert, *Et. ép. phil.*	———. *Etudes épigraphiques et philologiques.* Paris 1938.
Robert, *Op. min. sel.* I–VII	———. *Opera Minora Selecta* I–VII. Amsterdam 1969–90.
Robert, *Villes*	———. *Villes d'Asie mineure*^{2}. Paris 1962.
Samuel, *Chronology*	A. E. Samuel. *Greek and Roman Chronology.* Munich 1972.
Schlesinger, "Asylie"	E. Schlesinger. "Die griechische Asylie." Diss., Giessen 1933.
Schmitt, *Untersuchungen*	H. H. Schmitt. *Untersuchungen zur Geschichte Antiochos' des Grossen.* Wiesbaden 1964.
Schroeter	F. Schroeter. *De regum hellenisticorum epistulis.* Leipzig 1932.
Schürer II	E. Schürer, *History of the Jewish People in the Age of Jesus Christ* II. Translated by G. Vermes and F. Millar. Edinburgh 1979.
Seyrig, *Ant. syr.* I–VI	H. Seyrig. *Antiquités syriennes* I–VI. Paris 1934–66.
Seyrig, *Notes*	———. *Notes on Syrian Coins.* NNM 119. New York 1950.
Seyrig, *Scripta numism.*	———. *Scripta numismatica.* Paris 1986.
Seyrig, *Scripta varia*	———. *Scripta varia.* Paris 1985.
Seyrig, *Trésors*	———. *Trésors du Levant anciens et nouveaux.* Paris 1973.

Walbank, *Comm.* I–III	F. W. Walbank. *A Historical Commentary on Polybius* I–III. Oxford 1957–79.
Wilhelm, *Beiträge*	A. Wilhelm. *Beiträge zur griechischen Inschriftenkunde.* Sonderschr.Österr.Arch.Inst. 7. Vienna 1909.
Wilhelm, *Kl. Schr.* I–II	———. *Kleine Schriften:* I, *Akademieschriften zur griechischen Inschriftenkunde* 1–3. Leipzig 1974. II, *Abhandlungen und Beiträge* 1–2. Leipzig 1984.
Will, *Histoire* I–II	E. Will. *Histoire politique du monde hellénistique*[2] I–II. Nancy 1979–82.

Introduction

A modern commonplace holds that Greek civic religion after the fourth century B.C. was an empty shell, traditional forms followed without emotion, and that the Greeks' true longings expressed themselves in the mystery religions and other novelties or in philosophy—in phenomena at once more personal and more universal than the cults of the old gods. This view owes much to hindsight, our desire to explain the rise of Christianity. An enduring source of strength of pagan cults was precisely their local and formal character: the gods of one's own city and country watched over places familiar and significant, bound up with the life cycle of the individual and the group. The holy places of one's land had each been touched by a particular god for reasons known to the community. Here were powerful roots, with which the new religions of Roman times offered little to compete, until the rise of the cult of saints. Civic religion, polytheism, would decline only with civic life itself in late antiquity.

In the Hellenistic period, certain places, either temples with their precincts or whole cities with their territories, were declared by foreign states to be "sacred and inviolable" in honor of the city's tutelary god. This episode in the history of Greek civic religion and Greek diplomacy is the concern of the present volume.

SACRED SPACE

Est locus ... The literature of the Greeks and Romans provides rich testimony to their emotional response to sacred places, where ritual, myth, dedicatory objects, or even natural setting[1] betokened the presence or past action of a god.

1. *Stat vetus et multos incaedua silva per annos; credibile est illi numen inesse loco* (Ov. *Am.* 3.1–2; cf. *Fast.* 3.295–296).

Many religions, in separating the sacred from the profane,[2] apply this distinction to space; places attributed to the divine are in some measure under the god's authority, and in them mortals may be bound by rules that do not pertain in secular space. In ancient Greece this boundary was especially strong: as we see in many anecdotes from both life and literature, anyone who entered a temple precinct or clasped an altar or even achieved some other physical connection with sacred space[3] was to be immune from violence, for he had put himself at the discretion of the god rather than of man.[4] Anyone could do it, at any sacred place. Other religions can be cited in which this barrier is less forceful or more selective. In Republican Rome such a "right of asylum" was an anomaly, specially conceded to only one or two temples: immunity from secular intrusion was not automatically a property of sacred space. Similarly, in pharaonic Egypt, temples seem not to have enjoyed immunity from the civil authorities. So is it also in the modern West: the rise of the secular state was accompanied by the gradual, and often disputed, rejection of the late antique and medieval tradition of the right of asylum of Christian churches.[5] Today in the United States, a fugitive from the law will gain no immunity by fleeing to a church, synagogue, or mosque.

In A.D. 22, Roman authorities feared that the right of asylum practiced in their Greek provinces posed a threat to civic tranquility. Moderns might well sympathize; exemption from the power of the state seems on its face subversive to good order. It is worth observing, therefore, that selective territorial immunity from the law is a widely attested practice, despite which the needs of public order are successfully met. Early modern London had various neighborhoods that served as debtors' asylums, from which the instruments of public authority were excluded. These areas were left to govern themselves, and they maintained strict admissions policies; the last of them was abolished by act of Parliament in

2. For Greek vocabulary on the distinction see W. R. Connor, *AncSoc* 19 (1988) 161–188. For the distinction in Christianity see R. A. Markus, *JECS* 2 (1994) 257–271.

3. For example by a rope: so the Cylonian conspirators (Plut. *Sol.* 12.1); of places: Ephesus (Hdt. 1.26; cf. Polyaen. 6.50; Ael. *VH* 3.26); Rheneia (Thuc. 3.104.2).

4. See, for instance, U. Sinn, "Greek Sanctuaries as Places of Refuge," in *Greek Sanctuaries,* ed. N. Marinatos and R. Hägg (London/New York 1993) 88–109.

5. For the case of England see I. D. Thornley, in *Tudor Studies . . . A. F. Pollard,* ed. R. W. Seton-Watson (London 1924) 182–206. Eventually Tacitus' description of the review of A.D. 22 (*Ann.* 3.60ff.) could be invoked to argue that there was no absolute right of asylum, that this was rather a gift of the state subject to limitations in the public interest. The Roman Senate's argument in A.D. 22 is not unlike that of Henry VIII in 1519 (who could now know the Tacitus passage): the original grantors did not intend asylum "to serve for wilful murder or for crime committed out of the sanctuary *sub spe redeundi.* He would have that reformed which had been encroached by abuse, and would reduce the privilege to the original plan of its founders" (Thornley 201).

the 1720s.[6] The University of Heidelberg maintained its own judicial and prison system for its students until the beginning of the twentieth century. Modern embassies offer an analogy to the ancient Greek temple, places in which the host state has no sovereignty, sometimes with embarrassing consequences for the rule of law.

Greek temples were held to be automatically immune from war and all acts of violence. So the Boeotians told the Athenians who seized and exploited the temple of Apollo Delius.[7] Pausanias knew stories about the vengeance of the Cabeiri upon soldiers who entered their temple (9.25.10), and Antiochus III would apologize for the violence his troops did to the temple of Artemis at Amyzon (below, p. 336). For this immunity several terms were available, ἄσυλος being by no means the most common. From the classical period to the end of antiquity, the boundary stones of sacred property illustrate the fact.[8] A fifth-century boundary of a temple in Corinth uses the word for what could be said of any Greek temple at any time (*Corinth* VIII.1 22 [*LSCG* Suppl. 34]): [hόρος ἱαρὸς?] ἄσυλος· μὲ καταβιβασσκέτο· ζαμία ||||||||.

In the Hellenistic period, by contrast, Greek states began to declare some spaces in other states to be "inviolable" (of temples) or "sacred and inviolable" (of the whole city and territory), in honor of the relevant god. The documentary testimony for these declarations is voluminous. The inscriptions constitute a significant fraction of our epigraphical evidence for foreign affairs in the Hellenistic period. Most are civic decrees or royal letters declaring a temple or city to be inviolable; they reveal the form and something of the historical circumstances of such declarations. Because in some quarters of the Hellenistic world it became fashionable to inscribe civic titles on coins, we also have as evidence the coinages of dozens of cities. These let us place pins on a map, often with dates, and thus are crucial for tracing the spread of the civic title "sacred and inviolable."

A purely documentary definition of our topic—places that were declared "inviolable," ἄσυλος—will reveal a coherent historical episode: the material record shows no such declaration before the 260s B.C. and none after the senatorial review of the status in A.D. 22–23, and more than ninety in between. A few earlier instances are alleged in our literary sources; these will be seen to have served as precedents for the Hellenistic institution. Citations of the title after A.D. 22 were probably survivals of grants of Hellenistic date.

6. See Paul Haagen, "Imprisonment for Debt in England and Wales" (Ph.D. diss., Princeton University 1986) 270–311.

7. Thuc. 4.97–98; the Athenians in response do not dispute the rule but claim that their actions are defensive, in light of Boeotian violence against temples, and in any case under compulsion. Cf. Robert A. Bauslaugh, *The Concept of Neutrality in Classical Greece* (Berkeley 1991) 38–39; Nock, *Essays* I 487–488.

8. Cf. M. Guarducci, *Epigrafia greca* IV (Rome 1978) 57–73.

DECLARED INVIOLABILITY

These declarations ought in principle to cause surprise: all temples had always been inviolable, and cities that chose to remain out of hostilities had always had the claim of justice on their side in insisting upon their neutrality. Peace was the state of nature, and it was war that was supposed to be declared.[9] The gesture is intrinsically enigmatic. What did these declarations add or accomplish?

Early scholars followed the Romans[10] and took this to be a legislated "right of asylum," which is indeed what Tacitus portrays concerning the Hellenistic grants. Since Ezekiel Spanheim, however, the declarations, at least when applied to a city, have been taken as "neutralization," granting immunity from war. In the ancient authors the one articulated account of the phenomenon is Tacitus' description of the Senate's review under Tiberius in A.D. 22 and 23 (see pp. 580–586): many Greek cities now sought confirmation of their previously granted privileges of inviolability; the Senate confirmed these, but with limitations so that religion could not be used as a mask for self-aggrandizement. This is certainly the same matter that we know from the Hellenistic documents, for most of the cities and the cults Tacitus mentions are so recorded in the inscriptions. Tacitus leaves no doubt about the substance, logic, and legal source of the privilege: it was the "right of asylum" of a temple, immunity of sacred space from civil law, and it was granted by that sovereign who controlled the city.

Tacitus' portrait is at variance with the Hellenistic grants in two essential ways: in the documents the grantors of *asylia* are not confined to the relevant sovereign (if in fact there was one); and the recipients are not only temples but also whole cities with their territories. In general, the Hellenistic evidence

9. For sacred space, see, e.g., Lys. 12.98; Dio Chrys. 31.88: "It is not customary to harm even evildoers if they have taken refuge," invoking "the inviolability which such places [temples] provide to criminals" (μηδὲ τοὺς κακὸν δράσαντας ἐάνπερ καταφύγωσιν ἔθος ἐστὶν ἀδικοῦντες and τὴν ἀσυλίαν ἣν παρέχουσι τοῖς φαύλοις οἱ τοιοῦτοι τόποι); Jos. *AJ* 15.90, the robbing of temples and tombs by Antony, who thought no temple too inviolable (οὔθ' ἱεροῦ τινος οὕτως ἀσύλου δόξαντος ὡς μὴ περιαιρεθῆναι τὸν ἐν αὐτῷ κόσμον). Praise of the exemplary behavior of Alexander at Thebes: Polyb. 5.10.6–8. Cf. the complaint of the suppliant under attack in Achil. Tat. 8.2: καὶ τοῖς μὲν πονηροῖς αἱ τῶν ἱερῶν ἀσφάλειαι διδόασι καταφυγήν (contrast Lycurgus' opinion, cited below). As to cities, see generally Bauslaugh, *Neutrality*; cf. G. Nenci, *Il veltro* 22 (1978) 495–506, to the effect that neutrality was in Greek eyes the state of nature and did not need to be declared or legislated. For Onasander (*Strat.* 4.1–3) the first principle in war is that "it must be clear to all that one is fighting with justice," which, he explains, will win the favor of gods and men, and just wars are defensive.

10. The locus classicus is Servius ad Verg. *Aen.* 2.761 (the "asylum of Juno" at Troy): "This right is not for all temples, only those to which it has been granted by a law"; the first was at Athens, a temple founded by the Heracleidae when they fled there (he cites Stat. *Theb.* 12.497ff., then compares that of Romulus); summarized ad *Aen.* 8.342.

reveals an affair of international relations among sovereign states, while Tacitus describes the domestic governance of temples.

The first critical assessment of the civic title "sacred and inviolable" was offered by Spanheim,[11] and his analysis has guided all informed discussion since. Spanheim realized from the coins that this status could be possessed by cities as well as temples; he invoked in support of the coins the Oxford Stone for Smyrna and the literary testimonia for Delos, which show inviolable cities. The context of the status, he saw, was an especially revered shrine.[12] Although gods owned their property, the right to receive refugees was enjoyed only by temples of special veneration,[13] a right formally granted by the king or the Amphictyonic Council, as Tacitus says. But the "sacred and inviolable" cities known from so many coins of Hellenistic and imperial date cannot have been places to which criminals or slaves could flee; even temples were restricted on this score, and the Romans would not have permitted such a situation. The solution, he concluded, is found in Polybius' description of the primitive Eleans, who were declared by the Greeks sacred and inviolable so that they were immune from war and free to administer the Olympic games. Civic inviolability was such an immunity from war ("spoliationis militaris periculo immunes") and from σῦλαι, raids at will. Thus these grants were a tool of foreign relations.

Logically these two interpretations (a temple's asylum, a city's neutrality) are not incompatible, and many have seen the second, Hellenistic "neutralization," as an outgrowth of the first, the traditional right of asylum of Greek temples. But the modern understanding, neutralization, affects profoundly the historical interpretation of the phenomenon: rather than arising from a desire to protect suppliants in various cities, the grants are seen as an effort to limit war. The effort arose amid the growing violence and anarchy of the Hellenistic age and limited as well the "right of reprisal" that was part of Greek interstate relations. It ended when the Roman peace made such special exemptions from

11. *Dissertationes de praestantia et usu numismatum antiquorum.* I have not seen the first edition (Rome 1664). In the second (Amsterdam 1671), 778–783, he cites Suetonius' bald statement (*Tib.* 37) that Tiberius abolished *iura asylorum*, and protests that the privilege is still attested by coins of imperial date; adding various literary testimonies (Strabo on Ephesus, the two *asyla* of Rome, and others), he speaks of the extension of the right of asylum beyond the temple proper but is thinking still of the right to receive fugitives, as in Tacitus. It is in the third edition (editio nova, London 1706), I 659–674, that he makes his case instead for military neutralization. On Spanheim (1629–1710) see H. von Petersdorff in *Allgemeine Deutsche Biographie* 35 (Leipzig 1893) 50–59. The discussion (for example) of E. Chishull, *Antiquitates Asiaticae* (London 1728) 124 (his introduction to the decrees for Teos), is scholarly but brief, and conventional in holding that the declaration created places of refuge. An important summation at J. Eckhel, *Doctrina numorum veterum* IV.2 (Vienna 1828) 306–309.

12. Spanheim 665: "ob peculiarem Numinis, quod apud eos colebatur, dicatique eidem Templi sanctitatem ac religionem, cum IERAI, tum ASULOI . . . dicerentur."

13. Citing Livy 35.51 (the Delium in Boeotia; cf. p. 83).

war unnecessary.[14] Historians of the Hellenistic period invoke the grants as evidence for the breakdown of order in the third and second centuries B.C., and especially for the rise of piracy. This alleged context and motive require examination.

DEGREES OF SACREDNESS

Sacredness might naturally be thought an absolute. Yet it is a familiar fact of religious consciousness that some things are more sacred than others: Lourdes is in some sense more sacred than one's neighborhood Catholic church and is the object of pilgrimage; so too Apollo's temple at Delphi, as distinct from a hundred other temples of Apollo. Such places might well be felt to be more promising in times of need, whether need of miraculous intervention or of refuge. Diodorus' account of the cult of Hemithea in Caria illustrates the growth of sacredness and its vocabulary: the temple eventually obtained such increase (αὔξησις)[15] that Hemithea was honored not only by the locals and their neighbors but by those living afar, who brought sacrifices;

> τὸ δὲ μέγιστον, Πέρσας ἡγουμένους τῆς Ἀσίας καὶ πάντα τὰ τῶν Ἑλλήνων ἱερὰ συλῶντας μόνου τοῦ τῆς Ἡμιθέας τεμένους ἀποσχέσθαι, τούς τε λῃστὰς τοὺς πάντας διαρπάζοντας μόνον τοῦτο ἀφεῖναι παντελῶς ἄσυλον, καίπερ ἀτείχιστον ὑπάρχον καὶ ἀκίνδυνον ἔχον τὴν ἁρπαγήν.
>
> . . .
>
> The greatest thing is that the Persians, when they ruled Asia and were plundering all the temples of the Greeks, held off from the precinct of Hemithea alone, and the pirates, who were seizing everything,[16] left this one quite unviolated, even though it was unwalled and plundering was free of risk.[17]

14. So, for example, D. Magie, *Roman Rule in Asia Minor* (Princeton 1950) I 504.
15. So too Strab. 8.3.30 (353) of the cult at Olympia by virtue of the crowned games.
16. For the sentiment ("unharmed even by" the worst of men) compare Cicero on Juno of Malta (below, p. 33 n. 14), Diod. 31.34.1 (temple of Zeus at Mt. Ariadne), and Strab. 8.6.14 (374); cf. on **185**.
17. Diod. 5.63; cf. J. M. Cook and W. H. Plommer, *The Sanctuary of Hemithea* (Cambridge 1966); Blümel, *I.Rhod.Per.* 401, 451–458. Cf. Diod. 11.89 on the *temenos* of the Palici in Sicily, with its geysers: it was held in such awe that oaths are sworn here and claims settled; this precinct has remained unviolated/inviolable from time immemorial (ἔστι δὲ τοῦτο τὸ τέμενος ἔκ τινων χρόνων ἄσυλον τετηρημένον), a great aid to slaves with cruel masters, who cannot remove fugitives by force but only upon a pledge of good treatment—no violation of this being on record (καὶ τοῖς ἀτυχοῦσιν οἰκέταις καὶ κυρίοις ἀγνώμοσι περιπεπτωκόσι πολλὴν παρέχεται βοήθειαν· τοὺς γὰρ εἰς τοῦτο καταφυγόντας οὐκ ἔχουσιν ἐξουσίαν οἱ δεσπόται βιαίως ἀπάγειν). Compare the shock when Enna in Sicily was plundered by the Romans in 214 B.C.: it was distinguished *vel ob insignem munimento naturali locum vel ob sacrata omnia vestigiis raptae quondam Proserpinae . . . non hominem tantum sed etiam deorum sedem violatam esse* (Livy 24.39.8). Again, because of the story that Persephone was abducted at Etna, people

But for this obvious fact of popular sentiment—that some places are holier than others—the Greeks had no term and no institutional recognition. Pleonasm is a feature of religious praise—"the Lord is in His holy temple." So too a Greek could underscore sacredness, with ἄβατος, for example, or ἅγιος[18]—or with ἄσυλος: one spoke of "an inviolable temple," ἄσυλον ἱερόν,[19] for emphasis, without implying some special grant or status. This is the rhetoric of praise, not a legal category of temple.[20] The superlative ἱερώτατος is common enough, at least in poetic and rhetorical contexts—the elative;[21] but the comparative

---

"honor and respect the place as inviolable and do not attack animals that pasture there" (Plut. *Mor.* 917F: τιμῶντες καὶ σεβόμενοι τὸ χωρίον ὡς ἄσυλον οὐκ ἐπιτίθενται τοῖς ἐκεῖ νεμομένοις).

18. E.g., Hdt. 2.41.5, 2.44.1: ἱερὸν ἅγιον; cf. Androsthenes *FGrHist* 711 F 2 (Strab. 16.3.2); Theoc. 25.22; *Etym. Magn.* 542.54; also Pl. *Cri.* 11 C: ἱερὸν ἅγιον . . . ἄβατον (cf. *Lach.* 183B, Spartans defending their country reckon Lacedaemon to be an ἄβατον ἱερόν); Plut. *Mor.* 290C: τῶν ἀσύλων καὶ ἁγίων ἱερῶν ἀσφαλῆ καταφυγὴν τοῖς ἱκέταις (of the Acropolis and Delos); Ael. Arist. *Sacr.* 4.3: ἱερὸν . . . ἅγιον καὶ ὀνομαστόν; Poseidonius 87 F 33 (Strab. 4.1.13): τὸ ἱερὸν ἦν ἅγιον, τιμώμενον σφόδρα ὑπὸ τῶν περιοίκων (and therefore a secure place to store money). These terms connote the negative, like the Hellenistic formula "sacred and (therefore) inviolable"; for the negative connotation of ἅγιος see E. Benveniste, *Indo-European Language and Society* (Coral Gables 1973) 466.

19. One flees to a (secular) person or place "as to an inviolable temple" in Polyb. 16.13.2 and Philo *Moses* 1.34; cf. Iambl. *Myst.* 7.5 (259.3 Parthey), preserve ancient prayers "as though inviolable temples"; Liban. *Declam.* 32.9, let the house be, "as though an inviolable and untouchable (ἄψαυστον) temple."

20. A pleonasm that seems to reflect the influence of Latin is found in a bilingual advertisement from Panormus in Sicily: ναοῖς ἱεροῖς / *aidibus sacris* (*CIL* X 7296).

21. One apparently literal superlative—a representative is to be designated in the most holy temple in each *ktoina* of Camirus: ἐν τῶι ἱερῶι τῶι ἁγιωτάτωι ἐν τᾶι κτοίναι κατὰ τὸν νόμον τὸν τῶν Ῥοδίων (*T.Camir.* 109.14–15 = *Syll.*³ 339, III B.C.); cf. Paus. 1.26.6 (cited below, p. 87). By contrast: in a hymn to Athena and Athens, ὦ πολιοῦχε Παλλάς, ὦ τῆς ἱερωτάτης ἁπασῶν . . . χώρας (Ar. *Eq.* 581–582); at Callim. *Hymn.* 4.3 islands that are ἱερώταται correspond (275ff.) to ἁγιωτάτη and the absence of war. Cf. Dionysus in Limnae, τῷ ἀρχαιοτάτῳ ἱερῷ τοῦ Διονύσου καὶ ἁγιωτάτῳ ([Dem.] 59.76); the temple of Athena Lindia, ἀρχαιότατόν τε καὶ ἐντιμό[τα]τον (*Syll.*³ 725.3); at Tithorea in Phocis, ἄδυτον ἱερὸν Ἴσιδος, ἁγιώτατον ὁπόσα Ἕλληνες θεῷ τῇ Αἰγυπτίᾳ πεποίηνται (Paus. 10.32.13; cf. 7.24.5); similarly the temple of Aphrodite on Cythera was ἁγιώτατον καὶ . . . ἀρχαιότατον of the temples of Aphrodite in Greece (3.33.1); in Rome, the temple of Jupiter Optimus Maximus is τὸ ἁγιώτατον καὶ φρικωδέστατον ἐν τῇ πόλει τῶν ἱερῶν (Plut. *Ti. Gracch.* 21.5); for σεβασμιώτατος used of emperors or their temples, see Preisigke, *Wörterbuch* III 199. No formal distinction is at issue in the ἱερώτατος δῆμος often met in the Roman East: e.g., Nicopolis (*IGR* I 581, 582, 591), Ephesus (*I.Ephesos* III 625), the deme Pyleitae near Tralles (Nollé, *EpigAnat* 15 [1990] 124; Herrmann, 19 [1992] 115–116), the σεμνότατος δῆμος (Nollé, *Side* I nos. 28, 29)—a variation on ἱερὸς δῆμος (p. 36). At Pliny *HN* 30.2.6 Telmessus is *urbs religiosissima*, meaning "most superstitious" (the context is magic); *sanctissimus deus* (Cic. *Verr.* 2.1.49), *etiam delubra omnia sanctissimis religionibus consecrata* (1.1.14), *maximum et sanctissimum Dianae sacellum* (*Har. resp.* 32). ἀσυλώτατος in *Anth. Gr.* 8.250 of a buried corpse

ἱερώτερος, whereby one would seriously draw distinctions in degrees of sacredness, is exceedingly rare.[22] Indeed, ἱερός was a broad word,[23] applied to cities by poets and orators from Homer ("holy Ilium") to the end of antiquity.[24] Gregory of Nazianzus wrote to a friend of a visit to a villa near the Halys in the hills of Galatia:

> I am writing you this letter from "holy Vanota," if I do not wrong the place in calling it as they do locally; I say wrong the place, because it has no elegance in its nickname, and the great charm of the site is not displayed in this Galatian cognomen.

(He proceeds to describe its beauty at length.)[25]

Such emotive expressions need to be excluded from the evidence on places formally declared sacred and inviolable—not always an easy task. Likewise, a Greek temple might be so august that popular sentiment would hail it as a "common temple of the Greeks": this was most often said of Apollo of Delphi, but a partisan might make the claim of lesser shrines.[26]

("utterly unplunderable" because poor, with nothing to steal). The word ἀσύλωτος was expunged by Woodward from an inscription from Perge (below, p. 450), and accordingly from LSJ. Adler prints ἀσύλωτον at *Suda* τ 553: wrongly, for the word that makes sense there is in fact what was written in the source of the *Suda*, Theoph. Sym. 3.16.5, ἀσύλωτατον (the common happiness of mankind is a glorious and most inviolable treasure).

22. Plut. *Mor.* 350A, the battle of Mantinea made the twelfth day of Scirophorion more sacred (than before); 750C (what is more sacred than marriage? cf. 758B); various metaphors at Ael. Arist. 35.37, 39.6, 44.12 Keil. A more serious comparison at Paus. 3.10.8, but using a different term: in the view of the Spartans the cult of Apollo at Amyclae is more distinguished (ἐπιφανεστέρα) than that at Thornax, as is proved by their dedications (so already Polyb. 5.19.3, but there ἐπιφανέστατον). At Paus. 4.33.6, the mysteries at Andania are second in solemnity only to Eleusis (δεύτερα . . . σεμνότητος); Cic. *Nat. d.* 3.50: a hero *sanctius colunt quam quemquam nobilium deorum.* Compare Benveniste 456, that *sacer* admits of a superlative but not a comparative.

23. It can mean no more than "great," as ancient readers realized: Ath. 284C (μέγαν); at Opp. *Hal.* 3.544 Μασσαλίην ἱερήν the scholiast explains μεγάλην. Cf. Benveniste 456–461.

24. Not just cities, but Euboea (*Il.* 2.535), threshing floors (5.499), etc. After Homer: e.g., Pind. *Nem.* 9.53; Ar. *Pax* 1036; "sacred Talmis" in the hymn to Mandulis (Nock, *Essays* I 365). See S. Scully, *Homer and the Sacred City* (Ithaca, N.Y./London 1990) 16–40; Robert, *Etudes anat.* 387 n. 1; *Bull. épigr.* 1954, 54. Rome as *sacrosanctam istam civitatem:* Apul. *Met.* 11.26.

25. *Ep.* 20.1: ἐκ τῶν ἱερῶν Οὐανώτων, εἴ γε μὴ ἀδικῶ καλῶν ἐπιχωρίως τὸν τόπον . . . μηδὲν ἔχει γλαφυρὸν ἡ ἐπωνυμία, καὶ ἡ τοσαύτη τοῦ τόπου χάρις οὐ συνεμφαίνεται τῷ Γαλατικῷ τούτῳ προσρήματι; subsequently he calls it simply Vanota without ornament or apology. W. Ramsay, *Historical Geography of Asia Minor* (London 1890) 288, thought that Gregory means that the name Vanota is Galatian. Rather, his apology is a Christian's for the word "holy." Nothing else is known of the place: E. Honigmann, *RE* 8A (1955) 347–349.

26. Aeacus' temple on Aegina, in the time of legend, ἱερὸν κοινὸν τῶν Ἑλλήνων (Isoc. 9.15; cf. Paus. 2.29; Wilamowitz, *Kl. Schr.* VI 107); the temple of Apollo at Naupactus (Phlegon *FGrHist* 257 F 36.iii.6; W. Oldfather, "Naupaktos 1," *RE* 16 [1935] 1998).

The Hellenistic declarations of inviolability will endow this popular sensibility with an institutional form.

DEDICATION

There was of course a quite familiar way in which the secular could become sacred, by the act of dedication. Any object, including land,[27] once given to the god, was sacred and therefore protected from violence under the law of *hierosylia*. The Hellenistic declarations of inviolable places can resemble the language of dedication. As a noun, the status is καθιέρωσις καὶ ἀσυλία; in summary statements after the fact we find καθιερόω applied to Teos and Miletus, ἀφιερόω to Xanthus (**164**). More often the recognizers "accept/approve" or "grant" (ἀποδέχομαι, ἀφίημι) the sacredness and inviolability of the place.

Historians, naturally seeking the political import of these declarations, have pointed to similarity with the "sacred manumissions" of slaves:[28] there one "dedicates" the slave to the god, so that he is henceforth free and not to be treated like a slave. He is "untouchable, unplunderable by all" (ἀπὸ πάντων, as in *FD* III.2 230.17, a phrase that sometimes occurs in the *asylia* decrees) and other synonyms (including once ἀφορολόγητος, as in the declarations for Teos, *IG* IX.1^2 96). Those who have focused on the intentions of sovereigns, primarily the Seleucids, have seen in this analogy support for *asylia* as the waiving of some degree of sovereignty.[29] This account, however, if valid at all, could apply to the king alone and would not explain the Panhellenic recognition.

HIKESIA

The legal immunity of a Greek temple is a negative fact, the absence of secular jurisdiction; so too the legal immunity of a city with respect to other sovereign states, which had no say about what went on within its boundaries. There was,

27. So sacred land was to be farmed only by the god or his delegates; violation of this occasioned Delphi's Sacred Wars. Cf. in a Cretan land dispute of 112/1 B.C., χῶρα ἱερὰ καὶ ἀγεώργητος (both "unfarmed" and "unfarmable": *I.Cret.* III IV 9.73–78). The people of Lista in Italy, expelled from their country by war, "declared the land sacred" (ἱερὰν ἀνῆκαν ... τὴν γῆν) and invoked curses upon any who might farm it (Dion. Hal. *Ant. Rom.* 1.14.6).

28. See O. Benndorf in *Beiträge zur alten Geschichte, Festschrift O. Hirschfeld* (Berlin 1903) 77–78.

29. We find the notion in the story of Alexander's dealings with Indian Nysa: he is asked to "grant the city to the god," ἀφεῖναι τῷ θεῷ τὴν πόλιν (Arr. *Anab.* 5.1.3) = ἐᾶσαι σφᾶς ἐλευθέρους τε καὶ αὐτονόμους αἰδοῖ τοῦ Διονύσου (5.1.5), for the citizens since their origin ἐλευθέραν τε οἰκοῦμεν τὴν Νῦσαν καὶ αὐτόνομοι καὶ ἐν κόσμῳ πολιτεύοντες (5.1.6), which Alexander grants (δίδωσιν ἐλευθέρους τε εἶναι ... καὶ αὐτονόμους). Cf. Polyb. 13.9.5, some barbarians had been given peace and freedom by the gods, which Antiochus III granted now. Compare the common expression for manumission, ἐλευθέρους ἀφεῖσον (e.g., Dem. 36.14).

however, a positive gesture, supplication (ἱκεσία).[30] A human being in need of protection might put himself at the discretion of another, god or man, by ritual action—clasping the knees of the person or statue, sitting at the hearth or altar. Like other rituals in Greek religion, this act was portable and not restricted to sacred space (the locus classicus is *Od.* 22.330ff.: to supplicate an altar or Odysseus?).[31] The one supplicated, however, was free to choose: he might give the ritual response, "raising up" the suppliant and agreeing to protect him, only if persuaded of the rightness of the appeal. In practice, therefore, escaping to a temple was not enough for a fugitive from the law: the god or the god's priest could refuse him. And in general, Greek cities had their means for dealing with the practical difficulties that supplication might pose for public order.[32] Commonly, one who took refuge in a temple was required by the temple to undergo a kind of trial to determine whether his flight was "just."[33] The god was not obliged to accept and protect every suppliant, only those who had a just claim. The founder of the cult at Andania in the 90s B.C. stipulated that the place was to be a refuge for slaves (τοῖς δούλοις φύγιμον[34] ἔστω τὸ ἱερόν, καθὼς ἂν οἱ ἱεροὶ ἀποδείξωντι τὸν τόπον, *Syll.*^{3} 736.80), but his point was to define procedure (no one to aid the fugitive, the priest to decide whether the flight is just). In cases of supplication doubtless Zeus Xenios was watching,[35] and the decision was not idle. But no foreign government had a say in this matter.

30. See G. Freyburger, *Latomus* 47 (1988) 501–525, with references to the extensive scholarly literature; Thuc. 8.84 is an informative instance.

31. The same analogy, refugees to a city and to a god are equally *hiketai*, is found at Hdt. 1.159. Cf. Eur. *IA* 911 and 973–974, Clytemnestra's οὐκ ἔχω βωμὸν καταφυγεῖν ἄλλον ἢ σὸν γόνυ, and Achilles' answer ἀλλ' ἡσύχαζε· θεὸς ἐγὼ πέφηνά σοι μέγιστος, οὐκ ὤν. A public debate on the subject at Diod. 11.92 (Syracuse).

32. On the famous law at Cyrene see J. Servais, *BCH* 84 (1960) 112–147; cf. V. Kontorini, Ἀνέκδοτες ἐπίγραφες Ρόδου II (Athens 1989) 17–29 no. 1 [*SEG* 39.729]. Refusal: e.g., Apul. *Met.* 6.2–3.

33. On this men disagreed. Note the Athenian statesman and religious thinker Lycurgus on Callistratus: exiled from Athens, Callistratus was told by Apollo that he would receive lawful treatment (τεύξεται τῶν νόμων) if he returned; he did so, taking refuge at the Altar of the Twelve Gods, but was nonetheless executed—"Justly: for lawful treatment for wrongdoers is punishment, and the god rightly returned the guilty man to those wronged for punishment. It would be a terrible thing if the same signs were manifested to the pious and to evildoers" (*Leoc.* 93). Lycurgus does not indicate by what procedure Callistratus was removed from the altar. At 128 he approves of the starving of Pausanias in the temple of Athena at Sparta (cf. Hdt. 9.10): this proves that the gods do not help traitors. Compare Eur. *Ion* 1314–1315.

34. Cf. Plut. *Mor.* 166E: ἔστι δούλῳ φεύξιμος βωμός; the adjective recurs at Delphi (p. 48), Chalcedon (**62**), and Sardes (**214**).

35. To quote an instance from the third century B.C.: ἀλλ' ἱκέτας ξείνους Διὸς εἵνεκεν αἰδέσσασθε Ξεινίου Ἱκεσίου (Ap. Rhod. 2.1131–1132). See O. Weinreich, in Roscher, *Lex.* 6.522–525 (*Ausgew. Schr.* II 549–554).

As to cities, in ancient law as in modern there was no such thing as a "right" of extradition:[36] the transfer of a person from the jurisdiction of one state to that of another can take place only by consent of both powers, that is, by a treaty of extradition. A pursuer might argue or demand that a city that received the fugitive surrender him, threatening war—whence a political and religious dilemma. There are famous episodes of this problem (Cyrus demanding Pactyes from the Cymaeans [Hdt. 1.157ff.], Alexander Harpalus from the Athenians, the Romans Hannibal from Prusias and Mithridates from Tigranes) and less famous (e.g., Hdt. 9.86; Polyb. 30.8–9; Tac. *Hist.* 3.48); and this dilemma is a theme in Greek literature from its beginnings, so the Danaids at Argos. Thus a declared immunity from war might be conceived as establishing a "right" of asylum, but only if the flight were held to be "just" by both parties—a point on which parties tend to disagree.

In accounts of the grants of *asylia* in the Seleucid kingdom, it is conventional to invoke a story about the island of Aradus off the Phoenician coast: during the conflict between Seleucus II and Antiochus Hierax, Aradus sided with Seleucus and made an agreement with him whereby refugees from his kingdom were permitted to come to Aradus and not be surrendered against their will (but they could not leave without his permission); Aradus obtained much profit from these wealthy refugees, especially after they returned home, in particular in terms of property on the mainland.[37] Whatever the details or the credibility of this arrangement, it is a form of subjection to the crown, not independence; we would better compare Antipater, after Lamia, allowing exiles to remain in Greece (Plut. *Phoc.* 29.3), or the Romans acknowledging cities of exile in Italy (p. 30). In any case, this story portrays a bilateral treaty, and a phenomenon that is entirely secular in character. The inscribed declarations of territorial *asylia* are neither.[38]

EKECHEIRIA

We must distinguish too the "sacred truce" (ἐκεχειρία or σπονδαί) that pertained for the Panhellenic festivals and many lesser games: participating states were not to engage in warfare during the time specified.[39] A clear legislated instance

36. Contra: Bickerman, *Institutions* 150; Bickerman considered that *asylia* was the partial restoration of juridical autonomy by the king to his conquered cities; again, even if one accepted this, it would not explain the declarations of inviolability as a whole, which are not confined to the Seleucids or to kings.

37. Strab. 16.2.14 (754) (*Staatsvertr.* III 491); cf. Kahrstedt, *Syrische Territorien* 76; Bickerman, *Institutions* 155; A. Heuss, *Stadt und Herrscher des Hellenismus,* Klio-BH 39 (Leipzig 1937) 176.

38. Aradus never put "sacred and inviolable" on its coins, although we shall see that such silence proves nothing; compare Tarsus, for example.

39. G. Rougemont, *BCH* 97 (1973) 75–106; F. J. Fernandez Nieto, *Los acuerdos belicos en la antigua Grecia* I (Santiago de Compostela 1975) 147–184.

derives from classical Athens, defining the dates of the σπονδαί for attendance at the Mysteries (*IG* I^3 6B). On its face, the effect is the same as with inviolability. But this was conditioned upon time rather than space,[40] and many of those Hellenistic grants of *asylia* of a place that simultaneously accept crowned games grant ἐκεχειρία for the games.[41] Thus the two items, one old and a regular condition of great games, the other a novel title for a place, apparently were not felt to overlap or compete. Some scholars hold that this was the purpose of granted territorial *asylia*, the security of visitors to Panhellenic games.[42] This does not account for the instances (the large majority) where no such games are present.

THE SACRED LIFE

Every city had its tutelary god,[43] to whom the place might be called sacred in the rhetoric of praise or in antiquarian writings.[44] Such statements prove nothing singular about the community or its status. But it was a common notion in ancient Greece that, just as sanctity of person is accompanied by immunity from violence, a community of such people might live a "sacred life," characterized by neutrality. I give two examples, which sum up the cluster of expectations that went with the sacredness of such a community, expectations that may well be pertinent to the Hellenistic phenomenon of declaring cities "sacred and inviolable." Herodotus describes the Scythian Argippaeans: "No one of mankind wrongs (ἀδικέει) these people, for they are said to be sacred (ἱροί); nor have they possessed themselves of any weapon of war. Furthermore, it is they who settle disputes for their neighbors, and whoever takes refuge (φεύγων καταφύγῃ) with them is wronged by no one."[45] He regards them as strange

40. Demosthenes (21.10) even speaks against exercising the right of reprisal on holy days of the Athenian sacred calendar.

41. So regularly for Magnesia; cf. in Boeotia **3** and **4**, and at Cos inviolability for the temple and for those who come to the games (**9**).

42. E.g., Gauthier, *Symbola* 226–230; but see 276 (in the absence of games, the goal of *asylia* is to protect the inhabitants from pirates).

43. E.g., Plut. *Thes.* 6.1: Ποσειδῶνα γὰρ Τροιζήνιοι σέβονται διαφερόντως, καὶ θεὸς οὗτός ἐστιν αὐτοῖς πολιοῦχος. A double patronage for Galen of Pergamum: τὸν πάτριον θεὸν Ἀσκληπιόν, οὗ καὶ θεραπευτὴν ἀπέφαινον ἐμαυτόν (*Libr. propr.* 2, XIX 18–19 K.).

44. E.g., Strab. 8.6.14 (373): Τροιζὴν δὲ ἱερά ἐστι Ποσειδῶνος, ἀφ' οὗ καὶ Ποσειδωνία ποτὲ ἐλέγετο; Dio Chrys. 38.87: the entire city of Rhodes is sacred (ἅπασα μὲν ἡ πόλις ἐστὶν ἱερά), yet the Rhodians mistreat even those statues that are in temples (cf. Manil. 4.765: *domus vere Solis, cui tota sacrata est*); Julian. *Or.* 4, 150C (with Seyrig, *Ant. syr.* IV 132): Ἔμεσαν . . . ἱερὸν ἐξ αἰῶνος Ἡλίου χωρίον; Cic. *Verr.* 2.4.106: *insulam Siciliam totam esse Cereri et Liberae consecratam*, with arguments from myth. Note, however, the similar statement about Cos, which had been declared inviolable (p. 111).

45. 4.23; whence Pliny *HN* 6.13: *sacros haberi narrant inviolatosque esse etiam feris accolarum populis nec ipsos modo sed illos etiam qui ad eos confugerint*; Mela 1.117 on Scythians with *iustissimi mores . . .*

people. Again, Oppian (*Hal.* 2.642–660) says that all fish are in a perpetual state of war except the grey mullet, which is most gentle and righteous: they harm no one and eat no living thing, being a holy tribe (ἁγνὰ γένεθλα); so other fishes give them honorable respect (τίμιον αἰδῶ) and do not eat their young, which shows that justice is honored everywhere (this observation leads him to praise the Roman peace, which ended the state of war among men). More generally, legend told of various peoples who were especially given over to the honoring of some god—a life that Greeks felt was rather exotic.[46] These ideas were common coin and are part of the backdrop to the Hellenistic institution of declared inviolability.

EXPLANATIONS

An attempt at a comprehensive list of places declared inviolable was made by B. Barth in 1888;[47] the fullest treatments of language and legal forms are those of E. Schlesinger (1933) and P. Gauthier (1972). The goal of modern scholars has been to place these declarations in a historical context;[48] the most important contributions have come from U. Kahrstedt, C. B. Welles, E. J. Bickerman, H. Seyrig, and M. I. Rostovtzeff.[49]

---

sacri itaque habentur, adeoque ipsos nemo de tam feris gentibus violat, ut aliis quoque ad eos confugisse pro asylo sit.

46. Three examples from Diodorus: in India, farmers, regarded as the common benefactors of mankind, are sacred and inviolable and not molested by war and are exempt from military service and other liturgies (2.36.6–7, 40.4 [Megasth. *FGrHist* 715 F 4]); in Arabia a city "sacred to Apollo," where the inhabitants spend their time honoring him (2.47.3); in Africa a city considered sacred (ἱερᾶς δ' εἶναι νομιζομένης), which was conquered by the Amazons (3.53.6).

47. B. Barth, *De asylis Graecorum* (Strasbourg 1888). C. Fontana, *RIN* 90 (1988) 63–82, surveys the coin evidence on the basis of Eckhel and Mionnet; Schlesinger dealt only with textual evidence and not coins and hence said nothing on the many cases of *asylia* outside the Aegean area.

48. An early effort, often cited, is H. Usener, *RhM* 29 (1874) 38–39 (*Kl. Schr.* III 399–402). Without mentioning Spanheim, he listed cases of declared inviolability, invoked as the model the purification of Delos in 426/5 B.C., and thought this invented neutralization of Hellenistic times a Seleucid device for protecting their cities from attack by the Ptolemies—hence its extensive use in Syria and Phoenicia. He added that neocoria, flattery of the emperor, succeeded *asylia*. Other surveys of the topic: Heuss, *Stadt und Herrscher* 145–159; M. P. Nilsson, *Cults, Myths, Oracles, and Politics* (Lund 1950) 119–122; C. Préaux in *Rec. Soc. Jean Bodin* VI *La Ville* (Brussels 1954) 113–118; P. Ducrey, *Le traitement des prisonniers de guerre* (Paris 1968) 304–311; W. Ziegler, "Symbolai und Asylie" (Diss., Bonn 1975) 89–101; J. K. Davies, *CAH* VII.1^2 (1984) 288–289; P. Debord, *Aspects sociaux et économiques de la vie religieuse dans l'Anatolie*, EPRO 88 (Leiden 1982) 271–286; L. Boffo, *I re ellenistici e i centri religiosi dell'Asia Minore* (Pavia 1985) 53–79; W. K. Pritchett, *The Greek State at War* V (Berkeley 1991) 125–132.

49. I will not attempt to list the scholars who mention "neutralization" in more general accounts of the Hellenistic world or of Greek rules of war; or those who, unaware of the

Our inscriptions leave no doubt that these declarations were first and foremost a religious gesture, increasing the honor of the god.[50] In strict logic, they do not seem necessary: all temples were supposed to be inviolable, and for a city the option of military neutrality was always there, without need of someone else's declaration.

Concerning temples, the prevailing solution in the nineteenth century was to save the phenomena by distinguishing two levels of immunity: all temples had *hikesia*, the power to give fugitives temporary sanctuary and a hearing, but only a few had *asylia*, the right to protect permanently even guilty fugitives.[51] This allowed scholars to believe the Roman claim about granted immunity even in the face of the abundant anecdotal evidence that any Greek sacred place might receive refugees. But this view presumed (with Tacitus) some overriding legal authority that told Greek cities what their permitted usages might be; it ignored (or exploited selectively) the conflicting opinions expressed in Greek literature about the propriety of protecting a particular suppliant (cf. p. 10); and in order to determine which temples enjoyed *asylia*, not just *hikesia*, scholars were drawn into an idle debate about which individuals in those anecdotes were "truly guilty." H. Usener's essay in 1874 reasserted Spanheim's treatment of the inviolable cities as a phenomenon of foreign policy, and Barth's work in 1888 reminded scholars of the geographical and legal range of the title (cities as well as temples); after this the debate over *asylia* as the proper treatment of suppliants largely ended, and the topic became (quite rightly) an item in the study of interstate relations.

These declarations of inviolability have often been taken to be compensations for a loss of piety and a decline of traditional religion held to be characteristic of the Hellenistic age:[52] with the loss of religious faith, special enactments were

---

scholarship, think that the Hellenistic grants created a "right of asylum" in the Roman manner, or merely summarize what Tacitus says.

50. So already Spanheim; G. Radet, *BCH* 14 (1890) 227: "L'ἀσυλία appartenait toujours aux sanctuaires les plus célèbres, à ceux dont les divinités étaient les plus fameuses et les plus vénérés"; cf. Robert, *Laodicée du Lycos* 289 n. 3.

51. E.g., H. A. Wallon, *Du droit d'asyle* (Paris 1837); J. Jaenisch, *De Graecorum asylis* (Göttingen 1868) 14–36 (cf. 5–6, treatments of the topic from 1801 to Jaenisch's own day); E. Caillemer, "Asylia," *DarSag* I (1877) 501–510. Their ability to disagree about the implications of Polyb. 4.35.3 for the "status" of Athena Chalcioecus at Sparta is illuminating (see Jaenisch 28).

52. Schlesinger, "Asylie" 64–65; W. Günther, *Das Orakel von Didyma in hellenistischer Zeit*, IstMitt-BH 4 (Tübingen 1971) 82 n. 86 (that *hierosylia* became more common in the Hellenistic period); Ducrey 309 (declared inviolability "is explained by the decline of religious sentiment which accompanied the wars and turmoil of the end of the third century B.C. and brought countless violations of sanctuaries and temples"); cf. A. J. Holladay and M. D. Goodman, *CQ* n.s. 36 (1986) 151–160 (Greeks before Alexander took seriously religious constraints on warfare).

needed to sustain what had been the traditional immunity of sacred or of neutral places.[53] The decline of religious scruples (whether this was historical or not)[54] is admittedly an ancient claim. Polybius says that in ancient times people declared war and gave notice of battle, but now that is considered poor generalship, and only Romans preserve a bit of the ancient practice.[55] Diodorus (3.5.3–4) has the story that in earlier times the Ethiopian kings, owing to their superstition, obeyed the priests (who would order the king's suicide), until in the third century one king, who had a Greek education, entered the *abaton* with troops and killed the priests. At *Anthologia Graeca* 8.198, *formerly* these things were inviolable (ἄσυλα): a god, a corpse.

But it is easy to find contradictions to such elegies about the morally superior past—violations of classical date[56] and moral indignation against such acts in the Hellenistic period. Thus a denunciation of an undeclared war and of sacrilege: Μεσημβριανῶν πόλεμον ἀνεπάγγελτον ἡμῖν ἐξενεγκάντων καὶ πολλὰ καὶ μεγάλα ἀσε[β]ησάντων εἰς τὸ ἱερὸν τοῦ Ἀπόλλωνος.[57] The Alexandrians rioted when royal agents pulled a suppliant out of a temple (Polyb. 15.27.2–3, 29.8–14, 33.8). Polybius himself expresses outrage at sacrilege (11.7)—not surprisingly, for this sentiment is of a piece with lamenting moral decline. In Hellenistic times as before, one was expected to show "piety toward gods, justice toward men."[58]

Moreover, to predicate declared inviolability upon a decay of religion is to hold that people who had lost their religious scruples were being asked to obey an ad hoc declaration that one should have religious scruples. Why would marauders who were pointedly indifferent to an ancient and inherited taboo that protected temples or peaceful cities honor such an artificial declaration of holiness?

53. Gauthier, *Symbola* 228–229, convincingly rejects this argument, pointing out both violations of sanctity in the classical period and outrage voiced against them in the Hellenistic.

54. This view of Hellenistic indifference to religion, often found in historians of Hellenistic political life, must surprise many historians of religion in the same period.

55. 13.3.5–6; contrast the polemic at 7.14.3 against Philip V, who both despoiled the gods and broke the laws of war; 9.30.2: τῆς μὲν γὰρ εἰς τὸ θεῖον ἀσεβείας. . .τῆς δ' εἰς ἀνθρώπους ὠμότητος.

56. E.g., Hdt. 5.46; Ducrey (295–304) gathers instances of respect and disrespect for suppliants, ambassadors, etc.

57. *IGBulg* I 388 bis; cf. *T.Calymnii* 64 (= *Syll.*^{3} 567), a war inflicted "unjustly" (without explanation: by Hierapytna upon Cos); *I.Priene* 17.9ff., Gauls' raids on temples; Diod. 19.63.5, suppliants removed from a temple and killed "contrary to the common conventions of the Greeks" (παρὰ τὰ κοινὰ τῶν Ἑλλήνων νόμιμα).

58. *Fouilles d'Amyzon* no. 35.8–9. Other expressions of outrage at *hierosylia*, often noting the gods' vengeance: Livy 29.8–9; Diod. 27.4 ἐπιφανέστατον τῶν κατὰ τὴν 'Ιταλίαν ἱερῶν . . . καὶ διὰ πάντος ἁγνὸν ὑπὸ τῶν ἐγχωρίων τετηρῆσθαι: Persephone of Locri), 28.3, 29.15 (Antiochus III in Elymais), 31.45 (Cretans at Siphnos), 32.21 (murder of Prusias in a temple of Zeus).

A variant theory of moral decline assumes a class distinction: ordinary soldiers were superstitious and so would respect declared *asylia*, even though their educated and cynical commanders knew better.[59] Against this we must set the experience of the ages, that it is the troops of the line who ignore fine moral principles and loot what they can, and their commanders who then must apologize for the troops; an ancient example is Antiochus III's letter to Amyzon.[60] Another variant is the assumption that Hellenistic kings did not acknowledge the inviolability of temples under their rule.[61] That may be true and relevant in some situations (perhaps the Seleucids and non-Greek temples), but it cannot account for declared inviolability outside the kingdoms, or recognitions voted by cities rather than kings, or recognitions of cities as distinct from temples.

A different answer to this dilemma is force majeure: the grants of *asylia* were promises to provide collective defense if the place recognized were attacked.[62] For this there is support in the texts themselves: the several Cretan and Aetolian prohibitions of violence, and most specifically the Cretan promises to come in aid if Teos is attacked. Against it speak three facts: so far as we know, no such defense ever happened; most of the recognizers would not have been useful as defenders; and, in contrast to military treaties, which are seriously meant, no grant of *asylia* contains an oath to bind future behavior. Thus, if in 242 B.C. the Coans had stood in genuine fear for their Asclepieum, they need not have applied for protection to (for example) Naples (**46**): the Ptolemaic fleet would have been sufficient. Welles's formulation is more consistent with the evidence: that the requests were a general appeal to "Greek public opinion" to defend the inviolable place (*Royal Corres.* p. 58). We might better call this wishful thinking, or rather admit that religion, like diplomacy, involves not so much belief as hope.

The goal of these recognitions is normally held to be the limitation of violence in an increasingly chaotic age—especially protection against piracy. Some scholars have written, erroneously, that the grants of *asylia* come mostly

59. So Seyrig, *Notes* 21: "A deep religious fear was attached to such violation, perhaps less by some cynical generals or condottieri, than by their simpler minded troops."

60. *Fouilles d'Amyzon* no. 9 (see p. 336); cf. *P.Tebt.* II 781.4, a temple damaged ὑπὸ τῶν παρ' Ἀντιόχου (Epiphanes' invasion of Egypt); *FD* III.1 22, Delphian thanks to a Messenian who came to protect the temple and the city and who kept his troops εὐτάκτους καὶ ἀνενκλήτους; Plut. *Dem.* 30.1, troops moved from Ephesus in order to prevent them from looting the Artemisium.

61. Welles, *Royal Corres.* pp. 57–58; Bickerman, *Institutions* 150; Rey-Coquais, *IGLSyrie* VII p. 63. Perhaps the best support for this is *Royal Corres.* 55: "As the χωρίον is sacred it absolutely must be taken" (Eumenes II on Pessongi).

62. Seyrig, *Notes* 20 n. 48: the recognitions were not sought from pirates but to bring upon offenders "some sort of reprisals on the part of the states which had recognized that privilege."

from Aetolians and Cretans, notorious pirates.[63] The charge of piracy calls for some caution, as would any such blanket characterization of peoples. Perhaps our third-century evidence reveals more acts of seizure than we hear of earlier.[64] But in general, inscriptions of the third century are more numerous and informative than earlier. Many of the seizures on record, moreover, arise as part of war or the right of reprisal. Freebooting, sailing "against all flags," was perhaps not so widespread as some scholars have thought, at least before the decline of Rhodes after 166 B.C. Nor are our literary sources unbiased; our one connected narrative on the third century is stridently anti-Aetolian. What would our history of the fifth century look like if it had been written by a Spartan or a Melian rather than an Athenian? Pirates collect tribute (φορολογεῖν, Diod. 28.1), of which the Athenians have left us some revealing lists.[65] When one reads the modern claim that fifth-century Athens kept the Aegean clear of pirates, one is tempted to emend: *other* pirates; no one likes competition. If Aetolia, a significant power, acted like one, that was nothing new. If Polybius had been an Aetolian, we might today be assessing the difficult question of the "popularity of the Aetolian Empire."

Was there in fact more violence in the third century B.C., and (more important) were Greeks so conscious of this as to devise a novel protection against it? It may be that the acceleration of the spread of *asylia* late in the third century owes something to such consciousness, as has been claimed. But can such a concern explain the beginnings of the gesture—the grants to the Itonium in the 260s, to Smyrna and the Coan Asclepieum in the 240s? About this one may remain doubtful.

Finally, it is common to treat *asylia* as a metaphor or charade for some other situation: fiscal autonomy, legal autonomy,[66] the right to act as a mediator, the holding of Panhellenic games, etc. These are circumstantial approaches, none of them universally applicable to the attested recipients. And kings were perfectly capable of granting autonomy, tax freedom, etc., under their proper names: why would they resort to an ambiguous façade for the same status?

63. E.g., D. van Berchem, *MusHelv* 17 (1960) 23: "It is certain . . . that the peoples whose acts of recognition were solicited were in the majority of cases pirates." On Hellenistic piracy see most recently H. Pohl, *Die römische Politik und der Piraterie* (Berlin/New York 1993).

64. See the list in Pritchett V 324–348. An impressive list, however, could be compiled from the fourth-century orators.

65. Note μήτε φόρον φέροντι among the provisions of the Second Athenian Confederacy (*Staatsvertr.* II 257.23).

66. In most detail, Bickerman, *Institutions* 149–155; cf. Schlesinger, "Asylie" 68 (the meaning of *asylia* faded until in the Roman Empire it was, like autonomy, merely a formal designation of a free city).

JURISDICTION

This volume does not concern the legal protection of a god's property—in both Greece and Rome, severe penalties applied for theft or damage (e.g., to trees in a sacred precinct)—or the exclusions that attend ritual purity (e.g., childbirth, death, or iron excluded from sacred space). These matters were the concern of the individual city. Who granted territorial inviolability?

It is commonly claimed that seekers of *asylia* applied to pirates, or at any rate to powers who were to be feared.[67] Such a focus may well be present in several cases (Teos, Tenos, Claros, Mylasa). But for the phenomenon as a whole, a glance at the map will disprove this account; and it is unreasonable to think that those who already ignored the norms of society would be dissuaded by a religious appeal. Rostovtzeff (*SEHHW* 845) made the realistic deduction that they must have been paid, that the *asylia* decrees were in effect purchased with protection money. To the contrary: when we hear of money changing hands, it is going in the other direction, a donation to the god by the grantor (e.g., **56**.7).

In fact, the scope of the grantors is Panhellenic, as the inscriptions show. Tacitus could not imagine this juridical situation: for him, the right of asylum is granted by the ruler of the place. But the Romans attributed to the Greeks their own juridical notion. So Livy (35.51), aware of the Greek origin of the word *asylum*, says that it applies only to certain temples; troops of Antiochus III attacked Roman forces even though these were in an asylum and war had not been declared (*in fano lucoque ea religione et eo iure sancto, quo sunt templa quae asyla Graeci appellant, et nondum aut indicto bello aut ita commisso*). This claim is repeated in late authors (see p. 4), and often enough in modern times.

The Panhellenic character of the grantors also excludes the Roman notion of a sovereign state waiving its sovereignty within now-sanctified space, an intention that scholars attribute also to the Seleucid state. When in 242 B.C. the citizens of Naples declared the temple of Asclepius on Cos inviolable, they could not have meant that a person could henceforth, but not before 242, take refuge in that temple: such an act was none of the Neapolitans' business. And if a malefactor in Naples wanted to escape punishment, he did not need to go the Coan Asclepieum:[68] like Medea, he needed only to leave for some other city, where Neapolitan jurisdiction automatically failed.

Thus territorial inviolability was normally a creation of the Greek people, at least in the third and early second centuries (from which we have inscribed

67. E.g., R. B. McShane, *Foreign Policy of the Attalids of Pergamum* (Urbana, 1964) 52: "*Asylia* was not usually sought from nearby friends but rather from the more distant and dangerous powers."

68. Except to the extent that taking refuge in the temple might help persuade the *Coans* not to expel him; so a number of stories: e.g., Paus. 3.5.6 and 3.7.10 on Spartans at the temple of Athena Alea in Tegea.

recognitions). To this scope there are several probable exceptions. The several extant recognitions of Boeotian temples all are decrees of the Delphian Amphictyony; it may be that in the beginning of our phenomenon, the Amphictyons (and the Boeotians) felt that this was a sufficient representation of the Greek people. The later grants in Syria-Palestine may well derive exclusively from the relevant king, as no external recognitions are attested; certainly this was the case in Egypt. And with Roman provincial rule, Roman decisions supplanted Greek public opinion as the source of civic status.

THE UNITY OF THE EVIDENCE

What defines the boundaries of this topic and this corpus? First, places versus persons: as Schlesinger saw, the difference between personal and territorial inviolability is fundamental.[69] In terms of documents, a corpus on personal inviolability would begin in the archaic period and extend through the Roman Empire. Greek cities granted to select individuals and groups of individuals ἀσυλία, immunity from the right of reprisal (σῦλον), often as one in a string of privileges—so for *proxenoi*, and for benefactors of various sorts. Such awards to whole citizen bodies are rare in the classical period, but not unheard of.[70] More date from the Hellenistic period, most famously the Aetolian grants of *asylia* to the citizens of a number of cities.[71] These are acts of individual states and do not derive from a Panhellenic quest by the recipient. They make no mention of cult or of piety, concerned as they are simply to extend to a person or persons some of the privileges that came with citizenship. This was no religious gesture, and there was nothing sacral about the privilege or the person; it gave the recipient the right to seek redress in the grantor's courts. By contrast, the documents recognizing territorial inviolability begin in the 260s B.C. and stop with a decision in Rome in A.D. 22; they speak of piety and the honor of the god. They are not to be confused with grants of personal inviolability, even the collective grants to communities of foreign citizens.

Our concern here is the declared inviolability of places. It must nonetheless be admitted that some grantors themselves confuse the two: the Aetolians and Cretans, with their active use of personal inviolability, seem more than once to

69. Schlesinger, "Asylie" 53; cf. Robert, *BCH* 54 (1930) 330 n. 2 (*Op. min. sel.* I 149), carefully distinguishing inviolability of temples and lands from that granted by the Aetolians to citizen bodies.

70. E.g., *Staatsvertr.* II 146 (Oeantheia and Chaleium), without using this noun (cf. Gauthier, *Symbola* 222–226); *CIDelph* 13 (= *LSCG* Suppl. 41), a grant of collective *asylia* from Delphi to Sciathos (fourth century B.C.); A. Chaniotis, *Chiron* 21 (1991) 247–252, ἀσφάλεια for the Melians restored in a Cretan decree.

71. H. Benecke, *Die Seepolitik der Aitoler* (Hamburg 1934) 17–31; Ziegler 168–263 (not distinguishing personal and territorial grants).

have granted this when in fact they had been asked to recognize the inviolability of a place.

Second, temples and cities. Some scholars have thought that the inviolability of a temple must be distinguished from that of a city and its territory, that these are different acts in substance and were prompted by different motives. So Spanheim accepted that a temple so recognized was to be an asylum in the Roman sense, a place of sacred refuge, whereas a city and its territory were to be immune from war. The inscriptions, however, by their language, geography, and chronology imply that *asylia* of temple and city was the same. In one historical setting, the Aegean from the 260s to the 180s, certain Greek cities sought through sacred ambassadors (*theoroi*) these Panhellenic recognitions in honor of their chief divinity. Whether the object of the grant is the temple or the city and country, the diplomatic procedures, the vocabulary, and the envoys' arguments are identical; the particular boundaries of the place in question are only a detail. Accordingly I follow the many scholars who have treated these acts as a single phenomenon, declarations of the inviolability of a place, whether a temple alone or the entire city and territory. A regular usage emerged quickly in the third century: a ἱερόν alone is declared ἄσυλον; the entire πόλις καὶ χώρα is declared ἱερὸς καὶ ἄσυλος. A ἱερόν is already ἱερόν and cannot be declared so;[72] even verbally, therefore, these declarations are identical. We have no instance in which a temple first was declared inviolable, and later this was expanded to include the city and country.

Louis Robert recognized a regular feature in a city's choice whether to ask for *asylia* for a temple alone or the entire city and country: with few exceptions, it is the temple when this stood outside the city proper, the whole city and territory when the temple was inside the city.[73] A partial exception is Smryna in the 240s, the first extant declaration of a city rather than a temple. But here too the Smrynaeans write with great care: the Greek world is asked to "accept the temple of Aphrodite Stratonicis as inviolable and the city as sacred and inviolable" (p. 98). That temple was in the city proper, and the Smyrnaeans are asking that inviolability encompass more than the temple. I suggest that the language and the substance here are transitional. The Smyrnaeans are not asking that their entire territory be encompassed in the *asylia*, only the city in which the temple stands. The more ambitious gesture has not yet in the 240s been attempted, and the formula for it has not yet emerged. "City and country sacred and inviolable" is first met with certainty at Magnesia in 221 B.C., and probably already at Miletus somewhat earlier.

72. As was observed by P. M. Fraser, *BCH* 78 (1954) 63.

73. *Hellenica* V (1948) 67 n. 1. Exceptions certain or probable: Thebes, Tenos, Miletus, Xanthus, Anaphe, Aphrodisias.

Third, there may be differences in times and places. With rare exceptions, from the old Aegean world we have grants, from the Greek East we have titles—inscriptions from the 260s to the 180s B.C. in the Aegean area, mostly coins from the 140s on in the East. The inscriptions reveal clearly the procedures and the ideology that led to inviolability: honors voted for a divinity and his place by the Greek people. From the title on eastern coins ("of Tyre the sacred and inviolable") it cannot be proved that the same procedures and arguments pertained: usually we are not told who declared the place inviolable or to what god, if any.[74] Do these two largely separate bodies of evidence constitute one subject, and if they do, can we yet discern an evolution in this subject?

A distinction has been drawn on the basis of historical context. Scholars have long treated the eastern declarations of inviolability as part of the disintegration of the Seleucid kingdom as rivals struggled for the allegiance of cities; from the point of view of the cities, the recognitions are seen as a step toward civic autonomy and liberty. No one will doubt the reality of both trends. The Aegean recognitions, where the religious motive is so visible in our inscriptions, have not been read as emblems of royal decline; but the role of competition seems evident there as well. Here again I have treated this phenomenon as one—as is traditional, although scholars have tended to see quite different motives for the grants in these different times and places (immunity from pirates in the third-century Aegean, partial freedom from the crown in late Seleucid Syria). Vocabulary is consistent (the title "sacred and inviolable"), and continuity is suggested by the pins on the map: the last epigraphically attested declaration in the Aegean area, Pergamum in 182, is soon followed by the spread of the title of inviolability on eastern coins, first seen at Tyre in 141/0.

In obvious ways Egypt stands apart, as does the Seleucid recognition **218**, which shares with the Egyptian material both its late date and the fact that it does not derive from the world of the Greek city-state. In Egypt the inscriptions make substance clear: *asylia* is a religious honor certainly, but granted by an internal decision of the Ptolemaic state, not by Panhellenic recognition, and the substance is immunity from intrusion by the state—a "right of asylum" in the Roman sense and ours. I have included these inscriptions, if only to err on the side of inclusiveness—all Greek acts declaring places inviolable—and because the map suggests continuity with the Panhellenic phenomenon: our first Ptolemaic declaration dates to 96 B.C.

Finally, the Roman grants for places in their eastern provinces present decided differences from the recognitions (including Roman recognitions) down to 182 B.C.: under Roman rule only temples are in question, and what they receive is the right of asylum as Romans understood it, the right to take refuge within the

74. The exceptions are Mopsuestia and Antioch, where the cults are specified and the authors of the grant are the Seleucid king (Antioch) or "the kings" (Mopsuestia).

boundaries of a temple; on this Tacitus and the inscribed Roman confirmations are consistent. Tacitus' account guarantees that this is a continuation of the Hellenistic title; but the substance is different. The Greek people claimed no authority concerning whether some temple might receive refugees, but the Roman government did.

HONOR

It remains to be seen what the declarations of territorial *asylia* meant and did. I see two reasons to think that this gesture never brought a recipient anything but honor, and that for most of its history no more than honor was intended by grantor or recipient.

First, the declarations are inherently contradictory or redundant. The oddity of the request is betrayed openly by two of the earliest recognitions, among those for the Asclepieum on Cos in 242 B.C.: Aegira says "the temple is to be inviolable from all, as it is in fact the policy of the city and the Achaeans that temples are inviolable" (**18**); Pella grants "inviolability as for all other temples" (**23**). Taken at their word, these decrees accomplish and alter nothing—they admit to making a grant that promises no new behavior. They betoken, in my view, surprise at such an anomalous request.

Moreover, it seems that different interpretations could be put on the gesture by the grantors. The Aetolian League repeatedly responded to such requests with the formulas it used in its program of granting personal inviolability. The League believed, in other words, that it was being asked to take legal responsibility for attacks by Aetolians on foreign persons and their property. For the Romans, the request was interpreted as being for a "right of asylum." And yet the Greeks continued to want the grant, indifferent to what might have been the grantor's intent or any practical consequences.

Second, the declarations protected no one from war. We have no record of the title thwarting an attacker, or even being invoked in an effort to ward off attack. This is an argument from silence, but a strong one; most of the recipients of *asylia* were important places, and it is their military history that we know best. We have abundant evidence that "sacred and inviolable" cities took part in war, as aggressor or victim, and without comment or criticism in our sources. To give one example out of many: in the 180s B.C. Miletus and Magnesia fought a war against each other; the elaborate provisions of the settlement that survives (*Syll.*^{3} 588) make no reference to the fact that both places had recently been declared inviolable, a fact that thus seems to have had no bearing on the definition of peace.

Rostovtzeff, with his acute sense of the real world, admitted that in the end, inviolability did not work (*SEHHW* 194); to this I would add only that it did not work in the beginning either. In 200 recognitions, moreover, no one ever adds an oath to bring aid in case of war, the sine qua non of a serious military intent.[75] The willingness with which the grantors acceded to these requests adds to this suspicion: contrast the number of surviving *asylia* inscriptions with the very few inscribed grants of autonomy or tax exemption by kings. It has fairly been doubted, moreover, whether the kings or Rome would have allowed their subject cities to recognize inviolability if this had entailed a real military commitment.[76]

There were unambiguous means of seeking neutrality or military protection; in such an important matter an ambiguous request seems pointless. Thus an embassy could be sent to ask that the city be left alone in a prospective war: ἥ τε φιλί[α κ]αὶ ἡ εἰρήνη διατηρῆται καὶ μηδ' ὑ[φ'] ἑνὸς περι[σ]πωμένη ἡ πόλις.[77] And a state could promise not to attack a place, without declaring it "sacred and inviolable."[78] Or again, when Iasus asked Rhodes for aid in order to remain "free and autonomous," Rhodes responded with diplomatic, not military, help, and without an oath.[79] Greek cities had at their disposal clear diplomatic paths to security, of which the most familiar was the defensive alliance.

Thus, to describe crudely "sacred neutralization" as it has been envisaged: in the Hellenistic period the Greeks, realizing that they had lost their religion and were acting badly, in order to improve their behavior toward some places invented a pseudoreligious constraint on war—which they proceeded to ignore.

A pragmatic reading of these recognitions seems then to be fraught with difficulties. Scholars are understandably skeptical that strenuous effort might be devoted to gaining an "empty title"; it frustrates our desire to be tough-minded. Hence, especially regarding the cities' clamor for Roman confirmation, the speculation that wealth accrued to places that were allowed to receive fugitives, as in the Aradus story.[80] Of this proposition we may tough-mindedly ask for a cost accounting. How much money did a city spend in sending ambassadors through the Greek world, or later merely to Rome, in order to seek *asylia*, and how much money did it make from any "neutrality" that followed or from fugitives who actually opted to flee there?[81] In our assessment of what motivated a Greek civic government, profit seems a meager possibility; and profit to whom

75. For the continuing force of oaths in the Hellenistic period see Wörrle, *Chiron* 13 (1983) 310–313.

76. A. Giovannini in *Ancient Macedonia* II (Thessalonica 1977) 467–478.

77. *Syll.*^{3} 547.7–9, Athens to the Aetolians and to Philip V.

78. So *IG* II^2 1130 (= *I.Cret.* II xxx 3), so far as can be seen from its fragmentary state.

79. *I.Iasos* 150. On Hellenistic Rhodes as a neutral mediator see S. L. Ager, *Historia* 40 (1991) 10–41.

80. E.g., Magie I 505; Herrmann, *Chiron* 19 (1989) 155–156, doubting that prestige can be an adequate explanation.

81. When Henry VIII established eight "cities of refuge" for debtors (with strict limits and procedures) as a palliative to the more general abolition of privileges of asylum, first Manchester and then others of them protested vehemently against this unwanted burden, and the project was soon abandoned (see Thornley 204).

in the city? In default of a clear advantage deriving from the recognition, we might better take the inscriptions at their word, that the purpose was to add to the honor of the god and the city.

The phrase "merely honorific" would have struck most Greeks as paradoxical and bewildering.[82] There is no such thing as an empty title: words have meanings, whether they invoke the realm of economics or that of religion; and every title betokens a diplomatic success over one's rivals. The eager quest for civic titles so richly documented among the Greeks under Roman rule had to start somewhere and sometime; I am suggesting that it started here, in the first attested civic title "sacred and inviolable." We see the spirit of the thing in A.D. 22: when the Greek representatives appeared before the Senate, the Romans were embarrassed by the rivalries (*studiis certabatur*) and turned the matter over to a committee. The rivalries were among the cities themselves, their competing claims about the antiquity and dignity of their cults. The tone and substance of the debate are audible in the opening presentation by the provincial capital Ephesus (*non, ut vulgus crederet*, etc.); this shows clearly enough the locus of the sentiment for *asylia*—not military security or financial profit, but honor.

But against these objections to the view that *asylia* genuinely intended neutralization may be brought the charge of logic chopping, and the answer that human motives are complicated; nor should we be surprised that people do not practice what they preach. Logical inconsistency proves nothing: it is a fact of life, especially in religion. If tragedy and comedy are the forms of expression most appropriate to acknowledge and explore contradiction,[83] documents of state diplomacy, like the *asylia* inscriptions, are the least; in this arena one expects polite avoidance of probing or embarrassing questions. Inflated claims prove nothing: in California and Italy are cities that have proclaimed themselves "nuclear-free zones," a gesture not realistically enforceable by the civic authorities. A law or declaration causes problems only if someone tries to enforce it; experience in the United States shows that laws do not matter until they have been tested by the courts, and that legislatures are willing to pass laws that they know will not stand up in court. The universality and unanimity of the grantors of *asylia* prove nothing: compare the nuclear nonproliferation accord, urged upon all countries whether or not they might seriously be expected to acquire nuclear weapons. Redundancy proves nothing: the world of diplomacy is filled with many routes to the same end.[84] We may put a twist on Eisenhower's

82. Athens, we are told, from its beginnings had competed for primacy, honor, and glory: ἀεὶ περὶ πρωτείων καὶ τιμῆς καὶ δόξης ἀγωνιζομένην (Dem. 18.66, repeated at 203). Montaigne, *Essays* II 7, has it right.

83. See H. S. Versnel, *Inconsistencies in Greek and Roman Religion* I (Leiden 1990) 1–35, esp. 25.

84. On the juridical ambiguities in war and peace see Bickerman, *RPhil* 9 (1935) 21–22 (*Religions* 123–124). V. Ilari, *Guerra e diritto nel mondo antico* I (Milan 1980) 357–372, provides a roster of citations of rules of war, arranged by his categories.

dictum: every peace will astonish you. UNESCO maintains a World Heritage List of places whose historical monuments make them worthy of international protection. In 1992 the committee added Dubrovnic to the "In Danger" section in the hope that this might protect the city. The gesture proved ineffective, but it did not arise out of a random intention of adding honor to Dubrovnic.[85]

Let us admit therefore that religion and diplomacy are alike fraught with hope,[86] and also susceptible to frequent reinterpretation. To read the minds of all seekers and grantors of *asylia* at all dates is doubtless beyond our capacity. I would stress, however, both the ancients' own uncertainty about the "true" force of these declarations, as is illustrated by their successive interpretations of the title, and the common theme of honor seen throughout its history. I offer the following survey.

BEFORE HELLENISM

The roots of the quest for *asylia* lie not in the decay of morality or in military anarchy, but in some specifics of literature and myth. Spanheim saw the crucial passage but took it as part of a historical continuum rather than a classical literary exemplum that was exploited in a later and more self-conscious age. The juridical form, the vocabulary, and the logic of the Hellenistic grants echo the old story about Elis and the Olympic games. But the new usage was triggered by a real military event.

The only place that the Greeks declared immune from war in the classical period was Plataea in 479, and the intent of that gesture was subject to conflicting interpretation already in the fifth century, as we know from Thucydides. Similar stories of recognized immunity came to be fabricated about primeval Elis, Delphi, and Delos. Thus by the time of Alexander, it was traditional lore that certain peoples who presided over places of great sanctity, "common temples of the Greeks," had been granted by the Greeks to be allowed to live a sacred life,

85. This bears comparison with our topic both for its form and thought and for its intrinsic contradictions. See M. Batisse, *Environment* 34.10 (1992) 13–32, esp. 16: "Parties to the convention share responsibility for protection of the listed sites. This idea is particularly innovative in international law, especially because it involves immovable property. Thus, the convention expresses the revolutionary view that the whole of humanity must act as trustee for all the great landmarks of the natural and cultural history of the globe"; cf. 17 on the "awkward situation" that arises when a requesting national government overvalues or undervalues a place in the judgment of the committee. Dubrovnic was the first case of intervention by the committee without being requested by the relevant government.

86. Among the arguments that a Hellenistic historian attributed to Demosthenes for why Athens would win the war against Philip, the first is that "you will have the gods as your greatest allies and helpers, whose guarantees he has ignored and whose oaths he has violated by unjustly breaking the peace" ([Dem.] 11.2 = Anaximenes *FGrHist* 72 F 11b). This historian, one may add, knew that Philip won the war.

free of war. These peoples performed unique religious services for the Greeks, and the nearest example chronologically, the Plataeans, could by then be seen as conforming to an old pattern: their city marked the place of the salvation of Greek freedom, and they maintained the graves of those who fell against the Persians.

It is a feature of all these stories that the status no longer actually affected real life and the necessities of war and peace. Hence its replication and dissemination in Hellenistic times need not inconvenience anyone.

The Aegean Area, 260s to 182 B.C.

After Delphi was saved from the Gauls by the Greeks and their gods in 279 B.C.,[87] these classical precedents suggested a new institution, declared territorial inviolability. We see it first in Boeotia in the 260s under Delphian influence, the Amphictyony's declaration for the temple of Athena Itonia. To many this may well have been at first a seriously meant experiment in the complex world of war and peace. Our capacity for hindsight should not blind us to others' capacity for hope. But sooner or later most Greeks will have seen the military inconsequence of the recognitions, and what will have loomed larger was the visible diplomatic success that it entailed. In effect, the gesture became a form of civic honor, contemporary and parallel with the vogue for new Panhellenic games;[88] this was the first in what would become a long list of civic titles.

Geographically, the recipients are in the old Greek world and its fringe—the Aegean area and the great Hellenized cities of western Anatolia; the grantors are the whole of the Greek people, which came to include Rome in the early second century B.C.[89] The last directly attested recipient in this stage is the temple of Athena Nicephorus of Pergamum in 182 B.C. Through the third century B.C., this honor went mostly to temples; but early on, in the 240s, the mold was broken when the city of Smyrna, not just its temple of Aphrodite, was declared sacred and inviolable.

In this period the recognition of Panhellenic games often accompanied the recognition of *asylia*; here was a clear and tangible emblem of the Panhellenic patronage of a cult. At Miletus the two are expressly linked in the diplomatic argument (p. 175); the initial failure of Magnesia in 221 B.C. suggests that there was by then a felt standard by which to judge requests for *asylia*. Like the cities

87. "A crisis like the Celtic invasion in the third century B.C. could evoke a fresh awakening of religious emotion," A. D. Nock, *Conversion* (Oxford 1933) 22; cf. 279.

88. The spread of "crowned" games in the Hellenistic period is surveyed by Robert, *Op. min. sel.* VI 710–719.

89. In 228 B.C.the Romans had been allowed to participate in the Isthmian games, which in effect declared them to be Greek (Polyb. 2.12.8; cf. *I.Délos* 1660: Ἀθηναίων καὶ Ῥωμαίων καὶ τῶν ἄλλων Ἑλλήνων). But their recognition of *asylia* does not seem to have been sought until Rome became involved seriously in Anatolia in the 190s.

that today compete annually for the title "All-America City" or seek to host the Olympic Games, the petitioner had to make a case, and apparently most cities chose not to make that effort.[90] Where games were wanting, sometimes we can see other items that bespeak more than local patronage: at Teos, the presence of the Artists of Dionysus, themselves inviolable; at Tenos, possibly elevation to the meeting place of the League of the Islanders. Often, however, no such concrete emblem of wide patronage is evident to us; the earliest such instance is Smyrna, already in the 240s.

This age had opened with the rebuilding of Thebes, the "refoundation" of the Panhellenic Eleutheria at Plataea, and the defense of Delphi against the Gauls, but also with the flow of power and opportunity to a new colonial world in the East. In the civic title "sacred and inviolable," which in effect asserted that one's own place was comparable to Olympia and Delphi and Plataea, a "common temple of the Greeks," we can see a spirit of self-assertion on the part of the Greek city-states in the face of this new situation of relative powerlessness. We may regard this quest as plucky or pathetic, depending on our own view of what is important in the historical process. In practice the declarations cost no one anything, and the irrelevance of the political alignments of grantors and recipients has long been noted with interest:[91] mortal enemies were unanimous in these recognitions. The one refusal on record is stated to reflect the inadequacy of the Magnesians' proposed honors for Artemis (**66**).

The Hellenistic East after 141 B.C.

Around 170 B.C. Antiochus IV of Syria allowed a good many cities in his kingdom a municipal bronze coinage, on which they put their ethnics. Not one of the cities here claims inviolability or any granted title.[92] Likewise Alexander Balas (150–145) granted local coinage rights to a smaller number of cities, and these still have no titles—including Seleuceia, which was to display ἱερᾶς καὶ ἀσύλου in 139/8. In view of the subsequent eagerness of the cities of this region to display their titles, these bronzes under Antiochus and Alexander supply a reliable terminus post quem for the arrival of inviolability in Syria-Phoenicia: the status did not exist there before 145 B.C.

The honor spreads thereafter through Syria and Palestine and Cilicia, accelerating toward the end of the second century B.C. As our evidence for this

90. Some omissions deserve speculation. Athens and Rhodes, well documented in the inscriptions, evidently never sought *asylia*, despite having arguably worthy cults (Eleusis, Athena Lindia); perhaps this reflects conservatism, an unwillingness to participate in a new fad (cf. Robert, *Op. min. sel.* V 149, on their not using foreign judges; C. Habicht, *Vestigia* 49 [1995] 91, on Athens' refusal to bury Marcellus inside the city walls).

91. Robert, *Op. min. sel.* II 781; Bickerman, *REA* 40 (1938) 373; Bousquet, *BCH* 64/5 (1940/1) 106; Nachtergael, *Les Galates* 335.

92. See p. 37, however, for the case of Byblos.

period consists primarily of titles and not the actual grants, we cannot be sure of the identity of the grantors. Probably they were only the relevant rulers of these cities, and not the Greek people approached by *theoroi*; for such missions might be expected to have left some trace in the abundant epigraphy of Delphi, as they had earlier. The link with Panhellenic games frequently seen in the Aegean area is not visible now. In this period we also begin to see granted inviolability in Egypt, where the inscriptions show that only the king was the grantor (as does the one Seleucid grant for a temple not in the territory of a city but on royal land, **218**).

The sequence of honor makes it clear that "sacred and inviolable" was a lesser prize than "autonomy": it is obtained earlier and on the coins yields its place to autonomy when space is lacking. It is questionable whether the granting of inviolability constituted a real loss of power to the king. The traditional reading of civic inviolability as betokening the decline of Seleucid power is valid in this sense: the title spreads in the context of the competition of the rival monarchs for the loyalty of the cities; but it was that competition, not some significant waiving of authority by the declaration of *asylia*, that caused the Seleucid decline. I suggest that what the kings were granting was honor, not power. We may compare the inflation in court titles in the late Hellenistic monarchies ("first friend," etc.): these titles reveal the king's favor and perhaps the recipient's influence at court, but they surrendered no specified power.

The Republican Provinces

With the coming of Roman provincial administration, Rome supplanted Greek public opinion as the highest source of law and became final arbiter of questions of status. Romans, when asked for confirmation, granted what they thought *asylia* meant—a temple's right of asylum, temporary refuge from civil law; and accordingly that is what it did mean henceforth, as far as the Roman authorities were concerned. The extant acts now are almost all confirmations, not new rights, and by Rome alone.[93] It seems therefore that the Romans were already uneasy about the matter once they found themselves responsible for the consequences; the Senate in A.D. 22 was enlarging upon an old uneasiness.

Support of Mithridates in the 80s B.C. cost many Greek cities their privileges, including the *asylia* of temples; the great dynasts of the last generation of the Republic, acting as benefactors to their Greek supporters, restored much of these losses, most systematically the dictator Caesar in the 40s through the agency of Servilius Isauricus in Asia.[94] At Ephesus in the time of Augustus the *asylia* of

93. A probable exception on both scores is the temple of Hecate at Stratoniceia in 81 B.C., which Panhellenic recognition rendered inviolable; Aphrodisias, with its special relationship with Rome, may also represent a new grant in the first century B.C.; and Soli-Pompeiopolis in Cilicia and Nicopolis in Epirus may owe their titles to their founders.

94. Cf. J. and L. Robert, *Hellenica* VI (1948) 37–42.

Artemis was felt to cause a problem for public order; this attracted the emperor's strictures and perhaps established a precedent for the review of A.D. 22.

The Roman Empire

Inviolability continues to be seen in Greek civic titulature into the late third century—as long as civic coinage lasts. But we can claim no certain addition to the list of inviolable places in imperial times: no new recognition is extant on stone, and the title "sacred and inviolable" on coins, because it is displayed so selectively, is not adequate evidence to show a new privilege as distinct from a traditional one intermittently advertised. I conclude that in A.D. 22 the Senate ratified existing rights but forbade the creation of new asylums. This has been my assumption in interpreting the Roman material: but it cannot be excluded that some emperor broke with tradition and granted the title anew—Hadrian, for example, under whom we see so many places advertising *asylia* for the first time (though I take this as a by-product of the expanded right of coining), or some emperor in the third century.[95]

As to refuge, the Roman government may in effect have abolished this in Greek cities. That would be a surprising intrusion by the central government into the legal affairs of the cities; but in fact attestations of flight to a temple in the Roman Empire are quite few. There was moreover the palliative of statues of the emperor. And there soon came to be a further palliative in the new civic title *neokoros*. This might be said to succeed and to upstage *asylia* in two senses: the neocorate temples, because they housed the cult of the emperor, had the right of asylum; and as an honor and object of competition, the *neokoria* came to be the new religious entitlement to seek, to be selected as the province's host for the provincial temple of the emperor, a cult of more than local patronage for a god honored by all the Greeks.

This matter ended with paganism.[96] But in late antiquity imperial legislation granting the right of asylum to Christian churches became part of the legal inheritance of medieval Europe and was often cited by the church in order to guard its jurisdiction over its own properties against intrusion by secular government.

95. Attractive possibilities for a new grant in imperial times are Aezani, Trajanopolis, Capitolias, Dura-Europus. It is well known that the second century A.D. witnessed a classicizing affectation (see Nilsson, *GGR* II 721, for its religious side); but this archaism cannot tell us whether signaling the title on coins indicates the new acquisition of it, imperial renewal of a title formerly enjoyed, or merely the local advertising of an ancient title that had never been lost.

96. For us, it virtually ends with the cessation of Greek civic coinage in the 270s A.D. and our best evidence on civic titulature; but see the case of Perge.

The Documents

TERMINOLOGY

Thanks above all to the work of Schlesinger and of Gauthier, the Greek terminology for legal immunity is well studied and well understood. I focus here on what is pertinent to the inviolability of places. In Latin the meaning and use of the key term are straightforward: there is only the noun, *asylum*, with only one meaning, a sacred place in which one can take refuge from pursuers. The noun is concrete, not abstract: *ius asyli* is a genitive of analogy, "the right of an asylum," comparable to *ius Latii*. There is no cognate adjective; what served to render ἱερὰ καὶ ἄσυλος, the formula that emerges suddenly in Greek in the third century B.C., was *sanctus et inviolatus / inviolabilis*.[1]

The word itself was of course borrowed from Greek; but Greek usage was different and more complicated. To express "refuge," καταφυγή and its verb were conventional and versatile, applicable to the place or the act, and to the sacred or the profane; less common was ἀποστροφή (e.g., Xen. *An.* 2.4.22). When the Septuagint translators wanted a special word to designate the "cities of refuge" prescribed in Numbers, they coined φυγαδευτήριον; they did not avail themselves of the phrase "sacred and inviolable" that was spreading among eastern cities in their own time.[2] Neither does Polybius when he describes the treaty relationship that some cities had with Rome whereby they could receive

1. An early instance at Caes. *BGall.* 3.9.3, of envoys. A mannered writer, wanting to echo the Greek more literally, used a quite recherché term, *inspoliatus* : [Sall.] *Resp.* 1.2.7, in the civil war men fled to Pompey "as debtors use a sacred and inviolable temple," *quasi sacro et inspoliato fano debitores usi* (for this analogy cf. Cic. *QRosc.* 30: *sicut in aram confugit in huius domum*). *Inspoliatus* means "unplundered," not "unplunderable," at Verg. *Aen.* 11.594 and Quint. 7.1.33. Cf. Tac. *Hist.* 4.58.6: *castra incorrupta et intemerata servari.*

2. LXX Num. 35:6: "You will give the Levites six cities of refuge (ἓξ πόλεις τῶν φυγαδευτηρίων) which you will give to the murderer to flee there"; 11–15 (only unintentional

Roman exiles with impunity: ἑκούσιον ... φυγαδεῖαν· ἔστι δ' ἀσφάλεια τοῖς φεύγουσιν ἔν τε τῇ Νεαπολιτῶν καὶ Πραινεστίνων ἔτι δὲ Τιβουρίνων πόλει καὶ ταῖς ἄλλαις πρὸς ἃς ἔχουσιν ὅρκια.[3] Such a treaty relationship, not sacred inviolability, is also what the Seleucid monarchy is said to have established with Aradus (for which Strabo offers no noun; see above, p. 11).

The privative of συλᾶν, to "plunder," is first attested in the adjective, ἄσυλος. Widely applied, it is not of itself a religious term,[4] and it can be either descriptive or prescriptive, "unviolated" or "inviolable." The earliest occurrence is in the Naupactians' law on land tenure around 500 B.C.: "Whatever someone plants, he is to be inviolable" for it, not subject to legal seizure.[5] In literature it appears first in Parmenides' poem, applied to Being, which cannot be increased or diminished: ἐπεὶ πᾶν ἐστιν ἄσυλον, οἷ γὰρ πάντοθεν ἶσον.[6] Medea calculates where she might find a γῆν ἄσυλον to which to flee; it did not need, or prove, to be literally sacred land, only Athens.[7] For her, as for any number of refugees, safety was gained by crossing a political boundary, so long as her host agreed not to send her back.

The noun ἀσυλία is abstract and has no Latin parallel: one grants, recognizes, *asylia*.[8] This was a privilege commonly granted to a foreigner by a city, immunity

---

murder is thus protected from the avenger, with trial guaranteed), 32 (refuge not to be purchased); cf. Deut. 4:41–43, 19:1–7; Josh. 20–21; 1 Chron. 6:57, 67.

3. Polyb. 6.14.8; bibliography at Walbank, *Comm.* I 682–683.

4. The people of Toulouse achieved ἀσυλία for their gold by putting it at the bottoms of lakes: Poseid. *FGrHist* 87 F 33. Cf. Theoph. Sym. 2.7: χώρους τινὰς ... οὐχ ἥκιστα ἀσύλους owing to their fortifications.

5. *IG* IX.1^2 609.6–9 (= M./L. 13; R. Koerner, *Inschriftliche Gesetzestexte* [Cologne 1993] 47).

6. 8.47–48 D.-K. For "unalterable" compare the famous poem from Rome concerning the sacred precinct established by Herodes Atticus: ἱερὴν ἀνὰ γαῖαν ἔηκε ... ἀνδράσιν ὀψιγόνοισιν ἀκινήτην καὶ ἄσυλον ἔμμεναι (*IGUrbRom* III 1155.71–74). Antiochus I of Commagene, dedicating villages to the gods, stipulates that the revenue is "an inviolable possession of the gods" (κτῆμα ἄσυλον δαιμόνων, *IGLSyrie* I 1.199–200 = *OGIS* 383), just as his statement is written in inviolable letters on sanctified pillars (8) or inviolable steles (110). Cf. Theodoret Cyr. *Rel. hist.* praef.: ἄσυλος ἔμενε ... ἡ μνήμη (*PG* 82.1284B).

7. Eur. *Med.* 386–388: τίς με δέξεται πόλις; τίς γῆν ἄσυλον καὶ δόμους ἐχεγγύους ξένος παρασχὼν ῥύσεται τοὐμὸν δέμας; answered at 728 (μενεῖς ἄσυλος) and in the lyric praise of Athens at 825–826 (ἱερᾶς χώρας ἀπορθήτου τε). "Unviolated" at Eur. *Hel.* 61 and 1587 and Pl. *Leg.* 866D; cf. Moretti, *I. stor. ellen.* II 76, officials praised because they rendered the meeting place of the Amphictyony secure, τὴν] Πυλαίαν ἄσυλον καὶ ἀσφαλῆ παρεσκεύ[ασαν.

8. An exception is found at Jos. *AJ* 16.168: in an (apocryphal) edict of Agrippa to Ephesus, those who steal the sacred moneys of the Jews and flee into *asyliai* (καταφεύγοντας ... εἰς τὰς ἀσυλίας) can be seized, by the same law as for *hierosyloi*. An expression "right of *asylia*" (e.g., τὰ δίκαια τῆς ἀσυλίας) would be redundant and does not seem to occur in Greek. Schol. Ar. *Thesm.* 224, ἄσυλον γὰρ εἶχον οἱ καταλαμβάνοντες τὰ ἱερὰ τῶν Ἐρινύων, may reflect a late date and Latin influence; but J. Jaenisch (*De Graecorum asylis* [Göttingen 1868] 27 n. 1) would emend to ἀσυλίαν.

from reprisal and seizure, often phrased as the right to import and export ἀσυλεὶ καὶ ἀσπονδεὶ in war and peace.[9] This meant that when a foreign city had some claim against his own, or when the two states were at war, he was nonetheless immune from seizure by the foreign city. This was not a technical term, and one used synonyms easily.[10] Nor was there any connection with cult in this privilege—that is, there is nothing religious about it: a merchant (say) granted *asylia* was in no way sacred, and the consequence of the grant was purely juridical: access to the courts of the foreign city.

A literal equivalent of the Latin *asylum*, a concrete noun τὸ ἄσυλον meaning a τόπος ἄσυλος, is altogether rare,[11] and virtually confined to Ptolemaic Egypt; the Latin term can be reckoned an instance of Egypt's prominence in the Hellenism of Rome. We find some part of the temple of Poseidon outside Carystus in Euboea called the ἄσυλον,[12] but this can have no bearing on the Panhellenic declarations of *asylia* for entire sites; perhaps it is merely the "holy of holies" that many temples had, under various names, or some adjunct building.[13]

By contrast, a new phrase emerges suddenly in documents of the third century B.C., when, in a novel diplomatic gesture, places are declared inviolable. Normal usage in these documents is that a temple is declared ἄσυλον, a city

9. For the right of reprisal and the problems it raises for the historian see Gauthier, *Symbola* 209–284; B. Bravo, *AnnPisa* X.3 (1980) 675–987, with Gauthier, *RHD* 60 (1982) 553–576.

10. Thus in otherwise identical decrees honoring soldiers in 208 B.C., Lilaea uses ἀσυλία and ἀσφάλεια interchangeably (ἀ. πολέμου καὶ εἰρήνης, *FD* III.4 132–135; cf. Gauthier, *Les cités grecques et leurs bienfaiteurs* [Paris 1985] 164–169; O. Masson, *REG* 106 [1993] 163–167). So too the Amphictyonic decree *IG* II^2 1132: ἀσυλία (9), ἀσφάλεια (12; cf. Daux, *Delphes* 357 n. 3; Flacelière, *Aitoliens* 121 n. 3). In the treaty of friendship between Sardes and Miletus *Staatsvertr.* III 407, movement ἀσυλεὶ καὶ ἀσπονδεί (8) is then called ἀσφάλεια (14); in *IG* VII 302 (Oropus) ἀσυλίαν καὶ τὴν λοιπὴν ἀσφάλειαν πᾶσαν.

11. Themist. *Or.* 15.190c (I 275.22 Downey), εἰς τὰ ἄσυλα τῶν ἱερῶν, reflects Roman law, for by now it was true that only some temples had the "right of asylum"; cf. Philostorg. 12.3: εἴς τε τῶν ἀσύλων ἱερὸν καταφυγεῖν (A.D. 408); HA *Heliog.* 2.3: *in templum dei Heliogabali confugisse, velut in asylum.* See also on Amyzon and Stratoniceia, and p.90.

12. T. W. Jacobsen and P. M. Smith, *Hesperia* 37 (1968) 189: decree to be erected ἐν τῶι ἱερῶι τοῦ Ποσειδᾶνος τοῦ Γεραιστίου ἐν τῶι ἀσύλωι. On the temple see R. W. M. Schumacher, in *Greek Sanctuaries*, ed. N. Marinatos and R. Hågg (London/New York 1993) 77–80 (citing Γεραίστιοι καταφυγαί at Eur. *Cyc.* 295). At Megalopolis, in a fragmentary context, ἐ]ν τῶι ἀσύλ[ω]ι (*Syll.*^{3} 665.29); at Chrysippus *SVF* II 1000 (Gell. 7.2.13) *perfugiunt ad fati necessitatem tamquam in aliquod fani asylum.*

13. E.g., Dion. Hal. *Ant. Rom.* 1.69.1: νεών τε καὶ ἄδυτον; glossed by 67.1: ναοῦ χωρίον ἔχοντος ἄβατον; cf. 69.3: ἐν ἀβάτῳ; Polyb. 16.12.7: τὸ τοῦ Διὸς ἄβατον (Arcadia); in Egypt *P.Lond.* VII 1975 (of Demeter); *OGIS* 56.59: ἐν τῶι ἁγίωι and *OGIS* 90: ἄδυτον (those who clothe the statue can go into the *adyton*; cf. *I.Sardis* 22); cf. Robert, *Op. min. sel.* V 498–500. The inner sanctum, however, would be a strange place to publish an inscription; a decree of Callatis was inscribed εἰς τὸν ἐπιφανέστατον τοῦ μυχοῦ τόπον (*Dacia* 1 [1924] 139 no. 2.41–42), but the character of this "interior" is uncertain. On Plot. 1.6.7.4 (τὰ ἅγια τῶν ἱερῶν) see E. R. Dodds, *Pagan and Christian* (Cambridge 1965) 94 n. 4.

and its territory ἱερὰ καὶ ἄσυλος.[14] The pair became a catch phrase by the end of the Hellenistic period, applied metaphorically to many things praised as sacrosanct. Philo is exceedingly fond of the phrase; a Roman of Martial's time had a pair of slaves named Hierus and Asylus;[15] in the third century a city in Lydia claimed to have a "sacred and inviolable worldwide festival."[16] Synonyms found in the authors, such as ἀπόρθητος,[17] are almost unknown in the documents.

Modern scholars often call these texts "treaties" and seek some pragmatic motive on the part of a grantor for establishing such a relationship with the other state. In fact, in both form and vocabulary, the documents are not treaties and are not bilateral. They are unilateral "recognitions" of a fact, the inviolability of a place. This, we sometimes are told, is "added to the laws" of the grantor; like laws, these acts contain no oaths to guarantee the behavior of the grantor. At least in the third century B.C., the grants were usually obtained from as wide a spectrum of the Greek people as the recipient could canvas; hence the identity and "motive" of any one grantor cannot be invoked as the occasion or explanation of the act. The recipient initiated these doings.

PROBLEMATIC EVIDENCE

Ordinary Greek respect for sacred space is not the subject of this book: it is not therefore a collection of every episode in which someone takes refuge in a temple, whether successfully or not. Our topic is *declared* inviolability. Various difficulties, however, attend the proper definition of the evidence for this.

14. The order "inviolable and sacred" is found in **163**; cf. **100**.33–34; **129**.18; **154**.32; **157**.13. So too Plut. *Ti. Gracch.* 21.5 (of the tribune of the plebs; the usual order at 14.4 and 15.2); *Arist.* 21.2 (Plataea); *Mor.* 604A (the isolation of an exile can be an "inviolable and sacred life"), 270F–271A (the wall of Rome is ἀβέβηλον καὶ ἱερόν = ἱερόν = ἄβατον καὶ ἱερόν τόπον); cf. 760C (defend lovers "as though inviolable and untouchable temples," ὥσπερ ἱεροῖς ἀσύλοις καὶ ἀθίκτοις). In Latin, Cic. *Verr.* 2.4.103: the temple of Juno on Malta *tanta religione semper fuit ut non modo illis Punicis bellis . . . sed etiam hac praedonum multitudine semper inviolatum* ("unviolated") *sanctumque*; Sil. Ital. 16.16: *inviolabile . . . sacrumque caput*; Gell. 6.18.1: *inviolate sancteque.*

15. *Ep.* 9.103, with *CIL* VI 280 and 30728. The personal name Ἄσυλος: in Latin, citations at *TLL* II 991, where it is called a slave name. See, however, *IG* II^2 3799 (an Athenian doctor) and *SGDI* 2057 (a citizen of Amphissa), both late Hellenistic.

16. Malay, *I. Manisa Museum* 48: panegyriarch of τῆς ἱερᾶς καὶ ἀσύλου οἰκουμενικῆς πανηγύρεως τῶν Κερδανετῶν.

17. E.g., Aesch. *Pers.* 349 ("Is the city of the Athenians still unplundered?"); Eur. *Med.* 825–826, quoted above (p. 31); *Hell. Oxy.* 16.3 (not the region previously attacked but "another one that was unplundered"); *Anth. Gr.* 9.151.7 (at Corinth only the Nereids are unplundered); Dion. Hal. *Ant. Rom.* 1.68.4 (Troy unplunderable thanks to the Palladium); Diod. 36.5.3 (Lilybaeum an impregnable city); Marin. *V.Procli* 27 (temple of Asclepius still unplundered). For φύξιμος see p. 48.

1. Many cases of *asylia* are known to us only through titles seen on coins, and these often date only from the Roman imperial period. Inscribing civic titles on coins came to be a habit in the East in the second century B.C., and it spread elsewhere only in imperial times and often halfheartedly. What is the import of this sort of evidence for the date of the recognition?

First, the silence of coins needs to be carefully assessed. It is clear that cities might be selective in their display of titles, and the selections tend to exhibit a hierarchy.[18] In late Hellenistic times, a city that is first "sacred and inviolable" and later "autonomous" will give all three words when there is space, but when there is not will abbreviate the first title, so as to produce "sacred and autonomous," or omit it entirely and inscribe only "autonomous." This represents not the loss of inviolability but the fact that "sacred" alone will serve for the whole title when space is wanting,[19] and when not even that much will fit the more prestigious title was displayed. In a city of the Roman Empire, neocoria is more prized than *asylia*, and colonial status more prized than both: a colony will typically supplant all previous Greek honors with the emblems and language of Rome. And in Roman times traditional titles inscribed on coins can appear and disappear in successive years or even the same year; this is not evidence for changes in status.

Hellenistic coins are more consistent in their advertising, when indeed cities had fewer honors among which to select. But even in the Hellenistic period we find occasional silences that are meaningless, or abbreviations or condensation that can obscure the evidence. A clear instance of abbreviation is Tyre between 140 and 126; of omission, Beirut, and probably Antioch between 93 and 48 B.C.

The tendency to abbreviate is usually unproblematic for us: when on the coins of some city ΙΕΡΑΣ or even ΙΕΡ alternates indifferently with ΙΕΡΑΣΥ or ΙΕΡΑΣΥΛ, we can easily recognize all these as abbreviations for ἱερᾶς καὶ ἀσύλου. Some scholars have treated these as two titles, distinct and separable.[20] Seyrig, who has been widely followed, argued that they were in fact sequential as well as distinct: that a city must first be declared "sacred" by its sovereign and

18. Seyrig, *Scripta numism.* 262; cf. *Ant. syr.* IV 74 (autonomy tends to take precedence). Cf. A. Houghton and S. Bendall, *ANSMN* 33 (1988) 72 n. 4 (silences are meaningless by the late first century B.C.).

19. Ascalon is unique in sometimes omitting "sacred" rather than "inviolable." In the inscribed recognitions sometimes only one of the two words is used (e.g., **88**.37, and often in the Tean material).

20. In particular Bickerman, *Institutions* 154–155; Rostovtzeff, *SEHHW* 845 ("by becoming 'holy' the city perhaps acquired certain privileges in respect of royal taxation; by being *asylos* it may have been exempted from royal jurisdiction"); recently, see, for example, A. Mastrocinque, *AttiVen* 135 (1976–77) 18; G. Dagron and D. Feissel, *Inscriptions de Cilicie* (Paris 1987) 73 ("le double privilège de consécration et d'asylie").

then would seek from the rest of the Greek world recognition as "inviolable."[21] He thought to prove this from several instances where ΙΕΡΑΣ seems to be found earlier than ΙΕΡΑΣΥ or the like. But the instances that he alleged are of dubious chronology, and his thesis ignored the extent and randomness of abbreviation.[22] More important, there is no inscribed example of the procedure that he envisaged; in particular, he was mistaken in thinking that Seleucid kings did not declare their own cities "inviolable," only "sacred." To the contrary, inscriptions by the score make explicit that "sacred and inviolable" is one item, granted in a stroke, and not two recognitions distinct in substance, juridical origin, and date. The phrase means "sacred and (therefore) inviolable," and where space was lacking on a coin, "sacred" was sufficient to imply the whole.[23]

The habit of putting titles on coins started in one region, Syria-Phoenicia, and never became universal even in Roman times. Not a few cases of *asylia* are known only by coin evidence of Roman date, sometimes quite late—typically in areas where inscriptions are few and also coins of Hellenistic date. This silence too I take as meaningless, for in several instances the chance survival of an early inscription reveals that the grant of inviolability dates to the Hellenistic period and is not new when we first see it on the coins centuries later (e.g., Soli-Pompeiopolis). Likewise, some cities exhibit inviolability on coins after a hiatus of even centuries after first signaling it in the Hellenistic period; such silences cannot safely be taken to represent abolition and restoration of the title. By contrast, the many inscriptions of the Roman Empire have revealed no new grant of inviolability. Accordingly my assumption is that the review of A.D. 22/3 led to the ending of new grants of *asylia*, and that all known instances of the title derive form Hellenistic grants; but I would stress that for many cases this cannot be demonstrated.

We have seen the traditional rhetorical flourish of calling a city "holy." At a few cities, it happens that no more than ΙΕΡ or ΙΕΡΑΣ is ever found on

21. *Syria* 12 (1939) 35–39 (*Ant. syr.* III 1–5); accepted: e.g., Bickerman, *RPhil* 65 (1939) 339 n. 3 (*Religions* 219); Gauthier, *Symbola* 224–226; contra: Herrmann, "Antiochos" 129. Seyrig's examples were Seleuceia, Ascalon, and Sidon. (Aware that some cities did not have sovereigns, Seyrig thought that these would declare themselves sacred. Were it so easy, what city would not?)

22. The best evidence for distinguishing the two terms is in fact verbal: Dagron/Feissel 134 no. 86: ὁ δῆμος Ἀδριανῶν Μοψεατῶν τῆς ἱερᾶς καὶ ἐλευθέρας καὶ ἀσύλου καὶ αὐτονόμου (below, p. 470); **153**.20: ἱεράν, καθὼς καὶ νῦν ἐστιν, καὶ ἄσυλον.

23. Cf. **88**.37. An epigraphical example from a different institution: a tribune of the plebs is frequently called "sacred and inviolable" in Greek, but in *Mon.Anc.* 5.17 Augustus is voted tribunician power ἵνα ἱερὸς ὦι / *sacrosanctus ut essem* ; compare Dion. Hal. *Ant. Rom.* 9.1.4, where the tribune is simply ἱερὸν ὄντα. Here too the implication is that the full phrase has the logic "sacred and therefore inviolable."

the coins.[24] I have included these as representing declared inviolability, but it is possible that this is no more than that flourish, which is not confined to literature but can be found in inscriptions of imperial date. Where there is ambiguity, I have left the text in majuscules, as ΙΕΡΑΣ might be either ἱερᾶς or ἱερ(ᾶς) ἀσ(ύλου). I have not, however, included in the corpus the instances in which political organs are called "sacred": the sacred *boule* or *demos*,[25] or indeed "sacred" of the imperial house; these reflect the rhetoric of the age and do not derive from some formal declaration.

Second, the referent of the adjective is a problem. Inscriptions are of course explicit in recognizing either the temple or the city and country. Most coins apply the title of inviolability to the city-state; for example, Σελευκέων τῆς ἱερᾶς καὶ ἀσύλου, where the implied feminine noun is taken to be πόλεως.[26] How literally should we take this? The great god of Antioch, Apollo of Daphne, had his temple outside the city proper; the usual Hellenistic practice would suggest that the temple, not the city and country, was declared inviolable, and Malalas supports this. But the coins later show Ἀντιοχέων τῆς ἱερᾶς καὶ ἀσύλου καὶ αὐτονόμου. Moreover, what the Roman Empire allowed to be inviolable were temples, not whole cities with their territories: the coin legends in imperial times simply cannot be literal, because all rights of asylum, whatever their form before Roman rule, had been reduced to the relevant temple precinct. The case of Mopsuestia is explicit: before and during Roman rule, the coins show Μοψεατῶν τῆς ἱερᾶς καὶ ἀσύλου; but a Roman confirmation inscribed on stone reveals that what enjoyed *asylia* by then was a temple of Isis, not the city and country. Thus the civic title does not allow us to deduce with confidence the form of the original grant—temple versus city and country. That the phrase is ambiguous on this score, whether the grant of inviolability was to temple or to city and country, testifies to the unity of the topic. Note, however, that no definitive instance of overlap is on record—namely, where we have both the original grant on stone (Mopsuestia is a Roman renewal, Antioch is on the dubious authority of Malalas) and later coins that give τῆς ἱερᾶς καὶ ἀσύλου.

The possible exception is the unusual application of the adjective directly to the god—"inviolable Artemis," for instance (so at Ephesus, Nicaea, Perge, Side, and Sillyum; cf. Aphrodisias). This may be an explicit statement that the right

24. So Epidaurus, Nicopolis in Cilicia, Hyde, Selinus, Mallus, Olba, Damascus, Byblos, Raphia, Nicopolis in Epirus.

25. ἱερὸς δῆμος: e.g., Hadrianeia (*von Aulock* 1130–1131), Hadrianotherae (1147), Aezani (3336), Cadi (*BMC Phrygia* 117–118), Acmoneia (*von Aulock* 8311), Daldis (8223), Laodicea on the Lycus (8414), Aphrodisias (2444), Tralles (3281–3283), Tabae (*La Carie* II pp. 139, 146), Apollonia Salbace (*La Carie* p. 267). Perge may be exceptional, cf. p. 451. On this usage see J. H. Oliver, *The Sacred Gerousia*, Hesperia Suppl. 6 (Athens 1941), esp. 28–38.

26. Note, however, at Nysa-Scythopolis Νυσαέων τῶν καὶ Σκυθοπολιτῶν τῆς ἱερᾶς καὶ ἀσύλου . . . ἡ πόλις (p. 538).

pertained from the start to the temple rather than to the city and country; but as no instance of this usage dates from before Roman rule, when only temples come into the question, caution is in order.

Byblos in Phoenicia presents a special problem. The convention of using civic titles seems to have originated in Phoenicia. Among the municipal coinages granted by Antiochus IV ca. 170 B.C., Tyre, Sidon, and Byblos show titles in Phoenician, the first in the history of money: Tyre is "mother of the Sidonians"; Sidon is "mother of Cambe, Hippo, Citium, and Tyre"; Byblos is "the holy" ("in Gebal the holy"). This last may pertain to our topic, and I have included Byblos in the corpus. Later, Byblos put Βύβλου ΙΕΡΑΣ on its coins; this may well mean ἱερ(ᾶς) ἀσ(ύλου), but the consistent use of the form ΙΕΡΑΣ and the attested Phoenician precedent are suggestive: this title may reflect a different origin from the Hellenistic Greek declared title "sacred and inviolable." The alternative would be troubling: if the Phoenician inscription indeed represents declared inviolability, then little Byblos would be the first city outside the Aegean to win it, anticipating great cities like Tyre and Seleuceia. I think it more likely that, like Tyre and Sidon in 170, Byblos is making a claim rooted in Phoenician history and myth, which only accidentally looks like the granted Greek title that (to judge from the rest of our evidence) began to spread in this area only a generation later.

Finally, the coins are silent on another score—cult. In the recognitions preserved on stone, it is repeatedly explicit that *asylia* depends upon a cult and marks the special sacredness of a place; this cannot be proved for most of the cases in the Greek East, where normally all that we see is the use of the civic title "sacred and inviolable." We have explicit instances of the cultic connection only at Mopsuestia and (probably) at Antioch. In commenting on each case I have remarked on the chief cult of the city, but the relevance of this, and the correct identification of the god honored by the title, is in most cases suppositious. No one would deduce from the coins or any other testimony that *asylia* at Mopsuestia came in honor of Isis, as the inscribed recognition shows.

2. In some instances of the phrase ἱερὸν ἄσυλον, it is difficult to be confident whether or not this betokens the Panhellenic declaration. I have included **228**, thinking that in a Ptolemaic edict the word ἄσυλον would not be idle, but have relegated **230** among the doubtful cases. These two foundation texts are quite similar; and there is no other instance in the corpus of a new temple obtaining inviolability, which normally marks a cult of established and widespread patronage. If these two have an affinity that sets them apart from other recognitions, that may be consistent with the suggested literary origin of **228**.

A speech found in Polybius presents a similar problem. The Acarnanian at Sparta in 211 alleges that "inviolable temples" were plundered by the evil Aetolians (9.34.8–10):

οἵ γε καὶ τοῖς ἀσύλοις ἱεροῖς ἐτόλμησαν προσάγειν τὰς χεῖρας. ὧν Τίμαιος μὲν τό τ' ἐπὶ Ταινάρῳ τοῦ Ποσειδῶνος καὶ τὸ τῆς ἐν Λούσοις ἱερὸν Ἀρτέμιδος ἐσύλησε, Φάρυκος δὲ καὶ Πολύκριτος, ὁ μὲν τὸ τῆς Ἥρας ἐν Ἄργει τέμενος, ὁ δὲ τὸ τοῦ Ποσειδῶνος ἐν Μαντινείᾳ διήρπασε.

. . .

These dared to lay their hands even upon inviolable temples: Timaeus plundered that of Poseidon at Taenarum and the temple of Artemis at Lusi, Pharycus robbed the precinct of Hera at Argos, Polycritus that of Poseidon at Mantineia.

Does this mean temples of a certain legislated class, or just "holy temples," that is, all temples?[27] The claim here is partisan and inflammatory, and I believe that this list must be regarded with caution as testimony for declared inviolability. Elsewhere Polybius may make an explicit reference to such declarations (4.18.9–12): the temple of Artemis at Lusi "is considered inviolable among the Greeks" (ἄσυλον δὲ νενόμισται παρὰ τοῖς Ἕλλησιν); and an extant Aetolian decree of personal inviolability for the Lusiates may be relevant. I discuss Lusi and Taenarum (on which there is other evidence) in the corpus but have not taken Polybius' list as sufficient evidence for the other two.

Again, writers on Pompey's campaign against the pirates preserve a tradition about their depredations.[28] According to Plutarch (*Pomp.* 24.4–5) they took 1,000 ships and 400 cities and plundered temples that had heretofore been unviolated, which he lists:

τῶν δὲ ἀσύλων καὶ ἀβάτων πρότερον ἱερῶν ἐξέκοψαν ἐπιόντες τὸ Κλάριον, τὸ Διδυμαῖον, τὸ Σαμοθρᾴκιον, τὸν ἐν Ἑρμιόνῃ τῆς Χθονίας νεὼν καὶ τὸν ἐν Ἐπιδαύρῳ τοῦ Ἀσκληπιοῦ καὶ τὸν Ἰσθμοῖ καὶ Ταινάρῳ καὶ Καλαυρίᾳ τοῦ Ποσειδῶνος, τοῦ δὲ Ἀπόλλωνος τὸν ἐν Ἀκτίῳ καὶ Λευκάδι, τῆς δὲ Ἥρας τὸν ἐν Σάμῳ, τὸν ἐν Ἄργει, τὸν ἐπὶ Λακινίῳ.

Is this to be treated as a list of temples that had been declared inviolable? A literal rendering makes this doubtful: "temples that had previously been unviolated and untouched." Certainly there is overlap with cases of declared *asylia* known independently, as one might expect: Apollo of Claros, Hera of Samos, Apollo of Didyma, possibly others. But I would conclude that Plutarch's list of victims cannot be relied on to argue for granted *asylia*.[29]

It happens that the Roman law of 58 B.C. (see p. 52) granting tax exemption to Delos makes a similar claim about the pirates, but without listing victims (apart from Delos) and without attributing any special status to these temples: *praedones, quei orbem te[r]rarum complureis [annos vexarint* (?), *fan]a delubra simu[la]cra deorum*

27. 16.13.2 presents the phrase as a metaphor (above, pp. 7 n. 19, 30 n. 1).

28. See the comments of Flacelière and Chambry, eds., *Plutarque Vies* VIII (Paris 1973) 293–295.

29. Compare the list at Eur. *Cyc.* 290–296, Greek sacred places protected against Trojan raids.

inmor[t]aleium loca religio[sissuma devast]arint. Here it is evident that we have the elative, not a legislated class of temple.

3. On Melos in the time of Nero a priest of Zeus dedicated to Zeus and the heavenly gods a wall that he had built around τὸ ἱερὸν καὶ ἄσυλον Σεβαστῆον (*IG* XII Suppl. 165). Rather than reflecting a specially granted title, this is partly the rhetoric of praise, comparable to the punning σεβασμιώτατον of temples of the emperor (above, p. 7 n. 21), partly one man's articulation of the fact that any temple of the emperor had the right of refuge and thus might appropriately be described with this now-traditional phrase.

4. "Inviolable" boundaries (like that quoted above, p. 3) are evidence of traditional sacred land, not of some granted extra inviolability; the term occurs in this context as early as the fifth century B.C. and therefore must be regarded as inconclusive as evidence for declared inviolability when we find such boundaries in the Hellenistic age. Inscriptions themselves may be dedicated and thus become sacred; for example, *IG* IX.1^2 138: ὁ δὲ πίναξ ἱαρὸς ἔστω τᾶς Ἀρτέμιδος; and they may be the object of inflated rhetoric like the "inviolable steles" of Antiochus of Commagene (p. 31 n. 6).

5. It is possible that a story about the "sacred life" of some city of the remote past, told in later times, reflects an actual declaration of inviolability in the Hellenistic period that has left no trace in the documentary evidence. Thus the cases of Dodona and some others in old Greece are suggestive, but no more; I have mentioned them briefly in what follows.

6. I have included the Ptolemaic declarations for temples, different as these appear from the Panhellenic recognitions of the Greek world (to exclude them would have meant also excluding **218**, the Seleucid declaration for Zeus of Baetocaece), and inevitably the Roman confirmations, whose substance is much like the Ptolemaic grants. I have not included the late imperial grants of asylum to Christian churches,[30] a phenomenon that recreated the traditional immunity of pagan Greek temples but seems to have no connection with the Hellenistic declarations studied here.

Under these restrictions, a coherent body of evidence emerges, and a coherent historical episode.

THE CORPUS

In presenting the evidence I have given numbers to the documents that change the status—recognitions and confirmations—but not to secondary references to the existing status. These last, whether inscriptions, coins, or literature, I have quoted as fully as seemed useful. This limitation is made necessary by the more abundant coinages: it would be distracting and pointless to describe every coin

30. *Cod. Theod.* 9.45; L. Wenger, *Philologus* 86 (1931) 426–454.

of Tyre inscribed Τύρου ἱερᾶς καὶ ἀσύλου; for such data, tabulation will serve. But for cities whose titles are attested quite meagerly, I have presented such secondary references in rather more detail. The order of the recipients is first by geographical regions (mainland Greece, the Aegean and western Anatolia, the remainder of Anatolia, Syria, Egypt, Rome); within these, by date, and from more certain instances to less. The grants are highly formulaic; I have provided translations only selectively, where this seemed most helpful to the reader or the most efficient way to indicate my interpretation.

In the lemmas I have tried to confine bibliographical citations to specific treatments of the individual texts; more general historical comments are cited in the course of the discussion. The equals sign refers to inscriptions, not editions: it is meant as a convenience for readers, to signal other places where an inscription may be read.

Sigla

[ ]	a restoration
⟨ ⟩	a modern correction of an ancient error: addition of an omitted letter when unexplained in the apparatus, correction of an ancient error when the latter is given in the apparatus
( )	a modern expansion of an abbreviation
{ }	ancient material but superfluous, to be deleted
[[ ]]	an ancient deletion
*	a modern correction of an early modern copy, when the stone is lost

Before Hellenism

Several episodes from the classical past can be understood as the historical precedents and models for declared inviolability in the Hellenistic period. As Spanheim first saw, the legend of Elis shows clearly that "sacred and inviolable" means immune from war. The recognitions for Elis and Plataea, whose genesis is described in some detail, have in common an association with Panhellenic games, as does Delphi by implication; this was to be the most common associate of declared *asylia* also in the third century. All three episodes, however, include an oath sworn by the grantors: this is in striking contrast to Hellenistic practice, when our documents never contain an oath.

Elis

The Hellenistic Greeks were much impressed with the story of the sacred life of the primitive Eleans: after the Heracleidae returned to the Peloponnesus, Elis was declared sacred and inviolable so that the Eleans, to be custodians of the Olympic games, could lead a sacred life, immune from war—although this lapsed in historical times. Ephorus supplied a version, which Strabo retells; a rather different version is given by Diodorus; and Polybius comments more generally on the matter. I summarize the passages:

Ephorus *FGrHist* 70 F 115 (Strab. 8.3.33): the Aetolians, ancestrally from Elis, helped the Heracleidae return and then won from the Epeians Elis and the oversight (ἐπιμέλειαν) of the temple at Olympia. With the consent of the Heracleidae, "all readily took an oath that Elean territory is to be sacred to Zeus and that whoever should come against this land in arms is accursed (συνομολογηθῆναι ῥᾳδίως ἐκ πάντων μεθ' ὅρκου τὴν 'Ηλείαν ἱερὰν εἶναι τοῦ Διός, τὸν δ' ἐπιόντα ἐπὶ τὴν χώραν ταύτην μεθ' ὅπλων ἐναγῆ εἶναι), accursed also are any who fail to defend Elis to the best of their ability. As a result those who later founded the city of the Eleans left it unwalled." Armies passing through the country relinquished their weapons; and Iphitus held the Olympic contest, "the Eleans being sacred" (ἱερῶν ὄντων τῶν 'Ηλείων). Hence the increase in population, for while others had wars the Eleans and their guests enjoyed πολλὴν εἰρήνην. As the Eleans possessed no weapons "on account of the peace" (διὰ τὴν εἰρήνην), they could not prevent the forcible intrusion of Pheidon of Argos;[1] after which they took up arms and with Spartan help expelled him.

Diod. 8.1: "The Eleans being populous and well governed, the Spartans became suspicious of their increase (αὔξησιν) and joined in arranging their common life, so that they would enjoy peace and have no experience of the works of war. They dedicated them to the god, with almost all Greeks joining in the grant (καθιέρωσαν αὐτοὺς τῷ θεῷ συγχωρησάντων σχεδὸν ἁπάντων τῶν Ἑλλήνων). Hence the Eleans did not join in the war against Xerxes[2] but were excused because of their tendance of the god's honor (ἀφείθησαν διὰ τὸ ἐπιμελεῖσθαι τῆς τοῦ θεοῦ τιμῆς). And domestically, in the civil wars of the Greeks, no one troubled them, as all were eager to preserve their country and city as sacred and inviolable (διὰ τὸ πάντας τὴν χώραν καὶ πόλιν σπεύδειν ἱερὰν καὶ ἄσυλον φυλάττειν). But many generations later they both joined in campaigns and themselves initiated wars."

Polyb. 4.73.9–74.1: the rural, prosperous, and just character of the Eleans reflects above all "the sacred life they once practiced, when, having received a grant from the Greeks for the sake of the Olympic contest, they inhabited Elis sacred and unplunderable, so that they were inexperienced of any catastrophe or military difficulty" (διὰ τὸν ὑπάρχοντά ποτε παρ' αὐτοῖς ἱερὸν βίον, ὅτε λαβόντες παρὰ τῶν Ἑλλήνων συγχώρημα διὰ τὸν ἀγῶνα τῶν 'Ολυμπίων ἱερὰν καὶ ἀπόρθητον ᾤκουν τὴν 'Ηλείαν, ἄπειροι παντὸς ὄντες δεινοῦ καὶ πάσης πολεμικῆς περιστάσεως). Later, when they had been attacked by Arcadia over possession of Lasion and the Pisatis[3] and "forced to defend their land and change their way of life, they no longer had the least care to recover from the Greeks their ancient and ancestral inviolability but remained in the same condition" (μεταλαβεῖν τὰς ἀγωγὰς τῶν βίων, οὐκέτι περὶ τοῦ πάλιν ἀνακτήσασθαι παρὰ τῶν Ἑλλήνων τὴν παλαιὰν καὶ πάτριον ἀσυλίαν οὐδὲ τὴν τυχοῦσαν ἐπιμέλειαν ἔσχον, ἀλλ' ἔμειναν ἐπὶ

1. Mentioned by Pausanias (6.22.2, under the eighth Olympiad).

2. Cf. Strab. 10.2.25 (Ephorus F 123), explaining why the Acarnanians did not participate in the Trojan War—a story they told the Romans in order to win autonomy.

3. The events of 365–363 B.C.: cf. Swoboda, "Elis," *RE* 5 (1905) 2403–2405; Walbank, *Comm.* I 526.

τῶν αὐτῶν)—unwisely, says Polybius, who proceeds to describe the blessings of peace.

Phlegon's book on the Olympic Games (*FGrHist* 257 F 1; Parke/Wormell no. 489): after the establishment of the games, the Peloponnesians entrusted the Eleans to conduct them and to proclaim the sacred truce (*ekecheiria*). Later, when the Eleans wanted to help the Spartans besiege Helos,[4] the Pythian oracle was consulted: "Leaders of the Eleans, keeping straight the custom of your fathers, protect the fatherland and abstain from war, maintaining common friendship for the Greeks each time the benevolent fifth year comes" (πολέμου δ' ἀπέχεσθε, | κοινοδίκου φιλίης ἡγούμενοι Ἑλλήνεσσιν, | εὖτ' ἂν πενταετὴς ἔλθῃ φιλόφρων ἐνιαυτός). In the face of this oracle "they abstained from war and took care of the Olympia" (τοῦ μὲν πολεμεῖν ἀπέσχοντο, τῶν δὲ Ὀλυμπίων τὴν ἐπιμέλειαν ἐποιοῦντο).

Compare Diod. 37.7.1: Sulla got lots of booty here, because the temple had remained ἄσυλον ἐξ αἰῶνος, "unviolated/inviolable from time immemorial."[5]

It has long been recognized that this claim of primitive Elean neutrality is a fiction of the classical period, with a political motive.[6] Our versions disagree as to the date at which Elis abandoned its neutrality—the seventh century (Ephorus, Phlegon), the fourth (Polybius), "many generations" after the Persian Wars (Diodorus). More to the point, we know that Elis was not neutral in early times; we have the Eleans' military alliance with Heraea in the sixth century (*Staatsvertr.* II 110). And in fact their involvement in the Persian Wars is (and was) well known (Hdt. 9.77; M. /L. 27.9), as is their participation in the Peloponnesian War.

This fiction reflects the Panhellenic aspirations of the late classical period.[7] Pausanias, by contrast, reports extensively on the early history of Elis and the Olympia; informed by local sources and with no thesis to argue, he knows nothing of immunity from war and mentions Elean participation against the Trojans and the Persians (see especially 5.4).

In Ephorus/Strabo, the word *asylia* does not occur: ἱερός is sufficient to signal immunity from war, evoking the traditional image of a "sacred people." The story in Phlegon associates abstention from war (a permanent condition) with

4. At the mouth of the Eurotas; the date is toward the seventh century B.C., if this is the initial Spartan conquest recorded at Paus. 3.2.7.

5. Cf. Diod. 31.34: Orophernes of Cappadocia plundered a temple of Zeus that "was from of old inviolable/unviolated": ἱεροσυλῆσαι τὸ τοῦ Διὸς ἱερόν . . . ἄσυλον δ' ἦν ἐκ παλαιῶν χρόνων. Compare Thuc. 8.24.3 (ἀπαθῆ), Macrob. 3.67 (Delphi).

6. References at Walbank 526, seeing it as anti-Spartan propaganda. E. Meyer, *Geschichte* III^2 (Stuttgart 1937) 342, suggested as ultimate source the book of Hippias of Elis on the Olympia (*FGrHist* 6 F 2).

7. On the Panhellenism of Ephorus see P. Gauthier, *REA* 68 (1966) 25–31.

the sacred truce or *ekecheiria* that pertained only every four years on the occasion of the games. It is suggestive, finally, that Polybius offers no contemporary example of this inviolable status to hold up in criticism of the Eleans.

Delphi

Inviolability at Delphi is known to us from diverse and in part contradictory testimonies—most fully, the Romans' confirmation of Delphi's privileges. The Amphictyonic recognitions of Boeotian temples as inviolable give us a sure terminus ante quem in the 220s (which is hardly surprising) for the belief that Pythian Apollo's temple already had this status, since the status is invoked in them as analogy and precedent.[8] We have no evidence of a Panhellenic declaration of Hellenistic date, despite the unrivaled wealth of Delphian epigraphy. The claim to inviolability surely rested upon earlier traditions, for Apollo's was of old a "common temple of the Greeks,"[9] and the goal of the "sacred wars" of earlier times.

The temple of Apollo at Delphi is in the city proper, at its highest point (Paus. 10.9.1). It is unnecessary to recount the stories of Apollo receiving and protecting refugees of various stripes; Orestes and Ion come to mind. Familiar too is the noninvolvement of Delphi in war, and the several wars to free the temple from interference by other powers.[10] The foundation legend for the protected status of the temple is given by Aeschines: the Amphictyonic cities swore to come in aid if anyone should plunder the god's property (συλᾷ τὰ τοῦ θεοῦ, 2.115) and to leave the sacred land unworked (3.109). In Hellenistic times it was said that the Amphictyony had been founded to serve the Greeks as a common bulwark against the barbarians and a forum for resolving their differences and maintaining unity (Dion. Hal. *Ant. Rom.* 4.25). Given this reputation, the Delphians apparently did not feel the need to seek the recognitions that became

8. **3**.7, **4**.22. The silence of the Amphictyons in **1** of the 260s is unprobative, as this is merely a summary of a decree and no such details could be expected. And such analogies are absent from the much fuller Amphictyonic decrees for Smyrna, Alabanda, and Pergamum. For Teos, the analogy invoked by the Amphictyons and the Aetolians was not the temple at Delphi but the Artists of Dionysus (**132**, **133**).

9. So the Soteria decrees of 246 B.C.: τὸ τοῦ Ἀπόλλωνος ἱερὸν τὸ κοινὸν τῶν Ἑλλήνων (Nachtergael, *Les Galates* 435–447); Ael. Arist. *Panath.* 190 Behr: τὸ κοινὸν τῶν Ἑλλήνων ἱερὸν τὸ ἐν Δελφοῖς.

10. See Bauslaugh, *Neutrality* 39–43, on the traditional exemption from war of peoples with Panhellenic sanctuaries; for Delphi he sees no historical violation of this (in contrast to Olympia).

fashionable in the Hellenistic period; probably that would have been demeaning rather than an increase in honor. To the contrary: the Hellenistic fashion may have been prompted by the actual demonstration of Delphi's inviolability in the repulse of the Gauls in 279 B.C.

As for formal recognitions: the Athenian-Spartan truce of 423 B.C. began with a provision guaranteeing all parties access to Delphi (Thuc. 4.118.1):

> περὶ μὲν τοῦ ἱεροῦ καὶ τοῦ μαντείου τοῦ Ἀπόλλωνος τοῦ Πυθίου δοκεῖ ἡμῖν χρῆσθαι τὸν βουλόμενον ἀδόλως καὶ ἀδεῶς κατὰ τοὺς πατρίους νόμους.
>
> ...
>
> Concerning the temple and oracle of Pythian Apollo, we agree that anyone who wishes may use it openly and without fear, in keeping with the ancestral laws.

Two years later the Peace of Nicias likewise began by stipulating unhindered access to "the common temples" and then specifically guaranteed the "autonomy" of Apollo's temple and of the Delphians (5.18.2):

> περὶ μὲν τῶν ἱερῶν τῶν κοινῶν, θύειν ἐξεῖναι καὶ μαντεύεσθαι καὶ θεωρεῖν κατὰ τὰ πάτρια τὸν βουλόμενον ... ἀδεῶς. τὸ δὲ ἱερὸν καὶ τὸν νεὼν τὸν ἐν Δελφοῖς τοῦ Ἀπόλλωνος καὶ Δελφοὺς αὐτονόμους εἶναι καὶ αὐτοτελεῖς καὶ αὐτοδίκους ...
>
> ...
>
> Concerning the common temples, anyone who wishes may sacrifice and consult and visit in keeping with tradition ... without fear. The sanctuary and temple of Apollo at Delphi and the Delphians are to enjoy their own laws and taxes and justice ...

This is not yet the Hellenistic gesture, or "inviolability" at all, but rather a guarantee of access and independence. Granting "autonomy" to the temple as well as to the Delphians is odd.[11] But this is echoed in the Romans' confirmation of the privileges of Delphi,[12] just as "the common temple of the

11. Despite the special pleading of the commentators: J. Classen, *Thukydides* V (Berlin 1882) 86: "Uebrigens verbindet sich der Tempel mit den Bewohnern von Delphi, wie zu einer unzertrennbaren Gemeinde"); G. Daux, *Delphes au IIe et I^e siècle* (Paris 1936) 259 n. 1 ("L'un ne va pas sans l'autre; le sort du dieu et le sort de la ville sont intimement liés"); A. W. Gomme, *Historical Commentary on Thucydides* III (Oxford 1956) 667 ("The shrine and the community of Delphians are almost one, at least so bound with one another that one could not be free without the other"). Stranger still is the phrase "sanctuary and temple"; νεώς is regularly the physical building, and always so in Thucydides. I wonder if the words καὶ τὸν νεὼν τὸν ἐν Δελφοῖς are an intrusive gloss. Commentators invoke 4.90.2, τάφρον μὲν κύκλῳ περὶ τὸ ἱερὸν καὶ τὸν νεὼν ἔσκαπτον, but it is proper so to describe the ditch around the temple of Apollo Delius.

12. Roman absorption of the ideology of Delphi and its temple is obvious in Sherk, *Roman Documents* 40 (quoted below), denouncing Perseus' intervention and invoking the Gauls' attack.

Greeks" was invoked in the enlargement of the Soteria to Panhellenic status in commemoration of the defeat of the Gauls.

Granted *asylia* at Delphi is first seen epigraphically in the Romans' confirmation of the status in 190 B.C. When Manius Acilius Glabrio liberated Delphi from the Aetolians in 191, he was approached by the city for favorable treatment on a number of matters—status, control of property, domestic political tensions.[13] His own response and the subsequent ones from other Roman authorities are preserved by several fragmentary inscriptions.

Concerning counterclaims that worried the Delphians, Glabrio wrote:[14]

[περὶ δὲ]
[τ]ῶν κατὰ τὸ ἱερόν, ἐάν τε Θεσσαλοὶ ἐάν τε ἄλλοι τινὲς πρεσβεύωσι, πειράσο[μαι ἐν Ῥώμῃ? κατὰ]
[τ]ὰ ἐμ[α]υτοῦ φροντίσαι ἵνα ὑμῖν κατάμονα ἧι τὰ ἐξ ἀρχῆς ὑπάρχοντα πάτρ[ια τὰ περὶ τῆς]
τῆς πόλεως καὶ τοῦ ἱεροῦ αὐτονομίας.

. . .

Concerning the affairs of the temple, if the Thessalians or any others send embassies, I shall try [in Rome(?) to] the best of my ability to take care that the ancestral usages concerning the autonomy of the city and the temple remain in force for you.

Various disputed matters were indeed referred to the Senate. In 189 the consul Spurius Postumius wrote to the Delphians and to the Amphictyons advising them of the Senate's favorable action with regard to the status of city and temple:[15]

[οἱ Δελφῶν πρεσβευ]-
ταὶ Βούλων, Θρασυκλῆς, Ὀρέστας περὶ τῆς ἀσυλίας τοῦ ἱεροῦ κα[ὶ] τῆς πόλεως καὶ τῆς [χώρας διαλεχθέντες]
καὶ περὶ τῆς ἐλευθερίας καὶ ἀνεισφορ[ί]ας ἠξίουν ὅπως αὐτοῖς ἐπιχωρηθῇ πα[ρὰ τοῦ δήμου τοῦ Ῥωμαίων·]
γινώσκετε οὖν δεδογμένον τῆι συγκλή[τ]ωι τό τε ἱερὸν τοῦ Ἀπόλλωνος τοῦ Πυθίο[υ ἄσυλον εἶναι καὶ]
τὴν πόλιν τῶν Δελφῶν καὶ τὴν χώραν, καὶ Δ[ελφοὺ]ς αὐτονόμους καὶ ἐλευθέρους κ[αὶ ἀνεισφόρους, οἰκοῦν]-
τας καὶ πολιτεύοντας αὐτοὺς καθ' αὐ[τοὺς καὶ] κυριεύο[ν]τας τῆς τε ἱερᾶς χώρ[ας καὶ τοῦ ἱεροῦ λι]-
μένος, καθὼς πάτριον αὐτοῖς ἐξ ἀρχῆς [ἦν·]

. . .

13. See Holleaux, *Etudes* V 249–294; Daux 225–270.

14. *Roman Documents* 37.A.7–10; a further fragment of the list of properties is published by J.-P. Michaud in *Etudes delphiques,* BCH Suppl. 4 (Paris 1977) 125–136.

15. *FD* III.4 353.8–14 (*Roman Documents* 1). I have collated the surviving fragments; I quote here from the letter to the Amphictyons, better preserved than that to the Delphians.

> The Delphians' envoys Bulon, Thrasycles, and Orestas [spoke] on the inviolability of the temple and the city and [country] and on their freedom and tax exemption, asking that it be granted them by the Roman people. Know that the Senate has decided the temple of Apollo Pythius [to be inviolable and] the city and country of the Delphians, and the D[elphian]s to be autonomous and free [and tax exempt], living and governing themselves by them[selves[16] and] in control of the sacred land[17] [and the sacred har]bor, as was ever their ancestral right.

On the same stone as these two letters are the remains of a later senatorial decree, probably of 165 B.C., in which we read (17–19):

> [περὶ ὧν] Δ̣ελφοὶ λόγους ἐπο[ιήσαντο περὶ ἱεροῦ]
> ἀσύλου, πόλεως ἐλευθέρ[ας καὶ αὐτονόμου καὶ ἀνεισφόρου·] περὶ τούτου τοῦ π[ράγματος οὕτως]
> ἔδοξεν· καθὼς πρότερο[ν - - - ἡ σύγκλητος?] ἐκεκρίνει, ἐκείνω[ι τῶι κρίματι ἐμμέ]νειν ἔδοξεν.
>
> . . .
>
> Concerning the Delphians' [case about the temple being] inviolable, the city free [and autonomous and tax exempt]: on this matter it has been decided thus: as previously [- - - the Senate(?)] had judged, it has been decided to remain with that judgment.

These several texts attest a strange mixture of grants, and strange phraseology. Glabrio in 191 spoke of the autonomy of the city and the temple; Hellenistic texts offer no parallel for the "autonomy" of a temple—but the Peace of Nicias does. Postumius in 189 responded to an embassy that spoke on two items, the *asylia* of temple and city and country, and the freedom and tax exemption of the Delphians; the actual decision maintained this distinction and added "autonomy" in the second element. So there can be no doubt that the Romans recognized the inviolability of the temple and city and country. For this fullness there is no neat analogy, but some similarity at Smyrna, Anaphe, and Tenos. The later senatus consultum, if it is rightly restored, and allowing for its odd asyndeton, further defines matters by reserving *asylia* for the temple and freedom for the city, a logical distinction and consistent with the later Roman understanding of the nature of asylum as a category of temple.

We have some possible secondary references to *asylia*. The Roman letter ca. 171 B.C. denouncing Perseus was restored by Nikitsky so as to invoke the inviolability of Delphi (*Roman Documents* 40.30–33):

16. For the phrase cf. Diod. 14.17.3: εἴασαν καθ' αὑτοὺς πολιτεύεσθαι (the Thebans for Oropus, ca. 400 B.C.). In the Athenian guarantees for Samos in 405 we have πολιτευομένος ὅπως ἂν αὐτοὶ βόλωνται (*IG* I³ 127.13; cf. M. Ostwald, *Autonomia: Its Genesis and Early History* [Chico 1982] 45).

17. On this see U. Kahrstedt in *Studies . . . D. M. Robinson* II (Baltimore 1953) 749–757.

[οὐδὲν φροντίσας οὐδὲ]
[τῆς παρὰ τοῦ] θεοῦ πᾶσιν τοῖς παραγινο[μένοις πρὸς αὐτὸν δεδομένης ἀσφαλείας οὐδὲ ἐν λόγωι ποιησά]-
[μενος, ὅτι ὑπά]ρχ[ε]ι ἡ παρὰ πάντων ἀνθ[ρώπων νενομισμένη καθιέρωσις καὶ ἀσυλία τῆς πόλεως τῶν Δελφῶν]
[τοῖς τε Ἕλλησιν] καὶ βαρβάροις ἐκ παντ[ὸς χρόνου - - -]
...

[He paid no attention to the security granted by] the god to all those who come [to him nor did he take into account that the sacredness and inviolability of the city of the Delphians recognized] by all mankind [for both Greeks] and barbarians from all [time . . .]

Livy's account of the speech of Eumenes II to the Senate in 172 (Livy 42.11–15; cf. 40) lies behind the restoration of the text, but Livy does not there refer to the *asylia* of the temple or city.

In advanced imperial times we find in several honorific inscriptions ἡ ἱερὰ Δελφῶν πόλις;[18] but this is the rhetorical flourish typical of the age. A different item is more pertinent. On the western section of the peribolos wall of the sixth century B.C. a boundary statement was eventually inscribed (*FD* III.4 512: A with broken bar, large O, open Ω):

ὅρος·
φύκτιμον
τὰ ὑποκάτω.

This seems to mean "Boundary: place of refuge with respect to the parts below." For the adjective compare the Delphian decree for Chalcedon (**53**.5), Caesar's edict for Sardes (**214**.48), Plutarch *Mor.* 166E (ἔστι δούλῳ φεύξιμος βωμός) and *Rom.* 9.3 (ἱερόν τι φύξιμον τοῖς ἀφισταμένοις, Romulus' asylum on the Capitolium), and a rock-cut inscription in Laconia (*IG* V.1 1325: φύγιμον).

The wall is at the high side of the temple of Apollo; it cannot be determined which way the stone originally faced, eastward toward the building or toward the open area to the west. Neither editor of this text has ventured a date; the writing seems late Hellenistic or imperial. If this was inscribed under Roman rule, it will reflect the Romans' recognition of the temple as an asylum and will be consistent with a Roman understanding of the law, as allowing a place of refuge.

At Delphi as at Elis, we have the traditional portrait of a city wholly taken up with the maintenance of its temple. As the treaties of the 420s suggest, the Panhellenic character of the temple is already associated with neutrality and open access. It seems that the Delphians told the Romans that their temple and city and country were traditionally inviolable and autonomous—an unusual

18. Statue bases of the second half of the third century and the early fourth: listed by T. Drew-Bear, *REA* 82 (1980) 168–169.

amalgam that was made possible by the complex traditions about Delphian sacredness and neutrality and also by the absence of any recognition of Hellenistic date and manner that would have used the standard formulae. The Romans at first responded accordingly but then clarified their thinking and restricted the *asylia* to the temple. Thus we can see them, already in the second century B.C., groping toward the application of their own notion of an asylum.

Plataea

The altar of Zeus Eleutherius was already "the common altar of the Greeks" in the dedicatory poem attributed to Simonides (*Anth. Gr.* 6.50; Preger, *IGMetr.* no. 78); so later Aelius Aristides (*Panath.* 190 Behr): κοινὴν ἔχον παράκλησιν τοῖς Ἕλλησιν εἴς τε ὁμόνοιαν καὶ τὸ τῶν βαρβάρων καταφρονεῖν. Plataea is the one precedent known to us from historical times for the declared inviolability of a secular place.

According to Thucydides, the Plataeans of his day maintained that the Greeks who defeated the Persians at Plataea in 479 made solemn promises about the future security of Plataea:

> Pausanias, ... after he had made sacrifice in the agora of Plataea to Zeus the Liberator, summoned all the allies and conceded to the Plataeans their territory and city to possess, living by their own laws, and no one was ever to wage war against them unjustly or for enslavement: if anyone did, the allies there present were to bring aid to the best of their ability (ἀπεδίδου Πλαταιεῦσι γῆν καὶ πόλιν τὴν σφετέραν ἔχοντας αὐτονόμους οἰκεῖν, στρατεῦσαί τε μηδένα ποτὲ ἀδίκως ἐπ' αὐτοὺς μηδ' ἐπὶ δουλείᾳ).... We say to you, do not harm the Plataean territory or violate the oaths, but let us live by our own laws as Pausanias decided (γῆν τὴν Πλαταιίδα μὴ ἀδικεῖν μηδὲ παραβαίνειν τοὺς ὅρκους, ἐᾶν δὲ οἰκεῖν αὐτονόμους καθάπερ Παυσανίας ἐδικαίωσεν).[19]

19. Thuc. 2.71, the Plataeans' speech to the Spartans; on ἀπεδίδου, "concede," see N. G. L. Hammond, *JHS* 112 (1992) 145; cf. Daux, *FD* III. 3 218.B.6 with p. 185 n. 3; contra: E. Badian, *From Plataea to Potidaea* (Baltimore 1993) 119–120 ("restore"). In their defense at 3.53–59, the Plataeans do not repeat this claim of immunity from war, nor do they perceive an inconsistency in their seeking συμμαχία with Thebes or Athens (55.1; cf. the Athenian garrison at 2.6.4); they do invoke "the common gods of the Greeks" (θεοὺς τοὺς ὁμοβωμίους καὶ κοινοὺς τῶν Ἑλλήνων) and urge the Spartans to honor their fathers' oaths and not neglect these suppliants (ἱκέται) at their ancestral tombs (59.2). The Spartans answer that the Plataeans broke the oath when they joined in attacking Aegina (64.3), and did not keep quiet in accord with the old truce (κατὰ τὰς παλαιὰς ... σπονδὰς ἡσυχάζειν) and remain open to both sides (κοινοὺς εἶναι κατ' ἐκεῖνα, 68.1). For ἡσυχάζειν as the converse of going to war

Herodotus does not mention this oath; and in the lore concerning Plataea retailed in [Dem.] 59, which derives from more sources than Thucydides alone,[20] there is no trace of the declared neutrality of the place.[21]

We see again the themes of a common cult of the Greeks and military neutrality. In fact, an oath "not to wage war unjustly[22] or for enslavement" anticipates already the central paradox of *asylia* in the Hellenistic period: for as no one admits to waging an unjust war, the oath could have no practical effect. Nor is it clear what this adds to the mutual defense pact of 481 that applied to all the Greek allies. Finally, there is no practice of military inaction either here or in the Spartans' interpretation (that the oath meant that the Plataeans must help them free the Greeks from Athenian domination). It should be noted, however, that the Spartans took special precautions before investing Plataea, assuring the gods that they were not the first to do wrong (Thuc. 2.74–75).[23]

When Plutarch came to tell this story, he used the formulae that had been made standard by the Hellenistic recognitions, and the event itself has been compounded: the Greeks not only declared Plataea sacred and inviolable but also founded Panhellenic games, the Eleutheria:[24]

---

cf. 1.120.3; in the partisan claim of the Second Athenian Confederacy, ἐῶσι τὸς Ἕλληνας ἐλευθέ[ρ]ος [καὶ] αὐτονόμος ἡσυχίαν ἄγειν (*Staatsvertr.* II 257.9–11).

20. Cf. J. Trevett, *CQ* n.s. 40 (1990) 407–420.

21. On the question see P. A. Brunt, *Historia* 2 (1953) 153–156; F. R. Wüst, *Historia* 3 (1954/55) 144; W. K. Pritchett, *The Greek State at War* III (Berkeley 1979) 178–181. Ostwald (16–22) has argued that the term αὐτόνομος is anachronistic, a buzzword of the later fifth century; T. Figueira, *BICS* 37 (1990) 63–88, while disputing Ostwald's view of the word, does not comment on this point regarding Plataea. The more famous oath before the battle of Plataea, reported at Hdt. 7.132.2 and alleged in detail by a fourth-century inscription (Tod II 204), includes a provision that no one is to destroy Athens, Sparta, Plataea, or any of the other allied cities. This provision has been recognized as a late borrowing from the Amphictyonic "rules of war" (see Tod p. 307); but the specification of Plataea may derive from the story of its special inviolability in Thucydides. G. A. Sheets, *AJP* 115 (1994) 51–73, urges the reality of legal constraints in this affair but does not address the status of Plataea.

22. Badian (110) glosses "i.e., a war of aggression." In any case, the adverb would not seem in such a legal context to be mere pleonasm. Contrast Xen. *Hiero* 4.18: because of their need for money, tyrants are habitually forced to plunder unjustly both temples and men (οἱ τύραννοι τοίνυν ἀναγκάζονται πλεῖστα συλᾶν ἀδίκως καὶ ἱερὰ καὶ ἀνθρώπους). Ptolemy wrote to Cyrene ἐπεὶ οὖν σπουδάζομεν μηθένα τῶν ὑπὸ τὴν βασιλείαν τασσομένων παρὰ λόγον σκύλλεσθαι, "so we are eager that no one under our rule be harassed beyond reason" (*SEG* 9.5.52–54).

23. Pritchett III 322–323, cites the few parallels. On the implications see Badian 112.

24. *Arist.* 21.1–2; cf. Eust. 269.15–17 (I 411 Erbse): ἱδρύσαντο Ἐλευθερίου Διὸς ἱερὸν καὶ τοὺς ἐν μάχῃ τελευτήσαντας δημοσίᾳ θάψαντες ἀγῶνα γυμνικὸν στεφανίτην ἀπέδειξαν τὰ Ἐλευθέρια. On Plutarch's use of Thucydides see C. B. R. Pelling, in *Plutarch and the Historical Tradition,* ed. P. A. Stadter (London/New York 1992) 10–40 (not addressing this passage).

> At the common assembly of the Greeks, Aristeides proposed a decree that each year counselors and *theoroi* from Greece gather at Plataea, and that they celebrate a quadrennial contest, the Eleutheria. . . . And to declare the Plataeans inviolable and sacred, as they sacrifice to the god in behalf of Greece (Πλαταιεῖς δ' ἀσύλους καὶ ἱεροὺς ἀφίεσθαι τῷ θεῷ θύοντας ὑπὲρ τῆς Ἑλλάδος).

In fact, the Eleutheria are not attested in the classical period and did not exist then, but they are well known in the Hellenistic age.[25] Plataea was destroyed after Leuctra in 371 and refounded by Alexander in 335,[26] an age rich in historical fictions about Panhellenism. The games—and Plutarch's version, whatever his source—were created in this second period of the city's history, to be a partner to the status of immunity from war described in Thucydides.

Delos

Delos was invoked already by Spanheim in explaining the Hellenistic sacred and inviolable cities.[27] It was traditionally the "sacred island," hence the Athenians' several purifications of it and the federal Ionian festival (Thuc. 3.104, 5.1). Herodotus (6.97) portrays the agent of Xerxes promising not to harm the city: ἄνδρες ἱροί, . . . ἐν τῇ χώρῃ οἱ δύο θεοὶ ἐγένοντο, ταύτην μηδὲν σίνεσθαι, μήτε τὴν χώρην μήτε τοὺς οἰκήτορας αὐτῆς. This passage was later rephrased by the author of the *Axiochus* (371A): ὅπως τηρήσειε τὴν νῆσον ἄσυλον ἐν ᾗ οἱ δύο θεοὶ ἐγένοντο. At Callim. *Hymn.* 4.275ff. Delos is the holiest of islands (ἁγιωτάτη), whence the absence of war, and all cities send choruses each year (which are well documented in the Hellenistic age). In inscriptions of Roman imperial date we have ἐν τῆι ἱερᾶι [νήσωι (Durrbach, *Choix* no. 177 and p. 266) and ἐπ[ι]μελητὴς τῆς ἱερᾶς Δήλου (no. 182); cf. Verg. *Aen.* 3.73 *sacra tellus*.

25. Etienne and Piérart, *BCH* 99 (1975) 63–68; cf. Robert, *Op. min. sel.* VI 323–326; N. Robertson, *Hesperia* 55 (1986) 88–102 (esp. 102, "life imitating literature"). The earliest reference to the games is Posidippus frag. 31 K.–A. (ca. the 280s B.C.). Compare Diod. 15.53.4 calling the Basileia at Lebedeia "crowned" from their foundation in 371 B.C.: a Hellenistic expansion has been projected onto the origins of the festival.

26. Alexander proclaimed at the Olympia that in the Persian Wars the Plataeans had presented their territory to the Greeks: Plut. *Arist.* 11.9, with L. Prandi in *La Béotie antique* (Paris 1985) 211–217.

27. See above p. 5; so too Usener, *RhM* 29 (1874) 38–39 (*Kl. Schr.* III 399–402).

Scholars have debated whether Delos in fact enjoyed a "sacred neutrality" that made it a safe port, and whether this immunity was abused by pirates.[28] For us is only the narrower question, Was Delos ever declared sacred and inviolable?

The Aetolian League in the mid-third century B.C. granted Delian citizens collectively "security" (*IG* IX.1² 185):

> δ ό γ μ α Α ἰ τ ω λ ῶ ν·
> Δαλί[οι]ς εἶμεν ἀσφάλειαν τὰ
> ἀπ' Α[ἰτω]λῶν καὶ τῶν π̣ο̣[λιτευόντων - - -]

This gesture, well known in Aetolian foreign policy of the period, is not a religious act and is not to be confused with territorial *asylia* (see above, p. 19).

This apart, we know of no declarations. The blessings of peace are sometimes seen, but not arising from a Panhellenic stipulation in historical times. Around 200 B.C. military measures were taken to see that warships did not use Delos as a base of operations (*Choix* no. 67 = *Syll.*³ 582). In 168, we are told, the sanctity of the temple and island rendered its military visitors inviolable; so Romans, Macedonians, and the allies of Eumenes mingled freely in the temple, the religion of the place supplying them a truce (Livy 44.29.2: *sanctitas templi insulaeque inviolatos praestabat omnes. itaque permixti Romanique et Macedones et Eumenis navales socii in templo indutias religione loci praebente versabantur*). Again, "Delos was a market for the Greeks and seemed to offer security (ἄδειαν) to merchants on account of the god"; but Mithridates' forces attacked it, Delos being unwalled, and plundered the sacred properties, killed people, and razed the city; Apollo, however, exacted his revenge (Paus. 2.33.3).

By a law of 58 B.C. the Roman people exempted Delos from Roman taxes.[29] A general sentiment on the good sense of honoring the gods was followed by a specific evocation of the cult of Delian Apollo (lines 27ff.):

> *fanum A[pollinis – – – antiquissum]um ac religiosissumum sit constitutu[m – – –] sanctitatem caerimoniasq(ue)*, then a historical argument, *in qua insula Apollinem et Dianam n[atos esse arbitrantur?], vecteigalibus leiberari, quae insula post hominum me[moriam semper fuit?] regum, ceivitatium nationumque imperieis sacra leib[era immunis?]*, then an appreciation of the defeat of the pirates, who had been plundering all the most sacred places: now that there is peace, Delos is to be restored to its ancient splendor, and *ill]am insul[a]m nobilissumam ac sa[nc]tissum[a]m deis inmo[rtalibus restitui? et i]nsulam l[ei]berari.*

28. F. Durrbach, *Choix d'inscriptions de Délos* (Paris 1921) p. 92 ("sacred neutrality" made Delos a safe port and open to all); cf. Nachtergael, *Les Galates* 329; contra: Tarn, *JHS* 44 (1924) 141–147 (sacred but not neutral). Surveyed: W. A. Laidlaw, *History of Delos* (Oxford 1933) 279–282.

29. Text and commentary in C. Nicolet et al., *Insula Sacra* (Paris 1980) (= *Choix* no. 163; *I.Délos* 1511).

The tax immunity now provided Delos is represented as the norm before the war of Mithridates.

The only evidence suggesting that Delos may ever have received a formal declaration of *asylia*, whether in the Hellenistic period or in lore about earlier times, is the one phrase in the piracy law just cited, the familiar formula for recognition "by kings, cities, nations" as sacred, free, and immune (?); but when the Romans thought this to have happened is uncertain. I think it unlikely that there was a Hellenistic grant; the Delians, like the Delphians, will have told the Romans about older traditions.

Greece: Boeotia

In the history of *asylia*, pride of place goes to Boeotia. In Plataea the Boeotians possessed the first site that the Greeks in historical times had declared inviolable—so went the story (cf. p. 49). The first extant decree of inviolability honors the Boeotians' federal temple, the Itonium. Sheer volume, moreover, sets Boeotia apart: at least four places declared inviolable in the third century B.C., while the rest of mainland Greece has little or nothing to show.

The surviving evidence for Boeotia is coherent in that we find only temples granted *asylia*, not cities; and the grants come only from the Delphian Amphictyony, with which Boeotia had close ties in legend and in recent history. The substantially preserved acts (**3**, **4**) both invoke the temple of Apollo at Delphi as precedent for the declarations. The Artists of Dionysus played an important role in these Boeotian cults, and the new status of the temples is associated with their quest for personal inviolability.

Boeotian patriots and scholars linked the cult at Delphi with the great migration of the Boeotians from Thessaly after the Trojan War: the Council was founded by Amphictyon, son of Poseidon and Arne (or of Deucalion and Pyrrha).[1] Of Amphictyon's two sons, Aetolus fathered the Aetolian nation,[2] and Itonus established the temple of Athena at Coroneia; Itonus' son was Boeotus.

1. See variously *FGrHist* 324 F 58, 376 F 5, 378 F 1; Paus. 9.1.1; Diod. 4.67 (Boeotus directly the son of Poseidon and Arne); schol. Eur. *Or.* 1094 (I 204–205 Schwartz). On the Amphictyony see especially F. R. Wüst, *Historia* 3 (1954/55) 129–153.

2. The Aetolians' account of themselves was understandably quite different. They reckoned themselves not Boeotians from Thessaly but the original inhabitants of Elis in the Peloponnesus: Ephorus *FGrHist* 70 F 122; cf. 115; schol. *Il.* 13.218 (*FGrHist* 65 F 1); cf. Wilamowitz, *Kl. Schr.* IV 544–546; H. Pomtow, *Klio* 18 (1923) 297–298; S. Bommeljé, *Historia* 37 (1988) 301 n. 11, 311 n. 49. I assume that this belief in Elean kinship is the truth behind Polyb. 4.9.10 (Aetolians have always cultivated Elean friendship in order to be able to plunder the Peloponnesus). Note Aetolian assistance of Elis against the Spartans ca. 400 B.C. (Diod. 14.17.9;

Such tales are consonant with the close if uneasy relations of Boeotia with Delphi and the Aetolians in the third century B.C. The stories emphasize the primacy of the temple of Athena Itonia among Boeotians, and its ties with that of Apollo of Delphi; the two might be called sister temples. If the Itonium was in fact the first place declared inviolable in Hellenistic times, Delphi played an important role, for the model was the great temple of Apollo.

Temple of Athena Itonia, Coroneia

In the 260s B.C. the Delphian Amphictyony declared inviolable the temple of Athena Itonia—the earliest declaration extant on stone. Athena Itonia had two famous temples, one at Iton in southern Thessaly,[3] the other, which the Boeotians believed to be an offshoot of the Thessalian cult, in Boeotia in the territory of Coroneia. It is possible that the Thessalian temple of Athena Itonia is in fact the subject of **1**.[4] Certainly it had attributes often associated with inviolable temples: this was a federal temple of the Thessalian League; Athena was a military goddess in costume, her name served as the password of the early Thessalian army (Paus. 10.1.10), and to her were dedicated the spoils of defeated invaders of Thessaly.[5] The federal games, the Itonia, were famous.[6] Nevertheless, Bousquet surely was right to refer the *asylia* decree **1**

nothing suggests that these Aetolians were mercenaries, pace R. Unz, *GRBS* 27 [1986] 33), and the Aetolian commanders of Elean armies in the Hellenistic period (Polyb. 5.30.2, 91.3, 94.2).

3. On this cult, known already to Hecataeus (*FGrHist* 1 F 2), see F. Stählin, "Iton," *RE* 9 (1916) 2371–2373; *Das hellenische Thessalien* (Stuttgart 1924) 176; Robert, *BCH* 59 (1935) 209 (*Op. min. sel.* I 277); Walbank, *Comm.* III 276; *Deltion* 20.II.2 (1965) 311–313; 22.II (1967) 295–296; A. Moustaka, *Kulte und Mythen auf thessalischen Münzen,* Beitr.z.Arch. 15 (Würzburg 1983) 23–30; B. Helly, *RN* VI.8 (1966) 7–32 (the federal coins with their images of Athena in battle).

4. This possibility was suggested by Pouilloux (*FD* III.4 p. 28); J. and L. Robert, *Bull. épigr.* 1977, 226, noted the relevance of the Panhellenic games at Iton. Polybius (25.3.2) writes without further specification that the amnesty edict of Philip V was to be posted at "Delos, Delphi, and the temple of Athena Itonia"; Walbank ad loc. takes this to be the Thessalian one on the grounds of proximity.

5. A. S. F. Gow and D. Page, *Hellenistic Epigrams* (Cambridge 1965) I 195 (Theodoridas no. 17 [*Anth. Gr.* 9.743]), Illyrian invaders; 137 (Leonidas no. 95 [*Anth. Gr.* 6.130]), Gauls defeated by Pyrrhus (the spoils from the Macedonian invaders he dedicated in his own showplace, Dodona: Paus. 1.13.3 [Preger, *IG Metr.* no. 96]); Polyaen. 7.43 (Thracian invaders, and violation of the sacred truce).

6. A Coan delegation in the third century B.C.: Boesch 28; M. Segre, *RivFil* 62 (1934) 180. Callim. *Hymn.* 6.74–75 describes an international attendance at the Thessalian Itonia in mythic times.

to Boeotia, the only part of mainland Greece that is certain to have obtained such recognitions.

The Boeotian Athena Itonia, often seen on the coins of Coroneia, was federal and military, like her Thessalian counterpart.[7] Her temple, near Lake Copais in the plain below Coroneia,[8] was the religious center of the Boeotian League. Whereas the federal council met at the grove of Poseidon at Onchestus, the great religious gathering of the Boeotian people was the festival and games held each October[9] beside the temple of Athena, the Pamboeotia. Here in Hellenistic times the Boeotarchs presided over military competitions among teams sent by the member cities. The federal character of the shrine and games may well be as old as the League itself.[10] Athena's statue was by a student of Phidias (Paus. 9.34.1). The Boeotian-Aetolian treaty of the early third century is to be inscribed at the temples of Poseidon at Onchestus, Athena Alalcomeneis, and Athena at Coroneia.[11] Many of the surviving decrees of the League derive from the Itonium.

At the battle of Coroneia in 394 B.C., some eighty Boeotian soldiers and allies took refuge by the temple; Agesilaus respected their immunity and let them retreat. Xenophon felt it sufficient to refer simply to "the temple"

7. A. Schachter, *Cults of Boeotia* I, BICS Suppl. 38.1 (London 1981) 117–127; P. Roesch, *Etudes béotiennes* (Paris 1982) 220–224; D. Knoepfler in *Comptes et inventaires* (Neuchâtel/Geneva 1988) 276 n. 36. A Hellenistic decree of Coroneia refers to Ἀθάνας τᾶς κατεχώσας [πεδὰ τῶν ἄλλων Ὀλ]υμπίων ἐξ ἀρχᾶς τὰν πόλιν (Robert, *Et. épigr. phil.* 12 n. 1; *TrGF* I pp. 41–42). Alcaeus frag. 325: Ἀθανάα πολεμάδοκε ἅ ποι Κορωνήας μεδ[έοισα. On the Pamboeotia see Moretti, *I. agon. gr.* pp. 101–103; J. and L. Robert, *Bull. épigr.* 1973, 213; 1978, 210. The event εὐοπλίη at the games (*SEG* 3.355) supports Robert's attribution of ὁπλοφανίαι to the Thessalian cult (*Op. min. sel.* I 277), as does *FGrHist* 8 F 1 (ὁπλομαχική of the Thessalian Athena).

8. T. G. Spyropoulos, *AAA* 6 (1973) 385–392 and *Prakt* 1975.2, 392–414, may have found the building, nearer to the city proper than is usually thought; see further J. M. Fossey, *Topography and Population of Ancient Boiotia* (Chicago 1988) 331; P. Krentz, "Athena Itonia and the Battle of Koroneia," in *Boiotika,* ed. H. Beister and J. Buckler, Münch.Arb.z.Alt.Gesch. 2 (Munich 1989) 313–317.

9. In Pamboiotios, the tenth month: cf. B. Latischew, *AM* 7 (1882) 31–39. The annual period is questioned by Schachter (I 124 n. 3), who invokes the biennial festival of Dionysus, the *trieteris,* at Thebes. But Dionysus traditionally had *trietereis* (e.g., *Hymn. Hom.* 1.11–12; Diod. 3.65.8, 4.3.1–3; Artem. *Oneir.* 4.39; further at A. S. Pease, *Publi Vergili Maronis Aeneidos liber quartus* [Cambridge, Mass. 1935] 280–281), while nothing suggests that the Pamboeotia were other than annual.

10. Cf. L. Ziehen, "Pamboiotia," *RE* 18 (1949) 288; J. Ducat, *BCH* 97 (1973) 59–73, esp. 60–61 on the archaic character of the games. Earliest mention of the contest is Pind. *Parth.* 2.41–42 (frag. 94b S.-M.).

11. *Staatsvertr.* III 463.a.4–6: ἐν δὲ Βοιωτοῖς ἐν τῶι ἱερῶι [τοῦ Ποσει]δ̣[ῶ]ν̣ος ἐ̣ν̣ Ὀγχηστῶι καὶ ἐν Ἀλαλκομενείωι καὶ ἐγ̣ Κο[ρωνείαι] ἐν τῶι ἱερῶι τῆς Ἀθηνᾶς. On the treaty see Roesch 357–359.

in describing the event, ὁ ναός; it is later authors who gloss this as the Itonium.[12]

At the start of the Social War in 220, the Achaeans complained that the Aetolians had plundered the temple of Athena in time of peace (συλήσαιεν τὸ τῆς Ἀθηνᾶς τῆς Ἰτωνίας ἱερὸν εἰρήνης ὑπαρχούσης, Polyb. 4.25.2) and had violated the truce of the festival (παρασπονδήσαντος τὴν τῶν Παμβοιωτίων πανήγυριν, 4.3.5; cf. 9.34.11). Nicostratus is named as the man responsible; apparently he led a raid on the Boeotian forces marshaled at the temple. So our partisan informant. Polybius assigns no date to the violation, but it seems recent and surely cannot be as much as fifty years before the complaint.[13] This violation must therefore have happened after the extant declaration of inviolability in the 260s. Yet Polybius mentions no special or enacted security of the Itonium: it was enough that it was a temple, with the added outrage that the festival, with its sacred truce, was in progress, and that there was no war—this was mere Aetolian piracy. We should not conclude from his notices that Polybius would have found nothing wrong in the Aetolian attack if it had happened in wartime, or again not during the sacred truce; nor does he use this occasion to say that the Aetolians had violated a specific recognition of inviolability. As in 394 B.C., proper respect was due a temple. On the other hand, we have Livy 36.20, recording a Roman attack on the temple's land or vicinity in 191 B.C. (*circumiectum templo agrum*); Livy does not seem to see this as a sacrilege.[14]

The Amphictyonic grant of inviolability, in the year of the archon Pleiston, can be dated within limits. The membership of the Council places the decree in the 260s, and the meeting is during the Pythia: therefore September of 266 or 262, and attractive reasons have been offered for the later date.[15] A great deal hangs on the choice, for the act is either at the beginning of the Chremonidean War or else near its end. Athens still has a seat on the Council, so (on the common assumption) the war is not yet over, and Athens has not fallen to Antigonus Gonatas. As Flacelière noticed, however, it would be surprising if Athens could observe such solemn normalities as a meeting of the Council while

12. Xen. *Hell.* 4.3.20 (*Ages.* 2.13); cf. Plut. *Ages.* 19.1–2; Paus. 3.9.13. Roesch (221), taking this as evidence of an early grant of *asylia*, considers that **1** might be a confirmation rather than a grant; but the text is unambiguously a grant, and Agesilaus' respect was what was due any temple.

13. Dated 229/224: Feyel, *Polybe* (Paris 1942) 137–138, followed by Walbank, *Comm.* I 452; Roesch 222. Ca. 220: B. Niese, *Geschichte der griechischen und makedonischen Staaten* II (Gotha 1899) 409; Flacelière, *Aitoliens* 289; Klaffenbach, *IG* IX.1^2 xxv.65ff. and *DLZ* 69 (1948) 98 (rejecting Feyel's argument).

14. Cf. M. Sordi, "Acilio Glabrione e l'Atena Itonia," in *La Béotie antique* (Paris 1985) 265–269.

15. R. Etienne and M. Piérart, *BCH* 99 (1975) 59–62, arguing for the greater consistency of the membership if 262. For the beginning of the war in 267 see D. Knoepfler, *BCH* 117 (1993) 327–341.

under siege (*Aitoliens* 195 n. 2). This objection would point to 266 rather than 262. Pouilloux, by contrast, has invoked the Panhellenic spirit of Greece in the aftermath of the Chremonidean War.

In either case this was a period of close relations between the Boeotians and Aetolians (cf. Feyel, *Polybe* 79). Aetolia remained neutral but profited from the allies' efforts against Macedonia; the role of Boeotia is unclear. The allies in the war saw themselves as engaged in rallying Greece to a new effort to ward off the Macedonians of the north. Two other gestures of Panhellenic solidarity may be relevant. In the spring following their recognition of the Itonium, the Amphictyons recognized the Ptolemaia in Alexandria as crowned, agreeing to send *theoroi* to the first new Panhellenic contest of the Hellenistic age.[16] And from a Pythia probably in the same period—so perhaps the same meeting that produced **1**—dates the Amphictyonic decree indicating the success of recent missions to Ptolemy and Antigonus to obtain safe passage for those attending the Pythia.[17]

1. Amphictyonic Council

Delphi, temple of Apollo. Two joining fragments of a small marble stele. Inv. 1641 (lines 1–10) found in 1895 west of the Syracusan tripods; inv. 7577 (lines 11–14) found in 1957 south of the terrace of the Siphnian Treasury. The lower left quarter is lost, other margins preserved; combined dimensions: h. 0.35, w. 0.34, th. 0.07. Blockish letters (h. 0.008, intersp. 0.009) with slightly curving strokes, O usually small and suspended, right hasta of N fully descended, Σ with somewhat splayed arms.

Lines 1–10: A. Jardé, *BCH* 26 (1902) 250 no. 6 (copy of Bourguet); Flacelière, *Aitoliens* 393–394.

Complete: J. Bousquet, *BCH* 82 (1958) 74–77 [*SEG* 18.240; Moretti, *I. stor. ellen.* II 74]; J. Pouilloux, *FD* III.4 358. *Collation.*

Photograph: Bousquet fig. 10; Pouilloux pl. 5.

Πλείστωνος ἄρχοντος ἐν Δελ-
φοῖς, ἱερομνημονούντων Αἰτω-
λῶν Μάχωνος, Ξεννία, Οἰκιάδα,
Στρατάγ[ου], Ἀλεξιμάχου, Εὐνί-
κου· Βοιωτῶν Ἐνδίου, Εὐρυφάον-
τος· Φωκέων Χηρία, Δαφναίου,

16. Moretti, *I. stor ellen.* I 75. Why this recognition comes so long after that of the Island League in 283/2 remains a mystery; for this date see L. Nerwinski, "The Foundation Date of the Panhellenic Ptolemaea" (Ph.D. diss., Duke University 1981). It may be that in 283 Ptolemy invited only his allies. C. Habicht, *Gottmenschentum und griechische Städte*² (Munich 1970) 259, considers the gesture of the 260s to represent a rapprochement between the Aetolians and Ptolemy in connection with the war.

17. Moretti, *I. stor ellen.* II 76; cf. Will, *Histoire* I 230.

Δημητρίου· Ἀθηναίων Εὐθυδί-
κου· Ἱστιαιέων Καλλιχάριδος·
Δελφῶν Ἰασιμάχου, Ἐπιχαρί-
δου· γρα[μματεύο]ντος Καλλι̣-
[. . . . . . Αἰτωλοῦ· Π]υ[θ]ίοις· [ἔδο]-
[ξε τοῖς Ἀμφικτί]οσιν τὸ ἱερὸ[ν]
[τῆς Ἀθηνᾶς τῆς] Ἰτωνίας τὸ
[ἐγ Κορωνείαι ἄσυ]λον εἶναι.

vacat

7–8 Flacelière: Εὐθυδά|μου Jardé.

We have not the actual decree but a summary recording that the grant occurred.[18] The summary has omitted the preliminaries that would have mentioned the Boeotian embassy and its arguments, and hence we have lost the portion that might have revealed the historical setting or motivation of the grant. The Pamboeotia took place at the Itonium about a month later, and no doubt this recognition will have been announced there to the assembled Boeotians.

Temple of Apollo Ptoius, Acraephia

The cult of Apollo Ptoius with its oracular cave was famous and much patronized from earliest times. The shrine occupied three terraces on the western slope of Mt. Ptoius in the territory of Acraephia, at the eastern end of Lake Copais. The site has been extensively excavated, yielding a rich body of evidence, especially of the archaic period.[19] The Delphian Amphictyony recognized the inviolability of the temple in the 220s B.C. The background to this event is obscure, for the development of the shrine in the fourth and third centuries is poorly known. The date of the building itself, on the highest of the terraces, is not firmly determined—either the end of the fifth century or the late fourth.[20] Its inviolability is attested by inscribed texts of three sorts: an oracle of Trophonius, an Amphictyonic Council decree, and boundary stones.

The Amphictyonic decree (**3**) grants personal inviolability to Artists who compete in Apollo's games, the Ptoia; declares the temple inviolable, with

18. Compare *FD* III.4 155 (Delphian grant of *promanteia* to Smyrna); *IG* XI.4 1050 (Aetolian grant of *asphaleia* to the Delians, quoted p. 52); *IG* IX.1^2 175 (Aetolian grant of *asylia* to the Artists of Dionysus)—all mid-third century B.C.

19. Testimonia and bibliography at Schachter I 52–73; Fossey 271–273.

20. J. Ducat, *Les kouroi du Ptoion* (Paris 1971) 41 n. 2.

those who wrong the temple or its land made subject to prosecution before the Amphictyons; regulates the length of the festival truce; and approves the addition of the agonothete to the number of the administrators of the temple. The opening of the text is lost; determination of the date rests, as Holleaux saw, on the authority with which the Council instructs Ptoicles on the inscribing of the decree (**3**.17): therefore he must have been a Boeotian member of the Council, and a Boeotian of this name was such in the year of the Delphian archon Callias.[21]

The dates of this recognition and that for Dionysus of Thebes (**4**) must be addressed together.[22] The two are quite close in substance and language and have always been considered close in date. The decree for Thebes, passed in the autumn (**4**.30), very probably dates to the year of the Delphian archon Nicarchus. The two archons Callias and Nicarchus both belong to years when Aetolia had fourteen seats on the Council and Boeotia two. A third such year is attested; that year and that of Callias witnessed a celebration of the quadrennial Soteria, and so this period encompassed at least five archons. This distribution of seats probably began after the death of Demetrius II early in 229 and the Aetolians' victories in Thessaly and ended in 224 when the Boeotians again allied themselves with Macedonia against the Aetolians. Thus the two Soteria years of this period would be 229/8 and 225/4. To one of these two years should belong the decree for the Ptoium, dated by Callias. The two possible dates are at the extremes of the period in question, framing the year of Nicarchus and its decree for Thebes.

Which cult is likely to have been honored first? Feyel thought that the great city Thebes would be the initiator and Acraephia the imitator in this competition. But the Boeotian League, not just the city of Acraephia, spoke for the Ptoium, and the League may well have preceded Thebes in such a matter; the relation of Thebes to the League had been unstable and uneasy early in the century, Thebes joining definitively only in 288.[23] I tentatively give the Ptoium first place, therefore 229/8, with Dionysus of Thebes honored in a subsequent autumn but before 225/4. If their similarity indicates immediate proximity, then Apollo Ptoius (the season of this decree being unknown) may be spring 228 and Dionysus in autumn of the same year. But it remains possible to assign Thebes to any autumn in 228–225, and Acraephia to 225/4.[24]

21. Holleaux, *BCH* 16 (1892) 455; cf. Flacelière, *Aitoliens* 405–406; Feyel, *Contribution* 142–147.

22. See Feyel, *Polybe* 251–256; Nachtergael, *Les Galates* 283–289.

23. Cf. Roesch 421–439.

24. These considerations build on the several contributions of Flacelière, Feyel (*Contribution* 147 n. 1 for the priority of Thebes), Nachtergael, and R. Etienne and D. Knoepfler (*Hyettos de Béotie,* BCH Suppl. 3 [Paris 1976] 331–337), while modifying them somewhat. The period of fourteen Aetolian seats has traditionally (since Homolle) been placed in the early 220s. I have preferred this over Nachtergael's lower dating (his nos. 62–64: beginning later than 229/8,

In the course of 228 Antigonus Doson recovered much of what he had lost and Aetolia had gained in Thessaly in 229, driving the Boeotians to make common cause again with the Aetolians.[25] By mid-228, he had ravaged Doris and detached Phocis from the Aetolians; in spring 227 there was fighting between Macedonia and Boeotia (Polyb. 20.5).[26] This growing threat may be the context of the decisions by Acraephia and Thebes to seek inviolability for their chief temples. The Council's favorable responses can be seen as part of the restoration of good relations between Boeotia and Aetolia. If we place those decisions in 226 or 225, we are on the eve of the renewed defection of Boeotia from the Aetolians in 224. Earlier is perhaps more likely, with 228 spring and autumn possible for the pair; but it must be stressed how many variables affect all this.

As for the Ptoium, by the time of the Amphictyonic decree this was a federal temple, for the Boeotian League already shared in its administration; the burden of the decree on the score of administration is to add an agonothete to the number of the temple authorities (**3**.15). This suggests that the status of the god's games was now being increased. From other inscriptions we know that late in the third century the cities of Boeotia voted to increase the honors of Apollo by sending representatives to offer sacrifice at the Ptoia: that is, the games became Pan-Boeotian.[27] Feyel argued convincingly that this was the same occasion as our Amphictyonic decree. Perhaps the enlargement of the games was described in the lost portion of **3**, the Council being asked to approve the formal arrangements. In what survives of the Boeotian civic decrees accepting the Ptoia, however, there is no mention of the inviolability of the temple. It would seem that in Boeotia recognition by the Amphicytonic Council was regarded as authoritative and sufficient for *asylia,* and no civic recognitions were sought; whereas certainly the Amphictyony could not render the games Pan-Boeotian—the Boeotian cities themselves must agree to that.

An oracle of Trophonius (**2**) is inscribed below the decree: Trophonius says that Lebadeia is to be dedicated to Zeus and Trophonius, Acraephia to Apollo; and each is to "proclaim the holy contest" in every land. The stone evidently

---

down through 221/0), for it seems to me still possible in light of his commentary (pp. 286–289) on the added fifteenth Aetolian seat (which he places in 217/6); he dates Callias (**3**, the Ptoium) to 221/0 (**4**, not in a year of the Soteria, does not enter his discussion). P. Gauthier, *Nouvelles inscriptions de Sardes* II (Geneva 1989) 143–150, has argued for giving the Pythian year 226/5 to Alexandridas; see, however, Knoepfler, *MusHelv* 50 (1993) 40–42 (Alexandridas "soon after 214/3").

25. For the defection of the Boeotians from the Aetolians in the mid 230s and their restoration on the Amphictyony ca. 229, see Flacelière, *Aitoliens* 248–250; Etienne and Knoepfler 336–337.

26. F. W. Walbank, *ZPE* 76 (1989) 184–192; cf. Gauthier, *Bull. épigr.* 1989, 275; Etienne and Knoepfler 334–335.

27. The dossier at Feyel, *Contribution* 133–147; cf. *Polybe* 254–256; S. Lauffer, "Ptoion," *RE* 23 (1959) 1547–1553; Roesch 229–238.

was intended as a dossier of texts pertinent to the increase of Apollo's honors; a third text records a dedication of funds to the god. The physical arrangement need not reflect their chronological order. Most scholars have taken the oracle as the occasion of the increase in Apollo's honors, thus prior to the decree. The Acraephians may have inscribed the Amphictyonic decree first as being the decisive text, and the oracle as an attendant document, part of the case that persuaded the Amphictyony. Neither this decree (its first half lost) nor those accepting the Ptoia[28] mention any oracle; but such silences are common in the *asylia* inscriptions.

If the oracle is the earlier text, what was its intent? The god would seem at first to envision inviolability for the city of Acraephia: yet in the event only the temple was declared inviolable. I think, however, that the poetic language of an oracle should not be pressed. Presented with this statement, ambiguous on Lebadeia as well as Acraephia, the Acraephians seem to have interpreted conservatively and in accord with their institutions: *asylia* was sought for the temple alone, which was outside the city on Mt. Ptoius; the games were to be Pan-Boeotian, proclaimed in every city of Boeotia.

It is possible, however, that the oracle is later and represents a subsequent stage in the honors of the god. This implies a more literal reading, taking "sacred games" as this was commonly used in Roman times, "declare the contest Panhellenic" (so Roesch). If that is so, then Trophonius spoke later than the Amphictyons (thus in the order of the texts on the stone) and now urged yet greater honor for Apollo Ptoius—games not just Pan-Boeotian but Panhellenic, inviolability for not only the temple but also the city and country. These two statuses were never obtained, so far as we know; accordingly, I have assumed the oracle to come first, prompting the attested events.

The oracle was addressed by the Opuntian Calliclidas rather than by a citizen of Lebadeia or Acraephia; Roesch urged that he was acting on instruction of the Boeotian League and the oracle should date from a time when Opus was in the League (the dates of which are problematic).[29] But this question need not be material, for the oracle may well be older than the 220s, and the city's reaction slow or delayed, as we know could happen.[30]

2–3

Acraephia, temple of Apollo. Plaque of blue-grey marble broken at top and bottom, found in 1885 reused in a Byzantine tomb north of the temple, now in the museum at Thebes; h. 1.22, w. 0.58, th. 0.15. Three texts, a dossier on

28. Only one text is fully preserved, however, the decree of Oropus (*LSCG* 71).

29. Roesch 232–235; but see Etienne and Knoepfler (333), who deduce from Calliclidas' ethnic "Locrian" that Opus was not in the Boeotian League at this time.

30. Again, if Trophonius does mean to order Panhellenic games and an inviolable city, the oracle is later than the increase of the 220s and failed to be fulfilled.

the temple probably cut by the same mason (so Roesch 232): the uppermost is the Amphictyonic decree **3**, then the oracle **2**, then a dedication of money to Apollo (not included here).

Holleaux, *BCH* 14 (1890) 19–33 no. 10 [Dittenberger, *IG* VII 4135–4136; *Syll.*^{2} 557; Michel, *Rec.* 700; Prott-Ziehen, *Leg.Sacr.* II 70; Pomtow, *Syll.*^{3} 635; Sokolowski, *LSCG* 73].

Cf. Holleaux, *BCH* 16 (1892) 453–457, 472; A. Nikitsky, *ZhournMinistNarod Prosv* n.s. 38 (March 1912) 125–133; Feyel, *Contribution* 140–147; G. Klaffenbach, *Philologus* 97 (1948) 373–376; Etienne and Knoepfler, *Hyettos* 331–341; P. Roesch, *Etudes béotiennes* 60–68, 232–236; A. Schachter, *AJP* 105 (1984) 259–270.

2. Oracle of Trophonius

Καλλικλίδας Λοκρὸς ἐσς Ὀπόεντος καταβὰς ἐν Τρεφώ-
νιον ἀνάνγειλε Λεπάδειαν τοῖ Δὶ τõι Βασιλεῖι ἀνθέμεν
κὴ τõι Τρεφωνίοι, κὴ Ἀκρήφια τõι Ἀπόλλωνι τõι Πτωΐυ, κὴ μεὶ
4 ἀδικῖμεν μειδένα οὕτως· οὕτως [δ]ὲ ἀγιρέμεν ἀμφοτέ-
ρως τὰ ἱαρὰ χρείματα κυνῆ ἐφ' οὐγίῃ κατὰ πᾶσαν χώ-
ραν, κὴ τὸν ἀγῶνα ἱαρὸν καταγγελλέμεν· ὅστις δέ κα τῶ
Διὸς τῶ Βασιλεῖος ἐπιμελειθείει τῶ ναῶ, τὸν στέφανον
8 ὕσετη.

. . .

Calliclidas, Locrian from Opus, having gone down to Trophonius, proclaimed that Lebadeia is to be dedicated to Zeus Basileus and Trophonius, and Acraephia to Apollo Ptoius, and no one is to wrong these (peoples). They are both to collect sacred funds, for the common good, in every land, and proclaim the holy contest. Whoever repairs the temple of Zeus Basileus will wear the crown.

This is a complex answer to what may have been a series of questions, apparently posed at the behest of the Boeotian League, as the questioner is not from either Lebadeia or Acraephia.[31] The League approached the most respected oracle in Boeotia, the Trophonium in the territory of Lebadeia. The questions concerned how the two cities might best honor their chief gods; perhaps the cities had put these issues before the League, which sought divine sanction or adjudication. One can only speculate why the affairs of two cities were put before the oracle at one time. This need not reflect some collaboration between the two (on 6 ἀγῶνα see below); perhaps each had resorted to the League for guidance, which in turn pooled the requests in consulting the oracle.

1: The verb reflects the fact that the Trophonium was a cave (cf. καταβῆναι at Philostr. *VA* 8.19; other instances at Schachter 260 n. 11). On the oracle see G. Radke, "Trophonios," *RE* 7A (1939) 685–691.

31. Holleaux took Calliclidas to be a religious expert whose services were sought out.

4: Holleaux rightly took the second οὕτως as a pronoun;[32] an adverb (so Dittenberger) would refer back to nothing. But he took the pronoun to refer to the two gods rather than the two peoples. Schachter takes ἀμφοτέρως as "jointly," perhaps correctly. As to the collection of funds, Miletus in the third century consulted Delphi about a religious collection, asking "whether it will be pleasing to the goddess and advantageous to the people to conduct now and in the future collections for Artemis Boulophoros" (*LSAM* 47). Greek cities took care to regulate such religious solicitations, as Holleaux remarked, citing in addition Isis on Samos (*LSCG* 123.10) and Artemis Pergaia at Halicarnassus (*LSAM* 73.26); cf. Segre, *I.Cos* ED236.

6–7: I assume that two contests are in question, despite the singular ἀγῶνα; these two cities did not share a contest. The phrase κατὰ πᾶσαν χώραν can be taken to mean that the two contests were to become Panhellenic, "in every land" (cf. Dem. 20.76: πᾶσαν ἐπέλθων . . . χώραν; the Isis aretalogy, *IG* XII Suppl. p. 98: ἡ τύραννος πάσης χώρας); the Magnesians proclaimed their games κατὰ πᾶσαν τὴν Ἑλλάδα (**111**.25). But χῶρα is vague enough to allow a less ambitious interpretation, every region or city of Boeotia,[33] or "the entire land" of Boeotia.[34] The god thus can be taken to call for Pan-Boeotian games—at any rate this seems to be how the Acraephians took it.[35] A single increase happened now, and thus Trophonius' instruction to "dedicate" the city to Apollo and not harm the Acraephians is what prompted the Amphictyony to declare the temple inviolable and to regulate the games that the Boeotian cities would vote to share.

As to "sacred" in 7, Greek did not apply a word "Panhellenic" to festivals. The games that all Greeks shared, by sending *theoroi*, were identified circumstantially: "crowned," "equal to the Olympia," "triumphal," etc. By Roman times a favored term had emerged, "sacred" games (the prize was dedicated to the god). But that usage is a late development, and all games were sacred to some god.[36] Hence ἀγὼν ἱερός is found early on as a poetic effusion, without implying a contrast with ordinary games (*agon thematites* or *chrematites*, with a cash prize).[37] Of the technical usage, the earliest instance may be *I.Délos* IV 1957 (ca. 150–130 B.C.); cf. *SEG* 39.1243.I.7 (Claros, late II B.C.); *AM* 33 (1908) 409 no. 40 (a

32. Cf. W. Blümel, *Die aiolischen Dialekte* (Göttingen 1982) 267.

33. Compare Dem. 23.139, Charidemus' attacks κατὰ πάσης χώρας = many Greek cities in Thrace.

34. Cf. *Hell.Oxy.* 11.3: πάντες οἱ τὴν χώραν οἰκοῦντες (Boeotia); in poetry Ar. *Plut.* 773, honoring χώραν πᾶσαν Κέκροπος = Attica.

35. For Lebadeia see below; we do not know the status of the Basileia of Lebadeia in the third century B.C.

36. E.g., Plut. *Aem.* 17.9, vowing a hecatomb and ἀγῶνος ἱεροῦ τῷ θεῷ (Heracles).

37. This is probable in Pind. *Nem.* 2.4, 6.59; certain in Theoc. 16.47, 17.112 (a "sacred contest" of Dionysus at Alexandria; Gow ad loc. is wrong to think that this is trying to equate the contest with the Panhellenic games); *IG* II^2 11387 (of comedy).

statue from Pergamum, I B.C.?). We need not follow Roesch and Schachter in interpreting Trophonius to intend the technical usage, with the Acraephians instructed to seek Panhellenic games; I have argued above that the Acraephians did not interpret the oracle so.

7–8: I take this to mean στεφανηφορεῖν, "to be the priest"; compare *I.Scythiae* I 54.19–20 (= *Syll.*[3] 708): Διὸς τοῦ Πολιέως ἀναλαβὼν στέφανον καὶ ἱερησάμενος εὐαρέστως (Istria); *LSAM* 13.11–12: στεφανηφορεῖν αὐτῶν ἀεὶ τὸν ἔχοντα τὴν ἱεροσύνην (Pergamum). Schachter thought rather "to win a crown" as a reward for services; cf. Etienne and Knoepfler 341.

3. Amphictyonic Council

Inscribed above **2**.

[- - - - - - - - - πενθ' ἡμέρα]ς πορευομέ[νοις καὶ ἀπερχομέ]-
[νοις ἄλλας τοσαύ]ṭας καὶ ὡς ἂν ἡ πανήγυ[ρις γίνηται καὶ]
[αὐτοῖς καὶ τοῖς] ἀκολούθοις καὶ ἃ ἂν ἔχωσι [χρήματα παν]-
[ταχοῦ·] ἐὰν δέ τις [παρὰ] ταῦτα ἄγηι τινὰ ἢ ῥυ[σιάζηι,]
[ὑπ]όδικος ἔστω ἐν Ἀμφικτύοσιν· εἶναι δὲ καὶ ἄσυ-
λον τὸ ἱερὸν τοῦ Ἀπόλλωνος τοῦ Πτωΐου τὸ ἐν Ἀκραιφίοις ὡς ἂν
αἱ στῆλαι ὁρίζωσι καθάπερ τὸ ἐν Δελφοῖς, τὴν δὲ λοιπὴν χώ-
ραν τὴν ἱερὰν τοῦ Ἀπόλλωνος τοῦ Πτωΐου μὴ ἀδικεῖν μηδένα·
ἐὰν δέ τις ἀδικῆι, ὑπόδικος ἔστω ἐν Ἀμφικτύοσιν· τῆς δὲ
ἐκεχειρίας καὶ τῆς ἀσφαλείας ἄρχειν τὴν πεντεκαιδεκά-
την τοῦ Ἱπποδρομίου μηνὸς κατὰ θεὸν ὡς Βοιωτοὶ ἄγουσιν,
ὡς δὲ [Δ]ελφοὶ Ἀπελλαίου· κυρίους δ' εἶναι οἰκονομοῦντας
τὰ κατὰ τὸ ἱερὸν τόν τε προφήτην καὶ τὸν ἱερέα τοῦ Ἀπόλλω-
νος τοῦ Πτωΐου καὶ τὴν πόλιν τῶν Ἀκραιφιέων καὶ τὸ κοινὸν
τῶν Βοιωτῶν, καθὼς καὶ ἔνπροσθεν, καὶ τὸν ἀγωνοθέτην
τὸν εἰρημένον ἐπὶ τὸν ἀγῶνα τῶν Πτωΐων· ἀναγράψαι δὲ τὸ ψή-
φισμα ἐν στήλαις Πτωϊοκλῆν Ποταμοδώρου καὶ ἀναθεῖναι
τὴμ μὲν ἐν Δελφοῖς ἐν τῶι ἱερῶι τοῦ Ἀπόλλωνος, τὴν δ' ἐν Ἀ-
κραιφίοις ἐν τῶι ἱερῶι τοῦ Πτωΐου, τὴν δὲ ἐμ Πυλαίαι, ἀναθεῖ-
ναι δὲ καὶ τῶν ἄλλων ἱερῶν ὅπου ἂν δοκῆι ἐν καλλίστωι εἶν-
αι· ἐὰν δέ τι γίνηται ἀδίκημα παρὰ τὸ δόγμα τῶν Ἀμφικτυ-
όνων, ἀποτεισάτω ὁ ἀδικῶν δισχιλίους στατῆρας καὶ ὃ
ἂν καταβλάψηι, τὰ δὲ καταδικασθέντα χρήματα ἱερὰ ἔσ-
τω τοῦ Ἀπόλλωνος τοῦ Πτωΐου· ἀνενεγκεῖν δὲ τὸ δόγμα τοὺς
ἱερομνήμονας ἐπὶ τὰς πόλεις καὶ τὰ ἔθνη τὰ ἴδια ὅπως εἰδῶ-
σιν πάντες τὰ δεδογμένα τοῖς Ἀμφικτίοσιν.

The division in the opening lines is to a degree arbitrary; and line 5, though short, seems complete. 1–4 Feyel. 2 init. Klaffenbach: ἐπανερχομένοις δὲ - - - ἡμέ]ρ̣ας Feyel.

. . .

[(inviolability) . . . for five days] in coming [and as many in departing] and while the festival [takes place, both for themselves and their] attendants and their [property,

> everywhere.] If anyone contrary to this seize or rob anyone, let him be subject to prosecution before the Amphictyons. The temple of Apollo Ptoius in Acraephia is to be inviolable, as the boundaries define, as is the temple in Delphi; the other sacred land of Apollo Ptoius no one is to harm; if anyone does, he is to be subject to prosecution before the Amphictyons. The sacred truce and security are to begin on the fifteenth of Hippodromios by the moon as Boeotians reckon, of Apellaios as Delphians. Those in authority to administer the temple affairs are to be the prophet, the priest of Apollo Ptoius, the city of Acraephia, and the Boeotian League, as previously, and the agonothete elected for the contest of the Ptoia ... (provisions for inscribing) ... If any offense occur contrary to the decree of the Amphictyons, the wrongdoer is to pay 2,000 staters plus damages and the fine is to be dedicated to Apollo Ptoius. The *hieromnemones* are to report this decree to their respective cities or nations so that all may know what the Amphictyons have decreed.

1–4: Compare **4**.19–22, the two passages serving to restore each other; cf. 1 Macc. 10:34: τρεῖς ἡμέραι πρὸ ἑορτῆς καὶ τρεῖς ἡμέραι μετὰ ἑορτήν. The privilege voted the Artists, right of complaint to the Amphictyons if they are harmed, is to pertain only to the time of their travel and performance at the Ptoia. Cf. *IG* XII.9 207.63–64 (for the Artists on Euboea); for an individual, *I.Delos* 502.17–19. For excused absences cf. Wilhelm, *Jahresh.* 12 (1909) 140 (*Kl. Schr.* II. 1 362); parallels for their "attendants": J. and L. Robert, *Bull. épigr.* 1958, 261. For the inviolability of the temple, by contrast, no time limit is stated, and the analogy with Delphi implies that none was intended.

7: One of the few references to boundaries in a grant (outside of Egypt); compare Apollo Chresterius at Chalcedon and Athena at Pergamum. The precedent of the inviolability of the temple at Delphi is used also in **4**.22 from Boeotia, but nowhere else in the *asylia* inscriptions. Similar precedents are invoked in Ptolemaic Egypt and in the Roman province of Asia (pp. 19, 389)—closed legal systems in which a single authority rather than Greek public opinion is the source of the grant. This supports the idea that Boeotians felt the will of the Amphictyony to be sufficient to establish the status and did not seek recognition by the Greek world at large; such at least is the scope of the evidence extant.

The word λοιπήν indicates that Apollo owned other land, not contiguous with his temple on Mt. Ptoius;[38] this was nothing unusual, but the express inclusion of such land in the grant of *asylia* is not paralleled.

11–12: The calendric equation is useful.[39] The months were to be as reckoned by nature (κατὰ θεόν), by the sighting of the new moon, without regard for intercalary months or days. The law on performance in Euboea makes explicit the problem presented by intercalation: when an intercalary month has been

38. Cf. Rigsby, *AJP* 108 (1987) 733–734.

39. See Roesch 37, 60–68; cf. J. Pouilloux, *REA* 66 (1964) 211–213; Samuel, *Chronology* 68–69, 74.

inserted, the magistrates are to do whatever is necessary to guarantee synchronism (*IG* XII.9 207.49–51; cf. 61: κατὰ θεόν; compare on **25**.16–17). Apellaios was the first month at Delphi; Boeotian Hippodromios, their eighth month, is equated by Plutarch with Attic Hecatombaion (July/August). The Ptoia began on the 20th of Hippodromios (five days after the start of the truce, line 1), hence roughly mid-August.

12ff.: The Council evidently was asked to give its imprimatur to a change in the administrators of the "temple affairs" (for the phrase see Robert, *Op. min. sel.* I 562), to whom an agonothete was now added.[40] From this addition, some have concluded that no games were celebrated in Apollo's honor before now.[41] In my view the status of the agonothete is here increased along with that of the contest, which until now was local; for there is some evidence for the Ptoia earlier than the 220s.[42]

24ff.: The same provision is in the Amphictyonic decree *Syll.*^{3} 704E.43ff.

The excavators of the temple found two boundary stones (neither in situ), one by a fountain near the temple complex, the other just down the hill from the temple itself. I give here the text of the better preserved, underlining what is extant only on the other stone.

Holleaux (1890) 7–8 [*IG* VII 4153, 4154].

[ἄσ]ουλον τὸ ἱα-
[ρ̲]ὀ[ν̲] τῶ Ἀπόλω-
[ν]ο[ς] τ̣ῶ Πτωΐω
. . . . . . ΛΙΙ ὁρι-
.Ο.Ο. [Ἀ]πόλω-
[νι?]

The script, as reported, seems no older than the third century B.C. The text evidently was more elaborate than the chaste ὅροι ἄσυλοι of ordinary temples of the classical period, Hieracome, and the rest; it seems to have made a statement and likely reflects the decreed inviolability of the temple. Hence the markers probably are subsequent to **3** and respond to its intent. The findspot of the one stone might suggest that the limits of *asylia* stipulated at **3**.7 were to encompass only the terrace of the *naos* itself. But the Amphictyony adds that the rest of the land belonging to the god is not to be harmed (**3**.7–8), for Apollo owned other land in the territory of Acraephia; that too will have had boundary markers.

40. At **4**.24–26, however, the Council similarly approves the administrators of the games at Thebes, although it is not evident what is changed there.

41. References at Lauffer 1547.

42. See *AJP* 108 (1987) 729–740: probably in the 230s, a special competition for Athena held at the Ptoia, to which Acraephia invited neighboring Haliartus.

Temple of Dionysus Cadmeius, Thebes

Thebes had the distinction of being the birthplace of two sons of Zeus, Dionysus and Heracles.[43] The prominence of Dionysus in the legends of Thebes is well known; this was the home of Semele and the city that owed her son first honor. The prominence of Thebes in the affairs of Boeotia is equally familiar; refounded in 316 after its destruction by Alexander, it became one of the five members of the Boeotian League privileged to have an ἀφεδριατεύων on the federal council in the third century.[44] The festivals of Dionysus and of Heracles at Thebes had each obtained Panhellenic status by the early second century B.C.[45] The inviolability of Dionysus Cadmeius[46] is attested by an inscription at Delphi of the 220s: the Amphictyony defines the privileges and responsibilities of the Artists who perform at Dionysus' festival, and also declares the temple inviolable. Half a century later, the Artists would state that oracles of Apollo had persuaded the most pious among the Greeks to grant them personal inviolability because of their role in the contest of Dionysus at Thebes, among other festivals (*IG* XI.4 1061.16).

The temple has not been located with certainty; nonetheless Thebes seems to provide an instance of inviolability of a temple (rather than city and country) when the temple is inside the city.[47] Within the *temenos* of Dionysus was a σηκός (**4**.17, 28). The opening of Euripides' *Bacchae* (with θυγατρὸς σηκόν, 11) portrays the palace and Semele's tomb juxtaposed on the citadel of Thebes, where the lightning struck her. Pausanias was shown a ruined chamber (θάλαμος) of Semele[48] in the agora, together with an altar made by the sons of Praxiteles

43. Testimonia on Dionysus of Thebes are listed at Schachter I 185–187; add *FGrHist* 380 F 1 with Jacoby's comments, the tradition that Dionysus sent the Sphinx to Thebes. For Heracles, Schachter, *Cults* II, BICS Suppl. 38.2 (London 1986) 14–30. On the topography see F. Schober, "Thebai," *RE* 5A (1934) 1423–1452; for the temple, A. D. Koumanoudis, *Deltion* 3 (1917) 341–346; S. Symeonoglou, *The Topography of Thebes* (Princeton 1985) 57, 127.

44. P. Roesch, *Thespies et la confédération béotienne* (Paris 1965) 138.

45. See Roesch, *ZPE* 17 (1975) 1–7, with J. and L. Robert, *Bull. épigr.* 1976, 301; A. Schachter, "The Boiotian Herakles," *Teiresias* Suppl. 2 (1979) 39; D. Knoepfler, *Chiron* 22 (1992) 476.

46. Apart from **4** the only mentions of the cult epithet of Dionysus of Thebes are in an epigram a generation earlier (Kaibel, *Epigr.* 926.13–14) and at Paus. 9.12.3. Cf. *Anth. Gr.* 11.40.5 (A. S. F. Gow and D. Page, *The Garland of Philip* I [Cambridge 1968] 126, Antistius 3), referring to Dionysus simply as Καδμεῖε (corrected from Κάδμε).

47. The temple is usually identified with a structure near the Electra gate; cf. Fossey 204. In the *asylia* inscription, ἐν Θήβαις (**4**.14, 28) is too vague to be useful; so the rural Itonium could be ἐν Κορωνείᾳ (*FGrHist* 378 F 1; schol. Ap. Rhod. 1.551a; **1**.14; n. 11 above), the Ptoium ἐν Ἀκραιφίοις (3.6), the Sarapeum ἐν Μέμφει (Paus. 1.18.4); cf. Philostr. *VA* 4.1 (τοῦ Κολοφῶνι μαντείου and τοῦ περὶ τὸ Πέργαμον ἱεροῦ).

48. 9.12.3; compare ὁ τῆς Σεμέλης θάλαμος at Callixenus *FGrHist* 627 F 2.31 (Ath. 200B), Σεμέλης θάλαμος at [Ael. Arist.] 25.2 Keil; cf. J. and L. Robert, *Bull. épigr.* 1982, 298. For σηκός = ἡρῷον see Bourguet, *FD* III.1 p. 200.

and a statue of the god: here a log had fallen from heaven, which the Thebans adorned with bronze and called Dionysus Cadmeius. So there is good reason to think that Pausanias' *thalamos* is the *sekos* of the inscription (hence the restoration of Semele's name), and that the temple was in the center of Thebes. This evidence is not conclusive, however: Pausanias does not mention a temple, and he puts the tomb of Semele in the lower city to the northeast (μνῆμα, 9.16.7; Symeonoglou 190), in contrast to Euripides. Keramopoullos's suggestion that the temple was defunct and in ruins in Pausanias' day seems contradicted by the celebration of the games (though fused with the Heracleia) in imperial times.[49] So the possibility remains that Dionysus' temple stood outside the city (as did Heracles'), like most others declared inviolable.[50]

The festival at issue is here called the τριετηρίς rather than a proper name; a two-year period was typical for Dionysus (see above, p. 56). The contest was certainly old in the 220s, attested, for example, by the Pythocles epigram before the mid-third century.[51] The Amphictyons obviously envisage that the contest will become of more than local patronage—it is to be proclaimed "to the cities" (compare, on the Ptoia, **2**.5 and **3**.25). In fact games of Dionysus administered by Thebes and the Artists, the Agrionia, are attested as Panhellenic as early as 170 B.C. The name does not occur in our inscription of the 220s. Robert suggested that the present effort to increase the games to Panhellenic status failed and that subsequently the festival was reorganized and renamed as part of a new (and successful) effort (*Op. min. sel.* VII 778). Instead, it may be that the Panhellenic status of the games was indeed gained now and the Amphictyons' failure to call the *trieteris* the Agrionia is not significant: as a generic term, like *thysia*, *panegyris*, and *agon*, the word is often found substituted for the proper name of a festival (e.g., at Pergamum).[52] The Amphictyons will naturally have echoed the language of the embassy that made the request. I suggest however a third possibility: what is envisioned in the 220s is making the games only Pan-Boeotian. The absence of the Boeotian League from the administration of the cult perhaps speaks against this; but that the proclamation of the games is to be "to the cities" (and not "kings, dynasts, nations, cities," the conventional Panhellenic roster) suggests a restriction, surely to Boeotia. The revised terminology that Robert detected will have come about later, as he thought, when the games became Panhellenic; the present effort, however, was not a failure, merely less ambitious.

As to date, decree A to inscribe the previous enactments concerning Theban cult was passed in a subsequent Pythian year.[53] Of the two decrees then inscribed

49. On the reorganized Dionysia-Heracleia see Robert, *Op. min. sel.* VII 778–779.

50. For the Heracleum, Arr. *Anab.* 1.8.3–5, with J. G. Frazer, *Pausanias* V (London 1898) 46–47; Symeonoglou 133; Schober 1448–1449.

51. Kaibel, *Epigr.* 926, with Nachtergael, *Les Galates* 318–322.

52. See C. P. Jones, *Chiron* 4 (1974) 186–187.

53. Probably 214 B.C.; see Flacelière, *Aitoliens* 295 n. 4; Feyel, *Contribution* 143 n. 4.

below A, the second and better preserved, C, is dated to autumn of the Delphian archon Nicarchus; this decree alludes (31–33) to the substance of its predecessor, B, and regulates a further detail concerning the Artists. Feyel argued that this is an afterthought to decree B, responding to the same request and passed at the same Council session as B.[54] To this it can be added that C states not that the Amphictyony has declared the temple inviolable but that the Thebans have requested as much. If C was prompted by a different embassy sent later, surely the grant, the acquired fact of inviolability, rather than the request, would have been invoked. C thus seems to be a rider on current business, and so B, like C, dates to Nicarchus' year. The *asylia* of the temple of Dionysus thus would belong to an autumn of the years 228–225 (see above on Acraephia); I would prefer the earliest of these, autumn 228, in immediate proximity to that for the Ptoium at Acraephia and amid the events that led to war with Macedonia in 227.

The later decree (A) grants a request to inscribe the previous enactments concerning the cult of Dionysus. These earlier decrees have been abridged, for both lack their lists of *hieromnemones*, and B has no preliminaries describing the embassy and its petition. C alone reveals (31) that the embassy was a joint one by Thebes and the Artists—in keeping with their joint administration of the cult and proclamation of the games as stipulated in B (23–26; cf. 12, 15). As a rider voted on the same occasion, C adds penalties to enforce the provisions of B.

4. Amphictyonic Council

Delphi. Five fragments of two marble blocks, originally part of a wall of the Theban Treasury. Careful, somewhat crowded lettering (0.008–0.01; intersp. 0.009, diminishing) of the late third century B.C.: strokes slightly curving, occasional thickening at the ends; A with straight bar; Θ, O, Ω small and suspended; right hasta of N slightly raised. Word division is observed at the line ends.

Inv. 632, upper block, lines 1–15; h. 0.24, w. 0.242, th. 0.24; found built into the wall of a modern house, removed to the museum in 1893: E. Dodwell, *A Classical and Topographical Tour* (London 1819) 508 [Le Bas-Foucart, *Voyage* 842]; Boeckh, *CIG* 1689 (copy of Koehler); F. Thiersch, *Ueber die Topographie von Delphi*, AbhBerlin 3.1 (Berlin 1840) 68–70; J. L. Ussing, *Graeske og Latinike Indskrifter* (Copenhagen 1857) no. 30 (copy of Brøndsted); Baunack, *SGDI* 2532 (squeeze).

Inv. 632, +1142+4449 (lower block, broken in the middle, found by the Theban Treasury in 1894; combined h. 0.34, w. 0695 [slight upward taper], th. 0.82): E. Bourguet, *FD* III.1 351 and p. 199.

Inv. 632+1142+4449, +5084 (bottom center of upper block, Theban treasury; h. 0.087, w. 0.01, th. 0.037) +7705 (bottom center of lower block, Theban Treasury; h. 0.12, w. 0.18, th. 0.037): J. Bousquet, *BCH* 85 (1961) 78–88 [*SEG*

54. On the inconsistency of dialect between the two, he noted (*Contribution* 145 n. 1) that C is itself inconsistent, first Koine, then Doric.

19.379; Pickard-Cambridge, *Dramatic Festivals of Athens*² 309–310 (B and C); *SEG* 28.487 (from Robert 1977)].

Photograph: Bourguet pl. X (632+1142+4449); *FD* II *Trésor de Thebes* pl. 69 (1142); Bousquet figs. 8–11 (all but 1142).

Cf. Pomtow, *JahrbClPhil* 40 (1894) 548–558; 43 (1897) 806; Wilhelm, *Beiträge* 292; Nikitsky, *ZhournMinistNarodProsv* n.s. 38 (March 1912) 125–133; Flacelière, *Aitoliens* 409–410; Feyel, *Contribution* 140–147; Klaffenbach, *Philologus* 97 (1948) 373–376; Daux, *RA* 1950, 194–195 (copy of A. F. Sturtzenbecker [1784] and squeeze); Robert, *ArchEph* 1977, 195–210 (*Op. min. sel.* VII 765–780); D. M. Lewis ap. Schachter, *Cults* I 189 n. 2; J. Ebert, *Epigraphica* 45 (1983) 7–10.

A. [θεοί. τύχα. ἐπὶ 10-12 ἄρχοντος ἐν Δελφοῖς, ἱερομνημονούντων Αἰτωλῶ]ν Φι[λίπ]που Λαμιέος, Σιμάργου
[-]στα Προσχείου, Πολυξένου Λιμναίου,
[-]λαιέος, Μνασιλαίδα Ἀμβρακιώτα,
4 [- - - - - - - - - - - - - - - Χίων ? - - - - - - - - - - -]ταίνου· Δελφῶν Τελεδάμου, Ἐμμενίδα·
[Ἀθαμάνων ? -]ου Θαυμακοῦ· Πυθίοις· ἐπειδὴ παρὰ
[τᾶς πόλιος τῶν Θηβαίων ἀπολσταλεὶς - - - - - - - - - -] παρεκάλεσεν τοὺς Ἀμφικτίονας ὅπως ἂν
[ἐπιμέλειαν ποιήσωνται τᾶς ἀναγραφᾶς πάντων τῶν δεδογμένων ὑ]πὲρ τᾶν τριετηρίδων καὶ γένηται ἐν
8 [παραδόσει αὐτά· δεδόχθαι τοῖς Ἀμφικτιόνεσσι τὰ ὑπὲρ τᾶν τριε]τηρίδων ἀναγράψαι τὰ δόγματα τὰ
[ἐπὶ Νικάρχου ἄρχοντος δεδογμένα εἰς τὴν οἰκίαν τῶν Θηβαίων, εἶ]μεν δὲ αὐτὰ καὶ ἐν παραδόσει καθὼς
[παρακαλεῖ - - - τοὺς Ἀμ]φικ[τίονας. vacat] vacat

B. [ἐπὶ Νικάρχου ἄρχοντος ἐν Δε]λφοῖς, Π[υλαίας ὀπωρινῆς· ἔδοξεν τοῖς Ἀμφι]κτίοσιν, ὅπως ἂν ἡ θυσία τῶι Διονύσωι
12 [τῶι Καδμείωι καὶ οἱ] ἀγῶνες οὓς σ[υντελεῖ ἡ πόλις τῶν Θηβαίων καὶ τὸ κ]οινὸν τῶν τεχνιτῶν τῶν εἰς Ἰσθμὸν
[καὶ Νεμέαν συνπορευο]μένων γίνητ[αι ὡς κάλλιστα, ἐπιμελεῖσθαι] τοὺς ἱερομνήμονας οἳ ἂν ὦσιν ἐν τῶι
[ἐνιαυτῶι ἐν ὧι ἂν αἱ τ]ριετηρίδες κα[θήκωσιν τῶι Διονύσωι τῶι Κα]δμείωι ἐν Θήβαις ὑπὲρ τοῦ [τὴν]
[ἐκεχειρίαν ἄρχειν] ἐν τῆι ἡμέρα[ι ἧι ἂν ἡ πόλις τῶν Θηβαίων καὶ τὸ κ]οινὸν τῶν τεχνιτῶ[ν]
16 [ἐ]θελ[ήσω]σιν [-]α̣ναι ἐν τῶι
ἱερῶι παρὰ τὸν σηκ[ὸν τῆς Σεμέλης - - - - - - - - - - - - - - · εἶ]ναι δὲ καὶ ἀσφάλειαν
καὶ ἀσυλίαν πᾶσι το[ῖς τεχνίταις τοῖς νεμηθεῖσιν εἰς τὴν θυσία]ν τῶν τριετηρίδων
πένθ' ἡμέρας πορευ[ομένοις καὶ ἀπερχομένοις ἄλλας τοσαύτας κ]αὶ {ε}ὡς ἂν ἡ πανήγυρις

γίνηται, καὶ αὐτοῖς κ[αὶ τοῖς συνεργαζομένοις αὐτοῖς, πα]νταχοῦ· ἐὰν δέ τις παρὰ ταῦτα
ἄγηι τινὰ ἢ ῥυσιάζηι, ὑ[πόδικος ἔστω ἐν Ἀμφικτίο]σιν· εἶναι δὲ καὶ τὸ ἱερὸν τοῦ
Διονύσου τοῦ Καδμείου [τὸ ἐν Θήβαις ἀπὸ πάντων ἄ]συλον καθάπερ καὶ τὸ ἐν Δελφοῖς·
τὴν δὲ θυσίαν καὶ ἐκεχε[ιρίαν ἐπαγγέλλειν ἐ]πὶ τὰς πόλεις τήν τε τῶν Θηβαίων
πόλιν καὶ τοὺς τεχνίτας· κ[υρίους δ' εἶναι οἰκονο]μοῦντας τὰ κατὰ τὸ ἱερὸν τόν τε ἱερέα τοῦ
Διονύσου καὶ τοὺς ἐπιμελ[ητὰς τοὺς ὑπὸ τῶ]ν τεχνιτῶν εἰρημένους καὶ τὸν ἀγωνοθέτην
Θηβαίων· ἀναγράψαι δὲ τὸν [γραμματέα τόδ]ε τὸ ψήφισμα ἐν στήλαις δυσὶν καὶ ἀναθεῖναι
τὴν μὲν ἐν Δελφοῖς ἐν τῶ[ι ἱερῶι τοῦ Ἀπόλλωνο]ς ὅπου ἂν δοκῆι ἐγ καλλίστωι εἶναι, τὴν δὲ
ἐν Θήβαις παρὰ τὸν σηκὸ[ν τῆς Σεμέλης, ἀν]αθεῖναι δὲ καὶ τῶν ἄλλων ἱερῶν ὅπου ἂν
δοκῆι ἐν καλλίστωι εἶναι. [vacat] vacat
c. ἐπὶ Νικάρχου ἄρχοντος ἐ[ν Δελφοῖς, Πυλαία]ς ὀπωρινῆς· ἔδοξεν τοῖς Ἀμφικτίοσιν· ἐπειδὴ
ἁ πόλις τῶν Θηβαίων κα[ὶ οἱ τεχνῖται οἱ εἰς] Ἰσθμὸν καὶ Νεμέαν συντελοῦντες παρεκάλεσαν
τοὺς Ἀμφικτίονας τό τε [ἱε]ρὸν [τοῦ Διονύσου] ἄσυλον ποιῆσαι καὶ ἐπιμέλειαν ποιήσασθαι τᾶς
ἀ[σ]φαλείας καὶ τοῦ ἀγῶ[ν]ος, ὅπω[ς κα ἁ θυσία ἁ] τῶν τριετηρίδων ὡς κάλλιστα συντελῆται τῶι
Διονύσωι τῶι Καδμε[ίω]ι· δεδόχ[θαι τοῖς Ἀμφικτ]ιόνεσσι, αἴ τίς κα τῶν αὐλητᾶν ἢ τῶν χο-
ρευτᾶν ἢ τῶν τραγωιδῶν ἢ τῶν κω[μωιδῶν τῶν νε]μηθέντων εἰς τὰς τριετηρίδας ὑπὸ τῶν τε-
χνιτᾶν μὴ ἀγωνίζηται [τ]ὰς τριετηρίδα[ς συντελειμέ]νας κατὰ τὸν νόμον τᾶς πόλιος τῶν Θηβαίων,
ἀλλὰ ὑγιαίνων λίπη[ι τὸν] ἀγῶνα, μὴ ε[ἶμεν αὐτῶι ἀσφ]άλειαν μηδὲ τοῖς συνεργαζομένοις αὐτῶι μή-
τε πολέμου μήτε εἰρά[να]ς· αἴ κα μὴ ἀγ[ωνίζηται, καἴ] κα ζαμιωθῇ ὑπὸ τοῦ ἀγωνοθέτα, καὶ ἀγώγιμος ἔ-
στω πανταχόθεν· [αἴ κα] τις πόλις ἢ [ἀρχεῖον ἢ ἰδιώτ]ας [τ]ὰν ζαμίαν ἀφέληται τὸν ἐζαμι[ωμ]ένον

Text of Bousquet. Some letters once read have been lost to flaking; I have not indicated the losses. 1: ΝΙΙΣ ΟΥ Sturtzenbecker, Νικ[ίπ]που? Daux. 3: Αἰ]λαιέος or 'Ε]λαιέος. 4: Πλει]σταίνου or Ἀρι]σταίνου Pomtow. 5: γραμματεύοντος τοῖς ἱερομνάμοσιν Μενάνδρου] Pomtow. 6: Sturtzenbecker read the verb in full; παρα[γενόμενος πρὸς τὸ συνέδριον ὁ δεῖνα παρε]κάλεσεν Pomtow; πρὸς τοὺς ἱερομνήμονας ὁ ἀγωνοθέτης Θηβαίων παρε]κάλεσεν Bourguet. 7 ποιήσωνται Ebert (ποιήσωσι κτλ. Bousquet): [ὡς κάλλιστα συντελῆται ἁ θυσία τῶι Διονύσωι τῶι Καδμείωι] Bourguet. 8: ΤΗΡΙΔΩΝ Sturtzenbecker;

- - - ἡ θυσία τῶι Διονύσωι τᾶν τριετηρί]δων Pomtow; [ταῖς καθηκούσαις ἡμέραις ἁ πανήγυρις καὶ - - - ὁ ἀγὼν τῶν τραγωι]δῶν (or προστεθεὶς ἀγὼν τῶν κωμωι]δῶν, p. 198) Bourguet. 9:]ΔΙΕΝ Sturtzenbacker; εἶ]μεν Wilhelm; [πρότερον δεδογμένα αὐτοῖς ἐν Θήβαις, - - - μ]εν Pomtow; [περὶ τούτων και πρότερον δεδογμένα εἰς τὰν οἰκίαν τῶν Θηβαίων· εἶ]μεν Bourguet. 10: [τοῖς τεχνίταις συγκεχωρημένον ἦν] Pomtow; [παρακαλεῖ τὸ κοινὸν τῶν τεχνιτῶν] Bourguet. 11 Νικάρχου Feyel. 12 init. Robert: [- - - καθὼς παρακαλεῖ τὸ κοι]νὸν Pomtow; [τῶι Καδμείωι ὡς κάλλιστα συντελῆται, καθὼς π. τ. κ.] Bourguet; [ἡ τῶν τριετηρίδων κ. ο.] Bousquet. 14 Lewis:]ΑΜΕΙΟΙ Koehler; τ]αμεί⟨ω⟩ι Boeckhh; ἱερῶι καὶ ἀναγράψαι τὰ δεδογμένα αὐτοῖς ἐν τῶι τ]αμείωι Pomtow; [συνεδρίωι τῶν δογμάτων τῶν ἀναγεγραμμένων ἐν τῶι Κα]δμείωι Bourguet; [συνεδρίωι ὁπόταν αὖ τ]ριετηρίδες κα[ὶ οἱ ἀγῶνες συντελῶνται ἐν τῶι Κα]δμείωι Bousquet; [ἐνιαυτῶι ἐν ὧι ἂν Robert; κα[τασκευάζωνται or κα[ταγωνίζωνται Ebert. 14–15 Robert (or [ἀσφάλειαν and ταύτηι ἧι): ὑπὲρ τού[των | ὅπως Bourguet; [ὅπως ἕκαστα γίνηται] Bousquet. 16: τὸν ἀγῶνα τιθέ]ναι? Nikitsky; ἀναγραφῆ]ναι Bourguet. 18: [τοῖς ἐπὶ τὴν πανήγυριν καὶ τὴν θυσία]ν Bourguet. 19 Klaffenbach; {ε} del. Nikitsky: πορευ[ομένοις ἐν τούτοις ἐνγεγραμμένοις κριτηρίοις, κ]αὶ ἕως Bourguet. 20: [καὶ πᾶσι τοῖς (κτλ.) Bourguet; [καὶ τοῖς ἀκολούθοις καὶ ἃ ἂν ἔχωσιν Nikitsky. 21–22 Bourguet: ῥυσιάζηι [τι Nikitsky. 23 Nikitsky: ἀναγορεῦσαι Bourguet. 24 Nikitsky: κ[αὶ τοὺς ἀεὶ ο. Bourguet. 25 Nikitsky: ὑπὸ τοῦ κοινοῦ τῶ]ν Bourguet. 26–32 Bourguet. 33 Robert: · ὅπω[ς οὖν? Nikitsky. 34 Nikitsky: Καδμ[είωι καὶ γένηται ἐν ἁμέραις πλει]όνεσσι Bourguet. 35 Nikitsky: προσνε]μηθέντων Bourguet. 36 Ebert: ἀγωνίζητα[ι τοὺς προστεταγμένους ἀγῶν]ας Bourguet; τριετηρίδα[ς καὶ τοὺς ἀγῶν]ας Bousquet. 37: λίπη[ι, μὴ εἶμεν αὐτῶι μηδαμοῦ ἀσφ]άλειαν Bourguet. 38: εἰ[ρήνας, μηδὲ ἀσυλίαν, ἀλλὰ ὅπως κ]α Bourguet. 39: πανταχόθεν [εἰς Θήβας· καὶ μηδεμί]αν Bouguet; ⟨αἴ κ'⟩ [ἀ]φέληται τὸν ἐζαμ[ιωμ]ένον | [ἢ τῶν τούτου τι πόλις τις ἢ ἰδιώτας - - - Nikitsky.

A: In a Pythian year (214?) the Council grants a request by a single Theban envoy that the earlier decrees about the *trieteris* be inscribed on the Theban Treasury and put in the "tradition," the papyrus record of official acts that the annual magistrates passed on to their successors.[55] The original decree provided for an inscription (line 27); perhaps this was not carried out or was in a place too obscure to satisfy the Thebans. At Teos and Tenos it was felt worthwhile to send a special embassy around Crete to request that earlier *asylia* decrees be inscribed.

The two decrees B and C, like **3** for the Ptoium, define the administrative control of the cult and make the safety of the festival a legal concern of the Delphian Amphictyony; C, in effect a rider, stipulates the penalties for defaulting performers.

55. On the *paradosis* see Wilhelm, *Beiträge* 292. The form was perhaps the τόμος συγκολλήσιμος known from the papyri—each new document glued to the last until a roll was made up; cf. N. Lewis, *Papyrus in Classical Antiquity* (Oxford 1974) 81.

B: So that the sacrifice to Dionysus [Cadmeius and the] games c[onducted by the city of the Thebans and the] Isthmian-[Nemean] Artists may be [as fine as possible,] the *hieromnemones* of the [year in which the] *trieterides* are [held for Dionysus] Cadmeius in Thebes [are to see to it that the sacred truce begins] on the day [on which the Thebans and the Artists] wish. . . . All [Artists assigned to the sacrifice] of the *trieterides* are to have security and inviolability for five days in coming [and as many in leaving] and while the festival lasts, both themselves [and their assistants,] everywhere. If anyone contrary to this seize or plunder any of them, [he is to be subject to prosecution before the Amphictyons.] The temple of Dionysus Cadmeius [in Thebes] is to be inviolable [from all], like the temple in Delphi. The Thebans and the Artists [are to proclaim] the sacrifice and truce to the cities. [Those empowered to] administer the temple affairs are to be the priest of Dionysus, the overseers named by the Artists, and the agonothete of the Thebans. (Provisions for inscribing.)

C: Inasmuch as the Thebans and the Isthmian-Nemean [Artists] have asked the Amphictyons to make the temple of [Dionysus] inviolable and to take care of the security of the contest as well, so that the sacrifice of the *trieterides* for Dionysus Cadmeius may be conducted as finely as possible, [the Amphic]tyons decree that if any flutist, chorist, or tragic or comic actor assigned to the *trieterides* by the Artists should not compete in the *trieterides* conducted in accordance with the law of Thebes but, in good health, should miss the competition, neither he nor his assistants is to have security in war or peace. If he should not compete and is punished by the agonothete, he is to be subject to arrest everywhere. If any city or [magistrates or private person] should remit the fine . . .

14: For κα[θήκωσιν of games cf. **97**.25; **101**.35; Plut. *Dem.* 40.7: τῶν δὲ Πυθίων καθηκόντων. For κα[τασκευάζωνται Ebert adduced **100**.30 (τοὺς ἀγῶν[α]ς . . . συγκα[τα]σκευάζ[ων), but *Syll.*³ 690.3 (καταγωνίξασθαι . . . [τὸν ἀγῶνα]).

16: The provision for inscribing this decree begins only later (26ff.). The present passage comes after the statement that the date of the festival is to be at the organizers' discretion, and before the privileges for Artists who participate. Perhaps here was a provision that the date of the festival, when decided upon, is to be posted beside the *sekos* of Semele, perhaps on a temporary *leukoma*,[56] so παρεστ]άναι; but the usual verb is τιθέναι and its compounds (e.g., at Miletus: ἐκτιθέναι τὰ ὀνόματα αὐτῶν εἰς τὴν Ἀντιόχε⟨ι⟩ον στοάν).[57]

22: For the citation of the precedent see on **3**.7.

23–24: The city and the Artists are joint sponsors of the games (cf. 12); what they proclaim jointly "to the cities" (of Boeotia, in my view) was only the games

56. On the practice see Wilhelm, *Beiträge* 246–247, 273–274.

57. *Syll.*³ 577.29. Cf. *I.Ephesos* 4.21; *I.Priene* 59.36; Dem. 56.18; προ-: *IG* IX.2 1109.35; *SB* XIV 12144.15; κατα-: *I.Cret.* III IV 7.14; but *LSCG* 50.17: (the decree) ἐκκίμενον [ἧι . . .] πρὸ τοῦ ναοῦ; and Dem. 58.8–9.

of Dionysus, the "sacrifice and truce": like Acraephia, Thebes requested *asylia* from the Amphictyony, games from the cities.

24–26: At Acraephia the parallel passage brought about an innovation, the addition of the agonothete (**3**.15); here it is not made clear what is changed.

34ff.: For the privilege conditional upon fulfillment of a contract cf. *IG* XII.9 191.A.37–38: Chaerephanes and his laborers will enjoy *asylia* only so long as they are doing their work for the city. Again on Euboea, Artists who miss work are to be ἀγώγιμοι, 207.42–45; compare 62, ἀφεῖσθαι τῶν πρότερον ζημ[ιῶν], with line 39 here.

Unidentified Boeotian Temple

I place here a mention of inviolability for a temple that certainly was Boeotian and possibly was that of Dionysus at Thebes; its date is ca. 225–200 B.C.

5. Amphictyonic Council

Delphi, Theban Treasury (?). Two nonjoining fragments of white marble. Letters and intersp. 0.008: full-sized O, right hasta of Π almost fully descended, Σ with somewhat divergent bars; last quarter of the third century B.C. (Bousquet).

Inv. 1145, upper fragment; h. 0.20, w. 0.15, th. 0.18; found in 1894 probably by the Theban Treasury: H. Pomtow, *Klio* 14 (1915) 301 [Flacelière, *Aitoliens* 417].

Inv. 1145, +7664, lower fragment (find unrecorded); h. 0.11, w. 0.15, th. 0.165: Bousquet, *BCH* 88 (1964) 385–387 [*SEG* 22.450]; Roesch, *Etudes béotiennes* 10–11 [*SEG* 32.541].

Photograph: Bousquet fig. 5.

A. [θ ε ο] ị

[ἐπὶ - - - ἄρχοντος ἐν Δελφοῖς, Πυλαίας - - -] ἱερομν[αμονούντων Αἰτωλῶν - - -]

[-]λου Κοτ[ταέος - - - - - - - - -]

4 [- Μελι?]ταιέος̣ [- - - - - - - - - - - - -]

B. [- - - - - - - - - - - - - - - Ἀ]μ̣φι̣χ̣[τι - - - - - - - - - - - - - - - - - -]

[- - - - - - - - - - - - - - - ἄσυ]λον εἶμ[εν - - - - - - - - - - - - - - - - -]

[- - - - - - - - - - - - - μηνὸς Θει]λουθίου ὡς [Βοιωτοὶ ἄγοντι, ὡς δὲ]

4 [Δελφοὶ 'Ιλαίου, - - - - - - μηνὸ]ς ἱσταμένου· ἀ[ναγράψαι - - - τόδε]

[τὸ ψήφισμα ἐν τῶι ἱερῶι τοῦ Ἀ]πόλλωνος το[ῦ Πυθίου vacat?]

vacat

B. 1 Roesch: ψ]α̣φι̣[σμ - - - Bousquet. 4 'Ιλαίου Roesch; ἀ[ναγρ. δὲ τὸν γραμματέα κτλ. Bousquet.

We do not know how much is lost between the two fragments. A longer line than even Bousquet envisaged is possible; and B.5 may have gone on to provide for more than one copy. At B.1ff. Roesch suggested ἔδοξε τοῖς Ἀ]μφικ[τίοισι τὸ ἱερὸν or τὰν χώραν (name) ἄσυ]λον εἶμ[εν· ἔδοξε τῶι κοινῶι Βοιωτῶν, ἄρχοντος - - - μηνὸς Θει]λουθίου. Thus he assumed that the body of the Amphictyonic decree begins at B.1 rather than earlier and also ends there and that a different decree, of the Boeotians, begins at B.2; this reconstruction is arbitrary and improbable.

The month Thelouthios is exclusive to Boeotia (the seventh, ca. July).[58] From the color and grain of the stone as well as from the excavation records, Bousquet assigned the decree to the Theban Treasury[59] but found it incompatible in its lettering with any extant text from there. No city but Thebes is known to have inscribed its documents on the treasury.[60]

From the double date (B.3–4) I suggest that a sacred truce is being specified, as at **3**.11, with the games in Thelouthios. That excludes certain major Boeotian festivals whose season is known—the Pamboeotia in Pamboiotios, the Ptoia in Hippodromios (**3**.11), the Basileia of Lebadeia in Panamos.[61] We do not know the season of the Theban festival of Dionysus, and the Amphictyons had left the specific day to the discretion of the local authorities (**4**.15–16). The present decree might be a subsequent enactment about the same cult, expressly fixing, as was done for the Ptoia, the day and month on which the truce is to begin and mentioning (as **4**.31–32 does) the inviolability of the temple of Dionysus.

One might expect, however, that the Agrionia were held in Agrionios, the fourth month (April/May). Hence this may well be a new grant of *asylia* for another Boeotian shrine, possessed of an important festival whose month is not otherwise known to us—for example, the Mouseia at Thespiae[62] or the Amphiaraea at Oropus.

58. For the Boeotian calendar see Roesch, *Etudes* 3–87, who recognized the Delphian equivalent. F. Lefèvre, *BCH* 115 (1991) 586 n. 25, remarks the rarity of such equations in Delphian epigraphy.

59. He found the inventory numbers consistent with those of the Theban Treasury (rather than the Athenian Treasury, as in the excavation journal); accepted with caution by J.-P. Michaud, *FD* II *Le Trésor de Thèbes* (Paris 1973) 129.

60. A contrary statement has been restored at *FD* III.1 36.2: see, however, Robert, *Op. min. sel.* I 136.

61. Feyel, *Contribution* 74.

62. The Mouseia seem to have become Panhellenic late in the third century; cf. Feyel, *Contribution* 88–132; A. Schachter, *NC* VII.1 (1961) 67–70.

Temple of Amphiaraus, Oropus

The oracular and healing shrine of Amphiaraus stood in the frontier region between Attica and Boeotia.[63] The first great "increase" in the cult had occurred in the fourth century B.C., a tumultuous period during which Athens and the Boeotians disputed control of the sacred place. Much of its major construction dates from those years, and there is evidence that the number of pilgrims swelled. Already in the fourth century the *panegyris* and games of Amphiaraus were celebrated with greater pomp every fourth year (Ἀμφιαράϊα τὰ μεγάλα, ἡ πεντετηρίς).[64] The Hellenistic age, when the site was Boeotian (after 295/4), was more peaceful, and few events are known in the history of the shrine. Oropus, some three kilometers to the northwest of the temple, possessed the place, evidently without significant challenge;[65] and, as at some other important Boeotian temples, the Boeotian League seems to have played a role in its administration.[66] During this long period of stability the cult enjoyed an international patronage, visible in the many extant dedications—especially by Romans in the age of Cicero. The games of Amphiaraus may have become Panhellenic by the early second century B.C.[67]

No primary grant survives, and the inviolability of the Amphiaraeum is known to us only by a reference of Roman times. Sulla, during his brutal passage through Greece, besieged Athens in 87 and in the next year fought Mithridates' forces in Boeotia.[68] At the Amphiaraeum, we learn, he made a vow to add land to the *temenos* "so that that land too will be inviolable" (**6**.45)—a kindness at variance with his reported plundering of other temples in Greece. The term ἄσυλος here reveals an existing privilege of *asylia*, expanded now with the limits of the temple land, as Caesar would do at Didyma and Antony at Ephesus.

63. V. C. Petrakos, Ὁ Ὠρωπὸς καὶ τὸ Ἱερὸν τοῦ Ἀμφιαράου (Athens 1968), and Ἐπιγραφικὰ τοῦ Ὠρωποῦ (Athens 1980) (cf. *SEG* 31.418ff.); A. Petropoulou, *GRBS* 21 (1981) 39–63; cf. Schachter I 19–26. On the chronology of ownership of the shrine see D. Knoepfler, *Chiron* 16 (1986) 71–98; 22 (1992) 452.

64. *IG* VII 412.26, 414; Petrakos (1968) 196 no. 47; *Syll.*^{3} 287.13, 675.35.

65. Athens attempted to take possession in 156 B.C.; cf. *Syll.*^{3} 675, with Petrakos (1968) 37–39, 187–188.

66. In the 260s, we are told, the philosopher Menedemus, exiled from nearby Eretria, took up residence in the Amphiaraeum; but charged with stealing sacred vessels, he was required to leave by vote of the Boeotian League: Diog. Laert. 2.142; cf. K. von Fritze, "Menedemos 9," *RE* 15 (1931) 789–790; D. Knoepfler, *La vie de Ménédème* (Basel 1991).

67. Mentioned in Moretti, *I. agon. gr.* 45 (early II B.C.), a list of distinguished games, though not all Panhellenic.

68. On Sulla in Boeotia see P. W. Wallace, *Strabo's Description of Boiotia* (Heidelberg 1979) 176–177. For the possibility that he made a grant to Trophonius as well as to Amphiaraus, see below on Lebadeia.

The occasion of the original recognition we can only guess at. Other Boeotian instances, and perhaps Panhellenic status of the Amphiaraea by about 200 B.C., would suggest a date in the second half of the third century. But the silence of the rich material from the site, apart from Sulla's inscription, recommends caution. It may be that the local authorities foisted upon Sulla some claim of a right of asylum from more remote antiquity, and there was no recognition of Hellenistic date. Compare Delphi, and perhaps the Asclepieum at Epidaurus (cf. p. 90), which first flourished, like the Amphiaraeum, in the early fourth century and which apparently never sought a Hellenistic recognition of inviolability. At any rate, the harvest of inscriptions from the Amphiaraeum can show nothing of *asylia* before Sulla's visit.

The Sulla inscription contains the following:

A. a covering letter (lines 1–6) to Oropus from the consuls in October 73 conveying the following:

B. a report (lines 6–59) submitted to the Senate in October 74 by the consuls together with a committee of senators, rendering their opinion (16–34) and quoting from

 1. the *lex locationis*[69] as it concerns Sulla's power to dispose of sacred land (35–42)
 2. Sulla's declaration, in 86 B.C., of the fulfillment of his vow to Amphiaraus (42–51)
 3. the s.c. of 80 B.C. ratifying Sulla's acta (51–59)

C. an s.c. of October 73 (two days after A) reaffirming that of 80 (B.3) in light of the consuls' investigation (59–69)

The Oropian land in question (32–33, 65–66: περὶ χώρας Ὠρωπίας) is judged to be exempt from taxation because Sulla lawfully assigned it to the god Amphiaraus. Publicans had challenged the tax exemption,[70] on the argument that Amphiaraus was not a god.

As this is a secondary act, and one to which *asylia* is only incidental, I quote it here selectively, in chronological sequence (and indicating the outline given above).

6. Rome

Oropus, temple of Amphiaraus. White marble stele found in 1884 by the statue base of Sulla (*IG* VII 264); now in the local museum (inv. 452).

S. Vases, *ArchEph* 1884, 101–120 (from a squeeze by Leonardos) [Mommsen, *Hermes* 20 (1885) 268–287 (*Ges. Schr.* V 495–513); Viereck, *Sermo Graecus* 18;

69. ὁ τῆς μισθώσεως νόμος (25, 35, 66): strictly speaking, the *lex censoria* for his province; cf. Kornemann, *RE* 13 (1926) 935.

70. On the phenomenon see R. Bernhardt, *Polis und römische Herrschaft* (Berlin 1985) 194–197. For the question of the status of Oropus between the Roman conquest in 146 and Sulla see Knoepfler, *MusHelv* 48 (1991) 275.

E. de Ruggiero, *L'arbitrato pubblico* (Rome 1893) 25]; Dittenberger, *IG* VII 413 (collation by Lolling) [*Syll.*[2] 334; Bruns, *Fontes*[7] 42; Laum, *Stiftungen* 26 (lines 42–50); Hiller, *Syll.*[3] 747; Abbot and Johnson, *Municipal Administration* 18; Riccobono, *Fontes*[2] 36; Sherk, *Roman Documents* 23]. *Collation.* Photograph: C. Lanzani, Lucio Cornelio Silla (Milan, 1936) p. 172.

(B.2) The committee's description of Sulla's vow and dedication of 86 B.C. (lines 42–51):

Λεύκιος Κορνήλιος Σύλλας ἀπὸ συν-
βουλίου γνώμης γνώμην εἰρηκέναι δοκεῖ· τῆς εὐχῆς ἀποδόσεως
ἕνεκεν τῶι ἱερῶι Ἀμφιαράου χώραν προστίθημι πάντῃ πάντοθεν πόδας
χιλίους, ἵνα καὶ αὕτη ἡ χώρα ὑπάρχῃ ἄσυλος· ὡσαύτως τῶι θεῷ Ἀμφιαράωι
καθιερωκέναι τῆς πόλεως καὶ τῆς χώρας λιμένων τε τῶν Ὠρωπίων
τὰς προσόδους ἁπάσας εἰς τοὺς ἀγῶνας καὶ τὰς θυσίας ἃς Ὠρώπιοι
συντελοῦσιν θεῷ Ἀμφιαράωι, ὁμοίως δὲ καὶ ἃς ἂν μετὰ ταῦτα ὑπὲρ τῆς
νίκης καὶ τῆς ἡγεμονίας τοῦ δήμου τοῦ Ῥωμαίων συντελέσουσιν,
ἐκτὸς ἀγρῶν τῶν Ἑρμοδώρου Ὀλυνπίχου υἱοῦ, ἱερέως Ἀμφιαράου, τοῦ
διὰ τέλους ἐν τῇ φιλίᾳ τοῦ δήμου τοῦ Ῥωμαίων μεμενηκότος·

. . .

Sulla is found to have stated: "In fulfillment of a vow I attach to the temple of Amphiaraus land for one mile continuously in every direction, so that this land too be inviolable." Likewise it is found that to the god Amphiaraus have been dedicated all the revenues from the city and territory and harbors, for the games and sacrifices which the Oropians celebrate for Amphiaraus, likewise those which they will celebrate hereafter in honor of the victory and power of the Roman people—excepting the fields of Hermodorus son of Olympichus, priest of Amphiaraus, who has always remained in the friendship of the Roman people.

(B.3) Ratification of this by the Senate in 80 B.C. (lines 54–57):

ὅσα τε θεῶι
Ἀμφιαράωι καὶ τῶι ἱερῷ αὐτοῦ Λεύκιος Κορνήλιος Σύλλας ἀπὸ συ⟨ν⟩βουλίου
γνώμης προσώρισεν συνεχώρησεν, τὰ αὐτὰ ἡ σύνκλητος τούτωι τῶι θεῶι
δοθῆναι συνχωρηθῆναι ἡγήσατο.

(B) L. Domitius Ahenobarbus' protest in behalf of the publicans, as described by the committee (lines 25–29):

ἐπεὶ ἐν τῶι τῆς μισθώσεως νόμωι αὗται αἱ χῶραι ὑπεξειρημέναι εἰσὶν
ἃς Λεύκιος Σύλλας θεῶν ἀθανάτων ἱερῶν τεμενῶν φυλακῆς ἕνεκεν
συνεχώρησεν, οὔτε ὁ Ἀμφιάραος, ὧι αὗται αἱ χῶραι συνκεχωρημέναι
λέγονται, θεός ἐστιν, ὅπως ταύτας τὰς χώρας καρπίσζεσθαι ἐξῇ
τοὺς δημοσιώνας.

. . .

While in the *lex locationis* those lands are excluded which Sulla granted for the security of the sacred precincts of the immortal gods, Amphiaraus, to whom these lands are claimed to have been granted, is no god, so that it is permitted that the publicans enjoy these lands.

(C) The Senate's decree in 73 on the findings of the committee in favor of Amphiaraus (lines 65–67):

> ὡσαύτως τὴν Ὠρωπίων
> χώραν ὑπεξειρημένην δοκεῖν εἶναι κατὰ τὸν τῆς μισθώσεως νόμον,
> μὴ δοκεῖν τοὺς δημοσιώνας ταῦτα καρπίζεσθαι...

The issue here was not *asylia* but the tax status of land and of revenues that had formerly been secular and were now sacred. The publicans challenged the sacredness of the added land and the dedicated revenues, not a "right of asylum," which Sulla mentions only in passing.

According to Augustine (*De civ.D.* 4.27), the pontifex maximus Q. Mucius Scaevola (consul in 100 B.C.) had written that the general public ought not to be told that Asclepius and the like had been mortal, lest doubt be raised about their divinity. Cicero, who was a member of the committee that found against the publicans in the case of Oropus (lines 11–12), years later wrote complacently of the controversy, without mentioning the outcome or his own participation:[71]

> *an Amphiaraus erit deus et Trophonius? nostri quidem publicani, cum essent agri in Boeotia deorum inmortalium excepti lege censoria, negabant inmortalis esse ullos qui aliquando homines fuissent. sed si sunt hi di, est certe Erechtheus . . .*

Thus Sulla did two things in 86. He increased the god's land by adding one mile to the radius of the precinct,[72] and he diverted to the upkeep of the god's festival the taxes that the city of Oropus paid annually to Rome. The first entailed ownership, the second "enjoyment" (καρπίζεσθαι).

The topographical import of the first act is uncertain, for we do not know the original radius.[73] The narrow valley in which are crowded the temple and its attendant buildings is about four Roman miles from the city proper. Even before Sulla, the sacred land may well have extended to the coast. The harbor Delphinium, about a mile from the temple, Strabo calls "the sacred harbor";[74] if this usage is older than Sulla, the original sacred land may already have extended a mile from the temple.

As to the resignation of Roman taxes, nature and art combined to make the harbors of this coast very lucrative, and the Oropians are singled out for their

71. *Nat. d.* 3.49, with A. S. Pease ad loc. (II 1080–82). At *Leg.* 2.19 he has no doubt that Asclepius ought to be worshipped. For publicans' encroachments on sacred land see Rostovtzeff, *SEHHW* III 1526 n. 89.

72. Compare two miles at Didyma and Hieracome, and Antony's doubling at Ephesus.

73. The boundary stone *IG* VII 422 (IV B.C.?) is from the site itself, but precisely where is not recorded: ὅρος· μὴ τοιχοδομε͂ν ἐντὸς τῶν ὅρων ἰδιώτην.

74. Strab. 9.2.6 (403): ὁ ἱερὸς λιμήν, ὃν καλοῦσι Δελφίνιον; restored by Köhler at *IG* I^3 428.6: ἐν Ὀροπõι ἐν ἱερ[õι λιμένι - - -. Cf. Petrakos (1968) 11; Wallace 25, 43–45.

rapacious taxation of trade;[75] from Oropus one can see Eretria—the shortest passage between Attica and Euboea.[76] Taxes on sales and transit of goods and on land formed the bulk of any Greek city's revenue. By πρόσοδοι (47) are meant Rome's revenues, its tax on Oropus, and not the tax revenues of Oropus itself—the diversion of which to the god would have ruined the city. The god will now "enjoy" (not own) those resources, receiving the revenues that formerly went to Rome. Oropus, we know, hailed Sulla as savior and benefactor[77] and renamed the Panhellenic games the Ἀμφιαράϊα καὶ Ῥωμαῖα.[78] The taxes they had paid to Rome now would go to their god, to pay for games that would otherwise have been a substantial expense to the city. Alexander had done a similar favor for Artemis and the Ephesians when he assigned to the goddess the taxes that the city had paid the Persians.[79] Sulla himself assigned the income of half the territory of Thebes to repay the temples at Delphi, Olympia, and Epidaurus for the goods he had requisitioned of them.[80] The priest's property is exempted from the assignment to Amphiaraus (50); apparently this dignitary and friend of Rome[81] was already exempt from Roman taxation, and consequently from the transfer of that obligation to the god.

Temples of Zeus Basileus and of Trophonius, Lebadeia

In his oracle inscribed at the Ptoium in the 220s (**2**), Trophonius had as much to say about his own Lebadeia as about Acraephia, calling for its dedication

75. Heraclid. Perieg. 7 (p. 76 Pfister); see Robert, *Hellenica* XI–XII (1960) 265.

76. And traditionally Oropus' mother city: Nicocrates *FGrHist* 376 F 1. Knoepfler (above, n. 70) 278–280 suggests that Oropus did not in fact exist in the preceding generation, with the Amphiaraeum attributed to Eretria, and that Sulla reestablished Oropus. The silence of **6** about this reestablishment perhaps speaks against this idea.

77. *IG* VII 264 (Petrakos [1968] pl. 58b); cf. 372 for his wife.

78. On this and other Boeotian festivals in the age of Sulla see A. G. Gossage, *BSA* 70 (1975) 115–134, esp. 117–118 n. 6.

79. Arr. *Anab.* 1.17.10. Cf. Antiochus I of Commagene on the revenue of villages dedicated to the gods (*IGLSyrie* I 1.19, quoted p. 31 n. 6).

80. Plut. *Sull.* 12, 19; App. *Mith.* 54; Diod. 38.7.

81. Cf. A. J. Marshall, *AJP* 89 (1968) 52–53. We know or suspect other members of Hermodorus' family: an Olympichus was priest of Amphiaraus early in the third century B.C. (Petrakos [1968] 156 no. 12 = *IG* VII 336); toward 150 B.C. Hermodorus' father proposed the pro-Roman decree *Syll.*^{3} 675 (defense against Athens; cf. Knoepfler [above, n. 70] 276 n. 109); a probable descendant in *IG* VII 341 was the agonothete of the first of the new games after Sulla (Knoepfler 280 n. 127).

to Zeus Basileus and Trophonius, the proclaiming of a contest, and the repair of the temple of Zeus. As to *asylia*: if the Lebadeians did as the Acraephians, they will have sought inviolability for their temples of Zeus and of Trophonius, and at some date in the last quarter of the third century. We have, however, no evidence that they did so.[82] A text of the third century A.D. need reveal no more than the rhetoric of its age in speaking of "the holy city of Lebadeia," ἡ ἱ[ε]ρὰ Λεβα[δ]έων πόλις (*IG* VII 3105). As to the games, the facts are uncertain. As we have seen, the Acraephians probably responded to the oracle by making the Ptoia Pan-Boeotian, not Panhellenic, and possibly the Thebans did likewise in these years. At Lebadeia two festivals[83] come into the question because two gods are named. The Basileia, founded after Leuctra in 371, are first attested as Panhellenic at the end of the third century B.C., the Trophonia in the early second.[84] Thus we know only a terminus ante quem for each, but that much is consistent with their gaining the status as a result of this oracle, and thus in the last quarter of the third century.

Asylia for these two sacred places, which adjoin each other on a hill outside the city proper, would not have been untoward.[85] The cults of Zeus Basileus and Trophonius were famous. In the Boeotian-Aetolian treaty (early third century B.C.), the oath begins with Zeus Basileus.[86] A new temple of Zeus seems to have been begun toward the end of the third century and extensively repaired in the first half of the second, partly with funds from Antiochus IV; it does not seem ever to have been completed.[87] Apollo's son[88] Trophonius, who spoke from a cave, was the most respected oracular god in Boeotia, and much frequented. Pausanias gives examples of cities that are dedicated to gods: ἀνακεῖνται πόλεις ... Λεβάδεια Βοιωτῶν Τροφωνίῳ (1.34.2). The cult statue was by Daedalus (Paus. 9.40.3), and the fame of the oracle had spread beyond Greece already in archaic times (Hdt. 1.46, 8.134).

82. But see the unattributed **229**, where one might restore a reference to Zeus Basileus.

83. See Moretti, *I. agon. gr.* pp. 105–107.

84. References at D. Knoepfler, *Chiron* 22 (1992) 487. Diodorus (15.53.4) knew an oracle of Trophonius delivered upon the occasion of the founding of the Basileia in 371 B.C., stipulating that the games be Panhellenic (ἀγῶνα τιθέναι Διὶ Βασιλεῖ στεφανίτην); this certainly is anachronistic.

85. For "Zeus Trophonios" see E. Rohde, *Psyche* I (New York 1925) 107–108. Dicaearchus wrote a tract on the Trophonium: frags. 13–22 Wehrli.

86. *Staatsvertr.* III 463; cf. Roesch, *Etudes* 359–364. In the second century B.C. some Boeotians in Egypt made a dedication to "Zeus Basileus and the other ancestral gods" (*SB* III 6664).

87. Etienne and Knoepfler 337–342; Feyel, *Contribution* 67 n. 1. On the topography see E. Vallas and N. Phaklas, *AAA* 2 (1969) 228–233; Lee Ann Turner, "The History, Monuments, and Topography of Ancient Lebadeia" (Ph.D. diss., University of Pennsylvania 1994).

88. Hence perhaps Lactant. Plac. ad Stat. *Theb.* 7.345 on Lebadeia: *civitas Apollini sacrata.*

On the question of deified mortals, Cicero mentioned not only Amphiaraus but also Trophonius before citing the publicans' challenge to the tax exemption of fields "in Boeotia" (*Nat. d.* 3.49, cited above). Larsen concluded that Sulla made the same gesture to Trophonius at Lebadeia as to Amphiaraus at Oropus.[89] Feyel observed that the Basileia in the first century B.C. had more money than in the preceding century and that this derived now not from the cities of the League but from a tithe: this, he thought, reflected the assignment of Rome's tax burden to Trophonius as at Oropus.[90] But his case rests on an unjustified equation of the Trophonia and the Basileia.[91] So I leave open the question whether Sulla intervened in this way at Lebadeia, noting only that the assignment of tax revenues does not prove inviolability, as the two are distinct matters.

Temple of Apollo Delius, Tanagra

The Delium, the famous temple of Apollo that Tanagra possessed on its coast, some eight kilometers from the city,[92] is described as follows by Livy (35.51), in narrating the attack on a Roman army there by troops of Antiochus III in 192 B.C.:

ubi et in fano lucoque ea religione et eo iure sancto, quo sunt templa quae asyla Graeci appellant.

The Greeks and Flamininus, we are told, expressed outrage (Diod. 29.1). Roman troops gathered at the temple were attacked, Livy says, in spite of the sanctity of the place and the fact that there was not yet the formality of war. No doubt Livy's source was Polybius, who mentions the inviolability of a threatened temple in Arcadia, and who makes a similar complaint about an attack at the Itonium in time of peace (see pp. 57, 91). Hence this passage may be no more than partisan fulmination. But it is possible that at some time Tanagra laid before the Romans the claim and evidence that the temple had been declared inviolable; and indeed Livy's phrase has the ring of a Roman legal pronouncement. A brief statement by Appian about the Delium (*Syr.* 12: ἱερὸν δ' ἐστὶ τὸ χωρίον Ἀπόλλωνος) is too generic to decide the matter.

89. In T. Frank, ed., *Econ. Survey* IV (Baltimore 1938) 307–308, 365, 427; cf. Wallace 176–177.

90. Feyel, *Contribution* 86–87; cf. Knoepfler (above, n. 7) 294.

91. See Moretti, *I. agon. gr.* p. 105.

92. For references see Wallace 27–29; Fossey 62–66; Schachter I 44–47. Honors voted by Tanagra announced at the games of Apollo Delius and elsewhere: *IG* VII 20.12.

Alalcomenae

The temple of Athena Alalcomeneis stood on the south shore of Lake Copais, in the plain below Mt. Tilphossium.[93] Here Athena was born; the Boeotian month Alalkomenios and the legendary Alalcomeneus (Page, *PMG* 985) hint at the early importance of the cult. When Alexander attacked Thebes, the statue of Athena Alalcomeneis burst into flames (Ael. *VH* 12.57). The Boeotian-Aetolian treaty (early third century) was inscribed ἐν Ἀλαλκομενείωι as well as at the Itonium and Onchestus (*Staatsvertr.* III 463.a.5). Boeotians held that when Homer mentioned Ἀλαλκομενηὶς Ἀθήνη he meant their goddess, not, as others thought, "guardian Athena."[94] The temple suffered the depredations of Sulla, and in Pausanias' time it was in decline and overgrown; he was told little of local legend (9.33.5–7).

Strabo, with access to earlier and better sources than Pausanias, reports a local story and claim (9.2.36 [413]); this was an ancient temple of Athena, greatly honored, and here she was born:

> διὰ τοῦτο δ' ἴσως οὐδ' ἐν τῷ καταλόγῳ μέμνηται τῶν ἐνταῦθα ἀνδρῶν, ἐπειδὴ ἱεροὶ ὄντες παρεῖντο τῆς στρατηγίας. καὶ γὰρ καὶ ἀπόρθητος ἀεὶ διετέλεσεν ἡ πόλις, οὔτε μεγάλη . . . τὴν θεὸν σεβόμενοι πάντες ἀπείχοντο πάσης βίας . . .
>
> . . .
>
> This is probably why there is no mention of men from here in the Catalogue: for being sacred, they were exempt from the expedition. And in fact the city has always continued unplundered, although it is not large . . . for all men, respecting the goddess, have abstained from any violence.

Hence (he concludes) the Thebans fled to Alalcomenae during the war of the Epigoni. The story, certainly older than the time of Sulla, bears an obvious similarity to the fourth-century Elean explanation of their absence from early wars. It is possible that the tale reflects a formal grant of inviolability dating to the Hellenistic age, which has left no trace in inscriptions. But it seems more likely that the opposite is the case, and the story is a myth of classical date.

93. Schachter I 111–114; Roesch, *Etudes* 218–220; on the topographical problem see W. K. Pritchett, *Studies in Ancient Greek Topography* II (Berkeley/Los Angeles 1969) 86 n. 10; Wallace 143–144; Fossey 332–335.

94. *Il.* 4.8 = 5.908, with H. Erbse, *Scholia graeca* I (Berlin 1969) 446.

Greece: Doubtful Cases

In Greece apart from Boeotia, several instances of declared inviolability are possible, but all are subject to various kinds of uncertainty.[1] Most of these (Epidaurus, Calaureia, Taenarum, Hermione, Nicopolis) are on Plutarch's list of inviolable temples attacked by the Cilician pirates.

Athens

Athens cultivated the reputation of being the benefactor and savior of the Greeks and the protector of suppliants. In Roman times we know of an "Altar of Mercy" (*IG* II^2 4786; Paus. 1.17.1); Statius offers the fullest account, that the goddess Clementia founded an altar in Athens where all might take refuge, hence Athenian protection of suppliants from the Heracleidae on (*Theb.* 12.481–518).[2]

1. The famous temple of Hera at Argos is called an asylum in a late Latin source, as well as in the piracy list of Plutarch and the list in Polybius (p. 38): Ampel. *Lib. mem.* 8.6: *Iunonis templum magnifice ornatum, quod asylum vocant*; cf. Pomp. Mela 2.41: *templum Iunonis vetustate et religione percelebre.* I hesitate to press this as evidence for an earlier Greek belief or recognition. Likewise Pausanias when he remarks the particular capacity of various temples to receive suppliants: so 3.5.6, the "Peloponnesians" from earliest times held Athena Alea at Tegea in such awe that foreigners took refuge there and no one thought to demand their surrender (αὐτόθι ἱκετεύουσιν ἀσφάλειαν); cf. 2.13.4 on Hebe at Phlius (ἄδειαν ἐνταῦθα ἱκετεύουσι).

2. R. E. Wycherley, *Athenian Agora* III (Princeton 1957) 67–74, 122 (perhaps the Altar of the Twelve Gods); P. Bruggisser, *Romulus Servianus* (Bonn 1987) 175–183. On the individuality of the Statius passage see J. F. Burgess, *CQ* n.s. 22 (1972) 339–349; A. W. Verrall, *Collected Literary Essays* (Cambridge 1913) 225–226, argued that the notion of Athens as humane to refugees had first been developed in the second half of the fifth century.

Of declared inviolability at Athens, early or late, there is no clear proof. But some problematic material needs to be considered. It was a commonplace by Roman times, and often in modern, that in ancient Athens two holy places had the right to receive suppliants: the Theseum east of the Agora and the Grove of the Furies, the *Semnai Theai*, on the Areopagus. Not surprisingly, given Greek norms, there is quite explicit evidence that sacred places in classical Athens other than these two received suppliants.[3] I suggest that the reports of their special exemption are a projection of Roman notions onto the classical past.

THE THESEUM

Theseus had at least two temples in Athens, the Theseum on the north slope of the Acropolis and the depository of his bones by the Agora.[4] As to status, first the late evidence. Diodorus (4.62.4) states that for the bones of Theseus, brought back to Athens from abroad, the Athenians "made an inviolable precinct" (τέμενος ἄσυλον ἐποίησαν); Cimon brought the bones from Scyros in the 470s.[5] In the scholia to Aristophanes and Aeschines and in the lexicographers, the Theseum is explicitly a place where slaves can escape their masters; so too Plutarch: φύξιμον οἰκέταις καὶ πᾶσι τοῖς ταπεινοτέροις καὶ δεδιόσι κρείττονας (*Thes.* 36.4).

What items are old and cannot be attributed to the influence of Roman usage (selectively granted right of asylum)? We have Philochorus F 177, from the *Etymologicum Magnum*:

> Θήσειον· τέμενός ἐστι τῷ Θησεῖ, ὃ τοῖς οἰκέταις ἄσυλον ἦν ... ἢ ναὸς τοῦ Θησέως, ἐφ' ὃν οἱ ἀποδιδράσκοντες δοῦλοι προσέφευγον. Φιλόχορος δὲ οὐ μόνον τοὺς οἰκέτας τὸ παλαιόν φησι καταφεύγειν εἰς τὸ Θήσειον ἀλλὰ καὶ τοὺς ὁπωσοῦν ἱκετεύοντας.

Jacoby treated only the last sentence as from Philochorus, and indeed the first part of the entry looks much like the other statements in the late scholia and lexica. Strictly speaking, the correction ("in ancient times not only slaves fled

3. Lipsius, in Meier/Schömann, *Der attische Process*² II (Berlin 1883) 626 n. 382, listed various temples; he explained, however, that only the two had "the right of asylum," while the rest were merely used by fugitives (on this attempted distinction see above, p. 14).

4. S. Koumanoudes, *ArchEph* 1976, 194–216; cf. Jacoby on Philochorus *FGrHist* 328 F 177; Wycherley 113–119; Thompson and Wycherley, *Athenian Agora* XIV (Princeton 1972) 124–126; A. J. Podlecki, *JHS* 91 (1971) 141–143; H. Herter, *RE* Suppl. 13 (1973) 1223–1224; K. A. Christensen, *AJAH* 9 (1984) 23–32; H. A. Shapiro, *Art and Cult under the Tyrants in Athens* (Mainz 1989) 143–149. For the games of Theseus in late Hellenistic times see G. R. Bugh, *ZPE* 83 (1990) 20–37.

5. Plut. *Cim.* 8.5–6; *Thes.* 36.2; Paus. 1.17.6. See R. Garland, *Introducing New Gods: The Politics of Athenian Religion* (London 1992) 82–98. The sacred place was certainly older than the bringing of the relics; cf. Herter 1224.

to the Theseum but those with any sort of supplication") might come either from Philochorus or from the scholiast who has seen in Philochorus an instance of a nonslave taking refuge. If the correction is Philochorus', then the notion that the Theseum had a special status with regard to slaves is older than the early third century B.C. But that cannot be guaranteed from this passage.

By contrast, we have from the classical period some passages of comedy. Aristophanes used the word Θησειότριψ, meaning "someone who spends time at the Theseum" (frag. 475); and a slave is found to say: "Best for me to run to the Theseum and stay there until I find a sale," ἐμοὶ κράτιστόν ἐστιν εἰς τὸ Θησεῖον δραμεῖν, ἐκεῖ δ' ἕως ἂν πρᾶσιν εὕρωμεν μένειν (frag. 577, cited by Pollux as evidence that the Athenians had the same humane practice as the Romans for a slave with a cruel master); we find also the expression ἐν τῷ Θησέῳ καθήμενος in Pherecrates' *Doulodidaskalos* (frag. 46). Finally, at Aristophanes *Knights* 1311–1312 one of the Athenian ships, wanting escape from bad politicians, says: "I think we should sit [as suppliants], sailing to the Theseum, or at the Dread Goddesses" (καθῆσθαί μοι δοκεῖ εἰς τὸ Θησεῖον πλεούσας ἢ 'πὶ τῶν σεμνῶν θεῶν). Thus it was known in late fifth-century Athens that the Theseum was a good place to escape to.

None of these passages proves a peculiar legal status for the Theseum, less still that other temples could not receive suppliants. Philochorus may have known that the Theseum had a reputation for protecting slaves—which is no more than we see in the fifth-century comic writers. Perhaps, however, he considered this the intention of the founder Cimon, if Diodorus' ἄσυλον too derives from Philochorus. Only if that intention was Philochorus' belief do we have a notion, at the beginning of the third century, of a specially designated place of refuge. The comic authors of the fifth century offer no explicit support for such an institutionalized right of refuge, only for a popular sentiment.

THE GROVE OF THE FURIES

There was a grove of the Furies on the Areopagus.[6] One act of refuge is most pertinent, that of the Cylonian conspirators. Herodotus' brief account is almost without topography (5.71): Cylon occupied the Acropolis but, unable to prevail, "sat down as a suppliant at the statue" (ἱκέτης ἵζετο πρὸς τὸ ἄγαλμα);[7] officials "raised them up" (ἀνιστᾶσι) upon guarantee of their lives, but they were murdered. Thucydides adds a good many details, including topographical (1.126): besieged on the Acropolis, the conspirators "sat down as suppliants

6. E. Wüst, "Erinys," *RE* Suppl. 8 (1956) 128.

7. Certainly the statue of Athena Polias at the Erechtheum. Paus. 1.26.6: Athenians honor Athena most highly, for whereas each deme has its own divinities, all have one of Athena as well; "and the holiest thing, jointly worshipped many years before the unification of the demes, is a statue of Athena on the Acropolis; legend holds that it fell from heaven."

at the altar on the Acropolis" (καθίζουσιν ἐπὶ τὸν βωμὸν ἱκέται τὸν ἐν τῇ ἀκροπόλει); officials raised them up, promising security, when they saw them dying of starvation in the sanctuary (ἐν τῷ ἱερῷ), but led away and murdered them and "also did away with[8] some who were sitting at the altars of the Dread Goddesses on the way" (καθεζομένους δέ τινας καὶ ἐπὶ τῶν σεμνῶν θεῶν τοῖς βωμοῖς ἐν τῇ παρόδῳ ἀπεχρήσαντο). These are taken to be some of the group from the Acropolis, escaping to the Areopagus while being led away, for this is what we are told by Plutarch (*Sol.* 12.1: the rope they had attached to the statue of Athena broke near the altars of the Furies, to which some fled and where they were slaughtered).

The import of this story is that the temple of Athena on the Acropolis was the hoped-for asylum. Flight to the Grove of the Furies was an afterthought by a few persons in extremis.

We have another testimony for the asylum of the Furies. Pausanias says that during the Peloponnesian invasion that led to the death of Codrus, the invaders departed, abandoning some of their own; these, realizing their danger, fled to the altars of the Furies on the Areopagus; they were allowed to depart unharmed because of an oracle of Zeus of Dodona:[9]

> φράζεο δ' Ἄρειόν τε πάγον βωμούς τε θυώδεις
> Εὐμενίδων, ὅθι χρὴ Λακεδαιμονίους σ' ἱκετεῦσαι
> δουρὶ πιεζομένους· τοὺς μὴ σὺ κτεῖνε σιδήρῳ
> μηδ' ἱκέτας ἀδικεῖν· ἱκέται δ' ἱεροί τε καὶ ἁγνοί.
> . . .

> Watch the Areopagus and the smoking altars of the Eumenides, where Lacedaemonians, pressed by the spear, will supplicate you: do not kill them with iron, or harm suppliants; suppliants are sacred and holy.

Pausanias goes on to contrast the Athenians' later treatment of the Cylonians there.

Again the comic authors are crucial. A character in Aristophanes proposes flight εἰς τὸ τῶν σεμνῶν θεῶν (*Thesm.* 224); a scholiast explained ἄσυλον γὰρ εἶχον οἱ καταλαμβάνοντες τὰ ἱερὰ τῶν 'Ερινύων.[10] And Aristophanes in the

8. The verb, perhaps a euphemism current at the end of the fifth century for murder by deception, recurs at Ar. frag. 374 (the Lemnian women who killed their husbands) and at Thuc. 3.81 (the Corcyraean democrats killed [ἀπέκτεινον] all of the opposite party whom they could find in the city, and Messenian troops whom they had persuaded to board ships they then debarked and did away with [ἐκ τῶν νεῶν ὅσους ἔπεισαν ἐσβῆναι ἐκβιβάζοντες ἀπεχρῶντο]). Of those who had taken refuge as suppliants in the temple of Hera, fifty were persuaded to come out and stand trial, and were condemned; the majority, who refused, took their own lives in the temple.

9. Paus. 7.25.1–2; cf. H. W. Parke, *The Oracles of Zeus* (Oxford 1967) 130–131.

10. The noun ἄσυλον may reflect a late date and Latin influence; see above, p. 31 n. 8.

Knights (quoted above) links the Theseum and the Grove of the Furies as places of refuge: but which grove of the Furies is not said; the scholiast's plural suggests his own uncertainty.

CONCLUSION

What then can be said of a special status for these two shrines? It is the comic authors who need explanation—as was already felt in antiquity; and all the claims about the two as special *asyla* likely derive from scholarly attempts to explain Aristophanes.

We can imagine why shrines of the Furies by the fifth century had entered popular consciousness as a traditional place of refuge, for such were the stories—the Peloponnesian troops, the Cylonians, Oedipus, doubtless more. The more interesting question concerns Theseus' tomb, half a century old when Aristophanes wrote. I think it impossible that one temple in the 470s B.C. can have been formally declared to possess a "right of asylum," with the implication that others did not—that is a Roman notion. But how then did the Theseum come, by Aristophanes' time, to be seen as an especially good place for a slave to flee to? Plutarch's explanation may well be right (*Thes.* 36.4), "because he was of a protecting and helpful nature and attended generously to the requests of the weak": the comments in the comic writers reflect not some formal enactment but popular appreciation of the character of Theseus.

Dodona

Dionysius of Halicarnassus, writing of the age before the Trojan War, says that the residents of Dodona were sacred and thus no one would inflict war upon them; hence their kinsmen the Pelasgians took refuge with them: τραπόμενοι πρὸς τοὺς ἐν Δωδώνῃ κατοικοῦντας σφῶν συγγενεῖς, οἷς οὐδεὶς ἠξίου πόλεμον ἐπιφερεῖν ὡς ἱεροῖς (*Ant. Rom.* 1.18.2). Dodona flourished in the Hellenistic period, and it may have well have been declared sacred and inviolable then; but in the absence of more concrete evidence this is speculative.

Epidaurus

At Epidaurus was the first great pilgrimage shrine of Asclepius, situated in the countryside outside of the city. In imperial times the city is sometimes called

"Epidaurus the holy." The city so names itself in erecting a statue of Caracalla, ἡ ἱερὰ Ἐπίδαυρος (*IG* IV.1^2 611), comparable to monuments at Roman Delphi (p. 48). In the 40s A.D. the Athenian Areopagus and *demos* each voted a statue for a distinguished citizen who had died prematurely at Epidaurus (*IG* 82–84): his family had ranked with those of the finest cities of Greece—Lacedaemon, Argos, "Epidaurus the holy"—and statues of him are to be erected at Eleusis and "Epidaurus the holy" (copies of these two decrees are to be sent simply to "Epidaurus"). So too in the authors: Aelius Aristides was directed by a vision εἰς Ἐπίδαυρον τὴν ἱερὰν τοῦ θεοῦ (52.1); Plutarch says "holy Epidaurus" when alluding to Pericles' siege at the start of the Peloponnesian War (*Per.* 35.3: πολιορκήσας τὴν ἱερὰν Ἐπίδαυρον; see also Paus. 2.1.4: ἐν Ἐπιδαύρῳ τῇ ἱερᾷ; cf. 2.26.3: Ἀσκληπιοῦ δὲ ἱερὰν μάλιστα εἶναι τὴν γῆν). Plutarch (*Sull.* 12.3) says that Sulla "disturbed the asylums of Greece (ἐκίνει τὰ τῆς Ἑλλάδος ἄσυλα), transferring the richest dedications from both Epidaurus and Olympia." His use of the noun may suggest a Latin source. He also includes the Asclepieum in his list of inviolable places raided by pirates in the early first century B.C. (*Pomp.* 24.5). In poems, finally, we find ζαθέα Ἐπίδαυρος (*IG* 128.37, 692.5).

Such was the affectation of the time for a place possessed of a famous shrine—these phrases need not prove that there had been a formal recognition of *asylia*. It is more telling that the word appears on some bronze coins of the city under Antoninus Pius and Caracalla: ΙΕΡΑΣ Ἐπιδαύρου (*BMC Pelop.* 159). I would nevertheless urge that Epidaurus remains a doubtful case. The coins may reflect the rhetorical usage described above and need not attest to a declaration of inviolability, whether Hellenistic or legendary.

The great "increase" in the cult of Asclepius came in the first half of the fourth century B.C., 100 years before the beginnings of declared inviolability. Perhaps Hellenistic Epidaurus had some legend that, as for Olympia or Delphi, gave it the luxury of an early claim to the status and no need to seek formal recognition; but if that is so, it has left no trace in our literary evidence.

Calaureia

On the little island Calaureia was a well-known temple of Poseidon.[11] Strabo (8.6.14 [373]) calls it an asylum sacred to Poseidon or an inviolable temple of Poseidon (ἐνταῦθα ἦν ἄσυλον Ποσειδῶνος ἱερόν), who gained the island from

11. See Wilamowitz, *Kl. Schr.* V. 1 100–113; R. W. M. Schumacher, in *Greek Sanctuaries,* ed. N. Marinatos and R. Hågg (London/New York 1993) 74–76.

Leto in exchange for Delos.[12] He proceeds to quote Ephorus for an oracle that calls for the exchange and compares Calaureia to Delos but says nothing of *asylia*:[13]

> ἶσόν τοι Δῆλόν τε Καλαυρίαν τε νέμεσθαι
> Πυθώ τ' ἠγαθέην καὶ Ταίναρον ἠνεμόεντα.

The first part of this chapter of Strabo, with the word ἄσυλον, seems to be his own rather than from Ephorus in the fourth century (Ἔφορος δὲ καὶ ... λέγει).

The temple of Poseidon, much enriched by new constructions in the fourth century B.C., was the center of a religious amphictyony; it is in the list of those attacked by Cilician pirates. It was well known to Hellenistic and later authors because Demosthenes took refuge there,[14] and there his grave was shown; perhaps this moved Strabo to apply the word "asylum" to it.

Temple of Artemis, Lusi

According to Polybius, in 220 B.C. an Aetolian army pillaging Arcadia approached the temple of Artemis at Lusi, "which is between Cynaetha and Cleitor and is considered inviolable among the Greeks (ἄσυλον δὲ νενόμισται παρὰ τοῖς Ἕλλησιν), and threatened to seize the flocks of the goddess and the other things that belonged to the temple; but the Lusiates, by prudently giving them some of the furnishings of the goddess, averted the impiety of the Aetolians and suffered nothing serious" (4.18.9–12). Again, in the anti-Aetolian speech of the Acarnanian at Sparta in 211 (cf. p. 38), Polybius includes this shrine among the "inviolable temples" plundered by the Aetolians (9.34.8–10): οἵ γε καὶ τοῖς ἀσύλοις ἱεροῖς ἐτόλμησαν προσάγειν τὰς χεῖρας. ὧν Τίμαιος μὲν τό τ' ἐπὶ Ταινάρῳ τοῦ Ποσειδῶνος καὶ τὸ τῆς ἐν Λούσοις ἱερὸν Ἀρτέμιδος ἐσύλησε; the alleged event is conventionally assigned to the 240s B.C. (cf. Walbank, *Comm.* I 483). Thus Polybius claims that the Aetolians plundered the temple on one occasion and extorted from it on another, even though it was "inviolable."

12. In the preceding sentence he had stated blandly that "Troezen is sacred to Poseidon, from whom it was once called Poseidonia"; this means no more than that Poseidon was the patron divinity; cf. above, p. 12. For other testimonia for the exchange of Delos and Calaureia see Parke/Wormell II 126 (earliest: Callim. frag. 593 Pf.).

13. *FGrHist* 70 F 150; Parke/Wormell no. 314. Paus. 2.33.2, quoting the oracle, comments: Ποσειδῶνος ἱερὸν ἐνταῦθα ἅγιον.

14. Plut. *Mor.* 846 (suppliant first at the temple of Aeacus on Aegina, then Poseidon on Calaureia); cf. 849B.

In fact we have an Aetolian grant of collective personal inviolability to the citizens of Lusi (*IG* IX.1^2 135, from Calydon):

[ἀγαθᾶι τύχαι· δόγμ]α Αἰτωλῶν· Λουσιά[ταις εἶμεν ἀσυ]-
[λίαν καὶ μὴ ἄγεσθαι] μηδὲ ὑφ' ἑνὸς Αἰτω[λῶν μηδὲ τῶν ἐν]
[Αἰτωλίαι κατοικ]ούντων μητὲ αὐ[τοὺς μητὲ χρήμα]-
[τα· εἰ δέ τίς κα ἄγηι] ἢ Αἰτωλὸς ἢ [τῶν ἐν Αἰτωλίαι κατ]-
[οικοῦντων Λουσιά]ταν ἢ τ[ὰ χρήματα αὐτοῦ - - -]
[- - - - - - - - - - - - - -]NTỌ[- - - - - - - - - - - - - -]

This decree belongs with the dozen or so Aetolian grants of personal inviolability, a kind of act that does not concern cult. And we may as easily restore ἀσφά|λειαν in 2–3, as in the Aetolian decree for the Delians (quoted p. 52). This grant should not be confused with the status of the temple,[15] whatever the value of Polybius' claim—yet just this equation has been the basis of dating the inscribed decree to the episode of 220 (Poulsen) "or soon after" (Klaffenbach), which strictly speaking would contradict Polybius, who portrays *asylia* as a fact already in 220. Indeed, the clipped formulary and the script of this decree seem to me rather earlier.

Thus the two items need have no connection. But Polybius' words may imply not merely an attitude on the part of the Greeks but a concrete declaration of Hellenistic date, and the Aetolians may be responding in their own manner—as they would do for Magnesia and Teos. But if that is so, they would here be departing even further from the usual formulary of territorial *asylia*, of which this decree shows no trace. So the question of *asylia* of this temple turns in the end on the credibility of Polybius when he denounces Aetolians—in my view, another non liquet.

The goddess was Artemis Hemera,[16] known already to Bacchylides (*Epin.* 11.92–112) and to Callimachus (*Hymn.* 3.233–236); her games, the Hemerasia, are attested in the second and first centuries B.C. The temple, a kilometer east of the city proper, was built toward 300 B.C., and the cult seems to have enjoyed its greatest prosperity in the third century. But this is not one of the greater cults of Arcadia, and we must doubt that Polybius' statement implies a recognition of *asylia* in the Hellenistic period. The city had ceased to exist by Pausanias' time (8.18.8).

15. E.g., P. Ducrey, *Le traitement des prisonniers de guerre* (Paris 1968) 310: "The sanctuary had received from the Aetolians the privilege of *asylia*."

16. See M. Jost, *Sanctuaires et cultes d'Arcadie* (Paris 1985) 419–425.

Temple of Poseidon, Taenarum

Cape Taenarum had a famous shrine of Poseidon.[17] Scholars sometimes have included it in their lists of Greek temples with the "right of asylum," and a notorious act of refuge occurred there.[18] We have seen above that Ephorus knew an oracle that set in parallel Delphi and Taenarum, Delos and Calaureia. Polybius, in the tendentious passage quoted above, applies to this temple the phrase ἄσυλον ἱερόν. The case for declared inviolability seems to me dubious.

Hermione

In late antiquity Hermione in the Argolid was reputed to be a special place of asylum; a phrase in Aristophanes perhaps gave rise to the several accounts that survive.

At Zenobius 2.22 we find the following: "ἀνθ' Ἑρμιόνος: the saying applies to those who save suppliants, since in Hermione in the Peloponnesus was a temple of Kore and Demeter that supplied security to fugitives (ἀσφάλειαν παρέχον τοῖς καταφεύγουσι); Aristophanes mentions this saying in *Babylonians* [frag. 89]." The *Suda* (α2459) calls Hermione a πόλις Κόρης καὶ Δήμητρος ἄσυλος, ὥστε σκέπην παρέχειν τοῖς ἱκετεύουσιν. Photius s.v. states: χωρίον ἄσυλον· ἢ πόλις ἡ ἐν Πελοποννήσῳ, ἔχουσα ἱερὰ Δήμητρος καὶ Περσεφόνης ἄσυλα.

Rather than a Hellenistic declaration, some episode in myth or history can easily lie behind this reputation, but our sources on the cult at Hermione do not seem to have preserved it. The cult of Kore Chthonia there had the usual trappings—the place where Kore was seized, an entrance to the underworld, and, perhaps most significant, in the Hellenistic period federal games called the Chthonia.[19]

Nicopolis

In 30 B.C. Augustus founded Nicopolis in Acarnania in commemoration of the battle of Actium. The evidence for *asylia* consists of the brief inscription on

17. F. Bölte, *RE* 4A (1932) 2037–2044; J. Ducat in *Mélanges Pierre Lévêque* I (Paris 1990) 183–187; Schumacher 72–74. The general statements are Strab. 8.6.14 (373): ἐνταῦθα ἦν ἄσυλον Ποσειδῶνος ἱερόν . . .; and Nepos *Paus.* 4.4: *quod violari nefas putant Graeci.*

18. Thuc. 1.128; cf. 1.133.

19. Bölte, *RE* 8 (1912) 840; Farnell, *Cults* III 320; Robert, *Et. épigr. phil.* 68.

the coins: we see the sporadic Νικόπολις ΙΕΡΑ (or the genitive) throughout imperial times.[20] As elsewhere where no more than ἱερά is guaranteed, this may be no more than rhetorical and may not reflect a granted title of inviolability.

The great god of the place was of course Apollo of Actium, who had brought victory to Augustus. From the point of view of Greek festivals, Nicopolis was unique in beginning life with Panhellenic games, the Actia. Originally a property of the city of Anactorium, the cult of Apollo was taken over by the Acarnanian League late in the third century B.C., and the Actia became their federal festival. The fate of the games in the difficult years of the late second and first centuries B.C. is unknown. At any rate, the first quadrennial celebration of the games, now Panhellenic, apparently took place in 28 B.C., the quadrennium after the victory, and the season is presumed to encompass 2 September, the day of the battle.[21]

It is possible that the temple of Apollo had been declared inviolable in the Hellenistic period and this is what brought the Roman city the title (so I have assumed, for example, for Aezani and Capitolias; cf. Paneas). This temple is in Plutarch's list of inviolable shrines attacked by the Cilician pirates. If that is both literal (reflecting granted *asylia*) and not anachronistic (Plutarch knowing the status in his own day), then its inclusion would imply a Hellenistic recognition of the temple's inviolability, which later was advertised by the new city that came to own the temple.

Little reliance, however, can be placed on the Plutarch passage, and it is possible that Augustus first declared the place inviolable when he founded Nicopolis. Pompey may have done the same for his foundation Soli-Pompeiopolis a generation earlier. Inviolability would be an unsurprising companion to the new Panhellenic games at Augustus' city.

20. M. Karamesine Oikonomidou, ἡ Νομισματοκοπία τῆς Νικοπόλεως (Athens 1975); cf. C. Kraay, *NC* VII.16 (1976) 237, on the one coin on which ἀσύλου was once read. No other titles occur, with the possible exception of *nauarchis* (once on an issue of the mid-third century attributed to Nicopolis: Karamesine Oikonomidou p. 147 no. 36).

21. See Moretti, *I. agon. gr.* pp. 205–206.

Smyrna and the Temple of Aphrodite Stratonicis

The case of Smyrna has a special importance in the history of *asylia*. It is the second known, some fifteen or twenty years after the grant to the Itonium and slightly before that to the Asclepieum on Cos. It is the first case about which we can gather some circumstantial detail from our texts, and the first grant for a city rather than for a temple alone.

In the 240s the Greek world declared inviolable both the temple of Aphrodite Stratonicis in Smyrna and the city itself. The Smyrnaeans had received an oracle of Apollo demanding this honor for the goddess, and so they put the request to King Seleucus II; presumably they had obtained the oracle on their own initiative—Smyrna, not Seleucus, was the instigator of this affair. Seleucus recognized the inviolability and in addition granted the city freedom and immunity from tribute; he also gave their envoys a letter asking the Greek world to join in the recognition of *asylia*. With this letter, the oracle, and their decree of request, the Smyrnaean ambassadors now set about their missions. Our evidence consists of the answering decree of Delphi[1] and a description of the event in a later Smyrnaean decree preserved on the famous "Oxford Stone"; the recognition appears to be mentioned also in a decree of Smyrna accepting the Soteria at Delphi as Panhellenic. Tacitus, finally, describes Smyrna among the petitioners of A.D. 22.

Aphrodite Stratonicis was the patron divinity of the Hellenistic city. Aelius Aristides probably is describing her temple at 17.10 K.: ναῶν τε ὁ κάλλιστος αὖθις τῆς εἰληχυίας θεοῦ τὴν πόλιν; he implies that it was near the acropolis, and Vitruvius (5.9) supports this by indicating that the stoa of the Stratoniceum was near the theater, which is at the foot of the acropolis. Probably it stood on the "sacred way," which Aristides says was one of the two main streets of

1. A decree of Athens has also been alleged; see p. 590.

Smyrna.[2] Smyrnaeans included the name of their goddess in their oaths; at her temple they put up some of their public inscriptions and honorific statues.[3] The goddess owned revenue-producing lands in the territory of Smyrna (*I.Smyrna* 723 and p. 377). In the second century A.D. Smyrna had occasion to defend before an emperor the "rights" of its temples (ἤριζεν ἡ Σμύρνα ὑπὲρ τῶν ναῶν καὶ τῶν ἐπ' αὐτοῖς δικαίων), which must therefore have been challenged by a provincial governor or a rival city; such rights were most likely *asylia* or neocoria.[4] The statue of Aphrodite Stratonicis is thought to be represented on Hellenistic coins that show an Aphrodite wearing a long chiton and a *polos* and bearing in her left hand a Nike who crowns her.[5]

Smyrna, founded by Theseus,[6] was destroyed by the Lydians early in the sixth century B.C., and its former citizens lived in villages (κωμηδόν) thereafter; they were reconstituted as a city only at the beginning of the Hellenistic age.[7] Thus Smyrna was in a sense a relatively new polity when it was declared inviolable. What claim to honor or antiquity could be made in behalf of the cult of Aphrodite Stratonicis? The epithet has been taken by many scholars to derive from Queen Stratonice, grandmother of Seleucus II.[8] The similarity of the names is obvious, and according to the Oxford Stone Seleucus told the Smyrnaeans that he benefited their city because of their piety toward the gods and their loyalty to his ancestors; he specifies that his father,

2. For the topography of Smyrna see the brief account by R. Naumann and S. Kantar, *IstForsch* 17 (1950) 69–75. The Stratoniceum is mentioned also in *Anth. Gr.* 11.97; cf. Robert, *Op. min. sel.* VI 418–419. A priestess of Aphrodite probable at Petzl, *I.Smyrna* 751 (I B.C.).

3. *I.Smyrna* 573.70, 83 (= *OGIS* 229; *Staatsvertr.* III 492; Ihnken, *I.Magnesia am Sipylos* 1: the Oxford Stone); 578.4.

4. Philostr. *VS* 539. For the neocorate temples of Smyrna see Petzl on *I.Smyrna* 594; Burrell, "Neokoroi" 334–361. In imperial times Smyrna had a magistrate called the ἐπὶ τοῦ ἱεροῦ, presumably the Stratoniceum (*I.Smyrna* 697, 771, 773, with p. 193). Aristides, describing a dramatic or choregic competition for Dionysus, seems again to assume the primacy of Aphrodite: "It is proper to hold celebrations for Dionysus, and indeed by Zeus for Aphrodite and all the other gods" (29.4 K.). For Aphrodite on coins of imperial date see C. P. Jones, *AJN* 2 (1990) 65–69; D. O. A. Klose had thought that the cult was then in decline (*Die Münzprägung von Smyrna* [Berlin 1987] 24–25).

5. R. Weil, *ZfN* 8 (1881) 337–338; J. G. Milne, *NC* V.7 (1927) 6; *SNG Copenhagen Ionia* 1183–1198, 1226–1232, 1327, 1335; *von Aulock* 2168, 2170, 2198.

6. For references see C. J. Cadoux, *Ancient Smyrna* (Oxford 1938) 47; Petzl on *I.Smyrna* 200.5–6.

7. Strab. 14.1.37 (646): reestablished by Antigonus and by Lysimachus. Cf. Tscherikower, *Städtegründungen* 24; Cadoux 94–104; R. Meriç and J. Nollé, *Chiron* 18 (1988) 230–232.

8. Dittenberger, *OGIS* 228 n. 5; Gebhard, "Stratonikis," *RE* 4A (1931) 325–326; Cadoux 111; M. Segre, *Historia* 5 (1931) 246–247; Robert, *Op. min. sel.* VI 418–419. Couve (*BCH* 18 [1894] 233) believed that Stratonice or Antiochus founded the cult of Aphrodite Stratonicis.

Antiochus II, and his grandmother Stratonice have been given divine honors at Smyrna.[9]

Nevertheless, one must question whether a goddess so new and artificial might become the patron divinity of a Greek city and then quickly be honored with inviolability. The Oxford Stone implies that Antiochus II and his mother were the first Seleucids to be worshipped at Smyrna; the city must have come into the Seleucid alliance after his accession in 261. His mother, Stratonice, died at Sardes in 254, Antiochus himself at Ephesus in 246. Smyrna's cults of Antiochus and Stratonice were founded during these years. Did the Smyrnaeans now also abandon a former chief divinity[10] for an invented "Aphrodite who is like Stratonice" or "founded by Stratonice"? This seems to me unlikely. Royal epithets added to gods are not common in civic cult;[11] assimilation and syncretism were more often literary and artistic extravagances than facts of cult.

As Nipperdey recognized, moreover, we should distinguish the divine honors of Antiochus and Stratonice from the cult of Aphrodite Stratonicis.[12] The former are a recent innovation, eliciting Seleucus' praise. That the latter cult is new is in no way implied in the Delphians' decree of acceptance (**7**), or in the Oxford Stone (lines 7–12):

> ἐτίμησεν τὴμ πόλιν ἡμῶν διά τε τὴν τοῦ δήμου εὔνοιαν καὶ φιλοτιμίαν ἣν ἐπεποίητο εἰς τὰ πράγματα αὐτοῦ καὶ διὰ τὸ τὸμ πατέρα αὐτοῦ θεὸν Ἀντίοχον καὶ τὴμ μητέρα τὴν τοῦ πατρὸς θεὰν Στρατονίκην ἱδρῦσθαι παρ' ἡμῖν τιμωμένους τιμαῖς ἀξιολόγοις... καὶ ἐβεβαίωσεν τῶι δήμωι τὴν αὐτονομίαν καὶ δημοκρατίαν, ἔγραψεν δὲ καὶ πρὸς τοὺς βασιλεῖς καὶ τοὺς δυνάστας καὶ

9. *I.Smyrna* 573.7–12, quoted below; see C. Habicht, *Gottmenschentum und greichische Städte*[2] (Munich 1970) 99–102. The month name Stratonikeon must derive from the queen rather than the goddess, in parallel with the months Antiocheon and Laodikeon (cf. Robert, *Op. min. sel.* II 786–791; *Bull. épigr.* 1971, 630).

10. Perhaps the Two Nemeses, so visible and honored at Smyrna in imperial times; references at Petzl, *I.Smyrna* 628 and 741; M. K. and J. Nollé, *ZPE* 102 (1994) 245 n. 17.

11. Cf. Aphrodite Laodice at Iasos in 193 B.C. (*I.Iasos* 4.80). The adjectival form: Zeus Philippios at Eresos (Tod II 191.5); Heracles Diomedonteios on Cos, founded by Diomedon ca. 300 B.C. (*Syll.*[3] 1106; S. Sherwin-White, *Ancient Cos,* Hypomnemata 51 [Göttingen 1978] 363–364); Zeus Antigoneios in Lydia (H. Malay, *Catalogue Manisa* 69–74); Apollo Leonteios (Corsten, *I.Bursa* II 1017). Zeus Seleukios, attested in Lydia (see *TAM* V.1 426), has been suggested as a royal conceit; cf. Nock, *Essays* I 156–157; but see J. and L. Robert, *Hellenica* VI (1948) 25, and H. Schwabl, *RE* 10A (1972) 358–359, for the pre-Hellenistic origin of the epithet (though no one will deny that the Seleucids came to look with favor on this god). See the cautious assessment by E. Badian in *Ancient Macedonian Studies . . . Edson* (Thessalonica 1981) 40–41.

12. Karl Nipperdey, *P. Cornelius Tacitus* I[9] (Berlin 1892) 228: "This goddess can be neither the same as Stratonice . . . nor named after her, as the words *ceteros obscuris – initiis niti* and *propiora Sardianos* etc. show. The epithet stands on its own" (citing Aphrodite Strateia, Nicephorus, and Venus Victrix).

τὰς πόλεις καὶ τὰ ἔθνη ἀξιώσας ἀποδέξασθαι τό τε ἱερὸν τῆς Στρατονικίδος Ἀφροδίτης ἄσυλον εἶναι καὶ τὴμ πόλιν ἡμῶν ἱερὰν καὶ ἄσυλον.

...

he honored our city because of our loyalty and zeal toward his kingdom and because of his father the god Antiochus and his father's mother the goddess Stratonice being founded among us, honored with conspicuous honors ... and he guaranteed to the people autonomy and democracy, and he also wrote to the kings, dynasts, cities and nations asking them to accept the temple of Aphrodite Stratonicis as inviolable and the city as sacred and inviolable.

The king's interest is not in Stratonice alone but also in his father Antiochus; and his stated motives are typical of the age, as are the Smyrnaeans' honors for his two ancestors. This was background and coaxing for their present request regarding the status of the city and the temple of Aphrodite, which is a different cult from that of Antiochus and Stratonice.

Tacitus says that the oracle the Smyrnaeans showed the Senate in A.D. 22 called for the foundation of the cult: "Others relied on origins obscured by age: the Smyrnaeans invoked an oracle of Apollo, on whose command they dedicated the temple to Venus Stratonicis.... The Sardians evoked more recent things, a gift of the victorious Alexander."[13] In this account the oracle with which the Smyrnaeans opened their case to the Romans was not the one that called for *asylia* in the 240s (**7**.5–6, 16) but a more remote one that established the cult itself—older even than the refounding of Smyrna in the time of the Successors.[14] There is much room for confusion here by Tacitus or exaggeration by the Smyrnaeans, but the implication of this report is that Aphrodite Stratonicis was worshipped at Smyrna already before the time of Alexander and thus well before Stratonice.

Accordingly, I follow those scholars who take the similarity of words, Stratonicis and Stratonice, as a happy accident. Aphrodite's epithet and cult were already in place; here as in some other cities she was a military goddess, "of the victorious army."[15] Possibly the cult was no older than the refoundation

13. *Ann.* 3.63; as Segre pointed out, however, the same sentence is applied to Tenos, whose cult of Poseidon seems to date from the fourth century B.C. (see p. 163); but he thought that the oracles were those calling for *asylia*.

14. Compare the cases of Samos and Cos. The oracles mentioned in **7** and Tacitus are equated by Gebhard, Segre, Cadoux, and Parke/Wormell (II 140): that is, a single oracle both called for a new cult of Aphrodite Stratonicis and demanded its inviolability. Segre and Couve held that Tacitus is simply wrong about the date of the oracle and that the Smyrnaeans in A.D. 22 exaggerated the age of the temple. (The Oxford Stone does not mention an oracle.)

15. After Nipperdey, Wilamowitz, *Nordionische Steine*, AbhBerl 1909.2 (Berlin 1909) 55 ("mit Rücksicht auf Stratonike umgedeutet"); Höfer, in Roscher, *Lex.* 4 (1915) 1551–1552. For images of Aphrodite in armor see Gow and Page, *Hellenistic Epigrams* II 334, 397. On the coins of Smyrna, however, there is nothing military about the image of Aphrodite, from which alone one would have deduced no more than the epithet *nikephoros*.

of the city at the end of the fourth century. But it is just as likely that the cult was maintained across the centuries when the inhabitants lived κωμηδόν and without civic institutions. The archaeological record of Old Smyrna shows that the temple of Athena there was rebuilt after the Lydian destruction of ca. 600 B.C.;[16] surely other cults were similarly kept up by the propertied families or by the villages—even or especially after the renewed destruction of the old site by the Persians ca. 545. If this view is correct, it bears the implication that the site for the refounded city was chosen with the temple of Aphrodite in mind, for the temple was at the center of the Hellenistic city (compare the Magnesians' choice).

The date of the grant to Smryna is subject to several controls:[17]

1. Seleucus' predecessor, Antiochus II, died at Ephesus in 246; Seleucus' accession was known in Babylon in August.[18]

2. The Delphian recognition of Smyrna's *asylia* (**7**.14ff.) provides that the *theoroi* sent to proclaim the Pythia are to praise Seleucus for his favor to Smyrna. The year 246 was a Pythian year, with the games occurring in August/September.

3. The Smyrnaean decree on the Oxford Stone opens with this account of Seleucus' movements at the start of his reign:

> previously at the time when King Seleucus crossed over into the Seleucis and many grave dangers were besetting our city and territory, our people maintained loyalty and friendship toward him, not disconcerted by the approach of enemies and not reckoning the loss of our possessions,[19] but counting everything second to holding to our policy and assisting his kingdom as much as we could, as we had undertaken from the start,

whence his gratitude and his grant of *asylia* and other benefactions (quoted above). Thus between the death of Antiochus and the Delphian recognition for Smyrna (**7**) there was time for Seleucus to pass from Ephesus to Syria, for the Smyrnaeans, having suffered at the hands of enemies, to report their loyalty to him, for his benefactions to be reported to Smyrna, and for Smyrnaean ambassadors to reach Delphi. If Antiochus died in the spring or summer of 246, all this cannot have happened before the Pythian *theoroi* departed to announce

16. E. Akurgal, *Alt-Smyrna* I (Ankara 1983) 75–79, 120–123; Meriç and Nollé 230–232.

17. See Nachtergael, *Les Galates* 209–241, 328–338; cf. Ihnken pp. 36–42; Will, *Histoire* I 257–258. The traditional crux is the date of the Athenian archon Polyeuctus; Nachtergael's case for 246/5 is given further support by M. J. Osborne, *ZPE* 78 (1989) 219.

18. A. J. Sachs and D. J. Wiseman, *Iraq* 16 (1954) 206; H. Heinen, *CAH* VII.1^2 (1984) 420–421, is mistaken in writing summer 245. Nachtergael (*Les Galates* 234 n. 141) admits the difficulty that the August 246 notice poses to dating the *asylia* of Smyrna to 246.

19. Seleucus' restoration of the Smyrnaeans' "ancestral territory" (**7**.8–9) perhaps undid the work of these enemies, whoever they were.

the games that would be celebrated in August/September of 246.[20] Either he died very early indeed in 246, or else the future Pythia mentioned in **7** were those of 242.

4. In the spring of 245 the Aetolians sought Panhellenic recognition of their Soteria; their *theoroi* were in Athens in April. A stone at Delphi seems to contain Smyrna's acceptance, which also mentions the acquisition of *asylia*:[21]

ται εὔξα{ξα}σθαι [- -]
τῶν Σωτηρίων [- -]
καὶ βασιλέα Σ̣[έλευκον - - - τό τε ἱερὸν τὸ τῆς Ἀφροδίτης τῆς Στρατονίκιδος ἄ]-
συλον καὶ τ[ὴν πόλιν ἱερὰν καὶ ἄσυλον - - - - - - - - - - - -]
δὲ ταῖς ε[- - - - - - - - - - - - - - - τῆι Ἀφροδίτηι τῆι Στρατο]-
[ν]ικίδι [- -]

The context of this citation is not easy to imagine, but it would appear to impose on the inviolability of Smyrna a terminus ante quem of spring 245.

The provision at **7**.14ff. that the next Pythian *theoroi* will praise Seleucus is a weak control, for it need not imply that the games are in the near future. The delay of a polite diplomatic gesture for months or even years, until some more weighty or regular business arose, is well attested;[22] the Delphians would naturally be reluctant to travel for the sole purpose of praising the king for his favor to another city. Pythian *theoroi* would eventually be in Smyrna, and it cost Delphi nothing to instruct them to praise Seleucus on that occasion.

Most scholars have preferred 246 for the recognition, relying on the mention of Smyrna's *asylia* in its acceptance of the Soteria in 245. This requires that we posit a rapid course of events. Thus Antiochus will have died in Ephesus

20. So A. Mastrocinque, *La Caria e la Ionia meridionale* (Rome 1979) 111, assigning the grant to Smyrna to 243; he does not notice the difficulty presented by *I.Smyrna* 574. In the fourth century the Pythian *theoroi* departed Delphi six months before the games, in Bysios (February/March): Rougemont, *CIDelphes* 10.46 (= *Syll.*^{3} 145), with *BCH* 97 (1973) 98.

21. *I.Smyrna* 574 (= *FD* III.1 483), restored by Robert (*Op. min. sel.* II 678–686); the dossier of acceptances of the Soteria is at Nachtergael, *Les Galates* 435–447.

22. So in the second century the Eleans vote that a letter to Miletus be delivered by the next *theoroi* to the Didymeia (*I.Olymp.* 39.40, with Robert, *Op. min. sel.* I 128 n. 2); here no more than a few months' delay is implied, if the quadrennial Didymeia occurred in the year after the Olympia (see p. 175)—for otherwise Olympic *theoroi* would take the letter to Miletus. Around 100 B.C. Samothrace votes to give a decree honoring a citizen of Priene to the next *theoroi* coming from there to the (annual) festival of the Samothracian Gods (*I.Priene* 68.9–11, with Robert, *Op. min. sel.* I 233). Ca. 250 B.C. the Aetolians grant citizenship to Heraclea, "and if any embassy should go to King Ptolemy," it is to urge him to be attentive to any requests of the Heracleans (*IG* IX.1^{2} 173 [Moretti, *I. stor. ellen.* II 77]). Cyme votes to convey a decree to the (not very distant) Attalid king by means of the next ambassadors who should happen to be sent to him (*SEG* 29.1216.16–17, with J. and L. Robert, *Bull.épigr.* 1980, 434, and *Fouilles d'Amyzon* I p. 194 n. 6).

at the beginning of the year. Seleucus went at once to Syria to make contact with loyal forces before trying to assure himself of the disaffected cities of western Anatolia.[23] Smyrna remained loyal, and their ambassadors told him so, surely the same ambassadors sent to congratulate him on his accession.[24] There were rival claimants to the throne, and Seleucus will have moved quickly. These events may have taken no more than the first three or four months of 246. As to the Babylonians, perhaps they simply waited to replace Antiochus' name in their records until it was clear which claimant would win. In Smyrna's acceptance of the Soteria in spring 245, their unusual evocation of the grant of *asylia* will reflect its recentness. But all this is difficult; its virtue is to salvage the simultaneity of the decrees accepting the Panhellenic Soteria.

An alternative: if we must rely on the Babylonians' date of the death of Antiochus, then the first half of 246 is excluded for the inviolability of Smyrna, and the Pythia mentioned at **7**.15 cannot be those of 246. The simplest solution then is Elwyn's, separating the Smyrnaean decree accepting the Soteria from the rest of the series.[25] In citing Smyrnaean inviolability that decree is decidedly more verbose than the other extant acceptances: we must place it later than spring 245, for whatever reason. In the one precedent for enlarged games, the Ptolemaia first held in 282, the two extant recognitions are separated by more than fifteen years, the Islanders' decree in 283/2, the Delphians' in the 260s. The Delphian recognition of Smyrna's inviolability will date before early 242 (when the Pythian *theoroi* of that year will have set out from Delphi), but it can be well before then. Even spring 245 might be too soon to accommodate the events described by the Oxford Stone; and in spring 245 Aetolian envoys, surely with Delphian help, were canvassing the Greek world for recognitions of the enlarged Soteria—a mission that might have been instructed to praise Seleucus at Smyrna, if Delphians were part of it and if **7** was voted as early as early 245. Hence better summer of 245 or indeed 244 or 243 for the inviolability of Smyrna.

I am uncertain how to choose between these alternatives—a very rapid set of events in the first half of 246, or an unhurried one that entails a delayed Aetolian approach to Smyrna about the enlarged Soteria. In either case, the Coans then had the fairly recent example of Smyrna when in 242 they set about their own quest for inviolability.

As at Teos a generation later, the Seleucid king's grant, while not exclusive, is prior to the Panhellenic recognition of the status, which the king and the city

23. See Will, *Histoire* I 249–250, for sources, especially Just. 27.1.1: "all the cities of Asia" opposed Seleucus. We now have a Ptolemaic letter from these uncertain months, from Kildara in Caria, but unfortunately not expressly dated: W. Blümel, *EpigAnat* 20 (1992) 127–133.

24. As did the Milesians: Welles, *Royal Corres.* 22 (cf. p. 174). This incidentally implies that Smyrna already had the oracle calling for increasing the honors of Aphrodite, as there seems insufficient time to seek one.

25. S. Elwyn, *JHS* 110 (1990) 177–180.

cooperated in seeking; and games are not involved in the grant.[26] Of subsequent developments nothing is known. There is no need here to recount the wars in which Smyrna engaged over the next two centuries.[27] The inviolability survived at least to A.D. 22, as we know from Tacitus.

7. Delphi

Delphi. Equestrian statue base of grey limestone found in 1894 west of the temple of Apollo (inv. 1338); h. 0.944, w. 0.642–648, th. 0.774. The first of four Delphian decrees[28] inscribed (by different hands) on one of the ends; letters 0.01, intersp. 0.005–0.012. A few letters have been lost to flaking since the first edition, which I do not mark here.

L. Couve, *BCH* 18 (1894) 227–235 no. 1 (copy of Homolle) [Baunack, *SGDI* 2733; Michel, *Rec.* 258; Dittenberger, *OGIS* 228]; Flacelière, *FD* III.4 153. *Collation.*

Drawing of the monument: F. Courby, *FD* II *La Terrace du Temple* 295 fig. 241.

Cf. B. Haussoullier, *Etudes sur l'histoire de Milet* (Paris 1902) 122 n. 2; G. de Sanctis, *AttiTor* 47 (1911–12) 967–968; Herrmann, "Antiochos" 120 n. 154.

[θ ε] ο ί
[ἔδοξε τᾶι πό]λει τῶν Δελφῶν· ἐπεὶ βασιλεὺς Σέλευκος βασιλέως
[᾿Αντιόχ]ου, ἀποστείλας γράμματα ποτὶ τὰν πόλιν, ἀξιοῖ τό τε ἱερὸν τὸ
[τᾶς] Ἀφροδίτας τᾶς Στρατονικίδος καὶ τὰν πόλιν τῶν Σμυρναίων
[ἱε]ρὰν καὶ ἄσυλον εἶμεν, αὐτὸς πρότερον πεπεισμένος τῶι τοῦ θεοῦ
χρησμῶι καὶ πεποιηκὼς ἃ καὶ τὰν πόλιν ἀξιοῖ, ἐπικεχώρηκε δὲ τοῖς [Σμυρ]-
ναίοις τάν τε πόλιν καὶ τὰν χώραν αὐτῶν ἐλευθέραν εἶμεν καὶ ἀφο[ρο]-
λόγητον, καὶ τάν τε ὑπάρχουσαν αὐτοῖς χώραν βεβαιοῖ, καὶ τὰν πάτρι[ον]
ἐπαγγέλλεται ἀποδώσειν, οἴονται δὲ δεῖν καὶ οἱ Σμυρναῖοι, πρεσβευτὰς ἀπο[στεί]-
λαντες Ἑρμόδωρον καὶ Δημήτριον, ἀναγραφῆμεν ἐν τῶι ἱερῶι, ὥσπ[ερ καὶ]
ὁ βασιλεὺς ἀξιοῖ, τὰ ἐπικεχωρημένα αὐτοῖς· δεδόχθαι τᾶι πόλει τῶν Δελ-
φῶν τό τε ἱερὸν τὸ τᾶς Ἀφροδίτας τᾶς Στρατονικίδος καὶ τὰμ πόλιν τῶν [Σμυρ]-
ναίων ἱερὰν καὶ ἄσυλον εἶμεν, καθάπερ ὅ τε βασιλεὺς ἐπέστελκε [καὶ]

26. Smyrna had a Panhellenic contest by the late second century B.C.: *Claros* I p. 64 [*SEG* 39.1244.II.32]. The Roberts were inclined to attribute this to Nemesis or the Two Nemeses, who had Panhellenic games in imperial times (p. 26); but these divinities, for all their importance in Roman Smyrna (κληροῦχοι τῆσδε τῆς πόλεως, Ael. Arist. 20.23 K.), are not attested in the Hellenistic period.

27. See Cadoux 128–170.

28. *FD* III.4 153–156. The second honors a citizen of Antioch on the Cydnus (Tarsus; archon Aristion, "256/5?" Daux); the third grants *promanteia* to Smyrna (240s B.C.); the fourth (same year) honors the dynast Lysias, who was an ally of Seleucus III. Four such statue bases stand in a row here behind the temple, and Pomtow took them all to be of Seleucid kings (*Klio* 16 [1920] 174; *RE* Suppl. 4 [1924] 1353–1356 no. 87); that next to ours was certainly the base of Antiochus III, inscribed with the Delphian decree for Alabanda (**163**).

ἁ τῶν Σμυρναίων πόλις ἀξιοῖ, ἐντείλασται δὲ καὶ τοῖς θεωροῖς τοῖ[ς τὰ]
Πύθια ἐπαγγελλόντοις ἐπαινέσαι τὸν βασιλέα Σέλευκον ἐπί τε το[ύτοις]
καὶ τᾶι εὐσεβείαι καὶ τῶι ἐπακολουθηκέναι τῶι τοῦ θεοῦ χρησμῶι,
καὶ θῦσαι τᾶι Ἀφροδίται· ἀναγράψαι δὲ τὸ μὲν ψάφισμα τόδε τὰν πόλιν
ἐν τῶι ἱερῶι τοῦ θεοῦ, τὰν δ' ἐπιστολὰν ἐν τῶι ἀρχείωι ἐν τῶι τοίχωι.

8 Haussoullier and de Sanctis: πατρί[δα] Couve. 15 Baunack, citing *SGDI* 2644.11: το[ῖσδε] Couve.

...

Inasmuch as King Seleucus son of King Antiochus has sent a letter to the city asking that the temple of Aphrodite Stratonicis and the city of the Smyrnaeans be sacred and inviolable, he himself having previously obeyed the oracle of the god and done what he is asking our city to do as well; and he has granted the Smyrnaeans that their city and country be free and exempt from tribute, and guarantees their existing territory and announces that he will restore their ancestral territory; and as the Smyrnaeans, having sent as ambassadors Hermodorus and Demetrius, also ask, as does the king as well, that what has been granted them be inscribed in the temple: it is decreed by the city of the Delphians that the temple of Aphrodite Stratonicis and the city of the Smyrnaeans be sacred and inviolable, just as the king has written and the city of the Smyrnaeans asks (etc.)

3–6: The operative phrase used here and at 12–13 abbreviates the full and logical statement made by the Smyrnaeans themselves subsequently in the Oxford Stone (*I.Smyrna* 573.10–12): ἀξιώσας ἀποδέξασθαι τό τε ἱερὸν τῆς Στρατονικίδος Ἀφροδίτης ἄσυλον εἶναι καὶ τὴμ πόλιν ἡμῶν ἱερὰν καὶ ἄσυλον. As remarked above (p. 20), a temple, ἱερόν, cannot logically be declared ἱερόν because it already is. Thus the Smyrnaeans' meticulousness of expression is consistent and compelling; this precision, which must have been in the Smyrnaean decree requesting inviolability, as it is in their decree on the Oxford Stone, evidently was lost on the Delphians, who condense matters so as to declare the temple and the city sacred and inviolable.[29] The Smyrnaeans' phrase is not closely paralleled, and I suggest that it is transitional; the Delphians' condensation of it in 7 perhaps reflects the unfamiliarity of the situation and the language. The Smyrnaeans' intent was that the whole city be declared inviolable, not just the temple;[30] so far as we know, this was a novelty in the 240s, and they may have felt obliged to state explicitly the physical continuity of temple and city. But I do not know why the "country," which later was regularly included, here was omitted; that more ambitious proposition perhaps had not yet been imagined. At any rate, in the extant evidence Smyrna sets the

29. Unless the word ἄσυλον has fallen out, as suggested by Herrmann, "Antiochos" 120 n. 154; but this error will have to have occurred twice, in 3 and 12.

30. Will, *Histoire* I 257, is mistaken in thinking that *asylia* had already been given the temple and was by this act extended to the city; the two inscriptions are explicit that a single act created the *asylia* of both temple and city.

immediate precedent (as opposed to the ancient one, Plataea) for the religious inviolability of a city, secular space.

The Delphians, however, also expand on what the Smyrnaeans later would state in the Oxford Stone: there Seleucus alone granted autonomy and democracy; everyone was to recognize the temple as inviolable and the city as sacred and inviolable, but the Smyrnaeans do not actually say that the king did the latter. The Delphians, by contrast, make plain that the king granted Smyrna inviolability:[31] Seleucus asked Delphi to recognize the *asylia* of Smyrna, "himself having previously obeyed the oracle and done what he is asking our city to do as well; *and* he has granted" freedom etc. This also implies that the oracle concerned only *asylia*, as was normal, and not the civic privileges that the king grants in addition. And the oracle was not about the creation of the cult, as has been thought by scholars who would equate it with that shown the Romans in A.D. 22.

At another point the Delphians' decree is at first misleading: their summary of the request implies that Seleucus asked for the *asylia* while the Smyrnaeans (and the king) asked merely for the inscribing of the texts at Delphi. It is only at line 14 that we learn that the Smyrnaeans also (as we would expect) requested Delphian recognition of the *asylia*.[32] The king sent only a letter, not ambassadors of his own: contrast the behavior of Eumenes II and Pergamum two generations later, when the king and not the city sponsored the theoric missions.

That the Delphians speak simply of "the oracle of the god" shows that the god was Apollo, but this need not prove that it was Apollo of Delphi—one might think too of Claros or Didyma.

7–9: Smyrna approached Seleucus, who was fresh on the throne, with a number of requests: inviolability, freedom and immunity from tribute, and restoration of lost territory. These are carefully distinguished; only the first appears to have been urged by the oracle, and only this is what was asked of the Greek world at large. The king had sole authority over those other matters, but not over inviolability. The Delphians say that the king granted freedom and exemption from tribute; the Smyrnaeans' account (*I.Smyrna* 573.10–12) used the words "democracy and autonomy." A tantalizing fragment (*I.Smyrna* 576, undated) refers to democracy(?), autonomy, ancestral (land or constitution), a request by someone, presumably to a Hellenistic king.

8: πάτρι[ον] is restored from *Syll.*^{3} 656.9; cf. Robert, *Hellenica* XI–XII (1960) 513, for further examples.

31. This was denied by Seyrig, who, relying only on the Oxford Stone, thought that the king did not himself grant *asylia* but only urged others to do it: *Syria* 20 (1939) 36–37 (*Ant. syr.* III 2–3); see above, p. 35.

32. W. Günther, *Das Orakel von Didyma*, IstMitt-BH 4 (Tübingen 1971) 83, states that only the king, and not Smyrna, made the request for inviolability; that is consistent with the silence of the Oxford Stone (see on 7.9) but overlooks 7.14.

9: Smyrna in the Oxford Stone mentions the king's letter but not any missions sent to the Greeks by the city itself (the context is praise of the king). The Delphian decree shows that such ambassadors were sent, as we would expect. The two envoys are not called *theoroi* here, probably because games were not in question.

17: The Pythian announcers will make a sacrifice to Aphrodite (compare the frequent slogan in the Cretan answers to Teos, "we too worship Dionysus"). I take it, therefore, that the *theoroi* in question are those to be sent to Smyrna, not to Seleucus—their praise of the king was not to his face.

17–18: The civic decree is indeed inscribed "in the temple," that is, in the precinct of Apollo, in this case behind the building itself; similarly a text inscribed on the Polygonal Wall nearby is "in the temple" (*Syll.*[3] 436). The (lost) royal letter, by contrast, was to be published in the city proper, on the wall of the archives building; this phrase does not recur at Delphi.

Temple of Asclepius, Cos

Asclepius, patron of Cos, had his sanctuary on a hill four kilometers southwest of the city, looking across town and sea toward the peninsula of Halicarnassus. The sacred place occupied two lower terraces and the plateau at the top and encompassed a cypress grove.[1] The city of Hippocrates was the home of a distinguished medical tradition,[2] and the Asclepieum of Cos became one of the great healing shrines of the Hellenistic world, rivaling Epidaurus and the Amphiaraeum, ultimately to be eclipsed by Pergamum in Roman times. The great flourishing of the cult occurred across the first half of the third century B.C., when a number of the sacred buildings were erected. How old the cult of Asclepius at Cos was we do not know; but the grant of inviolability in 242 was the crown to a systematic "increase" that was recent. Cos, a Ptolemaic ally, was the birthplace of Ptolemy Philadelphus and enjoyed the special favor of Egypt at its height.

The games of Asclepius were declared Panhellenic and his temple inviolable in 242 B.C. Cos has yielded the earliest extant archive of *asylia* decrees, parts of more than forty surviving; they have not yet been fully published, and the following presentation must be preliminary.[3] The quest was called for by an oracle, although this fact is mentioned only once (by Philippi, **27**.3). In their speech to one of the kings, the Coan *theoroi* cited the favorable decree of the Delphian Amphictyony (**8**.9). This implies that Cos had obtained that decree

1. See generally R. Herzog and P. Schazmann, *Kos* I (Berlin 1932); S. Sherwin-White, *Ancient Cos*, Hypomnemata 51 (Göttingen 1978) esp. 334–346 on the growth of the cult. Segre, *Iscr.Cos* ED177, τ]οῦ προκα[θηγε]μόνος θεο[ῦ] Ἀσκληπ[ιοῦ] (III A.D.); Plin. *HN* 2.9.4.

2. Privileges granted the Asclepiadae by Delphi already in classical times: *CIDelphes* I 11–12 and the Hippocratic *Presbeutikos* IX 415 Littré.

3. The chief publication is R. Herzog and G. Klaffenbach, *Asylieurkunden aus Kos,* AbhBerl 1952.1; see the comments of J. and L. Robert, *Bull. épigr.* 1953, 152. I have not seen R. B. Harlow, *Eine Dialektanalyse der koischen Asylieurkunden* (Dunedin 1972), cited by Risch (below, n. 50).

before its *theoroi* spread out across the Greek world. I assume that the Coans sent to Apollo of Delphi (though he is not specified in **27**) asking how best to honor Asclepius, and perhaps their ambassadors, upon obtaining the oracle calling for *asylia*, at once put that petition to the Amphictyony while they were still in Delphi. This may have been at the spring sitting of the Council, March/April 242, but an earlier event is possible. The numerous theoric missions probably all were armed with this precedent, even though it, like the oracle, is mentioned only once in the extant documents.

When in A.D. 23 Samos and Cos petitioned Rome to confirm the inviolability of the Heraeum and the Asclepieum, the Samians relied on an Amphictyonic decree dating from the time "when the Amphictyony regulated Greek affairs and when the Greeks by their foundations in Asia ruled the sea; the antiquity of the Coans' claim was as great" (Tac. *Ann.* 4.14). Tacitus does not say that the Coans also had an Amphictyonic decree, although his silence might be taken to imply as much. At any rate, what the Coans put before the Senate was claimed to date from the age of the great migrations, a forgery like the Cretan decree for Magnesia after the Trojan War.[4] If that was a pretended Amphictyonic decree, then that, rather than a contemporary act, might be what the Coans showed around in 242; but **8**.10 is explicit that the decree concerned the games and *asylia*. In fact the petitioners to Rome in 22/3 sowed with the whole sack, describing the history of their cults and honors from the beginning. Romans were impressed by antiquity of precedent, but this sentiment is little seen in the Hellenistic acts. I conclude that the decree evoked in 242 was new or recent rather than a forgery credited to the remote past. Thus by spring 242 Cos had from Delphi an oracle and an Amphictyonic decree; what the Coans told the Senate 300 years later took in the whole mythic history of the cult from its alleged foundation during the great wanderings.[5]

The archive offers only one date: the *theoroi* who made the long journey up the Greek mainland were in Macedonia during Gorpiaios of Antigonus Gonatas' 41st year, ca. August of 242.[6] The games to which they invited the world, the first Great Asclepieia, are to happen nine months hence (**25**.17), so in April/May 241. All the civic decrees, insofar as they are preserved in the right places, accept the new games and can be assigned to summer 242. Doubt has arisen only about some of the royal letters: since Herzog, scholars have thought that some of the royal letters are earlier than 242, maintaining that several make no mention

4. *I.Magn.* 20; cf. p. 181. H. Bürgel, *Die pyläisch-delphische Amphiktyonie* (Munich 1877) 76–77, already saw that this was the date claimed by Cos and that that excluded a genuine decree.

5. For ancient accounts of the establishment of the cult of Asclepius see Sherwin-White 335–340. The contemporary Herodas (2.95–98) says that the sons of Heracles brought it from Tricca in Thessaly.

6. **26**.2. On the regnal dates of Gonatas see M. Chambers, *AJP* 75 (1954) 385–394; cf. N. G. L. Hammond, *History of Macedonia* III (Oxford 1988) 582.

of the Asclepieia and that another (**13**) was written by Ptolemy II, who died in January 246—even though this king speaks of the Asclepieia. Decrees of inviolability, however, usually stem from a single occasion; we should not divide up the Coan material without strong reasons.

Letters **8** and **12** belong unmistakably in 242. Letter **8** accepts the "sacrifice and festival" of Asclepius; that this brief phrase denotes the Great Asclepieia of 242 is guaranteed by the mention of the Coans' theoric missions canvassing the world (line 11). And the garbled **12** speaks of *theoroi*, though in what is extant Asclepius is not named.

Letter **9** grants *asylia* to "those who come to the Asclepieia" (10), as well as to the temple. This is merely a periphrasis for the *ekecheiria*, the sacred truce, of a Panhellenic contest; it is reminiscent of *asylia* for Amphictyonic representatives on their way to a meeting (*FD* III.4 359) and performers at enlarged festivals in Boeotia (**3**, **4**). Several civic decrees, in recognizing the Asclepieia as Panhellenic, phrase this simply as "accepting the *ekecheiria*." This acceptance was an essential and evidently sufficient gesture in making a festival Panhellenic. Accordingly, the author of **9** is by this phrase joining in the Panhellenic recognition—that is, in 242.

As to **10** and **11**, the first is too fragmentary to reveal whether it mentioned games or not. Ziaelas of Bithynia (**11**), however, in his long discourse does not mention the Asclepieia. He does allude to and grant "the other benefactions" (7–8: ἀποδέχεσθαι ἄσυλον καὶ τὰ λοιπὰ φιλανθρωπεῖν; 48: καὶ τῶν ἄλλω[ν]). This letter is so idiosyncratic in manner that little reliance should be placed on its precision or thoroughness; his casual reference to other benefactions may well mean to encompass acceptance of the Asclepieia. Scholars have thought the letter early because the Coans have not had dealings before with Ziaelas, and the king invokes the memory of his father. But the date of his father's death cannot be established independently of this letter; and we know that Ziaelas had to struggle against his half brothers for an unknown time to gain the throne.[7] Cos may have had no occasion to approach him before 242 and therefore mentioned their dealings with his father. His letter, moreover, is linked to **9** (which accepts the Asclepieia) because the chief *theoros* to Ziaelas bears the same name as the *theoros* praised in **9** for speaking well in the Coans' interest—that is, the two missions had the same *architheoros*. This implies that Ziaelas too was approached in 242. Admittedly in 242 the city of Cius was visited by different *theoroi*, which might mean that the mission to Ziaelas was on another occasion. But it is possible that Ziaelas was not at the time in his capital Nicomedia nearby.

By contrast, **13**, which is attributed to Ptolemy II, is linked to the *asylia* recognitions only by virtue of mentioning the Asclepieia. Its substance and date

7. See G. Vitucci, *Il regno di Bitinia* (Rome 1953) 29–31.

are uncertain: it may not belong to this archive and hence is not a reliable control on the date of the archive contents.

Thus only the silence of Ziaelas about the festival and the inclusion of **13** as a recognition by Ptolemy II suggest a date earlier than 242, both doubtful points. If we defer to these two, we must conclude that Cos invited selected foreign friends to the local Asclepieia celebrated before 242 (an attested practice) and simultaneously asked for their recognition of the inviolability of the temple. I believe that this complication is unnecessary and that we have insufficient grounds for separating out any of the recognitions of *asylia* and assigning them an earlier date.

The quadrennial games first celebrated in 241 had most likely been preceded by a local and annual festival: this was the normal situation, and one of the Hippocratic letters speaks of an annual festival and procession to the cypress grove in honor of the god.[8] The Great Asclepieia are illustrated in the victor lists extant at Cos over the next hundred years, and occasionally in agonistic inscriptions elsewhere.[9] There was a procession, mentioned only once (**49**.31);[10] only the decrees of the Sicilian colonies and an unpublished fragment mention that the games are to be quadrennial and are to include both musical and gymnic competitions (**48**.15, **49**.14, inv. M86a).[11] The elaborate definition of a Panhellenic festival that is offered in the earliest such recognition, that of the Ptolemaia (*Syll.*³ 390.38ff.), and often thereafter, is given only by implication in the Coan archive. No title such as "crowned," "isolympic," or the like is directly applied to the Asclepieia. Rather, future Coan *theoroi* announcing the games will receive the same honors as those of the Olympia (**49**.32) or Pythia (**26**.15, **27**.16), or as "those who announce crowned games" (**21**.16, **23**.14). Under these

8. IX 324–326 Littré; cf. Sherwin-White 356–357. This text does not make clear, however, whether this was the state festival to the god, the Asclepieia, or some ceremony of the medical guild. The *asylia* decrees speak of the games in the present tense, with the exception of the future at **23**.8. From this last Klaffenbach deduced that there were no games before 242; but such a reading is needlessly literal—and the Panhellenic games now requested do lie in the future.

9. *Tit.Calymn.* pp. 10–11; *I.Didyma* 98.2 with Robert, *Op. min. sel.* III 1627; cf. T. Klee, *Zur Geschichte der gymnischen Agone* (Leipzig/Berlin 1918) 59–60, 118. In *OGIS* 42 Cos honors a Coan who has led his fellow Ptolemaic *theoroi* from Alexandria to Cos with a θυσία for Asclepius, presumably for the Great Asclepieia and thus 241 B.C. or later (cf. Sherwin-White 103 n. 107); evidently the same man, son of a doctor, was active in high Ptolemaic circles in 240 (*P. Mich.Zen.* 55; cf. C. Gorteman, *ChrEg* 32 [1957] 327; *Pros.Ptol.* VI 16614; E. Olshausen, *Prosopographie der hellenistischen Königsgesandten,* Stud.Hell. 19 [Louvain 1974] 315–316). In the second century B.C. the city of Aptera requested that its honors for a Coan doctor be announced at the Asclepieia (*I.Cret.* II III 3).

10. The sacred law *LSCG* 165 mentions processions to the cypress grove in honor of various gods (no mention of Asclepius extant).

11. The victor lists of the Asclepieia show by their ἵππιον that there were also equestrian competitions (references at Sherwin-White 357 n. 559).

terms, any variant of which was sufficient, the games were "accepted" and a *theorodochos* elected. The decrees mostly make no provision for sending *theoroi* to attend the Asclepieia; one has, in an uncertain context, [- - - τὴν] θυσίαν τοὺς συνθύσον[τας - - -] (**19**.8, but see too **12**.19). Thus the texts are strangely silent about the essential feature of a Panhellenic festival, the commitment to send *theoroi* to observe the games—this too apparently was assumed.

The decrees for Cos exhibit greater diversity of formulary than later *asylia* decrees or archives. It is evident that individual letters were written by the Coans to the several kings; and that a special letter was written to their colonies in Sicily, whose responses are quite similar to each other but not to those of the other cities. Yet even in the more uniform responses, we find a diversity of details not easily paralleled in later decrees of *asylia*. This reflects, I believe, the early date; the status itself was relatively new in 242, and the formulary of the act has not yet become rigid with use and familiarity. Another feature of the archive that in my view reflects its early date is the apparent surprise at the request expressed by two grantors (**18**.7, **23**.13).

There is no political *Tendenz* to be seen in the grantors; in a time of very difficult relations especially between Seleucus and Ptolemy, all the great powers "join in accepting" the inviolability of the Asclepieum (cf. on **23**.4–6).[12]

As to the later treatment of the Asclepieum, it is worth noting first that around 200 B.C. the Coans voted to take military measures "to protect the temples and city and country," probably from the forces of Philip V.[13] It seems to have been obvious to them that a declared status would not protect the sanctuary. The construction of a large new temple on the uppermost plateau is dated to the second century B.C. Cos sided with Mithridates, but the Coans assured the Senate in A.D. 23 that the Asclepieum protected Romans during the massacre of 88 B.C.[14] In 32 B.C. the Antonian admiral D. Turullius cut down much of the sacred grove of Asclepius; after Actium Octavian surrendered him to the Coans for punishment.[15] In circumstances that are not recorded, Cos lost its freedom in the Augustan period. Although this disadvantage lasted until the 70s A.D., the inviolability of the temple was not compromised, as we know from the investigation of A.D. 22–23.[16] Cos and Samos approached the Roman Senate

12. By contrast, Bengtson from the mere existence of the Sicilian decrees deduced that Rome and Ptolemy were friendly (*Historia* 3 [1954/55] 456–463 [*Kl.Schr.* 358–366]; followed by H. H. Schmitt, *Rom und Rhodos* [Munich 1957] 51, but not Will, *Histoire* I 323; cf. the skepticism of the Roberts, *Bull. épigr.* 1976, 522).

13. ποτὶ τὰν φυλακὰν τῶν ἱερῶν καὶ τᾶς πόλιος καὶ τᾶς χώρα[ς]: M. Segre, *RivFil* 61 (1933) 365 (= *Iscr.Cos* ED49), linked to the Cretan War. Cf. Holleaux, *Etudes* V 274–275; P. Baker, *Cos et Calymna* 205–200 *a.C.* (Quebec City 1991).

14. App. *Mith.* 23; Tac. *Ann.* 4.14; cf. Sherwin-White 138.

15. Dio 51.8.3; Val. Max. 1.1.19.

16. See Sherwin-White 145–149.

for the renewal of *asylia* not in A.D. 22 like the rest of the Greek cities but in 23. An inscription from Samos (**184**) suggests that this divergence in date is not a result of the hearings dragging over into the new year, for the decree is dated in September. Cos may have honored Tiberius after the success of this appeal.[17] Finally, in A.D. 53 on the request of the Coan doctor C. Stertinius Xenophon, the emperor Claudius persuaded the Senate to grant Cos immunity in honor of its famous medical tradition, "so that henceforth the Coans might inhabit an island that is sacred and subject only to the god" (*Coi sacram et tantum dei ministram insulam colerent*, Tac. *Ann.* 12.61); immunity was granted, but not yet liberty.[18]

Most of the texts are inscribed on steles of white marble, usually gabled opisthographic steles; three of the royal letters, however, are on a three-sided prism of blue-white marble. Inscriptiones Graecae in Berlin has a set of squeezes, which I have collated selectively. Diversity of script shows that several masons were employed. They are not consistent in their use of headings; several allow themselves the luxury of quite ragged right margins.

The excavations conducted by Herzog early in this century and later by the Italians have not been fully published. The exact findspot of many stones has not been stated, so that it is unclear where in the sanctuary the archive was inscribed, or what its order was. One principle of organization is revealed by **46**.1, ψηφίσματα ἃ ἐκόμισαν θεωροὶ ᾿Επιδαύριος (κτλ.): the texts were grouped according to the theoric missions that obtained them. Rather than a cartographic logic, the thinking was either bureaucratic, naming the ambassadors responsible, or chronological, wherein decrees were inscribed as they were brought to Cos by the several missions. There were exceptions to this grouping: the decree of Corcyra follows three from Macedonia. The individual decrees were not necessarily in the sequence of the itinerary (the mainland Greek ones seem to be, while Naples and Velia are not).

Thus there was no archive wall but rather a large number of freestanding steles; even the decrees on the prism stand apart from one another, obtained by different *theoroi* and inscribed by more than one hand. Probably mere reasons of space lie behind the exceptional placement of some documents.

17. A Coan inscription was fully restored to this effect by Herzog, *HZ* 125 (1922) 222 n. 2: [ὁ δᾶμος καθιέρωσε Τιβε]ρίωι Καίσαρι θεοῦ Σε[βαστοῦ υἱῶι | χαριστήριον τᾶς ἀσυλία]ς ἃς ἔχει παρ' αὐτο[ῦ βεβαιωθείσας· (κτλ.). Without a full publication it is difficult to be confident of the restorations.

18. Sherwin-White 149; at *I.Ephesos* VI 2055.4–5 (early III A.D.), ἐλεύθερον [καὶ αὐτόνο]μον. It has been suggested that *ministra* translates νεωκόρος: H. Furneaux, *The Annals of Tacitus* II^2 (Oxford 1907) 139; but this seems unlikely at this early date. For the sentiment of the god's place see p. 12.

COS: ASCLEPIEUM

These are Klaffenbach's texts except as noted, which he edited from Herzog's notes and squeezes and occasionally from notes from the Italian excavation.[19] I give the royal letters first, beginning with the one that mentions the existing Amphictyonic decree and the Panhellenic quest now in progress.

8. Ptolemy III (?)

Two joining fragments of a stele, right margin preserved. Lower right fragment (lines 9–20), found in 1902; h. 0.33, w. 0.245, th. 0.105. The other fragment is known only from a squeeze, and nothing is recorded about its discovery or dimensions. Letters 0.009–0.013, intersp. 0.005; same hand as **9** and **10** (on the prism).

Lower fragment: Herzog, *Hermes* 65 (1930) 463–471 [Schroeter p. 105 frag. 5; Welles, *Royal Corres.* 28].

Entire: Herzog/Klaffenbach, *Asylieurkunden* 2 [*SEG* 12.369].

Cf. Robert, *BCH* 54 (1930) 345 (*Op. min. sel.* I 164); Wilhelm, *Griechische Königsbriefe,* Klio-BH 48 (Leipzig 1943) 16–20; D. Musti, *AnnPisa* 26 (1957) 278–279; J. and L. Robert, *Bull. épigr.* 1966, 306.

[βασιλεὺς Πτολεμαῖος? Κώιων τῆι βου]-
[λῆι καὶ] τῶι δήμω[ι χαίρειν; ca. 7]
. . . ιν, ὅτι ἐπαγγέλλουσιν οἱ παρ' ὑ-
[μῶ]ν ἀρχιθέωρός τε Φαῖνις καὶ θεω-
[ροὶ] Φιλόφρων καὶ Ἀρχέπολις περὶ
[τῆ]ς θυσίας ἣν συντελεῖτε τῶι [Ἀσ]-
[κ]ληπιῶι καὶ περὶ τοῦ ἄσυλον εἶν[αι]
[τ]ὸ ἱερὸν τοῦ Ἀσκληπιοῦ· καὶ γάρ [φασι]
[τ]οὺς Ἀμφικτύονας ἐψηφίσθαι πε-
[ρὶ] τούτων καὶ πρὸς τοὺς λοιποὺς
[βα]σιλεῖς καὶ τὰ ἔθνη καὶ τὰς πό-
[λε]ις ἀφεστάλθαι τοὺς ἀξιώ{ον}-
[σο]ντας· τήν τε δὴ θυσίαν καὶ τὴν
[παν]ήγυριν καὶ τὴν τοῦ ἱεροῦ ἀσυλί-
[αν δε]χόμεθα μάλιστα μὲν διὰ τὸ[ν]
[θεόν, ἔπ]ειτα δὲ καὶ δι' ὑμᾶς· προσήγ-
[γειλαν δ]ὲ κα[ὶ ὅ]τι ἡ εἰκὼν ἕστηκεν
[ἡμῶν - - - - - -] καὶ τὸν ἀγῶνα ὃν τί-

19. I omit from this corpus Herzog, *Heilige Gesetze aus Kos,* AbhBerl 1928.6 no. 13 [Sokolowski, *LSCG* 158], assigned to the first half of the third century B.C. Of this fragment Herzog offered a complete restoration as a sacred law providing for the boundaries of the inviolability of the temple in accordance with an oracle of Apollo. The restorations seem to me groundless and unconvincing.

[θεμεν ἐν ʽΙερᾶι Νή]σωι ἀποδέχεσθε.
[ἔρρ]ωσθε.

I omit Herzog's extensive restorations (and Wilhelm's modifications of them); dismissed already by Robert and Welles, they were proved wrong by the upper fragment, which revealed a far shorter line. 1 init. J. and L. Robert. 17 init. Wilhelm. 18–19 J. and L. Robert: τε̣|[θεμεν τῶι Καθηγέμονι Διονύ]σωι Herzog, τί|[θεμεν τῶι Διονύ]σωι Klaffenbach.

. . .

[King Ptolemy (?) to the council and] people of Cos, [greetings. It is fitting (?)], what your chief *theoros* Phaenis and *theoroi* Philophron and Archepolis proclaim concerning the sacrifice which you are celebrating for Asclepius and concerning the temple of Asclepius being inviolable. For [they say] too that the Amphictyons have voted on these things and that requesters have been sent to the other kings and nations and cities. We accept the sacrifice and festival and the inviolability of the temple, especially for the sake of the god but next on your account. They have reported too that the statue [of us - - -] has been erected and that you accept the contest which we are cel[ebrating at Hiera Ne]sos. Farewell.

Inclusion of the Asclepieia should date this to 242 with the other texts. Herzog's attribution to the Attalid dynasty was based on elimination and on the restoration of Dionysus in line 19. But Eumenes never took the title of king, and Musti concluded that he cannot have alluded to "the other kings" (10–11). Dionysus, moreover, was not, as Herzog and others believed, an ancestor of the Attalids; he became prominent at Pergamum only in its later years, and because of his role in the Artists' guild rather than in the dynasty.[20] The only known Attalid festival that might have enjoyed more than local participation at this early date would be that of Athena (Polyb. 4.49.3).

The Roberts would restore in line 19 the toponym Hiera Nesos, in effect assigning the letter to a Ptolemy; although they did not publish their arguments, the attribution seems compelling. The author sponsored games to which he had invited the Coans. The only Panhellenic festival held by a king at this date was the Ptolemaia at Alexandria. But that festival seems excluded here, for the Coans would have accepted it a generation earlier.[21] A gesture of special friendship is evinced when a city shares in an otherwise local festival,[22] and for Cos this points to the Ptolemaic house. At Hiera Nesos, then the great center of Greek culture in the Fayum, the Ptolemies sponsored a lesser version of the Ptolemaia, τὸν ἐν ʽΙερᾶι νήσωι ἀγῶνα τῶν Πτολεμαιείων (*PSI* IV 364: 250 B.C.). The village

20. See Robert, *Etudes anat.* 25–26; *Op. min. sel.* VI 464–465 n. 42.

21. It is, however, a peculiar feature of our evidence for the Ptolemaia that the two extant acceptances derive from widely different dates, the Islanders' in 283/2 B.C. and the Amphictyony's in the 260s.

22. Thus around 220 B.C. Prusias of Bithynia invited his friends to share in his festival the Soteria at Nicomedia and thereby learned who his friends were (Polyb. 4.49.3).

is several times called Ἱερὰ Νῆσος Θεῶν Σωτήρων, marking the prominence there of the cult of Ptolemy I and his wife.[23] Our king avoids ambiguity with the Panhellenic Ptolemaia by naming the place rather than the festival.

Coan attendance at this local Ptolemaia is paralleled in a letter of Ptolemy III to Xanthus in the 240s: Xanthian *theoroi* have attended both the Ptolemaia and the Theadelpheia (*SEG* 36.1218). There the first festival, described only by name and without the geographical circumlocution of our letter, was the Panhellenic Ptolemaia at Alexandria. The second was a festival for the Theoi Adelphoi Ptolemy II and Arsinoe, attested several times;[24] it was not Panhellenic. Apparently the Xanthian visitors troubled to sacrifice at both, as would be appropriate to the close relations of their city with the Ptolemaic house.

Our letter is of a businesslike brevity, and that too might well be taken to suit a Ptolemy, whose dealings with the island must have been frequent—contrast the verbosity of the Bithynian and Spartocid(?) kings, who have never written to Cos before. For whatever reason, this is the only text in the archive that invokes the Amphictyonic decree and the Panhellenic quest.

Chambers (*AJP* 391–392) described the enlargement of the Asclepieia in 242 as an act of Ptolemy III commemorating his northern Aegean victories. In fact it was an act of the Coans commemorating Asclepius, and if this letter is rightly attributed, their action was news to him, as it was to all the others (nor does he know a Ptolemaic precedent for his favor to Cos: see below).

2: Klaffenbach suggested προσφιλὲς/προσῆκον ἐστ]ίν; or perhaps καλῶς ἔχον ἐστ]ίν as at **48**.17–18 (for parallels see Holleaux, *Etudes* III 236–238; Herrmann, "Antiochos" 75 n. 56).

4–5: These *theoroi* are not met again in the extant texts. Philophron was a common name at Cos (see Sherwin-White 542) as elsewhere; I assume that Philophron son of Dardanus who went with two others to Italy (**46**, **47**) was a different man.

13–14: The Great Asclepieia, therefore 242 B.C., must be meant by this phrase, given the Panhellenic quest described in the preceding lines.

16–19: The king had already made his own invitation to the Coans, and the *theoroi* now mention their city's favorable response as part of their appeal. This gesture of friendship was accompanied by voting the king a statue (which, again, the Byzantines refused to do for Prusias, Polyb. 4.49). Line 18 will have specified the location; ἐν τῶι ἱερῶι (Herzog) would suffice in this context.

9. Seleucus II (?)

On one face of a triangular prism of blue-white marble found in the Asclepieum in 1903; h. 1.15; letters 0.008. **10** and **11** are on another face; the third, which has suffered from use as a threshold, is undeciphered.

23. References in A. Calderini, *Dizionario dei nomi geografici* III (Milan 1978) 17.
24. J. Bingen, *ChrEg* 23 (1948) 208; J. Bousquet, *REG* 99 (1986) 27.

Herzog, *Hermes* 65 (1930) 463–471 [Schroeter 17; Welles, *Royal Corres.* 26].
Cf. Robert, *BCH* 54 (1930) 343–344 (*Op. min. sel.* I 162–163); Wilhelm, *Griechische Königsbriefe* 20; Rigsby, *Phoenix* 38 (1984) 103.

[τὰ ν]ο̣μ̣ι̣ζό̣μ̣[ενα συνετέ]-
λεσαν καὶ τὰ π̣[ερὶ τὰς θυ]-
σίας καὶ τὸν ἀγῶ[να παρέ?]-
θηκαν. ἀπὸ δὲ τού[των γε]-
νόμενοι ἀπήντων̣ [ἡμῖν]
καὶ διὰ πλεόνων ὑπέ[ρ τε]
τοῦ ἱεροῦ καὶ τῆς πόλεω̣[ς]
διελθόντες ἠξίουν ἀσυ-
λίαν τοῖς ἐπὶ τὰ Ἀσκληπί-
εια παραγινομένοις [[. . . . . .]]
καὶ αὐτῶι τῶι ἱερῶι παρ' ἡμῶν
ὑπάρξαι. ἡμεῖς δὲ τόν τε
δῆμον ἐπηνοῦμεν διὰ
τὴν πρὸς τοὺς θεοὺς εὐ-
σέβειαν καὶ ἐπὶ τῶι τὰ πρὸς
ἡμᾶς φανερὰ ποεῖν καὶ Διό-
γειτον ἀπεδεξάμεθα
διὰ τὸ ὑπὲρ τῆς πατρί-
δος ὁρᾶν πᾶν τὸ βέλτισ-
τον καὶ λέγοντα καὶ πράτ-
τοντα. παραδεχόμεθα
δὲ καὶ τὴν ἀσυλίαν καθό-
τι ὁ δῆμος ἠξίωσεν, καὶ εἰς
τὸ λοιπὸν δὲ πειρασόμεθα
τῶν καθ' ἡμᾶς ὄντων ἐν ἡ-
συχίαι μὴ ἀχαριστεῖν ὑμῖν'
ἐν τοῖς ἀξιουμένοις.
ἔρρωσθε.

3 Rigsby: [ἀνέ]θηκαν Herzog, [διέ]θηκαν? Robert. 4 the squeeze: τε Herzog.

The author accepts the Great Asclepieia and the date is therefore 242. Herzog assigned the letter to a Seleucid, hence Seleucus II, partly by elimination (having given **8** to the Attalid dynasty), partly because the same *theoroi* visited Ziaelas (**11**) and one wants therefore a king who ruled in Anatolia. Welles thought the clear and direct style impossible in a non-Greek ruler. If this is so, the choice lies between Eumenes I and Seleucus II: which, in the summer of 242, is the more likely to have stated cautiously that his affairs were now peaceful (25)? Eumenes' successor would soon be confronted with war against Antiochus Hierax and then the Gauls; but Eumenes himself, now in the last year of his life, is not known to have engaged in any military enterprise in his later years.[25] Seleucus, by contrast, toward 242 returned to Asia Minor from his largely successful Syrian campaign; at Sardes he now agreed to share power with Antiochus Hierax, and his treaty with Ptolemy followed in 241.[26] The reference to peace, not a banality, suits Seleucus' situation well.

1–4: The plural verbs show that there were several *theoroi*; Diogeitus, praised at 16ff., must have been their chief and spokesman, as he was to Ziaelas. In 3, as Robert and Welles saw respectively, it makes no sense for the Coan ambassadors either to "dedicate" or to "conduct" someone else's festival. But the object of the verb is τά: the sense should be "they performed the rites and contributed the things for the sacrifices and contest." For such a gesture in the course of diplomacy, compare *Aphrodisias and Rome* 4.15–16: τήν τε θυσίαν παρέστησαν.[27] I suggest the compound παρέθηκαν, thinking of the many instances of παράστασις ἱερῶν.[28] Perhaps ambassadors arrived while the king was presiding over some festival; as any Greek king from Nestor on would do (*Od.* 3.32ff.), he invited them to share in it, and they naturally made a contribution, presumably a sacrificial animal. We need not, therefore, look for Panhellenic games;[29] indeed in 242 there were none in Asia. It may be that these were games to which Coans had been specially invited, as Welles assumed; but that gesture is improbable of Seleucus for Ptolemaic Cos. It seems more likely that the Coans' arrival at the games was accidental.[30] Seleucus will most likely have been at Sardes. In any case, that a festival is in progress cannot tell us where the king was. As Philip (cf., for example, Dem. 18.192–193) and Alexander demonstrated, a king could celebrate one anywhere if circumstances called for it.

25. R. B. McShane, *Foreign Policy of the Attalids of Pergamum* (Urbana 1964) 42–47.

26. For the chronology see Beloch, *Gr. Gesch.* IV.2 541; cf. Will, *Histoire* I 257–261.

27. See, however, C. P. Jones, *EchCl* 29 (1985) 312, who takes the sacrifice in the Aphrodisias text to be spontaneous.

28. Also possible is ἐπέθηκαν, as at *LSAM* 37.1517: θύσει δὲ καὶ τὰς θυσίας ... καὶ λιβανωτὸν ἐπιθήσει (a priest's duties, Priene, II B.C.); also at Segre, *Iscr.Cos* ED236.4. The verbs are unfortunately lost at *IG* IX.1^2 187.16–18 (praise of a foreigner): τὰ κατὰ τὰς θυσίας συν[ετέλεσεν τοῖς θε]οῖς ὡς ποθῆκον ἦν, τά τε κατὰ τὸν ἀγῶνα τῶν Πυθίων ... κ[αλῶς διώικησεν (so Klaffenbach: ἐπεμελήθη Kern).

29. Herzog considered the games of Aphrodite at Smyrna or the Didymeia at Miletus; cf. Segre, *Historia* 5 (1931) 244 n. 9 (against the Didymeia). Contra: Welles p. 127 n. 3 on the silence of the *asylia* documents for Smyrna, and rightly rejecting the Didymeia; Welles observes that "it is possible also to think of special games as well as of periodic, games possibly in honor of Seleucus' recovery of Syria for which he received the epithet Callinicus" (p. 128).

30. Cf. *IG* II^2 1330.49: [ἐ]ὰν πρεσβεία τις ἔλθῃ παρὰ Ἀρια[ράθου ὅταν τὰ Διονύσια] γίνωνται (κτλ.).

7: A favorable attitude "to the temple and the city" is often praised in cities where a particular temple played a large role, as at Delphi, Delos,[31] Ephesus, or Samothrace.[32]

25–26: For guarded promises in diplomatic discourse compare **56**.7–9; Moretti, *I. stor. ellen.* I 14.30–31; *Syll.*³ 537.70 (= *IG* II² 916); Helly, *I.Gonnoi* 109.34–35.

10. Unknown king

On the other legible face of the triangular prism.
Herzog, *Hermes* 65 (1930) 463–471 [Schroeter 21; Welles, *Royal Corres.* 27].
Photograph: Herzog, *AM* 30 (1905) pl. 7.

[- - - ε]ἰς τὸν ἅπ̣α̣ν̣[τα]
[χρόνον..] καὶ ἔφασαν
[χαριεῖσθ]α̣ι̣ τῶι δήμωι
[συγκατ]α̣σκευάσαντα
[τὴν ἀσ]υλίαν. ἡμεῖς δὲ
[καὶ] δ̣ιὰ τὸν θεὸν καὶ διὰ
[τὴ]ν πόλιν προσδεδέ-
[γ]μ̣[ε]θα καθάπερ ὤιεσθε
δεῖν καὶ τοῖς ὑφ' ἡμᾶς τασσο-
μένοις παραδώσομεν ἄ-
συλον ἡγεῖσθαι τὸ ἱερὸν
ὡς τοὺς ὅρους τεθείκα-
τε. ἔρρωσθε.

1–2: [ὑπέμνησαν δὲ καὶ τοῦ ἡμετέρου πατρὸς τοῦ ποιησαμένου πρὸς ὑμᾶς φιλίαν καὶ συμμαχίαν ε]ἰς τὸν ἅπ̣α̣ν̣[τα χρόνον, ὃν] καὶ ἔφασαν Herzog. 3 Rigsby: [βοηθῆσ]α̣ι̣ Herzog, [χαρίσασθ]α̣ι̣ Welles.

Herzog assigned the letter to Ptolemy III, because he took the opening lines to invoke a previous grant by another king, therefore a predecessor (which he thought extant in **13**), and lines 9ff. to order administrative subordinates to observe the *asylia*, therefore the sovereign of Cos. But lines 9ff., as the parallels show, are a promise to order the cities subject to the king to recognize the inviolability.[33] As to the opening, συγκατασκευάζω, "join in establishing," is the usual verb for this act—join the Coans and the world,[34] not a predecessor as Herzog thought. A second recognition of *asylia* by the same dynasty would be unparalleled; here the matter rests finally on the tense of a restored verb. In line 3, it is more in keeping with the attested language of diplomacy to restore a future, alluding to the polite request: "They said that I would

31. C. Vial, *Délos indépendante* (Paris 1984) 92.
32. P. M. Fraser, *Samothrace* II.1 (New York 1960) 57 n. 5.
33. So Welles ad loc. and Sherwin-White 93.
34. For the force of συν- see Welles, *Royal Corres.* p. 150.

gratify the people by accepting the inviolability."[35] Moreover, the decree of Aenus (**28**), though earnestly expressing the city's loyalty to King Ptolemy, does not cite a Ptolemaic precedent or desire concerning the inviolability of the Asclepieum—not of Ptolemy III naturally, for that was only now being sought; but neither of Ptolemy II, which the Coans surely would have invoked had it existed.

Accordingly, nothing speaks for Ptolemaic authorship, which would be impossible if **8** is rightly assigned to Ptolemy III. Of the six letters for Cos, two are from non-Greek monarchs and two can be attributed with some probability to Ptolemy and Seleucus. Two major dynasties remain, the Attalids and Antigonids. On the situation of Eumenes I see above (p. 115). As to Antigonus Gonatas, we know that he joined in the recognition of the Asclepieum, and his favorable response, as promised here, was made known to the cities subject to him (**25**.10, **26**.14, **27**.14); this gesture, however, is too common to narrow the field (all the kings did this for Magnesia a generation later).[36] If this is Gonatas, we have no other letter of his to compare.[37] Presumably Gonatas was approached by the same ambassadors who canvassed Greece and Macedonia, and they seem to have found him at or near Pella, for the decree of that city (**23**) does not mention the king's favorable response, whereas the Macedonian cities subsequent on their route do.

1: Friendship for all time at **20**.7, but inviolable for all time at **35**.8.

4: The author mixes singular and plural, or else his singular here reflects the text of the Coans' request. Such mixing is common: *Royal Corres.* 1.65 with Welles's note; *Syll.*[3] 572.3 (Philip V); here, **11**.49.

7–8: προσδέχομαι recurs in the Coan material only in the decrees of Pella and Amphipolis (**23**.10, **26**.11); perhaps it was peculiar to the version of the Coan request sent to Macedonia.

11. Ziaelas of Bithynia

Inscribed below **10** by a different hand, letters slightly larger.

Herzog, *AM* 30 (1905) 173–182 [Hiller, *Syll.*[3] 456; Schroeter 20; Welles, *Royal Corres.* 25; Dörner, *TAM* IV 1].

Photograph: Herzog pl. 7.

35. Thus a civic request to a royal official for help, δηλοῦντες αὐτῶι ὅτι ταῦτα πράξας χαριεῖται τῶι δάμωι (*Syll.*[3] 644.26–27); a king [τα]ῦτα ποιῶν εὐχαριστήσει τοῖς Αἰτωλοῖς (Moretti, *I. stor. ellen.* II 77, with Robert, *DAM* 173–186); cf. *I.Magn.* 15b8; *OGIS* 329.30; *AM* 72 (1957) 242 no. 65.17; Robert, *Op. min. sel.* 33 n. 1. Welles (p. 130) envisioned this expression but thought that then ἠξίωσαν would be expected, which mistakes the formula. On the tone of the expression we have Theophr. *Char.* 24.13.

36. On the formula see Bickerman, *Religions* 218–219.

37. From his 36th year (248/7) we have a letter from his son Demetrius, *BSA* 40 (1939–40) 14–16 [*SEG* 12.311]; cf. Chambers pp. 390–391.

βασιλεὺς Βιθυνῶν Ζιαήλας
Κώιων τῆι βουλῆι καὶ τῶι δή{μ}-
μωι χαίρειν· Διόγειτος Ἀριστό-
λοχος Θεύδοτος οἱ παρ' ὑμῶν
παραγενόμενοι ἠξίουν τὸ ἱερὸν
τοῦ Ἀσκληπιοῦ τὸ ἱδρυμένον πα-
ρ' ὑμῖν ἀποδέξασθαι ἄσυλον καὶ
τὰ λοιπὰ φιλανθρωπεῖν τῆι πό-
λει, καθόπερ καὶ Νικομήδης ὁ
πατὴρ ἡμῶν εὐνόως διέκει-
το τῶι δήμωι. ἡμεῖς δὲ πάν-
των μὲν τῶν ἀφικνουμένω[ν]
πρὸς ἡμᾶς Ἑλλήνων τυγχάνο-
μεν τὴν ἐπιμέλειαν ποιούμε-
νοι, πεπεισμένοι πρὸς δόξαν οὐ
μικρὸν συμβάλλεσθαι τὸ μέρος
τοῦτο· πολὺ δὴ μάλιστα τῶν
πατρικῶν φίλων διατελοῦ-
μεν πολυωροῦντες καὶ ὑμῶν
διὰ τὴν πρὸς τὸμ πατέρα ⟨ἡ⟩μῶν
ὑπάρχουσαν πρὸς τὸν ὑμέτε-
ρον δῆμον γνῶσιν, καὶ διὰ τὸ
τὸμ βασιλέα Πτολεμαῖον
οἰκείως διακεῖσθαι τὰ πρὸς ὑμᾶς,
ὄντα ἡμέτερον φίλον καὶ σύμ-
μαχον· ἔτι δὲ καὶ τοὺς παρ' ὑμῶν
ἀπεσταλμένους φιλοτιμότε-
ρον ἀπολογίσασθαι τὴν εὔνοιαν
ἣν ἔχετε εἰς ἡμᾶς, ἔν τε τοῖς λοι-
ποῖς καθ' ὃ ἂν ἡμᾶς ἀξιῶτε, πειρασό-
μεθα καὶ ἰδίαι ἑκάστωι καὶ κοι-
νῆι πᾶσι φιλανθρωπεῖν καθ' ὅσον
ἡμεῖς δυνατοί ἐσμεν, καὶ τῶν
πλειόντων τὴν θάλασσαν
ὅσοι ἂν τυγχάνωσιν τῶν ὑμε-
τέρων προσβάλλοντες τοῖς
τόποις ὧν ἡμεῖς κρατοῦμεν,
φροντίζειν ὅπως ἡ ἀσφάλει[α]
αὐτοῖς ὑπάρχῃ· κατὰ ταὐτα [δὲ]
καὶ οἷς ἂν συμβῇ πταίματός [τι]-
νος γενομένου κατὰ πλοῦν
προσπεσεῖν πρὸς τὴν ἡμετέ[ραν,]
πᾶσαν σπουδὴν ποιεῖσθαι ἵν[α]
μηδ' ὑφ' ἑνὸς ἀδικῶνται. ἀποδ[εχό]-
μεθα δὲ καὶ τὸ ἱερὸν ἄσυλον κ[αθό]-
περ ᾤιεσθε δεῖν, καὶ Διογείτωι [καὶ]

Ἀριστολόχωι καὶ Θευδότωι πε[ρὶ]
τῶν τούτων καὶ τῶν ἄλλω[ν ὧν]
ἠβουλόμεθα ἐντέταλμαι ἀγ̣[αγ]-
γεῖλαι ὑμεῖν. ἔρρωσθε.

20: ΥΜΩΝ lapis.

These *theoroi* visited (probably) Seleucus at Sardes (**9**.16–17), but not the city of Cius on the Propontis (**32**), which would be on their way to Nicomedia; it may be that Ziaelas was not at the time in his capital. Perhaps the same men went on to South Russia for **12**.

Herzog placed this letter earlier than 242 B.C., but on flimsy grounds. Nicomedes had died between 255 and 246, leaving as king a son by his second wife; Ziaelas had to supplant this rival to become king, and how long that took is not known.[38] When Ziaelas speaks of his father's benefactions to the Coans at 9–11, he is surely echoing their request; evidently Cos has not previously had dealings with Ziaelas himself. He goes on to emphasize the continuity of his policy with that of his father. Like Seleucus II, who had been treated by his father in the same way,[39] Ziaelas had an interest in stressing the legitimacy of his position and might have done so for many years. The government of Cos is not likely to have had frequent occasion to address the Bithynian monarchy. Thus the letter need not be near the start of his sole rule, whenever that was; especially given the uncertain chronology of the dynasty, the date is best left at 242 B.C. with the rest of the Coan archive.

The letter is unusually discursive and shapeless (see Welles's comments on style). Ziaelas does not explicitly mention the Asclepieia, although this may be concealed in his reference to the "other benefactions" he is granting (8, 48). Together with many generalities, the king says as much about protecting Coan visitors as about the Asclepieum; the ambassadors had raised the question of the safety of merchants who landed or were wrecked on Bithynian shores (29ff.). In the course of all this we learn that Ziaelas is allied with Egypt (23).

1: By contrast with the practice of the civic decrees, this text (the only royal letter in the archive whose beginning is preserved) lacks a heading naming the author. Bickerman thought Βιθυνῶν intrusive and perhaps an addition by the Coan archivist;[40] Reynolds restored the ethnic at *Aphrodisias and Rome* 4.1, which may be another letter from a Bithynian monarch; but see Jones (above, n. 27) 317.

7: For πολὺ μάλιστα compare *Aphrodisias and Rome* 4.22 (adduced by Jones 313).

38. For details see C. Habicht, "Ziaelas," *RE* 10A (1972) 387–390.

39. Cf. Will, *Histoire* I 249–250. Compare *Royal Corres.* 22 (p. 174 below), which admittedly is from the start of Seleucus' reign.

40. *Mélanges I. Lévy* (Brussels 1955) 23–24 n. 1 (*Studies* II 34–35).

9ff.: Coan relations with the dynasty are reflected in *I.Cos* 35 (= *SGDI* 3635), a cult calendar of uncertain date that includes a sacrifice to King Nicomedes—but it is not clear which of the three (cf. Habicht, *Gottmenschentum* 126; Sherwin-White 137).

16: For τὸ μέρος, "this matter," see J. and L. Robert, *Bull. épigr.* 1965, 221.

23: A connection between the Bithynian house and Egypt is first seen in the fact that Ptolemy II was among those named in Nicomedes' will as guardians of his heirs—who did not include the exiled Ziaelas: Memnon *FGrHist* 434 F 1.14; Habicht, *RE* 389.

29ff.: The Coans, whose luxury goods were famous and whose amphorae are found throughout the eastern Mediterranean,[41] here made an issue of the safety of their merchants. For the dangers of an earlier time compare Xen. *An.* 6.4.2; but good relations with Sinope are evidenced by the decree at Segre, *Iscr.Cos* I pp. 26–27. Antigonus Monophthalmus had declared ἀσφάλεια τῆς θαλάσσης during his siege of Rhodes (Polyaen. 4.6.16); a similar concern at *I.Erythrai* 28.3–12.

36–37: "enter territory under our control," Welles; better "put in at [so LSJ] places we rule": τόποι usually were settled places. For Bithynian good treatment of the shipwrecked we have Nicolaus of Damascus *FGrHist* 90 F 113. The insecurity of which the Coans complained may have resulted from the Bithynian dynastic struggle in the 240s and diverse loyalties of the cities.

12. Spartocid king (?)

Four joining fragments; th. 0.1–0.15; letters 0.006–0.01, intersp. 0.003–0.004. The decree of Gela (**49**) is on the other side.

Herzog/Klaffenbach, *Asylieurkunden* 3 [*SEG* 12.370; F. P. Rizzo, *La Sicilia e le potenze ellenistiche,* Kokalos Suppl. 3 (Rome 1973) 15–20].

Cf. J. and L. Robert, *Bull. épigr.* 1953, pp. 156–157; Welles, *Gnomon* 25 (1953) 398; F. Piejko, *Gnomon* 57 (1985) 614.

η /[- -]
τω[- -]
δημ[- -]
προσδ[- -]
τι ἐν ἧμ[- -]
. αντων[- -]
. ε ἀκολούθ[ως αἷς εἶχον ἐντολαῖς τὴν ἐπαγ]-
γελίαν ἐποιή[σαντο τῆς τε θυσίας καὶ τῶν ἀγώ]-
νων τῆι διδασ[καλίαι χρώμενοι οὕτω καλῶς ὥστε]
θαυμάζειν ἐπῄει [ἡμεῖν - - - - - - - - - - - - - - - - - -]
ἀφ' οὗ τῆς βασιλεία[ς - - - - - - - - - - - - - - - - -]
. ίαν περὶ τούτων ὕσ[- - - - - - - - - - - - - - - - - σ]-

41. See Sherwin-White 229–243.

θε τηλικούτων καὶ το[ιούτων φιλανθρώπων προ]-
ϋπαρχόντων ἡμεῖν πρὸς [ὑμᾶς· ὄντων δέ τινων νῦν]
τούτοις ἐμποδίων, εἰ κα[ὶ οἱ θεωροὶ τοῦτο ἡμεῖν]
μέμψασ{α}θαι ἐφάνη{.}ν, πα[ρακαλοῦμεν ὅμως ὑμᾶς]
τοῖς καιροῖς ἴσως ἐπακ[ολ]ουθή[σαντας κρῖναι ἡ]-
μεῖν συγγνώμην ἐκτέον, ὅταν [- - - - - - - - - - - - - - - -]
κότες μὴ δυνώμεθα τὰς τούτω[ν τῶν ἀγώνων συντελείας]
θεωρεῖν· ἐγὼ δὲ καὶ ἡ ἀδελφ[ή] μ[ου - - - - - - - - - - - -]
καὶ οἱ ἡμέτεροι πολῖται τήν τε παρ' [ὑμῶν ἐπαγγε]-
⟨λ⟩ίαν γινομένην τῶι θεῶι καὶ τὴν ἀ[συλία]ν δεχ[ό]-
μεθα καὶ τὴν συγγένειαν οὖσαν ἀλ[η]θινὴν καὶ [ὑ]-
μῶν τε ἀξίαν καὶ ἡμῶν ἡδέως προσ[δε]δέγμεθα,
μαρτυρίας μεγίστης τῆς παρὰ το[ῦ ἡμ]ετέρου
πατρὸς προσγεγενημένης ἣν ἀπ[οπεφήν?]ατε
αὐτοῦ ἐκείνου ποιησαμένου· εἰ [δὲ καὶ τῶν λοιπῶν]
τινες Ἑλλήνων ἀρχὴν φιλί[ας ποιούμενοι ταύτ]ην
πρῶτον προσηγόρευον ἡμ[ᾶς συγγενεῖς, εὐ]λόγως
ἂν προσελαμβάνομεν τ[ούτους, τοιαύτη]ς φιλαν-
θρωπίας ἡμεῖν προϋπαρχ[ούσης πρό]ς γε τοὺς το[ι]-
αύτην συγγένειαν καὶ [τη]λικ[αύτην ἀ]ναγκαιότητα
ἀναμιμνήσκον[τα]ς κα[ὶ] ταύτ[ην δι]αφυλάττειν προ-
αιρουμένους π[ολ]λαπλασίως· κ[αὶ νῦν] τὴν εὔνοιαν ἀπ[ο]-
δεδέγμεθα [κα]ὶ τὰ μετ[ὰ] ταῦτα [π]ε[ι]ρασόμεθα δια-
[τ]ηροῦντε[ς τὰ ἐ]κ [π]αλαιῶν μὲν χρ[ό]ν[ω]ν συνεστη-
[κότ]α, ν[ῦν δὲ καλ]ῶς καὶ προσηκόντω[ς ε]ἰς τὴμ βελ-
[τίστην ἀνανέ]ωσιν ἠγμένα ὑφ' ὑμ[ῶν], εὖνοι φίλο[ι],
[φιλάνθρωπα τῶι] δήμωι ὑπάρχε[ιν καὶ ὑπ]ακούοντε[ς]
[τὰ ἀξιούμενα ἀεὶ χ]αρίζεσθαι εἰ[ς δύναμιν]. ἔρρωσθ[ε].

7 εἶχον Rigsby (cf. *Royal Corr.* 58.6): ἐλάβοσαν τοῖς καταχεχωρισμένοις Herzog. 9 middle: πάνυ κατέχοντες ἡμᾶς Herzog. 10–12: τοὺς ἄνδρας οὐχ εὑροῦσιν] ἀφ' οὗ τῆς βασιλεία[ς μετέχομεν τοιαύτην φιλολο]γίαν περὶ τούτων· ὕσ[τατα] δὲ ἡμᾶς εἰς θέαν ἐκαλεῖσ]θε Herzog. 14 end: οὐκ ὀλίγων Herzog. 16: ἐφάνη[σα]ν Herzog. 16–19: πα[ραυτίκα ὅμως ὑμᾶς] τοῖς καιροῖς ἴσως ἐπακ[ολ]ουθῆ[σαι βιαζομένοις ἡ]μεῖν συγγνώμην ἐκτέον, ὅταν [τούτοις ἐνδεδω]κότες μὴ δυνώμεθα τὰς τούτ[ου τοῦ ἀγῶνος θέας] Herzog; 17 Piejko: ἐπακ[ολ]ουθῆ[σαι ἡγούμενοι ἡ. Klaffenbach; 18: [ἐν τῶι πολέμωι ἐνεστη]|κότες Piejko; 19 συντελείας] Piejko: θεωρίας] Klaffenbach. 20: ἡ ἀδελφ[ὴ Δα]μ[αρέτη καθάπερ] Herzog. 22 ΑΙΑΝ lapis. 26: ἀσ[μένως ἠκού]σατε Herzog. 30 Rigsby: τ[οὺς τοιούτου]ς Herzog, τ[ούτους τῆς πάση]ς Klaffenbach. 31: εἶ]ς γε Herzog. 32: [φ]ιλικ[ὴν Herzog. 34: κ[αὶ] τὴν Herzog. 39–40: πᾶν ὑπ]ακούοντε[ς | ὅσον ἂν ὑμεῖν χ]αρίζεσθαι ἐξ[ῆι ἡμεῖν] Herzog.

. . .

. . . in accordance with [their instructions,] they made proclamation [of the sacrifice and games, using] their education [so beautifully that] wonder overcame [us . . .] since the time when [we acceded to?] our kingdom . . . concerning these things . . . so many and such long-standing [benefactions toward you. As there are just now certain things] standing in the way of these things, if [for this the *theoroi*] seem to find fault [with us, we ask you nonetheless to judge] that we are accommodating ourselves to the times, [reckoning] that indulgence is owed us, whenever . . . we should be unable to send *theoroi* to [the celebration] of these [games]. I and my sister . . . and our citizens accept both your [proclamation] that has been made for the god and the inviolability, and we also have accepted gladly the kinship as true and worthy of you and us, the best testimony being that of our father, which you have made clear he himself furnished. If any [of the other] Greeks, [making this] a start of friendship, should first proclaim us [kin], we would gladly approve them many times over, having full gratitude towards those who remember such kinship and blood ties and choose to preserve them. [And now] we approve your loyalty and in the future we shall try to maintain for your people the [benefactions] established in ancient times and now finely and suitably brought to the best [renewal] by you, loyal friends, and, heeding [your requests, always] to gratify you to [the best of our ability]. Farewell.

Because the decree of Gela is on the other side of this stone, Herzog assigned the letter to Hieron of Syracuse; Klaffenbach at first preferred his son Gelon but then realized (p. 30) that the placement of the texts is irrelevant. The author's odd expression "our citizens" (21) shows his urban base, which would be consistent with a tyrant of Syracuse.[42] As the Roberts remarked, however, his happiness that some Greeks have acknowledged his kinship with them (27ff.) shows that he was not Greek; their suggestion, a king of the Cimmerian Bosporus, has not been bettered.[43] For this dynasty's urban constituency see Diod. 20.24.4–5. In 242 this would be Paerisades II or one of his two sons.[44] From the author's reference to his father (14ff.) Seyrig concluded that he must be newly on the throne, therefore not Paerisades. This must be left open, however, for it is the Coans who introduced the father into the discussion, evoking some prior dealing with him that may have been years in the past (παλαιῶν χρόνων, 36).

With this clumsy and rambling letter there is little to compare, and it discourages restoration; rightly did the king marvel at the educated discourse of the Coans (9–10).[45] The sequence of thought is garbled, the apologetic emphasis on himself ungracious and pathetic. If rightly assigned, it is a precious document on the Hellenism of the Spartocid dynasty. In the first twenty lines I have given

42. Cf. Diod. 19.73.6, 20.24.4, 20.63.23.

43. *Bull. épigr.* 1953, pp. 156–157; accepted by Klaffenbach, *DLZ* 76 (1955) 737; Seyrig, *Scripta numism.* 12–13; D. M. Pippidi, *StClas* 7 (1965) 322–324; Gauthier, *Nouv.Inscr.Sardes* II 73 n. 83. Welles 398 had suggested Demetrius the Fair, who ruled Cyrene briefly ca. 250 B.C. (cf. Will, *Histoire* I 244).

44. R. Werner, *Historia* 4 (1955) 421–430; see *CIRB* 24, 25, 75, 822. Paerisades came to power in 284/3 (Diod. 20.100.7) and was alive as late as 250 (*IG* XI.2 287.B.126). That he died around 245 is merely Werner's guess that he cannot have lived much longer.

45. Welles 398: the letter "uses few of the usual chancery formulae."

Klaffenbach's conservative version of Herzog's reconstruction. Nevertheless, much is to be doubted.

9: διδασκαλία is normally "instruction" or a "lesson," not "education"; perhaps the king marveled at the lesson or presentation the Coans had offered about his ancestral connections with Cos.[46]

11: Some verb is needed for the king's accession; Welles (398) suggested ἤρξαμεν or ἀντελαβόμεθα.

12: Perhaps a form of ὑστερεῖν, if this passage looks forward to the author's excuse for not sending *theoroi* to the Asclepieia; cf. the contract of a contemporary flute player promising μηθεν[ὸ]ς δὲ ἀγῶνος ... ὑστερ[εί]τω (*CPR* XVIII 1.12–13).

15ff.: This reconstruction is only a possibility. The certain element is the phrase "whenever. . .we should be unable to send *theoroi*" (19–20). The reference is to the future, but the puzzling thing is that the envoys have already blamed the king for something, and this cannot be failure to send *theoroi* to past Asclepieia. Another possibility is that something has impeded the Coan *theoroi* (τούτοις, 15), for which he apologizes (these may be the same *theoroi* who complained to Ziaelas about Bithynian treatment of visitors, **11**.12).

20: "Sister" for the king's wife is a usage familiar in other Hellenistic kingdoms; see C. P. Jones, *GRBS* 34 (1993) 81–85. βασιλίσσα rather than ἀδελφή is found in the several dedications to the Bosporan royal family (*CIRB* p. 844).

23ff.: Legend traced the Coans to Thessaly; the Spartocids were Thracian (references at Werner 419), but what account they gave of themselves is unknown.

24: For ἡδέως see Gauthier, *I.Nouv.Sardes* II no. 2.17 with p. 73.

34: I am uncertain what the adverb modifies: I translate with προσελαμβάνομεν, but it might better go with what follows.

36: The good relations with Cos stem from "ancient times"; the envoys only reminded him of them, bringing about a fine "renewal." This suggests something older than the time of the king's father and may rest, like his Greek kinship, on the presentation of texts or arguments from the mythic past. But that would leave in doubt what the father "did" (line 27).

13. Ptolemaic king

Two joining fragments broken on all sides, found in 1903 and 1905; dimensions not stated; letters 0.01–0.013, intersp. 0.005.

Lines 3–8, 14–16: Herzog, *Hermes* 65 (1930) 465 [Schroeter p. 104 frag. 3; Welles, *Royal Corres.* 21].

Entire: Herzog/Klaffenbach, *Asylieurkunden* 1 [*SEG* 12.368].

[- - - - - - - - -]I/[- - - - - - - - - - - - - - -]
[- - - - - - - -]ΣΤΑΣ[- - - - - - - - - - - - -]

46. An inscribed example of such a discourse is *SEG* 38.1476.

[- - - - - τὰ πε]ρὶ τὰς θυσίας [- - - - - - -]
[- - - - - - -]ν μεθ' ἡμῶν ε|[- - - - - - - - -]
[- - - - - - τ]ῆς ἀδελφῆς Ἀρ[σινόης - - - -]
[- - - - - -]σαν καὶ ἐπεὶ προσ[- - - - - - -]
[- - - - - -] ἐνετύγχανον ἡ[μῖν - - - - - - - -]
[- - - - - τὴ]ν πανήγυριν καὶ τ[- - - - - - -]
[- - - - - -]αν ὑπὲρ ἡμῶν [- - - - - - - - -]
[- - - - - -]ε καὶ μετὰ τη[- - - - - - - - - -]
[- - - - - -]Λ̣ΡΓΙ̣...Τ...Λ[- - - - - - - - -]
[- - - - - - -]ΜΗΘΗ καὶ εἴ τισι τ[ῶν - - -]
[- - - - - - -]ειν καὶ παρ' ἡμῶν [- - - - - -]
[- - - - -] εἰς τὰ Ἀσκληπίεια νῦ[ν - - - - -]
[- - - - -]εσθαι· ἡμεῖς δὲ καὶ π[- - - - - -]
[- - - - -]ς ἐγράψαμεν περὶ [- - - - - - - -]
[- - - -]σθαι διὰ τὸ προαιρεῖσ[θαι - - - - -]
[- - - -]τινας τῶν ὑμετέρω[ν - - - - - - - - -]
[- - - φ]ανησόμεθα οἰκείως δ[ιακείμενοι - -]
[- - -] ἡμῖν καὶ τὴν σπουδ[ὴν - - - - - - - -]
[- - -]των βουλόμενοι κατα[- - - - - - - - -]
[- - -] τὰ εἰρημένα ὑπ' αὐτ[ῶν - - - - - - - -]
[- - - - - -]ς τοὺς πολίτα[ς - - - - - - - - - -]
[- - - - - -] παρέχοντες [- - - - - - - - - - -]
[- - - - - - πολ]ίταις τῶν [- - - - - - - - - - -]
[- - - - - - - -]μονον[- - - - - - - - - - - - -]
[- - - - - - - -] ἄλλη[- - - - - - - - - - - - -]
[- - - - - - - - -]μαλ[- - - - - - - - - - - - -]
[- - - - - - - - -]|ει[- - - - - - - - - - - - -]

3: [καὶ τὸν ἀγῶνα Herzog. 4: Welles suggested συνετέλεσα]ν μεθ' ἡμῶν. 8: τ[ὸν ἀγῶνα Herzog. 9: θυσί]αν Herzog. 10: τῆ[ς ἀδελφῆς? Herzog; ἠξίουν δ]ὲ καὶ μετὰ τῆ[ς πάσης σπουδῆς? Klaffenbach. 11: Ἀλεξάν]δρει[α? Klaffenbach. 12: ἐφιλοτι]μήθη? Klaffenbach. 14–15: νῦ[ν δὲ Herzog; perhaps ἀσυλίαν τοῖς παραγινομένοις] εἰς τὰ Ἀσκληπίεια νῦ[ν τε καὶ εἰς τὸ λοιπὸν γεν]έσθαι Welles. 15: π[ρὸς τοὺς Herzog. 15–16 [τοῖς ὑφ' ἡμᾶς τασσομένοι]ς Welles. 16: [τούτων Herzog. 18 ἀεὶ] and [ν πολιτῶν Herzog.[47]

All scholars have followed Herzog in thinking that the author is Ptolemy II (who died in 246), given the mention of "sister Ar[sinoe]" (5)—Arsinoe Philadelphus, who died in 268.[48] Earlier than 246 B.C., this recognition would be of the *asylia* of the temple but not yet the Panhellenic games of 242 (the games mentioned here would be still local). No one has thought that the letter

47. F. Piejko, *Epigraphica* 48 (1986) 9–15, restores an entire text; the result is a speculative pastiche, and I have not cited it here.

48. E. Grzybek, *Du calendrier macédonien au calendrier ptolémaique* (Basel 1990) 103–112; L. Koenen, in *Images and Ideologies* (Berkeley 1993) 51 n. 61.

can date from Arsinoe's lifetime; as Welles remarked, the passage would refer to some prior policy or benefaction by the king and his late sister. **10** was taken as a subsequent confirmation of Coan *asylia* by Ptolemy III. But this would be an astonishing gesture within a dynasty, and indeed no act of "confirmation" is attested before Roman times: the Panhellenic recognition was decisive.

That this is a Ptolemaic letter that refers to Arsinoe seems assured; what is not assured is that it is a recognition of *asylia*. The Coans joined in celebrating a royal festival (2–3; cf. **9**), and then (7) put a request to the king. That this request concerned *asylia* and the games and that this inscription belongs with our archive is suggested only by the mention of the Asclepieia (14; *panegyris*, 8). What little surives of a detailed response, with frequent mention of "your citizens," does not show the diagnostic phrases of a recognition of *asylia*.

The letter need not be written by Ptolemy II in order to contain a reference to the famous Arsinoe. The script looks to be of the mid-third century B.C. rather than earlier (or later: Ptolemy IV had a wife Arsinoe), and much like that of **8** and some others in the *asylia* archive. I suggest that it derives from Ptolemy III and that the occasion was a celebration of the Theadelpheia in Egypt, in honor of "my father Ptolemy and his sister Arsinoe" (who was not the mother of Ptolemy III); *SEG* 36.1218 shows *theoroi* from Xanthus attending this festival. The Coans may well have had reasons to discuss with Ptolemy III either foreign visitors to the enlarged Asclepieia or his own *theoroi* (like those honored in *OGIS* 42).

Thus the substance of this letter must be left in doubt. That it is a recognition of *asylia* is in my view improbable; it is impossible if **8** is rightly assigned to Ptolemy III.

14–18. Gabled stele broken across the middle but complete; reused as a threshold and badly worn; found in the North Hall on the uppermost plateau; h. 1.03, w. 0.475, th. 0.075–0.095; letters 0.009 for the headings, 0.006–0.008 for text, intersp. 0.005. Five decrees of Peloponnesian cities, the theoric mission of Aristolochus, Heraclitus, and Macareus.[49]

Herzog/Klaffenbach, *Asylieurkunden* 4 [*SEG* 12.371].

14. Sparta

Λ α κ ε δ α ι μ ο ν ί ω ν

Λακεδαιμονίων δόγμα, ἐφόρω Εὐξένω· δεξώμεσα τὰν ἐκεχη-
ρίαν τὰν τῶ Αἰγλαπιῶ ἀὴ τὰν τοὶ Κῶιοι ἐφενέποντι Ἀριστόλοχος
ἀρχιθέαρος καὶ Ἡράκλειτος καὶ Μακαρεύς· δῶμες τοῖς Κώι-
οις ἃ αἰτίοντι, ἄσυλον τὸ ἱερὸν τοῦ Ἀγλαπιῶ τῶ ἐν Κῶι.

. . .

49. Macareus' son is attested at the end of the century; cf. Sherwin-White 485.

Decree of the Lacedaemonians, in the ephorate of Euxenus: we accept the truce of the Asclepieia for all time which the Coan *architheoros* Aristolochus and Heraclitus and Macareus proclaim;[50] we give the Coans what they ask, that the temple of Asclepius on Cos is inviolable.

In 243/2 Agis IV, newly king, undertook a revolutionary program to restore "the ancient dignity of Sparta" (Plut. *Agis* 6.2) by returning the Spartans to the laws of Lycurgus, the δίαιτα of their ancestors (8.2). The ephor Lysander sponsored the program of land distribution and social reform, and in 242 the hostile king Leonidas was deposed. When the ephors of 242/1 opposed the program, they too were deposed and Leonidas exiled. Internal disputes and military pressure in the course of 241 put a stop to this first of Hellenistic Sparta's revolutions.[51]

The Coan *theoroi*, canvassing Greece in summer 242, will have arrived in the midst of these events. The Spartan civil year began ca. October;[52] hence the Coans must have arrived during the still unshaken regime of the revolutionary ephors of 243/2. Of these our literary sources name only Lysander.[53] The inscription gives us another, Euxenus, and reveals that he, not the leading partisan Lysander, was the senior and eponymous ephor.

Sparta grants the barest essentials, recognizing "the truce" of the games and the inviolability of the temple. The "laconic" manner[54] that the decree affects may well be a mannerism of the archaizing government rather than normal Spartan public discourse—we have no decrees of the third century to compare.[55] This text thus may well be drafted in a self-consciously "Lycurgan" manner.

50. On the force of the verb see E. Risch, *ZPE* 60 (1985) 1–9.

51. The events are surveyed by Will, *Histoire* I 333–338; B. Shimron, *Late Sparta* (Buffalo 1972) 14–27; L. J. Piper, *Spartan Twilight* (New Rochelle 1986) 32–41; G. Marasco, *Prometheus* 7 (1981) 35–42; P. Cartledge, *Hellenistic and Roman Sparta* (London/New York 1989) 43–47; none citing the present decree.

52. References at Andrewes, *HCT* IV 38.

53. Modern scholars sometimes include Lysander's supporters Agesilaus and Mandrocleidas among the ephors, but the sources do not make this explicit. References in A. S. Bradford, *Prosopography of Lacedaemonians*, Vestigia 27 (Munich 1977) 11, 273. H. Michell, *Sparta* (Cambridge 1952) 129–130, argued that Agesilaus (Agis' uncle) was the eponymous ephor of 242/1 (after the deposition of the first board of 242/1); that would be consistent with a date still in summer 242 for our decree with its different eponym.

54. Noted, for instance, by Herzog ad loc. and E. J. Bickerman, *Athenaeum* 41 (1963) 76 n. 22 (*Religions* 479). Loci classici are Hdt. 3.46, Thuc. 1.86, and Xen. *Hell.* 1.1.23.

55. Two proxeny decrees of the next century show nothing of this manner and are composed in conventional Hellenistic formulary (*IG* V.1 4–5). The dialectical forms in our decree are not consistently carried out (compare *Syll.*^{3} 594 n. 7) and may also be something of an affectation. Around 200 B.C. Nabis, who renewed the revolutionary program of Cleomenes, put the dialectic Βαίλέος Νάβιος on coins (so too the stamped tiles *SGDI* IV.4^{n}24.22 [p. 687]), with which

It is worth recalling that King Leonidas and his daughter took refuge in the temple of Athena Chalcioecus and did not come out until the new ephors took office in autumn 242 (Plut. *Agis* 11–12): thus they were there during the Coans' visit. In 241 Agis, defeated, took refuge there himself (16.3). Hence the Coans' request might have touched a nerve; no Spartan in 242 can have been unaware of the traditional respect of suppliants, and of the problems that this could cause. Evidently this was not thought relevant.

15. Messene

Inscribed below **14**.

Μ ε σ σ α ν ί ω ν
ἐπειδὴ Κῶιοι φίλοι ἐόντες καὶ συγγενεῖς τῶν Μεσσανίων ἀποσ-
τείλαντες ἀρχιθέωρον Ἀριστόλοχον καὶ θεωρὼς Ἡράκλειτον
καὶ Μακαρέα ἐπαγγέλλοντι τάν τε θυσίαν καὶ τοὺς ἀγῶνας
οὓς συντελοῦντι τῶι Ἀσκλαπιῶι καὶ ἐμάνυον τὰν {τὰν} εὔνοια[ν]
τὰν ὑπάρχωσαν αὐτοῖς ποτὶ τὰν πόλιν τῶν Μεσσανίων καὶ
{καὶ} παρεκάλων ὅπως τὸ ἱερὸν τῶ Ἀσκλαπιῶ τῶ ἐγ Κῶι ἄσυ-
λον ὑπάρχηι τὰ ἀπὸ Μεσσανίων καὶ τῶν ἐμ Μεσσάναι κατο⟨ι⟩κε[ύν]-
των, δεδόχθαι τοῖς Μεσσανίοις τὸ ἱερὸν τοῦ Ἀσκλαπιῶ ἄσ[υ]-
λον ἦμεν τὰ ἀπὸ Μεσσανίων καὶ τῶν ἐμ Μεσσάναι κατοικεύ[ν]-
των· διδόμεν δὲ τοῖς θεωροῖς δεκαπέντε δραχμὰς ἑκάστω[ι]
τᾶς ἁμέρας καὶ ἐφέστιον οἶν καὶ ἐνεκέχειρον μνᾶν· θεωροδόκο[ι]
δὲ Δαμόνικος Μαντικράτεος καὶ . . . Λ . ος Φιλοκλεῦς
ἐπαγγείλαντο τᾶς Κώιων πόλεως ἐσσεῖσθαι.

Another *asylia* decree of Messene is **93** a generation later. Messene may have been an ally of the Aetolians by the date of our decree.[56] Although the decree records the Coan request to accept the games and at the end provides for *theorodochoi*, it does not in so many words recognize the games, but only *asylia*.[57]

9: ἔδοξε τᾶι [πόλει τᾶι Μ]εσανίων in the contemporary *Staatsvertr*. III 495.9–10 (isopolity with Phigeleia); ἔδοξε τῶι δάμωι in *IG* V.1 1425.3 ca. 300 B.C.

11–12: For the daily allowance given the Coan *theoroi* compare **88**.57: αὐθαμέραν; presumably this was for the duration of their stay in Messene; contrast the arbitrary figure of ten days at **17**.9. The sheep was for sacrifice "at the (public) hearth" of Messene (cf. **17**.9, **18**.8); for joint sacrifices of magistrates and *theoroi* at the public hearth see **49**.33ff. On such donations to *theoroi* cf. Boesch 71–82.

contrast the issues of Βασιλέος Ἀρέος in the 260s: S. Grunauer-von Hoerschelmann, *Die Münzprägung der Lakedaimonier* (Berlin 1978) 126, 112; cf. A. Furtwängler, *Gnomon* 57 (1985) 639.

56. Polyb. 4.6.11; cf. Schmitt, *Staatsvertr*. III p. 184.

57. For such variations see Rigsby, *AJP* 108 (1987) 732.

13: As Klaffenbach notes, this may be a relative, possibly an older brother, of the Mnasagorus son of Manticrates who commanded some Messenian troops at Delphi toward the end of the third century (*FD* III.4 22.8).

16. Thelphusa

Inscribed below **15**.

Θ ε λ φ ο υ σ ί ω ν
ἐπειδὴ παραγενόμενο⟨ι⟩ πὰρ ⟨τ⟩ᾶι πόλι τῶν Κώι{ι}ων πὸς τὰν πόλιν τῶ[ν]
Θελφουσίων Ἀριστόλοχος Ζμένδρωνος [ἀ]ρχ[ιθ]έαρο[ς κ]αὶ θ[εα]-
4 ρ⟨ὸ⟩ς Μακαρεὺς Ἀράτου, Ἡράκλειτος Τιμαίθου παρεκάλεα[ν]
τᾶς τε θυσίας κοινανῆν τὰν θύονσι [οἱ Κῶι]οι τοῖ Ἀσκλαπιοῖ
καὶ τοῦ ἀγῶνος καὶ τᾶς ἐκεχηρίας τό τ[ε] ἱερὸν ἄσυλον ἦναι
τὸ ἰν Κῶι {οι} τῶ Ἀσκλαπιῶ, ἔδοξε τᾶι πόλι τῶ[ν] Θελφουσίων τᾶς
8 τε θυσίας κοινανῆν καὶ τῶ ἀγῶνος καὶ τᾶς ἐκεχηρίας, καθάπε[ρ]
ἀπαγγέλλονσι οἱ Κῶιοι· τὸ δὲ ἱερὸν τ[ῶ] Ἀσκλαπιῶ ἄσυλον ἦν[αι]·
δῶναι δὲ καὶ ξένια τοῖς θεαροῖς τὰ ἐς τοῖ νόμοι καὶ θεαροδό-
κον χηροτονῆσαι τᾶς πόλιος τῶ. . . . .σαι τὸς θεαρός. τύ-
12 χαι τἀγαθᾶι ἐχηροτονήθη Φίλων. . .ου.

4: ΡΩΣ lapis. 5 ΘΥΟΣΣΙ, corrected by the mason. 11: ΤΑΝ πόλιος, corrected by the mason; πόλιος τᾶς Κώιων τὸς θεαρός Herzog.

No other decree of Thelphusa in western Arcadia is extant; it is on record as having recognized the inviolability of Magnesia in 208 (**88**.67). On the road north from Heraea and Elis to Psophis and Achaea, Thelphusa was repeatedly drawn into the wars between Achaea and Aetolia. Little is otherwise known of its history.[58] The city had joined the Achaean League by about 238;[59] the decree is silent about the League (contrast Aegeira, **18**.7–8), which may suggest that Thelphusa was not yet a member in 242.

17. Elis

Inscribed below **16**.

Ἀ λ ε ί ω ν
ἐπεὶ τοὶ Κῶιοι ἀποστείλαντες ποτὶ τὰν πόλιν ἀρχιθέαρον
Ἀριστόλοχον καὶ θεαρὸ[ρ] Ἡράκλειτον καὶ Μακαρέα ἐπαγγέλ-
4 λοντι τὰν θυσίαν τοῖ Ἀσ[κλ]απιοῖ καὶ αἰ[τ]έοντι δῆν τὸ ἱερὸν
ἄσυλον ἦμεν, ἔδοξε τᾶι πόλει τάν τε ἐκε[χ]ηρίαν δέχεσθα[ι]
καὶ τὸ ἱερὸν τῶ Ἀσκλαπιῶ τὸ ἐν Κῶι ἄσυλο[ν] ἦμεν ἀπό τε Ϝαλ[εί]-
ων καὶ τῶν Ϝάλει κατοικεόντ[ω]ν [- - -] ἁλίασμα πο-
8 τὶ τό κα ἐὸν ὑπὸ ταμιᾶν [- - -]Λ.αν καὶ ξένι[α] το⟨ῖ⟩ρ θεα-
ροῖρ ἁμέρας δέκα, γ ἐφιστίοιρ τελείαρ δραχμᾶν ξ.

58. Polyb. 2.54.12, 4.60.3, 4.73.2, 4.77.5; E. Meyer, *RE* 5A (1934) 1618–1620; M. Jost, *BCH* 110 (1986) 633–645; *Sanctuaires et cultes d'Arcadie* (Paris 1985) 60–70.

59. Beloch, *Gr.Gesch.* IV.1 632.

8: τι τωι τὸν ὑποταμίαν αναδευρ - - - αννα ξένια Herzog.

This is our only third-century decree of Elis (which recognized the inviolability of Magnesia, **89**.49). The Eleans were now allied with the Aetolians, who around 244 had helped them annex Triphylia.[60] Of the constitution of Hellenistic Elis little is known.[61] The treasurers (line 8) are met in second-century texts (*I.Olymp.* 39.29, 52.26); ἁλίασμα is otherwise found only in the West, a "decree" of the *heliaia* (*IG* XIV 612.5, Rhegium) or a "meeting" (256.4 Gela, 952.7 Acragas, both in dating formulae).

1: As at Magnesia, these headings were added by the Coans and do not reflect the Elean dialect (6–7).

6–7: The meaning seems to be that the treasurers are to add the decree "to what exists," that is, as in other decrees, to add the *asylia* of the Asclepieum to the existing laws (cf. **48**.8).

8–9: "Sustenance for the *theoroi* for ten days, three adult sacrificial animals worth sixty drachmas"; cf. on **15**.11–12.

18. Aegeira

Inscribed below **17**.

Α [ἰ] γ ε ι ρ α τ ᾶ ν
πα[ρ]αγενο[μ]ένων παρὰ [τ]ᾶς [π]όλιος τᾶς Κώιων ἀρχιθεώρου
Ἀ[ρ]ιστ[ολόχου] καὶ θεαρῶν Μακαρέως καὶ Ἡρακλείτου καὶ ἀξι-
[ού]ντων τάν τε ἐκε[χ]ειρίαν δέχεσθαι [κ]αὶ τὰν ἀσυλίαν τοῦ ἱαροῦ
τοῦ Ἀ[σκλαπιοῦ] τοῦ πα[ρ'] αὐτοῖς, ἔδοξε τᾶι πόλει τῶν Αἰγειρα-
τᾶν δέ[χεσθαί τε τὰν] ἐκε[χ]ειρίαν καὶ τὸ ἱερὸν ἄσυλον εἶμε[ν] τ[ὰ] ἀ-
πὸ πάντ[ω]ν, [κα]θὼς καὶ [δόγ]μα ἐστὶ τᾶι τε πόλει καὶ τοῖς [Ἀ]-
χαιοῖς ἄ[συ]λα εἶμεν τὰ ἱερά· δόμεν δὲ καὶ ἐφίστιον κα[ὶ] σιτ[η]ρέσι-
ον τοῖς θεαροῖς δέκα δραχμὰς καὶ ἐπιβολὰν τῶι θεῶι δέκα
δραχμάς· ἐπαγγ[είλ]αντο δὲ κα[ὶ] θεαροδόκοι ἐσσεῖσθαι τᾶς
πόλιος τῶν Κώιων Κλέων Βίτωνος, Ἄγορις Ἀριστε[ί]δα.

2 ἀρχιθεώρου: an alpha was written above the epsilon in order to correct to Doric θεαρ. 8–9: Ἀ]χα[ιοῖς κοι]νὰ and δόμεν δὲ καὶ τοὺς [ταμίας εἰς ἐφ]έσ||[τι]ον Herzog.

Aegeira on the Corinthian Gulf was one of the original twelve Achaean cities and an early member of the revived League.[62] The city enters little into the historical record, but for the Aetolian attack on it in 219 B.C., to which we owe Polybius' detailed description of the site (4.57–58). A summary

60. Polyb. 4.77.5–10; Beloch, *Gr.Gesch.* IV.1 619–620.

61. Swoboda, *RE* 5 (1905) 2429–2430.

62. Joining the League ca. 272 B.C. (Beloch, *Gr.Gesch.* IV.1 574); see *IG* XII.9 1187 and *Syll.*^{3} 488 (Damosthenes' year at Delphi, in the 260s; cf. R. Etienne and M. Piérart, *BCH* 99 [1975] 59–62).

decree of the second century B.C. makes a similarly favorable reference to the Achaean League (*SEG* 24.337, a man praised for his devotion to the city and the League).

7–8: I take δόγμα as abstract, not a concrete "decree" that the Aegeirans are following: "as it is a belief of the city and of the Achaeans that temples are inviolable." Compare the Achaeans' statement about policy at **89**.24–27, which suggests that here too at Cos is meant an attitude rather than a decree. In my view this is an expression of surprise, not a piece of legal information, and as such it will reflect the rarity in 242 of the request for *asylia* (see p. 22).[63] Contrast the claim that the Achaeans in 235 B.C. became the first to ignore the inviolability of contestants going to the Nemean games (Plut. *Arat.* 28.4: ἡ δεδομένη τοῖς ἀγωνισταῖς ἀσυλία καὶ ἀσφάλεια).

9: The money for Asclepius, if truly only ten drachmas, would be offensively low; the *aparche* was typically sixty. Rather, by ἐπιβολή, an "addition" to the σιτηρέσιον they have just described, the Aegeirans would seem to intend an additional ten drachmas per *theoros* per day.

19–22. Stele found in 1933; left margin preserved; h. 0.38, w. 0.22, th. 0.085; letters 0.006–0.01, intersp. 0.005. Inscribed on both sides by the same hand; remains of two decrees on each side.

Herzog/Klaffenbach, *Asylieurkunden* 5 [*SEG* 12.372].

19. Thebes in Achaea Phthiotis

[Θηβαίων τῶν ἀπ' Ἀχαΐας τῆς Φθιώτιδος]
[παραγενομένων παρὰ τῆς πόλεως τῆς Κώιων ἀρχιθεώρου Ἀριστολ]όχου Ζμ[έν]-
[δρωνος καὶ θεωρῶν Μακαρέως Ἀράτου καὶ Ἡρακλείτου] Τιμαίθου ἐπαγ-
[γελλόντων - καὶ] τοὺς ἀγῶνας καὶ
[-] καὶ τὴν ἀσυλίαν τοῦ ἱε-
[ροῦ - ἔδοξεν τῆι] πόλει Θηβαίων τῶν ἀ-
[π' Ἀχαΐας τῆς Φθιώτιδος ἐπαινέσαι μὲν τὴν πόλ]ιν τὴν Κώιων καὶ δέξα-
[σθαι -] περὶ δὲ τῶν θεωρῶν τῶν
[- τὴν] θυσίαν τοὺς συνθύσον-
[τας - - - - - - - - προγράψασθαι? τοὺς ἄρχο]ντας εἰς τὴν ἔννομον
[ἐκκλησίαν τὴν - - - - - - - - - - - - - - - δοῦ]ναι δὲ αὐτοῖς τὸ θεωρικὸν
[- - - - - - - - - - - - - - - - - - καλέσαι δὲ κ]αὶ ἐπὶ ξένια τοὺς θεωροὺς
[εἰς τὸ πρυτανεῖον? vacat?] vacat

5: Klaffenbach suggested τοῦ Ἀσκληπιοῦ τοῦ ἐν Κῶι, ἀγαθῆι τύχηι, ἔδοξεν. 6: the name as at *IG* VII 288.5 Θ[ηβαῖον ἐξ Ἀχαΐ]ας τῆς Φθιώτιδος.

63. Contra: A. Giovannini in *Ancient Macedonia* II (Thessalonica 1977) 469–471, who argues that only leagues and not their member cities could recognize *asylia* (which is contradicted by **88** and **92**, Achaean cities recognizing Magnesia).

Thebans on the Greek mainland who offer a geographical specification (5) and do not speak Boeotian are necessarily the city in Phthiotis on the Gulf of Pagasae. Here as at Homolium (**22**), it is surprising to find them using Koine at this date: contrast *IG* IX.2 132, apparently of the second century B.C. Of the place we have a description in Polyb. 5.99; by 242 Thebes was probably an Aetolian ally (Flacelière, *Aitoliens* 199–200).

7–8: In the Coan archive this seems to be the only provision for sending *theoroi* to future Asclepieia (cf. **12**.19).

9: The verb is suggested from **100**.48.

10: Klaffenbach thought a chronological indicator was to be restored here; for the phrase in Thessaly see *IG* IX.2 11.11. Here too, as Klaffenbach notes, is our earliest attestation of θεωρικόν for the honorarium given *theoroi*, more often ἐκέχειρον or the more general ξένιον. Something like τὸ ἐκ τοῦ νόμου followed in 11 (cf. **21**.17).

20. Megara (?)

Inscribed below **19**.

[Μ ε γ α ρ?] ἐ̣ ω ν
[ἐπὶ βασιλέως - - - - - - - - ἐπειδὴ παραγεγέ]νηνται παρὰ τᾶς πόλιος τᾶς
[Κώιων ἀρχιθέωρος Ἀριστόλοχος Ζμένδρωνο]ς καὶ θεωροὶ Ἡράκλειτος Τι-
[μαίθου, Μακαρεὺς Ἀράτου ἐπαγγέλλοντες τ]ὰ Ἀσκλαπίεια θυσίαν τε καὶ
[ἀγῶνας οὓς συντελέοντι τῶι Ἀσκλαπιῶ]ι καὶ ἐκεχειρίαν, καὶ τὸ ἱερὸν ἀ-
[ξιέοντι ἄσυλον εἶμεν καὶ ἐμφανίζοντι τ]ά[ν] τ[ε] φιλίαν καὶ εὔνοιαν ἃν ἔχου-
[σα διατελεῖ ἁ πόλις ἁ Κώιων ἅπαντα τὸν χρό]νο[ν π]οτὶ τὸν δᾶμον τὸν Με-
[γαρέων - οἰκ]ειότατα, ἀγαθᾶι τύχαι
[δεδόχθαι τᾶι βουλᾶι καὶ τῶι δάμωι?· ἀποδέξασθαι τὰ]ν θυσίαν καὶ τὰν ἐκεχει-
[ρίαν καὶ - ἐπα]γγέλλοντι π[α]ρὰ τᾶς
[πόλιος τᾶς Κώιων -]

1: [Αἰτω?]λῶν Herzog. 9 init. Rigsby: ἔδοξεν τῶι δάμωι τῶι Μεγαρέων Klaffenbach.

Klaffenbach reckoned that a decree of a Dorian city Με- (7), not more than nine letters long, will be Megara; at the beginning of 1 he thought E more likely than Λ on the squeeze. The trace there is very faint and dubious, and the number of letters perhaps uncertain. One might think also of the far north of Greece, given the other contents of this stele; but the form ποτί (7) speaks against restoring Melitaea or Meliboea.[64]

21. Unknown city

Inscribed on the other side of the stele bearing **19–20**.

64. F. Bechtel, *Die griechischen Dialekte* I (Berlin 1921) 166.

Cf. J. and L. Robert, *Bull. épigr.* 1953, p. 45.

ἔδοξε[ν - παραγενομένων παρὰ]
τῆς πόλεω[ς τῆς Κώιων - - - - - - - - - - - - - - - - ἀρχιθεώρου Ἀριστολόχου]
Ζμένδρωνος κ[αὶ θεωρῶν Μακαρέως Ἀράτου καὶ Ἡρακλείτου Τιμαίθου ἐμφανι]-
4 ζόντων τήν τε [φιλίαν καὶ - τὴν ὑπάρ]-
χουσαν ταῖς πόλεσ[ιν ἐξ ἀρχῆς - καὶ]
τῶι ἄλλωι ἔθνει τ[ῶν - καὶ οἰομέ]-
νων δεῖν ἄσυλον Λ[-]
8 τὴν πανήγυριν καὶ [- τῶι]
Ἀσκληπιῶι δέξασ[θαι -]
ων τήν τε φιλίαν καὶ [-]
πρὸς τὴν Κώιων πόλ[ιν -]
12 καὶ τὸ ἱερὸν τοῦ Ἀσκλ[ηπιοῦ ἄσυλον -]
καθάπερ ἠξίουν διά τ[ε -]
καὶ τὴν συγγένειαν [- τοὺς ταμί]-
ας δοῦναι καθάπερ η[- τοῖς τοὺς ἀγῶνας]
16 τοὺς στ[ε]φανίτας ἐ[παγγέλλουσι - τὸ]
ἐκ τοῦ νόμου ξένιον. [vacat?]

Klaffenbach suggested the following exempli gratia: 2 πρὸς τὴν ἡμετέραν πόλιν, 8 [τοὺς ἀγῶνας οὓς συντελοῦσιν κατὰ πεντετηρίδα, 9 end δεδόχθαι τῶι δήμωι τῶι - - -]ων, 10 end διαφυλάσσειν, 15 ἡ [πόλις ἐψήφισται. 6 end Robb.: ἀπολογιζομέ?]νων Klaffenbach.

The Coans expressed their loyalty to the city and "the rest of the nation" (6) of which this city must have been a member. The Roberts suggested Demetrias, with its *ethnos* the Magnesians. The Thessalian League also comes to mind, but it is thought not yet to have come into being at this date. Whatever the city, Cos claimed kinship with its citizens (14), a claim not idle or universal.

22. Homolium

Inscribed below **21**.
Cf. J. and L. Robert, *Bull. épigr.* 1953, p. 45.

Ὁ μ ο [λ ι έ ω ν]
ἀγαθῆι τύχηι, ἐφ' ἱερέως [- ἐπιστα]-
τοῦντος δὲ Ἀνδρονίκο[υ - παραγενομένων πα]-
4 ρὰ τῆς πόλεως τῆς Κώι[ων - - - - - - - - - - - - ἀρχιθεώρου Ἀριστολόχου]
Ζμένδρωνος καὶ θε[ωρῶν Μακαρέως Ἀράτου καὶ Ἡρακλείτου Τιμαίθου ἐμφανιζόν]-
[των τήν τ]ε φιλίαν κ[αὶ - - - - - - - - - - - - - - - - - - - τὴν ὑπάρχουσαν ταῖς]
πόλεσιν ἐξ ἀρχῆς αυ[-]

2 end Robb.: προστα] Klaffenbach. Klaffenbach suggested the following exempli gratia: 4 πρὸς τὴν ἡμετέραν πόλιν, 7 αὔ[ξειν.

Homolium was the northernmost city of Magnesia. This text, our only decree, proves that Homolium escaped the incorporation into the new city Demetrias in the south that befell most other Magnesian cities in 293.[65] Of its institutions we learn (2–3) that a priest was eponymous (as often in Macedonia) together with (δὲ) what looks to be a royal governor. Close control by the Antigonid monarchy would not be surprising at this city. The priest might be of the royal cult rather than the city's chief god.

It may be at this point that the three *theoroi* divided. We know that only two of them went to Macedonia; the third may have taken ship to visit the northern islands or conceivably crossed west to Corcyra, whose decree (**45**) is inscribed with the Macedonian texts.

23–24. Gabled stele, broken at bottom, found in 1902; h. 0.365, w. 0.54, th. 0.075–0.85; letters 0.005–0.009, intersp. ca. 0.006. The decrees of Naples and Elea (**46**, **47**) are inscribed on the other side.

Herzog/Klaffenbach, *Asylieurkunden* 7 [*SEG* 12.374].

23. Pella

Π ε λ λ α ί ω ν

ἐφ' ἱερέως Ἀσκληπιοδώρου, Γορπιαίου· ἐπεὶ παραγενόμενος ἐκ Κῶ ἀρχιθέω-
ρος Ἀριστόλοχος Ζμένδρωνος καὶ θεωρὸς Μακαρεὺς Ἀράτου τήν τε οἰκειό-
τητα ἀνενεώσαντο τὴν ὑπάρχουσαν Κώιοις πρὸς Μακεδόνας καὶ τὴν εὔ-
νοιαν ἀπελογίζοντο ἣν ἔχουσα τυγχάνει ἡ πόλις ἡ Κώιων πρὸς τὸν βασιλέα
Ἀντίγονον καὶ πρὸς Πελλαίους καὶ τὴν λοιπὴν χώραν τὴν Μακεδόνων, καὶ ἐ-
πηγγέλλοσαν τὰ Ἀσκληπίεια τὰ γεινόμενα παρ' αὐτοῖς καὶ τοὺς ἀγῶνας
τοὺς ἐν τῆι πανηγύρει ἐσομένους καὶ τὴν ἐκεχειρίαν, ἠξίουσαν δὲ καὶ τὸ [ἱ]-
ερὸν τοῦ Ἀσκληπιοῦ τὸ ἐν Κῶι ἄσυλον εἶναι, ἔδοξε τῆι πόλει τήν τε ἐπαγγ[ε]-
λίαν τῶν Ἀσκληπιείων τὴν παρὰ Κώιων καὶ τὴν ἐκεχειρίαν προσδέξασθαι
καὶ ἐπαινέσαι αὐτοὺς ἐπί τε ταῖς τιμαῖς αἷς συντελοῦσι τοῖς θεοῖς καὶ
ἐπὶ τῆι εὐνοίαι τῆι πρὸς τὸν βασιλέα Ἀντίγονον καὶ πρὸς Μακεδόνας· ὑπάρ-
χειν δὲ καὶ τὴν ἀσυλίαν τῶι ἱερῶι καθάπερ καὶ τοῖς ἄλλοῖς ἱεροῖς· δοῦναι δὲ
κα[ὶ]
ξένια τοὺς ταμίας τοῖς θεωροῖς ἃ καὶ τοῖς τοὺς στεφανίτας ἀ[γῶνα]ς ἐπαγ-
[γ]έλλ[ο]υσι [δ]ί[δοτα]ι, καὶ θεωροδόκον ἑλέσθαι Κώιων. ᾑρέθη
Ἱππ[- - -]ου.

This is our only decree of the Antigonids' capital city. The month is the eleventh, placing the decree in August/September. Of the four Macedonian decrees for Cos, only Pella's fails to cite the favorable response of Antigonus Gonatas. The simple inference is that the *theoroi* reached Pella first of the four cities (as was inevitable if they were coming from the south) and that they

65. See Klaffenbach's references and F. Stählin, *AM* 54 (1929) 205; *Pagasai und Demetrias* (Berlin/Leipzig 1934) 181 n. 5.

addressed the city's assembly before they had their audience with the king.[66] The reason may be nothing more significant than the travels or schedule of Antigonus at the time. A famous instance is at Dem. 19.155.

The Macedonian decrees suggest the speed with which the *theoroi* moved: at Pella in Gorpiaios, at Amphipolis by the 19th of the same month; between these two stops they must have addressed Antigonus, presumably at or near Pella, and then Cassandreia. From Amphipolis they went on to Philippi, and possibly thereafter to Maroneia and Aenus.

1: The city's eponymous priest was perhaps of the royal cult, but compare Amphipolis (**26**.3).

4–6: At all the Macedonian cities the Coans stressed their loyalty to Antigonus; this sentiment, perhaps surprising in a Ptolemaic ally, points up the nonpartisan character of recognizing inviolability.[67] The expression of loyalty to the "land" of the Macedonians is strange; contrast the following decrees, which speak properly of loyalty to the Macedonians. But for χώρα evidently in the sense of "nation" or "community" required here, cf. **217**.13, 1 Maccabees 15.16, and *I.Labraunda* 42.10 (someone useful to the χῶρα of the Plataseis).

8: Klaffenbach thought the future implied that no games now exist; but strictly speaking no Panhellenic games now exist, and this has no implication for local ones.

11ff.: The phrases by which the Coans are praised are quite similar in all four Macedonian decrees; this must echo the particular Coan decree that the *theoroi* presented in Macedonia, which will have mentioned their good relations with Antigonus.

13: "inviolability for the temple as for other temples"; the Pellans, like the Aegeirans (**18**.7), seem surprised at a request for what is normal usage.

24. Unknown city

Inscribed below **23**.

[4–5]ιων

This is the heading of another civic decree. If also Macedonian, Pydna is a good possibility, as Klaffenbach suggested; but the other decrees (on the following stele) proceed from south to north, as the *theoroi* apparently did.

66. Bengtson, *Kl. Schr.* 365–366, citing only line 12 and not 6, was mistaken in writing that Pella, like Amphipolis (**26**.8), omits to include itself in the expression of loyalty, and that Amphipolis, like Pella, omits mention of the wishes of the king (see **26**.14). He concluded that these two cities were of a more independent legal status than Cassandreia and Philippi; his attempt to deduce differences of status from these decrees is refuted by J. J. Gabbert, "The Greek Hegemony of Antigonus II" (Ph.D. diss., University of Cincinnati 1982) 11–14, and F. Papazoglou in *Ancient Macedonia* III (Thessalonica 1983) 202–205.

67. Giovannini, however, takes the phrase to refer to a general edict of the king declaring temples inviolable, parallel to the "wishes of the king" in the other Macedonian decrees.

25–27. Stele with a cornice at the top, broken at bottom, found by the Italian excavators on Terrace 4; dimensions not reported; letters and intersp. ca. 0.007. Klaffenbach had a copy by Laurenzi, a bad squeeze, and a photograph. Remains of four decrees, three from Macedonia and that of Corcyra (**45**).

Herzog/Klaffenbach, *Asylieurkunden* 6 [*SEG* 12.373].

25. Cassandreia

Κ α σ σ α ν δ ρ έ ω ν
οἱ στρατηγοὶ καὶ οἱ νομοφύλακες εἶπαν· ἐπειδ[[δ]]ὴ παραγεγένηνται θεωροὶ πα-
ρὰ τῆς Κώιων πόλεως ἐπαγγέλλοντες τὰ Ἀσκληπίεια καὶ τοὺς ἀγῶνας
τοὺς συντελουμένους ἐν αὐτοῖς καὶ τὴν ἐκεχειρίαν, καὶ ἀπολογίζονται τὴν
εὔνοιαν τῆς αὐτῶν πόλεως ἣν ἔχουσα διατελεῖ πρός τε τὸμ βασιλέα Ἀν-
τίγονον καὶ τὴν Κασσανδρέων πόλιν καὶ πρὸς τοὺς λοιποὺς Μακεδόνας
πάντας, καὶ ἀξιοῦσιν τὸ ἱερὸν τοῦ Ἀσκληπιοῦ τὸ παρ' αὐτοῖς ἄσυλον εἶναι,
ἀγαθῆι τύχηι, δεδόχθαι τῆι βουλῆι δέχεσθαι τὴν ἐπανγελίαν τῶν Ἀσ-
κληπιείων καὶ τοὺς ἀγῶνας καὶ τὴν ἐκεχειρίαν καὶ εἶναι τὸ ἱερὸν τοῦ Ἀσκληπι-
οῦ ἄσυλον κατὰ τὴν τοῦ βασιλέως βούλησιν· ἐπαινέσαι δὲ τὴμ πόλιν τῶν Κώιων,
διότι διατελεῖ πρόνοιαν ποιουμένη τῶν πρὸς τοὺς θεοὺς συντελουμένων
καλῶς καὶ ἐνδόξως καὶ τὴν ὑπάρχουσαν αὐτῆι εὔνοιαν διαφυλάσσει
πρός τε τὸμ βασιλέα Ἀντίγονον καὶ τὴν ἡμετέραν πόλιν καὶ Μακεδόνας πάν-
τας· δοῦναι δὲ τὸν ταμίαν τοῖς παραγεγενημένοις ξένιον τὸ διάταγμα τὸ
ἐκ τοῦ νόμου· καλέσαι δὲ αὐτοὺς καὶ εἰς τὸ ἀρχηγέτειον· τὸ δὲ ἀνάλωμα
τὸ εἰς ταῦτα δοῦναι τὸν ταμίαν. οἵδε ἐπήγγειλαν· Ἀριστόλοχος Ζμένδω-
νος ἀρχιθέωρος, Μακαρεὺς Ἀράτου θεωρός· ἡ θυσία εἰς ἐνάτην σελήνην.

Several decrees are now known from Cassandreia in the Chalcidice (the former Potideia), the shipyard of the Antigonids.[68] Ours is a decree of the *boule* alone (8):[69] I assume that the Coans, pressing on with their travels, were unwilling to wait for a meeting of the assembly and contented themselves with the council's vote (see also on **27**.2).

2: *Nomophylakes* are found as high executive magistrates in several other cities founded or closely controlled by Hellenistic kings: thus at Athens under Cassander, at Demetrias, at Gonni (**83**.28), at Alexandria, and at Pergamum.[70]

10: The Coans now and hereafter could cite the favorable action of Antigonus, which they seem to have lacked as yet at Pella.

68. See M. B. Hatzopoulos, *Une donation du roi Lysimaque*, Meletemata 5 (Athens 1988) 19–21; and Meletemata 10 (1990) 135–148.

69. Cf. at Thessalonica *IG* X.2 1028, ca. 230 B.C.

70. See E. Ziebarth, *RE* 17 (1936) 832–833; a fuller list in A. P. Christophilopoulos, *Platon* 20 (1968) 134–143; cf. F. W. Walbank, *Philip V* (Cambridge 1940) 229.

14: As their honorarium (ξένιον) the *theoroi* receive "the disposition prescribed by law," equivalent, as Klaffenbach noted, to ὃ ἐν τῶι νόμωι διατέτακται. For this use of the noun the nearest parallel I find is in the Murabba'at papyri: τὸν ἐγ διατάγματος τόκ[ον], "the statutory interest" (*P.Mur.* 114.15–16 [*SB* 10304], II A.D.).

15: The *theoroi* are to be entertained at the founder's hall or temple, probably a cult place of the founder Cassander (cf. **28**.9). For parallels see Klaffenbach ad loc., who also considered Apollo Archegetes possible, and J. and L. Robert, *Bull. épigr.* 1953, pp. 45–46; for state entertainment at a temple, Robert, *DAM* 290 n. 49.

16–17: The Asclepieia were proclaimed for nine lunar months hence, around May of 241. This is a precious testimony on how *theoroi* coped with the diversity of local calendars in the Greek world in announcing the date of their festival: of necessity, they reckoned by the moon. See also **3**.11–12, **128**.5, **130**.9.

26. Amphipolis

Inscribed below **25**.

Ἀ μ φ ι π ο λ ι τ ῶ ν

βασιλεύοντος Ἀντιγόνου ἔτους ἑνὸς καὶ τεσσαρακοστοῦ, ἐπιστάτου Ξενί-
ου τοῦ Ὀργέως, ἐφ' ἱερέως Λυσιμάχου, ψηφίσματα Γορπιαίου ἐνάτηι ἐπὶ δέκα·
ἐπεὶ ὁ ἀποσταλεὶς ἀρχιθέωρος ὑπὸ τῆς Κώιων πόλεως Ἀριστόλοχος Ζμέν-
δρωνος καὶ μετ' αὐτοῦ θεωρὸς Μακαρεὺς Ἀράτου ἐπελθόντες ἐπὶ τὴν ἐκλη-
σίαν τήν τε οἰκειότητα ἀνενεώσαντο τὴν ὑπάρχουσαν Κώιοις πρὸς Μακε-
δόνας καὶ τὴν εὔνοιαν ἐνεφάνιζον ἣν ἔχουσα διατελεῖ ἡ πόλις πρός τε
τὸμ βασιλέα Ἀντίγονον καὶ πρὸς Μακεδόνας, ἐπηγγέλλοσαν δὲ καὶ τὰ Ἀσκλη-
πίεια τὰ γεινόμενα παρ' αὐτοῖς καὶ τὴν ἐκεχειρίαν καὶ ἠξίουν τὸ ἱερὸν τοῦ Ἀσ-
κληπιοῦ τὸ ἐν Κῶι ἄσυλον εἶναι, δεδόχθαι τῆι πόλει τῆι Ἀμφιπολιτῶν τήν τε
ἐπαγγελίαν τῶν Ἀσκληπιείων καὶ τὴν ἐκεχειρίαν προσδέξασθαι καὶ ἐπαι-
νέσαι αὐτοὺς ἐπί τε ταῖς τιμαῖς αἷς συντελοῦσι τοῖς θεοῖς καὶ ἐπὶ τῆι εὐ-
νοίαι τῆι πρὸς τὸμ βασιλέα Ἀντίγονον καὶ πρὸς Μακεδόνας· εἶναι δὲ καὶ τὸ ἱε-
ρὸν ἄσυλον, καθάπερ καὶ ὁ βασιλεὺς Ἀντίγονος προαιρεῖται· δοῦναι δὲ καὶ
τοὺς ἄρχοντας ξένιον τοῖς θεωροῖς ὅσον καὶ τοῖς τὰ Πύθια ἐπαγγέλλουσι
δίδοται· εἶναι δὲ καὶ θεωροδόκον τῆς Κώιων Διονύσιον Ἐπιγένου.
ἐψηφίσθη παραπάσαις.

This is one of the few decrees extant from Amphipolis on the Strymon.[71] Its preface contrasts with the other Macedonian decrees for Cos in such a way as to suggest that this city was more subordinate to the king than were the others,

71. I. Papastavru, *Amphipolis*, Klio-BH 37 (Leipzig 1936).

which cite only civic institutions: first a royal date and a royal overseer, then the civic facts, the eponymous priest (of Asclepius)[72] and the bureaucratic docket dating the decree to 19 Gorpiaios (late August). This provides our one date in the Coan material, late in the 41st year of Antigonus Gonatas, 243/2 B.C.

3: The name Orgeus I have found only of the father of two Thasians prominent ca. 480 B.C., one of whom took an interest in the coastal possessions of Thasos.[73] Perhaps our Amphipolitan was descended from Thasians.

The plural ψηφίσματα need not be taken literally[74] and can label this decree alone; but it might instead come from an archival heading in Amphipolis' record office, "decrees of 19 Gorpiaios" (compare **166**). This would mean that they organized their acts chronologically; see p. 73 on the τόμος συγκολλήσιμος form.

17: This records the count of votes (understand ψήφοις);[75] unanimity was not uncommon (e.g., *IG* XI.4 1057), especially as extant inscriptions tend to be about honors more than about policy—as was *asylia*, in my view. The adjective παράπας is not in LSJ; it occurs in a Byzantine doctor, Aetius Amid. 6.55 (*CMG* VIII.2 203.16): εἶτα παραπάσας τὰ ξηρά; but perhaps by error, for his source Galen shows εἶτα περιπάσας τὰ ξηρά (XII 420.13 Kühn). On the adverb παράπαν and synonyms see J. Nollé, *Chiron* 17 (1987) 363 n. 12.

27. Philippi

Inscribed below **26**.

Φ ι λ ί π π ω ν

ἱερῶν· ὑπὲρ τῆς ἐκ Κῶ θεωρίας· γνώμη τῆς ἐκλησίας, ἐπειδὴ ἡ πόλις ἡ Κώιων κατὰ
τὰ πάτρια καὶ κατὰ τὴμ μαντείαν τὸ ἱερὸν τοῦ Ἀσκληπιοῦ ἀπέσταλκεν ἀρχι-
4 θέωρον Ἀριστόλοχον Ζμένδρωνος καὶ θεωρὸν μετ' αὐτοῦ Μαχαρέα Ἀράτου
ἐπαγγέλλοντας τήν τε θυσίαν τῶι Ἀσκληπιῶι καὶ τὴν ἐκεχειρίαν, οἵτινες ἐπελ-
θόντες ἐπὶ τὴν ἐκλησίαν τὴν οἰκειότητα τὴν ὑπάρχουσαν τῆι πόλει τῆι Κώιων
πρὸς τὴμ πόλιν τὴν Φιλίππων καὶ πρὸς τὸμ βασιλέα Ἀντίγονον καὶ πρὸς τοὺς ἄλ-
8 λους Ἕλληνας καὶ Μακεδόνας ἐνεφάν[ι]σαν καὶ ἀνενεώσαντο, ἠξίουν δὲ
τὸ ἱερὸν ἄσυλον εἶναι, ἀγαθῆι τύχηι, δεδόχθαι τῆι ἐκλησίαι δέχεσθαι τὴμ πόλιν

72. For the priest and for *epistatai* in Macedonian cities see Moretti, *I. stor. ellen.* II p. 96 n. 2, 99 n. 6; D. Hennig, *Chiron* 17 (1987) 161 n. 66; Hatzopoulos, *BCH* 115 (1991) 347.

73. Hdt. 7.118; J. Pouilloux, *Recherches . . . Thasos* (Paris 1954) 264–265 no. 28.11.

74. See Welles, *Royal Corres.* p. 9 n. 9; Klaffenbach, *AbhBerl* 1958.2, 16; *Hesperia* 5 (1936) 422 no. 15.2; a neat example is *I.Magn.* 89.17 versus 18.

75. For such records in Greek decrees see P. Gauthier, "Quorum et participation civique," in *Du pouvoir dans l'antiquité,* ed. C. Nicolet, Cahiers du Centre Glotz 1 (Geneva 1990) 73–99, with 96 n. 95 on this text and **28**.

τήν τε ἐπαγγελίαν τὴν τῶν Ἀσκληπιείων τῶν ἐν Κῶι καὶ τὴν ἐκεχειρίαν κα-
θάπερ ἐπαγγέλλουσιν οἱ θεωρ[οί]· ἐπαινέσαι ⟨δ⟩ὲ καὶ τὴμ πόλιν τὴν Κώιων ἐπὶ ταῖς
τιμαῖς αἷς συντελεῖ τοῖς θεοῖς καὶ ἐπὶ τῆι εὐνοίαι τῆι τε πρὸς τὸμ βασιλέα Ἀντί-
γονον καὶ τὴμ πόλιν τὴν Φιλίππων καὶ τοὺς ἄλλους Ἕλληνας καὶ Μακεδόνας· ⟨εἶ⟩-
ναι δὲ καὶ τὸ ἱερὸν τοῦ Ἀσκληπιοῦ τὸ ἐν Κῶι ἄσυλο⟨ν⟩, καθάπερ καὶ ὁ βασιλεὺς Ἀντίγο-
νος προαιρεῖται· δοῦναι δὲ τὸν ταμίαν τοῖς θεωροῖς ὑπὲρ τῆς πόλεως εἰς ξένια
ὅσον καὶ τοῖς τὰ Πύθια ἐπαγγέλλουσιν δίδοται ἐν τῶι νόμωι γέγραπται· καλέσαι δὲ
τοὺς θεωροὺς καὶ ἐπὶ τὰ ἱερὰ ὑπὲρ τῆς πόλεως τὸν ἄρχοντα εἰς τὸ πρυτανεῖον· τὸν
δὲ ταμίαν δοῦναι τῶι ἄρχοντι ὑπὲρ ἑκατέρου αὐτῶν ἀργύριον τὸ ἐκ τοῦ νόμου· ὅπως
δ' ἂν ἀσφαλῶς ἀποσταλῶσιν εἰς Νέαν Πόλιν, τοὺς στρατηγοὺς συμπέμψαι αὐτοῖς
τοὺς ξένους ⟨σ⟩τρατιώτας τοὺς παρὰ τῆι πόλει μισθοφοροῦντας· εἶναι δὲ καὶ θεωροδόκον
[τ]ῆς ἐκ Κῶ παραγινομένης θεωρίας τὸν ὑποδεδεγμένον τὴν θεωρίαν Ἡρακ-
λεόδωρον Ἀριστίωνο[ς].

2: in ἐκλησίας H has been corrected by the mason from E. 11: ΛΕ lapis. 13–14: ΔΟΥ|ΝΑΙ and ΑΣΥΛΟΗ lapis. 16: ὅσον written in rasura; δίδοται either is redundant or should be δίδοσθαι.

Of Hellenistic Philippi little is known,[76] although we have from Appian a rather detailed description (*BCiv.* 4.105ff.). It was the easternmost city in Macedonia proper.

2: ἱερῶν appears to be Philippi's archival label, reflecting a formal agenda of the sort that Greek cities commonly had, with proposals classified under "sacred matters" coming first; there follows the label of the specific decree within this category.[77] Of a proposal sponsored by the entire assembly, odd as that seems, we have several examples;[78] it is of a piece with the unanimity of the Amphipolitans (**26**.17). It must be relevant that this was a decree of the assembly alone (9): I conclude that the *theoroi*, again wishing to press on, arrived in time for a meeting of the assembly and did not pass it by in order to wait for the council and then the next assembly; thus their request was dealt with by the assembly without a *probouleuma*.

76. P. Collart, *Philippes* (Paris 1937); Hatzopoulos, *BCH* 117 (1993) 315–326.

77. The Roberts, however, took ἱερῶν to designate the type of assembly: *Bull. épigr.* 1959, p. 214.

78. *Syll.*^{3} 589.10: γνώμη δήμου (Magnesia, 196 B.C.); others at Schulthess, *RE* 7 (1912) 1491–1492.

3: This is our only mention of an oracle for the Coans; but the anacoluthon shows that after μαντείαν something has fallen out of the text, so that the burden of the oracle is uncertain. Klaffenbach suggested ἱδρευμένη: this might then be the oracle shown the Romans in A.D. 23, which concerned the foundation of the cult.[79] But what is needed here is some act or attitude that is both ancestral and requested by an oracle, such as "making much of" or "honoring" the temple, for example, τιμοῦσα; cf. *IG* XII.5 802.35, XI.4 542.13ff., XII.8 156.5 (*Samothrace* II p. 39).

8, 13: Only the Philippians among these Macedonian cities add "Greeks" to Macedonians in describing themselves.[80] This may reflect the demographic facts of Philip's original foundation and the strong Thasian presence that preceded it; cf. Collart 133–166. The coins struck in the old Thasian peraea and in Philip's new city offer graphic testimony of continuity.[81] This may also be why this decree alone speaks of the οἰκειότης (6) of the Coans where the others (and here at 12) say "loyalty."

18–20: Ambassadors and foreign judges were often given a military escort to their next destination.[82] The port city Neapolis is sixteen kilometers distant.[83] These mercenaries evidently were civic troops, at the disposal of Philippi, and not royal.

28. Aenus

Stele broken above but complete below, found in 1922 reused in an altar on the middle terrace; h. 0.28, w. 0.475, th. 0.09; letters 0.001, intersp. 0.005.

Lines 3–11: Herzog, *Hermes* 65 (1930) 468.

Complete: Herzog/Klaffenbach, *Asylieurkunden* 8 [*SEG* 12.375].

[- ἐπαγ]-
[γ]έλλο[υσι -]
ἐκεχειρίας καὶ ἀγῶν[ας καὶ] αἶ[τοῦσι δέχεσθαι τὴν ἀσυ]-
λίαν τοῦ ἱεροῦ τοῦ Ἀσκληπιοῦ, ἀγα[θῆι τύχηι, δεδόχθαι]
τῆι βουλῆι καὶ τῶι δήμωι τά τε ἀγαθὰ ἃ ε[ὔχοντ]α[ι Κῶιοι]
δέχεσθαι ἐπὶ ὑγιείαι καὶ σωτηρίαι βασιλέως Πτο[λε]-
μαίου καὶ ⟨β⟩ασιλίσσης Βερενίκης καὶ τῶν τέκνων κα[ὶ]
τοῦ δήμου τοῦ τε Αἰνίων καὶ Κώιων· εἶναι δὲ καὶ τὸ
ἱερὸν τοῦ Ἀσκληπιοῦ τοῦ ἐγ Κῶι ἄσυλον· καλέσαι δ[ὲ]

79. Sherwin-White (341) refers the oracle to the construction of the new temple in the third century.

80. Compare a Thessalonican mentioning τοὺς λοιποὺς Μακεδόνας καὶ τοὺς ἄλλους Ἕλληνας (*IG* X.2 1031, ca. 143 B.C.).

81. Cf. Head, *HN*[2] 217; A. R. Bellinger, *ANSMN* 11 (1964) 29–30; G. Le Rider, *Le monnayage d'argent et d'or de Philippe II* (Paris 1977) 339 n. 4.

82. Boesch 53 n. 2; Robert, *Op. min. sel.* I 56 n. 1; expressly for security at *Delphinion* 152.13–14; *Syll.*[3] 614.33, 615.14, 679.23; and *IG* XII.7 44.

83. D. I. Lazaridis, Νεάπολις (Athens 1969).

καὶ τοὺς θεωροὺς ἐπὶ ξένια πρὸς τὸν ἱερέα τοῦ βασ[ι]-
λέως· δοῦναι δὲ αὐτοῖς καὶ εἰς ἀπαρχὴν τὸν ταμίαν
τὸ ἐκ τοῦ νόμου. προήδρευσαν πάντες.

6: ΚΑΙΚΑΣ lapis. 11: προ⟨σ⟩ήδρευσαν Klaffenbach.

If the *theoroi* with Aristolochus continued on across Thrace, they will have obtained the decrees of Maroneia and Aenus; but a different team may well have been sent north from Cos and canvassed Thrace from east to west. This region had only recently been conquered by Ptolemy III.[84] He is warmly invoked here, but, in contrast to most of the Macedonian cities, the Aenians do not yet know of their king's response to the Coans' request. That is to be expected, given the geography; what is more revealing (pertinent to **13**) is that they cite no response of Ptolemy II. The two decrees are close to each other in formulation; the Coans evidently offered an individualized decree and speech to their fellow allies of Ptolemy.

2: For the plurals compare **35**.5, 7, **50**.3; genitive singulars are also possible; cf. **16**.5–6.

4: The decree does not expressly accept the contest, except to the extent that this might be encompassed in the "good things," an expression frequently met in the *asylia* inscriptions and in other summations on religious matters (e.g., *IG* II^2 661.15, 668.6; Moretti, *I. stor. ellen.* I 15.17; *I.Stratonikeia* 14.5).

7: The singular δῆμος recurs in the decrees of the Coan colonies (**48**.24, **49**.25).

9: As at Cassandreia (**25**.15) the *theoroi* are entertained in some connection with the royal cult (cf. C. Habicht, *Gottmenschentum und griechische Städte* [Munich 1970] 122–123).

10: On the ἀπαρχή given to sacred ambassadors see Boesch 75–77.

11: Klaffenbach considered the text senseless and emended it so as to mean "all attended." This should be rejected. In a Greek assembly one might take a written vote to be sure of a quorum (see Gauthier [above n. 75]), but it would be unnecessary and unwieldy to reckon whether all eligible voters were in attendance (nor in practice would they ever be). Klaffenbach saw that the verb, emended or not, could not mean "voted for," indicating a unanimous vote as at **26**.17. I suggest rather that προήδρευσαν means that all "were *proedroi*": that is, there was no presiding committee at this meeting, for whatever reason, and the assembly served as a "committee of the whole."[85] One thinks too of the proposing of the decree (cf. **27**.2, proposal by the assembly as a whole); but even if the verb can mean that, here we have a decree of the council and people both.

84. References in R. S. Bagnall, *Administration of the Ptolemaic Possessions* (Leiden 1976) 159–168; Robert, *DAM* 289–294.

85. For placing such information at the end, compare statements of the source of the proposal in Delian decrees; cf. **80**.2; *Syll.*^{3} 644.11 from Argos.

29–30. Stele of grey marble (rather than the white of the others), the right margin preserved; h. 0.12, w. 0.18; same hand as **28**.

Herzog/Klaffenbach, *Asylieurkunden* 9 [*SEG* 12.376].

29. Maroneia

[- ἀγῶ]νας καὶ τοῦ ἱεροῦ ἀσ[υ]-
[λίαν, - - - ἀγαθῆι τύχηι, ἔδοξε τῆι βουλῆι καὶ τῶ]ι δήμωι τῶι Μαρω-
[νιτῶν - - - ὑπάρχειν μὲν τὸ ἱερὸν τοῦ Ἀσκληπιοῦ] τοῦ ἐγ Κῶι ἄσυλον,
[ἀποδέχεσθαι δὲ καὶ - - - - - - - - - - πανήγ]υριν καὶ σπονδὰς
[- - - - - - - - - καὶ τὰ ἀγαθὰ ἃ εὔχονται Κῶι]οι ἐπὶ ὑγιείαι καὶ
[σωτηρίαι τοῦ δήμου τοῦ τε Μαρωνιτῶν καὶ Κώιω]ν· δοῦναι δὲ
[τὸν ταμίαν τοῖς θεωροῖς εἰς ξένια καὶ εἰς ἀπαρχὴν τὰ ἐκ τ]οῦ νόμου.

The restorations of Herzog and Klaffenbach were exempli gratia, but they regarded 2–3 as complete and the length of line as certain; the effect would be to exclude the reference to Ptolemy that we find at Aenus. But a number of longer variations can be imagined at 2–3.

30. Unknown city

Inscribed below **29**.

[-]ς ἐπὶ

Letters somewhat larger than what precedes, so that Klaffenbach took this to be the heading of another decree, an ethnic with some geographical specification. But while some of the descriptive headings in the archive extend to the right margin, none runs over to a second line, as this seems to have done. So it may be that the variation in size is not significant and these letters belong to **29**.

31–32. Stele, broken on all sides, found in 1933; th. 0.09; letters 0.007–0.01, intersp. 0.005.

31. Unknown city

Herzog/Klaffenbach, *Asylieurkunden* p. 25.

Unpublished: the final seven lines of a decree in Doric.

32. Cius

Inscribed below **31**.

Herzog/Klaffenbach, *Asylieurkunden* 14 [*SEG* 12.381; Corsten, *I.Kios* 18].

Κ ι α ν [ῶ ν]

[- - - - - - - - - - - - ἐπειδὴ] Κῶιοι [φίλοι ὄντες ἀπεστάλκασι πρὸς]
[τὴν ἡμετέραν πόλιν? θεωροὺς Αἴ]σχρον [Θευδότου Ἐπικλῆ Ἀγορακρίτου]
[καὶ ἀρχιθέωρον Ἱππότην Εὐκ]ρίτου ἐπα[γγέλλοντες τήν τε θυσίαν]
[καὶ τοὺς ἀγῶνας οὓς συντε]λοῦσιν τῶι Ἀ[σκληπιῶι καὶ ἀξιοῦσιν τὸ ἱε]-
[ρὸν τοῦ Ἀσκληπιοῦ τὸ παρ' α]ὐτοῖς ἄσυλον [εἶναι, δεδόχθαι τῶι δήμωι]

[τήν τε θυσίαν καὶ τὴν ἐκεχ]ειρίαν δέχεσ[θαι· ὑπάρχειν δὲ τὸ ἱερὸν ἄ]-
[συλον, καθάπερ Κῶιοι ἀξιοῦ]σ[ι]ν· δοῦνα[ι δὲ τὸν ταμίαν τοῖς θεωροῖς]
[εἰς ξένια καὶ εἰς ἀπαρχὴν τὰ ἐκ τ]οῦ νόμ[ου. vacat]

Cius on the Propontis was not visited by the same *theoroi* who approached Ziaelas (**11**), whose capital Nicomedia was the next major city on the coast. The text so far as we have it makes no reference to the Bithynian monarch. Nicomedes had appointed the city as one of the guardians of his second set of children, Ziaelas' rivals (*FGrHist* 434 F 1.14); relations between Ziaelas and Cius may well have been difficult, and the city had an interest in maintaining its independence. A generation later, in unknown circumstances, Cius allied itself with the Aetolians; it was destroyed by Philip V in 202 (Polyb. 15.23) and given over to Prusias of Bithynia, who refounded it as Prusias ad Mare. A Coan proxeny decree for a Cian is extant from the third century (*I.Cos* 2).

The decree is rather abrupt; extant decrees of Cius a century earlier show elaborate preliminary formulae, which could not be restored here without assuming an improbably long line (*I.Kios* 1, 2, 25). These phrases may have been deleted by the Coan redactors.

4: The name Eucritus (see Sherwin-White 448) recurs at Cos only as one of the companions in Theocritus *Idyll* 7, which is widely viewed as describing historical personages. The respective dates would be consistent for identifying the father of the *theoros* with Theocritus' friend.

33–35. Stele in four fragments, three found by Herzog, the fourth (lower right) by Shazmann in 1922; Herzog associated the lower three, Klaffenbach added the uppermost; remains of three decrees; letters 0.01, intersp. 0.005; through **35**.5, written over an erasure.

33. Unknown city

Herzog/Klaffenbach, *Asylieurkunden* p. 25.
Unpublished; in Koine.

34. Unknown city

Herzog/Klaffenbach, *Asylieurkunden* p. 25.
Unpublished; in Aeolic. The *architheoros* is Hippotes, so probably the team that visited Cius.

35. Iasus (?)

Herzog/Klaffenbach, *Asylieurkunden* 15 [*SEG* 12.382; Blümel, *I.Iasos* 21].
Cf. Herzog, *Heilige Gesetze* p. 34.

[ ] Ἰασοῦ
[ἐπὶ στεφανηφόρου - - - - - - -]μου· ἐπειδὴ Κῶιοι φίλοι ὄ[ντ]ες ἀφεσ-
[τάλκασι θεωροὺς Αἴσχρον Θευδ]ότου, Ἐπικλῆ Ἀγοραχρ[ίτου] καὶ ἀρχιθέ-
[ωρον Ἱππότην Εὐκρίτου ἐπαγ]γέλλοντες θυ[σ]ί[αν τε καὶ] πανήγυριν

[τοῦ Ἀσκληπιοῦ καὶ ἐκεχειρίας] κα⟨ὶ⟩ ἀξιοῦσι τὸ [ἱερὸν τοῦ] Ἀσκληπιοῦ
[τὸ ἐν Κῶι ἄσυλον νομίζειν, ἀγαθ]ῆι τύχηι, δεδό[χθαι τῆι βο]υλῆι καὶ τῶι δ[ή]-
[μωι ἀποδέχεσθαι τὴν θυσίαν καὶ] τὰς ἐκεχ[ειρίας καὶ τὸ ἱ]ερὸν τοῦ Ἀσκλ[η]-
[πιοῦ ἄσυλον εἶναι, καθὼς ἀξιοῦσι Κ]ῶιοι, ε[ἰς ἅπαντα τὸ]ν χρόνον· ἐὰν [δέ]
[τις παραβαίνηι - - -] Ο [- - - - - - - - - - - - - - - ἔν]οχος ἔστω τ. . . .
[-]ν μήτε ει[- - - - - - - - - - - -]
[-]εἶνα[ι - - - - - - - - - - - - - -]

1: ἐξ] 'Ιασοῦ Herzog; vacat?] 'Ιασοῦ Klaffenbach. 5: ΚΑ Α lapis. 8: καθάπερ καθιέρωσαν Κ]ῶιοι ε[ἰς τὸν πάντ]α χρόνον Herzog. 9–10: τοὺς ὅρους τῆς ἀσυλίας, ἔν]οχος ἔστω τ[ῆι εἰς τὸν θεὸν ἀσεβείαι Herzog ("too short," Klaffenbach).

The attribution of this decree presents some difficulty. A singular toponym rather than the ethnic is unparalleled in the Coan archive, and the decrees of Hellenistic Iasus have a dating formula far too long to fit in line 2. As it is, the placement of the word in line 1 seems too far to the right to be centered; even with Herzog's addition it does not quite balance (better [παρὰ] 'Ιασοῦ). There is no change in letter size spacing or skipped line from **34** (so too M100), so that line 1 may be the end of the preceding decree; the present decree would then lack a heading (as does inv. M86a on the same stele, and apparently **39**).

5, 7: ἐκεχειρίαι unusually in the plural; cf. on **28**.2.

8: The "for all time" clause, as in a treaty, recurs only at Sparta (**14**, of the truce) among the decrees for Cos. Cf. on **10**.1.

8–9: A penalty clause, found at Cos also in **36**.11.

36. Unknown city

Three (?) fragments that Klaffenbach indicates are to be joined; complete at top.

Paton and Hicks, *I.Cos* 20, with bits of inv. M83, 85, quoted at Herzog, *Heilige Gesetze* p. 34, and Herzog/Klaffenbach, *Asylieurkunden* pp. 25, 26.

[ἐπὶ -] 'Επαμείνονος [- - - - - - -]
[ἐπειδὴ - - - - - - - - - - - - - - - - - Κῶιο]ι θεωροὺς ἀπέστε̣[ιλαν - - -]
[- 'Ιππότη]⟨ν⟩ Ε[ὐ]κρίτου καὶ Αἰ[σχρον]
[Θευδότου καὶ 'Επικλῆ Ἀγορακρίτου ἐπαγγέλλοντες? τὴν θυσ]ίαν καὶ τὸν ἀ[γῶνα]
[- - - - - - - - - - - - - - - - - - ὑπὲρ τῆς αὐτῶν πατ]ρίδος καὶ ἀ[ξιοῦντες]
[- αὐτο]ῖς ἄσυλον / ΑΟ[- - -]
[- δεδόχθαι τῶ]ι δήμωι δέ-
[χεσθαι μὲν τὴν ἐπαγγελίαν - - - - - - - - - - - - - - - - - ἀ]μφοτέρων
[- - - - - - - - - - - - τὸ ἱερὸν τοῦ Ἀσκ]ληπιοῦ· τὸν δὲ παραβαί[νοντα]
[- τῆ]ς ἀσυλίας τῶν ἐκ. .σαι ||[- - -]
[-]ων ἔνοχον εἶναι το. . . . οις ΕΠ
[- εἰς? τ]ὸ θεῖον ἀσεβοῦσι.

3 cf. Klaffenbach p. 25: Θε[ο]κρίτου Patton/Hicks. 4: a longer restoration is possible. 6 init.: εἶναι τὸ τέμενος Patton/Hicks. 10–12: [τοὺς ὅρους ("too short," Klaffenbach) τῆ]ς ἀσυλίας τῶν ἐκ [- - - ὁρμωμέν]ων ἔνοχον εἶναι το[ῖς νόμοις τοῖς κειμένοις ἐπὶ τοῖς τ]ὸ θεῖον ἀσεβοῦσι Herzog.

The same *theoroi* went to Cius. Line 11 shows a penalty clause, as does **35**.

37–40. Stele broken on all sides, found in 1906; th. 0.09; letters 0.008–0.01, intersp. 0.005.

Herzog/Klaffenbach, *Asylieurkunden* p. 26.

37. Unknown city

Unpublished: last two lines of a decree, possibly in Koine; chief *theoros* Herippidas.

38. Unknown city

Inscribed below **37**. Unpublished; a decree of ten lines, in Koine; same chief *theoros* as **37**.

39. Minoa on Amorgos

Inscribed below **38**.
Herzog/Klaffenbach, *Asylieurkunden* 16 [*SEG* 12.383].
Cf. J. and L. Robert, *Bull. épigr.* 1953, p. 159.

[γνώμη πρυτανέων·] ἔδοξεν τῆι βου[λῆι καὶ τῶι δήμωι· ἐπειδὴ παραγενόμενοι]
[παρὰ τῆς πόλεως τῆς] Κώιων ἀρχιθέωρ[ός τε Ἡριππίδας καὶ θεωρὸς - - -]
[ἐπαγγέλλουσιν ἐκεχ]ειρίαν καὶ θυσ[ίαν καὶ ἀγῶνας οὓς συντελοῦσιν Κῶιοι τῶι]
[Ἀσκληπιῶι, ἀξιοῦσ]ι δὲ καὶ ἄσυλον [ὑπάρχειν τὸ ἱερὸν τοῦ Ἀσκληπιοῦ ?εἰς πάντα]
[τὸν χρόνον τὰ ἀπὸ Μιν]οητῶν, ὅπ[ως -]

1 init. Rigsby, from *IG* XII.7 222.1. 5 Robb.: Ἀρσιν]οητῶν Herzog/Klaffenbach. 5f.: ὅπ[ως ἂμ φαίνηται ὁ δῆμος ὁ Ἀρσινοητῶν δια|φυλάττων τήν τε πρὸς τοὺς θεοὺς εὐσέβειαν κτλ.] Herzog/Klaffenbach.

The Roberts saw the authorship from the ending of the ethnic in line 5;[86] I restore line 1 accordingly. For other decrees of Minoa see Robert, *Op. min. sel.* I 563 n. 2. Klaffenbach's restorations seem for the most part filler; the length of line must remain uncertain, and indeed the name of the *theoros*. It is troubling too that as published, the decree lacks a heading (cf. on **35**).

40–41. Marble fragment with the remains of two decrees.

Herzog/Klaffenbach, *Asylieurkunden* pp. 27, 29.

86. See further *Hellenica* XI–XII (1960) 162–163 n. 2; accepted by Klaffenbach, *DLZ* 76 (1955) 737; Sherwin-White (114 n. 162) undecided.

40. Unknown city

Unpublished; in Doric, probably from Rhodes: last words quoted as ἐπ]ὶ ξένια εἰς τὸ ἱεροθ[υτεῖον.

41. Unknown city

Inscribed below **40**. Unpublished; in Doric, *theoroi* - - -]κόφρων Λυκ[- - -.

42–44

Stele with remains of three decrees of Cretan cities.

Unpublished; see Guarducci, *I.Cret.* I p. 100 n. 2; *RivFil* n.s. 21 (1944) 67–68; D. Musti, *AnnPisa* 32 (1963) 227; Herzog/Klaffenbach p. 29.

42. Phaestus

43. Hierapytna

44. Istron

The *theoroi* were Charippus, Dio, and Plato.

45. Corcyra

Inscribed below **27** (see on **25–27**).
Herzog/Klaffenbach, *Asylieurkunden* 10 [*SEG* 12.377].

[Κ ο ρ] κ υ ρ α ί ω ν ἔ χ ο ν ἐ π ί σ α μ ο ν γ ρ ῦ π α
[πρύτανις - - -,] μεὶς Πάναμος, ἁμέρα τρίτα ἐπὶ δέκα, προστάτας Νίκαρχος Τιμο-
[-] τῶν Κώιων τὰν θυσίαν καὶ
[- σ]ωτηρίαι τᾶς πόλιος [. . . . .]
[- τὰν ἀσυλίαν] τοῦ ἱε[ροῦ τοῦ Ἀσκλαπι]-
[οῦ -]

Another *asylia* decree of Corcyra is **94** for Magnesia.

1: Of the decrees from the Greek West, all whose beginnings survive offer a description of the seal on the papyrus;[87] perhaps the chief *theoros* in Sicily and Italy (Epidaurius) was devoted to this detail,[88] and he may have obtained **45** from Corcyra as well. Decree **45**, however, was inscribed apart from the decrees brought back by those *theoroi*, for the heading of their decrees is at the top of **46**. Decrees were legally binding documents and arrived sealed; so, for example, in the context of a boundary adjudication, ἐπιστολὰμ παρὰ Μιλησίων ἐσφραγισμέναν (*I.Olymp.* 52.12–13). Klaffenbach remarked that no griffon appears on the coins of Corcyra. Some coins of neighboring Dyrrachium

87. For references to these in inscriptions see Robert, *Monnaies antiques en Troade* (Geneva 1966) 52 n. 4; T. Ritti, *MemLinc* VIII.14 (1969) 261–360.

88. Another example at Cos, of a foreign decree: Herzog, *Koische Forschungen* (Leipzig 1899) 125–128 no. 190.24–25 (ζώιδιον γυναικεῖον).

are countermarked with a griffon head (*BMC Corinth* 101 nos. 14–15); these marks may derive from Corcyra. Assured Corcyraean countermarks, however, are the civic initials (*BMC Corinth* 112; *Thessaly* 153);[89] and the coins of Dyrrachium circulated widely in the Balkans.

46–47

On the other side of the stele that bears **23** (Pella). Letters as **23**, but line 1 larger (0.01). Two decrees of Italian cities; presumably the *theoroi* were traveling northwards, although the texts are not in that order on the stone.

Herzog/Klaffenbach, *Asylieurkunden* 11 [*SEG* 12.378].

46. Naples

ψαφίσματα ἃ ἐκόμισαν θεωροὶ Ἐπιδαύριος Νικάρχου, Φιλόφρων Δαρδά⟨ν⟩ου·
Ν ε ο π ο λ ι τ ᾶ ν ἔ χ ο ν ἐ π ί σ α μ ο ν ζ ώ ι δ ι ο ν ἀ ν δ ρ ε ῖ ο ν
ἐπειδὴ παρὰ τῆς πόλεως τῆς Κώιων ἀρχιθέωρος παραγενόμενος Ἐπιδαύριος Νικάρ-
χου καὶ θεωροὶ Φιλόφρων Δαρδάνου καὶ Σιμίας Τιμασιφῶντος ἀνανεοῦνταί τε τὴν ο[ἰ]-
κειότητα καὶ τὴν εὔνοιαν ἣν ἔχουσα ἡ πόλις ἡ Κώιων διατελεῖ πρὸς τὴν πόλιν τὴν Νε-
οπολιτῶν καὶ ἐπαγγέλλουσι θυσίαν τῶι Ἀσκληπιῶι καὶ ἀγῶνα καὶ ἀξιοῦσιν τὸ ἱερὸν
τοῦ Ἀσκληπιοῦ ἄσυλον παραδέξασθαι, τύχηι ἀγαθῆι, ἔδοξε τοῖς ἄρχουσι καὶ τῆ[ι]
συνκλήτωι καὶ τῶι δήμωι τήν τε οἰκειότητα καὶ τὴν εὔνοιαν τὴν τῆς πόλεως τῆς
Κώιων ἀποδέ⟨ξ⟩ασθαι καὶ τὴν θυσίαν καὶ τὸν ἀγῶνα τοῦ Ἀσκληπιοῦ συναύ-ξειν·
ὑπάρχειν δὲ καὶ τὸ ἱερὸν ἄσυλον· δοῦναι δὲ καὶ εἰς θυσίαν τῶι Ἀσκληπιῶι μνᾶς τρεῖς·
καλέσαι δὲ τοὺς θεωροὺς ἐπὶ ξένια.

1: ΑΗΟΥ lapis. 2: letters not so widely spaced as the headings of most other decrees (so too **47**.1). 9: Ι lapis.

Other extant decrees of Naples are of imperial date and much influenced by Roman usages. In 242 southern Italy and Sicily were in the last year of the First Punic War, which seems to leave no trace in these texts and the travels that they reflect. Naples and Elea were Roman *socii* and had lent Rome ships at the start of the war (Polyb. 1.20.14).

1: The heading names only two *theoroi*, yet a third was at Naples and the length of line guarantees that his name is to be restored in the decree of Elea

89. In Roman times, a dolphin or Zeus Casius: C. J. Howgego, *Greek Imperial Countermarks* (London 1985) nos. 356, 532.

that follows. His omission from the heading suggests that he diverted from his fellows along the route to canvass other cities and returned separately. A further oddity is that a different (and single) *theoros* accompanied Epidaurius in Sicily. Evidently the Coan travels in the west were complex, and they defy reconstruction.

2: A "male figure" at Naples, a "seated female figure" at Elea (**47**.1); I do not know whether the Coans mean to distinguish ζῷον and ζῴδιον. The two words appear successively at *IG* XI.2 161.74 and 76, without making clear a distinction. Both images will have been of human figures, given the specification of gender. Pugliese Carratelli (*ArchStorCalabLucan* 24 [1955] 1–7) suggested the man-faced bull seen on coins of Naples, perhaps Sebeithus; at Elea perhaps the nymph Elea or Persephone.

10: The sacrifice, worth 120 drachmas, is for Asclepius in Cos, not part of the honors for the *theoroi*; if we are to judge from **49**.30, this was a once-only donation and not a permanent commitment for a sacrifice to be offered by the Neapolitan *theoroi* to Cos at each Great Asclepieia.

47. Elea

Inscribed below **46**.

Ἐλεατᾶν ἔχον ἐπίσαμον Ζῶιον γυναικέον καθήμενον
ἔδοξε τοῖς ἄρχουσι καὶ τῶι δήμωι τῶι Ἐλεατῶν· ἐπειδὴ παρὰ τῆς πόλεως τῶν Κώιων
ἀρχιθέωρος παραγενόμενος Ἐπιδαύριος Νικάρχου [καὶ θεωροὶ Φιλόφρων Δαρδάνου καὶ Σιμί]-
4 ας Τιμασιφῶντος ἐπαγγέλλουσι τῶι Ἀσκλη[πιῶι θυσίαν τε καὶ ἀγῶνα καὶ ἀξιοῦσι τὸ ἱερὸν]
[τοῦ Ἀ]σκληπιοῦ ἄσυλον π[αραδέξασθαι -]

From Elea we have no other public acts. On the city see G. Radke, *RE* 8A (1958) 2399–2405; *PP* 21 (1966) 191–377, 25 (1970) 5–300.

Epidaurius and a different colleague toured Sicily, from which we have the decrees of Camarina and Gela, neighbors on the south coast. The *theoroi* in their speech appealed to these cities as colonies, whence we learn that Cos had participated in the refoundations of Timoleon.[90] The Sicilian cities maintain cults inherited from Cos and invite the Coans to their festivals (κατακαλεῖν **48**.20–22, **49**.21–23); they are united with the mother city by isopolity (**48**.11).[91] The decrees are so similar that these points must reflect the decree and speeches

90. Bibliography at Sherwin-White 80–81. Diod. 16.82.7 mentions Timoleon's intervention at Camarina; Plut. *Tim.* 35.2 at Gela. In the latter passage some scholars have thought to emend the origin of the colonist Gorgus from ἐκ Κέω to ἐκ Κῶ; discussion at R. J. A. Talbert, *Timoleon and the Revival of Greek Sicily* (Cambridge 1974) 204–205.

91. Cf. W. Gawantka, *Isopolitie*, Vestigia 22 (Munich 1975) 111–113.

of the *theoroi*, composed with these colonies in mind. The Sicilian decrees are alone in mentioning the program and period of the Asclepieia (**48**.15, **49**.14) and the procession (**49**.31), although these must have been specified also in the decrees presented to the other cities.

The Sicilian decrees are puzzling for their constitutional form. Each has two sections; what is granted in the first section does not recur in the second. Neither section reads as though it were a rider to the other in order to add points omitted inadvertently (an omission that is unlikely to have happened at both cities). This format seems to bespeak at both cities a division of jurisdiction. The first section (insofar as it survives) grants *asylia* and provides that this and the acceptance of the Asclepieia be added to the laws; in the second, the assembly votes only to accept the games (there is no mention of *asylia*) and to entertain the *theoroi*. The first section therefore is not a *probouleuma* and the second the decree (although there was a *probouleuma*; cf. **48**.8),[92] for the decree does not repeat the first section. Perhaps the first is instead a decree of *nomothetai*, reflecting the sort of distinction between a law and a policy decree that pertained in fourth-century Athens.[93] Yet in the first part both *asylia* and the acceptance of the games are "added to the laws" (**48**.6–8). Or possibly the distinction is fiscal, with the assembly voting funds for a policy decision made by the council.

48. Camarina

Stele broken at top and bottom, found in 1904; h. 0.43, w. 0.445–0.45, th. 9.5–10; letters 0.006–0.008, intersp. 0.004.

Herzog/Klaffenbach, *Asylieurkunden* 12 [*SEG* 12.379; G. Manganaro, *Historia* 13 (1964) 414–419; Rizzo, *La Sicilia* 10–11; Dubois, *IG dial. Sicil.* 117].

Photograph: Manganaro 1964; 1990 pl. 76.2.

Cf. Manganaro, *AnnPisa* 20 (1990) 391–408.

[- - -]ΛΟ . . . Α[- - - - - - - - - - - - - - - - - τῶγ Κα]-
μαριναίων τοῖς Κώιοις [- - - - - - - - - - - - - - - - - -]
συνοικιξάντεσσι, καθὰ ε||[- - - - - - - - - - - - - - - - -]
δεδόχθαι ἐπ' ἀγαθᾶι τύχαι καὶ ὁμο[νοίαι καὶ σωτηρί]-
αι τοῦ δάμου τῶγ Καμαριναίων καὶ τῶ[γ Κώιων· τὸ]
ἱερὸν ἄσυλον εἶμεν τοῦ Ἀσκλαπιοῦ, χωράξα[ι δὲ τάν]
τε ἀσυλίαν καὶ τὰν θυσίαν καὶ τοὺς ἀγῶνας εἰς
τοὺς νόμους. βουλᾶς φερούσας ἔδοξε τᾶι ἁλ[ίαι·]
ἐπειδὴ οἱ Κῶιοι συνοικισταὶ ἐγένοντο τᾶς πόλιος
ἁμῶν ὑπαρχόντων τε αὐτοῖς παρ' ἁμεῖν τῶν μεγίστων καὶ
ἀναγκαιοτάτων, συγγενείας τε καὶ οἰκειότατος καὶ ἰσοπο-
λειτείας, ἀποστείλαντες ἀρχιθέωρον Ἐπιδαύριον Νικάρχο[υ,]

92. A western example of this normal procedure is *IGUrbRom* 2.10: ἔδοξε τᾶι ἁλίαι καθὰ καὶ τᾶι συγκλήτῳ (Acragas).

93. See M. H. Hansen, *The Athenian Ecclesia* (Copenhagen 1983) 177–206.

θεωρὸν Σωσίστρατον Καφισίου ἐπαγγέλλοντι τὰν θυ-
σίαν ἃν θύοντ[ι] τῶι Ἀσκλαπιῶι καὶ τοὺς ἀγῶνας
οὓς τίθεντι μουσικὸν καὶ γυμνικὸν κατὰ πενταετηρ[ί]-
δα, καὶ ἀξιῶντι δεῖν κοινωνεῖν τὰν ἁμὰμ πόλιν ἐμφανί-
ζοντες τὰν οἰκειότατα καὶ εὔνοιαν ταῖς πολίεσσι, καλῶς
δὲ ἔχον ἐστὶ τάν τε ἐπαγγελίαν παρ' αὐτῶν δέχεσθαι κα[ὶ]
φανερὸν ποιῆσαι αὐτοῖς διότι μνάμαν ἔχοντες δια-
τελοῦμες τᾶς ὑπαρχούσας ποτ' αὐτοὺς συγγενείας [ἔν]
τε ταῖς πατρίοις θυσίαις ἃς παρελάβομες παρ' αὐτῶν κ[αὶ]
ἐν ταῖς παναγυρίεσσι κατακαλοῦντες αὐτοὺς καθ[ὰ]
καὶ τοὺς ἄλλους οἰκιστάς, δεδόχθαι ἐπ' ἀγαθᾶι τύχα[ι]
καὶ ὑγιείαι καὶ σωτηρίαι καὶ ὁμονοίαι τοῦ δάμου τῶν
Καμαριναίων καὶ τῶγ Κώιων δέξασθαι παρ' αὐτῶν τάν
τε θυσίαν ἃμ ποιοῦνται τῶι Ἀσκλαπιῶι καὶ τοὺς ἀγῶ-
νας· καλεῖν δὲ καὶ ἐπὶ ξένια τοὺς θεωροὺς τούτους τε
καὶ τοὺς ἀεὶ παραγινομένους πάσας τὰς ἁμέρας ἅς κα
ἐπιδαμέωντι.

1–3: ἀπε]λογ[ίξ]α[ντο? δὲ καὶ τὰν συγγένειαν τῶν Κα]μαριναίων τοῖς Κώιοις [τάν τε ἁμὰμ πόλιν καὶ Γέλαν] συνοικιξάντεσσι, καθὰ ἐμ[μαρτύρησε ἁμεῖν ὁ βασιλεύς? Herzog; καὶ ἐμφανίζοντι τὰν | συγγένεια]ν̣, ο[ἰκειότατα καὶ ἰσοπολιτείαν τῶγ Κα]μαριναίων τοῖς Κώιοις, [τὰν πόλιν σὺγ Κορινθίοις] συνοικιξάντεσσι, καθὰ ἐγ[γράφεται ἐν ἱστορίαις?] Manganaro 1964 (2 [τὰν πόλιν ἁμῶν καὶ Γέλαν] 1990). 4–5: or ὑγιεί]|αι; cf. 24 (Klaffenbach).

The inscription confirms Niese's view (II 187) that Camarina was not wholly destroyed in 258 B.C. The city's sorry condition, Klaffenbach thought, explains the fact that so little is done for the *theoroi*.

8: On ἁλία, frequent for "assembly" among the western Greeks, see Schulthess, *RE* 7 (1912) 2233–2241. φέρω apparently only here for the familiar ἐκφέρω or μεταφέρω when "transferring" a text from one body to another.

19: For such "remembering" of kinship (also **49**.19) see on **66**.27.

21: Sharing the same gods was a proof of kinship, according to Isocrates (4.43; cf. Jos. *AJ* 12.125–26, 257–60).

49. Gela

Inscribed on the other side of the stele bearing the royal letter **12**, and apparently by the same hand.

Herzog/Klaffenbach, *Asylieurkunden* 13 [*SEG* 12.380; Rizzo, *La Sicilia* 12–14; Dubois, *IG dial. Sicil.* 160].

Photograph: Manganaro pl. 77.

Cf. Manganaro, *AnnPisa* 20 (1990) 391–408.

[- - - - - - - δεδόχθαι ἐπ' ἀγαθᾶι τύχαι καὶ ὁμο]-
[νοίαι καὶ σωτηρίαι τοῦ δάμου τῶγ Γελώιων καὶ τῶν]
[Κώιων· τὸ ἱερὸν ἄσυλον εἶμεν τοῦ Ἀσκλαπιοῦ, χ]ωρά-

[ξαι δὲ τάν τε ἀσυλίαν καὶ τὰν θυσίαν καὶ τοὺ]ς ἀγῶ-
[νας εἰς τοὺς νόμους.] vacat
[βουλᾶς φερούσας ἔδοξε τᾶι ἁλίαι· ἐπει]δὴ οἱ Κῶι-
[οι συνοικισταὶ ἐγένοντο τᾶς πόλιος ἁ]μῶν Γέλας
[ὑπαρχόντων τε αὐτοῖς παρ' ἁμεῖν τ]ῶμ μεγίστω[ν]
[καὶ ἀναγκαιοτάτων, συγγενείας] τε καὶ οἰκιστ[εί]-
[ας καὶ ἰσοπολειτείας, ἀποστεί]λαντες ἀρχιθ[έ]-
[ωρον 'Επιδαύριον Νικάρχου, θ]εωρὸν Σωσίστρα-
[τον Καφισίου ἐπαγγέλλοντι τ]ὰν θυσίαν ἃν θύο[ν]-
[τι τῶι Ἀσκλαπιῶι καὶ τοὺς] ἀγῶνας οὓς τίθεντι
[μουσικὸν καὶ γυμνικὸν κα]τὰ πενταετηρίδα, καὶ
[ἀξιῶντι δεῖν κοινων]εῖν τὰν ἁμὰμ πόλιν
[ἐμφανίζοντες τὰν οἰκει]ότατα καὶ εὔνοιαν
[ταῖς πολίεσσι, καλ]ῶς δὲ ἔχον ἐστὶ τάν τε ἐ-
[παγγελίαν παρ' αὐ]τῶν δέχεσθαι καὶ φανερὸν
πο[ιῆσαι αὐτοῖς] διότι μνάμαν ἔχοντες διατε-
λοῦμ[ες τᾶς] ὑπαρχούσας ποτ' αὐτὸς συγγενείας
ἔν τε ταῖς πατρ[ί]οις θυσίαις αἷς παρελάβομες
παρ' αὐτῶν καὶ ἐν ταῖς παναγυρίεσσι κατακαλοῦν-
τες αὐτοὺς καθὰ καὶ τοὺς ἄλλους οἰκιστάς, δε-
δόχθαι ἐπ' ἀγαθᾶι τύχαι καὶ ὑγιείαι καὶ σωτηρίαι
καὶ ὁμονοίαι τοῦ δάμου τῶγ Γελώιων καὶ τῶν
Κώιων δέξασθαι παρ' αὐτῶν ⟨τάν⟩ τε θυσίαν ἃμ ποιεῦν-
ται τῶ[ι Ἀ]σκλ[α]πιῶι καὶ τοὺς ἀγῶνας· καλεῖν
δὲ καὶ ἐπὶ ξ[ένια τοὺς θ]εωροὺς τούτους τε καὶ
τοὺς ἀεὶ παρ[αγινομέν]ους πάσσας τὰς ἁμέρας
ἅς κα ἐπιδα[μέωντι· διδό]ντω δὲ αὐτοῖς καὶ οἱ πω-
λητῆρες εἰς [τε τὰν] θυσ[ίαν κα]ὶ τὰμ πομπὰν τῶι Ἀσ-
κλαπιῶι, ὅσσο[ν κ]αὶ τοῖς [τ]ὰ 'Ολύμπια περιαγγελ-
λόντεσσι, ἀρ[γυ]ρίου δοκίμου [δέ]κα μνᾶς· θυσάντω
δὲ καὶ οἱ θεωρο[ὶ μ]ετὰ τῶν ἱερ[ομναμόνω?]ν καὶ ἱερ[α]-
πόλων ἐπὶ τᾶς ἑστίας τᾶς κ[οινᾶς - - - - - - - - ἄρ]-
νας καὶ ἐν τῶι [Ἀσκ]λαπιείωι ἱε[ρεῖον τέλειον ὑπὲρ]
τοῦ δάμου τῶ[γ Γελώιων καὶ τῶν Κώιων· οἱ δὲ πωλη]-
τῆρες δ[όντω αὐτοῖς - - - - - - - - - - - - - - - -]

2: or καὶ ὑγιείαι; cf. 24 (Klaffenbach). 35: τρεῖς ἐτέλους ἄρ]νας Herzog.

The Gelans who survived the destruction of their city by the Mamertines ca. 280 maintained their identity when resettled at Phintias some sixty kilometers to the west.[94] Whatever others called them, their coins and inscriptions show that they continued to call themselves Γελῷοι. The specification of the toponym "Gela" in line 7 (contrast **48**.9–10) must reflect consciousness of the distinction between the old site and the new one.

94. Diod. 22.2.2, 23.1.4, and Klaffenbach's references; see generally Manganaro.

9–10: Klaffenbach considered οἰκιστείας an error for οἰκειότατος.

30ff.: The provisions for honoring the Coans are the most elaborate in the archive, and the amount for the sacrifice in Cos, 600 drachmas (33), is the largest. The contrast with Camarina is indeed striking. It is clear from αὐτοῖς (30) that this is a once-only donation given now to these *theoroi* (compare **56** for Tenos), not a provision for an ongoing commitment for sacrifices at future Asclepieia. The sacrifice at 33ff. is local, in the Gelans' Asclepieum, part of entertaining the present *theoroi* (see on **15**.11–12).

30–31: The *poleteres* of Gela (this form also at Delphi, *CIDelphes* II 32.88, 92) were obviously "treasurers" broadly; elsewhere *poletai* usually let contracts. The office was common in the Dodecanese, including Cos (T. Lenschau, *RE* 21 [1952] 1361; Manganaro 399–400), where their functions were similarly broad.

36: Compare the adult animal for Asclepius at Cos, *LSCG* 162.10–11.

50. Unknown city

Fragment of a marble stele; h. 0.25, w. 0.17, th. 0.08; letters 0.08, intersp. 0.07.
Segre, *Iscr.Cos* ED38. *Collation.*
Photograph: Segre pl. 12.

[- - - - - - - - - - - -]IPIAITO[- - - - - - - - - - - - - -]
[- - - - - - - - - - - -]IΩN δέχεσθ[αι - - - - - - - - - - -]
[- - - - - τάς τε θυσίας καὶ] τὰς ἐκεχειρία[ς καὶ τοὺς]
[ἀγῶνας - - - - εἶναι δὲ κ]αὶ τὸ ἱερὸν το[ῦ Ἀσκληπιοῦ]
[ἄσυλον - - - - - - - - - - - -]· δοῦναι δὲ τοῖ[ς θεωροῖς]
[- - - - - - εἶναι] δὲ αὐτοὺς καὶ π[ροξένους - - - - - - -]
[- - - - - - - -] τὸ δὲ ἀνάλωμα [εἰς - - - - - - - - - - - -]
[- - - - - - - -]ξιν ⟨δ⟩οῦναι τὸν [ταμίαν].
vacat

3–5: Segre treated the text as continuous; but the formulae can vary, so that the line length and line divisions must remain unknown. The nouns might be genitive singulars; cf. on **28**.2.

51. Unknown city

Fragment of white marble preserved at left; h. 0.09, th. 0.05; letters 0.01.
Segre, *Iscr.Cos* ED170.
Photograph: Segre pl. 47.

ἔδ̣[οξε - ἐπειδὴ]
Κῶιο[ι -]
θεωρὸς [ἀποστέλλοντες - - - ἐπαγγέλλοντι]
τὰν θυσ[ίαν - - - - - - - - - - - - - - - δεδόχθαι]
ἀποκρ[ίνεσθαι - - - - - - - - - - - - - - - - - -]

52. Unpublished

(a) Herzog/Klaffenbach, *Asylieurkunden* pp. 10–11 (18 incomplete lines): Herzog thought the hand the same as that of Ziaelas' letter and restored the text as a letter of Hieron II; Klaffenbach reserved judgment whether this is a letter or a decree; (b) p. 26 (inv. M 89): the same *theoroi* as to Cius; (c) p. 27: Priene? (d) various phrases cited at Herzog, *Heilige Gesetze* p. 34.

Tenos

The temple of Poseidon and Amphitrite on Tenos stood in a grove on the southern shore of the island two kilometers west of the city proper; it enjoyed its own small harbor. The complex has been partially excavated; there is no certain trace of cult activity before the mid-fourth century B.C., and the city itself seems to have moved from the interior to its coastal site only at about that time.[1] The first temple was built toward 300 B.C.; Philochorus, who died in 261, reports a famous sculpture of the two gods, the work of the Athenian Telesinus (*FGrHist* 328 F 176). There was a major project of expansion around 200 B.C. including a new temple, and another toward 100 B.C., which added a large stoa. The temple included an eating facility, a mark of a major pilgrimage shrine.[2] Games of Poseidon are attested at least as early as the quest for *asylia* (*IG* XII.5 802.25), but not their enlargement to Panhellenic status.

The evidence for *asylia* at Tenos presents grave difficulties. One decree has been assigned to the 270s or 260s B.C. (making it the earliest extant); others to the period 250–230; and yet others, which are reckoned to be renewals, to the early second century B.C. The texts are disparate also in content, and it is uncertain how to form a coherent picture from this material.[3]

53. Phocian League

Stele, preserved only at left, found built into a wall on the site of the temple of Athena Cranaea at Elatea; now lost. Writing "assez regulière," O and Ω smaller.

1. R. Etienne, *Ktema* 9 (1984) 205–211; *Ténos* I–II (Paris 1986–90).

2. Strab. 10.5.11 (487); cf. Nock, *Essays* I 434.

3. Boesch 128–132 (initial recognition, including Phocian, in the second half of the third century, renewal in the early second); cf. Guarducci, *RivFil* n.s. 28 (1950) 144–145 (Phaestus ca. 250, renewals early II B.C.). The list of inscriptions at Fiehn, *RE* 5A (1934) 524, is careless.

P. Paris, *BCH* 11 (1887) 332–337 no. 9 [*Elatée* (Paris 1892) 245–247 no. 57; Michel, *Rec.* 278]; Dittenberger, *IG* IX.1 97 (copy of Lolling) [Hiller, *IG* XII.5 p. xv; Schwyzer 352; Etienne, *Tenos* II 93–95].

[- - - - - - -] \ | | Λ [- - - - - - - - - - - - - - -]
[- - - τὰν ὑ]πάρχουσαν Τηνίοι[ς - - - - - - - -]
. . Η[- - - δ]εδόχθαι τῶι κοινῶι Φωκέων τ[ὸ] ἱε-
[ε]ρὸν τοῦ [Πο]τειδᾶνος καὶ τᾶς Ἀμφιτρίτας
ἐν Τήνωι καὶ τὰν νᾶσον ἄσυλα εἶμεν, καὶ
ἐν τὰν κατασκευὰν τοῦ ναοῦ τοῦ θεοῦ ἐπ̣ὶ
μὲν τοῦ̣ παρόντος [δ]όμεν πέντε μ[ν]ᾶς, ὕσ-
τερον δὲ γενομένων Φωκεῦσι τῶν πραγμάτω[ν]
καὶ τοῦ πολέμου κατὰ λόγον ἀποστεῖλαι
καταξίως τῶν θεῶν καὶ τᾶς ὑπαρχούσας
οἰκ̣ειότατος ποτὶ Τηνίους· ἐπαινέσαι δὲ καὶ
τὰν πόλιν Τηνίων ὅτι τοῦ τε ἱεροῦ τὰν ἐπιμέ-
λειαν ποιεῖνται καὶ τὰν ποτὶ Φωκεῖς οἰκειότα-
τα ἀνανεοῦνται, καὶ εἶμεν Τηνί̣οις ἰσοπολι-
τείαν πᾶσι δεδομέναν ἐμ Φωκεῦσι· δόμεν
δὲ καὶ Θεστ̣ίαι Διαίτου τῶι θεαρῶι μν̣ᾶν καὶ ἐ[πὶ]
ξένια καλεσάντων αὐτὸν τοὶ Φ[ω]κάρχαι· ἀν[α]-
γράψαι δὲ καὶ ἐν στάλας τρεῖς τὸ ψάφισμα κ[αὶ]
ἀναθέμεν τὰν μὲν ἐν τῶι ἱερῶι τᾶς [Ἀ]θάνας
ἐν Κράναις, τὰν δὲ ἐν τᾶι ἀγορᾶι ἐν Ἐλατεί[αι],
τὰν δὲ ἐν Δελφ[ο]ῖς· τὸ δὲ ἀνά[λ]ωμα δόμεν τ[οὺς]
Φωκάρχας καὶ τοὺς ἀρ̣[τ]ιστῆρας θέσθα[ι.]

vacat

Text of Dittenberger. 2–3: Τηνί[οις φιλίαν . . . | ἀγαθᾶι τύχαι δ.] Paris. 22–23: θέσθα[ι ἐν τοὺς | λόγους - - -] Paris.

. . .

(3ff.) the temple of Poseidon and Amphitrite on Tenos and the island are to be inviolable; toward the construction of the temple of the god, for the present to give five mnai, later when affairs and the war are in order for the Phocians to send in a manner worthy of the gods and the existing kinship with the Tenians; and to praise the city of the Tenians because they are taking care of the temple (etc.)

We have also the Phocians' recognition of Magnesia in 208 B.C. (**84**); in this decree, as in **84**, the last sentiment in the preliminaries is to invoke the friendship of the recipient (2, whatever nouns are to be restored). Only one ambassador, called a *theoros*, visited them, consistent with *IG* XII.5 802 (see below). Boesch concluded from the term *theoros* that games must also have been requested; but games are omitted also in the body of the decision, nor are they found in the other (admittedly fragmentary) *asylia* texts for Tenos.

Most scholars have followed Hiller in dating this decree to the period 278–261 B.C., hence the earliest extant recognition of *asylia*.[4] The argument is that the temple in question (6) was built by 261 (death of Philochorus, who mentions the statues) and that Phocis could not have put up an inscription at Delphi (21) before becoming a member of the Amphictyony in 278. But states not in the Amphictyony inscribed at Delphi; and line 6 might mean adornment (so Paris 335) rather than construction or might refer to the new construction of ca. 200 B.C. rather than the earlier one. Roesch in fact remarked that this decree can as well come from the second half of the third century and maintained that Phocarchs (22) were instituted only after 228.[5] In the early 220s Delphi honored a Tenian Diaetus son of Thestias, who already had ancestral proxeny:[6] this might be either the son of our *theoros* or his father, hence no help in dating this decree. In a catalogue we have Δίαιτος Ποσειδωνίου Θεστιάδης,[7] who Hiller thought might be the father of the *theoros*; but the date of the catalogue is doubtful, as is the relationship. As to when Phocians were at war (9), there are too many options. Accordingly the date of the Phocian recognition must be left open.

3–5: The terms of the recognition have no immediate parallel, but the intent is clear. The entire civic territory is to be inviolable; what is exceptional here is that the temple stood outside the city. In this circumstance the formula "city and territory sacred and inviolable" was avoided; but it would have been misleading to say τὸ ἱερὸν καὶ τὰν χώραν, "the temple and (its) territory." Therefore, I take it, "temple and island." The odd phrase might suggest an early date, before usages had become fixed.

9: For the sentiment compare *Delphinion* 141.32 (κατὰ καιρόν); on such reservations see Wilhelm, *Hermes* 41 (1906) 74–77.

14–15: *isopoliteia* with the League, not with its individual cities, according to E. Szanto, *Das griechische Bürgerrecht* (Freiburg 1892) 74.

54. Aetolian League

Stele of white marble with acroteria found in 1902 between the temple and the exedra, now in the local museum (no. 74); h. 0.84, w. 0.36, th. 0.06; writing of the mid-third century B.C. (so Klaffenbach; A with straight bar, Σ with somewhat splayed arms, Ω small and raised; small apices); the surface is extremely worn and hard to read throughout.

4. Most recently Etienne, *Ténos* II 95–96 (even as early as the 280s).

5. *Etudes béotiennes* (Paris 1982) 359–364.

6. J. Bousquet, *BCH* 82 (1958) 84–85 [*SEG* 18.187], with 83 (1959) 146 n. 1 and 84 (1960) 166 n. 1.

7. *IG* XII.5 872.109 (ca. 300 B.C.: Hiller, Wilhelm; ca. 200: Holleaux, Etienne [1984] 210). Θεστιάδης is a tribal affiliation.

H. Demoulin, *MusB* 8 (1904) 88 no. 15 (line 11); Hiller, *IG* XII.5 857 (copy of Demoulin; 7 lines); Graindor, *MusB* 14 (1910) 43–45 no. 22 (21 lines); Klaffenbach, *IG* IX.1² 191 (squeeze; selected lines) [*IG* XII Suppl. p. 135]. *Collation.*

(6–7 lines effaced)

[- - - - - - - - - - - - -] ἀσφ[ά]λειαν [- - - - -]
[-]
[- - - - - - - - -]Ι̣ΝΛΛΙ[- - - - - - - - - - - - -]
[- - - - - - - - -]ΑΙΛ[- - - - - - - - - - - - - -]
[- - - τοὺς πρεσβευ]τὰς τοὺς Τηνίων - - - -]
[- - - - - - - - - - -]ΚΟ[- - - - - - - - - - - - -]
[- - - - - - - -]ΝΣ . ΛΕΙΛΛΙ[- - - - - - - - -]
[- - - - - - - καὶ τ]ᾶς χώρας αὐτῶν [- - - - -]
[- - - τὸν στραταγὸ]ν ἀεὶ τὸν ἔ[να]ρχ̣ο̣ν̣ [- -]
[- - - - - - - - - -] στραταγοῦντ̣[ος - - - - - -]
[- - - - ἱππαρχοῦν]τος Τιμολόχου̣ [- - - - - -]
[- - - - γραμματεύ]οντος Δαμοκλ[έος - - - -]
[- - - - - - - - -]. Λ. ΧΣΟΥ[- - - - - - - - - -]
[- - - - - - - - δὲ] τοῖς Αἰτωλοῖς ΔΑΜΑ[- - -]
[- - - - - - - - Αἰ]τωλῶν ΤΟ[- - - - - - - - - -]
[- - - - - - - -]Μ̣Ε̣Θ̣ΟΝΑ[- - - - - - - - - - - -]
[- - - - - - - - -]ΙΣΠΛ[- - - - - - - - - - - - - -]
[- - - - - - - - - -]Ε̣[- - - - - - - - - - - - - - - -]
[- - - - - - - -]ΤΑ̣ΝΩΣΤΑ̣[- - - - - - - - - - -]
[- - - - - - - - -]ΤΑ̣[- - - - - - - - - - - - - - - -]
[-]
[- - - - - -]Τ . . ΣΤΡΑΤΑ̣[- - - - - - - - - - -]

Klaffenbach's text, plus the lines that Graindor reported; I could confirm only occasional phrases on the stone.

This is a white stele uninscribed on the back, rather than the grey opisthographic stones that held the archive (below). It was a long decree; the lettering suggests the third quarter of the third century B.C. Of the few words legible, line 8 would be consistent with a grant of inviolability for the city and country; but all that is assured in this text is "security" (1) and "territory" (8). This need not be an *asylia* decree.

55. Phaestus

Stele found reused at Miamu (ancient Leben) south of Phaestus, preserved at left and bottom; h. 0.68, w. 0.28, th. 0.24; letters 0.015–.02; now lost.

F. Halbherr, *MusItal* 3 (1890) 726–727 no. 178 (squeeze) [Blass, *SGDI* 5085; Guarducci, *I.Cret.* I XVII 1; *Staatsvertr.* III 562].

Drawing: Halbherr.

Cf. Graindor, *MusB* 10 (1907) 22–23; Guarducci, *RivFil* 71 (1943) 66–73.

μινων θε[-]
[-]
[- - - - - - - - - - - - - - εἶμεν δὲ ἰσοπολιτείαν Φαιστίοις καὶ]
[Τηνίοις καὶ τὸν Τήνιον ἐν Φαιστοῖ καὶ τὸν Φαίστιον ἐν Τήνωι]
[μετ]έχειν θ̣[ίνων καὶ ἀνθρωπίνων· καὶ ἄσυλον εἶμεν τὸ ἱερὸν τοῦ]
Ποτειδάων[ος καὶ τᾶς Ἀμφιτρίτας τῶι τῶν Φαιστίων ῥητῶι]
καὶ μηδενὶ [ἐξέστω ἀδικῆσαι τῶν Τηνίων μηδένα μη]-
δέν· αἰ δέ τ̣ί̣[ς τινα ἀδικήσηι τῶν Φαιστόθεν ὁρμιομένων]
Τηνίων, δικά[ζεσθαι -]
. ων τοῖς Τη[νίοις -]
. . . . ιαντο[- Φαι]-
[στ]ίων ἐν Τή[νωι - Φα]-
[ίσ]τιοι περὶ [-]
. πρόνοια [-]
πρόνοιαν [- - - - - - - - - ἐὰν δὲ συνδοκεῖ ταῦτα τῶι δήμωι]
τῶν Τηνίω[ν, ἀναγράψαι εἰς στάλαν λιθίναν τὸ δόγμα τῶν]
Φαιστίων [καὶ ἀναθεῖναι Φαιστίους εἰς τὸ ἱερὸν τῶ Ἀπέλλωνος τῶ]
Πυτίω, Την[ίους δὲ εἰς τὸ ἱερὸν τοῦ Ποτειδάωνος καὶ τᾶς Ἀμφιτρίτας].

Text of Graindor. 6 Guarducci (or δόγματι]): ἀπὸ τῶν Φ. ῥητῶ] Graindor.

Guarducci thought the lettering to date to the mid-third century or soon after. In what is otherwise reconstructed to be a decree of personal *asylia* intrudes a declaration for the temple, a restoration prompted by the name of Poseidon (6); at 11 might be [ἀσυλ]ίαν το[ῦ ἱεροῦ. **3** and **4** show a similar mixture; but Graindor's entire reconstruction must be regarded as uncertain.

If **54** and **55** are both responses to the Tenians' quest for inviolability of the temple, then the Aetolians and Cretans have responded in their manner and assumed that the Tenians' goal was personal inviolability; and the palaeography of these would dictate the date of **53**: the Tenian quest would be in mid-third century or soon after. But other constructions could be put upon both **54** and **55**.

An archive of decrees was inscribed on opisthographic steles of grey marble, the same stone as that used for the temple. Only for **57** can the length of line be estimated with some confidence, on the assumption that the headings were centered and that the text did not extend onto a neighboring block. These texts have been understood as subsequent "renewals" of *asylia* granted by "our ancestors" (**57**.9), like the second series for Teos. Normally, however, what one "renews" in Hellenistic diplomacy is friendship, and this is done by the initiator as a preliminary to the substance of the mission; the word in effect means "remind." In the several fragments, the mention of the temple of Poseidon comes so soon after the verb of "renewing" that (under the presumed line length) one must assume that the Tenians "renewed" *asylia*. For this phrase we have one parallel (**154**): ἀνανεώσασθαι τάν τε συγγένειαν καὶ τὰν προϋπάρχουσαν φιλίαν τά τε δεδομένα τίμια ὑπὸ τᾶς ἁμᾶς πόλεως ἐν τοῖς πρότερον χρόνοις καὶ τὰν καθιέρωσιν τᾶς πόλιος καὶ τᾶς χώρας τῶι Διονύσωι. But even in this passage, it is still the Teans who did the "renewing," not Aptera. Thus strictly speaking there is no parallel for a grantor "renewing" *asylia*. As to what the Cretans now vote, the nearest we come is in **59**.5: perhaps to inscribe the old grants, as for Teos.

In this sense I follow others in taking these texts as "renewals" of *asylia*; but with the caution that with a longer line one might instead restore the familiar renewing of *friendship*, as a preliminary to the request for *asylia*. That is, these texts all might be reconstructed as initial grants, thus presumably contemporary with the Phocian decree; but this seems less likely than a "reminder" of the sort the Teans sent to Crete.

In what survives, the ambassadors are called *presbeutai* rather than *theoroi*. That is perhaps the best evidence for separating out this archive from the assured grant (**53**) and deducing that this mission concerned inscribing rather than the status of the cult. It is only in this renewal series that we hear of an oracle (**57**.6); that is the case also at Teos. *IG* 802 shows a *theoros* bearing an oracle of Delphi, and that will surely be the same quest that produced the Phocian decree.

Some letters (especially in **59**, badly corroded) have been lost to flaking since the earlier copies, which I have not marked.

56. Gortyn

Four joining fragments of a stele with molding at top, now in the Tenos museum; h. 0.12, w. 0.37, th. 0.03; letters of the first third of the second century B.C., h. 0.008 (0.014 lines 1–2), intersp. 0.005.

P. Graindor, *MusB* 11 (1907) 20 no. 32 [Hiller, *IG* XII.5 867]; Guarducci, *I.Cret.* IV 196 (squeeze consulted by Klaffenbach). *Collation.*

Photograph: PLATE 1.

Cf. Graindor, *MusB* 14 (1910) 91; Halbherr ap. Maiuri, *RendLinc* V. 20 (1911) 666–667; H. van Muttelsee, *Verfassungsgeschichte Kretas* (Hamburg 1925) 48–49; H. van Effenterre, *La Crète et le monde grec* (Paris 1948) 138.

δ ό γ μ α τ α Κ ρ η τ[ῶ ν]
Γ ο ρ τ υ ν ί[ω ν]
[ἐπὶ τῶν Αἰ]ν̣α̣ώνων κορμιόντων Γόρτ̣[υνι - - - - - - - - -]
4 [- - μηνὸς - - δευτέ]ρ̣α̣ι φίνοντος· ἀπο[- - - - - - - - - - -]
(traces of one line)

1 van Effenterre, Guarducci: Κρητ[αιέων] Hiller, Muttelsee. 3 init. Halbherr, Maiuri.

The regional heading used by the Tenians suggests a more systematic grouping of the documents than is evident in other *asylia* archives; the Coan archive is only quasi-geographical, grouped by the theoric missions themselves. The restoration Κρητ[αιέων] ought strictly to mean the Cretan League, which would be inappropriate here. The heading also implies that other places than Crete were approached in this "renewal."

If the headings are centered, a far shorter line was used here than in the other decrees of this archive.

3: The reverse order at *I.Cret.* IV 184: Γόρτυνι κορμιόντων.

4: Perhaps ἀπο[στείλαντος τοῦ δάμου τῶν Τηνίων κτλ.; cf. *I.Cret.* IV 181.

57–58

Fragment of grey marble from Tenos, badly corroded, left edge preserved (Athens, National Museum, no. 11567); h. 0.42, w. 0.28, th. 0.06.

57. Unknown Cretan city and Tylissus

Graindor 21–22 no. 32 bis; Hiller, *IG* XII.5 868B [Guarducci, *I.Cret.* I xxx 2]. *Collation.*

(traces of one line)

[Τ υ] λ ι σ ί[ω ν]
[ἐπὶ κόσμων τῶν σὺν - - -] τ̣ῶ Καλλιδρόμω, μην[ὸς - - - - - - - -· ἐπειδὴ]
[Τήνιοι φίλοι καὶ συγγενέες ὑπάρχ]οντες ἀπέστειλα̣[ν ψάφισμά τε καὶ πρεσ]-
[βευτὰς ca. 12 Διόφαντον Νι]κύλλου, ἀνανεῶν[ται τε τάν ἀσυλίαν καὶ]
[τὰ λοιπὰ τίμια τῶ ἱρῶ τῶ Ποτειδάωνος καὶ τ]ᾶς Ἀμφιτρίτας κ[- - - - - -]
[- - - - - - - - - - - - καὶ τ]ὼς χρησμὼς τῶ Ἀπέλ[λωνος τῶ Πυτίω - - - - -]
[- - - - - καὶ ἐπελθόντες ἐπὶ τὰ]ν ἐκκλησία[ν] ἀπελο[γίξαντο περὶ - - - - -]
[- - - - - - - - - - - - - - - τᾶς πό]λιος· ὅπως ὧν ἁ πόλις [- - - - - - - - - - - -]
[- - - - - - - - - - - - - - - - - -] ὑπὸ τῶν [πα]τέρων [- - - - - - - - - - - - - - -]
[- - - - - - - - - - - - - - - τάν τ]ε ποτὶ τὼς θεὼς εὐσ[έβειαν - - - - - - - - - -]
[- - - - - - - - - - - - - - - - - -]χ̣α̣[. . .]Λ . . τα καὶ ε[- - - - - - - - - - - - -]
[- - - - - - - - - - - - - -]ΗΡΗ̣ . [. . . .]ν̣έ̣σ̣[. .] . [- - - - - - - - - - - - - -]
[.] Ι [- - - - - - - -] Ι Ι [- - -]ΙΚ[. . . .]γαπ̣[- - - - - - - - - - - - - - - - -]
[-]ν̣α̣θ[- - - - - - - - - - - - - - - - - - -]
[-]ΩΣΤ[- - - - - - - - - - - - - - - - - - -]
[- - - - - - - - - - - - - - - - - - -] ἐ̣λ̣ε̣γοσ̣[αν - - - - - - - - - - - - - - - - -]
[-]Ο̣Ι \ΕΠΙΓΕ[- - - - - - - - - - - - - - - - -]
[- - - - - - - - - - - - - - - - - -]ΓΩ̣[. . .]διὸ κ̣αὶ ἐπο̣ι̣[ησάμεθα - - - - - - - - -]
[-]Λ̣ΕΝ . ΕΛΥΤΟ̣[- - - - - - - - - - - - - -]

Text of Hiller. 4–5 Rigsby: ἀνανεῶν[ταί τε τὰν φιλίαν τὰν ὑπάρχωσαν | τῶι τε ἱρῶι τ. Π. Hiller; τε τὰν ἀσυλίαν τῶ ἱρῶ - - - Guarducci. 5–6: κ[ατὰ - - - Guarducci, κ[αὶ τᾶι πόλι - - - τᾶι | Τυλισίων κατὰ τ]ὼς Hiller.

The traces at the top are the end of another decree.

58. Aptera (?)

Inscribed below **57**; line 1 larger.

Cf. van Effenterre 138–139.

[Ἀ π τ α ρ ?] α ί [ω ν]
[ἐπὶ τῶν - - - κοσμιόντων τῶν σὺ]ν̣ Ἀ̣στώχῳ̣ [- - - - - - - - - - - - - -]
[- - - - - - - - - - - - - - - πρεσβ]ευτὰν [- -]
[- - - - - - - - - - - -]ΛΙ[- - -]ν Καραίῳ̣ [- - - - - - - - - - - - - - - - - -]
[- - - - - - - - - - - - - - - - - τὼ]ς Τη̣ν̣ί̣ῳ[ς - - - - - - - - - - - - - - - - - - -]
[- - - - - - - - - - - - - - - - -]Τ̣ΑΑ̣Γ̣[- -]

1, 2 van Effenterre, from the position on the stone and parallels to the personal names.

59–60

Fragment broken on all sides, found in 1881 built into a wall of a church near the city; the reverse side of **57–58**, into which it fits (Athens, National Musuem, no. 11568); h. 0.33, w. 0.23, th. 0.034; letters 0.008 (headings 1.2), intersp. 0.007.

A. Latischew, *BCH* 7 (1883) 247–250 [*SGDI* IV p. 1032 (**59** only)]; E. Georgantopoulos, Τηνιακά (Athens 1889) 42–43; Hiller, *IG* XII.5 868A [Guarducci, *I.Cret.* II XVI 2 (**59** only)]. *Collation.*

Photograph: Hiller (squeeze, **59**.10–**60**); PLATE 2.

59. Lappa

Cf. Hiller, *BCH* 24 (1900) 615.

[- - - - - - - - - - - - - - - - - - -]\ΙΩΝ̣[- -]
[- - - - - - - - - - - - - - - - - -]ε̣ γε̣γραμ̣[μ]εν[- - - - - - - - - - - - - - - - - - -]
[-]ε̣ ἀ̣[ν]ανέωνται τ̣[ε τὰν ἀσυλίαν καὶ τὰ]
[λοιπὰ τίμια τῶ ἱρω τῶ Ποτειδάωνος καὶ τᾶς Ἀ]μ̣φιτρίτας καὶ τὰν [τῶν πολίων φιλίαν?·]
[δεδόχθαι τῶι δάμωι ἀναγράψαι? καθότι] π̣αρακαλῶντι Τήν[ιοι τάν τε]
[ἀσυλίαν τῶ ἱρῶ τῶ Ποτειδάωνος καὶ τὰ λο]ιπὰ παρὰ Λαππαίων [δεδομένα]
[τίμια· ἐπαινῶμεν δὲ καὶ τὼς πρεσβευτ]ὰ̣ς καὶ τὸν συνεσδεδαμ̣[ηκότα]
[αὐτοῖς - - - - - - - - - - - - - - - - ἐπ]ὶ τᾶι ἀναστροφᾶι ἃν ἐπο[ιήσαντο]
[ἀξίως ἀμφοτερᾶν τε τᾶν πολίων καὶ αὐσα]υτῶν· ἐποιησάμεθα δὲ αὐτ̣[- -]
[- τῶ] θεῶ καὶ τοῖς πρεσβευταῖς [- - - - - -]
[- - - - - - - - - - - - - - - - -]ΙΕ καιρὸν καὶ ἐν τῶι κοινῶ[ι τῶν Κρηταιέων]
[- - - - - - - - - - - -]Ι τῶι θεῶι. εὐτυχεῖτε.

Latischew's copy of **59–60** is useful for confirming a few letters that Hiller dotted; Georgantopoulos's copy is not useful. 3–7 Rigsby: τ̣[ε τὰν ἀσυλίαν τῶ ἱρῶ | τῶ Ποτειδάωνος καὶ τᾶς Ἀ]μ̣φιτρίτας καὶ τὰν̣ [ὑπάρχωσαν ταῖς πόλεσι φιλίαν | καὶ συμμαχίαν? καὶ] π̣αρ̣ακαλῶντι Την[ίως ὅπως ἀποδέχωνται τὸν στέφανον? καὶ τὰ λο]ιπὰ παρὰ Λαππαίων [τίμια καὶ φιλάνθρωπα, ἐπαινῶντι Hiller. 7–9: αὐτοῖς γραμματέα | τὸν δεῖνα ἐπ]ὶ (κτλ.) καὶ α]ὑτῶν Hiller. 9: αὐτ̣[οὺς καὶ προξένους? Latischew. 11 init.: Δ̣Ε Latischew.

This becomes a letter in form, like many of the Cretan responses to Teos. Hiller's restoration of 3 has Lappa renew the *asylia* of the temple and call on the Tenians to accept a crown. But the "renewer" should be the Tenians in the preliminaries; the decree proper, I believe, begins in line 5, whatever action was voted by Lappa.

2: Perhaps ἀκολούθως τοῖ]ς γεγραμ[μ]έν[οις.

7: A secretary accompanying the ambassadors, quite regular for foreign judges, is unparalleled in the *asylia* decrees.

60. Axus (?)

Inscribed below **59**; line 1 larger (0.013).

Cf. Paris, *BCH* 1887, 336 n. 1; van Effenterre 139–140.

[Ἀ ξ ί ω ?]ν
[- - - - - - - - - - - - - - - - - -]ωνος, Ἀλέξανδρος Φιλοκλεῖος [εἶ]-
[πεν· ἐπειδὴ Τήνιοι φίλοι καὶ οἰκεῖοι κα]ὶ συγγενέες ὑπάρχοντες τᾶς [τε]
4 [πόλιος ἁμῶν καὶ τῶ κοινῶ τῶ Κρηταιέ]ων, ἀποστήλαντες ψάφισμά [τε]
[καὶ πρεσβευτὰς ca. 13 κ]αὶ Διόφαντον Νικύλλω, ἀνανẹ[ῶν]-
[ται τὰν ἀσυλίαν τὰν παρὰ? τῶ κοινῶ τῶ]ν Κρηταιέων τῶι τε ἱρῶι τ[ῶ Ποτει]-
[δάωνος καὶ τὰ λοιπὰ τίμια? τᾶς πό]λ̣εος καὶ τᾶν νάσω κατạ[- - - - - - - -]
8 [- - - τὼς χρησμὼς τῶ Ἀ]πέλλωνος τῶ Πυτί[ω - - - - - - - - - - - - - - - - -]
[- - - καὶ ἐπελθόντε]ς ἐπὶ τὰν ἐσκλη̣[σίαν ἀπελογίξαντο περὶ - - - - - - - -]
[- - - τᾶ]ι π̣α̣τ̣ρ̣ί̣δ̣ι̣ [-]

1 van Effenterre, from the position on the stone. 6–7 Rigsby. 8: κατὰ τὰν μαντείαν τῶ Ἀ.] Paris.

I am not at all confident of the restorations suggested in 6–7, which make a difficult transition from the temple in the dative to the city and island in the genitive (especially given τε in 6). In the fragments of the "renewal" archive, this is our only mention of "city and island" as the subject; but elsewhere in these Cretan decrees "temple" is only a restoration, while "temple and island" were the subject of the Phocian grant.

7: The singular article does not need correction; for terminal ν for ς cf. **138**; **161**.20; *I.Cret.* I XXIII 4; *I.Mylasa* 650; *Gortina* I (Rome 1988) p. 331; Bechtel, *Die griechischen Dialekte* II (Berlin 1923) 737.

61. Rome

Fragment of grey marble found in the sea by the temple; h. 0.14, w. 0.21, th. 0.03; dots between words.

Graindor, *MusB* 12 (1908) 5ff. no. 1 (copy and squeezes by Sakellion) [*IG* XII.5 test. 1381].

[- - - - - - - - - - - - -]*ṿiolạṇ . ṣ* [- - -] . . *ọ*[- - - - - -]
[- - - - - - - - - - - - - -]*e delubra quei ut impeṇ*[- - - - -]
[- - - - - - - - - - - - - - -]*e praesident non solum .* [- - -]
4 [- - - - - - - - - - - - - - *f*]*ugerint omnes sacṛạṣ ạn*[- - - -]
[- - - - - - - - - - - - - -]*ipsa qua lege quoqụẹ jụ*[*re* - - - -]
[- - - *templum Neptun*]*o consacratum est atqụ*[*e* - - - - -]
[- - - - - - - - - - - - - -]*q̣ue iuṛẹ ẹṣ*[*t .*] *ḅḷạ?*[- - - - - -]

This Roman decision about the temple may derive from the senatorial review of A.D. 22, or from the work of Servilius Isauricus (40s B.C.), who we know restored some statues to the temple (*IG* 917). The remains defy restoration. Line 5 shows the argument from analogy that we meet elsewhere in Roman confirmations of *asylia*.

Finally, we have the following secondary items:

IG XII.5 802: The Tenians praise a Byzantine, Nymphaeus son of Athenaeon, for helping their *theoros* who was sent to proclaim the *asylia*: ἐπειδὴ [5–7] ἀποσταλεὶς θεωρὸς ὑπὸ προσ[τατῶ]ν ὥστε ἀπαγγεῖλαι τὴν ἀσυλίαν [Βυζαντίοι]ς[8] τὴν τοῦ ἱεροῦ τοῦ Ποσειδῶνος [κατὰ] τὰς μαντείας τῆς Πυθίας; Nymphaeus exerted every effort for the god and the *theoros* in the assembly (ἐν τῶι δήμωι). This surely alludes to the quest that also produced the Phocian decree; but the present decree cannot be closely dated. If Phormio son of Nymphaeus, a Byzantine active in Egypt in the years 217–204 (*Pros.Ptol.* VI 14635), was the son of the *theoros*, that might date the Tenians' quest well before the end of the third century; but it need not, nor is the filiation necessary.

IG XII.5 860 (cf. Etienne, *ZPE* 39 [1979] 145–149 [I B.C.]): In a time of threats by pirates, a Roman is praised for his aid: ἡγησάμενος εὐσεβὲς καὶ μεγαλοπρεπὲς ὑπ[άρ]χειν ἑαυτῷ τὴν προσήκουσαν τῆς πατρίδος ἡμῶν ποιήσασ[θαι] φροντίδα, ἀρχαίας νήσου καὶ ἱερᾶς ὑπαρχούσης. This last description may be no more than vague and grandiloquent; but similar statements are made about Pergamum and Ephesus under Roman rule in possible allusion to their declared inviolability.

Tacitus *Ann.* 3.63: In A.D. 22 the Tenians showed the Senate an oracle of Apollo "wherein they were ordered to dedicate a statue and shrine to Neptune." This appears to be the foundation text of the cult rather than the oracle that called for *asylia*.

Certainty is out of reach, but I would urge that we have no intrinsic basis for dating the Phocian decree, our clearest text, and hence no reason to put it earlier than others. If **53** and **54** are indeed recognitions for the temple, then the probable date for the Tenians' quest is the period 250–225 B.C. But they need not be, and the quest and the Phocian decree then might well be as late as ca. 200, when Tenos became the center of the Island League. The "renewal" seen in the archive would seem to belong in the next generation.

8. Hiller and Etienne (*Tenos* II 95) considered the space too short to restore the Byzantines; but Klaffenbach from the squeeze thought it possible (*IG* XII Suppl. p. 134), and Gauthier (ap. Etienne) urged that only a citizen could have supported a foreign *theoros* in the assembly.

Chalcedon

In Roman times a visitor to Chalcedon remarked that among all the monuments in the city notable for age and history none was more marvelous than the oracular temple of Apollo, inferior to none of the greatest oracles in the world.[1] This shrine, the oldest of the Chalcedonians, was chosen by Cocconas, associate of Alexander the False Prophet, as the lucrative place in which to fabricate oracles of his own (Lucian *Alex.* 10). Around 250 B.C. the Istrians consulted the Chalcedonian god concerning the worship of Sarapis.[2] The epigrammatist Antiphilus of nearby Byzantium (first century A.D.) could evoke this oracle in the briefest terms: Φοῖβος ἐρεῖ.[3] Apolline types, such as the lyre and tripod, dominate the city's coins; one series shows the god seated on an *omphalos*.[4] An inscribed act of Hellenistic date is headed by the chief magistrates: βασιλεύς, ἱερομνάμων, προφήτης, νομοφύλακες; the third, obviously an important figure, must have served Apollo.[5] Boeckh first recognized the Chalcedonian Apollo as Pythian, arguing from the Pythian games mentioned on coins and from the cult of Apollo Πυθαεύς at Chalcedon's mother city Megara. The Pythia were Panhellenic in imperial times.[6] Thus many testimonies show that Chalcedon was the city of Apollo. But the two extant inscriptions concerning *asylia* at Chalcedon suggest that his worship was not simple in its history or its geography.

1. Dionysius of Byzantium frag. 67 (*GGM* II 93). Testimonia on Chalcedon are collected by Merkelbach, *I.Kalchedon* pp. 91–141.

2. Pippidi, *I.Scythiae* I 5 (= *SEG* 24.1091).

3. *Anth. Gr.* 9.551; cf. Gow and Page, *The Garland of Philip* (Oxford 1968) II 123.

4. *Recueil gén.* I.2 294ff.; Seyrig, *Essays . . . Stanley Robinson* (Oxford 1968) 196–197 (*Scripta numism.* 228–229); K. Hanell, *Megarische Studien* (Lund 1934) 165.

5. *I.Kalch.* 7; cf. 19, 42; a prophetess at 61; cf. Hanell 150; Robert, *RPhil* III.13 (1939) 188 (*Op. min. sel.* II 1341).

6. *IGR* I 802, IV 161; *MAMA* VIII 521.

Chalcedon city occupied a small peninsula (modern Kadıköy) jutting into the entrance to the Bosporus; a wall separated the city proper from its extensive mainland territory.[7] Some ruins were still visible in the sixteenth century, but all have yielded to modern construction. In fact **63–64** is the only inscription from the site that actually names the ancient city. So the topography of Chalcedon is in general obscure; but Dionysius and Lucian leave no doubt that the oracular shrine was in the city itself, not outside in its territory.

Our two inscriptions are a Delphian decree found at Delphi and a fragment of an archive of decrees found at Kadıköy. Discrepancies between the two inscriptions have given rise to not a little debate. In fact the differences are striking and decisive: Delphi (**62**) declares the temple of "Apollo Pythaeus in the Chalcedonia" to be inviolable and a refuge; Phocaea and Tenedos (**63–64**) declare the city of Chalcedon sacred and inviolable, and in the name of Apollo Chresterius. Lemerle took it that the Phocaeans wrote "Chresterius" (**63**.5; the Tenedians used no epithet) as an ignorant choice of their own, the true epithet being Pythaeus, as in the Delphian decree. Klaffenbach rightly countered that *asylia* decrees normally repeat the language of the request. Latte concluded that the original Megarian epithet "Pythaeus" was supplanted by "Chresterius" when the shrine became oracular—after **62** but before **63–64**;[8] so there would be two occasions, the *asylia* of the temple being extended to include the whole city. Klaffenbach, however, thought the dates too close to allow for a change in the cult title and assumed, like Lemerle, a single occasion: the god will have possessed both epithets, although Klaffenbach did not explain how the Delphians can have used one and the Phocaeans the other. We know now, moreover, that whatever the relative and absolute dates of the two inscriptions, the oracular power of Apollo is older than both, and thus the god cannot have changed his name between the two upon becoming oracular.[9]

The burden of these discrepancies is greater than has been realized.[10] The two inscriptions share no signficant phrase, precisely where (as Klaffenbach remarked) *asylia* decrees regularly echo the terms of the request. Thus the god's epithet is different; one inscription concerns the temple, the other the city; at Delphi we have the highly individual ἄσυλον καὶ φύκτιμον, in the other inscription the familiar ἱερὰν καὶ ἄσυλον. But the crucial difference is geographical: the Delphians' explicit and pointed τὸ ἐν τᾶι Καλχαδονίαι (**62**.4) must mean that the temple of Apollo Pythaeus was not in the city proper at

7. On the region see R. Janin, *EchOr* 21 (1922) 335–386; 22 (1923) 50–58, 182–198; 26 (1927) 287–303.

8. K. Latte, "Orakel," *RE* 18 (1939) 848.

9. Pippidi recognized this in publishing the Istrian inscription and adduced the coins as further early evidence; followed by Pouilloux.

10. For fuller discussion, especially on the Megarian background, see Rigsby, *GRBS* 28 (1987) 93–102.

Kadıköy but somewhere out in the territory[11]—as was usual when it was a temple that received the status. By contrast, it is expressly the city (and not the familiar "city and country") that Phocaea and Tenedos declare sacred and inviolable to Apollo Chresterius; and we know from the literary sources that the oracular shrine of Apollo was in the city itself.

We have therefore not merely two occasions but two sacred places: Apollo Pythaeus in the countryside, Apollo Chresterius in the city. This split in the worship of Apollo appears to reflect a similar split in the original cult of Apollo Pythaeus at Megara; and Miletus supplies a well-documented parallel. Of our two inscriptions, the Delphian is clearly the older, perhaps by a generation or more: as at Megara, first honor at Chalcedon went to the country god, whose epithet reflected still the Megarian origin of Chalcedon. The city god ranked second; his epithet changed when the oracular power of this shrine exhibited itself, at some date before the Hellenistic age (Apollo of Megara had no oracle). Both were important to the Chalcedonians, but owing to the growing popularity of the oracle the city temple has eclipsed the country temple in our literary evidence.[12] Thus Chalcedon was one of those few cities that eventually gained two recognitions of *asylia* for two places; so too Pergamum and Stratoniceia later.

Of topography we are not wholly ignorant. The archive fragment **63–64** was found (though not in situ) at Moda on the southern side of Kadıköy, the area thought to be the oldest part of the ancient city;[13] probably somewhere in this region we should place the temple of Apollo Chresterius. Of the chief temple, Apollo Pythaeus in the country, we can say only that it was not on the Bosporan coast, about which we are richly informed:[14] rather in the interior, which is little known—perhaps, like that of Apollo Pythaeus in the Megarid, at some high place within a day's walk of the city. One thinks of the pleasant heights of Big and Little Çamlica several miles northeast of Kadıköy, to which modern Istanbulers like to resort for picnics.

The two inscriptions thus seem to stem from two episodes, not one. The date and context of these events are problematic. On the basis of letterforms, the Delphian inscription has been assigned to the last third of the third century B.C., the archive fragment to the end of the third or the beginning of the second.[15] The former has A with straight crossbar; N and Π with right hasta only half descended; Θ, O, and Ω somewhat small and raised; Σ with splayed arms.

11. Such was the common usage of Greek; for Chalcedon see Hdt. 4.85, τῆς Καλχηδονίης, of a place at the northern end of the Bosporus.

12. The temple at Lucian *Alex.* 10 (ὅπερ ἀρχαιώτατόν ἐστι τοῖς Χαλκηδονίοις) is the city temple of Apollo; but his adjective need not be taken literally; cf. p. 7.

13. On Moda see Janin (1922) 354.

14. See Janin, and Oberhummer, "Bosporos 1," *RE* 3 (1899) 742–757.

15. So, on the Delphian stone, Pomtow, followed by Pouilloux; on the Chalcedonian, Laurent, followed by Klaffenbach, who nevertheless thought that the two must be contemporary.

It might be little later than the mid-third century. The Kadıköy inscription has small apices, A sometimes with broken crossbar, the hasta of N and Π further descended, arms of Σ quite parallel; it cannot comfortably be placed much earlier than ca. 200 B.C. The texts at Kadıköy show the fully evolved formulary of *asylia* decrees. The Delphian one is clipped and undeveloped, and its φύκτιμος unique in the decrees, as though the formulae have not yet become firm. The inviolability of the two temples might be separated by as much as half a century, though a much shorter hiatus is of course possible.

Greater precision is speculative. In the 220s the city cooperated with Byzantium in taxing traffic on the Bosporus, which led to the intervention of Rhodes.[16] In 202 Philip V compelled Chalcedon, which with Lysimacheia and Cius had recently joined the Aetolians, to abandon the alliance and join him (Cius, which refused, he destroyed).[17] Chalcedon's alliance with Aetolia is usually placed between the beginnings of the First Macedonian War ca. 215 and the start of Philip's invasion of Thrace ca. 204. We might imagine the first grant of *asylia* in a time of good relations with the Aetolians and the Amphictyony, the second a decade later during the negotiations with Philip. But these events and political ties need have no relation to *asylia* at Chalcedon.[18]

On each of our two occasions, an oracle prompted the quest for *asylia*. The Chalcedonians had no need to go abroad for their oracles, and at least on the second occasion the source was Apollo Chresterius himself (**63**.5, **64**.5). The latter decrees mention "oracles" in the plural (**63**.5, 9, 16; **64**.5, 10). This might be taken as further evidence for the two occasions; but in fact oracles often accumulated before they were actually fulfilled. Finally, in no text is there question of games of Apollo.

The odd vocabulary of the Delphian grant reflects, I believe, a relatively early date, perhaps not much after 250 B.C. What is odd in the second grant is the specification of the city alone, not the usual city and country. Smyrna offers a parallel, but I suggest that the explanation lies in the existing facts at Chalcedon. While Pergamum and Stratonicea would also receive two recognitions, these were for temples in the countryside, and there can have been no question of overlapping inviolable boundaries. When the Chalcedonians sought *asylia* for their city temple, the formula "city and country" was conventional for that situation; but the country place already had the status, and perhaps they limited

16. Polyb. 4.38ff., with Seyrig, *Scripta numism.* 215–235.

17. Polyb. 15.23.8; cf. Walbank, *Comm.* II 477–479; Schmitt, *Staatsvertr.* III 549 and *Untersuchungen* 234. Merkelbach (*I.Kalch.* p. 10) deduced from *Orac.Sib.* 3.434–435 ("Chalcedon . . . , you also one day an Aetolian child will come and plunder") that Aetolians attacked Chalcedon between 220 and 210.

18. See Flacelière, *Aitoliens* 312 n. 3, and Klaffenbach, against the precision of Pomtow (ca. 213–203 B.C.).

the honor for the city god to the city itself so as not to subsume or encroach upon the older honor of the country temple.

62. Delphi

Delphi, temple of Apollo. White marble stele found in 1894 north of the opisthodomos, near the steps of the theater; now in the Delphi museum (inv. 1906). Broken at the top; h. 0.275, w. 0.22 at bottom, 0.195 at top, th. 0.085; letters 0.007 (last two lines 0.006), intersp. 0.006. Lettering of the last third of III B.C. (see above).

H. Pomtow, *Klio* 15 (1918) 14–15 no. 38; *Syll.*[3] 550 [Schwyzer 330a; Merkelbach, *I.Kalchedon* p. 116]; Pouilloux, *FD* III.4 372. *Collation.*

Photograph: Pouilloux pl. 8A; PLATE 3.

[.....]ΙΟΝ εἶμεν, ἀγαθ̣ᾶ̣[ι τύχαι,]
[δεδ]όχθαι τᾶι πόλι τῶν Δελφῶ[ν]
[τ]ὸ ἱερὸν τοῦ Ἀπόλλωνος το[ῦ]
4 Πυθαίου τὸ ἐν τᾶι Καλχαδο-
νίαι ἄσυλον καὶ φύκτιμον ε[ἶ]-
μεν ἀπὸ πάντων, ὧι ταὶ στᾶ-
λαι ὁρίζοντι, κατὰ τὰν τοῦ
8 θεοῦ μαντείαν· ἀγγράψαι δὲ
τὸ ψάφισμα τόδε ἐστάλαν λ[ι]-
θίναν καὶ ἀνθέμεν ἐν τὸ ἱε-
ρὸν τοῦ Ἀπόλλωνος.
12 Ῥοδοκλῆς Ἡροδώρο Βοιώτιος
ἐπεμελήθη.

1: Hiller suggested [λῶιον καὶ ἄμει]ν̣ον, Pomtow [ἐπειδὴ - - - ἁ πόλις τῶν Καλχαδονίων - - - παρακαλεῖ, τὸ ἱερὸν τοῦ Ἀπόλλωνος τοῦ Πυθαίου ἄσυλον καὶ φύκτι]μ̣ον.

This is not a summary of a decree like **1**, but a decree of unaccustomed brevity. For what immediately preceded the extant text, the beginning of the formula of oracles (Hiller) has no place here, thus truncated and without the necessary dependent clause ("that it is better and more fitting *to recognize*," etc.). Pomtow's suggestion makes better sense but renders the whole strangely repetitious.

5: φύκτιμος recurs in our inscriptions only in a boundary of the temple of Apollo at Delphi (p. 48) and in Caesar's edict for Sardes (**214**.48). Plutarch applies the term to Romulus' asylum on the Capitolium (p. 576). Polybius uses it of a purely secular place of refuge (9.29.4, 13.6.9), like Medea's γῆν ἄσυλον (Eur. *Med.* 387). As old as Homer (*Od.* 5.359; cf. Ap. Rhod. 2.1147), the word evidently has a literary ring and is used here to expand on the bare *asylos*; I assume that it had occurred in the verse oracle that prompted the quest.

12: The name Rhodocles recurs in Boeotia at Lebadeia (three men in the first century A.D., *IG* VII 3077 and 3106). Rhodocles' role here is unclear. He has been invoked in order to date the act to a period when Boeotia had a seat on the Amphictyonic Council.[19] The Council does sometimes instruct one of its members to see to the inscribing of a text (cf. **3**.17); but this is a decree of the city of Delphi, and it includes a provision to inscribe the text. When Delphian decrees state who is to see to the inscribing, it is usually οἱ ἄρχοντες (e.g., *FD* III.3 120.19); a Boeotian can have had no formal role here. One assumes that the Council also recognized the inviolability of Apollo of Chalcedon; if Rhodocles was now a member, the Boeotian representative, perhaps he was ordered to see to the Council's inscription and volunteered to take care of that of the city of Delphi at the same time.[20] But this is an independent monument, small and not very finely written. It may be that Rhodocles was a private citizen acting as a friend to Chalcedon or to Delphi; if that is so, his gesture cannot help date this text.

63–64

Chalcedon. White marble slab found in rubble beneath a burned schoolhouse of the convent of Notre Dame-de-Sion, in the Moda district of Kadıköy; the stone has been reworked since antiquity for reuse; h. 0.635, w. 0.746; lettering of late III/early II B.C. (see above).

V. Laurent, *EchOr* 27 (1928) 24–44 [*SEG* 4.720 (Robert)]; Klaffenbach, *Varia epigraphica,* AbhBerl 1958.2 (Berlin 1958) 10–14 no. 4 (squeeze, photograph) [*SEG* 17.540]; Merkelbach, *I.Kalchedon* 5 (squeeze).

Photograph: Laurent p. 27, Merkelbach pl. 1.

63. Phocaea

[Φωκαέων]

[ἔδοξεν τῆι βουλῆι καὶ τῶι δήμωι· ἐπειδὴ Καλχηδόνιοι φίλοι τε καὶ εὔνοι]
[διὰ προγόνων] τ̣ῆ̣ι̣ [πό]λει ἡμῶ̣[ν ὑπάρχοντες ἀπεστάλκασι ψήφισμα καὶ πρεσ]-
[βευτὰς] Ἀντικράτη καὶ Δημύλο̣ν̣ [καὶ...]υ̣σιμ̣[- - - ἐμφανίζοντες πε]-
[ρὶ χρησ]μῶν αὐτοῖς ὑπὸ Ἀπόλλωνος τοῦ Χρηστ̣η̣ρ̣[ίου δεδομένων, ἐν]
[οἷς φησ]ιν τὴμ πόλιν τὴν Καλχηδονίων εἶναι ἑαυτοῦ καὶ ὑπάρχειν ἄπ̣[ασιν]
[ἀνθρώποι]ς ἱερὰν καὶ ἄσυλον, καὶ π̣αρακαλοῦσιν ἡμᾶς συναυξῆσαι τ̣[ὰς τοῦ]
[θεοῦ τιμά]ς, καθότι καὶ ἐπιβάλλει ἡμῖν, καὶ ἀποδεῖξαι τὴμ πόλιν τὴν Καλχηδ[ονίων]
[ἱερὰν καὶ ἄ]συλον κατὰ τὰς τοῦ θεοῦ μαντείας· ἐπελθόντες δὲ καὶ οἱ πρεσβ[ευταὶ]

19. Pouilloux points to 217–212 but is rightly skeptical about the role of Rhodocles for dating the event. According to Flacelière, *Aitoliens* (and there are many gaps in the evidence), there was a Boeotian seat in the years 245–235, ca. 229–219, 217–212.

20. Pomtow thought (mistakenly) that some of the forms in the decree are exclusively Boeotian, and attributed these to Rhodocles. Unless Rhodocles actually composed or carved the text, his own dialect is irrelevant.

[ἐπὶ τὴν βου]λὴν καὶ τὴν ἐκλησίαν διελέγησαν ἀκολούθως τοῖς ἐν τῶι ψηφίσ̣[ματι]
[γεγραμμέ]νοις, ἀγαθῆι τύχηι καὶ ἐπὶ σωτηρίαι τοῦ τε Φωκαέων δήμου καὶ τ̣[οῦ Καλ]-
[χηδονίω]ν, δεδόχθαι τῆι βουλῆι καὶ τῶι δήμωι ἀποκρίνασθαι Καλχηδον[ίοις διό]-
[τι ὁ Φωκα]έων δῆμος διά τε τὴν ἐκ προγόνων ὑπάρχουσαν αὐτῶι εὐ[σέβει]-
[αν πρὸς τ]ὸ θεῖον καὶ διὰ τὴν πρὸς Καλ[χ]ηδονίους εὔνο̣ιάν τε καὶ φιλίαν κ[αὶ βου]-
[λόμενος] συναύξειν τὰς τῶν θεῶν τιμὰς ἀποδέχεται τὴμ πόλιν αὐ[τῶν ἱε]-
[ρὰν καὶ] ἄσ[υ]λον καὶ ἀποδεικνύει κατὰ τὰς τοῦ θεοῦ μαντείας· τοὺ[ς δὲ]
[- - -]ους δοῦναι τοῖς πρεσβευταῖς ξένια τὰ ἐκ τοῦ νόμου.

Text of Klaffenbach. 3 init.: [ἐκ παλαιῶν χρόνων] Laurent. 3–4: ἀπέ|στειλαν Laurent, ἀποστεί|λαντες Robert. 4: [οἳ μὲν ε]ῦ̣ ση[μαίνουσιν?] Laurent. 5–6: [- - - ἀποφαίνον|τες ἡμ]ῖ̣ν Laurent, ἀποφαίνου|σιν Robert. 7–8 Laurent; cf. **64**.8: τῶν | θεῶν Merkelbach, from 15. 11–12 Robert: τ̣[ῆς πόλε|ως αὐτῶ]ν Laurent. 14–15 Robert: κ[αὶ φιλο|τιμίαν] Laurent. 16–17: ἐπι|[μηνί]ους Laurent, στρατηγ]οὺς? Merkelbach.

. . .

(4–9) [describing the oracles given] them by Apollo Chresterius in which he says that the city of the Chalcedonians is his and is for all [mankind] sacred and inviolable, and they call upon us to join in increasing [the honors of the god], as is in fact incumbent upon us, and declare the city of the Chalcedonians [sacred and] inviolable in keeping with the oracles of the god (etc.)

Hellenistic Phocaea is poorly documented; of decrees there is little to compare.[21] The city joined Attalus I in 218 (Polyb. 5.77) but had reverted to the Seleucid alliance before 191 (App. *Syr.* 22). It was favorably treated in the peace of 188, its ancestral constitution and territory restored (Polyb. 21.45.7). The tantalizing fragment from Delos mentioning Phocaea (*Staatsvertr.* III 550) is roughly contemporary with our decree.

2: Klaffenbach's restoration is doubtful; *I.Priene* 65 has γνώμη στρατηγῶν after the decree formula.

8: The recognition of inviolability is taken to be an obvious moral duty; cf. at Amorgos καθότι ἐπέβα[λλ]εν ἀ[ν]δρ[ὶ] καλῶ[ι καὶ ἀγαθῶι κ]αὶ τῶν ἀρίστων [γ]εγονότ[ι ζ]ηλ[ωτῆι (*IG* XII.7 231.5 for a doctor). For the sentiment compare Eumenes' urging to Cos, ὥσ]περ ὑμῖν ἁρμόζει (**176**.36), and the frequent response to the Teans, "we too worship Dionysus." The action is "declare" in the request, "accept and declare" in the response (15–16).

17: As Klaffenbach remarks, we do not know which magistrates at Phocaea were in charge of such expenditures. The Phocaeans make no provision for inscribing the decree.

21. Cf. *I.Priene* 65, with Robert, *RA* 1926 II, 180–181 (*Op. min. sel.* I 239–240).

64. Tenedos

Inscribed below **63**.

Τενεδίων

ἔδοξεν τ]ᾶι βόλλαι καὶ τῶι δάμωι, γνώμα τᾶς βόλλας· ἐπειδὴ Κα[λχαδό]-
[νιοι φίλ]οι ἔοντες κ[αὶ] οἴκειοι καὶ σύμμαχοι ἐκ παλαίων χρόνων τ[αῖς πόλι]-
4 [ος ταῖς Τ]ενεδίων ἀπεστάλκαισι ψάφισμα καὶ πρέσβεα Δήμ[υλον ἐμ]-
[φανίζ]οντες διότι ὁ Ἀπόλλων πὰρ αὔτοις ἐξενηνόχει χρήσμο[ις δι']
[ὧν ἀπ]οφαίνεται ταὶν πόλιν ταὶν Καλχαδονίων ἔμμεναι ἐαύ[τω καὶ]
[ὐπάρχ]ειν πάντεσσι ἀνθρώποις ἴραν καὶ ἄσυλον, καὶ παρκα[λείοισι]
8 [Καλχαδ]όνιοι τὸ⟨ν⟩ δᾶμον συναύξησαι ταὶς τῶ θέω τίμαις καὶ Α[- - -]
[ἀπόδειξα]ι ταὶν πόλιν ταὶν Καλχαδονίων ἴραν καὶ ἄσυλον κὰτ [τοὶς τῶ]
[θέω χρήσ]μοις, [κα]ὶ ὁ παρέων πὰρ αὔτοις πρέσβευς ἐπέλθων ἐπ[ὶ ταὶν]
[βόλλαιν καὶ τὸν δ]ᾶμον διελέχθη ἀκολούθως τοῖς ἐν [τῶι ψαφίσματι]
12 [γεγραμμένοις], σπούδαις καὶ φιλοτιμίαις οὖθεν ἐ[λλείπων, ἀγάθαι τύχαι]
[καὶ ἐπὶ σωτηρίαι,] δεδ[όχ]θαι τᾶι βόλ[λαι κ]αὶ τῶ[ι δάμωι - - -]

4: τῶν Τ]ενεδίων ἀπεστάλκασι Laurent. 5–6, or ἐν | οἷς Klaffenbach: οἳ δὲ ἡ|μῖν ἀπ]οφαίνοντα[ι] Laurent, καὶ ἡ|μῖν Robert. 7: the mason has corrected ΙΕΡΑΝ to Aeolic ΙΡΑΝ (likewise in 9); παρκάλ[ουσι] Laurent. 8: ΤΟΙΔ lapis. 8–9: ἀ[ποδεῖ|ξαι κα]ὶ Laurent, ἀ[πόδειξαι | {ἀπόδειξα]ι} Klaffenbach, ἀ[κολουθῶς?] Merkelbach. 9–10: κατ[ότι ἐν τοῖς | χρήσμ]οις Laurent, κατ[ὰ τοὶς χρήσμ]οις Robert. 12–13: κατ' οὐθένα τρόπον?·| ἀγαθᾶι τύχαι Laurent.

Other decrees of Tenedos are *IG* XII Suppl. 147–148 (II B.C.: both proposed by individuals rather than the council). The city was presumably Attalid;[22] the decree reveals that Tenedos was now an ally of Chalcedon (line 3). Only one ambassador, diverting from the other two in the party, visited the island, which perhaps was judged less important than Phocaea.

5: ἐκφέρω, to "divulge" an oracle to an assembly at Hdt. 5.79; cf. Diod. 1.27.6: τοὺς ἱερεῖς . . . μὴ βούλεσθαι τἀληθὲς ἐκφέρειν εἰς τοὺς πολλούς.

22. Cf. Livy 31.16.7. For its links with the mainland see L. Robert, *Etudes de numismatique grecque* (Paris 1951) 10–11; J. M. Cook, *The Troad* (Oxford 1973) 189–198.

Miletus

The chief god of the Milesians was Apollo, represented by the Delphinium in the city and the Didymeum in the country. The latter stands more than fifteen kilometers south of Miletus, linked to the city by a sacred way and also easily reached by sea.[1] Didyma, a large complex that included a village (οἱ τὸ ἱερὸν κατοικοῦντες),[2] was one of the great oracular shrines of the Greek world, patronized already by the eastern monarchs of early times (Hdt. 1.92, Croesus), and flourishing especially in the Hellenistic and Roman ages; the cult enjoyed the particular favor of the Seleucids, descended as they were from Apollo. His games, the Didymeia, became Panhellenic late in the third century B.C. In A.D. 26 the Milesians lost in the competition to host the provincial temple of Tiberius on the grounds that they seemed fully occupied with the worship of Apollo, as were the Ephesians with Artemis (Tac. *Ann.* 4.55.2: *caerimonia occupavisse*).

Tacitus' account of the senatorial review of A.D. 22 places the Milesians' claim of *asylia* for the Didymeum among the oldest, for "they relied on King Darius" (*Ann.* 3.63). The epigraphical record suggests instead the more familiar situation, Greek recognitions late in the third century B.C.: Tacitus' report is neither complete nor exact. The precedent of Darius might be a Hellenistic

1. W. Günther, *Das Orakel von Didyma in hellenistischer Zeit,* IstMitt-BH 4 (Tübingen 1971), and J. Fontenrose, *Didyma* (Berkeley 1988), both with further bibliography; cf. Robert, *Op. min. sel.* III 1622–1639, V 584–615; *Hellenica* XI–XII (1960) 440–489. The sacred way is richly documented by *I.Delphinion* 133; on the territory of Miletus see M. Piérart, *MusHelv* 40 (1983) 1–18; 42 (1985) 276–299. Note the Milesians' temple of Apollo at Naucratis (Hdt. 2.178; cf. A. B. Lloyd, *Herodotus Book II* II, EPOR 43.3 [Leiden 1988] 228) and a statue dedicated by some Milesians at Medinet Habu (τὸν πάτριον θεὸν Διδυμέα Ἥλιον Ἀπόλλωνα, *SB* 1530); Milesian sailors' dedications on Cos to Apollo Didymeus (Segre, *Iscr.Cos* EV14, 192); and Damodamas' altar on the Syr Darya (Pliny *HN* 6.49, with Robert, *DAM* 455–460).

2. References at K. Tuchelt, *Vorarbeiten zu einer Topographie von Didyma,* IstMitt-BH 9 (Tübingen 1973) 29–30.

forgery. But the Achaemenids were especially friendly to Apollo, and it seems more likely that the Milesians had a legitimate Greek text of some Persian benefit or immunity for the temple of the sort we know elsewhere.[3] In my view it cannot have been, at that early date, a grant of *asylia* isto nomine, but perhaps some fiscal immunity, which the Milesians will have evoked in their discourse on the traditional privileges of the temple. For this wide scope we may compare the arguments offered by the Ephesians.

Miletus contradicts the "rule" that rural shrines received *asylia* alone, urban ones the whole city and territory; for *Syll.*[3] 590 is explicit that "the city and country" of Miletus became inviolable in honor of Apollo Didymeus—the rural god. In the city proper was the temple of Apollo Delphinius, prominent in the life of Miletus, but not the honorand of the status. It is perhaps relevant that, at least in Roman times, some events of the Great Didymeia were celebrated in the city and others at the temple (*I.Didyma* 183). Inscriptions of imperial date attribute *asylia* to the temple alone; but that surely represents both the *interpretatio Romana* of asylum and the constriction that came after the punishment of the city for its Mithridatic stance.

In the 250s B.C. Antiochus II freed the Milesians of a tyrant and gave them freedom and democracy,[4] which they seem to have preserved for the rest of the century, maintaining effective independence from the competing monarchies.[5] From the second half of the third century comes a bilateral treaty of personal inviolability with the Aetolians.[6] In the third century Miletus fought a war with Priene (*I.Priene* 26), and in the 180s with Heracleia and with Magnesia on the Maeander, the latter settled without reference to the *asylia* of either Miletus or Magnesia;[7] evidently this relationship was not felt to overlap or compete with territorial inviolability. At the Peace of Apamea in 188 B.C., sacred land that Miletus had lost in war was restored to the city's possession (Μιλησίοις δὲ τὴν ἱερὰν χώραν ἀποκατέστησαν, ἧς διὰ τοὺς πολέμους πρότερον ἐξεχώρησαν, Polyb. 21.45.5). Didyma is in Plutarch's list of inviolable temples attacked by pirates in the first century B.C. For siding with Mithridates in the 80s Miletus was punished with the loss of the Didymeia.

3. Cf. Meiggs/Lewis no. 12, with discussion and parallels in L. Boffo, *BollIstDirRom* III.20 (1978) 267–303, esp. 273–274.

4. Rehm, *I.Didyma* 358; App. *Syr.* 65.

5. See M. Holleaux, *Rome, la Grèce et les monarchies hellénistiques* (Paris 1921) 91; *Etudes* IV 329–331 (cf. Gauthier, *Symbola* 266 n. 160; H. Müller, *Milesische Volksbeschlüsse,* Hypomnemata 47 [Göttingen 1976] 14–15; R. S. Bagnall, *Administration of the Ptolemaic Possessions* [Leiden 1976] 174), against the notion (based on the vague and inflated claims of the Adulis inscription, *OGIS* 54.13) that Miletus became Ptolemaic soon after 246 (e.g., Hiller, *RE* 15 [1932] 1607).

6. *Staatsvertr.* III 564, with Gauthier, *Symbola* 263–265; Ziegler (above, p. 13) 189–190.

7. *Syll.*[3] 633; 588, with R. M. Errington, *Chiron* 19 (1989) 279–288, for the date.

Upon his accession to the throne in 246, Seleucus II was approached by his allies with congratulations, as we have seen at Smyrna, and doubtless with requests for favors. We have most of his response to the Milesian embassy; it has been suggested that this response included a declaration of inviolability.[8] The king evokes the benefactions given Miletus by his ancestors because of the oracles of Apollo Didymeus and their kinship with the god and cites the crown the Milesians have brought him from the Didymeum; he approves their loyalty and then proceeds: "reckoning it of first importance to bring [your city] to a more distinguished standing ... benefactions ..." Holleaux's restorations make this an increase of their existing privileges:

> προθυμούμενοι καὶ ἐν τοῖς μεγίστοις ἡγούμεν[οι τὴμ πολιν ὑμῶν] εἰς ἐπιφανεστέραν διάθεσιν ἀγαγεῖν κ[αὶ τὰ ὑπάρχοντα ὑμῖν] φιλάνθρωπα ἐπίδ[οσιν λαβόντα ἣν προαιρεῖσθε ἐπαῦξαι - - -]

The final words restored ("to increase your present privileges in the way you desire," Welles) are questionable, and we must in any case doubt that *asylia* was what the king went on to recognize. He has said nothing about the Milesians' or his own piety, which we would expect in a grant of inviolability, nor does the surviving text suggest that the ambassadors made any request of him. Admittedly the Milesians were later to claim that the Greek world granted Miletus *asylia* "unasked" (see below), but that claim is intrinsically unlikely. In the final extant line the king may in fact be waxing more general rather than more specific, promising vaguely to seek to improve their condition in the future (so Ptolemy II to Miletus ca. 260, *Royal Corres.* 14). The verb ἐπιδιδόναι in public acts, when it is not "donate," is frequent with the reflexive, "devote oneself" to public good;[9] and we find this usage of promises for the future, thus **102**.64: ἀπαράκλητος ἑαυτὸν ἐπιδώσει. Such may have been the sentiment here, ἐπιδ[ώσομεν ἡμᾶς. And there are of course other possibilities, including Haussoullier's ἐπὶ δ[ὲ τούτοις - - -.

Accordingly, I do not include this letter as a grant of *asylia*.[10] This incidentally eliminates a chronological discrepancy, for **65** seems to be a generation later than Seleucus' letter.

Our fullest reference to the inviolability of Miletus comes from the Milesians themselves rather than from a foreign recognition. Between 218/7 and 206/5 the Didymeia were recognized as Panhellenic. We have the Milesian decree requesting that honor, in the version sent to Cos (*Syll.*[3] 590.4–18):

8. *Royal Corres.* 22 (= *I.Didyma* 493); cf. Günther 66–85.

9. E.g., *Royal Corres.* 75.6; *Syll.*[3] 591.4; *I.Priene* 108.147; cf. Robert, *Op. min. sel.* I 197.

10. That the stele was erected in the Didymeum is not evidence that the letter concerned the temple, for other public acts were inscribed there: e.g., *I.Didyma* 487 (honors for foreign judges), 492 (letters of Antiochus II concerning the property of Laodice). L. Boffo, *I re ellenistici e i centri religiosi dell' Asia Minore* (Pavia 1985) 181 n. 218, is properly cautious.

ἐπειδὴ τοῦ δήμου κατὰ τὰ πάτρια τάς τε πανηγύρεις καὶ τοὺς ἀγῶνας συντελοῦντος ἐν Διδύμοις τῶι Ἀπόλλωνι τῶι Διδυμεῖ, τῆς τε πόλεως καὶ τῆς χώρας καθιερωθείσης διὰ τὴν ἐν τῶιδε τῶι τόπωι Λητοῦς καὶ Διὸς μεῖξιν καὶ τὰς τοῦ θεοῦ μαντείας, ἐξ ὧν ἔθνη τε οὐκ ὀλίγα καὶ πόλεις καὶ τῶν βασιλέων οἱ τετευχότες τῶν μεγίστων τῆς παρὰ τοῦ θεοῦ συμβουλίας τήν τε καθιέρωσιν καὶ τὴν ἀσυλίαν ἀνηγόρευσαν ἀπαράκλητοι αὐτοί, τῶι τε θεῶι καὶ τῆι πόλει τὴν ἀξίαν περὶ τούτων ἀπονείμαντες χάριν . . .

. . .

inasmuch as the people by ancestral custom celebrate the festivals and games at Didyma for Apollo Didymeus, and as the city and country have been made sacred[11] on account of the joining of Leto and Zeus at that place and on account of the oracles of the god, in response to which not a few nations and cities and, of kings, those who have obtained the greatest things from the advice of the god, proclaimed unasked the sacredness and inviolability, rendering to the god and the city proper thanks for those things . . .

For these reasons Miletus, in keeping with the oracles, now seeks to enlarge the Didymeia to crowned status. As to the date,[12] the limits are suggested by *Delphinion* 143.9–10 [*Staatsvertr.* III 537] (Trallian *theoroi* specially sent to the annual sacrifice to Apollo Didymeus in 218/7) and *Syll.*^{3} 577.70–71 with *I.Didyma* 259.25 (quadrennial Didymeia already existing in 206/5 when Eudemus was honored). There is some reason to think that the Didymeia occurred in the year after the Olympia (like the Magnesian Leucophryeneia): Elis honors someone who has treated Olympian *theoroi* well, and the decree is to be sent with the next *theoroi* to the Didymeia.[13] This would place the first celebration in 215 or 211 or 207. Thus the Panhellenic Didymeia probably were in place in 207 B.C. at the latest, and the quest for the recognition must have occupied the preceding year; the recognition of *asylia* preceded that quest, by how long is unclear. I think it probable that both these honors for Miletus preceded those for its lesser neighbor and old enemy Magnesia in 208. If that is so, then it was in the years during which the Magnesians were smarting over their failure of 221 B.C. that Milesian Apollo inaugurated crowned games, in 215 or 211.[14] Inviolability was older, perhaps not long before 221 and prompting the Magnesians' first effort.

11. For the verb, see p. 9; Greek has no verb deriving from ἄσυλος (cf. **156**.12, **219**.4).

12. For Milesian chronology in this period see M. Wörrle, *Chiron* 18 (1988) 428–448; cf. Günther 100–107.

13. *I.Olymp.* 39. Hiller, *RE* 15 (1932) 1608, held that this was the local and annual Didymeia; apparently he relied on the excavators' earlier date for the inscription. See Robert, *Monnaies grecques* (Paris 1967) 42–45; Herrmann, *IstMitt* 25 (1975) 159.

14. For the possibility of dating the Milesian "Persic" silver drachmas to this period see P. Kinns, *NC* 146 (1986) 256–257.

It is interesting that the Milesians do not claim that the recognition of *asylia* is Panhellenic—rather, many nations and cities, some kings, "unasked." Of these recognitions we appear to have one fragment.

65. Aptera

Marble stele found at Aptera in Crete; preserved only on the right; h. 0.135, w. 0.23, th. 0.065; letters 0.005–0.01. The lettering is known only from the drawing published by Guarducci: A with broken bar, right hasta of N fully descended, of Π mostly so, bars of Σ only slightly splayed, Ω small and suspended, some thickening at the ends of strokes; "III B.C." Guarducci; I should think the last quarter.

Guarducci, *I.Cret.* II III 16.

Cf. Robert, *Hellenica* I (1940) 113–115; M. Segré in *Hellenica* V (1948) 123 n. 1; Günther 85 n. 100.

[- - - - - - - - - - - - - - - - - - -]ENIA - - - ΔΙΝΥ[- - -]
[- - - - - τὰν πόλιν καὶ τὰν χώρ]αγ καὶ τὰς νάσος ἱερὰς
[καὶ ἀσύλος εἶναι? τοῦ Ἀπόλλων]ος τοῦ Διδυμέως· καὶ ΕΙΗ
[- - - - - - - - - - - - - - - - τᾶι τοῦ δ]αιμονίω προνοίαι καὶ τᾶι
[- καὶ] π[ολ]έμ[ω κα]ὶ εἰράνας

(traces)

2 τὰν πόλιν Robert. 3 καὶ ἀσύλος εἶναι τοῦ Günther. 4 Robert: - - - Λακεδ]αιμονίω Guarducci.

Guarducci took this to be a treaty, perhaps with Miletus, referring to sacred land and islands of Aptera. Robert and Segré independently recognized a declaration of Milesian inviolability. The islands of Miletus were a substantial part of the civic territory and presumably were specified for that reason.[15] I think that the succession of topics in lines 3–5 requires a longer line than Günther's restoration of line 3: here instead may have been invoked oracles "of Apollo Didymeus"; hence the line length must be considered uncertain.

If this is indeed a decree of inviolability, then the event probably was in the last quarter of the third century, if we can judge from the script, and not earlier in the time of Seleucus II. If, however, we take the Milesians' own statement literally, then there was no Panhellenic quest,[16] and we may well be mistaken to seek a coherent occasion and date for the inviolability of Miletus. A complete decree of recognition would resolve these doubts by revealing whether Milesian *theoroi* in fact canvassed the Greek world for

15. On them see G. Manganaro, *Annuario* 41–42 (1963–66), esp. 293–295, and Piérart (1985) 276–292; the phrase "city and country and islands" is found in the *lex sacra I.Didyma* 488.19 (= *LSAM* 48) of 276/5. Compare at Itanos disputed "territory and islands," *I.Cret.* III IV 8.10–11, 9.44; at Calymna attack on the "city and territory and islands," *T.Calymnii* 64.9 (= *Syll.*[3] 567).

16. Benefactors who act "unasked": **102**.64; *OGIS* 194.11, 248.25.

the status, or by contrast governments recognized it casually in the course of other dealings with Miletus; this latter seems improbable behavior, and unparalleled.

The remaining evidence for inviolability at Miletus concerns Roman policy toward the temple at Didyma. Miletus was deprived of freedom in the 80s B.C. for supporting Mithridates; the Didymeia were abolished, and the temple was in some way separated from the city administratively (perhaps fiscally), for a distinct calendar now functioned there. The "festival and games" were restored in 63, and the city regained its freedom after the Parthian invasion in 40.[17]

Some cities punished by Rome in these circumstances lost their inviolability, only to have it restored in the 40s on Caesar's orders. At Miletus things were otherwise. The temple treasurer of the first semester of 44 B.C. stated that in his term "Caesar increased the existing *asylia* of the temple by two miles," προσεδόθη ὑπὸ Καίσαρος πρὸς τῆι προϋπαρχούσῃ ἀσυλίᾳ τοῦ ἱεροῦ μίλια δύο.[18] In effect, this will have been the work of Servilius Isauricus,[19] so active in this regard, and contemporary with Caesar's edict for Sardes (**214**); Caesar was of course dead before this treasurer went out of office and put up his inscription (hence perhaps the brief "Caesar"). The two miles is doubtless an addition to the radius, the sort of gesture attested at Ephesus, Oropus, and Hieracome. We do not know the original boundary to which this extension was added. Certainly the resulting perimeter cannot have approached the city proper and created the problems that the Romans observed at Ephesus, but (as Rehm saw) the south coast with its harbor Panormus is just over two miles from the temple and must now have come within the inviolable perimeter.

The temple, not the city and country, now possesses *asylia*. Perhaps in the 80s, rather than abolish the status, the Romans stripped it from the city and country but let it continue at the temple, which for a generation was in some degree treated separately from the city. This moreover would accord with Roman thinking about asylum, a property of temples and not cities. Caesar's favor on this topic accordingly had to be different here than elsewhere, an expansion of the boundaries rather than a restoration of the status.

In the time of Augustus a distinguished Milesian was honored because he obtained from the emperor "the inviolability of Apollo," αἰτησάμεν[ον τὴ]ν

17. See Rehm, *SBMünch* 1939.8; the relationship between city and temple in these years, about which Rehm wrote with caution, suggesting some fiscal separation (p. 41), remains obscure. For the status of the Panhellenic Didymeia in Roman times see Herrmann, *IstMitt* 25 (1975) 149–166 and 38 (1988) 309–313.

18. *I.Didyma* 391.II.A.7–10 (= *OGIS* 473), with Günther, *Gnomon* 63 (1991) 605. For the topography see Rehm (1939) 24 n. 1. The bare term "Caesar" is odd, but the date admits of no doubt (Haussoullier had thought the reference was to Caligula). Extensions of the boundaries of *asylia* are not attested after Augustus.

19. So Habicht, *GGA* 213 (1959) 152; cf. p. 28 above.

τε ἀσυλίαν τοῦ Ἀπόλλωνος.[20] Apparently the status was revoked or at least threatened at some moment after 44 B.C.; perhaps Caesar's expansion of the limits had provoked hostility and challenge on the part of some affected party such as publicans. On a later occasion the Milesians honored a citizen with a statue in the temple precinct; among his past services was an embassy to an emperor concerning the inviolability of the temple and the rights of the city, [πρεσβ]εύσαντα πρὸς τὸν Σεβασ[τὸν] ὑπὲρ τῆς ἀσυλίας τοῦ Διδυμέως Ἀπόλλωνος καὶ τῶν τῆς πόλεως δικαίων.[21] This may refer to the inquest of A.D. 22; the text is consistent with Tacitus, who says that the embassies were sent to the emperor, who deferred them to the Senate. Finally, we have a small fragment of a stele found near the temple; its script indicates a much later date, perhaps the third century A.D.:[22]

[- - - - - - -]ου καὶ μείλ̣ι̣α̣ β̣
[- - - - - - -] λιτουργίας, πρεσ-
[βεύσας - - -]ος ὑπὲρ τοῦ τῆς
[- - - - - συν]οικισμοῦ
[- - - - - - -]Λυρα λόφο-
[ν - - - - - -]α ὁ Σεβα-
[στὸς - - - -] . . . ω̣ς καὶ

The subject appears to be some repair to the temple or repopulation (συνοικισμός) of the sacred village, a change that apparently required the permission or generosity of the emperor. The mention of "two miles" might allude to Caesar's enlargement of the inviolable territory, but that is speculative.

20. Herrmann, *IstMitt* 44 (1994) 203–219.
21. *I.Didyma* 107.9–13 (= *OGIS* 472).
22. *I.Didyma* 304; on συνοικισμός (line 4) see Robert, *Op. min. sel.* III 1631; *Hellenica* XI–XII (1965) 463; *Amyzon* I p. 188.

Magnesia on the Maeander

Artemis Leucophryene was from earliest times famous as the *archegetis* of Magnesia, praised already by Anacreon as the shepherdess of the city.[1] Her epithet, "of the white brow," derives from the place Leucophrys where the temple stood and to which the city proper was moved early in the fourth century B.C.; already for Xenophon the temple was "of great sanctity" (μάλα ἅγιον, *Hell.* 3.2.19; cf. 4.8.17). The prominence of her temple among the Greeks of Asia is reflected in the Oxford Stone ca. 240 B.C., the treaty between Smyrna and the soldiers at Mt. Sipylus: Smyrna's copy is to be inscribed not only at Smyrna but also in the temple of Artemis at Magnesia (*Staatsvertr.* III 492.84). To build her Hellenistic temple the Magnesians employed the most famous architect of the age, Hermogenes (Vitr. 7 praef. 12). Artemis dominates the handsome civic tetradrachms of the mid-second century B.C.[2] In imperial times she is shown often on the civic bronze issues, accompanied by her two eagles and Nikes; and the one neocoria gained by Magnesia was held in the name of Artemis rather than of an emperor.[3]

1. Anac. frag. 1; cf. Nic. frag. 74.15–16 (Λεύκοφρυν ἀγασσαμένη). The testimonia on Magnesia are set out by Kern, *I.Magn.* pp. v–xviii. For description of the site and the remains see C. Humann, *Magnesia am Maeander* (Berlin 1904); A. Yaylali, *Der Fries des Artemisions von Magnesia,* IstMitt-BH 15 (Tübingen 1976); on the cult, R. Fleischer, *Artemis von Ephesos,* EPRO 35 (Leiden 1973) 140–146. Pausanias was shown on the Athenian Acropolis a statue of the goddess dedicated by the sons of Themistocles, who had been made tyrant of Magnesia (1.26.4: Μάγνητες γὰρ . . . Λευκοφρυήνην Ἄρτεμιν ἄγουσιν ἐν τιμῇ; on Magnesian honors for Themistocles see I. Malkin, *Religion and Colonization* [Leiden 1987] 223–228). On Arist. frag. 631 (Magnesians sacred to Apollo, being colonists of Delphi) see Wilamowitz, *Kl. Schr.* V.1 81–82.

2. N. F. Jones, *ANSMN* 24 (1979) 63–109. For the coins of Roman date see S. Schultz, *Die Münzprägung von Magnesia* (Berlin 1975).

3. Robert, *BCH* 101 (1977) 75 (*DAM* 33); *RPhil* III.41 (1967) 51–54 (*Op. min. sel.* V 391–394); Burrell, "Neokoroi" 323–326.

The temple of Artemis was in the heart of the city, facing the agora. In 1891–92 the excavators found what remains today the largest archive of texts deriving from a quest for *asylia*, inscribed on the perimeter walls of the agora. More than sixty decrees and letters survive; to judge from the distribution of the stones, this may represent little more than two-thirds of what was once inscribed. Subscriptions appended to fifteen of the decrees ("the following voted the same way") name more than 100 other cities whose decrees were not inscribed at all, their authors instead listed thus in short form.[4] Geographically, the attested grantors range from Sicily to Iran. The organization of the texts is not unlike that of a modern epigraphical corpus: some covering documents came first, then royal letters, then civic decrees in roughly geographical groups, beginning in central Greece and proceeding to the rest of the mainland, then the northwest, the Aegean, Anatolia, and the far west and the far east.

The most important item is the Magnesians' own account of events (**66**), which gives us their reasons and a chronology.[5] As a result of some sign, it seems, the Magnesians consulted old oracles of Apollo, in which the god spoke to them about "preserving their holy city." Later a manifestation of Artemis occurred, and the city sent to consult Delphi; Apollo ordered that he and Artemis be honored and the city and country of Magnesia be declared sacred and inviolable. In response the Magnesians in 221/0 sought recognition of inviolability and of a competition with cash prizes to which they invited the Greeks of Asia. But this quest failed: the Magnesians were "fobbed off" (**66**.24). So in 208 they decided to establish a "crowned" competition for all the Greeks, quadrennial and with prizes equal to the Pythia ("just thanks" to Artemis, as the grantors often say), and to renew their quest for *asylia* now in connection with the enlarged contest: this invitation was universally approved, with the city and country recognized as sacred and inviolable and the Leucophryeneia as Panhellenic.[6]

One text stands apart, a decree of the Aetolian League inscribed at Thermus and Delphi (**67**). The Aetolians recognize the *asylia* of Magnesia but do not mention the games or indeed Artemis. This act must derive from the Magnesians' first effort, in 221, before they added Panhellenic games to their request.

4. I hope to comment elsewhere on various aspects of these lists.

5. Overviews of the episode, from various perspectives: O. Kern, *Hermes* 36 (1901) 491–515; R. Laqueur, *Epigraphische Untersuchungen* (Leipzig 1927) 32–39; Robert, *REA* 38 (1936) 12–15 (*Op. min. sel.* II 775–778); Parke/Wormell I 371; Gauthier, *Symbola* 270–274.

6. The proper distinction is explicit at **102**.33–35, **105**.7–16, **120**.28–33, and **129**.17–19, to cite a few instances: the oracle urged *asylia* for Magnesia; the Magnesians added their own request for enlarged games. More often the grantors simply merge matters, implying that Apollo's oracles asked for both games and *asylia* (e.g., **112**.28). The Epirotes (**82**.6–14) seem to distinguish two divine orders, the oracles (μαντείας) that called for Panhellenic games (cf. **83**.12 and **131**.10) and the oracle (χρησμόν) that called for inviolability. Various oracles were recited in the context of narrating Magnesia's history and services (**85**.9, **86**.9, **96**.13–14, etc.).

The decree of request in 208, often cited in the responses, does not survive; it mentioned the epiphany and oracle and also the many benefactions of Magnesia to the Greeks, which included their aid against the Gauls in the invasion of 279 and their recent mediation of civil war in Crete.[7] The *theoroi* took with them texts that illustrated the antiquity, honor, and good deeds of their city.[8] Fragments of two of these survive inscribed with the recognitions: a history of the foundation of Magnesia and a (forged) decree of the Cretan League voting to assist the ancient Magnesians in their original emigration from the mainland to Asia.[9]

The embassies apparently left in spring, as was common,[10] and their travels spanned a summer, as is shown by several month names in the decrees. At least twenty teams of *theoroi* are attested.[11] The Leucophryeneia probably were held in the month Artemision, the goddess's month; this was very likely the last of the year, for the first celebration was to happen still within the same civic year (**66**.28), so in the spring of the next year.[12] Indeed, it was possible already in the decree of acceptance to elect the *theoroi* who would attend the first celebration (e.g., **115**.10–11): that is, this canvass for recognitions also served as the invitation to the first enlarged games. The canvass probably took place across 208 B.C., and so the first crowned games were held in spring 207. The games are thereafter attested only occasionally outside of Magnesian inscriptions, in victory lists of late Hellenistic or imperial date.[13] The Panhellenic status was still acknowledged as late as the third century A.D. (*I.Magn.* 193).

7. The Epidamnians alone specify these particulars (**96**.8–12); more vague allusions to Magnesian services to the Greeks and to the temple at Delphi are found in **85**.8, **86**.8, **94**.13, etc. Several Cretan inscriptions attest honors voted to Magnesians there in Hellenistic times: see *I.Cret.* III III 3.C, with Guarducci's notes.

8. In addition to their own poetic and historical texts, they were able to cite earlier decrees of other cities honoring them for Magnesia's services (**85**.9–10, **88**.22–29, and most specifically **96**.15–16: "honors and crowns"). The *theoroi* do not seem to invoke the other *asylia* decrees that they have themselves gathered (but see **94**.17).

9. *I.Magn.* 17, with J. Ebert, *Philologus* 129 (1985) 54–63; *I.Magn.* 20–21. Cf. Wilamowitz, *Kl. Schr.* V.1 78–99; Jacoby ad *FGrHist* 482; A. Chaniotis, *Historie und Historiker in den griechischen Inschriften* (Stuttgart 1988) 34–40.

10. Cf. Robert, *Op. min. sel.* II 777 n. 3. In arriving at spring 207 for the quest, he was assuming that the Magnesian year started in autumn; but see below, and on **87**.

11. See Kern, *Hermes* 499–504.

12. The month is suggested by the name itself and by the fact that a lesser and annual festival instituted at the temple in the second century B.C. was held on 6 Artemision: *Syll.*[3] 695.6–7, 56 (= *LSAM* 32); this decree also reveals that the annual elections took place on 2 Artemision (lines 77–79), as would suit the last month of the year. At neighboring Miletus the year began in spring, and its last month was Artemision. For all this see Ebert, *Philologus* 126 (1982) 212. Foreign *theoroi* attending the new games were to be sent in the month Posideion on Paros (**100**.49), on 18 Terpheios on Lesbos (**101**.38), and in Hyacinthios on Rhodes (**104**.23).

13. *IG* XII.1 73.b.6; *I.Didyma* 97.B.4; J. and L. Robert, *Bull. épigr.* 1972, 366; cf. *I.Priene* 108.160 (a *theoros* from Priene at Magnesia).

The bulk of the responses traditionally have been assigned to the period from 208/7 to 203.[14] But the year of the quest was most likely 208, for the Magnesians' phrase "the fourteenth stephanephorus" from Zenodotus in 221/0 (**66**.25) implies inclusive reckoning rather than exclusive. I assume as a working principle that all the extant responses date to 208 except those we have good individual reasons to place later (or, in the one case, earlier). These are the Aetolian decree of 221 (**67**), the Seleucid letters (**69**, **70**), and the appended decrees of some Attalid cities (**128–131**); and from Tacitus we know the Roman recognition of 189 B.C.

The Magnesians report that in 208 all who were asked accepted the games and the inviolability (**66**.30ff.). Among the extant decrees, however, several states accept the Panhellenic games but do not mention *asylia*: these are Attalus (**68**), the Seleucid kings (**69**, **70**), Argos (**90**), Sicyon (**91**), Chalcis (**97**, yet mentioning the epiphany), Delos (**99**), Rhodes (**104**), Antioch in Persis (**111**, yet mentioning the oracle), probably the Aetolian League and Delphi (**78**, **79**), and later than 208 an Attalid city (**131**).[15] Some doubt is possible. Thus we do not have the end of the letter of Attalus, who might have gone on to introduce *asylia*, although this seems unlikely. Rhodes, in its brief decree, "accepts the festival that the Magnesians are holding for Artemis, and the other things, and joins them in taking care to increase the things voted by them"; so too the Seleucid kings. These last vague phrases might be taken to encompass *asylia*, but that seems excluded by ἐψαφισμένα: these are the honors voted by Magnesia for Artemis (cf. **95**.25).

These omissions of *asylia* have been interpreted as deliberate refusals. In their own account of the initial quest (in 221) the Magnesians make clear that one might well refuse to recognize *asylia* (**66**.24)—a decision that in the nature of things normally leaves us no evidence. If the omissions are intentional, what do these states have in common? Of kings, Welles noted, only Ptolemy accepts *asylia* as well as the games: "Just the kings with territorial interests in the Maeander Valley . . . held aloof."[16] This, however, does not explain the silence of these cities (not all, for example, were allies of the aloof kings); nor was Ptolemy without territorial interests in the Maeander Valley.

A. Giovannini has offered the astute alternative that subject cities and league members did not have the freedom of foreign policy to recognize *asylia*; the league or the king spoke for them.[17] This is not, however, borne out consistently; thus Corinth and Megalopolis, members of the Achaean League, accepted *asylia* as well as the games, as does Antigonid Eretria (but not Chalcis). Giovannini's

14. Kern, *Hermes* 499–504; followed by Holleaux, *Etudes* IV 187 n. 1, among others.

15. At least: some texts are too fragmentary to allow for certainty.

16. *Royal Corres.* p. 147; further O. Picard, *Chalcis et la confédération eubéenne* (Paris 1979) 275, who states that independent cities recognized the *asylia* of Magnesia but the kings did not.

17. In *Ancient Macedonia* II (Thessalonica 1977) 465–472.

assumption was that *asylia* was a serious foreign policy decision with military implications, which would not have been permitted to a subordinate state.

Careless writing is a possible explanation: thus Corinth (**92**), Corcyra (**94**), and Tralles (**129**) in the preliminaries of their decrees cite the request for the crowned games, even referring (Corcyra at some length) to the Magnesian benefactions and the oracles, but do not mention *asylia*—yet each then grants *asylia* in the decree proper. Conceivably a complete omission in other texts might reflect no more than such an error. Cnidus (**105**) cites the request for *asylia* but in the grant proper abridges this to accepting "what they request, in keeping with the oracle."

Another explanation, equally unsinister, seems to me more likely. We have a decree of the Aetolian League (**67**, surviving only at Thermus and Delphi) that derives from the quest of 221; the Aetolians recognize *asylia* but of course not the games for the Greeks of Asia, to which they would not have been invited. The omitters of *asylia* in 208 may represent those states that had recognized the inviolability of Magnesia in 221, so that a recognition from them would be superfluous in 208. And in fact the decree of Gonni (**83**) describes the inviolability of Magnesia as a fact and proceeds to recognize only the games. The "omitting" states can hardly have been 10 percent of the extant archive; if that fraction had recognized Magnesian inviolability in 221, then we have a gauge on what the Magnesians regarded as being "fobbed off," as constituting failure—the Greeks' refusal was not total. If this is so (whatever the percentages), it would seem that the most active grantors of *asylia* in the Hellenistic period, the kings and Delphi and its patrons, hastened to recognize Magnesia in 221, but few others did. It may be objected that those putative early recognitions of *asylia* have not been found inscribed in the agora with the decrees of 208; but this applies as well to **67**, whose date in 221 is secure.

To the Senate in A.D. 22 the Magnesians stated that Scipio and Sulla had recognized the inviolability of the temple of Artemis. The first must be L. Cornelius Scipio at the beginning of 189 B.C., when after the defeat of Antiochus III he and his brother were approached by a number of Asian cities in their first diplomatic contact with Rome.[18] Magnesia surrendered to the Scipios and became one of the cities where the Roman army wintered (Livy 37.45). Sulla granted Magnesia freedom because the city had opposed Mithridates,[19] and also confirmed the inviolability, unless Tacitus here has merged the two in summarizing the Magnesians' survey of their Roman honors.

The Magnesians make no mention of a political or military background or motive in their quest for inviolability.[20] By their own account, their motives

18. See Sherk, *Roman Documents* p. 218; Jacoby ad *FGrHist* 434 F 18.6; M. Wörrle, *Chiron* 18 (1988) 427.

19. App. *Mith.* 61; cf. 21; Livy *Epit.* 81.

20. So also Kern, *Hermes* 511; M. P. Nilsson, *Griechische Feste von religiöser Bedeutung* (Leipzig 1906) 250. A political motive for the enlarged games, friendship with Philip V, is argued by

were religious: ordered to add inviolability to the honors of Artemis, they at first misjudged the character of the games that would be the fitting accompaniment for the status. Gods, however, tend to manifest themselves when they are needed. Possibly the sojourn and expulsion of Antiochus Hierax early in the 220s put the city in difficulty and moved the Magnesians toward the undertaking of 221 B.C.[21]

Why was it in 208 that they tried again?[22] The most pertinent fact seems to me to be the success of Magnesia's neighbor and enemy Miletus in obtaining first Panhellenic games and then inviolability. Until Michael Wörrle backdated a crucial set of Milesian *stephanephoroi*, it was thought that the *asylia* of Magnesia preceded that of Miletus by several years and inspired it.[23] It is altogether sensible that the great city came first and the lesser neighbor followed.[24] The envy will have been all the sharper if Miletus succeeded after Magnesia had first been rebuffed. There is reason to think that the Leucophryeneia were placed in the same year as the Didymeia (see p. 175), which would be an obvious convenience for the competitors and an aid to the success of the Leucophryeneia.

The city began issuing large denomination silver with local types at about this time, which may well have been prompted by the new honor;[25] similar gestures are likely at Alabanda, Teos, and perhaps Miletus.

Nothing suggests that the recognition protected Magnesia from war. In 201 the army of Philip V imposed requisitions (Polyb. 16.24.6). In the 180s Magnesia and Miletus fought a war against each other; the elaborate peace treaty that survives makes no mention of the inviolability of either city, as though this was irrelevant to matters of war and peace.[26] The Magnesians told the Senate in A.D. 22 that they had opposed Antiochus III in 190 and Mithridates a century later.[27] It is possible that the status was revoked at a later time and then restored by Caesar in 44 through the agency of Servilius Isauricus: for the Magnesians

S. Dušanić, *Epigraphica* 45 (1983) 11–48; cf. *Rec.trav.Fac.Phil.* (Belgrade) 15 (1985) 43–64 (non vidi: summarized at *SEG* 35.1127).

21. The outbreak of war in the Greek mainland in 220 may be relevant. Compare Wilamowitz, *Kl. Schr.* V.1 361, noting the special arrangements for security attested in 221/0 (*I.Magn.* 15.B.24–26); and Haussoullier, *Etudes* 143–144. But there was war in the Peloponnesus in 208, the Achaean League attempting to seize the Olympic games (Livy 28.7.15). And, in any Panhellenic undertaking, when will there not have been war somewhere?

22. Because of the threat of war: Wilamowitz, *GGA* 162 (1900) 575; the building of Hermogenes' temple: Kern, *Hermes* 495–499, and others.

23. So Rehm, *SBMünch* 1923.8, 22; Hiller, *RE* 15 (1932) 1608; W. Günther, *Orakel von Didyma* (Tübingen 1971) 100–101.

24. Cf. Strab. 14.1.40 (647) for Magnesia's subjection to Miletus in the seventh century.

25. Cf. P. Kinns in *Kraay–Mørkholm Essays* (Louvain 1989) 137–148; but note that the iconography (horseman | bull, conventional since the fourth century) shows nothing of Artemis.

26. *Syll.*[3] 588, with R. M. Errington, *Chiron* 19 (1989) 279–288.

27. Tac. *Ann.* 3.62.1 (*Antiocho ... Mithridate pulsis*). Cf. B. C. McGing, *The Foreign Policy of Mithridates VI* (Leiden 1986) 111 n. 110.

thanked Isauricus for his benefactions to the temple and city: δι[ὰ τὰς] . . . γεγενημένας εἰς [τὸ ἱερὸν] τῆς Ἀρτέμιδος τῆ[ς Λευκο]φρυηνῆς καὶ τὴν πό[λιν] εὐεργεσίας (*I.Magn.* 142).

The dossier is inscribed along the southern and western walls of the agora colonnade, facing in upon the agora (see Kern's Plate II); **114**.21 suggests that the Magnesians had decided in advance of the missions where they would inscribe the resulting decrees.[28] The lettering—mostly, it seems, in one hand—is ostentatiously handsome and regular, with split-end serifs, and sometimes punctuated by vacats (and in **66** by dashes; cf. **129**.14); the royal letters at the start of the archive are written somewhat larger than the rest. The majority of the blocks are in the Pergamon Museum in Berlin; a few were left on the site. Squeezes are in the care of the Inscriptiones Graecae in Berlin. I follow Kern in not reporting the dimensions of the blocks; the texts are Kern's except as indicated. I have collated stones and squeezes only selectively. For the most part I follow Kern's order of presentation (and retain his line numbers); I omit here the historical texts that were used in the quest for *asylia* but are not grants.[29] Finally, stones found at Thermus and Delphi preserve texts not extant at Magnesia (**67**, **78–79**).

66. Magnesia on the Maeander

Kern, *I.Magnesia* 16 [Dittenberger, *Syll.*² 256; Hiller, *Syll.*³ 557; Jacoby, *FGrHist* 482 F 2]; J. Ebert, *Philologus* 126 (1982) 198–216 (squeeze) [*SEG* 32.1147].

Photograph: Ebert pp. 214–215 (squeeze).

Cf. Wilhelm, *Jahresh.* 4 (1901) Beibl. 25 (*Kl. Schr.* II.1 153); *Hermes* 36 (1901) 493 n. 1; Haussoullier, *RevCrit* 35 (1901) 209 n. 1; Kolbe, *SBHeid* 1942/3.1, 16–17; Parke/Wormell no. 347.

[7–8]ες καὶ Ἀλεξάνδρεια | [ca. 20]
[8]ν̣ δύο δ[ο]θῆ[ν]αι καὶ τοιαύτης [ca. 18]
[7 α]ὐτοῖς τελε[ῖ]ν πάντας τοὺς προει[ρημένους ca. 8]
[7]ς ὁ θεὸς καθ' οὓς ἱερὰν τηρήσουσι τ̣ὴ̣μ̣ π̣[όλιν· ἐπειδὴ δὲ]
[ὕστε]ρὸν ἐπιφαινομένης αὐτοῖς Ἀρτέμι[δο]ς Λε[υκοφρυηνῆς ἔπεμ]-
[ψα]ν̣ Ἀγάριστον̣, χρηστηριάζει τάδε πρὸς τὴν ἐρώ[τησιν αὐτῶν·]
[λῶ]ιον εἶμεν καὶ ἄμεινον τοῖς σε[β]ομένοις Ἀπ[όλλωνα Πυθι]-
[ο]ν̣ καὶ Ἄρτεμιν Λευκοφρυηνὴν καὶ τὰ[μ] π[όλιν καὶ τὰν]

28. Cf. the honorific (but not *asylia*) decree of Cnossus inscribed among the archive texts: ἐς τ]ὰν στωιάν (*I.Magn.* 67.6 [*I.Cret.* I VIII 10]). I take it that **109**.b.18 and **125**.b.10 are simply ignorant and relying on formula in asking the Magnesians to place the decree in the temple of Artemis Leucophryene; cf. *I.Magn.* 89.82, stipulated for the temple but found in the southwestern part of the agora like the *asylia* inscriptions.

29. *I.Magn.* 17 (the foundation legend), 20–21 (Cretan assistance then). Cretan thanks for Magnesian help in settling the recent civil war also came to be inscribed on the agora wall (*I.Cret.* I VIII 9–10; IV 176). I omit also *I.Magn.* 29a–b, 51, 62, and 84, none of which contains a complete word.

[χ]ώραν τὰμ Μαγνήτων τῶν ἐπὶ Μαιάνδρ[ο]υ [ἱερὰν καὶ ἄσυ]-
[λ]ον νομιζόντοις· >—< ἐπιφανοῦς δὲ γενομένης [Ἀρτέμιδος]
προσδεξάμενοι >—< τὸγ χ[ρ]ησμὸν ἐπὶ στ[εφανηφόρου]
Ζηνοδότου, ἐν Ἀθήναις δὲ ἄρ[χο]ντος Θρασυφ[ῶντος, Πύθι]-
α δὲ κιθαρωιδοῦ νικῶντο[ς τ]ῶι προτέρωι ἔτ[ει - - -]
ου Βοιωτίου, Ὀλύμπια δὲ τῶι ὑστέρωι ἔτει τὴ̣ν̣ [ἑκατοστὴν]
κ̣αὶ τετταρακοστὴν Ὀλυμπιάδα νικῶντος [τὸ τρίτον]
[π]αγκράτιον Ἁγησιδάμου Μεσσηνίου, >—< πρῶτ[ον ἀργυρί]-
την ἀγῶνα θεῖναι τῶγ κατοικούντων τὴν Ἀσίαν [ἐψηφίσαν]-
το, τὴν ἐκδοχὴν τοῦ χρησμοῦ ταύτην λαβόντες, [ὅτι οὗτοι]
τιμήσουσιν οὕτως Ἄρτεμιν Λευκοφρυηνή[ν,] ἄλ[λως πρὸς]
τ̣ὸ θεῖον εὐσεβῶς ἔχοντες, ἐὰμ Μάγνησιν ἐπὶ τὸν ἀ̣[ρχαῖον ἐπό]-
μενοι βωμὸν Ἀρχηγέτιδι γέρα κεχαρισμέν[α ἀποδιδῶσιν,]
ἅτε καὶ τῶν ἄλλων ἀ[γ]ώνων τὴν ἀρχὴμ̣ μὲν ἐπ' ἀρ̣γ̣[υρίωι τε]-
θέντων, χρόνωι δὲ ὕστερον διὰ χρησμοὺς στεφαν[ιτῶν γεγο]-
ν̣ότων. >—< ὡς δὲ ἐπιβ[α]λόμενοι παρη̣λ̣κ̣ύσθησ[αν, ἐπὶ]
[σ]τεφανηφόρου Μοιραγόρου, ὅς ἐστιν τετταρα̣κ̣[αιδέκατος]
ἀ̣πὸ Ζηνοδότου καθ' ὃν αὐτοῖς ἐγέ̣νε[τ]ο̣ ὁ χ[ρη]σμ̣[ός, φιλιῶν μι]-
μ̣νησκόμενοι πατρίων καὶ ἄλλοις ἐ̣πέδειξα[ν πάνθ' ἃ ἐκέχρησ]-
τ̣ο· >—< στεφανηφοροῦντος δὲ Μοιραγόρου τὸ̣ν στεφαν[ίτην ἀγῶνα]
[ἰ]σοπύθιον, στέφανον διδόντες ἀπὸ πεντήκο̣[ντ]α̣ χρ[υσῶν, ἔθεσαν,]
ἀποδεξαμένων τῶμ βασιλέων [κ]αὶ τῶν ἄλλ[ων ἁπάν]-
τ̣ωμ πρὸς οὓς ἐπρέσβευσαν κατὰ ἔθνη καὶ πό[λεις ψηφισα]-
[μ]ένων τιμᾶν Ἄρτεμιν [Λε]υκοφρυηνὴν κα[ὶ ἄσυλον εἶναι]
[τ]ὴμ Μαγνήτωμ πόλιν καὶ χώραν διὰ τὴμ παρα[ίνεσιν τοῦ]
[θε]οῦ καὶ τὰς ὑπαρχούσας πρὸς πάντας α̣ὐτ[ῶν φιλίας]
[κα]ὶ οἰκειότητας ἐκ προγόνωμ Μάγνη[σιν - - -]

Text of Ebert. 1–2: [ὥστε αὐτοῖς καὶ χρυσοῦς στεφάνους | ὑπὸ Ἰώνω]ν vel Αἰτωλῶ]ν Hiller. 2 Kern: δ[.]θ[..]αι Ebert. 2–3: α]ὐτοῖς τε αε̣..ν Kern; [τιμῆς αὐτὸς ἔφη αἴτιος γε|νήσεσθαι α]ὐτοῖς τελέ[σω]ν Hiller; τελε[..]ν (but not enough space for [ΣΩ]) Ebert. 3–4 Kern: ἀγῶνας τούς | τε νόμου]ς Hiller. 4–5:]φον Kern, [πρότε]ρον Wilhelm, *Jahresh.*; μετὰ δὲ τὸν | ἀδελ]φὸν Hiller. 5–6: αγαριστοι Kern; τῶι | καὶ] Ἀγαρίστωι Haussoullier (accepted by Kern, *Hermes* 493); τῆι ἱ|ερεί]αι Ἀριστοῖ vel τῶι δεῖνι καὶ] Ἀγαρίστωι Hiller. 17 Kolbe. Kern: 10 [τῆς Α., 15 [ἀνδρῶν], 16 στεφανί]-, 17 [ἐπεβάλον]-, 18 [καθότι], 20 ἀ̣[γνὸν ἀφιγ]μένοι, 21 κομίσωσιν], 22 ἀρ̣γ̣[ύρωι τε]-, 24 παρη[κο]ύσθησα̣[ν, 25 τέτ{τ}αρ[τ]ος [καὶ δέκατος], 26 ἐγίνε̣[τ]ο̣ ὁ χ[ρη]σμ̣[ός, ἀναμι]-. 27: ἐ̣πεδείξα[ντο - - -] Kern, ἐ̣πεδεῖξαν τὸ [πάθος τοῦ]|το Hiller. Kern: 28 τοῦ Στεφάν[ου], 29 χρ[υσῶν], 30 Ἑλλήνων ἁπάν]-, 31 ἀποδεξα]-, 32 ἀ. νομίζειν]. 33 Wilhelm, *Hermes*, accepted by Kern 495: παρά[κλησιν Kern. 34: αὐτ[οῖς φ. Kern, αὐτ[οὺς φ. Dittenberger (accepted by Kern 495). 35 Dittenberger.

. . .

(4ff.) But when later, upon Artemis Leucophryene manifesting herself to them, they sent Agaristus, the god proclaimed in response to their enquiry: "It is better and more auspicious for those who honor Apollo Pythius and Artemis Leucophryene and recognize the city and country of the Magnesians as sacred and inviolable."

After the manifestation of Artemis had occurred and they received the oracle, when Zenodotus was stephanephorus, Thrasyphon archon in Athens, first year of the [Pythi]a in which [—] Boeotian won as cithara-singer, one year before Olympiad 140 when Hegesidamus Messenian won in pancration [for the third time], they first voted to hold a moneyed contest for those who live in Asia, making this interpretation of the oracle, that these (the Asians) would honor Artemis in this way, being in general piously disposed toward the divine, if accompanying the Magnesians to the [old] altar they should render gifts pleasing to the Foundress—inasmuch as other contests had been established originally with moneyed prizes, but later as a result of oracles became crowned. But when having undertaken this they were fobbed off, when Moeragoras was stephanephorus, the fourteenth from Zenodotus under whom the oracle was given them, remembering their ancestral [friendships] they revealed to others all that had been prophesied; and, in Moeragoras' year, they established the crowned contest, equal to the Pythia, giving a crown worth fifty gold staters, with the approval of the kings and all the other Greeks to whom they sent ambassadors, voting by nations and cities to honor Artemis and to make inviolable the city and country of Magnesia, because of the god's urging (etc.)

1–4: Hiller restored an allusion to earlier festivals and prizes. I suggest a different possibility, although the word order is clumsy: καὶ τοιαύτης [οὔσης τῆς ἐρωτήσεως ἐ|κέλευσε (or |ἔχρησεν) α]ὐτοῖς τελε[ῖ]ν πάντας τοὺς προει[ρημένους Μάγνησιν | χρησμοὺ]ς ὁ θεός, "Such being the question, the god ordered them to fulfill all the oracles that had already been given, according to which they would preserve the holy city."[30] This last was merely the familiar poetic phrase,[31] which then in 221 B.C. (lines 6ff.) was given a contemporary and literal reading when Apollo was consulted again and ordered that the city be declared sacred and inviolable. The repeated issuance of oracles, with growing clarity and insistence, is a familiar pattern; a graphic case is the famous Sarapis papyrus, *PSI* IV 435.

6: The only other Magnesian Agaristus on record is the father of one of the *theoroi* of 208 B.C. (see on **103**).

12ff.: The more precise date of this first quest was probably spring/summer 221; see on **67**. This text gives us one of the few externally dated archons of third-century Athens (listed by C. Habicht, *Untersuchungen zur politischen Geschichte Athens,* Vestigia 30 [Göttingen 1979] 113) and helps to anchor the list *IG* II^2 1706

30. For τελεῖν in Delphian oracles compare Parke/Wormell II nos. 292 (τ. σέβας) and 339 (τ. καθαρμόν).

31. Compare the verse oracle quoted in *I.Magn.* 215.13, Μαιάνδροιο λαχόντες ἐφ' ὕδασιν ἱερὸν ἄστυ, where "holy town" is merely poetic. This text, an "ancient oracle," is older than the mid-third century, as the date by a *prytanis* shows (see Hiller on *I.Priene* 2.4 and Kern on *I.Magn.* 5.11; cf. A. D. Nock, *Conversion* [Oxford 1933] 277), and thus earlier than the *asylia* declarations.

(cf. B. Meritt, *Hesperia* 23 [1954] 244). Zenodotus is named on civic coins, as is Moeragoras (line 25): H. Engelmann, *ZPE* 10 (1973) 278.

15: Kern's [ἀνδρῶν], about which he was doubtful, implied that the narrative was composed after 200 B.C., when the boys' category was added in pancration (Paus. 5.8.11; Kern, *Hermes* 494). The Olympia are identified by the pancratiast with the number of his victories (rather than by stadion) also at Thuc. 3.8 (tacitly) and 5.49.1.

16: Ebert's [ἀργυρί]την eliminates the self-contradiction that Kern's [στεφανί]την had involved.[32] The oracle did not specify what the proper honor for Artemis was, and the Magnesians had to interpret. They intended a gradual promotion of the contest, from local to Asian to Panhellenic, and from moneyed to "crowned." For the term (which Ebert, 202 n. 17, preferred because of the echo in 22) note the contrast at Ath. 584C (οὐ γὰρ στεφανίτης ὁ ἀγών ἐστιν ἀλλ' ἀργυρίτης); but χρηματί]την or θεματί]την are also possible.

17: The notion of the "Greeks of Asia" was of course old,[33] and it does not seem to have expanded in the Hellenistic period despite the many civic foundations in Asia by Alexander and later kings. That is, I suspect that the Magnesians in 221 did not invite to the games all the Greek cities from Ionia to Afghanistan, but rather, as we see in the Delphian *theorodochoi* list, the old Greek cities of Aeolis, Ionia, and the Dorian south.[34]

18: For the expression cf. Polyb. 22.7.6: λαμβάνειν ἐκδοχὴν ὅτι.

20: If Ebert's restoration is right, this is the original altar rather than the Hellenistic great altar (Humann 91–99), a distinction envisioned by Kern, *Hermes* 494. This implies that the extant great altar was in place by 208 B.C.; it is normally taken to be the work of Hermocrates and contemporary with his temple.

22: The Magnesians are defensive about their first interpretation of new honors for Artemis, which proved to be inadequate.

24: For ἐπιβάλλεσθαι of an oracular "undertaking," Robert adduced an example from Antioch by Cragus: μαντείαν ... περὶ ὧν ἐπιβάλλομαι (*Laodicée du Lycos* 306 n. 7). Ebert took παρηλκύθησαν to mean that the Magnesians "were slow in their undertaking" (to establish crowned games, which he believed to be their intention from the start), and that annual games for the Greeks of Asia

32. Hinted at already by Robert, *REA* 38 (1936) 13 n. 1 (*Op. min. sel.* II 776).

33. See R. Seager and C. Tuplin, *JHS* 100 (1980) 141–154.

34. Polybius often uses "Asia" of western Anatolia; thus 18.46.15 (the freedom of the Greeks in 196) and 21.17.12 with 21.18.2 (the peoples this side of the Taurus = "all those in Asia"). Cf. Arr. *Anab.* 1.20.1 (after Alexander took Miletus, the Persians no longer had a port in Asia); App. *Syr.* 3; M. Segre, *RivFil* 60 (1932) 446 (Eumenes II saved from the Galatians not only his own subjects but all the inhabitants of Asia). See Robert, *Op. min. sel.* I 336–337, on the geographical limits of the Delphian *theorodochoi*. The extant fragments of Nymphodorus' "Periplus of Asia" (ca. 200 B.C.?) all concern the Aegean (*FGrHist* 572 FF 4–8). See generally D. J. Georgacas, *The Names for the Asia Minor Peninsula*, Beitr.z.Namenforsch. n.F. 8 (Heidelberg 1971) 27–29.

were a reality down to 208.[35] He guessed that they were waiting on the new constructions of altar and temple for the final elevation of the games. This seems to me mistaken, and Kern's understanding of an initial failure correct. The passive παρέλκεσθαι ought not to mean "were delayed," with no moral tone, but "were turned aside," "fobbed off." That is regularly its meaning and tone in Ptolemaic papyri, where the word figures in complaints and petitions when one is being "stalled" or "fobbed off" (especially by debtors or by bureaucrats).[36] And the defensive tone of the passage does not suit the success story that Ebert deduces, a growth from local to Asian to Panhellenic games, with an apology only for its slowness. Rather, ἐπιβαλόμενοι is the undertaking of both the Asian games and (as specified in the oracle) *asylia*, and the Magnesians met with refusal of both in 221. Refusals will not normally have left any record. We evidently have one result from the quest of 221, the decree of the Aetolians (**67**).

25: The phrase "fourteenth stephanephorus from" 221/0 implies inclusive reckoning, as would be natural in counting eponyms in sequence, thus 208/7 rather than 207/6.[37] We have seen that the quest began early in the civil year, so spring 208.

27: So other cities "remember" their kinship and friendship with Magnesia (**84**.16, **88**.29, **102**.62; Ebert cites also *I.Cret.* III iii 3.C.2–4); cf. **12**.33, **48**.19, **49**.19, and the Xanthians being asked to remember (ἀναμνησθέντας) their kinship with Cytenium (*SEG* 38.1476.14).

28: The force of repeating the citation of Moeragoras is that he not only dates the year of invitations (ἐπέδειξαν) but was still stephanephorus when the enlarged games actually came to be celebrated (spanning spring to spring, in my view). The text thus speaks against the theory of Ferguson (see on **87**) that the Magnesian *theoroi* went out in 209 and Moeragoras merely dates their *return* to Magnesia.

35. He argued (205) from the detail of the Asians' sacrifice envisaged at the old altar, and from the annual contest attested in a decree of 221/0 (*I.Magn.* 15b.4–5), which he took as the Asian games. As to the latter text, surely there had long been a local and annual contest for the patron divinity, so that this passage (καθ' ἕκαστον ἐνια[υτὸν ἐν τῶι μουσικῶ]ι ἀγῶνι τῶν συντελουμένων παρ' ἡμῖν [Λευκοφρυηνῶν - - -]) is not proof of the existence of the contest for Asians between the local and the Panhellenic games. Ebert speculated that the vacat in 24 represents an erasure and that the mason intended οὕτως ... ἐπὶ δὲ and, having omitted δὲ by mistake, altered the conjunction.

36. So all three instances in *P.Enteuxis* (32.9, 55.14, 75.10); all seven in the Zenon papyri, listed at P. Pestman, *Guide* (*P.Lug.Bat.* 21) p. 698 s.v. Note especially *P.Cair.Zenon* 59355.108: [πλ]είω γὰρ χρόνο[ν π]αρειλκύσμεθ[α διὰ τὴν Φ]ι[λ]ωνος ἀγνωμ[οσύν]ην; cf. (all passive) *UPZ* 20.42, 57; 39.8 = 40.7.

37. Kern assumed exclusive reckoning. Inclusive: W. S. Ferguson (*Athenian Tribal Cycles* [Cambridge, Mass. 1932] 128); Welles (*Royal Corres.* p. 147 n. 9); Kolbe; Ebert (206). The discussion of W. B. Dinsmoor, *The Athenian Archon List* (New York 1939) 166–167 (cf. S. V. Tracy, *Hesperia* 41 [1972] 44–45) is confused.

32: Note that a single word (whether ἄσυλον or ἱερόν) is sufficient to evoke the status; compare the elliptical allusions in **88**.37 and **140**.7.

34: D. Musti, *AnnPisa* 32 (1963) 225–239, has argued for the increasing banality of the claim of kinship by the late third century B.C.; for "kinship with all," however, he cites (227–228) **27**.7–8 of 242 B.C.

67. Aetolian League

Copies at Thermus in Aetolia and at Delphi, not at Magnesia.

Thermus: inv. 57+86, found in 1897, inscribed with several other Aetolian acts; limestone stele broken at top; h. 0.63, w. 0.75, th. 0.39; letters 0.010–0.015, intersp. 0.007.

I.Magn. pp. xiv–xv (copy of Soteriades) [Dittenberger, *Syll.*[2] 923; Schwyzer 385; Soteriades, *EphArch* 1905, 83; Pomtow, *Syll.*[3] 554]; Klaffenbach, *IG* IX.1[2] 4.c.

Photograph: Kern, *Inscriptiones Graecae* (Bonn 1913) 34.

Delphi: inv. 60, a small fragment found ca. 1892, preserved only at bottom right; h. 0.13, w. 0.11, th. 0.038; letters 0.008, intersp. 0.003–4.

Bousquet, *BCH* 82 (1958) 90–91 [*SEG* 18.246].

Photograph: Bousquet fig. 18.

I give the Thermus copy, underlining the little that survives at Delphi.

στραταγέοντος Ἀγελάου Ναυπακτίου τὸ
δεύτερον, ἱππαρχέοντος Πολεμάρχου Θυ-
ρισχαίου, γραμματεύοντος Σκόπα Τριχονέος,
ἔδοξε τοῖς Αἰτωλοῖς· ἐπειδὴ Μάγνητες οἱ ἀ-
πὸ Μαιάνδρου ἀποστείλ̣α̣ντες πρεσβευτ̣ὰ⟨ς⟩
Μνασιπτόλεμον καὶ Ἱππόνικον τάν τε οἰκει̣ότα-
τα τὰν ποτὶ τ̣ὸ ἔθνος ἀνενεώσαντο καὶ τὰν εὔ̣-
νοιαν ἐνεφάνιξαν ἃν ἔχοντι ποτὶ τὸ κοινὸ̣ν
τῶν Αἰτωλῶν Μάγνητες, δεδόχθαι τάν τε̣ φιλί-
αν τὰν ποτ' αὐτοὺς διαφυλάσσειν καὶ τὰν π̣όλι-
ν αὐτῶν καὶ τὰν χώραν ἱαρὰν καὶ ἄσυλον εἶμεν, καθότι οἱ
πρεσβευταὶ ἐπαγγέλλοντι, καὶ μηθενὶ ἐξουσίαν εἶμ̣εν
Αἰτωλῶν μηδὲ τῶν ἐν Αἰτωλίαι κατοικεόντων ἄγε̣[ι]ν
μηθένα ἐκ τᾶς χώρας τᾶς Μαγνήτων μηδαμόθεμ̣ ὁρμ̣ω-
μένους μήτε κατὰ γᾶν μήτε κατὰ θάλασσαν· εἰ̣ δ̣έ τ̣ίς̣
κα ἄγηι, τὰ μὲν ἐμφανέα ἀναπράσσειν ἀεὶ τὸν στ̣ρατα-
γὸν τὸν ἔναρχον, τῶν δὲ ἀφανέων το⟨ὺ⟩ς συνέδρους κατα-
δικάζοντας ζαμίαν ἅν κα δοκιμάζωντι ὡς τὰ κοινὰ
βλαπτόντων καὶ ἐκπράσσοντας τὰς καταδίκας καὶ ἀποδι-
δόντας τοῖς ἀδικουμένοις κυρίο⟨υ⟩ς εἶμεν· δεδόσθαι δὲ αὐτοῖς
καὶ ψᾶφον ἱερομναμονικὰν ἐν τοὺς Ἀμφικτύονας· τὸ δὲ ψάφισμα τό-
δε ἀναγράψαι καὶ ἀναθέμεν ἐν Θέρμον καὶ ἐν Δελφούς.

5 ΒΕΥΤΑΝ, 17 ΤΟΥΣ lapis. 20 Dittenberger: ΚΥΡΙΟΙΣ lapis. 21 ΤΙΟΝΑΣ Delphi.

. . .

(4ff.) Inasmuch as the Magnesians on the Maeander, sending as envoys Mnesiptolemus and Hipponicus, have renewed their friendship with our people and made clear the loyalty they have toward the League, it is decreed to preserve our friendship with them, and their city and country are to be sacred and inviolable, as the ambassadors proclaim. No one of Aetolians or those living in Aetolia is permitted to seize anyone from Magnesian territory, operating from anywhere, by land or sea. If anyone does, the current *strategos* is to impound the visible property, while for that not visible[38] the *synedroi* are empowered to fix such fines as they deem fit, as upon those harming League affairs, and to collect the fines and pay them over to the victims. They are to be given as well a hieromnemonic vote in the Amphictyony.

At Thermus a subsequent Aetolian decree (*IG* IX.1^2 4.d) was inscribed below this one; it mentions King Philip, hence a terminus ante quem of 179 B.C. The text, mostly lost, was restored by Klaffenbach as a grant of a crown and citizenship to the Magnesians in thanks for their prior grant of these to the Aetolians, with a provision to include in the laws the decree under Agelaus. Most of this is speculative, and the act can provide no reliable guide for defining the occasion or date of **67**.

When was Agelaus *strategos* for the second time? Polybius names other men as the Aetolian *strategoi* of 221/0 and 220/219 (4.5.1, 4.27.1), and Agelaus in 217/6 (5.107.6)—but which time this was for him Polybius does not say. Agelaus was *strategos* again in 206/5 (*SEG* 38.1476.79, also unnumbered). Klaffenbach, treating the chronology of the *strategoi*, dated our decree to 224/3—thus before the first effort of the Magnesians in 221, which is impossible; Bousquet preferred to call 217/6 the first and 206/5 the third, with our text somewhere in between.[39]

The Aetolians here grant the Magnesians a seat on the Amphictyony. This seat is first seen with certainty in **133**, probably 202/1 B.C. (the Delphian archon Megartas). Flacelière assigned to the years from ca. 220 to Megartas as many as five Amphictyonic decrees that seemed to lack the Magnesian seat. Accordingly he placed this decree with the second quest, in 208. This too should be judged impossible, given the silences of the decree. The Delphian evidence seems in fact to be inconclusive on whether Magnesia had a seat during the period 220–202.[40] Moreover, we now have in **78** an Aetolian decree given to the Magnesian *theoroi*

38. That is, already disposed of.

39. Klaffenbach, *IG* IX.1^2 p.L (he put the first tenure in 231/0; he could not know about that of 206/5); J. Bousquet, *REG* 101 (1988) 26–27.

40. So also P. Fraser, *BCH* 78 (1954) 65. See Flacelière, *Aitoliens* 324–325, 409–412. Flacelière admitted (325 n. 1) that his I 42 and 43 were of quite uncertain date; I 40 and 41 are too fragmentary to show whether the Magnesians are absent; I 39, almost complete and certainly lacking the Magnesian seat, he assigned to 216/5 (archon Polycleitus): but 225–214 or 206–205 according to G. Daux, *Chronologie delphique* (Paris 1943) 48.

of 208, accepting the Leucophryeneia: that occasion could not have produced two Aetolian decrees. We must judge by the nature of the act itself and put it into the historical context defined by the Magnesians' account (**66**).[41]

The Magnesians send two ambassadors, not called *theoroi*, both otherwise unattested,[42] who speak on friendship; the Aetolians approve the friendship and declare the city and country sacred and inviolable, dwelling at length on penalty clauses of the sort regularly found in Aetolian grants of collective personal inviolability. This decree differs from those Aetolian grants only in making inviolable not the people but the city and country, which (the Aetolians add) is what the Magnesians are "proclaiming" (11–12). This territoriality, by contrast, is the only point that the present act shares with the recognitions of the inviolability of city and country that date from 208: there is no mention of Artemis, the oracles, the epiphany, games, or the piety and past benefactions of the Magnesians—the "case" that they would make in 208.

This decree, therefore, is a response to the first Magnesian effort, in which they asked baldly for inviolability without "revealing" all the oracular testimonia (**66**.27), and without requesting crowned games for Artemis; nor of course would they invite Aetolians to the games for the Greeks of Asia. The Aetolians responded by reading this request into their own conventional formulary for collective personal *asylia*, as they would for Teos later (**132**) and as the Cretan League would for Anaphe (**175**). Indeed in 221 B.C. the Aetolians may never before have been faced with a request for the *asylia* of an entire city and country.

The Magnesians say that they failed in their effort in 221: we can conclude that the Aetolians' recognition was exceptional. In 208 a number of Aetolian cities responded to the Magnesians by accepting at least the Panhellenic games (**77**): but not enough of that decree survives to indicate whether they granted *asylia* at the same time; likewise it is not certain that the Delphians (**79**) granted *asylia* in 208. All these may well have followed the League's lead in 221 and granted *asylia* then.

1: The date is Olympiad 139.4 = 221/0 (**66**.14). Aetolian *strategoi* served from autumn to autumn (Polyb. 4.37.2); another man is certain in 221/0 (Polyb. 4.5.1), so Agelaus' year, his second tenure,[43] must be 222/1.[44] Our decree must date from the last months of his term, in the summer of 221.

41. Beloch (*Gr. Gesch.* IV.2 417), Pomtow (ad loc.), and Daux (*JSav* 1939, 122) have all seen that this act must precede those of 208; cf. Gauthier, *Symbola* 273–274. Summary by Fraser, (above, n. 40).

42. The name Hipponicus is found again at the end of the Hellenistic period, *I.Magn.* 88.f and 346.

43. His term in 217/6, unnumbered at Polyb. 5.107.6, will be his third.

44. To this year Klaffenbach (p. 74) assigned Pantaleon's fourth tenure, but with much hesitation. He invoked Pomtow, who, however, said no more than "c.a. 220" (*Syll.*^{3} 522 n. 5) and "c.a. 222" (546.A n. 1).

16–17: On these terms for disputed property see J.-H. Michel in *Le monde grec* (Brussels 1975) 508–512.

18–19: For parallels for "harming" see Wilhelm, *WS* 29 (1907) 3.

68. Attalus I

To the left is inscribed the list of Cretan cities *I.Magnesia* 21, apparently the subscription to the forgery *I.Magnesia* 20.

Kern, *I.Magnesia* 22 [Dittenberger, *OGIS* 282]; Schroeter 23; Welles, *Royal Corres.* 34.

Cf. Wilhelm, *Jahresh.* 4 (1901) Beibl. 27 n. 6 (*Kl. Schr.* II.1 154); Holleaux, *Etudes* I 315; P. Roussel, *REA* 38 (1936) 229; R. E. Allen, *The Attalid Kingdom* (Oxford 1983) 169.

βασιλεὺς Ἄτταλος [Μα]-
γνήτων τῆι βουλῆι καὶ τῶι [δή]-
μωι χαίρειν· Πυθίων καὶ Λυκ[ο]-
μήδης οἱ παρ' ὑμῶν ἀνεκόμι-
σαν πρός με ψήφισμα καθ' ὃ πα[ρα]-
καλεῖτε τὸν ἀγῶνα ὃν τίθετẹ
τῆι Ἀρτέμιδι τῆι Λẹυκοφρυην[ῆι]
μουσικὸν καὶ γυμνικὸν καὶ ἱπ̣-
πικὸν ἀποδέξασθαι στεφανίτ[ην]
ἰσοπύθιον, καὶ αὐτοὶ διελέχθησ[αν]
ἀκολούθως τοῖς γεγραμμένο[ις·]
ἠξίουν δὲ καὶ τὰς ὑπ' ἐμὲ πόλει̣[ς]
ἀποδέξασθαι ὁμοίως. θεωρῶ̣[ν δὲ]
τὸν δῆμον μεμνημένον τῶν [ὑπ̣' ἐ]-
μοῦ γεγενημένων εἰς αὐτὸν εὐ[εργε]-
σιῶν καὶ ὁμιλοῦντ' ἀεị μοι̣ φι̣λ̣[οφρό]-
νως, τόν τε ἀγῶνα ὥσπερ παρα[καλεῖ]-
τε ἀποδέχομαι καὶ ἀπαρχὴν ἐγ[ὼ προσέτα]-
ξα δοῦναι, καὶ αἱ πόλεις δὲ αἱ π̣[ειθόμε]-
ναι ἐμοὶ ποιήσουσιν ὁμοίως· [ἔγραψα]
γὰρ αὐταῖς παρακαλῶν· κα[ὶ ἐν τοῖς ἄλ]-
λ̣οις δὲ καθ' ὅσον ὁ δῆμος [αἰτεῖται]
[συνα]υ̣ξήσω τὸν ἀγῶνα̣ [- - -]
[. . . . .] τ̣ὴν π[- - - - - - - - - -]

13 Dittenberger: δ' ἐγὼ] Kern. 16 ἀεị μοι̣ Roussel, φι̣λ̣[οφρό]|νως Rigsby: ὁμιλοῦντα ἐμ Μούσα̣ι̣[ς δει]|νῶς Kern ("pour moi un grand mystère," Holleaux); the Berlin squeezes reveal nothing after ΟΜΙΛΟΥ. 18 Holleaux: ἐγ[ώ τε ἔτα]|ξα Kern; or ἐπ̣[έτα]|ξα? (the squeezes are illegible in the right half of the line). 21–22 Wilhelm: Περγαμη]|νοῖς Kern (followed by Allen); the squeezes show the stone broken in the middle of omicron, so that Kern's nu was either lost after discovery or an error of recording.

. . .

> Your envoys Pythion and Lycomedes brought me a decree in which you ask me to accept as crowned and isopythian the musical, athletic, and equestrian contest you are holding for Artemis Leucophryene; and they themselves spoke in keeping with the text, and asked that also the cities under me accept it likewise. Seeing that your people are mindful of my past benefactions to them and are always friendly in their dealings with me (?), I accept the contest as you ask and have given orders to give a firstfruits sacrifice; and the cities that obey me will do likewise, for I have written them asking. And in all else, insofar as your people ask, I shall join in increasing the contest . . .

I place Attalus' letter first, for although he makes no allusion to the fact, Magnesia certainly was on some terms an Attalid city in 208.[45] Presumably they had been allies since the 220s and his defeat of Antiochus Hierax, who had held Magnesia.[46] Attalid rule over much of Caria would be ended for a time in 204 by the western campaign of Antiochus III.[47]

In what survives of the letter, Attalus does not mention the request for *asylia*. He alone among the kings specifies the categories of competition (8–9) and promises to provide a sacrifice for Artemis (18–19).

3: This pair of *theoroi* is not met again; the same number, rather than the usual three, were sent to Ptolemy (**71**). A Lycomedes visited some Anatolian cities (**125**, **126**), while perhaps a different one toured the Greek mainland (cf. on **73**); but the name was common at Magnesia.

16: Kern's text is unparalleled in a diplomatic context and dubious Greek,[48] hence Roussel's emendation ("ἀε(ί) μο(ι) avec un adverbe"). For the construction compare Origen *Cels.* 7.35: ὄψεταί τις αὐτοὺς . . . ἀεὶ τοῖς βουλομένοις ὁμιλοῦντας. One might instead have ἀ̣σ̣μ̣[έ]νως; compare ἀσμένως ἐντετύχηκά σοι at Philostr. *VA* 4.16.

19–21: "The cities subject to me will do likewise because I have written them asking" is revealing concerning παρακαλεῖν in the mouth of a Hellenistic king. The verb is common in the *asylia* decrees; when a recipient "calls upon" a grantor to recognize inviolability, that is a request to a sovereign state. Attalus' statement might be taken to imply that Magnesia was not among these obedient cities,

45. A tribe Attalis is attested soon after, *I.Magn.* 89.7. A. Mastrocinque, *La Caria e la Ionia* (Rome 1979) 154–156, from the fact that Ptolemy alone of the kings grants *asylia*, infers that Magnesia was Ptolemaic; Fraser, *BCH* 1954, 67, assumes that it was Seleucid (on his claim of an Amphictyonic recognition for Magnesia, see J. and L. Robert, *Bull. épigr.* 1955, 122).

46. Porphyry *FGrHist* 260 F 32.8; cf. Will, *Histoire* I 296–300.

47. The city is attested as Seleucid a generation earlier (*I.Magn.* 5.4; G. Le Rider, *BCH* 114 [1990] 543–551 [Antiochus II]; the last issues of the Seleucid royal mint come under Seleucus II; cf. Newell, *WSM* 290) and was so again by 201 (Polyb. 16.24.6).

48. Kern cited *IG* IX.1 235, a poem on an individual, its text uncertain; in honorific prose we have παιδείᾳ ὁμιλῶν at *OGIS* 505.7; compare εἰσὶν ἐν μούσαις ἀεί at Eur. *Hipp.* 452. With this sentiment δεινῶς would be jarring; and the phrase ὁμιλέω ἐν is not well supported by the parallels adduced by Welles.

rather an ally. Several Attalid cities are represented in the archive, and some recognized inviolability as well as the games (e.g., Teos, Colophon, later Tralles).

21ff.: As Welles (p. 151) remarks in support of Wilhelm's restoration, Περγαμηνοῖς makes no sense with συναυξήσω (and Pergamum surely would be reckoned among Attalus' subjects). The "other things" whereby he will help increase the games might be an indirect reference to inviolability, but this seems improbable, uselessly unspecific; compare the Seleucid letters (**69**.6, **70**.6), in which Magnesia has voted to establish "the contest and the other things."

69. Antiochus III

Kern, *I.Magnesia* 18 [Dittenberger, *OGIS* 231; W. Janell, *Ausgew. Inschr.* (Berlin 1906) 51]; Schroeter 25; Welles, *Royal Corres.* 31.

Photograph: Kern pl. III.2 (lines 1–15).

βασιλεὺς Ἀντίοχος Μαγνή-
των τῆι βουλῆι καὶ τῶι δήμωι χαί-
ρειν· Δημοφῶν καὶ Φιλίσκος καὶ Φέ-
ρης οἱ παρ' ὑμῶν πεμφθέντες πρὸς
ἡμᾶς θεωροὶ ἕνεκεν τοῦ ἐπαγγεῖ-
λαι τὸν ἀγῶνα καὶ τἆλλα ἃ ἐψήφισ-
ται ὁ δῆμος συντελεῖν τῆι ἀρχηγέ-
τιδι τῆς πόλεως Ἀρτέμιδι Λευκοφρυ-
ηνῆι, συμμείξαντες ἐν Ἀντιοχείαι
τῆς Περσίδος τό τε ψήφισμα ἀπέδω-
καν καὶ αὐτοὶ διελέχθησαν μετὰ σπου-
δῆς ἀκολούθως τοῖς καταχεχωρισμέ-
νοις ἐν τῶι ψηφίσματι, παρακαλοῦντες
ἀποδέξασθαι στεφανίτην ἰσοπύθιον
τὸν ἀγῶνα ὃν τίθετε τῆι θεᾶι διὰ πεν-
[τ]αετηρίδος. ἔχοντες οὖν ἐξ ἀρχῆς π̣[ερὶ]
τοῦ δήμου τὴν φιλανθρωποτάτην διάλ[η]-
ψιν διὰ τὴν εὔνοιαν ἣν τυγχάνει ἀποδε̣-
δειγμένος ἐμ πᾶσι τοῖς καιροῖς εἴς τε ἡ-
μᾶς καὶ τὰ πράγματα, καὶ βουλόμενοι φα-
νερὰν ποιεῖν τὴν ἑαυτῶν προαίρεσιν ἀπο-
δεχόμεθα τὰς ἐψηφισμένας ὑφ' ὑμῶν τ[ι]-
μὰς τῆι θεᾶι, πρόκειταί τε ἡμῖν συναύξειν
ταῦτα ἐν οἷς ἂν ὑμεῖς τε παρακαλῆτε καὶ
αὐτοὶ ἐπινοῶμεν· γεγράφαμεν δὲ καὶ
τοῖς ἐπὶ τῶν πραγμάτων τεταγμένοις,
ὅπως καὶ αἱ πόλεις ἀκολούθως ἀπο-
δέξωνται. ἔρρωσθε.

6 Welles: τ[ὰ] ἄλλα Kern.

Antiochus, engaged in his eastern expedition (211 to 205 B.C.), was found by the envoys at Antioch in Persis (9–10), whose decree also survives (**111**). Since

Kern (pp. 13, 15) this letter has been dated to 205.[49] Other reasons are doubtful, but the geographical argument for 205 and against 208 is strong. Antiochus wintered in Carmania in 206/5 (Polyb. 11.34.13) and was on the Persian Gulf by late 205 (13.9.4–5): he therefore passed through Persis in 205. His whereabouts during all of 208 are not certain,[50] but probably he defeated the Parthians in 209 and began his invasion of Bactria in 208 (Polyb. 10.48–49). It is very unlikely that he came as far south as Persis in between. If the Magnesians were willing to take the trouble to find him in Iran in 205 but not in the northeast in 208, that must reflect his engagement in his campaign, ended by 205. But this need have no bearing on the date of the non-Seleucid letters.

Of the Magnesian request he mentions the crowned games but not *asylia*, unless the latter is encompassed in "the other things" they have asked (6); what he goes on to approve is in fact rather vague, the "honors voted by you." If this mission was delayed until 205 (these *theoroi* do not recur in the archive), then the Magnesians apparently had no difficulty about addressing themselves to Seleucid cities in 208 (e.g., Laodicea on the Lycus, which does recognize *asylia*), before they had approached the king.

23–25: "It is our intention to join in increasing these things in whatever ways you might ask or we ourselves might conceive" (for ἐπινοεῖν see Gauthier, *Nouv. inscr. Sardes* II p. 77).

25–28: The reference to royal officials is generic, and no particular level of government is meant; their task, well illustrated in other Seleucid inscriptions, will be to convey down the chain of command a letter of the king signaling his decision about Magnesia. Attalus, by contrast, implies that he will write to his cities directly. None of the answers from Seleucid cities (notably that of Antioch in Persis, **111**) cites the king's opinion in this matter, except perhaps **110**.19—contrast such allusions to the Antigonid kings in decrees for Cos (**25–27**) and once for Magnesia (**97**). The reason, rather than constitutional, may be chronological: most had been approached in 208; or instead geographical: even if the Seleucid letters date to 208, the Magnesian *theoroi* had long scattered on their missions before this set found Antiochus in Iran and could report his answer to others. As to Antioch in Persis, it is possible that the *theoroi* received a hearing from the city before they could obtain one from the king; the same may have happened to the Coan envoys at Pella (cf. on **23**).

70. Antiochus son of Antiochus III

Kern, *I.Magnesia* 19 [Dittenberger, *OGIS* 232]; Schroeter 26; Welles, *Royal Corres.* 32.

49. Cf. Holleaux, *CAH* VIII 142; *Etudes* III 178 n. 4; Schmitt, *Untersuchungen* 28 n. 3; Welles and Will (*Histoire* II 65) for all the royal letters to Magnesia.

50. "We lose sight of him," Holleaux, *CAH* 141.

Cf. Wilhelm, *Jahresh.* 4 (1901) Beibl. 25 (*Kl. Schr.* II.1 153); Holleaux, *Etudes* I 315.

βασιλεὺς Ἀντίοχος Μαγνήτων
τῆι βουλῆι καὶ τῶι δήμωι χαίρειν· Δη-
μοφῶν καὶ Φιλίσκος καὶ Φέρης οἱ πα-
ρ' ὑμῶν πεμφθέντες πρὸς τὸν πατέ-
ρα θεωροὶ ἕνεκεν τοῦ ἐπαγγεῖλαι
τὸν ἀγῶνα καὶ τἆλλα ἃ ἐψήφισται
ὁ δῆμος συντελεῖν διὰ πενταετη-
ρίδος τῆι ἀρχηγέτιδι τῆς πόλεως
Ἀρτέμιδι Λευκοφρυηνῆι ἀπέδωκαν
καὶ τὸ πρὸς ἐμὲ ψήφισμα καὶ διελέχθη-
σαν μετὰ σπουδῆς ἀκολούθως τοῖς
ἐν τούτωι καταχεχωρισμένοις παρα-
καλοῦντες ἀποδέξασθαι στεφανί-
την ἰσοπύθιον τὸν ἀγῶνα ὃν τίθετε τῆι
θεᾶι. ἔχοντος οὖν τοῦ πατρὸς περὶ
τοῦ δήμου τὴν φιλανθρωποτάτην δι-
[άλη]ψ̣ι̣ν καὶ ταῦτα ἀποδεδεγμένου, θέ-
[λων κ]αὶ αὐτὸς ἀκολουθεῖν τῆι προαιρέ-
[σει αὐτ]οῦ, νῦν τε ἀποδέχομαι τὰς ἐψη-
[φισμένα]ς ὑφ' ὑμῶν τιμὰς τῆι θεᾶι καὶ
[τὸ λ]ο[ιπ]ὸ̣ν πειράσομαι κατακολουθῶν
[τῆι τοῦ π]α[τρ]ὸς ὑφηγήσει συναύξειν ὑμῖν
[ἐν οἷς ἂ]ν π[αρ]α̣καλῆτε ἢ καὶ αὐτὸς ἐπινοῶ.
ἔρρωσθε.

18 Dittenberger: θέ|[λω κ]αὶ Kern. 21 Dittenberger: [εἰς χρ]ό[ν]ον Kern, [εἰς τὸ λ]ο[ιπ]ὸν Wilhelm, Holleaux.

The eldest son of Antiochus the Great, born in 220, was co-regent by 209 and died in 193; he never ruled alone.[51] Evidently he accompanied his father on the eastern campaign, and it is visible that he has his father's answer before him; but it need not follow that he too was at Antioch in Persis (in whose decree the response of neither king is mentioned). That the Magnesians obtained a separate letter from him (contrast the letters of the joint rulers Theodore and Amynander to Teos and Claros) might suggest that the two were in fact not in the same place. And the Magnesians presented the decree and made their speeches "to me" (10), not to the two together.

4–5: For this simple citation of the parent see Aymard 86 n. 2, 93 n. 5. The son makes explicit that the ambassadors were sent "to my father" and not to himself.

51. For the dates see A. Aymard, *Etudes d'histoire anciennes* (Paris 1967) 217 n. 1, 267–268; Schmitt, *Untersuchungen* 13–20.

71. Ptolemy IV

The only inscription of the archive that was found exposed to the elements, its text was badly worn and had a furrow down the middle; the stone was left at the site. Kern derived more from the squeezes. The letters become increasingly crowded, so that the loss in the middle of each line is hard to estimate.

Kern, *I.Magnesia* 23 [Strack, *ArchPF* 2 (1903) 543; Schroeter 24; Welles, *Royal Corres.* 33].

Cf. J. De Decker, *RPhil* n.s. 29 (1905) 160 (squeeze).

[β]ασιλεὺς [Πτολε]μαῖ[ος]
Μαγνήτων [τῆι βουλ]ῆι καὶ
τῶι δήμωι χα̣[ίρειν· οἱ] παρ' ὑ-
μῶν ἀποστα̣[λέντες] π̣ρεσβ[ευ]-
ταὶ Διοπείθ[ης - - - - - - - - -]
καὶ 'Ιθαλίδης(?) [- - -]δήμο[υ]
τὸ ψήφισμά [μοι] ἀπέδωκαν ἐ̣ν ὧι
[. . . . .]τω[- - - - - -]ων π[. . .]
[ἀγ]ῶνα τῶ̣[ν Λευκοφρυηνῶν κ]ατὰ τὸν
χηρσμὸν τοῦ [θεοῦ ὃν συν]τελε[ῖτε]
τῆι 'Αρτέμιδ[ι τῆι Λευκοφρυ]ην[ῆι καὶ]
περὶ [τοῦ] νομί[ζειν τὴν πόλι]ν κ[αὶ τὴν]
χώραν ἱερὰν κα[ὶ ἄσυλον, παρεκλήθην? δὲ]
καὶ ἐγὼ ἀπο[δέξασθαι τὸν ἀγῶν]α̣ σ[τε]-
φανίτην [ἰσ]οπ[ύθιον ταῖς τιμ]αῖς οἷ-
[ο]ν ἡμῖν ἐπ[ηγγέλκατε αὐ]τόν· [οἱ δὲ παρ']
ὑ̣μῶν ἀπο[π]εμ[φθέντες καὶ α]ὐτοὶ δ[ιελέ]-
χθησαν μετὰ πά[σης σπ]ουδῆς [καὶ κατὰ]
τἆλλα ἐν τ[ῶι ψηφίσματι περὶ ὧν εἶχον]
[τ]ὰς ἐντολάς. [ἐγὼ μὲν οὖν τόν τε ἀγῶνα]
[στ]εφανίτην καθ[άπερ ἠξι]ο[ῦτε] ἀπο-
[δέ]δεγμαι καὶ τ[- - - - - - - - - - - - - - -]
. . . χο . . . . λο[- - - - - - - - - - - - - -]
. . . . . ὑμᾶς κ[- - - - - - - - - - - - - - -]

7 μοι Welles. 8: [ἀγγελέ]τω[σαν διὰ ἐτέ]ων π[έντε] De Decker. 13 end Welles: ἔγνωκα δὲ] Kern. 18 end, 19–21 Welles. 22–24: Welles suggested τ[ὴν πόλιν ἄσυλον εἶναι | συνε]χώ̣[ρησ]α̣ ὅ[πως φανερὰ γένοιτο πᾶσιν ἡ πρὸς] ὑμᾶς κ[αὶ τὸ θεῖον προαίρεσις].

Ptolemy alone of the kings explicitly recognizes the inviolability of Magnesia. These two *theoroi* are not met again. The name Ithalides (6) is unparalleled and has no evident Greek root; but the squeeze, faint as it is, seems to support Kern's reading. Perhaps correct to the heroic name Αἰθαλίδης, the herald of the Argonauts; the name Αἰθάλης is common enough (six known in Athens: Osborne/Byrne, *Lexicon of Greek Personal Names* II [Oxford 1994] s.v.).

72. Unknown king (Philip V?)

Small fragment, with large lettering as in the openings of the other royal letters; left at Magnesia.

Kern, *I.Magnesia* 24 [Schroeter p. 107 frag. 13].

βασιλ[εὺς - - - - - - - - - - - -]

Kern suggested Philip on the basis of elimination and of the mention of his favorable response at **97**.1–2; followed by Boesch 41, among others.

73. Boeotian League

Kern, *I.Magnesia* 25; Feyel, *Contribution* 5–14 (squeeze).

Cf. P. Roesch, *Thespies et la confédération béotienne* (Paris 1965) 82–84 (cf. J. and L. Robert, *Bull. épigr.* 1967, 524); R. Etienne and D. Knoepfler, *Hyettos de Béotie* (Paris 1976) 311–312 (squeeze); Knoepfler, *Chiron* 22 (1992) 427–428.

Two fragments, the upper (lines 1–2) in Berlin, the lower left at Magnesia and deciphered by Kern mostly from the squeezes.

παρὰ τοῦ κοινο[ῦ τ]ῶν
Βο[ιω]τ[ῶν]
[ἄρχοντος Βοιωτοῖς] Θίβρ̣[ωνος? - - - - - - - - - - - - - - - - - -]
[τῶ] ἀγ[ῶνος πὰρ Μα]γνή̣τ[ων Ἀπολλοφάνεις Ἡσχούλω, Εὔβου]-
[λο]ς Ἀναξ[αγόρα, Λ]υκομ[ήδης Χαρισίου τό τε ψάφισμα]
[ἀ]πέδωκαν [κὴ αὐ]τ̣υὶ διελέ[γησαν ἀκολούθως τοῖς ἐν τῶι ψα]-
[φίσμ]ατι γεγραμμένοις οὐθ̣[ὲν ἐλλείποντες σπουδᾶς, δηλοῦντες]
[τὰν ἐκ] προγόνων ὑκειότατα [τὰν ἐῶσαν τᾶι] πόλι τῶν [Μαγνή]-
[των τῶν] ἐπὶ Μαιάνδρου πὸτ τὸ κυνὸν Βοιωτῶν καὶ ἀπολο[γι]-
[ξάμενοι τ]άν τε τᾶς θεῶ Ἀρτέμιδος Λευκ[φρ]υηνᾶς ἐπιφ[άνει]-
[αν κὴ τὰς γ]εγενημένας ὑπὸ τῶν πρ[ογόνων] ἐν τὼς Ἕλλ[ανας]
[εὐεργεσίας, κὴ] παρεκάλεσαν μετὰ πάσας σπουδᾶς κὴ φι[λοτι]-
[μίας ἀποδέξα]σθη{ι} τάν τε θ̣[υσίαν κὴ] τὰν ἐκηχειρίαγ κὴ [τὸν]
[ἀγῶνα στεφανίταν ἰσοπούθιον ὃν] τ[ίθεντ]ι τᾶι Ἀρτ[έμιδι]
[καθὰ ἐν τῦ ψαφίσματι τῦ πὰρ αὐ]τῶν γέγρα[πτη, κὴ τὰν πόλιν]
[αὐτῶν κὴ τὰν χώραν ἱαρὰν] κὴ ἄσουλον [εἶμεν, καθὰ κὴ ὁ θιὸς]
[ὁ ἐν Βελφῦς ἔχρεισε αὐτῦς]· δεδόχθαι [- - - - - - - - - - - - - -]
[- - - - - - - κ]ὴ πὸτ τὸ θεῖογ κὴ [- - - - - - - - - - - - - - - - -]
[- - - - - - - - -]τῶγ Βοιωτῶγ [- - - - - - - - - - - - - - - - - -]
[- - - - - - - -]τάν τε υἱκιότατα σ̣[- - - - - - - - - - - - - - - - -]
[- - - - - - - - - Μα]γνήτωγ [- - - - - - - - - - - - - - - - - - -]
[- - - - - - - - - - -]θως ὑπὸ̣ . . νγ[- - - - - - - - - - - - - - - -]
[- - - - - - - - - - -]ητας ἐ̣ν̣ε̣χηρ̣ο[- - - - - - - - - - - - - - - -]
[- - - - - - - - - - - -]ω . . . ταγ[- - - - - - - - - - - - - - - - - -]
[- - - - - - - - - - -] ἀπεσταλμε̣ν[- - - - - - - - - - - - - - - - -]
[- - - - - - - - - - -]τογ β̣ . . . θιοσ[- - - - - - - - - - - - - - - -]
[ἐπηνέση δὲ κὴ τὼς θιαρὼς Ἀ]πολλο̣[φά]νειν [Εὔβουλον Λυκο]-
[μείδην φιλοτιμίας ἕνεκεν τᾶς τ]ε πὸτ τὰν θεὸν [κὴ τᾶς πὸτ τὰν]

[πατρίδα, τὺ δὲ Βοιωτάρχη καλεσάν]των ἐπὶ ξένια [αὐτώς - - -]
[- - - - - - - - - - -]ο . νο . . .ατιχ[- - - - - - - - - - - - - - -]
[- - - - - - - - - - - - -]καταθẹ . α̣ [- - - - - - - - - - - - - - -]
[- - - - - - - - - - - -]ουτον μẹμ[- - - - - - - - - - - - - - - - -]
[- - - - - - - - - - - - - -]αντα καὶ [- - - - - - - - - - - - - - -]
[- - - - - - - - - - - - - τ]όδε θέμ̣[εν - - - - - - - - - - - - - - -]
[- - - - - - - - - - - - - -]σουντας [- - - - - - - - - - - - - - -]

vacat

3 (ΘΙΒ clear on the squeeze) Kern, Roesch, Etienne/Knoepfler: [ἐπιδεὶ τὺ] θια̣ρῦ̣ [τὺ ἀπεσταμένυ οὑπὲρ τᾶς ἐπαγγελίας] (or ἐπὶ τῆ ἐπαγγελίῃ) Feyel; Νίκ̣[ωνος? Knoepfler. 4 Feyel. 14–17, 27–29 Feyel: 15 τῶν γεγρα[μμένων Kern. Feyel suggested: 17–19, τὰς μὲν | τιμὰς κὴ τὰν εὐσέβιαν κ]ὴ πὸτ τὸ θεῖον κὴ [πὸτ τὰν Ἄρτεμιν | σουναυξέμεν, καθὼς τῦ κυνῦ] τῶγ Βοιωτῶγ [καθῖκόν (πάτριόν) ἐστι? - - - τὰν δὲ φιλίαν] τάν τε υἱκιότατα σ[ουντειρέμεν | τὰν ὑπάρχωσαν πὸτ τὰμ πόλιν τὰμ Μα]γνήτωγ; 24–25, κὴ τὰμ πόλιν αὐτ]ῶ[γ κὴ] τὰγ [χώραν ἱαρὰγ κὴ | ἄσουλον εἶμεν, καθὼς τὺ] ἀπεσταλμέν[υ πὰρ αὐτῶν θιαρὺ | παρεκάλεσαν.

This decree of the Boeotian League, one of the few extant, was evidently long; Feyel saw essential points of its structure. At 17ff. the Boeotians acknowledge the piety and kinship they shared with Magnesia; at 22ff. they recognize the games and the inviolability; at 27ff. the *theoroi* are honored; 32ff., provision for inscribing. These *theoroi* canvassed central Greece (attested also in Euboea, Athens, and Phocis).

Feyel claimed (p. 15) that only the Boeotian League, and not individual Boeotian cities, could recognize *asylia*; so also Giovannini (above, p. 182), on the grounds that members of leagues were not free to decide the foreign policy matter of war and peace implicit in declaring inviolability. This assumes that the Boeotian League took a general constitutional posture about allowing these recognitions, and the general principle is contradicted by several civic decrees for Magnesia by members of leagues.

74. Unknown city

A heading, inscribed below **73**.
Kern, *I.Magnesia* 25c.

[παρὰ - - -]των[- - -]

75. Larisa (?)

The stone is badly damaged and difficult to read.
Kern, *I.Magnesia* 26.
Cf. A. Fick, *BeitrKundIndogermSpr* 26 (1901) 280–281.

[- - - - - - - -]ν[- - - - - - - - - - - - - -]
[- - - - ἐψάφιστ]ει ἐν ἁ[γ]ο[ρᾶ - - - - - -]
[- - - - - - - - - - - -]ν[- - - - - - - - - -]

[- - - - - - -]ο[- - - - - - - - - - - - - - - -]
[- - - - - -]ε θεοῖς [ο - - - - - - - - - - - -]
[- - - - - - -]ολλ [- - - - - - - - - - - - - - -]
[- - - - - - - - - - - - - -]δ [- - - - - - - - - -]
[- - -]α το[ῖς] μὰ Λευκοφ[ρ]υηνοῖ[ς - - - -]
[- - - ἰ]σ̣οπύ̣θιον σ̣τ̣εφ[ανίταν - - - - - - - -]
[- - -]ο̣μ - - θ - - σλ̣ - - αυ - - ου̣ν[- - - -]
[- - - ο]ἰκεί̣οις ἐπα̣ιν[έσαι] με̣[ν - - - - - - -]
[- - -]σ - - τος - - υ - - νσε - - τ[- - - - -]
[- - -]σ - τοις υ̣ - - - ν - - - α̣ν - - ε[- - -]
[- - -]αιχε - - - ν - -α[- - - - - - - - - - - -]
[- - -]τ̣ιδ - - - μμ - - - τι[- - - - - - - - - -]
[- - - -]νκε̣ι - - - ισσ̣[- - - - - - - - - - - - -]
[- - - - -]γε[γρ]α̣μμέν[- - - - - - - - - - - -]
[ἐν πα]σ̣τά̣[δα?] λιθίναν εἴσθ̣ετ[α. . . . .]α. .ο
[- - -] καὶ . . . . ξένια ἐν [τὸ] [π]ρ[υτα]νε[ῖον - -]
[- - - - -] ἱερὰ . . . θ. ετε. οισ̣ο . . . στοεσ[- - -]
[- - - - - -] τὸ [ψά]φι[σ]μα καὶ οἴκαδε . . . . . τους
[- - - - - -]ν τοῖς θεουροῖς πλοῖον καὶ α̣λ̣ι̣. ε̣
[- - -ψάφισ]μα στάσαντας ἔσσαμον παρὰ. .
[- - - - - - -]σ̣αι οὕς κ' ἐπιστ⟨άε⟩ται ὁ δᾶμος
[- - - - - - - - ο]ὐ̣ μόνον κὰτ τὰν ὁμογένειαν
[- - - - - ἀ]λ̣λ̣ὰ καὶ κὰτ τὰν ὅλαν ἄνγρασ̣ιν ἐ . η̣ς̣
[- - ψάφισ]μα ἐν στάλλαν ⟨λ⟩ιθίναν καὶ θ[έμ]ε[ν - -]
[- - - - - - -] πὰρ τὰν τοῖ βασιλέος εἰκόνα, τὸ [μὰ]
[ἀνάλουμα δό]μεν τὸς ταμία̣ς τό τε ἐν τὰν ὄγγρα̣ψ[ιν]
[καὶ τὰν θέσιν, ἑλ]έσθαι μὰ καὶ θεουροδόκον τὶς ὐ̣[ποδέ]-
[ξεται τὸς παρα]γινομένος θεουρὸς παρὰ Μ[αγή]-
[των. ἁιρέθη Σ]ουίδας Κασάνδρειος.

2, 18 Fick. 23 Fick: ἐς Σάμον? Kern. 24 Fick: ΕΑ̣ΤΑΙ lapis. 25, 26 Rigsby:]ι μόνον and]μα, ἄνγρα⟨ψ⟩ιν Kern. 27: ΑΙΘΙΝΑΝ lapis.

The dialect is Thessalian. Kern's suggestion of Larisa seems best. Our city had more than one treasurer (29), which is unusual in Thessalian cities but richly attested at Larisa.[52] The city seems to have supplied the Magnesian *theoroi* with a boat for some part of their voyage (22); Larisa had a harbor on the Peneius River, which was navigable,[53] and we can envisage a boat downriver to Homolion. Whichever was the city, its king (28) was Philip V.

The sequence of thought is difficult to make out. At 17–18 we seem to have a provision for making known the documents (γεγραμμένα) brought by the *theoroi* (so Fick), then for honoring the men (19) and sending them on their way (21–22).

52. Occasionally too in texts of Gonni, Crannon, and Hypata.

53. *IG* IX.2 517.42: ἐν τὸν λιμένα; cf. Plut. *Pomp.* 73, ποτάμιον πλοῖον at the mouth of the Peneius.

Perhaps in 23–24 the reference is to a request that the decree be inscribed in a conspicuous place in Magnesia; at 27–28 is the provision for inscribing the act locally, next to the statue of the king.

18: Probably the inscriber's error for Thessalian *ἔσσθετα, = ἔκθετα "set out, published" (so Fick; cf. error τὶς for Thessalian relative κὶς in 30).

23: "Erecting the decree in full view"; cf. F. Bechtel, *Die griechischen Dialekte* I (Berlin 1922) 206.

24–26: As I restore, "not only for their kinship ... but also for their whole policy." For ἄνγρεσις = αἵρεσις cf. *IG* IX.2 461.28, 504.4; *BCH* 59 (1935) 56 line 40; Bechtel 204. ὁμογένεια is nearly a hapax.[54] Rarity may intensify the implication of ὁμο-: this seems a stronger word than the familiar συγγένεια. That is perhaps especially apt for a Thessalian city addressing the Magnesians, whose ambassadors will have described their origins in the region (*I. Magn.* 17).

76. Unknown city

Kern, *I.Magnesia* 27.

[- ἀγῶ]να
[- - - - - - - - - - - - - - - - - ἐν τῶι? ἐ]πιφα-
[νεστάτωι τόπωι? - - - - - - - - ἐν τῶι ἱ]ερῶι
[- θ]εωρο-
[δόκος - - - - - - - - - - - - - - - - - - -]. ΙΩ

77. Calydon

Inscribed to the right of **76**.

Kern, *I.Magnesia* 28 [Klaffenbach, *IG* IX.1^{2} 186].

Cf. Wilhelm, *Jahresh.* 4 (1901) Beibl. 25–26 (*Kl. Schr.* II.1 153); Holleaux, *Etudes* I 315.

[- Αἰ]-
τωλοὶ ἄγοντι Μάγνητας [τοὺς ἀπὸ Μαιάν]δρο[υ - - - - - - - - - - - -]
προξένων καὶ εὐεργετᾶν· ὅπ[ως οὗν τὰ δεδ]ο̣γμέν[α κύρια ἧι ἐν]
τὸμ πάντα χρόνον, τοὺς νομο[γράφο]υ̣ς τᾶς πόλ[ιος καταχωρίξαι]
τόδε τὸ ψάφισμα ἐν τοὺς νόμους· θεαροδόκος ἁιρέ[θη Δαμόκριτος]
Στρατάγου· ἀναγραψάντω δὲ καὶ ἐν τὸ ἱερὸν τᾶς Ἀρτ[έμιδος τᾶς Λαφρί]-
ας ᾇ οἱ κτίσται τᾶς πόλιος ἐπὶ τᾶς βάσιος ᾆι ἁ Ἄρτεμις [- - - - - -]
κατὰ τὰ αὐτὰ δὲ ἐψηφίσαντο·

Πλευρώνιοι	Ἀμβρακιῶται	Σκα[ρφεῖς]
Τριχόνιοι	Ἀργεῖοι οἱ Ἀμφίλοχοι	Καλ[λιεῖς]
Αρσινοεῖς	Στράτιοι	Φυσ[κεῖς]

54. Posidonius *FGrHist* 87 F 105b (Strabo 16.4.27) uses it of three Arab tribes. See also Diosc. 1 prooem. 3, where the noun is prompted by long use of the adjective ὁμογενής in biology; whence a scientific tone in Epicur. frag. 36 Usener (of two perceptions); cf. Iambl. *In Nic.* 38.23 Pistelli.

Ἀμφισσεῖς	Ναυπάκτιοι	Ὑπα[ταῖοι]
Πολιεῖς	Ἡρακλεῶται	Θρο[νιεῖς]
Φυταιεῖς	Λαμιεῖς	Ἀ[ντικυρεῖς?]

vacat

1 ὡς Αἰ]- Klaffenbach. 3 end Wilhelm, Holleaux (or βέβαια, κατάμονα, or διαμένηι): φανερὰ ἦι Kern. 4 end Wilhelm, Holleaux: ἀναγράψαι Kern. 5 Klaffenbach. 13 end Klaffenbach: Θρό[νιοι] Kern. 14 end "arbitrary," L. Lerat, *RPhil* III.19 (1945) 185.

Attribution to Calydon, already envisaged by Kern (hence Artemis Laphria, 6) because it is absent from the subscription, was guaranteed by Klaffenbach's recognition of Damocritus in line 5, a Calydonian who was later a *strategos* of the League (cf. *IG* IX.1[2] 31.131). If I am right, the League decree **67**, granting *asylia* but not the crowned games, dates to 221 B.C. If individual members had been approached then, we should expect this decree of 208 to omit *asylia*, as having been already granted; but the substance is lost.

Swoboda argued that the list of Aetolian cities implies a date after the Aetolian loss of western Thessaly in 208/7 and before the Peace of Phoenice late in 205 (*Klio* 11 [1911] 450–456). But 208/7 reflects his date for the Delphian archon Babylus, whom Flacelière would place around 212/1 (*Aitoliens* 295–296).

2: It is difficult to see what sentiment would introduce the following genitives; perhaps ὡς ὑπὲρ].

6: On the cult of Artemis Laphria at Calydon see E. Dyggve, *Das Laphrion* (Copenhagen 1948); C. Antonetti, *Les Etoliens* (Paris 1990) 245–262.

78–79

Stele found at Delphi in 1936 (inv. 6163), complete only on the left, badly worn; h. 0.40, w. 0.19, th. 0.135; letters 0.004–.008, intersp. irregular; two decrees cut by the same hand.

H. van Effenterre, *BCH* 77 (1953) 168–176 [*SEG* 12.217]; J. Bousquet, *REG* 101 (1988) 27–28 (only **78**) [*SEG* 38.412]. *Collation.*

Cf. Bousquet, *BCH* 82 (1958) 91 n. 1.

78. Aetolian League

[- τὰ ψηφίσματα τὰ]
[πρότερον γεγονότα? αὐ]τοῖς περ[ὶ πάντων τῶν φιλανθρώπων κα]-
[τάμο]ν̣α εἶμεν καὶ ὥσπερ ἀξιοῦσ[ι νῦν οἱ πρεσβευταὶ δέχεσθαι τάν]
[τ]ε θυσίαν καὶ τὸν ἀγῶνα τᾶι Ἀρ[τέμιτι τᾶι Λευκοφρυηνᾶι στεφανί]-
ταν ἰσοπύθιον ταῖς τιμαῖς· καὶ ἀ̣[ναγράψαι τόδε τὸ ψήφισμα ἐστά]-
λ̣ας καὶ ἀνθέμεν ἔν τε Δελφοῖς [ἐν τῶι ἱερῶι τοῦ Ἀπόλλωνος καὶ]
ἐν Θερμῶι. στραταγέοντος Μα[- - - - - -, ἱππαρχέοντος δὲ - - - - -]
Φυσχέος, γραμματεύοντος δὲ [τῶν Αἰτωλῶν - - - - - - - - - - - - - -]
[.]ιεος, τῶν δὲ συνέδρων Μαρσ[ύα, Θερμικοῖς· ἔδοξε τοῖς Αἰτωλοῖς τὸ]
ψάφισμα τὸ γενόμενον ἐπὶ [- - - - καθὼς ἀξίουν Μάγνητες οἱ ἀπὸ]

Μαιάνδρου περὶ τοῦ ἀγῶνος [καὶ τᾶς θυσίας ἃν συντελέοντι τᾶι Ἀρ]-
τέμιτι τᾶι Λευκοφρυηνᾶι το[ὺς κατασταθέντας νομογράφους]
καταχωρίξαι ἐν τοὺς νόμους, [ἐπεί κα αἱ νομογραφίαι γίνωνται].

vacat

4 Bousquet 1988. 5 Bousquet 1958. 8 Θερμικοῖς Bousquet 1988. 9 Bousquet 1988: ἐπὶ ἀξιώσει Μαγνήτων τῶν ἀπὸ] van Effenterre. 10 συντελέοντι Bousquet 1988: συντίθεντι van Effenterre. 12 Bousquet 1988.

It happens that in the Magnesian archive decrees of the Aetolian League and Delphi have not survived. But the *theoroi* (**79**.6) are those attested in the Magnesian archive for northwestern Greece, so the occasion is certain. The Aetolians here manifestly recognized the crowned games, which their decree of 221 (**67**) had not done; nothing of what survives here suggests that the Aetolians granted inviolability again, which no doubt would have been felt superfluous.

We have two decrees, both addressing the games. Enough survives of the first (1–6) to reveal it as the League's initial acceptance of the games (3–4), however we reconstruct the first two lines. The second (6–12) is a summary text, stating a decision without the preliminaries that would have revealed the occasion; the provision is to incorporate their earlier vote on the Leucophryeneia into the laws—at the prompting of the Magnesians, if 9 is rightly restored. This act is a later rectification of an oversight in the initial decree; on Bousquet's understanding of line 9 (ἐπί with a previous *strategos*), it was passed at the same meeting as the decree it emends, the autumn meeting at which election of the new *strategos* took place.

1–2: Van Effenterre's restorations, based on **132**, assume reference to earlier decrees (which would include **67**); but this reconstruction must remain in doubt.

6: A second and subsequent decree begins here, which apparently provided only for the inclusion of the first in the laws.[55] A federal *strategos* Μα- is not otherwise known in the late third century (which is in fact rather full); if this is August/September of 208, then this man was *strategos* in 208/7, and his predecessor was named in line 9.

79. Delphi

Inscribed below **78**, after an interval.

[ἄρ]χοντος Ἀθανίωνος, βουλε[υόντων - - - - - - - - - - - - - - - - - -]
[Πρα]όχου, [- - -], Φιλίνου, [ἔδοξε τᾶι πόλει τῶν Δελφῶν ἐν ἀγο]-
[ρᾶι] τελεί[ωι σὺν] ψάφοις ταῖς [ἐννόμοις· ἐπειδὴ Μάγνητες οἱ]
[ἀπὸ] Μαιάνδρου οἰκεῖοι ὄντες [καὶ φίλοι τᾶς πόλιος τῶν Δελφῶν],
[θ]εωροὺς δ[ὲ] κα[ὶ] πρεσβευτ[ὰς Ἀριστόδαμον Διοκλέος, Ἀριστέ]-
[α]ν Φοργάσ[ο]υ, Ἀντάνορα Κωλ[ωτίωνος ἀποστείλαντες, τάν τε οἰκει]-
[ό]τατα κα[ὶ] τὰ ἄλλα τὰ ἔνδο[ξα -]

55. Compare *IG* IX.1^2 4.d (above, p. 191), which adds an earlier decree to the laws.

[.]ας . ΓΕΜ . [. . .] . αν ἀπελογίξ[αντο - - - - - - - - - - - - - - - -]
νουσας ὑπọ̀ ṭọῦ κοινοῦ τῶ[ν Μαγνήτων εἰς τὰν τῶν Δελφῶν πό]-
λιν καὶ εἰ̣ς πάντας τοὺς Ἕλ[λανας καὶ παρεκάλεσαν ἀποδέξασθαι τάς]
τε [θ]υσίας καὶ [ἐκ]ẹχει̣[ρί]αṇ κα[ὶ τὸν ἀγῶνα ὃν τίθεντι τᾶι Ἀρτέμιτι]
τᾶι Λ̣ευκ[οφρ]ụạνᾶι στεφạ[νίταν ἰσοπύθιον ταῖς τιμαῖς· δεδόχθαι]
[τ]ᾶι πόλει ἐπαινέσαι τὸν δ[ᾶμον τῶν Μαγνήτων ἐπί τε τᾶι πο]-
[τ]ὶ τοὺς θεο[ὺς] εὐσεβείαι καὶ [τᾶι ποτὶ τὰν πόλιν εὐνοίαι, καὶ στε]-
[φ]ανῶσαι τ[ὸ]ṇ δᾶμον τῶν Μα[γνήτων δαφνᾶς στεφάνωι τῶι παρὰ]
τοῦ θεοῦ καθὼ̣ς πάτριόν ἐστι Δ̣[ελφοῖς - - - - - - - - - - - - - - - - - -]
[τοῖς] Μάγνησι[ν] ἐν τῶι ἀγῶνι τῶ̣[ν -]
πάντα χρόνον εὐσεβείας ἕ[νεκεν καὶ φιλοτιμίας ποτὶ τὸν θεὸν]
[κ]αὶ τὰν πόλιν τῶν Δελφῶν· [δέχεσθαι δὲ τὸν ἀγῶνα ὃν συντε]-
[λέ]ον[τ]ι Μ̣ά̣[γν]ητ[ες ἀπὸ Μ]ạιάν[δρου στεφανίταν ἰσοπύθιον ταῖς τι]-
[μ]αῖς καὶ [δό]μ[ε]ν [εἰς ἀπ]ạρχὰ[ν -]
[- ?τὰν]
[δὲ πόλι]ṇ αὐτῶν καὶ τ[ὰν χώραν ἱερὰν καὶ ἄσυλον εἶμεν κατὰ]
[τὸν τοῦ θε]οῦ̣ χρησμόν· [ἑλέσθαι δὲ καὶ θεωροδόκους τοὺς ὑποδε]-
[ξομένους τὰς] ἀεὶ πα[ραγινομένας θεωρίας παρὰ τῶν Μαγνήτων]
[-]

The *theoroi* are those we know from the Magnesian archive to have traveled northwestern Greece, so the decree derives from the Magnesians' second quest, the summer of 208.[56] This fixes the Delphian archon Athanion to 209/8 or 208/7,[57] depending upon how quickly the *theoroi* reached Delphi (where the year began in early summer). The presence of both the Aetolian and Delphian recognitions on this stone at Delphi would suggest that the Aetolians' was obtained first; if it is rightly assigned to their autumn meeting, then the Delphians' is also autumn and Athanion's year was 208/7. The alternative, with the Magnesians traveling from east to west, is that the Aetolians' decree was sent on to Delphi before the Delphians had gotten around to inscribing their own decree.

There is not room to restore mention of a request for *asylia* in lines 7–8, which would in any case be too early in the text. If van Effenterre was right to restore the recognition at 23–24 (where nothing survives but an allusion to the oracle), then this decree is like those of Corinth and Corcyra in neglecting to mention the request in the preliminaries. It may be, however, that Delphi does not mention *asylia* at all but following the lead of the Aetolians had granted it in 221.

80. Unknown city

Kern, *I.Magnesia* 30.

56. Van Effenterre (175–176), with much the same argument as Swoboda, held the date to be 207, after the Aetolians' loss of part of Thessaly.

57. Thus Daux, *Chronologie* 45; "248–7?" in Flacelière, *Aitoliens* 463–464.

[δόμε]ν ἀπαρχὰς τὸ ἐκ [τοῦ] νόμου ϛτατῆρας δύο.
[ἐπεψ]ᾳφ[ι]ξε Τιμέ[α]ς.

From the Doric and the location in the archive, Kern surmised a city in the northwest, perhaps Oeniadae (which is absent from the list in **81**).

81. Acarnanian League

Inscribed below **80**.
Kern, *I.Magnesia* 31; Klaffenbach, *IG* IX.1 ^{2} 582.
Cf. Habicht, *Hermes* 85 (1957) 110 n. 2.

[στραταγ]οῦντος [τῶν Ἀ]καρνά[ν]ων Νικαίου τοῦ Ἐχε-
[. . . . . . Κ]οροντaίου, ἱππάρχα Κλεωνύμου τοῦ Λαμίσ-
[κου . . . .]ου, γραμματέος στραταγῶι Χέρσυος τοῦ
[. . . . .] Μεδιωνίου, συνεδρίου γραμματέος Ἀν-
[. . . . .] τοῦ Ἡρακλείτου Ἀνακτοριέος, προμνάμο-
[νος δὲ Ν]ικάνδρου τοῦ Λύκου Θυρρείου, μηνὸς Πα-
[νάμου ἕκτ]αι ἐπ' εἰκάδι, παραγενομένων πρεσβευτᾶν
[παρὰ Μαγ]νήτων τῶν ἐπὶ Μαιάνδρου Ἀριστοδάμου
[τοῦ Διοκ]λέος, Ἀριστέα τοῦ Γοργάσου, Ἀντάνορος τοῦ
[Κωλω]τίωνος καὶ διαλεγομένων περὶ τᾶς οἰκειό-
[τατ]ος τᾶς ὑπαρχούσας τοῖς Μάγνησιν ποτὶ τοὺς
[Ἀκ]αρνᾶνας, ἔτι δὲ καὶ τὰν φιλίαν ἀ[ν]ανεουμέ-
[ν]ων καὶ τὰς εὐεργεσίας ἀπολογιζομένων ἃς πεποίην-
ται τὸ κοινὸν τῶν Μαγνήτων ἐς τοὺς Ἕλλανας, ἀποδόντων
δὲ καὶ τὸ ψάφισμα καθ' ὃ παρεκάλουν δέχεσθαι τὰν ἐ-
κεχειρίαν χρήσαντος τοῦ θεοῦ τοῦ ἐν Δελφοῖς λώϊον
[εἶμ]εν καὶ ἄμεινον [τ]οῖς σεβομένοις Ἄρτεμιν Λευκοφρυη-
νὰν καὶ τὰν πόλιν αὐτῶν καὶ τὰν χώραν ἱερὰν καὶ ἄσυλον εἶ-
[μ]εν, διὸ καὶ τὸν δᾶμον ἐψαφίσθαι τᾶι εὐεργέτιδι τᾶς πόλιος
Ἀρτέμιδι Λευκοφρυηνᾶι διὰ πέντε ἐτέων θυσίας καὶ
πανάγυριν καὶ ἀγῶνα στεφανίταν ἰσοπύθιον μουσι-
κόν τε καὶ γυμνικὸν καὶ ἱππικὸν ποιεῖν, δικαίαν ἀποδι-
δόντας χάριν τᾶι εὐεργέτιδι, παρακαλούντ[ων αὐ]-
τῶν ὅπως οἱ οἰκεῖοί τε καὶ φίλοι μετέχ⟨ω⟩ντι τᾶν θυσιᾶν
τᾶν συντελουμενᾶν ὑπ' αὐτῶν, καὶ ἐμφανιζόντων τὰν
ἐπιφάνειαν τᾶς θεοῦ, δεδόχθαι τᾶι βουλᾶι τῶν Ἀκαρ-
νάνων καὶ τοῖς χιλίοις τάν τε θυσίαν καὶ ἐκεχειρί-
αν καὶ τὸν ἀγῶνα ποτιδέχεσθαι στεφανίταν ἰσοπύ-
θιον ταῖ[ς] τιμαῖς, εἶμεν δὲ αὐτῶν τάν τε πόλιν καὶ τὰν
χώραν ἱερὰν καὶ ἄσυλον, ἀποστέλλε[ι]ν δὲ καὶ θεω-
ροὺς τοὺς συνθύσοντας τὰν θυσίαν καὶ θεαροδόκους
καταστᾶσαι ἑκάσταν πόλιν τᾶν Ἀκαρνανίδων τοὺς
ὑποδεξομένους ἀεὶ τοὺς παραγινομένους θεωροὺς πα-
ρὰ τῶν Μαγνήτων· δόμεν δὲ Ἵππαρχον τὸν ταμίαν εἰς
ἀπαρχὰν τᾶι θεῶι εἰς τὰν θυσίαν ἀργυρίω δραχμὰς
ἑκατὸν πεντήκοντα, ἀνανεώσασθαι δὲ καὶ τὰν φι-

[λία]ν καὶ τὰν οἰκειότατα καθὼς παρεκάλουν· ὅπως
[δὲ] μεί[ν]ηι εἰς τὸν ἅπαντα χρόνον, ἀναγράψαι δὲ τὰ
[δεδ]ογμένα εἰς στάλαν λιθίναν Ἵππαρχον τὸν ταμί-
[αν] καὶ ἀναθέμεν ἐν τῶι ἱερῶι τοῦ Ἀπόλλωνος τοῦ
[Ἀκτ]ίου· εἶμεν δὲ προξένους καὶ εὐεργέτας τοῦ κοι-
[νοῦ] τῶν Ἀκαρνάνων κατὰ τὸν νόμον Ἀριστόδα-
[μον] Διοκλέο⟨ς⟩, Ἀριστέα Γοργάσου, Ἀντάνορα Κωλωτί-
[ωνος].
κατὰ τὰ αὐτὰ δὲ ἐψηφίσαντο·

Θυρρεῖς	Μεδιώνο[ι]
Λευκάδιοι	Παλαιρεῖς
Ἀνακτόριοι	[Φ]οκρεῖς
Ἀλυζεῖς	. . . λε[ῖς?]

3: perhaps Θυρρεί]ου, Klaffenbach in sched. IG, from *IG* IX.1^2 246–247. 24: XON lapis. 31: ΖΥΝΘΥΣ, then corrected by the mason. 48 end Habicht.

The Acarnanian League was at this time allied with Philip V against the Aetolians. For the constitutional details seen here we have a close parallel in *Staatsvertr.* III 523, a League treaty of about a decade earlier. The earlier text adds a nauarch to the roster of magistrates (in third position) and calls the two secretaries those of the council (βουλά) and magistrates. The Aetolian League likewise had two secretaries (cf. Klaffenbach ad *IG* 69.3–4).

8–10: Aristodamus, with varying companions but always named first, went on up the Illyrian coast; he had one set of companions on the southern mainland, another companion (who went on to Sicily) on the western islands (where he was second to his brother) and then Illyria. The brother later served as Magnesia's representative to the Amphictyony, and both were then honored by Delphi and the Aetolian League (*I.Magn.* 91 [*Syll.*^{3} 598; *IG* IX.1^2 187], 190s B.C.).

26–27: "The council and the Thousands" recur in the decree at P. Funke et al., *Klio* 75 (1993) 131–144; "the Thousands" are reported to have been mentioned in a now lost inscription of the early third century, *IG* IX.1^2 207. *Staatsvertr.* III 523 lacks the authorizing phrase; in later League decrees (listed at Habicht 90) we find τᾶι βουλᾶι καὶ τῶι κοινῶι τῶν Ἀκαρνάνων.

31–34: The League can order its member cities to elect *theorodochoi*; so too the Aetolian League (**178**.25). Presumably this is the same as ordering them to recognize the crowned games, as Attalus did with his subjects.

40–41: *Staatsvertr.* III 523 reveals that the temple of Apollo at Actium became a federal temple of the League only about a decade before the present decree.

82. Epirote League

Kern, *I.Magnesia* 32 [J. Pouilloux, *Choix d'inscriptions* (Paris 1960) 22].
Cf. Wilhelm, *Jahresh.* 4 (1901) Beibl. 26 (*Kl. Schr.* II.1 153).

[ἐπειδὴ Μάγνητες οἱ ἐπὶ Μαιάνδ]ρωι φίλο[ι ὄ]ντες καὶ

οἰκεῖοι̣ [τῶν Ἀπειρωτᾶν ψάφισμ]ά τε καὶ πρεσβευτὰς ἀποστείλαν[τες Ἀριστόδαμο]ν̣ Διοκλέος, Ἀριστέα Γοργάσου, Ἀντάν̣[ορα Κωλωτίων]ος τάν τε φιλίαν καὶ τὰν οἰκειότατα ἀ[νενεώσ]αντο καὶ παρεκάλουν τοὺς Ἀπειρώτας ἀποδέξασθαι τὸν ἀγῶνα ὃν τίθητι ἁ πόλις τῶν Μαγνήτων τᾶι Ἀρτέμιδι τᾶι Λευκοφρυηνᾶι κατὰ πενταετηρίδα μουσικόν τε καὶ γυμνικὸν καὶ ἱππικὸν ἰσοπύθιον ταῖς τιμαῖς κατὰ τὰς μαντείας τοῦ θεοῦ τοῦ ἐν Δελφοῖς, ἐνεφάνιξαν δὲ οἱ πρεσβευταὶ καὶ τὸγ χρησμὸν ἐν ὧι λώϊον ἦγ καὶ ἄμεινον τιμᾶν Ἀπόλλωνα Πύθιον καὶ Ἄρτεμιν Λευκοφρυηνὰγ καὶ τὰν πόλιν καὶ τὰγ χώραν τῶν Μαγνήτων ἱερὰγ καὶ ἄσυλον νομίζουσιν, ἀπελογίξαντο δὲ καὶ τὰν ἐπιφ̣άνειαν τᾶς θεοῦ καὶ τὰς γεγενημένας ἀπὸ τῶν Μαγνήτων εἰς τοὺς Ἕλλανας εὐχρηστίας τε καὶ εὐεργεσίας καὶ ἀξίουγ καὶ παρεκάλουν τοὺς Ἀπειρώτας ἀποδέξασθαι καὶ συναυξῆσαι τὰς ἐψηφισμένας τιμὰς τᾶι θεῶι· τα[ῦτ]α γὰρ ποιήσαντας ἀκόλουθα πράξειν τ⟨ᾶ⟩ι τοῦ θεοῦ μαντείαι, χαριεῖσθαι δὲ καὶ τῶι δάμωι· δεδόχθαι τοῖς Ἀπειρώταις τάν τε οἰκειότατα καὶ φιλίαν τὰν ὑπάρχουσαν τοῖς Ἀπειρώταις ποτὶ τοὺς Μάγνητας ἀνανεώσασθαι, καὶ τὸν ἀγῶνα ὃν τίθητι ἁ πόλις τῶν Μαγνήτων τᾶι Ἀρτέμιδι τᾶι Λευκοφρυηνᾶι ⟨π⟩οτιδέχε⟨σθ⟩αι στεφανίταν ἰσοπύθιον ταῖς τιμαῖς· καὶ τὰν [π]όλιν δὲ καὶ τὰν χώραν τῶν Μαγνήτων εἶμεν ἱερὰν κα[ὶ] ἄσυλον, καθίστασθαι δὲ καὶ θεαροδόχους τοὺς ὑποδεξομένους τοὺς θεωροὺς τοὺς ἑκαστάκις παραγινομένους καὶ ἐπαγγέλλοντας τὰν θυσίαν καὶ τὸν ἀγῶνα{ι} ἐκ τᾶς τῶν Μαγνήτων πόλιος, ἀποστέλλειν δὲ καὶ θεωροὺς τοὺς συνθύσοντας καὶ συναυξήσοντας τὰς τιμὰς τᾶι θεῶι, ὑπάρχειν δὲ καὶ τοῖς Μάγνησιν φίλοις καὶ οἰκείοις οὖσιν τὸ δίκαιογ καθάπερ καὶ τοῖς προξένοις τῶν Ἀπειρωτᾶν· ὅπως δὲ εἰς τὸν ἅπαντα χρόνον ὑπάρχηι φανερὰ τὰ δε[δ]ογμ̣ένα, ἀναγράψαι τ[ὸ] ψάφισμα ἐν Δωδώναι ἐν τῶι ἱερῶι τοῦ Διὸς τοῦ Νάου ἐν τῶι βήματι τῶι Ἀθηναίων ἀναθέματι, καὶ ἐπιμεληθῆμεν ὅπως γρα⟨φ⟩ῆι Κρίσωνα τὸν στραταγὸν καὶ τοὺς συνάρχοντας, τὸ δὲ ἀνάλωμα δόμεν Χαροπίδαν τὸν ἐπικαθιστάμενον γραμματῆ{ι} συνεδρίου· ἐπαινέσαι δὲ καὶ τοὺς πρεσβευτὰς Ἀριστόδαμον, Ἀριστέα, Ἀντ̣άνορα ὅτ̣ι παρ[ε]πεδάμησάν τε καὶ διελέγη[ν] περὶ πάντων ἀξίω[ς] τ̣ᾶς τε πόλιος τῶν Μαγνήτων καὶ τοῦ ἔθνους τῶν Ἀπειρωτᾶν, διὸ προξένους εἶμεν αὐτούς τε καὶ ἐκγόνους εἰς τὸν ἅπαντα χρόνον, ὑπάρχειν δὲ αὐτοῖς καὶ πολιτείαν καὶ ἀσφάλειαν π̣αρὰ Ἀπειρωτᾶν καὶ πολέμου καὶ εἰράνας καὶ ἀτέλειαν καὶ ἐντέλειαν καὶ τὰ ἄ̣λλα πάντα καθὼς [κ]α̣ὶ̣ τοῖς ἄλλοις Ἀπειρώταις, δόμεν δὲ καὶ ἐκέχειρον

48 [αὐτοῖς Χα]ροπίδαν τὸν [γ]ραμματῆ{ι} τῶν συνέδρ[ων]
[ὅσον καὶ τοῖς] τ̣ὰ̣ Πύθια ἐπ̣αγγέλ[λουσ]ιν ἐ̣ν̣ τ̣ο̣ῖ̣ς̣ ν̣[όμοις.]
[κατὰ τὰ αὐτὰ] δὲ̣ ἀπεδέξαντο
[Κα]σ[σ]ωπαῖοι.

11: τιμᾶ⟨σι⟩ν Schulze ap. Kern. 19: the mason wrote THI, then corrected to AHI (i.e., he misplaced the new letter). 24: NAIOTIΔEXETAI lapis. 37 Wilhelm: ΨHI lapis.

On the institutions and the extant decrees of the League see P. Cabanes, *L'Epire* (Paris 1976) 353–383; Gauthier, *RPhil* III.53 (1979) 120–128; Moretti, *I. stor. ellen.* II p. 129 n. 10. As Pouilloux remarks (p. 87), the Magnesian inscriber has omitted the constitutional mechanics that would have headed the decree. In 208 the League was already dominated by Rome; cf. S. I. Oost, *Roman Policy in Epirus and Acarnania* (Dallas 1954) 30–39.

31–33: On this collective grant of proxeny to the Magnesians see Gauthier, *Les cités grecques et leur bienfaiteurs* (Paris 1985) 163.

35–36: The oracular shrine of Zeus at Dodona became the federal temple of the Epirotes toward 230 B.C. As Kern saw, the *bema* of the Athenians must be the dedication mentioned by the fourth-century orators, called a bronze *trapeza* (Dem. 21.53) and an ornament of the throne of Dione (Hyper. *Eux.* 24).

37: Cabanes (364, 392; cf. 362 on συνάρχοντας) suggests that Crison may be the same as a man attested some years earlier whom he takes also to be a *strategos* (*SEG* 24.446, 451), hence here for the second time or more.

46: ἐντέλεια is often granted in Epirote proxeny decrees, always as one in a list of rights and therefore not easily interpreted; LSJ translate "full rights." Here the word seems to be more specific, and to balance ἀτέλεια. Perhaps the pair means "with tax immunity and liability" the same as of Epirotes.

83. Gonni

Kern, *I.Magnesia* 33 [Helly, *Gonnoi* no. 111].
Cf. Boesch, *Hermes* 52 (1917) 136–140.

ταγευόντων τῶν περὶ Εὔδημον τὸν Νικάνορος, Νίκαι-
ον τὸν Νικάρχου, Μίκυθον ⟨τὸν⟩ Παρμενίωνος, Γόρρασον
τὸν Ἀσάνδρου, Ἄσανδρον τὸν Ἐπίνου, ἔδοξεν τῆι
4 πόλει τῆι Γοννέων· ἐπειδὴ Μάγνητες οἱ ἐπὶ Μαιάν-
δρου φίλοι ὄντες καὶ συγγενεῖς Γοννέων, ἔχοντες
τὴν πόλιν καὶ τὴν χώραν ἱερὰν καὶ ἄσυλον τῆς Ἀρτέμι-
δος τῆς Λευκοφρυηνῆς καὶ αὔξοντες τὴν πρὸς τοὺς
8 θεοὺς εὐσέβειαν, ἀποστείλαντες ἄνδρας Διαγόραν
Κρατίνου, Ζώπυρον Ἑρμώνακτος, Διότιμον Λυκομήδου[ς]
τήν τε θυσίαν ἐπήγγελλον καὶ τὴν πανή[γυ]ριν καὶ τὸν
ἀγῶνα ὃν προκεχειρισμένοι εἰσὶν συντελεῖν τῆ[ι Ἀρτ]έ-
12 μιδι τῆι Λευκοφρυηνῆι κατὰ τὸν χρησμὸν τοῦ ἐν
Δελφοῖς θεοῦ στεφανίτην ἰσοπύθιον μουσικὸν καὶ

γυμνικὸν καὶ ἱππικόν, καὶ ἀνενεώσαντο τὴν ἐξ ἀρχῆς ὑπάρχουσαν φιλίαν καὶ οἰκειότητα Μάγνησίν τε καὶ Γοννεῦσιν, δεδόχθαι τῆι πόλει τήν τε θυσίαν καὶ τὴν πανήγυριν καὶ τὸν ἀγῶνα ἀποδέξασθαι ἰσ̣οπύθιον, καὶ τὸ ἐκεχείριον δοῦναι τοὺς ταμίας ἐκ τῶν κοινῶν προσόδων ὅσον καὶ τοῖς ἐπαγγέλλουσιν τὰ Πύθια, δραχμὰς Δημητριείους εἴκοσιν, δίδοσθαι δὲ καὶ τοῖς νικήσασιν Γοννέων τοὺς ἀγῶνας τού[τ]ο⟨υς⟩ ὅσον καὶ τοῖς τὰ Πύθια νικῶσιν δίδοται, ἀποστέλλειν δὲ καὶ θεωροὺς καθ' ἑκάστην σύνοδον τοὺς κοινωνήσοντας τῆς θυσίας· ἐπαινέσαι δὲ καὶ τοὺς ἀπεσταλμένους ἄνδρας Διαγόραν, Ζώπυρον, Διότιμον ἐπὶ τ̣ῆι φιλοτιμίαι ἧι πεποίηνται πρὸς τὴν πόλιν· ἀναγράψαι δὲ καὶ τὸ ψήφισμα τόδε εἰς τὰ κοινὰ γράμματα καὶ ἀνενεγκεῖν εἰς τὸ νομοφυλάκιον, ὅπως καὶ εἰς τὸν ἐνεσόμενον χρόνον ἀεὶ τοῖς ἀποστελλομένοις ὑπάρχωσιν τὰ τίμια πάντα ἀξίως [τ]ῆ[ς] θ[ε]ᾶς· ἀ[πε]δείχθη θεωροδόκος ἡ πόλις.

ἀκολούθως δὲ ἔδοξεν
ψηφίσασθαι
Φαλανναίοις

vacat

Gonni in Thessaly was a dependency of the Antigonids.

2: Micythus is attested as *tagos* in another decree (Helly no. 12 = Moretti, *I. stor. ellen.* II 104); cf. Helly I p. 108; Habicht in *Ancient Macedonia* I (Thessalonica 1970) 269.

5–7: "Having their city and country sacred and inviolable for Artemis Leucophryene and intending to increase their piety toward the gods," they are establishing the games: the Gonneis clearly state that Magnesia possesses inviolability already and do not describe this as part of the request, nor do they grant it. It is evident that this is not a refusal, but a presumption that that status already exists and what is at issue is the new games. I would conclude that they had granted inviolability already in 221 B.C.

11: For προχειρίζεσθαι of a contest see *Syll.*[3] 457.15 (the Mouseia of Thespiae).

20: "Demetrian drachmas" are silver of Demetrius Poliorcetes (†283), which the hoard evidence shows to have circulated throughout the third century B.C. and later.[58] No coinage has been attributed to Demetrius II (239–229 B.C.). Only bronze issues are known on the part of Gonni (Helly I 155–159).

23: For σύνοδος of a festival cf. *IG* XII.7 36.22, *OGIS* 326.25.

28: For *nomophylakes* in cities closely controlled by kings, see on **25**.2.

58. E.g., *Coin Hoards* 5 (1979) no. 42 (buried ca. 190 B.C.).

30–31: The city itself rather than a private citizen is made responsible for hosting future *theoroi.* Boesch (111–112) compares the city of Delphi serving as *proxenos* for Sardes in *Syll.*[3] 548 (on which see Gauthier, *Nouv. inscr. Sardes* II pp. 143–144).

34: Phalanna, about fifteen kilometers southwest of Gonni up the Europus River, presumably shared a border, as no city is known in between (cf. Helly I 34).

84. Phocian League

From line 13 on a lower block, from 30 on a third.
Kern, *I.Magnesia* 34.
Cf. Robert, *RPhil* n.s. 53 (1927) 114–115 (*Op. min. sel.* II 1069–1070).

παρὰ τοῦ κοινοῦ τῶν Φωκέων
ἐπε[ι]δὴ Μάγνητες οἱ ἐπὶ Μαιάνδρωι οἰκεῖοι ὄντες καὶ φί-
λοι Φωκέων ψάφισμα καὶ θεωροὺς [ἀ]πεστάλκαντι Ἀπολλοφά-
νην Αἰσχύλου, Εὔβουλον Ἀναξαγόρα, Λυκομήδ[η]ν Χαρι-
σίου, οἵτινες παραγενόμενοι ποτὶ τὸ κοινὸν τῶμ Φωκέων
ἀνενεώσαντό τε τὰν διὰ προγόνων ὑπάρχουσαν οἰκειό-
τατα καὶ φιλίαν ποτὶ Μάγνητας καὶ ἀπολογιξάμενοι διὰ
πλειόνων τάν τε τᾶς θεᾶς Ἀρτέμιτος {τὰν} ἐπιφάνειαν τᾶς
Λευκοφρυηνᾶς κὴ τὰς γεγενημένας ὑπὸ τῶμ προγόνων αὐτῶν
ἐν τοὺς Ἕλλανας [εὐ]εργεσίας παρεκάλεσαν μετὰ πάσας σπουδᾶς
καὶ φιλοτιμίας ἀποδέξασθαι τοὺς Φωκεῖς τὸν ἀγῶνα στεφα[νί]-
[ταν ἰσο]πύθιον ὃν τίθεντι τᾶι Ἀρτέμιτι τᾶι Λε̣[υκοφρυη]ν̣[ᾶι, καὶ τὰν]
πόλιν αὐ[τ]ῶν̣ [καὶ] τὰγ χώραν ἱερὰν [κ]αὶ ἄσο̣υλον εἶμεν, καθότι̣ [α]ὐτοῖς
καὶ ὁ θεὸς ὁ ἐν Δελφοῖς ἔχρησεν· ὅπως οὖν καὶ τὸ κοινὸν τῶμ Φωκέ-
ων φαίνηται τάν τε πὸτ τὸ θεῖον εὐσέβειαν καὶ τὰς τιμὰς συναύ-
ξειν, καθότι αὐτοῖς πάτριόν ἐστιν, μναμονεύοντες τᾶς οἰκειότα-
τος καὶ φιλίας ποτὶ Μάγνητας, δεδόχθαι Φωκεῦσι ἀποδέξασθαι
τὸν ἀγῶνα ὃν τίθεντι Μάγνητες τᾶι Ἀρτέμιτι τᾶι Λευκοφρυηνᾶι
στεφανίταν ἰσοπύθιον, κα[ὶ] τὰμ πόλιν αὐ̣τῶγ καὶ τὰγ χώραν ἱε-
ρὰν καὶ ἄσουλον εἶμεν, καθὼς κὴ [ὁ] θεὸς ἔχρησεν, καὶ τετάχθαι
τοῖς νικεόντοις {ἄθλοις} ἆθλα καὶ τιμὰς ἃς καὶ τοῖς τὰ Πύθια
νικεόντοις, ἀποστέλλειν δὲ καὶ θεαροὺς καὶ θύειν, καθά̣περ καὶ
ἐν τοὺς λοιποὺς ἀγῶνας, ὅ(κ)α παραγγέλλω[ν]τι Μάγνητες· ἐπαι-
νέσαι δὲ καὶ τοὺς θεαροὺς Ἀπολλοφάνην Αἰσχύλου, Εὔβουλον
Ἀναξαγόρα, Λυκομήδην Χαρισίου καὶ στεφανῶσαι αὐτοὺς δάφνα̣ς
στεφάνωι κατὰ τὰ πά̣τρια εὐσεβείας ἕνεκεν τᾶ̣ς ποτὶ τὰν θεὰν
καὶ τᾶς ἐν τὰμ πατρίδα φιλοτιμίας, καὶ εἶμεν αὐτ̣[οὺς] καὶ ἐκγό-
νους προξένους καὶ εὐερ[γέτ]α̣ς τοῦ κ̣οιν[οῦ τ]ῶ[μ Φωκέ]ων καὶ ἰσο-
πολίτας κ̣αὶ ὑπάρχειν αὐτ[οῖς πάντα τὰ φιλάνθρωπα ὅσ]α καὶ
[τοῖς π]ροξένοις καὶ εὐργέτ[α]ις Φωκέων· ἀναγράψαι δὲ καὶ τοὺς [Φ]ω-
κ̣ά̣ρχας [τ]ὸ ψάφισμ[α τ]οῦ[τ]ο ἐν στάλαι λιθίναι καὶ ἀναθεῖναι ἐ[ν] τ̣ὸ
ἱερὸν τᾶς Ἀθανᾶς τᾶς Κραναίας, τὸ δὲ ἀ̣νάλωμα δόμεν τοὺς [Φ]ω-
κάρχας καὶ τοὺς χρ[η]ματιστὰς τᾶς Τ̣ . Ο̣ . . Α̣Ι̣, καταχωρίξαι δὲ

τοὺς ν̣ομογράφους κα[ὶ] ἐν τοὺς νόμους [τ]ὸ ψάφισμα τοῦτο, [καλέ]-
σαι δὲ τοὺς Φωκάρχας καὶ ἐπὶ ξένια τοὺς θεαρούς.

23 Schultze ap. Kern: ΟΣΙΑ lapis. 33: so I read, most doubtfully, on the stone; the squeeze shows nothing here: τᾶς π[όλιος] Kern, τᾶς [Ἀθανᾶς] Robert, τᾶς Τφ̣[6] Α̣ Klaffenbach in sched. IG.

The only other Phocian decree extant is **53** for Tenos. In 208 the League was allied with Philip V and the Achaeans; Elateia was under Macedonian control from 217 to 197 (cf. F. Schober, *RE* 20 [1941] 490–494).

8: The word order seems garbled. Given his one error, I suspect that the mason realized that he had skipped ἐπιφάνειαν, and in inscribing it late included the article again by mistake; that is, the true text was τάν τε ἐπιφάνειαν τᾶς θεᾶς Ἀρτέμιτος τᾶς Λευκοφρυηνᾶς κτἡ.

32: The temple of Athena Cranaea, the federal temple of the Phocians, was atop a hill two miles southeast of Elateia; **53** was discovered in the ruins. For the excavations see P. Paris, *Elatée* (Paris 1892) 73–206.

33: Robert saw that the Phocians ought not to call themselves a city. On the squeeze I can see nothing; the stone yields faint traces, which I report with much uncertainty. Perhaps the mason meant to write τοῦ κοινοῦ.

85. Same

Kern, *I.Magnesia* 35.

[ἐπὶ] ἀρχόντων Λυκίνου τοῦ Λύκου, Φαλακρίωνος τ̣[οῦ . . . . . .]κράτου το[ῦ]
[Εὐ]ηθίδα, γραμματέος Τίμωνος τοῦ Σωτάκου, ἱερο[ποιοῦ Φι]λ̣ίσκου τοῦ Ἀν-
[δρ]ομήδους, πρεσβευτᾶν παραγενομένων παρὰ τοῦ [δ]άμου τοῦ Μαγνήτων
[τῶ]ν ἐπὶ Μαιάνδρου, τῶν δὲ αὐτῶν ἀρχιθεώρου Σω̣σικλέος τοῦ Διοκλέ-
[ο]ς καὶ θεωρῶν Ἀριστοδάμου τοῦ Διοκλέος, Διοτ[ί]μου τοῦ Μηνοφίλου,
[κ]αὶ τό τε ψάφισμα ἀποδόντων καὶ ἐμφανιζόντων τάν τε τᾶς Ἀρτέμι-
[το]ς ἐπιφάνειαν καὶ τὰς γεγενημένας ὑπὸ τῶν προγόνων αὐτῶν ἐν τοὺς
[Ἕ]λλανας εὐεργεσίας καὶ ἐν τὸ ἱερὸν τὸ ἐν Δελφοῖς διά τε τῶν τοῦ θεοῦ
[χ]ρησμῶν καὶ διὰ τῶμ ποιητᾶν καὶ διὰ τῶμ ψαφισμάτων τῶν ὑπαρχόν-
[τ]ων αὐτοῖς παρὰ ταῖς πολίοις καλῶν τε καὶ ἐνδόξων καὶ παρακαλούντων
ἀ̣ποδέξασθαι τάν τε θυσίαν καὶ τὰν ἐκεχηρίαν καὶ τὸν ἀγῶνα ὃν τίθεντι τᾶι Ἀρ-
τέμιτι τᾶι Λευκοφρυηνᾶι στεφανίταν ἰσοπύθιον ταῖς τιμαῖς, ἐμφανιξάντων
δὲ καὶ περὶ τᾶς οἰκειότατος τᾶς ὑπαρχούσας Μαγνήτοις ποτὶ Κεφαλλᾶνας
κατὰ τὰν συγγένειαν τὰμ Μάγνητος καὶ Κεφάλου τοῦ Δηΐονος μετὰ πάσας φιλο-
τιμίας· ὅπως οὖν καὶ ἁ πόλις τῶν Σαμαίων φαίνηται συναύξουσα τὰς τῶν θε-
ῶν τιμάς, καθὼς πάτριόν ἐστιν Σαμαίοις, δεδόχθαι τᾶι πόλει τῶν Σαμαίων,
ἐπαινέσαι μὲν τὸν δᾶμον τὸμ Μαγνήτων ἐπί τε τᾶι ποτὶ τοὺς θεοὺς εὐσεβείαι
καὶ ἐπὶ τᾶι ποτὶ τοὺς Σαμαίους εὐνοίαι, καὶ καλεῖν τὸν δᾶμον τὸμ Μαγνήτων

ἐμ προεδρίαν Διονυσίοις καὶ ἐν τὰν θυσίαν καὶ τὸν ἀγῶνα τοῦ Κεφάλου ὃν τίθη-
τι ἁ πόλις εὐσεβείας ἕνεκεν καὶ εὐεργεσίας τᾶς τε ἐν τὸ ἱερὸν τὸ ἐν Δελφοῖς
κ̣αὶ ἐν τοὺς ἄλλους Ἕλλανας, δέχεσθαι δὲ καὶ τὸν ἀγῶνα ὃν τίθεντι τᾶι Ἀρτέ-
μιτι τᾶι Λευκοφρυηνᾶι στεφανίταν ἰσοπύθιον ταῖς τιμαῖς, καθὼς ἐπάγγελλον
ὅ τε ἀρχιθέωρος καὶ οἱ θεωροί, εἶμεν δὲ αὐτῶν τάν τε πόλιν καὶ τὰν χώραν ἱερὰν
καὶ ἄσυλον καθὼς ὁ Ἀπόλλων ὁ ἐν Δελφοῖς ἀνιέρωσεν· ἀποστέλλειν δὲ καὶ θε-
ωροὺς ἐμ Μαγνησίαν, οἵτινες συνθυσοῦντι τὰν θυσίαν καὶ συναυξησοῦντι
τὰς τιμὰς τᾶι θεῶι· ἐπαινέσαι δὲ τόν τε ἀρχιθέωρον καὶ τοὺς θεωροὺς καὶ εἶ-
μεν προξένους καὶ εὐεργέτας τᾶς πόλιος τῶ[ν] Σαμαίων Σωσικλέα, Ἀριστόδα-
μον, Διότιμον, ἐπειδὴ διελέγ{ει}εν τε καὶ παρε[π]εδάμησαν ἀξίως τᾶς τῶμ Μα-
γνήτων πόλιος καὶ τᾶς τῶν Σαμαίων, καὶ ὑπάρχειν αὐτοῖς πάντα τὰ φιλάνθρω-
πα παρὰ τᾶς πόλιος ὅσα καὶ τοῖς λοιποῖς προξένοις καὶ εὐεργέταις, δόμεν δὲ τοῖς
θεωροῖς ἐνεκέχηρον ἀργυρίου ἡμιμναῖον καὶ ἐνέστιον οἶν, καλέσαι δὲ αὐτοὺς
καὶ ἐπὶ ξένια ἐμ πρυτανεῖον ἐπὶ τὰν κοινὰν ἑστίαν· ἑλέσθαι δὲ καὶ θεαροδόκον
τὸν ὑποδεξόμ̣ενον τὰς παραγινομένας θεωρίας παρὰ τῶμ Μαγνήτων· ἁ̣[ιρέ]θ̣η
[Κ]λευφάνης Σιμάκο[υ]· τὸ δὲ ψάφ[ι]σμα τοῦτο ἀναγράψαι ἐν στάλαν καὶ ἀνα[θέμε]ν
[τ]οὺς ἄρχοντας ἐν τᾶι ἀγορᾶι παρὰ τὸ ἱερὸν τᾶς Ἀρτέμιτος, καταχωρίξαι δὲ
καὶ ἐν τοὺς νόμους τούς τε ἄρχοντας καὶ τοὺς νομογράφους, παραπέμψαι
δὲ αὐτοὺς ἐν Ἰθάκαν.

κατὰ τὰ αὐτὰ δὲ ἐψηφίσαντο·
Παλεῖς, [Κ]ράνιοι, [Πρῶ]νν[οι]

These *theoroi* went on to Ithaca, Corcyra, Apollonia, and Epidamnus. This is the only extant decree from any of the four cities of Cephallenia; the subscription (38–39) indicates that the other three were successfully asked by the Magnesians. In these years the four were Aetolian allies and held a seat on the Delphian Amphictyony, which rotated among them (Flacelière, *Aitoliens* 284–285). Same alone resisted Rome in 189 and was destroyed (Livy 38.28–29).

9–10: These laudatory decrees of other states were not other grants of *asylia* that the *theoroi* had collected but earlier honors voted to the Magnesians for the services to Greece that they cited in their decree of request; see above, p. 181.

14: The Samaeans are unusual in specifying the basis of their kinship with the Magnesians. The hero Cephalus, eponym of the island, is seen on the coins of several of the cities: he was given the island for helping Amphitryon with his wars.[59] His father, Deion, was the brother of Magnes, whence the kinship.

59. Strab. 10.2.14 (456); Apollod. 2.4.7; schol. *Il.* 2.631 (I 315 Erbse).

The same *theoroi* at Ithaca apparently mentioned no kinship there, although Odysseus was great-great-great-grandson to Deion.

19: Collective *proedria* at the local games was also voted by neighboring Ithaca, **86**.16.

36–37: The provision of an escort was a common civility of Hellenistic diplomacy and does not (as Kern thought, *Hermes* 506) prove the political dependence of Ithaca upon Cephallenia; cf. Dittenberger, *Syll.*² 257 note 2. This gesture would seem to imply that Same was the last of the Cephallenian cities visited; at any rate, it was the closest to Ithaca.

86. Ithaca

Kern, *I.Magnesia* 36 [Dittenberger, *Syll.*² 257; Hiller, *Syll.*³ 558].

[ἐπ]ὶ̣ δαμιοργῶν Ἀρνίσκο[υ τοῦ - - -, Τ]ι̣μάνορος [τοῦ - - -,]
Ἀναξιλάου τοῦ Κλεομήδεος, [ἐκκλησία ἐν] τῶι Ὀδυσσεί̣[ωι, γραμματέος Ἀ]-
γλαοτέλεος, ἐπειδὴ Μάγνητες ο̣[ἱ ἀ]π[ὸ Μα]ιάνδρου οἰκεῖοι ὄντε[ς] κ[αὶ φίλοι]
τᾶς πόλιος τῶν Ἰθάκων πρεσβευ[τ]ὰς [ἀπ]οστείλαντες τοὺς δὲ αὐ[τοὺς]
καὶ ἐπαγγελτῆρας Σωσικλῆν Διοκλέος, Ἀριστόδαμον Διοκλέος, Διό[τι]-
μον Μηνοφίλου, οἵτινες τό τε ψάφισμα ἀπέδωκαν καὶ αὐτοὶ ἀπελογίξαν-
το τάν τε τᾶς Ἀρτέμιδος ἐπιφάνειαν καὶ τὰν γεγενη̣μένας ὑπὸ τῶν προγό-
νων αὐτῶν ἐν τοὺς Ἕλλανας εὐεργεσίας καὶ ἐν τὸ ἱερὸν τὸ ἐν Δελ̣φοῖς
διά τε τῶν χρησμῶν καὶ διὰ τῶν ποιητᾶν καὶ διὰ τῶν ψαφισμάτων
τῶν ὑπαρχόντων αὐτοῖς παρὰ ταῖς πολίοις καλῶν τε καὶ ἐνδόξων, παρανέ-
γνωσαν δὲ καὶ τὸν χρησμὸν ἐν ὧι καταχεχωρισμένον ἦν, λώϊον εἶμεν καὶ
ἄμεινον τοῖς σεβομένοις Ἄρτεμιν Λευκοφρυηνὰν καὶ τὰμ πόλιν καὶ τὰγ
χώραν ἱερὰν καὶ ἄσυλον νομιζόντοις, δεδόχθαι τᾶι ἐκκλησίαι ἐπαινέσαι
μὲν τὸν δᾶμον τὸμ Μαγνήτων ἐπί τε τᾶι ποτὶ τοὺς θεοὺς εὐσεβείαι
καὶ ἐπὶ τᾶι ποτὶ τοὺς Ἕλλανας καλοκἀγαθίαι καὶ καλεῖν τὸν δᾶμον τὸμ Μα-
γνήτων ἐν τὰν προεδρίαν τοῖς Ὀδυσσείοις, εἶμεν δὲ αὐτῶν τάν τε πόλιν καὶ
τὰν χώραν ἱερὰν καὶ ἄσυλον καθὼς ὁ Ἀπόλλων ὁ ἐν Δελφοῖς ἀνιέρωσεν,
δέχεσθαι δὲ καὶ τὰν θυσίαν καὶ τὸν ἀγῶνα ὃν τίθεντι τᾶι Ἀρτέμιδι τᾶι
Λευκοφρυηνᾶι στεφανίταν ἰσοπύθιον ταῖς τιμαῖς, δόμεν δὲ καὶ ἐν ἀ-
παρχὰν τᾶι θεᾶι δραχμὰς ἐπιχωρίας δεκαπέντε καὶ τὸ ἐνέστιον θῦ-
[μ]α οἶν, καλέσαι δὲ αὐτοὺς καὶ ἐπὶ ξένια ἐπὶ τὰν πάτριον ἑστί̣αν·
ἑλέσθαι δὲ κα̣ὶ θεαροδόχον τὸν ὑποδεξούμενον τὰς ἀεὶ παραγινομένα[ς]
θεαρίας παρὰ τῶμ Μαγνήτων· ἁιρέθη Ἰγέρτας Πραΰλου· ἐπαινέσαι δὲ̣
τόν τε ἀρχιθέαρον Σωσικλῆν καὶ τοὺς θεαροὺς Ἀριστόδαμον, Διό-
τιμον ἐπί τε τᾶι ὑπὲρ τᾶς αὐτῶν πατρίδος φιλοτιμίαι καὶ ἐπὶ τᾶι σπου-
δᾶι τοῦ μολεῖν ποθ' ἁμέ, καὶ εἶμεν αὐτοὺς προξένους καὶ εὐεργέτας τᾶς
πόλιος τῶν Ἰθάκων καὶ ὑπάρχειν αὐτοῖς παρὰ τᾶς πόλιος πάντα τὰ φιλάν-
θρωπα ὅσα καὶ τοῖς ἄλλοις προξένοις καὶ εὐεργέταις ὑπάρχει· ἀναγράψαι
δὲ τόδε τὸ ψάφισμα ἐστάλας δύο καὶ ἀναθέμεν τὰμ μὲν ἐν τῶι [Ὀδ]υσσείωι,
τὰν δὲ ἐν τῶι ἱερῶι τᾶς Ἀθάνας, ὁ δὲ ἐπιδαμιοργὸς Σωτίων τὰν ἐπιμέ-
λειαν ποιησάσθω.

The one decree of Ithaca extant. To judge from the space in 1–2, the eponymous *damiourgoi* numbered three; this magistracy was common in Dorian cities. The *epidamiourgos* (30) was by contrast rare; the same function, overseeing the inscription, is found at Chaleium in Locris.[60]

2: The Ithacans assembled in the Odysseum—doubtless they were not numerous. That the decree was inscribed in both the Odysseum and the temple of Athena (29–30) suggests that one of these was out in the countryside. This may have been the Athena temple, because it is named second and because the civic assembly met in the Odysseum; but perhaps rather the latter was the putative site of Odysseus' palace outside of the city.[61]

It is of course one of the engaging features of this decree that these partners from literature figure prominently in the cults of Hellenistic Ithaca (including games of Odysseus, 16); so too on the city's coins, which show only Athena and Odysseus (*BMC Pelop.* 105–106).

4–5: "ambassadors, and the same men as proclaimers"; ἐπαγγελτήρ seems to be a hapax, a recherché way of saying θεωρός. The formula is at **96**.5: πρεσβευτὰς τ[ο]ὺς δὲ αὐ[τοὺ]ς καὶ θια[ρ]ούς.

20: Hellenistic Ithaca is known to have struck only bronze, and that sporadically. Yet these "local drachmas" appear to be the gift to the present Magnesian *theoroi*, not money for the Ithacans who will attend the future festival and might be expected to use the "local" money there, that is, Magnesian silver.[62] Unless we have failed to recognize Ithacan money, the requirement would seem to indicate weight: every city of course had a definition of the drachma.[63]

87. Athens

Kern, *I.Magnesia* 37.
Cf. S. V. Tracy, *Hesperia* 41 (1972) 44–45.

[10–11 ἄρ]χοντος ἐ̣π̣ὶ τῆ[ς Ἱππ]οθωντίδος πέμ-
[πτης πρυτανεία]ς, Ἀρχικλῆ[ς Χ]αριδήμου Ἐρχιεὺς ἐγραμ-
[μάτευε, βου]λῆς ψήφισμα̣, Πυανοψιῶνος ἕκτει ἱσταμένου,
[ἑβ]δόμε[ι] τ̣ῆς πρυτανείας· βουλεῖ ἐμ βουλευτηρίωι· τῶμ προ-
έδρων ἐπεψήφιζεν Εὔβιος Νικάνορος Φαληρεύς καὶ συμπρό-
εδροι· Ἀγαθοκλῆς Διοφάνου Δεκλεεὺς εἶπεν· ἐπειδὴ Μάγνη-

60. *IG* IX.1² 740.35; cf. L. Lerat, *Les Locriens de l'Ouest* II (Paris 1952) 120.

61. It was certainly not the cave at Polis (S. Benton, *BSA* 35 [1934/5] 54). Corcyra had an apparently rural *temenos* of Alcinous, a vineyard (Thuc. 3.70.4).

62. Thus in the Zenon archive some visitors' ἐπιχώριον νόμισμα, "(their own) native money," as distinct from Ptolemaic (*P.Cair.Zenon* 59021.12). But once in the Milesian accounts "local drachmas" = "Milesian," evidently in opposition to Alexander drachmas (Rehm, *I.Didyma* 471.7, with p. 152); a scholiast to Thuc. 8.101.1 on Chian τεσσαρακοστάς explained ἀρχαῖα νομίσματα ἐπιχώρια.

63. Hultsch, "Drachme," *RE* 5 (1905) 1624, took the coins to be "local" to Greece and thought the phrase indicated a standard (Aeginetan).

τες οἱ ἐπὶ Μαιάνδρωι οἰκεῖοι καὶ φίλοι τοῦ δήμου τοῦ Ἀθηναίων ὄντες ψηφισάμενοι θυσίαν καὶ ἀγῶνα στεφανίτην ἰσοπύθιον μουσικὸν καὶ ἱππικὸν καὶ γυμνικὸν συντελεῖν τεῖ ἀρχηγέτιδι τῆς πόλεως αὑτων Ἀρτέμιδι Λευκοφρυηνῆι ἀφεστάλκασιν θεωροὺς Ἀπολλοφάνην Αἰσχύλου, Εὔβουλον Ἀναξαγόρου, Λυκομήδην Χαρισίου οἳ προσελθόντες πρὸς τὴν βουλὴν καὶ τὸν δῆμον ἀνενεώσαντο τήν τε προϋπάρχουσαν ταῖς πόλεσιν οἰκειότητα καὶ φιλίαν καὶ ἀπολογισάμενοι τὴν τῆς θεᾶς ἐπιφάνειαν παρεκάλεσαν μετὰ πάσης σπουδῆς καὶ φιλοτιμίας ἀποδέξασθαι τὸν ἀγῶνα στεφανίτην ἰσοπύθιον ὃν τιθέασιν τεῖ Ἀρτέμιδι τεῖ Λευκοφρυηνεῖ, καὶ τὴν πόλιν αὐτῶν καὶ τὴν χώραν ἱερὰν καὶ ἄσυλον ἀποδεῖξαι, καθότι αὐτοῖς καὶ ὁ θεὸς ὁ ἐν Δελφοῖς ἔχρησεν· ἵνα οὖν καὶ ὁ δῆμος φανερὸς ἦι ἐμ παντὶ καιρῶι τιμῶν τὸ θεῖον καὶ τὴν οἰκειότητα καὶ τὴμ φιλίαν τηρῶν τὴμ πρὸς Μάγνητας, ἀγαθεῖ τύχει δεδόχθαι τεῖ βουλεῖ, τοὺς προέδρους οἳ ἂν λάχωσιν εἰς τὴν ἐπιοῦσαν ἐκκλησίαν χρηματίσαι περὶ τούτων, γνώμην δὲ ξυμβαλέσθαι τῆς βουλῆς εἰς τὸν δῆμον, ὅτι δοκεῖ τ[ε]ῖ βουλεῖ δέχεσθαι τὸν δῆμον καὶ νῦν καὶ εἰς τὸμ μετὰ ταῦτα χρόνον τάς τε σπονδὰς καὶ τὰς θυσίας καὶ τὸν ἀγῶνα ὃν τιθέασιμ Μάγνητες τεῖ Ἀρτέμιδι τεῖ Λευκοφρυηνεῖ στεφανίτην ἰσοπύθιον, καὶ τὴν πόλιν αὐτῶν καὶ τὴν χώραν ἱερὰν καὶ ἄσυλον εἶναι κατὰ τὰς τοῦ θεοῦ μαντείας· ἐπαινέσαι δὲ καὶ τὸν δῆμον τὸμ Μαγνήτων καὶ στεφανῶσαι θαλλοῦ στεφάνωι εὐσεβείας ἕνεκεν, ἐπαινέσαι δὲ καὶ τοὺς παραγεγονότας θεωροὺς Ἀπολλοφάνην, Εὔβουλον, Λυκομήδην καὶ στεφανῶσαι ἕκαστον αὐτῶν θαλλοῦ στεφάνωι εὐσεβείας ἕνεκεν τῆς εἰς θεὰν καὶ τῆς εἰς τὴν πατρίδα φιλοτιμίας· καλέσαι δὲ αὐτοὺς καὶ ἐπὶ ξένια εἰς τὸ πρυτανεῖον εἰς αὔριον, ἀναγράψαι δὲ τόδε τὸ ψήφισμα τὸγ γραμματέα τὸγ κατὰ πρυτανείαν ἐν στήληι λιθίνηι καὶ στῆσαι ἐν τῶι ἱερῶι, τὸ δὲ γινόμενον ἀνήλωμα εἰς τὴμ ποίησιν τῆς στήλης καὶ τὴν ἀνάθεσιν μερίσαι τὸν ταμίαν καὶ τοὺς ἐπὶ τεῖ διοκήσει.

1: [Σωστράτου? Tracy.

In 208 Athens was free and neutral.[64] The other extant Athenian decree of *asylia* is **162** for Alabanda several years later.

The date of this text has spawned a substantial literature, conceived in the main as a conflict between the implications of **66** (with the missions commonly dated 207–205) and the Athenian tribal cycle (line 2: fourth position, implying

64. Cf. W. S. Ferguson, *Hellenistic Athens* (Cambridge, Mass., 1911) 255; Habicht, *Studien zur Geschichte Athens*, Hypomnemata 73 (Göttingen 1982) 137–138.

209/8).[65] In fact the Athenian year 209/8 is what we should expect from the Magnesians' account in **66** (with inclusive reckoning): the *theoroi*, leaving in spring or early summer 208, will likely have reached Athens before midsummer and the end of the Athenian year 209/8. The problem is not in the year but in the season.[66]

Pyanopsion in the fifth prytany requires us to assume an intercalary month earlier in the year,[67] making the season late autumn, well into November. This, however, is not the time we expect the Magnesians to be in Athens—certainly too early if we go by the tribal cycle and posit November 209, probably too late if we disregard the cycle and posit November 208. Chronologically, therefore, this text seems to me a non liquet, and I continue to rely on **66**.[68]

2–6: These Athenians are not otherwise on record. In 2, we expect ἧι before the secretary's name; in 4, βουλῆ.

39: Holleaux (*Etudes* I 316) thought that this unidentified temple must be that of the Demos and the Charites, where a number of Athenian decrees were inscribed in these years; cf. Habicht, *Studien* 85 n. 33. But the noun is at best ambiguous, for the usual expression is ἐν τῶι τεμένει τοῦ Δήμου καὶ τῶν Χαρίτων.

88. Megalopolis

A second column begins at line 41.

Kern, *I.Magnesia* 38 [Dittenberger, *Syll.*² 258; Hiller, *IG* V.2 p. XXV; *Syll.*³ 559; Maier, *Gr. Mauerbauinschr.* 34].

Photograph: Maier pl. 21 (lines 60–67 col. b).

Cf. Fick, *BeitrKundIndogermSpr* 26 (1901) 283–287; Wilhelm, *Jahresh.* 3 (1900) 58; 4 (1901) Beibl. 25 (*Kl. Schr.* II.1 74, 153); Laqueur, *Epigraphische Untersuchungen* 33.

65. Relying on the tribal cycle: Kirchner, *IG* II.4² p. 14 (but 222/1 B.C.); Ferguson, *Athenian Tribal Cycles* 36, 128–129 (209/8 B.C., with the return of the *theoroi* in 208/7 under Moeragoras); Meritt, *Historia* 26 (1977) 178; Habicht, *Studien* 171. Relying on the unity of the theoric missions: Robert, *Op. min. sel.* II 775–778; Nachtergael, *Les Galates* 224; Ebert (*Philologus* 1982, 208–209) follows a different numeration of the cycle to arrive at 205/4.

66. The 6th of Pyanopsion (line 3) was a sacred day for some purposes, but apparently no state festival obstructed the council from meeting; see J. D. Mikalson, *The Sacred and Civil Calendar of the Athenian Year* (Princeton 1975) 67–78, who cites this decree and *IG* II² 1014 for meetings on this day.

67. So W. K. Pritchett and O. Neugebauer, *Calendars of Athens* (Cambridge, Mass. 1940) 90, claiming other instances from the last quarter of the third century; Kern and Dinsmoor (*Athenian Archon List* 234) considered emendation necessary ("fifth" prytany to fourth, Dinsmoor). The usual intercalation was Posideon II, hence later than our decree; but a Hecatombaion II is attested (*IG* I³ 78).

68. Pritchett, *Greek State at War* III (Berkeley 1979) 173 n. 66, on a different problem, evokes erroneous month names in the prescripts of Attic decrees. In ours, however, name and number, even while incompatible, are each improbable for the travels of the *theoroi*, both being well into autumn.

πρεσβευτᾶν καὶ θεα̣[ρῶν π]α̣[ρ]α̣γεγο[νότων] π[αρὰ τᾶι πόλι] τῶμ Μαγνήτων τῶν ἐπὶ Μαιάνδρου Φιλίσκ[ωι τῶι Πυθα]γόρωι, Κόνωνος τῶι Διονυσίωι, Λαμπέτωι τῶ[ι Πυθαγό]ραι καὶ ἀποδόντων τὸ ψάφισμα ἰν οἷ κατακεχῴ̣[ριστο] ὁ χρησμὸς ὁ γεγονὼς ὑπὸ τοῖ Ἀπόλλωνι τοῖ ἰν Δε[λφοῖς] λώϊον ἶμεν καὶ ἄμεινον τοῖς σεβομένοις Ἄρτεμιν Λευκοφρυηνὰν καὶ τὰν πόλιν καὶ τὰν χώραν ἱερὰν καὶ ἄσυλον νομίζοσιν καὶ περὶ τῶν λοιπῶν πάν⟨τω⟩ν διαλεχθέσσι, καθὰ εἶχον τὰς ἰντολὰς παρὰ τᾶι ἰδίαι πόλι ⟨κ⟩αὶ ἁρμοζόντ⟨ω⟩ς τοῖς ἰν τοῖ{ς} ψαφίσματι γεγραμμένοις, ἰν⟨ε⟩φάνιζον δὲ καὶ τὰν τᾶς θεᾶς ἐπιφάνειαν καὶ τὰν γεγονῶσαν ὑπὸ τοῖς προγόνοις ἰν̣ τὸ{ι}ς Ἕλλανας εὐχρηστία⟨ν⟩ καὶ παρακαλέντω⟨ν⟩ ὡς ἀποδέχηται ἁ πόλις τὰν πανάγυριν καὶ ἐκεχειρίαν καὶ τὸν ἀγῶνα στεφανίταν ἰσοπύθι[ο]ν τόν τε μου[σικ]ὸν καὶ γυμνικὸν καὶ ἱππικὸν τὸν τιθεῖ τᾶι Ἀρ̣τέμιδι τᾶι Λευκοφρυηνᾶι ὁ δᾶμος τῶμ Μαγνήτων, καὶ τὰν πόλιν καὶ τὰν χώραν αὐτῶν ἱερὰν καὶ ἄσυλον εἶναι, τᾶι δὲ πόλι τᾶι ἁμετέραι πάτριόν ἐστιν μάλιστα μὲν τὰς τᾶν θεᾶν τιμὰς συν[α]ύξειν, ἔπειτα δὲ καὶ τοὺς συγγενέας καὶ φίλος ἀντευεργετῆν ἰν τὸ ἀπροφασίστος φαίνεσθαι εἶναι φίλος πρὸς πάντας τὸς καὶ ἁμὲ ἐαρημένος, τῶν δὲ Μαγνήτων τῶν ἀπὸ Μαιάνδροι ἐκ παλαιῶν μὲν χρόνω⟨ν⟩ ἐχόντ⟨ων⟩ εὐνόως πρὸς ἅμμε, συμφανὲς δὲ ποιησάντων τὰν ἔχοιεν ἐκτένειαν καὶ αἵρεσιν, ἁν⟨ί⟩κα παρεγέν⟨ον⟩το πὸς αὐτὸς πρεσβεύοντες Πρόξενος, Ἆγις, Ἀριστοπάμων· εὐνόως τε γὰρ ποσ[ε]δέξαντο οἱ Μάγνητες καὶ ἔδωκαν ἰν τὸν τειχισμὸν τᾶς πόλιος Δαρεεικὸς τριακοσίος τὸς ἐκόμισεν Ἀγαμήστωρ, διὸ ἁ πόλις μεμναμένα τᾶς τε συγγενείας καὶ φιλίας καὶ πάντων τῶν γεγονότων εὐγνωμόνων ὑπὸ τᾶι πόλι τᾶι Μαγνήτων ἀποδέχεται τὰ[ς] θυσίας τᾶς Ἀρτέμιδος τᾶς Λευκοφρυηνᾶς καὶ τὰν ἐκεχηρίαν καὶ τὸς ἀγῶνας στεφανίτας ἰσοπυθίος τόν τε μουσικὸν καὶ γυμνικὸν καὶ ἱππικὸν τὸν ποιένσι οἱ Μάγνητες, δικαίαν ἀποδιδόντες χάριν τᾶι εὐεργέτιδι καὶ καθαγεμόνι τᾶς πόλιος, καὶ τὰν πόλιν καὶ τὰν χώραν εἶναι αὐτῶν ἱεράν, καθὼς ὁ θεὸς ἔχρησεν καὶ ἀξίοσι[ν] οἱ παραγεγονότες πρεσβευταὶ καὶ θεωροί· τοῖς θεωροῖς τοῖς ἐπαγγέλλοσι τὰν θυσίαν καὶ ἐκεχηρίαν τᾶς Ἀρτέμιδος τᾶς Λευκοφρυηνᾶς δότω Σθενόλας ὁ ταμίας [- - - - - - - - - - - - -] σ̣υμφόροις ἰνίσ[τιον], καὶ τὰ [ἰν τοῖς ν]όμο[ις γεγρα]μ̣μένα ἦν δίδοσθαι, τὰ ἶσα γρα[φάτω ἰν τ]ὰν θεωρίαν, ἰν δὲ τὸ λοιπὸν τί δεῖ δίδοσθαι ταινὶ τᾶι θεαρίαι ἰνίσ[τ]ιο̣ν ἐ̣νεκέχειρον, οἱ νομογράφοι οἱ ἰν τᾶι ἐπὶ Λυκίν[ωι] ετείαι γράψαντες ἐπιδειξάντων τᾶι πόλει, ὡς οἱ πολῖται βωλεύ-

σ⟨ο⟩νται περὶ τοινί· χωρα⟨ξ⟩άντων δὲ οἱ νομογράφοι
ἰν τὸ{ι}ς νόμος καὶ ταννὺν τὰ[ν ἐ]κεχειρίαν, καὶ τὸς
ἀγῶνας τοσνὺν γραψάντων πὸς τὸς ἄλλος
στεφανίτας, ὡς συμφανὲς γίνητα[ι τ]οῖς Μάγνη-
σιν ὅτι ἁ πόλις τάς τε τῶν θεῶν θυσίας συναύξει
καὶ τὰ ὑπὸ τοῖς συγγενέσι καὶ φίλοις καὶ [εὐ]νοίοις
ἀξιωμένα ὑπακούει· θεαροδόκος κατεστάθη
Νικήρατος Ἀρκεσίλου· ἐδόθη τοῖς θεαροῖς ἐπὶ
τὰν κοινὰν ἱστίαν τᾶς πόλιος θῦσαι ὄϊς και τᾶι
θεοῖ ὅσον καὶ αὐτοὶ διδοῦσι, καὶ ξένια τοῖς θεαροῖς
τὰ ἐκ τῶν νόμων αὐθαμέραν.

ἀκολούθως δὲ ἔδοξεν ψηφίσασθαι
καὶ τοῖς ἄλλοις Ἀρκάσιν·

Τεγεάταις	Ὀρχομενίοις
Μεθυδριεῦσιν	Καφυιεῦσιν
Στυμφαλίοις	Φλεασίοις
Κλειτορίοις	Φενεάταις
Πελλανεῦσιν	Φιαλεῦσιν
Ἡραιεῦσιν	Ἀλεάταις
Ψωφιδίοις	Κυναιθεῦσιν
Θελφουσίοις	Καρυννεῦσιν
Λουσιάταις	Τριταιεῦσιν

1 end Laqueur, from **89**.2: π[αρὰ τῶι δάμωι] Kern; cf. line 9. 8 end Wilhelm (cf. **93**.11): ΠΑΝΣΙΝ lapis. 10 ΛΙΤΑΙ, ΖΟΝΤΟΙΣ, 11 ΙΝΙΦΑΝ, 13 ΣΤΙΑΣ and ΕΝΤΩΣ, 23 ΧΡΟΝΩΣ ΕΧΟΝΤΕΣ, 25 ΑΝΑΚΑ and ΓΕΝΕΤΟ lapis. 47 Wilhelm: ΣΑΝΤΑΙ, ΧΩΡΑΣΑΝΤΩΝ lapis. See Kern and Fick for the mason's errors in transcribing Arcadian.

The *theoroi* visited a number of Arcadian cities, but the Magnesian authorities chose to inscribe the decree of Megalopolis and merely list the others (58ff.). Authorship is established by lines 22–29, citing Magnesia's earlier contribution of 300 darics toward the building of the city walls; in Arcadia this can only be the famous walls of Megalopolis. The birthplace of Polybius was the most important member of the Achaean League and in 208 was allied with Philip V and Macedonia.

20–22: "to return favors to kinsmen and friends with a view to showing ourselves to be unstinting friends to all who have preferred us"; the participle seems an error for ἁιρημένος or ἀραιρημένος (Kern).

25–29: Able to name the Megalopolitan envoys who came to Magnesia in 369 B.C. and the Magnesian who returned, the *theoroi* obviously had consulted the old Magnesian decree voting funds. The literary evidence on the foundation of Megalopolis does not preserve a report of such a far-ranging quest for funds. Panhellenic donations aided the rebuilding of Thebes late in the fourth century (Holleaux, *Etudes* I 1–40). The use of darics, Persian gold staters, is to be expected at Magnesia in the fourth century; cf. the references at Hultsch, *RE* 4 (1901) 2182.[69]

37: "Sacred" seems to be thought a sufficient answer, even though "sacred and inviolable" was in the request (18).

45: Legislation fixing the amount to give future *theoroi* is to be drafted in the year of Lycinus—the next year, one assumes (although no introductory dating formulae are given at the beginning that would prove that this is not Lycinus' year). This specification reveals that we are near the end of the Megalopolitan year. There is some reason to think that their year began ca. September;[70] if that is so, then the Magnesians were in Arcadia in summer or late summer. In the second century B.C. the eponym of Megalopolis was the secretary of the *synedroi* (*IG* V.2 439ff.).

54: Descendants of Niceratus are known; cf. Habicht, *Chiron* 2 (1972) 115.

89. Achaean League

Kern, *I.Magnesia* 39.
Cf. Holleaux, *Etudes* I 316; De Decker, *RPhil* n.s. 29 (1905) 160 (collation).
From line 45, on a lower block.

πρεσβευτᾶ καὶ̣ θεαροῦ παραγεν̣ο̣[μένου παρὰ]
τᾶς πόλιος τῶ⟨ν⟩ Μαγνήτων τῶν ποτὶ τῶ[ι Μαιάν]-
δρωι Φιλίσκου τοῦ Πυθαγόρα ποτὶ τὸ κοιν̣[ὸν]
τῶν Ἀχαιῶν καὶ ἀποδόντος τὸ ψάφισμα ἐν ὧ[ι]
κατακεχώριστο ὁ χρησμὸς ὁ γεγενημένος
ὑπὸ τοῦ θεοῦ τοῦ ἐν Δελφοῖς λώϊον εἶμεν κα[ὶ]
ἄμεινον τοῖς σεβομένοις Ἄρτεμιν Λευκοφρ[υ]-
ανὰν καὶ τὰν πόλιν καὶ τὰν χώραν ἱερὰν καὶ [ἄ]συ-
λον νομίζουσιν, διαλεγέντος δὲ καὶ τὰ λοι-
πὰ ἀκολούθως τοῖς ἐν τῶι ψαφί̣σματι κατακεχω-
ρισμένοις καὶ ἀξίως τᾶς τε πόλιος τᾶς ἀποστ̣ει-
λάσας καὶ τοῦ κοινοῦ τῶν Ἀχαιῶν καὶ ἐμφανί-
ζοντος τὰν τᾶς θεοῦ ἐπιφάνειαν καὶ τὰς γεγε-
νημένας ὑπὸ τῶν προγόνων εὐχρηστίας ποτὶ
το[ὺς] Ἕλλανας καὶ παρακαλοῦντος τοὺς Ἀχαι-
οὺς ἀπ[οδ]έξασθαι τὰν πανάγυριν καὶ ἐκεχειρίαν
καὶ τὸν ἀγῶ[να] σ̣τεφανίταν ἰσοπύθιον τόν τε μου-
σικὸν καὶ γυμνικὸν καὶ ἱππικὸν ὃν τίθεντι τᾶι
Ἀρτέμιδι τᾶι Λευκο[φ]ρ[υ]ανᾶι καὶ τὰν πόλιν καὶ

69. This excludes the suggestion of T. Reinach, *BCH* 28 (1904) 13 n. 1, that the contribution may have been recent, after the destruction that followed the battle of Sellasia in 222 (Polyb. 5.93.5).

70. See Samuel, *Chronology* 97: Achaean usage, which was followed in some Arcadian cities in the second century B.C., had the seventh month equal to the tenth at Delphi (*SGDI* 1774 of 170/169), whose year started ca. June.

τὰν χώραν αὐτῶν ἱερὰν καὶ ἄσυλον, [κ]αὶ διότι ἐπα-
κολουθήσαντες τοῖς ἀξιουμένοις καὶ συναυξ[ή]-
σαντες τᾶς Ἀρτέμιδος τὰς τιμὰς ἀκόλου̣θ[α]
πράξοντι τᾶι τε τοῦ θεοῦ μαντείαι καὶ τῶν προ[γε]-
γενημένων ποθ' αὐτοὺς φιλανθρώπων, τοῖς δ[ὲ]
Ἀχαιοῖς πάτριόν ἐστι συναύξειν τάς τε τιμὰς
τὰς παρ' ἑκάστοις ὅσοι καὶ τοῖς Ἀχαιοῖς συν[αύ]-
ξοντι· δεδόχθαι τοῖς Ἀχαιοῖς ἀποδέξασθ[αι]
τάν τε θυσίαν καὶ τὸν ἀγῶνα στεφανίταν ἰσο-
πύθιον ὃν τίθητι ἁ πόλις τῶν Μαγνήτων τᾶι Ἀ[ρ]-
τέμιδι τᾶι Λευκοφρυηνᾶι, καὶ τὰν πόλιν
καὶ τὰν χώραν αὐτῶν εἶμεν ἱερὰν καὶ ἄσυλο[ν],
καθὼς παρεκάλει Φιλίσκος ὁ ἀποσταλεὶς π[ρ]εσ-
βευτὰς καὶ θεωρός· τοὺς δὲ δαμιοργοὺς τῶν [Ἀ]-
χαιῶν ἀναγράψαι τὸ ψάφισμα τὸ παρὰ τᾶς π[ό]-
λιος τῶν Μαγνήτων καὶ τὸ δόγμα τῶν Ἀχαιῶν
εἰς στάλαν λιθίναν καὶ ἀναθέμεν εἰς τὸ ἱερὸν
τοῦ Διὸς τοῦ Ἀμαρίου, ὅπως φανερὸν ἦι καὶ τοῖς
λοιποῖς Ἕλλασιν διότι οἱ Ἀχαιοὶ τοῖς ποτὶ τὸ θεῖ-
ον εὐσεβῶς διακειμένοις τὰν αὐτὰν αἵρεσιν ἔχον-
τες διατελέοντι ἀκόλουθα πράσσοντες τᾶι τῶν
προγόνων αἱρέσει, ἇι θέλοντι προάγειν καὶ συν-
αύξειν τά τε ἔνδοξα καὶ τὰς τιμὰς τὰς παρ' ἐκ[άσ]-
τοις τῶν φίλων· καταχωρίξαι δὲ κα[ὶ] τοὺς νομ[ο]-
γράφους τὸ δόγμα τῶν Ἀχα̣[ιῶ]ν εἰς [τοὺς ν]όμο[υς],
τοὺς πρώτους [ca. 7]ύς, [ca. 9]μ[ca. 6 χρη]-
ματίξαι τοῖς Ἀχα[ιοῖ]ς, δόμε̣[ν δὲ καὶ] ξένια τῶι [πρεσβευ]-
τᾶι Διοκλῆ τὸν ταμίαν τὰ μέγιστα ἐκ τῶν νόμ[ων.]
ὁμοίως δὲ ἀπεδέξαντο καὶ
Ἠλεῖοι

2: ΤΩΙΜΑΓ lapis. 45: Holleaux suggested πρώτους [οὓς αὐτο]ὺς [δεήσει νο]μ[ογραφήσαντας χρη]ματίξαι, citing **132**.16ff.; [καὶ ἱαρο]ύς, [τοὺς δὲ γρα]-μ[ματεῖς χ.] De Decker ("parait impossible," Robert ap. Holleaux).

The *theoroi* in the Peloponnesus divided their task; the three were together at Megalopolis, Messene, Argos, Sicyon (these two after the Achaean League had been addressed), and another city (**122**); but only one of them approached the League and another city (**124**), and a different one Corinth. This must reflect geographical convenience and is not (as Kern thought) evidence of some diminution of the importance of the Achaean League.

The provision (43–46) that "the *nomographoi* are to place this into the laws, the next ... to put matters before the Achaeans," suggests that we have here a decree of the federal council, which met with some frequency, whereas the full assembly met only when called.[71]

Lines 23–24 seem poorly formulated, as we expect a noun parallel to μαντείαι (cf. εὐχρηστία, **93**.15; βοήθεια, **96**.9). Arguing for the Magnesians' interpretation of the oracle, the ambassador told the Achaeans that "by acceding to the request and joining in increasing the honors of Artemis, they would be acting in accord with the oracle of the god and the benefactions already rendered to them." They respond with an observation of their own (δ[ὲ] ... ἐστι κτλ.), apparently not part of the genitive absolute that begins in line 1 and summarizes the ambassador's speech (cf. **93**.22, **96**.25, **98**.13, etc.): "It is ancestral to Achaeans to join in increasing honors among those who do so for the Achaeans." Compare **18**.7–8 about the Achaeans, which I take as a general sentiment.

27: At *Syll.*[3] 519.13 we find ἔδοξε τῶι κοινῶι τῶν Ἀχαιῶν. Our wording in its ambiguity may reflect that this is a decree of the Achaean council rather than the full assembly.

33: For the *damiourgoi* as executives of the League (e.g., *Staatsvertr.* III 452.3; *Syll.*[3] 519) see Larsen 221–223.

37: The temple of Zeus Amarios was a federal temple; the cult is also attested in Achaean colonies. This is the first god by whom the Achaeans swear in *Staatsvertr.* III 499.8 (a generation earlier). See Aymard, *Assemblées* 277–293; *Mélanges Navarre* (Toulouse 1935) 453–470; H. Schwabl, "Zeus," *RE* 10A (1972) 270–271.

45: Aymard (*Assemblées* 187 n. 2) and Lehmann (248 n. 28) took the phrase to be "into the first laws," which makes no sense. Holleaux saw that the adjective means "next," a prescription for the future, and modifies νομογράφους; for example: "the next [elected and empowered] to put business before the Achaeans ..." This would mean that entering decrees of the council into permanent law required approval by the full assembly.

48–49: Elis, appended by the Magnesian redactors in this subscription, was an enemy of the Achaean League.

90. Argos

Kern, *I.Magnesia* 40.

[- - - - - - - - - - - - - - - - - Μαγνή]τ̣ων τᾶι βουλ̣[ᾶι]
[καὶ τῶι δάμωι χαίρειν· οἱ παρ' ὑ]μ̣ῶν πρεσβευταὶ καὶ
[θεαροὶ παραγενόμενοι Φ]ιλίσκος Πυθαγόρου, Κόνων
[Διονυσίου, Λάμπετο]ς Πυθαγόρου τό τε ψάφισμα
[ἀπέδωκαν τῶι δά]μ̣ωι καὶ αὐτοὶ διελέγεν ἀκολού-

71. On the problems raised by Achaean political bodies see A. Aymard, *Les assemblées de la confédération achaienne* (Bordeaux 1938), esp. 80 n. 1 (rightly observing that the use of Ἀχαιοί does not establish which body passed this decree); G. A. Lehmann, *ZPE* 51 (1983) 237–261; in general, J. A. O. Larsen, *Greek Federal States* (Oxford 1968) 227–233.

[θως τοῖς ἐν τῶι] ψαφίσματι καταχεχωρισμένοις πε-
[ρὶ τοῦ ἀγῶνο]ς [τ]ῶν Λευκοφρυηνῶν· ὑπογεγράφαμες οὖν
ὑ̣μ̣ῖ̣ν̣ τὸ ἀντίγραφον τοῦ ψαφίσματος τοῦ δοχθέντος
τῶι δάμωι. ἔρρωσθε.
πρεσβευτᾶν παραγενομένων παρὰ τοῦ δάμου τῶμ
Μαγνήτων τῶν πρὸς τῶι Μαιάνδρωι Φιλίσχ̣ου τοῦ
Πυθαγόρου, Κόνωνος τοῦ Διονυσίου, Λαμπέτου τοῦ
Πυθαγόρου καὶ ἀποδόντων τὸ ψάφισμα καὶ διαλεγέν-
των ἀκολούθως τοῖς γεγραμμένοις, ἔδοξε τῶι δά-
μωι συντελεῖν τὰν θυσίαν κοινᾶι μετὰ τῶν Ἀχαιῶν
ἃν συντελεῖ ὁ δῆμος ὁ τῶν Μαγνήτων τῶμ̣ πρὸς τῶι Μαι-
άνδρωι τᾶι Ἀρτέμιδι τᾶι Λευκοφρυηνᾶι· δοθῆμεν δὲ
παρὰ τῶν ταμιᾶν καὶ ἐνεχέχειρα τοῖς ἐπαγγέλλονσι
ὅσον καὶ τοῖς τὰ Νέμεα ἐπαγγέλλοσσι δίδοται.

Argos, approached by the brother of the Magnesian who addressed the Achaeans, was a member of the League. The decree, preceded by a letter of transmittal, is of unusual brevity, containing almost no specifics of the action. It offers no description of the request, does not mention *asylia*, and deals with the crowned games not by description but by concurring with the Achaeans' vote and providing future Magnesian *theoroi* their due on analogy with the Argive Nemea. I hesitate to take such a clipped statement as evidence that Argos deliberately did not recognize *asylia*; perhaps this was not requested by the Magnesians (on the theory that Argos had recognized it in 221). The somewhat fuller decree of Sicyon (**91**) also is silent about *asylia*—yet both cities, in addressing the games, claim to be acting on the example of the Achaean League, which granted both games and *asylia*. Neither city, moreover, makes any provision for a sacrifice to Artemis or for sending their own *theoroi* to the games. We cannot deduce that the League arrogated these powers to itself (so Giovannini) and left to member cities only the right to receive Magnesian *theoroi* as they passed through, for the response of Achaean Megalopolis is lengthy and detailed and granted the full Magnesian request.

On the formulary of Argive decrees see P. Charneux, *BCH* 114 (1990) 395–415 (396 n. 7 on the several omissions here).

91. Sicyon

Inscribed below **90**.
Kern, *I.Magnesia* 41.
Cf. Holleaux, *Etudes* I 316.

[παρὰ] Σικυωνίων
[πρεσβευτᾶ]ν̣ καὶ θεαρῶν παραγενομένων παρὰ τῶν
[Μαγνήτων] Φ̣ιλίσκου, Κόνωνος, Λαμπέτου καὶ ἀνανε-
ο̣υ̣μ̣έ̣νων τὰν οἰκειότατα τὰν ὑπάρχουσαν αὐτοῖς
ποτὶ τὰν πόλιν καὶ τὰν φιλίαν καὶ ἐπανγελλόντων

τᾶι Ἀρτέμιδι τᾶι ἀρχαγέτιδι αὐτῶν τᾶι Λευκοφρυηνᾶι
τὰν θυσίαν καὶ πανάγυριν καὶ ἐκεχειρίαν καὶ ἀγῶνα
στεφανίταν [ἰ]σο[π]ύθιον μουσικόν τε καὶ γυμνικὸν καὶ
ἱππικόν, δεδόχθαι τῶ[ι δά]μωι ἀποδέξασθαι τὰν θυ-
σίαν κα[ὶ τ]ὰν πα[νάγυ]ριν καὶ [τὰ]ν ἐκεχειρίαν ἂν συντε-
λοῦντι οἱ [Μάγ]ν̣η̣τες κατὰ τὸ μαντεῖον τᾶι Ἀρτέμιδι
τᾶι Λευκοφρυ[ηνᾶ]ι, ε[ἶ]μεν δ̣ὲ̣ τὸν ἀγῶνα στεφαν̣ίταν
ἰσοπύθιο[ν] τ̣ό̣ν [τε] μ̣[ουσικὸ]ν̣ [κ]αὶ γυμνικὸν καὶ ἱππικόν,
καὶ τὰ ἆθλ[α καὶ ὑπάρχειν τοῖς] νικῶσι τοὺς ἀγῶνας ὅσα
καὶ ⟨εἰς τοὺς⟩ τῶν [Π]υ[θί]ω̣ν γέ[γραπται], κ[α]θὼς καὶ οἱ Ἀχαιοὶ ἀποδε-
δεγμένοι ἔντ[ι]· δ[ό]μ̣[εν δὲ κα]ὶ ἐνεκέχειρα τοῖς θεαροῖς
τὸν γροφῆ τᾶς βωλ[ᾶς] τ[ὰ ἐ]κ τᾶν πινακίδων, καταστᾶσαι
[δὲ θε]α̣ροδόχον· ὁ θεαρο[δ]όχος Γόργος Μενεκλεί[ο]υς·
[κατὰ τὰ] α[ὐ]τ̣[ὰ δὲ ἐψη]φίσαντο·
[- - - - - - - - - Κα]λλισταιε̣ῖς

14 Holleaux: ἆθλ[α καὶ τὰς τιμὰς τοῖς] Kern. 15 ⟨εἰς τοὺς⟩ add. Holleaux.

The only decree of Sicyon extant. It was a member of the Achaean League. In summer 208 its territory was raided by Roman forces and defended by Philip V (Livy 27.31.1–2, 27.32.2; Broughton, *MRR* I 287). Like the Argives, the Sicyonians evoke the League decree but do not mention *asylia*; but they are more detailed in dealing with the games.

17: Instead of ἐκ τοῦ νόμου, which reveals Sicyon published its laws on tablets (so Wilhelm, *Beiträge* 244, 287).

20: Another city may have been subscribed to the left, and the list may have continued on a block below. The coins of Callistae give the ethnic as Καλλιστατᾶν (cf. von Geisau, *RE* 10 [1919] 1673); but the Magnesians, in composing these subscriptions, several times got the ethnic wrong.

92. Corinth

Kern, *I.Magnesia* 42.

πρεσβευτᾶ παραγενομένου καὶ θεωροῦ παρὰ τοῦ δά-
μου τῶμ Μαγνήτων ἐπὶ Μαιάνδρου Λαμπέτου
τοῦ Πυθαγόρου καὶ ἀποδόντος τὸ ψάφισμα καὶ διαλεγο-
μένου ἀκολούθως τοῖς ἐν τῶι ψαφίσματι καταγεγραμ-
μένοις καὶ ἀνανεουμένου τὰν οἰκεότατα καὶ φιλίαν τὰν
προϋπάρχουσαν καὶ παρακαλοῦντος ἀποδέξασθαι
τὰν πόλιν τῶν Κορινθίων τὰν θυσίαν καὶ τὰν ἐκεχειρί-
αν καὶ τοὺς ἀγῶνας οὓς τίθητι ἁ πόλις ἁ τῶν Μαγνήτων
τᾶι Ἀρτέμιτι τᾶι Λευκοφρυηνᾶι τόν τε μουσικὸν καὶ τὸν
γυμνικὸν καὶ ἱππικὸν ἰσοπύθιον, ἔδοξε τᾶι ἐκκλησί[αι]
ἀποδέξασθαι τὰν ἐκεχειρίαν καὶ τοὺς ἀγῶνας ἰσοπυ-
θίους, καθὰ παρακαλεῖ, καὶ δόμεν ἐνεκέχηρον καὶ ἐνέσ-
τιον καὶ ξένια τῶι ἐπαγγέλλοντι ἃ καὶ αὐτοὶ δίδοντι τοῖς
τὰ Ἴσθμια ἐπαγγέλλουσι· δεδόχθαι δὲ καὶ τὰν πόλιν καὶ

τὰν χώραν αὐτῶν ἱερὰν καὶ ἄσυλον εἶμεν κατὰ τὸν χρησ-
μὸν τοῦ θεοῦ κατὰ τὸ ψάφισμα ὃ ἀπέδωκεν τᾶι πόλει·
ἑλέσθα[ι] δὲ καὶ θεαροδόκον. ἁιρέθη Πανταίνετος Μν[α]σικλείδα.

Corinth, a member of the Achaean League, was approached by only one of the *theoroi* for the Peloponnesus. Other extant decrees of Corinth are quite fragmentary (cf. *Corinth* VIII.1 pp. 2ff.). This decree is in general as brief as that of Sicyon; it does not mention *asylia* in its preliminaries yet proceeds to grant it as well as the games (the same omission in **94** from Corcyra). Like the Argives, the Corinthians use their own games rather than the Pythia as the analogy for the Leucophryeneia, voting reciprocal honors for the *theoroi* (13–14); Syracuse, a colony of Corinth, also cites the Isthmia (**120**.39).

93. Messene

Inscribed below **92**; from line 23, on a lower block.
Kern, *I.Magnesia* 43.
Cf. Holleaux, *Etudes* I 316–317.

παρὰ Μεσσηνίων
ἐπειδὴ παραγενόμενοι πρεσβευταὶ παρὰ Μαγνήτων
τῶν ἐπὶ Μαιάνδρου Φιλίσκος Πυθαγόρου, Κόνων Διο-
νυσίου, Λάμπετος Πυθαγόρου ἐνεφάνιζον τάν τε οἰ-
κειότατα καὶ τὰν φιλίαν τὰν προϋπάρχουσαν ποτὶ τὸ
κοινὸν τῶμ Μεσσανίων καὶ ἀπέδωκαν τὸ ψάφισμα ἐ-
[ν] ὧι κατεκεχώριστο ὁ χρησμὸς ὁ γενόμενος ὑπὸ τοῦ
Ἀπόλλωνος τοῦ ἐν Δελφοῖς λῷϊον εἶμεν καὶ ἄμεινον
τοῖς σεβομένοις Ἄρτεμιν Λευκοφρυηνὰν καὶ τὰν πόλιν
καὶ τὰν χώραν ἱερὰν καὶ ἄσυλον νομίζοντι, κα[ὶ π]ẹρὶ
τῶν λοιπῶν πάντων διαλεχθέντων, καθὰ εἶ[χον]
τὰς ἐντολὰς παρὰ τᾶς ἰδίας πόλεως ἁρμοζό[ν]τ[ως τοῖ]ς
ἐν τῶι ψαφίσματι καταγεγραμμένοις, ἐνεφά[νιζον]
δὲ καὶ τὰν τᾶς θεᾶς ἐπιφάνειαν καὶ τὰς γεγενημέ-
νας ὑπὸ τῶν προγόνων ἐς τοὺς Ἕλλανας εὐχρηστίας,
καὶ παρακαλούντων ὅπως ἀποδέξηται τὸ κοινὸ[ν τῶμ]
Μεσσανίων τὰν πανάγυριν καὶ ἐκεχειρίạṿ ḳ[αὶ τὸν ἀγῶ]-
να στεφανίταν ἰσοπύθιον τόν τε μ[ουσικὸν καὶ γυ]-
μ̣ṿι̣ḳọ̣ṿ καὶ ἱππικὸν ὃν τίθητι τ[ᾶι Ἀρτέμιτι τᾶι Λευκο]-
[φρυηνᾶι ὁ δᾶ]μος τῶμ Μαγν[ήτων, καὶ τὰν πόλιν καὶ
[τὰν χώραν αὐτῶ]ν ἱερὰν καὶ ἄ[συλον εἶμεν· ἐπεὶ οὖν τοῖς]
[Μεσσανίοις πάτ]ριόν ἐστι μάλ[ιστα μὲν τὰς τῶν θεῶν]
[τιμὰς συναύξειν, ἔπειτα δὲ καὶ τοὺς συγγενέας καὶ]
[φίλους -]
[- - - - - - - - - - - - -]ι̣ καὶ το[- - - - - - - - - - - - - -]
[δέχεσθαι τὰ]ς [θυσίας] τᾶς Ἀρτέμι̣τ̣ος τᾶς [Λευκο]-
[φρυηνᾶς καὶ τὰ]ν ἐκεχ[ειρί]αν καὶ τοὺς ἀγῶνας στ̣[εφα]-
[νίτας ἰσ]ο[π]υθίως τόν τε μουσικὸν καὶ γυμνικὸν κα̣[ὶ]

[ἱππικὸν οὗ]ς ποιόντι οἱ Μάγνητες καθὼς ὁ θεὸς ἔχρησε[ν·] [τοῖς δὲ θε]αροῖς τοῖς ἐπαγγελλόντοις τὰν θυσίαν καὶ ἐκε[χειρίαν] τᾶς Ἀρτέμιτος τᾶς Λευκοφρυηνᾶς δόντων οἱ ταμίαι ὅσα καὶ τοῖς τὰ Πύθια ἐπαγγελλόντοις.

10: singular participle for plural. 11, 16: the participles should be nominative, as Kern noted. 21–22 Holleaux: εἶμεν, τᾶι δὲ πόλει | τᾶι ἁμετέραι Kern.

Messene was an Aetolian ally in 208, and around this time Messenian troops are found helping to defend Delphi (*FD* III.4 21–24 = *Syll.*[3] 555–556). The request for *asylia* is mentioned twice in the preliminaries (by virtue of quoting both the oracle and the speech); unless the decree had an omission the reverse of that of Corinth and Corcyra, the grant must have come in the damaged lines 23–25.

16: For κοινόν as "government" see Robert, *Monnaies antiques en Troade* (Geneva 1966) 89–90.

94. Corcyra

Kern, *I.Magnesia* 44.

Cf. Wilhelm, *Jahresh.* 4 (1901) Beibl. 26 (*Kl. Schr.* II.1 153); Holleaux, *Etudes* I 317.

From line 43, on a lower block.

παρὰ Κορκυραίων

ἐπὶ πρυτάνιος Ἀνθρωπίσκου, μηνὸς Φοινικαίου ἁμέραι πέμπτα⟨ι⟩ ἐπ' εἰκάδι, προστάτας προβούλων Μνάσων Στράτωνος, ἀγαθᾶι τύχαι, ἐπειδὴ ἁ πόλις ἁ τῶμ Μαγνήτων πρὸς τῶι Μαιάνδρωι ὑπαρχούσας οἰκειότατος αὐτᾶι ποτὶ τὰν πόλιν τῶγ Κορκυραίων θυσίαν τε ποιεῖν ἐψάφισται κατὰ τὰν τοῦ Ἀπόλλωνος μαντείαν τᾶι Ἀρτέμιτι τᾶι Λευκοφρυηνᾶι καὶ πανάγυριν διὰ πενταετηρίδος καὶ ἀγῶνα μουσικὸν καὶ ἱππικὸν καὶ γυμνικὸν στεφανίταν ἰσοπύθιον ταῖς τιμαῖς καὶ ἀπέσταλκε πρεσβευτὰς καὶ θιαροὺς Σωσικλῆ Διοκλέος, Ἀριστόδαμον Διοκλέος, Διότιμον Μηνοφίλου, οἳ ποτελθόντες ποτὶ τὰν ἐπείσκλητον τό τε ψάφισμα ἀπέδωκαν τὸ παρὰ Μαγνήτων καὶ ἀπελογίξαντο τάν τε τᾶς θεᾶς ἐπιφάνειαν καὶ τὰν ὑπάρχουσαν οἰκειότατα ταῖς πόλεσιν καὶ τὰς γεγενημένας ὑπὸ τῶν προγόνων αὐτῶν εὐεργεσίας εἴς τε τὸ ἱερὸν τὸ ἐν Δελφοῖς καὶ εἰς τοὺς Ἕλλανας διά τε τῶν τοῦ θεοῦ χρησμῶν καὶ δία τῶν ποιητᾶν καὶ διὰ τῶν ψαφισμάτων τῶν ὑπαρχόντων αὐτοῖς παρὰ ταῖς πόλεσιν καλῶν καὶ ἐνδόξων, παρεκάλουν τε καὶ ᾤιοντο δεῖν παραδεξαμένους, καθὼς καὶ αἱ πόλιες αἱ Ἑλλανίδες, μετέχειν τᾶς τε θυσίας καὶ τοῦ ἀγῶνος καὶ ἀποστέλλειν θιαροὺς ἐπεί κα ἑκαστάκις ὁ χρόνος περιίκῃ τᾶς π[ε]νταετηρίδος, τοὺς κοινωνησοῦντας τᾶς τε θυσίας καὶ τῶν λοιπῶν τιμίων παρ' αὐτοῖς, δεδόχθαι τοῖς Κορκυραίοις παραδέξασθαι τάν τε θυσίαν καὶ τὸν ἀγῶνα τᾶς Ἀρτέμιτος τᾶς Λευκοφρυηνᾶς στεφανίταν ἰσοπύθιον ταῖς τιμαῖς ὃν τίθητι ἁ πόλις ἁ τῶν Μαγνήτων, καὶ τοῖς νικῶσι τῶν πολιτᾶν τὰς αὐτὰς εἶμεν τιμὰς παρὰ τᾶς πόλιος ἃς καὶ τοῖς τὰ Πύθια νικῶσιν· ἀποκρίνασθαι δὲ τοῖς πρεσβευταῖς καὶ θιαροῖς διότι ἁ πόλις ἁ τῶν Κορκυραίων αὐτά τε τιμῶσα διατελεῖ τὰν Ἄρτεμιν θυσίαις, καθὼς αὐτᾶι πάτριόν ἐστιν, καὶ Μάγνησι δὲ τοῖς παρακαλοῦσιν ἐπὶ ταῦτα προθύμως ἐπακολουθεῖ καὶ συναύξει τὰς τιμὰς τὰς ποτιγινομένας τᾶι θεῶι· ὅπως δὲ καὶ οἱ θιαροὶ αἱρεθῶντι καὶ ἀποσταλῶντι εἰς τ[ὸ]ν καιρὸν τὸν δέοντα προβούλους τοὺς γενομένους ἐν ἀρχᾶι κατὰ τὸν χρόνον τὸν συνίκοντα ἐπιμεληθῆμεν ὡς ἂν ἀποσταλῶντι, εἴ κα δυνατὸν ἦι τᾶι πόλει, δόμεν δὲ τοῖς τε νῦν παροῦσι θιαροῖς ἱερεῖον ἐνίστιον τέλειον καὶ ἐκέχειρον εἴς τε τὰν θυσίαν καὶ τἆλλα τὰ νομιζόμενα ἀργυρίου Κορινθίου δραχμὰς ἑκατὸν πεντήκοντα [ἐ]πεί κα τὰν ἐπαγγελίαν τοῦ ἀγῶνος ποιήσωνται, ὁμοίως δὲ καὶ τοῖς ἄλλοις ἀεὶ τοῖς παραγινομένοις, περὶ δὲ πάντων τούτων γράψαι τοὺς ἀιρημένους νομοθέτας καὶ κατατάξαι ἐς τοὺς ἱεροὺς νόμους· εἶμεν δὲ αὐτῶν τάν τε πόλιν καὶ τὰγ χώραν ἱερὰν καὶ ἄσυλον κατὰ τὸν τοῦ θεοῦ χρησμόν· ἐπαινέσαι [δὲ] καὶ τὸν ἀρχιθέωρον Σωσικλῆ{ι} καὶ τοὺς θιαροὺς Ἀριστόδαμον, [Διότι]μον εὐσεβείας ἕνεκεν τᾶς εἰς τὰν θεὸν καὶ τᾶς εἰς τὰν πατρίδα [φι]λοτιμίας, ὑπάρχειν δὲ καὶ προξενίαν αὐτοῖς καὶ ἐκγόνοις, καλέσαι δὲ κα[ὶ] [αὐτοὺς] ἐν τὸ πρυτανεῖον· εἶμεν δὲ καὶ θιαροδόκον Κλείδικον Ἀλεξικλέ[ος] [τὸν ὑποδε]ξούμε[νον τὰς ἀ]εὶ παρ[αγιν]ομένας θιαρίας παρὰ Μαγνήτων· τ[ὸ] δὲ ψάφισμ[α ἀναγραφὲν ἐν στάλα]ν ἀναθέμεν πρὸ τοῦ πρυτανείου, τὸ δὲ [εἰς τὰ προγεγραμμένα? γε]νόμενον ἀνάλωμα εἴς τε τὰν κατα[σκευὰν τᾶς στάλας?] [- -]

[ἀ]κολού[θ]ως [δ]ὲ ἔ[δοξεν ψηφίσασθαι καὶ]
Ὠ[ρ]ικί[οις]

2: ΠΕΜΠΤΑΣ lapis. 41 init. Wilhelm: [τὸν παραδε] Kern. 42–43 Holleaux.

Corcyra (like Apollonia and Epidamnus) had been a Roman *socius* since the time of the Illyrian War (Polyb. 2.11.6–8). This is one of the most detailed decrees from the Magnesia archive, and yet (like that of Corinth) it fails to mention the request for *asylia* in the preliminaries, although it then in fact grants it (35–36).

The formulary seen here differs in some details from that of the extant Corcyraean proxeny decrees of Hellenistic date. With line 20 contrast ἔδοξε τᾶι ἁλίαι at the beginnings of *IG* IX.1 685–688; with line 1 contrast πρύτανις Στράτων at *IG* 682, but also πρυτανεύοντος Ἀριστεμένεος in 694.[72] Line 3 explicates the bare προστάτας Γνάθιος of 682; the *probouloi* of Corcyra are elsewhere always coupled with *prodikoi*, responsible for inscribing decrees (683, 685, 686; also 688, adding *strategoi*).

2: Ambracia also had a month Phoinikaios; Athena Phoenice was honored at Corinth (Höfer, in Roscher, *Lex.* 3.2398–2399), and doubtless also in its colonies.[73]

72. Republished with legal commentary by A. Mannzmann, *Griechische Stiftungsurkunden* (Münster 1962); the date is uncertain.

73. See Wilhelm, *Kl. Schr.* I.1 447–451 (restoring Attic Thargelion, ca. May, as the synchronism at *IG* II^2 951.3).

3: A Straton is the *prytanis* of *IG* 682, which has been assigned to the end of the fourth century. We have Corcyraean amphoras stamped ἐπὶ Στράτωνος, also bronze coins (*BMC Thessaly* 149 nos. 525–526), of uncertain date.

10: LSJ take ἐπείσκλητος as an adjective, "(sc. ἐκκλησία), specially convened meeting," as in Athens an ἐκκλησία σύγκλητος.[74] To the contrary, in this context it is clearly a noun and must be western usage for "assembly." In fact we know how the Corcyraeans named a specially convened meeting: καρυκτὰ ἁλία (*IG* 694.53). Compare the noun σύγκλητος in Italy, also πρόσκλητος (= *consilium*, *IG* XIV 657, 660), ἔσκλητος (= the *prytaneis*? 612; Hesych. s.v. of a privy council at Syracuse).

17: While many grantors invoke the honorific decrees that cities have voted for Magnesia, this passage alone suggests that these might include the recognitions that were now being gathered; in practice a team of *theoroi* could know only those that they themselves had been given. But the aside may be generic rather than specific: "accept, as Greek cities do," rather than "as the Greek cities have."

25: With this pious sentiment compare many of the decrees for Teos ("we too worship Dionysus"); at Magnesia, only the Eretrians (**98**.11–13), but cf. **96**.24–25.

30: For a cautionary note about sending *theoroi* in the future ("so long as it is possible for the city"), compare **12**.15; **109**.b.6 and **120**.35 in the other decrees for Magnesia.

32: Payment in "drachmas of Corinthian silver" also in *IG* 694, and at Epidamnus (**96**.41); cf. *Staatvertr.* II 480.39, one "Corinthian stater" per day for a cavalryman in Aetolia and Acarnania in the 260s. Of course the phrase had long been in use for true Corinthian money (e.g., Thuc. 1.27.1). But Corcyra issued its own drachmas and didrachmas in abundance,[75] though by now bearing the types familiar from Corinthian coins (regularly the Pegasus reverses), with Corcyra's identity signaled merely by a monogram. This native money must be intended or at least included in "Corinthian silver."

33: The provision to give the present ambassadors their gifts when they make the proclamation of the contest reveals a two-stage process: the Magnesians made one speech to request the new status, and a second, only after that was approved, in order to invite Corcyraeans to the upcoming contest of 207. This legal nicety is clear otherwise only at Paros (**100**.42–45), another unusually detailed decree. Possibly it was true in all cases, and other texts merely condense the stages of the visit.

74. So G. Busolt, *Griechische Staatskunde* (Munich 1920) 444 n. 2, 447 n. 1; F. Ghinati, *PP* 15 (1960) 371, argued that the Corcyraean ἐπείσκλητος was an oligarchic assembly, between a council and a full assembly.

75. E.g., *BMC Thess.* 135–139 and *Hunterian Coll.* II 18; S. Fried, "The Autonomous Silver Coinage of Korkyra" (Ph.D. diss., University of Michigan 1982), stops with 229 B.C. and the end of the drachmas that give the ethnic Κερκυραίων in full (the exact date 229 is conventional).

46: In the late third century, Oricum, the harbor city on the Epirote mainland near the mouth of the Aous, was in a *sympoliteia* with Corcyra, as we know from a question put to Zeus of Dodona by the two cities jointly.[76]

95. Apollonia

From line 44, on a lower block.
Kern, *I.Magnesia* 45.
Cf. Boesch, Θεωρός 72 n. 1; De Decker, *RPhil* n.s. 29 (1905) 161 (collation).

παρὰ Ἀπολλωνιατῶν
πρυ[τ]α[νεύ]οντος Ἀριστομένεος, Ἁλ⟨ι⟩οτροπίου
τρίτᾳ, παραγενομένων πρεσβευτᾶν καὶ θεωρῶν
παρὰ τᾶς πόλιος τῶν Μαγνήτων τῶν ἐπὶ Μαιάν-
δρου Σωσικλέος τοῦ Διοκλέος καὶ Ἀριστο-
δάμου τοῦ Διοκλέος καὶ Διοτίμου τοῦ Μηνοφί-
λου καὶ κομιξάντων ψάφισμα παρὰ τᾶς πόλι-
ος ἐν ὧι κατεκεχώριστο ὅ τε χρησμὸς ὁ παρὰ
τοῦ θεοῦ τοῦ ἐν [Δ]ελφοῖς ὅτι λώιον εἴη καὶ ἄμει-
νον τοῖς σεβ̣ομένοις Ἄρτεμιν Λευκοφρυ[η]ν̣ὰν
καὶ τὰ[ν] π̣όλιν τῶν Μαγνήτων καὶ τὰν χώραν ἱ[ε]-
[ρ]ὰν κ[αὶ ἄ]σ[υ]λον νομίζουσιν, καὶ ὅτι ὁ δᾶμος τ[ῶ]ν
Μα[γνήτω]ν ἐψάφισται τᾶι εὐεργέτιδι τᾶς πόλι-
ος Ἀρ[τ]έμιδι Λευκοφρυηνᾶι διὰ πέντε ἐτέων θυ-
[σ]ίαν καὶ πανάγυριν καὶ ἐκεχειρίαν καὶ ἀγῶνα
στεφανίταν ἰσοπύθιον μουσικόν τε καὶ γυμνι-
κὸν καὶ ἱππικόν, διαλεχθέντων δὲ καὶ τῶν πε-
ρὶ Σωσικλῆ ἀκολούθως τῶι ψαφίσματι καὶ ἐμ-
φανιξάντων τάν τε τᾶς θεοῦ ἐπιφάνειαν καὶ
τὰν οἰκειότατα Μαγνήτων καὶ Ἀπολλωνιατᾶν
καὶ τ̣ὰ̣ς εὐεργε[σ]ίας τὰς προγεγεν̣ειμένας ὑπὸ
τῶν προγόνων αὐ[τ]ῶν εἴς τε τὸ ἱερὸν τὸ ἐν Δελ-
φοῖς καὶ εἰ τοὺς Ἕλλανας καὶ παρακαλούν[τ]ων
ἀποδέξασθαι τὸ[ν ἀ]γῶνα καὶ συναύξειν τὰς [ἐψα]-
[φ]ισμένας τιμὰς [τ]ᾶι θεῶι, ἔδο[ξ]ε τῶι δάμωι̣
τῶν Ἀπολλωνιατᾶν ἀποδέξασθαι τὰ ἐπαγ-
γελλόμενα παρὰ τῶν Μαγ[ν]ήτων καὶ τὰν πό-
λιν κ̣α̣ὶ τὰν χώραν αὐτῶν ἱερὰν κ̣αὶ ἄσυλον
νομίζειν, καὶ τοῖς [ν]ικῶσι τῶν π[ολιτ]ᾶν τὸν ἀγῶ-
ν̣α̣ τῶν Λευκοφρυ[η]νῶν [εἶ]μεν τ[ὰ]ς [αὐτὰς τιμὰς]
ἅς καὶ τοῖς τὰ Πύθια νι[κῶ]σιν, ἀ[ποστέλλειν]
δ̣ὲ παρὰ τᾶς πόλιος καὶ θεωρο[ὺς εἰς Μαγνησί]-
[α]ν ἐπὶ τὰν θυσίαν κ̣α̣ὶ̣ [τ]ὸν ἀγ[ῶνα καὶ τὰ]ν̣ π̣α̣[νά]-
[γυρι]ν̣, τοὺς δ̣ὲ̣ [- -]
[- -]

76. *SEG* 23.474; J. and L. Robert, *Bull. épigr.* 1971, 382; bibliography at Cabanes, *L'Epire* 315.

μιείου̣ [- - - - - - - - -] ἐπὶ [- - - - - - - - - - - -]
[π]ρυτανείωι καὶ τὰ λοιπὰ ἃ καὶ [τοῖς τὰ Πύθια ἐ]-
παγγέλλουσιν, καὶ καταταχθῆ[ναι ἐν το]ῖς
ν̣όμοις τόν τε ἀγῶνα καὶ τὰς τιμὰς τὰς ἐψαφισ-
μένας· ἐπαινέσαι δὲ καὶ τοὺς θεωροὺς Σωσι-
κλῆ{ι}, Ἀριστόδαμον, Διότιμον ἐπί τε [τῶι δια]-
λεχθῆμεν ἀξ[ίω]ς̣ ἀμφοτερᾶν τᾶ̣ν̣ [πολίων]
[καὶ -]
[- - - - - - - - - - - - - προξέ]νους τᾶς Ἀπολ-
[λωνιατᾶν πόλιος, δόμεν δ' αὐτοῖς] καὶ ξένια τὰ
[μέγιστα ἐκ] τ̣ῶν [νόμων κα]ὶ [κλ]η̣θῆμεν αὐτο[ὺς]
[εἰς τὸ πρ]υτανεῖο[ν ἐπὶ] τὰν [κ]οινὰν ἑστίαν·
[θεαροδόκ]ον εἶμεν Μ[αγν]ήτων Ἵππανθον Φ[- - -·]
[τοὺς] δ̣ὲ ταμίας ἐπιμέλει̣α̣ν π̣[οιήσ]ασ[θαι]
[ὅπως ἀναγρα]φῆ εἰς χάλκωμα τὸ ψάφισμ[α]
[καὶ ἀνατεθῇ εἰς τὸ] ἱερὸν τοῦ Ἀπόλλωνος.

2: ΑΛΟΤ lapis. 33–34 τὰ]ν̣ π̣α̣[νά|γυρι]ν̣ De Decker. 34–36: [ἐπαγγέλλοντας ἀεὶ τὸν ἀγῶνα | ἄγεσθαι εἰς τὸν δᾶμον ἐπὶ τὰ ξένια ἐκ τοῦ τα]|μιείου, [κληθῆναι δὲ αὐτοὺς] ἐπὶ [σίτησιν ἐν τῶι] De Decker. 47 Boesch: [ν εἰς] Kern.

The only extant decree of Illyrian Apollonia, whose coins, with those of Epidamnus, dominate the Hellenistic hoards of the Balkans; on the two cities see P. Cabanes, *Les Illyriens* (Paris 1988) 208–212. They and Corcyra had been allied with Rome now for two decades.

2–3: The month Heliotropios is attested otherwise only at Epidamnus (**96**); it must fall in summer, as Wilhelm saw (*Kl. Schr.* I.1 450), presumably linked to the summer solstice.

17ff.: In describing the speech of the *theoroi* the Apolloniates mention crowned games, but not *asylia*, which emerges only when they quote the oracle (cf. **100**). They then grant *asylia*, but not in so many words the games, which are in effect recognized as isopythian by defining the reward for victors (29–31).[77]

50: On the frequent use of bronze for inscriptions in this part of Greece see Robert, *Hellenica* X (1955) 289–290.

51: Apollo was naturally the patron god of Apollonia. An epigram names Phoebus as its founder;[78] the city kept a flock of sheep sacred to Helios (Hdt. 9.93–94).

96. Epidamnus

From line 44, on a lower block.

Kern, *I.Magnesia* 46 [Dittenberger, *Syll.*² 259; Hiller, *Syll.*³ 560].

77. So too **115** and **131**; cf. *AJP* 108 (1987) 732.
78. Paus. 5.22.3 (Preger no. 60): cf. *I.Olympia* 692.

Cf. Wilhelm, *Jahresh.* 4 (1901) Beibl. 26 (*Kl. Schr.* II.1 153); Holleaux, *Etudes* I 317; De Decker, *RPhil* n.s. 29 (1905) 161–162 (collation).

παρὰ Ἐπιδαμνίων

[.]δ[- - - - - - - - - - - -]ạλακρ[- - - - - - - - - -]φῶντος, μη[ν]ὸς Ἁλι[ο]-
τροπίου, [ἐπειδὴ Μ]άγ[νητες] οἱ ἐπὶ Μαι[ά]νδρ[ου] συγγ[ενεῖς] ὄντες καὶ φị̣λοι τῶν Ἐπị-
4 δαμνίων εὐ[σεβ]έως [διακείμ]ενοι ποτὶ τὸ θεῖον κα[ὶ τὰ κάλ]λιστα αἱρ̣[ούμ]ενοι τῷ̣[ν]
κατ' ἀνθρώπο[υς] ἀφεστά[λκα]ντ[ι] πρεσβευτὰς τ[ο]ὺς δὲ αὐ[τοὺ]ς καὶ θια[ρ]οὺς Σωσικ[λῆ]
Διοκλέος, Ἀρι[σ]τ[όδαμ]ον Διοκλ[έ]ọς, Διότιμον Μηνοφί[λου, ο]ἳ ποτελθόντες ποτὶ
τὰν βουλὰν καὶ [τὸν] δᾶμ̣[ον ἁμῶν τὸ ψά]φισμα ἀπέδωκα[ν καὶ αὐτ]οὶ διελέχθην μετὰ πά-
8 σας φ[ι]λοτιμία[ς] ἐμφανίξ[αντες τὰν] τᾶς Ἀρτέμι[δος ἐπιφάν]ειαν καὶ τὰν γεγενημέν[α]ν
βοάθειαν ὑπὸ τ[ῶ]ν π̣[ρ]ο[γόνων α]ὐτῶν [εἰ]ς τὸ ἱερὸν τὸ ἐν Δελφ[οῖς], νικ̣ασάντων μάχαι τοὺς
βαρ[β]άρους το[ὺ]ς ἐπιστ[ρατεύ]σ̣αντας ἐπὶ διαρπαγᾶι τῶ[ν το]ῦ [θ]εοῦ χρημάτων, καὶ τὰν
εὐε[ργ]εσίαν ἃν [συ]νετελέσαντο εἰς τὸ κοινὸ[ν] τῶν Κρηταιέ[ων] δι[α]λύσαντες τὸν ἐμφύλι-
12 ον πόλεμον, ἐνεφάνιξαν δὲ καὶ τὰς εἰς τοὺς ἄλλους [Ἕλ]λανας γεγενημένας
εὐε[ρ]γεσίας διά τε τῶν τοῦ θεοῦ χρησμῶν καὶ διὰ τῶ[ν π]οι̣ητᾶν καὶ διὰ τῶν ἱ[σ]-
τορ[ι]αγράφων τῶν συγγεγραφότ[ων] τὰς Μαγνήτων πρ[άξ]ει[ς], παρανέγνωσαν δὲ
καὶ τὰ ψαφίσματ[α] τὰ ὑπάρχοντα αὐτοῖς παρὰ ταῖς πόλ[ε]σιν ἐν οἷς ἦν καταγε-
16 γρ̣αμμ̣[έ]ναι τιμαί τ[ε] καὶ στέφαν[ο]ι εἰς δόξαν ἀν⟨ή⟩κοντ̣α ⟨τᾶι⟩ [πό]λ̣[ε]ι, τοῦ θεοῦ τοῦ ἐν
Δε[λ]φοῖς χρήσαντος λώϊον εἶμ[εν καὶ ἄ]μεινον τοῖς σε[βομέ]νοις Ἄρτεμ̣ιν Λευκο-
φ[ρυ]ηνὰν καὶ τὰν πόλιν καὶ τὰγ χώραν τ[ῶ]μ [Μαγ]νήτων ἱ[ερὰν κ]αὶ ἄσυλον νομιζόν-
τ[ε]σσι, τὸν δᾶμον ἐψαφίσθαι τᾶι ἀρχαγέτιδι τᾶς πόλιος [Ἀρ]τέμιτι συντελεῖν θυσ[ί]-
20 ạ[ν] τε καὶ πανάγυριν καὶ ἀγῶνα στεφανίταν ἰσοπύθιον μου̣[σι]κόν τε καὶ γυμνικὸν κα[ὶ]
ἱ[π]πικόν, παρεκάλουν δὲ καὶ ἁμὲ ὄντας οἰκείους καὶ φίλους [ἀ]ποδέξασθαι τάν τε θ[υ]-
[σί]αν καὶ τὰν ἐκεχ[ει]ρίαν καὶ τὸν ἀγῶνα στεφανίταν ἰσο[πύ]θιον ταῖς τιμαῖς,
[ἔ]δ̣οξε τᾶι βουλᾶι καὶ τῶι δάμωι τῶι Ἐπιδαμνίων τύχ[αις] ἐπ̣ὶ ταῖς ἀρίσταις
24 [κ]ρίνασθαι Μάγνησιν ὅτι ὁ δᾶμος ὁ τῶν Ἐπιδαμνίων [αὐτ]ός τε ποτὶ τὸ θεῖον εὐ-
σεβέως τυγχάνει διακείμενος, πά̣τ̣ριόν τέ ἐστιν ạὐ̣[τῶι] καὶ τὰς τῶν οἰκείων

τιμὰς συναύξειν, ἐπαιν[έσ]αι δὲ κ̣αὶ τ[ὸν] δᾶμον τὸμ Μαγ[νή]των ἐπί τε τᾶι ποτὶ
τοὺς θεοὺς εὐσεβείαι καὶ ἐπὶ τ[ᾶ]ι ποτὶ τοὺς [Ἕλλαν]ας εὐνοί[αι] καὶ ἐπὶ τᾶι εὐεργεσίαι
τᾶι τε εἰς τὸ ἱερὸν τὸ ἐν Δελφοῖς καὶ εἰ[ς] τ[οὺς] ἄλλους Ἕλλα[νας], δέχεσθαι δὲ καὶ τὸν
ἀγῶνα ὃν συντελοῦντ[ι] Μάγν[η]τες τᾶι Ἀρτέμι[τ]ι τ[ᾶ]ι Λ[ε]υκ[οφ]ρυηνᾶι στεφανίταν ἰσο-
πύθιο[ν, καθὼς] ἐπαγγ[έλλοντι ὅ τε ἀρ]χιθ[έ]ω[ρος καὶ οἱ] θε[ωροί], καὶ ὑπάρχειν τοῖς νικών-
τεσ̣[σι τοῦτον τὸν] ἀγ[ῶνα φιλάνθ]ρ[ωπα] ὅ̣σα κ̣[αὶ τοῖς τὰ Πύ]θια [νικ]ώ̣ντεσσι παρὰ τᾶς πόλι-
[ος δέδοται], ε̣ἶ̣μεν δ[ὲ τὰν πόλιν κα]ὶ τὰγ [χ]ώραν τὰ[ν Μαγ]ν[ήτ]ων ἱερὰν καὶ ἄσυ-
[λον καθότ]ι ὁ Ἀπόλλων ὁ ἐν [Δελφοῖ]ς ἔχρησεν· ἐπαινέ[σαι δὲ τ]όν τε ἀρχιθέωρον
[Σωσικλῆ] κ̣αὶ τ̣οὺς [θι]αροὺς Ἀριστόδαμον, Διότιμο[ν ἐπὶ τ]ε τᾶι ὑπὲρ τᾶς πατρί-
[δος φιλο]τιμί[αι καὶ] ἀ̣[ναστροφᾶι] ἇι ἐποιήσαν[το ἀξ]ίως ἀμφοτερᾶν τᾶν πο-
[λίων, καὶ εἶμεν] δ̣[ὲ̣ αὐτ]οὺς προξένους κα[ὶ εὐεργ]έτας τᾶς πόλιος τῶν
[Ἐπιδαμνίων· ὅπως δὲ τὰ ἐψηφισ]μένα μετὰ τᾶς τῶν θε[ῶν εὐ]νοίας νῦν τε καὶ εἰς
[τὸν ἀεὶ] χρό[νον ἐπ' ἀγαθῶι συντ]ελῆται τῶι [τ]ε Μα[γνήτων] καὶ Ἐπιδαμνίων, τὸμ
πρύ[τα]νιν [κατεύχεσθαι τᾶ]ι Ἀρτέμιτι τᾶι Λε̣[υοκοφρυη]νᾶι καὶ τᾶι Ἑστίαι, καλέ-
σαν̣τ̣α̣ δ' α[ὐτοὺς εἰς τὸ πρυταν]εῖο[ν ἐ]πὶ τὰν κοινὰν ἑστ[ίαν] ἱερεῖον θῦσαι ἐφέστι-
ον [καὶ δίδο]σ[θαι αὐτοῖς τὰ σ]κέλη̣ καὶ τὸ νάκος καὶ ἐ[νεχέχηρον] ἀργυρίου Κορινθίου
[ἡ]μιμναῖον, δόμεν δὲ καὶ τᾶι θεᾶι ἀργυ]ρ̣ίου ἡ̣μιμναῖον, [ὑπάρχεν] δὲ καὶ τὰ κατάλοιπα
[ὥσπερ καὶ τοῖς θιαροῖς τοῖς ἀεὶ ἡκόντεσσι]ν εἰς ἁ[μέ· ὅτε δέ κα] ἐς καιρὸν ἦι τᾶν συν-
[τελουμένων θυσιᾶν κ]α[ὶ τοῦ] ἀγῶνος, [ἀποστέλλεν τοὺς συνθύσοντας· ἵνα δὲ καὶ ἁ ὑποδοχὰ τῶν ἀεὶ]
[ἀποστελλομένων ἐ]γ Μαγνησίας ἀξία γίνηται τᾶμ [π]ολίω[ν ἀμφ]οτερᾶν, θεωρ[οδόκον]
[παρ' ἁμὶν ἑλέσθαι· ἀ]ναγράψαι δὲ καὶ τὸ ψάφισμα ἐμ βουλευτηρίωι.

2: - - - Φα]λακρ[ίωνος or Βα]λάκρ[ου? Kern; [ἔ]δ[οξε τῶι δάμωι ἐπὶ ἄρχοντος Φ]α̣λακρ̣[ίωνος τοῦ Καλλι]φῶντος De Decker. 16 ἀν⟨η⟩κοντα̣ Rigsby: ἀνίκοντα̣ Kern. 39 De Decker: [κατεύχεσθαι] Holleaux. 40 Holleaux: σ̣α̣ι̣ δ̣' α̣[ὐτοὺς Kern. 41 init. Holleaux: κ̣[αὶ καταλιπ]έ̣σ̣[θαι] α̣[ὐτοῖς] De Decker. 43–46: De Decker as modified by Hiller.

Our only decree of Epidamnus, this text provides unique details about the Magnesians' speech; lines 8–12 identify the services of Magnesia to the Greek people, so often cited in the abstract, as aid to Delphi against the Gauls in 279 and arbitrating civil war on Crete.

2–3: For Heliotropios see on **95**.1–2. In Apollonia on the third of the month, the envoys had passed through Epidamnus before its end, as we should expect.

5: For this description of the ambassadors see on **86**.4–5.

16: This sentence suggests, if only by its silence about the games and inviolability, that these decrees, cited elsewhere in more general terms, concerned past honors and are not the new recognitions. A unique verb (so LSJ ἀνίκω) is then followed by an emendation and a lacuna. I suggest therefore that further emendation is warranted here; for the common expression with ἀνήκω see the index, and on **102**.65.

24–25: For expressions of one's own piety see on **94**.25.

37–39: Apparently the *prytanis*, who was eponymous (cf. Robert, *Hellenica* X 289), is to pray to the Magnesian goddess and to the goddess of the Epidamnians' public hearth "that the things voted with the goodwill of the gods be fulfilled now and forever for the good of the Magnesians and Epidamnians." Such public prayer is a common enough stipulation in honorific decrees (in the *asylia* texts: **111**.53, **125**.b.13), but elsewhere it is done by priests rather than magistrates. In what follows the sentiments are clear but not the structure or details: the *prytanis* is to invite the *theoroi* to sacrifice at the hearth in the prytaneum, giving them a sheep, from which they get the legs and fleece, and some money as the sacrificial allowance, and in addition a half-mina of silver. This last is the amount of the *enekecheron* at **85**.31, but some second item seems to be intended here.

97. Chalcis

Kern, *I.Magnesia* 47 [Dittenberger, *Syll.*[2] 260; Ziebarth, *IG* XII.9 pp. 166–167; Hiller, *Syll.*[3] 561].

Cf. Wilhelm, *Jahresh.* 3 (1900) 58 (*Kl. Schr.* II.1 74); O. Picard, *Chalcis et la confédération eubéenne* (Paris 1979) 275.

[οἱ στρατ]ηγο̣[ὶ] εἶπαν· [ἐπειδὴ ὁ β]ασιλεὺς Φίλι[π]πος
ἔγρα[ψε]ν τῆι βουλῆι κ[αὶ τῶι] δήμ[ωι] περὶ [Μ]αγνή-
των τῶν ἐπὶ Μαιάνδρωι, οἳ [σ]υγγενεῖς ὄντες Μακε-
δόνων ἠξίουσαν̣ τ[ὸν] ἀγῶν[α ὃ]ν τιθέασι [τῆι] Ἀ[ρτ]έ-
μιδι τῆι Λευκοφρυηνῆι προσ[δέξα]σθαι στεφανίτην,
αὐτὸν μὲν οὖν ὑπα[κ]ηκόεν̣αι, [κ]α̣λ̣[ῶς] δὲ ποιήσειν̣ κα[ὶ]
τοὺς πολίτας προσ[δ]εξαμ[ένους] τοὺς ἄνδρας τοὺς
ἀπεσταλμένους ὑπὲρ τούτ[ων·] ἀκολούθως δὲ καὶ οἱ ἡι-
ρημένοι ὑπὸ Μαγνήτων περὶ τῆς ἐπαγγελίας τοῦ ἀγῶ-
νος Ἀπολλοφάνης Αἰσχύλου, Εὔβουλ[ος] Ἀναξαγό-
ρου, Λυκομήδης Χ[α]ρισίου πρόσοδον ποιη[σ]άμενοι

καὶ τὸ ψήφισμα ἀποδόντες καὶ ἀπολογισάμενοι
τήν τε τῆς θεᾶς ẹπιφάνειαν καὶ τὰς γεγενημένας
ὑπὸ τῆς πατρίδος εὐχρηστίας εἰς τοὺς Ἕλληνας
παρεκάλουν ἀποδεξαμ̣ẹ́νους τοὺς πολίτας συναύ-
ξειν τὰς ἐψ[ηφ]ισμένας τιμὰς τῆι Ἀρτέμιδι τῆι Λευκο-
φρυηνῆι· περὶ δὴ τούτων [δε]δόχθαι τῆι βουλῆι καὶ
τῶι δήμωι ἀποδέξασθαι τὸν ἀγῶνα τῶν Λευκοφρυ-
ηνῶν ὃν τιθέασι Μάγνητες ο[ἱ] ἐπὶ Μαιάνδρου τῆι Ἀρτέ-
μιδι τῆι Λευκοφρυηνῆι στε[φα]νίτην ἰσοπύθιον, καθά-
περ οἱ ἀπεσταλμένοι ὑπ' [α]ὐ[τῶν θ]εωροὶ ἐπαγγέλλουσιν,
καὶ τοῖς νικήσασιν Χαλκ[ι]δ[έων τ]ὸν ἀγῶνα τοῦτον διδό-
ναι τὰ ἴσα ἆθλα ὅσαπερ κ̣[αὶ] το[ῖς τ]ὰ Πύθια νικήσασιν
ἐκ τοῦ νόμου καθήκε[ι] δίδοσθ[αι], ἀποστέλλεσθαι δὲ καὶ
θεωροὺς παρὰ τῆς πόλεως, ὅτ[αν] καθήκωσιν οἱ ἀγῶνες
[τ]ῶν Λευκοφ[ρυ]ηνῶν, δίδο[σ]θ[αι] δ[ὲ] τὴν ἀπαρχὴν τοῖς ἀπο-
στελλομένοις θεωροῖς παρὰ [Μ]αγνήτων τὴν ἐκ τοῦ νόμου.

1 Picard: [περὶ ὧν ὁ β.] Kern. 6 Wilhelm: [τ]α̣ὐ̣[τὸ] δὲ Kern; the stone and the squeeze are too faint to decide.

Chalcis was the largest city on Euboea, and subject to the Antigonids, as is explicit here. The decree is brief and without verbal flourishes. It does not even provide for the inscribing of the act—and it makes no mention of *asylia*.

Lines 1–8 summarize the letter of Philip V to Chalcis (hence Μακεδόνων, reflecting the Magnesians' argument to Philip, not to the Chalcidians); in direct speech, "I have myself acceded, and you too would do well to accept the men sent concerning this"—that is, accept them favorably, as εὐνόως προσεδέξαντο at **88**.26. For the expression cf. *Royal Corres.* 13.13: καλῶς δ' ἂν ποήσαιτε ψηφισάμενοι. The deference to the king implied by this opening is striking and contrasts with the decrees of Macedonian cities for Cos, which mention the wishes of the king in brief and in the body of the decree. It contrasts too with the decree of Eretria (**98**), which does not mention Philip at all.

The Chalcidians speak of two prompting events, the royal letter and the Magnesians' visit. It would seem that the king's letter arrived before the *theoroi*, who are not said to have brought it. These are the men who canvassed central Greece, and unless they were traveling from north to south, they did not approach Philip; already others had done that, and early enough for his letter (of the sort promised in some extant royal letters) to reach Euboea before the *theoroi*.

1: The dating by *hegemon* that commonly precedes Chalcidian decrees has been omitted at Magnesia. A board of *strategoi* we see otherwise at *IG* XII.9 900.c.8. *Strategoi* commonly propose decrees at Eretria (whose Hellenistic epigraphy is more abundant than that of Chalcis).

3: Macedon and Magnes were brothers (Hes. frag. 7 M.-W.), whence this kinship. By contrast, neither the Chalcidians nor the Eretrians claim kinship with Magnesia.

98. Eretria

To the right of **97**.
Kern, *I.Magnesia* 48 [Ziebarth, *IG* XII.9 p. 162].
Cf. Robert, *Op. min. sel.* I 28.

[ἐ]π[ὶ] στρατηγ̣οῦ [- - - - - - - - - - - - - - - - ἐπειδὴ] Μάγ[ν]ητες
οἱ ἐπὶ Μαιάνδ[ρου φίλοι καὶ οἰκεῖοι ὑπ]ά[ρχοντες ἐκ π]ρο-
γόνων τοῦ δ̣ή[μου τοῦ Ἐρετριέων - - - ἀπεστάλκασι] ψήφισμα καὶ θε-
ωρ̣οὺς Ἀπολλ[οφ]ά[νη]ν Αἰσχύλου, Ε[ὔβου]λον Ἀναξα[γόρου, Λυκο]-
μήδην Χαρισίο[υ, οἵτ]ινες παραγενόμενοι ἀνενεώσα[ντο τὴν οἰ]-
κειότητα τὴν π[ρο]ϋπάρχουσαν καὶ ἀπελογίσαντο τὴ[ν τῆς θεᾶς]
Ἀρτέμιδος Λευ[κο]φρυηνῆς ἐπιφάνειαν καὶ τὰς γεγενημένας [εἰς]
τοὺς Ἕλληνας [ὑπὸ] τῶν προγόνων εὐεργεσίας καὶ παρεκάλουν [φιλο]-
τίμως ἀποδέξασθα[ι τὸ]ν ἀγῶνα στεφανίτην ἰσοπύθιον ὃν τιθέασιν τῆι Ἀρτέ-
μιδι τῆι Λευκοφ[ρυη]νῆι, καὶ τὴν πόλιν αὐτῶν καὶ τὴν χώραν ἱερὰ[ν καὶ]
ἄσυλον εἶναι κ[αθό]τι αὐτοῖς καὶ ὁ θεὸς ὁ ἐν Δελφοῖς ἔχρησ[εν], πά[τρι]-
ον δ' ἐστὶν Ἐρετρ̣[ιεῦ]σιν τά τε πρὸς τὸ θεῖον εὐσεβῶς διακεῖσθαι [καὶ μάλισ]-
τα πρὸς τὴν Ἄρτε̣[μιν] καὶ τὴν οἰκειότητα τὴν ὑπάρχουσαν πρὸς [τοὺς Μά]-
γνητας διαφυλά[σσει]ν· περὶ δὴ τουτῶν ἔδοξεν τῆι βουλῆι καὶ τῶι [δή]-
μωι ἀποδέξασθα[ι τὸν] ἀγῶνα τῆς Ἀρτέμιδος τῆς Λευκ[οφρυη]νῆς στεφα-
νίτην ἰσοπύθιον [καὶ τ]ὴν πόλιν καὶ τὴν χώραν αὐτῶν ἱε[ρ]ὰν καὶ [ἄ]συλον
εἶναι, καθὰ καὶ ὁ [θεὸς ἔχ]ρησεν, εἶναι δὲ καὶ τὰ ἆθλα καὶ τὰς [τ]ιμὰς
καθάπερ καὶ τοῖς [τὰ Π]ύθια νικῶσιν ὑπάρχει, ἀποστέλλειν δὲ καὶ θ[εω]-
ροὺς καὶ θυσίαν ε[ἰς τ]ὸν ἀγῶνα· ἐπαινέσαι δὲ καὶ τὸν δῆμον τὸμ [Μα]-
γνήτων ἐπὶ τῆι εὐ[σε]β̣είαι τῆι πρὸς τὸ θεῖον, στεφανῶσαι δὲ καὶ το[ὺ]ς
θεωροὺς θαλλοῦ [στ]ε̣φάνωι φιλοτιμίας καὶ σπουδῆς ἕνεκεν ἧς πεποί-
ηνται περί τε τῶν θ̣[ε]ῶ̣ν καὶ τῶν πολιτῶν, καὶ εἶναι αὐτούς τε καὶ ἐκγό-
νους αὐτῶν προξέ[ν]ο̣υς καὶ εὐεργέτας τοῦ δήμου τοῦ Ἐρετριέων, εἶναι
δὲ αὐτοῖς καὶ γ[ῆ]ς [καὶ] οἰκίας ἔγκτησιν καὶ πρόσοδον πρὸς τὴν βουλὴν
καὶ τὸν δῆμον, ἐάν [τι]νος δέωνται, πρώτοις μετὰ τὰ ἱερὰ καὶ προεδρίαν
ἐμ πᾶσι τοῖς ἀγῶσι[ν] οἷς ἡ πόλις τίθησιν καὶ ἀτέλειαν καὶ εἰσάγουσιν καὶ
ἐξάγουσιν, καθάπε[ρ κ]αὶ τοῖς ἄλλοις Ἐρετριεῦσιν, εἶναι δὲ αὐτοῖς καὶ ἀσ-
φάλειαν καὶ ἀσυλί[αν] καὶ πολέμου καὶ εἰρήνης παραγινομένοις εἰς τὴν
πόλιν καὶ τὴν χώρ[αν], ἐπιμελεῖσθαι δὲ αὐτῶν τοὺς ἄρχοντας τοὺς ἀ-
εὶ ἐν ἀρχῆι ὄντας, ὅπως μηδ' ὑπ' ἑνὸς ἀδικῶνται, καλέσαι δὲ αὐτοὺς καὶ
ἐπὶ ξένια εἰς τὸ πρυ[τα]νεῖον· ἑλέσθαι δὲ καὶ θεωροδόκον ἐκ πάντων Ἐρε-
τριέων· ἀναγράψα[ι δὲ] τόδε τὸ [ψ]ήφισμα εἰς στήλην λιθίνην καὶ στῆσαι
ἐν τῶι ἱερῶι τοῦ Ἀπό[λλω]νος τοῦ Δαφνηφόρου. [ἡ]ιρέθη θεωροδόκος
Ἀρίστιππος Ἀρχι[-]
ὁμοίως δὲ [ἀπ]εδέξαντο
Ἑστιαιεῖ̣ς

19 Robert: ἐ[πὶ Kern.

This decree of Antigonid Eretria, to which that of Histiaea is subscribed (36), makes no mention of the wishes of Philip V. Possibly we should deduce some more privileged condition than that of Chalcis; but perhaps an easier explanation is that the king's letter had not yet reached Eretria when the *theoroi* arrived. The tone seems a good deal friendlier to the Magnesians than that of the Chalcidians (cf. 12–13, and the elaborate honors for the *theoroi*). At any rate, Eretria grants *asylia* as well as the crowned games. For the *theoroi* they add a distinction (27–28) which enlarges upon the more familiar phraseology in the granting of personal inviolability: "They are to have inviolability and security in war and peace whenever coming into the city and country."

1: In the fourth century a board of *strategoi* commonly authored proposals (*IG* XII.9 205, 206, 208, 212), but here alone we see one as eponymous.

12–13: Cf. on **94**.25 for parallels. Eretrian honor of Artemis is richly illustrated in the inscriptions of the fourth century, all probably pertaining to the cult of Artemis Amarynthia east of the city; cf. W. Wallace, *Hesperia* 17 (1947) 134; D. Knoepfler, *CRAI* 1988, 382–421.

33: The temple of Apollo Daphnephoros was in the middle of the city; see *IG* p. 162 and P. Auberson, *Eretria* I (Bern 1968). A number of public acts were inscribed there, and the oath of *IG* 191 was sworn there.

99. Delos

Kern, *I.Magnesia* 49.

Cf. Wilhelm, *Jahresh.* 4 (1901) Beibl. 26–27 (*Kl. Schr.* II.1 153–154); Holleaux, *Etudes* I 325, with Robert in n. 4.

[ἔδο]ξε τῆι [β]ουλῆι καὶ τῶι [δήμ]ωι· Ἀρ̣ιστείδης
[Τηλεμ]νήστου εἶπεν· ἐπειδὴ παραγεγόνασιν παρὰ
[Μαγνήτ]ων ὄντων οἰκείων καὶ [φ]ι̣[λω]ν Δημήτριος,
[Μολοσσ]ός, Καλλικράτης ἐπαγ[γέ]λλοντες τὸν ἀγῶ-
[να] ὃν τ[ιθέ]ασι Μάγνητε[ς] τῆι Ἀ[ρτέμ]ιδι τῆι Λευκο-
[φρυ]η̣ν[ῆι σ]τεφανίτην [ἰ]σοπύθιο[ν], δεδόχθαι τῆι
β[ουλῆ]ι καὶ τῶι [δ]ήμωι [ἀποδέχεσθα]ι τὸν ἀγ[ῶ]να τῆς
Ἀρ[τέμι]δος, καθὰ παρακα[λοῦσι οἱ π]αραγε[γο]νότες
παρὰ [Μαγ]νή[τω]ν τύχηι ἀγ̣α̣[θῆι· καλέ]σαι δ̣ὲ [αὐ]τοὺς καὶ
ἐπὶ ξέ[νια καὶ] θ[υσίαν τοὺς ἄρχοντας εἰς τ]ὸ πρυτ[α]νεῖον, τὸ
δὲ ἀνάλω[μα δοῦναι τὸ ἐκ τοῦ νόμ]ου τοὺς ταμίας.
ἡι[ρ]έθη Ε̣πε . . . . ς [- - - - - - - - - - - - - - - - - -]

2 Wilhelm: [Πολυμ]νήστου Kern. 10 Robert: τὸν] θ[εωροδοκήσοντα Holleaux. 11 Holleaux.

The attribution to Delos was established by Wilhelm (confirming Kern's suggestion), who recognized Aristeides as the proposer of other Delian decrees (*IG* XI.4 704ff.). Delos is not in the list of Cycladic cities subscribed to the decree of Paros (**100**).

The decree is of the utmost brevity and does not grant *asylia.* Here as elsewhere, I suggest that the Delians were not motivated by military designs upon the Maeander Valley but rather had recognized *asylia* in 221.

100. Paros

Beginning below **99**, a second column from line 18, a third from 60.

Kern, *I.Magnesia* 50 [Dittenberger, *Syll.*^{2} 261; *IG* XII.5 1341 (excerpts); Hiller, *Syll.*^{3} 562].

Cf. Holleaux, *Etudes* I 326; Wilhelm, *Jahresh.* 3 (1900) 58–59, 4 (1901) Beibl. 27 (*Kl. Schr.* II.1 74–75, 154); *GGA* 165 (1903) 792; A. Oguse, *BCH* 53 (1929) 140; Fraser/Matthews, *Lexicon of Greek Personal Names* I (Oxford 1987) 326.

παρὰ Παρίων
ἔδοξεν τῆι βουλῆι καὶ τῶι δήμ[ωι, Κ]αλλιθεί-
[δ]ης Νήσιος ε[ἶπ]εν· ὑπὲρ ὧν οἱ ἄρχο[ντε]ς π̣ρ̣οε-
[γ]ράψαντο ὑπὲρ το[ῦ] ψη[φ]ίσματ[ο]ς τοῦ [ἐκ] Μ̣[αγν]ησί-
[α]ς [δ]εδό[χ]θαι τοὺς ἄρχοντας ἐπὶ τὸν δ[ῆ]μο[ν]
[ἄ]γειν τοὺ[ς θ]εωροὺς τοὺς ἀπ[ε]σταλμέν[ους ἀπὸ Μα-
[γ]νησίας ὑπὲρ τῆς ἐπαγγελίας τοῦ ἀγῶνος· Καλλ̣ιθ[εί]-
[δ]ης Νήσιος εἶπ̣εν· τὰ μὲν ἄλλα τ⟨ὴ⟩ν τῆς βουλῆς· ἐπει-
δὴ ⟨δὲ⟩ Μάγνητες οἱ ἀπὸ Μαιάνδρου φί[λοι] ὄντε[ς τ]οῦ δή-
[μ]ου [τ]οῦ Παρίων ἀπε[στά]λκασ[ι ψή]φισμα καὶ ἄνδρα[ς]
[Μ]ολοσσὸν Καλλιφῶντος, [Δημή]τριον Ἀμφιστρά]-
[τ]ου, Καλλικράτην [Ἰ]φικρά[του], οἵτινες ἐπε̣λ[θ]όν-
τες ἐπὶ τὴν [βουλὴν] καὶ τὸν [δῆ]μον καὶ ἐμ[φανίσα]ν-
τες τὴν τ̣[ῆς θεᾶς] ἐπιφάν[ειαν κα]ὶ ὅτι [- - - - - - -]
[-]
[-]
[-]
ἐ[ψήφισ]ται ὁ δῆμος [συντ]ε̣λεῖν τῆι ἀρχηγέτιδι τ̣[ῆς]
πόλεως Ἀρτέμιδι Λευκ[ο]φρυηνῆι διὰ πέντε ἐτῶν
θυσίας τε καὶ πανήγυριν καὶ ἐκεχειρίαν καὶ ἀγῶνα
στεφανίτην ἰσοπύθιον μουσικόν τε̣ καὶ γυμνικὸν
καὶ ἱππικόν, καὶ παρακαλοῦσιν καὶ ἡμᾶς κ[αὶ] ἀξιοῦ-
σιν ἀποδέξασθαί τε τὸν ἀγῶ[να κ]αὶ συν[α]ύξε[ιν τὰ]ς
ἐψηφισμένας τιμὰς τῆι θεᾶ[ι· ὅπω]ς οὖν καὶ [ὁ Παρί]-
ων δῆμος φαίν[ητ]αι τὴ[ν πρὸς τοὺς] θεοὺς ε[ὐσέβει]-
αν δ̣ι̣αφυλ̣άττων κ̣α̣ὶ̣ τὴν π[ρὸς τὴν πόλ]ιν̣ αὐτ[ῶν προ]-
ϋπάρχουσαν φ̣[ι]λ̣[ία]ν [ἐκ παλαι]ῶ[ν χρόν]ων
ἐπὶ πλεῖον αὔξων καὶ ἐπα̣κ̣ο[λουθῶν τοῖς ἀξιουμέ]-
νοις ὑπ᾿ αὐτῆς καὶ τοὺς ἀγῶν[α]ς ο[ὓς] τίθησι [τῆι Ἀρ]-

τέμιδι τῆι Λευκο[φ]ρ[υ]ην[ῆι] συγκα[τα]σκευάζ[ων· τ]ύ-
χηι οὖν τ̣ῆι ἀγαθῆι τῆς τε πόλ[εως τῆς ἡμετέ]ρα[ς καὶ]
τῆς Μαγνήτων δεδόχθαι τῶι δήμωι [δέχεσθαι]
τ̣ή̣ν τε ἀσυλίαν τῆς πόλεως καὶ τῆς χώρας τ[ῆς Μα]-
γνήτων καὶ τὴν καθιέρωσιν καὶ τὰς θυσίας [καὶ τὸν]
ἀγῶνα στεφανίτην ὃν τιθέ[α]σιν τῆι Ἀρτέ[μιδι Μά]-
γνητες [ἰ]σοπύθιον εἰς τὸν ἅπαν̣τα χρ̣ό̣νον, κ̣α̣ὶ̣ [ὑπάρ]-
χειν τοῖς νικῶσιν τὸν ἀγῶνα τοῦτον τὰς τιμ̣ὰς [τὰς]
ἐν τοῖς νόμοις γεγραμμένας τοῖς νικῶσιν τὰ Π[ύ]θια,
ἀναγορεῦσαι δὲ καὶ τὴν ἀσυλίαν καὶ τὴν καθιέρω[σιν]
τῆς τε πόλεως καὶ τῆς χώρας τῆς Μαγνήτων το[ὺς]
ἄρχοντας ἐν τῶι θεάτρωι ὅταν πρῶτον ἄγωμεν [τὰ Διο]-
νύσια τὰ μεγάλα τραγῳδῶν τῶι ἀγῶνι· ποιήσασθαι δ[ὲ]
καὶ τὴν ἐπαγγελίαν τοῦ ἀγῶνος καὶ τῆς πανηγύρ[ε]-
ως τοὺς παραγεγονότας Μολοσσόν, Δημήτριον, [Καλ]-
λικράτην· ἀποστεῖλαι δὲ τὸν δῆμ[ο]ν καὶ θεωρὸν ε[ἰς]
τὸν ἀγῶνα τὸν συντελούμενον ὑπὸ Μαγνήτων
τῆι Ἀρτέμιδι τῆι Λευκοφρυηνῆι, περὶ δὲ τῆς ἀποστο-
λῆς καὶ τοῦ ἀναλώματος τοῦ εἰς ταῦτα προγράψασ-
θαι τοὺς ἄρχοντας τοῦ μηνὸς τ̣οῦ Ποσιδεῶνος, ἑ̣λ[έσ]-
θαι δὲ τὸν πρό[ε]δρον καὶ θεωροδόκον ὅστις θεωροδ[ο]-
[κή]σει τοῖς ἐπαγγέλλουσιν τὸν ἀγῶνα τοῦτ[ο]ν καὶ ε[ἶ]-
[ναι] τῶ[ι α]ἱρεθέντι θ[εω]ροδοκίαν αὐτῶι καὶ ἐγγόνοις· δοῦ-
[να]ι [δ]ὲ τοῖς θεωροῖς [καὶ] ἐκέχειρ[ον τὸ]ν ταμίαν, τὸ δ[ὲ]
[- - - -]ι̣ον ε̣[- - - - - - -] δίδοσθαι τοῖς θεω[ροῖς],
ἐ[π]α[ινέσαι δὲ] καὶ το[ὺς θεωροὺς] Μολοσσὸν Κα[λλι]-
φ[ῶντος, Δημ]ήτρ[ιον Ἀμφιστ]ράτου, Καλλι[κρά]-
τ[ην] Ἰ[φικράτ]ου, [στεφανῶσαι δὲ κ]αὶ ἕκαστον [αὐτῶν]
[- - - - - - - - - - - - - - - - - - -]τους [. . . . .]
[-]
[. . . τ]ὴν θεὰ[ν -]
[. . . τρ]αγῳδῶν τ[ῶι ἀγῶνι - - - - - - - - - - -]
[. . . .] καὶ προξένους καὶ εὐεργέτας [εἶναι τῆς]
[πόλεω]ς Παρίων καὶ αὐτοὺς καὶ ἐγγόν[ους, καὶ]
[ὑπάρχει]ν αὐτοῖς πάνθ' [ὅσ]α κ[αὶ τοῖς] ἄ[λ]-
[λοις προξέν]οις ὑπάρχει· κ̣α̣λ̣έσ̣α̣ι̣ [δὲ καὶ]
τοὺς θεωροὺς ἐ[πὶ ξέ]νια τοὺς ἄρχοντα[ς]
[εἰς τὸ πρυταν]εῖον, [τὸ] δὲ ἀνάλωμα [εἰς ταῦ]-
[τα εἶναι] ἀπὸ τῆς π[αρα]στάσεως τῶν δη[μοσίων·]
[φυλάσσ]ειν δὲ καὶ τὸ ψ[ή]φισμα τὸ ἐγ Μαγ[νησίας]
ἐν τῶι δημοσίῳ [τοὺς] ἄρχοντας με[τὰ τοῦ]
[γρ]αμματέως, τὸν [δὲ α]ἱ̣ρεθέν[τα] θ[εωρὸν]
ἀξιοῦν Μ[ά]γνητας ἀ̣ναγρά[ψαι τ]όδ[ε τὸ ψή]-
φισμα κα[ὶ θ]εῖναι εἰς τὸ [ἱε]ρὸν τῆς Ἀρ[τέμι]-
[δ]ος [τ]ῆς Λευκοφρυηνῆ[ς. θε]ωρο[δόκος ἡι]-
[ρ]έθη Ἀλέξαρχος Νεο̣[μή]δου.

[κατὰ τὰ] αὐτὰ δὲ ἐψηφίσαντο·

[Ν]άξιοι	Ἄνδριοι
Ἀρσινοεῖς	Τήνιοι
Θηραιεῖς	Ἰουλῖται
Σάμιοι οἱ ἐμ Μινοίαι	Καρθαιεῖς
Σερίφιοι	Ἀρκεσινεεῖς
[Κ]ύθνιοι	Ἀσκληπιεῖς
Α[ἰ]γιαλεῖς	Οἰν[αῖοι ἐξ Ἰκάρου]
[?Μήλιο]ι	Κιμ[ώλιοι]
[- - - -]	Μυκ[ό]ν[ιοι]

3 Wilhelm, from line 48: καθε- Kern; the stone and squeeze are indeterminate. 8 Wilhelm: ΤΩΝ lapis. 9: ⟨δὲ⟩ add. Dittenberger. 14 Holleaux: δ]ιότι Kern. 27 Holleaux. 31: οὐρίῃι Kern, οὗ⟨ν τ⟩ῆι Dittenberger (the stone confirms N). 33 Holleaux: τ[ῶμ Kern. 67–68 Dittenberger. 75 Fraser/Matthews: Νεο[κύ]δου Kern. 84 [Μήλιο]ι Hiller.

For this long decree of Paros parallels are supplied by the decree found on Pharos: see Robert, *Hellenica* XI–XII (1960) 520–526. The names of a number of the Cyclades are subscribed, excluding, however, the Delians, whose decree was inscribed separately—and who did not vote *asylia* (**99**).

3–5: This procedure is seen at the start of other Parian decrees (Robert 520–524; L. Migeotte, *L'emprunt public* [Paris 1984] no. 62): "Concerning the matters which the archons proposed about the decree from Magnesia, it is decided that the archons are to introduce the *theoroi* to the assembly ..." In 8 the phrase resembles that by which a rider is added to a decree; Dittenberger deduced that the council had refused the Magnesian request but was overridden by the assembly (Wilhelm was skeptical of this). But this phrase occurs also in the Pharos decree; and there as here *probouleuma* and decree were proposed by the same man. The council, without dealing with the substance of the request, simply put this item on the agenda of the assembly and named the sponsors of the Magnesians' appearance there. Compare (in the realm of religious policy) *IG* II² 337, in which the council's role is confined to urging the assembly to discuss a request to establish a cult of Astarte.

14–17: The preliminaries as we have them do not mention *asylia*, so probably the oracle was quoted in these damaged lines and that was felt sufficient, as in **95**. Oguse suggested ὅτι [τοῦ Ἀπόλλωνος | τοῦ ἐν Δελφοῖς αὐτοῖς χρή]σαν[τος λώϊον εἶναι καὶ | ἄμειον τοῖς σεβομένοις Ἄρτεμιν Λευκοφρυηνὴν καὶ | τὴν πόλιν καὶ τὴν χώραν ἱερὰν καὶ ἄσυλον νομίζουσιν] | ἐ[ψήφισ]ται.

33–34 and 39: For the order "inviolable and sacred" see p. 33. For the provision in 39–42 to proclaim the inviolability to the public we have perhaps **109**.a.29; it is to be proclaimed only once (πρῶτον, the "next" Dionysia, 41). By contrast, the present *theoroi* are themselves to proclaim the upcoming Leucophryeneia immediately (43; cf. **94**.33); where we are not told. For a festival there was a schedule to be met, and real consequences, the participation of foreigners; Magnesia was employing one theoric visit both to seek Panhellenic recognition and to invite visitors to the first Panhellenic celebration. The Parian Great Dionysia (42) are known otherwise only at *IG* XII.5 129.34 (II B.C.).

49: The calendar of Paros (Wörrle, *Chiron* 1993, 352–357) is too imperfectly known to determine when in the year the archons were to make arrangements for the theoric mission to Magnesia. If their Posideon matched the Athenian month, then midwinter, which would be reasonable for a spring festival.

50: πρόεδρος might be used here because the *theorodochos* will introduce future Magnesian *theoroi* to the Parian assembly; the term does not recur in the governmental usages of Paros.

58ff.: Here probably was quoted the praise of the Magnesian ambassadors that was to be read out at the Dionysia (61).

68: For παράστασις as a state fund for buying sacrificial victims see Wilhelm 1901 and *JRS* 27 (1937) 146–148; cf. Robert, *Hellenica* XI–XII 126–131.

69–71: The Parians make provision to keep the Magnesians' decree of request in the record office, and to ask that their own decree be inscribed at Magnesia (two gestures that cost them nothing), but make no provision to inscribe either text at Paros. Their specification that the inscription be in the temple of Artemis at Magnesia (73) is simply formulaic and uninformed as to the Magnesians' intentions.

77ff.: Arsinoe is Coresia on Ceos, on which see Robert, *Hellenica* XI–XII (1960) 132–176. Robert, *REG* 46 (1939) 423–442 (*Op. min. sel.* I 549–568), argued cautiously that the Asclepieis are Thermae on Icaros, given both its warm springs and the next entry Oene on Icaros; but these lists are not arranged geographically.

101. Mytilene (?)

Kern, *I.Magnesia* 52.

Cf. A. Fick, *BeitrKundIndogermSpr* 26 (1901) 281–283; Wilhelm, *Jahresh.* 4 (1901) Beibl. 28 (*Kl. Schr.* II.1 154); Robert, *REG* 38 (1925) 41 n. 2 (*Op. min. sel.* II 733 n. 2); Hiller, *IG* XII Suppl. 138.

ἔγνω ὁ δᾶμος [περὶ ὧν οἱ στράταγοι προ]-
{ε}τίθεισ[ι καὶ ἔπηλθον· ἐπειδὴ ὁ δᾶμος]
ὁ Μα[γ]νήτ[ων -]
ωπ . . . Δ̣ιονύσιο[ν .]υ[- - - - - - - - - - - - - -]
τῶ Ἀ̣γ[- - -, οἶ ψάφισμα] ἀπέδωκ[αν ἐν τῶι ἐμφα]-
νίζοισ[ι] ὅτ[ι γνόν]τ̣ες χρῆσαι ἑαύτοισ[ι τὸν θέον]
τὸν ἐν Δέλφοισι λώϊον καὶ ἄμεινο[ν ἔμμε]-
ναι σεβομένοισ⟨ι⟩ Ἄρτεμιν Λευκοφυάνα[ν]
καὶ νομισσάντεσσι τάν τε πόλιν καὶ τὰν χ[ώ]-
ραν ἶραν καὶ ἄσυλον ἔμμεναι, ἐψαφίσμενοί
ε⟨ἶσ⟩ι συντελείην τᾶ ἀρχαγέτιδι τᾶς πόλιος

αὔτων Ἀρτέμιδι Λευκοφρυάνα διὰ πέντε ẹ-
τέων θυσίαν καὶ πανάγυριν καὶ ἐκεχειρίαν κα[ὶ]
ạ̔́γωνα στεφανίταν ἰσοπύθιον μούσικον καὶ
γụ́μνικον καὶ ἴππικον, δικαίαν ἀποδίδοντες
χάριν τᾶ εὐεργέτιδι, καὶ παρακαλείοισι τὸν δᾶ-
μον φίλον ἔοντα καὶ συγγένη⟨ν⟩ μετέχην τᾶν
θυσίαν καὶ τᾶς παναγύριος καὶ τᾶν ἐκεχει-
ρί[αν], διελέχθησαν δὲ καὶ οἰ πρέσβευται ἀκο-
λ[ού]θως τοῖς ἐν τῶι ψαφίσματι γεγραμμένο[ισι]
τᾶς [φι]λοτιμίας οὔδεν ἐλλείποντες· ὄπως οὖν
[ὀ δᾶ]μος φαίνηται ἐμ πάντι καίρωι τάν τε πρ[ὸς]
[το]ὶς θέοις εὐσέβειαν αὔξων καὶ τὰν πρὸς Μ[ά]-
[γ]νητας συγγένειαν καὶ φιλίαν διατηρ[έ]ων,
[ἀ]γ[ά]θα τύχα δέδοχθαι τῶι δάμωι ἐπαίνε-
[σ]αι [μ]ὲν Μάγνητας ἐπὶ τᾶ εὐσε[β]είαι τᾶ πρὸς
τ̣ὸ θ[ε]ῖον καὶ ἐπὶ τᾶι εὐνοίαι τᾶι πρὸς τὰν πόλι[ν],
δέχεσθαι δὲ πὰρ αὔτων ταίς τε θυσίας καὶ
τὸν ạ̔́γωνα ἰσοπύθιον, ἔμμεναι δὲ καὶ τὰν πό-
λιν καὶ τὰν χώραν ἴραν καὶ ἄσυλον καθά-
περ Μάγνητες ἀξίοισι, δίδωσθαι δὲ καὶ
τοῖς ἐπαγγελλόντεσσι θεώροισι πὰρ Μαγ̣ν[ή]-
των εἴς τε ἐνάρχαν καὶ ἐφέστιον κ[αὶ] ξ̣ένια
[ὄσ]σα καὶ τοῖς τὰ Πύθια ἐπαγγελλόν[τ]εσσι [ἐν]
[ν]όμω γέγραπται, καὶ ἐπεί κε καθήκη ὀ ἄγω[ν]
[κ]αὶ ἐπαγγέλλωσι οἰ θέωροι οἰ παρὰ Μαγνή-
[τ]ων, χειροτονήτω ὀ δᾶμος τῶ μ̣ῆννο[ς] τ̣ῶ
[Τε]ρφείω{ι} τᾶ ὀκτωκαιδεκάτα θεώροις δ[ύο ἐξ]
[ἀ]πάντων τᾶν πολίταν, δόμεναι δὲ καὶ ⟨ξέ⟩-
[νια] τοῖς πρεσβεύταισι τὰ ἐν νόμωι διακό̣[σια?].
[κ]ατὰ τὰ αὖτα δὲ ἐψηφίσαν[το]
[Μη]θυμναῖοι Ἀντισσαῖοι [7–9]

vacat

See Fick on the dialectical forms and the mason's errors (28, for θυσίαις; 36, for πὰρ; 39, for τῶν). 1–2 Robert, ΕΤ.ΘΕΙ confirmed by Klaffenbach from the stone, ΕΤΙ̣ΘΕ by Rigsby from the squeeze: επιθευς Kern. 3: e.g., ἔπεμψε vel sim. 4 Rigsby: ιο[ς Ε]ὐ Kern. 5 οἴ Rigsby. 11 the mason wrote ΕΝΤΙ (ἔντι). 17 ΓΕΝΗΑ lapis. 38 Wilhelm: [Ὀ]ρφείωι Kern. 39–40 Rigsby: ὄδ̣[ι|ον] Kern.

The author is either Mytilene or Eresus, as the other two cities of Lesbos are named in the subscription. The stone has been beveled off immediately to the right of Ἀντισσαῖοι (42); if a third ethnic was inscribed here, there is room for Ἐρέσιοι, but not for Μυτιληναῖοι.

3: Some verb for sending the *theoroi* is to be assumed.

17: As to kinship, Magnes had a brother Macar, who was founder of Mytilene (*Hom. Hymn. Ap.* 37; Paus. 6.21.11).

33: ἐν- for ἐπαρχή seems to be attested only here; perhaps a mason's error, as at **102**.12.

38: The season of Terpheios is unknown; there might be a parallel for specifying the day on which future *theoroi* are to be elected at **111**.69.

39–40: I cannot confirm on stone or squeeze Kern's ὄδ̣[ιον], a hapax for ἔφοδιον and incompatible with the plural τά that follows; Klaffenbach (in sched. IG) glosses this as an error. I have assumed the familiar ξένια.

102. Clazomenae

A second column begins at 44.

Kern, *I.Magnesia* 53 [Engelmann/Merkelbach, *I.Erythrai/Klazomenai* II 507].

Cf. Wilhelm, *Neue Beitr.* 4 (1915) 36–37 (*Kl. Schr.* I.1 210–211); B. Haussoullier, *Etudes sur l'histoire de Milet* (Paris 1902) 143–147.

[ἔδοξεν τῶι δήμωι· γνώμη τῶν πολ]ε̣μ̣ά̣ρχ[ω]ν καὶ τ̣ῶν σ̣[τρα]τ̣[η]-
[γῶν -] πρ̣[ὸς τ]ὴν [?ἐκκλ]ησ[ίαν]
[-]φ . ντες [ψ]ήφισμα ἀ . . . . .
[- - - - - - - - - - - χρήσαντος τοῦ Ἀπόλλω]ν[ος] λῷον εἶνα̣ι̣ κ̣[αὶ]
[ἄμεινον τοῖς σεβομέν]οις Ἄ[ρτεμιν Λε]υκο[φ]ρυηνὴν καὶ τὴν πόλ̣ι̣ν̣
[καὶ τὴν χώραν αὐτῶν] ἱερὰν [κ]αὶ [ἄσ]υλον νομίζουσιν, ὁ δῆμ[ο]ς ἐ[ψήφι]-
[σται συντελεῖν] τ̣ῆ[ι ἀ]ρχηγέτιδι τ̣[ῆς] πόλε[ω]ς Ἀρτ[έ]μ̣ιδι Λευκο-
φρυ[ην]ῆι̣ διὰ π[έ]ν[τ]ε ἐτῶν θυσίαν καὶ πα[ν]ήγυρ[ι]ν καὶ ἐ[κε]χειρίαν [καὶ]
ἀγῶνα στεφανίτην ἰσοπύθιον μουσικόν τ̣ε καὶ [γυ]μνικὸν [κ]αὶ
ἱπ[π]ικ[όν], δικαίαν ἀπ̣οδιδοὺς χάριν τῆι εὐε[ρ]γέτιδι, βούλεσθαι δὲ
καὶ τοὺς οἰκείους ⟨κ⟩αὶ φίλ[ο]υς τοῦ δήμου με[τ]έχ[ε]ιν τ[ῶν] συντε-
λουμένω̣ν θυσιῶν γενομένης αὐτοῖς ἐ⟨π⟩αγγελίας π[ερὶ] τού-
των, καὶ ἀξιοῦσιν ἡμᾶς ἀποδέξασθαί τε καὶ συναύξει[ν] τὰς ἐψη-
φισμένας τιμὰς τῆι θεᾶι· κατ̣ακολουθήσα[ν]τας γὰρ τοῖς ἀξιου-
μένοις ἀκόλουθα πρᾶξε[ι]ν ταῖ[ς τ]οῦ θεοῦ μαντείαις καὶ χαριεῖσ-
θαι τῶι δήμωι· ἐπελθόντες δὲ καὶ οἱ αἱρεθέντες ἄνδρες ὑπὸ Μα-
γνήτων περὶ τῆς ἐπαγγελίας τοῦ ἀγῶνος Διομέδων Διονυσί-
ου, Νέαιθος Νεαίθου, Μενεκράτης Πολυάρχου καὶ ἀπολογισά-
[με]νοι τήν τε τῆς θεᾶς ἐπιφάνειαν καὶ περὶ τῶν συνηντημένων
[ὑ]πὸ Μαγνήτω̣[ν] εἰς τοὺς Ἕλληνας εὐχαρίστων παρεκάλουν συν-
[ε]πι[λ]αβέσθαι τῆς τοῦ δήμου σπουδῆς καὶ φιλοτιμίας ἀκολούθως
[τ]οῖς προϋπάρχουσιν πρὸς αὐτὰς ταῖς πόλεσιν διὰ προγόνων φιλαν-
[θρώ]π[οι]ς, ἀγαθῆι τύχηι δεδόχθαι τῆι βουλῆι καὶ τῶι δήμωι
[ἐπαινέ]σαι μὲν τὸν δῆμον τὸν Μαγνήτων ἐπί τε τῆι πρὸς τοὺς
[θ]εοὺς [εὐ]σεβείαι καὶ φιλοδοξίαι καὶ τῆι πρὸς τὸν δῆμον εὐνοί-
αι, ἐπαιν̣έσαι δὲ καὶ τοὺς πεμφθέντας ὑπὸ Μαγνήτων Διομέ-
δοντα, Νέαιθον, Μ̣ενεκράτην ἐπὶ τῶι διαλεγῆναι περὶ ἑκάστων
μετὰ πάσης προθυμίας ἀξίως τῶν πόλεων ἀμφοτέρων καὶ
στεφανῶσαι τὸν μὲν δῆμον τὸν Μαγνήτων χρυσῶι στεφάνωι,
τοὺς δὲ ἀποσταλέντας στεφάνωι θαλλοῦ, τῆς δὲ ἀναγγ̣ελίας
[τ]ῶν στεφάνων ἐπιμεληθῆναι τὸν ἀγωνοθέτην τοῖς πρώτοις
Δ[ι]ονυσίοις ἐν τῶι θεάτρωι μετὰ τὰς σπονδάς, ἀπ̣ο̣δεδέχθαι δὲ καὶ

τ[ὸν] ἀγῶνα τὸν συντελο[ύμ]ενον ὑπὸ Μαγνήτων τῆι Ἀρτέμιδι καθά-
περ ἠξιώκασιν Μάγνητες, [κ]αὶ τὴν πόλι[ν] αὐτῶν καὶ τὴν χώραν ἱε-
[ρ]ὰν καὶ ἄσυλον ἀκολούθω[ς] τῆι τοῦ θεοῦ μαντεί[α]ι ἐπὶ σωτηρίαι
τῆ[ς τε] πόλεως τῆς ἡμετέρας καὶ τοῦ δήμου τοῦ Μαγνήτων, καὶ
ὑ[π]ά[ρχειν τ]οῖς ἀγωνισαμένοις τῶν πολιτῶν καὶ νικήσασιν τὰ
ἐκ τῶν ν̣ό̣[μων] ἆθλα καὶ τὰς τιμὰς [κα]θ[άπ]ερ καὶ τοῖς νι[κ]ήσασιν
τὰ Πύθ[ι]α, δ[ίδοσ]θαι δὲ καὶ τοῖς θεω[ρ]οῖς τοῖς ἑκάστοτε πορευομέ-
νοις ἐπὶ τὰς [ἐπα]γγελίας τὰς ἀπαρ[χ]ὰς καὶ τὰ ξένια καθάπερ
καὶ τοῖς τὰ Πύθ[ια ἐ]π̣αγγέλλ̣ουσιν δί[δ]οται· ἵνα δὲ καὶ τῆς προσ-
[η]κο[ύσης] ἐπιμελ[είας] τυγχάνω[σ]ι[ν], ἀποδεῖξαι θεω[ρο]δό[κον· τ]ὸ[ν] τ̣ι̣
[- - - - - - - - - - - -]το τοῦ δήμο[υ - - - - - - - - - - - - - -]
[-]
. . υς, [τῆς δὲ ?ἀποσ]τολῆς [- - - - - - - - - - - - - - - - -]
ἐπαγγέ[λλε]ιν τὸ[ν] ἀγῶ[να], ἀποκρίνα[σ]θαι δὲ Μά-
γνησιν [ὅτι] ὁ δῆμος παρηκολ̣ουθηκὼς τούς τε προγ[ό]-
νους α[ὐτ]ῶν ἕ[νεκ]εν εὐφημί[α]ς καὶ δόξης εἰς ἅπαν
τὸ συμφέρο[ν] τ[αῖ]ς δεηθείσαις τῶν πόλεων ἐπιδεδω-
κότας ἑαυτοὺς προθύμως καὶ πολλοὺς καὶ μεγά-
λους ἀγῶνας ἠγωνισμένο⟨υ⟩ς δ[ιὰ] τὸ διειλη[φέ]ναι
καλὸν εἶ̣ναι καὶ τίμιον τὰς παρὰ τοῖς πολλο̣ῖς ἀπο-
κειμέ[νας] αὐτοῖς εὐεργεσίας, κε[ί]νοις τε ἀξ[ί]ως
προσε[φέρε]το ἐν ἑκάστοις τῶν καιρῶν, καὶ νῦν θεω-
ρῶν Μά̣[γ]νητας καὶ αὐτοὺς ἀκόλουθα πράσσοντας
τῆι τῶν̣ [πρ]ογόνων αἱρέσει καὶ εὐσεβῶς ἔχοντας
καὶ φιλ̣[οδό]ξ[ω]ς πρὸς τὸ θεῖον, ἔν τε τῶι παρόντι
ἀποδέ[χε]τ[αι] τὰ τίμια βουλόμενος ἐ[πι]φανεῖς κα-
[θι]στάναι τὰς [τῆ]ς θεᾶς τιμάς, καὶ ἐπαινεῖ Μάγνη-
τας καλὴν καὶ πρέπουσαν ὁρῶν αὐτοὺς ἀπόδει-
ξιν ποιουμένους τῆς περὶ τὰ μέγιστα σπουδῆς,
καὶ εἰς τὸ λο[ι]πὸ[ν] δ̣ὲ ὁ δῆμος μεμνημένος τῶν
προϋπαρχόντων α[ὐ]τῶι πρὸς Μάγνητας οἰκείων
καὶ φιλανθρώπων ἀπαράκλητος ἑαυτὸν ἐπιδώσει
καὶ οὐθενὸς ἀποστήσεται̣ τῶν ἀνηκόντων τῆι πό-
λει τῆι Μαγνήτων πρὸς τιμὴν ἢ χάριτος ἀπόδοσιν·
πέμψαι δὲ καὶ ξένια παρὰ τοῦ δήμου Διομέδοντι
καὶ Νεαίθωι κα[ὶ Μ]ε[ν]εκράτει, τῆς δὲ ἀποστολῆς
τῶν ξενίων ἐπιμεληθῆναι τοὺς στρατηγοὺς
καὶ τοὺς πολεμάρχας καὶ τὸν ταμίαν, τὸ δὲ ἀνά-
λωμα δοῦναι τὸν ταμίαν ἐκ τῆς διοικήσεως· τὸ
δὲ ψήφ[ισ]μα ἀναγραψάτωσαν οἱ ἐξετασταί. θεωρο-
δόκο[ς ἡ]ι[ρέ]θη Ἑρ]μησίλοχος Ἑρμησιλόχου.

ὁμοίως δ[ὲ ἀπεδ]έξαντο·

Κολοφώνιο[ι οἱ τὴν]	Τήϊοι
ἀρχαίαν πόλ[ιν οἰ]-	Χῖοι
[κ]οῦντες	Ἐρυ̣θραῖοι
Κολοφώνιοι ἀ̣[πὸ]	Φωκαιεῖς

θαλάσσης	Π̣τολεμαιεῖς οἱ
Ἐφέσιοι	πρότερον καλού-
Πριηνεῖς	μενοι Λεβέδιοι
Σάμιοι	[Σμ]υρναῖοι

- -

11 ⊏AI, 12 ENAΓΓ (or ⟨ἀ⟩ναγγελίας; cf. 30 ἀναγγ̣ελίας), 51 MENOIΣ lapis.

. . .

(47–66) our people, acting in keeping with the example of our ancestors, who for the sake of good reputation and honor devoted themselves to everything that was advantageous to cities in need and who undertook many great struggles because of their understanding that their good deeds stored up among many were a fine and honorable thing, have always imitated them worthily on every occasion, and now, seeing that the Magnesians for their part are acting in keeping with the policy of their ancestors and are piously and honorably disposed toward the divine, on this occasion approve the honors and praise the Magnesians, seeing that they are making a fine and distinguished display of their zeal for the most serious things; and for the future our people, mindful of our traditional friendly and beneficial attitude toward the Magnesians, will devote ourselves without being asked and will stint in nothing of what befits the city of the Magnesians as regards honor and the rendering of thanks.

That the author is Clazomenae was suggested by Kern and supported by Wilhelm and Haussoullier. Of Ionian cities, only Miletus and Clazomenae are missing in the subscription. The name Hermesilochus (73) occurs on coins of Clazomenae, and *exetastai* (72) are known there but not at Miletus. Of decrees of Clazomenae we have also *I.Erythrai/Klazomenai* 503, of the early third century B.C.

These *theoroi* are not again attested, perhaps because they visited only Ionian cities, all of whose decrees have been reduced to the subscription. Different men, however, were sent to the Dionysiac Artists at Teos (**103**). Probably the Ionians, near neighbors of Magnesia but in opposite directions, were visited by several sets of *theoroi*.

The text is especially detailed and ornate and might fairly be reckoned an example of what would later be called the Asiatic style. The unusual passage at 47ff., a long account of the Clazomenians' motives, in effect explicates *philotimia* as a civic policy.

2: Kern's restoration is dubious, as Engelmann and Merkelbach note; this is not yet the moment to mention the approach of the *theoroi* to the assembly, which first occurs at 16.

14–16: The reasoning of the Magnesian decree is summarized: "for by acting in accord with these requests they will be acting in accord with the oracles of the god and will gratify our people." On the future χαριεῖσθαι see on **10**.3.

19: On συναναντάω see Holleaux, *Etudes* III 142–143.

29: The crowning of the city, and with a golden crown, is a substantial honor, and in the Magnesian archive a rare one—otherwise done by the Artists (**103**), and in gold at **107**.23 and perhaps **109**.b.27.

33–35: The decree carefully distinguishes that the games were requested by the Magnesians, the inviolability by the god.

65: For ἀνήκων see Robert, *Villes* 32 n. 2.

73: The name recurs of a mint magistrate on a Hellenistic bronze issue, *BMC Ionia* 27 no. 87, *Copenhagen Ionia* no. 101.

74ff.: With the author Clazomenae, these are the original thirteen Ionian cities, if we restore Miletus at the end. On Old and New Colophon (the latter is Notium) see Wilhelm, *Beiträge* 173; Robert, *Villes* 62.

103. The Artists of Dionysus

From line 45, on a lower block.
Kern, *I.Magnesia* 54.

[- -]
[- -]τους
[- - - - - - - - - - - - - - - - - ἀπεστάλκα]σ̣ιν πρε-
[σβευτὰς Πυθόδοτον Χαρισίου, Ἐπίκουρον Ἀγ]αρίστου,
[Πρύτανιν Πυρωνίδου, οἳ παρα]καλ[οῦ]σιν τὴν θυσί-
α[ν τε ἀπο]δέ[ξασθαι καὶ τὴν πανή]γυρ[ιν κ]αὶ τὸν ἀγῶν[α]
ὃν τιθέασιν [Μάγνητες μουσι]κὸν κ[α]ὶ γυμνικὸ[ν καὶ ἱ]π-
πικὸν τῆι ἀρχ[ηγέτιδι τῆς πόλεως Ἀρτ]έμ[ιδι]
Λευκοφρυηνῆι, ἀκο[λούθως] δὲ [καὶ αὐτοὶ διελέ]-
χθησαν τοῖς ἐν τῶι [ψηφίσ]ματι [γεγρα]μμέ[νοις ἀ]πο-
λογισάμενοι τὴν τ[ῆς θεᾶ]ς ἐπι[φά]νεια[ν κ]αὶ
τὰς γεγενημένας ὑπ[ὸ Μα]γνή[των εὐχρησ]τ[ίας ε]ἰς
τοὺς Ἕλληνας, ἐφ' οἷς [ὁ θεὸς ὁ ἐν Δελφοῖς ἄσυλον] ἐθέσ-
πισεν αὐτῶν εἶναι τῆ̣[ν πόλιν καὶ τὴν χώρ]αν καὶ
λώϊον καὶ ἄμεινον τ[οῖς σεβομένοις Ἀπό]λ̣λωνά
τε Πύθιον καὶ Ἄρτεμι[ν Λευκοφυρ]ηνήν· [ὅπως] οὖν καὶ οἱ
τεχνῖται φαίνωνται, [κα]θ̣ότι̣ πάτρι̣[ον] αὐτοῖς ἐ̣σ̣τιν,
ταῖς τοῦ θεοῦ μαντε[ίαις ἀκολουθοῦντες καὶ]
τὴν πᾶσαν ἀποδεικν[ύμενοι εὔνοιαν καὶ προ]-
θυμίαν εἰς τὴν πόλιν [τὴν Μαγνήτων συντελοῦν]-
τές τε τοὺς ἀγῶνας [καὶ συμπομπεύοντες,]
ἀγαθῆι τύχηι δεδό[χθαι τῶι κοινῶι τῶν περὶ τὸν]
Δ̣ιόνυσον τεχνιτῶν [ἀποδέχεσθαι μὲν τὴν θυσίαν]
καὶ τὰς ἐκεχειρίας κ[αὶ τὸν ἀγῶνα ὃν] τιθ[έασι Μά]-
γνητες στεφανίτην ἰ[σοπ]ύθιον [ἐπὶ σωτ]ηρίαι κα̣ὶ ὑ̣γι-
είαι καὶ ὁμονοίαι τῶ[ν τεχνι]τῶν [κ]αὶ τοῦ δήμου τοῦ
Μαγνήτων, εἶναι δὲ αὐ[τῶν τήν τε] πόλιν καὶ τὴν χώ-
ραν ἱερὰν καὶ ἄσυλο[ν κατὰ] τὸν τοῦ θεοῦ χρησμόν·
ἐπαινέσαι δὲ καὶ τὸν [δῆμον] τὸν Μαγνήτων καὶ στε-
φανῶσαι στεφάνωι τῶ[ι ἐκ] τοῦ νόμου ε[ὐ]σ[ε]βείας ἕνεκεν

τῆς εἰς τὸ θεῖον, ἀνα[γγεῖ]λαι [δὲ] τὸν στέφανον ἐν μὲν
τῆι πανηγύρει τῶν τ[εχνιτ]ῶν τὴν ἀναγγελίαν ποιη-
σαμένου τοῦ ἀγων[ο]θ[έτ]ου, ἐν δὲ [Μ]αγνησίαι ἐν τῶι
ἀγῶνι τῶι γυμνικῶ[ι· ἀποστ]έλλεσθαι καὶ θεωροὺς
νῦν τε καὶ εἰς τὸν [ἅπαντα] χρόνον ἐκ πάντων τῶν
τεχνιτῶν τρεῖς, [δοῦναι δὲ] α[ὐ]τοῖς τοὺς μερι[σ]τὰ[ς]
εἰς θυσίαν ὅσον [ἂν τάξηι ἡ] σύνοδος, οἱ δὲ χειροτονη-
θέντες ἀφικόμεν[οι εἰς Μαγν]ησίαν μετεχέτωσαν
τῆς πανηγύ[ρεως καὶ συμπ]ομπευέτωσαν [εἴς τε]
τ[ο]ὺς [ἀγῶνας καὶ τὴν θυσί]αν· ἐ[παινέσαι δὲ τοὺς]
πρέσβ[ει]ς Πυθό[δοτον Χαρισί]ου, Ἐπίκο[υρον Ἀγαρίστου,]
Πρύτανιν Πυρω[νίδου - - - - - - - - - - - - - - - - - -]
. . νων[-]
[-]
[προ]θ̣[υ]μ̣ί̣α̣ς διετέλ[εσαν - - - - - - - - - - - - - - - -]
[τ]ὸ κοινὸν τῶν περὶ τ[ὸν Διόνυσον - - - - - - - - -]
αὐτοὺς τῶν τεχ[ν]ιτ[ῶν - - - - - - - - - - - - - - - - -]
τοὺς πρεσβευτὰς [-]

The Ionian-Hellespontine branch of the guild of the Artists of Dionysus was headquartered at Teos. The decree shows that the guild was treated in international law as a Greek government, of like standing with the "kings, nations, cities" of the formula.

The *theoroi* are not those who visited Clazomenae (**102**), to whose decree the vote of Teos was subscribed. The present men are attested again (whence the restoration) in a second inscription pertinent to the Artists, when subsequently the three were sent by Magnesia to attend a sacrifice conducted by the Artists.[79] Epicurus is also named on silver didrachms and drachms: Kinns, *Kraay–Mørkholm Essays* 141.

13: Or perhaps [ὁ Ἀπόλλων ἱερὰν καὶ ἄσυλον], to be closer to the text of the oracle; but for a single adjective see **88**.37.

15: Otherwise only the Epirotes (**82**.11) mention that the oracle included honor to Pythian Apollo (**67**.7).

21: The procession that Kern restored is explicit elsewhere only in line 39; certainly there was one—each year, according to *I.Magn.* 100a.33. In the Coan archive only a single allusion survives to the procession for Asclepius (**49**.31).

34: I do not understand how the Artists can dictate the proclamation of their action in a contest at Magnesia, or why it is athletic rather than musical; the latter would seem more appropriate, at which too the Artists were subsequently granted *proedria* (*I.Magn.* 89.15).

79. *I.Magn.* 89, a stele, not part of the wall, and cut by a different hand, but apparently erected in the southwest corner of the agora near the *asylia* inscriptions (even though the stipulation was to erect it in the temple of Artemis, lines 82–84).

36: μεριστής = "treasurer" also at Istria; but μερίσαι is the usual verb for what treasurers do.

42ff.: Here will have been the provision to crown the envoys, mentioned in *I.Magn.* 89.

104. Rhodes

Kern, *I.Magnesia* 55.
Cf. Robert, *RPhil* n.s. 53 (1927) 115 (*Op. min. sel.* II 1070).

[ἔδοξε τᾶ]ι βουλᾶι κ̣[αὶ τῶι δ]άμωι· περὶ ὧ[ν]
Μάγνητες φ[ί]λοι ὑ[π]άρχοντες τοῦ δάμου
[τ]ὸ ψά̣[φισμα] καὶ τοὺς ἄ[ν]δρας ἀ̣π̣[έστε]ιλαν,
[οἳ δὲ παραγ]ενόμενοι παρ' α̣[ὐ]τῶν̣ Λάμπων,
Διαγόρας, Πυθόδημος τὰν ἀπογ[ραφὰ]ν ἐποι-
[ή]σ[αντ]ο κ[αὶ] ἐπε[λθόν]τες ἐπὶ τὰν βουλὰν καὶ
[τὰν ἐκκλ]ησία[ν] δ̣ι̣[ε]λέγεν μετὰ πάσας προθυ-
[μί]α[ς], ἀ̣ποκρίνασθαι αὐτοῖς ὅτ[ι ὁ] δᾶμος πρότε-
[ρόν τε] διετέλει πᾶσαν ἐπιμέλειαν ποιεύμε-
νο[ς π]ε̣[ρὶ ὧ]ν ἐπέστει[λα]ν [Μ]άγνητες, καὶ νῦν
[τά]ν τ[ε] θ̣[υσ]ί̣αν ἃν συντελε̣ῦντι τᾶι Ἀρτάμιτι
τ[ᾶι Λ]ευ[κο]φρυανᾶι καὶ τἆ̣λ̣λα φιλανθρώπως
ἀποδ[έχ]εται καὶ συνεπιμελεῖται τοῦ συν-
αύξεσθαι τὰ ἐψαφισμένα ὑπ' αὐτῶν κα[θ]άπερ
ἀξιοῦντι· ὅπως δὲ καὶ [συν]τ[ε]λῆται ὑπὸ τοῦ
δάμου τὰ ἀξιούμενα ὑπὸ Μ[αγ]νήτων, τύχαι
[ἀγαθᾶι οἱ] πρυτάνιες οἵ κα ἄρχωντι τὰν
[πράταν ἑξ]άμηνο̣ν ἐπὶ ἱ[ερ]έ̣ως Ἀριστωνί-
[δα καὶ οἱ] ἀεὶ ἔναρχοι εὕντες καθ' οὕς κα
χρόνου̣ς σ[υν]τελῶντι Μάγνητες τ[ὰν θυσίαν]
καὶ τοὺς ἀγῶνας τᾶι Ἀρτάμιτι τᾶι Λε[υ]-
[κοφ]ρυη̣ν̣ᾶι γράψαντες εἰσφερόντων ἐς τὰν
βου[λὰν] καὶ τὸν δᾶμον ἐμ μηνὶ Ὑακι[ν]θίωι,
καθότι ἁ θυσία ἀποσταλησεῖ ὑπὸ τοῦ δά-
μου κατὰ τὰ νομιζόμενα ἐπὶ σωτηρίαι
καὶ εὐτυχίαι ἀμφοτερᾶν πολίων·
τοὺς δὲ ἄνδρας τοὺς παρὰ Μαγνήτων
καλέσαι ἐπὶ ξένια εἰς τὸ ἱεροθυτεῖον.

11 Robert: τ' [ἑ]ο̣[ρ]τ̣ὰν Kern.

These *theoroi* went to Cos (?: **106**) and elsewhere (**107**), and one of them to Cnidus (**105**).

The Rhodians' decree is brief and unspecific; the preliminaries do not even mention the topic of the Magnesian embassy, and the substance accepts the festival "and the other things as they ask" but does not explicitly mention *asylia*. The decree serves to date to 208/7 or 207/6 the eponymous priest of Helios Aristonidas (line 18), who is also attested by amphora stamps.[80]

The few details are bureaucratic in tone. Where the *theoroi* would normally be said to have presented the Magnesian decree, here they "made their deposition" (5). The Rhodians, rather than electing a *theorodochos* and providing for the future honors for Artemis, establish the lines of authority for doing so and leave all specifics to the future (17ff.): "The prytanies who hold office in the first semester of the year of Aristonidas, and those who do so in future at such times as the Magnesians celebrate the sacrifice and games for Artemis, are to draft (a proposal) and bring it before the council and people in the month Hyacinthios so that the sacrifice may be sent" (a similar procedure at Cnidus, **105**.31ff.). It seems a conservative response, committing Rhodes to as few specifics as possible.

I take it from 18 that we are near the end of a year and the next eponymous priest of Helios, Aristonidas, is already known. The Rhodian year began in spring or summer (its two semesters were first summer and then winter). In Roman times Hyacinthios (line 23) was the ninth month, so perhaps early spring; but there are grounds for thinking that the calendar was reformed in the second century B.C. See Samuel, *Chronology* 108–110; C. Börker, *ZPE* 31 (1978) 193–218.

105. Cnidus

Kern, *I.Magnesia* 56 [Blümel, *I.Knidos* I 219].

Cf. Wilhelm, *Jahresh.* 4 (1901) Beibl. 28–29 (*Kl. Schr.* II.1 154–155); Holleaux, *Etudes* I 318; De Decker, *RPhil* n.s. 29 (1905) 162–163 (collation).

[ἔδοξε τῶι δάμωι, γνώμαι προστατᾶν,]
[ἐπειδὴ Μ]άγνητες [εὖνοι ὄντες τῶι δά]-
[μωι διὰ π]ο̣λλῶν ὑπ[αρχ]ό̣ντω̣ν οἰκείων
[ταῖς πόλ]ε[σ]ιν ποθ' αὑτάς, ἀποστείλαν-
[τε]ς ψ[άφι]σμα καὶ τὸν ἁιρημε̣νον ἐπὶ τὰν
ἐ̣π̣αγγ̣[ε]λίαν τοῦ ἀγῶνος Λ̣άμπωνα Φανί̣-
[ο]υ̣, τοῦ θεοῦ τοῦ ἐν Δελφοῖς χρήσαντος
λώϊον εἶμεν καὶ ἄμεινον τοῖς σεβομέ-
νοις Ἄρτα̣μιν Λευκοφρ[υ]α̣νὰν καὶ τὰν
πόλιν αὐτῶν καὶ τὰν χώραν ἱερὰν καὶ
ἄσυλον νομίζουσ̣ιν, ἐψαφίσθα̣ι ἀπο̣[τε?]-
λεῖν τᾶ̣ι Ἀρτάμιτι τᾶι ἀρχαγ⟨έ⟩τιδ[ι τ]ᾶς
πόλιος αὐτῶν διὰ πέντε ἐτῶν θυ̣σία[ν]
καὶ πανάγυριν καὶ ἐκεχειρίας κα[ὶ] ἀγ[ῶ]-
να στεφανίταν ἰσοπύ[θ]ιο̣ν γ̣υ̣μν̣ι̣κ̣[ὸν]
καὶ μουσικὸν καὶ ἱππικ[ό]ν, καὶ πα̣[ρακαλεῦν]-
τι τὸν δᾶμον ἀποδέξασθαι καὶ συ̣ν̣α[ύ]-

80. But the Aristonidas of these is dated to 222 B.C. by V. R. Grace, *AM* 89 (1974) 199.

ξειν τὰς ἐψαφισμένας ὑπ' αὐτῶ[ν] τ̣[ιμὰς]
τᾶι θεᾶι, διελέγη δὲ καὶ ὁ ἀπ[οσταλεὶς]
[παρ' αὐ]τῶν μετὰ π̣άσας σ̣π̣ου[δᾶς· ὅπως οὖν]
[φανερὸς ἦι ὁ] δᾶμος προαιρ[εύμενος διὰ]
παντὸς ποτὶ τὸ θεῖο̣[ν] εὐσ[εβεῖ]ν̣ [καὶ Μάγνη]-
τας φίλους ὄν̣τ̣ας α[ἰ]νέσ̣αι, [ἀγα]-
θᾶι τ̣ύχαι, δεδόχθαι τῶι δά̣[μωι ἐπαινέ]-
σ̣α̣ι Μάγνητας ἀρετᾶς ἕνεκε[ν καὶ εὐνοί]-
ας καὶ ἀποδέξασθαι ἃ ἀξιοῦ[ντι ἀκολού]-
θως τῶι τοῦ θεοῦ χρησμῶι· π[ερὶ δὲ τῶν ἄ]-
θλων καὶ τᾶν τιμᾶν ὅπως ἄρ[ωνται ἐς πάντα]
τὸν χρόνον τοῖς νικῶσι τὸν ἀ̣[γῶνα ὃν τιθέα]-
σι Μάγνητες καθάπερ τοῖς τ̣[ὰ Πύθια νικῶσι·]
καὶ περὶ θεωρίας ὅπως ἀπ[ο]στ[έλληται, οἱ]
νομογράφοι περὶ τούτω[ν] εἰσ̣α̣[γέτωσαν]
ἐν τοῖς χρόνοις τοῖς ἐκ τ̣[ῶ]ν̣ ν̣[όμων· Λάμπω]-
να δὲ καλέσαι ἐπ[ὶ ξ]έν[ι]α ε[ἰ]ς̣ [τὸ δαμιορ]-
γεῖον, πέμψαι δὲ αὐτῶ[ι] κα[ὶ ἐκέχειρα τοὺς]
στραταγοὺς μετὰ τῶν παρ' [ἁμῶν τιμίων ἃ]
ἐπιτήδεια εἶμεν [δοκ]ε̣[ῖ.]

1, 2–3 De Decker. 11 De Decker: αὐ̣[τοῖ]ς [τε]- Kern. 12: ΑΡΧΑΓΑΤΙΔ lapis. 22 Wilhelm, Holleaux: εὐσ[εβῶ]ς̣ [Μάγνη]- Kern. 23 (confirmed by De Decker): α[ὔ]⟨ξειν⟩ Wilhelm. 26 Blümel: ἀξιοῦ[σιν Kern. 28 ἄρ[ωνται De Decker: δ̣ο̣[θῆι Wilhelm, Holleaux. 35 ἐκέχειρα Holleaux. 36–37 De Decker: τῶν π[ροστατᾶν ὅσα δοκεῖ] | ἐ. ε. Kern.

As Kern saw, a Dorian city that entertains foreigners in the *damiourgeion* (34–35) is almost certainly Cnidus; cf. *I.Knidos* 59.7, 606.7; the *damiourgos* was eponymous at Cnidus. The preliminaries of the decree convey the Magnesian request in full, but the substance does not repeat this, merely providing "to accept the things they ask, in accordance with the oracle" (26–27), and then addressing what was entailed by the enlarged games.

2–3: On this restoration a verb is apparently lost, on which ἐψαφίσθαι (11) depends. Perhaps instead Μ]άγνητες [ἐπέστειλαν, μεμνημέ|νοι τῶν], "the Magnesians have written [cf. **104**.10, **106**.23], mindful of the many close connections our cities have with each other [cf. **102**.62], . . . that it has been decided by them . . ." But this seems clumsy and abrupt.

28–30: Cf. **106**.34ff. for the phrase and the structure.

106. Cos

Kern, *I.Magnesia* 57.

Cf. Wilhelm, *Jahresh.* 4 (1901) Beibl. 29–30 (*Kl. Schr.* II.1 155); Robert, *REA* 38 (1936) 17 (*Op. min. sel.* II 780).

[- - - - - - - - - - - - - - - - ἐπειδὴ Μάγ]νη̣τ[ες]

[- - - - - - - - - - - - φίλοι] καὶ οἰκ[εῖοί εἰ]-
σ[ι]ν̣ [- - - - - - - - - - - - - - - - -] προα̣ι̣-
ρεύμ[ενοι αὔξειν τὰς τιμὰς τᾶς] Ἀρτέμι-
τος τᾶ[ς Λευκοφρυανᾶς ψάφισμα] ἀ̣[πο]στεί-
λαντες [καθότι ἐψαφισμένοι εἰσ]ὶ̣ν διὰ πέν-
τε ἐτέω[ν συντελεῖν θ]υσίαν καὶ πανάγ[υ]-
ριν καὶ ἐκ[εχειρίαν κα]ὶ ἀγῶνα μουσι[κόν]
τε καὶ γυμνι[κὸν καὶ ἱ]π̣πικὸν ἰσοπυθίαι[ς τιμαῖς]
[π]αρακαλ[ε]ῦν[τι τὸ]ν̣ δᾶμον μετέχ̣ειν τῶν
συντελευμέ[νω]ν καὶ ἀποδεξάμενον τὰ
ἀ̣ξ̣ι̣ο̣ύμενα συ[να]ύξειν τὰς ἐψαφισμέ̣ν̣ας
τιμὰς τᾶι θε[ῶι, δ]ιελέγεν δὲ καὶ τοὶ ἀπο-
στ[α]λέ̣ντε[ς] π[αρ'] αὐτῶν Λάμπων, Διαγό-
ρας, Πυ[θ]ό[δ]ημ[ο]ς ἐπελθόντες ἐ̣πὶ τὰν βου-
λὰ̣ν̣ καὶ τὸν δᾶμ̣[ο]ν ἀκολούθως τοῖς ἐν τῶι
ψαφίσ[μα]τι γε[γρ]αμμένοις· ὅπως οὖν καὶ
ἁ τοῦ δάμου π[ρ]ο̣αί⟨ρε⟩σις ἂν ἔχει ἐμ̣ παντὶ
κ̣αιρῶι [πο]τί τε [τὸ] θ̣εῖον κ̣αὶ π̣οτὶ Μάγνητας
[φα]νερ̣ὰ γίνητ̣α̣[ι, τ]ύχαι τ[ᾶι] ἀγαθᾶι δε[δ]ό-
[χθα]ι ἀ[π]οκρί[νασθ]αι α[ὐ]τοῖς ὅτι ὁ δᾶμος ἔν τε
τῶι πρότερον χ̣ρ̣[ό]νωι τὰν πᾶσαν σπουδὰν
[καὶ προθυ]μ̣[ίαν ἐ]π̣οιεῖτο ὑπερ ὧν ἐπέστει-
[λαν Μάγνητες κ]α̣ὶ νῦν τὰν αὐτὰν αἵρεσι[ν]
[ἔχων ἀ]π[οδέχετ]αι τάν τε ἀσυλίαν καὶ τὸν
[ἀγῶνα καὶ τὰν θυσί]αν· ὅπως δὲ καὶ θεωρία καὶ
[θυσία ἀπ]οστέ[λλ]ηται τᾶι θεᾶι ὑπὲρ τοῦ δά[μ]ου,
ἁ [ἐκ]κ̣λ̣[η]σία α[ἱ]ρεί[σ]θω θεωροὺς ἐκ πάντων τρ̣εῖς· οἱ ⟨δὲ ταμίαι⟩
[ἐ]ν [ὧι κα χ]ρόνωι σ̣υ̣ντελῶντι Μάγνητες τὰν
[θυσίαν] τελεύντων τοῖς αἱρεθεῖσι ἐπὶ μ̣ὲ̣ν
τ̣ὰ̣[ν θυσ]ί̣αν δραχμὰς τριακοσίας καὶ μισ-
θὸ̣ν̣ [τὸν ε]ἰ̣ς πο[ρεῖ]ον ἁμερᾶν τριάκοντα
[διατετ]α̣γμέν[ον· π]ε̣ρὶ δὲ τῶν ἄθλων καὶ τᾶν
τιμᾶν ὅπως [δο]θ̣ῆ̣ι τοῖς νικῶσιν τὸν ἀγῶ-
να, οἱ ἄνδ̣ρες [ο]ἱ α̣ἱρ[εύμ]ενοι ἐπὶ τὰν διοί[κη]-
[σιν] τᾶς πόλι[ος π]ρ̣ο̣ν̣ο̣[είσθων·] δὲ οἱ ἐκ τῶ[ν]
π̣α̣ρ̣[- - - - - - - - - - - - - - - - - γ]ράψαντες εἰς
[τοὺς νόμους· τοὺς δὲ παραγενο]μένους παρὰ
Μαγνήτω[ν] κ[αλέσαι] ἐ̣π̣ὶ̣ [ξέν]ια [ε]ἰς τὸ πρ[υ]-
τανεῖο[ν.]

18: ΑΙΛΥΣΙΣ lapis. 28 ⟨δὲ ταμίαι⟩ add. Wilhelm: τρεῖς, οἳ | [ἐ]ν Kern. 30 Wilhelm: συν]τελεύντων Kern. 31 Robert: θεωρ]ίαν Kern. 32 πο[ρεῖ]ον Robert. 33 Pomtow in sched. IG: [. . . . . τετ] Kern.

As Kern saw, a Dorian city visited by these *theoroi* may well be Cos, and Wilhelm adduced some parallel phrasing in Coan decrees. This decree, while not mentioning *asylia* in the preliminaries (except perhaps in "the things asked," 12; cf. **105**.26, **107**.30), in fact grants it, though in the briefest possible terms (25: "the inviolability and the contest and sacrifice").

28: Wilhelm saw that a new clause, concerned with funds for the sacrifice, begins here and that its subject (ταμίαι if this is Cos; cf. S. Sherwin-White, *Ancient Cos* [Göttingen 1978] 210–211; or, for example, οἰκονόμοι) has been omitted by the mason.

32: Kern considered πόριον but lacked a parallel; for πορεῖον = "travel money" cf. *Delphinion* 152.65, 104; *I.Cret.* II III 3.18. A trip of thirty days is envisaged; contrast the period of five days before and after a festival in **3** and **4**.

36: A verb has been omitted by the mason.

107. Unknown city

I.Magn. 58 was in situ on the wall, while 73 was found detached; Oguse showed 73 to be the right side of 58.

Kern, *I.Magnesia* 58 and 73a; joined by Oguse, *RPhil* n.s. 54 (1928) 313–319 [Robert, *SEG* 4.502].

Cf. Holleaux, *Etudes* I 326; Robert, *RPhil* II.53 (1927) 115–116 (*Op. min. sel.* II 1070–1071).

[ἐπειδὴ Μάγνητες οἱ ἀπὸ Μαιάνδρου φίλοι καὶ οἰκεῖοι]
ὄντ̣ε̣ς [τοῦ δήμου ψήφισμα καὶ πρεσβευτὰς ἀποστείλαν]-
τες Λάμ̣πωνα̣ [Φανίου - - - - - - - - - - - - - - ἐπαγγέλ]-
λουσιν τήν τε [καθιέρωσιν καὶ τὴν ἀσυλίαν τῆς τε πόλε]-
ως καὶ τῆς χ[ώρας αὐτῶν καὶ τὴν θυσίαν καὶ τὴν πανήγυριν καὶ]
τὴν ἐκεχειρί[αν καὶ τὸν ἀγῶνα στεφανίτην ἰσοπύθιον μουσικὸν]
καὶ γυμνικὸν κα[ὶ ἱππι]κὸν [ὃν τιθέασιν τῆι Ἀρτέμιδι]
τῆι Λευκοφρ[υη]ν[ῆι καὶ παρακαλοῦσιν τὸν δῆμον συν]-
αύξειν τὰς [ἐ]ψηφ[ισμένας ὑπ' αὐτῶν τιμὰς τῆι θεᾶι· οἱ ἀπο]-
σταλέντες δὲ {ε̣} παρ' [αὐτῶν ἐπελθόντες ἐπὶ τὴν βουλὴν]
καὶ τὸν δῆμον καὶ δηλ̣[ώσαντες διὰ πλειόνων τὰς γε]-
γενημένας ὑπὸ τῶν προ[γόνων αὐτῶν εἰς τοὺς Ἕλληνας εὐ]-
χρηστίας καὶ [π]ερὶ τῶν [πολλῶν προϋπαρχόντων οἰ]-
⟨κ⟩ε[ίω]ν ἀμφοτέραις ταῖς π[όλεσι οὐθὲν ἐλλείποντες]
φιλοτιμίας π̣αρε⟨κ⟩άλ⟨ε⟩σ[αν ἡμᾶς - - - - - - - ὅσον]
ἐστὶν ἐφ' ἡμῖν προσπο[- - - - - - - - - - - - - - - - - -]
τῆι πόλει αὐτῶν τὴν σπου̣[δὴν - - - - - - - - - - - ἐπα]-
κολουθήσαντας γὰρ τ[οῖς ἀξιουμένοις] ἀ̣κ̣ό̣[λουθ]α̣ π̣ρά-
ξειν ταῖς τοῦ θεοῦ μαντ̣[είαις καὶ χα]ρ̣ιεῖσθ[α]ι τῶι δήμωι·
δεδόχθα[ι τ]ῶι δήμω[ι τύχαις ἐπὶ] τ̣αῖς ἀρίσταις στεφα-
νῶσαι̣ μ̣ὲ̣ν Μάγνητας [τῆς τε πρ]ὸς τοὺς θεοὺς εὐσεβεία[ς]
ἕνεκεν καὶ τῆς πρὸς τὸ[ν δῆμον] ε̣ὐνοίας χρυσέωι στεφάνω[ι]
ἀπὸ χρυσῶν ἑκατὸν ὅ[ταν πρ]ῶ̣τον Λευκοφ[ρ]υηνὰ σ[υν]τ̣ε̣-
[λ]ῶ̣σιν, καὶ ἀποκρίνασθ̣[αι αὐτοῖς ὅτι ὁ] δῆμος οὔτε πρότερο[ν ο]ὐ[θε]-
νὸ[ς] ἀπέστη τῶν χρησί[μων αὐτ]οῖς, νυνί τε καὶ [δ]ι̣ὰ̣ τὸ πρὸς

τὸ θεῖον ὁσίως καὶ εὐσε̣β̣[ῶς δι]α̣κεῖσθαι καὶ δι[ὰ] τ̣ὸ προα̣ιρεῖ[σ]-
θαι χα[ρί]ζεσθαι αὐτοῖς [οὐθ]ὲν ἐλλείψει{ν} τῆς ἐν τούτοι[ς]
σπουδῆς καὶ φιλοτ[ιμί]ας, τήν τε κ̣αθιέρωσιν τῆς τ̣ε̣
πόλεως αὐτ[ῶ]ν κα[ὶ τῆς χώρ]ας καὶ τὴν ἀσυλίαν προσδέδε-
κται καθότι ἠ̣ξίουν, καὶ [τὸ]ν ἀγῶνα̣ ἀποδέδεκται στεφα̣-
νίτην ἰσοπύθιον, καὶ ἐν τῶι καθήκοντι κα̣ιρῶι πέμψ[ει]
θυσίαν καὶ θεωροὺς [τοὺς] συνθύσ[ο]ντα̣ς καὶ τἆλλ[α] ⟨τ⟩ὰ ν⟨ο⟩-
μιζόμενα συντελ[ο]ῦ[ντ]α̣[ς] ἀ̣ξ̣ί̣[ω]ς ἀμφοτέρων τῶν̣ πόλ[ε]-
ων καὶ τὴν ἀνα[γγελλίαν τοῦ] στεφάνου ποιησομέν̣ους· εἰς [δὲ]
τὸ λοιπὸν ἀ[ποστέλλειν θεωρ]ούς τ̣ε καὶ θυσίαν κα̣ὶ̣ ⟨ἀ⟩παρχ̣[ὴν]
τῆι θε̣ᾶι κα[θ' ἕκαστα? Λευκοφρ]υηνὰ δ̣ραχμὰς ἑκατὸν ἑκάσ̣[τοτε· ἵνα]
δὲ καὶ τὰ δέο[ν]τα [μετὰ] τῆς τῶν θεῶν εὐνοίας νυν̣[ί] τ̣ε̣
καὶ εἰς τὸ[ν ἀεὶ χρόνον συν]τελῆται, τοὺς προέδρους
[?το]ὺ⟨ς⟩ [ἐπὶ] Θε[ο]τίμο[υ ἄρχον]τος προσαγ̣αγεῖν θ̣υ̣[σίαν]
[- -]τ̣οι εὔχοντα[ι]
[- -] ἐ̣πὶ π̣[. . .]

Text of Oguse. I omit here restorations attempted before the two fragments were joined (the join largely confirmed those of Holleaux and Robert); see Oguse for details. At 9–13 an ancient fault in the stone has caused the mason to skip several spaces, which I have not marked (e.g., 10 ΣΤΑΛΕΝ ΤΕΣ). 7: or συντελοῦσιν, better for the space. 13–14 Rigsby: - - -]|ρε . ν Kern. 14 end: ἐλλείποντες σπουδῆς καὶ] Oguse, which seems too long. 15: ΠΑΡΕΑΛΑ lapis. 18 end: τ]ὰ̣ ψη̣[φίσ]μ̣ατα Kern. 23 end: σ[τ]ε̣φα̣|[νῶσαι? Kern. 31 Robert's correction πεμ⟨ψ⟩ is confirmed by the squeeze: πεμφ[θῆναι] Oguse. 32 Robert: τἆλλ[α] πάντ̣[α τὰ νο]- Oguse (nothing visible on the squeeze). 34–35 Robert: εἰς | τὸ λοιπὸν ⟨δ⟩[ὲ πέμπεσθαι Oguse. 35: κα̣ὶ̣ παρα̣[Kern. 36 Robert. 39 init. Rigsby: . υρ. . Kern, προέδρους [τοὺς ἐπὶ . . . | ο]υ ⟨τ⟩[οῦ] Oguse; there is no space after προέδρους. 40: αὐ]τοὶ Kern.

Evidently the city was in the direction of southwestern Asia Minor; Lampon (3) was alone at Cnidus, and the full team was at Rhodes and Cos. The city spoke Koine and had *proedroi* (38); Oguse restored an archon as the eponym (39).

It is odd that the decision to crown Magnesia (a rarity in the archive in any case) is put before the response to the request. **108**.14 similarly declares a holiday before answering the Magnesians' request.

25: Parallels for ἀφίστημι at Holleaux, *Etudes* I 301.

39: Here as occasionally elsewhere, specifying the eponym under whom money is to be provided for the sacrifice implies that the city was near the end of its current year.

108. Unknown city

Inscribed to the right of **107**.

Kern, *I.Magnesia* 73b.

Cf. Boesch, Θεωρός 55 n. 3; Robert, *RPhil* III.10 (1936) 124 (*Op. min. sel.* II 1203).

[- - - - - - - - - - - -]α̣ι̣δ̣ [- - - - - - - - - - - - - - - - - -]
[τ]ὸ[ν δῆ]μον κ̣αὶ σ̣υ̣νθύειν ⟨τ⟩ὴ̣[ν θυσίαν καὶ συναύξειν]
τ̣ὰ̣ς̣ ἐ̣ψηφισμένας τιμὰς τῆ̣ι̣ [θεῶι, ἐπελθόντες δὲ]
οἱ [π]ρ̣εσ̣βευταὶ ἐπὶ τὴν ἐ[κ]κλησία[ν τὴν προϋπάρχουσαν]
ἡμῖν οἰκειότητα ⟨κ⟩αὶ φιλίαν πρὸς Μά̣[γνητας ἀπελογί]-
σαντο, διελέχθησαν̣ δὲ καὶ περὶ τῶν γ̣[εγονυιῶν? εὐ]-
[ερ]γεσιῶν [ὑ]πὸ Μαγνήτων εἰς τοὺς Ἕλλ[ηνας ἀκολού]-
[θω]ς τοῖς ἐν τῶι ψηφίσ[μ]ατι κατακεχωρ[ισμένοις· ὅπως]
[ο]ὖν καὶ ὁ δῆμος φαίνηται τήν τε πρὸς το[ὺς θεοὺς εὐσέ]-
[βε]ιαν διατηρῶν κ̣αὶ τὴν πρὸς Μάγνητας [οἰκειότητα]
[κα]ὶ φιλίαν ἐπ̣ὶ̣ π̣λεῖον αὔξων, ἀγαθῆι τύ[χηι καὶ ἐπὶ σω]-
[τ]ηρίαι δεδόχθαι τῆι βουλῆι καὶ τῶι δή̣[μωι, ἐπὶ τοῖς]
γ̣εγο[ν]ό⟨σι⟩ν ἀγαθοῖς Μάγνησιν κατὰ τ[ὰ] λό̣[για τοῦ]
θεοῦ τοὺς ⟨μὲ⟩ν ἱερεῖς καὶ τὰς ἱερείας ἀνοίξ[ειν τοὺς]
ναοὺς καὶ λιβαν̣ωτ[ὸν] ἐπιθυμιᾶν ἐπευ[χ]ομέ̣[νους γι]-
ν⟨ε⟩σ⟨θ⟩α̣ι τ̣ὰ̣ ἀ̣[γαθὰ τῶι τε] δ̣ή̣[μ]ωι ἡμῶν καὶ τῶ̣ι̣ Μαγν[ήτων]
. . . τ . ἀφ[ιέναι τοὺς] παῖδας ἐκ τῶμ μαθημά[των - - - - - -]
. . . . τ [. . . . . . κ]αὶ τὰς [ἐκ]ε[χ]ειρίας [κα]ὶ τὴν̣ [- - - - -]
[- - - - - - - - - - - - - - - - -]ν̣γρ̣ο̣[- - - - - - - - - - - - - - - - -]

2 Rigsby: σ̣υ̣νθύειν μὲ̣[ν - - -] Kern. 3 Boesch: παρελθόντες Kern. 5: ΣΑΙ lapis. 12–13 Robert: διὰ τὰ] γεγο[ν]ότα{ν} ἀγαθ⟨ὰ τ⟩οῖς. 14 corr. Robert: ΝΥΝ lapis. 15–16 Robert: - - - |νας κ̣α̣ὶ τ̣ὰ̣ς̣ [- - - Kern.

The substance of the decree begins with a declaration of a public holiday, of a sort found in some other honorific decrees but extravagant and rare in the *asylia* inscriptions (otherwise only **125**). It is strange too that this is the first item (cf. **107**); in **125**, as one would expect, these honors come after the Magnesians' request has been granted. The text then seems to proceed rather abruptly to the games (if ἐκεχειρίας is right in 18); in the context of the holiday one expects at least a statement of the occasion or date, for which there is scarcely room in lines 17–18.

109. Laodicea on the Lycus

Two columns (a, b), with some loss between.

Kern, *I.Magnesia* 59.

Cf. Holleaux, *Etudes* I 326–327; Robert, *RPhil* n.s. 53 (1927) 98, 116; III.10 (1936) 123–126 (*Op. min. sel.* II 1053, 1071, 1202–1205).

a.

[- -]σ̣υ̣ν̣ . .
[- Ἀπόλλ?]ων̣ι̣ κ̣α̣ὶ
[-] π̣α̣ρ̣' ἡμῶ[ν]

[-] τῆς θυσίας
[- - - - - - - - - συντε]λ̣ε̣[ῖν . . . . . . ὑ]πὲρ τῆς σωτηρί-
[ας - - - - - - - -, διδόν]αι δὲ κ̣α̣ὶ εἰς [ἀπ]α̣ρχὴν τῆι
[θεᾶι - - - - - - ὅσο]ν ἂν ὁ δῆμος τάξηι, συντελ . . .
[- - - - - - - - - ?θυσ]ίας καλέσ̣αι τοὺς πρεσβευτὰς
[εἰς τὸ πρυταν]ε[ῖο]ν [ἵν]α̣ συνθύωσιν καὶ συνῶσι ἐν
[- - - - - - -] ἐπηνῆσθ̣α̣ι δ̣ὲ̣ καὶ τοὺ[ς] πρεσ[β]ευ-
[τὰς τοὺς ἀ]ποστα[λ]έ̣ν[τ]ας παρ' αὐτῶν ἐπί [τε τῆι]
[πρὸς τὸ θεῖο]ν εὐσεβεία[ι] καὶ τῆ[ι] πε̣[ρὶ] τὴν πατρί-
[δα φιλοτιμί]αι· [ὑ]π̣άρχ[ε]ιν δὲ αὐτοῖς καὶ ἔφο̣[δο]ν̣ πρὸς
[τὸν δῆμον μετ]ὰ [τὰ ἱ]ερά, [κα]ὶ̣ ε̣[ἶ]ναι α̣[ὐ]τοὺ[ς πρ]οξέ[νους]
[τοῦ ἡμετέρου] δήμου, στεφ[α]νοῦ[σ]θαι δὲ αὐτοὺς
[καθ'] ἕ̣[καστον] ἐ̣ν̣ι̣αυτὸν ἐ̣ν̣ τῶι ἀγῶνι ὧι συντ[ε]-
[λοῦμεν] ἐν [τῶι μηνὶ] τῶ[ι Ἀ]ν[τιοχ]εῶνι χρ̣υ̣σῶι στε-
[φάνωι εὐσεβείας ἕ]ν̣[εκεν καὶ εὐ]νοίας τῆς πρ[ὸ]ς τὴν
[Ἄρτεμιν τε καὶ τὸν δῆμ]ο̣ν̣ ἡμῶν, περὶ δὲ̣ [τ]ῆ̣ς ἀναγο-
[ρεύσεως τοῦ στεφάνου ἐ]π̣[ι]μ̣έ̣λειαν ποιεῖσθαι
[τὸν ἀγωνοθέτην καὶ τοὺς πρυ]τάνεις κ̣α̣ὶ τὸν
[-]ς τὸν ταμί-
[αν -]α̣τον . . .
[- δίδ]οσθαι, ἐλ[έσθα]ι̣
[-] τι [ὑ]πάρ̣[χ]ε̣[ιν]
[- ὁ δῆμο]ς ὁ Λαοδικέ-
[ων - - - στεφανοῖ τὸν δῆμον τὸν Μαγνήτων? χ]ρυσῶι
[στεφάνωι -]σει . αὐ-
[- - - - - - - - - - - - τὴν πόλιν καὶ τὴ]ν χώραν τ[ῶ]ν
[Μαγνήτων ἱερὰν καὶ ἄσυλον - - - - - - - - - - - - - -]
[- θεω]ρούς
[-]
[-]δ .

b. [-]
[. . . κ]αὶ νῦν [ὁ δῆμος ἀκούσας? παρὰ τῶν πρεσβευτῶν]
[τ]ὰ συνηντημ̣[ένα Μάγνησιν ἀγαθὰ ὑπὸ τοῦ θεοῦ]
ἥ̣δεταί τε καὶ ν̣[-]
των προθύμως [- - - - - - - - - - - - - - - - - - - ὅσον]
ἦι δυνατὸς ὁ δῆμ̣ο̣ς, ο[ὐθενὸς λειπόμενος]
τῶν πρὸς δόξαν καὶ ἀ[ρετὴν ἀμφοτέραις ταῖς]
π̣όλεσιν ἁρμοζόντω[ν· τοὺς ἐξεταστὰς]
[τ]οὺς ἐσομένους ἐπὶ ἱερέ[ως τῆς Πόλεως Ἰα]-
τροκλείους ἀναγράψαν̣[τας τὸ ψήφισμα]
τόδε̣ καὶ τὸ παρὰ Μαγνή[των εἰς στήλην λευκοῦ]
[λί]θ[ου], ἣν στῆσαι ἐν τῆι [ἀγορᾶι ἐν τῶι ἐπιφα]-
νεστάτωι τόπωι· δοῦν[αι - - - - - - - - - - - - - - - -]
τ̣ε̣ [πά]ντα τὰ . . . ἀξι[ούμενα - - - - - - - - - - - - -]
. . εἰς τὸ ταμ̣ι̣εῖον ἀε̣ὶ - - -· [παρακαλέσαι δὲ τὸν δῆ]-

μον τὸμ Μαγνήτων [καὶ παρ' αὐτοῖς ἀναγράψαι]
τὸ ψή[φ]ισμα τοῦτο εἰς [στήλην λιθίνην, ἣν]
στῆσαι ἐν τῶι ἱερῶι τ̣ῆ[ς Ἀρτέμιδος τῆς Λευκο]-
φρυη̣ν̣ῆς, ἀν̣α̣γρ̣[άψαι - - - - - - - - - - τοὺς πρεσ]-
βευ̣τὰς τὰς εἰς [- - - - - - - - - - - - - - ἐν τῶι ἀρ]-
χείωι ἐτάγησαν̣ δ̣[- - - - - - - - - - - - - - - ἀργυ]-
ρίου̣ δίδοσ̣[θα]ι π[- - - - - - - - - - - - - - - - - -]
θεωρ̣οδόκον [- - - - - - - - -. ἡιρέθη - - - - - - -]
Ἀπελλιχ̣[ῶν]τος.
κατὰ τὰ [αὐτὰ δὲ ἐψηφίσαντο·]
Ἀ̣ν̣τιοχ̣ε̣ῖς [- -]
Εὐρωπεῖ[ς -]
Ἀλ̣ι̣νδ̣εῖς [- -]
Π̣τολ̣εμ[αι]ε[ῖς πρὸς - - - - - - - - - - - - - - - - -]
Κ̣α̣ . . . . . . ωι [- - - - - - - - - - - - - - - - - - -]

Klaffenbach confirmed on the stone Robert's emendations, except for a.8. a.8: ἄρχον]τ̣ας Robert (Kern's ΙΑΣ confirmed by Klaffenbach). 9 Robert: Πάνθ]ε[ο]ν Kern. 11–13 Robert: τ[ὴν] ἐκκλη̣|[σίαν διὰ τὴ]ν εὐσέβεια[ν κ]α̣ὶ τὴ[ν] πε̣[ρὶ] τὴν πατρί|[δα ἀρετήν· κ]αὶ Kern. 17 Robert: ἐν Π̣[αν]θ[έ]ω̣ι τῶ[ι Ἀ]ν̣τιο̣χέων̣ χ. Kern. 19 Ἄρτεμιν τε Rigsby. b.2–3 Robert. 6–10 Robert: 6 ὁ [Λαοδικέων - - -, 8 ἁρμοζόντω[ς - - -, 9 Πα?]-, 10 ἀναγράψαι̣ [Kern. 11–12 Holleaux: στήλην | λι]θ̣[ίν]ην, στῆσαι Kern. 16–17 Holleaux: - - - ἀναγράψαι] and [στήλην λιθίνην καὶ] Kern.

Kern saw from the subscription that this Laodicea must be in the vicinity of Caria, thus the city on the Lycus. Useful parallels are supplied by the decrees *I.Priene* 59 and *MAMA* VI 5. This Seleucid foundation makes no reference to the king, so far as we have the decree (contrast **110** and **111**). This was, however, a long text, and much is lost: we have the provisions for the sacrifice sent to Artemis and for honors for the Magnesians, which followed the recognition of the games (by a.5–6) and *asylia* (the latter is included in the announcement prescribed at a.29). All of the second column is taken up with provisions and requests for inscribing the text.

a.16: Annual crowning of individuals also in *I.Priene* 59 (foreign judges); the festival, not named here but implied by the month, was the Antiocheia (cf. Robert, *Laodicée du Lycos* pp. 251ff.).

a.27: Kern's restoration is uncertain; only the *theoroi* (a.15), not the Magnesian people, are voted a crown in what survives (the provision may have come in a.22–24). What follows concerns the Laodiceans' proclamation, whether at their own Antiocheia or by an ambassador elected (a.24) to travel to Magnesia for the purpose.

b.9: For the eponymous priest of the City see Robert, *Laodicée* p. 325. Here as occasionally elsewhere, we seem to be near the end of the civic year—the next eponymous magistrate is known.

b.20–21: Perhaps what were "assigned" were rewards for future *theoroi*, the verb used as at **84**.20 and Robert, *Op. min. sel.* V 354 (cf. 357 n. 2); a new sentence may begin with this finite verb.

b.30: Κα[λύνδ]ωι or Κα[ύν]ωι; cf. Robert, *Hellenica* VII 189–193.

110. Unknown city

Kern, *I.Magnesia* 60.

(four lines lost)

[- κ]α̣ὶ φι-
[λοτιμίας -]οι
[- ε]ἰς τὸ
[- -]π̣ρα-
[ξα - βα]σ̣ιλέως
[Ἀντιόχου - αὐ]τ̣ο̣ὶ διε-
[λέχθησαν ἀκολούθως τοῖς ἐν τῶι ψηφίσματι γε]γ̣ραμμέ-
[νοις -] τ̣ὸν ἀγῶνα
[- Μα]γνήτων ὑπὲρ
[- -] σ̣υντελεῖν θυ-
[σίαν καὶ πανήγυριν καὶ ἀγῶνα στεφα]γ̣ίτην ἰσοπύ-
[θιον ὃν τιθέασι τῆι Ἀρτέμιδι τῆι Λευκοφρυ]η̣νῆι ἀρχηγέ-
[τιδι τῆς πόλεως - - - - - - - - - - - - - - - - κα]ὶ τοῖς πολί-
[ταις - ἐ]π̣ὶ τῆι εὐνοί-
[αι - - - - - - - - - - - - - πρὸς τὸν βασιλέα Ἀ]ν̣τίοχον καὶ
[- -] καὶ τὴν ἡμε-
[τέραν πόλιν - - - - - - - - - - - -, ἐπηινῆσ]θαι δὲ καὶ τὸν
[-] αὐτῶν ἐψη-
[φισ- ἔγρ]α̣ψεν δοθῆ-
[ναι - ἀ]π̣αρχὰς πα-
[- δραχ]μὰς ἑκα-
[τόν, τοὺς δὲ θεωροὺς καλέσαι εἰς τὸ π]ρυτανεῖ-
[ον.]

The author was a subject of the Seleucids, making deferential references to Antiochus III (9, 19). If ἔγρ]α̣ψεν is right in 23 and the king or a subordinate is the subject (as in **97**.2), then the city has received instruction from him and this decree must date later than **69**—perhaps then later than 205 B.C. But too much is lost to be confident of this. What little we have preserves mention of the games but not of *asylia*.

111. Antioch in Persis

Inscribed to the right of **110**. A second column begins with line 57; on a second stone from lines 44 and 100.

Kern, *I.Magnesia* 61 [Dittenberger, *OGIS* 233].

Cf. Holleaux, *Etudes* I 318–319; Haussoullier in *Anatolian Studies Ramsay* (London 1923) 188; Oguse, *BCH* 53 (1929) 144; Robert, *Hellenica* VII (1948) 20 n. 2; *Laodicée* 330–331; *Fouilles d'Amyzon* 168 n. 40; F. Piejko, *Epigraphica* 50 (1988) 45.

[π]αρὰ Ἀντιοχέων τῶν Π[ερσίδος]
[ἐ]πὶ̣ ἱερέως Σελεύκου Νικάτορος καὶ Ἀντιόχου
Σωτῆρος καὶ Ἀντιόχου Θεοῦ καὶ Σελεύκου Καλλινί-
κου καὶ βασιλέως Σελεύκου καὶ βασιλέως Ἀντιόχου
καὶ τοῦ υἱοῦ αὐτοῦ βασιλέως Ἀντιόχου Ἡρακλείτου
τοῦ Ζωέους τῆς πρώτης ἑξαμήνου, δόγματα ἐκκλη-
σίας κυρίας τὰ ἀπενεχθέντα ὑπὸ Ἀσκληπιάδου τοῦ
Ἑκαταίου τοῦ Δημητρίου τοῦ γραμματέως τῆς βου-
λῆς καὶ τῆς ἐκκλησίας, μηνὸς Πανθέου τρίτηι φθίνον-
τος, ἔδοξε τῆι ἐκκλησίαι πρυτάνεων εἰπάντων, ἐπε̣ι̣-
δὴ Μάγνητες οἱ ἀπὸ Μαιάνδρου, συγγενεῖς ὄντες
καὶ φίλοι τοῦ δήμου καὶ πολλὰς καὶ ἐπιφανεῖς χρεί-
ας παρε̣ισ̣χημένο[ι] τ̣ο̣ῖ̣ς [Ἕλλ]ησίν [εἰσιν τῶν πρὸς δόξ]-
αν ἀνηκουσῶν, πρότ̣ερόν τε Ἀντιόχου τοῦ Σωτ̣ῆ̣ρ̣ος
φιλοτιμο̣[υ]μ̣ένου ἐπα[υξ]ῆσαι τὴμ πόλιν ἡ̣μῶν οὖσαν
αὐτοῦ ἐπώνυμον καὶ πέμψαντος πρὸς αὐτοὺς περὶ
ἀποικίας, καλὰ καὶ ἔνδοξα ψηφισάμενοι καὶ εὐχὰς καὶ
θυσίας ποιησάμενοι ἀπέστειλαν ἄνδρας πλήθει
ἱκανοὺς καὶ ἀρετῆι διαφέροντας, σπουδάζοντες
συναυξῆσαι τὸν τῶν Ἀντιοχέων δῆμον, διατηροῦν-
τές τε τὴν πρὸς ἅπαντας τοὺς Ἕλληνας εὔνοιαν
καὶ φανερὸν θέλοντες ποιεῖν ὅτι πᾶσιν τοῖς προσήκ̣[ου]-
σιν μεταδιδόασιν σπονδῶν τε καὶ θυσιῶν καὶ τῶν ἄλ-
λων τιμίων τῶν ἀνηκόντων εἰς τὸ θεῖον, ἐγδοθέντος
αὐτοῖς χρησμοῦ ἀνέδειξαν κατὰ πᾶσαν τὴν Ἑλλά-
δα συντελοῦντες τῆι ἀρχηγέτιδι τῆς πόλεως θυσί-
ας καὶ πανήγυριν καὶ ἐκεχειρίαν καὶ ἀγῶνα στεφανί-
την διὰ πενταετηρίδος μουσικόν τε καὶ γυμνικὸν
καὶ ἱππικόν, δικαίαν ἀποδιδόντες χάριν τῆι εὐεργέ-
τιδι, καὶ πρὸς τὸν δῆμον ἀπεστάλκασι πρεσβευτὰς
Δημοφ⟨ῶ⟩ντα Λυκιδέως, Φιλίσκον Φιλίου, Φέρητα
Φέρητος, οἳ καὶ ἐπ̣ελθόντες ἐπί τε τὴν βουλὴν καὶ
τὴν ἐκκλησίαν ψήφισμά τε ἀπέδωκαν παρὰ Μαγνή-
των καὶ ἀνανεωσάμενοι τὴν συγγένειαν καὶ τὴν φι-
λίαν ἀπελογίσαντο διὰ πλειόνων τήν τε τῆς θεᾶς ἐ-
πιφάνειαν καὶ τὰς χρείας ἃς παρέσχηνται Μάγνητες
πολλαῖς τῶν Ἑλληνίδων πόλεων καὶ παρεκάλουν
ἀποδέξασθαι τὸν ἀγῶνα στεφανίτην ὃν συντελοῦ-

σιν Ἀρτέμιδι Λευκοφρυηνῆι κατὰ τὸν τοῦ θεοῦ χρησμόν·
ὁ δὲ δῆμος σεβόμενος μὲν τοὺς κοινοὺς θεοὺς αὑτοῦ τε
καὶ Μαγνήτων, προαιρούμενος δὲ αὔξειν τ̣ὴν ἑ[αυτοῦ]
εὔνοιαν πρὸς τοὺς συγγενεῖς καὶ ἄλλω̣ν̣ ⟨τ⟩ε̣ π̣όλεω̣ν̣
[καλὰ καὶ ἔνδοξα π]ρ̣οε̣ψ[η]φ[ισ]μ̣έν̣ω̣ν̣ [τοῖς Μάγνησιν τὸ α̣ὐ]τὸ
[ποι]ε̣ῖ̣ν̣ πρὸ π̣α̣ν̣τ̣ὸ̣ς̣ οἴεται δεῖν καιρὸ[ν μηδένα] παρα̣[λεί]-
πε[ιν πρέ]ποντα ἐν ὧι [καὶ] καθ' ἰδίαν ἑκ[άστωι κ]α̣ὶ κοινῆι πᾶ-
σιν ἐ[να]π̣οδείξεται τὴ̣ν̣ σπουδὴν ἣ̣[ν ἔχ]ων διατελεῖ
[εἰς τὸ συ]μφέρον τὸ τῶν Μαγνή[των·] ἀγαθῆι τύχη̣[ι],
[δ]ε[δ]ό[χθα]ι τῆι βουλῆι καὶ τῶι δή̣μω̣[ι ἐπαι]ν̣έσαι μὲν Μά-
γ̣νητας τῆς τε πρὸς τὸ θεῖον εὐσεβείας ἕνεκεν καὶ τῆς
πρὸς τὸμ βασιλέα Ἀντίοχον φιλίας καὶ εὐνοίας καὶ
τὸν δῆμον τὸν Ἀντιοχέων, καὶ δ[ι]ότι τοῖς ἰδίοις ἀγαθ[οῖς]
καὶ τῆι εὐημερίαι [τ]ῆς πόλεως καλῶς χρώμενοι δι[αφ]υ-
λάσσουσιν τὴμ πάτριον πολιτείαν̣, ε̣ὔξασ[θ]αι δὲ τ̣οὺς
ἱερεῖς θεοῖς πᾶσιν καὶ πάσαις διαμένειν Μ[άγ]ν̣ησιν
εἰς τ̣ὸ[ν] ἅπαντα χρόνον ἐπὶ τύχη̣ι ἀγαθῆι τὴ[ν] πολε[ιτεί]-
αν· ἀπ̣[ο]δ̣έ̣ξασθαι δὲ τὴν θυσίαν καὶ τὴν πανήγυρι[ν]
καὶ τὴν ἐκεχ̣[ειρίαν καὶ τὸν ἀγῶνα στεφανίτην ἰσοπύθιον]
τόν τε μου[σικὸν καὶ γυμνικὸν καὶ ἱππικὸν ὃν]
συντελοῦ̣[σι Μάγνητες τῆι Ἀρτέμιδι τῆι Λευκοφρυηνῆι]
διὰ τὸ πάτρ̣ι̣[ον -]
φίλων τίμια̣ [-]
καὶ τὰ λοιπὰ ἃ [-]
καὶ τῆι Μαγνήτ̣[ων πόλει - - - - - - - - - - - - - - - - - - -]
καθ' ἑκάστην [- - - - - - - - ἀποστεῖλαι δὲ καὶ θεωρούς]
εἰς Μαγ̣ν̣ησία̣[ν τοὺς θύσοντας Ἀρτέμιδι Λευκο]-
φρυηνῆι ἐπὶ σωτηρ̣ί̣α̣[ι τοῦ τε βασιλέως καὶ ἀμφοτέρων τῶν]
π̣όλεων, δίδοσθαι δὲ α[ὐτοῖς καὶ ἐφόδιον ἐκ τοῦ δημοσίου]
ὅσον ἂν ὁ δῆμος ψηφ[ίζηται ἱκανὸν εἶναι καὶ πρέπον]
[τῆ]ι πόλ̣[ει· αἱρεῖσθαι δὲ τοὺς θεωροὺς τῆι - - - τοῦ Ἡρα]-
κλείου μηνὸς [ὅταν καὶ αἱ ἄλλαι ἀρχαὶ αἱ πολιτικαὶ]
σταθῶσιν, τοὺς δὲ [αἱρεθέντας ἀποστέλλεσθαι]
ἀπὸ τῆς ἑστίας τῆς [κοινῆς τοῦ δήμου· τοῖς δὲ παρα]-
γινομένοις θεωροῖ[ς ἐκ Μαγνησίας πρὸς ἡμᾶς δίδοσ]-
θαι ὑπὸ τῶν ταμιῶν ἐ[κ τοῦ δημοσίου ξένια ὅσα δίδο]-
ται καὶ ταῖς παρὰ Ἀρ[τέμιδος τῆς Ἐφεσίας θεωρίαις?·]
συνθυέτωσαν δὲ οἱ θ[εωροὶ - - - - - - - - - τῆι Ἀρτέμι]-
[δι τῆι Λευκ]οφ[ρυ]ηνῆι τὰ [- - - - - - - - - - - - - - - - - -]
τοῖς δὲ νικῶσιν τῶ̣ν̣ [πολιτῶν τὸν ἀγῶνα τῶν Λευκο]-
φρυηνῶν εἶναι τὰς α[ὐτὰς τιμὰς καὶ τὰ φιλάνθρωπα παρὰ]
τῆς πόλεως καθὰ κ[αὶ τοῖς τὰ Πύθια νικήσασιν ἐκ τῶν]
νόμων ὑπάρχει, τὰ α[-]
κου ἐφιέμενοι, πειρώ[μενοι δὲ - - - - - - - - - - - - - - ἄ]-
γεσθαι τοὺς ἀγῶνας [-]

ε . σε . . καὶ τῶν παρα[- - - - - - - - - - - - - - - - - - - -]
αἱ τιμαὶ τῶι νικήσαν̣[τι -]
καὶ τοὺς πρε̣σβευτὰς [- - - - - - - - - - - - - - - - - - - ἔτα]-
ξεν ὁ ἐπὶ τὴ[ν κ]οινὴν [διοίκησιν ἡιρημένος - - - - - - - -]
τοὺς πρυτάνεις ἀεὶ [- - - - - - - - - - - - - - - κατὰ τὰ ὑπὸ]
τοῦ δήμου ἐ̣[ψ]ηφισμ[ένα - - - - - - - - - - - - - - - - οἱ ἀφι]-
κνούμενοι παρὰ Μα[γνήτων - - - - - - - - - - - - - - - - - -]
πάση̣ς̣ προεδρ[ία]ς τ[- -]
ἵνα καὶ ἡ φιλία ταῖς πό[λεσιν ὑπάρχηι εἰς τὸν ἅπαντα]
χρόνον· αἱρεθῆναι δ[ὲ καὶ θεωροδόκον ὑπὸ τοῦ δήμου]
ὅστις ὑποδέξεται τ[οὺς θεωροὺς τοὺς παραγενομένους πα]-
ρὰ Μαγνήτων, εἶνα[ι δὲ -]
τὸν θεωροδόκον ε[- -]
δέδεκται ὁ δῆμος [- -]
προεψηφισμένο[ις - - - - - - - - - - - - - - - - - - ἐπὶ - - - -]
ἱερ[έως ἡιρ]έθ[η - - - - - - - - - - - - Ἡγ]η̣σά̣ν[δρου?]
ὁμο[ί]ως δὲ ἔδοξεν καὶ
Σελευ̣κεῦσιν τοῖς [- - - - - - - - - - -]
πρὸς [τ]ῶι Τίγρει [- - - - - - - - - - -]
Ἀπαμεῦ̣σιν τοῖς [- - - - - - - - - - -]
[π]ρὸς τῶι Σελείαι [- - - - - - - - - - -]
Σελευκεῦσιν τοῖς Ἀν[τι]ο̣[χεῦσιν τοῖς]
πρὸς τ̣ῆι Ἐρυθρᾶι πρὸς [- - - - - - -]
θαλάσσηι Ἀλ[εξανδρεῦσιν τοῖς]
Σελευκεῦσιν τοῖς [- - - - - - - - - - -]
πρὸς τῶι Ε̣ὐ̣λαίωι [- - - - - - - - - - -]
Σ[ε]λευκ[εῦσι]ν τ[οῖς] [- - - - - - - - - - -]
π[ρὸ]ς τῶ[ι Ἡδυφῶντι] [- - - - - - - - - - -]

1 Robert, *Hellenica*: Π[ερσικῶν] Kern. 13 Holleaux: εὐδοξί]|αν Dittenberger. 31: ΦΙΟΝ lapis. 42–44 Piejko: δ̣ε̣ (delta is clear on the squeeze) π̣όλεω̣ν̣ | [πολλῶν τὰ αὐτὰ π]ρ̣οε̣ψ̣[η]φ̣[ισ]μ̣ε̣ν̣ω̣ν̣ [- - - -]το | . σ̣ι̣ν̣ Kern. 45 πρέ]ποντα and [καὶ] Holleaux, Dittenberger. 54: πάσαις ⟨αὐτὴν⟩ add. Holleaux. 55–56 Dittenberger: τῆ[ς] πόλε[ως], | ἀναπ̣[ο]δ̣ε̣ξ̣ασθαι Kern. 59, 64, 65 middle, 67–74 middle Dittenberger. 66: or τ. β. ἀξίως ἀ. τ.] Oguse. 74 ὅσα Robb., *Amyzon*: καθὰ δ. Kern. 75 Robb.: ἀρ[χόντων καὶ πόλεων πρεσβείαις] Dittenberger. 79–80, 82 end, 86–89, 93 end, 95 Dittenberger. 111 Haussoullier.

This is the fullest decree we have from a Seleucid subject city or royal city, a city both founded and governed by the Seleucid crown. See generally the Roberts' remarks at *La Carie* II pp. 300–302; Robert intended a commentary on this decree (*Op. min. sel.* V 392 n. 7). Antioch in Persis is not again attested, and its exact location is disputed.[81] Here the Magnesian *theoroi* found Antiochus III (**69**.9–10), yet in what survives there is no mention of an instruction from the

81. See C. Rouché and S. Sherwin-White, *Chiron* 15 (1985) 9 n. 18.

king to the city concerning their request. Although the Antiochenes mention the oracle (25), they apparently relate it only to the crowned games and (like the Seleucid kings) do not mention inviolability. The king's presence there seems to guarantee that the year is 205 B.C., his return from his long and successful campaign in the northeast; but it is striking that he is not here given the appellation Antiochus the Great, which that campaign had occasioned (Holleaux, *Etudes* III 162).

1–6: On dating by the priest of the royal cult see J. and L. Robert, *Amyzon* p. 168. The calendar, with division into semesters and the months Pantheos and Herakleios (69–70),[82] is not Macedonian, nor does the city use the Seleucid era (see *La Carie* II 301 n. 6; Bickerman, *Institutions* 206). It is interesting that the son (cf. **70**) has not only the royal title but also a cult.

7–10: An archival docket, "the decrees of the major assembly submitted [to the record office; cf. *Syll.*[3] 665.15] by the secretary." Compare the heading at **26**.3, and the heading of Lampsacene decrees interpreted by J. and L. Robert, *Bull. épigr.* 1954, 209.

14–20: As at Megalopolis, the Magnesians were able to cite a historical connection that gave them a special claim on this city's favor: "When previously Antiochus Soter [281–261 B.C.] did us the benefaction of increasing our city, which was named for him, and sent to them about a colony, they passed a fine and honorable decree, made prayers and sacrifices, and sent men sufficient in number and distinguished in virtue, as they were eager to join in increasing the people of Antioch." Apparently Antioch already was in existence, whether founded by Nicator or Antiochus. We know also that Magnesia at some date sent colonists to Antioch in Pisidia (Strab. 12.8.14 [577]: ταύτην δ' ᾤκισαν Μάγνητες οἱ πρὸς Μαιάνδρῳ)—the only colonists there mentioned by Strabo.[83] Dittenberger in fact considered the possibility that the latter is our city, with Π[ισιδικῆι] in line 1; that is excluded if **125** is from Antioch in Pisidia (cf. Boesch, Θεωρός 66 n. 1).

40–41: In general the sentiment here is like that expressed by so many Cretan cities to Teos, "we too worship Dionysus." But certainly the Magnesian colonists will have brought some of their own cults with them to Antioch.

51–53: "and because they have used well their private prosperity and the well being of their city and have preserved their ancestral constitution"—the solicitude of a colony for its mother city; cf. Robert, *Laodicée* 331 n. 4.

75: The Roberts' restoration is on the assumption that Ephesians had also joined in the colony (cf. *Laodicée* 330), not that Ephesus had crowned games (although that is possible at this date).

108: On Seleuceia on the Eulaeus see Robert, *Op. min. sel.* II 982–985.

82. Literary evidence of Roman date attributes the same two months to the original Seleucid capital, Seleuceia in Pieria (Samuel, *Chronology* 174); but two inscriptions from there use Seleucid dates (*IGLSyr* 1183–1184: II B.C.).

83. On Hellenistic colonization see P. Briant, *Klio* 64 (1982) 83–98.

112. Unknown city

From line 36, on a lower block.

Kern, *I.Magnesia* 62.

Cf. Wilhelm, *Jahresh.* 4 (1901) Beibl. 30 (*Kl. Schr.* II.1 155); Holleaux, *Etudes* I 319–320; Oguse, *BCH* 53 (1929) 141; Robert, *Sanctuaire de Sinuri* (Paris 1945) 23 n. 2.

[- - - - - - - - - - - - ?τοῖς σεβομένοις Ἄρτεμιν Λευ]-
[κοφρυηνὴν καὶ τὴν πόλιν καὶ τὴν χ]ώρα[ν αὐτῶν]
[ἱερὰν καὶ ἄσυλον νομίζουσι, καὶ διὰ ταῦ]τ̣α τὸν̣ δῆ[μον]
[ἐψηφίσθαι συντελεῖν τῆι ἀρχηγέτι]δι τῆ[ς π]όλεως
[διὰ πέντε ἐτῶν θυσίαν καὶ πανήγυ]ριν κ̣α̣[ὶ] ἐ̣κεχει-
[ρίαν καὶ ἀγῶνα στεφανίτην ἰσοπύ]θιον μουσικόν
[τε καὶ γυμνικὸν καὶ ἱππικόν, ἐλθόν]τες δὲ̣ ἐπὶ τὴν
[βουλὴν καὶ τὸν δῆμον οἱ π]εμφθέντες ὑπ' αὐ-
[τῶν πρεσβευταὶ ἀπολογισ]ά̣μενοι τήν τε [τ]ῆς
[θεᾶς ἐπιφάνειαν καὶ τὰς γ]εγενημένας ὑπ[ὸ] τῶν
[προγόνων πρὸς τοὺς Ἕλληνα]ς εὐχρηστία[ς κ]αὶ τὴν
[εὔνοιαν τῆς πόλεως τῶν] Μ̣α̣γνήτων ἣν ἔ[χ]ε̣ι πρὸς
[τὴν πόλιν ἡμῶν, παρα]καλοῦσιν καὶ ἀ̣ξιοῦσιν̣ τὸν
[ἡμέτερον δῆμον] προσδέξασθαι τὰ ἐψη[φ]ισ-
[μένα· ὅπως οὖ]ν καὶ ὁ δῆμος φαίνηται αὐτὸς
[εὐσεβῶς διακείμ]ε̣νος πρὸς τὸ θεῖον, καθάπερ
[πάτριον αὐτῶι], καὶ Μάγνησιν ὑ̣πακούειν̣
[πρόθυμος ὤν, τύχ]ηι ἀγαθῆι, δ̣εδόχθαι
[τῶι δήμωι ἐπαινέσ]αι μὲν τὸν δῆμον τὸμ Μ̣α-
[γνήτων, ὅτι εὐσεβῶ]ς διακείμενος πρὸς τὸ θεῖ-
[ον καὶ καλῆς καὶ ἐνδ]όξου αἱρέσεως ἀνθ̣ε̣ιλημμέ-
[νος ἐπαύξησε τὰς τ]ῆς Ἀρτέμιδος τιμὰς μεμνη-
[μένος τῶν γ]ε̣γενημένων ὑπ' αὐτῆς ἐπιφα-
[νειῶν εὐεργε]τημάτων, ἀποκρίνασθαι δὲ αὐ-
[τοῖς ὅτι ὁ δῆμος] καὶ πρότερον μὲν διετέλει
[εὐνόως διακείμε]νος τῆι πόλει τῆι Μαγνήτων,
[νῦν δὲ προαιρούμε]νος συναύξειν τὰ ἐψηφισμέ-
[να τῆι Ἀρτέμι]δ̣ι τίμια ἀποδέχεταί τε κατὰ
[τὴν τοῦ θεοῦ μαντεί]α̣ν τὸν ἀγῶνα τῶν Λευχ̣ο̣φρ̣[υη]-
[νῶν στεφανίτην ἰσο]πύθιον μουσικὸν καὶ γυ̣[μνι]-
[κὸν καὶ ἱππικὸν ἐφ' ὑγιεί]αι καὶ σωτηρίαι τοῦ τ[ε]
[ἡμετέρου δήμου καὶ τοῦ τῶν Μαγν]ήτων, καὶ τὴμ πόλιν
[καὶ τὴν χώραν ἱερὰν καὶ] ἄσυλον νομίζει· ὑπάρ[χειν]
[δὲ καὶ τοῖς νικ]ῶσιν τὸν ἀγῶνα τ[ῶν Λευκοφρυηνῶν]
[τὰ ἴσα ἆθλα ὅσαπερ καὶ] τοῖς τὰ Πύθια νι[κῶ]-
[σιν ἐκ τῶν νόμων δίδο]τ̣α̣ι̣· ἐπαινέσαι [δὲ καὶ]
[- -]
χον Ἱππ̣ί̣αν [ἐπὶ τῶ]ι μετ̣[ὰ] π[άσης σπουδῆς καὶ φι]-

λοτιμίας ἀπολε̣λογίσθαι πε̣[ρὶ τῶν τῆς θεᾶς τιμῶν,]
καθότι προσή̣κ̣ει πράσσειν το[ῖς ὑπὸ τῆς πατρίδος]
περὶ τῶν εἰς τὸ θ̣ε̣ῖο̣ν̣ [πι]στε[υο]μ̣[ένοις καὶ πεμπο]-
μένοις, δοῦναι δὲ καὶ ξένιον [- - - - - - - - - ἑκάστωι αὐ]-
τῶν τὸ ἐκ τοῦ μερισμοῦ [- - - - - - - - - - - - - - - - -]

1–4 Oguse: 1 [ἄμεινον εἶναι τοῖς τὴν π. κ. τ. χ., 2 [ἱ. κ. ἄ. ν., ὑπακούσαν?]τ̣α, 3 [ταῖς τοῦ θεοῦ μαντείαις τ. ἄ. Kern. 20–23 Holleaux: 20 διατελεῖ καὶ τῆς φιλοδ]όξου, 21 δέχεσθαι δὲ τὰς τ]ῆς, 22 [μένους, 23 [νῶς Kern. 32 init. Rigsby: [τῶν Μαγνήτων ἱερὰν Kern; fin. Wilhelm: ὑπάρ[ξειν] Kern. 33–34 Rigsby (cf. **97**.23): τ[ῶν | Λευκοφρυηνῶν ὅσα καὶ] Kern. 38–40 Holleaux: 40 [εἴ]ς τε [τὴ]μ [πόλιν ἀνηκόντων? - - -] Kern.

No detail survives to identify the author; the *theoroi* (37) are not met elsewhere.

42: μερισμός is frequent enough of cult distributions but unusual of a fund of the state; cf. μερισταί at **103**.36.

113. Unknown city

Inscribed to the right of **112**.

Kern, *I.Magnesia* 63.

Cf. Wilhelm, *Jahresh.* 4 (1901) Beibl. 30 (*Kl. Schr.* II.1 155); Holleaux, *Etudes* I 320; De Decker, *RPhil* n.s. 29 (1905) 163 (collation).

[- - - ψήφ]ισ̣μ̣[α καὶ] ἄ̣νδρας [- - - - - - - - - - - - -]
[- - - - - -]α̣ρχου τ[οῦ] Παρμενίω[νος - - - - - - - -]
[- - - - - τ]ὸν θεὸν τὸν ἐν Δελ[φοῖς χρῆσαι, λώϊον]
[εἶναι καὶ ἄμ]εινον τοῖς σεβομέ̣[νοις Ἄρτεμιν Λευκοφρυ]-
ηṇ[ὴν καὶ τὴμ] π̣όλιν αὐτῶν καὶ τ[ὴν χώραν ἱερὰν καὶ ἄσυ]-
λο̣ν̣ [νομίζο]υσιν καὶ διὰ ταῦτ[α ἐψηφίσθαι αὐτοῖς συντε]-
λεῖ[ν τῆι ἀρ]χ̣ηγέτιδι τῆς [πόλεως Ἀρτέμιδι Λευκοφρυηνῆι]
διὰ π̣[έντε ἐ]τῶν θυσίαν [καὶ πανήγυριν καὶ ἐκεχειρίαν καὶ]
ἀγῶν̣[α στ]ε̣φανίτην ἰ[σοπύθιον μουσικὸν καὶ γυμνικὸν καὶ]
ἱππικ[όν, κ]α̣ὶ οἱ π̣[αρ]αγενόμ̣[ενοι πρε]σ̣[βευταὶ πρὸς τὴν]
βουλὴ̣[ν κα]ὶ τ[ὸ]ν δῆμ̣[ον] ἀ̣πελ̣[ογίσ]α̣ντο [τὴν ἐπιφάνειαν]
τ̣ῆς [θεοῦ κ]α[ὶ] τὰς γ̣[εγεν]ημένας ὑπὸ τῶ[ν Μαγνήτων]
ε̣ἰ̣ς [τοὺς Ἕλ]λην̣α̣[ς] εὐχρηστίας καὶ τὴν [φιλίαν τοῦ δήμου]
τ[ῶν] Μα[γν]ήτων ἣν ἔχει πρ̣ὸ̣ς τὴμ πόλιν̣ ἡμ[ῶν, καὶ πα]-
ρακαλ̣[οῦσ]ιν κ̣α̣ὶ̣ [ἀξ]ι̣ο[ῦ]σιν τ̣ὸν δῆμον πρ[ο]σδέ[ξασθαι τὰς ἐψη]-
φι[σ]μέ[νας τ]ιμ̣[ὰς] τ̣ῆ̣ι̣ [θε]ᾶι μ[ετ]ὰ πάσης σπου[δῆς τοὺς λόγους ποι]-
ούμεν̣[οι]· ὅπ[ως] οὖ[ν κ]αὶ ὁ [δῆ]μος εὐσεβῶς φαίν̣ηται [διακείμε]-
νος [μὲν π]ρὸς τὸ θεῖ[ον, κ]αθ[άπ]ερ αὐτῶι πάτ[ρ]ιόν ἐ[στι, Μάγνη]-
σι δ̣' [ὑπα]κ̣ούω̣ν̣ εἰς τὰ ἀξιούμενα, τύχηι ἀγαθ[ῆι, δεδόχθαι τῆι βουλῆι]
κ̣α̣ὶ̣ τ̣[ῶι δήμ]ωι ἀποκ[ρίν]α̣σθ[α]ι Μάγνησιν ὅτι ὁ δῆμ[ος καὶ πρότε]-
ρο[ν ἀεὶ] δ̣ι̣ε̣τέλει [οἰ]κε̣ίως διακείμενος κοιν̣[ῆι τε τῶι δήμωι]
τῶ[ν Μαγνή]των κ̣α̣ὶ ἰδίαι̣ τοῖς ἀφικνουμέν[οι]ς, καὶ νῦν [βουλόμενος]
κ̣α̣[τὰ δύναμιν] σ̣υ̣ν̣[α]ύξ[ει]ν τὰ ἐψηφισμένα ὑπ' αὐτῶ̣[ν τίμια τῆι θεᾶι]

ἀ[ποδέ]χε̣[ται καὶ τὴμ π]ό̣λιν [κ]αὶ τὴν [χ]ώραν [ἱ]ε̣ρὰν καὶ ἄσ[υ]λ̣[ον
τ . . . . α . . . . ν [. . . . . . . κ]α̣ὶ τἆλλα κ̣αθότι Μάγνητε[ς - - -]
ω . . . . ι· ἐ̣π̣[αιν]έ̣[σ]αι δὲ [καὶ τ]οὺς ἥκον[τ]ας ἄνδρας [ἐπὶ τῶι τὰ συμφέ]-
ρο[ντα π]επ[ολυ]ωρῆσ[θ]αι, [κ]αὶ καλέσαι αὐτοὺς τὸν ἱε[ρ- - - - - - - - - - -]
εἰ̣[ς . . . .] ἐ̣πὶ ξέν[ια . . . .], περὶ δὲ τῆ[ς] αἱρέσεως τῆς [- - -]
[- - - - - - - - - - - - - - - -] τῶν ἄλλων εἶναι κ̣αθότι [- - - - - - - - - - - - -]

vacat

12–13: M. εἰς πά|ντας τοὺς Ἕλ]λην[ας] De Decker. 14: ἡμ[ῶν ἀεί, κ. π.] De Decker. 15 [ἀξ]ι̣ο[ῦ]σιν Wilhelm, Holleaux, supported by the squeeze (Ι̣Ο . ΣΙΝ): κ̣αὶ̣ [ἁρ]μ̣ό[ζ]ειν Kern, [ὁμ]ό[σ]ειν Oguse. 16–17 Holleaux. 19–20: δεδόχθαι | τῶι δήμωι] ἀ. De Decker. 20–21: καὶ ἐν τοῖς ἔμπ]|ρο[σθεν] δ. Holleaux. 22–23 Holleaux: [προ|αιρού]μ[ενος] σ. De Decker. 25–26: init. τ[όν τε] ἀ[γῶνα ἰσοπύθιον κα]ὶ; fin. ἠξί]|ω[σαν, ἐπαινέσ]αι De Decker. 26–27: τῶι μετὰ | π]ρο[θυμίας ἀ]π[ολελογί]σ[θαι Holleaux; τῶι πα]|ρό[ντ]α̣ς̣ [εὖ ἐπιδημεῖ]σθαι De Decker. 27–28: ἱε[ροκήρυκα / ἱε[ρέα] | ε̣ἰ̣[ς τὸ πρυτανεῖον] ἐπ[ὶ ξενισμόν Holleaux. 28–29: α. τ̣[οῦ θε|οροδόκου καὶ π]ε[ρὶ πάντω]ν̣ [τ]ῶν ἄ. De Decker.

The *theoros* (2) is unknown, and the city unidentified. If the acceptance of the games was expressed in line 25 (as De Decker restored), this was with unaccustomed brevity; if not, the substance of the decree grants *asylia* but not expressly the Panhellenic games, although both are cited in the preliminaries and there appears to be provision for electing a *theorodochos* (28).

114. Unknown city

Kern, *I.Magnesia* 64.
Cf. Boesch, Θεωρός 9 n. 4, 79 n. 4, 97 n. 3; Oguse, *BCH* 53 (1929) 142–144.

(three lines lost)

[- - - - - - - - - - - - - - πρ]ογόνων ε̣[- - - - - -]
[- - - - - - - - - - - - - πεντ]αετηρίδα π̣α̣[- - - -]
[- - - - - - - - - - - - - -]ον καὶ τῆι Ἀρ̣τ̣[έμι]-
[δι - - - - - - - - - - - - - -]τατα εὐ[- - - - - - - -]
[- - - - - - - - - - - - - - - -]ους μελ̣[- - - - - - -]
[- - - - - - - - - - - - - - -]ὅ̣σοι καὶ [- - - - - - -]
[- - - - - - - - - - - - -]ον παρε̣κάλουν δ̣[- - - -]
[- - - - - - - - - - - - - σ]υγγένειαν τας [- - - - - -]
[- - - - - - - - - - - - - -] τῆι Ἀρτέμιδι τ[ῆι - - - -]
[- - - - - - - - - - - - - - -]τ̣ων τῆ̣ι βουλῆι [- - - - -]
[- - - - - πρεσβευτὰς τοὺς] δὲ α̣ὐ̣τοὺς καὶ θεωρο[ὺς]
[- - - - - - - - - - - - - -] ψή[φ]ισμα ἀποδώσου[σιν - -]
[- - - - - - - - τὴν θυσίαν κ]αὶ τἆλλα [τ]ὰ νομιζ[όμενα]
[- - - - - - - - - - - - - - -] τῶν κοινῶν σωτή̣[ρων]
[- - - - - - καὶ ἀμφοτέρ]ων τῶν πόλεων οἳ κα̣[- - -]
[- - - - - - - - - - - - - -]σουσιν μετὰ τῶν ἄλ[λων]
[- - - - - - - - - - - - - εἰς δὲ] τὸν ἄλλον χρόνον, ὅταν

[- - - - - - - - - - - συν]τ̣ελοῦντες τὸν ἀγῶνα τῶι
[- - - - - - - - - - - καὶ] Ἀρτέμιδι ἀρχηγέτιδι· παρα-
[καλέσαι δὲ Μάγνητας ὄντ]ας [φ]ίλους καὶ συγγενεῖς προν̣[ο]-
[ῆσαι ὅπως τὸ ψήφισμα τόδε ἀν]αγραφῇ ἐν τῆι στοᾶι αὐτῶν·
[- - - - - - - - - - - - - - - - θεω]ροὺς καθάπερ καὶ τῶν ἄλ-
[λων - - - - - - - - - - - - - - Με]νέας Λυσιμάχου Μενεσ-
[- -]

vacat

11, 13 init. Boesch. 10–14: Oguse suggested δεδόχθαι - - -]των τῆι βουλῆι [καὶ τῶι δήμωι· ἑλέσ|θαι πρεσβευτὰς τρεῖς? τοὺς] δὲ α̣ὐ̣τοὺς καὶ θεωρο[ὺς, οἵ|τινες παραγενόμενοι τό τε] ψή[φ]ισμα ἀποδώσου[σιν καὶ | τήν τε θυσίαν συντελέσουσιν κ]αὶ τἆλλα [τ]ὰ νομιζ[όμενα | ὑπὲρ - - -]. 15–16: [κ. ὑπὲρ or καταξίως ἀ. and κα̣[ὶ τῶν ἱερῶν καὶ τοῦ | ἀγῶνος τῶν Λευκοφρυηνῶν μεθέ]ξουσιν μετὰ τῶν ἄλ[λων | Ἑλλήνων - - - Oguse. 17 Rigsby. 20–21 Oguse: 20 end προς Kern; ὅπως ἀν]αγραφῇ Boesch. 22: [ἐπιμελεῖσθαι τοὺς θεω]ροὺς Boesch.

The city was kin to the Magnesians (8) and perhaps had common gods (14), unless the latter refers to the Seleucid kings (cf. Herrmann, "Antiochus," no. 1.51).

10–14: In keeping with the future ἀποδώσου[σιν, Oguse took the substance of the decree to begin with the election of future *theoroi* to the Leucophryeneia (cf. **115**.4–5; **130**.15).

11: On this formula for the *theoroi* cf. on **86**.4–5.

17: For this phrase in a cult law cf. *I.Magn.* 99.8 [Sokolowski, *LSAM* 34].

115. Unknown city

Inscribed to the right of a decree of Cnossus.[84]
Kern, *I.Magnesia* 66.

[- -]
[- - - - - -]σιν Ἀ[ρτέ]μιδι [- - - - - - - - - - - - - - - - -]
[- - - τύχηι] ἀγαθῆι καὶ ἐπὶ [σωτ]ηρίαι το[ῦ τῶν Μαγ]-
νή[τω]ν δή[μ]ου καὶ τοῦ ἡμ[ετ]έρου δήμου,
ἑλέσθαι θεωροὺς τοὺς συντελέσοντας τὰν [θυ]-
σίαν καὶ τῶν ἱερῶν καὶ τοῦ ἀγῶνος μεθέ̣ξ̣οντα[ς]
μετὰ τῶν ἄλλων Ἑλλήνων, τὴν δὲ ἐσομέ-
νην δαπάνην εἰς τοὺς θεωροὺς καὶ τὰν̣ θυ-
σίαν δότωσαν οἱ ταμίαι ἀφ' ὧν χειρίζου-
σιν προσόδων· ᾑρέθησαν θεωροὶ Πυθόνικος
Ἀπολλωνίου, Διονύσιος Ἀριστέου.

84. *I.Magn.* 65b [*I.Cret.* I VIII 9], honoring Magnesian arbiters of Cretan hostilities; nearby were found 65a+75 [IV 176], Gortyn similarly, and 67 [I VIII 10], Cnossus honoring two Magnesians (cf. II III 7.c) for unspecified favors. These decrees probably were carried by the *theoroi* in illustration of Magnesian services to the Greeks.

If 3–4 are the transitional phrase that introduces the substance of the decree, then this city responded only to the request for games and did so rather offhandedly, merely providing for the future representatives. Alternatively, 3–4 refer to a prayer appended to the preceding action (acceptance of the games and *asylia*); but then we should expect ἑλέσθαι δὲ.

116. Unknown city

Inscribed to the right of the Cnossian honorific decree *I.Magn.* 67.
Kern, *I.Magnesia* 68.

[τήν τ]ε θυσίαν καὶ τἆλλα [τ]ὰ νομιζό-
μενα συντελείτωσαν ἀκολούθως τῆι
τοῦ δήμου [α]ἱρέσει· τὰ δὲ γενόμενα
εἰς ταῦτα δαπανήματα δότωσαν
τοῖς θεωροῖς οἱ ἐνεστηκότες ταμιε[ύειν?]
[ἀπ]ὸ ṭῶṿ τῆς πόλεως· ἡρ[έθη]σạṿ
[- - - Κλ]εάρχου, [Κλ]έαρχος Μίκκου.

The *theoroi* appear to be father and son; compare the pair of brothers who canvassed western Greece for Magnesia, those sent to Tralles, and those who traveled through central Greece for Alabanda.

117. Unknown city

Inscribed to the right of **116**.
Kern, *I.Magnesia* 69.

καὶ τοῖς θεω[ροῖ]ς ὅ[πως - - -]
εἰδῆτε περὶ ἑκάστω[ν - - - - -]

Part of a covering letter to a decree; cf. **90**.

118. Unknown Cretan city

Kern, *I.Magnesia* 70 [Blass, *SGDI* 5156].

[ἐπειδὴ Μ]ạ́γν[ητες -]
[. . . . . . .] συγγ[ενεῖς - - - - - - - - - - - - - - - - - -]
[. . . . . π]ολλὰ [-]
[. . . . .]ριοντẹṣ [-]
[φιλά]νθρωπα α[- - - - - - - - - - - - - - - - - - - ψάφισ]-
μά τε καὶ πρε[σβευτὰς - - - - - - - - - - - - - - - - - -]
των Θεόδοτ[ος καὶ - - - - - - - - - - οἵ τό τε ψάφισμα]
ἀπέδωκαν καὶ δ[ιελέγεν - - - - - - - - - - - - - - - σπου]-
δᾶς καὶ φιλοτιμία[ς -]
το· ὅπαι ὦν κἀ πόλις [- - - - - - - - - - - - - - - - - -]
πορτὶ Μάγνητα⟨ς⟩ ẹσ̣[- - - - - - - - - - - - - - - - - ἀν]-
θρώποι[ς,] δεδόχθαι̣ [- - - - γράψαι - - - - - - - - πρὸς]
τὸν δᾶμον τὸμ Μαγ[νήτων ὅτι - - - - - - - - - - - - - -]

νων προίσταται καθά[περ τοὶ πρεσβευταὶ αὐτῶν ἐπαγ]-
γέλλοντι, τῶν Λευκο[φρυηνῶν τὸν ἀγῶνα καὶ τὰνς θυσί]-
ανς ἀποδεχόμ[ε]θ[α] κ̣[αὶ - - - - - - - - - - - - - - - - - -]
οντι ἀποδεδεγ[μέν]οι [-]
καὶ τὰ ἀνθρωπ[-]
[κ]ὰτ τὴν τᾶι πόλ̣[ι -]
ἀεί τι ἀγαθὸν τ[ῶι] δ[άμωι - - - - - - - - - - - - - - - - -]
μον καὶ κ[ο]ινὰν ἱσ[τίαν - - - - - - - - - - - - - - - - - - -]
ον αὔξηται [-]
τανς· [εἰ] δὲ μὴ [- - - - - - - - - - - τοῖς πορτὶ τὰν ἰδίαν?]
πατρίδα στρατε[υσαμένοις - - - - - - - - - - - - - - - - -]

7: Θεόδοτ[ος Ἀριστόμαχος (κτλ.) Kern. 11: HTAN lapis, but see p. 162.

7: A Theodotus and Aristomachus obtained from Hierapytna in Crete a decree to inscribe various ancestral privileges enjoyed there by Magnesians (*I.Cret.* III iii 3.c). Although the Hierapytna decree is probably later than 208 B.C., the privileges listed do not include territorial inviolability, which apparently was not a concern. Guarducci, who assigned the script of the Hierapytna decree to the early second century B.C., rightly remarked that nothing guarantees the name of Aristomachus at **118**.7. Note, however, the second visit to the Artists at Teos by the three *theoroi* of 208 (cf. on **103**).

23–24: Here seems to have been a provision for the military defense of Magnesia, parallel to those in Cretan recognitions of other cities but not in the other decrees for Magnesia.

119. Unknown city

Kern, *I.Magnesia* 71.

[-]
[- - - - - - - - - - - - - - - ἀκόλου]θα [- - - - - - -]
[- - - - - - - - - - - - - - -]ν̣ . ς ἐ̣[π]αγγ[ελίας . .]
[- - - - - - - - - - - - - - - - - - -] δημο . . . σ . .
[- - - - - - - - - - - - - - - -] τὸ [ψ]ή[φ]ι[σμα] τ[ὸ]
[- - - - - - - - - - - - - - ἀπέδ]ωκαν καὶ ἀ̣π̣ε̣[λογί]-
[σαντο - - - - τὴν τῆς Ἀρτέ]μι[δος] ἐπ[ι]φάνε[ιαν]
[- - - - - - - - - - - - - - - δ]ήμου̣ ἀνα[. . . . . .]
[- - - - - - - - - - - - - - - - - -]υ θε . ε . . ημ . . .
[- - - - - - - - - - - - - - - - στ]ε[φα]νίτην ἰσοπύθιο̣ν
[- - - - - - - - - - - - - Ἀπόλ]λωνος τοῦ ἐ̣ν Δελφοῖς
[- - - - - - - - - - - - - τὴν] ἐ[πι]φάνειαν καὶ τὰς [τι]-
[μὰς τὰς ἐψηφισμένας] ὑ̣π̣ὸ [τ]οῦ δήμου· ἡμεῖς δὲ
[εὐνόως πρὸς ὑμᾶς] δ̣ι̣α̣κ̣είμενοι τόν [τ]ε ἀγ[ῶ]-
[να ἀποδεχόμεθα ὃν ἐπ]αγ[γέ]λλετε [κ]α[ὶ] τὴμ πόλ̣ι̣ν̣
[καὶ τὴν χώραν ἱερὰ]ν κ̣α̣ὶ [ἄ]σ[υ]λον νομίζομε̣ν̣
[ἀκολουθοῦντες τὴν μαντεί]αν του̣ ἐν Δελφοῖς̣

[θεοῦ - - - - - - - - - - - - - -] δ' ῦ̣πὸ τῶν . μ̣ .
[- -] ὁ ταμίας
[- -]α̣π̣ . α̣ . . .

17 Rigsby: [κατὰ τὴν τοῦ Ἀπόλλωνος μ. Kern.

Line 15 shows that this was a letter in form.

120. Syracuse

Kern, *I.Magnesia* 72 [Dubois, *IG dial. Sicil.* 97].
Cf. Holleaux, *Etudes* I 327–328 (squeeze); Wilhelm, *Beiträge* 181–183.

ἐπι Πολυξενί[δ]α τοῦ Φιλοξένο[υ, - - - - - - - - - - - - - -]
νους [Τι]μ[ασα?]γόρα, Ἐπικύδης Ξεν[οκλέος? - - - - - - -]
εκτα· δόγμα τᾶς σ[υ]γκλήτου, Ἀπο[λλωνίου - - - - - - -]
ἱσταμένου· προστάτας Ἀρτεμίδ[ωρος . . . . προγράψας]
⟨πρό⟩πεμπτα ὑπὲρ πρ̣εσβε⟨υτᾶ⟩ν καὶ θε̣[αρῶν ἐπαγ]-
γελλόντων τὰ[ν θ]υσ̣ίαν καὶ τὸν ἀγῶ̣ν̣[α Ἀρτέμιτι Λευκο]-
φρυηνᾶι· ἔδ[ο]ξε τᾶι σ[υ]γκλήτωι καθὰ κ[αὶ τᾶι βουλᾶι, εἰ]-
⟨π⟩άντων τῶν π̣ροσγραφέντων Ὑπερ[- - - - - - - - - - - -]
στογένου, Φιλοκράτεος, Σωσιπάτρ[ου, - - - - - - - - - - -]
Δάμωνος, Σω[σ]ανδ̣ρίδα{ς}, Σιμωνίδα, [παραγενομένων πρεσ]-
βευτᾶν καὶ θεαρῶν παρὰ τοῦ δάμου τ[ῶν Μαγνήτων ἀπὸ]
Μαιάνδρου Διοτίμου τοῦ Μηνοφίλο[υ - - - - - - - - - - -]
Ἀριστέος καὶ τ̣ό τε ψάφισμα ἀ[π]οδόν[των - - καὶ ἀπολογι]-
ξαμένων τάν τε τᾶς θεᾶς ἐπι[φ]άνεια[ν καὶ τὰς γεγενημέ]-
νας ὑπὸ τῶν π[ρ]ογό[ν]ων [α]ὐτοὶ ἔδειξαν ε̣[ὐχρηστίας]
δικαια - - - - - - - δ -
- -
. ον τί̣μια . . . ς κα . . . . . ε - - - - - - - - - - - - - - -
παρακαλεόντω[ν ἀποδέ]ξα̣σθαι τὰν [θυσίαν καὶ τὸν ἀγῶ]-
να ὃν τίθεντι τᾶι Ἀρτέμιτι τᾶι Λε̣[υκοφρυηνᾶι στεφανί]-
ταν ἰσοπύθιον τ[α]ῖ̣ς τιμαῖς, ἀπολογιξ̣[αμένων δὲ ὑπάρχον]-
[τ]ας φίλους [κ]α[ὶ] συ[γγενέα]ς [διὰ προγόνων τᾶς πόλιος ἁ]-
[μ]ᾶς Μ̣άγ[νητας -]
[Σ]υρακοσίω[ν -]
τ̣ι̣α ὑ̣π̣[- - - - - - - - - - - - - - - - - - δεδόχθ]α[ι τᾶι συγκλή]-
[τ]ωι τῶν Συρακοσίων καὶ τ[ᾶι βουλᾶι? - - - - - - - ἐπαινέ]-
σ̣αι μὲ̣ν̣ τὸν δᾶμον τῶν [Μαγνήτων ἐπὶ - - - - - - - - - - - -]
[καὶ] εὐσεβείαι ν[- - - - - - - - - - - - - - - - - ἀποδέ]-
ξασθαι δὲ καὶ τὸν [ἀγῶνα ὃν συντελέοντι Ἀρτέμιτι]
Λευκοφρυηνᾶι στεφ[ανί]ταν ἰσο[πύθιον, καθότι]
ἐπαγγέλλοντι οἱ πρ[ε]σβευταὶ [καὶ θεαροί, νομίζειν δὲ καὶ]
τάν τε πόλιν καὶ τὰν χώρα[ν] ἱ[ερὰν καὶ ἄσυλον κατὰ τὸν]
τοῦ θεοῦ χρησμόν, ἀποστέλλειν δ[ὲ καὶ ἄνδρας εἰς Μαγνσί]-
αν τοὺς συνθύσ⟨ο⟩ντας καὶ [συναυξήσοντας τὰς τιμὰς τᾶι]
θεᾶι, καθώς κα δυνατὸν ἦι τᾶι π̣[όλει· ἐπαινέσαι δὲ καὶ τοὺς]

πρ̣εσβευτ[ὰς] καὶ θεαροὺ[ς Δ]ιότιμο[ν - - - ἐπὶ τῶι ἀ]-
πολογίξασθαι ἀξίως [τ]ᾶς τε πό[λιος αὐτῶν καὶ τᾶς ἁμᾶς]
πόλιος, δόμεν δὲ αὐτοῖς ὅσον κα̣[ὶ τοῖς ἐπαγγέλλουσι]
τὸν ἀγῶνα τῶν Ἰσθμίω[ν], ἐ̣ξ⟨εῖ⟩με[ν δὲ αὐτοῖς καὶ θῦσαι ἱε]-
[ρ]εῖα τέλεα δύο ἐνίστι[α] π̣ρ . . δ[- - ὁσάκις κα παρεπιδαμῶν]-
τι παρ' ἁμῖν, καλέσαι δὲ α[ὐ̣]τ[οὺ]ς [- - - - - - - καὶ εἰς τὰν]
κοινὰν ἱστίαν· ἐλέσθαι δὲ καὶ θεαρ[οδόκον. ἁιρέθη]
[Ἐ]πιμενίδας Μνε[-]

Written in rasura; the squeeze is too faint at most points to control readings. 2–5 Wilhelm: 2 νους. . μμ. ργόρα , 3 ἕκτα̣, 5 τριτα πέμπτα[ι] and πρεσβείων Kern; at 5 init. the squeeze suggests TPỌTA, so perhaps π̣ρ̣ό̣{τα}πεμπτα. 7–8 Wilhelm: - - -]|σάντων Kern; τῶι δάμωι/τῆι ἁλίαι προαγορη]σάντων Holleaux. 10 Wilhelm: [- - - ἡκόντων? π.] Kern. 21–23 Holleaux: 21–22 - - - ὄν|τ]ας Kern. 25–26 Holleaux: τῶι δά|μ]ωι Kern. 26 βουλᾶι Rigsby, cf. 7: τ[ᾶι συγκλήτωι Kern; τᾶι συγκλή|τ]ωι and τ[ῶι δάμωι or τ[ᾶι ἁλίαι Holleaux. 31 [καὶ θεαροὶ Holleaux: [αὐτῶν Kern. 33 ἄνδρας Holleaux (or θεαρούς). 34: ΘΥΣΑΝ is clear on the squeeze; fin. Holleaux: [συμπομπεύσοντας τᾶι] Kern. 39 Holleaux (reading EΞME): ETME, ε⟨ἶ⟩με[ν Kern. 40 Holleaux: δ[ὲ] ὁ ἐνίστι[ος] Kern. 41: some magistrate, e.g., [τὸμ προστάταν (Holleaux).

The only extant decree of Syracuse, and passed three years after the city was sacked by M. Claudius Marcellus. Of the *theoroi*, Diotimus canvassed western Greece with the two sons of Diocles (and was not the chief of that mission); he is paired here with a different man, otherwise unknown.

Lines 4–7 seem to be a docket rather than part of the decree proper, for they summarize the act so far as to omit where the *theoroi* came from. The preliminaries reveal an elaborate attention to the *probouleuma* (as do the Sicilian decrees for Cos **48**, **49**). A committee of ten drafted the bill and put it before the assembly.

1: The eponym of Syracuse is reported to have been the priest of Zeus Olympius (Diod. 16.70.6).

25–26: See Dubois ad loc. for bibliography on the problem of constitutional forms. I have assumed a simple pair, council and assembly.

39: The Panhellenic games most in honor at Syracuse are those of its mother city, Corinth (cf. **92**.14).

121. Ap–

Found near **111**.
Kern, *I.Magnesia* 74.

παρὰ Ἀπ[- - - - - -]

A heading, from an Apamea or an Apollonia (Kern).

122. Unknown city

Inscribed to the right of the Gortynian decree *I.Magn.* 65a+75; the stone was found near **113**.

Kern, *I.Magnesia* 76.

καὶ δ̣ [- - - - - - - - - - - - - - - - - -]
Λά[μπετρ̣ος Πυθαγόρου, Κόνων Διο]-
νυσ[ίου, Φιλίσκος Πυθαγόρου? καὶ]
δια̣λ̣[εχθέντες - - - - - - - - - - - - - ἀ]-
κο[λούθως - - - - - - - - - - - - - - -]

Kern restored the names of the *theoroi* who canvassed the Peloponnesus.

123. Unknown city

Kern, *I.Magnesia* 77.

[- - - - - - - - - - -]ς . . . . ο[- - - - - - - - - -]
[- - - - - - - - - - -]ν̣λ̣[- - - - - - - - - - - - - - -]
[- - - - - - - - - - - -]τατη[- - - - - - - - - - - - -]
[- - - - - - - - - - -]αλωσι[- - - - - - - - - - - - -]
[- - - - - - - - - - χ]ρόνοις [- - - - - - - - - - - -]
vacat

124. Unknown city

Found near **130**.

Kern, *I.Magnesia* 78.

Cf. Boesch, Θεωρός 27 n. 2.

[- -]
[- - - - - - - - - - - -]ξ[- -]
[Φιλίσκος Πυθ]αγόρου Μαγνη[τ- -]
[- - - - - - - - -]ο . . . . . φη̣μ[- - - - - - - - - - - - - - - - - - - -]
[- - - - - - - - - - - - - Μάγ]νητ[ες? - - - - - - - - - - - - - - - -]
[- - - - - - - - - -] Ἀρισ[- -]
[- - - - - - - - -] Ἀριστομέν[- -]
[- - - - - - - - ἰσοπύ]θ[ι]ον μου[σικὸν - - - - - - - - - - - - - - - - -]
[- - - - - - - -] τὸν [ἀγῶ]να [- -]
[- - - - - - - - - - - - -]νο . εμ̣[- -]
[- - - - - - - - - - - - - - -]αυ . α[- - - - - - - - - - - - - - - - - - - -]
[- - - - - - - - - ἰσοπύ]θιον ὃν τί[θ]ησι [- - - - - - - - - - - - - - - -]
[- - - - - - - - - - - -]δε[- - - Ἀρτ]αμιτε[- - - - - - - - - - - - - - - -]
[τὰμ πόλιν] κ̣α̣ὶ̣ τὰγ χώραν τὰν Μαγνή[τ]ω̣ν [ἱ]ε̣[ρὰν καὶ ἄσυλον]
[- - - κ]αθὼς ἐπαγγέλλει Φιλίσκος ὁ ἀποστα̣λ̣[εὶς - - - - - - - -]
[- - -]α̣ι· δόμεν δὲ καὶ τοὺς ἱερομνάμονας [- - - - - - - - - - - - -]
[- - -] τῶι ἐπαγγέλλοντι Φιλίσκωι πρεσ[βεῖα - - - - - - - - - - -]
[- - -κ]οντα δραχμὰς Ἀλεξανδρ̣είας [. . . . . .]δ[- - - - - - - -]

[- - -] ἐπὶ ξένια εἰς τὸ πρυτανεῖον καλέσ[αι· εἶμεν δὲ καὶ θεαρο]-
[δόκ]ους Ζωΐλον καὶ Λέοντιν τοὺς Μα[ν]δ[ρο]δώρου.

vacat

26–27 Boesch: - - - τοὺς | θεωρ]οὺς Kern.

The city was Dorian. Philiscus toured the Peloponnesus—sometimes alone as here (23), sometimes with others. Boesch saw that the pair at 27 were not his subordinates but the foreign city's *theorodochoi*. The city's executive or fiscal magistrates were *hieromnemones* (23), a rarity in the Peloponnesus; we know the office at Roman Sparta, and they were eponymous at Hellenistic Lusi (*IG* V.2 393–394).

125. Antioch in Pisidia (?)

Kern, *I.Magnesia* 79+80.

Cf. Wilhelm, *Jahresh.* 4 (1901) Beibl. 30 (*Kl. Schr.* II.1 155); Holleaux, *Etudes* I 320–321; Robert, *RPhil* n.s. 53 (1927) 116–117, III.10 (1936) 123–124 (*Op. min. sel.* II 1071–1072, 1202–1203); Oguse, *BCH* 53 (1929) 129–140, 148–150.

a. [-]
[- - - - - - - ?ἐπειδὴ Μαγνήτων τῶν ἀπὸ Μαιάνδ]ρου ὁ δῆμος, [τοῦ θεοῦ]
[τοῦ ἐν Δελφοῖς χρήσαντος λώϊον εἶναι καὶ ἄμεινον τ]οῖς σεβομένοις [Ἄ]ρτε-μι[ν]
[Λευκοφρυηνὴν καὶ τὴν πόλιν καὶ τὴν χώραν ἱε]ρὰν καὶ ἄσυλον ε[ἶν]α[ι νομί]-
[ζουσιν, ἐψήφισται συντελεῖν - - - - - - - - - - τῆι] ἀρχηγέτιδι τῆς [πό]λε[ως]
[Ἀρτέμιδι Λευκοφρυηνῆι διὰ πέντε ἐτῶν θυσίαν κα]ὶ πανήγυριν κα[ὶ] ἐχεχειρί-
[αν καὶ ἀγῶνα στεφανίτην ἰσοπύθιον μουσικὸν κ]αὶ γυμ[ν]ικὸν καὶ ἱπ[πικόν,]
[δικαίαν ἀποδιδοὺς χάριν τῆι εὐεργέτιδι, καὶ] πρὸς ἡμᾶς πρεσβε[υτὰς Λυκο]-
[μήδην Λυκομήδου, Δημήτριον Δημο]φῶντος, Διονύσαρ[χον Ἀνα]-
[ξαγόρου ὅπως - - - - - - - - - - - - τὰ]ς γεγενημένας τοῖς [Μά]γν[η]-
[σιν παρὰ τοῦ θεοῦ μαντείας - - - ἀ]πολογίσωντα[ι] καὶ τὸν ἡμέτερον
[δῆμον - - - - - - παρακαλέσωσ]ι συναύξειν τὰς ἐ[ψ]ηφ[ι]σμέ[ν]ας
[τιμὰς τῆι θεῶι, καὶ ἐπακλουθοῦντα το]ῖς [ἀξιου]μένοις ἀκόλο[υ]θα πρᾶξαι
[ταῖς τοῦ θεοῦ μαντείαις καὶ χαριεῖσθ]αι τ[ῶι] δή[μωι] αὐτῶν, διελ[έ]γησ[αν δὲ κ]αὶ
[-] τῆς σ[υγ]γενείας καὶ περὶ τ[ῶ]ν παρα . επ .
[- - - - - - - - - - - - - - - - - - - τ]οῖ[ς] γεγραμμένοις φιλοτιμίας ο[ὐ]θὲν ἐλ[λεί]-
[ποντες - - - - πρὸς τὸν ἡμέτε]ρον δῆμον τάς τε τοῦ Ἀπό[λλων]ος μαν[τ]ε[ί]-
[ας - - - - - - - - - - - - -] τιμὰς συν[α]ύξοντα ἐμ π[α]ντὶ [και]ρῶι . . . . . .
[- - - - - - - - - - - - - -]ον Μαγν[ή]τ[ων] ἀποδέξασθα[ι . . . .]α . . . .
[- - - - - - - - - - - - - - - - πανη]γυρι[ν] καὶ [τὴ]ν ἐκεχειρίαν κα[ὶ τ]ὸν [ἀγῶ]να
[- - - - - - - - - - - - - - - - -] κατ[ὰ τ]ὴ[ν] σ[υγ]γέν[ε]ιαν τὴν ὑ[π]ά[ρχ]ουσα[ν]
[- - - - - - - - - - - - - - - -]τ . τ[- - - ἀγ]αθῆι τύχηι, δε[δόχθαι τῆι] βο[υ]λῆι
[ἀποδέχεσθαι μὲν τὰ ἀξιούμενα] ὑπὸ Μ[α]γ[νή]τ[ων] ἐπὶ σωτη[ρίαι τῶν τ]ε [Μ]αγνή-
[των -]π[- - -] πόλιν ὁ δ[ῆμος] τῶν Μαγ-

[νήτων - - - - - - - - - - - - - - ἀμφοτέρων τῶ]ν πόλεων . . . . καὶ τὴν [π]ό-
[λιν - - - - - - - - - - - - - - -]ε[- - - - τῆς Ἀ]ρ̣τέμιδος [τ]ῆς [Λευκ]ο[φ]ρυηνῆς
[- το]ὺς θε[ο]ὺς [εὐσ]εβ[- - - - - - - - - -]
[-]ς τὸν ε . . . . ορ . . . . οις
[-]ρι . . , κα[λ]έ̣[σ]αι τ̣[οὺ]ς δ[ὲ . . .]
[-]ιτ[- - - - - - - - - -]πο . . η . . .
[-]ος . . . . . . δ . . . . δίδο[σθαι] δὲ κ̣α̣[ὶ]
[- - - - - - - - - - - - - - - - - - -]ε̣ω[- - - - - - ἀ]μ[ε]ιβο̣ . . . . . . με̣-
[- - - - - - - - - - - - - - - - - -]ε[- - - - - - - - - -]η̣δο̣ . . . .
[- - - - - - - - - - - - -]χ . . . .να[- - - - - - - - -] τὸ̣[ν] δῆ̣[μον . . . . . .]
[- - - - - - - - - - - - - - - - - -]ε . . . κλ̣[- - - - - - - δεδό]χθαι . . . .
[- - - - - - - - - - - - - - - - - - Διον]υσ[ί]ο[ις ἀνακηρύσσε]σθαι τὸμ̣ . . . .
[- - - - - - - - - - - - - - - - - - -]νον τῆι . . λ[- - - - - - -]ται [το]ῖ̣ς θεω̣[ροῖς]
[Μαγν]ήτων [κ]αὶ ἐ[π]α̣γγ̣[έλλοντε]ς [-]
εἰ[ς] Μαγν[η]σίαν . . . . . ε̣[-]
[- -]ρ . αχ . . οτι[- - - - Ἀρτέ]μ̣ιδι [-]
[- - - -]ρι[- - - - - - - - - - -]ο̣[-]
[-]

b. [-]
ἀκο[υσ]αντ . . πρεσβευτῶν τοὺς ἀ[π]ο[λογισμοὺς? καὶ τὰ συνηντημένα Μάγνησιν]
ἀγαθὰ̣ ὑ[πὸ τ]οῦ θεοῦ ἥδεταί τε κ[α]ὶ προ[-]
το̣ὺ[ς ἱερεῖς καὶ] τὰς ἱερείας, καὶ εἰς τὸ [λ]ο[ι]π[ὸ]ν̣ [- - - - - - - - - - οὐδενὸς]
ἀ[πο]στήσ[ε]ται τ[ῶν] πρὸς . υ̣[. . . ?ὑ]πὸ τούτων [- - - - - - - - - - - - - - -]
[διατ]ε[ιν]όντ[ων?·] τ̣[ο]ὺς δ̣ὲ̣ [σ]τρατ]ηγοὺς [μετ]ὰ τ[ῶν γραμματέων ἐπι̣μέλειαν ποι]-
ή[σασ]θαι ὅπως ἀ[ντι]γραφῇ τὸ [ψή]φισμ[α] τοῦτ[ό τε] καὶ [τὸ παρὰ Μαγνήτων εἰς σ]τ̣ή-
λην μαρμαρ[ίνην] καὶ στ̣[αθῆι ἡ σ]τήλη{ι} τῆς [ἀγ]ορᾶς ἐν [τῶι ἐπιφανεστάτωι τόπ]ωι,
ἀξιῶσα[ι] δὲ κ[α]ὶ τὸν Μαγ[ν]ή̣των [δ]ῆμον ἀνα[γ]ράψαι κ̣α̣[ὶ παρ' αὐτοῖς τὸ ψήφισμα] τοῦ̣-
το ε[ἰ]ς στήλ[η]ν [μ]αρμαρ[ίν]ην καὶ στῆσαι ἐν τῶ[ι ἱ]ερῷ[ι τῆς Ἀρτέμιδος τῆς Λευκοφρυ]-
ην[ῆ]ς, ἵ̣ν̣[α] φαν[ε]ρὸ[ν ᾖ]ι πᾶσ[ιν] ὅ̣τι [ὁ δῆ]μος ἡμῶ[ν] εὐσεβῶς κ̣[αὶ φι]λ̣[οδ]ό-[ξως πρὸς τοὺς]
θ[εοὺ]ς ἔ[χων δ]ιατ[ηρ]εῖ τ̣ή̣[ν τε] συγγ[έ]νειαν καὶ τὴν οἰκ[ε]ι[ό]τητα [κα]ὶ φ[ιλίαν τὴν ὑ]πάρχου-
σ[αν] τ[ῆ]ι πόλει [τῶν] Ἀντ[ιοχ]έων [π]ρὸς [τὴ]ν πόλιν τὴν [Μ]αγνήτω[ν·] τ̣ο̣[ὺ]ς δὲ ἱερεῖ]ς καὶ τὰς
ἱ̣ε̣ρε[ί]ας ἀνο[ῖ]ξ̣α̣ι̣ τοὺς να[οὺ]ς κ̣α̣ὶ ε̣ὔ̣ξασθαι καὶ Μάγν[ησιν . . . .]σχηνται [- - -]
εἰς τὸ[ν ἀε]ὶ [χρόνον γίνε]σθ[α]ι κοιν[ῆ]ι πάντα τὰ ἀγαθ[ὰ] Ἀ[ντιοχεῦ]σ̣ίν τε καὶ Μάγνη-

σιν, ἀφ[ιέ]ναι δὲ [κ]αὶ [τ]οὺς [π]αῖδα[ς κ]α[ὶ] τ⟨ὰ⟩ς παῖδας ἐκ τῶ[ν] μ[α]θ[ημάτων ἐ]ν τῆιδε τῆι
ἡμέ[ρ]αι, ποιεῖν δὲ [κ]αὶ [τ]ὸ αὐτὸ τοῦτ[ο ε]ἰς τ[ὸ λοι]π̣όν, ὅτα[ν ὑποδεχώμεθα] παρὰ Μαγνήτ[ω]ν
τ[ὸ]ν θεωρὸ[ν] τὸν α[ὐτῶν]· τοὺς [δὲ] στρα[τηγ]οὺς καὶ βουλ[ευτὰς μετά] τε τῶν γρα⟨μ⟩μα-
τέων [κ]αὶ τοῦ ἐξε̣[τα]στ̣[οῦ] κ̣α̣τὰ μ̣ῆ[να] θ̣ύσασ[θ]αι τοῖς Θε[σ]μ[οφό]ρ̣οις καὶ Ἀρτέμι-
δι Σωτείρ[αι κ]αὶ Ἀρτέμ[ιδι Λε]υκ[οφ]ρ[υην]ῆι· καλέ[σ]αι δὲ [καὶ εἰς τὴν κοι]ν[ὴν] ἑστίαν τοὺς
π[αρ]ὰ Μαγν[ήτ]ων [θεωρο]ύ[ς], ὅπ[ως π]ρῶτ[οι] μετάσ[χωσι θυσίας μετὰ] τούτων, τοὺς
δ[ὲ] τ̣[α]μίας εἰ[ς τὴν θ]υσίαν [τὰ μὲ]ν ἱ̣ε̣ρ̣εῖα χορηγ[ῆ]σ[αι, ξένια δὲ δοῦναι ὅσα τοῖς ἄλλοις?]
πρεσβ[ευτ]αῖς [δίδοται] δραχμ[ὰς] τ[ρι]άκ[ον]τα. ἀπεδε[ίχθη θεωροδόκ]ος Φ[ι]λ[ί]νος
Δ[η]μ̣έ[ου].

a: 2–6, 8 init. Oguse doubtfully; 4 καὶ τὴν πόλιν, 7 στεφανίτην, 8–9, 13 καὶ ἐπακολουθοῦντα, 14, 23 init. Robert. b: 2 init. Robert: ὑπ]|ακο[υσ]αντ.. ⟨τῶν⟩ π. Kern; ἀ[π]ο[λογισμοὺς? Holleaux; fin. Robert: - - - πάντα τὰ] Kern. 5 τ[ῶν] Holleaux: τ[οῦ] Kern. 6 init. Holleaux. 7 fin. Robert: καὶ [ἀναγραφῆι εἰς Holleaux. 9 παρ' αὐτοῖς Wilhelm, Holleaux: [- - - ψήφισμα καὶ] Kern. 16: ΤΟΥΣ. 17 ὑποδεχώμεθα Holleaux. 21 Holleaux: τῶν θυσιῶν] τούτων Kern. 22 [τὰ μὲ]ν ἱ̣[ε]ρ̣εῖα Holleaux, which the squeeze confirms: . . . . νη . ρ̣εια Kern. 22–23 Holleaux: - - - δοῦναι τοῖς] | π. [ξένια] δ. Kern.

The text is in two columns, with only one line lost at the top of b; Kern envisioned that his 80 might continue 79 rather than begin below 79, and Robert urged that the two columns are in fact one decree. This seems quite probable, because there can have been little space below a to start a new decree that completes its grants before turning (by the top of b) to the attendant celebrations.

The *theoroi* are the same as in **126**, inscribed below b. Their leader might be the same Lycomedes who went to Attalus, but need not be (cf. on **68**.3). Both cities were named Antioch; Kern urged Pisidian Antioch (cf. Robert, *Laodicée* 330). Our city gave special honor to the Thesmophoroi and Artemis Savior (b.19–20)—widespread usages. Robert's restoration of a.23 makes this a decree of the council alone (cf. **25**).

What is most striking in this decree is its effusive honors for Magnesia, including public prayers and a public holiday on the occasion of the future visits of the *theoroi* (b.12ff.). That may point to Antioch in Pisidia, which Magnesia had helped colonize (Strab. 12.8.14 [577]); in what survives, the Leucophryeneia are accepted, but *asylia* is not mentioned, which is consistent with the better-preserved response of the colony Antioch in Persis. Both were very long decrees, as might befit colonists for a mother city.

126. Antioch in ?

Inscribed below the second column of **125**.
Kern, *I.Magnesia* 81.

ἐ̣[π]ὶ στρα̣[τ]η̣γ[οῦ - - - - -] Λ[υκ]ομή̣δη̣ς Λυκομ[ή]δου τοῦ [. . . .]ου ἀρχιθ[έ]ωρος
κ̣[αὶ Δ]η̣μ̣ήτρι[ο]ς Δ[ημοφῶ]ν̣τ[ο]ς, Δ[ιο]ν̣ύσα̣ρχο[ς] Ἀ[ν]αξ[α]γόρου θεωροὶ οἱ [π]αρὰ Μαγνή-
[τ]ω[ν] τῷ[ν ἀπὸ Μαιάν]δρ[ου] ἐπα[γγέλλ]ουσιν τή[ν] τε θυσίαν καὶ τὴν ἐ[κ]ε-[χει]ρίαν
καὶ [τοὺς ἀγῶνας ἅτιν]α̣ συ[ν]τε[λοῦ]σι[ν] Μ̣άγ[νη]τες Ἀρ[τέμ]ιδι τᾶι Λ[ε]υ-κοφρυηνῆι
κ[ατὰ πεντετηρίδα, ἀγα]θῆι [τύ]χηι, δεδόχθ[αι τῆι] βου[λῆι] καὶ τῶι δήμωι δέχεσθαι
[- - - - - - - - - - - -]ενε . . . υμ . δι[- - - - - - - -]ωνωι . α[. . . . θ]εωρο[ὺς]
[- - - - - - - - - - - - - - Μαγν]ήτω[ν - - - - - - - -]κω . μ̣[ηνὸς] Σμισ[ιῶ]νος
[- - - - - - - - - - - - - - -] τ̣έκνων καὶ γ[υναικῶ]ν̣ [- - - - - - - -]ους [- - -]
[- - - - - - - - - - -] τ[ῶ]ν πόλεων τ̣οὺς δ . ε[- - - - -]αι τοῖς Θ[εσμοφ]ό[ροις?]
[- - - - - - - - -]σαι . . ιας· τὸν δὲ ἀρ[χ]ι[θέωρ]ον [καὶ] τοὺς θ[εω]ροὺς [- - -]
[- - - - - - - -]ν̣τ[. ἑκατ]ὸν̣ δρ[αχ]μ̣ῶ[ν . .]ς . . . θεμ . . . εν . . ν̣ ετ̣ωι . η[- - -]
[- - - - - - -]σε[- - -]ο[- - -] ὁ δ[ῆμ]ος ὁ Ἀντιο[χέω]ν ἀποσ[- - - - - - - -]
[- - - - - - -]δικ̣[-]

Inscribed immediately after **125**, this decree was obtained by the same *theoroi*. The decree was evidently short, and in what survives there is evidence of games but not *asylia*. The city dated its acts by a *strategos*. The month Smision (7) is attested otherwise only at Magnesia itself, so this passage may state a synchronism (for the sending of future Magnesian *theoroi*?) rather than a month of the author.

127. Unknown city

Found near **110–111**; inscribed by a different hand from that of the rest of the archive.
Kern, *I.Magnesia* 82.
Photograph: Kern pl. v (lines 7–16).

[-]
[. .] θ̣[υσ]ίαν καὶ [- - - καὶ τὴν παν]ήγυ̣ρ̣ιν
[καὶ τὴ]ν ἐ̣[κ]εχειρίαν [καὶ τὸν ἀγῶνα στεφ]ανίτ[ην]
[ἰ]σ̣οπύθ[ι]ον μουσικ[ὸν καὶ γ]υμνικὸν κ[α]ὶ ἱ[π]-
[πικ]ὸν τὸν συντελο[ύμεν]ον{ενο̣ν̣} Ἀρτέμιδι
[Λε]υκοφρυηνῆ̣[ι] δι[ὰ πεντ]ε̣τ̣ηρίδ[ος . . . .] ὃν
[ἐπ]αγγέλλουσιν οἱ [παρ]ό[ν]τες πα[ρὰ] τοῦ [δ]ή-
[μο]υ τοῦ Μαγν̣ή[των θε]ω̣ρ̣οὶ Φ̣[ι]λ[ή]νωρ Ζηνο-
[δό]του, Πρύτανι[ς Πυρωνίδ]ου· ⟨δοῦ⟩[ναι δ]ὲ καὶ τοῖς

[θεω]ροῖς τὸν [τ]αμία[ν τ]ῆς πόλ[εω]ς εἰς ἀπαρ-
[χ]ὴ[ν] τῆι Ἀρ[τέ]μι[δι τῆι] Λευκοφρυηνῆι δρα-
[χμὰ]ς Ἀλε[ξα]νδ[ρείας] εἴκοσι, ἀποσταλῆ-
[ν]αι δὲ αὐτ[οῖ]ς̣ καὶ [ξέν]ια, [κα]λέσαι δὲ αὐ-
[τ]οὺς ἐπὶ τ[ὸν δ]όρπ[ον τὸ]ν ἀποδεδειγμένον
[ὑ]π̣ὸ τοῦ [δ]ήμου· τοὺς [δ]ὲ στρατηγοὺς ἐπιμε-
[λ]ηθῆνα[ι τῆ]ς παραπο̣μπῆς α[ὐ]τῶν.

Prytanis was one of the *theoroi* to the Artists at Teos (**103**), a relatively short trip, so that he was perhaps available at once for another mission. As the fragment begins the city is accepting the games; mention of inviolability does not survive. The invitation to "dinner" (δόρπον) is the most individual item (14); as occasionally elsewhere, an escort is provided for the departing *theoroi* (16).

128. Attalid city

Inscribed to the right of **127**, but in the script of the majority of the archive.
Kern, *I.Magnesia* 83.
Photograph: Kern pl. v (lines 5–14).
Cf. Holleaux, *Etudes* I 321–322.

. . . . . . υ[- - - - - - - - - - - - - - - - πρὸς ἡ]-
μᾶς [πεμ]φθέν[τες - - - - - - - - - - - - - - - - -]
κομι[ζ]ομ[-]
Ἄρ[τε]μ̣ι̣ν Λ[ευκο]φ[ρυηνὴ̣ν - - - - - - - - - -]
εἰς σελήνην [- - - - - - - - - - - - - - - - - - -]
με̣τ̣έχειν ἡμ[ᾶς - - - - - - - - - - - - - - - - - -]
δεδόχθαι τῆι βο[υλῆι καὶ τῶι δήμωι ἀποδε]-
δέχθαι τὴν ἐπ̣[αγγελίαν τῆς θυσίας ἐπὶ σωτηρί]-
αι τ⟨οῦ⟩ βασιλέως Ε̣ὐ̣μ̣[ένους καὶ τῆς μητρὸς αὐ]-
τοῦ βασιλίσσης̣ Ἀ̣π̣ο̣[λλωνίδος καὶ τῶν ἀδελ]-
φῶν καὶ τοῦ δήμο[υ τοῦ - - - - - - - - καὶ τοῦ]
δήμου τοῦ Μαγνήτ[ων· - - - - - - - - - - ἀπαρ]-
χὴν τῆι θεᾶι Ἀρ[τέμιδι - - - - - - - - - - καὶ ξέ]-
νια ἑκατέρω[ι τῶν θεωρῶν, καλέσαι δὲ αὐ]-
τοὺς καὶ εἰς τὸ [- - - - - - τοὺς δὲ στρατη]-
γοὺς προνοιῆσαι [τῆς παραπομπῆς αὐτῶν?]
εἰς Μαγνησία[ν - - - - - - -]

8 Holleaux (or ἐπ[ηγγελμένην θυσίαν). 9 Holleaux: ΤΗΣ lapis. 9–10 Holleaux from the photograph: γυναικὸς αὐ]τοῦ βασιλίσση[ς Στρατονίκης Kern. 16 Rigsby, from **127**.16.

Although this decree appears to have been inscribed by the same mason who did the rest of the archive, Kern assigned it to the reign of Eumenes (197–159 B.C.), noting its placement to the right of **127**; and if Holleaux was right in seeing the queen mother rather than Stratonice, the date is before Eumenes married Stratonice.

In 208 Attalus had promised that his subjects would respond favorably (**68**); this decree, like those that certainly are under Eumenes, may derive from a city acquired by the Attalid dynasty only in 188 B.C. But in general I do not see why the Magnesians would have failed to canvass these cities in 208 (especially their neighbor Tralles), no matter who the cities' ruler had been at that time. Two ambassadors made up this team (14). Line 6 shows that the games were accepted; no trace survives about *asylia*.

5: "by the moon"; the season of the Leucophryeneia is here defined in terms of the local calendar, as "in the second month" at the Attalid city of **130**.9.

8–10: It seems the formula was like that found in the decrees of Attalid cities that certainly are later than 208 B.C. (**130**.16, **131**.15), hence Holleaux's emendation of ΤΗΣ.

129. Tralles

Inscribed by a different mason, who also carved **130** and **131**.

Kern, *I.Magnesia* 85 [Poljakov, *I.Tralleis* 21].

Photograph: Kern pl. v (lines 1–10).

Cf. Wilhelm, *Jahresh.* 4 (1901) Beibl. 30 (*Kl. Schr.* II.1 155); Holleaux, *Etudes* I 322–323, 330; De Decker, *RPhil* n.s. 29 (1905) 164–166 (collation); Robert, *RPhil* III.3 (1929) 122 n. 1 (*Op. min. sel.* II 1088).

παρ[ὰ Τ]ραλλιανῶν

[ἔδοξε τῶι δήμωι· στρατηγῶν γν]ώμη Διοκλείους, Ποσιδέου, Ἀριστέου, Οὐλιάδου, Π̣[- - -]

[- - -]ρίνου [γ]ραμμ[α]τέω[ς] δή[μ]ου· ἐπειδὴ Μάγ̣νητε[ς] φίλοι καὶ ἀστυ[γείτονες ὄντες τοῦ δήμου τοῦ]

[Τραλλιανῶν π]ολλὰς ἀποδε[ί]ξεις ἐμ πᾶσι τοῖς καιροῖς σπουδῆς καὶ ἐκτενεία[ς ἐποίησαν, καὶ ἐν τῶι παρόντι]

[ἀκολούθως τῆ]ι τοῦ Πυθίου Ἀπόλλωνος μαντείαι κατὰ πενταετηρίδα τῆ ἀρχηγέτ[ιδι τῆς πόλεως Ἀρτέμιδι]

[Λευκοφρυη]νῆι θυσίαν τε καὶ πανήγυριν καὶ ἀγῶνα στεφανίτην ἰσοπύθιον γυμν[ικὸν καὶ ἱππικὸν καὶ μουσικὸν]

[πε]ποι[ήκ]ασιν καὶ πρὸς ἡμᾶς ψήφισμά τε καὶ πρεσβευτὴν Νικόδημ[ο]ν Μανδροκλ[είους πέμψαντες, ἔτι δὲ Νικό]-

[δη]μόν [τ]ε Μανδροκλείους νεώτερον καὶ Ἰσαγόραν Διαγόρου τοῦ Διαγόρου τοὺς παραγ[ενομένους θεωροὺς σὺν αὐτῶι, ἀξιοῦ]-

[σι σ]υναύξειν τὰς ἐψηφισμένας τῆι θεᾶι τι[μὰς] ἀκολούθως τῶι τοῦ θεοῦ χρησμῶι, καὶ ο[ἱ θεωροὶ ἐπ]-

[ελ]θόντες ἐπὶ τὸν δῆμον διελέγησαν ἀ̣ξίως τῆς τε Ἀρτέμιδος τῆς Λευκοφρυηνῆς καὶ τοῦ αὐτῶν καὶ [τοῦ ἡ]-

[μ]ετέρου δήμου πᾶσαν σπουδὴν καὶ φιλοτιμίαν εἰσενεγκάμενοι καὶ τὴν ἀναστροφὴν ποι[ησάμενοι μετὰ πάσης)]

[εὐκο]σμίας· ὅπ[ω]ς οὖν κα̣ὶ ἡ τοῦ [δή]μου πρός τε τ[ὴ]ν θεὰν ὁσιότης τε καὶ σπουδὴ ἔγδηλ[ος γένηται καὶ ἡ πρὸς]
[Μ]άγνητας ὑπάρχουσα ἐκ παλ[αι]ῶν χρόνων εὔνοιά τε καὶ φιλία πολλαπλασιόνως [πᾶσι φαίνηται, ἀκολού]-
θως τῆι ἀμφοτέρων τῶν πόλε[ων φιλοτι]μίαι >—< τύχηι ἀγαθῆι δεδόχθαι ἐπηνῆσθαί τε τὸ[ν δῆμον τὸν Μαγνήτων]
[ἐ]πὶ τῆι καλοκἀγαθίαι καὶ τῆι [πρὸς] τ̣ὴν Ἄρτεμιν τὴν Λευκοφρυηνὴν καὶ τοὺς ἄλλο[υς θεοὺς εὐσεβείαι]
τε καὶ σπουδῆι καὶ τῆι πρὸς τὴν ἡμετέραν πόλιν καὶ τοὺς Ἕλληνας εὐνοίαι καὶ ἀ[ποδέξασθαι τήν τε]
θυσίαν καὶ τὴν πανήγυριν καὶ τοὺς ἀγῶνας ἰσοπυθίους καθότι ἐπηγγέλκασιν [οἱ θεωροὶ καὶ]
τὴν ἀσυλίαν καὶ τὴν καθιέρωσιν τῆς πόλεως καὶ τῆς χώ[ρ]ας αὐτῶν κατὰ τὴν [τοῦ θεοῦ μαντείαν],
[ὑπ]άρχειν δὲ τοῖς νικῶσιν τῶν πολιτῶν ἆθλά τε καὶ σιτηρέσια καὶ τἄλλα τίμια ὅ[σαπερ καὶ τοῖς νικῶσι]
τοὺς ἰσοπυθίους ἀγῶνας ὑπάρχει· ἐπηνῆσθαι δὲ καὶ Νικόδημον καὶ Ἰσαγόρα[ν καὶ Νικόδημον τοὺς ἥκοντας]
πα[ρ'] αὐτῶν ἄνδρας ἐπί τε τῆι καλοκἀγαθ[ί]αι καὶ τῆι πρὸς τὴν πατρίδα σπουδῆι κα[ὶ δοθῆναι ἐκ τῶν πόρων]
ὑπὸ τῶν ταμιῶν εἰς ἀπαρχὴν τῆι θεᾶι δραχμὰς ἑκατόν, πεμφθῆναι δὲ τοῖς θεωροῖς κα[ὶ ξένια τὰ ἐκ τῶν νόμων,]
[κληθ]ῆναι δὲ αὐτοὺς καὶ ἐπὶ τὴν κοινὴν ἑστίαν τοῦ δήμου· κατ̣ασκευασθῆναι δὲ καὶ φ[ιάλην ἀπὸ δραχμῶν]
[- - - - -]ạκοσίων ἣγ καὶ ἀναθέτωσαν οἱ ἀποσταλησόμενοι ὑπὸ τ[ῆ]ς πόλεως θεωροὶ [εἰς τὸ ἱερὸν τῆς Ἀρ]-
[τέμιδος τῆς Λευκοφρυηνῆ]ς ἐπιγράψαντες ὅτι ὁ δῆμος ὁ Τραλλιανῶν Ἀρτέμιδι Λευκοφρυ[ηνῆι ἀνέθηκεν]
[- - - - - - - - - - - - - - - - - ἡ εἰ]ς τὴν θεὰν εὐσέ[βε]ια καὶ ἡ πρὸς Μάγνητας εὔ[νοια - - -]
[- - - - - - - - - - δοῦναι τοῖς] θεωρ[οῖ]ς ἀπαρχὴν δραχμὰ[ς - - - - - - - - - -]

Text of De Decker (somewhat longer line than Kern's). 2 punctuation Robert: Kern assumed patronymics. 2–3 Robert: ὑπάρχοντες | τῆς πόλεως Kern. 3: Χα?]ρίνου Merkelbach ap. Poljakov. 4–5: πεποίηνται | καὶ νῦν ἐπὶ τῆ]ι Kern, πεπ. καὶ νῦν ἀ|κολουθοῦντες τῆ]ι Holleaux. 5 fin. αὐτῶν Ἀρτ.] Kern. 7 πέμψαντες, 9 ο[ἱ θεωροὶ Holleaux: ο[ὗτοι Kern. 13: ἐ[παύξηται ἀ. Holleaux. 16: καὶ [φιλοτιμίαι, δεδέχθαι τε τὴν] Kern. 17 Holleaux: [τὴν ἐκεχειρίαν καὶ] Kern, [οἱ θ., εἶναι δὲ] De Decker. 19: ο[ἷα καὶ εἰς] Kern. 20 Kern: Ἰσαγόραν [τ]οὺ[ς παραγεγενημένους] De Decker (the mason omitting the third name). 24–25 Holleaux. 27 init. Merkelbach.

In 208 B.C. Tralles would still have been called "Seleuceia"; it reverted to its original name after the defeat of Antiochus III in 190 and the end of Seleucid power in western Anatolia. This confirms the implication of the common hand that wrote **131** in the time of Attalus II, that the Trallian decree was obtained later than the rest of the archive.

These ambassadors do not recur in Magnesian inscriptions; but Diagoras son of Isagoras, evidently the ambassador's son, moved the decree for a new statue of Artemis in the second half of the second century B.C. (*I.Magn.* 100).

The games but not inviolability are mentioned in the preliminaries (although the oracle is); but both are granted in the decree proper. The letter of Attalus I (**68**) does not include *asylia.*

1: The proposal is by the college of executive magistrates; *strategoi* were frequent in Attalid cities, often numbering five, as at Pergamum (cf. **131**; see Allen, *Attalid Kingdom* 104–109).

3: Magnesia and Tralles shared a border, Tralles being the next city up the Maeander Valley.

18: For the order "inviolable and sacred" see p. 33.

20: In 208 B.C. there would have been few "isopythian" games that could have been invoked; the comfortable analogy used here reflects the later date, for Panhellenic festivals proliferated in the late third and early second centuries.

23ff.: Such a specification of a dedicatory object to be presented to Artemis by the first Trallian *theoroi* is unique in the *asylia* inscriptions.

130. Attalid city

Same mason as **129** and **131**.

Kern, *I.Magnesia* 86.

Cf. Holleaux, *Etudes* I 323; Wilhelm, *Jahresh.* 4 (1901) Beibl. 30 (*Kl. Schr.* II.1 155); Klaffenbach, *Asylieurkunden aus Kos* p. 17; Robert, *BCH* 59 (1935) 494 n. 7 (*Op. min. sel.* I 307).

[- -]
[- -]
[. . . . . ἔδοξε τῶι δή]μωι̣ [- -]
4 [- - - - - - - - - ψη]φίσματι προφερ̣[- -]
[- - - -] καὶ θεωροὺς τόν τε προγ̣[εγρα]μμένο[ν .]α[- - - - - - - - - - - -]
[ἐ]πὶ τὴν ἐκκλησίαν τήν τε τῆ[ς θε]ᾶς ἐπιφ[άνειαν ἐνεφάνιζον καὶ τὰς τῶν προγόνων εἰς τοὺς Ἕλλη]-
ν̣ας εὐεργεσίας ἀπε̣[λογίσα]ν̣τ̣ο κα̣[ὶ π]αρεκάλουν ἡμᾶς ἀποδέ[χεσθαι τ]ὴν [π]α̣[νήγυριν καὶ τὴν θυ]-
8 σίαν καὶ τὸν ἀγῶνα στεφανίτην ἰσοπύθιον μ̣ο̣υσικὸν γυμνικ[ὸν] ἱππικὸν ὃν τι[θ]έασ̣ι̣ [- - -]
εἰς σελήνην δ̣ε̣υτέρα̣ν̣ [τοῖς ἀ]φικνουμένοις ἐπ' ἀσ[φ]αλείαι τε καὶ ἀσυ[λίαι -]
κατευξάμ[εν]οι τοῖς θ[εοῖ]ς̣ καὶ τἆλλα τὰ προγεγραμμέ[να - - - - - - - - - -]
[ὁ δὲ] δ[ῆ]μ̣ος [ποιούμενος] π̣ρόνοιαν ἕνεκεν τοῦ συνα̣[ύξειν τὰς συντελ]ουμένα[ς] τ̣ιμὰς ὑπὸ τῆ[ς πόλεως]
12 [τῆι θεᾶι, το]ὺς δὲ Μάγνητας μὲν μάλιστα δὲ [- - -]ς ἔ[χ]ων ἐκτενῆ{ι} καὶ πρό[θυμο]ν ἑα[υ]-
[τὸν πρὸς τ]ὰ π[α]ρα[καλούμ]ενα παρέχεται, ἀ[γαθῆι τύχηι - - -]ητ[. . . . ἐ]παγγ[έλ]-

λουσι, ἐπηνῆσθ[αι Μά]γ[ν]ητας ἐπί τε τῆ[ι πρὸς τοὺς θεοὺς εὐσεβείαι κα]ὶ πρὸς τὸν δῆμον ἡμ[ῶν] ε[ὐνοί]-
[αι κ]αὶ [εὐθέως ἐ]λέ[σθαι θεω]ρ̣οὺς οἵτινες ἀφικόμ[ενοι τ]ήν τε θυσίαν ἐπιτελέσωσιν καὶ τὰ ἄλλα [τ]ὰ νομιζ[ό]-
[με]να [ἐπὶ σωτηρίαι τοῦ τε] βασιλέως Εὐμένου Σωτῆρος καὶ Εὐεργέτου καὶ βασιλίσσης Στρατονίκ[ης καὶ]
[τῶ]ν [ἀδελφῶν τοῦ] β[ασι]λέως καὶ τῶν φίλων καὶ τῶν δυνάμεων [κ]αὶ [τῶ]ν [σ]υμμάχ[ω]ν [καὶ τοῦ] δήμ[ου]
[ἡμῶν κ]αὶ τοῦ Μ[αγ]νή[τω]ν· δοῦναι δὲ καὶ τοῖς παραγεγον[όσιν - - - - - - -]
[. . . . . ἀποσταλῆν]αι δὲ αὐτοῖς καὶ ξένια τὰ ἐκ τοῦ [νόμου - - - - - - - - -]
[- - - - - -]αι[- - - - - - - -] ἐκτενῶς καὶ προ[θύμως - - - - - - - - - - - - - - -]
[-]ι δὲ τὰ π[- - - - - - - - - - -]
[- εἶν]αι δὲ αὐ[τοῖς - - - - - - - - -]
[-]
[-]
[-]νκ[- - - -]
[-]

6 Wilhelm: [- - - τὰς πρὸς τοὺς Ἕ. Kern. 7 Wilhelm: ἀπ̣ε[δείξα]ν̣τ̣ο Kern. 9 Klaffenbach: δευτέραι Kern. 15 εὐθέως Holleaux. 17 [καὶ τοῦ] δήμου Robert: [τοῦ] Kern.

Inscribed by the same mason as the other two late decrees of Attalid cities, this dates explicitly under Eumenes II Soter (197–159). Inviolability is not mentioned—but the epiphany is (6), and in fact little of the text survives; **129** omitted *asylia* in the preliminaries but recognized it in the decree proper, which here is mostly lost.

The roster of the royal house is quite full, like that of **131** under Attalus II (cf. **128**), more than in **129**. In line 9, the phrase for "for security and inviolability" seems to apply to "those who come" to the games (cf. **9**.10) rather than to territorial inviolability. In 9, the date of the Magnesians' festival appears to be reckoned by the moon.

131. Attalid city

Same mason as **129** and **130**.
Kern, *I.Magnesia* 87 [Dittenberger, *OGIS* 319].

[ἔδοξε τῶι δήμωι· στρα]τ̣ηγῶν γνώμη Λυκόφρονος τοῦ Ἀρτεμιδ̣[ώρου . . . .]
[- - - - - - -]ι̣μου, Βοήθου τοῦ Σίμωνος, Γα̣λ̣έστου τοῦ Διονυσίο[υ . . . . .]
[. . . . . . προέ]δρου καὶ γραμματέως τοῦ δήμου Πόλ[λι]δος τοῦ Ἀπολλοφά-
νου· ἐπειδὴ [Μ]άγν[ητ]ες οἱ ἐπ[ὶ Μ]αιάνδρου εὐνόως διακείμενοι τῶι δήμωι καὶ ὄν-
τες οἰκεῖοι καὶ φίλοι πρότερόν τε φιλανθρώπως προσεφέροντο τῆι πόλει καὶ νῦν
ἀφεστάλκασ[ι]ν ψήφισμά τε καὶ πρεσβευτὰς καὶ θεωροὺς Λεοντίσκον καὶ Ἀ-πολλώνιον, παρακαλοῦντες προσδέξασθαι τ[ή]ν τε θυσίαν καὶ πανήγυριν
καὶ ἐκεχειρ[ίαν κα]ὶ ἀγῶνα στεφανίτην ἰσοπύ[θι]ον μουσικόν τε καὶ γυμνικὸν

καὶ ἱππικὸ[ν] ὃν συντελοῦσιν τῆι ἀρχηγέτιδι τ̣[ῆς] π[όλ]εως Ἀρτέμιδι Λευκοφρυ-
ηνῆι διὰ πέντε [ἐτῶ]ν κατὰ τὰς τοῦ θεοῦ τοῦ ἐν Δελφοῖς μαντείας, καὶ οἱ πρεσβευ-
ταὶ καὶ [θεωρ]ο̣ὶ ἐλθόντες ἐπὶ τὴν ἐκκλησ[ί]αν διελέγησαν ἀκολούθως
τοῖς ἐν [τῶι ψη]φίσματι καταχεχωρισμένοις, σπουδῆς καὶ φιλοτιμίας [οὐδ]ὲν
ἐλλείποντε[ς], καὶ τ̣ὴν καταγγ[ε]λίαν ἐποιήσαντο πρεπόντως, τύχηι ἀγαθῆι
δεδόχθαι ἀποκρίνασθαι Μάγνησιν ὅτι ἀποδέ[χε]ται ὁ δῆμος τὰ ἐπηγγελμέ-
να ἐπὶ σωτηρ[ί]α[ι] τοῦ τε βασιλέως Ἀττάλου Φιλαδέλφου καὶ Ἀθηναίου τοῦ
ἀδελφοῦ το[ῦ β]ασιλέως καὶ βασιλίσσης Στρατονίκης καὶ Ἀττάλου τοῦ υἱοῦ
τοῦ βασιλ[έω]ς Εὐμένου καὶ τοῦ ἡμετέρου δήμου καὶ τοῦ Μαγνήτων, πέμπε[ιν]
[δ]ὲ καὶ τὸν δῆμο[ν] καθ' ἑκάστην πενταετηρίδα θεωροὺς τοὺς συντελέσ[οντ]ας
[τὴν θυσίαν καὶ τὰ] ἄ̣λλα τὰ νομιζόμενα πάντα, διδόναι δὲ καὶ τοῖ[ς ἐπ]αν-
[γ]έλλουσι τὰ [Λευκοφρυ]ηνὰ εἰς ἀπαρχὴν τῆι θεῶι δραχμὰς ἑ[κ]ατόν, ἑλέσθαι
δὲ καὶ θ̣ε̣ω̣ρ̣ο̣δ̣όκο[ν] τ̣ούτοις ⟨τοῖς⟩ [π]αραγινομένοις [θεω]ροῖς [πα]ρὰ Μαγνήτων,
ὑπάρχ[ειν δὲ τοῖς νικ]ῶσιν τ[ὰ] Λευκοφρυ[ηνὰ] ὅσ[α] καὶ [το]ῖς [τὰ] Πύθια νι-
κήσασι· [ἐπηνῆ]σθαι δὲ καὶ τοὺς ἀπεσταλμένους [ὑπ' αὐ]τῶν πρεσβευ-
τὰς κα[ὶ θεω]ρ[οὺς ἐπὶ τῆι] ἐπιδη[μ]ίαι ἧι ἐποι[ήσ]α[ν]το ἐν τῆι πόλ[ε]ι [μ]ετὰ πά-
σης ε̣[ὐκο]σ̣μ̣ία[ς καὶ ἐπι]στροφῆ[ι] τ̣οῖς β̣α̣σιλεῦσι, [τῆι] τε περὶ το[ῦ]
δήμου καὶ [τοῦ ἡμετέρο]υ καὶ [τ]ο̣[ῦ τῶν Μαγνήτων ἐπιμελείαι· δοῦναι δὲ]
ἑκατὸν [δρ]α[χμὰς ἀργυρί]ου [ἐκ το]ῦ δη[μοσίου - - -]εου

25–27 Dittenberger.

The city was ruled by Attalus II (159–138). Its executive magistrates were five *strategoi*, as was common in the Attalid kingdom (see on **129**.1). The personal names are mostly too widespread to point to a region for this city. For the rare "Galestes," Dittenberger cited an Alexandrian (*Pros. Ptol.* VI 14904); cf. the Galestes prominent at Stratoniceia in the first century A.D. (*I.Straton.* I p. 141); at Pergamum, *AM* 27 (1902) 122. There is no mention of *asylia*; but, as in **129**, the oracle is mentioned, here for the games but not inviolability.

The Magnesian *theoroi* are not otherwise known. Dittenberger and others have suggested that the decree was not obtained in 208 because the city had then not yet been founded; but that theory cannot account for the lateness of Tralles' decree. Kern (ad *I.Magn.* 83) considered that the Magnesians originally sent *theoroi* to Attalus I alone and relied upon his letters to obtain the civic recognitions, but then sent out *theoroi* to cities after the new king came to power.

Teos

The patron god of the Teans, their *archegetes*, was Dionysus.[1] Local legend held that the god was born here, and a miraculous fountain of wine was shown in evidence; Dionysiac motifs dominate the coins of Teos from the fourth century B.C. on.[2] Doubtless the prominence of the cult had a part in attracting the Ionian-Hellespontine Artists of Dionysus to choose Teos as their residence in the third century.[3] The god's epithet at Teos, about which the inviolability texts are silent, is uncertain;[4] the frequency of the cithara on Tean coins suggests that he was especially honored in his musical aspect, and certainly music was the focus of the Artists.[5] His temple was in the midst of the city, 400 meters south of the acropolis and theater.[6] For the new building the Teans recruited Hermogenes, the most famous architect of the time.

1. References at W. Ruge, "Teos," *RE* 5A (1934) 560; Robert, *Etudes anat.* 20–37 (24: τὸν προε[σ]τῶτα τῆ[ς] π[όλεω]ς ἡμῶν θεὸν Διόνυσον); Magie II 899 n. 113.

2. Diod. 3.66.1–2. *BMC Ionia* 313–322; *SNG Copenhagen Ionia* 1444–1533; *von Aulock* 6.2264–2273.

3. By the 220s; see Herrmann, "Antiochos" 102 n. 105, on the date of *SEG* 2.580.

4. Σητάνειος is usually cited: C. Picard, *Ephèse et Claros* (Paris 1922) 406, Ruge 560, from Le Bas-Waddington 106: οἱ τοῦ Σητανείου θεοῦ Διονύσου μύσται. But this epithet is doubtful in text (only Hamilton's copy preserves the whole word) and meaning (Farnell, *Cults* V 123; Zwicker, *RE* 2A [1923] 1895–1896; W. Kroll, *AJP* 60 [1939] 105–107). Deriving from a rhetorical utterance of imperial date on the part of a private *thiasos*, this need not be the title of the civic cult.

5. Dithyrambic competitions at Teos: Le Bas-Waddington 93; *BCH* 4 (1880) 176–177 (II B.C.). The Tean ambassadors of the second *asylia* series, who surely were also Artists, sang poems of Timotheus with cithara (*I.Cret.* I VIII 11.7–11, XXIV 1.6–9).

6. On the sporadic excavations (from 1775 on) see Y. Béquignon and A. Laumonier, *BCH* 49 (1925) 282–283; Y. Boysal, *TürkArkDerg* 14 (1965) 231–233.

Teos was declared inviolable by Antiochus III and the Greek world toward 203/2 B.C.[7]

The major festival of Teos was the Dionysia; the games may well have been Panhellenic by imperial times,[8] but certainly no such increase accompanied the recognition of Tean inviolability,[9] for the decrees make no mention of games and nowhere call the Tean envoys *theoroi.* Neither do the grants expressly envisage the building of a new temple (cf. **53**), although Hermogenes' work may have followed soon after.[10] In their decree thanking Antiochus III (quoted below) the Teans allude to grave fiscal problems before his arrival; we may conclude that whatever the dates of Hermogenes and of the enlarged Dionysia they are subsequent to the declaration of inviolability. Probably one of their arguments for Panhellenic honors for Tean Dionysus was the presence of the Artists, whose personal inviolability, already granted by the powers at Delphi, was evoked there as the analogy for the inviolability of Teos (**132**.15, **133**.18, **134**.11).

Teos had gone over to the Attalid house in 218 B.C., abandoning Achaeus.[11] The occasion of the recognition of inviolability was the reassertion of Seleucid power in western Anatolia during 204–202 B.C., as was revealed by the inscriptions discovered in 1963.[12] The Teans now voted Antiochus III and Laodice elaborate cultic honors in gratitude for his benefactions, and their description of these is the fullest external account of a grant of *asylia* after that of the Magnesians (**66**):[13]

κοινὸς [εὐ]-
[ἐργέτης πρ]οείρηται γίνεσθαι τῶν τε ἄλλων Ἑλληνίδωμ [πό]-
[λεων καὶ τ]ῆς πόλεως τῆς ἡμετέρας, καὶ πρότερόν τε ὑπάρ-
[χων] ἐν τῇ ἐπέκεινα τοῦ Ταύρου πολλῶν ἀγαθῶν ἐγίνετο παραί-
τιος ἡμῖ[ν] καὶ παραγενόμενος ἐπὶ τοὺς καθ' ἡμᾶς τόπους ἀπο-
κατέστησε τὰ πράγματα εἰς συμφέρουσαν κατάστασιν καὶ ἐ-
πιδημήσας ἐν τῇ πόλει ἡμῶν καὶ θεωρῶν ἐξησθενηκότας
ἡμᾶς κα[ὶ] ἐν τοῖς κοινοῖς καὶ ἐν τοῖς ἰδίοις διά τε τοὺς συνεχεῖς

7. L. M. Gluskina, *VDI* 139 (1977) 82–94, argues on grounds of probability that Antiochus was confirming an Attalid recognition. A. Mastrocinque, in *I santuari e la guerra,* ed. M. Sordi (Milan 1984) 142–163, seeks a political context.

8. Ruge 560; the victory list at Segre, *Iscr.Cos* p. 228 (in part *Syll.*[3] 1065: Cos, Augustan date) includes the Dionysia at Teos among contests at least some of which were Panhellenic.

9. Pace Sherk, *Roman Documents* p. 215.

10. References for Hermogenes and Teos at P. Gros, *Vitruve* III (Paris 1990) 110–112; Herrmann, "Antiochos" 33.

11. Polyb. 5.77.5; cf. Herrmann, "Antiochos" 101. R. E. Allen, *The Attalid Kingdom* (Oxford 1983) 45–57, attributing mere "influence" to Attalus (49) and then Antiochus (50), is too vague to be convincing.

12. In addition to Herrmann's detailed commentary, see J. and L. Robert, *Bull. épigr.* 1984, 365.

13. Herrmann, "Antiochos" 34–35 no. 1.6–29.

πολέμου[ς] καὶ τὸ μέγεθος ὧν ἐφέρομεν συντάξεων καὶ βουλόμενος
τά τε πρὸς τὸν θεὸν εὐσεβῶς διακεῖσθαι ὧι καθιέρωσεν ἡμῶν τὴν πόλιν
καὶ τὴν χώραν ⟨καὶ⟩ θέλων χαρίζεσθαι τῶι τε δήμωι καὶ τῶι κοινῶι τῶν
περὶ τὸν Δ̣ι̣όνυσον τεχνιτῶν, παρελθὼν εἰς τὴν ἐκκλησίαν αὐτὸς
ἀνῆκε τὴ[ν] πόλιν καὶ τὴγ χώραν ἡμῶν ἱερὰν καὶ ἄσυλον καὶ ἀφορολό-
γ̣η̣τ̣ον κ[αὶ] τῶν ἄλλων ὧν ἐφέρομεν συντάξεων βασιλεῖ Ἀττά-
λωι ὑπεδέξατο ἀπολυθήσεσθαι ἡμᾶς δι' αὐτοῦ, ἵνα γενομένης ἐ-
παυξήσ[ε]ως τῶν κατὰ τὴν πόλιν μὴ μόνον εὐεργεσίας λάβῃ τὴν
ἐπιγραφ[ὴ]ν τῆς τοῦ δήμου, ἀλλὰ καὶ σωτηρίας· ἐπεδήμησε δὲ καὶ
ἐν τῇ πόλει μετά τε τῶμ φίλων καὶ τῶν ἀκολουθουσῶν αὐτῶι δυνά-
μεων ἀπόδιξεν ποιούμενος μεγίστην τῆς προϋπαρχούσης αὐτῶι πίσ-
τεως πρὸς ἅπαντας ἀνθρώπους, καὶ μετὰ ταῦτα πολλῶν ἀγαθῶν πα-
⟨ρ⟩αίτιος δ[ι]ατελεῖ γινόμενος ἡμῖν παράδειγμα πᾶσιν ἐκτιθεὶς τοῖς Ἕλλη[σι]ν ὃν
τρόπον προσφέρεται πρὸς τοὺς εὐεργέτας καὶ εὔνους ὑπάρχοντας αὐτῶι, κα[ὶ τ]ὰ
μὲν συ[ν]τελεῖ τῶν ἀγαθῶν δι' ὧν εἰς εὐδαιμονίαν παραγίνεθ' ἡ πόλις ἡμ̣[ῶ]ν,
τὰ δ' ἐ[πι]τελέσει· (κτλ.)

. . .

he proclaims himself to be the common benefactor of other Greek cities and of ours; previously, while on the far side of the Taurus, he was responsible for many good things for us, and on coming into our region he restored his kingdom to a favorable condition; and visiting our city[14] and seeing us weakened in public and private on account of the continual wars and the burden of contributions we were paying, and wishing to act piously toward the god to whom he has dedicated our city and country,[15] and wanting to gratify the people and the guild of Artists of Dionysus, he came in person into the assembly and declared our city and country sacred and inviolable and exempt from tribute, and he promised that through him we would be relieved of the other contributions that we had been paying to King Attalus, so that, with the affairs of the city improved, he would have the credit not merely for benefiting the people but for saving them. He stayed in the city with his friends and the troops that were with him, making the greatest demonstration of his goodwill toward all mankind. Thereafter he has been responsible for many good things for us, setting an example to all the Greeks of how he conducts himself toward his benefactors and those well disposed toward him; he is accomplishing the good things through which our city is coming to a happy state, and he will go on accomplishing them . . .

Antiochus now invited a Tean embassy to be sent to him and announced to them that the relief from the tribute they had paid the Attalids would be permanent (rather than for a stated period of recuperation, as was common). Statues are therefore voted of the king and queen, whose action (now a joint action) is again described (47–49):

14. Compare his personal appearance at Thebes, App. *Syr.* 13.
15. Not some separate act prior to the declaration described next, but a generic reference to it.

ἀφέντες τὴμ πόλιν καὶ τὴν χώραν ἱερὰν
καὶ ἄσυλον καὶ [π]αραλύσαντες ἡμᾶς τῶμ φόρων καὶ χαρισ[ά]μενοι ταῦ-
τα τῶι τε δήμ[ω]ι καὶ τῶι κοινῶι τῶμ περὶ τὸν Διόνυσον τεχνιτῶν (κτλ.)

...

who declared the city and country sacred and inviolable and released us from tribute[16] and thus benefited both the people and the Artists ...

A second decree, inscribed in the same hand and probably voted soon after the first, summed up the royal benefactions yet again (Herrmann, "Antiochos" no. 2.50–53):

οὐ μόνον εἰρήνην ἡμῖν ὁ βασιλεὺς παρέσχεν ἀλλὰ καὶ
[τῶν] βαρέων καὶ σκληρῶν ἐκούφισεν εἰς τὸ μετὰ ταῦτα τελῶν παραλύ-
[σας] τῶν συντάξεων καὶ λυσιτελεῖς τὰς ἐν τῇ χώραι μετ' ἀσφαλεί-
[ας π]εποίηκεν ἐργασίας καὶ τὰς καρπείας (κτλ.)

...

the king furnished not only peace[17] but also a lightening for the future of the heavy and harsh taxes, by releasing us from the contributions,[18] and he has made work and agriculture in the countryside profitable by virtue of security ...

Our documents on inviolability at Teos say nothing about the genesis of Antiochus' declaration. No initial Tean embassy to him is mentioned. Yet it seems unlikely that the new honor for Dionysus was an unprompted whim of the king; and the Teans do not claim, as others sometimes did, that the king acted "unasked," ἀπαράκλητος. The ambassadors of the second series of requests, at least at one city, supported the inviolability of Teos by citing oracles from Delphi and Didyma (**157**.9): perhaps the initial quest did likewise, and these have been passed over in silence, as happened at Cos. But it is possible too that, as at Alabanda, the oracles were acquired only once the quest had begun and Tean envoys passed through Delphi and Didyma. Antiochus' recognition clearly preceded all others; for those powers that could in principle subject cities to tribute—other monarchs and Rome—follow Antiochus in adding ἀφορολόγητος to their grants of *asylia*.[19]

16. The phrase is synonymous with ἀφορολόγητος and replaces it; this element, tax relief, clearly was a separate item from the grant of inviolability.

17. Cf. the praise of Antiochus at *I.Iasos* 4.43, τὴν εἰρήνην παρέχοντος, and in connection with Alabanda (**163**).

18. Cf. *I.Iasos* 3.12: σύνταξιν φέρειν.

19. On the term see Herrmann, "Antiochos" 138–145. Readers of the Roman letter have often expressed puzzlement, since Rome did not collect taxes in Teos; see variously A. Heuss, *Die völkerrechtlichen Grundlagen der römischen Aussenpolitik*, Klio-BH 31 (Leipzig 1933) 95; W. Dahlheim, *Struktur und Entwicklung des römischen Völkerrechts* (Munich 1968) 103; P. Klose, *Die völkerrechtliche Ordnung des hellenistischen Staatenwelt* (Munich 1972) 188—none of whom cite the Athamanian letter (nor Klose the Antiochus documents). But unlike τέλος, φόρος is morally loaded; loyal subjects and citizens pay "taxes," defeated enemies pay "tribute" (Polyaen. 4.7.1:

The chronology of these events is subject to several limits.[20] The Delphian and Aetolian eponyms establish a lower date of about 200 B.C. Tean envoys were on the Greek mainland near the start of a Julian year, for they obtained the Aetolians' decree at the Panaetolica (**132**.2), held at Naupactus ca. March;[21] they were at Delphi later (**133**.13). So they will have left Teos by about the first of the year at latest—and, presumably, not long after Antiochus' visit and declaration, which ought therefore to be assigned to the latter months of a Julian year. The king was fighting in the East well into 205, in Syria during 201 and perhaps already in 202; the Carian campaign was in between. His benefaction to Teos accordingly occurred in the late months of 204, 203, or 202.

The Tean decree thanking Antiochus gives the impression, perhaps accurate, that the king and his army swept victoriously through Caria and reached as far as Teos, where his generosity won over the city from Attalus—a single and rapid campaign. But the account given is schematic, and it is possible that the campaign was slow and difficult.

Amyzon, seventy miles southeast of Teos, had been conquered from Ptolemy by May 203, when Antiochus wrote the city offering reparations for the misdeeds of his troops—the earliest known date in Antiochus' Carian campaign. Seleucid benefactions to Amyzon then continued over several years: decrees in response date from late 202 and late 201.[22] Teos, before the king's arrival, had suffered from "the continual wars." These might be, as Herrmann suggested (105), local wars among cities or some involvement in the Cretan War; but we should consider too the Seleucid invasion itself and the inevitable responses of forces loyal to Ptolemy, Attalus, or Philip to defend their territorial interests (leading

---

τῆς τούτων χώρας κρατήσομεν καὶ φόρους οἴσουσιν); φορολογεῖν is also what pirates do (Diod. 28.1); it is prohibited by the terms of a manumission, ἐλευθέραν εἶμεν καὶ ἀνέφαπτον ἀπὸ παντὸς ἀνθρώπου καὶ ἀφορολόγητον (*IG* IX.1² 96). The word, like "sacred and inviolable," is a promise not to treat a city hostilely; compare earlier Thuc. 8.37.2; *Staatsvertr.* II 257.21–23 (the Second Athenian Confederacy); Tod II 185.13 (Alexander and Priene); *I.Iasos* 2.30 (314 B.C.); and Polyb. 21.45.5 (the Peace of Apamea). In the *asylia* inscriptions this recurs only at Mylasa, texts of uncertain character, and at Smyrna.

20. Wilhelm, *GGA* 160 (1898) 219–220; Holleaux, *Etudes* IV 178–203; Herrmann, "Antiochos" 66, 93–100 (who considered 204 B.C. too early); Gauthier, *Symbola* 281. The attempt by F. Piejko, *Belleten* 55 (1991) 13–69, to redate Antiochus' grant to 197/6 B.C., later than the recognitions of the mainland states, is arbitrary and unconvincing; in my view it is excluded by the Athamanians' use of Antiochus' word ἀφορολόγητος (**135**); for further reasons see C. P. Jones, *GRBS* 34 (1993) 80–88. The attempt by H. R. Rawlings, *AJAH* 1 (1976) 17–19, to date the first series of Cretan decrees to the 190s is rightly rejected by S. Kreuter, *Aussenbeziehungen kretischer Gemeinden* (Munich 1992) 60; cf. E. S. Gruen, *The Hellenistic World and the Coming of Rome* I (Berkeley 1984) 182 n. 150.

21. Holleaux, *Etudes* I 219–227; J. A. O. Larsen, *TAPA* 83 (1952) 7, 30; Pomtow (*Syll.*³ 563 n. 2) thought precisely at the vernal equinox, in parallel with the autumn Thermica (Polyb. 4.37.2). The Amphictyony met around March/April; cf. F. Lefèvre, *BCH* 115 (1991) 579–594.

22. *Fouilles d'Amyzon* nos. 9, 14, 15; see below, p. 336.

finally to Philip's personal intervention in 201). Alabanda was the immediate eastern neighbor of Amyzon, and we might have expected Antiochus to make his grant to Alabanda at about the same date (spring 203: in fact it is two years later) and then move on to Teos. A close grouping of events, therefore, does not seem required. At any rate, it seems hard to envision the king in Teos already in the latter half of 204; but this cannot be excluded.

A crucial fact is that the inviolability of Alabanda and that of Teos were voted at Delphi under different Delphian archons—Megartas for Teos (season unrecorded), Philaetolus for Alabanda (autumn meeting). The latter, following upon a celebration of the Soteria, is probably the autumn of 201, so Philaetolus' year was 201/0. Hence Antiochus' grant to Alabanda must have been made earlier in 201—and in absentia, for he was by then in Palestine. The king's personal appearance at Teos cannot be later, so Megartas' year at Delphi was 202/1 or earlier.

We have also the uncertain chronology of the Fifth Syrian War. The thesis, argued by Holleaux and widely held, that the war began in 202 rests in the main on the impression given by Polybius (15.25.13ff.) that the war began soon after the accession of Ptolemy V (apparently summer 204; see Herrmann, "Antiochos" 96). The Scythopolis archive (*Bull. épigr.* 1970, p. 471) shows the Holy Land already reconquered from Ptolemy before October 201; the successful siege of Gaza at the southern extreme of Palestine was completed in 201. It seems we must follow Edouard Will (*Histoire* II 102) in leaving open the choice between 202 and 201 for the first hostilities in Syria. Hence it is in theory possible that Antiochus was at Teos as late as the last months of 202. But that seems the less likely date, for no one will be comfortable with having to fit into roughly one year the conquest of all Palestine down through Gaza, where the siege reportedly was long. This leaves 203 as the most likely for Antiochus' visit.

If then Antiochus was in Teos late in 203, the Tean ambassadors were at Naupactus and obtained the Aetolian decree toward March of 202 (this makes Alexander the Aetolian *strategos* in 203/2; cf. **132**.2); if they went on at once to Delphi for the spring sitting, as has long been assumed,[23] then Megartas' year was 203/2. But it is possible that they now made their tour of the northwest, including Athamania, and came back by way of Delphi in autumn, so that Megartas' year was 202/1; but this seems less likely.

If, on the other hand, Antiochus was in Teos late in 204, all these dates are earlier by a year and the Teans' quest was in 203. My guess, however, is that Antiochus' appearance in Teos is better placed in late 203, and that the Tean envoys canvassed the Greek world during 202.

By contrast, the Roman recognition of Tean inviolability (**153**), obtained by Antiochus' envoy Menippus from the praetor M. Valerius, dates to 193 B.C., for

23. Pomtow, *RE* 4 (1901) 2631; Holleaux IV 179 n. 2.

we know independently that Menippus was in Rome at the start of 193[24] and that M. Valerius Messalla was then praetor peregrinus.[25] This delay of about ten years after the initial series of grants is in principle disquieting—though the Teans' use of a royal envoy rather than one of their own underscores the separation of this Roman act from the others. Holleaux's explanation (IV 200–203) was that Teos, while subject (as he thought) to Philip, would not have approached Philip's enemy Rome ca. 203; but that in 193 relations between Antiochus (in control of Teos since 197) and Rome were nominally friendly, hence an appropriate time to make good the omission. We know now, however, that Teos became Seleucid in 204/3; while in 193 relations between Antiochus and Rome were by no means cordial, with both actively preparing for war after several years of negotiations.[26] Here as elsewhere, the attempt to see political motives in the recognition of inviolability, reflecting relations between sovereigns, is dubious: even mortal enemies are found joining in the recognition of the *asylia* of places. *Asylia* was created by common consent of the Greek people (here see **154**.51–52). In 228 B.C. the Romans were in effect declared Greek and allowed to participate in the Isthmian games (Polyb. 2.12.8); but that declaration by Corinth evidently was not widely taken seriously, at least in Asia, before Roman intervention in Asia in the 190s. At any rate, separate and subsequent recognition of *asylia* by Rome is certain at Magnesia and possible at Claros; evidently it did not occur to these cities to include Rome in a Panhellenic quest until Rome's presence in Greek affairs made this inclusion a polite necessity.

In 190 Teos was storing supplies for Antiochus; a Roman army ravaged its territory in order to extort the supplies (Livy 37.27–28). We might conclude that the Romans reckoned that Teos had given up its neutrality by helping Antiochus. But no such fine calculation is likely, and in Livy's brief account of the praetor's demands and the Teans' deliberations there is no mention of *asylia*.

The tenor of the Tean decree of request can be seen from the responses. The envoys invoked the good relations of Teos with the grantor, and, where possible, kinship.[27] They described the sanctification and inviolability of Teos to

24. With Hegesianax and Lysias: Livy 34.37; Diod. 28.15; cf. E. Olshausen, *Prosopographie der hellenistischen Königsgesandten*, Stud.Hellen. 19 (Louvain 1974) 190–193.

25. Livy 34.55.6. Explicitness is needed here because the M. Valerius who authored **153** might well have been M. Valerius Falto, one of the praetors of 201 and so nearer to the original declaration.

26. The paradox is noted by E. Badian, *Studies in Greek and Roman History* (New York 1964) 138; R. M. Errington, *ZPE* 39 (1980) 279–284, deduces from the Roman recognition in 193 elaborate and self-interested designs on the part of both Rome and Antiochus.

27. So the Athamanians and Cretans but not the Aetolians, Amphictyons, and Delphians. Little should be trusted to silence, however: if we are to judge from silence, we would conclude that the Teans never mentioned Antiochus' declaration (even when in the presence of his

the *archegetes* Dionysus, and the other distinctions and honors: "By voting these for the god you will yourselves join in increasing them and become responsible for some benefit to the people; and in so doing you will be acting piously toward the divine and will be doing the greatest favor for our people" (**139**, **148**, **150**, more briefly **149**, **151**).

Eventually the Teans could cite oracles from Delphi and Didyma, although no decree of the first series mentions them. No extant decree expressly identifies Antiochus as having made the recognition first (contrast the first Seleucid case, Smyrna). Yet the Athamanians and Romans include the king's ἀφορολόγητος, and one Cretan city uses his authoritative ἀνίημι and the Athamanians use συνχωρέω (cf. δίδομεν at **142**.22).[28] These terms doubtless reflect the Tean decree of request, which in turn will have reflected the king's language. Antiochus is said by the Teans to have "granted" the privileges (ἀνῆκε, ἀφέντες, Herrmann, "Antiochos" no. 1.18, 47, quoted above). The verb is there used in the context of a liberation from taxes as well, where it is more appropriate than ἀποδέχομαι and the like.

It seems evident that the envoys invoked the presence of the Artists of Dionysus and their personal inviolability in asking for the recognition. The first Tean decree for Antiochus couples Teans and Artists as joint beneficiaries of his action (Herrmann, "Antiochos" no. 1.17). The states of the Aetolian orbit (**132–134**) make explicit the analogy of the personal *asylia* of the Artists for Teos, and several Cretan decrees assimilate the grant for Teos to one of personal inviolability by adding penalty clauses against harming Teans.

The civic grantors respond, often in letter form, with greater legal precision than is usual, and in greater detail. Agreeing to join in honoring the god ("we too worship Dionysus," the Cretans often say),[29] they make the security of Teos and the Teans an explicit matter of law. Those in the Aetolian group, who had already recognized the Artists' personal *asylia*, could invoke this as an analogy (and this was sufficient for the Delphians and Amphictyons; the Aetolians, like the Cretans, add provisions against the seizure of persons and property). This analogy is lacking in the Cretan decrees, but details are of the same sort: property stolen from Teos or a Tean may be seized by any citizen or Tean and claimed in the local courts by the rightful Tean owner (**139**, **141**, **151**). The privilege of access to the courts and the right of seizure on foreign soil were substantial matters, should the need have arisen. But their inclusion is peculiar to the

---

envoy Hagesander). Note the disparity of the responses to Alabanda concerning Antiochus: praise and honors from Delphi (**163**); silence, apparently, from Athens (**162**).

28. Welles (p. 155) urged the difference between "granting" and "accepting" the status and suggested it reflected Teos' lesser importance than Cos or Magnesia. ἀναδείκνυμι occurs at Teos, Alabanda, and Pergamum, where royal initiative was important; but also **111**.25.

29. Perhaps thinking of the several traditions that connected the god specially with Crete (Farnell, *Cults* V 117). Oenopion, father of Athamas (see on **135**.9–11), was a son of Dionysus.

Aetolian and Cretan acts, where such strictures had become a traditional tool of foreign policy.

Two embassies, each consisting of two men, are known to us—one in northern Greece (two brothers) and the other in Crete. The Teans organized the inscribing in accordance with the embassies that obtained the decrees, as at Cos, for the texts are otherwise inscribed in no geographical order. It is possible therefore that the later envoys to Crete brought back a decree of Cnidus (**158**), where they will have passed on their voyage. But the attested range of grantors does not seem to reflect the mere accident of the survival of stones (those decrees that happen to derive from the Cretan and northwest Greek embassies), for the second series has exclusively Cretan decrees, though inscribed later by a different mason; and the grants for Claros show much the same distribution—the Aetolian orbit, the Athamanians, and Crete. Scholars have accordingly drawn the inference that the Tean quest was selective, addressed to pirates.[30] This is cast in doubt by the apparent exceptions—Cnidus for Teos, as Thessaly for Claros; and the piracy of Athamania is especially hard to prove. It is possible instead that we have before us a set of military allies, though this was not so at Alabanda. If I am right that the Tean recognitions span the year 202, this was a period of alliance between Macedonia and Syria against Egypt, dating from 203.[31]

The ambassadors to Crete were seconded by two royal agents; for a parallel among the recognitions of inviolability, we have the case of Pergamum.[32] At one city, in fact, a royal agent alone and not the Teans addressed the assembly (**141**). The Rhodian Hagesander, a friend of Antiochus "sent to resolve the war,"[33] accompanied the Tean envoys to two cities; the Macedonian Perdiccas, "an ambassador sent by" Philip V who has also been granted citizenship in Teos, accompanied them to seven; in two decrees neither is mentioned, and at one city both men appeared (**149**); the other decrees are too fragmentary to reveal whether either agent was present. Five cities accede to the Teans' request "wishing to please Perdiccas." Because the political allegiance of Teos is no longer in doubt,[34] the question to be asked is why an Antigonid agent has any

30. E.g., Welles p. 154; P. Brulé, *La piraterie crétoise hellénistique* (Paris 1978) 94; Kreuter 58; Errington (282) adds that in 193 Rome was feared, like pirates.

31. See the cautious assessment by Holleaux IV 198–199.

32. Cf. *IG* II² 844.15–17, the Cretan Eumaridas who aided Athenian envoys to Crete by serving as their fellow ambassador to some cities and writing letters to others.

33. So only **149**.15. On the Cretan War see Brulé 29–56; on Hagesander, S. L. Ager, *Historia* 40 (1991) 19. A decade or so later he and his brother dedicated a statue of their father as priest of Athena Lindia: *I.Lindos* 158, with Robert at Holleaux, *Etudes* 191 n. 1.

34. Holleaux offered reasons (rejected by Bickerman, *Hermes* 67 [1932] 68 n. 4 [*Religions* 60]) for thinking that Teos was Antigonid (and the Cretan decrees therefore from 201 B.C., upon Philip's Asian expedition and somewhat later than the Tean mission to the Greek mainland); the finds of 1963 confirmed the view of Ruge.

role here. The answer is probably the political influence that Philip V achieved in Crete after 218.[35] At this moment in 203/2, to judge from the joint appearance at Eleutherna (and indeed from the appearance of the Seleucid agent anywhere), we may guess that relations were good between Antiochus and Philip. No doubt, as Holleaux argued, Hagesander was in Crete primarily on other business for Antiochus (resolving the Cretan War) and not for the sole purpose of helping the Teans. But that does not explain Perdiccas, or in general the unusual behavior of these Tean envoys. The state of war in Crete may itself lie behind the use of royal escorts by the ambassadors. Again, their self-effacement is perhaps paralleled by the absence of any Tean from the request to Rome in 193.

At some later date the Teans sent a new pair of envoys to at least Crete. These canvassed the cities and obtained a number of "renewals" of *asylia*—that is, reminders: for the granting cities had not let the status lapse,[36] and the substance of what they now voted was to inscribe the former decrees granting *asylia*, as the Teans expressly requested (**154**.13). These decrees commonly add to the earlier substance the provision that if anyone harm the Teans or their land, the grantor will come with such military aid as is possible—a formula from defensive alliances, although here not backed up by any oath. What the Teans now asked was that the old decrees be inscribed; and indeed most of those extant from the first series have no provision for publication. Two do (Arcades and Biannus), however, though the request of the second series was put to them as well. The burden of the Tean embassy seems therefore to have been a reminder. And two cities apparently felt nothing new was necessary, and simply praised the Tean envoys for their culture without mentioning *asylia*; the envoys, obviously Dionysiac Artists, had given recitals about the traditional relations of Crete and Teos.[37]

Tenos may also have approached cities, and apparently not only Cretan ones, to "renew" its inviolability; and Athens had occasion to remind various Cretan cities of the existing *philanthropa*, in order to assure the safety of Athenians (*IG* II^2 844).

What occasioned this reminder? On its date, guesses have ranged down to 131 B.C.;[38] the only internal marker is that the Cretans' "ancestors" had first recognized Tean *asylia*, which since Waddington has usually been taken to

35. Polyb. 4.55, 7.11.9, 7.14.4; cf. Holleaux 187; Kreuter 55–61.

36. Contra Gauthier, *Symbola* 280 (the privileges "étaient peu à peu devenus lettre morte"); Kreuter (58) postulates "continual violations" of inviolability in the interim. S. Şahin, *Epigr. Anat.* 23 (1994) 1–36, a pirate attack on Teos in the third century, may be relevant.

37. Cnossus (*I.Cret.* I VIII 11) and Priansus (I XXIV 1), not included here, though in the second case this is probable evidence that Priansus was among the grantors on the first occasion.

38. Listed at Ruge 550. The only published photographs are of **160** and **161**; I agree with Guarducci (*I.Cret.* I p. 28) in thinking the script to be of the first rather than the second half of the second century (note especially the unbroken bar of A).

require a date after about 170 B.C. Several decrees state plainly that the status had not lapsed. Several add more pointed promises about the defense of Teos. There is no hint that the Cretans themselves had violated the territory of Teos, and this would be a very roundabout way of addressing such an act (cf. **154**.41).

Some other royal letters to Teos (Herrmann, "Antiochos" 157–159) may be relevant to this later mission. In one a king has received a Tean embassy offering him a crown; he mentions honors and his ancestors, then turns to his present benefactions (7–13):

[- - - - - - προσδέδεγμα]ι̣ δὲ καὶ τὸν στέφανον
[- - - - - - - - - - - - -] αἵρεσιν καὶ ἐπὶ ταῖς
[- - - - - - - - - - - - τὴν] δημοκρ̣ατίαν ὑμῖν
[- - - καὶ τὴν πόλιν καὶ] τὴν χώραν ἱερὰν καὶ
[ἄσυλον - - - - - καθά]περ καὶ οἱ πατέρες καὶ
[ἐγὼ - - - - - - - - - -]ν εὐνοίας ἀεί τινος
[ἀγαθοῦ παραίτιος - - -]ι. ἔρρωσθε.

A second letter on this stone, from a king and his sister, similarly confirms existing privileges in response to an embassy (16–19):

[- - - - - - - - - - - -]οις καὶ ἐμὲ καὶ τὴν ἀ-
[δελφὴν - - - - - - τὰ ψ]ηφίσματα καθ' ἃ ἐτετι-
[μήκειτε ἡμᾶς - - διότι - - τὴ]ν ἐλευθερίαν καὶ τὴν
[- - - - - - καὶ τἆλλα φιλ]άνθρωπα τῆι πόλει

Another letter on a different stone makes reference to the author's "brother"; apparently the author is the sister mentioned in the second letter.

These letters have quite reasonably been taken to derive from Antiochus and Laodice, hence within ten or twelve years of the grant of inviolability and alluding to the benefactions of ca. 203. But Antiochus was first to grant *asylia* to Teos and was the last of his dynasty to control the city; it is hard to see how any Seleucid's "fathers" can be invoked on the topic of the *asylia* of Teos. Herrmann reports that the script of these texts is far different from those of ca. 203. I have wondered whether these letters are Attalid: perhaps after their reversion to Attalid rule in 188 the Teans felt it expedient to seek confirmation of a title they owed to the usurpation by Antiochus, and on the same occasion sent out envoys to Greek cities with their reminder. But again the "fathers" of an Attalid king did not initiate *asylia* at Teos. Hence, for either dynasty, these ancestors must be invoked here in allusion to a policy of past good relations, not specifically the granting of *asylia*; the letters likely are from Antiochus and Laodice, adding further benefactions to the *asylia* of ca. 203. Similar gestures spanned several years at Amyzon.

The Romans' attitude has left no direct trace. The worship of the emperor Tiberius came to be associated in some way with the temple of Dionysus, as happened also at Claros.[39] This may reflect Roman confirmation of the privilege of asylum in A.D. 22, despite the silence of Tacitus about both places.

So far as we know, Teos issued gold money only once in its history, of which a single specimen has survived. It shows a running griffon on the obverse and a lyre and the magistrate Πολύθρους on the reverse.[40] A Polythrous was one of the two Tean ambassadors to Antiochus, and Herrmann (86) did not fail to note the several bronze issues that also give this name as a magistrate. Surely the occasion of this rare and commemorative gold is the liberation from Attalid rule, *asylia*, and the "lightening of burdens," and on this coin at least it is the same man as the ambassador; as Herrmann remarked, he is also very likely the founder of a school known in a famous inscription from Teos.

The *asylia* decrees for Teos were inscribed on blocks of the blue-grey marble quarried east of the city[41] and used to build Hermogenes' temple of Dionysus; the "renewals" of the status voted in the second century specify only that the decree would be inscribed "in the temple." Most of the stones, like other Tean inscriptions, were early scattered, used to build the monuments, walls, and tombs of the surrounding Turkish villages—Seğacık, the port town on the north side of the Tean peninsula four miles from the city, Tepecik and Araka some miles to the east, and Gesusler to the northeast. Waddington reported that the Roman edict and the Cretan decrees of the first series were inscribed in "exactly similar letters";[42] if this means the same hand, then possibly the Teans waited at least a decade to inscribe their archive, perhaps on the new temple of Hermocrates. But such a vague assessment of style is dubious, and such a delay seems improbable.

The general order of the Tean archive cannot be reconstructed, although the relative positions of texts on the same stone have been respected here (in this I follow Waddington); I divert from this only in following the Delphian rather than Tean order of the decrees known also in a Delphian copy (at Delphi, the Aetolians preceded the Amphictyony, the actual chronology; at Teos the reverse).

39. Robert, *Etudes anat.* 34–35 (*LSAM* 28.12); *Op. min. sel.* VI 540.

40. G. K. Jenkins, *BMQ* 29 (1965) 91–92, who thought that style placed the coin in the third century B.C. Publishing simultaneously, Jenkins could not know the Antiochus inscriptions nor Herrmann the gold coin.

41. So Richard Chandler recognized in 1764: *Travels in Asia Minor and Greece* I (Oxford 1825) 122.

42. From Chishull (p. 102) until Wilhelm it was therefore assumed that the grants were all contemporary with the dated Roman recognition, 193 B.C.; but note that the epigraphic copy printed by Le Bas shows a different sigma in the Roman text, with straight rather than flaring arms. The flaring letters (especially pi) portrayed by Le Bas are those we see in the Antiochus inscriptions published by Herrmann.

A number of the texts were copied by Sherard in 1709,[43] with some known to us from other early sources.[44] Le Bas added to this substantially, and the archive was put in order and discussed by Waddington, who had Le Bas's copies and squeezes.[45] The French excavation after World War I contributed two more decrees.[46] Finally, it was the spectacular discoveries of the Turkish excavators in 1963 that showed the occasion of the grants. From Delphi come copies of the Aetolian and Delphian decrees, and of an Amphictyonic decree not extant at Teos. The texts printed here are Waddington's (and the majuscules Le Bas's) except as indicated.

132. Aetolian League

Two copies, at Delphi and Teos. I give the text and line divisions of the Tean copy, which was virtually undamaged.

Teos: block found by Sherard reused at Seğacık.

E. Chishull, *Antiquitates Asiaticae* (London 1728: copies of Sherard) 104–107; F. Hessel, preface to *Antiquae inscriptiones* by M. Gude (Leeuwarden 1731) no. 72 (copy of H. van der Horst) [Boeckh, *CIG* 3046];[47] Le Bas-Waddington 85 [Cauer 96; Cauer² 238; Dittenberger, *Syll.*² 280; Fick, *SGDI* 1411; Michel, *Rec.* 68; F. Bleckmann, *Gr.Inschr.z.gr.Staatenk.* (1913) 6; Pomtow, *Syll.*³ 563; Schwyzer 387; Klaffenbach, *IG* IX.1² 192].

Delphi: found in 1893 on the inward face of the north anta of the Athenian Treasury (on which are a number of non-Athenian texts), containing **132–134**

43. The botanist William Sherard, resident in Smyrna from 1703 to 1716, whence Chishull's edition. It is for the sake of simplicity that I bracket *CIG* as merely derivative from Chishull; in fact Boeckh, through the agency of C. O. Müller, consulted Sherard's manuscript, from which he often corrected Chishull's printed texts.

44. Chandler, during his tour of 1764/5, examined a number of the inscriptions with Chishull's edition in mind but printed none; of two readings he offered corrections, both wrong (**139**.1 ΚΥΔΩΝΙΩΝ, **140**.1 ΝΑΞΙΩΝ): R. Chandler, *Inscriptiones antiquae* (Oxford 1774) p. iii. Pococke in 1739 saw the block with **158** and following and recorded a few letters: *Inscriptionum antiquarum liber* (London 1752) 17 no. 8, here **158** (ΚΑΤΑΨΙ and ΤΙΟΥ) and **159**.1.

45. The early copies occasionally show a more convincing text than Le Bas's, which makes one suspect that Waddington did not or could not always control the text from Le Bas's squeezes.

46. Béquignon and Laumonier, *BCH* 49 (1925) 308, mention finding fragments of other *asylia* decrees, which have not been published.

47. The Tean inscriptions in the Gude volume were copied at Seğacık in February 1719 by two members of the Belgian consulate in Smyrna—most by the consul himself J. de Hochepied, the Aetolian decree by his aide H. van der Horst; they passed on their copies to C. A. Duker, who sent them to Hessel (I note this because of the frequent confusion in subsequent editions about the genesis of these copies; Hessel's "addenda to the preface" of Gude's book is unpaginated; his explanation of his sources is placed after his no. 73 of this series of texts).

and a Delphian proxeny decree for the ambassadors.[48] Three blocks associated by Homolle (inv. 439: h. 0.44, w. 0.90; 471: h. 0.377, w. 0.97; 493: h. 0.365, w. 0.53) and a small piece (436: h. 0.042) of the block that lay between the upper two, added by Pomtow; letters 0.008, intersp. 0.007. Copied by Bourguet (439, 436), Couve (471), and Homolle (the three large blocks).

Jardé, *BCH* 26 (1902) 281–286 no. 23; G. Colin, *FD* III.2 134a.

Cf. Wilhelm, *GGA* 160 (1898) 216–220.

I give the Tean copy; the Delphian preserves diminishing amounts of lines 1–7.

Αἰτωλῶν
στραταγέοντος Ἀλεξάνδρου Καλυδωνίου, Παναιτωλικοῖς·
ἐπεὶ Τήϊοι πρεσβευτὰς ἀποστείλαντες Πυθαγόραν καὶ Κλεῖτον τάν τε οἰκειότατα
καὶ τὰν φιλίαν ἀνενηοῦντο καὶ παρεκάλεον τοὺς Αἰτωλοὺς ὅπως τάν τε πόλιν
αὐτῶν καὶ τὰν χώραν ἐπιχωρήσωντι ἱερὰν εἶμεν καὶ ἄσυλον τοῦ Διονύσου·
δεδόχθαι τοῖς Αἰτωλοῖς, ποτὶ τοὺς Τηΐους τὰν φιλίαν καὶ οἰκειότατα τὰν ὑπάρχουσαν
διαφυλάσσειν, καὶ τὰ ψαφίσματα τὰ πρότερον γεγονότα αὐτοῖς περὶ πάντων τῶν φιλαν-
θρώπων κατάμονα εἶμεν· ὑπάρχειν δὲ αὐτοῖς παρὰ τῶν Αἰτωλῶν τᾶς τε πόλιος καὶ τᾶς
χώρας τὰν ἀνιέρωσιν καὶ ἀσυλίαν, καθὼς καὶ οἱ πρεσβευταὶ ἀξίουν, καὶ μηθένα Αἰτωλῶν μηδὲ
τῶν ἐν Αἰτωλίαι κατοικεόντων ἄγειν τοὺς Τηΐους μηδὲ τοὺς ἐν Τέωι κατοικέοντας μηδαμόθεν
ὁρμωμένους, ἀλλὰ τὰν ἀσφάλειαν καὶ ἀσυλίαν εἶμεν αὐτοῖς τὰ ἀπ' Αἰτωλῶν καὶ τῶν ἐν Αἰ-
τωλίαι κατοικεόντων· εἰ δέ τίς κα ἄγηι ἢ αὐτοὺς ἢ τὰ ἐκ τὰς πόλιος ἢ χώρας, τὰ μὲν ἐμ-
φανῆ ἀναπράσσειν τὸν στ[ρ]ατα[γὸν] καὶ τοὺς συνέδρους ἀεὶ τοὺς ἐνάρχους, τῶν δὲ
ἀφανέων ὑποδίκους εἶμεν τοὺς ἀχνηκότας, γινομένας τοῖς Τηΐοις τᾶς ἐγδικάσιος
καὶ τᾶς λοιπᾶς οἰκονομίας, καθὼς καὶ τοῖς Διονυσιακοῖς τεχνίταις ὁ νόμος τῶν
Αἰτωλῶν κελεύει· ὅπως δὲ καὶ εἰς τοὺς νόμους καταχωρισθῆι ἁ ἀνιέρωσις καὶ ἁ ἀσυλία
τοὺς κατασταθέντας νομογράφους καταχωρίξαι, ἐπεί κα αἱ νομογραφίαι γίνωνται,
ἐν τοὺς νόμους.

48. This text (*FD* 134d [*Syll.*^{3} 564]) does not survive at Teos and may not have been inscribed there, although noninviolability decrees were at Teos (see n. 37) and in the Magnesian archive.

1: θεοί instead at Delphi. 2: Delphi omits Παναιτωλχοῖς. 3: Delphi adds the patronymic Κλείτου after at least the second name, possibly also after the first. 4: ἀνανεοῦντο Delphi.

2: Alexander was Aetolian *strategos* for the second time in 196/5, for the third in 185/4; here, without number, is his first tenure, and 203/2 if my reasoning is correct. See Klaffenbach, *IG* IX.1^2 pp. xxxiii and 51 (who assigned Alexander to 204/3 on the basis of Pomtow's date for Megartas at Delphi). The season of the Panaetolica was early spring, ca. March.

7–8: These *philanthropa* already granted Teos by the Aetolians are unknown to us; possibly personal inviolability, as in the case of Miletus (p. 173). The analogy is weaker with Magnesia, with its close ties to Aetolia and a seat on the Amphictyonic Council.

9–16: The Aetolians give a clear exposition of their understanding of the Teans' objective: personal *asylia*, against seizure of movable goods, including persons:

> no Aetolian or resident of Aetolia operating from anywhere is to seize Teans or residents of Teos; rather they shall have security and inviolability with respect to Aetolians and Aetolian residents; if anyone seize either them or their property from city or country, the general and *synedroi* in office are to confiscate the visible goods, while for those not visible[49] those who committed the seizure are subject to trial, right to prosecute[50] and other procedures being available to the Teans, as Aetolian law stipulates also for the Artists of Dionysus.

Their analogy with the Artists, who had no territorial state, underscores the assimilation of this act to a grant of personal inviolability, which is what the Artists enjoyed. Thus the Aetolians choose to focus on the Teans rather than on the place Teos, and they say next to nothing of Dionysus. What they grant the Teans, in effect, is access to Aetolian courts.

14: The unaspirated ἀγνηκώς at **181**.5.

133. Delphian Amphictyony

At Delphi, inscribed below **132**; no Tean copy extant.
Lines 3–9: L. Couve, *BCH* 18 (1894) 240–241 [Baunack, *SGDI* 2530].
Entire: Jardé no. 23; Colin, *FD* III.2 134b; Pomtow, *Syll.*^{3} 564.

[θ ε ο] ί
[ἐπὶ Μεγάρτα ἄρχοντος, Πυλαίας ἠρινῆ]ς, ἱερομναμονού[ν]-
[τ]ων Αἰτωλῶν Ἀριστάρχου Ἀμφισσέος, Φιλλέα Ν[αυπακτί]-
ου, Λαμίου Οἰ⟨χα⟩λειέος, Ξενοκράτεος Στρατίου, Λεοντ[ο]-
μένεος Φυταιέος, Βουθήρα Ἀρσινοέος, Ἀγοραίου Ὑπα-

49. I.e., already disposed of; cf. on **67**.16–17.

50. Cf. *FD* III.2 205.10, ἐκδικασαμένου of someone who "filed charges" before the Amphictyons.

ταίου, Πυρρία Θηβαίου, Ἁρμόστου Λαμιέος, Δαμοκρά[τεος]
Εἰτεαίου, Λαμίσκου Ἀργείου, Κεφαλλάνων Σωτάκ[ου ?Σαμαί]-
ου, Δελφῶν Πραόχου, Πατρέα, Χίων Πλειστία, Μαγ[νήτων . . . .]
γένεος, Ἀθηναίων Ἀμύκλα· ἐπεὶ παραγενόμενο[ι πρεσβευ]-
ταὶ παρὰ τοῦ δάμου τοῦ Τηΐων ποτὶ τὸ κοινὸν τ[ῶν Αἰτω]-
λῶν Πυθαγόρας Κλείτου καὶ Κλεῖτος Κλείτου, [καὶ νῦν ἐλθόν]-
τες ποτὶ τοὺς ἱερομνάμονας ἐνεφάνιξαν τ[ὰ δεδομένα]
παρὰ τῶν Αἰτωλῶν φιλάνθρωπα καὶ τίμια [τῶι δάμωι]
τῶι Τηΐων· ἔδοξε τοῖς Ἀμφικτιόνοις τὰμ π[όλιν καὶ τὰν]
χώραν τῶν Τηΐων ἱερὰν εἶμεν καὶ ἄσυλον Δι[ονύσου ἀπὸ]
πάντων, καὶ ὑπάρχειν τοῖς Τηΐοις καὶ τοῖς ἐν Τέω[ι κατοι]-
[κ]εόντοις παρ' Ἀμφικτιόνων τὰ φιλάνθρωπα καὶ τίμι[α]
[πάν]τα ὅσα καὶ τοῖς Διονυσιακοῖς τεχνίταις δέδοτα[ι]
[παρὰ] τῶν Ἀμφικτιόνων.

Text of Colin. 3 fin. Pomtow (who had first thought [Οἰναί]ου). 4 Couve: ΟΙΚΥΛ lapis. 7 end Pomtow. 11: [καὶ ἐπελθόν]-Jardé.

10: The *theoroi* evidently were traveling from west to east, Naupactus to Delphi. The Council makes explicit that the Teans have already obtained the vote of the Aetolian League, and indeed this decree reads like a précis of the Aetolians' decision, including even the citation of earlier Aetolian, not Amphictyonic, *philanthropa*. In the preliminaries the Council does not even say what the Teans wanted, not mentioning friendship or *asylia*, as do the Aetolians and Delphians.

134. Delphi

Copies at Teos and Delphi, the Delphian inscribed below **133**, the Tean (h. 0.40, w. 1.175) seen by Le Bas built into the fort at Seğacık, by Wilhelm in 1891 in Izmir.

Delphi: Jardé no. 123; Colin, *FD* III.2 134c.

Teos: Le Bas-Waddington 84 [Michel, *Rec.* 67; Cauer^2 208]; Wilhelm, *GGA* 160 (1898) 216–220 [Baunack, *SGDI* 2675; Pomtow, *Syll.*^{3} 565; Schwyzer 331].

I give the Tean copy, more complete, underlining what survives only at Delphi.

Δελ[φῶ]ν
[ἔδοξε τᾶι πόλει ἐν ἀγορ]ᾶι τελείωι σὺμ ψάφο⟨ι⟩ς {Ο} ταῖς ἐν[νόμοις· ἐπειδὴ Τή]-
[ϊοι πρεσβευ]τὰς ἀποστείλαντες Πυθαγόραν Κλείτου κ[αὶ Κλεῖτον]
[Κ]λ[είτ]ου τάν τε οἰκειότατα καὶ τὰν φιλίαν ἀνενεώσαν[το καὶ παρεκά]-
λεον τὰν πόλιν ὅπως ἅ τε πόλις καὶ ἁ χώρα αὐτῶν ἐπιχ[ωρηθῆι ἱερὰ εἶ]-
μεν καὶ ἄσυλος τοῦ Διονύσου· δεδόχθαι τᾶι πόλει τάν τ[ε φιλίαν καὶ τὰν οἰ]-
κειότατα τὰν ὑπάρχουσαν ποτὶ τοὺς Τηΐους διαφυλάσ[σειν καὶ ἐπὶ πλεῖ]-
ον αὔξειν, καὶ εἶμεν αὐτῶν τάν τε πόλιν καὶ τὰ[ν χώραν]
ἱερὰν καὶ ἄσυλον τοῦ Διονύσου καθὼς καὶ οἱ πρεσβε[υταὶ παρεκά]-
λεον, καὶ εἶμεν αὐτοῖς τὰν ἀσφάλειαν [κα]ὶ ἀσ[υλίαν καὶ]

τοῖς ἐν Τέωι κατοικεόντοις καθὼς καὶ τοῖς [Διονυσιακοῖς]
τεχνίταις· ὅπως δὲ διαμένηι τόδε τὸ [ψάφισμα]
ἐν τὸ[μ] πάντα τὸν χρόνον, ἀναγράψαι το[ὺς ἐνάρχους]
βουλευτὰς ἐν τῶι ἱερῶι. ἄρχοντος Μεγάρτ[α, βουλευόντων]
Μνασιθέου, Πρωτάρχου, Ἀθάμβου, Φιλί[νου, Νικοβούλου.]

1: θεοί instead at Delphi. 2: init.]ΛΗΣΙΑΙΤΕΛ, then ΨΑΦΟΣΟ at Teos. 15: Delphi reverses the order of Πρωτάρχου and Ἀθάμβου.

135. Athamanian kings

Inscribed below **134** (Tean copy); broken below line 14, with one or two lines lost before the second column begins.

Le Bas-Waddington 83; Wilhelm, *GGA* 160 (1898) 216–220 [Welles, *Royal Corres.* 35].

Ἀθαμ[ά]ν̣ων̣
[β]ασιλεὺ[ς Θ]εόδωρος [κα]ὶ Ἀμύνανδ[ρο]ς Τ[η]ΐων τῆι βουλῆι [κ]αὶ τ[ῶ]ι
δήμωι
χαίρειν· Πυθαγόρας καὶ Κλεῖτος οἱ ἀποσταλέντες πα[ρ' ὑ]μῶν π[ρ]ε[σ]-
βευταὶ τό τε ψήφισμα ἀπέδωκαν [καὶ αὐ]τ[οὶ δι]ελέγησ[αν πρὸς ἡμᾶς π]ε[ρὶ]
τοῦ συγχωρηθῆναι παρ' ἡμῶν τήν τε πόλιν καὶ τὴν χώραν ἱερὰν τῶι
Διονύσωι καὶ ἄσυλον καὶ ἀφορολόγητον· ὧν [δι]ακούσαντες προθύ-
μως ἅπαντα τὰ ἀξιούμενα ὑπακηκόαμεν καὶ σ[υ]γχωροῦμεν εἶναι καὶ τὴν
πόλιν ὑμῶν καὶ τὴν χώραν ἱερὰν καὶ ἄσυλον καὶ ἀφορολόγητον· καὶ τοῦτο
πράσσομεν καὶ διὰ τὸ πρὸς ἅπαντας μὲν τοὺς Ἕλληνας οἰκείως
ἔχοντες τυγχάνειν, ὑπαρχούσης ἡμῖν συγγενείας πρὸς αὐτὸν τὸν
ἀρχηγὸν τῆς κοινῆς προσηγορίας τῶν Ἑλλήνων, οὐχ ἥκιστα δὲ καὶ δι-
ὰ τὸ πρὸς τὴν πόλιν ὑμῶν φιλόστοργον διάληψιν ἔχειν, ἔτι
δὲ καὶ μέλλοντες ἅμα καὶ ὑμῖν τοῖς ἠξιωκόσιν τὴν χάριν διδόναι
καὶ τὴν παρὰ τοῦ θεοῦ εὐμένειαν ὡς ὑπολαμβάνομεν περιποιεῖσθαι
- -
[-]ειν παν
[-]ν τῶν πολ
[-]ορισμένα τοῖς πα . .
[-] ἀκριβεστέραν τὴν
[- εἰ]ς τὰ μετὰ ταῦτα ὑπε-
[-]ΙΛΕΙ[- - - - - - -] ἔρρωσθε.

Text of Wilhelm, who recognized this as a royal letter. 1 [ἐπει]δὴ? [Πυ]θόδωρος, 3–4 [παρὰ τῶν | Τηΐων], 4–5 [καὶ δι]ελέγησ[αν ἀκολούθως τῶι ψηφίσ|μα]τι σ. Waddington.[51]

51. 15ff.: a continuous and complete text has been composed by F. Piejko, *Epigraphica* 50 (1988) 41–46 [*SEG* 32.1227].

The Athamanian pair[52] also recognized the inviolability of Apollo of Claros; they may appear too in the tantalizing fragment *Staatsvertr.* III 550.12—texts all close in date. An Amynander son of Machaus made a donation to Melitea (where Hellenus was buried); there too he is not called king.[53] But Polybius calls the king of the Athamanians in 220 B.C. "Amynas" (4.16.9). Theodorus is known otherwise only in the Delian temple inventories: his daughter Phila made dedications there before 225 B.C.: Φίλα βασιλέως Θεοδώρου.[54] Other literary sources know only Amynander as king of the Athamanians: if he is rightly identified with the donor at Melitea, then Theodorus cannot be his father. Perhaps Theodorus was now in effective retirement, being old enough to have begotten a daughter well before 225.

The Athamanians, having been independent of Epirus for a generation by now, were at various times allied with the Aetolians and may well have been in 203/2.

9–11: The Athamanians' uneasy insistence on their Greek descent may reflect the view of others that they were barbarians (Strab. 7.7.1 [321]). They cite their kinship with all Greeks, as Athamas was a descendant of Hellenus (a tale otherwise unrecorded, as Waddington remarked). According to a legend as early as the fifth century (Pherecydes *FGrHist* 3 F 102), Teos itself was founded by Minyans led by Athamas, grandson of Athamas. An account at least as old (Ion, 392 F 1; cf. Jacoby's note 44) held that Oenopion and his son Athamas came from Crete to Chios, and the son may then have been taken to be the founder of Teos (F 3). Moderns have distinguished the Minyan and the Cretan Athamas, but the Teans seem to have found it convenient to merge them, at least when they dealt with the Cretans.[55]

136–143 on two once adjacent blocks (above and below), found reused at Seğacık.

136. Cnossus

J. Kennedy Bailie, *Fasciculus inscriptionum* (Dublin 1846) 127–130 no. 154; Le Bas-Waddington 61 [Blass, *SGDI* 5165; Guarducci, *I.Cret.* I VIII 8].

Cf. W. Aly, *Der kretische Apollonkult* (Leipzig 1908) 13.

[τάν τε πόλιν καὶ τὰν χώραν ἦμεν ἱ]ερὰν καὶ ἄσυλον

52. On them see Moretti, *I.stor.ellen.* II pp. 5758; on Amynander, S. I. Oost, *CP* 52 (1957) 1–15; W. Welwei, *Historia* 14 (1965) 252–256; M.-F. Baslez in *L'Illyrie méridionale* (Clermont-Ferrand 1987) 167–173.

53. *IG* IX.2 208; Strab. 9.5.6 (432); Oost 13 n. 9.

54. *I.Délos* 338Bb.29; 369A.6–7; 442B.13, 184, 213.

55. See Jacoby ad loc.; Pfeiffer ad Callim. frag. 49; G. Huxley, *GRBM* 10 (1984) 149–152; D. C. Braund, *CQ* n.s. 32 (1982) 350–353; on the Boeotian Athamas who reared the infant Dionysus, see H. Fuhrmann, *JdI* 65–66 (1950–51) 105–107.

[δίδομεν, καὶ τὰ λοιπὰ τὰ ὑπάρχοντα ὑ]μῖν ἔνδοξα καὶ
[τίμια συνδιαφυλαξίομεν ἀπροφασίστω]ς ἐφ' ὅσον κ' ἴωμεν
[δυνατοί, καὶ εἴ τινές κα τῶν ὁρμιομένω]ν Κνωσόθεν κεῖ-
[σε ἀδικήσωντί τινα Τηΐων ἢ τῶν πα]ροίκων ἢ κοινᾶι
[ἢ ἰδίαι παρὰ τὸ γραφὲν δόγμα περὶ τᾶς ἀ]συλίας ὑπὸ τᾶς
[πόλεως τῶν Κνωσίων, ἐξέστω τῶι π]αραγενομένωι
[Τηΐων ἢ τῶν παροικιόντων ἐπιλαβ]έσθαι καὶ τῶν σω-
[μάτων καὶ τῶν χρημάτων, εἴ τίς κα ἄγηι· οἱ δὲ] κόσμοι οἱ τόκ' ἀεὶ
[κοσμίοντες τοῖς ἀδικημένοις ταῦτα ἀ]ποδίδοντες
[κύριοι ἔστων ἀζάμιοι ἰόντες καὶ] ἀνυπόδικοι· ἀγγρά-
[ψαι τὸ δόγμα ἐς τὸ ἱερὸν τῶ] Ἀπέλλωνος τῶ{ι} Δελ-
[φιδίω τὸν γραμματέα τᾶς πόλ]εως· δοθῆμεν δὲ καὶ ξέ-
[νια τοῖς πρειγευταῖς τὰ ἐκ τ]ῶ νόμω· ἦμεν δὲ καὶ προ-
[ξένος τᾶς πόλεως Ἀπολλό]δοτον Ἀστυάνακτος καὶ Κω-
[λώταν Ἑκατωνύμω καὶ] αὐτὸς καὶ ἐγγόνος.

13 Aly: Δελ|[φινίω Waddington.

The envoys of the second Tean mission visited Cnossus and sang of Tean-Cretan relations but obtained only honors for themselves, without mention of *asylia* (*I.Cret.* I VIII 11; so too at Priansus, of which no decree survives from the first mission: I XXIV 1). Unless this was a polite refusal, the Cnossians may be thought to have kept their earlier grant inscribed, although no provision for inscription occurs in **136**.

5, 8: πάροικοι is merely what others would call κατοικοῦντες, the other inhabitants of Teos besides citizens; the same term recurs in the decree of Sybrita (**141**.20).

137. Polyrrhenia

Inscribed below **136**.

Lines 1–5: Chishull pp. 121–122 [Boeckh, *CIG* 3054; Kennedy Bailie has line 1 (his no. 154.17)]. Complete: Le Bas-Waddington 62 [Cauer 49; Cauer² 126; Blass, *SGDI* 5166; Michel, *Rec.* 52; Guarducci, *I.Cret.* II XXIII 3].

Πολυρρηνίων
Πολυρρηνίων οἱ κόσμοι καὶ ἁ πόλις Τηΐων τῶι δάμωι
καὶ τᾶι βωλᾶι χαίρειν· κομισάμενοι τὸ ψάφισμα τὸ παρ'
ὑμῶν ἀνέγνωμεν καὶ τῶν πρεσβευτᾶν Ἀπολλοδό-
τω{ι} καὶ Κωλώτα{ι} διακούσαμεν παρακαλούντων μετὰ
πάνσας σπουδᾶς καὶ φιλοτιμίας ἀκολούθως τοῖς ἐν τῶι
ψαφίσματι κατακεχωρισμένοις· περὶ δὴ τούτων δεδό-
χθαι Πολυρρηνίων τοῖς κόσμοις καὶ τᾶι πόλει ἀποκρίνασ-
θαι Τηΐοις διότι τὸν Διόνυσον καὶ αὐτοὶ σεβόμεθα καὶ δίδο-
ται τῶι θεῶι [παρ' ἁ]μῶν τάν τε πόλιν καὶ τὰν χώραν ἀνιέμεν
ἱερὰν καὶ ἄσυλον νῦν τε καὶ εἰς τὸν ἅπαντα χρόνον· ἦμεν δὲ
καὶ [πάνσι τ]οῖς ἐν Τέῳ ἀσφάλειαν καὶ κατὰ γᾶν καὶ κατὰ
[θάλασσ]αν ἐ[ς] τὸν ἅπαντα χρόνον. ἔρρωσθε.

12: [παροίκοις τ]οῖς Cauer.

Polyrrhenia was in the western extreme of Crete. The decree is short, and to the recognition of territorial inviolability it appends personal inviolability, called simply ἀσφάλεια, for residents of Teos, irrespective of their location.

9–10: It is conventional to construe an infinitive ἀνιέμεν dependent on δίδοται ("it is given to the god from us to recognize" etc.). This is clumsy at best, and I suspect that a phrase has fallen out, the true subject of δίδοται (as in **139**.20–21 etc.): the god first is given his honors and then "we grant" inviolability, thus δίδοται τῶι θεῶι [παρ' ἁ]μῶν ⟨τὰ καλὰ καὶ τίμια καὶ Τηΐων⟩ τάν τε πόλιν καὶ τὰν χώραν ἀνίεμεν (or whatever the word order).

138. Rhaucus

Second column.

Chishull pp. 116–117 [Boeckh, *CIG* 3051]; Kennedy Bailie no. 155; Le Bas-Waddington 63 [Cauer 50; Cauer² 127; Michel, *Rec.* 53; Blass, *SGDI* 5167; Schwyzer 188; Guarducci, *I.Cret.* I xxvii 1].

Cf. K. Meister, *IGForsch* 18 (1905/6) 200.

῾Ραυκίων

ἔδοξε ῾Ραυκίων τοῖς κόσμοις καὶ τᾶι πόλει· ἐπειδὴ παραγε-
νόμενοι πρειγευταὶ παρὰ τῶ δάμω{ι} τῶ Τηΐων πορτὶ ῾Ρω-
κίονς Ἀπολλόδοτος Ἀστυάνακτος, Κωλώτας ῾Εκατωνύμου
ἐπελθ{ι}όντεν ἐπὶ τὰν ἐκκλησίαν ἐνεφάνιξαν τάν τε
οἰκειότατα τὰν ὑπάρχονσαν ῾Ραυκίοις ποθ' αὐτόνς,
καὶ περὶ τᾶς ἀσυλίας τᾶς τε πόλεος καὶ τᾶς χώρας πα-
ρεκάλεσαν, ἔτι δὲ καὶ τῶ παρ' Ἀντιόχω τῶ βασιλέος πρει-
γευτᾶ ῾Αγησάνδρω παρακαλέσαντος μετὰ πάνσσαν
σπουδᾶς καὶ φιλοτιμίας, ὁμοίως δὲ καὶ τῶν παρὰ [Τηΐων]
πρειγευτᾶν ἐμφανιξάντων τὰν αὐτῶν εὔνοιαν καὶ
προθυμίαν, δεδόχθαι ῾Ραυκίων τοῖς κόσμοις καὶ τᾶι πό-
λει ἀποκρίνασθαι Τ[η]ΐοι[ς] ὅτι ἅ τε καθ[ιάρωσι]ς [τῶι Δι]ονύ-
σωι τᾶς πόλεος καὶ τᾶς χώρας αὐτῶν ἅ τε ἀσυλία καὶ
τὰ ἄλλα ἔνδοξα καὶ τίμια παρ' [ἁμῶν ὑπάρξει αὐτοῖς]
νῦν τε καὶ τὸν ἄλλον χρόνον πάντα.

3 Chishull: ΠΡΕΣΒΕΥΤ Le Bas. 10–12 Chishull: 10 παρ' ἁμῶν, 11 τὰν ὑμ[ῶ]ν εὔνοι[άν τε κ]αί, 12 [κόσμοι]ς [καὶ τᾶι] πο- Le Bas-Waddington; 11 τὰν ὑμ[ὰ]ν Meister. 14: ΤΑΣΤΑΣΠΟΛΕΩΣ Chishull, Kennedy Bailie, ΤΑΣΠΟΛΕΟΣ Le Bas; ΑΥΤΩΝ Chishull, Kennedy Bailie: ΑΥΤΟΙΣ Le Bas; ΤΑΝΤΕΑΣΥΛΙΑΝ Chishull, Kennedy Bailie. 15 ΤΙΜΙΑ[ΠΑΡΔΕΧΟΜΕΘΑ] Chishull.

The only extant decree and almost the only inscription of Rhaucus, a small city in the Heraclion valley. Here, as with Axus and Eranna (and Allaria in Polybius), the spelling of the name apparently varies (line 3). The city was partioned by Cnossus and Gortyn in 166/5 B.C. and ceased to exist: Guarducci p. 291; Rigsby, *TAPA* 106 (1976) 316.

5, 9: Terminal ν for ς; cf. on **60**.7.

10–12: Here, among all the decrees for Teos, the early copies raise a question of substance. I have relied on Chishull's text:[56] as the ambassadors have stressed Tean friendship with Rhaucus and called for *asylia*, with Hagesander zealously calling for this too and the *Tean* ambassadors likewise stressing their loyalty and devotion, it is decreed to answer (etc.). On Le Bas's reading: as the Tean ambassadors have called for *asylia*, upon Hagesander calling for it and "*our* ambassadors stressing your loyalty," it is decreed (etc.). The implication of this last would be that some *Rhaucian* ambassadors had passed through Teos—in the course of dealing with the Seleucid government, Waddington deduced (followed by Holleaux 192, Herrmann, "Antiochos" 135). Chishull's version, though clumsy and to a degree redundant (mentioning the Teans' speech twice, but for rather different arguments), eliminates this extra embassy from little Rhaucus, for which the other decrees for Teos offer no parallel.

139. Cydonia

Inscribed below **138**, with line 14 beginning the third column.

Lines 1–2 init., 27 end: Chishull 122 [Boeckh, *CIG* 3055]. Lines 14–26: Kennedy Bailie no. 156. Complete: Le Bas-Waddington 64 [Cauer 51; Cauer[2] 124; Michel, *Rec.* 54; Blass, *SGDI* 5168; Schwyzer 203; Guarducci, *I.Cret.* II x 2].

Κυδωνιατᾶν

Κυδωνιατᾶν ἁ πόλις καὶ οἱ ἄρχοντες Τηΐων τᾶι βωλ[ᾶι]
καὶ τῶι δάμωι χαίρειν· ἐπειδὴ [Τή̈ι]οι φίλοι καὶ συγγενεῖς
ὑπάρχοντες διὰ προγόνων τᾶι πόλει ψάφισμα καὶ πρεσ-
βευτὰς ἀπεστάλκαντι Ἀπολλόδοτον καὶ Κωλώταν, οἳ
ἐπελθόντες ἐπὶ τὰν ἐκκλησίαν τό τε ψάφισμ⟨α⟩ ἀπέδω-
καν καὶ αὐτοὶ διελέγην ἀκολούθως τοῖς γεγραμμένοις,
τὰν ἐκτενεστάταν σπουδὰν καὶ φιλοτιμίαν ποιιόμε-
νοι περὶ τῶ γενέσθαι τὰν καθιάρωσιν τῶι Διονύσωι τᾶς
τε πόλιος καὶ τᾶς χώρας τᾶς Τηΐων καὶ τὰν ἀσυλίαν, ἔτι
δὲ καὶ τἆλλα τὰ ὑπάρχοντα αὐτοῖς ἔνδοξα καὶ τίμια εἰς

56. I put little faith in Kennedy Bailie's copies (Waddington p. 30 was mistaken in stating that these derived from Borrell): more than others, he seems to normalize spelling and dialect and "see" restorations, or again to reproduce with suspect exactitude already published readings; on p. 130 he makes clear that the majuscules he prints are emended versions of the copies he made. At any rate, here his text gives ΠΟΤΙΡΑΥ at 3 end, ΑΥΤΟΥΣ in 6, ΒΑΣΙΛΕΩΣ in 8, ΠΟΛΕΩΣ in 14; at 9 after ΜΕΤΑ he gives ΠΑΣΑΣ where Chishull printed dots and Le Bas ΠΑΝΣΣΑΝ. At 10ff. he duplicates Chishull but with ΠΑΡΑΤΗΙΩΝ where Chishull had printed ΠΑΡΑτηιων, i.e., παρὰ [Τηΐων]. Note, however, **139**.15–17, where Kennedy Bailie is the sole authority.

τὸν θεὸν ψαφιξαμένος καὶ αὐτὸς συναύξεν καὶ αἰεί τι-
νος ἀγαθῶ παραιτίος γενέσθαι τῶι δάμωι, καὶ ὅτι ταῦτα
ποιήσαντες ἀκόλουθα πράξομεν τᾶι τε [?συγγενείαι καὶ τᾶι]
ποτὶ τὸ θεῖον εὐσεβείαι καὶ τὰ μέγιστα χαριξιόμεθα τῶι
δάμωι· ἀποκρίνασθαι Τηΐοις φίλοις καὶ οἰκείοις οὖσιν δι-
ότι τὸν Διόνυσον καὶ αὐτοὶ σεβόμεθα καὶ τὸν Τηΐων δᾶμον
συγγενέα ὄντα ἀσπαζόμεθα καὶ ἐπαινῶμεν δ[ι]ό[τι] ̣κ[α]-
λῶς καὶ ἐνδόξως καὶ καταξίως τῶ{ι} θεῶ{ι} προεστάκαντι,
ἕνεκα ὧν καὶ παρ' ἁμῶν τὰ καλὰ καὶ τίμια δίδοται τῶι θεῶι
καὶ Τηΐων τάν τε πόλιν καὶ τὰν χώραν ἀνίεμεν ἱερὰν καὶ
ἄσυλον νῦν τε καὶ εἰς τὸν ἄλλον χρόνον πάντα, καὶ πει[ρα]-
σόμεθα αἰεί τινος ἀγαθῶ παραίτιοι γίνεσθαι τῶι δάμωι
καὶ κοινᾶι καὶ ἰδίαι· εἴ κά{ι} τινες ἄγωντι Τηΐος ἢ τὸς κατοικόν-
τας παρ' αὐτοῖς, οἱ κόσμοι καὶ ἄλλος ὁ λῶν Κυδωνια-
τᾶν ἢ Τηΐων ἀφελόμενοι καὶ διδόντες τοῖς ἀδικη-
μένοις κύριοι ἔστωσαν. ἔρρωσθε.

2 ΑΡΧΟΝΤΕΣ Le Bas: ΚΟΣΜΟΙ Chishull (but Sherard's copy ends with ΚΑΙ). 15–17: the line ends are reported by Kennedy Bailie (16–17: ΟΥΣΙΝ | ΔΙΟΤΙ) but not Le Bas; 16 οἰκε[ίοις ὑπάρχονσι] Blass, οἰκε[ίοις ἐῶσιν δι]- Guarducci. 20: ΕΝΕΚΕΝ Kennedy Bailie. 21: ΧΩΡΑΝΑΥΤΩΝΕΜΕΝ Kennedy Bailie. 24, 25 Cauer: καί and ὅλων Waddington.

Cydonia in the west, modern Chania, was reckoned the third city of Crete (Strab. 10.4.7). Its decree is one of the more detailed in this series; the penalty clause (24ff.) empowers any Cydonian or Tean to "seize and restore" goods to the victim (cf. Allaria, **151**).

8ff.: If I have understood this morass, the envoys "showed the most earnest zeal and public spirit about establishing the sacredness to Dionysus and inviolability of the city and country of the Teans, and about us voting to join in increasing the other existing distinctions and honors they enjoy on account of the god and being always ready with some good for their people, and that by doing these things we would be acting in keeping with piety toward the divine and would greatly gratify their people." Cf. **148**, **152**, and more briefly **149**.11ff., **150**.11ff. (this last passage is clearest for sorting out the two parties in the sentence).

14: The parallel passage in **148** has nothing of the phrase restored here.

19: Cf. on **145**.

24: Cauer's correction is doubtful; we expect καὶ εἴ κά τινες.

140. Axus

Beginning below **139** in the third column; 16ff. on another block (in Izmir: seen by Wilhelm in 1891, and again by Robert).

Chishull pp. 114–116; Hessel no. 6 (copy of J. de Hochepied: only lines 16–24) [Boeckh, *CIG* 3050]; Le Bas-Waddington 65 [Cauer 52; Cauer² 122; Michel, *Rec.* 55; Blass, *SGDI* 5169; Guarducci, *I.Cret.* II v 17].

Cf. Wilhelm, *GGA* 160 (1898) 215 (autopsy); Robert, *Hellenica* I (1940) 118 n. 4 (autopsy, Le Bas's squeeze).

Ϝαξίων

ἔδοξεν Ϝαξίων τοῖς κόσμοις καὶ τᾶι πόλει ψαφιξαμένοις
κατὰ τὸν νόμον· ἐπειδὴ Τήϊοι διὰ προγόνων φίλοι καὶ συγ-
γενεῖς ὑπάρχοντες τᾶς ἁμᾶς πόλεως ἀπέστειλαν ψά-
φισμα καὶ πρειγευτὰς Ἀπολλόδοτον καὶ Κωλώταν,
οἳ καὶ ἐπελθόντες ἐπὶ τὰν ἐκκλησίαν καὶ τὸ ψάφισμα
ἀποδόντες διελέγεν πεδὰ πάνσας σπουδᾶς καὶ φι-
λοτιμίας περὶ τῶ{ι} γενέσθαι τὰν καθιέρωσιν τῶι Διονύ-
σωι τᾶς τε πόλεος αὐτῶν καὶ τᾶς χώρας καὶ τὰν ἀσυ-
λίαν τά τε ἄλλα τὰ ὑπάρχοντα αὐτοῖς ἔνδοξα καὶ τίμι-
α διαφυλάδεν καὶ συνεπαύξεν ἐς τὸν ἀεὶ χρόνον, περ[ὶ]
δὲ τῶν αὐτῶν διαλεγέντος καὶ Περδίκκα τῶ παρὰ τῶ βα-
σιλέως Φιλίππω πρειγευτᾶ· δεδόχθαι Ϝαυαξίων τοῖς
κόσμοις καὶ τᾶι πόλει ἐπαινέσαι μὲν τὸνς πρειγευτὰνς
διότι καλῶς καὶ συμφερόντως διελέγεν περὶ τᾶς οἰκειότατος
τᾶς ὑπαρχόνσας αὐτοῖς πορτ' ἁμὲ καὶ τῶν λοιπῶν ἐνδό-
ξων καὶ τιμίων, ἀποκρίνασθαι δ⟨ὲ⟩ ὅτι ὁ δᾶμος ὁ Ϝαυξίων δια-
φυλάδων τὰν πορτὶ τὸ θεῖον εὐσέβειαν καὶ τᾶι πόλει τῶν
Τηΐων εὐχαριστεῖν βωλόμενος τάν τε καθιέρωσιν τῶι Δι-
ονύσωι τᾶς τε πόλεως τῶν Τηΐων καὶ τᾶς χώρας ἀναδεί-
κνυντι καὶ παρδέχεται ἱερὰν καὶ ἄσυλον καθότι παρκα-
λεῖ ὁ δᾶμος ὁ Τηΐων, ὑπάρξει δὲ καὶ τὰ ἄλλα τίμια
Τηΐοις πὰρ τᾶι πόλει τῶν Ϝαυξίων νῦν τε καὶ εἰς
τὸν αἰεὶ χρόνον. ἔρρωσθε.

13 Robert: ΣΑΘΑΞΙΩΝ Sherard, ϜΑΥΞΙΩΝ Le Bas. 17 Blass: ΔΙΟΤΙ the copies. 23 after τε Chishull, Robert, and Le Bas's squeeze: καὶ αἰεί Waddington.

Axus was an important city, situated at the foot of Mt. Ida west of the Heraclion valley. The crucial phrase (19ff.) is unusually full: the city "declares the sanctification to Dionysus of the city and country of the Teans and accepts it as sacred and inviolable."

141. Sybrita

On the second block, beginning below **140** end; second column begins with line 19.

Lines 1–9 and 19–27: Chishull pp. 113–114; Hessel no. 6 (copy of de Hochepied) [Boeckh, *CIG* 3049]. Complete: Le Bas-Waddington 66 [Cauer 53; Blass, *SGDI* 5170; Guarducci, *I.Cret.* II xxvi 1].

Cf. Holleaux, *Etudes* IV 183; M. Muttelsee, *Die Verfassungsgeschichte Kretas* (Hamburg 1925) 12 n. 4.

Συβριτίων

Συβριτίων ἁ πόλις καὶ οἱ κόσμοι Τηΐων τᾶι βωλᾶι καὶ τῶι
δάμωι χαίρειν· παραγενόμενος Περδίκκας ὁ παρὰ βασι-
λέως Φιλίππου πρεσβευτὰς τό τε ψήφισμα ἀπέδωκεν
ὃ ἔφερον οἱ παρ' ὑμῶν πρεσβευταὶ ἐπεὶ αὐτοῖς συνε-
[πρέσβευσεν], ἐν ὧι ἐγράψατε ἁμῖν περὶ τᾶς οἰκειότα-
τος καὶ τᾶς φιλίας καὶ ὅτι καλῶς κα ποιήσαιμεν προσ-
δεξάμενοι τάν τε ἀνιέρωσιν τῶι Διονύσωι καὶ τὰν ἀσυ-
λίαν τᾶς τε πόλιος καὶ τᾶς χώρας [ὑμῶν - - - - - - - - -]
[. . . . .]πράσσειν· διελέγη δὲ [καὶ Περδίκκας ὁ ὑμέτερος]
[πολί]τας ἀκολούθως τοῖς γ[εγραμμένοις μετὰ πάσας]
σπουδὰς καὶ φιλοτιμίας· πρό[θυμοι οὖν καὶ ἀπὸ προ]-
γόνων πρὸς πάντα τὰ [θεῖα διακείμενοι - - - - - - - τὰν]
ἀνιέρωσιν τῶι Διονύσωι κ[- - - - - - - - - - - - - - - -]
[. .] βουλόμενοι ὑμῖν π[- - - - - - - - - - - - - - - - - -]
[καὶ τ]ἄλλα τίμια [καὶ ἔνδοξα - - - - - - - - - - - - - -]
[καὶ τὰ]ν ἀσυλίαν [τᾶς πόλιος καὶ τᾶς χώρας - - - - -]
[. . . . .]ιο[-]
πάντα· εἰ δέ τινές κα τῶν ὁρμισμένων ἐξυβρίτας ἀδι-
κήσωσίν τινα Τηΐων ἢ τῶν παροίκων ἢ κοινᾶι ἢ ἰδίαι πα-
ρὰ τὸ γραφὲν δόγμα περὶ τᾶς ἀσυλίας ὑπὸ τᾶς πόλεως
τῶν Συβριτίων, ἐξέστω τῶι παραγενομένωι Τηΐων
ἢ τῶν παροίκων τῶν ἐν Τέωι ἐπιλαβέσθαι καὶ τῶν σω-
μάτων καὶ χρημάτων, εἴ τίς κα ἄγηι· οἱ δὲ κόσμοι οἱ τόκα
ἀεὶ κοσμίοντες ἐπαναγκαζόντων ἀποδιδό-
μεν τοὺς ἔχοντας, ἀζήμιοι ὄντες καὶ ἀνυπόδι-
κοι πάσας ζαμίας. εὐτυχεῖτε.

6 Boeckh from Sherard's copy (line omitted by Chishull and Hessel): init. Holleaux: συνέ|[βη ἅμα ἐπιδημεῖν] Waddington; τᾶς τ' Boeckh, T omitted by Le Bas. 9–10: [καὶ παρακαλεῖτε | περὶ τούτων] Waddington. 10 end Muttelsee: ὑ|μῶν Waddington. 13 [θ. δ. καὶ τὰν], 14 κ[αὶ Περδίκκαι χαρίζεσθαι], 15 γ[ε τὰ λοιπὰ τὰ ὑπάρχοντα καὶ], 16 [κ. ἔ. διαφυλάξομεν ἀπροφασίστως], 17–18 χ. καὶ τὰν ἀνιέρω|σιν τῶι Δ]ιο[νύσωι δίδομεν νῦν τε καὶ ἀεὶ εἰς τὸν λοιπὸν χρόνον] Waddington. 19: ΟΡΜΙΣ Sherard, Hessel, Le Bas, ΟΡΜΩ Chishull, ὁρμι⟨ο⟩μένων Boeckh; ΒΡΙΣΤΑΣ Hessel, ΒΡΙΤΙΑΣ Chishull.

Sybrita, at the western foot of Mt. Ida, has left little trace in the historical record; Polybius, in a lost passage, had occasion to mention the city under the year 206/5 (*I.Cret.* p. 289, from Steph. Byz. s.v.). Only here in the archive does a royal agent speak for the Teans.

19ff.: The terms of the penalty clause are unusually elaborate and somewhat redundant (cf. **142**.24ff.): "If anyone operating from Sybrita wrong any Tean or resident of Teos contrary to the decree of inviolability written by the city of the Sybritans, the Tean or resident of Teos is empowered to come and take both persons and property, if anyone has seized them; the annual *kosmoi* are to force restitution by those in possession, acting with impunity and immune from any prosecution."

142. Lato

Below **141**, with line 19 beginning the third column.

Lines 1–6 init., 19–31: Chishull p. 122; Hessel no. 7 (copy of de Hochepied) [Boeckh, *CIG* 3058]. Complete: Le Bas-Waddington 67 [Cauer 54; Blass, *SGDI* 5171; Guarducci, *I.Cret.* I XVI 2].

Λατίων
ἔδοξε Λατίων τοῖς κόσμοις καὶ τᾶι πόλει· ἐπειδὴ
Τήϊοι συγγενεῖς καὶ φίλοι διὰ προγόνων ὑπάρχον-
τες ψάφισμα καὶ πρειγευτὰνς ἀπέσταλκαν Ἀπολ-
λόδοτον καὶ Κωλώταν, οἱ δὲ ἐπελθόντες ἐπὶ τὸ κοι-
νὸν τὸ Λατίων τό τε ψάφισμα ἀπέδωκαν καὶ αὐτοὶ
διελέγεν ἀκολούθως τοῖς γεγραμμένοις τὰν ἐκτε-
[νεστάταν σπουδὰν καὶ φιλοτιμίαν ποιούμενοι] περί τε
[τῶ γενέσθαι τὰν καθιέρωσιν τῶι Διονύσωι τᾶς] πό-
[λιος καὶ τᾶς χώρας τᾶς Τηΐων καὶ τὰν ἀσυλίαν,] ἔτι
[δὲ καὶ τἄλλα τὰ ὑπάρχοντα αὐτοῖς ἔνδοξα καὶ] τ̣ί̣μι[α διὰ]
[τὸν θεὸν, -]Ι

5 lines lost

[- - - - - - ὅτι πρότερον ἁ πόλις καὶ νῦν δ' ἐμ πᾶσιν]
εὐχαριστεῖ, καὶ μεμναμένοι [τὰν πρ]οϋπάρχονσ[αν τᾶι]
πόλει συγγένειαν τάν τε καθιέρωσιν τῶι Διονύσωι τάν [τε]
πόλιν καὶ τὰν χώραν ἦμεν ἱερὰν καὶ ἄσυλον, βωλόμε[νοι]
χαρίζεσθαι Περδίκκαι, δίδομεν, καὶ τὰ λοιπὰ τὰ ὑπάρχον-
τα ὑμῖν ἔνδοξα καὶ τίμια συνδιαφυλαξίομεν ἀπρο-
φασίστως ἐφ' ὅσον κ' ἴωμεν δυνατοί, καὶ εἴ τινές κα τῶν
ὁρμιομένων Λατόθεν ἀδικήσωντί τινα Τηΐων ἢ κοινᾶι
ἢ ἰδίαι παρὰ τὸ γραφὲν δόγμα περὶ τᾶς ἀσυλίας τᾶς τε
πόλεος καὶ τᾶς χώρας, ἐξέστω τῶι παραγενομένωι
Τηΐων ἐπιλαβέσθαι καὶ σωμάτων καὶ χρημάτων, εἴ τίς
κα ἄγηι· οἱ δὲ κόσμοι οἱ τοκ' ἀεὶ κοσμίοντες ἀναγκαζόν-
των ἀποδιδόμεν τὸς ἔχοντας, ἀζήμιοι ὄντες καὶ ἀν-
υπόδικοι· ἀγγράψαι δὲ καὶ τὸ δόγμα ἐς τὸ ἱερὸν τᾶς Ἐλευθυίας.

9–12 Blass. 18–19 Blass: προαιρούμενοι οὖν ἐμ πᾶσιν]| εὐχαριστεῖ⟨ν⟩ Waddington.

Lato stood on a high saddle looking west across the Gulf of Mirabello and the harbor town Ayios Nikolaos. We learn from **152** that a distinct "Lato by Camara" existed at Ayios Nikolaos, apparently in sympolity with Lato proper. See generally E. Kirsten, *RE* Suppl. 7 (1940) 342–365.

5–6: For κοινόν as "assembly" (here also at Istron and Arcades) or "government" see Robert, *Monnaies antiques en Troade* (Geneva 1966) 90.

20ff.: The recognition is clumsily phrased, but parallel to **150**.29: "We grant the sanctification to Dionysus and that the city and territory be sacred and inviolable, wishing to please Perdiccas."

31: Eleithyia was clearly the patroness of Lato. Other inscriptions were set up in her temple (*I.Cret.* 35), and the Latoans tooks oaths by her as well as by the national Cretan goddess Britomartis (5.75). One of the two promontories of Lato is occupied by a temple, perhaps hers: P. Ducrey and O. Picard, *BCH* 94 (1970) 567–590.

143. Lappa

Below **142** (third column).

Lines 1–6 init.: Chishull p. 122; Hessel no. 8 (copy of de Hochepied) [Boeckh, *CIG* 3056]. Complete: Le Bas-Waddington 68 [Guarducci, *I.Cret.* II XVI 3].

Cf. Holleaux, *Etudes* IV 189 n. 2.

Λαππαίων
ἔδοξε Λαππαίων τοῖς κόσμοις καὶ τᾶι πόλει· ἐπειδὴ
παραγενόμενοι πρεσβευταὶ παρὰ τοῦ δήμου τοῦ Τη-
ΐων Ἀπολλόδοτος Ἀστυάνακτος, Κωλώτης Ἑκατω-
νύμου ἐπελθόντες ἐπὶ τὴν ἐκκλησίαν ἐνεφάνισαν
τήν τε οἰκειότητα τὴν ὑπάρχουσαν Λαππαίοις πρὸς
αὐτούς, καὶ περὶ τῆς ἀσυλί[ας] τῆς τε πόλεως καὶ
τῆς χώρας [παρεκάλ]εσα[ν, ἔτι δὲ καὶ] τοῦ παρ' Ἀντιόχ[ου]
[τοῦ βασιλέως πρεσβευτοῦ Ἁγησάν]δρου παρα-
[καλέσαντος μετὰ πάσης σπουδῆς καὶ] φιλοτιμίας, δε-
[δόχθαι -]ιαροι
[- - - - - - - - - -]θιε[- - - - - - -]υξου . οστι .
[- - - - - - -]α[- - - - - - - -] ἀσυλία . λ[- - -]
[- - - - - - - - -]χ[- - - - - -]λλ[- - -]ο[- - -]

8 Holleaux, Guarducci: [καλῶς διελεγ]ήσα[ντο, καὶ] Waddington. 14: perhaps ἄ]λλ[ον χρ]ό[νον Guarducci.

Lappa was in the western part of the island; as Guarducci remarks, little trace of the Cretan dialect remains in this decree.

144–146 are known from an eighteenth-century copy that included also **147**; Waddington accordingly placed them here.

144. Hierapytna

A. Torres y Ribera, *Antiquitates Cretenses* (Venice 1805) 39 no. 1 (copy of Maffei); S. A. Naber, *Mnemosyne* 1 (1852) 118–125 no. 4 (copy of Cobet) [Le Bas-Waddington 68a; Blass, *SGDI* 5172; Guarducci, *I.Cret.* III iii 2].[57]

[τάν τε καθιέρωσιν τῶι Διονύσωι τᾶς τε πόλιος]
καὶ τᾶς χώρας [ὑμῶν δίδομεν καὶ ἐφ' ὅσον κα δυ]-
νατὸν ἦ̣ι̣ οὐκ ἐπιτ⟨ρ⟩άψομεν οὐδενὶ ἀδικὲν ἐν τᾶι
ὑμᾶι χώραι, τάν τε̣ [φι]λίαν ἁρμοστὰν ἐῶσαν δι-
ακαθεξίομεν ⟨ν⟩ῦν τε καὶ εἰς τὸ⟨ν⟩ λοιπὸν χρόνον
πάντα· εἰ δὲ τ[ινές κα] τ̣ῶν ὁρμωμένων ἐξ Ἱα[ρα]-
πύτνας [ἀδικήσωντί τι]ν̣α Τηΐων ἢ κο[ι]ν̣ᾶι ἢ ἰδί-
αι, ἐξέ̣[στω τῶι παραγεν]ομένωι̣ [Τηΐων] ἐπιλα-
βέσθαι καὶ [τῶν σωμάτ]ων καὶ ⟨χ⟩ρ[ημάτων, εἴ τίς]
κα ἄγηι· οἱ δ[ὲ κόσμοι οἱ τ]όκ' ἀεὶ κ[οσμίοντες ἐπα]-
ναγκαζόντων ἀποδιδόμεν τὸς ἔχοντας, [ἀζάμιοι]
ἐόντες καὶ ἀνυπόδικοι πάσας ζαμίας. ἔρρωσθε.

2 ΝΙΒΟ, 3 ΤΑΝΤΑ, 5 ΔΩΝ, 7 ΜΕΝΟΔ, 9 fin. ΑΕΝ Naber.

Hierapytna, the important city in the southeast of Crete, is richly documented.

3: "We shall hold to our friendship because it is fitting" is a recherché expression for a familiar sentiment in Hellenistic diplomacy.

145. Aptera

Torres y Ribera; Naber no. 5 [Le Bas-Waddington 68b; Blass, *SGDI* 5173; Guarducci, *I.Cret.* II iii 1].

καὶ τὸν Τηΐω̣[ν δᾶμον συγγενῆ ἐόντα - - - - - - - - - -]
[ἀσπα]ζόμεθα καὶ [ἐ]παινῶμεν διότι κ[αλῶς καὶ ἐνδό]-
ξως καὶ καταξίως [τῶ θ]εῶ [προ]εστάκαντ[ι·]
[ἕνε]κεν ὧν καὶ παρ' ἁ[μῶν τὰ καλὰ] καὶ τί[μια δίδοται]
τῶι θεῶι καὶ Τηΐ[ων τάν τε πό]λιν καὶ [τὰν χώραν]
[ἀν]ίεμεν ἄσυλον νῦν τε καὶ εἰ[ς τὸν ἄλλον χρόνον]
πάντα, καὶ πειρ[άξ]ομεν ἀεί τινος ἀγαθῶ παραίτι[οι]
γίνεσθαι τῶι δάμωι καὶ [κ]οινᾶι καὶ ἰδίαι· ἐὰν δέ τι-
ν̣ες ⟨κ'⟩ ἄγωντι Τ̣ηΐος ἢ τὸς κατο̣ικόντας π[αρ'] αὐτοῖ[ς]
οἱ κόσμοι καὶ ἄλλ⟨ο⟩ς ὁ βουλόμενος Ἀπτεραίων [ἢ Τη]-
ΐων ἀφελόμενοι καὶ ἀποδίδοντες [τοῖς ἀδικημέ]-
νοις κύριοι ⟨ἔ⟩στων. ἐψήφιστ[αι ἐπὶ κόσμων τῶν μετὰ]
Βορθίω, μηνὸς Δ[ι]κτ[υ]νναίω [- - - - - - - - - - - - - -]

57. I have not seen the book of Torres (on it see S. Ricci, *MonAnt* 2 [1897] 79; Guarducci, *I.Cret.* III p. xii). The copies were obviously poor, confusing Ε/Σ, Κ/Ν, Ο/Ω, etc., which I have not marked; omissions too were probably due to the copyist.

1: ΤΙΝΑ. 6 Guarducci: λοιπὸν χ.] Naber. 8: ΜΙΝ. 9 ⟨κ'⟩ add. Blass; ΘΗΙΟΣ; ΚΑΤΑΙ. 10: ΑΛΑΣ. 12: ΡΥΟΙΣΤ.

Aptera stood atop the ridge overlooking Suda Bay and bordered Cydonia, whose decree (**139**) this one closely resembles; for both, the Teans "have conducted themselves worthily of the god" (cf. **151**.22; διεξάγω is a synonym at **149**.24). A subsequent decree is also extant (**154**). Aptera omits "sacred" from the recognition (6) but in the later decree refers to the present act as "sanctification."

146. Biannus

Torres y Ribera; Naber no. 7 [Le Bas-Waddington 68c; Blass, *SGDI* 5174; Guarducci, *I.Cret.* I VI 1].

[καὶ τὰ λοιπὰ τὰ ὑπάρχοντα ὑμῖν ἔν]-
δοξα καὶ τίμια, καὶ διαφυλάξομεν ἀπ̣[ρο]-
φασ⟨ί⟩στως ἐφ' ὅσον κα ἴωμεν δυνατοί, καὶ εἴ τι-
νες ἐγκαθορμιζόμενοι Βιαννόθεν ἀδικήσω[ν]-
τί τινα Τηΐων ἢ κοινῆι ἢ ἰδίαι παρὰ τὸ γραφὲν δό-
γμα τᾶς ἀσυλίας ὑπὸ τᾶς πόλιος τᾶς Βιαννί-
ων, ἐξέστω τῶι παραγενομένωι [Τ]ηΐω[ν] ἐπι-
λαβέσθαι καὶ σωμάτων καὶ χρήματα, εἴ τις κα
ἄγηι· οἱ δὲ κόσμοι οἱ τοκ' ἀεὶ κοσμίοντες ἐ{υ}παναγ-
καζόντων ἀποδιδόμεν τὸς ἔχοντας, ἀζάμι-
οι ἐόντες καὶ ἀνυπόδικοι· ἀναγράψαι δὲ κ[αὶ]
τὸ δόγμα τόδ' ἐς τὸ ἱαρὸν τῶ Ἄρεος.

2: ΡΑΣΣΤΩΣ.

Biannus was in the south of Crete, though at some remove from the coast. A decree is also extant in the second series (**156**), even though the present one makes provision for being inscribed.

7: The aberrant accusative is not a mason's error, for as Guarducci notes it recurs in **148**.37.

11: The binding of Ares by Otus and Ephialtes (*Il.* 5.385ff.) occurred at Biannus, where one of the brothers was buried and the Hecatomphonia were celebrated in honor of Ares (Steph. Byz. s.v. Βίεννος; Guarducci p. 29).

147–149 on a block at Seğacık.

147. Apollonia

Torres y Ribera; Naber no. 6; Le Bas-Waddington 69 [Blass, *SGDI* 5175; Guarducci, *I.Cret.* I III 1].

[εἰ δέ τινές κα τῶν ὁρμιομένων ἐξ Ἀπ]ολ⟨λ⟩ωνίας ἀ-
[δικήσωντί τινα Τηΐων παρὰ τὸ] γραφὲν δόγμα
[περὶ τᾶς ἀσυλίας ὑπὸ τᾶς πόλιος] τᾶς̣ Ἀπολλωνι-

[ατᾶν, ἐξέστω τῶι παραγενομένω]ι Τηΐων ἐπιλαβέσ-
[θαι καὶ σωμάτων καὶ χρημάτων, εἴ τίς] κα ἄγηι· οἱ
[δὲ κόσμοι οἱ τόκ' ἀεὶ κοσμίοντες ἐπα]ναγκαζόν-
[των ἀποδιδόμεν τὸς ἔχοντας, ἀζή]μιοι ἰόντε[ς]
[καὶ ἀνυπόδικοι· ἀγγράψαι δὲ] τόδε τὸ δόγμα εἰς
[τὸ ἱερὸν τοῦ Ἀπόλλωνος τ]οῦ Δεκαταφόρου τὸν
[γραμματέα τᾶς πόλιος· ἐξ]ενοτροφῆθεν δὲ καὶ οἱ
πρεσγευταὶ καθὼς καθέσταται.

3 ΤΑΙΑΠ. 9 Δεκαταφόρου, 10 Blass.

Guarducci urged that this is the Apollonia that was a port city west of Cnossus (*Historia* 7 [1933] 363–367); the other Apollonias that ancient authorities place in Crete are obscure and unlocated.

9: Apollo "who receives a tithe" is known at Hierapytna (*I.Cret.* III iii 9) and at Megara (Paus. 1.42.5).

10: Hospitality for the envoys is for some reason rare in this first series of Cretan decrees for Teos. This word applied to guests (rather than mercenaries) is unusual; compare the noun ξενοτρόφιον at **197**.6; cf. ξενισμός at **155**.49 and **156**.36.

148. Istron

Inscribed below **147**, continuing to a second column at line 18.

Chishull 110–113 [Boeckh, *CIG* 3048]; Le Bas-Waddington 70 [Cauer 55; Cauer² 123; Blass, *SGDI* 5176; Michel, *Rec.* 56; Guarducci, *I.Cret.* I xiv 1].

Ἰστρωνίων
ἔδοξεν Ἰστρωνίων τοῖς κόσμοις καὶ τᾶι πόλει· ἐπει-
δὴ Τήϊοι φίλοι καὶ συγγενεῖς ὑπάρχοντες διὰ προ-
γόνων τᾶι πόλει ψάφισμα καὶ πρεσβευτὰς ἀπε-
σταλκαν Ἀπολλόδοτον καὶ Κωλώταν, οἵ ἐπελθόν-
τες ἐπὶ τὸ κοινὸν τὸ Ἰστρωνίων τό τε ψάφισμα ἀπέ-
δωκαν καὶ αὐτοὶ διελέγην ἀκολούθως τοῖς γε-
γραμμένοις, τὰν ἐκτενεστάταν σπουδὰν καὶ
φιλοτιμίαν ποιούμενοι περὶ τοῦ γενέσθαι τὰν κα-
θιέρωσιν τωι Διονύσωι τᾶς τε πόλιος καὶ τᾶς χώρας
τᾶς Τηΐων καὶ τὰν ἀσυλίαν, ἔτι δὲ καὶ τἆλλα τὰ ὑπάρ-
χοντα αὐτοῖς ἔνδοξα καὶ τίμια διὰ τὸν θεὸν ψαφισα-
μένους καὶ αὐτοὺς συναύξειν καὶ ἀεί τινος ἀγαθοῦ
παραιτίους γίνεσθαι τῶι δάμωι, καὶ ὅτι ταῦτα ποιή-
σαντες ἀκόλουθα πραξίομεν τᾶι τε πορτὶ ⟨τὸ⟩ θεῖον
εὐσεβείαι καὶ τὰ μέγιστα χαριξιόμεθα τῶι δάμωι·
περὶ δὲ τῶν αὐτῶν διαλεγέντος μετὰ πάσης σπου-
δᾶς καὶ προθυμίας καὶ τ[οῦ παρ]ὰ τοῦ βασιλέως Φι-
λίππου πρεσβευτᾶ{ι} Περδίκκα{ι}· ἀποκρίνασθαι τῶι
δάμωι τῶι Τηΐων ὅτι πρότερόν τε ἁ πόλις διακει-
μένα φιλικῶς καὶ εὐνόως ποτὶ τὸ πλᾶθος τὸ

Τηΐων ἔν τε τοῖς ὑπεράνω χρόνοις οὐδενὸς ἀπέστα τῶν συμφερόντων, καὶ νῦν δὲ καθότι παρακαλεῖ ὁ δᾶμος ὁ Τηΐων καὶ Περδίκκας ὁ πολίτης αὐτῶν, προαιρούμενοι οὖν ἐμ πᾶσιν εὐχαριστεῖν καὶ μεμναμένοι τᾶς προϋπαρχούσας ταῖς πόλεσι συγγενείας, τάν τε καθιέρωσιν τῶι Διονύσωι τᾶς τε πόλιος καὶ τᾶς χώρας ὑμῶν, ἔτι δὲ ἱερὰν καὶ ἄσυλον εἶναι, βουλόμενοι χαρίζεσθαι Περδίκκαι, δίδομεν, καὶ τὰ λοιπὰ τὰ ὑπάρχοντα ὑμῖν ἔνδοξα καὶ τίμια συνδιαφυλαξίομεν ἀπροφασίστως ἐφ' ὅσον κ' ἔωμεν δυνατοί· εἰ δέ τινές κα τῶν ὁρμιομένων ἐξ Ἴστρωνος ἀδικήσωντί τινα Τηΐων ἢ κοινᾶι ἢ ἰδίαι παρὰ τὸ γραφὲν δόγμα περὶ τᾶς ἀσυλίας ὑπὸ τᾶς πόλιος τᾶς Ἰστρωνίων, ἐξέστω τῶι παραγενομένωι Τηΐων ἐπιλαβέσθαι καὶ τῶν σωμάτων καὶ χρήματα, εἴ τίς κα ἄγηι· οἱ δὲ κόσμοι οἱ τόκα ἀεὶ κοσμοῦντες ἐπαναγκαζόντων ἀποδιδόμεν τοὺς ἔχοντας, ἀζήμιοι ὄντες καὶ ἀνυπόδικοι· ἀναγράψαι δὲ καὶ τὸ δόγμα εἰς τὸ ἱερὸν τὸ τᾶς Ἀθάνας τᾶς Πολιάδος τοὺς γραμματέας τᾶς πόλιος.

15 ⟨τὸ⟩ ad. Cauer. 18 Blass: ΚΑΙΤ . . . ΑΙΟ - - - Chishull, καὶ τ[οῦ] ἀπο[σταλέντος παρὰ βασιλέως Boeckh, ΚΑΙ . . . . ΤΟΣΒΑΣ (κτλ.) Le Bas, καὶ [κελεύσαν]τος Waddington, καὶ [τοῦ ἀποσταλέν]τος ⟨παρὰ⟩ Cauer.

Istron was a small city south of Lato on the Gulf of Mirabello. The decree gives an unusually detailed representation of the Teans' speech and is unusually deferential to Perdiccas (for the phrase at 30 cf. **142**.22).

8ff.: The same intricate sentiment at Cydonia (**139**).

28ff.: This clumsy expression amounts to a gloss: "Wishing to please Perdiccas, we grant the sanctification to Dionysus of the city and country, that they be sacred and inviolable"; which is simply *asylia* at 35.

37: Here is a clear instance of Chishull tacitly correcting Sherard's copy: Sherard and Le Bas give χρήματα (and cf. **146**.7), Chishull χρημάτων. So too at **149**.5 the two give ἐσκλησίαν, and Chishull prints ἐκκλησίαν.

149. Eleutherna

Third column; the opening lines had deteriorated by Le Bas's day, so that Chishull's text is more complete.

Chishull 108–110 [Boeckh, *CIG* 3047]; Le Bas-Waddington 71 [Cauer 56; Blass, *SGDI* 5177; Michel, *Rec.* 57; Guarducci, *I.Cret.* II XII 21].

Cf. Wilhelm, *AEM* 20 (1897) 88; *GGA* 160 (1898) 215.

Ἐλευθερναίων

ἐπειδὴ Τήϊοι φίλοι καὶ συγγενεῖς διὰ προγόνων

ὑπάρχοντες ψάφισμά τε καὶ πρεσβευτὰς ἀπεστάλ-
καντι̣ παρ' ἁμὲ Ἀπολλόδοτόν τε καὶ Κωλώταν, οἵ-
τινες ἐπελθόντες ἐπὶ τὰν ἐσκλησίαν τὰν φι-
λίαν καὶ τὰν συγγένειαν τὰν ὑπάρχουσαν
ποτ' αὐτοὺς καὶ τἄλλα διελέγησαν [καλῶς καὶ] ἐν-
δόξως περί τε τῶ θεῶ καὶ τᾶς καθιερώσεως τᾶς πό-
λεως καὶ τᾶς χώρας, ἀκολούθως ἀπολο[γιζόμενοι]
τοῖς ἐν τῶι ψαφίσματι κατακεχωρισμένοις
τάν τε φιλίαν καὶ τὰν εὔνοιαν διαφυλάσσειν καὶ [ἀεί]
τινος ἀγαθῶ παραιτίους γίνεσθαι καὶ τὰ π̣[αρακαλώ]-
μενα ἐπὶ πλέον συναύξειν, ὁμοίως δὲ παρεκάλ[εσε]
καὶ Ἁγήσανδρος Εὐκράτευς Ῥόδιος ὁ παρὰ τῶ βασι-
λέως Ἀντιόχω πρεσβευτὰς ἐπὶ τὰς τῶ πολέμω
διαλύσεις ἀποσταλείς, οὐθὲν ἐλλείπων σπου-
δᾶς καὶ φιλοτιμίας κατ' οὐθένα τρόπον· ὡσαύτως δὲ
καὶ Περδίκκας ὁ παρὰ τῶ βασιλέως Φιλίππω πεμ-
φθείς· δεδόχθαι τοῖς κόσμοις καὶ τᾶι πόλει τῶν Ἐλευ-
θερναίων ἀποκρίνασθαι Τηΐοις φίλοις καὶ οἰκείοις
οὖσιν διότι τά τε περὶ τὸν Διόνυσον καὶ αὐτοὶ σεβό-
μεθα καὶ τὸν ὑμὸν δᾶμον ἀσπαζόμεθά τε κή-
παινίομεν διότι καλῶς καὶ ἱεροπρεπῶς καὶ κατα-
ξίως τῶ θεῶ διεξάγοντες οὐ μόνον καθῶς πὰρ τῶν
προγόνων παρέλαβον διαφυλάσσοντες, ἀλλὰ καὶ
πολλῶι μᾶλλον προσαύξοντες· ἕνεκεν ὧν καὶ παρ' ἁ-
μίων τὰ σεμνὰ καὶ τίμια δίδοται τῶι θεῶι καὶ Τηΐοις
καὶ τάν τε πόλιν αὐτῶν καὶ τὰν χώραν ἱερὰν καὶ ἄσυ-
λον ἀποδείκνυμεν καὶ πειρασόμεθα συναύξειν.

1–4 derive almost entirely from Sherard's copy. 4 init.: ΣΑΝΤΕΣ Sherard, ΣΑΝΨΟΣ Chishull. 7 [καλῶς W. Blümel by communication, from **151**.8: [εὖ καὶ] Boeckh. 9 Blass: ἀπο[τεινόμενοι? Boeckh, ἀπολο[γισάμενοι] Wilhelm. 11 [ἀεί] Wilhelm. 12–13 Wilhelm: [τὰ γεγραμ]μένα Chishull, γ[ενό]μενα Waddington, π̣[ρογενό]μενα Blass.

This is the one city where the two royal agents appear together; it is the only text to state Hagesander's purpose, and it is relatively quiet about Perdiccas. Holleaux (IV 197–198), who believed that every appearance of Perdiccas proved Antigonid alliance, concluded from his being mentioned briefly and second that Eleutherna has just now been brought to reconciliation with Rhodes and the Seleucids.

7: Boeckh considered that ἐνεφάνισαν (or ἀνενεώσαντο, Wilhelm 1898) has fallen out after αὐτοὺς.

27: The formula is varied with σεμνά. For the abrupt ending compare **138**.

150–152: block found at Tepecık by Le Bas.

150. Arcades

A second column begins at line 30.

Le Bas-Waddington 72 [Cauer 57; Michel, *Rec.* 58; Blass, *SGDI* 5178 (in part); Guarducci, *I.Cret.* I v 52].

Ἀρκάδων
ἔδοξεν Ἀρκάδων τοῖς κόσμοις καὶ τᾶι πόλει· ἐ-
πειδὴ Τήϊοι φίλοι καὶ συγγενεῖς ὑπάρχοντες
διὰ προγόνων τᾶι πόλει ψάφισμα καὶ πρειγευ-
τὰς ἀπέσταλκαν Ἀπολλόδοτον καὶ Κωλώ-
ταν, οἳ ἐπελθόντες ἐπὶ τὸ κοινὸν τῶν Ἀρκάδων
τό τε ψάφισμα ἀπέδωκαν καὶ αὐτοὶ διελέγεν
ἀκολούθως τοῖς γεγραμμένοις, τὰν ἐκτε-
νεστάταν σπουδὰν καὶ φιλοτιμίαν ποιούμε-
νοι περὶ τῶ γενέσθαι τὰν καθιέρωσιν τῶι
Διονύσωι τᾶς τε πόλεως καὶ τᾶς χώρας τᾶς
Τηΐων καὶ τὰν ἀσυλίαν, ἔτι δὲ καὶ τἆλλα τὰ ὑ-
πάρχοντα αὐτοῖς ἔνδοξα καὶ τίμια διὰ τὸν
θεὸν ψαφιζομένος καὶ αὐτὸς συναύξεν καὶ
ἀεί τινος ἀγαθῶ παραιτίος γίνεσθαι τῶι δάμωι,
καὶ ὅτι ταῦτα ποιήσαντες ἀκόλουθα πράξομεν
τᾷ τε πρὸς τὸ θεῖον εὐσεβείᾳ καὶ τὰ μέγιστα χα-
ριξόμεθα τῶι δάμωι· περὶ δὲ τῶν αὐτῶν διαλε-
γέντος μετὰ πάσης σπευδῆς καὶ τοῦ παρὰ τῶ
βασιλέως Φιλίππου πρεσβευτᾶ Περδίκκα· ἀ-
ποκρίνασθαι τοῖς πρειγευταῖς ὅτι ἁ πόλις δια-
κειμένα φιλικῶς καὶ εὐήθως ποτὶ τὸ πλῆθος [τὸ]
Τηΐων ἔν τε τοῖς ὑπεράνω χρόνοις οὐθενὸς ἀ-
πεστάτουν τῶν συμφερόντων καὶ νῦν δὲ
καθότι παρακαλεῖ ὁ δᾶμος ὁ Τηΐων καὶ Περ-
δίκκας ὁ πολίτας αὐτῶν, προαιρεόμενοι οὖν
ἐμ πᾶσιν εὐχαριστεῖν καὶ μεμναμένοι τὰν
προϋπάρχωσ⟨α⟩ν ταῖ⟨ς⟩ πόλεσι συγγένειαν, τάν
τε καθιέρωσιν τῶι Διονύσωι τᾶς τε πόλιος
καὶ τᾶς χώρας ὑμέων, ἔτι δὲ ἱερὰν καὶ ἄσυλον
ἦμεν, βουλόμενοι χαρίζεσθαι Περδίκκαι, δί-
δομεν, καὶ τὰ λοιπὰ τὰ ὑπάρχοντα ὑμῖν ἔνδο-
ξα καὶ τίμια διαφυλάξομεν ἀπροφασίστως
ἐφ' ὅσον ἠμὲν ἐν δυνατῶι· καὶ αἴ τινες τῶν ὁρμι-
ομένων ⟨ἐξ⟩ Ἀρκάδων ἀδικήσωντί τινα Τηΐων
ἢ κοινᾶι ἢ ἰδίαι πὰρ τὸ γραφὲν δόγμα περὶ τᾶς
ἀσυλίας ὑπὸ τᾶς πόλιος τᾶς Ἀρκάδων, ἐξ-
έστω τῶι παραγενομένωι Τηΐων ἐπιλαβέσ-
θαι καὶ τῶν σωμάτων καὶ χρημάτων, αἴ τίς κα
ἄγηι· οἱ δὲ κόσμοι οἱ τότε ἀεὶ κοσμέοντες ἐ-
παναγκαζόντων ἀποδιδόμεν τὸς ἔχοντας,

ἀζάμιοι ἰόντες καὶ ἀνυπόδικοι· ἀγγράψαι δὲ
καὶ τὸ δόγμα ἐς τὸ ἱαρὸν τῶ Ἀσκλαπιῶ τὸγ γραμ-
ματέα τᾶς πόλεος, δοθῆμεν δὲ καὶ ξένια
τοῖς πρειγευταῖς τᾶ ἐν τῶι νόμωι. ἔρρωσθε.

22 [τὸ], 35 ⟨ἐξ⟩ ad. Blass.

Arcadia was an important city at the eastern extreme of the Messara; on the problem of the site see D. Viviers, *BCH* 118 (1994) 232–234.

43: The major festival was the Asclepieia; cf. *Staatsvertr.* III 512.9 of about this date.

151. Allaria

After **150**, continuing to a third column at line 13.

Le Bas-Waddington 73 [Cauer 58; Blass, *SGDI* 5179; Michel, *Rec.* 59; Guarducci, *I.Cret.* II 1 1].

Ἀλλαριωτᾶν
ἐπειδὴ Τήϊοι φίλοι καὶ συγγενεῖς διὰ προ-
γόνων ὑπάρχοντες ψάφισμα καὶ πρεσβευ-
τὰς ἀπέστειλαν{τες} παρ' ἁμὲ Ἀπολλόδο-
τον καὶ Κωλώτην, οἳ καὶ ἐπελθόντες ἐπὶ
τὰν ἐκκλησίαν τάν τε φιλίαν καὶ οἰκειότα-
τα τὰν ὑπάρχωσαν ἁμῖν ποτ' αὐτὸς ἀνενη-
ώσαντο καὶ τἆλλα διελέγησαν καλῶς καὶ
ἐνδόξως περὶ τῶ θεῶ καὶ τᾶς καθιερώσιος
τᾶς τε πόλιος καὶ τᾶς χώρας ἀκολούθως τοῖς
ἐν τῶι ψαφίσματι κατακεχωρισμένοις, καὶ ἀξί-
ων τάν τε φιλίαν καὶ τὰν εὔνοιαν διαφυλάσσοντ⟨α⟩ς
ἀεί τινος ἀγαθῶ παραιτίως γίνεσθαι τῶι δάμωι
καὶ τὰ παρακαλώμενα ἐπὶ πλέον συναύξεν· ὁμοί-
ως δὲ παρεκάλει καὶ Περδίκκας ὁ παρὰ τοῦ βασι-
λέως Φιλίππου πρεσβευτὰς οὐθὲν ἐλλείπων
σπουδᾶς καὶ φιλοτιμίας· δεδόχθαι τοῖς κόσμοις
καὶ τᾶι πόλει τῶν Ἀλλαριωτᾶν ἀποκρίνασθαι
Τηΐοις φίλοις καὶ οἰκείοις ἐῶσιν διότι τὸν Διόνυ-
σον καὶ αὐτοὶ σεβόμεθα καὶ τὸν Τηΐων δᾶμον συγ-
γενῆ ἐόντα ἀσπαζόμεθα καὶ ἐπαινῶμεν διότι
καλῶς καὶ ἐνδόξως καὶ καταξίως τῶ θεῶ προέσ-
τακεν· ἕνεκεν ὧν καὶ παρ' ἁμῶν τὰ καλὰ καὶ τίμι-
α δίδοται τῶι θεῶι, καὶ Τηΐων τάν τε πόλιν καὶ τὰν
χώραν ἀνίεμεν ἱερὰν καὶ ἄσυλον νῦν τε καὶ εἰς
τόν ἄλλον χρόνον πάντα καὶ πειρασόμεθα ἀεί
τινος ἀγαθῶ παραίτιοι γίνεσθαι καὶ κοινᾶι καὶ ἰ-
δίαι· ἐάν τέ τινες ἄγωσιν Τηΐως ἢ τὸς κατοικόν-
τας παρ' αὐτοῖς, οἱ κόσμοι καὶ ἄλλος ὁ βωλόμενος
Ἀλλαριωτᾶν ἢ Τηΐων ἀφελόμενοι καὶ ἀποδι-

δοντες τοῖς ἀδικημένοις κύριοι ἔστων.

4 Blass: ΑΠΕΣΤΕΙΛΑΝΤΕΣ. 12 Blass: ΤΕΣ. 14: error for προγενόμενα? Blass.

Allaria has not been located but was probably in the west of Crete. Polybius had occasion to mention the city under the year 206/5 (book 13: Steph. Byz. s.v.), no doubt the same passage that mentioned Sybrita.

152. Lato by Camara

After **151**, continuing to the fourth column on the stone at line 11.

Le Bas-Waddington 74 [Cauer 59; Cauer² 125; Blass, *SGDI* 5180 (in part); Michel, *Rec.* 60; Guarducci, *I.Cret.* I XVI 15].

Λατίων τῶν πρὸς Καμάραι
ἔδοξεν Λατίων τοῖς κόσμοις καὶ τᾶι πόλει· ἐπει-
δὴ Τήϊοι συγγενεῖς καὶ φίλοι διὰ προγόνων ὑπαρ-
χοντες ψάφισμα καὶ πρειγευτὰν⟨ς⟩ ἀπέσταλκαν Ἀ-
πολλόδοτον καὶ Κωλώταν, οἱ δὲ ἐπελθόντες ἐπὶ τὸ
κοινὸν τὸ Λατίων τό τε ψάφισμα ἀπέδωκαν καὶ αὐ-
τοὶ διελέγεν ἀκολούθως τοῖς γεγραμμένοις, τὰν
ἐκτενεστάταν σπουδὰν καὶ φιλοτιμίαν ποιού-
μενοι περὶ τῶ γενέσθαι τὰν καθιέρωσιν τῶι Διονύ-
σωι τᾶς πόλιος καὶ τᾶς χώρας τᾶς Τηΐων καὶ τὰν
ἀσυλίαν, ἔτι δὲ καὶ τἆλλα τὰ ὑπάρχοντα αὐτοῖς
ἔνδοξα καὶ τίμια διὰ τὸν θεὸν ψαφισαμένος
καὶ αὐτὸς συναύξεν καὶ ἀεί τινος ἀγαθῶ πα-
ραιτίος γίνεσθαι τῶι δάμωι, καὶ ὅτι ταῦτα πράξαν-
τες ἀκόλουθα πραξίομεν τᾶι τε πορτὶ τὸν θεὸν
εὐσεβείαι τᾶι μεγίσται καὶ χαριξιόμεθα τῶι δά-
μῶι· περὶ δὲ τῶν αὐτῶν διαλεγέντος μετὰ πάσας
εὐνοίας καὶ προθυμίας καὶ ⟨τῶ⟩ παρὰ τῶ βασιλέος Φιλίπ-
πω πρειγευτᾶ Περδίκκα{ι}· ἀποκρίνασθαι τῶι δά-
μωι τῶι Τηΐων ὅτι πρότερον ἁ πόλις καὶ νῦν δ' ἐ[μ]
πᾶσιν εὐχαριστεῖ καὶ μεμναμένοι τὰν προϋπάρ-
χονσαν τᾶι πόλει συγγένειαν, τάν τε καθιέρω-
σιν τῶι Διονύσωι τάν τε πόλιν καὶ τὰν χώραν ἦμεν
ἱερὰν καὶ ἄσυλον, βωλόμενοι χαρίζεσθαι Περδίκ-
και, δίδομεν, καὶ τὰ λοιπὰ τὰ ὑπάρχοντα ὑμῖν ἔνδο-
ξα καὶ τίμια συνδιαφυλαξίομεν ἀπροφασίστως
ἐφ' ὅσον κ' ἴωμεν δυνατοί· καὶ εἴ τινές κα τῶν ὁρ-
μιομένων Λατόθεν ἀδικήσωντί τινα Τηΐων
ἢ κοινᾶι ἢ ἰδίαι παρὰ τὸ γραφὲν δόγμα περὶ τᾶς ἀ-
συλίας τᾶς πόλιος καὶ τᾶς χώρας, ἐξέστω τῶι
παργενομένωι Τηΐων ἐπιλαβομένωι καὶ σω-
μάτων καὶ χρημάτων, εἴ τίς κα ἄγηι· οἱ δὲ κόσμοι
οἱ τόκα κοσμίοντες ἀναγκαζόντων ἀποδιδό-
μεν τὸς ἔχοντας, ἀζάμιοι ὄντες καὶ ἀνυπόδικοι·

γράψαι δὲ καὶ τὸ δόγμα ἐς τὸ ἱερὸν τᾶς Ἐλευθυίας.

4 Blass: TAN Le Bas, τὰ⟨ς⟩ Cauer. 5: ΟΙΔΙΕΠ; οἱ δ' ἐπ. Waddington; or οἱ ⟨κ⟩αὶ ἐπ.? 9: περί ⟨τε⟩ τῶ Guarducci. 16: error for καὶ τὰ μέγιστα, unless this is iotacism. 18 ⟨τῶ⟩ ad. Blass. 20 δ' ἐ[μ] Blass: δὲ Waddington. 30: τᾶς ⟨τε⟩ πόλιος Guarducci. 31: error for ἐπιλαβέσθαι (Blass). 33: ἀεὶ may have been omitted after τόκα.

The distinction "Lato by Camara" is made only in the Teans' heading added to this decree, not in the decree itself. Evidently the two Latos are in sympolity. No two decrees in the archive are so similar (but note Istron and Arcades). Both moreover are to be inscribed in the temple of Eleithyia; I take it this was a single temple shared by the two. One thinks of the two Colophons, obliged to ratify each other's decrees (Robert, *Villes* 62). The separation probably was brief; several lists of Cretan cities extant (admittedly incomplete) know only one Lato—*Staatsvertr.* III 582.38 (260 B.C.); *I.Cret.* IV 179.a.6 (183 B.C.). Xenion by contrast knew Camara as a city that used to be called Lato.[58] Evidently the harbor city flourished at the expense of the hill site in late Hellenistic times. On all this see E. Kirsten, *RE* Suppl. 7 (1940) 357–358.

153. Rome

A block found in the cemetery at Araka near Seğacık.

Chishull pp. 102–104; Hessel no. 1 (copy of de Hochepied) [Boeckh, *CIG* 3045]; Le Bas-Waddington 60 [Dittenberger, *Syll.* 204, *Syll.*[2] 279; Viereck, *Sermo graecus* 2; Michel, *Rec.* 51; Hiller, *Syll.*[3] 601; *IGR* IV 1557; Sherk, *Roman Doc.* 34].

Cf. S. Accame, *Il dominio romano* (Rome 1946) 51–52; Schmitt, *Untersuchungen* 97.

Ῥωμαίων
Μάρκος Οὐαλάριος Μάρκου στρατηγὸς καὶ
δήμαρχοι καὶ ἡ σύνκλητος Τηΐων τῆι βουλῆι καὶ τῶι
δήμωι χαίρειν· Μένιππος ὅ τε παρ' Ἀντιόχου τοῦ βα-
σιλέως ἀποσταλεὶς πρὸς ἡμᾶς πρεσβευτής, προ-
χειρισθεὶς καὶ ὑφ' ὑμῶν πρεσβεῦσαι ὑπὲρ τῆς πόλεως,
τό τε ψήφισμα ἀνέδωκεν καὶ αὐτὸς ἀκολούθως τούτωι
διελέχθη μετὰ πάσης προθυμίας· ἡμεῖς δὲ τόν τε ἄν-
δρα ἀπεδεξάμεθα φιλοφρόνως καὶ διὰ τὴν προγεγενη-
μένην αὐτῶι δόξαν καὶ διὰ τὴν ὑπάρχουσαν καλοκά-
γαθίαν περί τε ὧν ἠξίου διηκούσαμεν εὐνόως· καὶ ὅτι
μὲν διόλου πλεῖστον λόγον ποιούμενοι διατελοῦ-
μεν τῆς πρὸς τοὺς θεοὺς εὐσεβείας, μάλιστ' ἄν τις στο-
χάζοιτο ἐκ τῆς συναντωμένης ἡμεῖν εὐμενείας
διὰ ταῦτα παρὰ τοῦ δαιμονίου· οὐ μὴν ἀλλὰ καὶ ἐξ ἄλ-

58. *FGrHist* 460 F 7. This speaks against Ziegler's suggestion to date Xenion before Polybius and even in the fourth century B.C. (*RE* 9A [1967] 1479–1480).

λων πλειόνων πεπείσμεθα συμφανῆ πᾶσι γεγονέναι τὴν ἡμετέραν εἰς τὸ θεῖον προτιμίαν, διὸ καὶ διά τε ταῦτα καὶ διὰ τὴν πρὸς ὑμᾶς εὔνοιαν καὶ διὰ τὸν ἠξιω[μέν]ον πρεσβευτὴν κρίνομεν εἶναι τὴν πόλιν καὶ τὴγ χώραν ἱεράν, καθὼς καὶ νῦν ἐστιν, καὶ ἄσυλον καὶ ἀφορολόγητον ἀπὸ τοῦ δήμου τοῦ Ῥωμαίων καὶ τά τε εἰς τὸν θεὸν τίμια καὶ τὰ εἰς ὑμᾶς φιλάνθρωπα πειρασόμεθα συνεπαύξειν, διατηρούντων ὑμῶν καὶ εἰς τὸ μετὰ ταῦτα τὴν πρὸς ἡμᾶς εὔνοιαν. ἔρρωσθε.

4: Le Bas did not report τοῦ. 6 ὑπὲρ Chishull, Hessel: περὶ Le Bas. 16: Le Bas did not report πᾶσι. 17: προ⟨θυ⟩μίαν sugg. Sauppe ap. Viereck. 18: ἡμᾶς Chishull.

. . .

(4ff.) Menippus the ambassador sent to us by King Antiochus, and already elected by you to serve as ambassador in behalf of your city, presented your decree and himself spoke with all zeal in keeping with it. We received the man gladly because of the reputation he had established and because of his manifest excellence, and we heard his requests favorably. And that we take the greatest account of piety toward the gods one may easily guess from the favor we have consequently obtained from the divine. For many other reasons besides we are persuaded that our primacy in honoring the divine is clear to all. So for this reason and out of loyalty toward you and because of your worthy ambassador, we judge your city and country to be sacred, as it in fact now is, and inviolable and immune from tribute as regards the Roman people, and we shall try to join in increasing honors for the god and privileges for you, if you also hereafter preserve your loyalty to us.

1–2: The date in 193 is given by the combination of Menippus and the praetor M. Valerius (see above, p. 286). The intervention of a praetor, in the absence of the consuls, to present foreign envoys to the Senate is well attested in this period (e.g., *Roman Doc.* 1, 4, 7, all covering letters to senatus consulta). The list of authors here is comparable to two other acts of the early second century (*Roman Doc.* 38, 39): a consul (or praetor), the tribunes of the plebs, the Senate. I do not know whether the tribunes had an actual role in these proceedings, all of which concern foreign policy.[59]

Evidently no Tean came to Rome in 193; but it is explicit that the Seleucid envoy Menippus carried with him a decree of Teos and was chosen by the city to do so. Presumably he had passed through Teos in the immediate past, but it is not clear whether this was a new decree or the same one that the Teans had circulated a decade earlier. Note that Valerius nowhere mentions Dionysus.

7: On the verb see Holleaux, *Etudes* I 357.

59. Perhaps as a redaction committee for the Senate, according to O'Brien Moore, *RE* Suppl. 6 (1935) 698. Mommsen (*Ges. Schr.* II 314 n. 1; cf. III 655 n. 3, 1027) thought the tribunes were mentioned simply in order to include a nonpatrician office; it may be more pertinent that tribunes were not in the Senate.

20: The phrase "sacred, as it now is, and inviolable" might suggest a two-tiered process consistent with Seyrig's theory (above, p. 35) that the king granted "sacred" and foreigners "inviolable"; but that is expressly excluded for Teos, as we know the terms of the king's recognition. The phrase here probably reflects merely the later date of the Roman recognition.

24: Picard (*Ephèse et Claros* 148 n. 3) considered that in this clause the Romans imposed a condition that Teos remain loyal, hence their attack on Tean territory in 190 (Livy 37.27–28) was justified;[60] Errington (n. 26: 282) held that the reservation was calculated, given the circumstances of 193. Compare the Senate's answer to Demetrius I of Syria in 160 B.C. (Polyb. 32.3.13): ἐὰν τὸ ἱκανὸν ποιῇ (cf. Diod. 31.30: ἀπόκρισιν σκολιὰν καὶ δυσεύρετον).

In the second series of civic decrees, the order on the Tean stones, so far as that is known, again does not appear to be geographical; and one decree (**158**) does not seem to come from Crete. The script is more blockish than that of the first series.

154–157: block found at Tepecik.

154. Aptera

The second column begins at line 30, the third at 58.

Le Bas-Waddington 75 [Cauer 60; Cauer² 128; Michel, *Rec.* 61; Blass, *SGDI* 5181; Schwyzer 204; Guarducci, *I.Cret.* II III 2].

Cf. Robert, *Hellenica* I (1940) 118 n. 4.

Ἀπτεραίων
Ἀπτεραίων οἱ κόσμοι καὶ ἁ πόλις Τη-
ΐων τᾶι βωλᾶι καὶ τῶι δάμωι χαίρειν·
παραγενόμενοι οἱ παρ' ὑμέων πρεγγευ-
ταὶ Ἡρόδοτος Μηνοδότω, Μενεκλῆς
Διονυσίω τό τε ψάφισμα ἀπέδω-
καν ἐν ὧι ἐγράψατε ἀνανεώσασθαι
τάν τε συγγένειαν καὶ τὰν προϋ-
πάρχωσαν φιλίαν τά τε δεδομένα
τίμια ὑπὸ τᾶς ἁμᾶς πόλεως ἐν τοῖς
πρότερον χρόνοις καὶ τὰν καθιέρωσιν
τᾶς πόλιος καὶ τᾶς χώρας τῶι Διονύ-
σωι, παρεκαλεῖτε δὲ καὶ ἀναγράψαι
τὸ πρότερον δόγμα ἐν ὁποίῳ κα κρί-
νωμεν ἱερῶι· διελέγην δ̣ὲ̣ καὶ οἱ παρ' ὑ-
μῶν πρεγγευταὶ ἀκολούθως τοῖς ἐν
τῶι ψαφίσματι ἀποφαίνοντες τάν

60. J. Briscoe, *Commentary on Livy Books CCCIX–CCCVII* (Oxford 1981) 331, offers neither argument nor citations: he notes the Roman recognition of *asylia* to Teos, "but that of course would not protect it on the present occasion."

τε πόλιν εὐσεβῶς διακειμέναν
πρὸς πάντας τὸς θεός, μάλιστα δὲ
πρὸς τὸν Διόνυσον ὄντα ἀρχαγέταν
τᾶς πόλεως ὧι καὶ καθιερῶσθαι συν-
βέβακε τάν τε πόλιν καὶ τὰν χώραν,
ὑπέρ τε τῶν λοιπῶν πᾶσαν σπου-
δὰν καὶ φιλοτιμίαν ποτάγοντες δι-
ελέγην· διὸ καὶ δεδόχθαι {ἀποκρίνασθαι}
τῶι δάμωι τῶι Ἀπτεραίων ⟨ἀποκρίνασθαι⟩Τηΐοις
οὖσιν συγγενέσι καὶ φίλοις διό-
τι ἔν τε τοῖς πρότερον χρόνοις τυγ-
χάνομεν εὐσεβῶς διακείμενοι πο-
τὶ πάντας τὸς θεὸς θ' ἡμῶν [μάλιστα δὲ]
καὶ τὸν Διόνυσον δι' ὃν καὶ πρότερον τάν
τε ἀσυλίαν ὑμῖν ἐδώκαμεν καὶ καθι-
ερώσαμεν τὰν χώραν καὶ τὰν πόλιν,
τετηρηκότες δὲ τὰ προδεδομένα ὑ-
μῖν φιλάνθρωπα μέχρι τοῦ νῦν πειρά-
ξομεν καὶ εἰς τὸν λοιπὸν χρόνον
διαφυλάσσειν ἀν⟨α⟩νεωσάμενοι ἃ
παρεκαλεῖτε διὰ τοῦ ψαφίσματος, καὶ
οὐκ ἀδικέομεν Τηΐος συγγενέας
καὶ φίλος ὑπάρχοντας οὔτε πολέμου
οὔτ' εἰράνας, καθότι οὔτε πρότερον,
πειράξομεν δὲ καὶ ἐάν τινες ἀδικῶν-
τι Τηΐος ἢ κατὰ κοινὸν ἢ κατ' ἰδίαν ἢ κα-
τὰ γᾶν ἢ κατὰ θάλασσαν ἐόντας ἱα-
ρὸς καὶ ἀσύλος, βοαθεῖν αὐτοῖς καθότι
ἂν ὦμεν δυνατοί, καὶ ἐάν τινες ὁρμι-
όμενοι ἐξ Ἀπτέρας ἀδικήσωντι Τη-
ΐος, εἶναι αὐτὸς ἐνόχος τῶι τῆς ἱερο-
συλίας νόμωι· ἀγγραψάτωσαν δὲ καὶ
Τήϊοι τὰν ἀνανέωσιν ἐς τὸ ἱερὸν
τῶ Διονύσω, ὅπως φανεφὰ ἦ πᾶσι τοῖς
Ἕλλησι ἡ τῶν Ἀπτεραίων εὐσέβεια
πρὸς πάντας τὸς θεός· ἀναγραψῶμεν
δὲ καὶ ἁμὲν τό τε πρότερον δόγμα
καὶ τὰν ἀνανέωσιν ἐς τὸ ἱερὸν τὸ
τᾶς Ἀρτέμιδος τᾶς Ἀπτέρας· ἐκαλέσα-
μεν δὲ καὶ ἐπὶ ξένια τοὺς πρεγγευτὰς
[- - - ἐπὶ τὰ]ν κοινὰν ἑ[στίαν]. ἔρρωσθε.

15 Cauer: HNANKAI Le Bas, διελέγησαν καὶ Waddington, διελέγην ἂν Michel, διελέγη⟨σ⟩αν ⟨δὲ⟩ Blass. 25–26 Robert: the verb has been misplaced. 30 Wilhelm ap. Schwyzer. 37: ANEN. 58: [ἐς τὸ πρυτανεῖον ἐ. τ. Waddington.

The earlier decree of Aptera (**145**) makes no provision for being inscribed. Here lines 34–35 are explicit in claiming that the status has not lapsed, and 41 that it has not been violated by Aptera. Like a number of these later decrees, the Apterans offer more lengthy protection clauses than in the first series; perhaps the second Tean decree had mentioned this feature of the earlier Cretan acts. Lines 44–45 explictly apply the territorial formula to persons, recognizing the Teans themselves as sacred and inviolable (cf. **160**.5).

30: For honoring all the gods cf. 53 and **159**.11; but "all our gods" is a strange expression, as Blass saw, and not paralleled in **159**.

33: For the order "country and city" see **156**.27. 56: Artemis Aptera only here; see Guarducci p. 9 for the possible meanings of the epithet.

155. Eranna

Below **154**, continuing on to the fourth column on the stone at line 28.
Le Bas-Waddington 76 [Cauer 61; Michel, *Rec.* 62; Blass, *SGDI* 5182].
Cf. Wilhelm, *GGA* 160 (1898) 216.

'Ερασνίων
[ἐπειδ]ὴ ὁ δᾶμος ὁ Τηΐων ἐκ παλαιῶν
[χρόνων] συγγενὴς ὑπάρχων καὶ φίλος
[δι]ὰ προγόνων τᾶς τῶν 'Ερασνίων πόλιος
ἐξαπέσταλκεν ψάφισμα καὶ πρεγ-
γευτὰς Ἡρόδοτον καὶ Μενεκλῆν, πα-
ρακαλίων ἁμὲ συντηρεῖν τὰ δεδομέ-
να τίμια ὑπὸ τῶν προγόνων ἁμίων καὶ
ἐπὶ πλεῖον αὔξειν, καὶ ὅπως ἀναγρα-
φῇ τὸ πρότερον δόγμα ὃ κατεβάλοντο
οἱ πρόγονοι περὶ τᾶς ἀσυλίας καὶ καθιε-
ρώσιος τᾶς τῶν Τηΐων πόλιος καὶ τᾶς
χώρας, ἐν ὁποίωι κα κρίνωμεν ἱερῶι, περὶ
ὧν καὶ οἱ πρεγγευταὶ διελέγησαν ἀκο-
λούθως τοῖς ἐν τῶι ψαφίσματι κα-
τακεχωρισμένοις μετὰ πάσης φιλο-
τιμίας· ἀγαθᾶι τύχαι ἔδοξεν 'Ερωνίων
τοῖς κόσμοις καὶ τᾶι πόλει ἐπαινέσαι
τὸν δᾶμον τὸν Τηΐων ἐπὶ τῶι πρός
τε τὸς θεὸς εὐσεβῶς διακεῖσθαι καὶ
μεμνᾶσθαι τῶν φίλων καὶ συγγενέων,
καὶ ἀποκρίνασθαι ὅτι ἁ πόλις τῶν 'Ερωνίων
καὶ πρότερον τετήρηκεν τὰν πρὸς Τη-
ΐους φιλίαν καὶ εὔνοιαν, καὶ νῦν δὲ
μένουσα ἐπὶ τᾶς αὐτᾶς αἱρέσιος τό τε
δόγμα τὸ πρότερον γραφὲν ὑπὸ τῶν προ-
γόνων περὶ τᾶς καθιερώσιος καὶ ἀσυ-
λίας τᾶς πόλιος καὶ τᾶς χώρας τᾶς Τη-
ΐων ὁμοίως δὲ καὶ τὸ νῦν ἀναγράψ(ε)ι ἐς τὸ

ἱαρὸν τὸ τοῦ Ἀσκλαπιοῦ καὶ τηρήσει
τὰν φιλίαν καὶ ἐπὶ πλεῖον αὐξήσει, καὶ ἐ-
άν τις ἐπὶ τὰν πόλιν τὰν Τηΐων ἢ τὰν
χώραν τὰν καθιερωμέναν τῶι Διονύσωι
τῶι ἀρχαγέται τᾶς πόλιος αὐτῶν στρα-
τεύηται ἢ κατὰ γᾶν ἢ κατὰ θάλασσαν,
βοαθήσει ὁ δᾶμος ὁ Ἐραννίων καθότι ἂν
ᾖ δυνατός· ὅπως δὲ εἴδωντι Τήϊοι
τὰν Ἐραννίων εὔνοιαν ἃν ἔχοντι πορ-
τ' αὐτός, δεδόχθαι ἦμεν Τηΐους πολίτας
Ἐραννίων, εἶναι δὲ αὐτοῖς καὶ ἀτέλειαν
καὶ ἔνκτησιν γᾶς καὶ οἰκίας· ἐπαινοῦ-
μεν δὲ καὶ τοὺς πρεγγευτὰς Ἡρόδοτον
Μηνοδότω, Μενεκλέα Διονυσίω ἐπί τε
τῶι σπεύδειν ὑπὲρ τᾶς πατρίδος φιλο-
τίμως καὶ τὰν ἐνδαμίαν πεποιῆσθαι
ἀξίως ἀμφοτερᾶν τᾶν πολίων, ἦμεν
δὲ αὐτὸς καὶ προξένος τᾶς τῶν Ἐραν-
νίων πόλιος, καλέσαι δὲ αὐτὸς καὶ ἐπὶ
ξενισμὸν ἐπὶ τὰν κοινὰν ἑστίαν.

29 Wilhelm: ΓΡΑΨΑΙ.

The earlier decree is not extant; the city of is attested also in the list of Cretan allies of Eumenes II in 183 B.C. (*I.Cret.* IV 179.a.6: Ἐρώνιοι, as twice here). It may have been in the Lasithi; cf. P. Faure, *Kadmos* 32 (1993) 69. Evidently Asclepius was their chief god; cf. the Arcades (**150**.43, **159**.34).

10: They are asked to inscribe the decree that their ancestors "set down": the verb is unusual and perhaps implies that the first decree had not been publicly inscribed.

11: On the order "inviolable and sacred" (contrast line 27; cf. **157**.13, **159**.32) see p. 33.

23ff.: Eranna is rather less explicit than Aptera in claiming that the status has continued in force. The protection provision concerns the place Teos, and there is no confusion with personal *asylia*; when granting honors to the Teans as persons Eranna turns quite properly to citizenship rights (so too Biannus).

156. Biannus

Below **155**, continuing to the fifth column on the stone at line 7, the sixth (which has longer lines) at 35.

Le Bas-Waddington 77 [Cauer 62; Michel, *Rec.* 63; Blass, *SGDI* 5183; Guarducci, *I.Cret.* I VI 2].

Wilhelm, *GGA* 160 (1898) 216.

Βιαννίων
ἔδοξεν Βιαννίων τοῖς κόσμοις καὶ τᾶι
πόλει, ἐπειδὴ Τήϊοι φίλοι καὶ συγγενεῖς
ὑπάρχοντες διὰ προγόνων ψάφισ-
μα καὶ πρεγγευτὰς ἀπέστειλαν Ἡρό-
δοτον Μηνοδότου καὶ Μενεκλῆν Διονυ-
[σίου, οἳ καὶ ἐ]πελθόντες ἐπὶ τὸς κόσμος
καὶ τὰν ἐκκλησίαν διελέγησαν ἀκολού-
θως τοῖς ἐν τῶι ψαφίσματι κατακε-
χωρισμένοις, ἀποδεικνύοντες τὰν
πόλιν ὑπὸ τῶν προγόνων ἁμῶν κα-
θιερωμέναν τῶι Διονύσωι καὶ ἄσυλον γε-
γενημέναν· διὸ καὶ ἔδοξεν τοῖς κόσμοις
καὶ τᾶι πόλει τῶν Βιαννίων ἀποκρίνασ-
θαι Τηΐοις διότι καὶ ἐν τοῖς πρότερον χρό-
νοις ἀπ' οὐθενὸς ἀπέσταμεν τῶν συμ-
φερόντων ὑμῖν, καὶ νῦν δ' ἐς τὰ παραχ̣αλού-
μενα ὑφ' ὑμίων συνεμβάντες διά τε
τὰν συγγένειαν καὶ τὰν φιλίαν τὰν
προϋπάρχουσαν καὶ διὰ τὸν θεὸν ὧι
καθιέρωται ἅ τε πόλις καὶ χώρα ὑμί-
ων, ἀναγράψομεν δὲ τό τε πρότερον
δόγμα ἐστάλαι λιθίναι καὶ ἀναθήσο-
μεν ἐς τὸ τοῦ Ἄρεος ἱερόν, ποιοῦμεν
δὲ ὑμᾶς καὶ ἰσοπολίτας καὶ ἀτελεῖς
καὶ πολέμω καὶ εἰράνας, καὶ ἐάν τινες
ἐπὶ τὰν χώραν τὰν καθιερωμέναν
καὶ ἐπὶ τὰν πόλιν ἐπερχόμενοι πολεμῶ-
σιν ἢ ἀφαιρῶνταί τι ὑμῶν, βοαθήσο-
μεν καθότι ἂν ὦμεν δυνατοί· ἔν τε
τοῖς λοιποῖς πειρασόμεθα αἰεί τινος
ἀγαθῶ ὑμῖν παραίτιοι γίνεσθαι· ἐπαι-
νοῦμεν δὲ καὶ τοὺς πρεσβευτὰς
Ἡρόδοτον καὶ Μενεκλῆν ἐπὶ τῶι
σπεύδειν ὑπὲρ τᾶς πατρίδος καὶ τὰ[ν ἐνδαμίαν πεποιῆσθαι ἀ]-
ξίως ἀμφοτερᾶν ⟨τᾶν⟩ πολίων, ἐκαλέσα[μεν δ' αὐτοὺς ἐπὶ ξενισ]-
μὸν ἐς τὸ πρυτανεῖον ἐπὶ τὰν κοινὰν ἐ̣[στίαν· εἶναι δὲ]
αὐτοὺς καὶ {τοὺς} προξένους ⟨τᾶς⟩ πόλιος τᾶ[ς Βιαννίων. ἐπὶ]
κόσμου Δεξίου τοῦ Γλαύκου, μηνὸς Ἐλε[υσινίου.]

7 Rigsby: [οἳ δὲ ἐ.] Waddington. 17 Wilhelm: ΑΒΑΛ. 35 Blass: τᾶ[ς πόλιος ἁμίων Waddington. 36: ⟨τᾶν⟩ add. Blass. 37 fin. Blass: [ἑστίαν τὰν ἁμὰν] Waddington. 38 Blass; fin. ἐψηφίσθη ἐπὶ] Waddington. 39 fin. Guarducci.

The earlier decree of Biannus (**146**) had contained a provision for inscription; in fact the present decree does not specify what the Teans now requested, but proceeds to grant a new inscription.

11: καὶ τὰν χώραν has been omitted or rather was felt superfluous (cf. **148**.35, **157**.7).

15: As at Eranna (**155**.23), a rather foggy assurance that the status has not lapsed.

18: For συνεμβαίνω, "join in an enterprise," as a civic virtue cf. *IGLSyrie* III 1183.7–10: ἕν τε πλείοσιν τῶν τῆι πόλει συμφερόντων καὶ κοινῆι τοῖς πολίταις καὶ ἰδίαι ἑκάστωι συνεμβαίνοντος ἀπαρακλήτως (Seleuceia, 186 B.C.).

157. Malla

Below **156** (still in the sixth column). Le Bas reckoned five lines at the end to be inaccessible, the stone being set into a modern structure; the stone is now dislodged and in Ireland, and W. Blümel will publish the five lines.

Le Bas-Waddingon 78 [Blass, *SGDI* 5184; Guarducci, *I.Cret.* I XIX 2].

Cf. Wilhelm, *Griechische Königsbriefe,* Klio-BH 48 (Leipzig 1943) 30.

⟨Μ⟩αλλαίων

ἔδοξε ⟨Μ⟩αλλαίων τοῖς κόσμοις καὶ τ[ᾶι πόλει· ἐπειδὴ Τήϊοι φίλοι]
καὶ συγγενεῖς ὑπάρχοντες διὰ [πρ]ογ[όνων ψάφισμα καὶ πρεγ]-
γευτὰς ἀπέσταλκαν Ἡρόδοτον Μην[οδότω, Μενεκλῆν Διονυσίω,]
οἳ καὶ ἐπελθόντες ἐπὶ τὰν ἐκκλησίαν [τό τε ψάφισμα ἀπέδωκαν]
καὶ αὐτοὶ διελέγην ἀκολούθως τοῖς ἐν [τῶι ψαφίσματι κατακε]-
χωρισμένοις, ὑπέρ τε τοῦ εἶναι ἱερὰν κα[ὶ ἄσυλον τὴν πόλιν, καὶ δ]
συνέστησαν διά τε τῶν χρησμῶ[ν τῶν δοθέντων τὰ μαντεῖα τὰ ἐν]
Δελφοῖς καὶ ἐν Διδύμοις, ὑπέρ τε τ[ῶν ἄλλων τῶν συμφερόντων ἀμφοτέ]-
ραις ταῖς πόλεσιν διελέγησαν μετὰ π[άσας σπουδᾶς καὶ φιλοτιμίας·]
ἔδοξεν ⟨Μ⟩αλλαίων τοῖς κόσμοις καὶ τᾶι πόλει ἀ[ποκρίνασθαι]
Τηΐοις διότι καὶ ἐν τοῖς πρότερον χρόνοις δεδωκό[των τῶν προ]-
γόνων ἡμῶν τὴν ἀσυλίαν καὶ καθιέρωσιν, εἰς στή[λην γράψαντες]
ἀναθήσομεν ἐς τὸ ἱερὸν τῶ Ζηνὸς τῶ Μοννιτίω· δ[ίδομεν δὲ αὐτοῖς]
καὶ ἀτέλειαν καὶ ἰσοπολιτείαν· καὶ ἐάν τινες ἀδικ[ῶσι Τηΐους ἢ τὴν]
χώραν παραιρῶνται τὴν καθιερωμένην, [βοα]θήσ[ει ἁ πόλις ἁ]
⟨Μ⟩αλλαίων ὡς καὶ ὑπὲρ τῆς ἰδίας πατρίδος, ἔν [τε τοῖς λοιποῖς πει]-
ρασόμεθα αἰεί τινος ἀγαθοῦ παραίτιοι ε[ἶναι· ἐπαινοῦμεν δὲ καὶ]
τοὺς πρεσβευτὰς ἐπ[ὶ] τῶι ΤΗ[- - -]

The Tean mason wrote the city's name Παλλαίων throughout. 7 πόλιν Rigsby, καὶ Wilhelm, δ Blass: ἄ. τ. χώραν αὐτῶν] Waddington. 8 fin. Wilhelm: τῶν ἀναγγελθέντων ἐν] Waddington, τῶ Ἀπόλλωνος τῶ ἐν] Blass. 10 fin.: ΜΕΤΑΡ[. 13 Blass: τὸ δόγμα] Waddington. 15 Blass: ἀδικ[ήσωσιν ὑμᾶς ἢ τὴν] Waddington. 17 Blass: [πᾶσι δὲ καὶ ἡμεῖς π. Waddington. 19: Blümel confirms Guarducci's suggested restoration.

Malla was a small city south of the Lasithi, facing the south coast; its earlier decree does not survive.

8: This is the only mention of an oracle in the Tean material. For συνίστημι, "demonstrate," see Welles, *Royal Corres.* p. 367.

14: On the god see Guarducci pp. 232–233.

16: παραιρέομαι for the more common ἀφαιρέομαι; note χώραν without πόλιν (hence Waddington's restoration at 7; cf. **159**.39, **160**.7; but the formulae of the recognition are not those of the protection clause); "city" alone at **156**.11 (the recognition).

158–159. Block found in the cemetery at Gesusler.

158. Cnidus (?)

Chishull 118; Hessel no. 16 [Boeckh, *CIG* 3052.12]; Le Bas-Waddington 79 [Blümel, *I.Knidos* 802].[61]

ἐψαφίσθη ἐπὶ δαμιουργοῦ Φίλωνος μηνὸς Ἀρτα-
μιτίου νευμηνίαι.

Boeckh thought the lines centered and a heading for the Arcadian decree that follows; Waddington saw that we have the end of a different decree. He invoked the eponymous *damiourgos* to suggest Cnidus as author; neither this office nor the month Artamitios is found in Crete. Possibly it was inscribed in this group because the Tean ambassadors to Crete passed through Cnidus on their way there or back.

159. Arcades

Below **158**, continuing on to the second column at line 29; below are inscribed the decrees of Cnossus and Priansus praising these envoys but not mentioning *asylia*.[62]

Lines 1–11 init., 28–50: Chishull 118–120; Hessel no. 16; Pococke 17 no. 8 [Boeckh, *CIG* 3052.3–55]. Complete: Le Bas-Waddington 80 [Cauer 63; Michel, *Rec.* 64; Blass, *SGDI* 5185; Guarducci, *I.Cret.* I v 53].

Cf. Wilhelm, *GGA* 160 (1898) 216.

Ἀρκάδων

ἔδοξεν Ἀρκάδων τοῖς κόσμοις καὶ τᾶι πόλει· ἐπει-
δὴ Τήϊοι φίλοι καὶ συγγενεῖς καὶ εὔνοοι ὑπάρχοντες
τᾶι πόλει διὰ προγόνων ψάφισμα καὶ πρεσβευτὰς
ἀπέσταλκαν Ἡρόδοτον Μηνοδότου, Μενεκλῆν Δι-
ονυσίου, οἳ καὶ ἐπελθόντες ἐπὶ τὸ κοινὸν τῶν Ἀρ-
κάδων τό τε ψάφισμα ἀπέδωκαν καὶ αὐτοὶ διελέ-
γεν μετὰ πάσας σπουδᾶς καὶ φιλοτιμίας ἐνφανί-
ζοντες τὰν εὔνοιαν τοῦ δάμου ἃν ἔχει πρὸς Ἀρ-
κάδας καὶ τοὺς λοιποὺς Κρ̣η̣[τα]ι̣έ̣ας, τάν τε εὐσέ-
βειαν ἃν ἔχετε πρὸς πάντας τοὺς θεοὺς μά-

61. Pococke saw the stone; see above, n. 44.

62. Hessel no. 16 reports only the headings of these three decrees, and also (preceding them) another, ΑΤΤΑΛΩΝ.

λιστα δὲ πρὸς τὸν Διόνυσον τὸν ἀρχαγέταν ὑμέ⟨ων ὧι⟩ ἅ τε πόλις καὶ χώρα ὑμῶν καθιερῶται, περί τε τῶν ἄλλων τῶν συμφερόντων ταῖς πόλεσιν διελέγησαν ἀξίως ἀμφοτερᾶν τᾶν πόλεων, παρεκάλεον δὲ ἁμὲ καὶ ἀναγράψαι τὸ πρότερον δοθὲν ὑμῖν δόγμα περὶ τᾶς ἀσυλίας ἐν ὁποίωι τε κρίνωμεν ἱερῶι· δε[δ]όχθαι ἀποκρίνασθαι τοῖς πρεσβευταῖς τῶν [Τ]ηΐων καὶ τᾶι πόλει διότι τὸ κοινὸν τῶν Ἀρ[κά]δων καὶ ἐν τοῖς πρότερον χρόνοις ἀπ' οὐδε[νὸς] ἀπέστα τῶν συμφερόντων τῶι δάμωι [τῶι] Τηΐων, διά τε τὸν Διόνυσον τὸν ἀρχαγέταν [ἔοντα] τᾶς πόλεως καὶ διὰ τοὺς λοιποὺς θεούς, [καὶ ἀνανεω]σαμένων τῶν παρ' ὑμῶν πρεσβευ[τᾶν τάν] τε φιλίαν καὶ συγγένειαν καὶ ἀποδει[ξαμένων] τὰν εὔνοιαν ἃν ἔχετε διὰ παντὸς [ἐς τοὺς Κρ]ηταιεῖς πάντας καὶ τὸ κοινὸν τῶν Ἀρκάδων· βωλόμενοι οὖν καὶ ἡμεῖς τοῖς εὐνόως διακειμένοις ἐν χάριτος μέρει μὴ λείπεσθαι, τό τε πρότερον δόγμα ὃ ἔχετε παρ' ἡμῶν περὶ τᾶς ἀσυλίας καὶ τᾶς καθιερώσιος τᾶς τε πόλιος καὶ τᾶς χώρας ἀναγράψομεν, καθότι παρακαλεῖτε διὰ τοῦ ψαφίσματος, εἰς τὸ ἱερὸν τοῦ Ἀσκλαπιοῦ, καὶ συντηρήσομεν τὰ δεδομένα ὑμῖν φιλάνθρωπα· παρακαλεσάντων δὲ ἁμὲ τῶν πρεσβευτᾶν δοῦναι ὑμῖν ἰσοπολιτείαν καὶ ἔνκτησιν γᾶς καὶ οἰκίας καὶ ἀτέλειαν, ταῦτά τε δίδομεν ὑμῖν, καὶ ἐάν τινες ἀδικῶσιν ὑμᾶς ἢ τὰν χώραν παραίρωνται τὰν καθιερωμέναν τῶι Διονύσωι καὶ πολεμέωσιν κατὰ γᾶν ἢ κατὰ θάλασσαν, βοαθήσομεν ὑμῖν καθότι ἂν ἔωμεν δυνατοί· εἶναι δὲ καὶ τὰ φιλάνθρωπα Τηΐοις παρ' Ἀρκάσι πάντα ὅσα καὶ Ἀρκάσιν ἔσται· ἐπαινέομεν δὲ καὶ τὸς πρεσβευτὰς Ἡρόδοτον καὶ Μενεκλέα ἐπὶ τῶι σπεύδειν ὑπὲρ τᾶς πατρίδος ἐκτενῶς καὶ τὰν παρεπιδαμίαν πεποιῆσθαι ἀξίως ἀμφοτερᾶν τᾶμ πόλεων, δοθῆμεν δὲ αὐτοῖς καὶ ξένια τὰ ἐκ τῶν νόμων, εἶναι δὲ Ἡρόδοτον Μηνοδότω καὶ Μενεκλῆ Διονυσίω προξένος τᾶς πόλεος ἁμῶν.

ἔρρωσθε.

8: ΠΟΛΛΑΣ Chishull, ΠΟ[Sherard, ΠΑΣΑΣ Le Bas. 10: ΚΑΙ . . ΤΑΝ Chishull, Κ[ρήτας] Boeckh, Π . . Ο . ΥΓΑΣ Le Bas, [Κρῆτ]ας Waddington, [Κρηται]έας Blass. 13 ⟨ὧι⟩ ad. Wilhelm, ὑμέ⟨ων⟩ Blass: ὑ|μέτερον, ἅ Le Bas-Waddington. 18: τε where we should have κα. 24: [ὑμέων] Blass. 25 Blass: [κ. ἐνφανι] Waddington, ἀπολογι] Wilhelm. 27 Blass: [ξαντες] Waddington, [ξάντων] Wilhelm. 28 Blass: [πρὸς τ. Waddington. 43: ΕΣΤΙΝ Sherard.

The Arcadians voted **150**, which was to be inscribed in the same temple as this decree now provides again (34). They are "unwilling to be behind with regard to those who are faithfully disposed on the score of gratitude" (29–30). At 36 they say quite explicitly that *isopoliteia* and other civic rights were requested by the Teans. In the penalty clause (39) they merge the protection of persons and territory (restored in **157**.15, expanded in **160**.5).

160. Hyrtacina

Block found by the acropolis in 1924; h. 0.49, w. 0.42, th. 1.36; letters 0.01, intersp. 0.005.

Y. Béquignon and A. Laumonier, *BCH* 49 (1925) 298–303 no. 1; cf. 482 [*SEG* 4.599; Guarducci, *I.Cret.* II xv 2].

Photograph: Béquignon and Laumonier pl. 10.

Cf. Robert, *RPhil* 53 (1927) 97–99 (*Op. min. sel.* II 1052–54).

[- - - - - - - - - - - - πρὸς] τὸς θεὸς ε[ὐ]-
[σεβ - - - - - - - - - - - - - -]ων εἰς τὸν
[- - - - - - ποιῆσαι Τηΐος] ἰσοπολίτας [καὶ]
[ἀτελεῖς καὶ πολέμω καὶ εἰρ]άνας, καὶ αἴ τίς
[κα ἀδικήσηι αὐτὸς] συγγενέας καὶ ἱερὸς
[ἐόντας ἢ πολε]μῆι ἢ κατὰ γᾶν ἢ κατὰ θάλα-
[σσαν καὶ παραιρῆ]ται τὰν χώραν τὰν καθιερωμέ-
[ν]αν, βοα̣[θή]σει ὁ δᾶμος ὁ Ὑρτακινίων καθὼς ἂν
δύναται μάλιστα· ἀναγράψαι δὲ τὰν ἀνανέ-
ωσιν εἰς τὸ ἱερὸν τὸ τᾶς Ἥρας· ὑπάρχειν δὲ
καὶ προξένος Ὑρτακινίοις Ἡρόδοτον Μη-
νοδότω, Μενεκλῆν Διονυσίω τὸς τῶν
Τηΐων πρεγγευτάς· ἐπαινέσαι δὲ α̣ὐ̣τ̣ὸ̣ς̣
ἐπὶ τᾶι ἐνδαμίαι καὶ τᾶι λοιπᾶι ἀναστροφᾶι
ᾶι πεποίηνται ἀξίως τᾶς πόλιός τε τῶν Τηΐων
καὶ Ὑρτακινίων πόλιος καὶ αὐσαυτῶν· κα-
λέσαι δὲ καὶ ἐπὶ ξένια τὸς πρεγγευτὰς
ἐπὶ τὰν κοινὰν ἑστίαν ἐς τὸ Δ[ελφ]ίνιον. ἔρρωσθε.

18 Robert.

Hyrtacina was in the southwest of the island.

4: The request has been merged with personal inviolability. For the phrase, here oddly applied, cf. **156**.26.

5: Cf. **154**.44.

7: Cf. **157**.16.

18: On the envoys' entertainment in a temple see Guarducci, *SMSR* 13 (1937) 162–163.

161. Unidentified Cretan city

Block found by the acropolis in 1924; h. 0.49, w. 0.48, th. 1.30; letters 0.01, intersp. 0.004.

Béquignon and Laumonier 303–305 no. 2; cf. 482–483 [*SEG* 4.600].

Photograph: Béquignon and Laumonier pl. 11.

Cf. Robert, *BCH* 50 (1926) 491 n. 3 (*Op. min. sel.* I 55).

[- - - - - - - - - παρακαλέων ἁμὲ] καὶ ἀν[α]-
[γράψαι τὸ πρότερον δοθὲν δόγμα] παρ' αὐτοῖς,
[ἵνα τούτων συντελεσθέν]των ὑπόμνη[μα]
[ὑπάρχηι τοῦ τοὺς 4–5]ας ἄξια τῶν προγό[νων]
[φιλάνθρωπα τοῖς Τη]ΐ̣οις χαρίζεσθαι· ὅπαι ὧν
[κατακολουθίοντες] τοῖς ὑπ' αὐτῶν παρκαλιομέ-
[νοις τάν τε ποτὶ] τὸς θιὸς εὐσέβειαν καὶ τὰν ποτὶ
[Τηΐος συγγένει]αν φαινώμεθα συντηρίοντες, δε-
[δόχθαι ἀπ]οκρίνασθαι αὐτοῖς διότι καὶ πρᾶτα περὶ
[ὧν ἐ]πέστελλον Τήϊοι πᾶσαν ἐτιθέμεθα πρόνοιαν
[ἐ]ς πάντα συνεπιδιδόντες αὐτὸς γνησίως,
καὶ νῦν ἐπὶ τᾶς αὐτᾶς αἱρέσιος ὄντες τῶν τε
πρεγγευτᾶν διακούσαμεν μετ' εὐνοίας καὶ βω-
λόμενοι τοῖς προϋπαργμένοις ἐξ ἁμίων φιλαν-
θρώποις πὸτ τὰν τῶν Τηΐων πόλιν ἀκόλουθα
πράσσεν ἀννεώμεθα μὲν τὰν ὑπάρχωσαν ἁμῖν
[ποτ'] α̣ὐτὸς συγγένειαν καὶ φιλίαν καὶ εὔνοιαν· ἀν[αγρά]-
[ψαν]τες δὲ καὶ τὰ προεψαφισμένα τίμια περὶ τᾶ[ς]
[καθι]ερώσιος τᾶς πόλιος καὶ τᾶς χώρας αὐτῶν [τῶι]
[ἀρχα]γέται Διονύσωι καὶ τὰν ἀσυλίαν εἰς τὸ ἱε[ρὸν τὸ]
[τᾶς Ἀ]θαναίας συντηρησίομεν καὶ εἰς τὸ λοιπ[ὸν]
[καθὼ]ς {ἂν} ἁμὲ παρακαλίοντι· ὅπαι δὲ συμβαί[νηι τὰν]
[ποτ' ἀ]λλήλους οἰκειότητα καὶ φιλίαν ἐπὶ πλ[εῖον]
[αὔξ]εσθαι κατὰ πάντα τρόπον, ἁμίων ΕΥ̣[- - -]

3 Wilhelm (*SEG*): [ἵνα - - - τού]των Béquignon and Laumonier. 4 Wilhelm: - - - ἀξίων ἁμ]ᾶς B./L. 6 Blümel by communication: [- - - αὐ]τοῖς B./L. 10 Robert: ἀ]π. B./L. 24: or ΕΧ; perhaps εὐ[χαριστεῖν βωλομένων Robert (*SEG*).

The only hint toward identifying the city is the cult of Athena, too common to be useful. The name is to be supplied in 4. At 9ff.: "Both previously (πρῶτον = πρότερον) we exercised every care for the things about which the Teans have written, joining in devoting ourselves nobly in every way, and now, holding to the same policy, we have attended to the envoys favorably, and wishing to act in keeping with the benefactions already established by us toward the city of the Teans, we renew" etc. In 20 the accusative appears to be an error for the genitive (but cf. p. 162).

Alabanda

Alabanda stood over the valley of the Marsyas River and the road that connected southern Caria to the Maeander Valley. The city was rich and important in the Hellenistic age and enjoyed an enduring relationship with the Seleucid dynasty. Refounded as "Antioch of the Chrysaorians" around 260 B.C., it maintained the royal name throughout the troubled generations that followed, reverting to "Alabanda" only after the defeat of Antiochus III in 190. This was one of the few cities of Caria south of the Maeander that became free after 188, excluded from the gift to Rhodes.[1]

The inviolability of the city and country, attested by decrees of Athens and the Delphian Amphictyony, was recognized in the wake of the western expedition of Antiochus III (204–202 B.C.).

The recognition was made in the names of two gods, Zeus Chrysaoreus and Apollo Isotimus. The first was patron of the League of the Chrysaoreans, of which many cities of Hellenistic Caria, including Alabanda, were members;[2] they met at the temple of Zeus Chrysaoreus at Stratoniceia.[3] Thus there is nothing surprising in finding this god honored also at Alabanda, although in fact the two *asylia* decrees are our only testimony.

1. Magie II 993–995; J. and L. Robert, *Fouilles d'Amyzon* I p. 17. On the names, Holleaux, *Etudes* III 141–157; Robert, *Op. min. sel.* I 22–23 and *BCH* Suppl. 1 (1973) 435–466 (refuting the traditional chronology that dated the refoundation to the end of the third century). Some limited excavation was carried out in 1904–5; the remains have deteriorated greatly since then: Edhem-Bey, *CRAI* 1905, 443–459; 1906, 407–422; H. Lauter, *BJb* 171 (1971) 134–139; G. Bean, *Turkey beyond the Maeander* (London 1971) 80–89. Freedom: Polyb. 30.5.15; Livy 43.6.5; cf. P. M. Fraser and G. E. Bean, *The Rhodian Peraea* (Oxford 1954) 107–108; Seyrig, *Trésors* 55; M. Errington, *Chiron* 17 (1987) 101.

2. Robert (1973, 452–453) notes that the coins allude to the city's membership by the emblem of Pegasus, the horse of Chrysaor (Hes. *Theog.* 281); cf. *Amyzon* p. 224.

3. Strab. 14.2.25 (660); cf. A. Laumonier, *Cultes indigènes en Carie* (Paris 1958) 200–211.

As to Apollo, his temple was identified by means of dedicatory texts inscribed on two columns in Roman times: θεοῖς Σεβαστοῖς καὶ Ἀπόλλωνι Ἰσοτίμωι καὶ τῶι δήμῳ and Ἀπόλλωνι Ἰσ[ο]τίμωι.[4] This Ionic temple, in the northern part of the city, was the largest building observed on the site. It seems to date from the later second century B.C.; part of the frieze survives, showing an Amazonomachia. Vitruvius, discussing pseudodipteral temples, mentions first the Magnesians' by Hermogenes of Alabanda, then that of Apollo by "Menesthes";[5] the second temple is usually taken to be that at Alabanda, which is in fact pseudodipteral.

In the two decrees Apollo is named second after Zeus. The civic coins, however, make clear that Apollo, not Zeus, was the patron of Alabanda.[6] The abundant Hellenistic issues, which begin ca. 200 B.C., show on the obverses only Apollo; the reverses show Pegasus (the horse of Chrysaor), or on smaller silver and on bronze Apolline types (cithara, tripod) among others. His epithet Ἰσότιμος marks him as being "of equal honor"—equal, apparently, to his father, Zeus. Clearly this was Apollo's official title, used even when he is named without Zeus, as on the columns from the temple precinct.

The epithet has been variously interpreted: as an act of Hellenism, Greek Apollo given equal honor with Carian Zeus (so Dittenberger); or as a reflection of contemporary politics, the Seleucid ancestor given equal honor with the city's traditional patron Zeus upon the royal refoundation (so Robert).[7] But the beginnings of the cult cannot be dated and need not be credited to Seleucid rule. A reading of the epithet that holds the chief civic cult to be no more than an expedient and temporary political fiction is in my view unlikely and unnecessary. The sentiment expressed by Apollo's epithet—equality of honor asserted against some challenge—is readily paralleled in the religious sphere and need not be taken as a metaphor from contemporary politics. Thus Poseidon

4. Edhem-Bey 1906, 419; Laumonier, *BCH* 58 (1934) 298–299; cf. *Cultes* 436–437.

5. Vitr. *De arch.* 3.2.6 (*a Menesthe facta*). The architect is not otherwise on record; the name, though known in myth (*Il.* 5.609; *FGrHist* 328 F 111), is not common (a Euboean, *IG* XII.9 1220; an Alexandrian, *I.Cret.* II XVI 8). I suggest that this is an error for the more familiar name Menestheus, especially popular at Carian Aphrodisias, where it is found in one family of artists (Lippold, *RE* 15 [1931] 852), and also of a mint magistrate at Alabanda (C. Boehringer, *Zur Chronologie mittelhellenistischer Münzserien* [Berlin 1972] 188–189).

6. For the sequence of the coins see Boehringer 9–11, 186–189; Seyrig, *Trésors* 54–55; N. Waggoner in *Kraay–Mørkholm Essays* (Louvain 1989) 283–290; M. J. Price, *The Coinage in the Name of Alexander* (London/Zurich 1991) 308–310.

7. Robert 1973, 460; *Amyzon* p. 141. Laumonier, *Cultes* 434–435, envisioned this only to reject it, though on the dubious grounds that only an old and indigenous god would have been thought worthy of inviolability, and that Ἰσότιμος may conceal some non-Greek epithet. Farnell, *Cults* IV 176, took it to mean "the god of equal civic rights," comparing Apollo Eleutherius at Alabanda (followed by Adler, *RE* 9 [1916] 223).

once heatedly asserted his equality with Zeus, μ' ὁμότιμον ἐόντα,[8] and Apollo's son Branchus was *patrio aequalis honori.*[9] The epithet Ἰσότιμος may derive from some local myth about a past rivalry of the two gods for the city, with Apollo winning the role as patron and acknowledged as equal to his father. The cult and cult title may well be older than Seleucid rule, although doubtless the Alabandans, like others, exploited their cult of Apollo in their dealings with the Seleucids.

I suggest that if there is anything "political" about the pair of gods honored in the *asylia* quest, it is rather Zeus Chrysaoreus who is the polite addition, named first in deference to the League of the Chrysaoreans. So too at Amyzon, where Artemis is seen to dominate before and after Antiochus' conquest, Apollo's name was placed first in its *asylia* documents—probably in deference to the Seleucids (see p. 335).

Two gods are named, but we have only one occasion and request. Was one cult place in question or two? The Pergamenes, for example, eventually came to have two inviolable temples on their territory, as did Stratoniceia and apparently Chalcedon, but these as a result of separate requests at different times. Because the Alabandans make a single request, and because the recipient of the status is the whole city and territory, I assume that only one sacred place is at issue, and within the city: therefore the large temple inscribed as Apollo's and mentioned by Vitruvius. Perhaps the precinct contained a *sekos* of Zeus Chrysaoreus, whom the Alabandans felt it expedient to mention on this occasion.

The date is controlled by the eleven Aetolian seats on the Council and the Delphian archon Philaetolus (**163**: end of the third century), the thirteen Athenian tribes (**162**.26: before 200), and the role of Antiochus III (whose similar actions at Amyzon, Labraunda, Nysa, and Teos were part of his western expedition, 204–202 B.C.). At Delphi the Alabandan envoy competed in the Panhellenic Soteria (**163**.31–32: ca. August) before attending the autumn meeting of the Amphictyony; if Nachtergael's reckoning of the cycle of the Soteria is correct, this must be August of 201 (*Les Galates* 232–235, 342 n. 182). The envoys probably set out from Alabanda in the spring; so the king's recognition would be late in 202 or early in 201.[10]

8. Hom. *Il.* 15.186. Cf. *Hymn. Hom. Merc.* 172–173, Hermes ἀμφὶ δὲ τιμῆς κἀγὼ τῆς ὁσίης ἐπιβήσομαι ἧς περ Ἀπόλλων, with E. Benveniste, *Indo-European Language and Society* (Coral Gables 1973) 463–464; Theoc. 17.16–17: Ptolemy Soter ὁμότιμον ἀθανάτοις; Callim. frag. 84 dieg.: τὸ μὲν ἄγαλμα τ[οῦ Εὐ]θυκλ[έο]υς κατ' ἴσον τῷ τοῦ Διὸς ἐτ[ίμη]σαν; Diod. 4.24.1: τιμηθεὶς ἐπ' ἴσης (Heracles).

9. Stat. *Theb.* 3.478; cf. Varro *Rer. div.* ap. Lact. Plac. ad *Theb.* 8.198 (p. 389 Jahnke): *et Apollini et filio pariter consecrat sunt templa.* Compare Ov. *Fast.* 5.18: *par erat omnis honos* among the primeval gods.

10. See Habicht, *ZPE* 69 (1987) 87–89.

Scholars have sometimes dated the grant to Alabanda to 203, contemporary with the king's dated letter to Amyzon concerning his army (p. 336).[11] And in 201 Antiochus was certainly not in Caria but engaged in the Syrian war. The cycle of the Delphian Soteria, on which I have relied, is admittedly debatable. But Seleucid control of this region lasted down to 190, and precisely from Amyzon we have evidence of negotiations between crown and city over several years following his western expedition (letters dated to 202/1 and 201/0). Antiochus' dramatic personal appearance at Teos in recognizing *asylia* there need not have been duplicated at other cities and was of course unusual. His several reported benefactions to Alabanda—democracy as well as *asylia*—may have emerged from slow diplomacy (as may have gone on at Teos even after his grant there),[12] perhaps spanning 203 to 201 and certainly not requiring his presence in Caria. But if instead this was a single gesture, the event should be dated ca. winter 202/1, with the Alabandans sending out their *asylia* envoys to the Greek world in spring 201.

Only one embassy is known to us, a pair of brothers: both appear at Athens, one at Delphi.[13] Thus they probably were in Athens first and parted thereafter in order to canvass different parts of the mainland. The two are called *presbeis*, not *theoroi*, probably because games were not in question at Alabanda (so too at Teos). The Alabandans' decree of request mentioned their Greek descent[14] and their piety, also the favor of Antiochus in protecting the city's democracy and peace (as he did at Teos, p. 284, and perhaps at Amyzon, *Amyzon* no. 9.4). He is not stated to have recognized inviolability, but the same silence is found in the many acceptances for Teos. The Amphictyony states that an oracle of Apollo of Delphi supported the request of Alabanda; it is explicit, however, that this oracle was obtained only now by the ambassador during his visit and did not initiate the quest.

It seems therefore that the quest for *asylia* recognitions occupied the spring and summer of 201. In late summer or early autumn, Philip V of Macedonia ravaged the land of the Alabandans "as enemy territory" (Polyb. 16.24.8):[15] certainly this was subsequent to Antiochus' recognition of inviolability, and possibly subsequent to the return of the ambassadors from their various missions. Polybius portrays Philip as excusing his action by claiming his army's need for provisions; but the excuse is prompted by Philip's alliance with Antiochus, not by the inviolability of the place, which Polybius does not mention. In 197 B.C.

11. Cf. H. R. Rawlings, *AJAH* 1 (1976) 2–3.

12. Cf. p. 284; Herrmann, "Antiochos" pp. 157–159.

13. A Dionysicles son of Iatrocles of Alabanda, possibly a third brother, was granted proxeny by Delphi in the year of Eucles, who, however, has been placed a generation earlier: discussion at Flacelière, *Aitoliens* 462–463.

14. Perhaps from equating the two heroes named Kar, one the founder of Alabanda, the other of Megara (see Eitrem, *RE* 10 [1919] 1924).

15. Cf. F. W. Walbank, *Philip V* (Cambridge 1940) 125–126, 309.

a battle between forces of Philip V and Rhodes may have been fought on Alabandan territory.[16] In 189, troops of Cn. Manlius Vulso, at the Alabandans' request, expelled from one of their fortresses a dissident faction and restored the fortress to the city (Livy 38.13.2). In 167 Alabanda participated in the war against Rhodes (Livy 45.25.13; Polyb. 30.5.15). In 40 B.C. the city resisted the Parthians without success (Dio 48.26.3–4).[17]

162. Athens

Two joining fragments of a stele of Hymettian marble, found in the Agora in 1970 and 1976 (Agora Museum I 7182); broken at top and bottom; h. 0.952, w. 0.544–0.578, th. 0.141; letters 0.006–7; the names at bottom are in inscribed crowns.

R. L. Pounder, *Hesperia* 47 (1978) 49–57 [*SEG* 28.75]; J. Osborne, *Naturalization in Athens* I (Brussels 1981) D 95. *Collation.*

Cf. Osborne, *ZPE* 38 (1980) 99–101.

Photograph: Pounder pl. 8.

[- - - - - - - - - - - - -]αντο καὶ [-]
[- - - - - - - - - - - - -]ο ἐπαυξηθῆνα̣[ι - - - - - - - - - - - - - - - - -]
[- - - - - - - - - - τ]ὴν πόλιν τὴν Ἀντι[οχέων - - - - - - - - - - - - -]
[- - - - - - - - - -]ούντων αὐτῶν̣ [-]
[- - - - - -]ΑΝΕΥΤ̣ΟΥΜΕΝΟΣΥ̣[- - - - - - - - δεδόχθαι τῆι βου]-
[λῆι τοὺς λ]αχόντας προέδρους εἰ]ς τὴν ἐπιοῦσαν ἐκκλησίαν χρηματί]-
[σαι περὶ τού]των, γνώμην δὲ συμβάλλε[σθαι τῆς βουλῆς εἰς τὸν
δῆμον ὅτι]
[δοκεῖ] τεῖ βουλε̣ῖ̣ ἀποκρίνασθαι [-]
[- - - - - - - -]τιων εἰσὶν οἱ πρέ[σβεις - - - - - - - - - - - - - - - - -]
[- - - - - προγ]εγονότα φιλάνθρω[πα - - - - - - - - - - - - - - - - - -]
[- - - - - - - -] μηδένα καιρὸν α[-]
[- - - - - κατὰ τ]ὴν ἑαυτοῦ δύναμιν [- - - - - - - - - - - - - - - - -]
[- - - - ἐπαι]νέσαι δὲ καὶ τὸν δ[ῆμον τὸν Ἀντιοχέων καὶ στεφανῶσαι]
[χρυσῶι στε]φάνωι κατὰ τὸν ν̣[όμον εὐνοίας ἕνεκα καὶ φιλοτιμίας εἰς]
[τὸν δῆμο]ν τὸν Ἀθηναίων [καὶ ἀναγορεῦσαι τὸν] σ̣τέφανο[ν Διονυσίων]
[τῶν ἐ]ν ἄστει καινοῖς [τραγωιδοῖς τῶι ἀγῶνι κ]αινῶι καὶ Παναθηνα[ί]-
[ων] καὶ Πτολεμ[α]ίων τ[οῖς γυμνικοῖς ἀ]γῶσιν· τῆς δὲ ποιήσεως τ̣[οῦ]
[στεφ]άνου καὶ τῆ̣[ς ἀναγορεύσε]ως ἐπιμεληθῆναι τοὺς στρατ̣η̣-
[γοὺς] κα[ὶ] τὸν τα[μίαν τῶν] στρατιωτικῶν· δεδόσθαι δὲ Ἀντιο-
χε̣ῦσιν καὶ πολ[ιτείαν κα]τὰ τὸν νόμον τὸν περὶ τῶν δωρεῶν κ[είμε]-

16. Livy 33.18.7; but the geography is surprising, and the Roberts have questioned the text (*La Carie* II 379 n. 4).

17. On the fate of Alabanda in the Mithridatic war see C. Marek in *Alte Geschichte und Wissenschaft, Festschrift für K. Christ* (Darmstadt 1988) 285–308, addressing in particular a decree of Alabanda concerning φόροι and ἀφορολογησία from Rome.

νον· καὶ εἶν[αι τ]ὴν πόλιν αὐτῶν καὶ τὴν χώραν καθιερωμένην τῷ[ι]
[Δ]ιὶ τῶι Χρυσ[αο]ρεῖ καὶ τῶι Ἀπόλλωνι τῶι Ἰσοτίμωι καὶ ἄσυλον
δ[ια]-
[μέ]νειν εἰς τὸν ἅπαντα χρόνον, ὅσον ἐστὶν ἐπ' Ἀθηναίοις· εἶνα[ι δὲ]
[αὐτ]οῖ[ς] καὶ προεδρίαν ἐν πᾶσι τοῖς ἀγωσιν οἷς ἡ πόλις τίθησ[ιν]
[καὶ] πρόσοδον πρὸς τὴν βουλὴν καὶ τὸν δῆμον πρώτοις μετὰ τ[ὰ]
[ἱερά· ἐ]πιμελείσθω δὲ καὶ ἡ βουλὴ οἱ ἑξακόσιοι καὶ πεντήκοντ[α]
[καὶ οἱ] σ[τρατη]γοὶ τῶν ἐπιδημούντων Ἀντιοχέων ὅπως ὑπὸ μηθε-
νὸς ἀδικῶνται· ἐπαινέσαι δὲ καὶ τοὺς παραγεγονότας πρέσβ[εις]
Παυσίμαχον Ἰατροκλέους, Ἀριστοφάνην Ἰατροκλέους καὶ στ[ε]-
φανῶσαι ἑκάτερον αὐτῶν θαλλοῦ στεφάνωι· καλέσαι δὲ αὐτοὺ[ς]
καὶ ἐπὶ δεῖπνον εἰς τὸ πρυτανεῖον εἰς αὔριον· ἀναγράψαι δὲ τόδ[ε]
τὸ ψήφισμα τὸν γραμματέα τὸν κατὰ πρυτανείαν ἐν στήλει λιθί-
[ν]ει καὶ στῆσαι ἐν ἀγορᾶι· τὸ δὲ γενόμενον ἀνάλωμα εἰς τὴν ποίη-
σιν τῆς στήλης καὶ τὴν ἀνάθεσιν μερίσαι τὸν ταμίαν καὶ τοὺς
[ἐ]πὶ τεῖ διοικήσει.

ἡ βουλή	ἡ βουλή	ἡ βουλή
ὁ δῆμος	ὁ δῆμος	ὁ δῆμος
Παυσίμαχον	τὸν δῆμον	Ἀριστοφάνην
Ἰατροκλέ-	τὸν Ἀντιο-	Ἰατροκλέ-
ους	χέων	ους

In a few restorations I have modified the line divisions of Pounder or Osborne. 5: Ṭ is possibly I. 13 Osborne: στεφανῶσαι αὐτὸν] Pounder. 20 Osborne: πολ[ιτείαν δοκιμασθεῖσι κα]τὰ Pounder. 20–21 Osborne: κ[αι]|νόν Pounder.

The Amphictyonic Council (**163**) would praise Antiochus III with some vigor for his favor to Antioch-Alabanda. In what survives the Athenian decree does not mention him at all. This might reflect the accident of what is preserved;[18] but from the crowns at the end it is certain that Athens did not crown Antiochus, as the Council did (**163**.26). Ptolemy's traditional friend Athens here accedes to a request occasioned when Antiochus deprived Ptolemy of his Carian cities; we are on the eve of the war in which Antiochus and Philip V would cooperate to deprive the Ptolemies of their overseas possessions. If the Athenians, while honoring Alabanda as was expected, omitted to mention Antiochus, that may reflect what was for them a delicate situation.

2ff.: Here apparently was talk of increasing the honors of Zeus and Apollo (or perhaps those of the Alabandans: so, for example, **155**.9), then of the *asylia* of the city and country.

8ff.: The Athenian answer first spoke well of the envoys, then cited the existing good relations between the two cities, then expressed the hope of losing no occasion for improving them to the extent of their ability.

18. So Habicht suggested, *Chiron* 19 (1989) 11 n. 17.

20: Citizenship for an entire city is an extraordinary honor at Athens; Osborne's catalogue indicates that the only precedents known are for Plataea and Samos long before, and subsequently only a grant of *isopoliteia* to Rhodes around 200 B.C. (Polyb. 16.26.9).

23: "in so far as it is in the Athenians' power," a polite caution of a sort found in some other grants of *asylia*, especially the Cretan decrees for Teos offering protection "so far as it is in our power" (e.g., **142**.24); for the phrase compare Isoc. *Arch.* 8: καθ' ὅσον ἐστὶν ἐπ' ἐμοί; Dem. 23.11: ὅσον ἐστὶν ἐν ὑμῖν; *FD* III.2 48.14: η[ὔ]ξησαν ὅσον ἐφ' ἑαυτοῖς; here, **107**.15–16.

26: The thirteen tribes reverted to twelve early in 200 B.C. (W. K. Pritchett, *TAPA* 85 [1954] 162–164), hence a terminus ante quem.

29: The name Pausimachus, while widely attested, seems to have been especially popular in Caria: *I.Magnesia* 3 (Alinda); *IG* XII.9 1187.24 and *Demetrias* V 307 (Halicarnassus); *I.Iasos* 271.40=272.41; *Amyzon* no. 28.26–29; cf. Klee, *Agone* p. 15 line 57 (Cos); App. *Syr.* 23 (Rhodes). So too Iatrocles; cf. Gauthier, *Bull. épigr.* 1989, 255.

163. Delphian Amphictyony

Marble base of a statue of Antiochus III[19] (cf. line 33) found in 1893 west of the temple of Apollo at Delphi (inv. 635); h. 0.81, w. 0.58, th. 0.72; letters 0.006, intersp. 0.006.

L. Couve (with copies by Homolle and Bourguet), *BCH* 18 (1894) 235–247 [Baunack, *SGDI* 2529; Michel, *Rec.* 252; Dittenberger, *OGIS* 234]; Flacelière, *FD* III.4 163. *Collation.*

Photograph: PLATE 4.

Cf. Wilhelm, *GGA* 160 (1898) 224–225; Pomtow, *Syll.*[3] II p. 7.

θεοί

ἄρχοντος ἐν Δελφοῖς Φιλαιτώλου, Πυλαίας ὀπωρινῆς, ἱερομνα-
μονούντων Αἰτωλῶν Τελεσάρχου Ἀπιρίχου, Λέωνος Ναυπα-
κτίου, Στομίου Μαχετιέος, Θεοδώρου Ἀργείου, Νικοβούλου Θηβαίου,
Εὐρυμάχου Θαυμακοῦ, Δορυμένεος Ὑπαταίου, Θεοδώρου Κοττα-
έος, Λαττάμου Βουκατιέος, Εὐδάμου Ἀρσινοέος, Λαμίου Ἀπολλω-
νιέος· Κεφαλλάνων Οἰνανθίου· Δελφῶν Ἀριστομάχου, Καλλικρά-
τεος· Ἀθηναίων Ἀριστοκλέος· Βοιωτῶν Φόξου, Καλλικράτεος·
Μαγνήτων Πολεμαίου· Χίων Μητροφάνεος· γραμματεύον-
τος τοῖς ἱερομνάμοσιν Μενάνδρου Θαυμακοῦ·
ἀγαθᾶι τύχαι, ἔδοξε τῶι κοινῶι τῶν Ἀμφικτιόνων, ἐπεὶ ἁ πόλις
ἁ τῶν Ἀντιοχέων τῶν ἐκ τοῦ Χρυσαορέων ἔθνεος, συγγενὴς ἐοῦσα
τῶν Ἑλλάνων, ἀποστείλασα πρεσβευτὰς ποτὶ πλέονας τέτευχε
πάντων τῶν τιμίων καὶ φιλανθρώπων, καὶ Παυσίμαχος δὲ ὁ πα-
ρ' αὐτῶν πρεσβεύσας ἐν ἐκείναις τε καλῶς καὶ ἀξίως τῶν Ἑλλά-
νων ἀνέστρεπται, καὶ νῦν ποτειληφὼς χρησμὸν παρὰ τοῦ θεοῦ,

19. Amid other equestrian statues, apparently of Seleucids: see on **7**.

κατακολουθέων {του} τούτωι, ποτελθὼν ποτὶ τὸ συνέδριον ἁμῶν, περί τε τᾶς ἰδίας πατρίδος πολλὰ κατευφάμηκε, ἐμφανίζων τὰν εὐσέβειαν αὐτᾶς καὶ τὰν ἀρετάν, ὁμοιως δὲ καὶ περὶ βασιλέος Ἀντιόχου τοῦ εὐεργέτα Ἀντιοχέων εὐλόγηκε εὐχαριστῶν αὐτῶι διότι τὰν δαμοκρατίαν καὶ τὰν εἰράναν {αν} τοῖς Ἀντιοχεῦσιν διαφυλάσσει κα[τ] τὰν τῶν προγόνων ὑφάγησιν· δεδόχθαι ἀποκρίνασθαι αὐτῶι ὅτι τὸ κοινὸν τῶν Ἀμφικτιόνων τὰν μὲν πόλιν τὰν Ἀντιοχέων καὶ τὰν χώραν ἀναδεικνύει ἄσυλον καὶ ἱερὰν τοῦ Χρυσαορ[έ]ως καὶ Ἀπόλλωνος Ἰσοτίμου, τὸν δὲ δᾶμον αὐτῶν καὶ βασιλῆ Ἀντίο[χον] ἐπαινεῖ, καὶ στεφανοῖ ἑκάτερον εἰκόνι χαλκέαι ὀκταπάχει ἐπὶ πᾶσι τοῖς προγεγραμμένοις· στᾶσαι δὲ τὰς εἰκόνας ἐν τῶι ἱερῶι τοῦ Ἀπόλλωνος τοῦ Πυθίου καὶ καρῦξαι ἐν τοῖς Πυθίοις· ἐπαινεῖ δὲ καὶ Παυσίμαχον Ἰατροκλέος καὶ στεφανοῖ χρυσέωι στεφάνωι ἀρετᾶς ἕνεκεν καὶ φιλοτιμίας τῆς εἰς τὰν αὐτοῦ πατρίδα, καὶ καρῦξαι τὸν στέφανον αὐτοῦ ἐν τᾶι πατρίδι, ὅταν εἰσάγηι τὸν τῶν Σωτηρίων στέφανον· ὅπως δὲ καὶ ὑπόμναμα ἦι εἰς ἅπαντα χρόνον, ἀναγράψαι τόδε τὸ ψάφισμα ἐν τᾶι βάσει τᾶι τοῦ βασιλέως Ἀντιόχου ἐν τῶι ἱερῶι τοῦ Ἀπόλλωνος τοῦ Πυθίου καὶ ἀποστεῖλαι ποτ' Ἀντιοχεῖς σφραγισαμένους τᾶι κοινᾶι τῶν Ἀμφικτιόνων σφραγῖδι.

A few letters have been lost to flaking since earlier editions; I have not indicated these losses. 4 cf. Dittenberger n. 3: Μα⟨κ⟩ετιέος Couve. 6 Pomtow: Λατταμίου Couve. 6 Baunack: Βου⟨χ⟩ατιέος Couve. 17 Flacelière: δὲ τούτωι Couve. 21 Wilhelm: AN, ἐν Couve.

2: The date of Philaetolus (201/0 on my reasoning): 205–202 Pomtow (cf. Holleaux, *Etudes* III 144 n. 2); ca. 202/1 Flacelière, *Aitoliens* 412–413 (rightly remarking that line 28 does not show that the year is Pythian and therefore 202/1); cf. Daux, *Chronologie* 45.

13–17: The case was argued on the basis of Greek kinship, the precedent of other honors, and now an oracle: Alabanda, "having sent ambassadors to many (cities), has obtained all the honors and benefactions; and their ambassador Pausimachus has conducted himself among them excellently and worthily of the Greeks, and now having in addition obtained an oracle from the god and obeying this . . ." The oracle will have urged other Greeks to join in the recognition; evidently the Alabandans originally had no oracle to argue from—at least no oracle of Delphi. Similarly, in their detailed account of Antiochus' visit, the Teans claimed no oracle, which is then mentioned only in the second series of grants.

21–22: At Alabanda Antiochus guarantees not only democracy but "peace"—in the context of the king's expedition, surely peace with other states, as was urged by Dittenberger and Robert (1973, 448), not domestic harmony. So too at Teos: peace and tax relief (p. 283: line 50) sum up what the king stated as inviolability and tax relief (lines 18–19). Consistent with Seyrig's view of *asylia*, this decree does not actually state that the king granted the status; but compare the ellipsis in the Delphian decree for Smyrna (p. 104). Here, by εἰράναν the Council may mean precisely the recognition of inviolability. For ὑφήγησις as the "example" set by a king's ancestors see Robert, *REG* 94 (1981) 351 n. 60.

24: As at Teos, one "grants" (here ἀνανδείκνυμι) rather than "accepts" the inviolability; here too this may reflect the king's choice of words in his own recognition. The word order "inviolable and sacred" is rare (see p. 33); this reversal, which is not in the Athenian decree and probably was not in the Alabandan request, seems to aim at the recherché, as does κατευφημεῖν (18).[20] The omission of the name of Zeus is surprising. "The Chrysaorean" seems not enough information for a foreigner; inasmuch as the Athenian decree does name Zeus, he was likely named in the Alabandan decree, and we may suspect a mason's error at Delphi, omitting Ζηνός (Holleaux III 141 n. 2 considered that πόλεις was omitted by mistake at 13).

26: These honors are quite substantial—colossal statues of both Antiochus and the Demos of the Antiochenes, as well as golden crowns; the Athenian honors (citizenship for all Alabandans, **162**.20) are substantial in a different way, but they may not have extended to the king.

31–32: As Dittenberger saw, Pausimachus has won a prize at the Soteria at Delphi, and on this visit, for he has not yet "brought home the crown"; for the phrase see Robert, *RPhil* III.4 (1967) 17 (*Op. min. sel.* V 357). The season is consistent: the Soteria occurred in August, in the weeks before an autumn sitting of the Amphictyony. And he was in Delphi long enough to consult Apollo, reportedly possible only on the seventh of each month (Callisth. *FGrHist* 124 F 49; cf. Plut. *Alex.* 14). As remarked above, if Nachtergael's chronology of the Soteria is right, the year is 201 B.C.[21]

20. The verb occurs in verse in the Jewish epigram Bernand, *I.métr.Egypte* 16.12 (imperial date).

21. Nachtergael, however, does not apply his own chronology to this particular case, repeating from Daux (*Chronologie* 45) "dernières années du 3e siècle ou 199/8" (474).

Temple of Artemis, Amyzon

The small Carian city Amyzon stood in relative isolation high in the area of Mt. Latmus south of the Maeander.[1] The Amyzonians' temple of Artemis looked over this mountainous country from its large terraces. Votive statuettes of the Carian goddess who came to be seen as Artemis are found as early as 500 B.C., Hellenistic inscriptions refer repeatedly to the temple of Artemis,[2] and Artemis dominates the coins; Apollo was a Hellenistic addition who remained secondary.

The main structures of the temple go back to the mid-fourth century B.C., under the Hecatomnids. A peribolos wall, entered by a monumental propylaeum, surrounded the sacred terraces, which included a theater and a fountain. The excavators found no public center apart from this complex, and no public buildings of a secular nature.[3] The citizens of Amyzon evidently lived in their villages scattered across the territory, and their public resources, no doubt meager, must have gone mostly to maintaining the cult of Artemis. The Seleucid governor of Amyzon was called ὁ ἐπὶ τοῦ Ἀρτεμισίου ἐπιστάτης (*Amyzon* no. 15.7); a decree of 321/0 B.C. lists as the chief magistrates the eponymous *prostates*, a committee of three archons, the head of the mountain patrol, and the "treasurer of the goddess" (no. 2). Thus the Artemisium dominated the civic life of Amyzon. The inscriptions indicate that it was the temple, not the city and country, that was declared inviolable.

When in 204/3 Antiochus III swept through Caria and reestablished Seleucid rule, his troops did extensive damage to this site, as surely happened elsewhere;

1. J. and L. Robert, *Fouilles d'Amyzon en Carie* I (Paris 1983).

2. *Amyzon* nos. 3.17, 15.7, 16.9; cf. 2.6. The sequence "Artemis and Apollo" seen under the Ptolemies (no. 3.13) becomes "Apollo and Artemis" under the Seleucids (nos. 10, 21)—a politic gesture. See *Amyzon* pp. 123, 167, 251.

3. It may be significant that the early decrees are of "the people"; a council is not mentioned until after 190 B.C. (no. 22).

his work of restoration has left us a number of documents, first put into context by Wilhelm.[4] Those that may be pertinent in some way to the inviolability of the Artemisium can be tabulated as follows.

Amyzon no. 9. In a letter to the people of Amyzon written in May 203, Antiochus encouraged them to remain in place, promising security, reconstruction, and the same rights they had enjoyed under the Ptolemies; he concludes: [- - - μηθένι ἐπιτρέπωσιν ἐ]νοχλεῖν ὑμᾶς. He does not mention the temple or *asylia* in what survives of this letter.

No. 13. A fragmentary royal letter confirming privileges does mention the temple:

[. .] α̣δικῆι [. . . . . . τ]ῶι ἱερῶι χ[- - - - - - - -]
[.]οις· ἐπιχωροῦμεν δὲ καὶ τὴμ π[- - - - - - - -]
[ὑ]μῖν καθάπερ καὶ πρότερον εἴθισ[ται - - - - - -]
[τ]ῶν ἐξ ἀρχῆς ὑμῖν κεχυρωμένω[ν - - - - - - - -]
[. μ]εν, ἀλλ' ἐῶμεν πάντα ἐπιχ[- - - - - - - - - -]
[. . .]αι τὸ ἱερόν. ἔρρωσθ[ε].

1: . ΔΙΚΗΙ, ἀ]δικῆι? Robb.; the alpha seems visible on the photograph.

The letterforms are quite similar to those of nos. 9 and 10. The Roberts suggest that at lines 2–4 the traditional constitution (πολιτεία) was guaranteed.[5] The brevity with which the Artemisium is invoked in 6 suggests that the temple was mentioned earlier in the letter; or else this may be a general evocation of prior benefactions granted "to the city/people and the temple."

No. 10. Antiochus also wrote to his army, giving some instruction about the temple, of which only the opening words survive: τὸ ἱερὸν τοῦ Ἀπόλλω[νος καὶ τῆς Ἀρτ]έμιδος τὸ ἐν [Ἀμυζῶνι - - -].[6] Presumably he ordered them not to molest it, and the letter may well have contained a statement that the temple was inviolable—perhaps baldly here in the first sentence: ἐν [Ἀμυζῶνι ἄσυλόν ἐστι - - -]. This cannot be the recognition itself, which will have been addressed to the people of Amyzon.

No. 11. A Seleucid official, certainly the viceroy Zeuxis, wrote a letter to the city, some phrases of which were copied in the nineteenth century. These include

4. *AnzWien* 57 (1920) 40–57 (*Kl. Schr.* I.2 39–56).

5. F. Piejko, *Gnomon* 57 (1985) 613, restores the text whole cloth, although nothing assures the line length; at 5–6: ἐπιχ[ωρηθέντα φιλάνθρωπα διαμένειν καὶ ἄσυλον | εἶν]αι τὸ ἱερόν—a strange sequence of Greek.

6. Piejko 612 restores [Ἀμυζῶνι ἄσυλον εἶναι (προαιρούμενοι/βουλόμενοι), an odd sentiment: kings did not need to wish for a place to be inviolable, or to explain their policies to their troops.

τὸ ἱερὸν ἄσυλον - - - [τὴν τοῦ] βασιλέως εὔνοιαν - - - καὶ μηθένι ἐνοχλεῖν ὑμᾶς.

Honorific decrees: no. 14 (October 202) for the royal governor of neighboring Alinda who had aided Amyzonian embassies to Zeuxis in obtaining some decision favorable to the city's σωτηρία in the recent war; no. 15 (November 201) for the royal *epistates* of the temple for his assistance in winning favor with Zeuxis, and for helping restore to the place persons who had been driven away (προσκαλούμενος εἰς τὸν συνοικισμὸν τοῦ Ἀρτεμισίου); no. 18 for a citizen who went on an embassy to the king himself to gain the return of sacred slaves; no. 19 for a military unit that raised a siege of "the fortress" (τὸ χωρίον; cf. no. 25); no. 22 for an ambassador to Zeuxis who won some *philanthropa* for the city.

No. 1. An inscription on the architrave of the temple itself shows that Zeuxis, acting in his own name, dedicated or secured land for the cult: Ζεῦξις Κυνάγου Μακεδὼν τοὺς ἀγροὺς τω[- - -].[7]

No. 12. A small column, inscribed in rather large letters, makes a summary statement about the action of Antiochus III and his son:

[ο]ἱ βασιλεῖς
[ἀ]πέδωκαν
[τὸ ἱερ]ὸν ἄσυ-
[λον . .]. ΗΛ

The script looks to be ca. 200 B.C. The Roberts describe this as a boundary. The pertinent formulae are lost, however, and given its findspot within the temple complex itself, this column may instead have been an element of the temple, inscribed with a brief statement of the royal benefaction such as adorned the gate of Xanthus in Lycia (**164**). As the Roberts note, the verb suggests restoration rather than the creation of a new status. I am unsure whether ἄσυλον is a second predicate, "restored the temple (to be) inviolable," or a simple adjective, "restored the inviolable temple" [to the goddess, people, vel sim.].[8]

No. 20. A civic decree honors one Hierocles who went on an embassy, presumably to the royal authorities, "concerning those who were plundering . . . the asylum, and destroyed the bandits":

6 [- - -] πρεσβεύσας πρὸς [- - - - - - - - - - - - -]
[- - - π]ερὶ τ[ῶ]ν λειστευόντων τὴν [?ἱερὰν χώραν]
[καὶ] τὸ ἄσυλον ἐπανείλετο τ[οὺς - - - - - - - ῥαι]-

7. Cf. *SEG* 35.1476.9–10: ἀ̣[γ]ρ̣ο̣[ὺ]ς(?) ἱερῶσαι (the Failaka letter).

8. Piejko 613 restores and reads from the photographs ἄσυ[λον, ὡς ἡ σ]τή̣λ[η | περιορίζ]ε̣ι, a surprising use of the singular.

9 [διο]υργοὺς (κτλ.)

7/8 Rigsby: [χώραν/πόλιν ἡμῶν] is also possible; τὴν [χώραν - - -] τὸ ἄσυλον Robb.

The script appears to be of the late third or early second century. Here is a rare instance of ἄσυλον as a noun. If this restoration of 7/8 is correct and the verbs are not exaggerations, not only land but the temple itself suffered attack some time under Seleucid rule—as had happened in 204/3.[9]

It is evident that Antiochus' benefactions included recognizing the inviolability of the Artemisium. It is worth stressing, however, that none of the extant texts is demonstrably such a grant; the obvious candidate is the lost beginning of no. 13. Nor do these several testimonies establish with certainty whether the inviolability of the Artemisium was newly granted now or merely confirmed by Antiochus in 203—a new status or the continuation of a Ptolemaic privilege. Several passages (in 13, 10, 12) might suggest such continuity, while the analogy of Antiochus' actions at Teos, Alabanda, and Xanthus points to a new status.

9. The natural thought that the two events are one—that the "brigands" were Seleucid troops and the embassy was to Antiochus III and prompted his intervention at Amyzon—seems excluded by the claim that Hermogenes "destroyed" the malefactors. But I do not understand the relation between the embassy and this act of destruction, unless this last was in fact accomplished by the king (i.e., Hierocles "brought about the destruction" of the malefactors).

Xanthus

Xanthus, the greatest city in Lycia, gave first honor to Leto and her children.[1] Here Leto came for rest after the birth of Apollo and Artemis. Their temple complex stands on a hill across the river, five kilometers downstream from the city proper. The excavators of the Letoon have found that the sacred place flourished from the Achaemenid period through the Roman. The largest of the temples, Leto's, appears to derive from the late third century B.C. or soon after; that of Artemis was funded by a Ptolemaic officer in the years between 205 and 197.[2] Mithridates was deterred by a dream from cutting trees in the Letoon (App. *Mith.* 27). The Lycian philosopher Proclus had a good education in the musical arts because he received it at his home city, τὴν ἱερὰν τοῦ Ἀπόλλωνος Ξάνθον (Marin. *V.Procli* 6).

Xanthus is the one certain case of declared *asylia* in Lycia.[3] The grant is known from one inscription, a secondary reference but seemingly contemporary with the recognition itself.

164. Antiochus III

Limestone block (h. 2.0, w. 0.91) forming the right pillar of the southern gate of the city; the text, which was subsequently erased, faces across the passageway.[4] Monumental letters of early second century B.C., 0.018, intersp. 0.013, A with

1. Strab. 14.3.6 (666): μεγίστη τῶν ἐν Λυκίᾳ; P. Demargne and H. Metzger, *RE* 9A (1967) 1375–1408; C. Le Roy, *RA* 1974, 322–333.

2. *TAM* II 263 (= *OGIS* 91); cf. *Pros.Ptol.* VI 15203.

3. Roman Tlos, praising itself as the site of a cult of Livia newly instituted by the Lycian League, offers an elative: "They designated the most holy city of the Tloans, because of its race of good men, its zeal in every undertaking, and its distinction for justice and loyalty," [καὶ ἀποδει]ξάμενοι πόλιν ἱε[ρωτάτην] τὴν Τλωέων (*TAM* II 549: ἡγη]σάμενοι πόλιν ἱε[ρὰν εἶναι] Boeckh). This is not evidence that Tlos had been declared inviolable.

4. Contrast *TAM* 264 and 265, facing outward.

broken bar, right hasta of N and Π half descended, Σ with fully parallel bars.

O. Benndorf, *Beiträge zur alten Geschichte, Festschrift O. Hirschfeld* (Berlin 1903) 77–78 (copy and squeeze made by Heberdey and Zingerle in 1898) [Dittenberger, *OGIS* 746; Kalinka, *TAM* II 266]. *Squeeze* (Vienna).

βα̣σιλεὺς μ̣έ̣γ[α]ς Ἀ̣ν̣τί̣ο̣χο̣ς
ἀφιέρωσεν τὴν πόλι̣ν
τῆι Λητῶι καὶ τῶι Ἀπόλ̣λ̣ων̣ι̣
4 κα̣ὶ̣ τῆ̣ι̣ Ἀρτέμ̣ι̣δι διὰ τὴν
πρὸς αὐτοὺς συνά̣πτουσαν̣
συνγένειαν̣.

Benndorf took the occasion to be Antiochus' Lycian expedition of 197 B.C. He considered that the king, failing to take Xanthus, "dedicated" it as a face-saving compromise on the analogy of freeing a slave by dedicating him to a god.[5] But as Schmitt saw (*Untersuchungen* 287), the king's campaign in Ptolemaic Lycia in 197 was largely successful, and it is at least as likely, on the analogy of *asylia* elsewhere, that the grant is a favor to a city that the king in fact won over, whether as conqueror or friend; and the recognition may have come only after longer negotiations, like the favors to Amyzon and perhaps Teos, and so perhaps somewhat later than 197. In any case, a decree of Xanthus of late 196 (*Amyzon* 15b) reveals a Seleucid city, dating its acts by the Seleucid calendar and the priest of the royal cult, but doing its own business as a Greek polis. This decree, if it is subsequent to the declaration of inviolability, offers neither support nor contradiction to the notion of *asylia* as equivalent to fiscal (or other) independence from the crown.

Like Miletus, Xanthus seems to be an exception to the rule that the temple alone received inviolability if it stood outside the city proper. In this summary statement on the gate, the mention of the "city," without the territory, need not be taken to reflect the terms of the recognition; compare "city" alone in the oracle for Cyzicus (**165**.7–8 but **168**.8). It is interesting, in the context of the parallels we have, that the king alone is credited with the recognition, not a Panhellenic quest; but we should put little reliance on this brief text.[6] The stated motive, Seleucid descent from Apollo, is the same one seen at Miletus.

2: The compound ἀφιερόω (instead of καθ-) is rare before the Roman period: e.g., a manumission (*IG* VII 3332) and a dedication (*I.Délos* 1757; cf. 1753).

5. This has been widely accepted; cf. J. and L. Robert, *Fouilles d'Amyzon* I p. 161; doxography at L. Boffo, *I re ellenistici e i centri religiosi dell' Asia Minore* (Pavia 1985) 322–323.

6. Seyrig, *Ant. syr.* III 4, adduced this inscription in arguing that "sacred" was an act of the king and "inviolable" an act of the Panhellenic community.

Cyzicus

Cyzicus, the great city on the Propontis, was given by Zeus to Kore as her dowry upon her marriage to Hades, and there she was held in first honor.[1] She defended her city against the Giants, and again in 73/2 B.C. when she destroyed the siege engines of Mithridates.[2] Her image is regularly shown on the coins already in the fourth century, labeled Σώτειρα;[3] later her torch marks the pseudo-Lysimachean tetradrachms issued by Cyzicus,[4] and she continues to dominate the coins in Roman times. The Mysteries of Kore are mentioned often in the inscriptions.[5] The exact location of her temple is not known, but it was certainly within the city proper: this is explicit in Appian's account of the siege by Mithridates; we hear also of a "sacred agora," and a statue of a poet was set up "in the precinct of blooming Kore, so that boys born later may have in the

1. App. *Mith.* 75: καὶ σεβοῦσιν αὐτὴν οἱ Κυζικηνοὶ μάλιστα θεῶν. The rape occurred at Cyzicus, according to Propertius (3.22.4) and perhaps *Priapea* 75.13. Cf. F. W. Hasluck, *Cyzicus* (Cambridge 1910) 210; Robert, *BCH* 102 (1978) 460–477 (*DAM* 156–173); M. J. Price and B. Trell, *Greek Coins and Their Cities* (Detroit 1977) 109–116. Kore is probably the *patrios thea* mentioned in *I.Didyma* 504; cf. Robert, *DAM* 167.

2. *FGrHist* 472 F 2. App. *Mith.* 75; Plut. *Luc.* 10; Porph. *Abst.* 25; cf. B. C. McGing, *Phoenix* 38 (1984) 12–18, for the date.

3. *BMC Mysia* 124–133; *SNG Copenhagen Mysia* 53–55; *von Aulock* 1217–1226. Bronzes of imperial date with Κόρη Σώτειρα: *BMC* 175–179, 200–201, 209; *Copenhagen* 99–102; *von Aulock* 1252–1253. Cf. Robert, *DAM* 168–169.

4. Seyrig, *Centennial Publication of the ANS* (New York 1958) 618 (*Scripta numism.* 207); M. J. Price, *The Coinage in the Name of Alexander* (Zurich/London 1991) 207; torch on late Hellenistic bronzes: *BMC* 146, 160–167; *Copenhagen* 79–84; *von Aulock* 1234, 1238–1243.

5. Hasluck 212–213. Neanthes of Cyzicus (early III B.C.) wrote a tract Περὶ τελετῶν, in which the Cyzicene rites no doubt had a place: *FGrHist* 84 F 15; cf. 37 (Neanthes exiled for impiety).

city a testimony to hospitality and an incitement to wisdom."[6] In the western part of the city Kore had a monumental altar,[7] probably commemorating her assistance in some Cyzicene victory.

Around 200 B.C. Cyzicus obtained inviolability and Panhellenic games, the Soteria, in honor of Kore. In testimony we have (with various degrees of probability) an oracle of Apollo of Delphi urging the quest, isolated decrees of Rhodes and of Dium in response to the Cyzicene request, and a fragment of an archive of recognitions by cities in northwestern Greece.[8]

The oracle (**165**) is known through copies at Delos and Delphi. At Delos the oracle is followed on the stone by a Delian decree granting space for the inscribing of Apollo's oracle, as requested by three Cyzicene *theoroi*. This title shows that their primary mission was not this simple request of Delos: rather they must have been religious emissaries returning from Delphi, sent either to obtain the present oracle or to proclaim the games and inviolability that the oracle had called for. Because no Delian decree of inviolability is on this stele, and the Cyzicenes invoke only the oracle and no recognition from Delphi, I believe the first option is more likely: these are not the proclaimers of the new honors, but the men who had been sent earlier to consult Apollo. The extant Delphian copy of the oracle seems to be later in script than the Delian; apparently it was a reinscribing of the inscription that is mentioned in the Delian decree, done when a gathering of texts pertinent to Cyzicus was made. Thus one control on the date of the inviolability of Cyzicus is the script and prosopography of the Delian inscription—hence the end of the third century or the beginning of the second.

We have, I believe, two segments of the archive of decrees of acceptance that must have been inscribed at Cyzicus. The two fragments are consistent in date with each other and with the oracle, ca. 200 B.C. A decree of Rhodes (**166**), found at Cyzicus, has not been recognized as a grant of *asylia*, because the substance of what was requested does not survive. At the prompting of three Cyzicene *theoroi*, Rhodes "accepts the proclamation" and praises the Cyzicenes for their piety: given these phrases, their request can only have concerned Panhellenic games or territorial inviolability; and Apollo had told Cyzicus to proclaim both.

Not content but attribution is at issue with the archival fragment, an inscription that Viscount Strangford acquired in the East, now in the British Museum (**167–170**). Strangford stated that it came from Megara. Foucart in

6. *CIG* 3671 [Kaibel, *Epigr.* 880; *IGR* IV 164]: ὀψίγενοι περ ἐν ἄστει παῖδες ἔχοιεν. The sacred agora: E. Schwertheim, *ZPE* 29 (1978) 213–228 [*SEG* 28.953.58] and Ael. Arist. 26.14 K. For the topography of Cyzicus see Hasluck 1–16.

7. See *I. Samothrace* 29, with J. R. MacCredie, *ArchDelt* 26 (1971) Chron. II 443 and pl. 438.

8. The fragments *FD* III.3 359–361 (with Robert, *DAM* 173 n. 116) may be relevant, as they mention games and the goddess; Cyzicus has voted to send ambassadors, not *theoroi*, to Delphi, so this is probably not the mission seeking the games and inviolability; perhaps instead merely to request space for inscriptions.

brief and Holleaux in detail argued that the subject of the decree of Megara is the cult of [Kore] Soteira (**170**.6) at Cyzicus, whose honors were known from the oracle. Robert, however, who established that the inscription contains distinct decrees and derives from an archive, concluded that Megara must be the source of the request and the home of the *theoroi*, where alone such an archive would be inscribed; and that the Megarian goddess Artemis Soteira was the honorand.

In my view, his attribution to Megara is improbable. The Greek mainland has little to show of *asylia* outside of Boeotia, and Robert already saw other objections to his attribution. The great god of Megara was Apollo Pythaeus; an Artemis Soteira we know only from two mentions of Roman date.[9] Nor should a Megarian envoy bear an Ionic name (**170**.4).[10] Robert's recognition of the archival character of the inscription is inescapable, but so too is the attribution of this goddess Soteira to Cyzicus. The error lies rather with Strangford.

Attributions in the Strangford Collection have several times proved false,[11] for good reason. The antiquities that Viscount Strangford eventually donated to the British Museum he collected while he was British ambassador in Constantinople from 1821 to 1824.[12] These were the first years of the Greek war of independence, which early on effectively removed the Peloponnesus from Ottoman control. Strangford, so far as I can determine, never left Constantinople during his tenure as ambassador.[13] He arrived toward June 1821, after the fighting had begun; on 10 April 1822 one of his entourage, William Hamilton, could write to Robert Gordon in Vienna: "From the Morea we hear the most contrasting reports."[14] Thus it seems certain that Strangford acquired our inscription (**167–170**) in Constantinople and could have no personal knowledge of its origin. His attribution can be no better than his informant, this in a time of great turmoil in Greece. We might reckon a Peloponnesian origin in fact rather unlikely, given the circumstances of the 1820s. By contrast, many stones over the

9. For Apollo of Megara see Rigsby, *GRBS* 27 (1986) 93–102; Artemis Soteira: Paus. 1.40.2 and the priestess at *IG* VII 112.

10. For the opposite, the affecting of Doric in names, see J. and L. Robert, *Fouilles d'Amyzon* I 100 n. 26.

11. R. A. McNeal, *Archaeology* 20 (1967) 263; B. Cook, *JourJPGettyMus* 1 (1974) 35; Rigsby, *GRBS* 16 (1975) 405 n. 8.

12. I owe to Brian Cook, Keeper of Greek and Roman Antiquities, the information (derived from the record of donation) that all the material in the Strangford Collection, though donated to the museum years later, was gathered during his diplomatic mission, an important fact that does not seem to be in the public record.

13. On Percy Clinton Sydney Smythe (1780–1855), sixth viscount of Strangford, see *Dict. Nat. Biog.* 18.603–605; E. Barrington de Fonblanque, *Lives of the Lords Strangford* (London 1877) 107–203. My immediate remarks are based on unpublished correspondence, now in the British Library, deriving from the years in Constantinople.

14. British Library MS 43213 f. 167, quoted by permission.

years have found their way from Cyzicus to Constantinople; to quote Bernard Ashmole, Cyzicus, "close to the sea and a few hours' sail from Constantinople, invites spoliation."[15] Hasluck was able to assign to Cyzicus several unattributed inscriptions in the Strangford Collection.[16]

I suggest that the present inscription is another such, and its reported attribution to Megara is the result of confusion or mendacity. It is the weakest piece of information we have about the stone, whereas the arguments of Foucart, Holleaux, and Robert are compelling. The inference is that this is a part of an *asylia* archive from Cyzicus. The script dates this inscription to the late third century or early second. The Rhodian decree does not survive to compare on the score of script. The decree found at Dium in Macedonia, which was of course Dium's copy rather than a wandering piece of the archive at Cyzicus, is not yet published.

To these honors for Kore of Cyzicus we have another Hellenistic reference. Toward 120 B.C. the explorer Eudoxus of Cyzicus visited Alexandria as a θεωρὸς καὶ σπονδοφόρος τοῦ τῶν Κορείων ἀγῶνος.[17] This certainly is the Panhellenic Soteria urged by the oracle;[18] Posidonius says *Koreia* to indicate the Cyzicene games of Kore, where *Soteria* would have been ambiguous for his readers. The use of σπονδοφόρος, as for the Eleusinian Mysteries, shows that mysteries were a part of the Panhellenic festival. From the first century A.D. on, we hear instead of the Phersephassia and of the Mysteries—apparently the terms were interchangeable; at any rate no inscription uses both. This was the "sacred isopythian contest of Kore" attested in imperial times: ἱερὸν Κόρης ἰσοπύθιον ἐν Κυζίκῳ.[19] It seems probable that the Soteria lapsed late in the Hellenistic period, like many other Greek festivals, and was reorganized and renamed after civic life had revived in the Greek world during the early Empire.

Other testimonies to the status of the city and the cult are few. A friend of the Attalids, Cyzicus was declared a free city in the settlement of 188 B.C. (Polyb. 25.2.13). In the 130s B.C. a Cyzicene was praised for his embassies to the Roman authorities concerning, among other things, the safety and the "rights" of the city.[20] In 73 the miracle of Kore persuaded Mithridates to abandon

15. *JWarb* 19 (1956) 81. Examples: *CIG* 3657; Robert, *Op. min. sel.* III 1581–1583; *DAM* 148–156; *Bull. épigr.* 1966, 254; 1971, 419; 1972, 287; R. Demangel, *Contribution à la topographie de l'Hebdomon* (Paris 1945) 33. Marbles from Cyzicus helped build Hagia Sophia: Codinus, *De S. Sophia* 132.9–10 (65B Bonn).

16. Hasluck 266 on *CIG* 3661 and 6851; cf. Robert, *Etudes anat.* 187 n. 4.

17. Posidonius *FGrHist* 87 F 28 (Strab. 2.3.4 [98]); cf. *Pros.Ptol.* VI 16258; P. M. Fraser, *Ptolemaic Alexandria* I (Oxford 1972) 182–184, 200.

18. So Robert, *DAM* 166, with references to earlier discussion, and for the evidence on the games of Kore in Roman times. Plutarch (*Luc.* 10) calls the festival Phersephassia in reference to the events of 73, but perhaps anachronistically.

19. *AEM* 8 (1884) 219–220 no. 49 (Perinthus-Heraclea), a list of victories.

20. *IGR* IV 134; cf. D. Magie in *Anatolian Studies Buckler* (Manchester 1939) 181 n. 2; E. V. Hansen, *Attalids of Pergamum*^{2} (Ithaca, N.Y., 1971) 155.

the siege of Cyzicus, "inasmuch as it is sacred" (ὡς ἱερᾶς).[21] Tacitus does not mention the city in his notice on the appeals of A.D. 22–23 concerning *asylia*.

165. Oracle of Apollo of Delphi

The Delian copy is the older, dated by its script to the late third or early second century; it is followed on the stone by a Delian decree granting space for inscribing the oracle.[22] The Delphian copy is on a stone with two other oracles pertinent to Cyzicus,[23] inscribed by the same hand—a gathering of texts, cut later in the second century B.C.

Delian copy: two fragments (inv. 123 A, B) of a white marble stele, A found in 1878 north of the temple of Apollo, B in 1879 south of the temple, joined by Homolle; broken at top, right, and bottom; h. 0.54, w. 0.315, th. 0.083; letters 0.007 (the heading Κυ[ζικηνῶν] larger).

T. Homolle, *BCH* 4 (1880) 471–477 [Michel, *Rec.* 852; Dittenberger, *Syll.*^{2} 791]; Roussel, *IG* XI.4 1298 [Hiller, *Syll.*^{3} 1158].

Delphian copy: the upper left corner of a marble statue base near the statues of Attalus I and Eumenes II (see Daux, *FD* III.3 pp. 295–297), inv. 4953 + 2247 + 2423; letters and intersp. 0.008.

G. Daux, *BCH* 59 (1935) 92–94; *FD* III.3 342 [P. Amandry, *La mantique apollinienne* (Paris 1950) 163 no. 18; Parke/Wormell II 138–139 no. 341]. *Collation.*

Cf. Wilhelm, *Neue Beitr.* III (1913) 22–27 (*Kl. Schr.* I.1 144–148); Robert, *Et. épigr. phil.* 295 n. 4; Daux, *BCH* 63 (1939) 171–172; Robert, *BCH* 102 (1978) 460–477 (*DAM* 156–173); Daux, *BCH* 103 (1979) 467–471; Merkelbach, *ZPE* 34 (1979) 70.

I give the Delian copy, underlining what survives only in the Delphian.

ὁ θεὸς ἔχ[ρησε Κυζικηνοῖς, οἳ]
ἐπιτετελέκα[ντι κατ' ἐνιαυτὸν?]
τὰ Σωτήρια πρᾶτ[οι τᾶι Κόραι]
τᾶι Σωτείραι καλῶς [καὶ εὐσεβέ]-
ως καὶ εὐτυχῶς, λῶιον [εἶμεν]
καὶ ἄμεινον ἐπαγγελλόν[τεσ]-
σιν ἐς ἀνθρώπους ἱερὰν τὰν π[ό]-
λιν οὖσαν κατὰ τοὺς χρ[η]σμοὺς
καὶ τὰν θυσίαν τᾶς θεᾶς.

. . .

The god prophesied to the Cyzicenes, [who] first have [annually?] celebrated the Soteria for Kore Soteira well and piously and happily, that it is better and finer

21. App. *Mith.* 75, though nothing of this is at Memnon *FGrHist* 434 F 28.

22. *IG* XI.4 1027; the same proposer moved 710 and 1026, both dated late III/early II.

23. *FD* III.3 343–344: these, quite fragmentary, were probably not pertinent to the *asylia* of Cyzicus, for they were not included at Delos; I do not include them here. The same base also contains a manumission (337) cut by another hand.

that they proclaim to mankind their city as sacred, in accordance with the oracles, and the sacrifice to the goddess.

The Delian version has a heading Κυ̣[ζικηνῶν]; the decree that is below, passed at the request of three Cyzicene *theoroi*, provided space for a stele εἰς ἣν ἀναγραφήσεται ὁ δεδομένος χρησμὸς Κυζικηνοῖς ὑπὸ τοῦ Πυθίου Ἀπ[όλ]λωνος καθ' [ὅ]τι καὶ ἐν τῶι ἱερῶι τῶι ἐν Δελ[φοῖς] ἀναγέγραπται. The Delphian version, arranged in four lines, is headed by A[- - -]I; Daux considẹred the space wrong for ἀ[γαθᾶι τύχα]ι. At the end is added [τ]ύχαι τᾶι ἀγαθᾶι [τ]ᾱ̣[ς πόλιος]. 1–3 Robert 1978: ἔχ[ρησε ὅτι τὰς θυσίας] ἐπιτετελέκα[τε τὰς πατρίας?] τὰ Σωτήρια πράτ[τοντες Κόραι?] Homolle; ἔχ[ρησεν τάδε· ἐπειδὴ] ἐπιτετελέκα[τε τὰν θυσίαν καὶ] Dittenberger, followed (without τάδε) by Daux (but ἐπεὶ) and Merkelbach (but εἰ). 3: πράτ[τοντες Homolle; πρᾶτ[ον Dittenberger, Merkelbach; πρᾶτ[οι ἁπάντων] Hiller. 5 Homolle: [ἔσσεται] Dittenberger.

The text is problematic. In line 2 we should not have the redundancy of the "sacrifice" in parallel with its name (Homolle); Robert's suggestion corresponds to the facts (a local and thus annual festival to become Panhellenic), although it seems prosaic and lends an odd emphasis. As in the oracle on Acraephia (**2**), the usage is loose and poetic, not the language of a decree: by "city" I assume that the god means city and country (so **168**.8; cf. **164** for Xanthus); by "sacred," sacred and inviolable. The Cyzicenes, who were first to honor Kore the Savior with annual games, have asked how to add to her honors, having oracles that need interpretation; they are told to proclaim to all people the sacredness of their city, in accordance with the oracles, and the sacrifice—that is, to seek Panhellenic recognition of the inviolability of Cyzicus and of the games of Kore.

166. Rhodes

A stone broken at right and bottom, copied near Cyzicus by Pococke in 1739, now lost.

R. Pococke, *Inscriptionum antiq. graec. et lat. liber* (London 1752) p. 27 [Boeckh, *CIG* 3656; P. Müllensiefen, *SGDI* 3752].

Cf. C. Schumacher, *De republica Rhodiorum commentatio* (Heidelberg 1886) 49; Hiller, *AM* 20 (1895) 390.

ἐπὶ Ἀριστάνδρου τοῦ Ἀ̣π̣ολλοφ̣[άνου· ἀρχιθέωρος Ἀπα[τούριος]
Σωσιβίου καὶ θεωροὶ Οἰνόβιος Εὔνεω, Ἱκέσιος Διονυσίου ἀποσ[ταλέντες ἀπέδωκαν τάδε τὰ]
ψηφίσματα. παρὰ Ῥοδίων· ἐπ' ἱερέως Ἀρατοφάνευς, Σμινθίου πρ⟨ά⟩ται ἐξ ἰ[κάδος,]
4 ἔδοξε̣ν̣ τῶι δάμωι· ἐπειδὴ Κυ̣ζικανοὶ φίλο̣ι̣ καὶ εὖνοι καὶ σύμμαχοι ὑπ[άρχοντες]
τῶι δάμωι ἀπεστάλκαντι ψάφισμα καὶ ἀρχιθέωρον Ἀπα[τούριον]
καὶ θεωροὺς Οἰνόβιον κα̣ὶ̣ Ἱκέσιον, οἳ τάν τε καταγγελία̣ν̣ ἐποήσ[αντο καὶ αὐτοὶ]
διελέγεν ἐπελθόντες ἐπὶ τὰν βουλὰν καὶ τὰν ἐκκλη⟨σί⟩αν ἀκ̣[ολούθως]

τοῖς ἐν τῶι ψαφίσματι καταχεχ⟨ω⟩ρισμένοις, σπουδᾶς καὶ [φιλοτιμίας]
οὐθὲν ἐλλείποντες, ἐποιήσαντο δὲ καὶ τὰν ἐπιδαμίαν ἀξίως [ἀμφοτερᾶν]
τᾶν πολίων· ἀποκρίνασθαι αὐτοῖς ὅτι ὁ δᾶμος τάν τε π[οτὶ] τοὺ[ς θεοὺς]
εὐσέβειαν περὶ πλείστου ποιούμενος καὶ τὰν Κυζικα[νῶν φιλίαν]
διατηρῶν τάν τε καταγγελίαν ἀποδέχεται μετὰ πάσας [προθυμίας]
καὶ ἐπαχ̣ολ̣ουθῶν τοῖς ὑπὸ Κυζικανῶν ἀξιουμέ[νοι]ς ΧΟΣΤ[- - -]
ε̣ὔνους εὔντας· ὅπ[ω]ς δὲ καὶ συ⟨ν⟩τελεσθ[ῆι] τὰ π̣αρὰ [Κυζικανῶν? - - -]

Text of Boeckh. 3 Schumacher, with Hiller: ΠΡΥΤ Pococke; Σμινθίου, πρυτα-[ν]ε[ύοντος - - -] Boeckh. 7 end: ΕΙΟΚΛΗΑΝΧ\Σ. Pococke. 10 end: ΤοΥΤΟΥ[Pococke.

Line 3 shows that this is the beginning of one section of an archive of decrees of acceptance, organized, as at Cos and perhaps Tenos, by theoric missions. Only the preliminaries of a Rhodian decree survive. It is unfortunate that the Rhodians do not actually say what the Cyzicenes requested; but the references to piety and to a proclamation by *theoroi* (11–12) are sufficient to indicate games or inviolability.

The decree is dated by the priest of Helius, Aratophanes. Of these we know two, distinguished and approximately dated by the amphora stamps of Rhodes; the earlier is named on a series assigned to ca. 210–175, the later ca. 100 B.C.[24] Our decree must belong to the earlier, in order to be consistent with the other texts.

Cyzicus and Rhodes were now allies (line 4). The basic stance of Cyzicus in this period was allegiance to the Attalids, and this placed Cyzicus and Rhodes on the same side in several wars, for example during the years 201–199.[25] When toward 220 Rhodes fought Byzantium over the latter's Bosporan tariff, Cyzicus can hardly have remained neutral.[26] But a rigorous date for the *asylia* of Cyzicus must await the clarification of Rhodian chronology.

1: The eponymous magistrate of Cyzicus was the hipparch. In the second century B.C. a hipparch Apollophanes son of Ar[istander] was served by a fiscal magistrate Aristander son of Apollophanes;[27] the names were popular at Cyzicus, but these may be the son and grandson of our hipparch. An Aristander

24. V. R. Grace in *Délos* XXVII (Paris 1970) 290–291, 313. To the later priest must be assigned the decree *ASAtene* n.s. 1–2 (1942) 156–161 no. 18 (revising *SEG* 3.674). In a letter of 24 May 1976 Miss Grace kindly wrote: "I would now suggest a date slightly after 180" for the earlier priest.

25. Polyb. 16.31.3; Livy 31.17.6; cf. Walbank, *Comm.* II 505; Will, *Histoire* II 124, who notes that this alliance may be older than 201. The two cities fought on the same side again in 180 and in 156 (Polyb. 25.2.13, 33.13.2).

26. Polyb. 4.50.5, with Holleaux, *Etudes* IV 236 n. 2. For Cyzicene trade through the Bosporus see Rostovtzeff, *SEHHW* I 587–589. For a list of other Rhodian alliances see S. L. Ager, *Historia* 40 (1991) 11 n. 9. Rhodes and Cyzicus were among the mediators (with Byzantium and Aetolia) between Ptolemy and Antiochus in 219 (Polyb. 5.63.5).

27. Robert, *Etudes anat.* 199–201.

son of Apollophanes proposed the honorific decree *CIG* 3657, which cannot be closely dated.

2: On the name Εὔνεως at Cyzicus see J. and L. Robert, *Bull. épigr.* 1966, 158.

3: Boeckh, not punctuating after ψηφίσματα, was puzzled by the plural and considered emending ψήφισμα τ⟨ὸ⟩ παρὰ. I punctuate here because the *theoroi* will have gone to more than one city, and accordingly the plural ψηφίσματα should be taken literally (see by contrast on **26**.3): this is an archival entry, followed then by a heading for the present decree.

The festival of Kore appears to have been held in early spring (the sacrifice that Mithridates' siege interrupted),[28] as would befit Persephone. There is some reason to think that the Rhodian month Sminthius fell in early spring,[29] and it follows that the Cyzicene *theoroi* began their mission about a year before the Panhellenic festival.

167–170

Two nonjoining fragments of white marble obtained by Viscount Strangford in the 1820s, allegedly from Megara; now in the British Museum. A: h. 0.44, w. 0.15, th. 0.02; B: h. 0.395, w. 0.15, th. 0.02. Letters 0.01–0.013 (except the headings: 0.015 at **168**.1 and **170**.1), intersp. 0.01–0.013. Writing of the late third century (so Klaffenbach) or early second: flaring strokes with serifs, A with crossbar either straight or broken, O and Θ sometimes smaller and suspended, Ω full-sized, N with elevated right hasta, Π with right hasta half descended, Σ with divergent and curving arms.

Boeckh, *CIG* 1052b (copy of Brønsted);[30] Newton, *IGBM* II 136 [Dittenberger, *IG* VII 16; Holleaux, *REG* 11 (1898) 267–273 (*Etudes* I 211–217)]; Robert, *Et. épigr. phil.* 70–76 (squeeze); Klaffenbach, *IG* IX.1^2 388 (squeeze: only **168**). *Collation.*

Photograph: Robert pl. 6 (squeeze).

Cf. P. Foucart in *IG* VII p. 742; Wilhelm, *Beiträge* (1909) 268; P. Charneux, *BCH* 90 (1966) 176 n. 2; Rigsby, *GRBS* 16 (1975) 405.

Parts of either three or four Doric decrees, depending on whether **168** carried over to fragment B; I number them as four. The *theoroi* Oenopion, Dionysas, and -nthodemos toured northwestern Greece, for they visited Medion. Given the various formulae possible, the length of the lines is uncertain and the line division arbitrary.

167. Unknown city

Fragment A, lines 1–7.

28. For the chronology see Broughton, *MRR* II 101 and 106–108; McGing (esp. Plut. *Luc.* 33.3).

29. C. Börker, *ZPE* 31 (1978) 193–218, esp. 201.

30. P. O. Brønsted (1780–1842), Danish classical scholar and ambassador to the Vatican, visited England in 1824, 1826, 1828, and 1831: K. F. Johansen and M. C. Gertz, *Dansk Biografisk Leksikon* 4 (Copenhagen 1934) 295–302.

[- - - - - - - - - - - - - -]Ι̣ΟΝΟΥ̣ΟΣΕ̣[- - - - - - - - - - - -]
[- - - καθὼς? ἔδ]οξε τᾶι πόλει· [- - - καλέσαι δὲ τοὺς πρεσ]-
[βευτὰς εἰς τὸ πρυ]τανεῖον ἐπὶ τ[ὰν κοινὰν ἑστίαν - - - - καὶ]
[δόμε]ν αὐτοῖς ἐκέχει[ρα τὰ ἐκ τοῦ νόμου· - - - - - - - - - -]
[εἶμεν δὲ] καὶ προξένους [τᾶς πόλιος - - - - - - - - - - - τοὺς]
[πρεσβευτὰς Οἰνοπ]ίωνα, Διονυσᾶν, [- - - νθόδημον - - - -]
[ἀγγράψαι δὲ τόδε τὸ ψ]άφισμα ΕΙΤΟΙΧ[- - - - - - - - - - -]

1 end, the lower left corner of E or B: ΟΝΟΙΟΣ Newton, πρόγ]ονοι οσ[Holleaux. 2–3 Dittenberger; καθὼς Rigsby: [ἐπαινέσαι τοὺς δεῖνας - - - καλέσαι δὲ αὐτοὺς καὶ ἐπὶ ξένια? Newton. 4 Wilhelm: ἑστίαν τοῦ | δάμου, καὶ εἶμε]ν αὐτοῖς ἐκεχει[ρίαν καθάπερ αἰτοῦνται Dittenberger. 7 Dittenberger: εἰ⟨ς⟩ τοῖχ[ον, ἔνθαπερ καὶ τὸ γεν|όμενον περὶ τῶν Μ]εδιωνίων Dittenberger; εἴ τοι χ[ρησμοὶ καὶ τὰ ψαφίσματα | τὰ περὶ Μ.] Wilhelm.

We are here in the final provisions, inviting the *theoroi* to the prytaneum; accordingly I follow Robert's suggestion (75 n. 2) that ἔδοξε τᾶι πόλει belongs with what precedes.

168. Medion

Fragment A, lines 8–20.

[Μ]εδιωνίων
[παραγενομένων π]ρεσβευτᾶγ κ[αὶ θεωρῶν - - - - - - - - - - - - - - - παρὰ τᾶς]
[πόλιος τᾶς Κυζικαν]ῶν Οἰνοπίωνος, [Διονυσᾶ, -νθοδήμου - - - - - - - - - -]
[ἐπαγγελλόντων] τὰς θυσίας καὶ [τὸν ἀγῶνα τῶν Σωτηρίων - - - ὃν τίθεντι]
[Κυζικανοὶ τᾶι Κορᾶι?, καὶ] διαλεγομένου [τοῦ ἀρχιθεώρου? Οἰνοπίωνος περὶ - - -]
[καὶ παρακαλέοντος? ἀποδέ]χεσθαι τὰν ἐκε[χειρίαν - - - - - - - - - - - - - -]
[- - - τοῦ ἀγῶν]ος καὶ ἀνανεώσ[ασθαι τὰν φιλίαν - - - - - - - - - - - - - - - - ,]
[τὰν πόλιν] δὲ καὶ τὰν χώρα[ν αὐτῶν - - - - - - - - - - - - - - - ἀποδέχεσθαι?]
[ἱερὰν ἀπὸ πάν]των καὶ ἄσυλο̣ν [-]
[- - - - - - - -]ΝΤΙ̣ΚΟΙ̣Ν[-]
[- - - - - - - -]ΟΥΜΕΝ[-]
[- - - - - - - - -]Λ̣ΤΕΤΩ[-]
[- - - - - - - - - -]Τ[-]

The continuous text restored through 9 by Klaffenbach assumes a needlessly short line and contains some improbable phrases. 1 Dittenberger (before Robert established that a new decree begins here); see on **167**.7. 2–3 Holleaux: Μεγαρέ]ων Robert. 4–9: [ἐπαγγελλόντων] τὰς θυσίας καὶ [τὸν ἀγῶνα ὃν τίθεντι | τᾶι Ἀρτέμιδι καὶ] διαλεγομένου [τοῦ ἀρχιθεώρου καὶ | παρακαλέοντος δέ]χεσθαι τὰν ἐκε[χειρίαν καὶ τὰς θυ|σίας τᾶς Ἀρτέμιδ]ος καὶ ἀνανεώσ[ασθαι τὰν ἐξ ἀρχᾶς | φιλίαν, δέχεσθαι] δὲ καὶ τὰν χώρα[ν καὶ τὰν πόλιν ὑπ|άρχειν ἱερὰν αὐ]τῶν Klaffenbach. 5 τοῦ ἀρχιθεώρου Robert ap. Holleaux 212 n. 1. 6 Robert. 7 init. Rigsby. 8–9 Rigsby: φιλίαν, | ἀποδέχεσθαι] δὲ καὶ τὰν χώρα[ν - - | - - ἱερὰν αὐ]των Dittenberger. 10ff. are in rather larger letters (0.013). 10: ἀ]ντὶ κοιν[ῶν ἀγαθῶν? Newton.

The only extant decree of Medion in central Acarnania. Only the structure of the text is suggested; the formulae could be padded out to any line length.

169. Unknown city, or Medion

Fragment B, lines 1–4.

[- - - - - - - - Δ]ιονυσιο[- - - - - - - - -]
[- - - - - - - - - -]ΣΕΝΚ. [- - - - - - - - - -]
[- - - - - - - - ἐ]κέχειρα [- - - - - - - - - - -]
[- - - δραχμὰς ε]ἴκοσι καὶ τοῖς θ̣[εαροῖς - - -]

3: ἐ]κεχειρ[ί]α Boeckh; μετε]κέχειρα Newton. 4: θ̣[εαροῖς τοῖς ἐπανγελλόντεσσι τὰν θυσίαν καὶ τὸν ἀγῶνα τῶν Κο]ραίων Holleaux.

It is uncertain whether **169** is part of a new decree or the continuation of **168**.

170. Unknown city

Fragment B, lines 5–18.

[Κερκυ?]ραίων
[ἐπεὶ Κυζικανοὶ φ]ίλοι ὄντες κ[αὶ συγγενεῖς - - - τᾶς ἁμετέρας πόλιος]
[ἐξαπέστειλαν ποθ' ἁμὲ πρεσβευτὰς καὶ θεαροὺ]ς Οἰνοπίωνα [- - -, Διονυσᾶν - - -]
[- - - - - - - - -]νθόδημον Π[- - - - - - - - - - - - - - - -]
[- - - - - - - -]ΣΤΕΙ̣ΡΟΥΚΑΙ̣ΤΟ[- - - - - - - - - - - - -]
[τᾶι Κορᾶι] τᾶι Σωτείραι [- - - - - - - - - - - - - - - - - -]
[- - - ?παρεκάλ]ουν καὶ τὰν πό[λιν ἁμῶν - - - - - - -]
[ὁ τοῦ Ἀπόλλων]ος χρησμὸς [- - - - - - - - - - - - - - -]
[- - - - - - - -]ους τοῖς ἐν τοῖ[ς - - - - - - - - - - - - - - -]
[- - - - - - - - τ]άν τε συνγέ[νειαν καὶ τὰν φιλίαν - - -]
[- - - - - κατ]ὰ τὰ προγεγρ[αμμένα - - - - - - - - - - - -]
[- - - - - - - -]σιν αὐτὰς καὶ κ[- - - - - - - - - - - - - - -]
[- - - - - - - - -]Ι̣ πεποιειμέν[ους? - - - - - - - - - - - - -]
[- - -?γραμματεύον]τος Φιλίππ[ου - - - - - - - - - - - -]

1 Dittenberger; or [Παλαι]ραίων Charneux. 2–3 Holleaux: κ[αὶ σύμμαχοι Dittenberger. 6 Holleaux: Ἀρτέμιδι Newton. 7 Robert. 8 Foucart. 10 Dittenberger: συνγε[γραμμέναν? Newton. 14 Dittenberger.

13: The form -ειμένος, which worried Dittenberger in Megarian Doric, is normal in the northwest.

171. Dium in Macedonia

Unpublished decree found at Dium; announced by D. Pandermalis in 1994.

Temple of Apollo of Claros, Colophon

In a narrow valley in the territory of Colophon was one of the great oracular shrines of the Greek world, Apollo of Claros. Apollo was the "lord and savior" of Colophon.[1] The cult is most richly documented in the second century A.D. but was praised already in the *Homeric Hymns* (1.40, 8.5) and by the poet Nicander, a priest of Apollo (*Ther.* 958; *Alex.* 9–11). The temple was a mile up the valley from the sea, amid a sacred grove. A new building was completed between the middle and the late years of the third century B.C. Excavations by Picard and Macridy-Bey early in the century, by the Roberts in the 1950s, and now continuing have revealed some of the history of the sacred place.[2] The finds are for the most part unpublished, and only a schematic notice can be given here on the *asylia* of the temple.

From an archive of grants of inviolability inscribed at the temple[3] have come the remains of a letter of the Athamanian kings Theodorus and Amynander (Ἀθαμ[άνων·] στραγηγοῦντος ἐν Ἀ[θαμανίαι?); decrees from Thessaly, Crete, and unidentified places; and a letter of the Scipio brothers (190/189) (**173**). The last was quoted by Picard in a footnote; the others are listed briefly by Robert.

1. καθηγεμόνος καὶ σωτῆρος, L. and J. Robert, *BCH* 106 (1992) 279; cf. καθηγεμόνι τῆ πόλεως, *SEG* 39.1244.II.26.

2. T. Macridy-Bey and C. Picard, *BCH* 39 (1915) 45–52; Picard, *Ephèse et Claros* (Paris 1922) 138–155; Robert, *Op. min. sel.* VI 523–549; cf. IV 154, 184; J. de la Genière, *CRAI* 1992, 195–208.

3. Robert, *Op. min. sel.* VI 538–539; *TürkArkDerg* 10 (1960) 4. The Athamanian letter is quoted at C. Picard, *BCH* 39 (1915) 46 n. 2; cf. *Ephèse et Claros* (Paris 1922) 143. Also R. Demargne and A. Laumonier, *BCH* 47 (1923) 378 no. 6:

ἡ π̣[όλις τῶν Κολοφω]-
νί[ων]
ἀσυ̣[λίαν]
ἐμ̣ [πολέμωι.]

The restorations are rightly rejected by Robert, *SEG* 4.572.

No physical description of these inscriptions has been published; but another, copied at the turn of the century, has been described and published (**172**).

Apollo's games, the Claria, became crowned late in the third century B.C. (*Claros* I pp. 52–53); **172** shows that *asylia* was gained on the same occasion, at the prompting of a manifestation of the god. The Roman letter dates to late 190 or early 189: as at Magnesia and Teos, the Roman grant was sought only after Rome became involved in Anatolia in the 190s.

As for later developments, this is one of the inviolable temples listed as devastated by pirates early in the first century B.C. The worship of the emperor Tiberius was incorporated into the temple during his reign, as it was at the temple of Dionysus at Teos (Robert, *Op. min. sel.* VI 540); this may respond to Roman confirmation of the privilege in 22/3, despite the silence of Tacitus about both cities.

172. Unknown city

White marble stele; h. 0.26, w. 0.28, th. 0.05; copied at Notium by Benndorf in 1897 and by Keil in 1905.

H. Engelmann, *EpigAnat* 2 (1983) 21–22 no. 1 [*SEG* 33.973].

[- - - - - - - - - - - -]π̣ομ̣π[- - -]
[- - - - - - - - - - - -]χ . . ο̣[- - -]
[. . . .] παραγενόμενοι π̣α̣ρ' α̣[ὐτῶν? πρεσ]-
βευταὶ Ποσῆς Εὐπόρου, Ζη̣ . . [- - - τό]
τε ψάφισμα ἀπέδωκαν καὶ ἀπ̣[έφηναν? - - -]
τοῦ ἱεροῦ καὶ τας ἐπιφανειας [- - - Ἀ]-
πόλλω τὸγ Κλάριον καὶ πρω̣[- - - -]
χεον τὸν ἀγῶνα τε ἔθηκαν̣ [- - - γυμνικόν τε]
καὶ μ̣[ου]σικὸν ἐπὶ θυμέλας [- - - -]
[π]εντ̣αετηρίδα τῶι θεῶι [- - - - - -]
[. . . .]ε περὶ τᾶς ἀσυλία[ς - - - - -]
[- - - - -]α̣ι καὶ ἐπισ . [- - - - - -]
[- - - - - -]μ̣ο̣ . [- - - - - - - - -]

4: Engelmann suggests the name Ζήνης.

The city was Doric but has left no further trace of its identity.

8: Cf. the unpublished text quoted at Picard, *Ephèse et Claros* 143: [ἀγὼν γυ]μνικὸς καὶ μουσικὸς ἐπὶ θυμ[έλας.

173. Rome: L. and P. Cornelius Scipio

Fragment of a wall (which also contains the Athamanian letter); writing of the early first century B.C.

Picard, *Ephèse et Claros* 145 n. 5 [*SEG* 1.440; *ArchEph* 1925, 107; Sherk, *Roman Documents* 36].

Cf. Holleaux, *RivFil* 52 (1924) 29–44; Robert in Holleaux, *Etudes* VI (1968) 34–35.

[παρὰ Ῥωμαίων· Λ]εύκιος Κ[ορνήλιος Πο]-
[πλίου στρατηγὸ]ς ὕπατος Ῥωμαίων καὶ [Πό]-
[πλιος Κορνήλιος] ἀδελφὸς Κολοφ⟨ω⟩νίων τῆ[ι]
[βουλῆι καὶ τῶι δή]μωι χαίρειν· ἐνέτυχο[ν]
[ἡμῖν οἱ παρ' ὑμ]ῶν πρέσβεις Ἀγαμήδης καὶ
[ca. 8 ἄνδρε]ς καλοὶ κἀγαθοὶ ⟨οἳ⟩ τό τε
[ψήφισμα ἀπέδω]καν καὶ αὐτοὶ διελέγη-
[σαν ἀκολού]θως τοῖς ὑφ' ὑμῶν δεδογμέ-
[νοις, οὐδὲν ἐλ]λείποντες φιλοτιμίας, καὶ
[- - - - - - εἶ]ναι τὸ ἱερὸν ἄσυ[λον - - -]

Text of Holleaux but line divisions of Robert, who saw that the loss is mainly on the left. 3: φον Picard. 9–10 Robert: καὶ [?περὶ τοῦ | διαμεῖ]ναι and ἄσυ[λον ἠξίουν ἡμᾶς | πρόνοιαν ποιήσασθαι vel sim. Holleaux.

The consul Lucius and his famous brother Scipio Africanus (his legate) landed in Asia in spring 190 in order to confront Antiochus III. The king put pro-Roman Colophon-Notium under siege but abandoned this in late summer when his fleet was destroyed off Myonnesus by the praetor Aemilius Regillus. The Scipios' victory at Magnesia followed; they left Asia by spring of 189.[4] Colophon-Notium was rewarded with tax exemption (Livy 38.39.8).

The Colophonians' embassy was probably later than the lifting of the siege, and perhaps later than the battle of Magnesia: they may have sent their embassy only after fighting was done and the outcome was clear, the last months of 190. The successful repulse of the siege would be a fitting occasion to seek Roman honors for the god.

The same pair of Romans wrote to Heraclea by Latmus (*Roman Doc.* 35, its opening formulae identical with ours) thanking the city for its support and granting liberty and sending a military contingent to provide protection. Here too the precise date in relation to the campaign is uncertain; Heraclea sent a far larger embassy (eight men as against Colophon's two).

The text is a reinscription—Picard (*Ephèse et Claros* 146) speculated that after the destruction of Claros by the pirates, the temple was rebuilt under the favor of Sulla, as Colophon had opposed Mithridates.

4. Livy 37.26, 31; cf. Broughton, *MRR* I 356ff.

Unidentified City (Bargylia?)

A Hellenistic inscription seen by Pococke on Samos in 1739 contains two texts concerned with *asylia* and games. Pococke was told that the stone had been brought there from Mylasa, but concluded that Bargylia in Caria (line 1) was the more likely origin. The recipient of the recognition has not been convincingly identified.

The first text, a letter to Bargylia, was reckoned by Boeckh to be from the recipient of the recognition, a vote of thanks sent to the grantor for its recognition, which follows on the stone (hence in reverse chronological order). This implies a rather elaborate exchange of courtesies. Graindor thought instead that the letter was the initial request, and that the recipient was thus a Doric city seeking these honors for a goddess, specifically Telos (25: τοὺς Τ⟨η⟩[λίους) for the Persian goddess (6: περί τε τᾶς θεοῦ τᾶς Περσ]ικᾶς). In 1975 I argued for Cnidus and Artemis Hyacinthotrophus; a fragmentary decree at Delphi showed her games recognized as Panhellenic in the late third or early second century after a miraculous intervention (perhaps during the siege by Philip V in 201).[1] A well-preserved invitation and response on the enlarged Hyacinthotropheia have since been published, however, and there is no recognition of *asylia*.[2] The identity of the recipient is therefore in the air.

There is a different possibility, however: we may have the normal documentary situation, a fragment of an archive containing two recognitions of *asylia*, the first in letter form, like so many for Teos. If that is so, then the recipient

1. Polyb. 16.34, with Wörrle, *Chiron* 18 (1988) 442–443. The prominence there also of Aphrodite is well known; but Ael. Arist. 38.13, Κνίδον τὴν τῆς Ἀφροδίτης ἱεράν, is inconclusive as evidence for declared *asylia*.

2. After Pugliese Carratelli's publication, Blümel, *I.Knidos* 220 (= *SEG* 38.812).

was necessarily Bargylia with its chief goddess Artemis Kindyas.[3] What speaks against this is line 2, "we have sent to you," followed soon after by the names of the *theoroi*. The grantor's letter might open by saying that they have sent this through the agency of the Bargylian *theoroi*; but normally that goes without saying, and I do not know a parallel (this is not a covering letter for a separate decree, like **90**).

The decrees cannot be convincingly reconstructed:[4] in the second, clearly a grant, too many variant phrases are possible, while a recipient's letter of invitation (if that is what the first text is) would have too few parallels to work with (**176**, **177**). Hence the line length cannot be established. The second decree seems to move too quickly in the short line postulated by Boeckh and Graindor.

174. Unknown city or cities

R. Pococke, *Inscr. ant. liber* (London 1752) 44 [Boeckh, *CIG* 2670; P. Graindor, *MuséeB* 7 (1903) 296–300; Blümel, *I.Iasos/Bargylia* 606].

Cf. Rigsby, *GRBS* 16 (1975) 403–409; G. Pugliese Carratelli, *PP* 233 (1987) 110–123; Gauthier, *Bull. épigr.* 1989, 269.

[- - - - - - - - - - - - - ἄρχον]τες Βαργυλιατῶν τᾶι πόλι [χαίρεν·]
[- - - - - - - - - - - - - - - - - - ἀπε]στάλκαμες πὸθ ὑμὲ το[- - -]
[- - - - - - - - - - - - - - -]ΕΜΕΩΝ ἀρχιθέωρον Δαμάτ[ριον - - -]
[- - - - - - - - - - - - - - - -] Δαμοκράτη Ἀσστυτέλε⟨ο⟩ς, [- - -]
[- - - - - - - - - - - - - - - - - -] _Σ αὐτοῖς ἐντολὰς πρεσβε̣[υ- - -]
[- - - - - - - - - - - - - - - - - -]ικας καὶ περὶ τᾶς ἀσυλία[ς - - -]
[- - - - - - - - - - - - - - - - - - κ]α̣ὶ περὶ τᾶν τιμᾶν καὶ τα[- - -]
[- - - - - - - - - - - - τοῦ] ἀγῶνος ὃ⟨ν⟩ ἀποκατέστα[σεν ἁ πόλις?]
[- - - - - - - - - - - - - - - - - - τ]ῶν λοιπῶν Ἑλλάνων [- - - - - -]
[- - - - - - - - - - - - - - - τού]τους φιλοτίμως καὶ κ[αλῶς ? - - -]
[- - - - - - - - - - - - - - - - πό]λιος ἀξίως καὶ τᾶς θεο[ῦ - - - - -]
[- - - - - - - - - - - - - - - - -]ν πὸτ ἀμὲ ΡΟΙΝΟ.ΕΣΓΑΥ[- - - -]
[- - - - - - - - - - - - - - - - - -]ι περὶ τούτων ἐπιμέλε[ιαν - - - - -]
[- - - - - - - - - - - - - - - - - -]ατα τῶν θεαροδόχ̣ων [- - - - - -]
[- - - - - - - - - - - - - - - - - - ἀ]ναγράφωντι ἐν στ[άλαι λιθίναι·]
[- - - - - - - - - - - - πάντα τὰ τ]ίμια ἃ καὶ τοῖς πρ[οξένοις - - -]
ἔρρωσθε.
[ἐπειδὴ οἱ - - - - - - - - ε]ὖνοι καὶ συγγενεῖς ὑπά[ρχο- - - - - -]
[- - - - - - - - - - - - - - - κ]αὶ πρεσβευτὰς ἀποστ̣[έλλουσι Δαμά]-

3. For the city and the goddess see, in addition to Blümel's corpus, Robert, *Etudes anat.* 459–465. A tetradrachm of the early second century B.C. preserves an arresting image: a quite Hellenic Artemis standing beside an archaic statue of herself wearing a *polos*: G. Le Rider, *Greek Numismatics and Archaeology: Essays ... Margaret Thompson* (Wetteren 1979) 155–157.

4. As Robert observed, *BCH* 49 (1925) 236 n. 5 (*Op. min. sel.* I 30), criticizing Graindor's full restoration.

[τριον - - - - Δαμοκρ]ά̣τη Ἀστυτέλεος σ[- - - - - - - - - - - -]
[- - - - - - - - - - - -] πρὸς τὸν δῆμον ὑ[- - - - - - - - - - - - -]
[- - - - - - - - διελέχθησαν] δὲ καὶ περὶ τῆς ἀσυ[λίας - - - - -]
[- - - - - - - - - - ὁμοίω]ς δὲ καὶ τοῦ ἀγῶνο[ς - - - - - - - - - -]
[- - - - - - - - - -]αι στεφανίτην μετὰ [τῶν λοιπῶν Ἑλλήνων?]
[- - - - - - - - - - - - - - -] τὸν δῆμον τουστε[- - - - - - - - - -]
[- - - - δέχεσθαι τὰς] πρεσβευομένας ὑ[π' αὐτῶν - - - - - - -]
[- - - τιμάς - - - τῆ]ς ὑπαρχούσης [- - - - - - - - - - - - - - - -]
[- - - - - - - - - - - κ]α̣ὶ φιλίας, ἀξιου[- - - - - - - - - - - - -]
[- - - - - - - - - - - - - -]ΝΤΑΣ τῆς [- - - - - - - - - - - - - - -]

1: ἁ πόλις καὶ οἱ ἄρχον]τες Boeckh. 2–3: [ἐπειδὴ τό τε ψάφισμα ὃ ἀπε]στάλκαμες πὸθ ὑμὲ το[ῦτο φιλο|φρόνως ἐδέξασθε καὶ τὸν παρ' ἁ]μέων Boeckh, πὸθ ὑμὲ τό[ν τε παραγι|νόμενον παρὰ τᾶς πόλιος] Graindor. 4–5: [οὓς ἀ|πεστάλκαμεν ποθ' ὑμέ, δόντ]ε̣ς and πρεσβ[ευσομένοις Boeckh (ΠΡΕΣΒ|[Pococke), [- - - καθὰ ἐδώκαμ]ε̣ς and πρεσβε[υομένους Graindor. 8: ΟΤΕΑΠΟ; end Boeckh. 10 Boeckh. 12: [ὑπεδέξασθε, ὡς ἀπάγγειλα]ν πὸτ ἀμὲ οἱ [πρ]εσ[βε]υ[ταί Boeckh. 13: δέδοκται τᾶι πόλ]ι? and ἐπιμέλε[ιαν ποιήσασθαι τοὺς Boeckh. 14: με]τὰ Boeckh. 15 Boeckh. 16: [δόμεν δὲ καὶ αὐτοῖς (κτλ.) Boeckh. 18–19: ὑπά[ρχουσι | τῆι πόλει ὑμῶν διὰ προγόνων κ]αὶ π. ἀπ[ε]σ[τάλκασι Boeckh; ὑπά[ρχοντες ἐκ προγό|νων ἡμῖν ψήφισμα κ]αὶ Graindor. 20: σ[υμπρεσβευτάν? Boeckh. 21: οἳ καὶ προσελθόντες] π. τ. δ. ὑ[πὲρ Boeckh, οἵτινες ἀνενεώσαντο τὴν] π. τ. δ. ὑ[πάρχουσαν φιλίαν Graindor. 22 Boeckh; ἀσυ[λίας τῆς πό|λεως καὶ τῆς χώρας - - - Graindor. 23 init. Graindor: ὡσαύτω]ς Boeckh. 23–24: ὃν ἀπε|κατέστησαν Boeckh, ὃν παρεκά|λεσαν τοὺς Βαργυλιήτας δέχεσθ]αι Graindor. 24 Boeckh. 25–27: [ἀγαθῆι τύχηι δεδόχθαι μετέχειν] τ. δ. τοῦ στε[φανίτου | ἀγῶνος, δέχεσθαι δὲ καὶ τὰς Boeckh, [δεδόχθαι τῶι δήμωι· ἐπαινέσαι] τ. δ. τοὺς Τ⟨η⟩[λίους? ἐπὶ τῆι | προαιρέσει καὶ δέχεσθαι τὰς] π. ὑ[π' αὐτῶν περὶ τῆς | θεοῦ τῆς Περσικῆς τιμάς, διὰ τῆ]ς Graindor. 27–29: [πρὸς ἀμφοτέρας τὰς | πόλεις - - - οἰκειότητος κ]αὶ φιλίας, ἀξιοῦ[ντες ὅτι δίκαιόν | ἐστιν τὸν δῆμον τὸν ἡμέτερον συναύξει]ν τὰς τῆς [θεοῦ τιμὰς - - -] Graindor.

Graindor restored the second half of the first text:

[περί τε τᾶς θεᾶς τᾶς Περσ]ικᾶς καὶ περὶ τᾶς ἀσυλία[ς τᾶς πο]-
[λιος καὶ τᾶς χώρας ἔτι δὲ κ]α̣ὶ περὶ τᾶν τιμᾶν καὶ τᾶ[ν θυσιᾶν]
[καὶ τᾶς παναγύριος καὶ τοῦ] ἀγῶνος ὃ⟨ν⟩ ἀποκατέστα[σεν ἁ πόλις?]
[ἁμέων στεφανίταν μετὰ τ]ῶν λοιπῶν Ἑλλάνων [παρακαλοῦν]-
[τας προσδέξασθαι, τού]τους φιλοτίμως καὶ κ[αλῶς καὶ τᾶς]
[φιλίας τᾶς πὸτ ἀμετέρας πό]λιος ἀξίως καὶ τᾶς θεο[ῦ ὑποδέξασθε·]
[δεδόχθαι τῶι δάμωι· εἶ̣μ̣ε]ν πὸτ ἀμὲ ⟨πολίτας ἐπ' ἴ⟩[σαι καὶ ὁμοίαι]
[τοὺς Βαργυλιάτας? - - -]ι περὶ τούτων· ἐπιμέλε[ιαν καὶ ὁμοίαι]
[- - - - - - ὅπως τὰ ὀνόμ]ατα τῶν θεαροδόχ̣ων [τῶν ὑφ' ὑμετέρας]
[πόλιος ἀιρεθέντων πατρόθεν ἀ]ναγράφωντι ἐν στ[άλαι λιθίναι·]
[δόμεν δὲ καὶ αὐτοῖς πάντα τὰ τ]ίμια ἃ καὶ τοῖς πρ[οξένοις ὑπάρχει.]

6: Graindor assumed that the relevant divinity (female, line 11) was named here, as did I (suggesting Ἀρτάμιτος τᾶς Σωτε]ί⟨ρ⟩ας rather than the Persian

Goddess). But the name may have come later (in 8 or 9), and other words are possible here, for example, reference to a victory or to a periodic festival or sacrifice (πενταετηρ]ικᾶς).

8: A "restoration" of the games is the most individual feature, which may serve finally to identify the recipient. One thinks, however, of ὅτε ⟨κα⟩ ὁ κατεστα[μένος χρόνος ἵκηι; cf. **94**.18: ἐπεί κα ἑκαστάκις ὁ χρόνος περιίκῃ.

12: Perhaps κοινωνεῖν αὐ[τούς.

29: Perhaps μετέχο]ντας.

Temple of Apollo, Anaphe

In order to give safe anchorage to the Argonauts, Apollo caused Anaphe to rise up from the sea east of Thera—whence the name, from its sudden appearance (ἀναφαίνω); above the harbor the Argonauts established a precinct sacred to Apollo Αἰγλήτης (Ἀσγελάτας in the Hellenistic inscriptions), named for the flash of his bow when he revealed the island.[1] In this eastern part of the island, beside a good harbor some three kilometers from the height of the ancient city, his temple may still be seen in large part, incorporated into the monastery Panaghia Kalamiotissa.[2] Apollonius describes an altar in a grove in the time of the Argonauts; the temple building we see is Hellenistic but not closely dated. The chief festival of the Anaphiotes was the annual *panegyris* called the Asgelaia, known to the ancient authors for the ribald participation of women.[3] The Strangford Apollo may be the cult statue.[4]

The one document revealing *asylia* at Anaphe is of exceeding brevity: there is no mention of an Anaphiote embassy, nor is the god identified—yet surely it can only be Apollo. The decree is one of the few extant of the Cretan League and dates to the first half of the second century B.C. Too little is known of the history of Anaphe to speculate about the occasion.

This decree is the best candidate we have for an extension of inviolability from the temple to the whole city and country (but see on 14–15); if indeed the Cretans are expanding the boundaries of an existing privilege, that might explain the lack of detail.

1. Callim. frag. 7.19ff. (from the *Aetia*); Ap. Rhod. 4.1701ff. (1715: ἄλσει ἐνὶ σκιερῷ τέμενος σκιόεντά τε βωμόν); Theophr. in *SVF* I 106; Conon 49; Apollod. 1.26.1. Cf. Farnell, *Cults* IV 139.

2. See Hiller in *Thera* I (Berlin 1899) 351–358.

3. E.g., Conon 49; *IG* XII.3 249.21–22; cf. 25–27: ἱερομηνίαι celebrated at times in the city, at times in the country.

4. R. A. McNeal, *Archaeology* 20 (1967) 254–263.

175. Cretan League

White marble stele from the temple. As first seen, h. 0.63, w. 0.245, th. 0.085; letters 0.01, intersp. 0.005; first half of the second century B.C. Below, in a different hand, an Anaphiote proxeny decree for a citizen of Lyttus in Crete.[5] In 1976, a section at left and below had been slivered off and was not located; nothing was legible after line 22, and the stone breaks off at 25 (thus losing the proxeny decree).

K. S. Pittakis, *ArchEph* 2 (1840) 372–373 no. 477 (with facsimile); E. Legrand, *BCH* 16 (1892) 144–147 no. 35 [Michel, *Rec.* 439]; Hiller, *IG* XII.3 254 [Blass, *SGDI* 5146]; Guarducci, *I.Cret.* IV 197 (collation of squeeze in Berlin by Klaffenbach). *Collation.*

PLATE 5.

Cf. Wilhelm, *GGA* 160 (1898) 233; *Beiträge* (1909) 172; *Neue Beitr.* VI (1921) 14–19, *AnzWien* 1924, 154–156 (*Kl. Schr.* I.1 305–310, I.2 196–198); A. Maiuri, *RendLinc* V.19 (1910) 45–46, 112; Guarducci, *RivFil* 61 (1933) 232–233; Daux, *BCH* 59 (1935) 94–96; 61 (1937) 439–440; Hiller, *IG* XII Suppl. p. 83; H. van Effenterre, *Crète et le monde grec* (Paris 1948) 148 n. 4.

[ἔδοξ]ε τοῖς συνέδροις καὶ τῶ[ι]
[κοινῶ]ι τῶν Κρηταιέων Κνω-
[σοῖ ἐ]ν τῶι συνλόγωι, κορμι-
4 [όντω]ν ἐν Γόρτυνι μὲν ἐ-
[πὶ τῶ]ν Δυμάνων τῶν σὺν
[. . . . .]ίωι τῶι Ἀλλοδάμω
[ὄκα] τὸ δεύτερον μηνὸς
8 [Καρ]ν̣ήιω τετράδι, Κνωσο[ῖ]
[δὲ ἐ]π̣ὶ τῶν Αἰθαλέων κο[ρ]-
[μιόντ]ων τῶν σὺν Κυψέλω[ι]
[τῶι . . .]ρέτω μηνὸς Ἀγυή̣[ι]-
12 [ω τετρά]δι· ἄσυλον ἦμεν [Ἀ]-
[ναφαίων] τὰν πόλιν κα[ὶ]
[τὰν χώρ]α̣ν καθὼς καὶ τὸ [ἱ]-
[ερὸν ὑ]π̣άρχει ἄσυλον
16 [τῶι τῶ κ]οινῶ τῶν Κρητα[ι]-
[έων ῥη]τῶι· εἰ δέ τίς τι-
[να συλά]σηι Ἀναφαίων τῶν
[ἐκ Κρήτ]ας ὁρμιομένων,
20 [ἢ ἐκ τ]ᾶ̣ς πόλεως ἢ ἐκ τ[ᾶς]
[χώρα]ς, ὑπόδικος ἔστω [δί]-
[καν ἔν] τε Ἀναφαίοι[ς]
[ἅν κ' α]ὐ̣τοὶ προστάξ̣ω[ντι,]
24 [κ' ἐν κ]οινοδικίωι ἀπρ[όδι]-
[κον κ' ἀπ]άρβολον, καὶ κ[υ]-

5. On this decree see Robert, *RN* VI.4 (1962) 13–17 (*Op. min. sel.* II 1040–1044).

[ρία ἁ] πρᾶξις ἔστω κὰτ [τὸ]
[διάγρ]αμμα.

3 Wilhelm 1898: Κνω[σ|ίων] Legrand. 6: ['Ερτα]ίωι? Guarducci. 6 Wilhelm 1898: ἀλλοδάμω[ν χορμι|όντων] Legrand. 7 Guarducci 1933: [κατὰ] Hiller; [ἔ|τος] Blass. 8 init. Guarducci. 11: 'Ενα]ρέτω? Kaibel (*IG*). 11 end Guarducci, 12 Legrand, Maiuri: [A]ὐδου|[ναίω ἱκά]δι Wilamowitz (*IG*). 14–15 Wilhelm 1898. 16–17 Wilhelm 1909: [ἀπὸ τῶ κ]οινῶ Wilhelm 1898. 17 ῥη]τῶ Hiller. 17–18 Wilhelm 1898: τι [ἀφαι|ρέ]σει Legrand, τι[να | ἀδική]σηι Hiller. 20 init. Blass, Daux 1935: [ἤ τι ἔκ τινο]ς Wilhelm 1898, [ἢ ἔκ τινο]ς Wilhelm 1924, Daux 1937. 20–21 Wilhelm 1898: τ[ῶ | ἱερῶ] Hiller, τ[ῶν | ναοῶν] van Effenterre. 21–24 Guarducci: (23) πρὸς τὰς ω[Legrand, ἔστω |[τᾶι] τε 'Αναφαί[ων πό|λει ἐκ] τῶ προστακῶτ[ο]ς | [τῶι τε κ]οινοδικίωι Hiller; τ]ῶι προστάγ[τι δίκαν ἐν τῶι κ.] Wilhelm 1921. 24–25 Wilhelm 1921: δέκα | Legrand, δέκα [τά|λαντα πά]ρβολον Hiller.

...

(12ff.) The city and [country of the Anaphiotes] is to be inviolable just as the [temple] is already inviolable according to the law of the Cretan League. If anyone operating from [Crete] should seize any Anaphiote, from either city or [country], he is to be subject to trial both among the Anaphiotes, whatever trial they should order, and in the League court without preliminary arbitration or security deposit; and the exaction is to be binding in accordance with the law.

There is no talk of cult, beyond the mention of the temple (without naming the god). Like many of the Cretan civic decrees for Teos, this act of the League leaves no doubt that the Anaphiote request was understood to concern personal inviolability: the declaration about the place is glossed by the statement that persons are not to be seized from it and those who are will have access to the Cretan tribunal for redress. Taken literally, the combining of personal and territorial inviolability—mostly closely paralleled in the Aetolian grants for Teos and Pergamum—means that Anaphiotes seized by Cretans elsewhere (e.g., in Crete or on the high seas) are not included and have no recourse.

For the import of this text for the constitution of the League see M. Muttelsee, *Verfassungsgeschichte Kretas* (Hamburg 1925) 47–50; M. van der Mijnsbrugge, *The Cretan Koinon* (New York 1931) 17–20; Guarducci, *RivFil* 78 (1950) 148–154; Gauthier, *Symbola* 324; S. L. Ager, *JHS* 114 (1994) 1–18.

14–15: "just as the temple is inviolable in accordance with Cretan law"; this can be taken to indicate that a previous grant to the temple is now being enlarged to encompass the whole island. But it seems to me equally likely that this is merely a statement of the normal, such as we find of Cos (cf. p. 22), saying that in Cretan law temples have this immunity—a generic fact cited as explanation and analogy rather than a concrete enactment cited as historical precedent.

20: The restoration turns on whose city and country are in view, Anaphe or Crete; I follow those who prefer the former, consistent with what is voted at 13.

24–25: Restored from *I.Cret.* IV 175: [δίκαν] ἀπρόδικον κ' ἀπάρ[βολον (see Maiuri 45–46); δίκη πρόδικος as arbitration in lieu of a public trial at Aristophanes frag. 278 K.-A. Cf. Gauthier 329.

27: On διάγραμμα see Guarducci's references at *I.Cret.* IV 169; it seems to mean "law code" at I xvi 1.36–38; cf. the δικαστικὸν διάγραμμα at Cyrene (*SEG* 9.5.56).

Pergamum

The two great divinities of Pergamum were Athena and Asclepius, in that historical sequence.[1] In Roman times Asclepius came to surpass Athena as the city's chief god, but the two could still be invoked as joint patrons of Pergamum as late as the third century A.D.[2] The two temples of interest to us were out in the territory, not in the city itself, and it was the temples, not the city and country of Pergamum, that were declared inviolable. The inviolability of the Nicephorium was gained at the request of Eumenes II in 182 B.C., that of the Asclepieum later, but before 88 B.C.; both entitlements probably were abolished after the Roman Vespers in 88. That of Asclepius was restored by Caesar ca. 45; Athena's restoration is doubtful—Tacitus does not mention it, but it may be referred to in Caesar's edict on Sardes (**214**). This honor of two *asyla* in one city is rare, preceded by Chalcedon (if I am right about its two temples of Apollo) and followed by Stratoniceia. The Attalid kings were closely involved in the institutions of their capital city, and they shared in the sponsorship of the great festivals. The unusual, even ostentatious, quest for two inviolable temples doubtless reflects the peculiar eminence and ambition of the Attalids in world affairs in the second century B.C.

1. E. Ohlemutz, *Die Kulte und Heiligtümer der Götter in Pergamon* (Giessen 1940) 16–59, 123–173; C. P. Jones, "Diodoros Pasparos and the Nikephoria of Pergamon," *Chiron* 4 (1974) 183–205.

2. The two together on a coin under Herennius Etruscus: G. Le Rider, *RN* VI.15 (1973) 75 with fig. 9. Cf. the relief published by E. Boehringer, *AA* 81 (1966) 467–469 with pl. 44: Athena and Asclepius, flanked respectively by Zeus and Hygieia, crown a seated female; Boehringer thought the date early Hellenistic. A law on the priesthood of Asclepius is to be inscribed in the Asclepieum and in the temple of Athena on the acropolis (*I.Perg.* 251.38–39 [*LSAM* 13], II B.C.).

Temple of Athena Nicephorus

Whatever the importance of Athena at Pergamum before the Hellenistic period, the founder of the Attalid dynasty set out to make her the visible patroness of a second Athens. Her temple was on the terrace that overlooks the theater, near the royal palace. Early Hellenistic texts regularly give her no epithet. Later, when there was need to distinguish her cult from the newer one of Athena Nicephorus in the country, she is called Athena Polias; perhaps this title was old, but it was used only when necessary.[3] Great antiquity was credited to her worship at Pergamum: Auge, Heracles' victim, brought the cult statue from Tegea when she came with their son Telephus from Arcadia to Asia.[4]

As early as the mid-third century Athena had a public festival of first importance, the Panathenaia.[5] Probably it was to this festival, a "contest of Athena," that Byzantium sent participants (συνθύσοντας) at the invitation of Attalus I in the 220s.[6] Despite the presence of these foreigners, Pergamum did not have Panhellenic games in the third century; evidently the Byzantines were among friends or allies of Attalus specially invited[7] to a local festival (the Nicephoria passed through a similar stage forty years later). It was to Athena (without epithet) that Attalus dedicated the spoils of his defeat of the Gauls,[8] and that victory may be the occasion, with Attalus inviting his allies.

The cult of Athena Nicephorus was distinct from that of Athena on the acropolis. The Nicephorium was a sacred grove outside the city, not yet located by the excavators of Pergamum.[9] It was without defenses, and we first hear of Athena Nicephorus when in 201 Philip V ravaged the place, cutting down

3. See, however, Fränkel, *I.Perg.* I pp. 76–77; Ohlemutz 24–25. *I.Perg.* 251.39 makes the explicit location ἐν τῶι ἱερῶι τῆς Ἀθηνᾶς ἐν ἀκροπόλ[ει].

4. *I.Perg.* 156; cf. Robert, *REG* 40 (1927) 212–213 (*Op. min. sel.* I 453–454). Ohlemutz (20–22) argued that in fact the cult and image did not come into being until about 300 B.C.

5. *OGIS* 267 (= *Royal Corres.* 23): on advice of Eumenes I, Pergamum honors its five *strategoi* for their distinguished service; he has announced his own decision to crown the five at the Panathenaia (17: αὐτοί τε διεγνώκαμεν τοῖς Παναθηναίοις στεφανοῦν αὐτούς), which thus was an affair of the king as much as of the city.

6. Polyb. 4.49.3 (when the Byzantines angered Prusias of Bithynia by refusing his invitation to his festival, the Soteria). Many scholars follow Holleaux (*Etudes* II 61–62) in seeing the Pergamene festival as the Nicephoria (cf. Ohlemutz 34; Jones 184). For the Panathenaia: W. Kolbe, *Hermes* 68 (1933) 445; Walbank, *Comm.* I 503; E. V. Hansen, *Attalids of Pergamum*[2] (Ithaca, N.Y., 1971) 448.

7. For such a discrimination cf. the Cnidian decree enlarging the Hyacinthotropheia by asking their "friends and allies to share in the sacrifice and the games" (Blümel, *I.Knidos* 220).

8. *OGIS* 273–279; see R. E. Allen, *The Attalid Kingdom* (Oxford 1983) 194–199, on the problem of the date.

9. Generally thought to be near the "Red Hall"; cf. H. Müller, *Chiron* 22 (1992) 201; bibliography in Walbank, *Comm.* II 501; cf. Hansen 242. In the *asylia* inscriptions Eumenes and his respondents call the sacred place a τέμενος, an appropriate term for a rural precinct with

the grove and damaging the sacred buildings.[10] While the statue of Athena placed by Auge in the city temple was doubtless Greek, possibly archaic or archaistic, that of Athena Nicephorus was of an oriental style; on some coins of Pergamum she poses in the manner of Artemis of Ephesus, wearing a *polos*, veil, pectoral, and bracelets.[11] Her cult was linked to that of Athena Polias to the extent that, at least under Roman rule, a single priestess regularly served both goddesses.[12]

It is debated how long before 201 the sacred grove of Athena was established; and the date of her epithet (and thus what victory it commemorates) is perhaps a separate question. In his letter of 182 B.C. Eumenes seems to claim personal credit for the epithet (προσηγορεύκαμεν, **176**.6); the natural interpretation is that the goddess has acquired the epithet thanks to the victory over Prusias of Bithynia in 183.[13] How she might have been called earlier would then be a question—but the same ignorance applies to Athena in the city, whose Πολιάς is not attested until after the epithet Νικηφόρος was in use for the country shrine.

The date of the inviolability of the rural shrine and the Panhellenic Nicephoria, however, is fixed with certainty in 182.[14] The Aetolians (**178**.26) voted their recognition under the *strategos* Proxenus (183/2), the Amphictyony (**179**.1) in the archonship of Demosthenes (182/1). It follows that the Amphictyons voted at their autumn sitting of 182, in connection with the Pythia in September; the Aetolians had acted earlier, for they instruct the individual cities to submit the names of their new *theorodochoi* to Proxenus at the upcoming Pythia (**178**.24–26). The Aetolian decree possibly was voted at the regular League meeting, the Panaetolia, in March; but an extraordinary meeting (these were frequent), nearer in time to the Pythia, seems more likely (see on **177**.11).

a grove (cf. *AJP* 108 [1987] 734), though the respondents then revert to the more general term ἱερόν (**178**.28, **179**.23).

10. Polyb. 16.1.6: τὸ Νικηφόριον ἐλυμήνατο, τὸ μὲν ἄλσος ἐκτεμνών, τὸν δὲ περίβολον διαρρίψας, τούς τε ναοὺς ἐκ θεμελίων ἀνέσκαψε, πολλοὺς καὶ πολυτελεῖς ὑπάρχοντας; cf. 18.2.2; Livy 32.33.5.

11. Le Rider 69–70; O. Mørkholm in *Festschrift für Leo Mildenberg* (Wetteren 1984) 187–192.

12. *I.Perg.* 226 (113 B.C.), 489–525; for a parallel in Syria cf. *IGLSyrie* III 1184, with *TAPA* 110 (1980) 236.

13. This would mean that Polybius is anachronistic in calling the grove the "Nikephorion" in 201 (above, n. 10). Segre (in *Hellenica* V [1948] 119) thought that "Nikephoros" commemorated the victory at Chios in 201 and took Polybius' use to be anachronistic; this was denied by J. and L. Robert, *Bull. épigr.* 1952, 127; Klaffenbach, *MdI* 3 (1950) 102 n. 10; Walbank, *Comm.* I 503. On the problem see D. Musti, *AnnPisa* II.26 (1957) 279–282.

14. Robert, *BCH* 54 (1930) 332–338 (*Op. min. sel.* I 151–157), recognizing Proxenus rather than a *proxenos*; Jones 183–205, with *Bull. épigr.* 1974, 466 (p. 268).

Thus the Pergamene *theoroi* were canvassing Greece during 182, and the first quadrennial[15] Nicephoria were held in 181. Writing in 182, Eumenes reminded the Coans that they had twice before attended the Nicephoria at his invitation. This must refer to local celebrations, as Segre saw (urging 197 and 189 B.C.), and the Coans evidently were invited as a gesture of special friendship. These celebrations, however, will have been annual, and I suggest that the invitations were not sporadic but occurred in 183 and 182: thus the Nicephoria were indeed founded to commemorate Eumenes' defeat of Prusias early in 183.[16] If this chronology is correct, it implies that the festival was held in the spring:[17] that is, immediately upon the defeat of Prusias, Eumenes invited his allies, who included the Coans,[18] to join in celebrating the new Nicephoria at Pergamum in the spring, repeated this gesture to his allies for the celebration in 182, and then decided to seek Panhellenic recognition.

Eumenes is said to have planted the Nicephorium with a grove (Strab. 13.4.2 [624]). Conceivably he did this at the start of his reign (197), repairing the damage done by Philip in 201. But the occasion may instead have been the attention paid the sacred place in the 180s (see on **176**.19).

Athena Nicephorus, like some other gods, issued coins in her own name (Ἀθηνᾶς Νικηφόρου), struck from bullion belonging to herself.[19] Two sorts are known: silver tetradrachms bearing Medusa on the obverse and a standing Athena on the reverse; and small denominations in silver and bronze, with the helmeted head of Athena on the obverse and various reverses. The tetradrachms are known from only three examples, which used two obverses and three reverses; two were found in a hoard buried ca. 165. Only moderately worn, they cannot be much older than that, and Le Rider is surely right that they were issued soon after the elevation of the status of Athena's cult in 182.[20] It is a reasonable assumption that this was a festival coinage, struck on the occasions of the Nicephoria and

15. Jones has demonstrated that the Panhellenic games were from the start quadrennial, and his discussion makes it unnecessary to recount here previous efforts to make sense of the *asylia* inscriptions under the theory that the festival was biennial.

16. Habicht, *Hermes* 84 (1956) 90–100, established the dates of the battle and subsequent treaty.

17. This in turn implies that the Aetolian decree was not voted at the Panaetolica ca. March, which would be too early for the Pergamenes to have visited; but see on **177**.11.

18. For other testimonies of the alliance between Cos and the Attalids in the second century see S. Sherwin-White, *Ancient Cos* (Göttingen 1978) 132–133.

19. See Le Rider for the two hoard tetradrachms and a survey of the small issues, Mørkholm for the third tetradrachm; for the date, M. J. Price in *Kraay-Mørkholm Essays* (Louvain 1989) 233–243. Sacred revenues of Athena Nicephorus: *Syll.*[3] 982.

20. So too Mørkholm; Price (239–240) suggests instead that the coins are associated with the threat of Gallic invasion in 168. I pass over the use of the Attic standard of the tetradrachms for purposes of dating, as the relevant Pergamene royal issues are not yet securely dated. See Le Rider, *JSav* 1989, 163–190, esp. 175–176; H. Nicolet-Pierre in *Kraay-Mørkholm Essays* 203–216.

thus at four-year intervals. The three extant tetradrachms, struck from different dies and obviously (from their rarity) in numbers insufficient to wear out the dies quickly, should probably be assigned to three different festivals, from among those of 181, 177, 173, and 169. It seems that the first Panhellenic celebration was accompanied by a decision to honor the goddess with a coinage of her own. Evidently there was never much silver available for the coins of Athena, for the tetradrachms are rare in the extreme, and even they were given up, on present evidence, after the first several festivals. The smaller coinage, which cannot be closely dated, perhaps was subsequent to these first ambitious efforts. In this respect the coinage of Athena Nicephorus contrasts sharply with the voluminous issues of Artemis Pergaea or even Athena Iliensis.

At Pergamum the word *panegyris* is often applied to the Nicephoria. It is seen first at **176**.10 and 16, where Eumenes mentions the two celebrations previously held and the coming Panhellenic one. The games and temple were probably associated physically with the "panegyric gymnasium," where competitors in Panhellenic games exercised.[21] The Nicephoria survived the Mithridatic war (or were soon after revived), still a Panhellenic festival.[22] A text of the 70s or 60s B.C. names the major festivals of Pergamum in what appears to be a descending order of importance: προεδρία[ν] ἐμ πάσαις ταῖς πανηγύρεσιν[23] καὶ τριετηρίσιν (the Dionysia) καὶ Παναθηναίοις καὶ τοῖς ἄλλοις ἀγῶσιν.[24]

The Pergamenes, however, had sided with Mithridates, and they massacred Romans who fled to the Asclepieum for refuge (see below); the city lost its freedom and privileges. This is the obvious occasion for the revocation of the *asylia* of both temples. In the review of A.D. 22 the Pergamenes, as Tacitus reports the event, spoke only of the Asclepieum and not the temple of Athena; possibly they put their better case forward, a cult dear to Romans. The Nicephoria survived, attested once in Severan times (*I.Perg.* 525), but there is no hint that the games were still Panhellenic—witness the silence of the many victor lists of imperial date.[25]

176. Letter of Eumenes II; decree of Cos

From Cos, two joining fragments of a white marble stele, the lower found in 1907 built into a modern house in the city, the upper found in 1938 built into a Turkish tomb at Koumournou, eight kilometers from the city; joined now in the

21. Robert, *Monnaies antiques en Troade* (Paris 1965) 46; distinguished from the gymnasium of the *neoi* in *IGR* IV 294.5, 28.

22. So expressly the 29th, presumably 69 B.C., *IGR* IV 293.I.50; *theoroi* at 294.12.

23. The Nicephoria at least, but perhaps also the Soteria/Heracleia, called *panegyris* in *IGR* IV 300 (as is a festival for the emperor later in *I.Asklep.* 36.6).

24. *IGR* IV 292.33, with Jones 187 on the terminology; 293.II.25ff. neatly distinguishes the *panegyreis* and *trietereis* (μέν/δέ) and assigns the latter to Dionysus.

25. J. and L. Robert, *Bull. épigr.* 1974, 466 (p. 268).

city's museum (inv. 255). Broken at right and bottom; h. 0.79, w. 0.24, th. 0.13; letters h. 0.013 with large apices, irregular and increasingly crowded.

Lower fragment (lines 21–45): R. Herzog, *Hermes* 65 (1930) 455–463 [Schroeter 40; Welles, *Royal Corres.* 50; Allen, *Attalid Kingdom* 216–217].

Complete: M. Segre in Robert, *Hellenica* V (1948) 102–128.

Photograph: Segre pl. 1.

Cf. G. Klaffenbach, *MdI* 3 (1950) 99–106; J. and L. Robert, *Bull. épigr.* 1952, 127; 1974, 466; D. Musti, *AnnPisa* II.26 (1957) 279–282.

[β]ασιλεὺς Εὐμένης Κ[ώιων τῆι βουλῆι καὶ]
τῶι δήμωι χαίρειν· τὴν Ἀ̣[θηνᾶν μὲν τιμῶμεν]
μάλιστα τῶν ἄλλων θε[ῶν διὰ τὸ πολλὰς καὶ]
μεγάλας ἡμῖν περιτεθε[ικέναι εὐημερίας ἐν]
παντοδαπαῖς περιστάσ[εσιν καιρῶν, Νικηφόρον]
τε προσηγορεύκαμεν, [καλλίστην νομίζον]-
τες εἶναι καὶ οἰκειοτάτη[ν τὴν προσω]-
νυμίαν ταύτην, καθάπερ [καὶ πρότερον ἐγράψαμεν·]
δὶς γὰρ ἤδη παρακληθέ[ντες ὑφ' ἡμῶν τάς τε]
πανηγύρεις ἃς τότ̣[ε κατηγγείλαμεν ἀπεδέξασθε]
φιλοφρόνως, καὶ πέμψ[αντες θεωροὺς ἐκοινω]-
[ν]ήσατε τῶν ἱερῶν ὁ[σίως καὶ εὐσεβῶς· καὶ νῦν]
[ἐ]παύξειν δὲ βουλόμ[ενοι τὰς τιμὰς αὐτῆς]
[κ]αὶ μείζω χαριστή[ρια τῶν κατὰ πόλεμον ἀγώνων]
[ἀ]ποδιδόναι, διεγ̣ν[ωκότες δὲ συντελεῖν αὐτῆι πα]-
[ν]ήγυριν τε διὰ πέν[τε ἐτῶν καὶ στεφανίτας μουσι]-
[κο]ὺς καὶ γυμνικοὺς [καὶ ἱππικοὺς ἀγῶνας, ἀνα]-
[δεδ]ε̣ι̣χότες καὶ τὸ π[ρὸς Περγάμωι ἱερὸν αὐτῆς ἄσυ]-
[λον], ὧι θήσομεν αὐ[τοὶ τὰ ὅρια, καλῶς δὲ ἔχον κε]-
[κρικότες ταῦτα] ὑπὸ̣ [θεωρῶν καταγγέλλεσθαι,]
[ὥστε τ]οὺς ἀγῶνα[ς τούτους συντελεῖσθαι σὺν]
[ἅπα]σ̣ι̣ τοῖς ἐκτενεσ[τάτοις τῶν Ἑλλήνων, ἐπι]-
[τε]υγμάτων μεγάλω[ν χαριστήρια τῆι Ἀθηνᾶι,]
π̣επόμφαμεν θεωρ[οὺς πρὸς ὑμᾶς τὸν - - - - - - -]
ρέα, τυγχάνοντα παρ' [ἡμῖν τιμῆς τε τῆς πρώτης καὶ προ]-
ε̣δρίας δι⟨ὰ⟩ τὴν καλοκ̣[ἀγαθίαν, καὶ τὸν - - - - -]
Μυριναῖον καὶ Μέγων[α Ἐφέσιον, τῶν φίλων τῶν προ]-
τιμωμένων παρ' ἡμῖν, [καὶ - - - καὶ Κάλαν Περγα]-
μηνούς, καὶ ὑφ' ἡμῶν μὲ[ν κρινομένους ἀξίους, ὡς]
δὲ πολίτας τετευχ[ότας κατὰ τὴν ἡλικίαν τῶν προση]-
κόντων, προκεχειρισ[μένους δὲ καὶ ὑπὸ τῆς πόλεως]
διὰ τὸ καταγγέλλε[ιν μεθ' ἡμῶν τὰ Νικηφόρια· καλῶς]
οὖν ποιήσετε πρῶ̣[τον μὲν διὰ τὴν θεόν, ἔπειτα δὲ]
καὶ δι' ἡμᾶς τῶν ἀνδ[ρῶν τε φιλοφρόνως διακούσαν]-
τες καὶ ἀποδεξάμεν[οι τά τε Νικηφόρια καὶ τὴν ἀσυλίαν ὥσ]-
περ ὑμῖν ἁρμόζει· ταῦτ̣[α γὰρ πράξαντες τὰ μὲν ἐκείνης τί]-
μια φανεῖσθε συναύξ̣[οντες, ἡμᾶς δὲ ἀκολούθως τῆι]

παρ' ἡμῶν ὑπαρχούσῃ[ι πρὸς τὸν δῆμον ὑμῶν εὐνοίαι]
ὡς ἐνδέχεται μάλισ[τα προθύμους ἕξετε τὸ λοιπὸν κατὰ]
πάντα καιρὸν πρὸς τ[ὰ συμφέροντα ὑμῖν· τὰ δὲ πλείονα]
περὶ τῶν κατὰ μέρος [ἀκούσετε παρ' αὐτῶν τῶν θεω]-
ρῶν. ἔρρωσθε. [ἔδοξε τᾶι βουλᾶι καὶ τῶι δάμωι·]
γνώμα προστατᾶν· [ἐπειδὴ βασιλεὺς Εὐμένης ἀποστέλλων]
θ̣ε̣ω̣ροὺς [παρ' αὐτοῦ τε καὶ παρὰ τᾶς πόλιος τᾶς Περγαμηνῶν]
ἐ̣παγ[γέλλει -]

1–23 Segre. Klaffenbach attributed the earlier actions (8–10) to Attalus I: 8 [καὶ ὁ πατὴρ ἡμῶν], 9 ὑπ' αὐτοῦ, 10 κατήγγειλε; see contra Musti. 12: εὐσεβῶς πάντων·] Klaffenbach. 16 J. and L. Robert 1974: πεν[ταετηρίδος Segre, πέν[θ' ἡμερῶν Klaffenbach. 17–19 Klaffenbach: γυμνικοὺς [ἀγῶνας, καὶ τὸ ἱερὸν ἀνα|δεδ]ε̣ι̣χότες καὶ τὸ π[ερὶ αὐτὸ τέμενος ἄσυλα, | καθ'] ὧι θήσομεν αὐ[τῶν Segre. 20–21: καὶ νῦν διεγνωκότες στεφανί|τας τ]οὺς ἀγῶνα[ς τῶν Νικηφορίων Welles. 22 Klaffenbach: ἡμῖν τῶν Welles. 22–23: - - - τετευχότες ἐπι(?) |τευ]γμάτων μεγάλω[ν τὴν ἀνανέωσιν τῶν θυσιῶν καὶ] Herzog, μεγάλω[ν κατὰ τοὺς πολέμους γεγονότων] Welles. 24–25 Segre: Μάγνη]|τα Herzog. 26 ΔΙΤΗΝ lapis. 29 Welles: κρινομένους, φιλοτίμους] Herzog. 41 Welles: [ἀκούσεσθε Herzog. 43 Segre: ἀπέσταλκε] Herzog.

. . .

King Eumenes to the council and people of the Coans greetings: [we honor Athena] most of all the gods [because of her] bestowing upon us [many and] great [successes on] all sorts of [occasions], and we have dubbed her [*Nikephoros*, consider]ing this to be a most [beautiful] and appropriate epithet, as [we wrote you before]; for twice already, when you were invited [by us to the] *panegyreis* which at that time [we proclaimed, you accepted] in friendly fashion, and send[ing *theoroi* you shared] in the sacrifices [properly and piously; and now], wishing to increase [her honors] and render greater thanks [for our contests in war], we have decided [to celebrate for her] a *panegyris* every fourth [year and crowned musical] and gymnic [and equestrian contests,] and we have [declared her temple at Pergamum inviolable,] for which we shall set [the boundaries]; and judging it proper that these things [be proclaimed by *theoroi*, so that these] games [will be celebrated with all] the most devoted [of the Greeks, as a thank offering to Athena] for great successes, we have sent *theoroi* (etc.)

Eumenes' two letters of 182 B.C. give us our only extant request for *asylia* (see, however, **174**). The king speaks of the festival, indeed of the cult itself (τιμῶμεν, 2), as his own rather than Pergamum's; he has sent the *theoroi* (24), and he will himself set the boundaries of the Nicephorium (19). As the Aetolians tell it (**178**.6–7, 16), the king decided to celebrate the festival, and his brothers and Pergamum join him in the celebration.[26] The city joins in the

26. Contrast *I.Perg.* 223: the games of 129 B.C., probably the first after the end of the dynasty, are described pointedly as ἀχθεῖσιν ὑπ' αὐτοῦ (= τοῦ δήμου). For the sharing of festivals by the royal family and the city of Pergamum cf. *OGIS* 248.50–51.

announcement as well (**176**.31, **177**.5), and on his approval (**176**.29, cf. **177**.3) some elected Pergamene citizens join the courtiers whom he sends as *theoroi*.[27] The king in effect gives them a letter of introduction. An unusually large team went to Cos; only the courtier Megon and one Pergamene visited Iasus (?: **177**).

4: Parallels for εὐημερία at J. and L. Robert, *Fouilles d'Amyzon* I p. 204 n. 9.

6–8: The implication would seem to be that Eumenes himself named the goddess *Nikephoros*, and explained his choice of name to the Coans in his earlier letter. This suggests that the epithet dates from 183 and commemorates the victory over Prusias (see, however, n. 13).

16–18: The king does not specify the status of the several competitions, as do the extant recognitions: these details must have been included in the explanatory speech of the *theoroi* (cf. 41).

19: The responses echo Eumenes' talk of boundaries. In the recognitions of *asylia* the mention of boundaries is unusual; an inevitable feature of any sacred place, they were simply assumed as a given. Here that may not be so, for Eumenes' future θήσομεν suggests that the boundaries are to be changed, presumably expanded. The king is said by Strabo (624) to have planted the grove of the Nicephorium; the new honors for the goddess in the 180s may have been the occasion (cf. Segre 111), perhaps accompanied by an expansion of the sacred precinct.

36: "as befits you"; for the moral obviousness of granting *asylia* compare the Phocaeans' response to Chalcedon: καθότι καὶ ἐπιβάλλει ἡμῖν (**54**.8).

177. Letter of Eumenes II; decree of Iasus (?)

White masonry building block found "in Ionia" and acquired by the French School at Athens ca. 1885; now in the Louvre; h. 0.39, w. 0.565, th. 0.34–0.40; letters h. 0.01, intersp. 0.08–0.01, with large apices.

S. Lambrino, *RA* V.29 (1929) 107–120 [Herzog, *Hermes* 65 (1930) 459–463; Schroeter 39 (lines 1–11)]; Welles, *Royal Corres.* 49 [W. Blümel, *I.Iasos* 6; Allen, *Attalid Kingdom* 215–216].

Photograph: Lambrino pl. 1.

Cf. Holleaux, *RA* V.29 (1929) 390; Robert, *REG* 42 (1929) 433, *BCH* 54 (1930) 338–343 (*Op. min. sel.* I 221, 157–162); Segre in *Hellenica* V (1948) 105; Wilhelm, *Griechische Königsbriefe*, Klio-BH 48 (1943) 41–43.

[βουλόμενοι δὲ καὶ ὑμᾶς μ]ετ̣[έ]χειν τῶν θυσιῶν κ̣α̣ὶ̣ [τῶν ἀγώνων πεπόμφα]-
[μεν θεωροὺς Μ]έ̣γωνά τε τῶν φίλων 'Εφέσιον, ἐν τιμῆι [τῆι πρώτηι ὄντα, ὁ]-
[μοίως δ]ὲ̣ κ̣αὶ Κάλαν Περγαμηνόν, κρινόμενον καὶ ὑφ' ἡ[μῶμ μὲν ἄξιον, ὡς
δὲ πολί]-

27. Robert suggested that the extensive involvement of the Attalids in cult at Pergamum reflects the civic rather than Macedonian origin of the dynasty: *RPhil* 58 (1984) 14–15 n. 42 (*Op. min. sel.* VI 464–465).

4 [την] τ̣ετευχότα κατὰ τὴν ἡλικίαν τῶν προσηκόντω[ν, καὶ προκεχειρισμέ]-
[νον] ὑπὸ τῆς πόλεως διὰ τὸ καταγγέλλειν μεθ' ἡμῶν τ[αῦτα· καλῶς οὖν]
[πο]ιήσετε πρῶτομ μὲν διὰ τὴν θεόν, ἔπειτα δὲ καὶ δι' ἡ[μᾶς τῶν ἀνδρῶν τε φι]-
[λοφ]ρόνω̣ς διακούσαντες καὶ ἀποδεξάμενοι τά τε Ν[ικηφόρια καὶ τὴν ἀσυλίαν·]
8 [τ]α̣ῦτα γὰρ πράξαντες τὰ μὲν ἐκήνης τίμια φανεῖσ[θε συναύξοντες, τὸ δὲ λοιπὸν]
[ἡμᾶς] ὡ̣ς ἐνδέχεται μάλιστα προθύμους ἕξετε κατὰ τ[ὸ δυνατὸν εἰς πάν]-
τ̣α τὰ συμφέροντα τῶι δήμωι· τὰ δὲ πλείονα περὶ τούτων ἀκο[ύσετε παρ' αὐτῶν·]
ἔρρωσθε. ἀπέδωκεν Μέγων, Ἀνθεστηριῶνος ἕκτηι. vacat
12 ἐπὶ στεφανηφόρου Ἀπολλωνίου τοῦ Διογένου, Ἀνθεστηριῶν[ος ἕκτηι ἱσταμένου?·]
[ἔ]δ̣ο̣ξ̣ε̣ν̣ τῆι βουλῆι καὶ τῶι δήμωι· πρυτάνεων γνώμη· ἐπει[δὴ βασιλεὺς Εὐμένης]
[βασιλ]έ̣ω̣ς Ἀ̣τ̣τ̣άλ[ου] καὶ βασιλίσσης Ἀπολλωνίδος φίλος κ[αὶ εὔνους καὶ εὐεργέτης]
[διὰ προ]γ̣ό̣ν̣ω̣ν̣ ὑ̣π̣ά̣ρ̣χων τοῦ δήμου γέγραφεν πρὸς τὴν βουλὴ[ν καὶ τὸν δῆμον ὅτι]
16 [τιμᾶι μὲν τὴν] Ἀθηνᾶν μάλιστα τῶν ἄλλων θεῶν διὰ τὸ πολλὰς κ[αὶ μεγάλας ἐν παν]-
[τοδαπαῖς περιστάσε]σ̣ι̣ν̣ καιρῶν εὐημερίας αὐτῶ[ι] περι[τ]εθειχ[έναι, Νικηφόρον τε]
[προσηγόρευκε]ν καλλίστην νομίζων εἶναι κα̣ὶ οἰκειοτάτην τ[ὴν προσωνυμίαν]
[ταύτην, νῦν δ]ὲ αὔξειν τε βουλόμενος τὰς τιμὰς αὐτῆς καὶ μ[είζω χαριστήρια]
20 [τῶν κατὰ πόλεμον ἀ]γ̣ώ̣ν̣ω̣ν̣ ἀπ̣ο̣[διδ]ό[ναι] καὶ διεγνωκὼς σ̣[υ]ν[τ]ελ[εῖν - - -]

1–14 Welles. 1 init.:] Λ . . ΞΑ . . ΩΙΝ Lambrino, τὴν ἀνανέω]σιν? Herzog. 1–2: - - - ἐπέμψαμεν | οὖν πρὸς ὑμᾶς] Lambrino, [πεπόμφαμεν θεω|ροὺς πρὸς ὑμᾶς] Herzog. 2–3: [τ. π. παρ' | ἡμῖν ὄντα] Lambrino, [τ. π. τεταγμένον | παρ' ἡμῖν] Herzog. 3–4: ἡ[μῶν καὶ τῶν τι|μίων] Lambrino, ἡ[μῶμ μὲν, φιλότιμον δὲ πο|λίτην] Herzog. 4–5: οἱ ἀπεδείχθη|σαν] Lambrino, προκεχειρισμένον δὲ | καὶ] Herzog. 5: τ[ὰς θυσίας· κ. ο.] Lambrino, τ[ὰ Νικηφόρια Herzog. 6 Herzog, Robert: ἡ̣[μᾶς τούτων τε φι]- Lambrino. 7 end Lambrino. 8–9: μεθ' ἡμῶν συναύξοντες, | ἡμᾶς δὲ] Lambrino, συναύξοντες, ἡμᾶς δὲ τὸ | λοιπὸν?] Herzog. 9 Lambrino: π̣[αντα καιρὸν Herzog. 10 Lambrino: ἀκο[ύσεσθε Holleaux, Herzog. 14: κ[αὶ οἰκεῖος καὶ εὔνους] Lambrino. 15–20 Segre: 15–16 δ. ὅτι τὴν | Νικηφόρον Ἀ] Lambrino; 16–17 μ. κατὰ πᾶ|σαν περίστασιν κ]αιρῶν Lambrino; 17–18 ἀπ' ἀρχῆς ἐτί|μα αὐτὴ]ν Lambrino, καὶ πρότερον μὲν διε|τέλει τιμῶ]ν Herzog, καὶ νῦ]ν Robert, καὶ πρότερον ἐτί|μα καὶ] ν̣ῦ̣ν̣ Welles; 18–19 τ[ῶν Περγαμηνῶν ἀρχηγε|τίδα Lambrino, τ[αύτην τῆς χάριτος ἀπό|δοσιν Herzog, τ[ὴν ἡμέραν ἐν ἧι Γαλά|τας (Βιθύ|νους) ἐνίκησ]ε Robert, τ[ὴν τῆς θεᾶς θρησκείαν Wilhelm. 19–20 μ[ετέχειν ἀξιῶν τοὺς Ἕλ|ληνας τῶν ἀ]γ̣ώ̣ν̣ω̣ν̣ ἀπ̣ά̣[ντο]θ[εν?] Herzog. 20 end: ἀγῶνας στεφανίτας | δύο - - - Lambrino, αὐτοὺς στεφανίτας Herzog.

In relation to Eumenes' letter to Cos, this version is abbreviated in occasional phrases. The *theoroi* sent to Cos have split up, but the combination of a royal and a civic representative remains. The identity of this city, which the king perhaps regarded as less important than Cos, is uncertain. The delegation remained together until it had passed Cos, and so the two *theoroi* here may well have gone on to the Carian coast and Iasus. The chief reason for Lambrinos' attribution is that the assemblies of Iasus were held on the sixth of each month. But the docket stating that the *theoros* "presented on the sixth" (line 11) is perhaps ambiguous: this might refer to his presentation of the letter to the magistrates, or presentation to the council rather than to the assembly (for such dockets see Robert, *Op. min. sel.* I 125). And as Robert observed (I 157 n. 3), the reference to an *epistates* that is regularly found in decrees of Iasus is missing here.

11: This is the usual verb for "presenting" a decree or letter to a foreign city or a king. That only one man is said to do it suggests a physical action, whether presenting the decree or making the speech. Anthesterion was usually a month of early spring (e.g., at Athens, Ephesus, Miletus). Eumenes undertook his quest in 182 before late summer (the Pythia of **178**.26) but (on my assumption) after the second annual Nicephoria in spring; if this is so, then Anthesterion at this city cannot be so early as early spring.[28] Robert, however, may have been right to press this as evidence for spring and to assign **178** to the Panaetolica in March, dating the quest early in the Julian year (*Op. min. sel.* I 154).

14: The king's parents (and his brothers; cf. **178**.12) must have been discussed in the speech of the *architheoros*, for they are absent from Eumenes' letter.

178. Aetolian League

Delphi: temple of Apollo. Two fragments of the base of the statue of Eumenes II dedicated by the Aetolians.[29] Letters 0.007, intersp. 0.004.

B. Haussoullier, *BCH* 5 (1881) 372 no. 3 [Cauer[2] 236; Dittenberger, *Syll.* 215; *Syll.*[2] 295; Fick, *SGDI* 1413; Michel, *Rec.* 291]; Pomtow, *Syll.*[3] 629 (squeeze); Klaffenbach, *IG* IX.1[2] 179 (squeeze); Daux, *Delphes au II*[e] *et I*[e] *siècle* (Paris 1936) 298–302; *FD* III.3 240 [Allen, *Attalid Kingdom* 212–214].

Cf. Wilhelm, *GGA* 162 (1900) 104; 165 (1903) 795; Holleaux, *REA* 5 (1903) 210 (*Etudes* I 367); Robert, *BCH* 54 (1930) 332–338 (*Op. min. sel.* I 151–157); Daux, *Mélanges Gustave Glotz* I (Paris 1932) 290–291.

[θ ε] ό ς. [τ ύ] χ α.

[ἔδοξε τοῖς] Αἰτωλοῖς· [ἐπ]εὶ βασιλεὺς Εὐμένης ὑπάρχων φίλος καὶ σύμμαχος διὰ προγόνων τὰν οὖσα[ν ἐκ πα]-

28. The late antique calendric lists allege that at Perinthus Anthesterion matched September; see Samuel, *Chronology* 88–89.

29. For the monument see E. Bourguet, *REG* 25 (1912) 18–19; drawings: F. Courby, *FD* II *La Terrasse du temple* 275–277 and fig. 221; in general, Daux, *FD* III.3 p. 231, who in *Delphes* 298–302 added a detached fragment (inv. 3277: ends of 16, 26–29, 32–33).

[λαιῶν χρόνων ε]ὔνοιαν ἐμ παντὶ καιρῶι φανερὸς γίνεται συναύξων καὶ πολλὰς καὶ μεγάλας ἀποδείξε[ις]
[πεποίηται τ]ᾶς ἐν τὸ ἔθνος εὐνοίας καὶ τοὺς ἄλλους Ἕλλανας, ἀεὶ τὰ συμφέροντα διαπρασσόμενο[ς],
[σπουδᾶς καὶ] φιλοτιμίας οὐθὲν ἐνλείπων, γεγονότων τε αὐτοῖ πολλῶν καὶ μεγάλων εὐαμερημά[των]
[κατὰ τοὺς π]ολέμους ἐπαυξηκὼς τὰμ βασιλείαν καὶ ἐν τὰν καλλίσταν διάθεσιν ἀγνηκὼς κέκρικε
[συντελεῖν] ἀγῶνας καὶ θυσίας τᾶι Ἀθάναι τᾶι Νικαφόρωι μετὰ τῶν ἀδελφῶν καὶ τοῦ δάμου τῶν
[Περγαμηνῶ]ν, περὶ πλείστου ποιούμενος τὰν ποτὶ τοὺς θεοὺς εὐσέβειαν, παρακαλεῖ [δ]ὲ καὶ το[ὺς]
[Αἰτωλοὺς ἐ]ξαπ[ε]σταλκὼς θεωροὺς Πέρσαν, Θεόλυτον, Κτήσιππον ἀποδέξασθαι τοὺς ἀγῶνας
[τῶν Νικαφ]ορίων στεφανίτας, τὸμ μὲν μουσικὸν ἰσοπύθιον, τὸν δὲ γυμνικὸν καὶ ἱππικὸν ἰσολύμπιον,
[καὶ ὡσαύτ]ως ἄσυλον τὸ τέμενος τᾶς Ἀθάνας τᾶς Νικαφόρου· δεδόχθαι τοῖς Αἰτωλοῖς [ἐπ]αινέσαι
[μὲν βασιλέ]α Εὐμένη καὶ τοὺς ἀδελφοὺς αὐτοῦ Ἄτταλον, Φιλέταιρον, Ἀθήναιον καὶ βασίλισσαν
[Ἀπολλωνίδα] τὰμ ματέρα αὐτῶν καὶ τὸν δᾶμον τῶν Περγαμηνῶν ἐπὶ τᾶι ποτὶ τοὺς [θεοὺ]ς εὐσεβεί[αι]
[καὶ στεφανῶ]σαι ἕκαστον αὐτῶν εἰκόνι χρυσέαι, τὸμ μὲν βασιλέα ἐφ' ἵππου, τοὺς δὲ ἄ[λλους πεζικᾶι],
[ἀρετᾶς ἕνεκε]ν καὶ εὐνοίας τᾶς ἐ⟨ν τὸ ἔθνος⟩, ἀποδεδέχθαι δὲ καὶ τοὺς ἀγῶνας τῶ[ν Νικαφορίων οὓς]
[συντελεῖ βασ]ιλεὺς Εὐμένης [σ]τεφανίτας, τὸμ μὲν μουσικὸν ἰσοπύθιον, τὸν δὲ γυ[μνικὸν ⟨καὶ ἱππικὸν⟩ ἰσολύμπιο]ν,
[εἶμεν δὲ] κα[ὶ] τοῖς νικεόντοις τῶν Αἰτωλῶν τὰς τιμὰς καὶ τὰ λοιπὰ πάντα τὰ ἐν τ[οὺς νόμους περί τε τῶν]
[Πυθίων κ]αὶ Ὀλυμπίων {τὰ} κατακεχωρισμένα, καὶ καθάπερ ὁ βασιλεὺς Εὐμένης ἀνα[δεικνύει] τὸ τέμ[ενος]
[τᾶς Ἀθά]νας τᾶς Νικαφόρου τὸ ποτὶ Περγάμωι ἄσυλον, καθώς κα ὁρίξῃ, συναποδεδέχθαι τοὺς Αἰτω[λοὺς]
[ἄσυλον] εἶμεν αὐτὸ τὰ ἀπ' Αἰτωλῶν καὶ τῶν ἐν Αἰτωλίαι κατοικεόντων καὶ μηθένα ἄγειν μηδὲ ῥυσ[ι]-
[άζειν ἐ]ντὸς τῶν ὁρίων· εἰ δέ τίς κα ἄγῃ ἢ ῥυσιάξῃ ἢ ἀποβιάξαιτο ἢ διεγγυάσῃ, ὑπόδικον εἶμεν ἐν τοῖ[ς]
[συνέδρ]οις τῶι ἀδικηθέντι καὶ ἄλλωι τῶι θέλοντι ἐν ταῖς ἐκ ποτιστάσιος δίκαις· ἀποστέλλειν δ[ὲ]
[θεωρ]οὺς ἐν Πέργαμον ἐπε[ί] κα ἁ θυσία καθήκηι τᾶι Ἀθάναι τᾶι Νικαφόρωι· τᾶς δὲ ἐκπονπᾶς ἐπι-
[με]λεῖσθαι τὸν στραταγὸν ἀεὶ τὸν ἔναρχον· τοῖς δὲ θεωροῖς τοῖς ἐπαγγελλόντοις τοὺς ἀγ[ῶνας]
[τῶν Ν]ικαφορίων καταστᾶσαι τὰς πόλεις ἑκάστας θεωροδόκους τῶν ἰδίων πολιτᾶν καὶ ἀνενεγ-

[κεῖ]ν τοὺς ἄρχοντας τοὺς ἀπὸ τᾶν πολίων τῶι στραταγ[ῶ]ι Προξένωι ἐν τὰ Πύθια, διδόμεν δὲ
[ἐκέχει]ρον καὶ ξένια ὅσα καὶ τοῖς τὰ Ὀλύμπια ἐπαγγελλόντοις θεωροῖς δίδονται· ὅπως δὲ καὶ ἐ[ν]
28 [τοὺς ν]όμους καταχωρισθῆ ἅ τε ἀποδοχὰ τῶν ἀγώνων καὶ τοῦ ἱεροῦ ἁ ἀσυλία καὶ ἁ τῶν θ[ε]ωροδόκων
[κατάστ]ασις καὶ τὰ ἄλλα τὰ ἐν τῶι ψαφίσματι καταχεχωρισμένα, ἐπιμέλειαν ποιήσασθαι τὸν στραταγὸν
[Πρόξενον] καὶ τοὺς ἄλλους ἄρχοντας· ἐπαινέσαι δὲ καὶ τοὺς θεωροὺς Πέρσαν Δ[ιο]νυσίου Συρακόσιον,
[Θεόλυτον] Ἀρίστωνος Αἰγινάταν, Κτήσιππον Δαματρίου Περγαμηνόν, καὶ εἶμεν αὐτοὺς προξένους
32 [καὶ εὐεργέτ]ας τῶν Αἰτωλῶν· ἔγγυος τᾶν προξενιᾶ[ν ὁ γ]ρ[αμματ]εύς· ἀναγράψαι δὲ καὶ τὸ ψάφισ[μ]α
[τόδε ἐν στ]άλαις λιθίναις δύο καὶ ἀναθέμεν τὰν μίαν ἐν Θέρμο[ν], τὰν δὲ ἐν Δελφούς· τὸ δὲ γενόμεν[ο]ν
[ἀνάλωμα] δόμεν τὸν ταμίαν τᾶς κωλ[. . .] κ [.] λ [.] ι [.] ρι [.] ε [. . . .] ς [. . . .] λ [. .]ιλι τὸν γραμματῆ τῶν
[- - -]ιαν. vacat

Text of Haussoullier. 3 Klaffenbach: πρότερον ε.] Haussoullier. 4 Holleaux ap. Robert 151: [ποιούμενος Haussoullier; the mason corrected EM to EN. 6 Wilhelm 1900: [διὰ τοὺς Haussoullier. 7 Klaffenbach: [τιθέναι] Haussoullier. 11 Klaffenbach: [κ. ὁμοί]ως Haussoullier. 12 [μὲν Klaffenbach. 14 end Daux: ἀ[δελφοὺς π.] Haussoullier. 15 corr. Daux: εἰς τοὺς θεούς lapis. 16 init. Klaffenbach: [ἔθηκε Haussoullier; ⟨καὶ ἱππικὸν⟩ add. Pomtow. 17 Holleaux ap. Robert, τε Klaffenbach: τ[οὺς νενικηκότας Haussoullier, τ[οὺς ἀγῶνας Dittenberger. 18 τὰ del. Dittenberger; ἀνα[δεικνύει] Holleaux 1903, Wilhelm 1903: ἀνα[καλεῖ] Haussoullier. 20–21 Daux: ῥυσ[ιάζειν | τινὰ Haussoullier, ῥ. | μηθαμὰ Klaffenbach. 26 Robert: [ἧ] προξένωι Haussoullier. 27 Wilhelm 1900. 30 Klaffenbach. 35: [συνέδρων - - - Pomtow.

2: The alliance between the Attalids and the Aetolians was at least as old as 211 B.C. (Livy 26.24.8; *Staatsvertr.* III 536); cf. Polyb. 4.65.6, with R. B. McShane, *Foreign Policy of the Attalids of Pergamum* (Urbana 1964) 101.

10, 16: For such a differentiation in defining competitions, compare the Panhellenic Soteria at Delphi, isopythian in the musical competitions but isonemean in the athletic and equestrian (Nachtergael, *Les Galates* 435–444). These details, absent from Eumenes' letter, must have been included in the speech of the *theoros.*

14: The identity of the monument is confirmed by a separate inscription, *FD* III.3 230 (= *Syll.*^{3} 628).

18ff.: "Just as King Eumenes designates the precinct of Athena Nicephorus at Pergamum inviolable, as he defines the boundaries, the Aetolians join in recognizing it to be inviolable with respect to Aetolians and those living in Aetolia, and they are not to seize or plunder anyone inside the boundaries; if anyone should seize or plunder or take by force or seize as security, he is to be subject to trial before the council by the victim or anyone who wishes, in trials with open admission."

Although penalty clauses are frequent in Aetolian grants of personal *asylia*, this one is unusually rich. To the usual terms for seizure ἄγειν and ῥυσιάζειν are added ἀποβιάζεσθαι and διεγγυᾶν. The former normally has the general sense of "do violence." Here, however, it might mean to force someone out of the sacred space so that he can be despoiled; the verb and its cognates appear in the Ptolemaic texts for inviolable temples. διεγγυᾶν is yet more esoteric, here to "take pledges" most literally, "seize as security" for debt—the effective meaning of ἄγειν; compare κατεγγυᾶν in the charter of the League of the Greeks in 302 B.C., protecting League personnel μηδὲ ἀνδροληπτεῖν μηδὲ κατεγγυᾶ[ν]; in Vespasian's grant of personal *asylia* to doctors and teachers, against ὑβρίζειν ἢ κατεγγυ[ᾶν.[30] I do not think that fine legal distinctions are intended by the several terms, only two of which were thought necessary in lines 20–21; for the Amphictyony, ἄγειν ἐκ τοῦ τόπου was felt sufficient to convey the same meaning (**179**.25).

I think it improbable that Eumenes stood in genuine fear that his allies the Aetolians would plunder the temple of Athena but for the protection of this decree; the Aetolians are waxing eloquent in their manner, importing the formulae of their grants of personal inviolability. A real legal fact is being established, however, in granting a foreigner access to Aetolian courts. I have followed Dittenberger in translating ποτίστασις (22) to indicate the permission needed by a foreigner to use a court.

24–27: It is interesting to find this peremptory instruction to member cities to appoint *theorodochoi* (cf. the Acarnanian League, **81**.32), although they are not instructed to accept the games; it is as though the League decree to that effect spoke for all and what remains is the mechanical convenience of providing local *theorodochoi* and the usual emoluments for the Pergamene *theoroi*. I do not know what need the League would have of the resulting list of *theorodochoi*, which would obviously be of more use to Eumenes and the Pergamenes; of course the list would show that the member cities had done what they were told.

30–31: The *theoroi* were two courtiers and a Pergamene citizen, so a mixture as at Cos and Iasus. Aegina had been an Attalid possession for a generation; it is more noteworthy to find a Syracusan in Attalid service. Cf. E. Olshausen, *Prosopographie der hellenistischen Königsgesandten,* Stud.Hellen. 19 (Louvain 1974) 329–333.

30. *Staatsvertr.* III 446.64–65; Oliver, *Greek Const.* 38.6–7. Cf. *P.Dion.* 12.18 (108 B.C.): ἐὰν ὁ ἐνκαλούμενος ἐπ̣ι̣χείρῃ κατεγγυᾶν με αὐτοῖς, μὴ παραλαμβάνειν με (κτλ.); *Claros* I p. 64 [*SEG* 39.1244.38], the city freed from κατεγγυήσεις, compulsory sureties.

179. Delphian Amphictyony

Delphi: temple of Apollo. On the base of the statue of Attalus I (near the monument of Eumenes II),[31] seven fragments recognized by Bourguet in 1907 and constituted and published by Holleaux, an eighth (inv. 1955, lower left) later recognized by Bourguet and by Pomtow. Maximum preserved dimensions h. 1.15, w. 1.60; letters 0.02, intersp. 0.01, with moderate apices.

Seven fragments: M. Holleaux, *Philologie et linguistique, Mélanges offerts à Louis Havet* (Paris 1909) 187–196 (*Etudes* II 63–72).

Entire: E. Bourguet, *REG* 25 (1912) 19–20; Pomtow, *Delphica* III (1911) 114–116 (= *BPW* 32.14 [6 April 1912]); *Syll.*[3] 630; Daux, *Delphes* 293–298; *FD* III.3 261 [Allen, *Attalid Kingdom* 214–215].

Photograph: Daux, *Delphes* pl. 3 (lines 1–26); *FD* pl. 7; Daux, *BCH* 77 (1954) 371 (lines 21–26).

Cf. Robert, *BCH* 54 (1930) 346 n. 3 (*Op. min. sel.* I 165); Wilhelm, *Griechische Inschriften rechtlicher Inhalt* (Athens 1951) 48–51 (*Kl. Schr.* I.3 442–445); Daux, *BCH* 77 (1954) 370–371.

[ἄρχοντος ἐν Δελφοῖ]ς Δημοσθένου, δόγμα Ἀμφικ[τιόνων· ἐπειδὴ βασιλεὺς]
[Εὐμένης παρειληφ]ὼς παρὰ τοῦ πατρὸς βασιλέως Ἀττάλο[υ τήν τε πρὸς τοὺς θεοὺς]
εὐσ[έβειαν καὶ τὴ]ν πρὸς τοὺς Ἀμφικτίονας εὔνοιαν καὶ διατ̣η̣[ρῶν τὴν πρὸς Ῥωμαίους]
φιλίαν ἀεί [τινος ἀγ]αθοῦ παραίτιος γινόμενος διατελεῖ τοῖς Ἕλλησ[ιν καὶ μετεσχηκὼς]
τῶν αὐτῶν κ[ινδύ]νων ὑπὲρ τῆς κοινῆς ἀσφαλείας πολλαῖς τῶ[ν Ἑλληνίδων] πό[λεων]
δωρεὰς δέδ[ωκ]εν ἕνεκεν τοῦ διατηρεῖσθαι τὴν ὑπάρχουσ[αν αὐτον]ομίαν, δι' ἣν
αἰτίαν καὶ Ῥω[μαῖ]οι θεωροῦντες αὐτοῦ τὴν προαίρεσιν ἐπευξ[ήκασιν τ]ὴμ βασιλείαν
νομίζοντες [δεῖ]ν καὶ τῶμ βασιλέων ὅσοι μὲν ἐπιβουλεύουσιν [τοῖς Ἕλλ]ησιν τυγχάν[ειν]
τῆς καθηκού[σης] ἐπιπλήξεως, ὅσοι δὲ μηθενὸς γίνονται κακοῦ [παραίτιο]ι τούτους τ[ῆς]
μεγ[ί]στης [ἀξιο]ῦσθαι παρ' ἑαυτοῖς πίστεως· ἀπέσταλκεν δὲ κ[αὶ θε]ωροὺς τοὺς
παρακαλέσ[οντ]ας τοὺς Ἀμφικτίονας ὅπως τὸ τῆς Ἀθηνᾶς τῆς Ν[ικηφό]ρου τέμενος
συναναδε[ίξωσι]ν ἑαυτῶι ἄσυλον, καὶ τοὺς ἀγῶνας οὓς διέγ[νωκε] συντελεῖν
στεφανίτα[ς τό]ν τε μουσικὸν ἰσοπύθιον καὶ τὸν γυμνικὸν κα[ὶ ἱππι]κὸν ἰσολύμπιον
ἀποδέξων[ται· ἀ]πελογίσαντο δὲ καὶ οἱ θεωροὶ τὴν τοῦ βασιλέως [εὔ]νοιαν ἣν ἔχων

31. See Daux, *FD* III.3 pp. 231–232, with drawing by A. Martinaud.

δ[ια]τελεῖ κ[οινῆι τ]ε πρὸς ἅπαντας τοὺς Ἕλληνας καὶ καθ' ἰδίαν π[ρὸ]ς τὰς πόλεις·
[ὅπως οὖν καὶ οἱ Ἀμ]φικτίονες φαίνωνται ἐπακολουθοῦντες το[ῖς] ἀξιουμένοις
[καὶ τιμῶντες τ]ῶν βασιλέων ὅσοι διατηροῦντες τὴν πρὸς Ῥωμ[αί]ους τοὺς κοινοὺς
[εὐεργέτας φιλία]ν ἀεί τινος ἀγαθοῦ παραίτιοι γίνονται τ[οῖς] Ἕλλησιν, τύχηι
[ἀγαθῆι, δεδόχθα]ι τοῖς Ἀμφικτίοσιν ἐπαινέσαι βασιλέα [Εὐ]μένη βασιλέως
[Ἀττ]άλου καὶ σ[τε]φανῶσαι δάφνης στεφάνωι τῶι ἱερῶι τ[οῦ Ἀ]πόλλωνος τοῦ
[Πυ]θίου ὧι πάτρι[όν] ἐστιν στεφανοῦν τοὺς ἑαυτῶν εὐεργέ[τ]ας, ἀρετῆς ἕνεκεν
καὶ εὐνοίας τῆ[ς] εἰς τοὺς Ἕλληνας, στῆσαι δὲ αὐτοῦ καὶ εἰκ[ό]να χαλκῆν ἐφ' ἵππου
ἐν [Δ]ελφ[ο]ῖς, ἀναδεδεῖχθαι δὲ καὶ τὸ ἱερὸν τῆς Ἀθηνᾶς τῆς Ν[ικ]ηφόρου τὸ πρὸς
Περγάμ[ω]ι ἄσυλ[ο]ν εἰς ἅπαντα τὸν χρόνον καθ' ἃ ἂν ἀφορίσ[ηι] βασιλεὺς Εὐμένης,
καὶ μηθ[έ]να ἄγ[ει]ν ἐ[κ] τοῦ περιωρισμένου τόπου μήτε πολέμ[ου] μήτε εἰρήνης
πρὸς [μηθὲ]ν [ἔγκλημα]· ἀποδεδέ[χθ]αι δὲ [κ]α[ὶ] τοὺς ἀγῶ[να]ς [τοὺ]ς στεφανίτας
[τῶν Νικηφορίων οὓς συντελεῖ βασιλεὺς Εὐμένης, καὶ εἶνα]ι καὶ τα[ῖς τιμαῖς καὶ τοῖς]
[λοιποῖς πᾶσι τοῖς ἐν τοῖς νόμοις γεγραμμένοις τὸμ μὲν μ]ουσικὸν ἰσ[οπύθιον, τὸν δὲ]
[γυμνικὸ]ν καὶ ἱπ⟨π⟩ικὸν ἰσ[ολύμπιον· ἀναγράψαι δὲ τὸ ψήφ]ισμα ἐν Δ[ελφοῖς εἰς τὴν]
[βάσιν το]ῦ ἀνδριάντος τ[οῦ πατρὸς βασιλέως Ἀττάλο]υ καὶ ἐμ Π[εργάμωι ἐν τῶι]
[ἱερῶι τῆ]ς Ἀθηνᾶς τῆς Νικη[φόρου· κηρῦξαι δὲ τὸν στέ]φανον το[ῦ βασιλέως κ]αὶ τὴν
[ἀσυλί]αν τοῦ ἱεροῦ ἐν τοῖς ἀγ[ῶσι τῶν Πυθίων καὶ Σωτηρί]ων.

Text of Holleaux. 6 Robert: αὐταῖς εὐν]ομίαν Holleaux. 9 Daux: [αἴτιο]ι Holleaux. 12 Daux: διέγ[νω] Holleaux. 17 Roussel in *FD*: [προνοούμενοί τε τ]ῶμ Holleaux. 26 init. Daux 1954: πρὸς [ἴδιον συμβόλαιον?] Pomtow; [ἴδι]ο̣ν [σύμβολον] Daux, *FD*; [ἔγκλημα μηθὲν] Wilhelm; end: [δύο] στεφανίτας Holleaux. 27 Daux: [καθὼς ὁ βασιλεὺς ἀξιοῖ, κ. ε.] Holleaux. 27–28: τα[ῖς ἡλικίαις καὶ ταῖς τίμαις ταῖς τοῖς νική|σασιν ὑπαρχούσαις] Pomtow. 29 ΙΠΙΚ lapis. 31–32 Bourguet: τὸ[ν δεδομένον τῶι βασιλεῖ κ]αὶ τὴν [εἰκόνα ἐν τῶι ἀγῶνι τῶν Πυθί]ων[Holleaux, δ. τὸν προστάτ]αν Pomtow, *Delphica*.

At the beginning the text evidently has been condensed for inscribing, for it lacks a register of the Council members.

The Council displays a historical (and partisan) consciousness of Eumenes' role in world affairs that is absent from the king's letter and rather less specific in the Aetolian decree; this was a theme of the ambassador's speech (cf. 14). "Always ready to be the source of some good for the Greeks, he has shared their dangers in behalf of the common security for the greater part of Greek cities, and has given gifts to the end that their established autonomy be preserved: for which reason the Romans, seeing his policy, have increased his kingdom, considering it necessary that those of the kings who plot against the Greeks obtain fitting censure, while those responsible for no evil are worthy of their highest trust." Holleaux (*Etudes* II 70–72) deduced that the enemies of Philip and friends of Rome now dominated the Council membership, and that a letter of the king helped shape the decree. The decree does not trouble to name the ambassadors.

Temple of Asclepius Soter

The Asclepieum of Pergamum is situated two kilometers southwest of the city proper, among the hills on the far side of the Selinus River. Of its inviolability no primary grant survives, rather a fragment of a Roman confirmation ca. 45 B.C. (Servilius Isauricus: **181**). Tacitus reports that in the investigation of A.D. 22 Pergamum had rather more recent and credible proofs for the inviolability of the Asclepieum than those offered by some cities, which could cite only oracles or remote grants by Darius or Alexander; this may well mean that the Pergamenes had a Roman document to show the Senate. Isauricus was acting within the framework of Caesar's restoration of the privileges of Pergamum; a fragment of a letter of Caesar to Pergamum mentions inviolability (**180**), but here the identity of the possessor of the status—the Nicephorium, the Asclepieum, or the city and country—is lost.

The benefactions to Pergamum are invoked in a series of statue bases, which show that the city's honors were now restored after a lapse, not granted for the first time. Pergamum had entered Roman rule in 129 B.C. as a free city, its privileges intact.[32] The occasion on which the *asylia* of the Asclepieum and the Nicephorium was abolished was surely the Roman Vespers of 88, when in fact Romans who took refuge with Asclepius were killed by the Pergamenes.[33]

In 48 Caesar pursued Pompey to Egypt after the battle of Pharsalus, passing along the coastal cities of Asia Minor.[34] During the several weeks of his progess

32. For the status of Roman Pergamum see Habicht, *I.Asklep.* pp. 4–6, 23, and Jones 203.

33. Cic. *Flac.* 57; App. *Mith.* 23; Plut. *Sull.* 11. In 85 Fimbria fled to the Asclepieum before committing suicide (App. *Mith.* 60).

34. H. Hepding, *AM* 34 (1909) 335–340; A. E. Raubitschek, *JRS* 44 (1954) 65–75; Robert, *Hellenica* X (1955) 257–260.

he was hailed and honored by the cities of Asia. The Pergamenes erected a statue of him dated by his second consulship (which lapsed in December 48): calling him their patron and benefactor and the savior and benefactor of the Greeks, they praise him for his piety and justice (*IGR* IV 305). On this occasion, therefore, Caesar merely pardoned Pergamum for its support of Pompey and did nothing more positive to which the Pergamenes could allude. By contrast, statues dated by his second dictatorship (November 48 to April 46) reflect a different visit, during his tour of Asia late in the summer of 47, after Mithradates of Pergamum had saved his life in Alexandria.[35] Now, doubtless at the prompting of Mithradates, Caesar announced as a policy a major "restoration" of the city's status. **180** must stem from this decision; Isauricus, arriving in Asia some months later at the beginning of 46, was left to carry out details; he was in Asia until mid-44.[36]

Caesar apparently ordered the general restoration of the lost rights of Pergamum, including its "ancestral constitution" and the inviolability of at least the Asclepieum. Isauricus will have taken time to sift through what claims were ancestral and therefore legitimate; and evidently he had to address conflicting interests. We have a fragment of a decision by him about the Asclepieum—certainly favorable because it was inscribed by the Pergamenes at the temple—after its *asylia* was challenged (**181**). Evidently there were those who were disadvantaged by this status; the case of Oropus suggests that the inviolability of the Asclepieum may have been challenged by publicans, as tax status was in question.

Statues at Pergamum commemorating all three men date to the period 46–44 B.C. Mithradates has "restored to the ancestral gods the city and country," ἀπο[κα]ταστήσαντα τοῖς πατρῴοις θεοῖς τήν τε πόλιν καὶ τὴν χώραν.[37] Isauricus is savior and benefactor for "giving back to the city its ancestral constitution and its democracy unenslaved," ἀποδεδωκότα τῆι πόλει τοὺς πατρίους νόμους καὶ τὴν δημοκρατίαν ἀδούλωτον.[38] The text on Caesar's two statue bases is more problematic; he is Pergamum's savior and benefactor for restoring the city and country to the gods (I quote the better preserved, underlining what is preserved only in the other):[39]

[ὁ δῆμος]
[ἐτίμησε] τὸν ἑαυτοῦ σ̣[ωτῆρα καὶ εὐεργέτην]

35. On Mithradates see Rostovtzeff, *SEHHW* 1527–1528; Bowersock, *Augustus and the Greek World* (Oxford 1965) 9.

36. R. Syme, *Anatolian Studies Buckler* (Aberdeen 1939) 307–308 (*Roman Papers* I 127–128). On Caesar's program of restoration in Asia, carried out by Isauricus, see J. and L. Robert, *Hellenica* VI (1948) 37–42.

37. Two statue bases: Hepding 330–331 [*IGR* IV 1682]; cf. Robert, *Etudes anat.* 53.

38. *I.Perg.* 413 [*OGIS* 449; *IGR* IV 433; *ILS* 8779]; for Isauricus' daughter, *I.Perg.* 414.

39. *I.Perg.* 379 and 380, with Hepding 336–337 [*IGR* IV 1677]; cf. Passerini 276; Robert, *Op. min. sel.* I 614, V 581; *Hellenica* X 253; Magie II 1259.

[Γάιον Ἰού]λιον Γαίου ὑὸν Καίσ[αρα τὸν αὐτοκράτορα καὶ]
4 [ἀρχι]ερέα καὶ δικτάτορα τὸ [β πάσης ἀρετῆς καὶ εὐνοίας]
[ἕνεκ]εν ἀποκαταστήσα[ντα τοῖς θεοῖς τήν τε πόλιν]
[καὶ τὴ]ν χώραν ο[ὖ]σαν ἱερὰ[ν - - -]

To restore at the end either the name of a god (ἱερὰ[ν Ἀθηνᾶι Fraenkel; or some other, Segre 126) or ἱερὰ[ν καὶ ἄσυλον καὶ ἀφορολόγητον] (Hepding) contradicts what we know about Pergamum (but see on **180**.b.15–16): it was not the city and country of Pergamum that had been declared inviolable, but two of its temples.[40] One might deduce that the status had later been extended to the whole city and territory. There is no parallel, however, for the Romans doing that in their provinces; in fact they seem everywhere to have done the opposite, restricting *asylia* to temples. And at Pergamum, Isauricus' subsequent confirmation of the *asylia* of the Asclepium alone would be meaningless if the status were possessed by the city and country as a whole, nor in such a circumstance could the status of the temple be isolated and challenged.

The language of these statue inscriptions (especially Mithradates') must therefore be taken as rather hyperbolic rhetoric, hailing all the acts of Caesar and Isauricus as the restoration of their ancestral laws, and of their city and country to their gods (whatever we restore in line 6). We have a Hellenistic precedent for such comprehensive language at a Bithynian city conquered in the second century B.C., where a helpful citizen "asked the king to restore to the people the laws and ancestral constitution and sacred precincts and funds (etc.) that they had always possessed."[41] The plural θεοῖς might be taken to mean that Caesar restored the *asylia* of the Nicephorium also, and this may be supported by his edict for Sardes (**214**). But it may also simply be vague; Romans had a special fondness for healing gods, and the Pergamenes both now and in A.D. 22 may have been content to put their better case forward.

The original recognition of Asclepius' inviolability is most likely later than that of Athena, for she was the chief divinity of the Hellenistic city; and we might otherwise expect some mention of the *asylia* of Asclepius in the lengthy documents of 182 B.C. It should date therefore to the intervening century, either from the later Attalids or from the first forty years of Roman rule. The latter seems to me the less likely time, for new grants of *asylia* under Roman rule are quite few.

By contrast, we have substantial evidence of the later Attalids' special devotion to Asclepius. Attalus II established a contest in honor of Asclepius Savior and Heracles (who was the ancestor of the Pergamenes and their kings), the Σωτήρια

40. But cf. *I.Straton.* 512.21–22: τοὺς ἀ]σεβήσαντα[ς εἰς τὴν | χώρα]ν ἡμ[ῶν οὖσ]αν ἱερ[ὰν κ]αὶ ἄσυλον.

41. Corsten, *I.Prusa* II 1001.9–11: ἠξίωσεν τὸν βασιλέα ἀποδοθῆναι τούς τε νόμους καὶ τὴν πάτριον πολιτείαν καὶ τὰ ἱερὰ τεμένη καὶ τὸ εἰς τὰ ἱερὰ καὶ πόλεως διοίκησιν ἀργύριον καὶ τὸ τοῖς νέοις ἔλαιον καὶ τὰ ἄλλα ἅπερ ἐξ ἀρχῆς ὑπῆρχεν τῶι δήμωι. For parallels see Robert, *Op. min. sel.* V 580–581; and p. 163 above on Tenos.

καὶ Ἡράκλεια, celebrating the defeat of Prusias II in 155/4.[42] Prusias had invaded the territory of Pergamum, ravaging the Nicephorium and robbing the Asclepieum, only then to see his forces ruined by disease and by storm, the work of Asclepius and Heracles.[43] The royal house was much involved with this festival; the agonothete at the second celebration was the prince Athenaeus, who defeated Prusias.[44] In the 130s Pergamum honored Attalus III for a victory with a statue in the *naos* of Asclepius Soter, whose priest would hereafter lead a procession annually, on the day of the king's triumphal return, from the prytaneum in the city to the Asclepieum.[45] The Σωτήρια καὶ Ἡράκλεια lapsed during a subsequent war—either Aristonicus or Mithridates—but were then restored (*IGR* IV 300). The festival is not heard of thereafter; perhaps this last text is to be assigned to the first years of the province and the games were abolished after 88 B.C. When the civic and religious life of Roman Pergamum revived, it was Asclepius alone who acquired Panhellenic games (around the time of Domitian), the Attalid ancestor Heracles no longer so honored.[46]

Like Athena, Asclepius in the second century B.C. inaugurated a festival coinage (inscribed Ἀσκληπιοῦ Σωτῆρος or Ἀσκληπιοῦ καὶ Ὑγιείας), small change similar to the small denominations of Athena and similarly difficult to date precisely.[47]

In light of these things, I suggest that the inviolability of the Asclepieum was originally granted in the last Attalid generation, perhaps on the same occasion as the foundation of the Soteria/Heracleia ca. 153 B.C.

180. Rome: Julius Caesar

Two fragments, now lost, of a dossier of Roman acts, which included the s.c. on the territory of Pergamum,[48] inscribed on marble building blocks in the

42. See Robert, *RPhil* 58 (1984) 7–18 (*Op. min. sel.* VI 457–468).

43. Polyb. 32.15 (θεοπέμπτου); Diod. 31.35 (παραλόγῳ). Cf. Robert, *Etudes anat.* 111–118; Müller, *Chiron* 22 (1992) 195–226.

44. *I.Asklep.* 3. The peace was established in summer 154. Robert (*Op. min. sel.* VII 461) took the games to be Panhellenic and quadrennial, which is by no means assured, and reckoned 149 or 148 as the date of this inscription (Eumenes' brother Athenaeus presiding over the second celebration). If in fact the festival was not annual, its cycle was surely so fixed as to avoid the Nicephoria (153, 149, etc.). Note the victory of Attalus II commemorated at the Nicephoria of 149 (*OGIS* 299), probably his final defeat of Prusias (Hansen 137–138; Jones 183–189).

45. *OGIS* 332, with Robert, *BCH* 108 (1984) 472–489, 109 (1985) 468–481 (*DAM* 460–477, 522–535), and Müller.

46. On the Asclepieia see the references at Habicht, *I.Asklep.* p. 8 n. 21; on civic titles, 158–161. For Asclepius on the Pergamene cistophori of Hadrian see W. Metcalf, *The Cistophori of Hadrian*, ANS NumismStud 15 (New York 1980) 9–11.

47. See Le Rider (above, n. 2) 68–70. Revenues of the temple mentioned at *OGIS* 332.19 (ἀπὸ τοῦ πόρου τοῦ Ἀσκληπιείου).

48. *I.Smyrna* 589 = *Roman Doc.* 12.

agora of Smyrna. Frag. a: h. 0.36, w. 0.12; b: h. 0.33, w. 0.19; irregular letters, h. 0.01–0.015, of the first century B.C.

A. Passerini, *Athenaeum* n.s. 15 (1937) 273–277 (from a photograph) [Sherk, *Roman Documents* 54 (frag. a)]; Petzl, *I.Smyrna* 590 (squeeze of frag. b).

Photograph of squeeze (frag. b): Petzl, *I.Smyrna* II pl. 2.

Cf. M. Segre, *Athenaeum* n.s. 16 (1938) 119–127; Robert, *Anatolian Studies Buckler* (Manchester 1939) 227–230 (*Op. min. sel.* I 611–614).

a. [Γάιος Ἰούλιος Καῖσαρ] αὐτοκ[ράτωρ, ἀρχιερεὺς καὶ δικτάτωρ τὸ β? Περγαμηνῶν ἄρχουσι]
[βουλῆ δήμωι χαίρει]ν· εἰ ἔρρω[σθε, εὖ ἂν ἔχοι· ὑγίαινον δὲ καὶ αὐτὸς μετὰ τοῦ στρατεύματος·]
[ὑμῖν ἀντίγραφον τ]οῦ ἐπικρίμα[τος ὑπέγραψα? - - - - - - - - - - - - - - - - - -]
[- - - - - - - - - - - - π]ερὶ ὧν Μιθ[ραδάτης Μηνοδότου πολίτης ὑμέτερος καὶ φίλος μου]
[λόγους ἐποιήσατ]ο περὶ τούτ[ου τοῦ πράγματος οὕτως ἐπέκρινα· - - - - - -]
[- - - - - - - - - - - - Π]έργαμον καὶ χ[- -]
[- - - - - - - - - - - - ἐ]κτὸς βασιλικο[ῦ -]
[- - - - - - - - - - - -] τε εἶναι δοκε[ῖ -]
[- - - - - - - - - - - -]ας τε τούτων [- -]
[- - - - - - - τῶν Ῥ]ωμαίων δημ̣[- -]
[- - - - - - - - - - - - -]τε φαίνεται θε[- βασιλεὺς]
[Ἄτταλος βασιλέως] Εὐμένους υἱὸ̣[ς -]
[- - - - - - - - - - - - -]σ̣αν ἅς τε ἀσυλ[- -]
[- - - - - - - - - - - - -]ων ὑφέστησαν̣ [- -]
[- - - - - - - - - - - ἔγ]ραψαν ἔκρεινάν [τε -]
[- - - - - - - - - - ὑ]πὲρ τῶν ἱερῶν η̣[- -]
[- - - - - - - - - - - -]ι ὅσα τε ἄλλα π̣[- -]
[- - - - - - - - - - το]ύτων ἁπάντ[ων -]
[- - - - - - - - - - -]κρισις τοῦ μ[- -]
[- - - - - - - - - - -]ν̣ο̣π̣ωτα[- -]

b. [- - - - - - - - - - -] χ̣ώρ̣[α -]
[- - - - - - - - - - -]ασπ̣[- -]
[- - - - - - - - - - -]α τούτω̣[- -]
[- - - - - - - - - - -] χώρας [- -]
[- - - - - - - - χ]ώρας Ἐλα̣[ῑτικῆς -]
[- - - - - - - - - -]ς τὰ προσ[- -]
[- - - - - - τῶν Ἐλ]αειτῶν ἕω̣[ς -]
[- - - - - - - - - -]ε̣ται ἐκεῖθεν̣ [- -]
[- - - - - - - - - -]ν χώρας, ἥτις τα̣[- -]
[- - - - - - - - - -] ἐκεῖνον τὸν [- -]
[- - - - - - - - - -] ἀρχαίας εἰς τ[- -]
[- - - - - - - - - -] . Ι ὅριον χώρα[ς -]
[- - - - - - - - Πέργ]αμον μέρη ε[- -]
[- - - - - - - - - -] Γαΐου Ἰουλίο[υ Καίσαρος -]

[- - - - - - - - -] τὴν πόλιν κα[-]
16 [- - - - - - - - -]αν τοῖς θεοῖς ἀ[-]

vacat

Text of Passerini as emended by Segre; but the line length remains uncertain, as variant formulae are possible. 1 end: Σμυρναίων ἀ.] Passerini. 2 καὶ (or κἀγὼ) Rigsby; σὺν τῷ στρατεύματι Passerini. 3–4: ἀπέσταλκα τοῦ γεγονότος περὶ ἐκείνων τῶν πραγμάτων π]ερὶ Passerini, ἀπέσταλκα τοῦ γεγονότος περὶ τῆς χώρας τῆς ὑμῖν προσωρισμένης· π]ερὶ Segre. 4: Μιθ[ραδάτης? ἐμοί λόγους ἐποιήσατο - - - Passerini. 5: ὃ αὐτ]ὸ and πράγματος ἀπέσταλκα Passerini. 6–7: τήν τε πόλιν Π]έργαμον καὶ χ[ώρας ὅσον βασιλεὺς Ἄτταλος βασιλέως Εὐμένους τῇ πόλει | προσώρισεν, ἐ]κτὸς βασιλικο[ῦ κήπου vel παραδείσου Segre; βασιλικο[ῦ ὁρίσματος? Passerini. 7–8: - - - ἐλεύθερα αὐτόνομα ἀνείσφορα | ἀφορολόγητά] τε Segre. 10: τοῦ τῶν ῾Ρ]ωμαίων δήμ̣[ου Passerini. 11: θέ[λειν Passerini, an unlikely statement in an edict. 13 Rigsby: σαναστε ἀσυλ[ία Passerini. 15 Rigsby: προύγ(?)]ραψαν Passerini. 16: or ν̣[όμων? Robert. 17 Petzl: ῾Ρωμα]ῖος ἅτε ἄλλα π̣[άντα Passerini. 18 Petzl: α]ὐτῶν Passerini. b.6: τὰ ὅρια τῆς χώρα]ς Passerini. 8: λέγ]ε̣ται Passerini. 9: ὅριο]ν Passerini. 10: κατ'] ἐ. τ. [χρόνον? Passerini. 11: πόλεως?] Passerini. 15–16: κα[ὶ τὴν χώραν - - - καθιέρωσ]αν Passerini; κα[ὶ τὴν χώραν ἱερὰν καὶ ἄσυλον | καὶ αὐτόνομον οὖσ]αν τοῖς θεοῖς ἀ[ποκατέστησεν? Petzl.

Attribution to Caesar as dictator in 47 rests upon the consistency of the hand with the rest of the late Republican texts from this archive at Smyrna, and to Pergamum (as Segre and Robert saw) upon the mention of Caesar's Pergamene friend Mithradates (a.4).

The substance is beyond recovery. Segre took it to be lands added to Pergamene territory by Attalus' will, reasoning from a.12 (Attalus III, adopted son of Eumenes II). Little that he restored carries conviction; the phrase "the city Pergamum and territories" (6) is impossible, both for the simple toponym and the lack of an article before χώρας. After mention of the king (12), we have ἀσυλ- and then ἱερῶν. It is possible that King Attalus is cited not for his will but as grantor of the *asylia* of the temple.

The diagnostic fact about frag. a would seem to be the string of plural aorist active verbs at 13–15. Frag. b might not continue the same document; in an archive, identity of hand does not guarantee that. Here at least the land of Elaea on the coast was in question, evidently a boundary dispute.

a.3: To assume that a copy is mentioned here may be mistaken. It would be odd for a Roman magistrate to write a covering letter for his own act.

18: Cf. ἀντὶ το[ύ]των ἁπάντων ἀρέσκει in Caesar's edict on Sardes (**214**.43–44).

19: Perhaps ἀπό]κρισις, as at *Roman Doc.* 38.20.

20: Perhaps the beginning of a dependent clause, ὁπ⟨ό⟩τα[ν.

b.15–16: Strictly speaking, Passerini's καθιέρωσ]αν would be inconsistent with the statue bases; if the subject is the Roman authorities (rather than an ancient act of "the kings" or "the Greeks") we would expect ἀποκατέστησ]αν. Petzl's restoration has the merit of being consistent with the statue base of Julius Caesar and reflects Hepding's restoration; but I doubt whether that florid utterance of the Pergamenes belongs in an edict of Caesar.

181. Rome: Servilius Isauricus

White marble plaque found in the Asclepieum in 1927, now in the local museum (inv. 1927 no. 2). Broken at bottom; h. 0.28, w. 0.42, th. 0.12; letters h. 0.007–0.008 (line 2: 0.012), with large apices.

T. Wiegand, *Zweit.Ber.Pergamon 1928–1932*, AbhBerl 1932.5 (Berlin 1932) p. 32 [*AEpigr* 1933, 260; Sherk, *Roman Documents* 55]; Habicht, *I.Asklep.* 1.

Photograph: Habicht pl. 1.1.

Cf. M. Segre, *MCl* 3 (1933) 485–488; 4 (1934) 71.

ἀγαθῆι τύχηι
ἐπίκριμα περὶ τῆς ἀσυλίας
[Πό]πλιος Σεροίλιος Ποπλίου υἱὸς Ἰσαυρικὸς ἀνθύπατος
ἄρχουσι βουλῆ δήμωι Περγαμηνῶν χαίρειν·
Κλεῖτος Τείμωνος πρύτανις, Ἀσκληπιάδης Μάτρω-
νος ἱερεύς, Μοιροφάνης Μητροδώρου, Μενέμαχος
Ξενοκλέους, Ἡρώδης Ἡρώδου, Νέων Μελεάγρου,
Ἀπολλοφάνης Ὀρέστου ἄρχοντες, Περσεὺς Περσέως
τοῦ Δίωνος γραμματεὺς δήμου, Κρίτων Μηνοδώρου
γυμνασίαρχος, ὁμοίως τε πρεσβευταὶ ὑμέτεροι, ἄν-
δρες ἀγαθοί, ἐμοὶ προσῆλθον ὑπὲρ τῶν τοῦ Ἀσκλη-
πιοῦ ἱερῶν νόμων ἀσυλίας τε. ἥτις ὑμεῖν ἀντίστα-
σις ὑπὲρ τῶν τοῦ ἱεροῦ δικαίων πρὸς Μάρκον Φάννιον
Νεμερίου υἱὸν Τηρετείνᾳ ὑπῆρχεν· ὑπὲρ τούτου [τοῦ]
πράγματος τῆς ὑποθέσεω[ς ἐκ ἀντικαταστάσεως ὑφ' ἑ]-
κατέρων ῥηθείσης Γ[- - - - - - - - - ἐπέκρινα· περὶ]
ὧν Μάρκος Φά[ννιος Νεμερίου υἱὸς Τηρετείνᾳ ἐνε]-
φάνισεν [- -]
. ΟΝΓ [- -]

15 Segre 1933: ἀκριβέστατα ἑκατέρων Wiegand. 17 end Segre 1934: - - - ἀπε]φάνισεν Wiegand.

The substance of Isauricus' edict is clear from the title (2) and from the fact that it was inscribed at all:[49] the inviolability of the Asclepieum, challenged by a Roman citizen, is confirmed as the Pergamene envoys request. The envoys "approached me concerning the sacred laws and *asylia* of Asclepius. Your counterplea against M. Fannius in behalf of the temple privileges has

49. Segre thought the dispute might have involved a slave seeking refuge or else some physical desecration; Sherk that the subject is uncertain but important and that the outcome "may have been favorable" to Pergamum.

been received(?). On this matter, when the [opposing] speeches had been delivered by each party. . . ." This last is restored from Jos. *AJ* 14.246 (Servilius), διακούσας ἐγὼ λόγων ἐξ ἀντικαταστάσεως γενομένων ἐπέκρινα (κτλ.), and *Roman Doc.* 70.7.

Marcus Fannius is not known. Wiegand noted the Fannius who would be a legate of Cassius in Asia (App. *BCiv.* 4.72); but this dignitary seems improbable. For in what capacity did Fannius complain? The elaboration of his nomenclature and tribe, rather than an office, shows that he was a *privatus*, very likely a publican,[50] speaking for the interests of his group against the exemption of the Asclepieum and its lands. This had happened earlier to Apollo of Didyma (*I.Didyma* 367) and to Amphiaraus (**6**), and possibly the same argument was used here as against Amphiaraus, that Asclepius was a mortal and not a god.

5–10: The nine envoys constitute a roster of the Pergamene officialdom: the eponymous *prytanis*,[51] the hereditary priest of Asclepius, the five "magistrates" (Isauricus uses the generic term, as Roman texts often do: certainly these are the five *strategoi* familiar at Pergamum), the secretary of the assembly, and the gymnasiarch.

50. See R. Syme, *Historia* 13 (1964) 116 (*Roman Papers* II 594), followed by Habicht.

51. As Wiegand saw, Cleitus' wife is on record as priestess of the Meter Basileia (*I.Perg.* 481–483).

Temple of Artemis, Ephesus

The temple of Artemis of Ephesus stood about a mile distant from the Hellenistic city, across the Selinus River. There is no need to repeat here the testimonies concerning this famous shrine,[1] reputedly built by the Ionian people jointly (Livy 1.45; Dion. Hal. 4.25.4), more venerable than any other of Artemis (so Callim. *Hymn.* 3.237ff.), and a subject for scholarly investigation (*FGrHist* 267: third century B.C.). The goddess "whom all Asia and the world worships" (Acts 19:27; cf. Paus. 4.31.8) was honored among Greeks and barbarians alike, said the Ephesians, for her manifest miracles (*I.Ephesos* Ia 24.c.9–14). Her temple stands outside the city proper, and it was the temple, not the city and country, that was inviolable.

Despite the rich epigraphical record at Ephesus, no initial recognition has been found; with one possible exception (**182**), the extant evidence dates under Roman rule. It may well be that there was no Hellenistic grant, that the Ephesians invoked older traditions about refuge to persuade the Romans that the Artemisium was an asylum. The want of evidence can as easily be meaningless, however, for the site of the temple, where declarations would have been inscribed, was heavily exploited before modern times and has yielded few inscriptions.

Artemis of Ephesus was of old famous as ἱκεσία, protective of suppliants (*Etym. Magn.* s.v. Ἔφεσος), and myth and history show numerous acts of refuge

1. Assembled by R. C. Kukula, *Forschungen in Ephesos* I (Vienna 1906) 237–282; note Plut. *Mor.* 828D, in praise of frugality: ἡ μὲν γὰρ Ἄρτεμις ἡ ἐν Ἐφέσῳ τοῖς χρεώσταις, ὅταν καταφύγωσιν εἰς τὸ ἱερὸν αὐτῆς, ἀσυλίαν παρέχει καὶ ἄδειαν ἀπὸ τῶν δανείων· τὸ δὲ τῆς εὐτελείας καὶ ἄσυλον καὶ ἄβατον πανταχοῦ τοῖς σώφροσιν ἀναπέπταται, πολλῆς σχολῆς εὐρυχωρίαν παρέχον ἱλαρὰν καὶ ἐπίτιμον. See R. Fleischer, *Artemis von Ephesos*, EPRO 35 (Leiden 1973); B. L. Trell, *The Temple of Artemis at Ephesus*, ANS Monogr. 107 (New York 1945).

to her temple.[2] Achilles Tatius sets in the temple the scene of an elaborate proceeding to determine whether a suppliant had just claim on the goddess's protection (7.13; cf. 8.9). While in general I have ignored incidents of refuge as possible evidence for declared inviolability, the case of Ephesus may stand apart, because of the centrality of this lore to the identity of the temple and city.

First were the Amazons, who founded the temple (so the earliest version we have, Pind. frags. 173–176) or themselves took refuge there—whence the name Ἔφεσος, whether from the name of an Amazon or from Artemis' freeing them from danger when they fled before Dionysus to the temple (ἐφεῖναι, ἔφεσις/ἄφεσις).[3] Croesus tried by physical means (a rope) to attach the city to the sanctity of the temple (Hdt. 1.26),[4] and the Achaemenids respected its suppliants (Xen. *An.* 1.6.7). Some of the Ephesian oligarchs, on being overthrown by Alexander, took refuge in the Artemisium, but they were removed and stoned to death by the people (Arr. *Anab.* 1.17.10); on a later occasion Alexander ordered the Ephesians not to interfere with another suppliant (Plut. *Alex.* 42.1). In the mid-third century Ptolemy "the Son" took refuge in the Artemisium, only to be murdered by Thracian mercenaries, evidently not by due process (Ath. 593A). After the Roman Vespers in 88 B.C. at least one pro-Roman family fled from Rhodes to the Artemisium upon the approach of Mithridates (*Royal Corres.* 74); but when Ephesus later joined Mithridates, some suppliants were removed and executed (App. *Mith.* 23). Some of those defeated at Philippi fled to the temple; Antony on arriving let them depart with impunity, except for two who were involved in the murders of Caesar and Dolabella (App. *BCiv.* 5.4); later at Cleopatra's urging he had Arsinoe killed, who had taken refuge in the temple.[5] The temple was much used as a bank of deposit.[6]

At the senatorial review in A.D. 22, the claims of Ephesus, capital of the province of Asia, were heard first, and Tacitus reports the Ephesians' presentation in greater detail than the subsequent cases. They explained that the sacred grove was the birthplace of Apollo and Artemis—here, not on Delos, was Leto's olive tree.[7] At the temple Apollo made expiation for killing the Cyclopes,[8] and here the Amazons took refuge from Dionysus. Heracles as ruler of Lydia had

2. Quoted at *Forsch. Ephesos* I 258–260; a selection at C. Picard, *Ephèse et Claros* (Paris 1922) 139, 148–151.

3. *Forsch. Ephesos* I 239–241. For the epithet cf. Zeus Ἀφέσιος at Argos (*FGrHist* 156 F 16). For the statues of the Amazons that stood in the precinct, ranging in date from the classical age to the Augustan, see Brunhilde S. Ridgway, *AJA* 78 (1974) 1–17; *Proc.X.Internat.Congr.Class.Arch.* (Ankara 1978) 761–770.

4. Cf. D. van Berchem, *MusHelv* 17 (1960) 24–26.

5. Jos. *AJ* 15.89; Dio 48.24.2; cf. Magie 1279 n. 5.

6. References at *Forsch. Ephesos* I 261–262.

7. For the tree see Callim. *Hymn.* 4.209; Ov. *Met.* 6.335.

8. Cf. Eitrem, "Kyklopen," *RE* 11 (1922) 2333.

increased the sacrosanctity of the Artemisium, and Persians, Macedonians, and Romans had confirmed it.

This last statement implies that the Ephesian ambassadors cited documents: a privilege dating from mythic times was confirmed by various rulers (*auctam hinc concessu Herculis ... caerimoniam templo* etc.). The alternative view would be that they had in mind no more than the stories mentioned above, anecdotes in which kings respected suppliants of Artemis; but the specificness of *auctam* and *concessu* suggests formal grants. These need not all have concerned *asylia*, for the cities in A.D. 22 seem to have taken the opportunity to recite the histories of their temples and their privileges; the Ephesians surely cited benefactions of various sorts to the temple. Some Achaemenid benefaction to Artemis is credible and easily paralleled.[9] Several favors of Alexander are on record, one of them (the temple boundaries: see below) pertinent to *asylia*.[10] It is in fact Heracles' action, *aucta caerimonia*, that best echoes the terms of the Hellenistic recognitions. His rule in Lydia was his sojourn as Omphale's husband, whence the line of Heracleidae in Lydia that ended with Candaules.[11] Tacitus normally ignores Panhellenic recognition in favor of royal precedents, and in this he probably echoes the embassies of A.D. 22. The story of Heracles appears to have been shaped by Hellenistic practice, described as a formal recognition by a ruler.

A fragment of a Hellenistic decree of the Chrysaorean League or one of its members grants some request of an Ephesian ambassador; the substance is lost to us, but there was mention of a temple and of the close relations of the author with Ephesus (*I.Ephesos* IV 1388):

[-]. . η
[-]ειν νενομ-
[ισται/ισμένοις - - - - - - - - - - - - - - - - - τ]ὸ κοινὸν τῶν Χρυ[σ]-
[-] ἱεροῦ καὶ ὁ ἀποστ[α]-
[λεὶς - - - - - - - - - - - - - - πρὸς τὴν ἐκκλ]ησίαν διελέγη ἀκολού-
[θως τοῖς ἐν τῶι ψηφίσματι γεγραμμένοις μετὰ πάσ]ης σπουδῆς
[-] καὶ φιλοτιμ[ί]-
[ας - - - - - - - - - - - - - τὴ]ν ὑπάρχουσαν οἰκειότ[ητα - - - - - - -]
[- - - τ]ύχηι ἀγαθῆι δ̣ε̣[δόχθαι -]

This might be a recognition of *asylia*, but the diagnostic sentiments (piety, honoring the god) are not found in what little remains.

9. So the Milesians alleged to the Senate a recognition by Darius; cf. Meiggs/Lewis 12 (Darius for Apollo).

10. In addition, the taxes the city had paid the Persian crown henceforth go to the temple (Arr. *Anab.* 1.17.10); for such gifts of Alexander see T. Corsten, *Historia* 43 (1994) 112–118. The immunity of the temple from taxes and billeting is attested in an inscription of 302 B.C. (*I.Ephesos* V 1449.5). Compare the Seleucid favors to Zeus of Baetocaece, **218**.

11. Cf. Gruppe, *RE* Suppl. 3 (1918) 972–977.

Thus, in the current state of our evidence, it is not possible to determine whether the Ephesians extended back to the beginning of their history a status that was actually obtained by a Hellenistic grant of the usual sort, or instead relied on their reputation as a refuge and disdained to seek such a recognition in the Hellenistic period. If in fact the initial grant was Hellenistic (Tacitus' "Macedonians"), it was likely earlier than the Peace of Apamea in 188 B.C., when Ephesus was given over to the Attalid kingdom on rather unfavorable terms.[12] Hellenistic evidence for the privilege is confined to a boundary inscription of the second century B.C., whose text is uncertain.

182. Boundary

White marble block broken at right; h. 0.28, w. 0.415, th. 0.30; not in situ, reused in imperial times.[13] Letters, with small serifs, of the second century B.C.: A with broken crossbar, O and Ω smaller, Π with right hasta more than half descended, Σ with parallel bars; h. 0.025, intersp. 0.014.

Hicks, *IGBritMus* III 520 [Dittenberger, *Syll.*^{2} 574; *Forsch. Ephesos* I 280 no. 26; Hiller, *Syll.*^{3} 989; Sokolowski, *LSAM* 85; *I.Ephesos* V 1520]. *Collation.*

τὸ τέμενος τῆς Ἀ̣[ρτέμιδος ἄσυλον?]
πᾶν ὅσον ἔσω π[εριβόλου· ὃς δ' ἂν]
παραβαίνῃ, αὐτὸς α̣[ὑτὸν αἰτιάσεται?].

Text of Dittenberger. 1 end: a serif of a rising angular stroke, A or Λ. 2: Hicks added μὴ ἀδικεῖν exempli gratia. 3 end: part of a serif of a stroke that cannot be vertical, only A or Λ probable; [ἀπόλοιτο καὶ τὸ γένος] Hicks.

In 1 some synonym is possible instead, compare φύκτιμον at Delphi (p. 48). In 3 the restored words are easily paralleled,[14] but not with the nominative αὐτός.

The block derives from the perimeter wall of the temple. The sacred peribolos underwent a number of changes, especially in the first century B.C. (see below). But the script here seems older than that. The inscription may, as Hicks thought, derive from an otherwise unreported change in the boundaries of inviolability, in the second century B.C.; but it may equally have marked construction of a new wall along an old line or repair to the old wall. The script seems to me earlier than the beginning of Roman rule in 129 B.C., but that must remain uncertain. This text, however, is our best evidence for a terminus ante quem for the inviolability of the temple; but it might in fact state no more about the Artemisium than was true of any other temple.

The Romans' recognition of the status, attested from the age of Caesar on, may have occurred upon their earliest contact with Anatolia in the 190s, as at Claros, Teos, and Magnesia. In the 90s, according to Cicero, the quaestor of

12. References at *Phoenix* 33 (1979) 43.
13. *I.Ephesos* 1687.6 is on the reverse.
14. Cf. Robert, *Etudes anat.* 415–416.

the province, whose slave had taken refuge in the Artemisium, an asylum, was prevented by an Ephesian magistrate Pericles from seizing him; Pericles was brought to Rome to stand trial for this injustice.[15] Certainly the *asylia* of the temple will have been abolished as a result of the killing of Roman partisans who took refuge there in 88 B.C.

Our terminus ante quem for the restoration of the *asylia* of the Artemisium is 44 B.C., when the status was cited as precedent for the inviolability of the temple of Artemis at Sardes (**214**.47): τ̣[αὐτῶ]ι δικαίωι ὧι κα[ὶ] τ̣ὸ τ̣ῆ̣ς 'Εφεσίας Ἀρτέμι[δός. So again for Aphrodite at Aphrodisias in 39 (**212**.56–57): ἄσυλον [ἔ]στω τούτῳ τῷ δικαίῳ ταύτῃ τε δ⟨ε⟩ισιδαιμονίᾳ ᾧ δικαίῳ καὶ ᾗ δεισιδαιμονίᾳ τὸ ἱερὸν εἶτε καὶ τέμενος Ἀρτέμιδος 'Ε[φε]σίας ἐστὶν ἐν 'Εφέσῳ.[16] Thus the temple served as a legal precedent for *asylia* elsewhere in the province, perhaps because Ephesus was the capital; or possibly this shrine was the first in the province to regain the privilege after the Mithridatic interlude. In imperial times Ephesus paid divine honors to Servilius Isauricus, so it may have been Isauricus, as Caesar's agent in 45–44 B.C., who restored inviolability and other traditional rights, as he did elsewhere in Asia.[17]

Strabo gives this history of the fluctuating boundaries of the inviolable precinct (14.1.23 [641]):

> νυνὶ δὲ τὰ μὲν φυλάττεται τῶν νομίμων, τὰ δ' ἧττον, ἄσυλον δὲ μένει τὸ ἱερὸν καὶ νῦν καὶ πρότερον· τῆς δ' ἀσυλίας τοὺς ὅρους ἀλλαγῆναι συνέβη πολλάκις, Ἀλεξάνδρου μὲν ἐπὶ στάδιον ἐκτείναντος, Μιθριδάτου δὲ τόξευμα ἀφέντος ἀπὸ τῆς γωνίας τοῦ κεράμου καὶ δόξαντος ὑπερβαλέσθαι μικρὰ τὸ στάδιον, Ἀντωνίου δὲ διπλασιάσαντος τοῦτο καὶ συμπεριλαβόντος τῇ ἀσυλίᾳ μέρος τι τῆς πόλεως· ἐφάνη δὲ τοῦτο βλαβερὸν καὶ ἐπὶ τοῖς κακούργοις ποιοῦν τὴν πόλιν, ὥστε ἠκύρωσεν ὁ Σεβαστὸς Καῖσαρ.
>
> . . .
>
> The temple retains its rights, but some to a lesser degree. It remains inviolable now as before, but the boundaries of the inviolability have often been changed. Alexander increased them by a stadion. Mithridates shot an arrow from the corner

15. Cic. *Verr.* 2.1.85 (*in illud asylum confugisset*); cf. J.-L. Ferrary, *CRAI* 1991, 573. A Pericles was mint magistrate at Ephesus in 58 B.C., *BMC Ionia* 67.

16. For such a citation of precedent compare the evocation of Diana Aventina at *CIL* XII 4333 and elsewhere (cf. p. 578). For parallels for "the same status as" see C. Nicolet, *Insula sacra* (Paris 1980) 102 n. 46.

17. So Robert, *Hellenica* VI (1948) 41–42. Earlier Caesar had boasted of having twice protected the temple treasury (*BCiv.* 3.33, 105). In 56 B.C. Ptolemy XII appears to have taken up residence in or by the Artemisium (Dio 39.16.3: παρὰ τῇ θεᾷ διήτατο); but Ptolemy was not in flight from anyone, and this may be no more than a pretentious way of saying that Ptolemy resided in Ephesus (compare Libanius, below, p. 442).

of the roof and reckoned that it had gone somewhat beyond that stadion. Antony[18] doubled this and thus encompassed in the right of inviolability a part of the city; but this was deemed harmful, making the city over to wrongdoers,[19] and Augustus Caesar revoked it.

The topographical import of the extensions is uncertain. As the near wall of the Lysimachean city of Ephesus is about a mile, some eight stadia, from the temple, scholars have long insisted that Strabo's dimensions fall well short of intrusion upon the city. Benndorf concluded that the "city" Strabo meant was at Ayashuyuk just north of the temple and that this was the original site of Ephesus and still called "the city" in Augustan times.[20] Such an obscure usage by Strabo is unlikely, and I think unnecessary: for we must take into account the distance missing in Strabo, the original radius of the peribolos. This, the radius to which Alexander added a stadion and Mithridates a little more, we do not know. Nor does Strabo make clear whether the distance (τοῦτο) that Antony doubled was the whole radius or only the addition of Alexander and Mithridates. Sulla had added one mile to the radius of the Amphiareum at Oropus, Caesar two miles to that of the Didymeum at Miletus; I should guess that Antony's favor was similarly ostentatious, doubling the current radius rather than merely adding another stadion to it. If the primitive radius had been only three stadia (about 600 meters), Alexander's stadion and Antony's doubling will have brought the perimeter into the walled city.[21] Note finally that the population of Augustan Ephesus surely spread beyond the Hellenistic walls.

The question is not controlled as yet by the archaeological record. J. T. Wood found a corner of what seemed the Augustan peribolos, for it contained the inscriptions cited below; the corner is 460 meters from the temple. But we now know that the wall is of late Roman date and the inscribed blocks reused.[22] Even if we assume that this late wall followed the line restored by Augustus, Antony's doubling of that distance would not have extended the peribolos to the city walls.

18. Antony visited Ephesus in 42/1 after Philippi (App. *BCiv.* 5.4; Plut. *Ant.* 24; Dio 48.24) and again in 33 with Cleopatra (Plut. 56, 58), but probably too on other occasions during his long command in the East; a visit is mentioned in Sherk, *Roman Documents* 57.5, which is not otherwise dated; also Jos. *AJ* 14.304.

19. Echoed in one of the letters of Apollonius of Tyana, literary forgeries of later antiquity, in which Apollonius rebukes the Ephesians for this permitting of lawlessness: *Ep.* 65 (*Forsch. Ephesos* I 259 no. 295).

20. *Forsch. Ephesos* I 31–48.

21. The uncertainty is not resolved by the report of Mithridates' bow shot, which (if we accept the story) could have outstripped either Alexander's stadion or the original radius plus that stadion. The official world record at present is 851 yards, about four stadia: J. D. Latham and W. F. Paterson, *Saracen Archery* (London 1970) 109.

22. See W. Jobst, *IstMitt* 30 (1980) 241–260. For early relations between Augustus and Ephesus see P. Scherrer, *Jahreshefte* 60 (1990) 87–101.

183. Rome: Augustus

Ephesus: temple of Artemis

Two white marble blocks built into a late antique wall; they flanked a corner symmetrically, at a point 460 meters south of the temple (now in London and Berlin). Each ca. h. 0.44, w. 1.76.

MousSmyrn 1 (1873) 116 no. 14; J. T. Wood, *Discoveries at Ephesus* (London 1877) pp. 132–134 and app. I p. 2; Mommsen, *CIL* III 6070, 7118; Hicks, *IGBM* III 522 [Dessau, *ILS* 97; *I.Ephesos* V 1522].

Cf. Jobst 251–253.

Imp. Caesar divi f. Aug. cos. XII tr. pot. XVIII pontifex
maximus, ex reditu Dianae fanum et Augusteum muro
muniendum curavit, [[*C. Asinio Gallo procos.,*]] *curatore*
4 *Sex. Lartidio leg.*

Αὐτοκράτωρ Καῖσαρ θεοῦ υἱὸς Σεβαστὸς ὕπατος τὸ ιβ δημαρχικῆς ἐξουσίας τὸ ιη,
ἐκ τῶν ἱερῶν τῆς θεοῦ προσόδων τὸν νεὼ καὶ τὸ Σεβαστῆον τιχισθῆναι προενοήθη,
[[ἐπὶ ἀνθυπάτου Γαίου Ἀσινίου Γάλλου,]] ἐπιμελήᾳ Σέξστου Λαρτιδίου πρεσβευτοῦ.

The date is the first half of 5 B.C. The name of the governor has been erased (incompletely in one copy: I underline what survives there); Gallus (*PIR*^{2} A 1229) was disgraced and executed in the early 30s A.D.

Augustus' act here is described only as the building of a wall, not as an alteration of the boundaries of the Artemisium as described by Strabo. Yet even on its own terms it seems little favor to Artemis: the goddess, not the emperor, had to pay for this wall, and also (if Jobst is right) for a distinct wall surrounding the temple of Augustus in the new agora of the city.[23] On the same occasion and also through Lartidius, the emperor saw to the planning and repair of roads and a waterway leading to the temple.[24] Other benefactions of Augustus cannot be closely dated. Some dedications are on record, including perhaps the restoration of a statue by Myron stolen by Antony.[25] He guaranteed the boundaries of some land owned by Artemis well to the east in Ephesian

23. Jobst has argued for separating the two temples named in this inscription. The Augusteum wall is the περιτείχισμα mentioned in *Syll.*^{3} 818 (= *I.Ephesos* II 412) as needing repair in A.D. 79/80. For the two Augustea of Ephesus see H. Engelmann, *ZPE* 97 (1993) 279–289.

24. *I.Ephesos* V 1523–1524 (with *Jahresh.* 59 [1989] Beibl. 223–226), again duplicate inscriptions placed symmetrically in the late wall, and likewise of uncertain topographical import.

25. Pliny *HN* 34.58 (see, however, F. Münzer, *Hermes* 30 [1895] 595); Ridgway esp. *AJA* 1974, 14–15.

territory.[26] He also restored to her some funds the use of which had been usurped by private persons.[27]

Thus Augustus several times addressed himself to the well-being of the Artemisium. The wall built in 5 B.C. is to be placed among these examples of his concern. If this was the peribolos wall, 5 B.C. will be a terminus ante quem for the restoration of the boundary to its former situation before Antony's enlargement. But the building of this wall need not be the same act as changing the sacred boundary; the repudiation of Antony's change would seem more likely to belong early in Augustus' reign.

Ephesian coins show that the Artemisium, "the jewel of the whole province," as one governor called it, continued to enjoy *asylia* through the imperial period.[28] On occasional civic bronzes scattered in date from the late first century to the mid-third, we find on the reverse the image of the goddess and the label Ἄρτεμις Ἐφεσία ἄσυλος (PLATE 6) or Ἄρτεμις ἄσυλος.[29] But this notice is a rarity, in contrast to the frequent citation of the neocories with the image of the temple.

In conclusion, our authors may be right, and the Ephesians claimed inviolability for their temple from time immemorial. But it is possible instead (despite the silence of the epigraphical evidence) that the status of the temple followed the usual pattern: that is, that the *asylia* of the Artemisium was created by Panhellenic grant in the third century B.C.[30] In any case, it was abolished by the Roman authorities after 88 and restored later, perhaps in the 40s on Caesar's orders.

Strabo sees the *asylia* of the Artemisium in Roman terms: it was an asylum in which persons might take refuge, a privilege deriving from remote antiquity and old already in Alexander's day. I suggest that his source in this passage is the Roman decision on boundaries, made in Augustus' time, when the Ephesians, in the context of a complaint against them, contrived their case to satisfy Roman expectations and limitations.

Just as Artemis of Ephesus served Rome as the precedent for defining *asylia* in the province, she may also have served as the precedent for restricting that right in A.D. 22, for there is an obvious similarity in the problem perceived at

26. *I.Ephesos* VII 3501–3502, the first a substantial pillar found on the north slope of Mt. Mesogis, five hours' walk from the city. For other rural properties of Artemis guaranteed by imperial boundaries, see *I.Ephesos* VII 3506–3513; cf. II 566, simply ὅρος ἱερὸς Ἀρτέμιδος.

27. *I.Ephesos* Ia 18.b.5–7; cf. c.10–11, 19b.5.

28. *I.Ephesos* Ia 18.b.2–3. ἱερώτατος δῆμος at III 625 merely is the rhetoric of the age. The goddess took the place of the emperor in holding one of the neocories of the city: Robert, *RPhil* III.41 (1967) 48–50 (*Op. min. sel.* V 388–390); Burrell, "Neokoroi" 262–267.

29. See the list of types in S. Karwiese, "Ephesos," *RE* Suppl. 12 (1970) 331–361 (examples under Domitia, Antoninus Pius, Severus Alexander, Etruscilla, Philip Junior, and Otacilia Severa).

30. Artemis' games, the Ephesia, were Panhellenic by imperial times, but we do not know when they became so.

Augustan Ephesus, as described by Strabo, and during the Senate's inquiry under Tiberius.[31] The lawless behavior that resulted from Antony's enlarging the asylum at Ephesus (for a period that perhaps ended in 5 B.C. and thus lasted a generation, but that may have been far shorter) entered Roman legal lore as a grave objection to the right of asylum, on which the first princeps imposed limits at Ephesus. Augustus' solution there, however, was not so much legal as geographical: for at Ephesus the problem of public order was solved by restoring the precinct to its isolated remove from the city, an option not available in the diverse cases put before the Senate in A.D. 22.

31. See p. 29; B. Haussoullier, *RPhil* n.s. 23 (1900) 156.

Temple of Hera, Samos

The largest temple in Greece in the classical period was the Heraeum of Samos, situated on the south coast of the island about six kilometers from the city proper; seated in the middle of the plain, the temple faces Mt. Mycale across the strait.[1] "Autochthonous Hera," born at this site, was the patron divinity of the Samians.[2] Her aniconic cult statue, of great antiquity, was famous, and the temple and its dedications attracted scholarly interest in the Hellenistic age,[3] and the greed of Verres in 80 B.C. and of Antony later.[4]

In A.D. 23 the Samians offered the Roman Senate an Amphictyonic decree as authority for the inviolability of the Heraeum: "a decree of the Amphictyons, in whom resided chief judicial authority over all things, at the time the Greeks, through their founding of cities along Asia, ruled the shores of the sea" (Tac. *Ann.* 4.14). This appears to invoke the time after the Ionian migration in the Dark Ages, rather than the Hellenistic period.[5] Such a claim may have rested on an anecdote from a local history or on a forged document from such a book, such as we have in *I.Magnesia* 17 and 20.

1. Hdt. 3.60 for its size (cf. A. E. Furtwängler, *AM* 99 [1984] 97–103); the *temenos* encompassed a πέδον χθονὸς εὐρέος, according to the archaic poet Asius of Samos (frag. 13; cf. J. N. O'Sullivan, *GRBS* 22 [1981] 329–333). See in general H. Walter, *Das Heraion von Samos* (Munich 1976); H. Kyrieleis, *Führer durch das Heraion von Samos* (Athens 1981).

2. Ἥραν αὐτόχθονα: *Klio* 33 (1940) 164–170 (*FGrHist* 540 F 1: epigram, II B.C.); Paus. 7.4.4 on her birth. A famous early illustration of this *poliouchos thea* is the Attic stele *IG* II^2 1: O. Kern, *Inscriptiones Graecae* (Bonn 1913) 18. At *LSCG* Suppl. 81.15–16 [τῆς ἀρχηγετί]δος τῆς πόλεως Ἥρας. Note the Samians' temple of Hera at Naucratis (Hdt. 2.178).

3. *FGrHist* 536 F 3, with Jacoby's notes; 537 F 1; 540; 541; Paus. 7.4.7; Callim. frag. 100.

4. Cic. *Verr.* 2.1.50 (a temple *antiquissimum et nobilissimum*); Strab. 14.1.14 (637). For the statues by Myron, Antony's plunder, see E. Buschor, *AM* 68 (1953) 51–62.

5. So H. Bürgel, *Die pylaeisch-delphische Amphictyonie* (Munich 1877) 76–77, invoked by Herrmann, *AM* 75 (1960) 91 n. 73; see p. 107.

If there was a Hellenistic recognition of *asylia*, no remains of it have been found in the inscriptions. In the second half of the third century Samos was a Ptolemaic dependency. Ptolemy III (246–221) had occasion to regulate the treatment of suppliants in the Heraeum.[6] This is a most interesting intervention by the king into the legal and religious affairs of a city, but unfortunately little of the stone survives. A trial was to be held before the *hieropoiai*, who are to - - -]ονομεῖν; the case may have involved slaves (ὑπὲρ τῶν καταφευγόντων εἰς τὸ [ἱερὸν σωμάτων?]), the king laying down the conditions under which these may be handed over to their masters (παραδιδόνα[ι δὲ τοῖς κυρίοις αὐτ?]ῶν). A roughly contemporary law of Samos prohibits several categories of persons (slaves, soldiers, veterans, suppliants, indigents) from being employed in the shops established within the temple precinct;[7] here too trial will be before the *hieropoiai*, whose decision must be ratified by a civil court. From these texts it is clear that suppliants were an important part of the life of the temple in the third century B.C., and that the government of Samos imposed legal procedures on the phenomenon as did other Greek cities. What we see at the Heraeum need not be a consequence of a Hellenistic grant of *asylia*, as distinct from the usual Greek rights and regulations for suppliants, and the attraction for them of an especially honored and spacious temple.

The epigraphical evidence for declared *asylia* derives from the Roman confirmation in A.D. 23. We have a fragment of a decision concerning the Asclepieum on Cos and the Heraeum on Samos (**184**). And from the Heraeum come two statue bases of the consuls of 23, dedicated by the people of Samos;[8] presumably the consuls authored an advisory opinion to the Senate on the matter.

184. Rome

Stele of white marble broken on all sides, found on Samos reused in a church near the Heraeum; h. 0.45, w. 0.27, th. 0.095; letters 0.014, intersp. 0.01.

P. Herrmann, *AM* 75 (1960) 90–93 no. 5 [Sherk, *Roman Doc.* 32].

Photograph: Herrmann pl. 38.3.

[- - - - - - - - - - - - -]ΥΝ. [- -]
[- - - - - - - - - - - -]ΤΟ . Σ̣[- -]

6. C. Habicht, *AM* 72 (1957) 226–230 no. 59; cf. S. V. Tracy, "Hands in Samian Inscriptions," *Chiron* 20 (1990) 75; R. S. Bagnall, *Administration of the Ptolemaic Possessions* (Leiden 1976) 81 n. 8. In this same period donations were being collected from the citizens to pay for restoration work on "the great temple" (*SEG* 1.367: ἐπισκευ[ῆς τοῦ με]γ[ά]λου ναοῦ).

7. Habicht, *AM* 87 (1972) 211–225 no. 9 [*SEG* 27.545]; photograph: Tracy fig. 27, who attributes both inscriptions to the same mason. Commentaries by L. Koenen, *ZPE* 27 (1977) 211–216; L. Soverini, *Opus* 9–10 (1990-91) 59–121.

8. *AM* 44 (1919) 37 [*SEG* 1.389; *IGR* IV 1724]; cf. Herrmann 150; Habicht 1957, 228–229. A statue erected by the Samians to Tiberius may be from the same occasion (*SEG* 1.390); Herrmann compares the statue of Tiberius on Cos (above, p. 111).

[- - - - - - - - - - -]Δ̣ | | | ΝΕΙΣΔΟ[-]
[- - Γάϊος Στερτίνι]ος Μάξιμος κα̣[ὶ Γάϊος Ἀσίνιος Πολλίων ὕπατοι? - -]
[- - - - - - - - - -]αν πρὸ α εἰδῶν Σ[επτεμβρίων - - - - - - - - - - - - - - - -]
[- - - - - - - - - -] πρεσβευτῶν Κῴων [-]
[- - - ?τὸ παρ' α]ὐτοῖς Ἀσκληπιοῦ ἱ̣[ερόν -]
[- - - - - - - - -]| Ἥρας ὃ εὐσεβεστά[τοις? -]
[- - - - - - - - - κ]α̣ταστάντων καθὼ[ς -]

[- - - - - - - -] τῶι ἱερῶι τῆς Ἥρας τ̣[-]
[- - - - - - - -]υ̣τωι δικαιοτέραν [-]
[- - - - - - - ο]υ̣ ἐπι̣τυχεῖν π[-]
[- - - - - - - δεισι]δ̣α̣ιμονίας Λ̣[-]
[- - - - - - - - - τῆς] πόλεως κ[-]
[- - - - - - - - - - - -]ησαν. [-]
[- - - - - - - - - - - - - -]πιτ̣[-]

1: σ]υνκ̣[λητ-? Herrmann, perhaps κατὰ τὸ δόγμα τοῦ σ]υνκ̣[λήτου Sherk. 8 Rigsby: ὁ εὐσεβέστα[τος? Herrmann. 9: perhaps ἀποκ], Herrmann.

Herrmann thought that the first line might begin the inscription and be a heading. He suggested reasonably that we have a first text, the consuls' report, and a second (10ff.), the Senate's decree. If that is so, however, the letter seems to end rather abruptly and the decree to move rather swiftly into its subject. Perhaps instead a quotation (like the many in **6**) begins in line 10, introduced by words lost on the left in the one line between 9 and 10.

4: The consuls are those of A.D. 23, when Tacitus says the embassies of Samos and Cos were heard by the Senate. As is clear from 6–8, the two cases were addressed jointly, perhaps because in 22 they had been assigned to a committee whose report reached the Senate only in 23. But the date in September (line 5) suggests that these two cities appealed later than the others.

8: I suggest a relative clause, some such expression as *quod piissimis / sanctissimis caerimoniis*; cf. Cic. *Verr.* 1.14: *sanctissimis religionibus consecrata*; *Sest.* 56: *fanum ... sanctissimarum atque antiquissimarum religionum.*

13: Herrmann noted the parallel in the Roman grant to Aphrodisias, **212**.56.

Samothrace

The Samothracian Gods were widely honored; but only literature makes a claim of inviolability for their temple, attributing it to mythic times. The queen of the Amazons, obeying a dream vision, made this uninhabited island sacred to the mother of the gods (σαμοθρᾴκη meaning "sacred island" in Amazonian); here the goddess established her mysteries and ordained that the precinct be inviolable (τὸ τέμενος ἄσυλον νομοθετῆσαι)—so Dionysius Scytobrachion in the third century B.C.[1] From as early as the mid-third century, Greek *theoroi* were being sent to attend the celebration of the Mysteries on Samothrace. In the 280s B.C. the temple was pillaged by someone (*Syll.*[3] 372); and Samothrace is in the lists of temples plundered by the pirates in the first century.

Of declared *asylia* in Hellenistic times there is no trace. But there was a famous act of refuge in the temple, by King Perseus of Macedonia with his friends and his money in 168 B.C.[2] The extant sources on this episode attribute to the temple no more than a temple's ordinary capacity to receive a suppliant (Livy 45.4.3: *fani religione non viribus suis tutus esset*). What most nearly suggests a granted status is the Roman speech demanding the surrender of the king and his party (45.5–6): do we rightly understand that the island is sacred and entirely of revered and inviolable soil (*sacram hanc insulam et augusti totam atque inviolati soli esse?*); how then could the Samothracians allow there a man stained with crime (Evander who attempted murder at Delphi)? The Samothracians agree that Evander must stand trial at a hearing traditional for just such a purpose (*iudicia apud sese more maiorum*), or else leave the temple; Perseus himself then has

1. Frag. 4 Rusten (Diod. 3.55.8; *FGrHist* 32 F 7); a different account at Callistratus *FGrHist* 433 F 10. On the cult see S. G. Cole, *Megaloi Theoi*, EPRO 96 (Leiden 1984).

2. The testimonia at N. Lewis, *Samothrace* I (New York 1959) nos. 106–127. Arsinoe II fled to Samothrace in 280 (Justin. 24.3.9); Ptolemy was urged to in 170 (Polyb. 28.21).

Evander killed but realizes that he has thus violated the two most holy temples in the world, at Delphi and Samothrace (*duo sanctissima in terris templa ... violata*); he gives himself up to the Romans. The version of Plutarch says simply that the Roman commander allowed Perseus inviolability in deference to the gods, τὴν μὲν ἀσυλίαν παρεῖχε τῷ Περσεῖ διὰ τοὺς θεούς (*Aem. Paul.* 26.1).

Temple of Pluto and Kore, Nysa

Nysa in Caria looks across the Maeander Valley from the foothills of Mt. Mesogis. Its patron gods were Pluto and Kore, whose temple stood three kilometers west of the city proper in the ancient deme or village Acaraca, connected to the city by a sacred way.[1] Here was a grove consecrated to the two infernal gods; in the slope above was a cave sacred to Charon,[2] where each year the ephebes of Nysa sacrificed a bull (released into the cave, the animal died miraculously, untouched). By late Hellenistic times the Plutonium was a famous healing shrine, where the sick received healing dreams sent through the cave by Pluto, and where they could find men expert in medicine and in the interpretation of dreams. Nysa celebrated a Panhellenic festival, the Theogamia or "divine wedding" of Pluto and Kore.[3]

In this rural setting, we should expect that the temple, rather than the city and country, was declared inviolable, and the terms of the grants support this: συν[χωρ]εῖν. . .τῷ ἱερῶι (**185**.7–8); τὰ ἱερὰ γράμματα περὶ τῶν θεῶν καὶ τῆς ἀσυλίας αὐτῶν (**186**.10–11). Therefore I have placed with the adespota an inscription found at Acaraca, in which a lawyer (evidently from Nysa, as he is given no ethnic) is honored by a city that is ἱερὰ καὶ ἄσυλος; but this might

1. Strab. 14.1.43–48 (649–650); at 44 the MSS give Ἀχάραχα (for χ/χ see J. and L. Robert, *Fouilles d'Amyzon* I p. 201). The correct spelling, seen in the one inscription (n. 5 below), seems reflected in the *Etym. Magn.* s.v. Ἄχαρα ("later called Nyssa," with mention of the hero Athymbrus). See W. von Diest, *Nysa ad Maeandrum*, JdI-EH 10 (Berlin 1913); *PetMitt* 55 (1909) 174–177; for Pluto and Kore on the coins of Nysa and neighboring cities see Robert, *DAM* 32–33; *A travers l'Asie Mineure* (Paris 1980) 331–332; cf. *IG* XI.4 1235 (dedication on Delos by an Athymbrian, beginning with Pluto and Kore).

2. Some parallels for such caves at E. Des Places, ed., Iamblich. *Myst.* (Paris 1966) 147–148 n. 3.

3. Boeckh ad *CIG* 2949; von Diest 88–90; *Syll.*^{3} 1066 (Augustan); Robert, *Etudes anat.* 431; *Laodicée du Lycos* 297; Magie II 990.

after all be Nysa itself, given the looser usage of imperial times.[4] The great pilgrimage shrine dominated the lives of those Nysaeans who lived at Acaraca; "those who reside in holy Acaraca" they call themselves on a statue base of imperial date: [ο]ἱ κατοικοῦντες τὰ ἱερὰ Ἀκάρα[κα].[5] In this text ἱερά might allude to a juridical status of the village with respect to the city, but more likely it merely evokes a familiar fact of its daily life, the prominence of the temple.[6] Roman Nysa was exceedingly chaste in its advertising of titulature: occasional coins show it only as the "sixth" city of Asia, thus ahead of nearby Magnesia.[7]

In I B.C. an archive of old documents pertinent to the rights of the temple was inscribed there. Three substantial texts survive (together with the beginnings or endings of several more): a letter of Seleucus I and his son in 281 B.C. granting some privilege to the temple in response to an embassy from the city of Athymbra, which possessed the sacred place at this early date, before the Seleucid foundation of Nysa; another royal letter (**185**) confirming existing privileges, including *asylia*; and from I B.C. a decree of Nysa recording the success of a civic petition to the governor of Asia to permit the restoration of these texts to the city's record office, together with the beginning of the governor's letter (**186**).

The citizens' intent in I B.C. was the comprehensive restoration of privileges, such as are in fact listed in **185** and **186**: that is, the collected documents were not confined to recognitions of *asylia*. It seems to me certain that Seleucus' fragmentary letter of 281[8] is too early to be one, with Nysa anticipating cities like Smyrna or Cos. That Seleucus is granting a privilege to the temple (rather than the city) is clear from line 7, σὺν εὐ]σεβῆαι συναύξειν τὰς τῶν θε̣[ῶν τιμάς, and from the inclusion of the letter in this archive. At its beginning Hiller restored the list of privileges whole cloth from **185** and **186**:

2 [ἀποστειλάντων πρ]ὸς ἡμᾶς Ἀθυμβριανῶν περὶ τῆς [ἱκεσίας καὶ ἀσυ]-
[λίας καὶ ἀτελείας] Ἰατροκλέα (κτλ.)

This is not credible in its own right: for precisely here the temple needs to be named, and with this restoration it is not identified at all in the letter. Moreover, this indiscriminate list of privileges is in keeping with the relatively late date of

4. *BCH* 14 (1890) 224–225 no. 2; see pp. 36, 588.

5. *BCH* 232–233 no. 4 [*AM* 15 (1890) 282 no. 33]; photograph at *Deltion* 7 (1921/22) 81 fig. 65; cf. Robert, *Etudes anat.* 147 n. 3.

6. For such "sacred villages" see L. and J. Robert, *La Carie* II p. 295 (including Acaraca); cf. Strab. 10.1.10 (449) on the former city Tamynae in the territory of Eretria (πόλις ἦν Ταμύναι, ἱερὰ τοῦ Ἀπόλλωνος; cf. *FGrHist* 427 F 1).

7. Robert, *BCH* 101 (1977) 64–77 (*DAM* 22–35). In *I.Ephesos* Ia 22.48 (II A.D.) the Artists of Dionysus will erect an honorific inscription ἔν τε τῇ φιλοσεβάστῳ Νύσῃ πατρίδι of the honorand; the word is certainly their ornament rather than a granted title.

8. *Royal Corres.* 9 (addressed, like **218**, to a royal official rather than to the city); cf. W. Orth, *Königlicher Machtanspruch und städtische Freiheit* (Munich 1977) 32–36.

185 and **186**, the result of accumulation over time. Rather, here in 281 B.C. we likely have one of the rights found renewed later, coupled with the name of the god as is necessary: for example, τῆς [ἀτελείας? τοῦ ἱε|ροῦ τοῦ Πλούτωνος]. The last extant line (12) was restored by Hiller to refer to *asylia*: ἐπιτρέπ]ομεν πᾶσιν μὲν τοῖς ἱεροῖς τοῖς ἀσ̣[ύλοις . . ., "we permit to all temples that have inviolability . . ." This seems a strangely generic response to the ambassadors' petition about the Plutonium, a general policy prompted by a particular request. Strictly speaking it might also be at variance with the restoration of *asylia* in line 2, since the king now assumes that this temple has inviolability and proceeds to grant something further. Instead I suggest, we have here a statement of existing policy or attitude,[9] marked by μέν, which would have been followed (δέ) by a decision about the present request. As to how temples were characterized here, whatever weight is to be attached to the reading ΑΣ[, Welles's restoration, ἀ̣σ̣[υλίαν κεκτημένοις?, seems to me historically less credible than Hiller's, for it implies that in 281 B.C. there was in the Seleucid kingdom a class of temples treated as inviolable as distinct from those that were not (perhaps native temples). The case of Baetocaece in Phoenicia can be invoked for the distinction, but not for this early date. Hiller's text can be understood rather as the beginning of a polemic statement of policy: "We permit[10] to all inviolable temples," that is, to all temples.[11] Accordingly I omit this letter from the corpus, and also the surviving traces of other documents in the archive, as none can be shown to concern inviolability rather than some other honor to the temple.[12]

Our evidence, then, is confined to the two confirmations of the already-granted title; if I am right that **185** was written by Mithridates VI, then the original recognition occurred before 88 B.C. An obvious possible origin would be the Carian expedition of Antiochus III in 204–203;[13] and in fact there was mention of Antiochus at the end of the document written above **186**: (traces) [- - - Ἀντι]ό̣χου δε τοῦ μεγάλου [. But the original occasion must remain speculative.

The name of the author of **185** is lost in the first line. Hiller assumed Antiochus III, who is mentioned in the traces that precede. Welles showed that those traces belong to another letter, and also thought here an Attalid to be excluded by the space available and by the awkward style; he suggested some barbarian Ariarathes or Mithridates joining in the recognition of the *asylia* of

9. Cf. **18**.7, **23**.13.

10. If this was the verb; one thinks of βοηθήσ]ομεν, cf. the treaty between Philip V and Hannibal: βοηθήσομεν ἀλλήλοις εἰς τὸν πόλεμον (Polyb. 7.9.15).

11. Compare Polyb. 9.34.9, a persuasive piece in which τὰ ἄσυλα ἱερά are all the temples ravaged by the Aetolians (cf. p. 38).

12. *Royal Corres.* 43, a letter of an Antiochus found in the city rather than at the temple and not on the same stone as the temple archive, Welles thought nonetheless to be a grant of the three temple privileges; contra: L. and J. Robert, *La Carie* II p. 291 n. 9.

13. So the Roberts, *Amyzon* p. 144 n. 10, attribute **185** to Antiochus III, as had Hiller.

the temple. I have argued elsewhere that his authoritative decision shows that this king rules in Caria and is not joining in a Panhellenic recognition; he is not Seleucid, as he invokes the "previous kings" rather than his ancestors; and his mixing of authority and deference does not suit an Attalid dealing with either a subject or an ally. These features make sense if this is Mithridates VI of Pontus, after his conquest of the area in 88 B.C.;[14] the only extant letters of Mithridates come in fact from Nysa, documenting his antipathy to a pro-Roman citizen of Nysa, who eventually fled the city (*Royal Corres.* 73–74). By now the privileges of the temple have been gathered into a seemingly repetitious list, which we find again in the Roman confirmation in 1 B.C.—further evidence, I believe, for the lateness of **185**. That a governor's permission was needed to restore the documents to the temple indicates that its privileges had been revoked by Rome; presumably Nysa joined Mithridates, and it is easy to imagine that Roman partisans were killed in the temple, as occurred at Pergamum and Ephesus.

The archive was inscribed on blocks of white limestone, part of a wall or building associated with the temple at Acaraca. The lettering is large (h. 2.0 cm) and blockish, with apices.

185. Mithridates VI of Pontus?

Two joining blocks, the left (h. 0.71, w. 0.78, th. 0.34) found built into the mosque at Salavatlı (by ancient Acaraca), the right (h. 0.68, w. 0.59, th. 0.34) built into the mosque at Sultan Hıssar (by Nysa); now in the Izmir museum. Surface much worn; to the right, a vacat of ca. 20 cm to the end of the block.

Lines 9–14 left: G. Radet, *BCH* 14 (1890) 224–231 no. 1.

Entire: Hiller in *Nysa ad Maeandrum* 62–69 (copies of Kubitschek, Oehler, Pringsheim) [Schroeter 29]; Welles, *Royal Corres.* 64 (squeeze).

Cf. Wilhelm, *Jahresh.* 24 (1929) 195; *Griechische Königsbriefe*, Klio-BH 48 (Leipzig 1943) 59–60; Robert, *Laodicée du Lycos* 289 n. 3; B. Lifshitz, *ZPE* 6 (1970) 60–61; F. Piejko, *Chiron* 18 (1988) 61.

[βασιλεὺς Μιθραδάτης? Νυσαέων τῆι β]ουλῆι καὶ τῶι δήμωι χαίρειν·
[συμμείξαντές μοι ἐν - - - Ἀρ]τεμίδωρος, Βασιλείδης, Μι-
[. . . . οἱ πρεσβευταὶ πεμφθέντες ὑφ' ὑ]μ̣ῶν ἀπέδωκάν μοι τὸ ψήφι[σ]-
[μα παρ' ὑμῶν καὶ αὐτοὶ διελέχθησαν] μ̣ὲ̣ν̣ μ̣ε̣τ̣ὰ̣ [φιλοτιμ]ίας
[?ἀκολούθως τοῖς γεγραμμένοις περὶ] τῆς ἱκεσίας καὶ ἀσυλίας
[καὶ ἀτελείας, παρακαλοῦντες καὶ ἐμ]ὲ ἶσον τι (?) συν̣[χωρ]εῖν καθότι
[συνεχωρήθη καὶ πρότερον ὑπὸ τῶν ἔμπρ]οσθεν βα[σι]λέων τῷ ἱερῶ[ι]
[?τῶι παρ' ὑμῖν Πλούτωνός τε καὶ Κόρης.] βουλόμενος [οὖ]ν ἐπαύ-
[ξειν τὴν πρὸ]ς̣ ἡ̣μ̣ᾶ̣ς̣ φιλ̣[ίαν καὶ ἐκ] τῶ̣ν̣ ἀποδειχθέντων μοι ὑπὸ
τῶν πρεσβευτῶν θεωρῶν ἀπ[ὸ παλ]αιῶν χρόνων ὑπάρχουσαν τὴν
ἱκεσίαν καὶ ἀσυλίαν καὶ ἀτέλειαν, συνεχώρησα ὡς οἱ περιεστη-
λωμένοι ὅροι ὑπὸ τῶν ἔμπροσθεν βασιλέων ⟨ὥρισαν⟩, καὶ τὰ
ἄλλα δὲ πάντα φιλάνθρωπα καὶ τείμια ὅσα οἱ πρὸ ἡμῶν βασιλεῖς συν-

14. *TAPA* 118 (1988) 149–153. Orth (34) thought Eumenes II the probable author.

εχώρησαν ἐπιτρέπω, καὶ εἰς τὸ λοιπὸν π[ει]ράσομαι ἀεί τινος ἀγαθοῦ π[αραί]-
[τι]ος γείνε[σθαι ἐπὶ τῶι συμφ]έροντι ὑμῶ[ν.]

Text of Welles. 1 Rigsby: Ἀντίοχος Hiller. 2: [οἱ ἀφικόμενοι παρ' ὑμῶν πρέσβεις Ἀρ] Wilamowitz ap. Hiller. 4: μὲν κ[ατ]ὰ τῆς ἀτελήας Hiller. 6: ΕΙΣΟΠΩΣΥΙ ΑΡΧΕΙ Kubitschek. 9: τὴν πρόσο]δόν τε φρο[υρεῖν ἐκ] Hiller; πρὸ]ς ὑμᾶς Wilhelm 1943; τὰς τῶν θεῶν] τιμ[ὰς καὶ ἐκ] Piejko. 12 corr. Wilhelm 1943: συνεχώρησα lapis; - σα⟨ν⟩ Wilamowitz. 15 Wilhelm 1929.

...

(5ff., the envoys spoke) concerning the rights of supplication, inviolability, [and tax exemption, asking me as well] to grant roughly the same as what [had been granted also previously by the] kings before me to your temple [of Pluto and Kore.] Therefore, wishing to increase your friendship toward us and seeing from the things shown me by the ambassadors that the rights of supplication, inviolability, and tax exemption have existed from ancient times, I grant it as ⟨defined⟩ by the boundary stones established by the previous kings; and all other benefactions and honors such as the kings before us granted I permit, and for the future I shall try always to be ready with some good to your advantage.

By the time of this letter, the inviolability of the Plutonium was old (explicit at line 10) and is subsumed here in a list of privileges; by now the Nysaeans could speak of them in the same broad terms with which they addressed a Roman governor in 1 B.C. If the author is Mithridates in the 80s B.C., his emphasis on continuing exactly what "previous kings" had granted may be intended to annul the acts of the Roman government since the end of the Attalids. The invocation of precedents (9–10), other than one's ancestors, is unusual in the royal letters;[15] an example of the insistence on such proofs on the part of a minor and ephemeral ruler is *I.Labraunda* 42 (Eupolemus granting *ateleia*).[16] It is quite rare in the *asylia* documents because of their Panhellenic scope: once granted, the recognition did not need to be confirmed, until the coming of the Romans.

One must of course wonder whether an act of Mithridates would be submitted in evidence to the Roman government (so Gauthier, *Bull. épigr.* 1989 p. 408). The letter may have been included on the argument that "even Mithridates" respected the inviolability of the Plutonium—as he did that of the Asclepieum on Cos (S. Sherwin-White, *Ancient Cos* [Göttingen 1979] 138); compare the claims at Diod. 5.63.1 and Cic. *Verr.* 2.4.103 (quoted, pp. 6, 33).

2: If Welles's restoration is right, this king was not in his normal residence but on the move.

5–6: The gods may have been named in line 5 rather than 8. The list of privileges is repeated in the decree of 1 B.C., in an altered order (**186**.10ff., "texts

15. E.g., *Royal Corres.* 15.9; see *TAPA* 1988, 151–152.
16. On Eupolemus see now R. A. Billows, *ClAnt* 8 (1989) 173–206.

about the gods and their inviolability" etc.); this is not the rigorous precision of primary recognitions of earlier times. A comparable amalgamation of rights is found in **218** for Baetocaece, also of a late date. The word ἱκεσία does not recur in the documents of inviolability earlier (of Roman Stratoniceia, p. 418); it is not obvious how it might differ from ἀσυλία, and I believe that here it is merely part of the murkiness and redundancy that characterize the whole letter. Grants of tax exemption to temples for their economic activities are by contrast well attested in the Hellenistic kingdoms (see on **218**.26).

12: Klaffenbach (ap. Welles) saw that the mason has slipped and repeated the verb from the preceding line. Lifshitz defended the existing text; cf. J. and L. Robert, *Bull. épigr.* 1971, 617.

186. Rome: Gn. Lentulus Augur

Copied by Pococke at Nizili, the village by ancient Mastaura twenty kilometers east of Acaraca; the stone is lost.

R. Pococke, *Inscriptionum liber* (London 1752) p. 13 [J. M. Gesner, *Comm. Gotting. Ant.* 5 (1782) p. 7; Boeckh, *CIG* 2943; Viereck, *Sermo Graecus* 24 (lines 15–16); Hiller in *Nysa ad Maeandrum* 64–65; *Syll.*^{3} 781; Ehrenberg-Jones, *Documents . . . Augustus*^{2} 316; Sherk, *Roman Documents* 69].

Cf. Robert, *Etudes anat.* 519 n. 5.

[ἱ]ερέως Ῥώμης καὶ Αὐτοκράτορος Καίσαρος Σεβαστο[ῦ Ἡρα]-
[κλ]είδου τοῦ Ἡρακλείδου Μασταυρείτου, στεφανηφόρου
Διομήδους τοῦ Ἀθηναγόρου τοῦ Διομήδους, ἱε[ρέ]ως
[Δ]ιὸς Καπετωλίου διὰ βίου, μηνὸς Γορπιαίου ἐννεακαιδε-
κάτῃ, πρὸ μιᾶς εἰδῶν Αὐγούστων, Κόσσῳ [Κ]ο[ρ]νηλίῳ Λεντύλῳ
καὶ Λευκίῳ Πείσωνι ὑπάτοις, ἐπὶ γραμματέως τοῦ δήμου Ἡλι-
οδώρου τοῦ Μαιανδρίου τοῦ Θεοδότου, ἱερέως Τιβερίου Κλαυ-
δίου Νέρωνος διὰ βίου· Ἀρτεμίδωρος Δημητρίου Παπᾶς, τῶν
τῆς πόλεως στρατηγῶν, ἐπιμεληθεὶς ἀποκατέστη-
σεν εἰς τὸ γραμματῆον τὰ ἱερὰ γράμματα περὶ τῶν θεῶν
καὶ τῆς ἀσυλίας αὐτῶν καὶ τῆ[ς] ἱκεσίας καὶ τῆς περὶ τὸ ἱε-
ρὸν ἀτελήας, ἐμφ[α]νίσας Γνήῳ Λέντλῳ Αὔγορι τῷ ἀνθυπ[ά]-
τῳ καὶ ἀποδοὺς ⟨τ⟩ὴν ὑπογεγραμμένην ἐπιστολή⟨ν⟩.
ἐπὶ Διομήδους τοῦ Ἀθηναγόρου μηνὸς Δαισίου ιζ·
[Γ]ναῖος Λέντλος Αὔγουρ ἀνθύπατος Νυσαέων ἄρχουσιν
χαίρειν· Ἀρτεμίδωρος Δψμητρίου Παπᾶς πρεσβευτὴς

Text of Boeckh; I do not indicate the trivial errors in Pococke's copy (e.g., confusions of O and Ω, Γ and T, and E, H, N, Π); evidently the stone was hard to read. 12 end: ΑΝΘΥΠΙ Pococke. 13: T and N omitted by Pococke, who reported a leaf at the end of the line (unique in the archive), which may in fact be the required N. 15: ΑΥΤΟΥΠ Pococke (Π a typesetter's error?). 15–16 Robert: ΣΙΕΑ | ΗΡΟΤΕΙΗ Pococke; ἄρχουσι· ἐ[π]|ηρ[ώ]τ[ησε] Boeckh (a nonsyllabic division, as Viereck noted). 16 end Rigsby: ΑΡΧΩΝΙΧΙΗΖ Pococke, ἄρχων ⟨ε⟩ἰ χ⟨ρ⟩ή? Boeckh.

. . .

(8–13) Artemidorus Papas, son of Demetrius, one of the generals of the city, oversaw the restoration to the record office of the holy documents about the gods and their inviolability and right of supplication and the tax immunity belonging to the temple, after appearing before the proconsul Gnaius Lentulus Augur and bringing back the following letter.

The city's text, insofar as we have it, is not a decree ("inasmuch as . . .") but a statement of fact, a heading for the governor's letter. Our inscriptions will be copies of the papyrus documents that Artemidorus restored to the record office in Nysa city (line 10; called τὰ ἀρχεῖα at *CIG* 2950.4). The privileges of the temple must have been revoked by Rome; if, as Hiller thought (p. 65), mere physical damage is being repaired, there would be no need to seek the governor's consent, nor could damage to old inscriptions explain why the relevant papyri were not in the archives—unless we assume the accidental destruction of both the inscriptions at the temple and the papyri in the city. I assume that they or copies had been kept privately over the intervening years by interested parties. The alternative is that *grammateion* here means the archival wall at the temple.

In 1 B.C. Artemidorus submitted to Nysa the governor's letter of answer in May (line 14); some three months later in August (lines 4–5) the work of restoring the papyri to the civic archives and setting up the appropriate monument and inscribing the texts at the temple was completed.

1ff.: The preliminaries are an extravagant display of pro-Roman sentiment: mention of priests of Rome and Augustus, of Jupiter Capitolinus, of Tiberius (now in exile on nearby Rhodes), the consular year.[17] I take it that this is an affectation,[18] offered in the context of seeking Roman restoration of the temple's rights; the true eponym of Nysa was the *stephanephoros* (cf. *CIG* 2950.4), who alone is cited in line 14. It is surprising, given the apparent gravity of the affair, that only one man seems to have gone on the embassy to the governor and presented the case (12: ἐμφανίσας).

2: I do not understand why a citizen of Mastaura, Nysa's neighbor to the east, is serving as Nysa's priest of Rome.[19] On Mastaura see J. and L. Robert, *Amyzon* pp. 25–26 n. 3.

14: The date is local. I am uncertain whether this line is the heading of the governor's letter, as has been thought (cf. *Roman Doc.* 61.22), or rather goes with what precedes (ἀποδούς) and dates the presentation of the letter to the civic

17. Already in the 20s or 10s B.C. Nysa had renamed several of its tribes for members of the imperial house: see Hiller p. 68. This suggests a campaign to make friends in Rome, of which the present rehabilitation may be seen as a result. The patron of Nysa in the preceding generation is known to have been Ti. Claudius Nero (*RE* no. 254), Livia's first husband (Cic. *Fam.* 13.64.1). For priests of Tiberius in the Greek world see W. Orth, *Die Provinzialpolitik des Tiberius* (Munich 1970) 134.

18. Cf. Robert, *Laodicée* 326, on Roman affectations in dating Greek documents.

19. At *I.Stratonikeia* 1317 a *strategos* of Stratoniceia is taken to be a citizen of Iasus, Ἰα(σεύς).

authorities; if the latter, there should be no punctuation at the end of 13, where Pococke's leaf may be the missing N.

15: On Lentulus see Syme, *Augustan Aristocracy* (Oxford 1986) 284–299.

16: ἄρχων seems too vague a term here, and it would need to be followed by ὑμῶν; we expect an ambassador, and it seems to me possible to recognize the word in Pococke's copy.

Mylasa

The ruins of Mylasa, the old Hecatomnid capital,[1] have yielded fragments of decrees of Cretan cities that resemble those for Teos and Tenos. I include these texts here, although they may well be military alliances and not declarations of inviolability.[2]

The texts certainly were inscribed in archival form; but possibly they represent more than one archive, for the reported lettering and stones are diverse (as they are, however, at Cos). There is talk of war and of peace, and reference to Mylasa as "immune from plundering," "at peace," or "inviolable." The Mylasan ambassadors, like those of the second Tean mission, included literary demonstrations of their historical links to Crete. The date, to judge from the script, is the second century B.C.; the historical context is lost to us. Mylasa was attacked by Philip V in 201 and by Rhodes in 167 (Polyb. 16.24.7, 30.5.15). The city honored above all Zeus Osogo.

The stones were found reused in various houses of Milas.

187. Unknown city

Le Bas-Waddington 380 [Blass, *SGDI* 5157; Blümel, *I.Mylasa* 641].

[- - -] ἀλλήλ[οις -]
[- - -]ΘΕΝ παρὰ [-]
[- - - τοῖς κόσμ]οις καὶ τᾶ[ι π]ό[λει·] ἐπειδὴ Μυλασεῖ[ς - - -]
[- - -]ΣΙ ὑπάρχοντες ΦΡΟΝΩΝ ἁμίων τε [- - - - - - - - - - -]
[- - -]ΟΝ Κρηταιέων συνγενεῖς ἀπό τε [- - - - - - - - - - - - -]

1. Ruge, *RE* 16 (1933) 1046–1064.
2. So Holleaux, *Etudes* III 155–156, followed by Ruge 1052.

188. Unknown city

Le Bas-Waddington 381 [Blass, *SGDI* 5158; Guarducci, *I.Cret.* IV 177; Blümel, *I.Mylasa* 642].

[- - -]ΣΕ[- - -]ΤΟΥ ΕΝ[- - -]Α[- - - - - - - - -]
[- - -]ΑΝ οἷοι ἐς Κρήταν [- - -]Δ[- - - - - - - -]
[- - - ?πρότερο]ν καὶ νῦν φίλοι ΚΕΙ[- - - - - - - -]
[- - - Κρηταιέ]ας ἅπαντας ἔπεμ[ψαν - - - - - - - - -]
[- - - Γορτ]υνίος καὶ [Κν]ωσίος [- - - - - - - - - -]
[- - - τῶ]ν ἐλη[λ]υ[θ]ότων [- - - - - - - - - - - - -]
[- - - Γο]ρτυνίων καὶ ΠΟΡΤΑ[- - - - - - - - - - -]
[- - -]Σ καὶ πορτὶ τὰς ἄλ[λας - - - - - - - - - - -]
[- - - μετὰ πάν]σας σπουδᾶς κ[αὶ φιλοτιμίας - - -]
[- - -]ΕΝΟΙ παρεκάλιον ΛΑ[- - - - - - - - - - - -]
[- - -]ΕΣ τῶ πολέμω ΔΥΣ[- - - - - - - - - - - -]
[- - -]Σ ἀγαθὰ [- - -]ΤΟ[- - -]Τ[- - - - - - - -]
[- - -]ΩΣ[- - -]ΟΛΙ[- - -]Ε[- - - - - - - - - - -]
[- - -]ΛΓΛ[- - -]ΣΤΑ[- - -]ΕΙΑ[- - - - - - - -]
[- - -]μεθα Μυλασε[- - - - - - - - - - - - - - - -]
[- - -] ἀποστολαὶ [- - - - - - - - - - - - - - - -]
[- - -]ΝΟ[- - -]ΙΟ[- - -]Λ[- - - - - - - - - - - -]

189. Unknown city

Le Bas-Waddington 382 [Blass, *SGDI* 5159; Blümel, *I.Mylasa* 643].
Cf. Wilhelm, *Kl. Schr.* II.3 479–480 [*SEG* 13.489].

[βοαθῆν Μυλασεῦσι παντ]ὶ σθένει καὶ τὸς ἐν
[τᾶι νάσωι Κρηταιέας] καὶ τὸς ἔξω τᾶς νά-
[σω οἰκίοντας ὡς αὐτᾶς] τᾶς Κρήτας πολεμω-
[μένας? - - - - - - - - - -] ἀδικίωντι Μυλασέας
[- - - - - - - - - - - - - -] τούτοις μὴ ἦμεν ἐπι-
[- - - - - - - - - - - - - - -] τὰ μέγιστα ἀσεβή-
[ματα ? - - - - - - - - -]ẠΙ δαμοσίως καὶ αὐτῶν
[- - - - - - - - - - - - πρε]ιγεύεν δὲ καὶ ποτὶ τὸς
[- - - - - - - - - - - - - -]σσων καὶ τὸς δυνάστας
[- - - - - - - — - - - - - - τὰς] πόλιας, ὅπως ἐν εἰ-
[ρήναι - - - - - - - - - - ἀφορ]ολόγητοι ἔωντι τάν
[τε πόλιν καὶ τὰν χώραν] αὐτῶν ἱαρὰν ἐξ ἀρχᾶς
[- - - - - - - - καὶ ἦμεν π]ρόξενον καὶ εὐεργέταν
[τᾶς πόλιος - - - - - - -]Ν πάντων ἁμῶν μετε-
[- - - - - - - - - - - - - ἀνθρ]ωπίνων ἀρετᾶς ἕνεκα
[καὶ εὐνοίας ποτὶ τὰν πόλι]ν τ[ε καὶ πο]τὶ τὸ Κρη-
[ταιέων - - -]Γ[- - - - - - - - - - - - - - - - - - -]

I follow Blümel's conservative text rather than Wilhelm's complete restoration.

190. Unknown city

Fragment of limestone.
Le Bas-Waddington 383a [Blass, *SGDI* 5160a; Blümel, *I.Mylasa* 644].

[- - -] . . [- - -]Λ[- - - - - - - - - - - - - - - -]
[- - -]ΩΡΙΟ[- - - -]Ι̣ΟΙΣ Μυλασέων ἢ χ[ώρ]αι̣
[- - - - - - - - - - -]Ν βοαθῆν Μυλασεῦσι παντὶ
[σθένει καὶ τὸνς ἐ]ν τᾶι νάσωι Κρηταιέανς καὶ
[τὸνς ἔξω τᾶς νάσω Κρ]ή̣τανς πάντανς τὸνς ϝοικίον-
[τανς - - - - - -]ΤΑΣ, ὡς αὐτᾶς τᾶς Κρήτας πο-
[λεμωμένας - - - - πρ]εσβεύειν δὲ καὶ πορτὶ τὸνς
[- - - - - - - - - - - - -]ΤΩΝ καὶ τὸνς δυνάστανς καὶ
[τὰνς πόλιανς ὅπως εἰρήν]αν τε ἔχωντι καὶ ἀφορολό-
[γητοι ἔωντι τάν τε πόλι]ν καὶ τὰν χώραν [αὐ]τ[ῶν].

191. Unknown city

Column written to the right of **190**.
Le Bas-Waddington 383b [Blass, *SGDI* 5160b; Blümel, *I.Mylasa* 645].

[τάν] τε πόλ[ιν - ἀδι]-
κῶντι ἐξ Α[-]
καὶ αἴ κά τιν[ες - - - - - - - - - - - - - - - - - πράσσων]-
τι πολέμια Τ[-]
Μυλασέων ἢ [χώραι -]
βοαθεῖν Μυλ[ασεῦσι παντὶ σθένει - - - ὡς αὐτᾶς τᾶς]
Κρήτας πολε[μωμένας - - - - - - - - - πρεσβεύειν δὲ]
καὶ πορτὶ τὸν[ς -]
καὶ ΠΡΟ[-]

192. Unknown city

Le Bas-Waddington 384a [Blass, *SGDI* 5161]; Blümel, *I.Mylasa* 646 (copy of Szanto).

[- - -]Σ[- - - - - - - - - - - - - - - -]ΕΣ
[- - -]Ι τε Τ[- - - - - - - - - - - - - - - - - π]ορ-
[τὶ? - - - Κρητ]αιέα[ς - - - - - - -] τῶ πο-
[λέμω? - - -]Ν τῶι [- - - - - - -] ἐπὶ τὰν
[- - -]ΑΣΙΝΕΙ[- - - - - - -]Α̣Ν ποιήσαθ-
[αι - - - Μυλασέ]ων ἰόντων συγγενίων καὶ
[φίλων - - - -]ΩΣ τάν τε πόλιν ἀσφαλίως
[- - - κα]ὶ ἄσυλον ἴατ̣[τα]ν· καὶ εἴ κά τι-
[νες -]

193. Unknown city

Column to the right of **192**.

Le Bas-Waddington 384b [Blümel, *I.Mylasa* 647].

ΙΩ[- - - -]
ΔΑ[- - -]
ΠΕΡ[- - -]
ΣΕΙ[- - -]
ΦΙΛΟ[- - -]
ΤΟΣ[- - -]
ΛΕΙΑ[- - -]
ΣΕΩ[- - -]

194. Unknown city

Cousin and Diehl, *BCH* 12 (1988) 8–11 no. 1; Blümel, *I.Mylasa* 648 (copy of Hula).

[- - - - -]Σ τὰ ἱερ-
[- - - ἔς τ]ε τῶ Διὸς
[- - - - - - - - -]ΙΣ

195. Unknown city

Inscribed below **194**.
Cousin and Diehl, 8–11 no. 1 [Blass, *SGDI* 5162a; Blümel, *I.Mylasa* 649].

[ἔδοξε - - - - - - - - - τοῖς κόσμοις καὶ τᾶι πό]λει· ἐπειδὴ
[Μυλασέεν ὑπάρχοντες συγγενίεν καὶ φίλοι δι]ὰ προγόνων
[τᾶς ἁμᾶς πόλιος πρειγευτὰς ἀπέστειλαν μετὰ] τῶ ψαφίσ-
[ματος - λ]αβόντας
[-]Η καὶ τὰ
[- ἀλ]λάλονς
[- - - - - - - - - - - - - - - - καὶ ἀνανεώσασθαι] τὰν ἐξ ἀρ-
[χᾶς φιλίαν -] ὅπως τὸ
[-]ΡΙΟΝ ἐν
[-]ΩΝ καὶ
[- εὔνο]ιαν τὰν
[-]ΟΝΤΩΝ
[- τῶ ἔθ]νιος
[- ?ὁμ]οίως
[-]ΘΑΘΑΙ

196. Unknown city

Column to the right of **195**.
Cousin and Diehl, 8–11 no. 1 [Blass, *SGDI* 5162b]; Blümel, *I.Mylasa* 650.

ἀγαθᾶι τύχαι· ἔδοξε [- - - - - - - - - - - - τοῖς κόσ]-
μοις καὶ τᾶι πόλι· ἐπε[ιδὴ Μυλασέεν ὑπάρχοντες]
συγγενίεν καὶ φίλοι δ[ιὰ προγόνων τᾶς ἁμᾶς πόλιος]
καὶ τῶν ἄλλων Κρηται[ιέων - - - - - - - - - - - - - -]

ως μόνοι παρὰ τὸς ἄλλ[ος - - - - - - - - - - - - -]
ται περὶ τᾶς κοινᾶς εἰρ[ήνας - - - - - - - - - - -]
τῶ ἔθνιος ἐμπ̣ε̣τόντ[ος - - - - - - - - - - - - - πό]-
λεμος Κρηταιέων πά[ντων - - - - - - - - - - - -]
σον κοινὰν καὶ ἴσαν ε[ὔνοιαν καὶ φιλοστοργίαν]
περὶ παντὸς τῶ κοινῶ [- - - - - - - - - - - - σύ]-
σταμα συνᾶκται Κρητ[αιε - - - - - - - - - Μυλα]-
σέεν ἄξιοί ἐντι μεγαλ̣[- - - - - - - - διαφυλάτ]-
τεν ἐς Κρηταιέας πάν[τας τὰν ὑπάρχονσαν]
εὔνοιάν τε καὶ φιλοστ[οργίαν - - - - - - - -]
ἐπαινῆσθαι τὸμ Μυλασ[έων δᾶμον καὶ στεφα]-
νῶσθαι αὐτὸν μετ' ἀνα[γορεύσιος - - - - - -]
καὶ εὐεργεσίαι θείων [τε καὶ ἀνθρωπίνων πάν]-
των μέτοχον ἀρετᾶ[ς ἕνεκα καὶ εὐνοίας - - -]
τᾶς ἐς Κρηταιέας καὶ [- - - - - - - - - - - - -]
ον ὃ καὶ μὴ Μυλασεῦσι [- - - - - - - - - - - -]

197. Unknown city

Marble fragment.
Doublet and Deschamps, *BCH* 14 (1890) 618–620 no. 17 [Blass, *SGDI* 5163a; Blümel, *I.Mylasa* 651].

[- - - - - - - - - - - - - - -]Ν δια[λ]εγέντας
[- - - - - - - - - - - - ψαφ]ίσματι καὶ ἐπιδαμή-
[σαντας - - - - - -]ΙΝ καὶ ἁμὲν ἁμῶν προ-
[- - - - - - - - - - - - -] Μυλασέων καὶ τὸς
[- - - - - - - - - - αὐτ]οῖς καλοκἀγαθίας ἕνε-
[κεν - - - - - - - - - - ἐ]ς τὸ ξενοτρόφιον καὶ
[- - - - - - - - - - - ἐ]κ τῶ νόμω περὶ δὲ τᾶς
[- - - - - - - - - - -]ΩΝΤΙ Μυλασεῖς τὸ κοι-
[νὸν - - - ἀποκρίνασ]θαι αὐτοῖς ἁμέ, ὅτι ΑΙ-
[- - - - - - - - - - - - -]ΕΝ συμμάχων ἐπὶ τῶι
[- - - -]ΝΤΙ[- - - - -]ΝΕΣ δὲ οὐχ ὑπομε-
[- - - - - - - - - - - - - -]Ε τὰν ἐθνικὰν συνθή-
[καν - - - - - - πόλ]εμον ἦμεν· διὸ καὶ ἁμὲν
[- - - - - - - - - - - -]ΙΣ διατηρῶντες τὰ πα-
[- - - - - - - - - - - - παρα]δεδομένα ἐπιμέλει-
[αν - - - - - - - - - - -] συμφερόντων τᾶι νά-
[σωι - - - - - - - - - - - πε]ρὶ τούτων σαφέως

198. Unknown city

Column to the right of **197**.
Doublet and Deschamps, 618–620 no. 17 [Blass, *SGDI* 5163b; Blümel, *I.Mylasa* 652].

ἀξιολόγωμ πο[ιητ]ᾶν τε [καὶ συγγραφέων? - - -]
καὶ Θαλήτα τῶ Κρητὸς καὶ Ζ[- - - - - - - - - - -]

προξένος καὶ γένος αὐτῶν [- - - - - - - - - - -]
νομιζόμενα ξένια· περὶ δὲ [- - - - - - - - - παρα]-
καλέοντι Μυλασέες, οἱ πρε[ιγευταὶ - - - ἐμφα]-
νιξάτωσαν αὐτοῖς ἃ παρα[- - - - - - - - - - - - -]
γὰρ χαρίξασθαι Μυλασεῦσ[ι - - - - - - - - - - - -]
ας ὑπόμναμα{μα}ὑπάρχηι ποτὶ Μ[υλασέας - - -]
τὸ ψάφισμα τόδε παρὰ μὲν ἁ[μὶν ἐς τῶι ἱαρῶι τῶ]
Ἀπέλλωνος Πυτίο, παρὰ δὲ [Μυλασεῦσι - - - -]
αὐτῶν ἔς τε τῶ Ζανοποτε[ιδᾶνος καὶ τῶ Διὸς]
τῶ Λαβραύνδω· καὶ ἐς τὰ Ε[- - - - - - - - - - -]

2: On the singing of Thaletas' songs (cf. **199**.8) see A. Chaniotis, *ZPE* 71 (1988) 154–156.

199. Unknown city

Fragment of limestone.
Blümel, *I.Mylasa* 653 (copy of Hula).

[- - - - - - - - -]ες τε κρη-
[- - - - - - ?πατρ]ίδα μετὰ
[- - - - - - - - - - -] ἐπὶ τῶι
[- - - - - - - - - - -]ΤΑΣΑΝ
[- - - - - - - - - συ]γγενει-
[- - - - - - - Κρητ]αιέας πίσ-
[τεως - - - - - - - ἀξι]ολόγων
[- - - - - - - - κ]αὶ Θαλήτα
[τῶ Κρητὸς - - - α]ὐτὸς καὶ

200. Unknown city

Fragment of grey marble.
Judeich, *AM* 15 (1890) 262–263 no. 16 [Blass, *SGDI* 5164; Guarducci, *I.Cret.* IV 178; Blümel, *I.Mylasa* 654].

[- - -]ΑΙΑ κọιν[- - -]ΟΕΣ[- - - - - - -]
[- - -] ẹὐνομίας α[ἱ]λιομε[ν - - - - - - -]
[- - -]ΙΩ τὸμ πόλεμον [- - - - - - - - - -]
[- - -]. ΙΣ τῶ βωλομμέ[νω - - - - - - - -]
[- - - κ]ạὶ ἁμὲν καὶ Κνώσιοι [- - - - - -]
[- - - συ]ṇτηρίοντες τὰ νομι[ζόμενα - - -]
[- - - τὰ]ν δ' ἐπιμέλειαν ποι[- - - - - - -]
[- - -]ΟΣ πάνσι Κρηταιεῦσι [- - - - - -]
[- - -]ένων καὶ οὐχ ἐρ[- - - - - - - - - -]
[- - -] ταῖς κοινα[ῖς - - - - - - - - - - - - -]

201. Unknown city

Hula and Szanto, *SBWien* 132 (1895) II 13 no. 4 [Blümel, *I.Mylasa* 655].

ΚΑΙ[- - -]Τ. [- - - - - - - - - - - - - - - - - - - -]
ΝΩΙ τὰν ΔΑ[- -]
στεφάνωι [- -]
άσονς τῶ [- - - - - - - - - - - - - - - - - - - Ἀρισ]-
τέαν Ἰατροχ̣[λεῦς - - - - - - - - - - - - - - - - - -]
ΕΜΕΚΑΚΑΙΕ[- - - - - - - - - - - - - - - - - - -]
καὶ τὰν αὐτω[- - - - - - - - - - - - - - - - - - - -]
ἀνανεώσα[σθαι τὰν ἐξ ἀρχᾶς φιλίαν - - - - - - -]
αν· ἵνα δὲ καὶ [- - - - - - - - - - - - - - - - - - ἐς]
τὸν ἀεὶ χρόν[ον -]
ψάφισμα πὰ[ρ μὲν ἁμὶν ἐς - - - - - - - - - - - - ?ἱ]-
αρῶι, πὰρ δὲ [Μυλασεῦσι - - - - - - - - - - - - - - -]
αὐτῶν ἔς τε [τῶ Ζανοποτειδᾶνος καὶ τῶ Διὸς τῶ]
[Λ]αβραένδο [- -]
[τ]ῶν ἰόντω[ν -]
[- - -]ΑΦΑΝΙΤΤ[- - - - - - - - - - - - - - - - - -]

202. Unknown city

Blümel, *I.Mylasa* 656 (copy of Hula).

[- - -] . . [- - - - - - - - - - - - - - - - - -]
[- - - σ]τεφανο[- - - - - - - - - - - - - - -]
[- - - Ἰά]σ̣ονος τῶ Διοτ[ίμω - - - - - - -]
[- - - Ἰ]ατροκλείους τῶ Οὐλ[ιάδα - - - -]
[- - - ἕν]εκεν καὶ ΣΟΤΑΤ̣Ο̣[- - - - - -]
[- - -]. Σ τε τὰν ἁμὰ[ν - - - - - - - - - -]
[- - -] πατρίδα καὶ εἰσ[- - - - - - - - - -]

203. Unknown city

Fragment of limestone.
Blümel, *I.Mylasa* 657 (copy of Hula).

[- - -]Α Μυλασεῖ[ς - - - - - - - - - - - - - - - - - - -]
ἄριστον ὑπάρχειν δὲ καὶ [- - - - - - - - - - - - - - - - -]
τα φιλάνθρωπα ἃ καὶ το[ῖς ἄλλοις? - - - - - - - - - - -]
εἰθ̣ίσται· ἵνα δὲ καὶ τοῖς Ε̣[- - - - - - - - - - - ἐς τὸν ἀ]-
ε̣ὶ χρόνον τῶν φιλανθρώ[πων - - - - - - - - - - - - - - -]
ΟΛΕΣΕΙΝ ὑπόμνανα ὑ[πάρχηι ποτὶ Μυλασέας - - - τό]-
δε τὸ ψάφισμα παρὰ μὲ[ν ἁμὶν - - - - - - - - - - - - - - -]
χ̣αὶ πρότερον ἀνεγέ̣γ̣ρ[απτο - - - - - - - - - - - - - - - -]

204. Unknown city

Fragment of bluish stone.
Blümel, *I.Mylasa* 658 (copy of Hula).

[- - - τ]ύχαι Μυλα[σε - - - - - - - - - -]
[- - -]Ι εὐνοίαι καὶ φ[ιλοστοργίαι - - -]

[- - -]ΝΣ ὅτι ὅσον. [- - - - - -]
[- - - ἀποστ]αλέντας παρὰ [- - -]
[- - -] καὶ ἁ ὁμόνοια Π̣[- - - -]
[- - -]. τῶ πολέμω Ι[- - - - - -]
[- - -] ταύται κατ̣[- - - - - - - -]

205. Unknown city

Fragment of limestone.
Blümel, *I.Mylasa* 659 (copy of Hula).

[- - -]ΔΑ[- - - - - - - - - - - - -]
[- - -]Σ αὐτο[- - - - - - - - - - -]
[- - - κ]αὶ τὰν πα[τρίδα - - - - -]
[- - -]Ν δ' ἀναγγ[ε- - - - - - - -]
[- - - δᾶμ]ος ὁ Μυλασ[έων - - -]
[- - -]ΩΝ ἀγῶσι Κ[- - - - - - -]
[- - - ἀνα]γόρευσιν Κ[- - - - - -]
[- - -]ξιων Δ̣ιο[- - - - - - - - - -]

206. Lappa

Two fragments of white marble; letters 0.014–.015, intersp. 0.01.
Blümel, *EpigAnat* 19 (1991) 14–15.

[- - - - - - -] . ροντος
[- - - - -] τ̣ε καὶ τῶν
[- - - - - -]τ̣ειρουσα
[- - - ?συγγ]ενέας ἐόν-
[τας - - -] ἐοῦσαν ἀρ-
[- - - - Λ]αππαίων καὶ
[- - -]οσιν καὶ τᾶς οἰ-
[- - -]ομεν διὸ καὶ ὑπε-
[- - -]αν καὶ τᾶς κτη-
[- - - -]ασθαι τε τὸν
[- - - -] . ξον ὑπὸ Λα-

207. Unknown city

Column to the right of **206**.
Blümel, *EpigAnat* 13 (1989) 5–6 (left side), 19 (1991) 12 (left and right).

[- - -]Ν. [-]
ἀφ[ορολόγητοι ἔωντι τάν τε] πόλιν καὶ τὰν̣ [χώραν - - -]
αὐτ̣[ῶν ἱαρὰν ἐξ ἀρχᾶς - - -] οἰκιόντων· ἐπ̣[αινέσαι]
δὲ καὶ τ[ὸνς - - - πρειγευτὰς] Διονύσιον καὶ Ἀ[πολ]-
λώνιον [- - - καλοκἀγαθίας ἕν]εκα καὶ ἐπὶ τῶι δια[- - -]
μεν ὑπε[- - - - - - - - - - - - - - ἀ]ξίως Κρηταιέων καὶ τᾶς
αὐτῶν [πατρίδος· πολλὰ δὲ κ]αὶ ἔνδοξα προφερομέ-
νων κα[τὰ τὰν διὰ προγόνων] ὑπάρχονσαν συγγέ-

νειαν [καὶ εὔνοιαν καὶ φιλία]ν πορτὶ Κρηταιέας
πάντ[ας - - - - - - - - - τ]ὸνς μετὰ πάνσας ἐπι-
μελε[ίας - - - - - - - - -]Σ διαλεγέντας τε Α-

208. Unknown city

Blümel, *EpigAnat* 19 (1991) 13.

[- - -]σε̣ι̣ν̣ κ̣α[-]α
[-]α ὑπαρ-
[χ - ?τέσ]σ̣α̣ρ̣ας
[-]η καὶ
[- ἀφο]ρολόγη-
[τοι ἔωντι τάν τε πόλιν καὶ τὰν χώραν αὐ]τ[ῶ]ν ἱαρὰν
[ἐξ ἀρχᾶς - - - - - - - - - - - - - - - - ἐπ]αινέσαι δὲ καὶ
[τοὺς πρειγευτὰς Διονύσιον καὶ Ἀπολλ]ώνιον καλογκἀ-
[γαθίας ἕνεκα - - - - - - - - - - - - - ?πά]ντας Κρηταιεῖς
[- ?συλ]λύσεων ἀξί-
[ως Κρηταιέων - - - - - καὶ τᾶς αὐτῶν πα]τρίδος πολλὰ
[δὲ καὶ ἔνδοξα προφερομένων κατὰ τὰν δι]ὰ προγόνων ὑ-
[πάρχουσαν συγγένεαν καὶ - - - - - εὔνοια]ν̣ καὶ φιλίαν
[πορτὶ Κρηταιεῖς πάντας - - - - - - ?πολλο]ὺς τρόπους
[-]μ̣ενους
[-]Λ̣Ι

209. Unknown city

Column to the right of **208**.

Blümel, *EpigAnat* 19 (1991) 13–14.

πολε[μ]ω[μ]ε[ν -]
ΑΣΗΤΑ τῷ Μ[υλασέων δάμῳ ? - - - - - - - - - ὡς αὐτᾶς]
τᾶς Κρήτας [πολεμωμένας - - - - - - - - - - - - - - - - - - -]
ρα καὶ δαμο[σίως - πρει]-
γεύεν δὲ κα[ὶ ποτὶ τὸς -]
καὶ τὸς δυν[άστας καὶ - - - - - - - - - καὶ τὰς πόλιας, ὅπως]
ἐν εἰρήναι τ[ηρίωντι καὶ ἀφορολόγητοι ἔωντι τάν τε πόλιν]
καὶ τὰγ χώρ̣α̣[ν αὐτῶν ἱαρὰν ἐξ ἀρχᾶς - - - - - - - - - - - -]
οἰκιόντων [- τὸν]
Μυλασέων δ̣[ᾶμον? - - - - - - - - - - - - - - εὐεργεσίαι θεί]-
ωγ καὶ ἀνθρ[ωπίνων πάντων μέτοχον - - - - - - - - - - - -]
ποτὶ πᾶν τὸ [- - - - - - - - - - - - - - - - - - ἐπαινέσαι δὲ καὶ]
τὸς πρειγε[υτὰν - καλο]-
κἀγαθίας ἕ̣ν̣[εκα -]
Κρηταιέ[α]ς Ι̣[- ἑού]-
σας πίστεος [-]
σθαι αὐτὸς [-]
Υ[- - -]Ω̣[-]

Tralles

Tralles in Caria, "Seleuceia" until the end of Seleucid rule in 188 B.C., was the next city up the Maeander from Magnesia. The great god of the Trallians was Zeus Larasius, whose temple stood in the middle of the city proper, on a plateau looking south across the river.[1] His games, the Dieia, were Panhellenic in the second century B.C.;[2] prominent men held the priesthood (Strab. 14.1.42 [649]). Zeus appears frequently on the coins, often with his epithet (Διὸς Λαρασίου).[3]

The evidence for declared *asylia* is weak. We may begin with a famous inscription, if only to exclude it. A stone said to have been found on the site of Tralles was inscribed in the first century A.D.

Robert, *Coll. Froehner* 96 [Sokolowski, *LSAM* 75; Poljakov, *I.Tralleis* 3].

ἔτεος ||||||, μηνὸς ἐββδόμω,
βασιλέοντος Ἀρταξέσσε-
ω, ἐξσατραπεύοντος Ἰδριέ-
ως· ὅσα ἐψηφίσαντο Τραλ-
δεῖς· ἱκετηρίην εἶναι Διο-
νύσωι Βακχίωι τῶι δημοσί-
ωι· ἱκέτην μὴ ἀδικεῖν.

ὅρος ἱερὸς ἄσυλος Διονύσου
Βάκχου· τὸν ἱκέτην μὴ ἀδικεῖν
μηδὲ ἀδικούμενον περιορᾶν·
εἰ δὲ μή, ἐξώλη εἶναι καὶ αὐτὸ[ν]
καὶ τὸ γένος αὐτοῦ.

1. Ruge, *RE* 6A (1937) 2117–2118; Robert, *Op. min. sel.* II 1186; *Etudes anat.* 406–407; *BCH* 105 (1981) 356 (*DAM* 266).

2. Habicht, *Olympia VII Bericht* 221 [*SEG* 22.350.27]; on the Olympia of imperial date see Robert, *Op. min. sel.* II 1133–1135.

3. F. Imhoof-Blumer, *Lydische Stadtmünzen* (Geneva 1897) 168–180.

The text is conventionally assigned to the mid-fourth century B.C.; it was reinscribed in the first century A.D. To the Senate in A.D. 22, more than one city invoked Persian precedents for the inviolability of a temple. But as Robert saw, this text cannot derive from such an invocation, because no authority but the city stands behind the act. Moreover, a Greek city does not normally declare that one of its temples could receive suppliants—any temple could do that. Perhaps a private cult, of the sort so well known for Dionysus, is here being made public, and its sacral rights are being affirmed by the city for the first time; so for the new cult at Andania the right of refuge was stipulated in order to state its limits (cf. p. 10. The burden of the law, therefore, may be to specify the penalty for violation of a suppliant at a new temple. The inscription seems to combine two texts (1–7, 8–12), which in part repeat each other. This stone apart, the worship of Dionysus has left little trace at Tralles (a statue at *I. Trall.* 5); and there is no implication that this was the chief god—that was Zeus. Finally, it is not certain that the inscription comes originally from Tralles. But whatever its source and burden, the fact that this law was reinscribed in Imperial times might suggest that the city cited it to the Romans, who we know were uneasy about this privilege.

The material more clearly pertinent to declared inviolability at Tralles concerns Zeus, as we would expect. In the third century A.D. Tralles cites among its titles "sacred to Zeus Larasius by decree of the Senate":

> [τῆς] λαμπροτάτη[ς μητρο]πόλεως τῆς [Ἀσίας καὶ] νεωκόρου τῶ[ν Σεβαστῶν] καὶ ἱερᾶς τοῦ [Διὸς τοῦ Λα]ρασίου κ[ατὰ τὰ δόγματα] τῆς ἱερωτά[της συνκλή]του. (*I. Tralles* 81, A.D. 215–217; the same titles fully preserved at 74, but omitting "metropolis of Asia")

One might discount "sacred" in a late list like this,[4] but for the pointed addition "by decree of the Senate"; this suggests a granted title, and of late Republican date if I am right that no such grant occurred after A.D. 22. This honor may have been new under Republican rule but was more likely a Roman confirmation of a Hellenistic privilege. One could only speculate on an occasion.[5] Nothing emerges about Tralles from the evidence on the Carian expedition of Antiochus III in 204–203; the city flourished under the Attalids. It supported Caesar against Pompey; repaired with imperial aid after the earthquake of 26 B.C., it became Caesarea Tralles. Tiberius spoke in favor of the Trallians at a hearing before Augustus; its topic, however, is unknown (Suet. *Tib.* 8).

4. So ἱερὸς δῆμος sometimes on coins of Tralles: e.g., *BMC Lydia* 342 no. 105.

5. F. Piejko, *Chiron* 18 (1988) 55–69, restores in *Royal Corres.* 41 (concerned with tax relief) a confirmation of inviolability of a temple of Apollo at Tralles; he attributes the letter to Eumenes II and the original recognition to Antiochus Soter (281–261). The text he composes is arbitrary and at points impossible; see instead the important comment of Pleket at *SEG* 38.1170.

Stratoniceia

Stratoniceia was one of the great cities of the interior of Caria, "autochthonous and mother-city of Caria."[1] Founded probably in the 270s by Antiochus II through the synoecism of smaller cities, it possessed a large territory. Controlled variously by the Seleucids and Rhodes over the next century, Stratoniceia was liberated from Rhodes with the rest of Caria in 166. The city cultivated the goodwill of Rome: we are not told how the Stratoniceians regarded Aristonicus,[2] but in 81 B.C. their loyalty to Rome was said to be ancestral;[3] unlike many in Asia, they opposed Mithridates in 88 (unsuccessfully) and the Parthians in 40 (successfully), gaining high regard at Rome.[4] After 40 a consul-designate saw to the restoration of their "ancestral freedom and constitution" (ἀποκαθεστακότα . . . τὴν πάτριον ἐλευθερίαν τε καὶ πολιτείαν, *I.Straton.* 509).

Two temples in the territory of Stratoniceia came to be recognized as inviolable, Hecate at Lagina and Zeus at Panamara. Pergamum supplies a parallel for this double achievement, and perhaps Chalcedon. In imperial times the inviolable status of the two was evoked with pride:

> τὴν πόλιν ἄνωθεν τῇ τῶν προεστώτων αὐτῆς μεγίστων θεῶν [προνοίᾳ Διὸς Π]ανημε[ρίου καὶ Ἑ]κάτης ἐκ πολλῶν καὶ μεγάλων καὶ συνεχῶν
> κινδύνων σεσῶσθαι, ὧν καὶ τὰ ἱερὰ ἄσυλα καὶ ἱκετικὰ ἡ ἱερὰ σύνκλητος δόγματι σε[σήμασθαι δι' ἃς ὑπὲρ] τῆς τῶν κυρίων Ῥωμαίων ἀρχῆς
> ἐποιήσαντο προφανεῖς ἐναργείας·

1. Şahin, *I.Straton.* 15.2; parallels at Robert, *Etudes anat.* 304.

2. Robert, *Villes* 261, assigned Aristonicus' last stand to the Stratoniceia in the Caicus Valley.

3. *I.Straton.* 505.3–5 (Sulla): [οὐκ ἀγνοοῦμεν ὑμᾶς] διὰ προ[γ]όνων πάντα τὰ δίκαια [πρὸς τὴν ἡμετέρα]ν ἡγεμ[ον]ίαν πεποιηκότας καὶ ἐν [παντὶ καιρῶι πρὸς] ἡμᾶς πί[σ]τιν εἰλικρινῶς τετηρηκότας.

4. App. *Mith.* 21; Dio 48.26 names Stratoniceia alone as resisting the Parthians, although besieged.

...

> our city has from the start been preserved from many and great and continual dangers by the providence of its very great presiding gods Zeus Panemerios and Hecate, whose temples the sacred Senate by decree designated as inviolable and having the right of asylum because of the manifest miracles they accomplished in behalf of the rule of the great Romans... (*I.Straton.* 1101.2–4, ca. A.D. 200; cf. 512, quoted below)

In A.D. 22 the Stratoniceians appealed to the Senate concerning both temples:

> the Aphrodisians and Stratoniceians offered an edict of Caesar the dictator on account of ancient services to his faction, and a more recent one of the deified Augustus in which they were praised because they bore the Parthian invasion without wavering in their loyalty to the Roman people...[5]

Stratoniceia's extraordinary honor of two inviolable temples seems to have been linked in both cases to the city's loyalty to Rome in the first century B.C.

The Temple of Hecate at Lagina

Strabo knew the temple of Hecate as the most distinguished in the territory of Stratoniceia (ἐπιφανέστατον).[6] Lagina was a fertile plain seven kilometers north of the city; its life was dominated by the temple of Hecate, the inhabitants constituting a deme called the Ἱεροκωμῆται.[7] Eventually legend traced the name Λάγινα to the act of refuge in Hecate's temple by a hare.[8] The walled precinct, some 150 m by 135 m, was large enough to accommodate permanent dwellers, οἱ ἐν τῷ περιπολίῳ (or ἱερῷ) κατοικοῦντες (Laumonier 346). From the temple itself much of the sculptured frieze survives, illustrating elements of Carian legend, including Hecate's defeat of the Giants.[9] This temple dates from the late Hellenistic period, perhaps after the Roman favor of 81 B.C.,[10] and little material evidence from the site is older than about 200 B.C. The cult is first

5. Tac. *Ann.* 3.62.2; cf. p. 585. Augustus' edict does not survive, but he is known to have helped with the reconstruction of the temple of Hecate (*I.Straton.* 511).

6. 14.2.25 (660). The cult is surveyed by A. Laumonier, *Cultes indigènes en Carie* (Paris 1958) 344–425; cf. T. Kraus, *Hekate* (Heidelberg 1960) 24–56.

7. Robert, *Etudes anat.* 555–561; M. Şahin, *The Political and Religious Structure in the Territory of Stratonikeia* (Ankara 1976), with J. and L. Robert, *Bull. épigr.* 1979, 466.

8. Steph. Byz. s.v. Ἑκατήσια, with Laumonier 345.

9. A. Schober, *Der Fries des Hekateions*, IstForsch 2 (Baden 1933); Robert, *Etudes anat.* 552–555; *Etudes de numismatique grecque* (Paris 1938) 101–104.

10. So Robert, *Etudes anat.* 427 n. 2; after 129 B.C. according to Laumonier 357.

mentioned in a text dating under Rhodian rule (197–166 B.C.): a priest of Hecate is restored by the council to the priesthood of Helios and Rhodes.[11]

The inviolability of the temple is unusual in being a new grant under Roman rule. Mithridates, actively opposed by the Stratoniceians (*I.Straton.* 505.80–82), had to take the city by force and imposed on it a substantial tribute. Sulla's victory brought grave hardship upon most of the cities of the province but rewards to the few that had remained loyal to Rome. And it seems clear that Hecate herself had intervened against Mithridates. In the documents of 81 B.C. she is Ἑκάτη Σώτειρα Ἐπιφανής: these epithets are specific and pointed, implying a miraculous appearance in time of danger—as Zeus of Panamara would do a generation later.[12] There followed the recognition, by all the Greeks and by Rome, of her temple as inviolable and her games the Hecatesia as a quadrennial Panhellenic festival. The enlarged games were combined with the Rhomaia, as at Oropus, Xanthus, and elsewhere during this period.[13]

Sulla left Asia in 84; given the fighting in Italy, it was not until March 81 that the Senate, prompted by ambassadors from Stratoniceia, ratified Sulla's benefactions to their city. Stratoniceia is the one sure example of a city *in solo provinciali* seeking *asylia* from the Greek world at large and not just Rome. The new political reality seems reflected, however, in the fact that only Rome's recognition was inscribed on the temple wall, the Greek grantors being reduced to a list.

We have the remains of two letters of Sulla to Stratoniceia, a senatus consultum, and a decree of the city; this complex inscription, because most of it does not concern *asylia*, will not be reproduced here in extenso. Fragments listing the Greek grantors reveal that more than one copy of this list was made.

210. Rome

Fragments of thirteen blocks containing five columns of writing; parts were copied as early as the mid-nineteenth century, and the whole was constituted by Cousin and Diehl in 1885.

Şahin, *I.Stratonikeia* 505 (= Dittenberger, *OGIS* 441; Sherk, *Roman Doc.* 18).

The first letter (lines 1–14), of uncertain date, praises the Stratoniceians for their ancestral loyalty to Rome and now again in the war against Mithridates

11. *I.Straton.* 504. The episode probably reflects the hostility engendered by Rhodian rule and its symbols; compare the Stratoniceian exiles' complaints to the Senate (Polyb. 30.21.3, 30.31), and the known acts of rebellion in Caria and Lycia (Robert, *RN* VI.19 [1977] 32–33 [*Op. min. sel.* VI 194–195]). Possibly an allusion to the cult as early as the fourth century B.C.: Robert, *Etudes anat.* 570.

12. See especially Robert, *Etudes anat.* 521.

13. "Hecatesia" alone in *Syll.*³ 1066, a list of Panhellenic victories (cf. L. and J. Robert, *Claros* I 52 n. 259). See R. Mellor, ΘΕΑ ΡΩΜΗ, Hypomnemata 42 (Göttingen 1975) 176–177, for the omission of the Rhomaia here. A list of priests begins with "the first *pentaeteris* held after the war" (against the Parthians), *I.Straton.* 609.

and mentions a civic embassy. The second (15–17) briefly conveys to Stratoniceia a decree of the Senate. This decree, proposed by Sulla as dictator and dated late in March of 81, describes the Stratoniceian ambassadors, who have brought a crown to the Senate, and their city's steadfast loyalty to Rome (18–48), and grants that the city enjoy the same laws and privileges as in the past and that it possess those places that Sulla added to its territory (49–58); the temple of Hecate is to be inviolable (59–61):

[τό τε ἱερὸν τῆς] Ἑκάτης ἐπιφανεστά[της καὶ μεγίστης θεᾶς, ἐκ πολ]-
[λοῦ τε τι]μώμενον καὶ πολλα[- -]
[τό τε τέμεν]ος ὅπως τοῦτο ἄσυ[λον ὑπάρχηι·]

and the governor is to make good the losses suffered by the city during the war, including the restoration of captives (60–66). After first praising the serviceable actions of the Stratoniceians (67–86), the Senate confirms these things, with rather greater detail on the right of Stratoniceia to tax those places added to its territory (103–109), but briefly on the temple (115):

τὸ [ἱερ]ὸν τῆς Ἑ[κάτης] ὅπως ἦ[ι ἄσυλον·]

The civic decree that follows on the stone provides for drafting and inscribing a list of those who have recognized the inviolability of the temple and the Panhellenic games of Hecate, with allowance for latecomers to be added (*I.Straton.* 507.1–8):

[τῶν πόλεων καὶ βασιλέων καὶ δυνασ]-
τῶν καὶ ἐθνῶν προγράψας πρόγραμμον τόν[δε]·
αἵδε ἀπεδέξαντο τῶν πόλεων καὶ βασιλέω[ν]
καὶ δυναστῶν τήν τε ἀσυλίαν τοῦ ἱεροῦ καὶ τὸ[ν]
ἀγῶνα τὸν τιθέμενον κατὰ πενταετηρίδα
Ἑκάτηι Σωτείραι Ἐπιφανεῖ καὶ Ῥώμηι θεᾶι Εὐερ-
γέτιδι· ὁμοίως δὲ ἀναγραψάτω τὰ ὀνόματ[α]
καὶ τῶν ἀποδεδεγμένων ἐθνῶν· (κτλ.)

Of the list of recognizers (*I.Straton.* 508) three fragments survive, one of which (B) is a second copy inscribed by another hand (cf. *BCH* 9 [1885] 473 n. 1):

A:

[- - -]ς
[Μύ]λασα
[Κ]αῦνος
4 [Β]αργύλια
Ἡράκλεια ἡ ἐπὶ
τῶι Λάτμωι
Ἄλινδα
8 Ἀμυζών
Εὔρωμος
Ὑδισός
Κῶς
12 Στρατονίκεια
ἡ ἐν Μακεδονίαι
- - -
- - -
16 [Μίλη?]τος
Ἰασός
Ἔφεσος
Μαγνησία
20 Τράλλεις
Ἄβυδος
Δάρδανον

Ἀλεξάνδρεια
Τρωιάς
Δελφοί
Ναύπακτος
Ἦλις
Ἡραία
Μεγάλη πόλις
Λακεδαίμων
Ἄργος
Ἀθῆναι
Μέγαρα
Σύρος
Αἴγινα
Ἄβδηρα
Τένεδος
[- - -]εια
ἡ ἐν Μακεδονίαι
Ἀντιγόνεια ἡ ἐν
Μακεδονίαι
Ἀνθηδὼν
τῆς Βοιωτίας
Θῆβαι
Κορώνεια
[- - -]
Λά[ρισα]
Ὠρω[πός]
Νῦσα
Ἀφροδεῖ[ται]
Τεγέαι
Πάτραι
Φλεοῦς
Δύμη
Σικυών
Ἀντιγονίη
Αἴγιον
Αἴγιρα

B:
[.]σ̣ι̣ω̣αι
Λάρισα
Ὠρωπός
Νῦσα
Ἀφροδεῖται
Τεγέαι

C:
Ἀπάμεια ἡ πρ[ὸς]
[τῶι] Μαιάνδρωι
Πάταρα
Ξάνθος
Πίναρα
Τλώς
Λίμυρα
[Μ]ύρα
Ἀλάβανδα
Δημητριάς
Σελεύκια [ἡ π]ρὸς
τῶι Ἰσσικῶ[ι κ]όλπωι
Κελένδερι[ς]

There is some geographical grouping; as Robert observed, simple proximity can account for the early appearance of cities in Caria.[14] If the Stratoniceians began their Panhellenic quest at once upon Sulla's declaration (around 84), such a list might have been drawn up as part of their argument before the Roman Senate in 81, as precedent and as proof of their worth.[15]

Finally, some inscriptions derive from the aftermath of the Parthian attack of 40 B.C. In one (*I.Straton.* 512), because of their piety the people have been repeatedly saved from dangers and have become free and autonomous (ἐλεύθερος καὶ αὐτόνομος ἐγένετο)[16] and possessed of the greatest good things, for Hecate has stood by them in all these dangers (τῆς Ἑκάτης ἐν πᾶσι τούτοις συν-

14. *BCH* 108 (1984) 526 n. 159 (*DAM* 514).
15. A similar list of cities, whose object is lost, has been found on Andros (p. 589).
16. In imperial times an embassy to Rome obtained the restoration of the city's freedom, ἐπιτυχὼν [τὴν] ἐλευθερίαν (*I.Straton.* 220a).

παρισταμένης); there is reference to "those who committed impiety against our land (?) which is sacred and inviolable," τοὺς ἀ]σεβήσαντα[ς εἰς τὴν | ?χώρα]ν ἡμ[ῶν οὖσ]ạν ἱερ[ὰν κ]αὶ ἄσυλον;[17] the miraculous power of the goddess (τὴν τῆς θεᾶς ἐνάργειαν) is clear to all men. In another (511), damage to the temple (τῆς θεᾶς Ἑκάτης ἀσεβηθείσης) was made good by Augustus. And there was now a restoration of land sacred to Hecate (510).

The Temple of Zeus at Panamara

The temple of Zeus at Panamara was discovered in 1886 on a hilltop by modern Bağyaka, twelve kilometers southeast of the city proper.[18] A complex site with attendant shrines (of Hera, Artemis, and others), it has a situation typical of the mountain temples of Zeus in Caria. With its substantial walls, the sacred place was a virtual fortress; it had a special *epistates* under both Philip V and the Rhodians.[19] The god was called both Zeus Karios and Zeus Panamarios (with variant spellings).[20] No inscription seems earlier than the late third century B.C. In the earliest we hear of a biennial festival of Hera (*I.Straton.* 1); the annual Panamareia of Zeus and the Mysteries are first attested only under the Empire. Philip V visited the temple himself in 201 and made a dedication (*I.Straton.* 3). In Roman times it was said that "Zeus of Panamara, greatest and most manifest, protects the city always, and the most pious and patriotic men wish to serve as his priests."[21] Foreign cities were by then invited to attend the Mysteries of Zeus, and some of these invitations survive.[22]

The date of the inviolability of the temple is unclear. The likely occasion is the aftermath of the Parthian invasion in 40 B.C.; but several texts that seem earlier refer to the "asylum."

A. Decree of Stratoniceia?

Complete at left; "petites lettres de bonne époque" (Cousin).

17. Compare *I.Priene* 17.17: εἰς τὸ θεῖον ἀσẹβοῦντας (the Gauls).

18. For a general survey see Laumonier 221–343.

19. *I.Straton.* 4 and 9 (called a χωρίον here and in 10). Compare the situation at Amyzon with its royal *epistates* (*Amyzon* no. 15.7).

20. Laumonier 241; "Zeus Panamarios" is attested also at neighboring Hyllarima already in the second century B.C.; cf. Robert, *Etudes anat.* 513–515.

21. *I.Straton.* 15.3–4: ὁ μέγιστος καὶ ἐπιφανέστατος Ζεὺς Πανάμαρος σώζει τὴν πό[λιν διὰ πάντος χρόνου, θέ]λουσι δὲ καὶ οἱ εὐσαβέστατοι καὶ φιλοπάτριδες ἄνδρες [ἱ]ερᾶσθαι αὐτοῦ.

22. *I. Straton.* 22–39; cf. L. and J. Robert, *Claros* I pp. 53–55.

J. Hatzfeld, *BCH* 51 (1927) 58 no. 1 (copy of Cousin) [*SEG* 4.243; Şahin, *I.Straton.* 19].

[- - -]τουμ[- -]
[- - -]ουνουμ[- -]
[- - -] Ἀριστολαο[- -]
[- - -] Λέανδρον ε[- -]
καὶ ὁ δῆμος ὁ Σ[τρατονικέων - - - - - - - - - - τὸ ἱερὸν τὸ ἐν]
Παναμάροις ὑπ[- -]
εἶναι δεῖ τὸ ἄσυ[λον? - στήλην]
τε ἀνατεθῆναι ἐν [τῶι ἱερῶι τοῦ Διὸς ἐν τῶι ἐπιφανεστά]-
τωι τόπωι, ἐφ' ἧς κα[ὶ ἀναγραφήσεται τὸ ἀντίγραφον τοῦδε]
τοῦ ψηφίσματος κ[αὶ - ὁ ἱε]-
ρεὺς στοιχῶν ἐν τ[- τὴν στή]-
λην ἀναστήσειν κα[ὶ -]
[- - - ταῖς ἰδί]αις δαπά[ναις -]

4: or Κ]λέανδρον (*SEG*). 8: Διὸς τοῦ Καρίου Hatzfeld. 9 ἀναγρ. Wilhelm (*SEG*). 11: τ[ούτοις τῆι ἑαυτοῦ εὐνοίαι ἐπηγγείλατο τὴν στή]λην Hatzfeld. 12: κα[ὶ τὴν ἀναγραφὴν τοῦ ψηφίσματος ποιήσειν Ziebarth (*SEG*). 13 init. Hiller (*SEG*): καὶ τ]αῖς δαπά[ναις προνοήσειν αὐτόν Hatzfeld.

The date is uncertain ("s. III[a]?" *SEG*). The elaborate provisions for inscribing show that this is not a foreign recognition of *asylia* but a decree of Stratoniceia or the deme Panamara. The act may have nothing to do with inviolability; at any rate it would be subsequent to recognition of the status. Line 7 as restored, "the asylum must be . . .," is an odd sentiment and odd word order. The noun *asylon* is found only rarely outside of Egypt (cf. p. 32).

11: Compare ἐστοιχηκότας τῆι πρὸς ἑατὸν εὐνοίᾳ in a decree of Odessus (*BCH* 55 [1931] 44 lines 23–24 [I B.C.]).

B. Decree of Stratoniceia?

Complete at right; h. 0.23, w. 0.21, th. 0.065; "petites lettres, graveure soigneuse" (Cousin): 0.01, small apices, A with crossbars both straight and broken, Π with right hasta fully descended, Θ and Ω full-sized.

Hatzfeld 58–59 no. 2 (squeeze and copy by Cousin) [*SEG* 4.244; Şahin, *I.Straton.* 20].

Cf. Robert, *Etudes anat.* 520 n. 3.

[- - - - - - - - - - - - - - - - - -] εσει κ[- - -]
[- - - - - - - - - - - - - - - - - -] τοῦ Διὸς τοῦ
[Καρίου - - - - - - - - - - - - τὰς ἐν]αργεῖς ἐπι-
[φανείας - - - - - - - - - - - - -]ι τῆς κατὰ τὴν
[- - - - - - - - - - - - τῆ]ς πρὸς τὸν θεὸν εὐσε-
[βείας - - - - - - - - - -] πρὸς τιμὴν καὶ σεβασ-
[μὸν τοῦ θεοῦ - - - - τοῦ] ἀρχαιοτάτου καὶ ὑπο
[- - - - - - - - - - - - - -]οῦ καὶ ἀσύλου καὶ ἀτε-

[λοῦς - - - - - - - - - - - -] τῶν ὑπ' αὐτῶν ἀνηγο-
[ρευμένων - - - - - - - - -]οσιωθέντων καὶ ὄντων
[- - - - - - - - - - - - - - -]ιων ἐν τῶι περισταθέν-
[τι καιρῶι - - - - - - · τῶ]ν δὲ ἀντιγράφων αὐτ[οῦ]
[- - - - - - - - - - - - π]αρὰ Δίωνι νεωκόρω[ι - - -]
[- - - - - - - - - - - - - - -]ν ἀναγραφῆναι τ[όδε τὸ]
[ψήφισμα - - - - - - ἐν] τῶι ἱερῶι τοῦ Διὸς το[ῦ Κα]-
[ρίου - - - - - - - - - - - - τοῦ πρυ]τ̣άνεω[ς - - - - - -]
[-]π̣α̣ρ̣[- - -]

7–8: - - - ἱερ]οῦ Hatzfeld; τοῦ θεοῦ καὶ τοῦ ἐν Παναμάροις] α. κ. ὑπὸ [πάντων ἀνθρώπων τετιμημέν]ου? Hoeg (*SEG*). 12 Şahin: κινδύνωι Hiller. 13: [τὸ μὲν ἀνατεθῆναι ἐν τῶι ἱερῶι Hatzfeld. 14: εἰς δὲ στήλην λιθίνη]ν Hatzfeld. 15: [ψ. ἐν στήλαις λιθίναις δυσίν, ὧν καὶ ἀνατεθῆναι μίαν ἐν] Şahin. 16: ΓΑΝΕΩ Hatzfeld; πρυ]τανε(ί)ω[ι Hiller; [- - - τὴν δὲ ἑτέραν ἐν - - τοῦ πρυ]τ̣άνεω[ς Şahin.

The date is again uncertain: "époque macédonienne" (Hatzfeld), "s. II^{a}?" (*SEG*). Here too the provisions for inscribing exclude a foreign recognition. There is talk of miracles, of someone's piety toward the god, of the most ancient and inviolable and tax-exempt temple, and of a proclamation, with little space remaining for the substance of the decree. Perhaps therefore the city merely approves and inscribes something that has been proclaimed by delegates from the deme of Panamara, for that important deme is found once addressing itself to the city by means of a decree and a delegation (*I.Straton.* 7, below). Inviolability seems already to be a fact; the praise of the temple, which has the ring of Roman imperial date, will have been background to some addition or restoration of honors of the god.

C. Decree of Stratoniceia

At some date one Leon, a former priest of Zeus,[23] persuaded the city to enlarge the festival of Zeus and seek the participation of some foreign cities (τινας δήμους). He showed the people a decree of Panamara and quoted from old books to illustrate the previous honors and inviolabilities enjoyed by Zeus and the Panamarans (*I.Straton.* 7.3–6):

[- - - - - ψή]φισμα ἀποδοὺς καὶ παραθεὶς ἔκ τε [τ]ῶ[ν]
[ἱστοριῶ]ν καὶ τῶν ἀρχαίων γραμμάτων καὶ συστησά[με]-
[νος τὰς ἄν]ωθεν τιμὰς καὶ ἀσυλίας ὑπαρχούσας τῶι Δ̣ι̣ὶ̣
καὶ Παναμαρεῦσιν

23. Nilsson, *GGA* II 2 54 n. 2, thought of the historian Leon (*FGrHist* 278), of Hellenistic or Roman date; but he reportedly came from Alabanda, whereas this man seems to be Stratoniceian, the local priest.

The date is once more uncertain (second century B.C., Laumonier 237). The association of enlarged games and inviolability is familiar, here sequential as at Miletus. The plural ἀσυλίαι apparently is occasioned by the two possessors indicated, the place and the people.

During the Parthian invasion Stratoniceia stood by Rome, and Zeus intervened to protect Panamara and drive off the enemy; a famous inscription describes the miracle.[24] In 39 B.C. the Romans rewarded the city by confirming earlier privileges.[25] The substance of one fragment of the s.c. is almost entirely lost (*I.Straton.* 11 = *Roman Doc.* 27). But an s.c. on another stone, whether a part of the same act or of a subsequent one, included a provision for the temple of Zeus.

211. Rome

Two fragments of a white marble stele at Panamara, preserved at left; h. 0.32, w. 0.55, th. 0.095; lettering badly worn.

Hatzfeld, *BCH* 51 (1927) 59–61 no. 3 (squeeze and copy by Cousin) [*SEG* 4.246; Sherk, *Roman Doc.* 30; Şahin, *I.Straton.* 12].

ΑΤΑ[- συνε]-
χώ̣ρησαν τῆς πόλεω[ς αἰτούσης? - - - - - - - - - - - -]
τὰς δὲ ετο . υι . ε[-]
τῇ ἀρχαίᾳ τῆς ψυχῆς [εὐνοίᾳ ἐξοχωτάτῃ τε πίστει τοῖς]
δημοσίο̣ις πράγμασιν το[ῖς ἡμετέροις - - - βοηθή]-
σαντες χωρὶς πάση̣[ς] κα[κίας πρὸς τοὺς Πάρθους]
παρετάξαντο· τούτου δ[ὲ - - - - - - - - - - - - - - - - - -]
ἐξέβαλεν, ἐν ᾧ πολέμῳ τά τ[ε] μέ[γιστά εἰσι κεκινδυνευ]-
κότες· διὰ ταύτας τὰς αἰτίας δισσὰς [- - - δεδόχ]-
θαι, ἅτινα ἔπ[α]θλα ἅτινα [φι]λάνθρωπα [πρότερον τῷ]
δήμῳ Στρατονικέων δεδομένα προσμ[εμερισμέ]-
να τέ ἐστιν, ταῦτα πάντα δικαίως ἀξίως τ[ε αὐ]-
τοῖς δεδομένα προσμεμερισμένα [τε εἶναι καὶ]
πάντα κύρια ἔχειν· ὁμο[ίως] δὲ ᾧ καὶ ο[- - -]
[ἐξοχ]ωτάτης πίστεως α[ὐτῶν· τὸ δὲ] ἱε[ρὸν τοῦ Διὸς]
[τοῦ ἐν Παναμ]άροις κύκ[λῳ τε τοῦ ἱεροῦ? εἴτε τέμενος]
[εἴτε ἄλσος ἐστίν, ἄσυλον εἶναι - - - - - - - - -]

1–2 Ziebarth (*SEG*): 2 ΧΟΡΗ Cousin and squeeze. 3 init. squeeze: ΑΤΑΣ Cousin. 4–6 Şahin: 5 ΣΙΑΣ Cousin, ΣΙΑ Σ squeeze. 7: δ[ὲ γενομένου Crönert (*SEG*). 8–9 Hiller (*SEG*). 10–13 Hatzfeld. 14 Şahin, and suggesting ⟨δ⟩[ικαίῳ τῆς]. 15–16 Hatzfeld. 16–17 εἴτε (κτλ.) Şahin.

As restored at 15–17 (inspired by the s.c. for Aphrodisias, **212**), this could be either initial recognition of inviolability or confirmation of a traditional right. If

24. P. Roussel, *BCH* 55 (1931) 70–116 [*I.Straton.* 10]; on the episode see, for example, Pritchett, *Greek State at War* III (Berkeley 1979) 6–7.

25. See also above for *I.Straton.* 511 and 512 from Lagina.

it is the initial grant, then the three decrees cited above ought to be subsequent to 39 B.C., which seems difficult but possible. But the s.c. might rather be enlarging the perimeter of an existing right of asylum, as at Ephesus and Miletus and Oropus: for example (15), τοῦ δὲ] ἱε[ροῦ τοῦ Διὸς τοῦ ἐν Παναμ]άροις κύκ[λῳ εἰς τὸ πάντη μέχρι (number), ἐκεῖνος ὁ τόπος ἄσυλος ἔστω]. Some statement of distance is needed,[26] whether at 16 end or in what follows.

Fragments of a list of ethnics survive at Panamara, inscribed in monumental letters 2 cm high (*I.Straton.* 21):

(traces)

Μειλήσιοι
[Ἀπολλωνι]ᾶται Ἀφροδει[σιεῖς] Ταβηνοί Ἡρακλε[ῶται Ὑλλαριμε]ῖς Βαργασην[οί]

The date is again unknown. These cities may be the recognizers of the inviolability of the temple of Zeus or of the enlarged games later.

So the question remains, When did the *asylia* of Zeus first originate? The silence of Tacitus about acts before the Roman grant of 39 B.C. is uncompelling. Perhaps more significant is the silence of Sulla about Zeus in his long statement in favor of Stratoniceia; he recognizes the inviolability of Hecate but also addresses generally the good services of the city. Hecate, however, had intervened against Mithridates and was gaining a new honor in 81; if the *asylia* of Zeus was at that time traditional, the citizens might not have needed to raise the matter of the honors of Zeus. Still, we might expect Sulla to cite Zeus of Panamara as precedent for Hecate if his temple was already inviolable. Efficiency of information, moreover, would suggest that Zeus became inviolable after his epiphany against the Parthians in 40 B.C., as had Hecate in the 80s. Finally, there is the matter of priority: the cult of Zeus flourished more in imperial times; for Strabo, Hecate was the great divinity of the territory of Stratoniceia—he does not mention Zeus of Panamara. Perhaps then Hecate is more likely to have been the first honored with inviolability, and Zeus only in 39 B.C.

The consequence, however, is that the civic inscriptions cited above should be of imperial date. If by contrast these have been rightly assigned to the Hellenistic period, then we probably should place the original grant to Zeus of Panamara amid the competition for control of Caria between the end of the third century B.C. and the beginning of the Roman province in 129. I believe the first option to be more probable, with Hecate in 81 and Zeus in 39, and the inscribed allusions to his asylum later.

26. So Herrmann, *Chiron* 19 (1989) 144 n. 41.

Temple of Aphrodite, Aphrodisias

Aphrodisias in eastern Caria naturally gave first honor to Aphrodite; a Roman governor once promised to visit the city and sacrifice to their πάτριος θεά.[1] Her cult statue was of a hieratic manner similar to that of Ephesian Artemis. The temple was in the city proper, north of the agora; the extant building, repeatedly adorned in imperial times, seems to date from the first century B.C. It was the temple, not the city and country, that obtained *asylia*; this would be consistent with a grant originating under Roman rule and Roman thinking—an earlier recognition we might expect to be of the whole city and territory.

Of the Hellenistic history of the sacred place little is known. The city is first attested only in the second century B.C., then standing in sympolity with Plarasa. The cult is mentioned first in the time of Sulla: warned in a dream by a military Aphrodite, he sent an axe and crown to be dedicated here, for he had an oracle identifying a "great city of the Carians named for Aphrodite."[2] Caesar dedicated an Eros in the temple, which was stolen later when the Parthians plundered the city in 40 B.C. (Reynolds no. 12.13–15). Games of Aphrodite are attested only in imperial times, when the wealth of the goddess is well documented (Laumonier 483–485).

Aphrodisias is probably to be counted among the few instances of *asylia* that began under Roman rule; the near analogy is Stratoniceia. A recognition of the inviolability of the temple of Aphrodite came from Caesar, whose act

1. Joyce Reynolds, *Aphrodisias and Rome* (London 1982) no. 48.13–14; cf. *MAMA* VIII 413a: τὴν [προεσ]τῶσαν τῆς πόλε[ως ἡμ]ῶν ἐπιφανεστά[την θ]εὰν Ἀφροδίτην; 424.8: τὴν ἐπώνυμον τῆς πόλεως θεόν; *I.Didyma* 92: τὴν πατρίαν θεόν. See generally Laumonier, *Cultes* 478–504; on the temple, J. de La Genière and D. Theodorescu in *Aphrodisias Papers* I (Ann Arbor 1990) 49–74; on the cult statue, Robert, *JSav* 1971, 93 (*Op. min. sel.* VII 171); for Aphrodite on the coins, D. J. MacDonald, *Aphrodisias Papers* II (1991) 173.

2. App. *BCiv.* 1.97; bibliography at Reynolds p. 3. For the axe in Carian cults see Laumonier 85–95.

was confirmed by the Senate in 39 B.C. In A.D. 22, according to Tacitus, the Aphrodisians were able to show the Senate an edict of Caesar that spoke of their loyalty to Rome (probably in the time of Aristonicus or of Mithridates), and one of Augustus praising them for resisting the Parthians. He mentions nothing older, but his silences are not to be trusted. The relatively late development of Aphrodisias might suggest that *asylia* is unlikely before the second century B.C. or indeed before Roman rule; and the great favor that the city enjoyed at Rome also points to a Roman origin of the grant. But if this is so, in contrast to Stratoniceia, no reference survives to a Panhellenic recognition.

Neither of the edicts mentioned by Tacitus survives,[3] but rather the senatorial confirmation of 39 B.C., inscribed on the theater wall. Because this complex text concerns *asylia* only in brief, it is reproduced here only in the relevant sections.[4]

212. Rome

Reynolds, *Aphrodisias and Rome* nos. 6–8.

In 39 Octavian as triumvir wrote to the city in response to their ambassador, sending them copies of an edict from him and Antony and a senatus consultum (ἐπικρίματος καὶ δόγματος καὶ ὁρκίου καὶ νόμου, 6.26–30). Fragments of the edict and of the s.c. survive. The Senate confirms privileges and immunities granted by Caesar to Aphrodisias-Plarasa: the city is a friend and ally of Rome, immune from taxes and requisitions (8.60: πάντων πραγμάτων ἐ[λ]εύθεροι ἀτελεῖς τε καὶ ἀδημοσιώνητοι); this last shows that encroachment by publicans on inviolable land occasioned the Aphrodisian petition, as at Oropus. Of inviolability the Senate declares (38–42):

> [- - - ἥν τε ἀσυλίαν? - - -άτ]ω̣ρ τῇ παρ' αὐτοῖς οὔσῃ συνε̣[χώρησεν], τ̣α̣ύ̣τ̣η̣ν̣ δ̣[ικαίως]
> [συνκεχωρῆσθαι? - - - καὶ κατὰ? τὴν το]ῦ δήμου τοῦ Ῥωμαίων εὐσέβειαν τῇ σ[υνκλήτ]ῳ φαίνεσθα̣ι̣ [εἶναι?]
> 40 [- - - ἀρ]έσκειν τε ἐκεῖνο τὸ ἱερὸν ἄσυλον καὶ τῷ αὐτῷ δ̣[ι]κ̣αίῳ εἶναι ᾧ δ̣ικαίῳ
> [τὸ ἱερὸν Ἀρτέμιδος Ἐφεσίας ἐν Ἐφέσῳ ἐστί]ν̣ τά τε λοιπὰ ὅσα θεὸς Ἰούλιος περὶ ἐκείνων τῶν πραγμάτων διετάξατο
> [πάντα κύρια διαμένειν? - - -]

The scope of the grant is then specified (55–58):

> ὃ ἱερὸν εἴτε κ[αὶ] τέμενος θεᾶς Ἀφροδείτης ἐν πόλει Πλαρασέων καὶ Ἀφροδεισιέω[ν] ἐστίν, ἐκεῖνο τὸ ἱερόν, ἐκεῖνο τὸ τέμε-
> 56 νος ἄσυλον [ἔ]στω τούτῳ τῷ δικαίῳ ταύτῃ τε δεισιδαιμονίᾳ ᾧ δικαίῳ καὶ ᾗ δεισιδαιμονίᾳ τὸ ἱερὸν εἴτε καὶ τέμενος Ἀρ-

3. See Reynolds p. 80, and p. 585 below.

4. The added fragments and Reynolds's magisterial edition make it superfluous to give here a lemma with earlier publications (which include *OGIS* 453–455 and *Roman Documents* 28).

τέμιδος ᾿Ε[φε]σίας ἐστὶν ἐν ᾿Εφέσῳ, κύκλῳ τε ἐκείνου τοῦ ἱεροῦ, εἴτε τέμενός ἐστιν, εἰς τὸ πάντη μέχρι ποδῶν ἑκατὸν εἴκο-
σι, ἐκεῖνος ὁ τόπος ἄσυλος ἔστω·

. . .

The temple/precinct of the goddess Aphrodite that exists in the city of Plarasa-Aphrodisias, that temple/precinct is to be inviolable with the same law and religion as is the temple/precinct of Artemis Ephesia in Ephesus; and in a circle from that temple/precinct in all directions for 120 feet, that area is to be inviolable.

Strictly speaking, this does not make clear whether the privilege is a new creation, a confirmation of an old one, or an expansion of the boundaries of an old one. The analogy and precedent offered for the right of asylum is the case of Artemis of Ephesus, in the capital city of the province, which Caesar himself had probably restored as inviolable.

This is the only inscribed grant outside of Egypt that specifies the dimensions of the asylum; perhaps this too should be taken as evidence for the Roman origin of the privilege. The size stipulated is small compared with the mile or more at Ephesus, Oropus, or Didyma in the first century B.C. The site itself suggests that an inviolable perimeter of 120 feet from the building will have extended to no significant building in the vicinity. The temple had of course a peribolos wall; to the west of the building lie traces of wall about 120 feet distant, to the east perhaps nearer.[5]

Two boundary stones of the temple precinct survive from the Augustan period, unfortunately neither found in situ; Robert recognized the character of the text. I give the better preserved (A), underlining what survives only in the other.

213. Temple of Aphrodite: boundary

A: Block copied in 1893 by Kubitschek; h. 0.6, w. 0.62, th. 0.32; letters 0.025.

J. M. R. Cormack, *BSA* 59 (1964) 22 no. 16 [Robert, *AntCl* 35 (1966) 401–413 (*Op. min. sel.* VI 25–37)].

B: Marble block now in the Aphrodisias Museum; h. 0.36, w. 24, th. 0.34; letters 0.02.

Reynolds no. 35.

Photograph: Reynolds 24.2.

Cf. Herrmann, *Chiron* 19 (1989) 137 n. 15, 154 n. 75.

[? Ἀφροδίτης̣ ἱερὸς ἄσυ]-
[λος ὡς ἔκριναν ὁ μέγας]
[Καῖσαρ? ὁ δικτ̣άτωρ καὶ ὁ υἱὸς]
4 [αὐτοῦ? Αὐτοκράτωρ Καῖσαρ]

5. See Reynolds p. 84; more recent excavation has shown that the precinct was more symmetrical; cf. de la Genière and Theodorescu.

καὶ [ἡ σ]ύ̣ν̣κ̣λητ[ο]ς καὶ ὁ δ[ῆμος]
ὁ Ῥωμαίω[ν] καθὼς καὶ τὰ φιλάν̣-
θρ[ω]πα [καὶ] δ̣[ε]λτογραφήματα
κ[αὶ] ἐ̣πικ[ρίμ]ατα περιέχει, ἀνέσ-
τησεν δὲ τ[οὺ]ς [ὅρου]ς Γάϊος
[Ἰο]ύλ[ιο]ς [Ζ]ώ̣[ιλ]ος ὁ ἱερεὺς τῆς Ἀ-
φροδίτης.

1 Ἀ. Herrmann: ?οὗτος ὁ τόπος Reynolds.

The famous Zoilus was priest of Aphrodite for life (Reynolds no. 30); but his fixing of the sacred boundaries probably followed soon upon the stipulation in the s.c. of 39 B.C. He also sponsored some construction or repair of the temple itself (no. 37).

As at some other places where the temple alone and not the city enjoyed the title, we find the adjective applied to the goddess herself: in the third century A.D. a statue is to be placed in the temple παρὰ τῇ ἀσύλῳ θεῷ.[6] Robert has suggested that another inscription may relate to the right of inviolability, as it seems to forbid binding in chains within some perimeter: κωλύει ὁ τόπος τοῦ σιδήρου τὴν δέσιν ΕΠΙ.[7] Finally, we have from the third century A.D. the base of a statue of the Demos that gives the titles of Aphrodisias:[8]

τ̣ὸ̣ν̣ [. . . . .]τ̣ατον δ[ῆμον]
σύμμαχον Ῥωμαίων
τῆς λαμπροτάτης φ[ι]-
λοσεβάστου ἐλευθ[έ]-
ρας καὶ αὐτονόμου κ̣[α]-
τὰ τὰ δόγματα τῆς ἱ[ε]-
ρωτάτης συνκλήτο[υ]
καὶ τὰ ὅρκια καὶ τὰς θε[ί]-
ας ἀντιγραφὰς Ἀφροδ[ι]-
σιέων πόλεως
ἀσύλου
κ̣αθιέρωσεν
(κτλ.)

This would be straightforward, but line 11, with the word crucial to us, has been written somewhat smaller; the mason has been taken to have added this as an

6. Robert, *Etudes anat.* 299 n. 2.

7. *MAMA* VIII 430, with Robert, *Hellenica* XIII (1965) 172. But the exclusion of iron from temples is a well-attested item of ritual purity (cf. Sokolowski, *LSCG* Suppl. p. 115), and no more than that may be involved here.

8. Reynolds no. 43. Several other texts state the titles of Aphrodisias, but none mentions *asylia* (nos. 9, 42); the fragmentary no. 49 shows the city defending its traditional privileges before an emperor: [- - - τὰ δεδομένα φιλάνθρω]πα ὑπό τε αὐτοκρατόρ[ω]ν κ̣α̣ὶ συ̣ν̣κ̣λ̣ήτου δ̣[ή]μ[ου Ῥωμαίων - - -].

afterthought. The resulting word order is indeed strained, but the published photograph shows that the writing is only slightly smaller and has not been fitted in between existing lines; it cannot be a later addition. Applying the word to the *polis* is an apparent contradiction of the fact that it was the temple that enjoyed *asylia*. But this is paralleled in the civic titles seen on coins of imperial date (see p. 36).

Sardes

Sardes, the seat of Lydian kings and Persian and Seleucid governors,[1] was the city of Artemis. Already under the Achaemenids, there was a special link with Artemis of Ephesus.[2] Her temple was at the western foot of the acropolis, facing across the Pactolus River. In Roman times, at least, the temple was not within the city walls. This was the great monument of Hellenistic Sardes.[3] Built between 270 and 220, the temple escaped major damage in the decisive event in the history of Hellenistic Sardes, the siege of 215–213. The goddess possessed substantial lands and other wealth (*I.Sardis* 1); a text of 1 B.C. mentions "those who reside in the temple of Zeus Polieus and Artemis" (8.134); her priestess was prominent in the life of the city (50–54, statue bases). Under the Attalids we find a supervisor of the temple appointed by the crown (*I.Sardis* 4).

Achaeus' capital was plundered and burned by Antiochus III, who then undertook to repopulate and rebuild the city.[4] Around this time the structure of the temple was substantially altered, when a second cella was added to accommodate the cult of Zeus. It may be to Antiochus' program of reconstruction that we should attribute the original recognition of *asylia*, as at Amyzon a decade later. But in the several inscriptions that survive from this program there is no mention of inviolability. No Greek grant survives, in fact; we have rather an act of Caesar, dated eleven days before his murder, and the brief mention in Tacitus.

The coins and inscriptions of imperial date reveal various other titles, but not explicitly *asylia*: "metropolis of Asia, Lydia, and Greece" (through Pelops);

1. G. M. A. Hanfmann and J. C. Waldbaum, *A Survey of Sardis* (Cambridge, Mass. 1975); *Sardis from Prehistoric to Roman Times* (Cambridge, Mass., 1983).

2. *I.Ephesos* 2; Ar. *Nub.* 598–600; Autocrates frag. 1; architectural similarities of the two temples: *Survey* 75–76.

3. See *Survey* 53–87; 79 on the uncertain date of remodeling; 109 on Building L; cf. *Sardis* 119–120.

4. P. Gauthier, *Nouvelles inscriptions de Sardes* II (Geneva 1989).

"first"; "neocoros"; "friend and ally of Rome"; "autochthonous"; "sacred to the gods."[5] This last, despite its vagueness, might well reflect granted inviolability. Tacitus, who does not name the god in question, shows us the Sardians in A.D. 22 adducing "a grant by the victorious Alexander." We know that in 334 Sardes surrendered voluntarily to Alexander, who accordingly allowed the city freedom and "the use of the traditional laws of the Lydians" (Arr. *Anab.* 1.17.4). Perhaps this grant was the prime text put before the Senate in defense of the traditional rights of Sardes; for the Sardians' purpose Alexander's favor need not have concerned *asylia* isto nomine, and in my view cannot have done so at that early date. Tacitus' silence does not prove that the Sardians did not also cite later authorities that addressed *asylia* directly; and indeed it would be surprising if they did not cite Caesar's edict.

The inscription makes clear (line 2) that Caesar expanded the boundaries of an existing right of *asylia*; this was not a new grant but a confirmation and enlargement. Sardes had opposed Mithridates in 88 B.C. (Oros. 6.2.8) and probably never lost its privileges, as did cities that acted otherwise.

214. Rome: Julius Caesar

Marble stele, badly worn, found 500 meters from the temple of Artemis on the road to the city; h. 2.02, w. 0.45–51, th. 0.28; letters 0.014–17 in lines 1–10, 0.011–13 in lines 30ff.

P. Herrmann, *Chiron* 19 (1989) 127–164 [*AEpigr* 1989, 684; *SEG* 39.1290]. *Squeeze* (from Herrmann).

Photograph: Herrmann pls. 1–6.

ὅρος ἱερὸς ἄσυλος Ἀρτέμιδος
Σαρδιανῆς, ὃν προσώρισεν
ἐν Ῥώμηι Γάϊος Καῖσαρ αὐτοκρά-
τωρ καὶ ἀρχιερεύς, ὕπατος τὸ
πέμπτον, δικτάτωρ διὰ βίου,
πρεσβευσάντων ἐ̣[κ] τοῦ ἰδίου
[βί]ου Λυσιμάχου τοῦ Μηνοφίλου,
φ̣ύσει δὲ Μηνοφάντου, Δημητρ[ί]-
ου τοῦ Μενάνδρου, φ̣ύσει δὲ Δη-
μητρίου, Ναθείους. vacat
[[Twenty lines erased, stray letters legible (at 11 end, Ἀ̣ν̣τνωνίου)
]] δελτογράφημα·
[Γ]ά̣[ϊ]ο̣[ς Κα]ῖ̣σ̣αρ αὐτοκράτωρ καὶ ἀρχιερεὺς δικτάτω[ρ]
[τ]ε διὰ βίου ἐπέκρεινεν πρὸ ἡμερῶν τεσσάρω[ν]

5. See especially Head, *BMC Lycia* cvi–cix; *I.Sardis* 13.12 (αὐτόχθων καὶ πρεσβίστη), 63–68, with Robert, *Hellenica* I (1940) 56–59 (αὐτόχθων καὶ ἱερὰ τῶν θεῶν); Herrmann, *Chiron* 23 (1993) 238–243; cf. Nonnus 41.356 (Sardes the oldest of cities). Autochthony and freedom were linked by Lycurgus (*Leoc.* 41). Burrell ("Neokoroi," 376–379) considers that the second neocoria was for the temple of Artemis.

γ̣ωνῶν Μαρτίων· ἐπεὶ συνφωνεῖται τ[ὴν]
πο[λ]ιτε̣ίαν τῶν Σαρδιανῶν ἐν τῆι φιλί̣[α]ι̣ τοῦ δ[ή]-
μου τοῦ ῾Ρ̣ωμαίων διὰ παντὸς γεγονέναι
κ̣αὶ τὴ̣[ν - - - - - - - - - - - -]ν̣ πίστιν το[ῖς]
τοῦ δήμο̣υ̣ π̣ράγμασιν̣ κ̣α̣ὶ̣ τῆι̣ συκλήτωι παρ⟨α⟩σχ[ῆσ]-
θ̣αι [-] Λυσίμαχο[ς]
Μηνοφίλου, [φύσει δὲ] Μηνοφάντου, καὶ Δημή-
τριος Μενάνδρου, φήσ[ει δὲ Δη]μητρίου, Νά̣[θ]ης
. ΣΤΕΑ̣[-]ν̣τες πολλά[ς]
τε ἐν[-] πεπραγ[μέ]-
νων εἰς τὴν ἡγεμονίαν [῾Ρω]μ̣αίων· ἀντὶ το[ύ]-
των ἁπάντων ἀρέσκ̣ει α̣ὐ̣τ̣ο̣ῖς συνχωρεῖν ἃ ἐ-
νεφάνισαν. τὸ ἱερὸν Ἀρτέμιδος Σαρδια-
ν̣ῆς. . . . . ἄσυλον εἶναι τ̣[αὐτῶ]ι δικαίωι ὧι κα[ὶ]
τ̣ὸ τ̣ῆς ᾽Εφεσίας Ἀρτέμι[δός ἐσ]τ̣ι̣ν καὶ τὸν να[ὸν]
φύξι̣μ̣[ο]ν̣ ὄντα̣ [τῆς] Ἀ̣[θ]η̣νᾶ̣ς Νικηφόρου κ[αὶ]
Τ[ca. 5]Ο̣Υ[ca. 5]Λ̣[2–3] ἅτινά ἐστιν ἐν τῆι πό[λει?]
[ca. 7]Ι̣ΤΟ[ca. 19] ἐν Κολό[ηι?]
[- - - - - - - - - - -]Ρ̣Λ̣[.]ΙΕ̣[- - -]ΤΛ̣[. .]ΛΙΚ[. .]
[- - - - - - - - - - -]Α[- - - - - -]Τ[. . . .] ἐ̣στ̣ὶ̣ν̣ ἕν τε
[- - - - - - - - - - - - - - - - -] τ̣[ῆς] Σ̣αρδιαν̣ῆ̣ς ὅροις οἷς
[- - - - - - -]ΟΥ[. .]Ν τε̣ ε̣ἶναι Διὶ Μεγίστωι κ[. .]
[- - - - - - - - - - - - - - - - -]τω̣ι Χ . . Λ . .ηρίωι ὧι τ[.]
[-] Α̣Ρ̣Α̣ ἐ̣σ̣τὶν ὡς ἐν
[- - - - - - - - - - - - - - - -] ? Ἀ̣π̣ό[λ]λωνι συνεχώρησε
[- - - - - - - - - - - - - - - -] ἐ̣στὶν ἐν ὄρει Τμώλωι Ο[.]
[. . .]Ω[. . . .]ΜΕΝΞ[. . . . .] καὶ ἱερὸν Νυμφαῖον
[- - - - - - - - - - -]Ε . Τ[- - -]Ε̣Π̣Ι̣ΜΕ . ΙΛ̣Ι Σαρδιανο[.]
[- - - - - - - - - - - - - - - -] ἐ̣π̣ὶ̣ το̣ῖ̣ς α̣ὐ̣τοῖς δικαίοις οἷ[ς]
[-]Ν τούς τε δημοσιών[ας?]
[- - - - - - - - - - - - - - - - -]Μ̣Ι̣Ω. κ̣ατ᾽ ἐνιαυτὸν τελ[. .]
τ[υν]χάνω[σι - - - - - - - - - - - - -] ἐ̣π̣ώφειλον τοῖς τ[.]
[-]Α̣Ι Σαρδιανοῖς συνε-
[-]ΝΟΥΣ τε τοῦ Σαρδια-
ν̣ῶν [- - - - - - - - - - - - - - - - -]Ν̣ καὶ ῥ̣άβδων ἠλευθ[έ]-
[ρ]ωσε̣[- - - - - - - - - - - - - - - - - - -] ἀντάρχοντας οἳ
[- - - - - - - - - - - - - - - - -]Ξ . . . . Σ ἔσονται ταῦ̣-
[τα . . . . .] κ̣α̣[θι]έ̣ρ̣ω̣σ̣ε̣ν ἔδωκεν συνεχώρ[η]-
[σεν - - - - - - - - - - - - - - - -]Ε αὐτῶν ἀμύνεσθα[ι]
[- - - - - - - - - - - - - - -]Ε[. . .]Α ἀρέσκ̣ει μήτε ὑπεναν̣-
τ̣[ί]ως ᾦ̣ι̣? Γάϊος Κ̣α[ῖσα]ρ̣ αὐτοκράτωρ καὶ ἀρ[χ?]-
[ιερ]ε̣ὺς δικτάτωρ τε διὰ βίου συνεχώρη-
[σε]ν ἔδωκεν καθιέρωσεν ἔστησεν
[ποι]ε̣ῖ̣ν̣ μήτε γίνεσθαι ἐᾶν.

37: ΠΑΡΕΣΧ lapis. 46: possibly ΩΣ or ΟΙΣ ἄσυλον Herrmann.

The Sardians have inscribed several documents: their statement of the boundary of inviolability (1–10); a second text that was subsequently erased (11–30), which seems to have introduced the third, Caesar's decision allowing inviolability (31–76). The last, written in the third person, may derive in some way from Caesar's unexecuted *acta* or papers; the erased text may come from Antony. The Sardians' embassy most likely was prompted by the taxing of sacred land by publicans (62–64), as at Oropus. On this difficult inscription Herrmann's detailed commentary should be consulted in its entirety. I note several matters as they pertain to *asylia*.

In the crucial passage (45–50) Herrmann's reconstruction is supported by the s.c. for Aphrodisias (**212**: ἐκεῖνο τὸ τέμενος ἄσυλον [ἔ]στω τούτῳ τῷ δικαίῳ ταύτῃ τε δεισιδαιμονίᾳ ᾧ δικαίῳ καὶ ᾗ δεισιδαιμονίᾳ τὸ ἱερὸν εἴτε καὶ τέμενος Ἀρτέμιδος Ἐ[φε]σίας ἐστὶν ἐν Ἐφέσῳ). The passage implies that Caesar addressed himself to the inviolability of at least four or five temples in Sardes simultaneously, not just that of Artemis. Perhaps in 49 we should restore τὰ ἄ]λ̣[λα], ἅτινα (κτλ.), the other temples that are in the city, followed by some in the country. Such a collection of inviolable temples in one city is unparalleled, however.

I suggest therefore another possibility, that the temples listed after Artemis of Ephesus are other foreign precedents rather than Sardian recipients. I have imagined a text as follows:

ν̣ῆ̣ς· [πάντ]ω̣ς̣? ἄσυλον εἶναι τ̣[αὐτῶ]ι δικαίωι ὧι κα[ὶ]
τ̣ὸ τ̣ῆς Ἐφεσίας Ἀρτέμι[δός ἱερὸ]ν καὶ τὸν να[ὸν]
48 φύξιμ̣[ο]ν̣ ὄντα̣ [τῆς] Ἀ̣[θ]η̣ν̣ᾶ̣ς̣ Νικηφόρου κ[αὶ]
τ[ὸ ἱερὸν τ]ο̣ῦ [Ἀσκ]λ̣[ηπιοῦ] ἅτινά ἐστιν ἐν τῆι πό[λει]
[Περγάμωι κα]ὶ̣ τὸ [τοῦ Ἀπόλλωνος τὸ] ἐν Κολο[φῶνι]

On this theory, these temples were cited by the Sardians as examples of *asyla* that had been recognized by the Roman authorities. Asclepius is so recorded, and Apollo of Claros; but we do not know independently that Rome confirmed the *asylia* of Athena of Pergamum. This logic—precedents rather than a massive grant to Sardes—would be attractive, whichever cults and cities are restored. I make this suggestion with much hesitation.[6] These restorations of 49 and 50 init. seem too long; at 49 middle Λ (?) seems too far to the right to fit with Ἀσκληπίου. The grammar of this reconstruction is discomforting, with the precedents as accusatives following upon Caesar's declaration. And the passage that then follows certainly concerns Sardes (53, 58), and it mentions more gods, whose *asylia* is not on record in other

6. The photographs and squeezes, generously shown me by Professor Herrmann, reveal nothing at 47 middle; in 50 middle I seem to see on the squeezes ΛΛ. N, but quite doubtfully. It should be stressed that Herrmann worked repeatedly with the stone itself, reading with carbonized water.

cities.[7] We should have to posit a new theme, not the *asylia* of Artemis, beginning at line 52. Clearly this was a complex and detailed decision by Caesar, and it may well be that the *asylia* of a number of Sardian temples was addressed here.

2: The verb implies that Caesar increased the boundaries of inviolability, a gesture attested elsewhere (cf. Herrmann 137). If the findspot of the stone is at all near its original place, the result was not a large perimeter, certainly less than a Roman mile.

48: The Roberts postulated a cult of Athena Nicephorus at Sardes: *Hellenica* IX (1950) 7–25. In inscriptions the adjective φύξιμος recurs in various forms at Delphi, Chalcedon, and Andania (above, p. 48).

50: Herrmann reasonably suggested the important cult of Artemis at Koloe in Sardian territory to the north of the city.

67: Possibly the city or the temples are "freed from the fasces"; cf. Herrmann 151–153 on the difficulties here.

7. Zeus Megistos (54) is surely Sardian; cf. Herrmann 147–148.

Temple of the Persian Goddess, Hieracome-Hierocaesarea

Hieracome in the Hyrcanian Plain,[1] Hierocaesarea after A.D. 17, was famous for its cult of "the Persian Goddess." Anaitis, eventually seen as Artemis, arrived in Lydia with the settlement of Persians in Achaemenid times, and her worship is widely attested in the region.[2] Her image dominates the coins of Hieracome;[3] one of the city gates was dedicated to θεοῖς Σεβαστοῖς καὶ Ἀρτέμιδι Περσικῆι καὶ τῶι δήμωι (*TAM* V 1244). Her games, the Great Artemisia, are attested in Roman times (*Hellenica* 43–48). The very name of the city suggests that the cult dominated the life of the people.[4] In the Hellenistic period we hear of ἱερόδουλοι (*TAM* 1253; cf. 1252).

Tacitus describes at unusual length the appeal of the Hierocaesareans in A.D. 22: these presented an older case, a temple of Persian Diana dedicated by King Cyrus; and they cited acts of Perperna, Isauricus, and many other commanders, who had granted the same sanctity not just to the temple but for two miles around. Perperna was the victor over Aristonicus in 129, Isauricus Caesar's agent in rehabilitating the rights of the cities of Asia; an expansion of two miles is what Caesar did for the Didymeum (p. 177). The success of the appeal in 22 may have been the occasion of the erection of a statue of the Senate as a "goddess manifest" (*Hellenica* 50–52; *TAM* 1264).

The ambassadors in A.D. 22 emphasized, as was typical, ancient beginnings and Roman confirmations; but in between there may well have been a Hellenistic recognition, the real origin of *asylia*, left unmentioned by Tacitus. Too little is

1. See J. and L. Robert, *Hellenica* VI (1948) 27–55; Herrmann, *TAM* V pp. 444ff.

2. J. Keil in *Anatolian Studies Ramsay* (Manchester 1923) 250–251; Robert, *Op. min. sel.* V 502–509, VI 140–141.

3. Imhoof-Blumer, *Lydische Stadtmünzen* (Geneva 1907) 5–20 (labeled simply Περσική, never Artemis).

4. Cf. *La Carie* II pp. 294–295.

known of the Hellenistic history of the city to afford speculation about an occasion for the grant. Philip V visited the city in 201 B.C.,[5] and Prusias of Bithynia plundered the temple in 155.[6]

Apart from Tacitus, we have as evidence an inviolable boundary stone of Artemis, and possibly also a confirmation of her inviolability.

215. Temple of Artemis: boundary

Marble stele found reused in a modern house less than a mile from the ancient city; h. 0.43, w. 0.49, th. 0.15; large letters 0.05.

J. and L. Robert, *Hellenica* VI (1948) 33–42 no. 5; Herrmann, *TAM* V 1251.
Photograph: *Hellenica* pl. 21.3.

ὅρος
ἱερὸς
ἄσυλο[ς]
4 [Ἀ]ρ̣τ̣έ̣[μι]-
[δος.]

The editors did not venture a date, and writing this large is difficult to assess; I should think this square script not earlier than the late Hellenistic period. Given the findspot of the stone, either the temple of the goddess was in the city proper or the stone has been moved from elsewhere (which the Roberts doubted) or else it defined some other property of the goddess. I prefer the last option; even if her shrine was rural, she no doubt kept a place in the city itself.

We have also an inscribed grant, which was once ascribed to Artemis of Hieracome, but which the Roberts (58–59) urged pertains to a neighboring city. In it a ruler confirms the *asylia* of the Persian Goddess, and simple efficiency had led to its attribution to the cult of Hieracome described by Tacitus. The inscription was found at Sarıçam twenty-three kilometers west of the city, a substantial stone at a substantial place with other public inscriptions; the Roberts thought the stone unlikely to have been brought there from Hieracome and considered Sarıçam to be the site of an independent city as yet unidentified, with its own temple of the Persian Goddess. This seems to me unnecessary. Certainly there were more cities in Anatolia than we hear about and can name;[7] and the silence of Tacitus about another Lydian city is uncompelling. But it strains belief that an unknown city next to Hieracome might receive like Hieracome a Hellenistic declaration of *asylia* for the Persian Goddess.

To the contrary, the two-mile expansion of the perimeter described by Tacitus implies that Hieracome's temple was in the countryside, not the city proper, as

5. Polyb. 16.1.8; *TAM* 1261 (statue base).

6. Polyb. 32.15.11: τὸ τῆς Ἀρτέμιδος ἱερὸν τῆς ἐν Ἱερᾷ Κώμῃ μετὰ βίας ἐσύλησεν; cf. Holleaux, *Etudes* IV 250–251; Robert, *Etudes anat.* 112–114.

7. See in particular J. and L. Robert, *Bull. épigr.* 1976, 595 (p. 533).

does the raid by Prusias: I suggest that it stood at Sarıçam.[8] Similarly Didyma was a substantial place with public inscriptions, fifteen kilometers from its city. Hence I place this inscription here with Hieracome, on the theory that Sarıçam belonged to that city and was the location of its famous temple.

216. Rome

Brought from Sarıçam to the house of a stonemason at Manisa, where it was seen by Fontrier in 1886 (seen again, reused, by Keil and von Premerstein in 1906); h. 0.69, w. 0.95, th. 0.115; lettering monumental and "thick," h. 0.04.

Fontrier, *Mouseion Smyrna* 5.2 (1886) 28 no. φς′; Foucart, *BCH* 11 (1887) 81–84 no. 2 (Fontrier's squeeze) [Michel, *Rec.* 48; Dittenberger, *OGIS* 333; Schroeter 51; Welles, *Royal Corres.* 68; Herrmann, *TAM* V 1396].

Cf. Robert, *REA* 36 (1934) 525 (*Op. min. sel.* III 1574); Rigsby, *Asia Minor Studien* 17 (1994) 77–83.

ἀσυλίαν τῆς παρ' ὑμεῖν Περσικῆ[ς θεᾶς]
ἐπὶ τούτωι βεβαιῶ ὑμεῖν{ν} ἐφ' ᾧ μ[ηδὲν]
ἐν τῆι δωρεᾷ ταύτηι ἀλλαγῆνα[ι τὴν]
συνήθειαν ἣν ἔχετε, εἴπερ ἀληθ[ῶς τὰ]
γραφέντα λαβόντες παρά τε τ[ῶν βασιλέων]
καὶ τῶν ἐμῶν προγόνων ταύτη[ι χρῆσθε.]
δύο δὲ ὄντων ψηφισμάτων ἅ μ[οι ἔδωκαν]
οἱ ὑμέτεροι πρέσβεις καὶ σχεδὸν [ὁμοίων,]
μίαν πρὸς αὐτὰ ὑπηγόρευσα ἐπιταγ[ήν, ἣν]
γραφεῖσαν τύπῳ τοῖς δυσὶν ὑμῶν [πρέσβεσιν]
ἐκέλευσα δοθῆναι καὶ τὰ ὀνόματα [τὰ τῶν]
συμπρεσβευσάντων αὐτοῖς [ἐγγραφῆναι.]

Foucart's restorations, except the following: 2 Dittenberger: μ[ηδαμῶς] Foucart. 4: Rostovtzeff ap. Welles: ἀληθ[ινῶς] Foucart, ἀληθ[ῆ ἐστιν ἃ] Dittenberger. 5 Rigsby: τ[οῦ πατρὸς] Foucart, τ[ῶν πρόσθεν] (or τ[ῶν ἄλλων]) Dittenberger. 6 Dittenberger: ταύτη[ν ἔχετε] Foucart. 12 Dittenberger.

. . .

The inviolability of the Persian [Goddess] among you I confirm for you on this condition, that by this grant what is traditional among you is in no way altered, provided that you enjoy this because you have actually received written statements from the [kings] and from my ancestors. As there were two decrees [given] to me by your envoys which were nearly identical, I have dictated one order in answer to them, and have commanded that it be written out in a *typos* and given to your two [ambassadors] and that the names of their fellow ambassadors [be written there].

8. This is argued in more detail at *Asia Minor Studien* 17 (1994) 77–83. We do not know the westward extent of the territory of Hieracome; but Thyateira stood only sixteen kilometers to the north (*TAM* 859), and the long narrow territory implied by this attribution is a difficulty.

Earlier scholars thought the author to be a Hellenistic king; Robert preferred a Roman emperor but did not give his reasons. The crux is in line 5; I summarize here the case argued in *Asia Minor Studien.* The chief worry of the author, and the argument that convinced him, was precedent. That is a common theme of emperors (whose "ancestors" were their predecessors) but rare in the letters of Hellenistic kings. If we restore βασιλέων in 5, the author is drawing the familiar distinction between the Hellenistic kings and the Roman emperors, as Valerian does at **218**.10–12.

Other features seem to be Romanisms: ecthesis of the two sentences, ἐπιταγή (9) (cf. *iussus*), the reference to dictation, and ἀσυλίαν without article (1). τύπος (10) should not be a "summary" as Welles thought (which would be of little use to the recipient)[9] but may render *exemplum*, hence a Latin double dative ("written out as a copy for your ambassadors"). The undiplomatic and bureaucratic manner is not that of a king concerned to keep the loyalty of his cities, but of an emperor amid his paperwork.

A village four kilometers from Sarıçam has yielded a certainly Roman enactment from the time of Claudius (*Hellenica* 61–62; *TAM* 1404); its lettering can well be described as "thick." It may have been carried there from Sarıçam, as was a dedication to Claudius (*TAM* 1398). Claudius therefore had dealings with this place, and it is possible that he is the author of our letter.

10: Foucart's notion that there were two embassies has caused heavy weather. Welles suggested that one came from the city and one from the temple.[10] That is constitutionally impossible; in fact there were merely two ambassadors. The question rather is why the city passed two decrees; but second thoughts and second decrees must have been common enough in Greek government—Thucydides offers some famous examples.

9. The letter has been truncated in that it lacks the greeting and farewell; but that was done by the inscribers at Hieracome rather than by the author.

10. Followed by L. Boffo, *I re ellenistici e i centri religiosi dell' Asia Minore* (Pavia 1985) 95.

Nicomedia

Nicomedia was founded in the 260s B.C. to be the capital of the Bithynian kings, incorporating ancient Astacus and its vicinity. The site, at the head of the Olbian Gulf of the Propontis, has yielded a good many inscriptions; but public documents remain few, and almost nothing survives of Hellenistic date.[1]

The city's chief divinity was Demeter. Libanius, who visited in the 340s, contrasts Nicomedia "the city of Demeter" with Nicaea "the city of Dionysus."[2] Arrian of Nicomedia served as priest of Demeter and her daughter, "to whom the city is dedicated";[3] he reports the civic myth that the Mysteries of Demeter and Kore originated here, spread thence by the local hero Iasion, who had become their κάτοχος.[4] The Mysteries have left some trace in the inscriptions,[5] and Demeter is often seen on the civic coins, holding her torch. A festival Demetria was held in imperial times, Panhellenic by the third century.[6] I assume that inviolability was in her honor.

In the 220s B.C. Prusias I of Bithynia was angry with the Byzantines for sending *theoroi* to the Pergamene games of Athena but disdaining his festival, the Soteria; neither festival, it seems, was Panhellenic, and the Byzantine gesture betokened

1. F. Dörner, *TAM* IV.1 (1978). Cf. W. Ruge, "Nikomedeia," *RE* 17 (1936) 468–492; S. Şahin, "Neufunde von antiken Inschriften in Nikomedeia" (Diss., Münster 1973).

2. *Or.* 1.48; cf. 1.51: he lived five years ὑπὸ τῇ Δήμητρι, i.e., at Nicomedia.

3. *FGrHist* 156 T 4 (from Photius): ἱερέα τῆς Δήμητρος καὶ τῆς παιδὸς αὐτῆς, αἷς καὶ τὴν πόλιν ἀνακεῖσθαί φησιν; the earlier phrase at Arr. *Cyneg.* 35.2: Δήμητρι καὶ τῇ παιδὶ αὐτῆς. His priesthood is mentioned in a purported inscription, thought to be spurious: *TAM* IV 402.

4. Arrian *FGrHist* 156 F 107; he makes Iasion and Dardanus descendants of Priam and brothers of Harmonia, whom Cadmus later married (F 64).

5. *TAM* IV 42: ἀρχιμύστης; 262: μυστηριάρχης.

6. *Recueil général* I.3 553 nos. 281–282, Ἀντώνια Δημήτρια with agonistic crown (under Elagabalus).

special friendship for the Attalids and a corresponding insult to Prusias.[7] We do not hear again of Soteria at Nicomedia; perhaps the festival commemorated some royal victory and did not survive the dynasty. It need not have honored the chief divinity of Nicomedia; Demeter is not known anywhere with the epithet Soteira (although Kore was so called at Cyzicus).

One of the civic tribes was named Ἱερά; this may have been the tribe in whose district the temple of Demeter stood.[8] That the temple was in the heart of the city we know from the *Life* of Saints Indes and Domna, martyrs under Diocletian, which reports that a very great temple of Demeter, the greatest goddess among the Nicomedians, was next to the theater.[9] The theater could be seen from the Nicaea road—from the south (Liban. *Or.* 61.10); it must have stood against the south slope of the hill behind the modern city, with the temple beside it.[10]

The earliest coins of Nicomedia, under the late Republic, offer no titles, as is usual in Hellenistic Asia Minor; those of imperial date proclaim only the city's neocories and its titles "first" and "metropolis," but not *asylia*.[11] Two inscriptions, however, give its titulature more fully than any coin, and these are our only evidence of the inviolability of Nicomedia:

> In or after the time of Commodus (A.D. 180–192) Nicomedia erected at Delphi a statue of a famous citizen, the flutist T. Aelius Theodotus (*FD* III.6 143; *TAM* IV 34): ἡ μητρόπολις καὶ πρώτη Βειθυνίας Πόντου Ἀδριανὴ νεοκόρος Νεικομήδεια, ἱερὰ καὶ ἄσυλος, φίλη καὶ σύμμαχος ⟨ἄ⟩ν⟨ω⟩θεν τῷ δήμῳ τῷ Ῥωμαίων.
>
> At Nicomedia itself the city dedicated a statue of Julia Domna, who wintered there in A.D. 214/5 (copied by Count Vidua in 1817: *Inscriptiones antiquae* [Paris 1826] tab. 5 [*CIG* 3771, *IGR* III 6, *TAM* IV 25]): ἡ με[γίστη] μητρόπολις καὶ πρώτη Βειθυνίας τε καὶ Πόντου Ἀδριανὴ Σεουηριανὴ δὶς νεωκόρος Ν[ει]κομήδεια, ἱερὰ καὶ ἄσυλος, φίλη πιστὴ καὶ σύμμαχος ἄνωθε τῷ δήμῳ τῷ Ῥωμαίων.

A third inscription, heavily damaged, probably gave much the same titles.[12]

7. Polyb. 4.49.3; for games to which allies are invited see *Staatsvertr.* III 537, and p. 363.

8. *TAM* IV 258, with J. and L. Robert, *Bull. épigr.* 1974, p. 297.

9. So the version of Symeon Metaphrastes (Migne, *PG* 16.1073B: προσῳκοδόμητο μὲν τὸ θεατρὸν μέγιστον ἱερὸν Δήμητρος τῆς παρ' αὐτοῖς μεγίστης θεᾶς); the rather fuller recension published by Kleopas-Koikylides, Βίοι τῶν Παλαιστινῶν Ἁγίων (Jerusalem 1907) 77, does not add to the topographical information on this point (τῷ δὲ θεατρῷ τῷ μεγάλῳ ἐγειτνίαζεν ἱερὸν μέγιστον τῆς παρ' αὐτοῖς λεγομένης θεᾶς Δήμητρος). The martyr is then ordered to be taken out of the city, ἔξω τῆς πόλεως.

10. C. Bosch, *Die kleinasiatischen Münzen* II.1 (Stuttgart 1935) 216–218, offers a reconstruction of the central city, placing the temple facing south across the agora, where a dedication to Demeter was found (*TAM* IV 54).

11. On the competition for titles between Nicomedia and Nicaea see Robert, *HSCP* 81 (1977) 1–39 (*Op. min. sel.* VI 211–249; 238–239 on the two inscriptions).

12. M. Zahrnt, *ZPE* 36 (1979) 215–218 [*SEG* 29.1345].

Thus for the date we have no better than a terminus ante quem toward the end of the Antonine period. The origin of the status may lie in the rivalry of the Bithynian kings with Pergamum in the late third or the second century B.C., or in the first century B.C. amid the competition of Roman commanders. Military history is as usual unedifying. In 149 B.C. the Nicomedians, besieged by an Attalid force seeking the overthrow of Prusias II, allowed in a contingent who found and killed the king in a temple of Zeus (App. *Mith.* 7); and in 86 the city was plundered by the troops of Fimbria (Diod. 38.8.2).

Nicaea

Nicaea, the great neighbor and rival of Nicomedia, was the city of Dionysus.[1] Dionysus had founded the city, naming it for the nymph Nicaea; both are frequently seen on the coins.[2] As at Nicomedia, evidence of Hellenistic date is slight. In the imperial age Panhellenic Dionysia are attested; and by the time of Hadrian the city held neocories in the names of Dionysus and of Heracles, as we know from several inscriptions that list various civic titles, but not inviolability: ἡ εὐσεβεστάτη νεωκόρος τῶν Σεβαστῶν ἀπὸ Διονύσου καὶ Ἡρακλέους, πρώτη Βιθυνίας καὶ Πόντου, ἡ μητρόπολις.[3]

Inviolability at Nicaea is attested by a single bronze coin of the second century A.D.:

> M. Aurelius as caesar | Dionysus standing with thyrsus, pouring a libation on an altar; Διονύσῳ ἀσύλῳ ἐφεστίῳ Νικαιεῖς.[4]

Here, as at Ephesus and in Pamphylia, the adjective attaches to the god rather than to the city or ethnic. I take this to mean that it was the temple rather than the city and country that originally received the status; perhaps therefore

1. Liban. *Or.* 1.48; perhaps also 39.8, προπάτωρ τῆς πόλεως, although the coins show that Heracles too was regarded as a founder (*Recueil général* I.3 p. 396). See generally Ruge, "Nikaia 7," *RE* 17 (1936) 226–243; S. Şahin, *Museum Iznik* (IK IX–X).

2. References at Ruge 228, 239.

3. *Museum Iznik* nos. 29, 30, 30a (Hadrianic); emphasizing ties with Rome: *AEpigr* 1939, 295 (Severan). On titles and the competition with Nicomedia, Robert, *HSCP* 81 (1977) 1–39 (*Op. min. sel.* VI 211–249; on these inscriptions, 218–219, 236). For the games see C. Bosch, *Jahrb.f.Kl.Forsch.* 1 (1950/51) 80–99, esp. 88.

4. *Recueil général* 414 no. 125; cf. Robert, *A travers l'Asie mineure* (Paris 1980) 225. The dedicatory structure (nominative and dative) is found with several other gods on Nicene coins (e.g., nos. 168, 209, 220).

the temple stood outside the city proper, amid the vineyards that surround Nicaea's lake.[5]

Of the Nicenes' temple of their chief god, nothing further is known. The epithet ἐφέστιος is puzzling. The adjective can bear some rather distinct meanings[6] and as a divine epithet is found primarily of Zeus as guardian of hearth and home.[7] Here, however, the word is illustrated by the image and invokes the god "at the hearth" or altar.[8] Probably this was not the god's formal cult title (no more was ἄσυλος) but rather reflects an aspect of the story of Dionysus as founder of Nicaea, a possible occasion for the unusual situation of a god offering a libation. A label is here offered for the particular image, which may well derive from a statue or painting in the temple.[9] It was told already at the beginning of the Hellenistic age that Dionysus had fled Hera to an altar in Phrygia, where he was purified by Rhea.[10]

As with Nicomedia, we are rather well informed on other titles of Nicaea, which appear to have outweighed *asylia* in the minds of these competing cities in Roman times: we learn of this status only through the rarest of documents. I assume that the grant was not new at the time of our one testimony but derives from the Hellenistic age, whether under the Bithynian kings or the Romans of the late Republic.

5. On the topography of Nicaea, of which little is known, see Ruge 240–242.

6. Of a suppliant at Plut. *Mor.* 299D; a house guest at Plut. *Arat.* 49.1. Plato *Leg.* 931A says that a statuette is the more potent for being placed on the hearth (ἐφέστιον ἵδρυμα).

7. Cf. Jessen, *RE* 5 (1905) 2823; H. Schwabl, *RE* 10A (1972) 312.

8. For ἑστία = altar see Robert, *RPhil* 84 (1958) 32–33 (*Op. min. sel.* V 172–173); so at Herodas 4.10–11 the conceit ὅσοι θεοὶ σὴν ἑστίην κατοικεῦσιν καὶ θεαί for οἱ συμβώμιοι θεοί.

9. Parallels for Dionysus pouring a libation: E. Simon, *Opfernde Götter* (Berlin 1953) 47–57 (vase paintings of classical date); Nilsson, *Dionysiac Mysteries* (Lund 1957) 99–106; a statue carried in the famous procession of Ptolemy II (Ath. 198C; *FGrHist* 627 F 2); cf. Ath. 471C. Apollo is so portrayed on coins of Side, and cf. M. Cremer, *IstMitt* 38 (1988) 181–182.

10. Callixenus *FGrHist* 627 F 2; Apollod. 3.5.1; cf. E. E. Rice, *The Grand Procession of Ptolemy Philadelphus* (Oxford 1983) 99–102. Expiation is one context in which we hear of gods sacrificing: e.g., Plut. *Mor.* 418B (Apollo for killing Python).

Aezani

The great city of northern Phrygia was Aezani, "well-born and ancient," as a Roman governor called it, its citizens claiming Arcadian descent.[1] As befits Arcadians, their chief god was Zeus, whose sanctuary faced on the agora; the extant building, of Hadrianic date, is the best-preserved temple in Turkey.[2] Zeus was born here, and the city held a neocoria in his name; we hear of a panegyriarch in Roman times.[3] Additions to the god's lands made by kings Attalus and Prusias were confirmed by the Romans.[4]

The coins of Aezani, while rich in their testimonies to the city's cults and traditions, never mention *asylia.* The title is known to us from two inscriptions on statue bases dedicated by the city in the third century A.D.:

> Le Bas-Waddington 875 [*IGR* IV 581], a statue erected by the council and people of [τῆς ἱερᾶς καὶ] ἀσύλου καὶ [νεωκόρο]υ τοῦ Διὸς [Αἰζανει]τῶν πόλεως.

> Le Bas-Waddington 988 [*IGR* IV 567], a statue of Caracalla erected by ἡ βου[λ]ὴ καὶ ὁ νεωκόρ[ος] τ̣ο̣ῦ̣ Δ̣ιὸς ἱερὸς καὶ ἄ̣[σ]υ̣λ̣ος Α̣ἰζα̣[νειτῶ]ν δῆμος.

The city of Aezani was founded only ca. 20 B.C., later than the last new grant of *asylia* that we know of. This need not prove that the privilege was of imperial origin, for the temple was widely honored in the Hellenistic period, and these Severan inscriptions may merely transfer the title of inviolability from temple to city, as do the coins of so many cities in the Roman Empire. I assume that the original grant dates from the Attalid period or the Republican province.

1. *IGR* IV 572: ἰδὼν δὲ πόλιν εὐγενῆ τε καὶ ἀρχαίαν; cf. Robert, *Etudes anat.* 301–305; *BCH* 105 (1981) 331–360 (*DAM* 241–270). An overview by B. Levick in *Sociétés urbaines, sociétés rurales dans l'Asie Mineure et la Syrie* (Strasbourg 1987) 259–270.
2. H. Weber, *AM* 84 (1969) 182–201.
3. Le Bas-Waddington 984 and *IGR* IV 584, with Robert, *Hellenica* XI–XII (1960) 17–18.
4. U. Laffi, *Athenaeum* n.s. 49 (1971) 3–53.

We do have an earlier text, but it is of doubtful relevance. In the Julio-Claudian age the governor C. Norbanus Flaccus wrote to Aezani (*MAMA* IX 13), citing a letter of Augustus that the city's envoys had shown him.[5] He responded to their petition favorably (9–10); but his description of the matter at issue is a difficult passage, of which the editors offered only a tentative reconstruction:

οἱ πρεσβευταὶ ὑμῶν
ἀνέδωκάν μοι Σεβαστοῦ Καίσαρος ἐπιστολὴν ἐν ἧι
ἐγέγραπτο· συνκεχώρηκεν ἀσυ[λ]ί̣α̣[ν καὶ ἀ]λ̣η̣σ̣ί̣αν
8 ΣΥΠΑΓ[. .]ΟΦΙΛΑΒΙΟΙΩΙΟΝΕΠΩΡΟ[. .]Σ[.]Ω[11–12]
ἐγὼ οὖν συναύξειν βουλό[μ]ε̣ν̣[ο]ς̣ [τ]ὰ̣ [φ]ιλ[άνθρω]-
πα τ̣ῆ̣ς̣ π̣όλεως ὑμῶν, ἐπιτρέπω κατὰ το[- - - - - -]
. . .

your ambassadors presented to me a letter of Augustus Caesar, in which he wrote: "he has granted inviolability and immunity (?) . . ." Accordingly, wishing to increase the privileges of your city, I grant, in keeping with . . .

Line 7 is troubling (Υ[.]Π̣Ι̣[. . . . .]Λ lapis). LSJ's ἀλ̣ησία is cited from the *Etym. Magn.*, which gives ἀλήσια as from ληΐζεσθαι and comparing the paroxytone ἀσυλία. But there the word might well want emendation: ἀλ̣ήστεια, in light of the attested noun λ̣ηστεία and adjective ἀλ̣ήστευτος. In any case ἀλ̣ησία, if it existed, does not belong in the formulary of a document. Finally, one expects a direct quotation to be in the first person. I wonder then if Augustus' statement might have been συνκεχώρημ̣εν δ̣ὲ̣ ὑ[μ]ῖ̣ν [παραπ]λήσια ν[, "We have granted you nearly . . ." If that or something like it is so, then nothing survives to suggest that this document concerned inviolability.

5. I assume the consul of A.D. 15 rather than his father (who governed Asia ca. 12 B.C.), because a ruling of Augustus seems more likely to have needed citation after his death than before. If that is so, his governorship will certainly have been subsequent to the Senate's review of *asylia* in A.D. 22/3 (cf. Syme, *Roman Papers* IV 350).

Perge

Perge in Pamphylia was the city of Artemis, whose temple was among the most famous in the world.[1] Callimachus calls Perge her chief city (*Hymn.* 3.187); Cicero calls the temple "the oldest and most holy of Artemis" (*Verr.* 2.1.20). A hymn in mixed dialect sung at her service was famous (Philostr. *VA* 1.30). The goddess was oracular (*unde fata petuntur*) and informed Artemidorus of Perge, the Ptolemaic official on Thera, that he would live to be ninety.[2] The scholar Polemon describes the pilgrims who came to the temple seeking help.[3] The worship of Artemis Pergaea spread to a number of other cities, and we hear of wandering mendicants in the service of the goddess.[4] The temple was rich with votive offerings, and the goddess issued an abundant coinage in silver and bronze in her own name, Ἀρτέμιδος Περγαίας.[5]

1. B. Pace in *Anatolian Studies ... Ramsay* (Manchester 1923) 297–314; H. Oppermann, "Pergaia," *RE* 19 (1937) 683–689; A. Akarca in *Excavations and Researches at Perge*, TTKYay V.8 (Ankara 1949) 62–68; Robert, *BCH* 102 (1978) 541 (*DAM* 237); I. Kaygusuz, *TTKBelleten* 44 (1980) 249–256 (an early inscription); T. S. MacKay, *ANRW* XVIII.3 (1990) 2048–2078. Artemis and Athena represent Perge and Side on *homonoia* issues, *BMC Lycia* 141–142. On the city generally, K. Lanckoronski, *Städte Pamphyliens und Pisidiens* I (Vienna 1890) 33–63; W. Ruge, *RE* 19 (1937) 694–704; S. Jameson, *RE* Suppl. 14 (1974) 375–383; A. M. Mansel, *AA* 1975, 57–96; Seyrig, *RN* VI.5 (1963) 38–51 (*Scripta numism.* 42–55). The inscriptions are reproduced in Merkelbach and Şahin, *EpigAnat* 11 (1988) 97–170; an important collection of coins, Y. Akyay, *IstArkMüzYill* 13–14 (1967) 246–286.

2. Ps.-Ascon. 237 Stengl; *IG* XII.3 1350; cf. O. Palagia in Φιλολάκων, *Lakonian Studies ... H. Catling* (London 1992) 171–177.

3. Robert, *Hellenica* V (1948) 64–69.

4. See Oppermann 687–689 for references; on Cos, Segre, *Iscr.Cos* ED236, EV179.

5. The dedications: Cic. loc. cit.; Philostr. *VS* 2.6; Migne, *PG* 117.568 (a menologium deriving from a lost life of two Pamphylian martyrs, whose decisive act was to overturn "the idols" in the temple of Artemis; that this is the temple at Perge is an old assumption). The

Perge held the valley of the Cestrus River, or at least its right bank. The city itself was some twelve kilometers from the coast. The temple of Artemis was elsewhere, "near the city on a high hill" according to Strabo (14.4.2 [667]); the site has yet to be discovered. Because the adjective ἄσυλος is repeatedly applied to the goddess herself rather than the city, we may suspect that inviolability was granted to the temple rather than the city and country, as was typical of a rural shrine.

Our evidence for *asylia* at Perge is all of imperial date.[6]

Under Domitian (A.D. 81–96) a tower in the countryside (at Lyrboton Kome) was built by a priestess of Demeter and dedicated to the emperor and to Artemis, who is called Ἀρτέμιδι Περγαίᾳ ἀσύλῳ.[7]

In the early second century a statue was erected of a priestess of Artemis, ἱερείαν τῆς προε[σ]τώσας τῆς πόλεως ἡμῶν θεᾶς Ἀρτέμιδος ἀσύλου.[8]

Between 198 and 214 a nymphaeum in the city was dedicated to Artemis and the imperial family: τῇ Ἀρτέμιδι Περγαίᾳ ἀσύλῳ καὶ τοῖς αὐτοκράτορσι.[9]

At an uncertain date a prominent citizen, who begins the list of his services with the priesthood of Artemis, obtained by his embassies to Rome the restoration of something for Artemis:

τρ[ὶς πρ]ε[σβεύ]σαντα δω[ρ]εὰ[ν] εἰς Ῥώμην κα[ὶ]
κατ[ορ]θωσάμενον [τῇ Περ]γαίᾳ Ἀ[ρ]τέμιδι τὴ[ν ?ἀσυλί]αν καὶ
τῷ δήμῳ τὰ μέγιστα [κ]αὶ συνφέροντα.[10]

If Wilhelm's restoration is correct, this loss and recovery of *asylia* still need not date before Domitian (as Woodward thought), for such losses might be quite short-lived. Nor does the omission of Perge from Tacitus' account of the appeals of A.D. 22/3, given the many other omissions, prove that the original grant of *asylia* occurred later than 22/3.[11]

On coins, Roman Perge was more disposed to advertise its neocories. As noted above, many issues are labeled Ἀρτέμιδος Περγαίας already in the Hellenistic period, and in imperial times as well. We first see the fuller Ἀρτέμιδος Περγαίας ἀσύλου in the 240s A.D. and thereafter intermittently into the 260s (near the end of

---

coins: *BMC Lycia* 119ff. On the date and character of the Hellenistic issues: Seyrig, *Scripta numism.* 47–52; Robert, *Monnaies antiques en Troade* (Paris 1966) 45–46.

6. See generally A. M. Woodward, *CR* 46 (1932) 9–11.

7. As interpreted by Woodward (*SEG* VI 672; McCrum/Woodhead, *Documents of the Flavian Emperors* no. 144; Merkelbach/Şahin 158 no. 151).

8. Lanckoronski no. 39 [*IGR* III 797; Merkelbach/Şahin 127 no. 48], found reused in a church in the city.

9. Mansel 69–70 [Merkelbach/Şahin 112 no. 14].

10. Lanckoronski no. 33 (restoring στό]αν), emended by Wilhelm, *AEM* 20 (1897) 65–66 [*IGR* III 796; Merkelbach/Şahin 127 no. 47].

11. So C. P. Jones, *HSCP* 80 (1976) 236 n. 43; see E. Bosch in *Vorlaeufiger Bericht . . . Side 1947*, TTKYay V.11 (Ankara 1951) 69, who observes that Tacitus' omissions are meaningless.

the civic coinage).[12] In some types that give the ethnic Περγαίων rather than the name of the goddess, ἄσυλος is inscribed in the gable of the temple.[13]

An unusual literary testimony: in the *Acts* of Saint Ariadne, set at Prymnessus in Phrygia, the civic benefactions of the saint's master are portrayed, as Robert saw, in language apparently borrowed from an inscribed honorific decree; these include his sacrifices to τῇ παρθένῳ Ἀρτέμιδι Περγαίᾳ ἀσύλῳ Δικαιοσύνῃ.[14] Robert reckoned the phrase to be a pastiche, with παρθένῳ a scribe's addition and Δικαιοσύνῃ taken from the cult of Artemis at Prymnessus, but Περγαίᾳ ἀσύλῳ accurately echoing that at Perge.

Some testimonies, however, imply that the city rather than the temple possessed the title:

A series of acclamations in praise of Perge inscribed under the emperor Tacitus (A.D. 275–276) begins αὖξε Πέργη ἡ μόνη ἄσυλος.[15]

Several texts apply "sacred" to the city, as one of a string of epithets (but not "inviolable"). Its force might be no more than rhetorical: τῆς ἱερᾶς καὶ ἐνδόξου καὶ νεωκόρου Περγαίων πόλεως;[16] ἡ ἱερὰ καὶ λαμ(πρὰ) καὶ ἔνδοξ[ος] νεωκόρος Περγαίων πόλις;[17] on some coins, ἱερὰ λαμπρὰ ἔνδοξος Πέργη πρώτη.[18]

Artemis of Perge was honored with games, surely already in the Hellenistic period if her coinage was federal; Strabo mentions an annual *panegyris*. Coins of the third century A.D. show a link between the games, by now Panhellenic and equal to the Pythia, and the goddess's epithet ἄσυλος: the adjective ἀσύλεια serves to identify the games of Artemis, thus Ἀσύλια Πύθια Περγαίων εἱερά;[19] a prize crown labeled Πύθια resting on a table labeled Ἀσύλια;[20] a crown resting on a table labeled Ἀσύλιος with ἱερός inscribed below (viz. ἀγών; *von Aulock* 4757); crowns resting on a table labeled Περγαίων with Ἀσύλεια Αὐγούστεια above and ἱεροὶ οἰκουμενικοί below (4715). Finally, an inscribed acclamation has εἷς ἀγὼν Ἀσύλια Πύθια.[21] We can see, amid these attendant adjectives,

12. *BMC* 129ff.; on some issues Ἀρτέμιδος Περγαίας is inscribed around the border while ἀσύλου is in the architrave of the temple portrayed (e.g., *BMC* no. 51; Imhoof-Blumer, *RevSuisse* 4 [1908] 66 no. 3; *SNG von Aulock* 4731–4732).

13. Imhoof-Blumer, *Kl.M.* 333 no. 35; *von Aulock* 4759.

14. *A travers l'Asie Mineure* (Paris 1980) 248–256.

15. Kaygusuz, *EpigAnat* 4 (1984) 1–4 [Merkelbach/Şahin 115 no. 22]; commentary by C. Roueché, *CambrPhilolSoc* Suppl. 16 (1989) 206–228; P. Weiss, *Chiron* 21 (1991) 353–392.

16. Lanckoronski no. 34 [*IGR* III 793; Merkelbach/Şahin 126 no. 46].

17. Lanckoronski no. 10 [Merkelbach/Şahin 125 no. 43].

18. *Inv. Waddington* 3409; *NC* III.19 (1899) 105 no. 30; Imhoof-Blumer, *Kl.M.* 332 nos. 32, 34; *von Aulock* 4729, 8529.

19. *RevSuisse* 66 no. 4.

20. *BMC* 136 no. 84, with Woodward 10 n. 9.

21. Quoted, Merkelbach/Şahin 116.

that the games were called the "Asyleia," a neologism deriving from the habitual epithet *asylos* applied to Artemis of Perge, which indeed we might even capitalize, "Asylos."

Thus the status is applied to the goddess rather than to the city and country by most testimonies. The apparent exceptions come in highly rhetorical settings: the acclamations recorded in the late third century, and the word "sacred" amid laudatory as well as official (granted) titles. I think that these exceptions are rhetorical exaggeration; certainly the claim to be the "sole inviolable" city is not to be taken literally, but the elative μόνος.[22] I would conclude that the original and formal grant of *asylia* was expressly for the temple and not the city and country.

For the date, we have no better than a terminus ante quem late in the first century A.D. I assume the Hellenistic period; but Pergaean evidence of that date is quite meager: the temple coinage shows no titles, but that is to be expected in Hellenistic Anatolia (compare the issues of Athena of Pergamum). The city apparently was free after the end of the Attalid kingdom, but little of its history is known.

22. Roueché, however, takes this to mean "only" in Pamphylia (cf. J. Nollé, *Side in Altertum* I, IK 43 [Bonn 1993] 90); for such elatives in acclamations see H. S. Versnel, *Inconsistencies in Greek and Roman Religion* I (Leiden 1990) 224, 243.

Side

The rich harbor city of Side occupied a small peninsula, walled where it joins the mainland; the port, although artificial and poor, was much used as one of the few possible anchorages along the coast of Pamphylia. The region flourished especially in the third century A.D., with the growth of Roman military commitments in Syria.[1] While the founder Apollo was prominent, the true patron divinity of Side was Athena, called τῇ προκαθεζομένῃ Ἀθηνᾷ πενταετηρίδι in an inscription of the third century.[2] Strabo, whose account of Pamphylia occupies a single paragraph, is content to report: "Side, a colony of Cyme; it has a temple of Athena" (14.4.2 [667]). The goddess, in military dress, dominates the coins from the fifth century B.C. to the end of antiquity; she normally represents the city on the *homonoia* coins of imperial date.[3] The evidence of the third century pointedly illustrates, here as at Perge, the city's Panhellenic games granted by Gordian,[4] as does Athena's epithet πενταετηρίς.

Inviolability at Side is revealed by two documents. First, a bronze coin of the time of Aurelian (A.D. 270–275):

> Bust of Aurelian | Athena of Side, helmeted, in her left hand a palm, with her right holding a token over an amphora, Ἀθηνᾷ ἀσύλῳ Σιδητῶν (PLATE 7).[5]

1. A. M. Mansel, *Die Ruinen von Side* (Berlin 1963); *RE* Suppl. 10 (1965) 879–918; J. Nollé, *Side*. Cf. Robert, *Hellenica* V (1948) 69–76; Seyrig, *RN* VI.5 (1963) 57–64 (*Scripta numis*. 61–68); Nollé, *Chiron* 16 (1986) 204–206.

2. Bean and Mitford, *DenkschrWien* 102.3 (1970) no. 19.7 (Nollé, *Side* p. 195).

3. For the coinage see S. Atlan, *TTKYay* V.23 (1967) on the earliest; *TTKBelleten* 31 (1967) 483–511 on the Alexanders; 39 (1975) 575–611 on the coins of Amyntas.

4. Cf. P. Weiss, *Chiron* 11 (1981) 317–346, with J. and L. Robert, *Bull. épigr.* 1982, 450.

5. *BMC Cilicia* 296 no. 128A; cf. Imhoof-Blumer, *Kl. Münzen* p. 347. For the agonistic type see Robert, *Hellenica* VII (1949) 107–108; *RPhil* 32 (1958) 21 (*Op. min. sel.* V 161).

The palm and amphora evoke the games and prizes of Athena. Second, in the third century Side erected a statue of the Roman Senate; most of the inscription on the base is occupied with naming the organs of government responsible, together with their titles (Nollé, *Side* no. 26):

ἡ λαμπρ[οτάτη]
βουλὴ καὶ ὁ εὐσταθὴ̣[ς δῆ]-
μος καὶ ἡ σεμνοτάτ[η καὶ]
[φ]ιλοσέβαστος καὶ κρ[ατίστη]
[τ]ῆς λαμπροτάτης κ[αὶ ἐνδό]-
[ξ]ου ἑξάκις νεωκό[ρου Σιδη]-
[τ]ῶν πόλεως ἱερὰ κα[ὶ μεγάλη]
[γε]ρουσία νεωκοροῦ[σα Ἀθηνᾷ]
[τῇ θ]ε̣ῷ ἀσύλῳ καὶ νεω[κοροῦσα θε]-
ῷ Διονύσῳ τῷ ἐν τῷ ἱε[ρῷ]
αὐτῆς δειπνιστηρίῳ.

Concerning the status and titles of Side, the coins are rather modest. No title of any sort appears before Gallienus; thereafter coins mostly advertise the neocories, but occasionally their alliance with Rome and their "mystic" contest. The inscriptions on stone are also reticent, showing usually πρώτη, λαμπροτάτη, and ἔνδοξος.[6] One approaches the detail of that quoted above, without, however, calling Athena "asylos" (*Side* no. 44): [ἡ φίλη] σύμμ[αχος πι]στὴ Ῥωμαίω̣ν [Σίδη μ]ύστι[ς] καὶ ν̣[εωκοροῦσα τῷ πατρ]ῴῳ θ[εῷ] κτ[ίσ]τῃ Ἀπόλλ[ωνι κ]αὶ νεωκοροῦ[σ]α [θεῷ Ἀθηνᾷ.

The application of the adjective to the god rather than the city would suggest that the temple alone was so recognized, and it therefore may have been outside the city proper; such was the usage at Ephesus and at neighboring Perge. On the seaward extreme of the peninsula of Side, side by side facing east, stand two contemporary temples, one somewhat larger than the other. Mansel dated them to the second half of the second century A.D. and reasonably suggested that they belonged to the two great civic gods, Athena and Apollo.[7] If I am right, however, the inviolable temple of Athena is to be sought elsewhere.

Given especially the reticence of the coins, their silence is unprobative.[8] Here as at Perge, I assume that the recognition derives from the Hellenistic period.

6. Cf. Mansel, *RE* 886; Nollé, *Side* 88–91.

7. Mansel, *Ruinen* 77–86. On the temple of Apollo, see *CP* 91 (1996) 78–80.

8. Nollé (90; cf. 316), taking seriously Perge's claim to be "sole inviolable," limits that claim to Pamphylia and suggests that the original grant for Side came later, in A.D. 272/3.

Sillyum

Sillyum in Pamphylia stood some ten kilometers from the sea at the beginning of higher ground, on a bluff east of the Cestrus River overlooking the coastal plain.[1] The plateau itself is approachable only from the west; Alexander failed to capture the city (Arr. *Anab.* 1.26.5). The extant inscriptions reveal little about cult—Apollo and Tyche, a "priestess of Demeter and all the gods and *hierophantis* of the ancestral gods."[2] The chief divinity of Sillyum is revealed rather by the coins (almost all of imperial date): the moon god Men, shown in various poses, dominates.[3]

Here as at Side, the civic coinage signals *asylia* only quite late (under Aurelian, A.D. 270–275) and sparsely; we have two issues:

Aurelian | Men bust, or Men on horseback; Σιλλυέων, θεοῦ Μηνὸς ἀσύλο(υ).[4]

As elsewhere in Pamphylia, the title goes to the god rather than to the city. This suggests that the temple of Men rather than the city and country of Sillyum had received the recognition, and possibly that the temple was not in the city itself on the plateau but down in the plain. If the original grant occurred in the late Hellenistic period as I would prefer, it is interesting that this came in the name of a non-Greek god. A certain parallel is Mopsuestia with its inviolable temple of Isis (**217**).

1. Lanckoronski, *Städte Pamphyliens* I 64–84; cf. G. Bean, *Turkey's Southern Shore* (New York 1968) 59–66 with pls. 13–18.

2. Lanckoronski nos. 57, 58, 60.

3. Conveniently collected by E. N. Lane, *Corpus . . . Dei Menis* II, EPRO 19 (Leiden 1975) 134–151. Tyche is seen most frequently after Men. The nude male pictured on some of the rare Hellenistic issues (e.g., *BMC Cilicia* 165 no. 1) is perhaps the hero-founder Mopsus: compare *BMC* 108 no. 24 from Mopsuestia; for Mopsus in Pamphylia see Kruse, "Mopsos 2," *RE* 16 (1933) 242; R. D. Barnett, *JHS* 73 (1953) 142; for a statue of him at Sillyum, Bean p. 60.

4. Lane 151 nos. 53, 54; cf. Robert, *AntCl* 36 (1966) 411 n. 5 (*Op. min. sel.* VI 135).

Hyde

Hyde was a city of some importance in southern Lycaonia.[1] It appears to have struck coins on only one occasion in its history, some half dozen issues in the early 160s A.D. (obverses of M. Aurelius, Faustina, and Verus). The reverses show Cybele, a standing Hermes, or a river god, and are inscribed Ὕδης ΙΕΡΑΣ, κοινὸν Λυκαονίας.[2] I am uncertain whether we are to take this as ἱερ(ᾶς καὶ) ἀσ(ύλου) and the granted title, or as a rhetorical flourish, "Hyde the sacred."

1. See G. Laminger-Pascher, *DenkschrWien* 232 (1992) 94–98; H. von Aulock, *Münzen und Städte Lykaoniens,* IstMitt-BH 16 (Tübingen 1976) 40–41, 86, 93–95. The city is on record consulting Apollo of Claros: J. and L. Robert, *Fouilles d'Amyzon* I p. 34.

2. The second element, which is variously abbreviated, recurs at nearby Barata and Dalisandrus. It may imply that the occasion of these coins was the hosting of games of the League.

Tyana

Tyana in southern Cappadocia, the home of the seer Apollonius, stood above the valley of the Lamus River and the main road from central Anatolia to the Cilician Gates and was an important city already in Xenophon's time.[1] Hellenistic evidence for its history is slight.[2] Strabo's report that the city's dynastic name was "Eusebeia under Taurus" (12.2.7 [537]) would indicate refoundation by the Cappadocian kings in the second century B.C.; the name is not found in our several documents. Inscriptions of any date are few, and the earliest coins are imperial and never numerous.

The few autonomous bronzes, unfortunately not datable, give the city no titles, Τυανέων;[3] likewise an isolated issue under Nero.[4] The city reckoned an era from A.D. 116/7 and began under Trajan to issue coins regularly; from the first of these the city boasts of being inviolable and autonomous:

Τυανέων τ(ῶν) π(ρὸς) τ(ῷ) Τ(αύρῳ) ἱερ(ᾶς) ἀσύ(λου) αὐτο(νόμου)

This is seen, variously abbreviated, on all issues down to Caracalla, when the last extant coins of the city show these titles supplanted by the dignity of colonial status.[5]

1. Xen. *An.* 1.2.20. See Ruge, *RE* 7A (1943) 1630–1642.

2. We have a list of gymnasiarchs in the time of Ariarathes VI of Cappadocia (ca. 130–118 B.C.): *SEG* 1.466.

3. *BMC Galatia* no. 1; *Copenh.* 34.315; H. C. Lindgren and F. L. Kovacs, *Ancient Bronze Coins of Asia Minor and the Levant* (San Mateo 1985) 92.

4. *RPC* I 3659–3660 ("year 12").

5. *BMC Galatia* 96–98. Once (*BMC* no. 9) the three adjectives are written out in full within a wreath; an issue under Trajan (*BMC* no. 3; *von Aulock* 6536) omits the titles to make space for the name of the governor. *Von Aulock* 6537 under Hadrian shows no titles, but the coin is small and the strike partly off the flan.

We should deduce nothing from the silence of the few coins before Trajan, or of the colonial issues; Tyana probably had the title of inviolability throughout the imperial period. This region was annexed by Rome only in A.D. 17—not long before the Senate's review of *asylia*. At Tyana as elsewhere, I suggest that the status was older than the Roman Empire, granted probably by one of the Cappadocian kings in the late second or the first century B.C. Of cult, we see Zeus, Athena, Perseus, and Asclepius on the coins, as well as the predictable Tyche. In the 270s A.D., it was claimed, the city was saved from molestation by an epiphany of Apollonius.[6]

6. *HA Aurel.* 24.3; the miracle is absent from the account at *FHG* IV 197.

Comana in Pontus

Comana, in the fertile valley of the Iris River, claimed to be the daughter city of Comana in Cappadocia, and like the Cappadocian city it honored above all the goddess Enyo-Ma.[1] The city came under Roman rule in A.D. 34 and became eventually Hierocaesarea-Comana. With one exception the coins show no titles. Inviolability is known from an inscription from the site and from one of the few pseudoautonomous bronze coins.[2]

The inscription is a dedication to the emperors made by the city in the 160s A.D.: the city describes itself as ἡ Ἱερ[οκαι]σαρέων Κομανέ[ων ἱερὰ] καὶ ἄσυλο[ς πόλις - - -].[3] The coin, being pseudoautonomous, cannot be easily dated:

> Dionysus (?) bust, Ἱεροκαισαρέων Κομανέων | Goddess standing, ΙΕΡΑ. . . .
> (*Rec. gén.*[2] I 108 no. 8; "time of Septimius Severus?")

The most active year of the mint was the local year 162 = A.D. 195/6,[4] during which the coins almost all show for the first time a monumental temple of a goddess, presumably Ma; but these give the city no title.

1. Ruge, *RE* 11 (1921) 1126–1127; B. Remy, *Pontica* I (Istanbul 1991) 104–107.

2. The other pseudoautonomous issues (*Rec. gén.* no. 7), which lack "Hierocaesarea" as well as any title, are assigned to the 30s A.D.

3. Ramsay, *JP* 11 (1882) 153 no. 14, from a local copyist [*IGR* III 106]. ἱερὰ Rigsby: νεωκόρος] Ramsay.

4. In the *Recueil*, eight of the nineteen issues come from this year.

Cilicia

The inviolable cities of Cilicia were numerous;[1] the status seems to arrive toward 100 B.C., somewhat later than in Syria-Palestine. Various of the cities were intermittently under Seleucid kings, often rivals of one another, or under the lesser dynasts after the collapse of Seleucid authority in Cilicia in the 90s,[2] and the title spreads amid their growing competition for the loyalties of the cities.

Aegeae

Aegeae held the fine harbor that looks eastward across the Gulf of Issus toward Alexandria/Iskenderun and the road through Mt. Amanus to Syria.[3] In imperial times this was the city of Asclepius, whose miracles attracted to his temple pilgrims from all the world.[4] The inviolability of Aegeae is attested

1. For *MAMA* III 65 see p. 589. See generally G. Dagron and D. Feissel, *Inscriptions de Cilicie* (Paris 1987), and F. Hild and H. Hellenkemper, *Kilikien und Isaurien,* TabImpByz V (= DenkschrWien 215) (1990), whose bibliographies should be consulted for all the cities that follow. On several Cilician civic festivals see R. Ziegler, *Städtisches Prestige und kaiserliche Politik* (Düsseldorf 1985) 19–57; and *Tyche* 8 (1993) 203–219 on civic eras.

2. No Seleucid mint seems to have operated in Cilicia later than 93 B.C.: A. Houghton in *Festschrift für Leo Mildenberg* (Wetteren 1984) 102.

3. See Robert, *JSav* 1973, 161–211; 1978, 145–150 (*Op. min. sel.* VII 225–282); P. Weiss, *Chiron* 12 (1982) 192–205.

4. Cf. *CIG* 5616, Asclepius and Hygieia the πολιοῦχοι θεοί; literary and numismatic testimonies at Robert, *Op. min. sel.* VII 248–268. Note, however, the puzzling "ancestral goddess," ἡ πάτριος θεά, mentioned in an inscription of the second century A.D. (Robert, *DAM* 77–90, at 84–85; line 24 of the inscription).

by coins of the late Hellenistic period; issues of imperial date show a good many other titles, but not *asylia*. These later titles reflect the patronage of individual emperors[5] and the legendary origins and political prominence of the city: εὐγενίς for their Argive descent through Perseus, and "Macedonian," also ναυαρχίς and πιστή, eventually νεωκόρος, and, almost unique among civic titles, θεοφιλής, "dear to god,"[6] presumably Asclepius. The games of Asclepius were made Panhellenic in the third century A.D.[7] Nevertheless, the image of Asclepius is not seen on the coins until imperial times, and it may be that some other cult occasioned the recognition of inviolability in the Hellenistic period.[8]

Of the numerous bronze issues of late Hellenistic date[9] some show Αἰγεαίων with no titles; these are followed by bronzes with the titles "sacred and inviolable," then "sacred and autonomous":

A. Tyche bust | Horse's head, Αἰγεαίων τῆς ἱερᾶς καὶ ασύλου.
Bloesch nos. 103–107.
B. Athena bust | Goat, inscription as A; a smaller denomination.
Bloesch no. 108.
C. Tyche bust | Horse's head, Αἰγεαίων τῆς ἱερᾶς καὶ αὐτονόμου.
Bloesch nos. 113–172, 204–208; Ziegler, *Münzen Kilikiens*, Vestigia 42 (Munich 1988) 171–172 nos. 1365–1368.
D. Athena bust | Goat, inscription as C; a smaller denomination.
Bloesch nos. 173–189; 209–210; Ziegler no. 1369.
E. Heracles bust | Club and bow, inscription as C; a still smaller denomination.
Bloesch nos. 190–203, 211–212.

Then titles vanish until the developed imperial age, when Aegeae begins to display other honors. A terminus ante quem for the end of the title of inviolability on the coins might be given by Hellenistic Aegeae's several extant silver issues, which are without titles, only Αἰγεαίων: we would expect the silver to exhibit

5. As elsewhere in Cilicia: J. and L. Robert, *Bull. épigr.* 1970, 407; Ziegler, *Prestige* 67–120.

6. Found also of Hermoupolis Magna in Egypt (ἀρχαῖα καὶ θεοφιλής, *BGU* III 924, 937; *CPR* VI 73; *SB* 9358). The word probably had an antiquarian and poetic ring (cf. Homeric φίλος ἀθανάτοισι θεοῖσι); it had been applied to cities in classical epinician; cf. LSJ s.v.; F. Dirlmeier, *Ausgewählte Schriften* (Heidelberg 1970) 99. Compare εὐσεβής as a title at Gaza, the superlative at Nicaea.

7. Robert, *Op. min. sel.* VII 251; Ziegler, *Prestige* 51.

8. So Robert, *Op. min. sel.* VII 225 n. 119, against K. Latte, *Kleine Schriften* (Munich 1968) 735 n. 10. But against Robert's view that the vogue for Asclepius was a late phenomenon, note Alexander's celebration of Asclepieia at Soli in Cilicia: Arr. *Anab.* 2.5.8; cf. Curt. 3.7.3.

9. Assembled by H. Bloesch, *ANSMN* 27 (1982) 53–96, who would assign most of A–E to the years 110 to 83 B.C., the remainder to "60/50–47." His chronology is artificial; and especially for the latter group (his meager Period 5, here the second citations under C–E) it seems to me to have little foundation.

titles if the city had any. These coins, dated by the Caesarean era, are first seen in 44/3 and come down to 30/29.[10]

An exception is found in two issues of bronze:

F. Bust of Alexander the Great | Bust of Julius Caesar, Αἰγεαίων τῆς ἱερᾶς καὶ αὐτονόμου, date (?) ζπ = 87 = A.D. 40/1.[11]
SNG Levante 1691, 1692; *RPC* I 4036.

If these are rightly dated, they contrast not only with the silence of the other coins of imperial date, which would not be significant, but also with that of the post-Caesarean silver. Perhaps therefore these two issues represent a genuine alteration of the titles of Aegeae, a brief restoration in the first year of Caligula (the heralding of Alexander and Caesar may be relevant). Or else we must take the silence of the silver as meaningless, or ZΠ as not a date.

For the initial grant of *asylia* the style of the bronzes (A–B) suggests a date of roughly 100 B.C., so perhaps in the context of the loss of Seleucid control in the 90s. If the distribution of extant issues is any evidence, the recognition of autonomy followed fairly quickly upon that of inviolability.[12] The silence of the silver should indicate that the city lost both *asylia* and autonomy toward the mid-first century: probably at the hands of Pompey rather than Caesar, since it is after Caesar that Aegeae is seen to enjoy both a new era and the right to strike silver. If this is so, then Aegeae gained *asylia* and then autonomy amid the dynastic rivalries of the late second or early first century and lost them in Pompey's settlement in the 60s.

Hierapolis-Castabala

Castabala, some thirty kilometers inland on the Pyramus River, was the city of the goddess Perasia, who is attested already in Achaemenid times. Originally a version of Cybele, eventually equated with Artemis by Greek authors, Perasia is regularly shown on the coins of Hierapolis; her priestesses attracted notice for

10. See O. Mørkholm, *ANSMN* 32 (1987) 57–60, and A. Houghton and S. Bendall, *ANSMN* 33 (1988) 71–85, refuting Bloesch's assignment to early I B.C. (when these coins would certainly have borne the titles of inviolability, like the bronzes of that period). A further example: *M&M* 569.17.

11. Levante's interpretation for the date, which must be called uncertain; one issue has MI left, ZΠ right; the other only ZΠ left.

12. Houghton and Bendall argue reasonably that autonomy came after the end of Seleucid rule and before the invasion of Tigranes, i.e., in the period 93–83 B.C.

their ritual dance on hot coals.[13] Robert suspected that the temple stood on the hill at the eastern end of the main street. It is uncertain when Castabala acquired the Greek name Hierapolis (it is already so on the earliest coins, under Antiochus IV ca. 170 B.C.); the name signals the importance of the cult to the life of the city. In the first century B.C. the city came to be the capital of the dynasty of Tarcondimotus.[14]

The civic bronzes with imperial obverses, and thus datable, attribute no titles to Hierapolis. The pseudoautonomous issues, not closely dated, seem to begin in the second century B.C. and may come down as late as the Roman Empire. Of the nineteen pseudoautonomous issues identified by Robert (*Déesse* pp. 66–99), six show the title of inviolability, with two images:

A. Tyche bust | Eagle, Ἱεροπολιτῶν τῶν πρὸς τῷ Πυράμῳ τῆς ἱερᾶς καὶ ἀσύλου.
Robert 67 nos. 3–6;[15] Ziegler, *Münzen* 160 nos. 1285–1287.

B. Tyche bust | Perasia seated on a throne, same inscription.
Robert nos. 7, 13; *SNG Levante* 1571–74.

We have two absolute dates. Hierapolis, like many other Seleucid cities, was allowed a pseudoautonomous coinage by Antiochus IV around 170 B.C. (Robert nos. 1–2), and as everywhere else, these coins claim no titles. A terminus ante quem, equally unsurprising, is provided by an inscription from the site, the base of a statue of Tarcondimotus as toparch:[16]

ὁ δῆμος ὁ Ἱεροπολιτῶν τῶ[ν]
πρὸς τῶι Πυράμωι τῆς ἱερᾶς κα[ὶ]
ἀσύλου Ταρκονδίμωτον Στράτων[ος]
υἱὸν τοπάρχην, τὸν εὐεργέτην
καὶ κηδεμόνα τοῦ δήμου.

Thus Hierapolis was sacred and inviolable before the 30s B.C., when Antony promoted Tarcondimotus from toparch to king. Tarcondimotus is first met,

13. Strab. 12.2.7 (537); cf. H. Taeuber, *EpigAnat* 19 (1992) 19–24 (a διαβατηρία Περασίας).

14. A. Dupont-Sommer and L. Robert, *La déesse de Hiérapolis Castabala* (Paris 1964); more inscriptions at M. Sayar, P. Siewert, and H. Taeuber, *SBWien* 547 (1989) 9–33 [*SEG* 39.1497–1516]. Tarcondimotus has been surveyed by W. Hoben, "Untersuchungen zur Stellung kleinasiatischer Dynasten" (Diss., Johannes Gutenberg-Univ., Mainz 1969) 195–211 (without knowing Dupont-Sommer/Robert); R. D. Sullivan, *Near Eastern Royalty and Rome* (Toronto 1990) 185–192.

15. Robert felt that his no. 6 did not contain καὶ ἀσύλου, and suspected therefore that it preceded the other five issues (in keeping with Seyrig's thesis that ἱερά represents the earlier of two titles). Even if that reading were correct, with no other control on the relative chronology of these coins we might think instead that ΙΕΡΑΣ abbreviates the whole; but we now have an obverse die link with Ziegler no. 1287, whose reverse reads ΙΕ[ΡΑΣ] ΚΑΙ [ΑΣΥΛΟΥ].

16. Heberdey and Wilhelm, *Reisen in Kilikien*, DenkschrWien 44.6 (1896) no. 63 [*IGR* III 901; *OGIS* 752; Robert p. 38]; *squeeze* (Vienna).

already an ally of Rome, at the end of the 50s (Cic. *Fam.* 15.1.2) and is thought to have owed his rule to Pompey's settlement ca. 64 B.C. The title does not recur in the several other inscriptions from the site; but such silence in inscriptions is common and is matched by the coins of imperial date, so that these silences need not have any chronological significance.

Accordingly, the recognition of the inviolability of Hierapolis occurred in the latter part of the second century or the first half of the first; greater precision would require a surer dating of the bronze coins. The grantor might be one of the rival Seleucids during their last twenty years in Cilicia, or one of the lesser dynasts thereafter, or indeed Pompey, who may have been the first benefactor of Tarcondimotus.

Elaeusa-Sebaste

Elaeusa was situated by a small harbor at the eastern extreme of Rough Cilicia; when in the first century B.C. the kings of Cappadocia ruled part of Cilicia, Elaeusa stood on their western frontier with the Roman province of Cilicia. From the 20s B.C. Archelaus I of Cappadocia developed the city as a royal residence, building a palace on the island in the harbor; he renamed the city Sebaste in honor of Augustus.[17] For us this is useful as a terminus ante quem for inviolability, which is first attested when the city was still under the name Elaeusa. For cults we rely mostly upon the coins; but the strongest hint of the city's patron is given by an inscription of imperial date: the penalty for violating a tomb is to be paid to τῇ ἐν Σεβαστῇ Ἀθήνᾳ and τῷ Σεβαστηνῶν δήμῳ.[18] Athena is often seen on the coins of Roman times; in the most unusual image, widely found in Cilicia and suggestive of the local myth, she attacks the serpent-footed giant Enceladus.

Elaeusa was seat of a Seleucid royal mint in the late second century, especially prolific under Seleucus VI (96/5 B.C.).[19] Some autonomous bronzes of late Hellenistic date are extant; these show simply Ἐλαιουσίων without titles and may be assumed to precede the grant of inviolability. The first testimony to *asylia* consists of four meager issues of silver tetradrachms of late Hellenistic date:

17. Strab. 14.5.6 (671). See Keil and Wilhelm, *MAMA* III pp. 220–228; F. Imhoof-Blumer, *RevSuisse* 8 (1898) 24–40; E. Kirsten, *AnzWien* 110 (1973) 347–363, and in *Mélanges Mansel* (Ankara 1974) II 777–802; H. Hellenkemper and F. Hild, *Neue Forschungen in Kilikien,* DenkschrWien 186 (1986) 69–85; Archelaus is surveyed by Hoben 179–194; Sullivan 182–185.

18. *JHS* 12 (1891) 231 no. 11.

19. See Houghton, *ANSMN* 33 (1988) 67–69, 85–89, for references.

A. Tyche bust | Goddess standing left with tiller, Ἐλαιουσίων τῆς ἱερᾶς καὶ αὐτονόμου.
Four issues: Houghton p. 86.

In imperial times, scattered bronzes of the late second to mid-third century A.D. cite *asylia*, while most issues omit this title and prefer others (emperors' epithets, "metropolis," ναυαρχίς, "loyal ally of the Romans"). I cite examples to illustrate the range of abbreviation:

B. Commodus | Athena attacking giant, Σεβαστὴ ἱερ(ὰ) ἄσ(υλος) αὐτ(όνομος) ναυ(αρχίς).
Imhoof-Blumer 39 no. 42; *BMC Lycaonia* 235 no. 13.
C. Septimius Severus | Nike, Σεβα(στὴ) Ι(ΕΡΑ) αὐτό(νομος) ναυαρχίς.
Ziegler, *Münzen* 78 no. 573.
D. Gordian III | Eagle, Σεβαστὴ ΙΕΡΑ ναυαρχίς.
SNG Levante 852.
E. Valerian | Asclepius standing, Σεβαστὴ ἱερ(ὰ) ἄσ(υλος) αὐ(τόνομος) ναυαρχίς, π(ιστή) σ(ύμμαχος) Ῥ(ωμαίων) δ(ωρεαῖς) ἐ(ξαιρέτοις) τ(ετειμημένη).
Imhoof-Blumer no. 45; Ziegler no. 577.

The sporadic citation and abbreviation of *asylia* on the imperial bronzes is obviously without political significance, and we can conclude that the city possessed the status throughout the imperial period.

The occasion of the original grant will depend on the date of the silver tetradrachms for a terminus ante quem. Imhoof-Blumer thought their style ca. 100 B.C.; Mørkholm found their weight standard to be in the range typical of the 80s and 70s;[20] Houghton has argued for the decade following the end of Seleucid rule toward 93 B.C. The grant thus probably came early in the first century B.C., as at Aegeae, and in the context of the Seleucid loss of the region.

Mopsuestia

Mopsuestia stood in a fertile plain some fifty kilometers up the Pyramus River from its mouth, founded by the seer Mopsus whose fire altar is so often seen on the coins.[21] An inscribed confirmation by Rome in 86 B.C. reveals that the cult

20. Mørkholm, *ANSMN* 32 (1987) 58 n. 4, and in *Studia Paulo Naster oblata* I (Louvain 1982) 139–149.

21. W. Ruge, *RE* 16 (1933) 243–250; T. S. MacKay, *ANRW* XVIII. 3 (1990) 2115–2116; on Mopsus, J. and L. Robert, *Bull. épigr.* 1966, 464; F. Bron, *Recherches sur les inscriptions phéniciennes de Karatepe* (Geneva 1979) 172–176; for the coins, H. von Aulock, *AA* 1963, 231–277; D. Metzler, *Kernos* 3 (1990) 235–250 (Mopsus on coins).

for which inviolability was granted was that of Isis and Sarapis. This is a surprise when one considers the coins, where the Egyptian gods are not represented—a cautionary lesson on the limitations of the coin evidence. The inscription also makes clear that, despite the title on the coins ("of the Mopsuestians the sacred and inviolable"), in Roman eyes it was the temple, not the city and country, that held the title of inviolability.

The political history of Mopsuestia in the second century B.C. is known mainly from its coins. Refounded as "Seleuceia" by Antiochus IV, the city was at times the seat of a royal Seleucid mint[22] and also issued bronzes in its own name. These coins are without titles; the civic bronzes show the name Σελευκέων τῶν πρὸς τῶι Πυράμωι, which eventually yields to Μοψεατῶν, the city reverting to its ancestral name at an uncertain date. Thus *asylia* is not attested while the city used the name "Seleuceia"; only after the reversion to Μοψεατῶν come the civic coins that reveal inviolability and then autonomy, while the inscription gives a terminus ante quem of 86 B.C. for inviolability. Seleucus VI died violently in Mospuestia in 95, and the city may have become free of Seleucid rule after that.[23]

It is convenient to begin with this Roman recognition. In the first letter a magistrate follows the recommendation of Lucullus in granting the inviolability of the temple of Isis; in the second Lucullus the quaestor writes to Mopsuestia stating his decision that the temple is inviolable and adding to the privileges of the priest Diodotus. Clearly this is in reverse chronological order, the definitive decision placed first when the two letters came to be inscribed. In 86 B.C. Lucullus, quaestor to Sulla, was sailing the eastern Mediterranean in search of military support for his commander, who was in Greece preparing for war with Mithridates; he returned from Phoenicia by way of Cyprus, thus coasting Cilicia. The inscription reveals that he was now approached by Mopsuestia; no embassy is mentioned, which may mean that he went inland to Mopsuestia in person. After his return to Greece, the commander Sulla ratified the *acta* of the quaestor—perhaps only after the defeat of Mithridates in 85 B.C. and the general settlement of affairs in Asia.

217. Rome: Lucullus and Sulla

Marble block in the Adana museum, preserved only on the left; h. 0.60, w. 0.38, th. 0.16; letters 0.01.

22. Assigned to Mopsuestia because of the emblem of the fire altar: Jenkins, *NC* VI.11 (1951) 19–21; von Aulock (1963) no. 4 (tetradrachm of Antiochus IX, 108/7 B.C.); cf. Bellinger, "End" 71–72 nn. 64, 70.

23. The statement in the Armenian translation of Eus. *Chron.* (123 Karst) that Antiochus and Philip now destroyed the city in retribution for Seleucus is weak testimony in its own right, and now contradicted by the Roman grant of 86 B.C.

M. H. Sayar, P. Siewert, and H. Taeuber, *Tyche* 9 (1994) 113–130. *Squeeze* (Vienna).[24]

Photograph: *Tyche* pls. 20–23.

Cf. Gauthier, *Bull. épig.* 1995, 601.

[- - -]α̣σαντ̣[-]
[- - - -]σ̣εως τῆς [-]
[. . .] τ̣ῆ̣ς Ἴσιδος ἀσυλ̣[- - - - - - - - - - , καθὼς?]
[τὸ] ἱερὸν ἣν ὑπὸ τῶν βασιλ̣[έων τετιμημένον? διὰ]
[τ]ὴν εὐσέβειαν τὴν πρὸς τὴ[ν θεάν· ἐγὼ οὖν τὴν]
πα[ρ]άκλησιν τὴν Λευκόλλου̣ [ταμίου ὑπακούσας?]
συνεχώρησα ἄσυλον εἶναι τὸ [παρ' ὑμεῖν ἱερὸν]
τῆς Ἴσιδος.

Λεύκολλος ταμίας καὶ ἀντιστρά[τηγος τοῖς]
Μοψεατῶν ἄρχουσι βουλῆι δήμωι [χαίρειν· τὸ]
ἱερὸν τῆς Ἴσιδος καὶ τοῦ Σαράπιδ[ος σεμνότα]-
τ̣ον κ̣α̣ὶ̣ ἔνδοξον ὑ̣π̣ά̣ρ̣χον, ἐν πάσηι τ[ε πόλει]
κα̣ὶ χ̣ώραι δοξαζ̣ό̣μ̣εν̣ον καὶ παρ' ὑμε[ῖν τει]-
μῆς τ̣ῆ̣[ς] μεγίστης κατηξιωμένον, κ[έκρικα]
καὶ αὐτὸς καθ' ἃ κα̣ὶ οἱ π̣[ρ]ο̣ ἡμῶν αὐ[τοκρά]-
τορες ἐ̣π̣έκ[ρι]ναν ἄ̣σ̣υ̣λ̣ον εἶναι· Διόδοτον [δὲ Διοδό?]-
του τοῦ Ἀθηνίωνος τὸν ἱερέα τοῦ Σα[ράπιδος]
κ̣αὶ τῆς Ἴσ[ιδ]ο[ς] κ̣α̣θ̣ει̣λ̣η̣φὼς ἄνδρα χρήσι̣[μον, ?θρησ]-
κωδέστ̣α̣[τα] ΕΙ̣. δ̣ιαφέροντα τοῖς τε θεο[ῖς λυσιτε]-
λέστατ̣[α πα]ρεδρεύοντα καὶ τὰς θεραπε[ίας ποιού]-
μενον εὐσεβεστάτας καὶ ἱεροπρεπέ[στατα τὰ τῶν]
θεῶν τείμια ἐ̣παύξοντα καὶ τὸν τόπ[ον ?τῆι ἰδι]-
αι ἐπιμελεία̣ κοσμοῦντα ἀποδεξάμε[νος τιμᾶν? αὐ]-
τὸν βούλομαι. ἐπείπερ καὶ αὐτοὶ τε[ίμιόν]
τι πεποιήκατε πολλῶι μᾶλλον κα[τάξιον]
χάριν τειμῆς καὶ καταλογῆς τῶι δή[μωι ἐν]
ταῖς διαπράσεσι τῶν ὠνῶν ποιοῦντ̣[ες πα]-
[ρ]αίρεσιν κεφαλῆς αὐτοῦ τε καὶ γυνα[ικὸς καὶ]
[υἱ]ῶν τριῶν καὶ τῆς ὑπαρχο⟨ύ⟩σης αὐ̣[τῶι οὐσίας]
[. . . . .]ΙΤ[. . .]ΟΥΡΙΟ[- - - - - - - - - - - -]

2: The editors suggest as possible περὶ τῆς ἀνανεώ]σ̣εως or προαιρέ]σ̣εως. 3 Rigsby: ἀσυλ̣[ίαν - - -] edd. 4 ἣν (ἣ̣ν] edd.) and τετιμημένον Rigsby. 5 Rigsby: θεὰν καὶ κατὰ τὴν] edd. 6 Rigsby: [τοῦ ταμίου ἐμοῦ? edd. 7 Rigsby: [ἱερὸν τὸ. . . . .] or [τέμενος τὸ] or το[ῦτο τὸ ἱερὸν] edd. 12 Gauthier: τ[ῆι edd. 22 end Rigsby. 29: ΟΨΗΣ.

. . .

24. I am most grateful to the editors for discussing this inscription with me in advance of publication.

(4ff.) [. . . as?] the temple has been [honored?] by the kings [on account of] their piety toward the [goddess. (?)Therefore I have listened to the] request of [quaestor] Lucullus and grant that [your temple] of Isis is to be inviolable.

Lucullus, quaestor pro praetore, to the magistrates, council, and people of Mopsuestia, [greetings. The] temple of Isis and Sarapis, being [most revered] and distinguished, famed in every [city] and country and found worthy of the greatest honor among you, I myself, in keeping with the decision of the commanders before us, [have decided] to be inviolable. Diodotus son of [Diodo]tus grandson of Athenion, the priest of Sa[rapis] and Isis, I have found to be valuable . . . distinguished, and I approve of him for attending to the gods most generously and [do]ing the most pious services and increasing most devotedly the honors of the gods and adorning the place [through his personal?] supervision; so I wish to [honor?] him. Inasmuch as you yourselves have granted him an honor far more worthy because of his dignity and renown with the people by providing, at the farming out of tax contracts, immunity on his person and his wife and three sons and the [property] he possesses . . .

Some features of this text have made me wonder whether it might be of imperial date (hence Flavian or later), an unknown provincial quaestor Lucullus acting for the legate and being ratified by the emperor. Lucullus uses only his cognomen, and his superior grants him no more (a humble gesture first on record of Agrippa, *Roman Doc.* 66);[25] line 15 might evoke as precedent "the emperors before us," the words emperors themselves often use. But the editors' assignment to the famous Lucullus and to Sulla is persuasive; and it is difficult to envisage a provincial governor (less still his aide) complacently granting *asylia* on his own authority rather than referring the question to the emperor. As to the cognomen, this is our one letter by a quaestor in the Republic: modesty befits quaestors.[26] And it ill befits any imperial magistrate to speak of "the emperors before us" (meaning our time), for fear of being thought to use the royal We. But which Roman "commanders" might have recognized *asylia* at Mopsuestia before 86 B.C. remains a problem.

2–3: E.g. περὶ | τῆς τῆ]ς Ἴσιδος ἀσυλ̣[ίας, or τὸ ἱε|ρὸν τῆ]ς Ἴσιδος ἄσυλ̣[ον.

4: For the structure cf. *I.Cret.*III IV 9.139 (with Kern, *I.Magn.* p. 253) οὐδὲ ὑπ' αὐ[τῶν 'Ι]τανίων ἦν τι αὐτοῖς δεδο[μένον? - - -].

5: So *Roman Doc.* 58.78; or else ἐγὼ δὲ, as at *Royal Corres.* 69.7.

25. Contrast the traditional usage of more dignified individuals under Augustus: *Roman Doc.* 66, 69, 71.

26. A magistrate in the 50s B.C. mentioned τοῦ αὐτο]κράτορος ἡμῶν (*Roman Doc.* 51.8, context lost), perhaps a quaestor of his commander. Lucullus' letter gives no hint that his decision is provisional and dependent on that of Sulla; but the Mopsuestians evidently understood that, for they waited until they had received Sulla's letter before inscribing both.

6: Cf. **135**.7: [ἐπ]ακούσαντες τὰ ἀξιούμενα ὑπακηκόαμεν καὶ σ[υ]γχωροῦμεν; *Syll.*^{3} 672.6: ἐπακούσας προθ[ύ]μως τὰ ἀξιούμενα. But the restoration is somewhat long.

8: For Sulla it is a temple of Isis, for Lucullus of Isis and Sarapis, while the priest is of Sarapis and Isis. Isis was served chiefly by priestesses, Sarapis by priests; in the present diplomatic dealings between the city and Rome, the male apparently took the lead.

15–16: For *imperator* generically of a field commander with imperium we have from Sulla's time *Roman Doc.* 23.36 (cf. **6**): αὐτοκράτωρ αὐτοκράτορές τ[ε] ἡμέτεροι (the Senate speaking). What Roman commanders earlier than 86 B.C. (and later than the mid-second century B.C., given the first appearance of *asylia* on the coins) recognized the inviolability of Isis of Mopsuestia? A province called "Cilicia" was first voted in 102,[27] and three commanders are known before 86, including Sulla himself in the 90s; but the apparent silence of his letter about this (unless we have ἀνανεώ]σ̣εως in line 2) suggests that he is not one of those who had already granted Mopsuestia's request. No province Cilicia was needed, however, for the Mopsuestians to approach a Roman with this request (compare Teos, Magnesia, and Colophon, long before a "province" of Asia—with Magnesia allegedly reconfirmed by Sulla); but what campaign, military or diplomatic, might have put Mopsuestia in contact with the Romans before 102 is not obvious.

18–19: Woodward, *JHS* 58 (1938) 111, on *IG* II^2 1074 suggested τὴ[ν πομπὴν? - - - ὡς εὐσεβέστατα καὶ θρη]σκωδέστατα σ[υντελέσαι - - -.

The Hellenistic bronze coins first show inviolability only after the city had reverted to the name Mopsuestia. At least some of the issues described under A–D will be earlier than the Roman confirmation of 86; but a more certain chronology remains to be found.

A. Zeus bust | Fire altar, Μοψεατῶν τῆς ἱερᾶς καὶ ἀσύλου.
Von Aulock (1963) no. 5 (six issues).

B. Apollo bust | Artemis, same inscription.
SNG Levante 1315–1316.

C. Numerous issues of the late Hellenistic period in several denominations with various types (Zeus | Fire altar; Tyche | Zeus; Apollo | Artemis), Μοψεατῶν τῆς ἱερᾶς καὶ αὐτονόμου.
Von Aulock nos. 7–10; *SNG Levante* 1308–1314, 1317–1318; Ziegler, *Münzen* 122 nos. 929–930.

D. King or hero | Tripod, same inscription.
Von Aulock no. 6 (eight issues); *SNG Levante* 1306–1307.

27. On the early province see P. Freeman in *The Defence of the Roman and Byzantine East*, BAR-IS 297 (Oxford 1986) I 253–275.

Under the Empire, pseudoautonomous bronzes, roughly mid-first through second century A.D., are without titles with the exception (as at Aegeae) of three issues of the mid-first century A.D.:

E. Zeus | Corybantes (?), Μοψεατῶν τῆς ἱερᾶς καὶ αὐτονόμου.
Von Aulock no. 12 ("time of Claudius"); *SNG Levante* 1323; *RPC* I 4055.
F. Tyche bust | Apollo, ηιρ = 118 = 50/1, same inscription.
Von Aulock no. 13; *SNG Levante* 1324; *RPC* I 4056.
G. Apollo | Artemis, θιρ = 51/2, same inscription.[28]
Von Aulock no. 14; *SNG Levante* 1325; *RPC* I 4057.

On bronzes with emperors on the obverse (Tiberius to Gallienus) the title of inviolability occurs only in A.D. 93/4 and 94/5:

H. Domitian | Standing male (Mopsus or Apollo), Μοψεατῶν τῆς ἱερᾶς καὶ ἀσύλου καὶ αυτονόμου, date αζρ = 161 = 93/4.
Von Aulock no. 27; *SNG Levante* 1326.[29]
I. Domitian and Domitia | Tyche, same inscription.
Von Aulock no. 30.
J. Domitian | Standing male, same inscription but date βζρ = 94/5.
SNG Levante 1328.[30]

The next issues come under Hadrian, when the first of the imperial epithets appears: Ἀδριανῶν Μοψεατῶν, later Σεουηριανῶν and others. Inviolability and autonomy do not recur after 94/5.

Thus the coins document the city's inviolability during the late Hellenistic period and in the first century A.D.; thereafter *asylia* is supplanted on the coins by the greater glory of titles indicating imperial favor. This silence of the later coins is supplemented by two inscriptions. In A.D. 140 the Mopsuestians made a dedication in Rome to Antoninus Pius, who had decided in their favor at a judicial hearing about the city's privileges (*IGUrbRom* I 24):

> τῷ εὐεργέτῃ καὶ σωτῆρι Ἀδριανῆς Μοψουεστίας τῆς Κιλικίας, ἱερᾶς καὶ ἐλευθέρας καὶ ἀσύλου καὶ αὐτονόμου καὶ φίλης καὶ συμμάχου Ῥωμαίων ... διὰ τῆς θείας αὐτοῦ δικαιοδοσίας βέβαια τηρήσαντος αὐτῇ τὰ ἐξ ἀρχῆς δίκαια.

Likewise a statue of Antoninus Pius erected in Mopsuestia (Dagron/Feissel 134 no. 86 = *IGR* III 915:

28. Von Aulock no. 15 (*RPC* I 4058), a smaller denomination of the same year, apparently lacks titles.

29. A smaller issue of the same year (von Aulock no. 28) has no titles.

30. Again contrast 1329 (von Aulock no. 29), a small denomination of the same year without titles.

ὁ δῆμος Ἁδριανῶν Μοψεατῶν τῆς ἱερᾶς καὶ ἐλευθέρας καὶ ἀσύλου καὶ αὐτονόμου, φίλης καὶ συμμάχου Ῥωμαίων.

We can conclude that the silence of coins after the first century is without meaning and Mopsuestia probably possessed inviolability throughout the Roman period.

As to the beginnings of the status, we cannot date closely the autonomous series A–B; any better date than the estimate from style will depend on identifying the kings on two possible royal issues. Von Aulock no. 1 (King? | Μοψεατῶν without titles) would give a terminus post quem for *asylia* if we could identify the king.[31] Again, von Aulock considered the bust on D to be a king, probably Antiochus X ca. 95 B.C.;[32] this would establish a terminus ante quem for both *asylia* and autonomy. But it is not at all certain that either of these images is of a king rather than a god or hero.

Whatever the exact date, the recognition of inviolability appears to have come after a significant relaxing of Seleucid authority over the city, marked by the city's abandonment of the royal name. The number of issues with only *asylia* suggests that at least several years separated the grant of inviolability from that of autonomy.

Soli-Pompeiopolis

Soli, to the east of Elaeusa and possessed of a good harbor, was an important city already under the Achaemenids, and a mint from quite early times. Tigranes of Armenia razed the city in 83 B.C. and transferred its population to Tigranocerta; Pompey refounded it as Pompeiopolis, which is seen to use thereafter an era of 66/5.[33] The coins reveal diverse cults, with none noticeably dominant. The Hellenistic bronzes under the name Soli claim no titles, giving only Σόλεων, and thus should constitute a terminus post quem for the recognition of *asylia*; but they cannot be closely dated—they may not extend as late as Tigranes in 83.

31. Von Aulock took the obverse to show Antiochus IV; but Mørkholm, *Antiochus IV of Syria* (Copenhagen 1966) 126 n. 35, thought the identification wrong and the coin later.

32. Hill (*BMC* 103) thought this Antiochus IV, Imhoof-Blumer Alexander Balas; either is impossibly early for the titles "sacred and autonomous." Levante suggests Mopsus. At least some issues of D are subsequent to some of C: cf. Robert, *Déesse* 96 n. 5 (on the countermarks).

33. W. Ruge, *RE* 3A (1927) 935–938; Hellenkemper/Hild 87–99. For Seleucid silver issued at Soli (down to the 130s B.C.) see O. Mørkholm, *ANSMN* 11 (1964) 58–62; H. Pfeiler, *SM* 19 (1969) 42–43; A. Houghton, *NC* 149 (1989) 15–32.

A terminus ante quem is given by the base of a statue of Pompey from the site, perhaps from 66/5 or at any rate before he left the East in 62:[34]

> τρὶς αὐτοκράτ[ορα] Πομπηιοπολιτῶν τῆς ἱερᾶς καὶ ἀσύλου καὶ ἐλευθέρας καὶ αὐτονόμου ὁ δῆμος τὸν κτίστην καὶ πατρῶνα τῆς πόλεως.

The coins stand in contrast: from the earliest issues of the proud new city[35] they show no titles throughout their history, with one exception:

> Julia Mamaea | Asclepius, Hygieia, Telesphorus, Πομπηιοπολειτῶν ἱερ(ᾶς) ἀσύλ(ου) αὐτονό(μου), date ηϘς = 298 = A.D. 232/3.[36]

Thus we have no evidence that the Hellenistic city Soli (isto nomine: down to 83 B.C.) gained inviolability. It is quite possible that "sacred, inviolable, autonomous" came whole cloth from Pompey upon the creation of his new city Pompeiopolis in 66/5 B.C. So too later Nicopolis upon its foundation by Augustus apparently was similarly honored.

Rhosus

Rhosus stands at the southern extreme of the Gulf of Issus, atop a hill projecting into the gulf from a fertile plain. Its harbor made it an easy point of crossing from Syria to Aegeae and the interior of Anatolia; myth also links the city to Cilicia rather than Syria. Demetrius Poliorcetes and Seleucus I conferred at Rhosus in 300 B.C.[37] In Hellenistic times, however, its fame was rather overshadowed by its neighbor to the north, Alexandria ad Issum, which lay nearer the road through Mt. Amanus into Syria. The ruins of Rhosus, described by Heberdey in 1892, have not been further explored.[38]

The earliest coins of the city have been assigned on the basis of style to the middle of the first century B.C. Two bronze issues are known, and both show already the title of inviolability:

34. *IGR* III 869; I have collated the squeeze in Vienna (letters 0.04 h.).

35. An early example is *BMC* 152 no. 48: Pompey | Athena Nicephorus, Πονπηιοπολιτῶν, date ἔτους ις = 16 = 51/0 B.C.

36. Imhoof-Blumer, *Zur gr.-röm. Münzkunde* (Geneva 1908) p. 220; cf. *Inv. Waddington* 4523 (reporting ΙΕΡΑΣΑΥΤΟΝ. . .).

37. Plut. *Dem.* 32. Earlier, the city had voted honors for Harpalus: Ath. 586C, 595D (*FGrHist* 115 F 254, 137 F 30).

38. *Reisen in Kilikien*, DenkschrWien 44 (1896) 20. For the coins and the civic era see Seyrig, *Syria* 27 (1950) 32–34 (*Ant. syr.* IV 98–101); E. Levante, *NC* 145 (1985) 237–243.

Either Tyche bust, or shield decorated with a walking bull | Draped hieratic male statue standing on a base, holding a thunderbolt and a knife or an ear of grain, flanked by bulls, Ῥωσέων τῆς ἱερᾶς καὶ ἀσύλου.[39]

The sporadic later coinage shows that Rhosus inaugurated a civic era in 42/1 B.C.; this would reflect a benefaction by Antony, who arrived in Syria in 41. And two documents dating soon after reveal that autonomy has been added, surely the benefaction commemorated by the era of 42/1:

In December 35 B.C. (year 8), Octavian wrote to the city: Ῥωσέων τῆς ἱερᾶς καὶ ἀσύλου καὶ αὐτονόμου ἄρχουσι βουλῆι δήμωι.[40]

A bronze issue of 27/6 B.C.: Tyche | The hieratic statue, Ῥωσέων τῆς ἱερᾶς καὶ ἀσύλου καὶ αὐτονόμου, year 16 (*RPC* I 4077).

Most of the coins of imperial date give Rhosus no titles.[41] A few are exceptional:

Tyche | The hieratic statue, Ῥωσέων τῆς ἱερᾶς καὶ ἀσύλου καὶ αὐτονόμου, year 177 = A.D. 135/6.[42]

Commodus | Either goddess bust or a seated Aphrodite, Ῥωσέων ΙΕΡΑΣ, both types year 219 = A.D. 177/8.[43]

Finally, an undated coin that might be late Hellenistic or imperial:

Zeus bust | Tyche bust, Ῥωσέων ΙΕΡΑΣ.[44]

On these last the full title of inviolability has been abbreviated; the undated issue is a small denomination, but those under Commodus are not.

Accordingly, Rhosus was declared sacred and inviolable before 42/1: around the middle of the first century if the style of the first coins is rightly estimated and if they coincide with the granting of the status. So far as can be seen from extant evidence, both *asylia* and autonomy continued without interruption through imperial times.

As to cults, the most distinctive image on the coins is of a draped male cult figure associated with bulls. This was probably the patron god of the Rhosians, apparently a descendant of the storm god, the bull Baal, who dominated the area of Mt. Amanus in the Bronze Age.

39. Imhoof-Blumer, *Monn. grec.* 440 no. 8; *SNG Copenhagen* 36.386–387; H. C. Lindgren and F. L. Kovacs, *Ancient Bronze Coins of Asia Minor and the Levant* (San Mateo 1985) no. 2117; *Hunterian* III 210 no. 1.

40. Sherk, *Roman Documents* 58.3–4, 86 (Seyrig's reading of the date).

41. Imperial obverses under Claudius, Trajan, Caracalla (see Seyrig *Ant. syr.* IV 99–100); a pseudoautonomous dated to 106/7 (*Weber* 7992; *Hunterian* no. 2).

42. Seyrig, *RN* VI.10 (1968) no. 273 (*Scripta numis.* 349).

43. *BMC Galatia* 268 no. 2; Seyrig *Ant. syr.* IV 100.

44. *BMC* no. 1 ("first century B.C.?").

Epiphaneia

Epiphaneia stood at the head of the Gulf of Issus and about ten kilometers inland. Its early history is unknown; its name is taken to reflect a refoundation by Antiochus IV Epiphanes (175–163).[45] A Pompeian era is evidenced by the coins, on which no cult seems to predominate. Issues are few before the time of Trajan (after which they show no titles). Inviolability is known from the following bronzes of the first century A.D.:

A. Antiochus IV | Artemis, Ἐπιφανέων τῆς ΙΕΡΑΣ, date θϙ = 99 = ca. A.D. 31.
SNG Levante 1805–1806.

B. Tyche bust | Zeus Nicephorus, Ἐπιφανέων τῆς ἱερᾶς καὶ ἀσύλου, same date.
Several issues: *Hunterian* III 198 nos. 1, 2; *BMC Galatia* 242 no. 1; *SNG von Aulock* 5551; *SNG Levante* 1807–1808; Lindgren/Kovacs, *Ancient Bronze Coins* no. 2050; *RPC* I 4067, 4070.[46]

C. Athena bust, helmeted | Nude standing Apollo, branch in right hand, left on column, inscription as B, undated.
BMC no. 2; *Copenhagen Lycaonia* 130.

D. Domitian | Tyche, Ἐπιφανέων τῆς ΙΕΡΑΣ, date αξρ = 161 = ca. A.D. 93.
Ziegler, *Münzen* 178 no. 1411.

Evidently the beginning of the coinage in the 30s occasioned a diverse celebration of the city; yet another issue of "year 99" shows Tiberius | Tyche and no civic titles (*RPC* no. 4066). The issue showing Antiochus IV (A) had been assigned to the Aradian era, thus 168 B.C.; Seyrig refuted this usage, and that date would in any case be too early for *asylia* in Cilicia—and the coincidence of two different years 99 improbable. Rather, the city is honoring its founder posthumously on this occasion.

I assume that inviolability is not new with the coinage in the 30s and derives from a late Hellenistic or Republican recognition.

45. At Gözeneler Harabeler; cf. Hellenkemper/Hild 102–104; see in general Heberdey's discussion at *Reisen* 17–24. Pliny *HN* 5.27.93 says the original name was Oeniandus; for Antiochus IV see V. Tscherikower, *Die hellenistischen Städtegründungen* (Leipzig 1927) 41. For attribution of the coins to Cilician rather than Syrian Epiphaneia and to a Pompeian era, see Seyrig, *Syria* 27 (1950) 25–26 (*Ant. syr.* IV 91–92).

46. At *Hunterian* no. 2 MacDonald reports a possible date "ζρ(?)" (107 = ca. A.D. 39), but he was quite dubious about the reading; it does not seem to be confirmed among the several specimens.

Tarsus

Tarsus, metropolis and "greatest city in Cilicia" (Diod. 14.20.2), stood on the Cydnus River at an important crossroads linking Anatolia and Syria.[47] The city issued coins already in Achaemenid times; it was honored by the Seleucids as "Antioch by the Cydnus" and eventually became capital of the Roman province of Cilicia. The Tarsians gave first honor to Heracles/Sandon, worshipped throughout Cilicia but one of the founders of Tarsus (Amm. Marc. 14.8.3). His ritual pyre is often seen on the coins.[48]

The city is rather modest in its display of titles on coins, which nowhere show *asylia*; we see regularly "metropolis," eventually two neocories, and the many epithets from individual emperors.[49] These are attested also in the inscriptions. For example, a monument to Severus Alexander gives an ambitious roster, without mentioning *asylia*; it ends, however, with an "et cetera" (*ZPE* 15 [1974] 32 no. 1 = *IGR* III 880; cf. 879):

> Ἀλεξανδριανὴ [Σεουηρια]νὴ Ἀντωνειανὴ [Ἁδριανὴ] Τάρσος ἡ πρώτη κα[ὶ μεγίστη] καὶ καλλίστη μητρ[όπολις] τῶν γ ἐπαρχειῶν Κιλι[κ]ίας Ἰσαυρίας Λυκαονίας προ[κα]θεζομένη καὶ β νεωκόρο[ς], μόνη τετειμημένη δημιουργίαις τε καὶ Κιλικαρχία[ις] ἐπαρχικῶν καὶ ἐλευθέρῳ κ[οι]νοβουλίῳ καὶ ἑτέραις πλε[ί]σταις καὶ μεγίσταις καὶ ἐξαιρέτοις δωρεαῖς.

Inviolability is revealed by two other inscriptions:

> Dagron/Feissel 73 no. 29 (lettering first century A.D.), statue of a benefactor erected by ὁ δῆμος ὁ Ταρσέων τῆ[ς] μ̣ητροπόλεω̣ς τῶν κατὰ Κιλικίαν τῆς [ἱε]ρᾶς καὶ ἀσ̣ύ[λ]ου.

> 74 no. 30 (under Severus Alexander), a dedication by [Ἀλεξανδριαν]ὴ Ἀντωνειανὴ Ἁδριανὴ Ταρσὸς ἡ πρώτη καὶ μεγίστη καὶ καλλίστη μητρόπολις τῶν τριῶν ἐπαρχειῶν [Κιλι]κίας Ἰσαυρίας Λυκαονίας προκ[αθεζο]μένη καὶ δὶς νεωκόρος ἱερὰ [καὶ ἄσυλος - - -].

I assume that the status, attested already in the first century A.D., derives from the late Hellenistic period.

47. Ruge, *RE* 4A (1932) 2413–2439.
48. See Philipp, *RE* 1A (1920) 2264–2268; C. P. Jones, *GRBS* 25 (1984) 177–181.
49. Ruge 2425–2426; Burrell, "Neokoroi" 491–495.

Seleuceia on the Calycadnus

The Calycadnus is the largest river emptying out of Rough Cilicia; the royal foundation Seleuceia stands at the point, several kilometers inland, where the river is crossed by the major road leading from the coast toward Iconium in the interior. This was the greatest city of Rough Cilicia, founded by Nicator himself.[50]

The coins do not suggest who might have been the chief divinity. A rich coinage is extant from the late Hellenistic period, royal silver down to ca. 94 B.C., and civic bronze that is not closely datable; Houghton takes the bronze to succeed the silver. Only the bronzes give the ethnic, and these show no titles: Σελευκέων τῶν πρὸς τῶι Καλυκάδνωι, or Σελευκέων alone. Then, at an uncertain date, the bronzes cease, and Seleuceia did not mint again until the time of Hadrian. From Hadrian to Commodus, Seleuceia issued both pseudoautonomous and imperial bronzes, which for the most part show no titles of any sort.[51] The testimonies for the title of inviolability are as follows:

A. Hadrian | Heracles, Σελευκέων τ. . τῆς ἱερᾶς καὶ ἀσ(ύλου) αὐτ(ονόμου).
SNG Switz. Levante Cilicia Suppl. 188.

B. Sabina | Io, Σελευκέων τῶ(ν) π(ρὸς) Καλυκάδνῳ τῆς ΙΕΡΑΣ αὐτ(ονόμου).
Inv. Waddington 4458.

C. Apollo and Artemis, ἔτους κ Αὐτ(οκράτορος) Καί(σαρος) Ἁδριανοῦ π(ατρὸς) π(ατρίδος) = A.D. 136/7 | Athena attacking giant, Σελευκέων τῶ(ν) πρ(ὸς) Καλυ(κάδνῳ) τῆς ἱερ(ᾶς) καὶ ἀσ(ύλου) αὐτ(ονόμου).
BMC Lycaonia 131 no. 17; *Inv. Waddington* 4457; Imhoof-Blumer, *Kl.M.* 575; *SNG Levante* 720.

D. Antoninus Pius | Athena Nicephorus, Σελευκ(έων) τ(ῶν) π(ρὸς) Καλ(υκάδνῳ) τ(ῆς) ΙΕΡ.
BMC no. 20; Ziegler, *Münzen* 62 no. 418; *SNG von Aulock* 5822.

These variations clearly are sporadic; ΙΕΡ and ΙΕΡΑΣ stand for the full title. More important, two silver issues under Pius (*BMC* nos. 18–19) are without titles. These few coins are sufficient to imply that Seleuceia possessed inviolability throughout imperial times—before Hadrian we have no coins, while the absence of the title on other issues is meaningless. Here as elsewhere, my assumption is that the status derives from the Hellenistic period. If that is so, and if the silence of Hellenistic issues can be trusted, then the recognition came after the end of the extant Hellenistic coinage. The last coins of Hellenistic Seleuceia thus give us our terminus post quem for *asylia*, probably the early first century B.C.

50. Keil and Wilhelm, *MAMA* III pp. 3–22; G. E. Bean and T. B. Mitford, *Journeys in Rough Cilicia,* DenkschrWien 102.3 (1970) 196–198; A. Houghton in *Kraay-Mørkholm Essays* (Louvain 1988) 77–98.

51. Apart from the four issues listed here, the only title attested at Seleuceia is ἐλευθέρας, which appears on many issues of the third century A.D.

Selinus-Trajanopolis

The site of Selinus, at the western extreme of Cilicia, is typical of the coastal cities of Rough Cilicia; its acropolis falls steeply to the sea, while the city itself spreads down into the valley to the west.[52] Of its cults and its Hellenistic history little is known. Selinus issued its earliest extant coins under Antiochus IV of Commagene (A.D. 38–72); the reverses show Σελινουσίων with no civic titles.[53]

After Trajan died here in August 117, the city was refounded as Trajanopolis, and both names appear on the fairly abundant bronzes that follow, down to the mid-third century. The city was granted *ius italicum*,[54] presumably on the occasion of its refoundation. The title of inviolability occurs only infrequently on these coins (and no other titles are claimed). The types show a temple of the god Trajan, and not surprisingly the Apollo of nearby Side; but otherwise no cult is clearly dominant. No more than τῆς ΙΕΡΑΣ is guaranteed by the coins, as at Mallus and Olba; and a number of issues across the whole period of the mint are without any titles. I cite a selection in order to illustrate the range of images and abbreviations:

A. M. Aurelius | Temple, with statue of Trajan, labeled θεοῦ Τραι(ανοῦ); Τραιανοπ(ολιτῶν) Σελινου(σίων) τῆς ΙΕΡ.
SNG Levante 460 (for the extreme abbreviation cf. *Inv. Waddington* no. 4486 under Macrinus).

B. Faustina Junior | Two goddesses standing, title τῆς ΙΕΡΑΣ.
Ziegler, *Münzen* 32 no. 178; *M&M* 325 (July 1971) no. 28 (for the type cf. *Inv. Waddington* no. 4485).

C. Caracalla | Standing Sidetan Apollo with raven, title τῆς ΙΕΡ (left) ΑΣ (right).
Imhoof-Blumer, *JHS* 18 (1898) 164 no. 7.

D. Herennia Etruscilla | Standing Dionysus, title τῆς ΙΕΡΑΣ.
SNG Levante no. 469; Ziegler no. 185.

If this inscription is more than rhetorical and implies a grant of inviolability, neither the cult nor the occasion for the grant is evident from the meager testimony of the coins. In the absence of earlier evidence we cannot discount a Hellenistic recognition of Selinus; but an obvious possibility is that the cult was in fact Trajan's and the occasion of the grant of *asylia* was the refounding of the city in his name—that Trajanopolis is possibly a new recognition in imperial times.

52. Wilhelm, *Reisen* 149–151; Bean/Mitford 153–155; E. Rosenbaum, G. Huber, and S. Onurkam, *Survey of the Coastal Cities of Western Cilicia*, TTKYay VI.6 (Ankara 1967) 29–35 with photographs.

53. Imhoof-Blumer, *Kl.M.* 486; *SNG Levante* nos. 456–458; Ziegler, *Münzen* 31.

54. *Dig.* 50.15.1.11, from which it is often claimed that Selinus became a Roman colony (Kornemann, *RE* 4 [1900] 552; von Premerstein, *RE* 10 [1918] 1240; Magie II 609); but there is no hint of colonial status in the coins, which like the inscriptions remain entirely Greek and which reveal an ἄρχων in the time of Caracalla (Imhoof-Blumer, *Kl.M.* 526).

Mallus

Mallus, the city of the hero Amphilochus, stood beside the Pyramus River twenty-five kilometers inland, bordering on Aegeae to the east and Tarsus to the west (Dio Chrys. 34.11, 43–46); in 1950 the site was discovered near Kiziltahta.[55] The finds have not been published, and the coins of Mallus, which begin in Achaemenid times, remain our best evidence for its cults. Its territory extended south to the coast and included the village Magarsus at the mouth of the Pyramus, with its temple of Athena Magarsis, who is often shown on the Hellenistic coins. This goddess figured prominently in the foundation legends of the region—Magarsus was built by Pamphylus, and the heroes Mopsus and Amphilochus were buried here.[56]

In Roman times, however, the great god of Mallus seems to have been the founder Amphilochus, son of Amphiaraus; his oracle, the truest in the world according to Pausanias, was of great repute, communicating by means of dream visions.[57] Amphilochus and the Mallians were Argive, so already Alexander, himself of Argive descent, in his passage made a point of sacrificing to the hero and to Athena.[58] The city became a Roman colony in the third century, and one subsequent issue has agonistic types and the inscription *Mallo colonia dei Amfilochi*.[59]

The Hellenistic coinage consists of Seleucid silver across the second half of the second century B.C. from Demetrius I to Antiochus IX (inscribed M or Μαλ) and some civic bronzes (Μαλλωτῶν), all without titles. The coins that suggest inviolability are all from A.D. 217/8:

A. Macrinus | Tyche with two river gods, Μαλ(λωτῶν) ἱερ(ᾶς) πόλ(εως) θεοῦ Ἀμφιλόχου, date ἔτ(ους) δπς = 284 = A.D. 217/8.
Several issues: Imhoof-Blumer, *JHS* 18 (1898) 163; *SNG Levante* 1284; 1283 (undated); Ziegler, *Münzen* 119 no. 907; 908 (undated).

B. Diadumenian | Amphilochus, nude, with serpent, same inscription and date.
Imhoof-Blumer, *JHS* 164; *SNG France* 2 *Cilicie* 1927.

C. Diadumenian | Temple with Athena, [Μαλ(λωτῶν)] ἱερ(ᾶς) πό(λεως) θεο(ῦ) Ἀμφιλόχου, same date.
SNG Levante 1285.

I am uncertain whether the phrase "sacred city of the god Amphilochus" should be taken as evidence of a granted status, inviolability, or merely as a

55. Ruge, *RE* 14 (1928) 916–917; H. T. Bossert, *Belleten TTR* 14 (1951) 664–666; L. Robert, *CRAI* 1951, 256–259; MacKay (n. 21) 2113–2115; A. Houghton, *Festschrift Mildenberg* 91–110.

56. Lycoph. *Alex.* 444.; Lucian *Alex.* 29, *Deor. conc.* 12; cf. Bethe, *RE* 1 (1894) 1938–1940.

57. Paus. 1.34.3; Plut. *Mor.* 434D; Dio 72.7.1; Clem. *Strom.* 1.34.4; cf. *Protr.* 2.11.2.

58. Arr. *Anab.* 2.5.9; Strab. 14.5.17 (676).

59. Hill, *BMC* p. cxxiv; *SNG Levante* 1296; Lindgren/Kovacs no. A1545B; Ziegler, *Prestige* 51, and in *Asia Minor Studien* 8 (1992) 181–183.

rhetorical expression that forms part of the evocation of Amphilochus, parallel to *colonia dei Amphilochi.*

Olba

Olba, home of Zeus Olbius, stood twenty-five kilometers from the sea, some 1,000 meters above sea level amid the spectacular gorges of Rough Cilicia. Legend traced its origin to Ajax of Salamis, who during his passage to Cyprus founded the temple of Zeus (at Uzuncaburc four kilometers west of Ura) and began the Teucrid dynasty that we meet first in the third century B.C.[60]

The coins exhibit only one title, and this for a brief time in the early first century A.D. The city Olba issued bronzes in the late Hellenistic period, which show emblems of Zeus and the ethnic Ὀλβεων without titles. Under Ajax, high priest and toparch, the coins are of the Lalasseis and Kennateis, with no mention of the city Olba. Then under his successor Polemon, dynast and king under Tiberius, these ethnics are preceded by another, Ὀλβεων τῆς ΙΕΡΑΣ. There follows a hiatus in the coins; by the end of the first century A.D., an independent city has been founded at Uzuncaburc, Diocaesareia.[61] Olba continued to exist (as did the *koinon* of the Lalasseis and Kennateis), striking coins from the time of Hadrian to that of Philip, which frequently show Zeus Olbius. Over time both cities came to enjoy various honors: the imperial epithets familiar in Cilicia (Hadrianoi, Antoninianoi), *colonia*, "metropolis"—but ΙΕΡΑΣ does not recur.

The great temple of Zeus that we see at Uzuncaburc appears to date from the early second century B.C. and may have been built under the patronage of Antiochus IV.[62] To judge from the archaeological record, Diocaesarea prospered at the expense of Olba once this area passed into the Roman province of Cilicia in the 70s A.D.

60. J. Fraser, *Golden Bough*[3] V (London 1914) 143–152, with an evocative description of the site; Wilhelm, *Reisen* 84–92; T. S. MacKay, "Olba in Rough Cilicia" (Diss., Bryn Mawr 1968); C. Borker, *AA* 1971, 37–54; A.-M. Vérilhac and G. Dagron, *REA* 76 (1974) 239–242. For the problems of the pre-Greek toponym Ura see R. H. Beal, *AnatSt* 42 (1992) 65–73. On the Lalasseis see Syme, *Roman Papers* VI 293. The coins: G. Hill, *NC* III.19 (1899) 181–207; G. M. Staffieri, *La monetazione di Olba* (Lugano 1978); *NumAntCl* 16 (1987) 229–249. A statue base from the site registers for some city the title of inviolability (see p. 589).

61. Probably sponsored by Tiberius, as he was given a statue as founder and savior of the city (Wilhelm, *Reisen* 84 no. 160, from the temple). See Kirsten, *AnzWien* 110 (1973) 347–363.

62. Caroline Williams, *AJA* 78 (1974) 405–414. Both Seleucid and Teucrid patronage is revealed by the inscription *Reisen* 85 no. 166 (late II/early I B.C.): one of the Teucrids, as high priest, renews roofing, apparently along the peribolos, that had been dedicated by Seleucus Nicator.

Thus the coins that suggest inviolability at Olba are bronzes of Polemon. If the years 10 and 11 are era dates rather than regnal, these coins date to A.D. 20–22; if regnal, probably in the period 28–35. All have the bust of Polemon on the obverse, and on the reverse the inscription Πολέμωνος δυνάστου Ὄλβεων τῆς ΙΕΡΑΣ καὶ Κεννάτων καὶ Λαλάσσεων. The reverse varieties, which all allude to the cult of Zeus, are as follows:

A. Throne, or thunderbolt; ἔ(τους) ι, ἐπὶ Νέωνος.
Hill 194–195 nos. 1–2; Staffieri nos. 29–30.

B. Thunderbolt; ἔτ(ους) ι, ἐπὶ Μ.Α.Νέων(ος).
SNG von Aulock 5792; Staffieri no. 31; Ziegler, *Münzen* 56 no. 370.

C. Throne, or thunderbolt; ἔ(τους) ια.
Hill nos. 3–4; *M&M Aukt.* 41 (June 1970) no. 569; Staffieri nos. 32–33.

Here as at Selinus and Mallus, I am unsure whether to take ΙΕΡΑΣ as more than a rhetorical flourish.

Phoenicia and Syria

Tyre

Tyre, the mother city of Phoenicia, and of Greece through Cadmus and the West through Dido,[1] was probably the first city outside the old Aegean world to be declared sacred and inviolable, gaining the title in 141/0 B.C.

The patron of the Tyrians was Heracles-Melqart.[2] No testimony explicitly links the city's inviolability to him, though some tesserae (described below) are suggestive; but Heracles is the obvious candidate.[3] Herodotus went to Tyre to see the famous temple, which he was told was 2,300 years old.[4] The colonies of Tyre annually sent firstfruits to this temple.[5] Alexander's first wish on approaching the city was to sacrifice in the world's oldest temple of his ancestor, and on taking the city he spared those who took refuge in the temple, and held victory competitions (as he did thoughout his campaign) here for Heracles, who had

1. Eissfeldt, *RE* 7A (1948) 1876–1908; M. Chéhab, *Tyr: Histoire, topographie, fouilles* (Beirut 1969); *MUB* 38 (1962) 13–40 on Roman Tyre; the coins: J. Rouvier, *JIAN* 6 (1903) 269–332. For Cadmus and Dido on the coins of Roman Tyre see Hill, *BMC Phoenicia* pp. cxli–cxlii; Sidon too claimed Cadmus (Kaibel, *Epigr.* 932, and its coins). On Tyre's rivalry with Beirut for titles, Robert, *HSCP* 81 (1977) 24–25 (*Op. min. sel.* VI 234–235). ἱερὰ Τύρος at Meleager *Anth. Gr.* 7.418.2 is merely poetic; cf. 419.5.

2. E.g., *I.Délos* 1519.15: ἀρχηγοῦ τῆς πατρίδος; M. G. Guzzo Amadasi, *Iscrizioni fenicie* (Rome 1967) 16 no. 1 (= *IG* XIV 600: Malta): ἀρχηγέτει, translating Phoenician "our lord of Tyre" (both II B.C.); cf. Strab. 16.2.23 (757); Diod. 20.14.1–2; Lucian *Syr. d.* 3. See C. Bonnet, *Melqart*, Stud.Phoen. 8 (Namur 1988). Nock found Heracles labeled ἅγιος only at Tyre: *Essays* II 923 n. 21. On the apparent counterindication at Eus. *Hist. eccl.* 9.7.7 (Zeus ὁ προκαθήμενος τῆς λαμπροτάτης ὑμῶν πόλεως), see S. Mitchell, *JRS* 78 (1988) 119.

3. This has long been assumed: e.g., Pomtow, *Klio* 15 (1918) 27.

4. Hdt. 2.44. Cf. Menander Eph. *FGrHist* 783 F 1 (temple of Heracles and Astarte built in the tenth century B.C.).

5. Arr. *Anab.* 2.24.5; Polyb. 31.12.11–12.

encouraged him in a dream.[6] The Seleucid Demetrius II, upon his defeat by Alexander Zabinas in 126, fled eventually to Tyre in order to "protect himself by the sanctity of the temple" but was killed as he debarked at the port.[7] In Heracles' honor Tyre held quadrennial games, first attested in the 170s B.C. when Jason sent from Jerusalem *theoroi* with 300 drachmas for sacrifices; the festival was Panhellenic in imperial times.[8] The club of Heracles marked the Seleucid silver issued by their mint at Tyre, and with the liberation of the city in 126/5 his portrait replaced that of the king on the obverse.

On the local bronzes permitted by Antiochus IV ca. 170 B.C., at Tyre as elsewhere there is no claim of inviolability; the Tyrians do, however, state in Phoenician "mother of the Sidonians."[9] During the second century B.C. Tyre was seat of a Seleucid royal mint: the silver issues are marked on their reverses by the club of Heracles surmounted by Ᵽ; royal bronzes have the inscription Τυρίων without titles as late as 143/2 (under Demetrius II).[10] But then on a silver tetradrachm of Demetrius dated to 141/0, the emblem Ᵽ is replaced by Τύρου ἱερᾶς καὶ ἀσύλου, written somewhat smaller than the king's name.[11] As Seyrig saw, this sudden bold assertion on royal silver, not repeated in this explicit way on the subsequent royal issues, must commemorate the winning of the status and is not merely a terminus ante quem.[12] In the period from 141/0 to 126/5, the royal silver reverts to using the civic monogram, but adds to the left $\overset{\text{Α}}{\text{ΡΕ}}$ ΙΕΡΑΣ or ΙΕΡ or ΙΕ, and to the right ΑΣ̌; Babelon recognized that these abbreviate ἱερᾶς (καὶ) ἀσύλου.[13] On the royal bronzes struck at Tyre in these years, the civic monogram is flanked by ΙΕΡ and ΑΣ̌ or (on the smaller denomination) ΙΕ and ΑΣ̌; or indeed these titles are omitted entirely.[14]

6. Arr. 2.15.7, 18.1, 24.5–6.

7. Justin. 39.1.7; Bellinger, "End" 64. The family of Pompey fled to the temple after Pharsalus, Dio 42.49.

8. 2 Macc. 4:18–19; *IGLSyrie* IV 1265, with Moretti, *I. agon. gr.* p. 209. Neither the quadrennial period nor Jason's *theoroi* need prove the games Panhellenic (but see Robert, *Op. min. sel.* VII 704); Jason's act might be an extraordinary gesture of diplomacy, like that of Antiochus VII at Jerusalem (Jos. *AJ* 13.236ff.; Plut. *Mor.* 184F).

9. *BMC Sel. Kings* 39 no. 55; Babelon, *Rois* 86 nos. 674–681; Rouvier nos. 1842–1844. "Sidonians" means Phoenicians, as in *FD* III.1 435 (Σιδωνίωι ἐγ Βαρυτέου, III B.C.) and probably the "Sidonians at Marisa" (*OGIS* 593). But it is also a nice insult to the Sidonians, who answered at length (cf. p. 492). Strabo (16.2.22 [757]) knew of their dispute about which was μητρόπολις Φοινίκων.

10. E. Rogers, *The Second and Third Seleucid Coinage of Tyre*, NNM 34 (New York 1927) p. 18; cf. Rouvier no. 1885; *SNG Copenhagen* nos. 288–289; *Coll.Houghton* no. 753.

11. Rogers nos. 39–40.

12. Seyrig, *Notes* 19–20. Terminus ante quem: e.g., Kahrstedt, *Syrische Territorien* 77.

13. Babelon, *Rois* cxxxiv; the fullest of these versions: e.g., *Coll.Houghton* no. 760 under Antiochus VII; the last royal issues, in 126/5: Rogers nos. 117–120; Rouvier no. 1942; *Coll.Dewing* no. 2625.

14. Rogers pp. 24ff.; no. 122 is a fractional bronze of 129/8 with ΙΕ but omitting ΑΣ̌.

In 126/5, with the death of Demetrius II (killed at Tyre) and the liberation of the city from Seleucid rule, the royal mint ended, and Tyre began its own silver coinage, dated by a civic era. This enduring and widely used money, showing Heracles-Melqart on the obverse and the Ptolemaic eagle on the reverse, runs with few interruptions from 126/5 to the 60s A.D. Without exception, the inscription is that seen in 141/0, Τύρου ἱερᾶς καὶ ἀσύλου. The civic bronze is more sporadic but continues longer; on it the titles are abbreviated to ΙΕΡ ΑΣ (or are omitted entirely). In A.D. 93/4 the title "metropolis" is added, either by compounding the Tyrian monogram to ΜΡ or by writing in full Τύρου μητροπόλεως. The metropolitan monogram sometimes is accompanied by the monograms for "sacred and inviolable," sometimes not; while the written form is sometimes expanded to Τύρου ἱερᾶς μητροπόλεως (or μητρόπολις ἱερά), sometimes not. All four of these variants are found in 93/4 and repeatedly thereafter: clearly these differing labels do not represent fluctuations in the city's status, but different options available to the die cutters. Thus the inscription Τύρου ἱερᾶς μητροπόλεως must imply the full "sacred and inviolable metropolis"; this variant is found as late as 195/6, our last allusion to Tyre's inviolability.[15] Thereafter the types of the new colonial status supplant the title of inviolability (although the Roman title "metropolis," as happens at other Roman colonies, continued to be advertised).[16]

Several inscriptions supplement the evidence of the coins. In the latter part of the second century B.C. Tyre sent a letter to Delphi to announce some great benefaction just gained; the author is Τύρου τῆς ἱερᾶς καὶ ἀσύλου ἡ [βουλὴ καὶ ὁ δῆμος. Pomtow took the occasion to be the liberation of 126/5, and Wilhelm restored an allusion to inviolability:[17]

[ἀεὶ προελόμενοι τὴν ἐς ὑμᾶς]
σύνκρασιν ἐπαύξειν καὶ ταῖς τ[ῶν βασιλέων εὐεργεσίαις μνημό]-
συνον αἰώνιον ὑπάρξαι, ἅμα δὲ [καὶ χρήσιμοι βουλόμενοι φαί]-
νεσθαι καὶ ὑμῖν καὶ τοῖς εἰς τ[ὴν πόλιν παραγινομένοις πρὸς τὸ]
καὶ μὴ ἀμετόχους εἶναι τοῦ κοιν[οῦ τε τῆς ἀσυλίας καὶ τοῦ νῦν]
ἐπιγενομένου φιλανθρώπου ἐ[λευθερίας τυχόντες ἐπιμελὲς]
ἐποιήσαμεν διασαφῆσαι [- -]

4 Crönert: τὴν πρὸς ὑμᾶς ὑπάρχουσαν] Wilhelm.

. . .

[. . . as we have always preferred] to increase our concourse [with you] and for there to be a lasting memorial to the [generosities of the kings,] and [wishing also to appear useful] to you and to those who [come to our city, so that] you not be without a share in both the common benefaction [of inviolability and the one

15. Rouvier no. 2204; *BMC* 264 nos. 328–330, with p. cxxxvi.

16. So also the inscription at Chéhab (1962) 19: Σεπτιμία κολ(ωνία) Τύρος ἡ μητρόπολις (III A.D.).

17. *AnzWien* 59 (1922) 11–13 (*Kl. Schr.* I.2 77–79) [*SEG* 2.330].

> that] has happened [now, our obtaining of freedom,] we have taken care to make clear . . .

This reconstruction is in my view strained and unconvincing; I suspect in 8 some more banal expression—for example, κοιν[οῦ τοῖς πολίταις τοῖς ἡμετέροις], "the common benefaction that has come about for our citizens." However this may be, the titles at the head suggest that inviolability is already a fact and not the new item that is now announced.[18]

At Didyma in A.D. 102 the Tyrians erected a monument to C. Julius Quadratus: τῶν Τυρίων ἱερᾶς καὶ ἀσύλου καὶ αὐτονόμου μητροπόλεως Φοινείκης καὶ τῶν κατὰ Κοίλην Συρίαν καὶ ἄλλων πόλεων καὶ ναυαρχίδος.[19] In A.D. 174 the Tyrian residents at Puteoli wrote a letter to Tyre, addressing their mother city with almost the same titles as in 102 (*IGR* I 421, omitting "Coele-Syria"). Finally, making a dedication at Puteoli, of unknown imperial date, Tyre calls itself ἱερὰ καὶ ἄσυλος κ[αὶ αὐτόνομος μητρό]πολις.[20]

The consistency of the silver coins and the information added by the inscriptions show that the silences and variations in the bronze are meaningless.[21] We can conclude that Tyre possessed inviolability from 141/0 B.C. to at least A.D. 195/6 with no known interruption. Nor need we doubt that the status continued into the third century when Tyre had been promoted to a colony.[22]

We have finally two bronze tesserae (diameters 2.9 and 2.7 cm), struck on both sides as though a coin, with a Phoenician inscription:[23] on one side, *l mlqrt* | *b ṣr*, "to Melqart in Tyre"; on the other, *hyrw* | *'sls*, which has no meaning in Phoenician. One tessera bears a date in Greek, L HN = year 58 = 69/8 B.C.[24] Seyrig convincingly argued that the second side transliterates the Greek title of

18. Cf. *Royal Corres.* 71–72 (Seleuceia: p. 486). A unique Tyrian double stater of gold is dated to 104/3: this is evidence for yet another great event, at this date probably aid from Ptolemy Lathyrus (so A. B. Brett, *AJA* 41 [1937] 456). The letter of Teos to Tyre *SEG* IV 601 gives Tyre no titles; this may be older than 141/0, however. The titles of Tyre do not appear in the two purported letters of Antony at Jos. *AJ* 14.314, 319, where we would expect them if the letters are genuine (cf. Octavian's letter to Rhosus, p. 473).

19. *I. Didyma* 151, with C. Habicht, *GGA* 213 (1959) 163–164, for the date.

20. *IGR* I 419, with J. and L. Robert, *Bull. épigr.* 1949, 196.

21. Note that no coin, silver or bronze, of any date has either αὐτονόμου or ναυαρχίδος. Strabo 16.2.23 (757) says that Tyre was granted autonomy by the kings (no doubt the liberation of 126/5 B.C.) and that the Romans (presumably Pompey) confirmed this grant.

22. On the types of the colonial coins see B. Servais-Soyez, in *Studia Phoenicia* I, Or.Lovan. Anal. 15 (Louvain 1983) 97–106.

23. A. Fuchs and J. Schwartz, *GNS* 30 (1980) 68–69 (dated); Seyrig, *Syria* 28 (1951) 225–228 (*Ant. syr.* IV 205–208), who, with the dated example not yet known, thought that the technique of his specimen placed it somewhat before 126/5.

24. Fuchs and Schwartz calculated instead from 141/0, which is not an attested usage of Tyre.

inviolability, linked by the Phoenician conjunction *waw*: "*hyr* and *asulos*."[25] We might take this as evidence for associating inviolability with the cult of Heracles; but strictly speaking the tesserae merely state the civic title when naming the city, as might be done in a context not associated with the god.[26]

Thus Tyre was declared sacred and inviolable in 141/0, soon after the usurpation of Tryphon.[27] Tryphon failed in his attempts to win over the great cities of Phoenicia: his enemy Demetrius II struck tetradrachms at both Tyre and Sidon throughout the years of Tryphon's rivalry.[28] It seems certain, therefore, that in 141/0 the status was granted by Demetrius, and surely as part of his effort to retain the loyalty of the city that was his effective capital.

Seleuceia in Pieria

Seleuceia at the mouth of the Orontes was the first city founded by Seleucus Nicator after his defeat of Antigonus Monophthalmus in 301, the seat of his first mint, the site of his tomb—in short, his capital city.[29] The rise of Antioch would come only in the generation of his son Antiochus; but apparently Seleuceia continued to be regarded as the *origo* of the dynasty.[30] The great god of the city was Zeus Olympius, whose emblem, the thunderbolt, is often seen on the coins.[31] On our present evidence, Seleuceia was at least the second (two years after Tyre) and possibly the first city outside of the Aegean to be declared inviolable.

In the mid-second century B.C. Alexander Balas allowed certain cities of the kingdom to issue bronze coins under their own names; those of Seleuceia (most showing on their reverses the winged thunderbolt of Zeus) give the city no titles, Σελευκέων τῶν ἐμ Πιερίαι.[32] These were issued as late as 147/6, which accordingly is a terminus post quem for the granting of the status. The evidence for the inviolability of Seleuceia can be summarized as follows:

25. A. Catastini, *RStFen* 13 (1985) 9–10, urged that *waw* be taken instead as part of what precedes and that the Greek so transliterated was ἱεροῦ ἄσυλος, which he translates "residence of the holy one"; this is not possible Greek.

26. Thus the letter to Delphi, and the civic titles of Seleuceia in *Royal Corres.* 71.

27. On the chronology see H. R. Baldus, *ZNG* 20 (1970) 217–239.

28. See Seyrig, *Notes* 11.

29. So E. Honigmann, *RE* 2A (1923) 1185–1186, followed by G. Downey, *History of Antioch in Syria* (Princeton 1961) 56–60.

30. See *Royal Corres.* 71.15, with Downey 59 n. 25.

31. Rigsby, *TAPA* 110 (1980) 233–238; note especially App. *Syr.* 58: θεὸν αὐτοῖς κεραυνὸν ἔθετο, καὶ θρησκεύουσι καὶ ὑμνοῦσι καὶ νῦν κεραυνόν.

32. *BMC Galatia* 269–270; *Coll.Houghton* (ACNAC IV) 410; cf. Rigsby 242–248.

A. Under Antiochus VII, Seleuceia was again allowed to strike pseudoautonomous bronzes; one issue is known, dated to Seleucid 184 = 139/8 B.C.: Antiochus VII bust | Seated Zeus, Σελευκέων τῶν ἐμ Πιερίαι τῆς ἱερᾶς καὶ ἀσύλου, date δορ (PLATE 8).[33]

B. Some smaller bronzes are undated: Zeus bust | Winged thunderbolt, Σελευκέων τῆς τῶν ἐμ Πιερίαι τῆς ΙΕΡΑΣ.[34]

Newell's brief remark on the style and date of these coins has guided subsequent scholars in the view that Seleuceia was declared sacred ca. 146–144 (B), inviolable in 139/8 (A). But style cannot establish such a fine distinction in date, nor is the inscription on the small coins (B) sufficient to show that the city possessed less than the full title of inviolability. Rather, whatever their exact date, I take the latter to carry an abbreviation for reasons of space; hence our earliest secure date is 139/8.

No coins of Seleuceia are explicitly dated in the generation after 139/8, although some or all of the undated bronzes (B) may belong in this period. Then comes an inscription:

C. On 29 Gorpiaios of Seleucid 203 (= 6 September 109 B.C.) Antiochus VIII or IX wrote to Ptolemy IX announcing the liberation of Seleuceia: [ἐκρίναμεν εἶ]ς τὸν ἅπανταν χρόνον ἐλευθέρους [εἶναι]. He refers to the citizens as Σελευκεῖς τοὺς ἐν Πιερίαι τῆς ἱερᾶς καὶ ἀσύλου (*Royal Corres.* 71).

D. From Seleucid 204 (= 109/8 B.C.)[35] Seleuceia reckoned a civic era, and an abundant new coinage is dated by it. Tetradrachms (Tyche bust | Enthroned thunderbolt) are extant between 106/5 and 84/3; of the rare fractional silver, the earliest dates probably to 107/6.[36] The bronzes, though quite sporadic after the 80s, come down

33. *ZfN* 29 (1912) 99 no. 27; an example (from Newell's collection) in the ANS in New York (pictured here). See Newell ap. Welles, *Royal Corres.* p. 292 (imprecise in implying that there is silver with the title as well as bronze); followed by Seyrig, *Notes* 13 n. 21 and 21 n. 49.

34. Seyrig, *RN* VI.8 (1968) 8 no. 265 (*Scripta numism.* 348); *Antioch-on-the-Orontes* IV.2 (Princeton 1952) p. 69 no. 726; H. C. Lindgren and F. L. Kovacs, *Ancient Bronze Coins* (San Mateo 1985) no. 2121; *BCH* 110 (1986) 406–407 nos. 78–79. Newell thought them stylistically closer to the issues under Balas and therefore placed them earlier than coin A of 139/8. The layout of this small bronze is, however, quite similar to that of the small silver dating to 97/6 (e.g., Seyrig, *Scripta* no. 267).

35. As the year 204 began almost one month after Antiochus' letter to Ptolemy, his decision about Seleuceia took a month or more to reach the city (for such delays see A. Aymard, *Etudes d'histoire ancienne* [Paris 1967] 223–226). Bellinger, "End" 69, assumed that the author was Antiochus VIII and that he was in Seleuceia, having been expelled from Antioch where Antiochus IX issued coins in 203 = 110/109. Antiochus IX replaced Antiochus VIII at Antioch in the course of 110/109 (A. Houghton, *SNR* 72 [1993] 91–92); note that Antiochus VIII also controlled Beirut in the Attic year (July/July) 110/109 (*I.Délos* 1551). We do not know where either brother was at the moment of this letter, but the author apparently was not in Seleuceia.

36. Tetradrachms: *BMC Galatia* 270–271; *SNG* IV *Fitzwilliam* 5959–5960, VII 1368; *Dewing Coll.* 2654; Seyrig, *Trésors* pl. 34; *ANSMN* 31 (1986) pl. 32.5; for the dates, Seyrig, *Syria* 27 (1950) 29 (*Ant. syr.* IV 95). Fractions: *BMC* no. 24 (year 3 = 107/6, if the date is placed as on the

to the time of Augustus.[37] And an isolated silver issue was struck under Augustus (Augustus | Thunderbolt).[38] These coins are inscribed Σελευκέων τῆς ἱερᾶς καὶ αὐτονόμου, with the exception of the fractional silver, which gives Σελευκέων τῆς αὐτονόμου,[39] certainly abbreviating for reasons of space (sometimes in the same year as tetradrachms with τῆς ἱερᾶς καὶ αὐτονόμου). The "autonomy" of the coins is obviously the "freedom" granted in the Seleucid letter of 109 B.C.

The early silver ends when it does because the victory of Tigranes of Armenia in 83 B.C., who was opposed by Seleuceia while supported by its neighbor Laodicea, altered the fortunes of the two cities.[40] But the titles on the bronzes, which extend later, show that Tigranes did not cancel the inviolability of Seleuceia; it may be that he never took the city.[41]

E. In A.D. 5/6 in Rome, perhaps at the Porticus ad Nationes, Seleuceia erected an honorific monument to Augustus:[42] [ὁ δῆμος τῆς πόλεως τῶν Σελευκ]έ̣ων ἐν Πειερίαι τῆς ἱ[ερᾶς] καὶ ἀσύλου καὶ α̣[ὐτονόμου καὶ] συμμά[χου Ῥωμαίων]. In two nonjoining fragments Alföldy restores [*Seleuciae Pieriae populus liber e*]*t sacer et ịnviola*[*bilib*]*us utens am*[*icitiaque p*(*opuli*) *R*(*omani*) *firmus*(?)], a reconstruction that must remain doubtful.

Of the later coins of Seleuceia (all bronzes), those with imperial obverses and therefore datable give the city no titles, normally Σελευκέων Πιερίας (*BMC* pp. 274–277). The few pseudoautonomous issues are otherwise:

F. Tyche, date ηπρ = A.D.79/80 | Enthroned thunderbolt, Σελευκέων τῆς ἱερᾶς καὶ αὐτονόμου (*BMC* no. 31, with *PIR*² C no. 603).

G. Tyche, ἱερ(ᾶς) ἀσύλ(ου) αὐτονόμου | Shrine of Zeus Casius, Σελευκέων Πειερίας, two issues dated by year 3 and year 5 of an emperor (*BMC* nos. 29–30; Antonine period?).

Thus Seleuceia was declared sacred and inviolable in the period from 147/6 to 139/8 B.C. In autumn 109 the city was also declared free; "autonomous"

---

tetradrachms); *Fitzwilliam* 5962; *ZfN* 3 (1876) 350–351; Seyrig, *Scripta numism.* 348 no. 267. Note that Demetrius III issued bronzes at Seleuceia ca. 92 B.C.: Babelon, *Rois* 207; *Coll.Houghton* no. 414; cf. Bellinger, "End" 75 n. 75.

37. *BMC* nos. 15, 25–28; more reported at Seyrig, *Ant. syr.* IV 95 n. 1.

38. *BMC* no. 32; *Auktion F. Sternberg* 25/6 Nov. 1976 no. 705.

39. Compare instances at Antioch and Laodicea.

40. Eutrop. 6.14.2: *non recepisset.* As Seyrig saw, the end of Seleuceian silver coincides with the arrival of Tigranes and the beginning of the tetradrachms of Laodicea (which like much of Syria welcomed him): *Ant. syr.* IV 95. Pompey restored Seleuceia to freedom for resisting Tigranes: διόπερ καὶ ἐλευθέραν αὐτὴν ἔκρινε Πομπήιος, ἀποκλείσασ⟨αν⟩ Τιγράνην (Strab. 16.2.8 [751], as emended by Bouché-Leclerq).

41. So Bellinger, "End" 81; Seyrig, *Ant. syr.* IV 94; Downey 137 n. 87.

42. I. Kajanto, *L'area sacra di Largo Argentina* I (Rome 1981) 108–111 no. 27; G. Alföldy, *Studi sull' epigrafia* (Rome 1992) 77–93, who also restores Seleuceia in an earlier dedication made jointly with Damascus (see p. 512 below).

supplanted "inviolable" on the coins thereafter, but the inscriptions on stone show that "sacred and autonomous" and "autonomous" are abridgments for "sacred and inviolable and autonomous." While only infrequently attested, these titles persist through imperial times with no known interruption.

The most important uncertainty is the date of the small bronzes with τῆς ΙΕΡΑΣ (B): if as Newell thought they precede A, they would show the status to be older than 139/8 B.C.; and Newell, Seyrig, and others have taken this as evidence for "sacred" and "inviolable" being distinct and sequential statuses.[43] The simple chronological question is of some consequence, for Tyre received the titles in 141/0: one or the other was the first city beyond those of the old Aegean to be declared inviolable and by its example began this competition in Syria-Palestine.

In the early 140s Seleuceia emerged as the effective capital of Alexander Balas and (after 145) of his widow and children (Jos. *AJ* 13.221). Seleuceia was the base of Demetrius II in his fight against the usurper Tryphon; when in 139 Demetrius was captured by the Parthians, his wife, still at Seleuceia, married and made king his brother Antiochus VII in fear that the city would go over to Tryphon.[44] Thus in 139/8, the date of A, Antiochus VII was in his first year; we have his coins too at Antioch and Tyre. That Seleuceia has no other dated coins from this generation (147/6–107/6) and none of this large size (the issues B are small and undated) suggests that A is a commemorative issue.[45] I regard it therefore as more than a terminus ante quem, but as marking the occasion itself: in the course of his first year, 139/8, Antiochus was prevailed upon to grant to his ancestral city an honor equal to that recently granted Tyre by his brother Demetrius. It was an appropriate moment for Seleuceia to seek a favor from the king.

Ptolemais

Ptolemais in Phoenicia, Akko/Acre, is strategic for its citadel, its fine harbor, and its access to the Galilee.[46] The place has often served as head-

43. Newell deduced from his chronology that "sacred" (146–144) was granted by Alexander Balas or Demetrius II, "inviolable" (144–138) by Tryphon or Antiochus VII (cf. Rostovtzeff, *SEHHW* 846: Demetrius and then Tryphon); Seyrig (*Notes* 21 n. 49) excluded Tryphon, for Seleuceia stood with the legitimate house.

44. See Bellinger, "End" 57.

45. Cf. Seyrig, *Notes* 13 (n. 21: "to congratulate him on his accession").

46. Schürer II 121–125; *Enc.Arch.Excav.* I (1975) 14–25; N. Kashtan, in *Mediterranean Cities,* ed. I. Malkin and R. L. Hohlfelder (London 1988) 37–53.

quarters for those who would control the Holy Land—thus Antiochus III in 218, Tryphon around 140, and repeatedly during the growing political turmoil of the late second century B.C. It owed its first Hellenistic name to Ptolemy Philadelphus, its second, "Antioch in Ptolemais," to Antiochus IV. Of its cults[47] we know too little to guess which god might have given the city a claim to inviolability.

Issues of the royal Seleucid mint at Ptolemais, which come down through 107/6 B.C., indicate the city by at most a monogram (and rarely that) and add no titles.[48] Civic bronzes permitted under Antiochus IV ca. 170 give the name as Ἀντιοχέων τῶν ἐν Πτολεμαΐδι without titles; so too pseudoautonomous coins, not readily datable, which Seyrig would assign to the same period.[49] Whatever the precise date of the latter and the length of the subsequent hiatus, in 126/5 the city began issuing bronzes that now have the title of inviolability.[50] These, in three denominations, show on the obverses the Dioscuri, Zeus, or Apollo, with suitable reverses of cornucopia, a standing Zeus, or a cithara; the inscription is Ἀντιοχέων τῶν ἐν Πτολεμαΐδι ἱερᾶς ἀσύλου. The dated coins are found from 126/5 through 118/7. An undated issue (still under the name Antioch) also shows the titles.[51]

One undated bronze (Dioscuri | Cornucopia) gives only ΙΕΡΑΣ.[52] Seyrig thought the style earlier than the "sacred and inviolable" coins (the flan is beveled as on the untitled issues) and concluded that this coin reveals a preliminary declaration, "sacred," some years before the addition of "inviolable"; he suggested that "sacred" derived from Tryphon ca. 140 B.C. The layout of the inscription is as on the untitled bronzes, with Ἀντιοχέων τῶν to the right of the cornucopia, ἐν Πτολεμαΐδι to the left, and now ΙΕΡΑΣ added below. Even if we follow Seyrig in placing this issue earlier than the "sacred and inviolable" issues, I would urge that ΙΕΡΑΣ implies the full titulature and that the artist merely has not yet solved the problem of adjusting the layout so as to fit on the coin the fully written title (name on the right, adjectives on the left). We need not assume Seyrig's interval of fourteen years: I suggest that this version, if in fact it came

47. Seyrig, *Syria* 39 (1962) 193–207 (*Ant. syr.* VI 100–114); a connection with Heracles: *FGrHist* 788 F 1; a dedication to Zeus Soter: *SEG* 19.904; to Hadad and Atargatis: *SEG* 18.622, with J. Teixidor, *The Pagan God* (Princeton 1977) 52–59.

48. Newell, *The Late Seleucid Mints in Ake-Ptolemais and Damascus*, NNM 84 (New York 1939) 2–40.

49. L. Kadman, *The Coins of Akko Ptolemais*, CNP IV (Jerusalem 1961); Seyrig, *RN* VI.4 (1962) 25–50 (*Scripta numism.* 261–287, at 263).

50. Seyrig, *Scripta numism.* 264–265; cf. 365 no. 411. Kadman no. 28, read by him as απρ = 181 = 132/1, has not been confirmed. His no. 29, γπρ = 130/129, was reread by Seyrig as γϙρ = 120/119; but note the report of another specimen dated γπ[ρ], *Auktion F. Sternberg* 25/6 Nov. 1976 no. 690 (the dies are not the same as Kadman no. 29).

51. Seyrig, *Scripta numism.* 266–267, who assigned it tentatively to the first century B.C.

52. Babelon, *Perses* no. 1506, with Seyrig, *Scripta numism.* 264, who first saw the title.

first, was quickly abandoned, immediately followed by the issues with the full title dated to 126/5.

The fate of the city's privileges over the next two generations is uncertain, and details must await a more reliable chronology of the coins. Royal silver down through 107/6 gives the civic name only in monogram, and in this situation, as earlier, there are no titles (Seyrig, *Scripta numism.* 265–266)—this does not indicate that the title had lapsed. Around 103 B.C., besieged by Alexander Jannaeus, the city appealed unsuccessfully to Ptolemy Lathyrus; it was then besieged and taken by Cleopatra III and severed thereafter from Seleucid rule (Jos. *AJ* 13.324–351). The Seleucid name was abandoned, and the title "autonomous" was gained, as we know from some bronzes of the first century B.C.and from an inscribed decree of Rhodes.[53]

The bronzes, dated "year 9" (L Θ), show on the obverse the Dioscuri, on the reverse Tyche and flanking her these monograms:

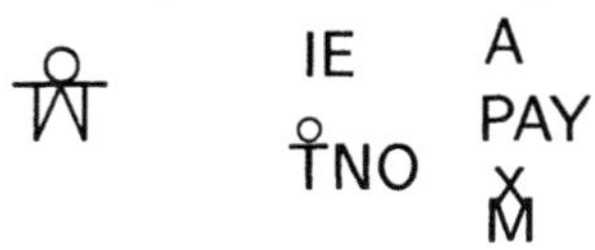

To the left is the familiar monogram of the city, regularly used in the second and first centuries whether the legal name was "Ptolemais" or "Antioch in Ptolemais"; the monogram on the right appears to contain IEPA αὐτονόμου.

The inscription concerns a Rhodian whose honors included being crowned by the city of Ptolemais: στεφανωθέντα ὑπὸ Πτολεμαιέων τᾶς ἱερᾶς καὶ ἀσύλου καὶ αὐτονόμου. This text, probably of the 60s B.C., guarantees that the monogram on the coins implies the full "sacred and inviolable and autonomous," as does ἱερᾶς καὶ αὐτονόμου on coins of various other cities.

The first half of the first century B.C. is obscure to us, with no coins securely dated.[54] Sporadic issues dated by the Caesarian era to the third quarter of the century display inviolability, ἱερᾶς καὶ ἀσύλου or as brief as ἱερᾶς ἀσύ(λου), but no longer autonomy (compare Ascalon, apparently deprived of autonomy by Pompey); these are found through the regime of Antony and Cleopatra (Seyrig, *Scripta* 270–271 no. 20) and down to 27/6 B.C. (*RPC* I 4743). The city was refounded under Claudius as Germanicopolis and soon after became a Roman colony:[55] the coins now show no titles. This might represent an abolition of *asylia* in the time of Augustus (again compare Ascalon), but more likely it is only

53. V. Kontorini, *RN* VI.21 (1979) 30–41; *Inscriptions inédites relatives à Rhodes* (Louvain 1983) no. 3 [*SEG* 33.644].

54. See the important article of Kontorini for the problems. We have also an issue still of "Antioch in Ptolemais the sacred and inviolable" and another of "Ptolemais the sacred and inviolable," each also from a "year 9."

55. Colony by Nero's time: *AEpigr* 1949, no. 142.

the selective advertising that is typical at cities that came to be honored with a Roman connection.

Strictly speaking, 126/5 is no more than a terminus ante quem for *asylia*. Before that year, however, Ptolemais had been the seat and mint of Demetrius II and Cleopatra Thea; but in 126 Demetrius was defeated near Damascus by Alexander Zabinas and repudiated by his wife, who closed Ptolemais against him (he fled to Tyre and was killed). She issued coins in her own name at Ptolemais and then found it expedient to associate with her rule her son Antiochus VIII; coins follow, still in 126/5, issued by the two jointly at Ptolemais. The declaration of the city's inviolability fits well in this period of competition, granted probably by Cleopatra alone, as she sought to assure herself of support.[56] These events, the same in which Tyre became free, are consistent with the first dated coins of Ptolemais showing inviolability.

Sidon

Sidon, the great rival of Tyre, paid special honor, like all Phoenicia, to the divine triad Baal, Astarte, and Eshmun.[57] At Sidon, however, first place seems to have gone to Astarte. In a rare early inscription the fifth-century king Ashmunazer displays his devotion to her (*ANET*^{3} 662). From the late second century B.C. to the time of Hadrian, one of the favored images on coins struck at Sidon is Astarte standing on a ship's prow and holding a crown, labeled "the goddess of Sidon," Σίδωνος θεᾶς.[58] The author of the Oxyrhynchus hymn to Isis, surveying the world, equates his goddess with Astarte at Sidon (*POxy.* XI 1380.116). It is a fair guess that when in the 120s Sidon was declared inviolable, Astarte was the honorand.

Seleucid issues struck at Sidon first show the civic name under Antiochus IV and sporadically thereafter during the next half century, in both Greek (Σιδωνίων

56. So Newell 20; Bellinger, "End" 63–64; Seyrig, *Scripta numism.* 265.

57. W. Baudissin, *Adonis und Esmun* (Leipzig 1911) 211–213. On the temple of Eshmun, M. Dunand, *MUB* 24 (1971) 19–25. Sidonians resident at Athens in the third century B.C. founded a temple of Baal (*IG* II^2 2946). Festivals of imperial date: Robert, *Op. min. sel.* II 1029–33, VII 703. On the city see E. Honigmann, *RE* 2A (1923) 2216–2229; the coins: J. Rouvier, *JIAN* 5 (1902) 99–134, 229–284.

58. The earliest example is of 133/2 (*BMC Phoen.* 181; Babelon, *Rois* no. 1174; Rouvier no. 1262), the latest at the end of the Greek coinage in A.D. 117/8 (Rouvier 1475). Bickerman, *Institutions* 153, misinterpreted θεᾶς in 133 as a civic title ("divine") and thought that "sacred" was added in 122/1; Seyrig, *Ant. syr.* III 4, wrote that at least two years separate "sacred" from "inviolable" at Sidon.

or abbreviated) and Phoenician. Under Antiochus IV, Sidon takes space to claim in Phoenician to be "mother of Cambe [Carthage], Hippo, Citium, and Tyre" (Rouvier 1213). But before 122/1 there is no claim of inviolability: Σιδωνίων as late as 134/3, ΣΙ in 128/7 (Rouvier 1269, 1265); Σίδωνος θεᾶς instead of the ethnic in 127/6 (Rouvier 1271). There is then a hiatus of several years, and when in 122/1 we next see a coin struck at Sidon, it bears the title of inviolability:

> Cleopatra Thea and Antochus VIII | Ptolemaic eagle, ΣΙΔΩ and ΙΕΡ left, ΑΣ̌ right = Σιδω(νίων) ἱερ(ᾶς) ἀσύ(λου); date αϙρ = 191 = 122/1 B.C.
> Babelon, *Rois* 1352; Rouvier 1272.

This title appears on the royal issues for as long as they continued to be struck at Sidon, regularly on the silver, but omitted on the bronzes that give "goddess of Sidon" in Greek in place of the ethnic.[59] Some undated silver under Antiochus VIII[60] omits the civic ethnic but still gives the title in the further abbreviation ΙΕ/Α.

Sidon inaugurated a civic era in 111/0, in the midst of the "war of the brothers."[61] Over the next 150 years, the rather sporadic coins of the city display the title of inviolability only occasionally (compare especially Antioch). On pre-Augustan bronze no titles are found; on the silver *asylia* is first evoked in 82/1 B.C. and last in A.D. 43/4:

> Tyche | Eagle on prow, Σίδωνος (or Σιδωνίων) τῆς ἱερᾶς καὶ ἀσύλου.[62]

A bronze of 6/5 B.C. gives Σίδωνος ἱερᾶς καὶ ἀσύλου (Rouvier 1450). On some bronzes in the 80s A.D. the "goddess of Sidon" type is augmented by civic titles:

> Tyche | Galley, Σίδωνος θεᾶς above, ἱερᾶς καὶ ἀσύλου καὶ ναυαρχίδος below.[63]

So when we see soon after Σίδωνος ΙΕΡΑΣ in A.D. 116/7,[64] this certainly abbreviates the full title "sacred and inviolable."[65] Most coins of imperial date give no titles at all. The mint was inactive for a century after A.D. 118, until

59. Rouvier 1279, 1280 (114/3, 113/2): Σίδωνος θεᾶς and the Phoenician ethnic, without titles.

60. Babelon 1413–1419; *BMC Sel. Kings* 88 nos. 9–12.

61. Seleuceia on the Orontes would be freed in September 109; cf. p. 486.

62. *BMC Phoen.* 158–161 nos. 104–117; Rouvier 1309–1328; Baramki, *Beirut Museum* 182 nos. 64–65. Silver issues without titles are extant in 107/6, 106/5, 100/99, 97/6 (*BMC* nos. 100–103; Rouvier 1305–1308; *RN* VI.10 [1968] 20). The civic bronze, untitled, is first seen in 110/109 (*BMC* no. 118; Rouvier 1329: Σιδωνίων and Phoenician, no titles).

63. Rouvier 1293–1297; *BMC Phoen.* nos. 193–196; Baramki nos. 164–168 (A.D. 80/1–87/8); other issues of 87/8 have this type but not the titles (*BMC* nos. 183–188).

64. Tyche | Chariot of Astarte: *BMC Phoen.* nos. 197–203; *SNG* IV 6059; Baramki nos. 195–198. Same inscription on *RPC* I 4604, where the reported date of 10/9 B.C. is uncertain.

65. Other issues of 116/7 have either Σίδωνος θεᾶς or Σίδωνος ναυαρχίδος: *BMC Phoen.* nos. 217–224; Rouvier 1469; Baramki nos. 216–233.

colonial status with its trappings was gained from Elagabalus (coins inscribed *colonia Aurelia Pia metropolis Sidon*, with no invocation of *asylia*).[66] Finally, a glass disk has been found inscribed in imitation of the coins, ηπρ (= A.D. 77/8) / Σίδωνος / ἱερᾶς καὶ ἀσύλου.[67]

The inviolability of Sidon thus was granted in the course of the war between Alexander Zabinas and Cleopatra Thea, with 122/1 as the terminus ante quem. We have no coins from Sidon between 127/6 (under Demetrius II) and 122/1 (under his widow Cleopatra and son Antiochus VIII) by which to narrow the date of the grant. Cleopatra operated in the 120s from Ptolemais, from which she excluded Demetrius after his defeat by Alexander in 126, and which was declared inviolable in 126/5. By late in the decade Alexander's fortunes were waning: in 123/2 Cleopatra gained Antioch and Ascalon, by 122/1 Damascus.[68] Without coins, we cannot know which faction was holding Sidon during these four years. If Alexander, then the inviolability seen under Cleopatra and Antiochus in 122/1 may mean that she won over the city in that year or soon before and precisely now granted it the title. But it is possible that she ruled Sidon earlier and 122/1 must remain only a terminus ante quem.

Beirut

Beirut in the Hellenistic age was one of the lesser cities of Phoenicia.[69] Its coinage is meager, and of its natives we are best informed about the merchants resident at Delos. In the second century B.C. Beirut bore the dynastic name "Laodicea in Phoenicia," and through much of the second century it was the seat of a royal mint issuing some silver and more bronze.[70] Some civic bronze, assigned by style to the second century B.C., shows in Phoenician "in Laodicea in Canaan" and ΛA^{O}_{Φ} = Λα(οδικέων) Φο(ινίκης); or else BH Φ. In the first century B.C. some coins give Βηρυτίων in full; and we find a civic era reckoned

66. Also ἡ σύμμαχος τῶν Ῥωμέων on a medallion of the same period: Seyrig, *Syria* 27 (1950) 249 (*Ant. syr.* IV 144). An exceptional issue in 193 under Pescennius Niger (Σιδωνίων without titles): Rouvier 1477.

67. D. Barag, in *Ann. 10e congr. hist. du verre* (Amsterdam 1987) 109–116, known to me only from *Bull. épigr.* 1991, 158.

68. Bellinger, "End" 64–65; A. Houghton and G. Le Rider, *BCH* 112 (1988) 404.

69. J. Lauffray, *ANRW* II.8 (1977) 135–163.

70. Rouvier, *JIAN* 3 (1900) 263–312; Wayne Moore, *GNS* 42 (1992) 117–125. Note both a "Beirutian" and a "Laodicean from Phoenicia" in a list from Rhodes: L. Migeotte, *BCH* 117 (1993) 351–352.

from 81/0 B.C., evidently reflecting benefactions of Tigranes.[71] No coin, whether of "Beirut" or of "Laodicea," shows any civic titles.[72] The city became a Roman colony around 15 B.C., and this limited the information displayed on its coins in imperial times. The great flourishing of Beirut was of course in later antiquity; Nonnus devoted his books 41–43 to its traditions.

As to cults,[73] Nonnus gives various details—Cronus was founder, Aphrodite visited Beirut first, it is the seat of Hermes, etc.—but it is Poseidon whose story dominates and who won the city, "and he brought to the dwellers in Beroe victory at sea in maritime war."[74] The Beirutians on Delos organized themselves around the worship of Poseidon, τὸ κοινὸν Βηρυτίων Ποσειδωνιαστῶν.[75] Poseidon with his hippocamps is shown often on the Hellenistic coins (*BMC* pl. 7).

The inviolability of Beirut is attested by a single inscription, found on Athenian Delos. In the archonship of Polyclitus at Athens (110/9 B.C.) the city erected a statue of its "benefactor and savior" Antiochus VIII, calling itself "Laodicea the sacred and inviolable":[76]

βασιλέα Ἀντίοχον Ἐπιφανῆ Φιλομήτορα
Καλλίνικον τὸν ἐγ βασιλέως Δημητρίου,
ὁ δῆμος ὁ Λαοδικέων τῶν ἐν Φοινίκῃ τῆς ἱερᾶς
καὶ ἀσύλου, τὸν ἑαυτοῦ σωτῆρα καὶ εὐερ-
γέτην Ἀπόλλωνι.
ἐπ' ἄρχοντος Πολυκλείτου, ἐπὶ ἐπιμελητοῦ δὲ
τῆς νήσου Διονυσίου τοῦ Νίκωνος Παλληνέως.

It happens that no coins of Beirut are extant for 110/9.

In itself this inscription need offer no better than a terminus ante quem for the recognition. But the statue must commemorate some royal benefaction, and the year 110/9 is suggestive. Here again, we are in the midst of the war of the

71. Seyrig, *Syria* 27 (1950) 38 (*Ant. syr.* IV 105).

72. So too a weight dated to 128/7: *RN* IV.1 (1897) 369. Strabo's statement that the city was destroyed by Tryphon (ca. 141 B.C.) and revived by the Romans is exaggerated at best, like many such claims in the ancient authors (16.2.19 [756]: κατεσπάσθη μὲν ὑπὸ Τρύφωνος, ἀνελήφθη δὲ νῦν ὑπὸ Ῥωμαίων); M. Dunand and R. Duru, *Oum el 'Amed* (Paris 1962) 182, invoke Strabo to cast doubt on the identity of the Laodicea of *CIS* I 7 (apparently of 133/2).

73. See Hill, *BMC Phoenicia* xlvii–xlix; Seyrig, *Syria* 20 (1939) 315–316 (*Ant. syr.* III 46–47: Roman divinities), 31 (1954) 71–72 (V 90–91: Dionysus), 87 (V 106: a Phoenician triad, rendered as Poseidon, Astarte, Eshmun/Asclepius).

74. 43.396–397; cf. Philo of Byblos *FGrHist* 790 F 2 (Eus. *Praep. evang.* 1.10.35), Cronus gave the city to Poseidon and others.

75. *I.Délos* IV 1772–1796; earlier (ca. 178 B.C.) they refer to themselves as οἱ ἐν Λα[οδικείαι] τῆι ἐν Φοινίκηι ἐγδοχεῖς καὶ να[ύκληροι, *IG* XI.4 1114.

76. *I.Délos* 1551; photograph at *BCH* 31 (1907) 445.

brothers, and at a moment evidently difficult for Antiochus VIII.[77] During the Seleucid year (October to October) 111/0 he had controlled Antioch and Tarsus; his brother ruled both in 110/9,[78] while Antiochus VIII apparently coined only at Ascalon; he was once again in control of Antioch in 109/8 (and also of Damascus as well as Ascalon). The Delian inscription reveals that in the Athenian year (July to July) 110/9, he held Beirut. It is possible, therefore, that, driven from Antioch in 110, he fled to Beirut, or at least won the city over (or kept its loyalty) by benefactions that included inviolability, and that this was itself the occasion of the statue on Delos.

Tripolis

Phoenician Tripolis, at modern Al-Mina, with a good harbor and a rich territory on the road into Syria, was important already in the fourth century B.C.[79] Of its cults we know very little—the coins show especially the Dioscuri, but also Astarte and Zeus Hagios.[80]

The city's privileges derive from the last years of the war of the brothers. Antiochus IX held the city ca. 106 B.C. (Jos. *AJ* 13.279) and issued tetradrachms there at least in 105/4.[81] At some point in the subsequent ten years, Tripolis began an era of liberty. Thereafter come occasional issues of silver tetradrachms; six such issues are known, each quite abundant, scattered from year 3 to year 32, that is, roughly from 100 to 70 B.C. They all have the same form:[82]

Dioscuri busts | Standing Tyche, Τριπολιτῶν τῆς ἱερᾶς καὶ αὐτονόμου.

77. See the chart at Bellinger, "End" 87. Since the first editor (Roussel), 110/9 has been thought the actual date of the grant; 122/1 at Bickerman, *Institutions* 153, is a lapsus (110/9 in n. 7).

78. In its adhesion to Antioch VIII, Beirut seems the exception among the several Phoenician cities whose loyalties we know: Antiochus IX held Ptolemais throughout these years, and Sidon in 113/2 and 111/0. See Bellinger 87 (but excluding Tripolis, which was not a royal mint: A. Houghton and G. Le Rider, *BCH* 112 [1988] 406–408); A. Houghton and W. Müseler, *GNS* 40 (1990) 60–61.

79. R. Dussaud, *Topographie historique de la Syrie* (Paris 1927) 75–78; Honigmann, *RE* 7A (1939) 203–207.

80. The coinage of Hellenistic Tripolis was put in order by Seyrig, *Syria* 27 (1950) 38–43 (*Ant. syr.* IV 105–110); cf. Rouvier, *JIAN* 6 (1903) 17–46.

81. A. Houghton and G. Le Rider, *BCH* 112 (1988) 406–408.

82. Some illustrated examples: *Weber* no. 8068; *Jameson* no. 1774 (year 3); *BMC Phoenicia* no. 4 (year 8); *BMC* no. 2; *Fitzwilliam* no. 9509; *SNG Salting* I.1 45 (year 11); *BMC* 5; Babelon, *Perses* no. 1874 (year 18); *SNG* IV 6066; Seyrig, *Scripta numism.* 357 no. 333 (year 30); *Glendining Sale Nov.* 25, 1953 no. 109; cf. *BMC* 7 (year 32).

While this silver does not fail to cite the titles of inviolability and autonomy, the several bronze issues that seem earlier than Pompey apparently omit them.[83]

In 64/3 or the next year, the city began a Pompeian era, and henceforth to the end of antiquity the coins of Tripolis display no titles,[84] with the exception of ναυαρχίδος in the third century A.D.[85] That this is mere chasteness on the part of the coins is proved by a statue of a provincial governor erected on the Acropolis in Athens around A.D. 130:[86]

> Τριπολιτῶν τῆς Φοινειχῆς τῆς ἱερᾶς καὶ ἀσύλου καὶ αὐτονόμου καὶ ναυαρχίδος οἱ ἄρχοντες καὶ ἡ βουλὴ καὶ ὁ δῆμος (κτλ.)

Thus, the coins are selective in their testimony. The silver gives a terminus ante quem of ca. 100 B.C. for inviolability and autonomy. It seems to me likely that at this relatively early date in this part of the world, inviolability preceded autonomy, as at Tyre, and the two honors were not granted simultaneously. Both the new era and the right to issue silver tetradrachms will reflect autonomy, hence granted between 105 and 95. Before that we are without evidence at Tripolis. Other examples from this last generation of the second century B.C. suggest that *asylia* might have preceded autonomy by some years. The competition of the brothers Antiochus VIII and IX is a possibility, as we have seen at Beirut ca. 110 B.C.

Antioch

Antioch, the Seleucid capital, was the city of Apollo, ancestor of the dynasty; the temple was in the sacred grove at Daphne outside the city. Here the royal house sponsored a *panegyris*, attended by foreign *theoroi*.[87]

83. Briefly treated by Seyrig, *Ant. syr.* IV 108 n. 3. *SNG* IV 6068 is dubiously read: [Τριπολιτῶν] ἱερ(ᾶς) αὐ(τονόμου) ἀσ(ύλου), year 9 = 90s B.C. At Babelon, *Perses* 1879, Τριπολιτῶν τῆς ΙΚΑ; taken as a date ∟ΤΚΕ by Rouvier (no. 1679).

84. Certainly the series dated by the Seleucid era and beginning in 30/29 is without titles (Seyrig, *Ant. syr.* IV 107; cf. *Scripta numism.* 357), likewise issues earlier under Cleopatra in 36/5 B.C. (*RPC* I p. 646).

85. E.g., *BMC* cxxii; 225 no. 133; *SNG* IV 6080. Neocoros has been alleged once, at Rouvier 1754.

86. *IG* II^2 4210.1–5 (I have collated a squeeze at the Institute for Advanced Study).

87. *FGrHist* 87 F 21; J. and L. Robert, *Bull. épigr.* 1955, 122; 1965, 436. Note, however, that in the first century B.C. when *asylia* was granted, the civic coins are entirely dominated by Zeus. On the cult of Zeus at Antioch (whose temple was in the city proper) see G. Downey, *History of Antioch* (Princeton 1961) 67–68, 75–76. Bibliography on the city at J. Lassus, *ANRW* II.8 (1977)

Around 170 B.C. the Jewish high priest Onias fled to the temple of Apollo for safety (ἀποκεχωρηκὼς εἰς ἄσυλον τόπον), only to be lured outside (ἐκ τοῦ ἀσύλου προελθεῖν) and killed by an agent of Antiochus IV—which caused an outcry among the Antiochenes.[88] The author of 2 Maccabees is here applying the language of Ptolemaic Egypt to the normal immunity of a Greek temple: his words should not be taken as evidence of some prior recognition of *asylia* (that would make Antioch by far the earliest instance outside of the Aegean area). Strabo, however, in describing the grove at Daphne with its ἄσυλον τέμενος καὶ νεώς of Apollo and Artemis (16.2.6 [750]), might well reflect the granted status, which by then had been confirmed by Rome.

Antiochus X expelled Seleucus VI from Antioch in 94 B.C.; during some of 93 he was in turn supplanted by Seleucus' brother Antiochus XI but succeeded in returning and holding the city until his expulsion and death in 92; in 92/1 the city was taken by Demetrius III.[89] That Antioch was an object of competition is obvious. For the development of civic privileges we have the following items:

A. According to Malalas (234), Antiochus XI (hence in 93 B.C.) built temples for Apollo and Artemis in the grove at Daphne, erected two gilded statues there, and "granted the privilege to whoever took refuge there not to be expelled from these temples," παρασχὼν προνόμια τοῖς καταφεύγουσιν ἐκεῖ πρὸς τὸ μὴ ἐκβάλλεσθαί τινα ἐκ τῶν αὐτῶν ἱερῶν. This account admittedly is murky, and we can hardly believe that Antiochus XI had the time (or the need) to build temples of the chief gods of Antioch; but the specific claim of the granted privilege looks to be a Roman way of saying that Antiochus declared the temple at Daphne inviolable.

B. In 92/1 Antioch obtained the right to issue bronze coins. These show only one title, Ἀντιοχέων τῆς μητροπόλεως, from 92/1 to 48/7.[90]

54–102; for the coins see Newell, "The Pre-Imperial Coinage," *NC* IV.19 (1919) 69–113; Seyrig, *Syria* 27 (1950) 5–15 (*Ant. syr.* IV 72–82).

88. 2 Macc. 4:33–34, with C. Habicht, 2. *Makkabäerbuch*, Jüd.Schr.hell.-röm.Zeit I.3 (Gütersloh 1976) 221. Queen Berenice fled to Daphne in 246 B.C. before being murdered (Justin. 27.1).

89. This chronology is a probable reconstruction; the relevant coins are not dated: Newell, "The Seleucid Mint of Antioch," *AJN* 51 (1918) 111–118. A coin of Cleopatra Selene and her son Antiochus XIII was struck probably in Antioch in 92 after the death of her husband Antiochus X: Bellinger, *ANSMN* 5 (1952) 53–55; but the mint and date are uncertain.

90. An example taken by Dieudonné as 103/2 B.C. would be exceptional and is surely mistaken (*RN* IV.30 [1927] 13, followed by Downey 130): the alleged Seleucid 210, ΣΙ, reads in the wrong direction, and *SNG Copenh.Syria* no. 70 with ΣΙΙ shows that it is not a numeral. Seyrig tacitly rejected Dieudonné's interpretation in omitting these coins from his account of the earliest issues of Antioch. Seyrig (IV 81) deduced from the absence of issues after 70/69 until 64/3 that coinage rights were abolished by Antiochus XIII when he replaced Tigranes in 69, and were restored by Pompey; but the activity of the mint is sporadic enough that this hiatus may be fortuitous. The city used a Pompeian era of 66/5.

C. Antioch sided with Caesar against Pompey. In June 47 Caesar visited the city; according to Malalas (216), before arriving Caesar issued an edict in which he declared the city free, προετέθη ἐν Ἀντιοχείᾳ ἡ ἐλευθερία αὐτῆς; Malalas claims to quote the opening words, ἐν Ἀντιοχείᾳ τῇ μητροπόλει καὶ ἱερᾷ καὶ ἀσύλῳ καὶ αὐτονόμῳ καὶ ἀρχούσῃ καὶ προκαθημένῃ τῆς ἀνατολῆς. This reads like a heading rather than the opening of a letter, and it appears to be an accretion of a later age or a literary context (so especially the final two titles, but also "autonomous" when this is the object of the edict). In any case, Malalas is specific in stating that what Caesar now granted was freedom, not inviolability.

D. Bronze coins extant from 48/7 to 41/0, dated now by a Caesarian era, show Ἀντιοχέων τῆς μητροπόλεως ἱερᾶς καὶ ἀσύλου καὶ αὐτονόμου; likewise a weight of year 7 = 43/2, from which no coins seem to survive (*IGLSyrie* III 1071.i). We find condensations: on the smallest denominations of 47/6 and 46/5, only τῆς μητροπόλεως (Newell nos. 4–10); on a coin of 42/1 Ἀντιοχέων τῆς μητροπόλεως αὐτονόμου (no. 12; *RPC* I 4222), yet the titles in full on other issues of this year (condensed again in 41/0, no. 13); similarly Ἀντιοχέων τῆς μητροπόλεως καὶ αὐτονόμου on a drachma of 47/6.[91] In these years Antioch also issued silver tetradrachms, the pseudo-Philips, which lack ethnic and titles but have the monogram ΑΤ, which might represent αὐτ(ονόμου).[92]

E. An issue dated suddenly again by the Seleucid era, 272 = 41/0, shows Ἀντιοχέων τῆς μητροπόλεως ἱερᾶς καὶ ἀσύλου (Newell no. 14). This reveals that when the Parthians conquered the city they revoked the autonomy and the era that derived from Caesar, but not inviolability or metropolis that derived from the Seleucids.

F. From 41/0 to A.D. 4/5 (*Copenh. Syria* no. 94), the coins have Ἀντιοχέων μητροπόλεως αὐτονόμου. This is merely a short form, and not evidence that inviolability has been canceled, for the same short form is found on the issue of 42/1 B.C., and Roman restoration of autonomy after the expulsion of the Parthians will not have been coupled with abolition of *asylia*. Different condensations occur in this period: an undated silver issue under Antony (*BMC* 157 no. 52 = *RPC* I 4135) and the bronzes of 31/0 (Newell nos. 20–22) omit αὐτονόμου; the smallest denominations of 25/4 and 23/2 omit instead μητροπόλεως (Newell nos. 35, 39; *RPC* I 4244); several issues under Augustus have no titles but the monogram ΑΤ.

G. From A.D. 11/2 (*Copenh.* no. 96) until the end of Antiochene coinage in the late third century, no title appears but "metropolis," and this rarely (e.g., *RPC* I

91. This last I owe to the kind advice of Arthur Houghton.

92. So Wroth (*BMC* 166) and Newell (72); MacDonald was skeptical (*NC* IV.4 [1904] 110 n. 11).

4162 of 35/6). Here as elsewhere the silence of these later coins should not be taken to imply the end of other titles.[93]

Thus Antiochus XI declared the temple of Apollo inviolable in 93 B.C., or else declared Antioch inviolable in honor of Apollo. The first option is consistent with Malalas and with the frequent pattern of rural shrines in declared inviolability. The right of bronze coinage came in the next year and simultaneously the title "metropolis"; this was a grant of Demetrius III, outbidding his rival for the loyalty of the city. Caesar added freedom, whence αὐτονόμου and the new era seen on the coins. This Roman addition was briefly canceled by the Parthians, but not Antioch's Seleucid titles of inviolability and metropolis.

This account requires that we discount the silence of the first generation of Antiochene coins about the acquisition of *asylia*, a surprising silence.[94] Antioch displayed a single title, Ἀντιοχέων τῆς μητροπόλεως, from 92/1 to 48/7; *asylia* is shown only from 48/7 to 41/0, and never again. But as we have seen, the Antiochene coins of the first century B.C. exhibit other omissions; contemporary Sidon is similarly modest in display. I suggest that the title "metropolis," familiar to us from imperial times but unprecedented in 92 B.C., was felt by the Antiochenes to outrank *asylia*, and so they put this alone on their coins until the time of Caesar and liberation, when for a few years everything was listed.

Larisa

Larisa stands some twenty-five kilometers southeast of Apamea, at the point where the middle Orontes valley comes to be closed in by hills.[95] The river emerges here from a sheer canyon, the left bluff of which served as the acropolis of ancient Larisa, later a medieval fortress. This was a strategic place; here the valley has its natural southern limit, and here the river, as it breaks from its winding gorge, is easily bridged. The site is attested already in the Bronze Age, under the name it still uses, Shaizar. The pastures of the Seleucid horse

93. So also Seyrig, *Ant. syr.* IV 81.

94. Seyrig, relying on the coins and not Malalas 234, held that Caesar declared Antioch "sacred, inviolable, and autonomous" in a stroke in 47 B.C.

95. R. Dussaud, *Topographie historique de la Syrie* (Paris 1927) 110, 200; *La Syrie* (Paris 1931) pl. 104; E. Honigmann, "Syria," *RE* 4A (1932) 1662; R. Mouterde and A. Poidebard, *Limes de Chalcis* (Paris 1945) 26 and 42 with pl. 7; M. Dunand, *De l'Amanus au Sinai* (Beirut 1953) 117–119; cf. J. L. Burckhardt, *Travels in Syria* (London 1822) 144. A writer from Apamea once specifies Λάρισα ἡ Θετταλική so as not to confuse his readers: Posidonius *FGrHist* 87 F 36 (Ath. 212A).

and elephant herds, which our sources associate with Apamea, will certainly have extended up river to Larisa. Of the history and the cults of Larisa little is recorded.[96] Its citizens, recruited and named from Thessaly in the time of Seleucus Nicator, were famous as horsemen. In the time of the usurpation of Tryphon, who came from Apamea, war broke out between the two neighbors, and both cities came to be used as bases by Tryphon.[97]

The only coins attributed with certainty to Syrian Larisa are some autonomous bronzes of the first century B.C., and these are our evidence for inviolability:

A. Zeus bust | Throne, Λαρισαίων τῆς ΙΕΡΑΣ, date ζκς (227 = 86/5 B.C.).
BMC Galatia 264 no. 1 (diameter 1.6 cm); Leake, *Numismatica Hellenica: Asiatic Greece* (London 1854) 75; Lindgren and Kovacs, *Ancient Bronze Coins* no. 2109.
B. Tyche bust | Horse's head, [Λαρι]σαίων [τῆ]ς ἱερᾶς καὶ αὐτονόμου.
Leake, *Supplement* (1859) 65.

A is a coin of small denomination; I assume that ΙΕΡΑΣ abbreviates the full title ἱερᾶς καὶ ἀσύλου. This provides a terminus ante quem of 86/5 for inviolability, hence before the regime of Tigranes, which so benefited Laodicea. Autonomy came subsequently, perhaps in fact from Tigranes.

Laodicea ad Mare

Hellenistic Laodicea was overshadowed politically and commercially by Seleuceia, its neighbor to the north; it has left little mark in history before the first century B.C., when it was promoted at the expense of Seleuceia by Tigranes of Armenia, who conquered the region in 83 B.C.[98] As to its cults, later evidence reveals several gods, none visibly dominant; the bronzes struck in the second century B.C. under Antiochus IV and Alexander Balas show Poseidon, appropriate to this harbor city.

Here as elsewhere, bronzes under Alexander Balas in the early 140s show no titles (Λαοδικέων τῶν πρὸς θαλάσσηι), and so too a civic weight of 106/5 B.C.,

96. In addition to the coins: *I.Syrie* IV 1378 (a priestess of some divinity, A.D. 201/2); Seyrig, *Syria* 42 (1965) 28–31 (*Ant. syr.* VI 144–147; a dedication to Artemis).

97. *FGrHist* 87 F 2; Strab. 16.2.10 (752); Diod. 33.4–5. Compare the deposition against the bishop of Apamea in A.D. 519, which details another battle between the two neighbors: E. Schwartz, *ACO* III (1940) p. 107.

98. Honigmann, *RE* 12 (1924) 713–718. On the political difficulties of the city in the 160s B.C. (murder of a Roman ambassador, threat of destruction) see C. Habicht, *ZPE* 74 (1988) 211–214.

which supplies a likely terminus post quem for the city's titles.[99] A civic coinage in silver and bronze, marked by a civic era, begins probably in 81/0.[100] These coins show from the start the titles "sacred and autonomous":

A. Tyche (silver) or Zeus bust (bronze) | Zeus Nicephorus (silver) or tripod or Artemis (bronze), Λαοδικέων τῆς ἱερᾶς καὶ αὐτονόμου; dates attested from year 1 to year 34 (81/0–48/7).[101] A unique hemidrachma of year 4 gives Λαοδικέων τῆς αὐτονόμου;[102] this certainly is an abridgment for reasons of space.

Two civic weights belonging to the same generation have the following inscriptions:

B. ἔτους θκ Λαοδικέων τῆς ἱερᾶς καὶ ἀσύλου καὶ αὐτονόμου μνᾶ (53/2 B.C.).[103]
C. Λαοδικέ[ων τ]ῆς ἱερᾶς κ[αὶ] αὐτονόμο[υ] ἔτους [.], ἀγορανομοῦντος Πολέμ[ω]νος ἡμιμναῖον.[104]

The second weight, half the size of B and with other matters to inscribe, has condensed the titles as do the coins.

With benefactions gained from Caesar in 48/7 B.C., Laodicea took a new name and began a new era: from now until the city gained metropolitan and then colonial status in the 190s A.D., the coins give no titles, only Ἰουλιέων τῶν καὶ Λαοδικέων.[105] But it is not believable that it can have lost its honorific titles at the same time as being honored by Caesar: the Caesarian name has merely usurped the space of the earlier titles. In fact a number of inscriptions on stone show that inviolability and autonomy survived.

D. A statue of Caesar's Cnidian friend Theopompus was erected by the Laodiceans at Cnidus; they call themselves [ὁ δῆμος] ὁ Ἰουλιέων τῶν καὶ Λαοδικέ[ων] τῶν πρὸς θαλάσσηι τῆς ἱερᾶς καὶ ἀσύλου καὶ αὐτονόμου (*IGBM* IV 801 = *I.Knidos* 58).

Their gratitude to Theopompus must have been incurred during the passage of Caesar and his entourage in summer 47 on their way to Egypt.

99. Babelon, *Rois* 118; *BMC Sel. Kings* 57. *IGLSyrie* 1271b: Λαοδικέων τῶν πρὸς θαλάσσηι, [ἐπὶ ἀγο]ρα[νόμου] Φιλοδάμου; but [τῆς ἱε]ρᾶ[ς, ἐπὶ] Φιλοδάμου must be considered a possibility.

100. See Seyrig, *Syria* 27 (1950) 26–32 (*Ant. syr.* IV 92–98); Mørkolm, *ANSMN* 28 (1983) 89–107.

101. Mørkholm 93. Most years are represented; Mørkholm reports a year 1; year 2 is represented in bronze by *BMC Galatia* 248 no. 10; for year 34 (48/7), Seyrig *Ant. syr.* IV 93 n. 2.

102. For this I am indebted again to Arthur Houghton.

103. Seyrig, *BMusBeyr* 8 (1949) 53 no. 3 with pl. 5 (*Scripta varia* 383) [*IGLSyrie* IV 1271c, by lapsus omitting ἀσύλου καὶ].

104. *IGLSyrie* IV 1271d; the one-digit year must have been 10, 20, or 30.

105. *BMC Galatia* 249ff., the earliest extant of year 2 = 47/6; on the late titles see Seyrig, *Syria* 40 (1963) 30–32 (*Ant. syr.* VI 132–134).

One coin shows a temporary change in year 7:

E. Tyche bust | Nike, Λαοδικέων τῶν πρὸς θαλάσσηι (Seyrig, *Ant. syr.* IV 97).

This attests the loss of the Caesarian name in 42/1, and probably also the titles, if we can treat this issue on a par with the "pre-Julian" issues that do give titles. In year 8 the coins revert to the normal Ἰουλιέων τῶν καὶ Λαοδικέων, still without showing titles.

F. In A.D. 109/110 the city erected at Ephesus a statue of A. Julius Quadratus, governor of Asia: Ἰου[λι]έων τῶν καὶ Λαοδικέων τῶν πρὸς θαλάσσῃ τῆς ἱερᾶς καὶ ἀσύλου καὶ αὐτονόμου ἡ πόλις (*I.Ephesos* III 614.10–13).

G. In A.D. 132 it erected a statue of Hadrian in Athens, our fullest list of its honors: ἡ πόλις Ἰουλιέων τῶν καὶ Λαοδικέων τῶν πρὸς θαλ⟨ά⟩σσῃ τῆς ἱερᾶς καὶ ἀσύλου καὶ αὐτονόμου, ναυαρχίδος συνγενίδος φίλης συμμάχου κοινωνοῦ δήμου Ῥωμαίων, ἐξαιρέτως τετειμημένη δωρεαῖς, καθὼς ἐν Καπετωλίωι δέλτοι περιέχουσιν (κτλ.).[106]

Accordingly, Laodicea had been declared sacred and inviolable and autonomous by the time of the earliest civic coins in 81/0; it probably lost these privileges along with its Julian name during 42 under the regime of Cassius, but these were restored by Antony upon his arrival in Syria in 41.

Certainly "autonomous" came with the civic era and the right to coin: it dates from 81/0. The question for us is the origin of its inviolability, for which the coins need give no more than a terminus ante quem. As Seyrig stressed, the victory of Tigranes changed drastically the respective fortunes of Laodicea and Seleuceia. After his arrival Laodicea, which had struck no civic money before, became the only source of silver tetradrachms in the region, when Tigranes made it the chief port of northern Syria. It is easily possible that, unknown to us for want of coins, *asylia* was gained before 81/0, preceding autonomy by some years, as was common; this seems more likely than that the two were granted in a stroke in 81. Even at that, *asylia* may yet derive from Tigranes, granted in 83 or 82; but little Larisa inland had the title by 86/5, and perhaps the *asylia* of Laodicea should also be placed earlier than Tigranes.

Apamea

On its strategic plateau overlooking the middle Orontes valley, Apamea was the military headquarters and one of the residences of the Seleucid kings.

106. *IG* II^2 3299.2–6 (ΘΑΛΣ); I have collated a squeeze at the Institute for Advanced Study. *Syngeneia* derives from the nomen Julia according to D. Musti, *AnnPisa* II.32 (1963) 237.

Here the kings pastured their horse and elephant herds; and the elephant is the most common emblem on the late Hellenistic coins of Apamea. The Belgian excavations have revealed much about the Roman city but little of its Hellenistic predecessor.[107] Seleucid Apamea is known mainly from its coins, which also are sole witness for the city's inviolability. Here as elsewhere in the region, in the 160s and 140s occasional local bronzes were allowed by the crown; these show on their reverses Zeus in armor and the ethnic Ἀπαμέων without titles.[108]

The more abundant civic coinage of Apamea, still in bronze, begins only toward the end of the Hellenistic period.[109] The types are predominantly Zeus bust | Elephant; but we find also Tyche, Athena, Demeter, and Dionysus. The first series runs from 76/5 to 68/7, with most years represented. Then after a hiatus of a generation, coins are extant again from 43/2 and continue sporadically into the 20s B.C. Thereafter they are less and less frequent, ceasing entirely in the early years of Tiberius, but for some issues (including a silver tetradrachm) under Claudius after the city was refounded under his name.[110] Thus the right to coin was granted by Tigranes of Armenia and then canceled by Pompey, whom Apamea resisted in 65/4.[111] The privilege was restored by Caesar, whose era is seen on the two issues extant before the Parthian invasion (43/2 and 42/1).

On all extant coins from 76/5 through 41/0 B.C., the inscription is Ἀπαμέων τῆς ἱερᾶς καὶ ἀσύλου. From 40/39 through 30/29 it is τῆς ἱερᾶς καὶ αὐτονόμου.[112] After 30/29 it reverts to "sacred and inviolable" and continues so until the end of this series in A.D. 14/5. The coins of "Claudia Apamea" are without titles, Κλαυδιέων Ἀπαμέων.

107. *IGLSyrie* IV 1311–1375; *Fouilles d'Apamée de Syrie* I– (Brussels 1968–); J. and J. C. Balty, *ANRW* II.8 (1977) 103–134; Burckhardt's description is still valuable, *Travels in Syria* (London 1822) 138–139; an evocative photograph of the citadel and its valley at M. Dunand, *De l'Amanus au Sinai* (Beirut 1953) 115; on foundation legends, A. S. Hollis, *ZPE* 102 (1994) 153–166.

108. With royal obverses: e.g., *SNG* VI 1105 (Alexander Balas, 150/149 B.C.); with autonomous (showing Tyche): *BMC Galatia* 233 nos. 1–2.

109. The sequence of issues, after a beginning by Seyrig, *Syria* 27 (1950) 15–20 (*Ant. syr.* IV 82–87), was established by M. El-Zein, "Geschichte der Stadt Apameia" (Diss., Heidelberg 1972) 138–197, and by *RPC* I pp. 631–634 without reference to El-Zein.

110. See the table at El-Zein 191–197; further examples at *SNG* IV 5948–5950. Before Claudius, the dates are by Seleucid era except at the beginning of the second series (coins of Caesarian 7 and 8 = 43/2 and 42/1); evidently the Caesarian era was abandoned after the Parthian invasion and the benefactions of Antony.

111. Jos. *AJ* 14.38. Seyrig attributed abolition of coinage to Antiochus XIII, who was installed in place of Tigranes in 69/8. But he was dead within a year (see Bellinger, "End" 83), probably before the issues of Apamea in 68/7; it is merely the sporadic character of striking that explains the absence of coins from 67/6 to the personal arrival of Pompey early in 64.

112. El-Zein 175; *RPC* I 4335.

Thus the city was declared sacred and inviolable in or before 76/5 B.C. As at Laodicea, the grantor may well have been Tigranes, in power here after 83 B.C. When in the 60s the city lost the right to coin, it may have lost the right of inviolability as well—we are without evidence from the generation that follows. If *asylia* was abolished, Caesar restored it in the 40s. In 40 Antony added autonomy, as reward to the Apameans for resisting the Parthian invasion.[113] In 29 Octavian canceled what Antony had added but no more (compare his treatment of Ephesus). The titles were supplanted by the imperial name under Claudius; this represents not abolition of the title but selectivity of display.

In Roman times the great god of Apamea was Bel. By the third century his shrine was oracular (*ILS* 4333); the priest Aur. Belius Philippus makes a dedication on the orders of τοῦ θεοῦ μεγίστου ἁγίου Βήλου.[114] The Hellenistic coins are dominated by Zeus in armor, an unusual image, who is probably the Bel of the imperial texts.

After the early start by the old capital Seleuceia (by 139/8), the other cities of the Orontes Valley obtained inviolability in rapid succession—Antioch (93), Larisa (by 86/5), Laodicea (by 81/0), Apamea (by 76/5); it is surprising that little Larisa to the south seems to have anticipated both Laodicea and its traditional enemy Apamea.

Temple of Zeus, Baetocaece

The temple of Zeus of Baetocaece in Phoenicia occupies a small upland valley, modern Husn Suleiman, east of the island of Aradus and some thirty-five kilometers inland.[115] The impressive ruins have been studied since the eighteenth century. The standing temple with its peribolos wall derives from Roman imperial times; traces of its predecessor, a smaller temple, cannot be closely dated.

113. Dio 48.25. The coins of 41/0 (still "sacred and inviolable") abandon the Pompeian era and revert to the Seleucid, reflecting Parthian control; some issues of years 2 and 3, "sacred and autonomous," are assigned to a brief civic era, 40/39 and 39/8, by *RPC*.

114. J. -P. Rey-Coquais, *AAAS* 23 (1973) 66–68; further references at *IGLSyrie* VII pp. 78–79; Seyrig, *Notes* 9; J. C. Balty, *JRS* 78 (1988) 94–95. The Apamean theophoric name Belius also at E. Schwartz, *ACO* III (1940) 109.23 (monastery of the blessed Belius, A.D. 518).

115. R. Krencker and W. Zschietzschmann, *Römische Tempel in Syrien* (Berlin/Leipzig 1938) 65–101; J.-P. Rey-Coquais, *Arados et sa pérée* (Paris 1974) 61–64, 108–121, and in *Sociétés urbaines, sociétés rurales*, ed. E. Frézouls (Strasbourg 1987) 191–198; the inscriptions are at Rey-Coquais, *IGLSyrie* VII 4028–4041.

The dozen dedications from the temple, all of imperial date, reveal by their occasional epithets (Keraunios, Olympios) a weather god, the local Baal-Shamin. He is called Zeus in our one Hellenistic document (**218**.18); in the later texts he is normally identified merely by the toponym "the most high god of Baetocaece."[116] Βαιτοκαικη probably means "the house of the castor oil tree" (*kiki*), which is cultivated in these hills. The inscriptions attest to the vitality of the *katochoi* of the god especially during the middle years of the third century A.D., the period when they obtained confirmation of the temple's rights.

This confirmation was commemorated by the most famous inscription from the site, a collection of acts displayed on the peribolos wall beside its main entrance. Four events are represented: the confirmation by Valerian of the traditional rights of the temple around 260 A.D.; a Seleucid memorandum granting inviolability and other privileges; a "decree of the city sent to Augustus" in which civic magistrates are forbidden to tax or requisition goods traded at the festival of Zeus; and the dedicatory statement of the *katochoi* of Zeus around 260.

Clearly the temple was widely patronized; its bimonthly fair (line 26) is characteristic of a popular rural shrine. Seyrig in fact thought it the federal temple of a league of cities. The evidence for this is weak, however, and at the times represented by the inscription, the silences are telling: in the Seleucid memorandum, the king alone controls the temple and village, which appear to be on royal land; in the civic decree, the city alone (Aradus, in Seyrig's view) controls it.[117]

The king Antiochus cannot be identified. For the date of his grant we cannot of course rely on palaeography. It has traditionally been assigned to the last years of the dynasty, as it was taken to betoken the enfeeblement of the central government. Whatever one thinks of that argument, a date in the late second or early first century[118] will be consistent with other grants of inviolability in the Hellenistic East; also with the existence of a satrapy of Apamea (line 21).

Antiochus' motive as stated is purely religious: he has been impressed by the "power," the miracles, of the god. The past owner of the village is dead or disgraced, and Antiochus, to increase the honor of the temple, gives the

116. The exception is at **218**.40, where perhaps the *katochoi* were influenced by the Hellenistic text that they were using.

117. Seyrig, *Syria* 28 (1951) 191–206 (*Ant. syr.* IV 170–200); *RN* VI.4 (1964) 28–47 (*Scripta numism.* 98–117). Rey-Coquais, *Arados* 125, invokes as possibly relevant a fragmentary inscription from Husn Soleiman that mentions "seven cities and seven villages"; this text does not appear to have been published as yet. Seyrig's assignment of the decree and hence Baetocaece to Aradus might be doubted. Aradus never put civic titles on its coins, so we do not know whether it claimed inviolability.

118. In defense of this date see Rigsby, *TAPA* 110 (1980) 248–254. Seyrig argued for a date early in the third century B.C., on the grounds that the temple is on Aradian territory and Seleucid rule ended there in 259 B.C. (the "era of Aradus"): but nothing suggests that Aradus owned the temple at the time of the Seleucid memorandum, which does not mention a city.

region over to the god rather than to another mortal.[119] The fiscal immunities seem the primary reward; the spirit of the act is not unlike that of Sulla for the Amphiaraeum at Oropus (**6**). Even the favor conjoined with making the temple inviolable, making the village immune from billeting, is mainly an economic benefaction. These fiscal benefactions do not amount to *asylia*; the same pair, exemption from taxes and troops, is met at the Artemisium of Ephesus at the end of the fourth century B.C. (*I.Ephesos* 1449). The specific meaning of *asylia* is not spelled out here. Because the king is not dealing with a sovereign state (a Greek city), it may be that here as in Egypt *asylia* meant the exclusion of the police powers of the crown—the right of asylum in the Roman sense.

Thus the grant to Baetocaece stands apart from other Seleucid recognitions and is similar instead to those in Ptolemaic Egypt: civic prestige is not at issue here, and what the temple gained was immunity from the royal authorities—police powers, royal taxes, billeting of royal troops. We are not in the legal world of the Greek polis. It seems that (at least by this date) the royal government here as in Egypt did not treat the temples on royal land as regularly immune. If this policy was relatively new, and we have no other evidence for the Seleucids, it may reflect the influence of the Ptolemies that was so pronounced in this last half century of the Seleucid dynasty.[120]

To round out the story I include the later documents, even though *asylia* does not come into the civic decree of Augustan date, whose economic emphasis, the fiscal independence of the temple from the city, is even more pronounced than in the royal memorandum. The temple has now passed into the territory of a city, perhaps upon the liquidation of the Seleucid monarchy by Pompey and the distribution of the crown lands. The present text reflects the tensions between the city and a temple that it had only recently acquired, perhaps by a Roman decision. Clearly some appeal from those involved with the temple has reached the governor, who likely consulted Augustus; the victory of the temple authorities was capped by their sending the city's decree of acquiescence to Rome.

218. Seleucid king

On the peribolos wall of the precinct, to the right of the main entrance, inscribed in an inset of h. 213, w. 105.

119. Cf. Bickerman, *Institutions* 181, for such assignments. Antiochus of Commagene stipulated that "the villages which I have dedicated to these gods it is wrong for anyone to appropriate or alienate or transfer or damage in any way, either these villages or the revenue, which I have dedicated as an inviolable possession of the gods" (*IGLSyrie* I 1.192–200 = *OGIS* 383).

120. Welles (p. 285) thought to see late features and Ptolemaic influence in the vocabulary: γενέσθω in line 17, προσφέρω and singular μοι in 18. The express θεός before the name of a god (18) is a usage more characteristic of imperial times than earlier.

R. Chandler, *Inscriptiones antiquae* (Oxford 1774) 88–90 [S. Donati, *Ad novum thesaurum* (Lucca 1765) 147; Franz, *CIG* 4474; Orelli, *Inscriptionum latinarum* II (Zurich 1828) 3657 (A, E); *CIL* III 184; *ILS* 540 (A, E)]; Waddington, ap. E. G. Rey, *Archives des miss. scient. litt.* II.3 (1867) 337 and pl. 3 (squeeze) [Le Bas-Waddington 2720a; Dittenberger, *OGIS* 262 (B–E); *IGR* III 1020]; H. H. Jessup, *Pal.Expl.Soc.Report* 2 (1873) 32–38 (poor copy of lines 1–21 by D. S. Dodge); H. Lucas, *BZ* 14 (1905) 21–25 (squeeze) [Laum, *Stiftungen* 209; Schroeter 61; Welles, *Royal Corres.* 70 (all B–C)]; Rey-Coquais, *IGLSyrie* VII 4028.

Photograph: Rey-Coquais pl. XI.

Cf. Seyrig, *Ant. syr.* IV 170–200; *Scripta numism.* 98–117; H. Kreissig, *Wirtschaft und Gesellschaft im Seleukidenreich* (Berlin 1978) 53–54; Rigsby, *TAPA* 110 (1980) 248–254; A. Baroni, "I terreni e i privilegi del tempio di Zeus a Baitokaike," in *Studi ellenistici* I, ed. E. Gabba (Pisa 1984) 135–167.

(A) *Imp. Caesar*
Publius Licin-
nius Valerianus
Pius Felix Aug. et Imp.
Caesar Publius Licinius
Gallienus Pius Fel. Aug. et Licin-
nius Cornelius Saloninus
Valerianus nobilissimus Caesar
Aurelio Marea et aliis:
regum antiqua beneficia, consuetu-
dine etiam insecuti tenporis adpro-
bata, is qui provinciam regit, remota
violentia partis adversae, incolumia
vobis manere curabit.

(B) ἐπιστολὴ Ἀντιόχου βασιλέως
βασιλεὺς Ἀντίοχος Εὐφήμῳ χαίρειν· ἐδόθη ὁ κατακεχωρισ-
μένος ὑπομνηματισμός. γενέσθω οὖν καθότι δεδήλωται περὶ ὧν δεῖ διὰ σοῦ
συντελεσθῆναι. (C) προσενεχθέντος μοι περὶ τῆς ἐνεργείας θεοῦ Διὸς Βαιτο-καιχης
ἐκρίθη συνχωρηθῆναι αὐτῷ εἰς ἅπαντα τὸν χρόνον ὅθεν καὶ ἡ δύναμις τοῦ
θεοῦ κατάρχεται κώμην τὴν Βαιτοκαι[κη]νήν, ἣν πρότερον ἔσχεν Δημήτριος
Δημητρίου τοῦ Μνασαίου ἐν Τουργωνα τῆς περὶ Ἀπάμιαν σατραπίας, σὺν τοῖς
συνκύρουσι καὶ καθήκουσι πᾶσι κατὰ τοὺς προϋπάρχοντας περιορισμοὺς
καὶ σὺν τοῖς τοῦ ἐνεστῶτος ἔτους γενήμασιν, ὅπως ἡ ἀπὸ ταύτης πρόσοδος
ἀναλίσκηται εἰς τὰς κατὰ μῆνα συντελουμένας θυσίας καὶ τἆλλα τὰ πρὸς αὔξη-
σιν τοῦ ἱεροῦ συντείνοντα ὑπὸ τοῦ καθεσταμένου ὑπὸ τοῦ θεοῦ ἱερέως ὡς εἴ-
θισται, ἄγωνται δὲ καὶ κατὰ μῆνα πανηγύρεις ἀτελεῖς τῇ πεντεκαιδεκάτῃ καὶ
τριακάδι, καὶ εἶναι τὸ μὲν ἱερὸν ἄσυλον τὴν δὲ κώμην ἀνεπίσ⟨τα⟩θμον μηδεμιᾶς

ἀπορρήσεως προσενεχθείσης· τὸν δὲ ἐναντιωθησόμενόν τισι τῶν προγεγραμμένων ἔνοχον εἶναι ἀσεβείᾳ· ἀναγραφῆναί τε καὶ τὰ ἀντίγραφα ἐν στήλῃ λιθίνῃ καὶ τεθῆναι ἐν τῷ αὐτῷ ἱερῷ. δεήσει οὖν γραφῆναι οἷς εἴθισται, ἵνα γένηται ἀκολούθως τοῖς δηλουμένοις.

(D) ψήφισμα τῆς πόλεως πεμ⟨φ⟩θὲν θεῷ Αὐγούστῳ ἐπάνανκες δὲ ἀνέρχεσθαι πάντα τὰ ὤνεια διὰ τῶν ἐνταῦθα καὶ ἐπὶ χώρας ἀγορητῶν πραθησόμενα καθ' ἑ[κ]άστην ἱερομηνίαν πρὸς τὸ ἀδιάλεπτα ὑπάρχιν πᾶσι τοῖς ἀνιοῦσι{ι}προσκυνηταῖς, ἐπιμελομένου τοῦ τῆς πόλεως ἀγορητοῦ μηδὲ ἐπιχειροῦντος ἢ ὀχλοῦντος προφάσει παροχῆς καὶ τέλους καὶ ἐπηρείας τινὸς ἢ ἀπαιτήσαιως· ἀνδράποδα δὲ καὶ τετράποδα καὶ λοιπὰ ζῷα ὁμοίως πωλείσθω ἐν τῷ τόπῳ χωρὶς τέλους ἢ ἐπηρείας τινὸς ἢ ἀπαιτήσαιως.

(E) οἱ κάτοχοι ἁγίου οὐρανίου Διὸς τῆς ὑπὸ τῶν Σεβαστῶν εἴς τε τὸν θεὸν εὐσεβείας καὶ τὸν τόπον ἐλευθερέας τὴν θείαν ἀντιγραφὴν ὑπὸ πάντων προσκυνουμένην προέταξαν.

. . .

(A) (10ff.) The ancient benefactions of the kings, which are supported also by the custom of subsequent time, he who governs the province will maintain intact for you, for the threats of the opposing faction have been set aside.

(B) Letter of Antiochus the king. King Antiochus to Euphemus, greetings. The following memorandum has been issued. Therefore let it be done as indicated as regards what must be carried out through you.

(C) Report having been submitted to me about the power of the god Zeus of Baetocaece, it was decided to grant to him for all time that from which the power of the god in fact arises, the village of Baetocaece, which formerly was held by Demetrius son of Demetrius son of Mnaseas in Tourgona of the satrapy of Apamea, together with all its appurtenances and properties according to the existing surveys and with the current year's harvest, so that the income from this (village) may be spent on the monthly sacrifices and the other things that contribute to the increase of the temple by the priest selected by the god as is customary, and so that tax-exempt festivals may be conducted each month on the 15th and the 30th. And the temple is to be inviolable and the village exempt from billeting, no objection having been reported. Anyone who contravenes any of the aforesaid is liable to prosecution for impiety. Copies are to be inscribed on a stone stele and placed in the same temple. It will be necessary accordingly to write to the accustomed persons so that things be done in keeping with what has been made clear.

(D) Decree of the city, sent to the deified Augustus. And all merchandise must be brought up through the agency of the local and rural *agoretai* in order to be sold at each monthly festival, so as to be at the uninterrupted disposal of the worshippers who come up, with the city *agoretes* to oversee and not to interfere or bother on excuse of requisition, tax, and any abuse or extortion; slaves, cattle and other animals are to be sold in the place on the same terms, without tax or any abuse or extortion.

(E) The *katochoi* of holy heavenly Zeus have posted the imperial rescript, to be respected by all, of the emperors' piety toward the god and liberality toward the place.

This composite inscription is rather like those from Ptolemaic Egypt, except that B–D are historical documents, part of the case made to the emperors in the third century. The chronological sequence is C, the king's decision; B, his letter of transmittal to a royal functionary (with a heading added by the *katochoi*, line 15); D, an extract from a civic decree under Augustus (with an added heading, 32); A, the imperial confirmation ca. 260; and E, the dedication of the inscribed monument. For various details and references see the valuable commentaries of Welles and of Rey-Coquais.

7–9: Saloninus was Caesar from 258 to 261: Wickert, "Licinius 46," *RE* 13 (1926) 238–239. "Aurelius Mareas and the rest" are presumably the *katochoi* who petitioned the emperor.

17ff.: A memorandum was submitted to the king, who responded with his own memorandum to a royal agent (references at Rey-Coquais p. 61). Such were the internal procedures of the Seleucid state, like the Ptolemaic. A city, by contrast, would have addressed the king through an embassy and been answered directly by his letter. It was not a city (Aradus or whichever) but the temple, on crown land, that initiated this event.

19–20: Attribution of the miraculous power of a god to the place itself is a familiar sentiment in all religions. Diodorus, on his native city, says of the precinct of Iolaus (4.24.5): "Such is the sanctity and awe of the precinct" that boys who do not perform the expected ritual become mute (τοσαύτη δ' ἐστὶν ἁγνεία καὶ σεμνότης περὶ τὸ τέμενος).

21: Most scholars have followed Wilamowitz in seeing Tourgona as a toponym.[121] I take the phrase about the satrapy of Apamea to go with the place rather than the person; but see Rey-Coquais p. 62. I imagine Demetrius to have been a courtier of some rank (he is given no ethnic), and I doubt that such persons were "registered" by satrapy, if indeed anyone was. Rey-Coquais cites a Ptolemaic document for the region, *C.Ord.Ptol.* 22 (πατρόθεν καὶ πατρίδος of those surveyed), but this means no more than their civic ethnics. The attested dates (meager evidence) for a satrapy of Apamea are between the mid-second century and the early first, before which we hear of the satrapy of the Seleucis (cf. Rigsby 253).

22: For parallels for "the appurtenant places" of a temple see on **223**.21 and Rey-Coquais p. 27.

23: Troubling to include assignment of the growing crops will have removed this important matter from any litigation.

121. F. Piejko, *Berytus* 30 (1982) 98–99, suggests an error for ἐλαιουργῶνα or ἐντὸς ὁρίων Ἀ(- - -).

25: That the priest was chosen by the god rather than by a city government is consistent with the absence of any civic authority over the place.

26: To Rey-Coquais's examples of tax exemption for festivals (62 n. 11) can now be added Wörrle, *Chiron* 18 (1988) 424 (Heraclea by Latmus); Gauthier, *I.nouv.Sardes* II 3.11 (Sardes).

27: Given a lunar calendar, Greek months often did not reach a 30th day.[122] But τριακάς can mean the last day of the month, even if it is in fact the 29th: so *IG* XII.1 4 (Rhodes). In any event, the thirty-day month was common parlance; see T. Heath, *Aristarchus of Samos* (Oxford 1913) 246; Pritchett, *Greek State at War* III (Berkeley 1979) 211.

29: Prosecution envisaged is before the crown, as no city-state comes into the question—important testimony that there was such a category of law in the Seleucid state just as in a city. The Ptolemaic state had laws concerning *hierosylia*, cf. *C.Ord.Ptol.* 53.5, 53 *ter*.5: ἱεροσυλίαις; *P.Köln* VII 313.A.5–6: τῶν ἐκ τ[ῶν ναῶν καὶ τ]ῶν ἄλλων [ἱερῶν καὶ ἱ]ερῶν ἀποδοχίων σεσυληκό[των].

32–33: The heading with θεῷ is anachronistic; either it was added when the documents were gathered (this is not the stele of line 30) and inscribed in the third century or it derives from a docket in the papyrus version kept by the temple. Few civic decrees have survived from Phoenicia. As inscribed this decree obviously is an extract, for it lacks any preliminaries and begins with δέ; hence precious constitutional information is lost to us, including certainty about the identity of the city.

35: The source of the conflict seems to be the coexistence of a city and a country magistrate claiming fiscal authority over the temple. This division may derive from the original condition of the temple, as not being in any civic territory.

40ff.: The sentence has troubled readers. Rey-Coquais (pp. 66–67) thought that its difficulties might reflect the modest education of the *katochoi* or the cultural decline of the third century A.D.[123] The solution lies in the word ἐλευθερία. The emperors do not in fact grant freedom to the place, and I suggest that the word renders *liberalitas* rather than *libertas* (whichever stood in the original Latin). Cf. earlier *UPZ* 62 (ἐλευθερία = ἐλευθεριότης); in the fourth century, Greg. Nys. *Hom.* 9 *Cant.* (VI 284.7 Jaeger): τὴν ἀνδρείαν καὶ τὴν ἐλευθερίαν; Basil *Ep.* 108 (*PG* 32.517A): τῇ σῇ ἐλευθερίᾳ. For confusion or equation of *libertas* and *liberalitas*,

122. Rey-Coquais, *Sociétés* 194 n. 13, deduces that the provision reflects a 365-day Roman calendar and must be a revision of the original text.

123. His translation, "le réscrit impérial de la liberté due à la piété des Empereurs envers le dieu et la localité," is properly rejected by Herrmann, *Gnomon* 45 (1973) 72, who understands "rescript through which the emperors showed their piety toward the god and granted the privilege of freedom for the place." B. Virgilio, *PP* 222 (1985) 218–222, argues for an omission in the text, and for a personified Pietas: εἴς τε τὸν θεὸν Εὐσεβείας καὶ τὸν τόπον, ⟨τῆς τοῦ τόπου⟩ ἐλευθρέας.

and both translated ἐλευθερία, see *TLL* VII 1299, 1318–1319; cf. A. U. Stylow, "Libertas und Liberalitas" (Diss., Erlangen 1972) 70–73 (imperial slogans in the third century).

Damascus

Damascus, the great oasis of Coele-Syria, appears to have prospered especially in the late Hellenistic period. It was the base of Demetrius III (96–88 B.C.), who was crowned king here, and the similarity of some coins of a city "Demetrias" to those of Damascus suggests that Demetrius III refounded the city.[124] Seyrig did not live to put its coins in order as he intended or to publish the many that remain unpublished;[125] this account of the numismatic evidence for *asylia* must be tentative.

Damascus was the site of a Seleucid royal mint from 138 until 69;[126] these coins do not name the city and thus reveal no titles. Three issues of civic bronzes, however, seem to derive from the first century B.C.;[127] the reverses show variously Tyche, Nike, or a standing male, all inscribed Δημητριέων τῆς ΙΕΡΑΣ.[128] Throughout the imperial age Damascus issued civic bronzes, in no

124. So R. Dussaud, *JA* X.3 (1904) 198–199. Newell, *The Late Seleucid Mints in Ake-Ptolemais and Damascus*, NNM 84 (New York 1939) 83, thought that ΔΗ on some Seleucid coins might indicate the royal name; this in fact appears already under Demetrius II in his last year 126/5 (no. 77), and still on the silver of Tigranes in 71–69 (nos. 148–149). The name was discarded before the 30s B.C., *SNG Copenh.* 36.419 Δαμασκηνῶν, and perhaps as early as the expulsion of Tigranes in 69 (cf. Newell p. 100). On the city see C. Watzinger and K. Wurtzinger, *Damaskus* (Berlin/Leipzig) 1921; J. Sauvaget, *Syria* 26 (1949) 315–358.

125. *Syria* 27 (1950) 34–37 (*Ant.syr.* IV 101–104).

126. See Newell 41–100; A. Houghton and A. Spaer, *GNS* 40 (1990) 1–5; Houghton and W. Müseler, *GNS* 40 (1990) 57–62. Tigranes' mint at Damascus: Newell 95–100; P. Bedoukian, *Coinage of the Artaxiads* (London 1978) 21.

127. Of the three obverses, one has Tyche; one a male formerly thought to be Antiochus XII (88–84 B.C.) but shown by Bellinger ("End" 78 n. 88) to be Apollo; one another male, once thought to be Demetrius III but suspected by Bellinger to be the Nabataean Aretas III, who was invited into the city upon the death of Antiochus XII. This identification is also dubious; and the Damascene coins of Aretas are undated (Newell 92). Hence we have no sure dates for these bronzes; see Newell 41–42. A poorly preserved issue attributed to Damascus: Lindgren and Kovacs, *Ancient Bronze Coins* no. A2138A, Zeus | Tyche, . . . ΙΕΡΑΣ(?).

128. *BMC Galatia* 289; *SNG* IV 5069. On one reverse, Tyche is offering an untied fillet, as Newell argued (94–95: rather than holding a sword); an unmistakable image of this gesture and object is at R. Ghirshman, *Fouilles de Châpour: Bîchâpour* II (Paris 1956) 43–44 and frontispiece; also, as a welcoming gesture, in the Palestrina mosaic; cf. Nike with untied fillet on the

great quantity. Apart from "metropolis" granted by Hadrian[129] and colonial status gained from Philip I, the only titles displayed on the coins come under Elagabalus:[130] the reverses have Δαμάσκου ΙΕΡΑΣ καὶ ἐνδόξου and within a wreath Σεβάσμια, the crowned games.[131]

Thus no more than ἱερᾶς is guaranteed by the coins. This I believe is sufficient to prove the full title of inviolability. Unfortunately, the Hellenistic issues cannot be dated with enough confidence to suggest, from their style, a terminus ante quem more precise than the mid-first century B.C. The reign of Demetrius III (96–88) is an obvious possibility for the original grant. We do not know how long after his death the city retained the royal name; Aretas or Pompey might rather be the source. The title recurs under Elagabalus after a long hiatus, but the intervening silence need not indicate an abolition of the status.

In 14 B.C. the people of Damascus honored the consul Crassus with a bilingual monument in Rome; the part that concerns us has been restored:[132]

[Δαμασκηνῶν τῆς ἱερᾶς καὶ] ἀσύλου καὶ α̣[ὐτονόμου καὶ συμμάχου τοῦ]
[δήμου Ῥωμαίων οἱ ἄρχοντες? κα]ὶ ἡ πόλις [πρεσβευσάντων - - -]
[τοῦ - - - καὶ Σελεύκου τοῦ Σ]ελεύκο̣[υ - - -].

Whatever the precise text to be restored, here is testimony for the inviolability of Damascus in the long period of the silence of the coins.

The famous god of Damascus, their θεὸς πατρῷος, was the Zeus known elsewhere as Jupiter Damascenus,[133] a Syrian Hadad associated with the bull and with agriculture. A late writer called Damascus "truly the city of Zeus and the eye of the whole East, sacred and greatest Damascus" (τὴν Διὸς πόλιν ἀληθινῶς καὶ τὸν τῆς ἑῴας ἁπάσης ὀφθαλμόν, τὴν ἱερὰν καὶ μεγίστην Δαμασκόν, [Julian.] *Ep.* 392c). The temple, dismantled to build the Umayyad palace, is in its Roman imperial version the largest temple attested in Syria. Zeus's consort Atargatis is represented in some detail on all the tetradrachms of Demetrius III, Zeus

early coins of Catane. A Damascene issue of Demetrius III showing a knotted diadem: Houghton/Spaer 2–3.

129. In addition to the coins, *SEG* 7.224.

130. De Saulcy, *Numismatique* 42; *BMC Galatia* 21.

131. The Sebasmia are mentioned on other coins of Damascus and at *IG* II^2 3169/70.29–30 (mid-III A.D.). ἔνδοξος of cities recurs in southern Asia Minor, at Side (see p. 454), Syedra (*BMC Lycaonia* 160–161), and Anazarbus (*BMC* 34ff.; *AnatSt* 2 [1952] 138, the *Acta* of Probus, Tarachus, and Andronicus).

132. L. Moretti, *MiscGrRom* 15 (1989) 209–211, and G. Alföldy, *Studi sull' epigrafia* (Rome 1992) 77–93, independently recognized Damascus; I have preferred Moretti's restorations where they differ.

133. See R. Dussaud, *Syria* 3 (1922) 219–250. This epithet is in the main peculiar to Italy (references at H. Schwabl, *RE* 10A [1972] 296); once, however, at Bostra (*IGLSyrie* XIII 9013). On an altar from the temple itself, rhetoric typical of the imperial age: θεῷ οὐρανίῳ πατρῴῳ τῷ κυρίῳ (*Syria* 6 [1925] 354–356).

himself then on those of Antiochus XII.[134] This cult, at the center of the city, was presumably the occasion of the inviolability of Damascus.

Dora

Dora was the southernmost city on the Phoenician coast, a well-fortified place at the foot of Mt. Carmel. It withstood the siege of Antiochus III (Polyb. 5.66), and here Tryphon fled and was besieged by Antiochus Sidetes.[135] Ultimately it was eclipsed by the foundation of Caesarea at the end of the first century B.C., twelve kilometers to the south.

The coins of Dora[136] show sporadically the title of inviolability. From the first civic issues in the 60s B.C. to the time of Trajan, the coins have no titles, merely Δωριτῶν (or abbreviated). Then a large number of issues were struck in the local year 175 = A.D. 111/2. Some show only the ethnic; one has a war galley and Δῶρα ΙΕΡΑ (a small denomination), another the hero Doros son of Poseidon and Δωρ(ιτῶν) ἱερ(ᾶς) ἀσύλ(ου) αὐτον(όμου) ναυαρ(χίδος). In 116/7 we find issues both with and without these various titles, and again in 143/4. Under the Severi, down to the last issues in 210/1, come issues with ΙΕΡΑ alone (two are large denominations) and some with ναυαρχ(ίς) alone.

Thus coins of the second century A.D. often cite the title of inviolability, often sharply abbreviated. If the grant is to be placed in the Hellenistic period (rather than 111/2), we can note that Dora was involved in the turmoil of the last decade of the second century B.C., taken by Jannaeus who freed the city from the tyrant Zoilus; Pompey removed it from Jewish rule, and it now began a new era (at 64/3). The original recognition of *asylia* may derive from that half century.

Samosata

Samosata controlled a fertile plain and a crossing over the Euphrates where major highways of northern Syria met; it became the seat of the kings of Commagene.[137] Although the site had been inhabited since the Bronze Age,

134. Newell 78–92; Houghton/Spaer 3–5.

135. Jos. *AJ* 13.223: φρούριόν τε δυσάλωτον; 1 Macc. 15:11–37. See Schürer II 118–120; *EncArchExc* I (1975) 334–337; E. Stern and I. Sharon, *IEJ* 37 (1987) 201–211.

136. Rouvier, *JIAN* 4 (1901) 125–131; Babelon, *Rois* cxxxix; Y. Meshorer, *INJ* 9 (1986/7) 59–72, with H. R. Baldus, *Chiron* 19 (1989) 477–480.

137. Babelon, *Rois* ccviii; Weissbach, *RE* IA (1920) 2220–2224; M. Mellink, *AJA* 95 (1991) 135–136; on the royal house, R. D. Sullivan, *ANRW* II.8 (1977) 732–798.

its name and foundation as a Greek city are thought to derive from the first of the kings, around 150 B.C. Little is known of the Hellenistic history of the place; it suffered sieges by the forces of Pompey in 69 B.C. and Antony in 38. The royal coins do not name Samosata, nor did the city itself issue coins in the Hellenistic period—hence we lack evidence about its status then.

Some autonomous bronzes, perhaps of the 30s B.C., feature variously a lion, Zeus, or the city Tyche, and are inscribed Σαμοσάτω(ν) πόλεως without titles (*RPC* I 3848–3851). In A.D. 72 the monarchy was dissolved, and Commagene was annexed to the province of Syria. The later civic coins show Samosata with the added name "Flavia" and an era reckoned from 71/2; these usages attest the settlement of troops and no doubt new construction ordered by Vespasian. These bronzes do not in fact begin until Hadrian, who evidently granted the right to coin, which continued into the third century.

The coins of the second and third centuries regularly show the title "metropolis of Commagene." But the abundant issues struck under Antoninus Pius and under M. Aurelius and L. Verus add to this inviolability and autonomy: Φ(λαουίων) Σαμ(οσατέων) ἱερ(ᾶς) ἀσύλ(ου) αὐτονό(μου) μητρ(οπόλεως) Κομ(μαγηνῶν), with the city Tyche seated over the river god Euphrates.[138]

Asylia surely will not have come early to this remote district (remote compared with Cilicia and coastal Syria-Phoenicia). If, as I assume, it is pre-imperial, it might derive from one of the two great eastern expeditions of Rome, Pompey's or Antony's; or if the autonomous bronzes are rightly dated to the 30s B.C. and if their omission of *asylia* is significant, then it will have been granted by the native kings, honoring their capital city.

Of civic cults we know no more than can be discerned from the coins; the most suggestive image is the association of Pegasus with the city Tyche in coins of the third century A.D., perhaps reflecting a foundation legend. It is a pity that Lucian tells us so little about his native place.

Nicopolis ad Issum

Nicopolis, founded by Alexander or by Seleucus I, was situated on the eastern slope of Mt. Amanus, on the road from Syria north into Cappadocia.[139] Little

138. *BMC* 118; *Hunterian* III.2 128 nos. 17–22; *Copenhagen* 36.19–20; *SNG* IV 5842; Baramki, *Coins . . . Beirut* (1968) 57 no. 187 (sometimes further abbreviated). Early scholars reported the titles also under Commodus and Septimius Severus (Mionnet V 120, Suppl. VII 93).

139. E. Honigmann, "Nikopolis 7," *RE* 17 (1936) 535–536; Jones, *Cities of the Eastern Roman Provinces*² (Oxford 1971) 244. The site is assured by the modern toponym Niboli and by the aqueduct inscription.

is known of its history. Tiberius paid for the construction of an aqueduct for the city (*IGLSyrie* 164). This is one of the cities said to have been burned by the Persians in the time of Valerian (Malalas 297).

Distinguishing the coinages of the several cities named Nicopolis—in Epirus, Pontus, Cilicia, Palestine (Emmaus)—is at times difficult. For the city by Mt. Amanus, the certain issues are three bronzes that bear an unambiguous geographical marker, "Nicopolis of the Seleucis," dating under Septimius Severus, Severus Alexander, and Philip I.[140] On the earliest of these the reverse presents, within a wreath, the ethnic Νειxοπολειτῶν, surrounded by τῆς Σελευxίδος τ(ῆς) ΙΕΡΑΣ. The other two give the ethnic and region without a title.

Thus a single issue in the time of Septimius suggests that Nicopolis was declared sacred and inviolable, although no more than "sacred" is assured. Of cults, the other two coins show Nemesis with her wheel and Tyche and another figure and a river god; the civic seals have a conventional picture of Tyche above a river god.

Dura-Europus

Dura-Europus, the fortress-city on the Euphrates, successively Macedonian, Parthian, and Roman,[141] is unique in the Greek East for the wealth of its documentation, represented in largest part by its papyri. The case of Dura is a cautionary tale. A small city of little consequence, it never struck a coin.[142] The harvest of inscriptions, unusually large for a Syrian city, yielded no mention of *asylia*. Only the chance survival of papyri has preserved the title of inviolability—

140. *BMC Galatia* 265 (no. 1 with title); Lindgren and Kovacs, *Ancient Bronze Coins* no. 2110. Some clay seals from papyri in the civic archives give the ethnic Νιxοπολειτῶν without a title: D. O. A. Klose, *JNG* 34 (1984) 63–76 (several bear a date "286," of whatever era); cf. Robert, *Hellenica* X (1955) 293–294.

141. Rostovtzeff, *Caravan Cities* (Oxford 1932) 153–219; A. Perkins, *The Art of Dura-Europus* (Oxford 1973); C. Hopkins, *The Discovery of Dura-Europus* (New Haven 1979). The recent work: S. Downey, *Syria* 63 (1986) 27–37; 65 (1988) 343–347; various authors in 69 (1992) 1–151.

142. Some Seleucid issues found in the excavation are attributed to a short-lived royal mint at Dura (270s B.C.): *WSM* 79–81, 402–406; cf. *Excavations at Dura-Europus: Final Report* VI *The Coins* (New Haven 1949) 109–110. A further caution concerning Dura is that some of the excavation records of the Hellenistic finds, from the 1935–36 and 1936–37 seasons, disappeared in the 1940s; we have the summary account at *Excavations at Dura-Europus: Preliminary Report, Ninth Season* I (New Haven 1944) 3–68, and see in particular the articles of Downey and Matheson in *Syria* 1992 (138 on the losses, concerning which I am also indebted to the advice of L. Richardson, Jr.).

and among the hundreds of papyri, only on one. How many other small cities of the Hellenistic-Roman world, which have left us few or no coins and few public inscriptions and of course no papyri, enjoyed this title?

The last dated papyrus from Dura is among the most surprising. On the heels of a number of inscriptions and papyri of the second and third centuries in which the city exhibits few pretentions, suddenly, in an otherwise unexceptional document of A.D. 254, we find a grandiose claim: a divorce settlement is registered ἐν κολωνείᾳ Εὐρω̣π̣[αίων Σελεύκου] Νει̣κ̣ά̣τ̣ο̣ρ̣ο̣ς [τ]ῇ ἱερᾷ [καὶ] ἀ̣[σύ]λ̣ῳ καὶ α̣[ὐ]τ̣ονόμ[ῳ] (*P.Dura* 32.4–5). We expect the name "Europeans,"[143] and "colony" has some other support; the rest is quite new.

No other papyrus mentions civic titles; but two inscriptions in the time of Caracalla (A.D. 212–217) were dedicated by the Αὐρηλ(ίων) Ἀντωνινιανῶν Εὐρωπαίων βουλή.[144] This is rather a sorry claim, the sort of imperial name that was so widespread in contemporary Cilicia; some benefaction by the emperor must lie behind it, but Welles's suggestion that Caracalla gave Dura the title of colony attested in the papyrus of 254[145] is contradicted by the silence of these two inscriptions on that score. Their concern is to flatter Caracalla, so their silence about inviolability has perhaps less weight. The phrase "colony of Seleucus Nicator" in the papyrus is strictly speaking a contradiction in terms, mixing a Roman technical term, *colonia*, with a Greek historical fact, the founder Nicator.[146] For this, however, we can compare *Mallo colonia dei Amphilochi* on coins of Mallus in Cilicia (p. 478).

However that may be, the title of inviolability is clear. The chief god of Dura is thought to have been Artemis, whose temple in the southern part of the city was one of the oldest and largest.[147] In the temple was

143. Welles's statement on the history of the name (*P.Dura* p. 5) is incomplete. In this same text individual citizens are called "Durenes," which came into popular use in the third century. But for the city as a whole the Macedonian toponym "Europus" was evidently the official usage throughout antiquity: Semitic "Dura" occurs in only one official text, *P.Dura* 129, and this one is official only in the sense that it derives from the Roman army, not from the city; and while individuals call themselves Durenes, this ethnic is not found applied to the citizens collectively.

144. *Preliminary Report, Third Season* (1932) 51–52; cf. *Fifth Season* (1934) 223–224 (Latin).

145. *P.Dura* p. 5; the other evidence is a dedication in the temple of Artemis (first half III) in which the dedicants call themselves κόλωνες βουλευταὶ καὶ ἱερεῖς [θ]εᾶς Ἀρ[τέμι]δος (Cumont, *Fouilles de Doura* 404 no. 50).

146. This was Youtie's reconstruction of the text. Welles had doubted that there is space in the lacuna for Σελεύκου: *Eos* 48 (1957) 467 n. 3. As the titles are dative, perhaps the toponym Εὐρωπ[ῷ rather than the ethnic. Rather than the founder, one might expect a geographic limit; other papyri show Εὐρωπὸς ἡ ἐν τῇ Παραποταμίᾳ or ἡ πρὸς Ἀραβίᾳ (*P.Dura* 18, 19, 22, 25), but the photograph in *P.Dura* does not support either of these against Youtie's reading.

147. See Cumont 195–204; Bellinger, *Third Season* 18–24; Perkins 17–18. The temple was enlarged in the early third century.

found a dedication to Ἀρτέμιδι καὶ Ἀπόλλωνι ἀρχηγοῖς—a revealing word order.[148]

When is Dura likely to have been declared sacred and inviolable? Welles (pp. 5, 167), given the silence of earlier documents, suggested that the grant came from Valerian for Dura's resisting the Persians in A.D. 253. I have regularly sought a pre-imperial origin; is that even possible here? Dura passed out of Seleucid control in the mid-second century B.C., before *asylia* had begun to spread even among the great cities of Syria. It remained under Parthian rule for more than 300 years, becoming Roman only in A.D. 164, long after the Senate had halted the spread of this status in A.D. 22. It may be that the title derives from a Parthian grant in this long period, and we should classify Dura with those cities made inviolable by the non-Greek kings—Tigranes of Armenia, the royal houses of Cappadocia and Commagene. But the silence of the earlier evidence is impressive, and the date 253 may be right.

Byblos

Byblos, Phoenician Gebal north of Beirut, was a significant city already in the Bronze Age, thanks to its good harbor.[149] The Phoenician kings issued coins there in the fourth century B.C., and the Seleucids in the second. The city is said by Strabo to be "sacred to Adonis" (ἱερά ἐστι τοῦ Ἀδώνιδος, 16.2.18 [755]); Adonis does not appear on the coins, however, which prefer the founder Cronus and others.[150] Lucian places the worship of Adonis in the great temple of Aphrodite,[151] which is illustrated on some of the imperial coins.

The first coins to show the civic name were the municipal bronzes under Antiochus IV around 170 B.C. Here as at Tyre and Sidon, the Phoenician inscription gives more than a name: "of Gebal the holy." This continues under

148. *Third Season* 63 (A.D. 1/2). The editors trace the word ἀρχηγοί to Seleucid tradition, which seems unnecessary and which does not account for the primacy of Artemis. Compare above on Amyzon (p. 335).

149. M. Dunand, *Byblos: Son histoire, ses ruines, ses légendes* (Beirut 1963); the coins at J. Rouvier, *JIAN* 4 (1901) 38–58.

150. See Hill, *BMC Phoenicia* lxi–lxv; Seyrig, *Notes* 12. Philo of Byblos *FGrHist* 790 F 2 (Eus. *Praep. evang.* 1.10.19, 35) for Cronus, who founded the city "and gave it to Baaltis who is called Dione"; cf. A. I. Baumgarten, *The Phoenician History of Philo of Byblos,* EPRO 89 (Leiden 1981) 223. A high priest of Dionysus (= Adonis?): Seyrig, *Syria* 31 (1954) 68–73 (*Ant. syr.* V 86–91). See J. Teixidor, *The Pagan God* (Princeton 1977) 46–48.

151. *Syr. d.* 6–9; cf. Nonnus 42.516, Aphrodite is πολιοῦχος at Beirut's neighbor, presumably Byblos. See B. Soyez, *Byblos et la fête des Adonies,* EPRO 60 (Leiden 1977).

subsequent kings, and also on most of the autonomous bronzes that begin in 102/1 and are found with this inscription as late as A.D. 14.[152] The inscription as a whole cannot be taken as the proper name of the city ("Holy Mountain"), because the royal issues of the fourth century B.C. show, for example, "Elpaal, king of Gebal": that is, the adjective does not appear on any issue before the second century B.C.

In imperial times the inscriptions are in Greek: only Βυβλίων on the few issues of the first and second centuries, then beginning with Commodus regularly ΙΕΡΑΣ Βύβλου until the end of the coinage fifty years later. Scholars naturally take this as ἱερᾶς Βύβλου, a translation of the Phoenician.

Is this granted inviolability, therefore the first instance outside of the Aegean? Byblos is unlikely for that role. The inscription first appears in rivalry with the different statements of Tyre and Sidon in 170 (p. 37) and must have been grounded similarly in some local myth; I do not believe that any of these was granted by the crown or by Panhellenic recognition. Rather we have an accidental convergence: the Phoenician label, presumably unreadable by the Seleucid and other authorities, resembles what later became a fashionable title of Hellenistic cities in the region, and Byblos was glad to keep it.

152. Rouvier nos. 650ff.; *BMC Phoen.* 17; cf. Seyrig, *Ant. syr.* V 92–94. "Holy" omitted: e.g., Rouvier 676 (17/6 B.C.), 668–669 (undated). A.D. 14: Rouvier 678, with Seyrig 92 n. 4.

Palestine

Ascalon

Ascalon was one of the five chief cities of the Philistines.[1] Here Herodotus saw the world's oldest temple of the "Heavenly Aphrodite" and was told how she had punished the Scythians for desecrating her shrine. This was the Philistines' Derceto, made known to Greeks under this name by Ctesias in the fourth century B.C.[2] Her sacred lake and fish attracted Jewish and Christian polemic, and her dove is frequently seen on the city's Hellenistic coinage. It was presumably in her honor that Ascalon was declared sacred and inviolable.[3] The coins show that inviolability was acquired in 112/1, autonomy and a civic era of liberation in 104/3.

Through much of the second century B.C. Ascalon was the seat of a Seleucid mint, issuing royal silver marked with the dove and ΑΣ or ΑΣΚΑ and dated by the Seleucid era.[4] These coins exhibit no titles until the "war of the brothers" at the end of the century. Antiochus IX took Ascalon from Antiochus VIII in the course of 114/3 (we have issues there of each brother) and held it during 113/2. As late as 114/3 under Antiochus VIII and 113/2

1. Jos. *AJ* 6.8. See Schürer II 105–107; *Enc.Arch.Exc.* I (1975) 121–130; de Saulcy, *Numismatique* 178–208.

2. Hdt. 1.105; cf. Paus. 1.14.7. *FGrHist* 688 F 1; cf. Lucian *Syr. d.* 14. On the doves of Derceto see Robert, *JSav* 1971, 96 (*Op. min. sel.* VII 174).

3. Note, however, one Ascalonite's dedication at Canopus, in A.D. 228, of a statuette of "my ancestral god Heracles Belus," θεὸν πάτρ[ιόν] μου Ἡρ[ακ]λῆ Βῆλον ἀνείκητον (A. Bernand, *Le Delta* I [Cairo 1970] 242–244 no. 14). Heracles first appears on the coins of Ascalon in Severan times (*BMC Pal.* 138–139); but the man's claim may be only private and familial.

4. A. B. Brett, *ANSMN* 4 (1950) 43–54; A. Spaer in *Festschrift für Leo Mildenberg* (Wetteren 1984) 229–239.

under Antiochus IX, Ascalon is without titles.[5] In 112/1, however, the city was again under Antiochus VIII, and now his coins show ΑΣ / ΙΕΡ / ΑΣΥ (or ΑΣ̌), thus (Ἀσ(χαλωνιτῶν) ἱερ(ᾶς) ἀσύ(λου); the title continues on the royal silver so long as this lasts, through 104/3.[6] So the royal issues; of the meager civic coinage under Seleucid rule, a single fractional issue of silver is extant: Tyche bust | War galley, with Ἀσ(καλωνιτῶν) above, ∟βς ΙΕΡΑΣ below (*BMC* no. 14). Given the date, 111/0 B.C., ΙΕΡΑΣ can only mean the full title ἱερ(ᾶς) ἀσ(ύλου). Some undated civic bronzes are also extant, with Ἀσ(καλωνιτῶν) and the same images, assigned by style to the late second century B.C. (*BMC* nos. 8–13). Only one of these issues adds ΙΕΡΑΣ; it will come at the end of this series of bronzes, in 112/1 or later, if the omission on the others is meaningful.

From 104/3 Ascalon reckoned an era of liberty, seen on the civic coins thereafter. In 103 various cities of Palestine invited Ptolemy Lathyrus to defend them against the ambitions of the new Jewish king Alexander Jannaeus. Scholars have deduced that Ascalon was threatened or taken by Jannaeus and then liberated by Ptolemy.[7] The silver coinage of Ascalon that follows[8] has the inscription Ἀσκαλωνιτῶν ἱερᾶς ἀσύλου αὐτο(νόμου), or further abbreviation, the most unusual being Ἀσκαλωνιτῶν ἀσύλου αὐτονό(μου). The title αὐτόνομος must derive from the events of 103; it is last seen in 64/3 B.C.[9] Thereafter we find only "sacred and inviolable," which last appears in 39/8.[10] Also to the period between 104/3 and 63/2 should belong some reported bronzes with ΑΣ(καλωνιτῶν) ΙΕΡΑΚΑΥ or ΙΕΡΑΣΚΑΥ, which must abbreviate all three words.[11] The city continued to coin into the third century A.D., with a long series of pseudoautonomous bronzes beginning in the 70s A.D. The coins of imperial

5. 114/3: Bellinger, "End" 89; Spaer no. B; 113/2: Brett no. 19; Spaer nos. 16–17; see also A. Houghton and W. Müseler, *GNS* 40 (1990) 60–61. The tetradrachm *Jameson* 1736 (= Brett no. 11) of 127/6 B.C. under Demetrius II gives only ΙΕ left, ΑΣ right, which might be "sacred . . . Ascalon." But in my view this is not a coin of Ascalon: ΑΣ is on the wrong side, there is no dove, and the eagle stands on a prow rather than a thunderbolt. All these features would point to Tyre, but for the lack of the Tyrian monogram and club of Heracles.

6. Spaer (235 no. 18) places one undated issue first, upon the occasion of Antiochus VIII acquiring the city and granting it *asylia.*

7. E.g., Hill, *BMC* p. xlix; Brett, *AJA* 41 (1937) 456; Bellinger, "End" 71.

8. Sporadic issues, with Ptolemaic obverses: Brett, *AJA* 452–463; Spaer 235, 237: the earliest in 99/8 B.C., Spaer nos. 50–51 (year 6).

9. *Auktion F. Sternberg* 25–6 Nov. 1976 no. 536.

10. Silver with Cleopatra on the obverse: Brett, *AJA* 455; *RPC* I 4866–4868.

11. De Saulcy, *Numismatique* 179 nos. 2–3. More problematic: his nos. 1 and 41 have obverse Apollo, reverse ΑΣΚΑ / ΙΕ / dove / ΡΑ, dates given as ⊏Λ? and ΕΛ, which may represent ∟Λ = 75/4 B.C.; cf. *BMC* no. 15, ΙΕΡΑΣ apparently dated ∟ΖΣ = 68/7. H. C. Reichardt, *NC* n.s. 2 (1862) 117 no. 56, reported an autonomous bronze inscribed ΙΕΡ ΑΣΥ and dated ΕΞΣ "265": probably an error for ∟ΕΣ or ∟ΖΣ = 108/7 or 106/5 B.C. A small bronze of 83 B.C. appears to omit titles: *INJ* 8 (1984/5) 6.

date are rich in their illustrations of the cult of Derceto (including images of her lake). No coin after 39/8 B.C., however, gives the city titles of any sort; but a papyrus contract drawn up at Ascalon in A.D. 359 has ἐν τῇ κολωνίᾳ Ἀσκ[άλωνι] τῇ πίστῃ καὶ ἐλευθέρᾳ (*BGU* I 316).

Thus Ascalon was declared sacred and inviolable by Antiochus VIII in 112/1, autonomous by Ptolemy Lathyrus in 103. It seems that autonomy was abolished in the settlement of Pompey in the 60s. Possibly inviolability was abolished in the 30s by Antony or Octavian; but the silence of the coins should not be trusted. In the case of Ascalon, no titles appear on coins of imperial date, even though the papyrus of 359 reveals both "free" and "colony," which must be older than the fourth century.

Gaza

Gaza city, some five kilometers from the sea, stands on a rise at the northern edge of the Negev at the beginning of arable land, where the roads from Aqaba and Petra reach the coast.[12] The best fortified of the coastal sites below Tyre, it guarded the road from Palestine to Egypt. The place enters history most often for its sieges. Pompey declared the city free, and his agent Gabinius as governor sponsored new construction to the south of the old city.

The ancestral god of the Gazaeans was Marnas,[13] who by the Hellenistic age had succeeded the Philistine Dagon as patron of the city. In late antiquity the fame of Marnas rendered his cult a rallying point for paganism; the destruction of his temple, which was in the city proper, was the theme of an imaginative hagiographer.[14] Hellenizing myth equated the god with Zeus[15] and traced him to Crete, taking "Marnas" to mean "Cretan-born"; the city is said to have been founded by Zeus, or by Minos. The Phoenician *mim* for Marnas (𐤌) signs much of the coinage of Gaza, and also a dedication by a priest of the god at Portus in Italy (*I.gr.Ital.Porto* 10).

12. Schürer II 98–103; *Enc.Arch.Exc.* II 408–415; Benzinger, *RE* 7 (1910) 880–886; C. A. M. Glucker, *The City of Gaza in the Roman and Byzantine Periods* (London 1987).

13. See Drexel in Roscher, *Lex.* 2.2378–2382; A. B. Cook, *Zeus* III (Cambridge 1940) 549–558.

14. The Neoplatonist Proclus wrote a hymn to Marnas (Marinus *V.Procli* 19); for references to the god in the *Historia Augusta* and Jerome see J. Straub, *Historia Augusta Colloquium* 1963 (Bonn 1964) 165–170. Location: Mark's *Life* of St. Porphyry, ed. H. Grégoire (Paris 1930) 19, 25, 45, 64, 79.

15. From Batanea east of the Sea of Galilee comes a dedication to Διὶ Μάρνᾳ τῷ κυρίῳ: Le Bas-Waddington 2412g; cf. D. Sourdel, *Les cultes du Hauran* (Paris 1952) 44–45.

The Ptolemaic and Seleucid royal coins struck at Gaza reveal no civic titles. The city's own coinage is meager in the Hellenistic period, consisting of bronzes scattered across the second half of the second century B.C.;[16] these show Marnas | Cornucopiae, or Tyche | Marnas. For some part of this time the civic name was "Seleuceia in Gaza," reflecting a refoundation after the Seleucids regained Palestine in 200 B.C. The civic bronzes are without titles, with one certain exception:

Marnas | Goddess wearing *kalathos*, with patera and cornucopiae, δήμου Γαζαίων, left IEP, right ΑΣ̌.
Two issues, one undated, one ∟ΙΓ = 210 = 103/2 B.C.: De Saulcy 211 no. 12; *BMC Pal.* 144 no. 6; Baramki, *Beirut Museum* no. 2; *BMC* no. 7.[17]

The year 103/2 puts the title in the same circumstances as the liberation of neighboring Ascalon. During 103 Gaza and other Palestinian cities called on Ptolemy Lathyrus for assistance against Alexander Jannaeus. After a successful campaign to the north, using Gaza as his base Ptolemy attacked his brother in Egypt; when this attempt failed, he wintered in Gaza—the winter of 103/2 or more likely 102/1. Subsequently he was driven from Palestine by his mother and Jannaeus, who put Gaza under siege and eventually sacked it.[18] Given our certain coin of 103/2, the inviolability of Gaza is likely to be a *philanthropon* of Lathyrus during his stay there, part of his effort to keep the support of the cities of Palestine.

The many bronze issues of imperial Gaza, which give rich illustration to the cult of Marnas, attribute no titles to the city, with a single exception alleged under Gordian III:

Gordian | Marnas seated, Γαζαίω(ν) IEP ΑΣ.[19]

Subsequent researchers have not confirmed this coin. Whatever its authority, however, we know that the Gazaeans dedicated at Portus at the mouth of the Tiber a statue of Gordian, the inscribed base of which was copied in the Renaissance; the city calls itself

16. See Hill, *BMC Palestine* pp. lxix–lxx.

17. Baramki no. 1 reports the same types and [δήμου] Γαζαίων, to right ΑΣ, date ∟ΕΓ = 108/7, described as struck somewhat off the flan at the left. I suggest that this is a poorly preserved example of the coin of 103/2 (where Baramki read ΑΣ̌ as ΑΣ).

18. Jos. *AJ* 13.356–364; *BJ* 1.87; upon the fall of the city the city council took refuge (without success) in a temple of Apollo (364), not that of Marnas.

19. Reichardt 122 no. 87. The seated pose of the god is unique here among the coins of Gaza. Other issues under Gordian (Rosenberger, *Coll.* I 75, 79) give no titles. We have evidence that Gaza acquired the title "colony," despite the silence of the coins, in a weight inscribed κολωνίας Γάζης (date uncertain): Le Bas-Waddington 1904 [*IGR* III 1212]. This may have been granted by Hadrian, who visited the city in 130; but see Glucker 77.

ἡ πόλις ἡ τῶν Γαζαίων ἱερὰ καὶ ἄσυλος καὶ αὐτόνομος, πίστη, ἡ εὐσεβὴς λαμπρὰ καὶ μεγάλη, ἐξ ἐγκ⟨ε⟩λ⟨ε⟩ύσεως τοῦ πατρίου θεοῦ.[20]

The statue was erected by the *epimeletes* of the temple—a temple of Marnas at Portus serving a local community of Gazaeans.[21] But Gaza itself commissioned the statue, no doubt in response to some benefaction of Gordian. Was this a renewal of *asylia*? On the title the civic coins had been silent for 300 years; but such silence is not unusual and need not prove that the status had lapsed since the Hellenistic age and was only now renewed by Gordian—especially given the silence of all coins about the autonomy mentioned in the inscription. Nevertheless, the Gazaeans' motive in honoring Gordian is religious and pertinent to Marnas, for they are acting on orders of the god. Whatever the titles of Roman Gaza had been before Gordian, it may be that here as elsewhere he guaranteed them after some challenge.

Sepphoris-Diocaesarea

Sepphoris in lower Galilee, on a height near Nazareth, possessed a large and populous territory that extended to Mt. Tabor fourteen kilometers to the southeast (Jos. *Vit.* 346). First attested when attacked by Ptolemy Lathyrus (Jos. *AJ* 13.338) and a strong place by nature, it was an important city in Roman times, famous for its rivalry with neighboring Tiberias for the primacy of Galilee (Jos. *Vit.* 9), its pro-Roman posture, and its Jewish learning.[22] The site was a prize of war both before and after our testimony for its inviolability.[23] Sepphoris struck no coins in the Hellenistic period.

Already upon the organization of the Roman province, Gabinius made Sepphoris the seat of one of the five *synedria* into which he divided Judaea. During the troubled times after 4 B.C., a Roman force destroyed the city and enslaved its population (Jos. *AJ* 17.289; *BJ* 2.68). Herod Antipas subsequently

20. Sacco, *I.gr.Ital.Porto* 5 (= *CIG* 5892; *IG* XIV 926; *IGR* I 387); cf. 10 (the same *epimeletes*) and 11 for the cult of Marnas at Portus.

21. This is denied by Straub (168–169), who believes that the temple and *epimeletes* were at Gaza. There would then be no reason for the dedication to be at Portus; and there is *I.gr.Ital.Porto* 10.

22. Honigmann, *RE* 2A (1923) 1546–1549; Schürer II 172–176; *Enc.Arch.Excav.* IV 1051–1055; S. S. Miller, *Studies in the History and Traditions of Sepphoris* (Leiden 1984); D. Adan-Bayewitz and I. Perlman, *IEJ* 40 (1990) 153–172. Coins: Y. Meshorer in *Greek Numismatics and Archaeology: Essays . . . Margaret Thompson* (Wetteren 1979) 159–171 (with C. M. Kraay, *ANSMN* 25 [1980] 56–57); Seleucid tetradrachms once attributed to Sepphoris: Bellinger, "End" 92–94.

23. Burned by a Roman force in A.D. 339: Miller, *Studies* 4.

rebuilt it to be "the showplace (πρόσχημα) of all Galilee," calling it Autokratoris (*AJ* 18.27) in honor of Augustus. In the fighting of A.D. 67/8 Sepphoris—alone in the region, according to Josephus (*BJ* 3.30–34)—remained loyal to Rome, fighting off attacks by the rebels and inviting in a Roman garrison. Some rare bronze issues show the city under the name Eirenopolis-Neronias-Sepphoris;[24] the two added names must reflect some benefactions from the imperial house, whether on this occasion or earlier. These are the earliest known coins of Sepphoris; the honorific names do not recur, and the city struck coins only sporadically thereafter—under Trajan, Antoninus Pius, Caracalla, and Elagabalus on present evidence.

Under Trajan come a large number of issues: their obverses, with Τραιανὸς αὐτοκράτωρ ἔδωκεν, reveal that Sepphoris had regained from the emperor the right to coin;[25] the reverses show Σεπφωρηνῶν, with no titles, and (depending on size) the city's name in a laurel wreath, a palm tree, a caduceus, or ears of grain. These images, already much used on Jewish coins elsewhere, are neutral on the score of cult, appropriate to a predominantly Jewish city. Under Hadrian there are no issues, and when the coins resume they reveal a significant event. Under Antoninus Pius and the Severi, the city has the new name Diocaesarea and unfailingly displays the titles of inviolability and autonomy: Διοκαι(σαρέων) ἱερ(ᾶς) ἀσύ(λου) καὶ αὐτο(νόμου) (or further abbreviations), with decidedly pagan iconography. We see a temple occupied by a standing Tyche with cornucopia, by a seated Zeus, or by the Capitoline triad Zeus, Hera, Athena; or a female with a patera, or a standing male; or a long inscription (within a wreath, and variously abbreviated) giving the civic name and titles and πίσ(της) φίλ(ης) συμμάχ(ου) ἱερ(ᾶς) βου(λῆς) σ(υγκλήτου) κ(αὶ) δ(ήμου) Ῥωμαί(ων), loyal friend and ally of the senate and people of Rome.[26]

Evidently Sepphoris took some part in the Jewish wars in the time of Trajan or Hadrian[27] and was refounded under a pagan name deriving from the cult of Zeus (like Jerusalem, Aelia Capitolina). It would seem that the pagans of Sepphoris, doubtless a minority but perhaps now augmented, were rewarded

24. Cornucopiae and caduceus, Εἰρηνόπολι(ς) Νερωνίας Σέπφωρ(α) without titles: Seyrig, *Scripta numism.* 461–469; *RPC* I 4850.

25. As recognized by Hill, *BMC* p. xii; for a critique of the evidence on coinage rights see J. Nollé, *RIN* 95 (1993) 487–504.

26. See Kraay 56–57. The Capitoline triad is shown also on coins of Samaria-Sebaste and Neapolis (*BMC* 64, 80).

27. A milestone dated to A.D. 130 apparently gives a terminus ante quem for the new name, ἀπὸ Διοκαισαρίας μίλια ι: B. Lifshitz, *Latomus* 19 (1960) 110–111 (provided the upper fragment with the date and the lower with the civic name are from the same stone, as the local discoverer thought). This was the year of Hadrian's progress through the region. By Hadrian's time there was a large imperial estate here, said to reach from Tiberias to Sepphoris: *Midrash Rabbach Lamentations* (London 1939) 159.

with control of the city in the aftermath of the war.[28] But do the privileges of which the refounded city now boasts—inviolability, autonomy, alliance with Rome—derive from this one occasion, or are they historical relics? Here as elsewhere, my assumption is that these titles are old, and that their omission on the coins under Nero and Trajan reflects selectivity. If that is so, we might think of the last Seleucids or the time of Pompey and Caesar for the recognition of *asylia*, or again the Herodian dynasty at the beginning of the first century A.D.; and of the settlement of Pompey for the treaty of alliance with Rome.

Caesarea-Panias

One of the sources of the Jordan rises in a grotto at the foot of Mt. Hermon; in antiquity this was a famous shrine of Pan, on the territory of Caesarea-Panias. In the walls of the cave have been found niches with votive inscriptions to Pan, whose image dominates the coins of the city.[29] Panhellenic games are attested in the third century A.D.[30] The city's inviolability, attested by coins of imperial date, presumably was in honor of Pan.

The sacred place is first mentioned in connection with the famous battle that gave the region to the Seleucids in 200 B.C., fought near τὸ Πάνιον (Polyb. 16.18.2). During the first century B.C. this area was subject to the Iturean dynasty of Chalcis, but in 20 B.C. Augustus transferred it to the kingdom of Herod of Judaea; in 3/2 B.C. his son Philip founded or refounded the city and named it for Augustus, the "Caesarea Philippi" of the Gospels. For a time Caesarea, like Sepphoris, also used the name Neronias.[31] We can only guess at the situation before 3 B.C.,[32] but it is possible that there was already a city here under some earlier name.

28. Cf. A. H. M. Jones, *JRS* 21 (1931) 82.

29. G. Hölscher, "Panias," *RE* 18 (1949) 594–600; Schürer II 169–171; Rey-Coquais, *Studi ellenistici* IV (Pisa 1994) 47–50; photograph at M. Dunand, *D'Amanus au Sinai* (Beirut 1953) 179. An epigram from the cave calls the god φιλευήχῳ Διόπανι (Kaibel, *Epigr.* 827).

30. Robert, *Hellenica* XI–XII (1960) 441–443.

31. *BMC* 239; Seyrig, *Scripta numism.* 464; A. Stein, *INJ* 8 (1984–5) 9–11; *RPC* I 4849–4850.

32. That Panias was not a city before 3/2 B.C. is often asserted on the basis of Polybius' words τὸ Πάνιον (e.g., E. Schwartz, *NAkG* 1906, 372). Robert, *Hellenica* IV (1948) 11, wondered whether a poem of Meleager of Gadara in the voice of Pan, "I will live in this city" (ἄστυ: *Anth.Gr.* 7.535), alludes to the future Caesarea Panias. Meleager wrote ca. 100 B.C.: A. Cameron, *The Greek Anthology* (Oxford 1993) 49–56.

Civic coins are extant from M. Aurelius to the end of the Severi.[33] Many give the name in full and leave no room for titles: Καισαρία Πανιάς or Πανιάδος. Just as many give the title of inviolability: Καισ(αρέων) Σεβ(αστέων) ἱερ(ᾶς) καὶ ἀσύ(λου) ὑπὸ Πανίῳ, with varying abbreviations. Coins with and without the title are found scattered throughout the life of the mint; only the amount of space available seems to dictate whether they appear. Of cults, we see most often Pan, either piping or standing in his grotto; but sometimes Zeus seated by a rock, or Tyche or other divinities. Thus, for as long as we have evidence on the status of the city (the duration of the coins), Caesarea-Panias possessed inviolability.

How much older is the status than the time of M. Aurelius? Certainly the shrine of Pan was old, attested already in 200 B.C.; if the temple then was, like Baetocaece, not in a civic territory, it was taken over eventually by Panias. As elsewhere, my supposition is that the recognition of *asylia* was pre-imperial, whether from one of the rulers of the first century B.C. or from the Herodian dynasty in the first half of the first century A.D.

Joppa

Joppa, where Perseus rescued Andromeda, was the port of Jerusalem, and while an important place, eventually Flavia Joppa, it issued few coins. The testimony for *asylia* here rests on a single coin described by de Saulcy, the attribution of which has been doubted:[34]

Tyche bust | Galley, above ΙΟΠ / Α Υ, below ΚΓ? ΙΕΡΑΣ.

Hill noted the similarity to some issues of Tyre.

33. De Saulcy, *Numismatique* 313–324; Y. Meshorer, *INJ* 8 (1984–5) 37–58. The few coins De Saulcy placed earlier than M. Aurelius have not been confirmed in modern literature; as described they display no titles. See also *RPC* I 4842–4846, tentative attribution to Panias of some Latin coins of the first century A.D.

34. De Saulcy, *Numismatique* 177 no. 2, with Hill, *BMC* p. xxiv. On the city see Schürer II 110–114; *Enc.Arch.Excav.* II 532–541; G. T. Radan, in *Mediterranean Cities*, ed. I. Malkin and R. L. Hohlfelder (London 1988) 74–86.

Raphia

Raphia was the southernmost city of Palestine; harborless, overshadowed by its neighbor Gaza to the north, it has left little trace of its history or cults. The city issued bronze coins sporadically from the late second century A.D. to the mid-third,[35] dated by a Pompeian era of about 60 B.C. and, except for one year, without titles. The most abundant year of its issues was "290" (ca. A.D. 230; obverses with Severus Alexander). The coins of this year show a diverse lot of gods, as do the others of the city. They differ from earlier and later issues in that all are inscribed IEPA Ῥαφία. Thus no more than "sacred" is assured; if this represents granted inviolability, I would look to the conflicts of the first century B.C. for the occasion.

Jerusalem

The inviolability of Jerusalem is a case apart, as the evidence is of uncertain credibility. We have a letter alleged in 1 Maccabees, and perhaps coins of the first Jewish war. The authenticity of the Seleucid and Roman *acta* cited in Maccabees and Josephus has attracted formidable scholarship,[36] and one enters this field with hesitation.

Jewish literature early contained expressions that learned readers of a later age might have taken as evidence for the declared inviolability of Jerusalem or the Temple. In the Torah the Temple is called ὁ ἅγιος τόπος,[37] and in the later books of the Bible Jerusalem is often ἡ ἁγία πόλις.[38] "The holy city" might well attract more grandiose claims.

First, in an account whose meticulous detail gives it the ring of truth,[39] 2 Maccabees reports that when an agent of Seleucus IV (185–175) attempted to seize moneys in the Temple, the high priest responded that one could

35. Y. Meshorer, *RN* VI.18 (1976) 57–68 (whose comments on the cults are uncompelling). On the city, Schürer II 169–171.

36. Rather than attempt a bibliography, I may cite two exemplary investigations: Bickerman, *Studies in Jewish and Christian History* II (Leiden 1980) 1–158; Habicht, *HSCP* 80 (1976) 1–18.

37. Exod. 29:31, repeatedly in Leviticus, etc. Applied also to synagogues in Roman times: Frey, *CIJ* II p. 153.

38. Earliest at Isa. 48:2; cf. Joel 3:17: ἔσται Ἱερουσαλὴμ ἁγία, καὶ ἀλλογενεῖς οὐ διελεύσονται δι' αὐτῆς οὐκέτι; the label in the Madaba mosaic: ἡ ἁγία Ἱερουσα[λήμ] (*IGLSyr* XXI 153.56); cf. App. *Syr.* 50: τὴν μεγίστην πόλιν Ἱεροσύλυμα καὶ ἁγιωτάτην αὐτοῖς. At Jos. *V.* 349, "the common temple of all."

39. See Bickerman, *Studies* II 159–191.

not wrong those who had entrusted their property to the *asylia* of the temple (3:12):

> ἀδικηθῆναι δὲ τοὺς πεπιστευκότας τῇ τοῦ τόπου ἁγιωσύνῃ καὶ τῇ τοῦ τετιμημένου κατὰ τὸν σύμπαντα κόσμον ἱεροῦ σεμνότητι καὶ ἀσυλίᾳ παντελῶς ἀμήχανον εἶναι.
>
> . . .
>
> That those who have trusted the sanctity of the place and the awe and inviolability of the temple honored throughout the whole world should be harmed is entirely impossible.

Despite the term used, this respect for the Temple did not stem from a concrete recognition of *asylia*, and the high priest makes no such claim; it was rather the respect that everyone, Jew or Greek, acknowledged was due to property deposited in a temple,[40] and the dispute concerned whether this money belonged to private persons or the crown. Both the event itself and the source, Jason of Cyrene writing around 150 B.C.,[41] are earlier than the arrival of declared inviolability in this part of the Hellenistic world.

1 Maccabees, by contrast, makes a far more specific claim. Composed originally in Hebrew ca. 100 B.C. and continuing later than the work of Jason and 2 Maccabees, the book recounts a formal declaration by the Seleucid Demetrius I in 151 B.C. Demetrius and Alexander Balas were competing for control of the kingdom. Demetrius made some concessions to Jonathan in Jerusalem; Alexander responded by appointing Jonathan high priest, in order to make Jonathan a friend and ally. Demetrius in turn responded with a letter to the Jews offering a long list of benefactions;[42] he frees the Jews from various taxes and then declares (10:31):

> καὶ Ἱερουσαλὴμ ἔστω ἁγία καὶ ἀφειμένη καὶ τὰ ὅρια αὐτῆς, αἱ δεκάται καὶ τὰ τέλη.
>
> . . .
>
> Jerusalem is to be holy and released, and its territory—the tithes and taxes.

This garbled Greek was translated from Hebrew by someone who did not know the Greek formulary of inviolability. What Greek phrase was the author of the lost Hebrew original trying to convey? When Josephus took up this passage, he transformed the language as follows (*AJ* 13.51):

40. So recently J. A. Goldstein, *II Maccabees* (Garden City 1983) 209.

41. See Habicht, 2. *Makkabäerbuch* (Gütersloh 1976) 175.

42. 10:25–45: the garrison in Jerusalem is withdrawn; all Jewish captives in the kingdom are released without ransom; inviolability; all Jewish festivals are tax-free for all Jews in the kingdom; Jewish troops are to be recruited and paid; Jews are to have their own leaders and laws; Ptolemais and its territory are given to support the Temple, to which the king adds cash of his own; right of refuge; money for construction.

καὶ τὴν Ἱεροσολυμιτῶν πόλιν ἱερὰν καὶ ἄσυλον εἶναι βούλομαι καὶ ἐλευθέραν ἕως τῶν ὅρων αὐτῆς ἀπὸ τῆς δεκάτης καὶ τῶν τέλων.

. . .

And Jerusalem I wish to be sacred and inviolable and free from the tithe and taxes to the limit of its boundaries.

This would be closer to attested documentary usage, but still odd: his added ἐλεύθερος is not normally said of taxes. I suggest that what Josephus has taken as "boundaries" was the civic territory (ὅρια = χώρα, frequent in the LXX and NT; and cf. 10:43) and is displaced in Maccabees, for mention of the territory should have preceded "sacred and inviolable"; last would come tax exemption. That is, the Greek that lay behind the original Hebrew might be τὴν πόλιν καὶ τὴν χώραν εἶναι ἱερὰν καὶ ἄσυλον καὶ ἀφορολόγητον. Against this, however, is not only the word order in Maccabees but also the specification of two kinds of taxes.[43] However this may be, the passage is clear in its claim that a king declared Jerusalem "holy," and that alone is sufficient to prove that the original author had in mind the phenomenon of granted *asylia*, whatever his wording was.

In the same letter Demetrius is said to grant security of property as well as person to debtors who take refuge in the Temple (10:43):

καὶ ὅσοι ἐὰν φύγωσιν εἰς τὸ ἱερὸν τὸ ἐν Ἱεροσολύμοις καὶ ἐν πᾶσι τοῖς ὁρίοις αὐτοῦ, ὀφείλοντες βασιλικὰ καὶ πᾶν πρᾶγμα, ἀπολελύσθωσαν, καὶ πάντα ὅσα ἐστὶν αὐτοῖς ἐν τῇ βασιλείᾳ μου.

. . .

And any who flee to the temple at Jerusalem and all its land because of owing royal or any debt are to be absolved, and all their property in my kingdom.

This shares elements with Strabo's story about Seleucid Aradus (see p. 11), especially in that a fugitive's property outside the place remained secure; but this does not add to its credibility. The author concludes by reporting that the Jews did not believe these things or accept them (10:46; Josephus omits this detail). I suggest that we should not either: the gifts seem too good to be true, and the refusal of them too convenient.

1 Maccabees (15:2–10) also produces a letter of Antiochus VII to the Jews at the start of his reign (139 B.C.): he confirms all previous privileges, and grants the right of coinage, freedom for the city and the temple (Ἱερουσαλὴμ δὲ καὶ τὰ ἅγια εἶναι ἐλεύθερα, 15:7), control of weapons and fortifications, and release

43. For discussion and bibliography see J. A. Goldstein, *I Maccabees* (Garden City 1976) 408, who takes the reasonable view that Josephus' ἄσυλον was his own expansion of ἱεράν and that the erroneous final nominatives in 10:31 were meant to go with the participle, "released from taxes." This would imply behind the Hebrew ἱερὰν καὶ ἀφορολόγητον, which is certainly possible.

from royal debts now and in future. Here too the favors seem too sweeping to be credible; "freedom" for a temple is unusual, though it finds a parallel at Delphi (p. 47). Finally, at 15:16–24 the author alleges a Roman document from the consul Lucius asking the Hellenistic states not to harm the Jews or wage war against them or form alliances with their enemies (ὅπως μὴ ἐκζητήσωσιν αὐτοῖς κακά, καὶ μὴ πολεμήσωσιν αὐτοῖς καὶ τὰς πόλεις αὐτῶν καὶ τὰς χώρας αὐτῶν, καὶ ἵνα μὴ συμμαχῶσιν τοῖς πολεμοῦσιν αὐτούς).[44] Certainly this could be construed as an invitation to grant neutrality, the consequence of being "sacred and inviolable"; but there are formidable arguments against its authenticity.

What is crucial for us is the claim in 1 Maccabees that Jerusalem was (almost) declared sacred and inviolable in 151 B.C.[45] If the letter is genuine, this would be the earliest attested recognition beyond the old Greek cities of the Aegean, anticipating great cities like Seleuceia and Tyre. These several letters seem to offer more than we should believe.

From the coins there is silence of two sorts: as a city-state Jerusalem itself struck no coins in the Hellenistic period, despite the alleged grant of 139 B.C. And coins of the Hasmoneans and their successors,[46] whether inscribed in Hebrew or Greek, make no claim of *asylia* for the city (none of these actually names Jerusalem, however). It is only in the first Jewish war, A.D. 66–70, that coins were given the Hebrew inscription "shekel of Israel" | "Jerusalem (the) holy."[47] This is polemic, like "redemption" or "freedom of Zion" on the bronzes.[48] I suggest that "Jerusalem the holy" reflects biblical usage rather than a granted title *more Graeco*, whether historical or even recollected now from the story in 1 Maccabees.

It seems to me improbable that Jerusalem and its god, among the less Hellenized of the important cities and cults of Palestine, achieved this honor

44. Picked up by Josephus at *AJ* 14.145–148, with much altered language: sent to the autonomous cities and the kings, ὑπὲρ τοῦ τὴν χώραν αὐτῶν καὶ τοὺς λιμένας ἀδείας τυγχάνειν καὶ μηδὲν ἀδικεῖσθαι. Josephus omits the name of the individual recipient (King Ptolemy in Maccabees) but completes that of the Roman as L. Valerius (now στρατηγός rather than ὕπατος). Bickerman (*Gnomon* 6 [1930] 357–361) assigned this to the consul of 142 B.C. Against authenticity: A. Giovannini and H. Müller, *MusHelv* 28 (1971) 156–171.

45. Kahrstedt (*Syrische Territorien,* 76) took this passage as historical and thought that its provisions were explicated by 10:43. Against this see Seyrig, *Scripta numism.* 104 n. 2, who rightly observed that "the whole passage involves an inextricable confusion between autonomy, *asylia*, and the concession of a temporary asylum." Also against authenticity, on various arguments: Schürer I (Edinburgh 1973) 178–179.

46. The earliest issues are those of Alexander Jannaeus ca. 100 B.C.: M. D. McLean, *ANSMN* 26 (1981) 153–161. For the few Seleucid royal issues attributed to Jerusalem see *SNG Houghton Sel.* 831–834 (Antiochus VII, 130s B.C.).

47. U. Rappaport in *Cambridge History of Judaism* I (1984) 49.

48. Cf. on the coins of Bar Kochba "redemption of Israel" and "freedom of Jerusalem / Israel"; but "Jerusalem the holy" does not recur.

at so early a date, before cities like Tyre or Seleuceia, or indeed at all. Rather, the letter of Demetrius I is a patriotic fiction composed after the time (the late second century B.C.) when inviolability acquired its vogue in this region and when its role as a *philanthropon* in dynastic struggles was common enough knowledge to be made an item in literary propaganda.

The Decapolis

In the region east of the Jordan River, Greek civic life seems to have prospered comparatively late.[1] The cities suffered damage from the campaigns of Alexander Jannaeus ca. 100 B.C. and were the objects of restoration by Pompey. No city of the Decapolis struck coins in the Hellenistic period with the probable exception of Gadara, and there only with the beginning of Roman rule in the 60s B.C. Our evidence for inviolability in this region is confined to Roman imperial times, and the original date is in every case unknown. I assume a Hellenistic origin for all and guess that Gadara, the richest and most famous of the recipients, was the earliest.

Gadara

Gadara of the Decapolis, at modern Umm Qeis, is some ten kilometers southeast of the Sea of Galilee on a plateau high above the Hieromykes (Yarmuk) River, a secure site in a rich land.[2] Its territory extended north across the Yarmuk to the Sea of Galilee and the territories of Tiberias and Hippus, south to that of

1. On the Decapolis see generally H. Bietenhard, *ANRW* II.8 (1977) 220–261; B. Isaac, *ZPE* 44 (1981) 67–81; I. Browning, *Jerash and the Decapolis* (London 1982) 18–58; E. Will in *Studies in the History and Archaeology of Jordan* II (Amman 1988) 237–241; some civic cults: Seyrig, *Syria* 36 (1959) 60–78 (*Ant. syr.* VI 34–53).

2. Benzinger, *RE* 7 (1910) 436–437; Schürer II 132–136; R. Janin and L. Stiernon, *Dict.hist.géog.eccl.* 19 (1981) 592–597. Alexander Jannaeus consumed ten months in besieging the place: Jos. *AJ* 13.356. It is in Josephus' list of cities ravaged by the Jewish rebels in the 60s (*BJ* 2.458: also Hippus, Nysa, Gerasa, Ptolemais, Ascalon, Gaza). For the remains, which include two theaters, see G. Schumacher, *Northern Ajlun* (London 1890) 46–113; cf. *ZDPV*

Scythopolis.[3] On the northern bank of the Yarmuk were the famous hot springs of Gadara.

Gadara was the great city of the Decapolis, the center of Hellenic culture in the Transjordan. It is called χρηστομουσία, "devoted to good music," in an epigram of imperial date;[4] the emblem chosen to indicate the city on the imperial tetradrachms was the three Graces (as on some civic issues).[5] At Gadara were born the satirist Menippus, the epigrammatist Meleager (who called it Ἀτθὶς ἐν Ἀσσυρίοις, *Anth.Gr.* 7.417.2), the Epicurean Philodemus, and the rhetorician Theodorus.[6] Its rich cultural life doubtless was supported by its role as an international resort, for the springs by the Yarmuk, considered second only to Baiae, attracted a cosmopolitan and educated clientele, and here the Gadarenes held an annual festival.[7]

The inviolability of Gadara is attested by coins of imperial date, usually stated in the form ΙΑΑΓ for ἱ(ερᾶς) ἀ(σύλου) α(ὐτονόμου) γ( ). Such extreme abbreviation was evidently a local mannerism, for it is attested otherwise only at neighboring Abila and Capitolias; probably these letters would be unintelligible farther afield. In fact the meaning of the fourth letter, Γ, which occurs also on the coins of Abila, remains uncertain.[8]

The coins of Gadara eventually show the name Πομπηιεῖς, and the city used a Pompeian era (of 64/3 B.C.); Josephus in fact singles out Gadara as a city that Pompey not only freed from Hasmonean rule but rebuilt, on the urging of his rich client Demetrius of Gadara.[9] The city evidently first issued coins under

---

49 (1926) 120–125; 82 (1966) 64–73; 94 (1978) 135–144; 96 (1980) 45–58, 158–162; 103 (1987) 78–100; *ADAJ* 34 (1990) 321–342.

3. Testimonies and discussion at M. Avi-Yonah, *RE* Suppl. 13 (1973) 426.

4. Peek, *Gr. Versinschr.* I 1070.2–3, πατρὶς δέ μου καὶ πᾶσι κοινὴ Γάδαρα χρηστομουσία—a hapax, but the verb is used with this meaning at Ath. 633B.

5. A. R. Bellinger, *Syrian Tetradrachms of Caracalla*, ANSNS 1 (New York 1940) 90–92.

6. Strab. 16.2.29 (759); it has long been recognized that Strabo here confuses the two Gadaras and misattributes his biographical information to Gadara Lysaniou, the Jewish city on the eastern fringe of the Holy Land (see Benzinger 438). The confusion persists in the Budé edition of *Anth.Gr.* 7.417 and that of Gow and Page (*Hellenistic Epigrams* II [Cambridge 1965] 607: "Ramoth-Gilead . . . a very distinguished record for so outlandish a community"). Γαδάρων θ' ἱερὰ χθών at Meleager 7.419.5 (so too 11.25.70), like his ἱερὰ Τύρος at 418.2, is merely poetic rather than the declared title.

7. Eunap. *V. Iamb.* 5.2.2 (459); Epiph. *Adv. haer.* 1.30.7 (*PG* 41.416C). E. L. Sukenik, *The Ancient Synagogue of El-Hammeh* (Jerusalem 1935) 18–23, collects the testimonia, to which can be added *SEG* 32.1502.

8. Eckhel, *Doctrina numorum* III^2 (Vienna 1828) 346, cites the opinions of N. F. Haym, γ(νώμη) = *decreto*, and of Belley (1757), γ(νωρίμου) cf. ἐνδόξου, λαμπροτάτης; I have not found a more recent suggestion.

9. *AJ* 14.75; *BJ* 1.155. In this region only Pella to the south is known also to have taken the name Pompeia, attested once under Elagabalus: *RN* IV. 39 (1936) 290; R. H. Smith, *Pella of the Decapolis* I (Wooster 1973) 56–57.

its own name in 47/6 B.C., thus after Caesar's passage through the region;[10] after a hiatus under Augustus, Gadara struck coins fairly regularly through the imperial age. Until A.D. 159/160 all coins lack titles, merely Γαδαρέων or the nominative.

In 159/160 we see added for the first time the Roman name Pompeia and civic titles: Πο(μπηιέων) Γαδαρ(έων) Κ(οίλης) Συ(ρίας) and ΙΑΑΓ (Spijkermann no. 31). Pompeia and the titles are seen added to the old ethnic sporadically thereafter, with Πομπηιέων appearing more often and later than ΙΑΑΓ. The fullest form of the titles given is ΙΕΑΣΑΓ = ἱε(ρᾶς) ἀσ(ύλου) α(ὐτονόμου) Γ (nos. 60–61, A.D. 178–180). Inviolability is last indicated on a coin of A.D. 218/9, which is unique both for its inscription, ΙΑΥ = Ι(ΕΡΑΣ) αὐ(τονόμου), and for its elaborate image of Heracles.[11]

With the exception of this last instance in 218/9, the titles of inviolability always accompany an image of Zeus Nicephorus seated in a tetrastyle temple—an image that itself first appears with the titles in 159/160, and that is seen only twice without ΙΑΑΓ (nos. 73 of A.D. 214/5, 90 of 239/240). This distribution may suggest that the inviolability of the city was held in honor of Zeus, the prominence of whose cult in this region is well known.

As to the date of the grant, obviously the name "Pompeia" was not new in A.D. 159/160 when we first meet it; the same, I suggest, applies to *asylia*, which may also date from the work of restoration under Pompey and Gabinius, or before.

Abila

Abila of the Decapolis, the eastern neighbor of Gadara, controlled the fertile plateau south of the upper reaches of the Yarmuk, famous for its vineyards.[12] The city proper stood on two hills, between which was the theater. Of the

10. A. Spijkermann, *Coins of the Decapolis* (Jerusalem 1978) 131 nos. 3–4. Seyrig, *Ant. syr.* VI 45–49, attributed to Gadara some bronzes whose only inscription is "year 1 of Rome," ∟Α Ῥώμης, thus 64/3: Spijkermann nos. 1–2; more examples at M. Rosenberg, *Coinage of Eastern Palestine* (Jerusalem 1978) 36.

11. Spijkermann no. 80: "Herakles, wearing short tunica and boots, lion's skin at back, standing r., l. hand resting on cysta placed upon column, from which two snakes emerge, r. extended, holding uncertain object, at r., lion jumping up against the column; at l., small animal, standing l."

12. Eus. *Onom.* 32.16 (οἰνοφόρος καλουμένη); scholars have remarked the grapes shown on some coins. See G. Schumacher, *Abila of the Decapolis* (London 1889); cf. *ZDPV* 49 (1926) 151–154; 76 (1960) 26; Schürer II 136–137; Spijkermann 48–57; M. J. Fuller, "Abila of the Decapolis" (Ph.D. diss., Washington University 1987).

Hellenistic city we know little beyond the fact of its dynastic name Seleuceia, Σελεύκ(εια) Ἄβιλα or Σε(λευκέων) Ἀβιληνῶν on coins of imperial date.

Abila struck coins sporadically from A.D. 161/2 to 218/9. After the familiar city Tyche, they show most often Heracles. The most unusual image is of the towered propylaea of a sacred precinct.[13] Civic titles appear on approximately half the issues, scattered from the first year of the mint to the last. The inscription most often takes the brief form seen also at Gadara and Capitolias: Σε(λευκέων) Ἀβιληνῶν ΙΑΑΓ Κο(ίλης) Συ(ρίας); in 218/9, however, we see ΙΕΑΣΥ = ἱε(ρᾶς) ἀσύ(λου) (nos. 23–24). The title of inviolability is not associated with one image more than another. The presence or absence of the title thus is not significant: we can say only that Abila had inviolability for as long as we have evidence to judge by. I would assume an origin in the first century B.C.

Capitolias

Capitolias was at Beit-Ras south of the Yarmuk, bordering on Gadara.[14] The coins show an era beginning in A.D. 97 or 98, and the city is not heard of earlier; clearly Capitolias was founded in one of those years, as all scholars have recognized. But its titles of inviolability and autonomy suggest (in my view) that the place had a Hellenistic history, that the Roman city absorbed an older temple that had been declared inviolable; and in this populous region, urbanized under the Ptolemies and especially the Seleucids, we might not expect to find an entirely new city created in the time of Trajan. In fact, Irbid five kilometers to the south has substantial remains older than the foundation of Capitolias in 97–98, and this may have been the previous urban center. This is taken to be Arbela, mentioned by Eusebius as a village in the territory of Pella.

A coin of the time of Commodus shows Alexander the Great and the inscription Ἀλέξ(ανδρος) Μακε(δὼν) γενάρ(χης); as Seyrig saw, this proves that Capitolias, like several other cities of the area, claimed Alexander as founder. This supports the idea that "Capitolias" is a new name for an older community, which claimed a Hellenistic past that is unknown to us.

The coinage of Capitolias began under M. Aurelius and extended, in modest abundance, over the next sixty years. On it the city is regularly Καπιτωλιέων ΙΑΑ, the abbreviation seen also at Gadara and Abila but without their Γ; it is on occasion expanded to ΙΕΡΑΣΑΥ and ΙΕΡΑΣΥΑΥ.

13. See Seyrig, *Ant. syr.* VI 34–35.

14. Schumacher, *Ajlun* 127–131; Spijkermann 96–107; C. J. Lenzen and E. A. Knauf, *Syria* 64 (1987) 21–46 on Beit-Ras; *RBibl* 95 (1988) 239–247 on Irbid.

The name of the city reflects a cult of Jupiter Capitolinus. The coins display two divinities. One is the city Tyche, her foot placed on a river god (the Yarmuk): of an oriental manner, she wears a short tunic like an Amazon and holds sometimes a globe, sometimes a scepter—a Hellenized Gad.[15] The other god is Zeus, seated in a monumental temple with an altar on the roof, surrounded by a massive walled precinct with corner towers, of a sort seen elsewhere in Syria.[16]

Antioch by Hippus

The city of Hippus was in the hills above the eastern shore of the Sea of Galilee.[17] Its royal name bespeaks a refoundation after the Seleucid conquest of Palestine in 200 B.C., probably by Antiochus III or IV. Antioch by Hippus suffered the fate of its neighbors, "destroyed" by Jannaeus and "freed" by Pompey from the Hasmoneans; its era is from 64/3 B.C. In the 60s A.D. the city was attacked and damaged by the Jewish rebels (Jos. *BJ* 2.459; cf. 478).

The cults and myths of "wise Hippus"[18] are not elaborately represented on the coins, which prefer the *type parlant* of a horse, often accompanied by the city Tyche, or of Pegasus—probably the city claimed a Hellenic origin deriving from the travels of Pegasus. The most individual item is Zeus of the Plow, Ἀροτήσιος, so labeled and showing him in a tunic standing in his temple (the only temple shown on the coins of Hippus);[19] this may be the Zeus who is shown facing Tyche on several coins (nos. 6, 22, 40).

The royal name appears to have been used interchangeably for a time with the original name: on its earliest coins (under Nero, Titus, and Domitian) the city is "Antioch by Hippus" on the larger denominations, "Hippus" (Ἱππηνῶν) on the smaller;[20] the latter is not found after the first century. No civic titles are shown on these few issues of the first century. The city next struck coins under Antoninus Pius (138–161); from this time until the end of

15. Cf. D. Sourdel, *Les cultes du Hauran* (Paris 1952) 49.

16. Seyrig, *Ant. syr.* VI 35–41.

17. G. Schumacher, *The Jaulan* (London 1888) 194–206; Schürer II 130–132; *Enc.Arch.Exc.* II 521–523; Spijkermann 168–179.

18. Peek, *Gr. Versinschr.* I 1070.4; the adjective is found applied also to Cotyaeum in Phrygia (Peek 1016; cf. Robert, *Op. min. sel.* VII 205).

19. Spijkermann nos. 14, 29–31, 33; cf. Seyrig, *Ant. syr.* VI 43–44.

20. Spijkermann 170–171; *RPC* I 4807–4808. Pliny (*HN* 5.71, 74) and Josephus use "Hippus," which is not unusual, as authors normally employ original names rather than later innovations.

the mint (last dated issue in 218/9), all coins give the city the title of inviolability: Ἀντιοχ(έων) πρ(ὸς) Ἱππ(ῳ) τῆς ἱερ(ᾶς) κ(αὶ) ἀσύλου or further abbreviation.[21]

The consistent appearance of the titles in the second century and their absence in the first might imply that the status was in fact granted in the period between Domitian and Pius. That I believe is unlikely; I take the silence of the few early coins as without significance and would look to the first century B.C. as the likely period of the original grant.

Nysa-Scythopolis

Beth-Shan occupied the rich land where the Jezreel Valley comes down to the Jordan; it is an important site, well documented from the Bronze Age through medieval times.[22] As a Greek city it was called Scythopolis, then Nysa after the Seleucid reconquest in 200 B.C.[23] It experienced the aggression of John Hyrcanus at the end of the second century B.C. (Jos. *AJ* 13.280; *BJ* 1.66), and the benefactions of Pompey and Gabinius; station of the fifteenth legion during the Jewish War, it was attacked by the rebels in A.D. 66 (*BJ* 2.458).

The city issued coins from the Julio-Claudian period to Gordian, under whom the mint was especially prolific. They show above all the worship of Dionysus, with particular reference to his childhood with his nurse Nysa; already Pliny knew the story that she was buried here (*HN* 5.74).

Inviolability is first invoked in A.D. 162/3 in its briefest form: Νύσας Κοί(λης) Συρ(ίας) ΙΕΡ.[24] The title appears on the majority of issues from Commodus on, most often abbreviated ἱερ(ᾶς) ἀσύ(λου).[25] The only other title on the coins is ΕΛ ΠΟΛ (nos. 15, 21). This is elucidated by a lone inscription that also spells out the title of inviolability: in the time of Marcus Aurelius the

21. Spijkermann 171–179. The two issues under Pius (undated) show the facing busts of Zeus and Tyche (no. 6) and Tyche with horse (7). The mint becomes decidedly more active under M. Aurelius; about a third of these issues are dated, all to A.D. 165/6.

22. Schürer II 142–145; *Enc.Arch.Exc.* I 207–229; B. Lifshitz, *ANRW* II.8 (1977) 262–294; Seyrig, *Syria* 39 (1962) 207–211 (*Ant. syr.* VI 115–119); M. Avi-Yonah, *IEJ* 12 (1962) 123–134; Spijkermann 186–209.

23. See Rigsby, *TAPA* 110 (1980) 238–242; at 241 I should have cited Nysa the daughter of Seleucus II attested at *FGrHist* 161 F 4.

24. Spijkermann nos. 7 (162/3), 12 (163/4), with a standing Dionysus; note no. 14 also of 163/4, the same image but without titles. The titles are next seen in 182/3: no. 17 ΙΕΑΥΣ (*sic*); *Aukt. F. Sternberg 25/6 Nov. 1976* no. 701 (with Tyche in a temple rather than Dionysus).

25. Name and unabbreviated title ἱερᾶς ἀσύλου in wreath: nos. 26 (A.D. 210/1), 34 (215/6), 52 (217/8).

city erected a statue of the emperor, on which it calls itself Νυσαέων τῶν καὶ Σκυθοπολιτῶν τῆς ἱερᾶς καὶ ἀσύλου τῶν κατὰ Κοίλην Συρίαν Ἑλληνίδων πόλεων ἡ πόλις.[26]

Here as elsewhere, the irregularity of usage suggests the occasional evocation of a traditional title rather than a privilege newly granted in 162/3.

Gerasa

Gerasa, "Antioch on the Chrysorrhoa," was at the eastern edge of the Decapolis; under the Antonines it prospered from the caravan trade.[27] The site has been selectively but carefully excavated; the result is many more inscriptions than from any other city of the Decapolis, and our record of the civic coinage may well be complete. No coin gives Gerasa any titles, which are known instead from a single Latin inscription erected on the occasion of a visit by Hadrian in A.D. 130.[28]

Early history is largely unknown. We have almost no texts of Hellenistic date: the inscriptions on stone begin under Tiberius, and the coins, never abundant, are quite few before Hadrian.[29] A claim to foundation by Alexander is made on some of the coins, as at Capitolias. This region reverted to the Seleucids after the battle of Panium in 200 B.C.; the royal name is assumed to derive from Antiochus IV.[30] Like its neighbors, Gerasa was attacked by Alexander Jannaeus and benefited by Pompey, whose era was later used. The great event as documented from the site itself was Hadrian's passage during A.D. 130, which has left a number of inscriptions and which apparently invigorated the local mint.

26. G. Foerster and Y. Tsafrir, *INJ* 9 (1986/7) 53–58, with P. -L. Gatier, *Syria* 67 (1990) 205–206. The coin abbreviation had previous been construed as ἐλ(ευθέρας).

27. C. H. Kraeling, *Gerasa, City of the Decapolis* (New Haven 1936), with Welles's edition of the inscriptions; Schürer II 149–155; *Enc.Arch.Exc.* II 417–428; Spijkermann 156–167; Browning, *Jerash*.

28. The complete silence of the coins is a caution for our subject; compare Tarsus.

29. Early testimonies: *I.Gerasa* 251 (with Seyrig, *Notes* 33), a weight Ἀντιοχέων τῶν πρὸς Χρυσ(ορρόαι), without titles, dated Seleucid(?) 180 = 143/2 B.C.; three coins reported from A.D. 67/8: Spijkermann nos. 1–3 (inscription Γέρασα). On the Hellenistic *I.Cos* 64 (not a Gerasene) see Seyrig, *Ant. syr.* VI 142.

30. In inscriptions, the royal name is first seen on the early weight (above, n. 29), then in A.D. 115 (*I.Gerasa* 56/57, dedication to Trajan as savior and founder), and regularly thereafter; never simply "Gerasa." On coins, first under M. Aurelius, usually Ἀν(τιοχέων) τῶ(ν) πρ(ὸς) Χρ(υσορόαι) τῶ(ν) πρ(ότερον) Γε(ρασηνῶν), as in the inscriptions; this alternates with "the Fortune of Gerasa is Artemis" and "Alexander the Macedonian founder of Gerasa."

Gerasa was the city of Artemis, the θεὰ πατρῴα.[31] A dedication to [θ]εᾷ Λακα[ίνῃ] ἐπηκόῳ Ἀρτ[έ]μιδι (*I.Gerasa* 43) suggests a myth deriving her from Artemis Orthia of Sparta and a civic claim of kinship with Sparta, like that of Jerusalem. She is regularly shown on the coins, many of which are inscribed with the religious acclamation Ἄρτεμις ἡ τύχη Γεράσων, "the Fortune of Gerasa is Artemis."[32] Her temple, with its peribolos, was the largest and most imposing monument in Gerasa, dominating the center of the city.[33] It seems a reasonable guess that the inviolability of Gerasa came in her honor.[34] In any case, our one testimony for the status is a dedication to Artemis found near the entrance to the precinct, erected in A.D. 130 by some cavalrymen in the retinue of Hadrian. The stone is lost; as reported, it began as follows (*I.Gerasa* 30.1–9):

Pro salute
Imp(eratoris) Caes(aris) n(ostri) Traian(i)
Hadriani Aug(usti) p(atris) p(atriae)
Deaniae Aug(ustae)
equites sing(ulares) eius qui
hibernati sunt Antioch[i]-
ae ad Chrysorhoan quae
et Gerasa hiera et asylo⟨s⟩ et au-
tonomos, quorum (etc.)

4: error, whether of mason or copyist, for *Dianae* (cf. *Deana[e]* at *IGLSyrie* VI 2949).

The cavalrymen wintering in Gerasa[35] acted to fulfill a vow, *v(otum) s(olverunt) l(ibentes) m(erito) honoris et pietatis causa* (16–17). It is of course interesting that the only extant evocation of the titles of Gerasa stems not from the city or one of its citizens but from some transient foreigners. The troops associate Artemis with the imperial house,[36] probably their own addition to her honor at Gerasa. It would seem that the Roman troops were given a rather full account of what to call the city, I take it an ancient privilege that the Gerasenes themselves did not normally bother to state.

31. *I.Gerasa* 27. Cf. Sourdel, *Cultes* 42.

32. First under Hadrian: Spijkermann nos. 4–7. For the collocation cf. at Palmyra the altar [Τ]ύχῃ [Ἀρ]τέμιδι (Teixidor, *Inv.Inscr.Palmyr.* XI no. 43). For the acclamation cf. at Dura-Europus μεγάλη τύ[χη] Δούρας (*YCS* 14 [1955] 145).

33. Browning 85–92; R. Parapetti, *Syria* 66 (1989) 1–39.

34. Welles (p. 31) thought instead of Zeus Olympius, on the grounds that someone is found taking refuge in his temple in A.D. 69/70. I hope to comment elsewhere on *I.Gerasa* 5–6.

35. Cf. H. Halfmann, *Itinera principum* (Stuttgart 1986) 206–207.

36. For *Augustus* as a divine epithet see Nock, *Essays* I 42–43, 156.

Egypt

From Greco-Roman Egypt come nearly a dozen grants of *asylia*, all dating from the first century B.C.[1] That the more abundant evidence of the third and second centuries has yielded no grant suggests that these edicts represent a new departure for the Ptolemaic crown around 100 B.C., at least in number if not as an absolute innovation. The map will suggest their continuity with the spread of the title in the Hellenistic East; but the substance that *asylia* took on in Egypt has little in common with the rest of the Greek world, and more with Rome. The Ptolemies granted asylum in the sense the Romans understood it, religious immunity from civil law; and surely it is from Egypt that the Latin word *asylum* comes, consistent in form and meaning with what we see in Egypt.

In these inscriptions we see a form already old before the Ptolemies' arrival. Since the end of the second millennium, benefactions granted to temples had been inscribed on limestone steles whose curved upper margin framed a painting of pharaoh honoring the god; made in four copies, these stones were placed around the temple "to the four winds."[2] The Ptolemaic *asylia* steles follow this form, except for the one that derives from a Greek city (**226**, PLATE 9); some preserve the painted scene, and the rest we may assume once had one. Probably we owe these stones to the practice of making multiple copies; a papyrus lies behind each, but no *asylia* edict has survived on papyrus.[3]

1. General treatments: F. von Woess, *Das Asylwesen Ägyptens* (Munich 1923), and in *ZSav* 46 (1926) 32–67; C. Préaux, *L'économie royale* (Brussels 1939) 483–488; Rostovtzeff, *SEHHW* 887–893, 1549–1550; F. Dunand in *Hommages Serge Sauneron* II (Paris 1979) 77–97; J. Bingen in *Egitto e storia antica* (Bologna 1989) 24–30. In what follows I am especially grateful to Ludwig Koenen for help on various points.

2. See D. Meeks, *Orient.Lovan.Anal.* 6 (1979) 605–687.

3. In Lenger's *C.Ord.Ptol.*, of the twelve items that begin with the first *asylia* decree in 96 B.C. nine are inscriptions, while three are papyri (from one archive); all the inscriptions are

Egypt is different juridically from the world of the Greek city-states. In Egypt *asylia* is requested only of the crown and is a matter of internal administration; there is no invocation of Greek public opinion, as the grant is not an affair of international law. Only temples are in question, not city and territory. These acts must be studied as one part of the evolution of the relations between the crown and the temples.[4] Did temples in Ptolemaic Egypt have, like those in the Greek world, the "right of asylum," automatic jurisdiction within their precincts? In 203 B.C. the Alexandrians were outraged when royal agents pulled a fugitive from a temple, a clear violation of Greek usage—but that was in a Greek city.[5] The temples of the *chora* bore a different relation to the crown.[6]

Pharaonic Egypt did not know the "right of asylum."[7] Herodotus reports a slave's right of asylum in the temple of Heracles at the Canopic mouth as something exceptional.[8] In general, fleeing to some holy precinct did not make a fugitive immune from arrest by secular officials. It is reasonable to suspect that the new Greek rulers would prefer to leave this useful fact in place.

Several Ptolemaic and Roman texts seem to classify temples. We find "first and second and third temples" in the Canopus and Rosetta decrees of the native priests, and elsewhere references to λόγιμα ἱερά, as though a special class.[9] These have sometimes been taken as legal distinctions, whether originating with the government or with the native priests; but apart from **219**.5 and **221**.9, where this classification may be invoked, it seems to play no role in the *asylia* edicts, or in the attested acts of flight to temples.

---

asylia grants. For the form and the themes of petitions to the Ptolemaic government preserved on papyrus see A. Di Bitonto, *Aegyptus* 57 (1976) 109–143.

4. See especially J. Quaegebeur, *Orient.Lovan.Anal.* 6 (1979) 707–729; J. E. G. Whitehorne, *JRelHist* 11 (1980) 218–226.

5. Polyb. 15.27.2–3; and their outrage was selective: cf. 15.29.8–14 and 15.33.8. In 216 B.C. a Capuan sought refuge in Cyrene at a statue of Ptolemy and was safely delivered to the discretion of the king in Alexandria (Livy 23.10.11).

6. W. Otto, *Priester und Tempel* II (Leipzig/Berlin 1908) 290–301.

7. The nearest analogy, attested as early as the Sixth Dynasty, is the granting of fiscal immunities (*nht*, the term to which **219** resorts in the Egyptian) to selected temples—usually exemption of the god's people from the corvée; references at A. Gardiner, *Egypt of the Pharaohs* (Oxford 1961) 92–93; Préaux, *L'économie royale* 488 n. 1. E. Lüddeckens, "Asylwesen," *LexÄgypt* 1 (1973) 514–516, has under this rubric no pre-Hellenistic material apart from Herodotus, but only the Greek texts surveyed here.

8. 2.113. Some scholars have thought that this privilege betokens a foreign origin for the cult; this is disputed by A. B. Lloyd, *Herodotus Book II, Commentary*, EPRO 43.3 (Leiden 1988) 43.

9. Otto I 18–19; Uxkull-Gyllenband, *BGU* V p. 81; properly cautious, W. Brashear, *BGU* XIII pp. 7–8 ("an unclarified concept"); cf. XV 2470.6.

Some acts of refuge in the *chora* are on record earlier than our first *asylia* edict in 96 B.C.:[10]

In the mid-third century, some farmers protested a property assessment: "Sitting down in the temple, they said they would not be assessed justly or unjustly" (*PSI* V 502.21, καθίσαντες εἰς τὸ ἱερόν, not further identified). It is not certain that this was an act of religious asylum.

Around the same time, a witness, in order to avoid testifying, ran off (ἀνεχώρησεν) to the Sarapeum at Memphis (presumably from the Fayum, not far), where he was being supplied food (*P.Cair.Zenon* 59620 [*C.Ptol.Sklav.* I 79]). This shows that the Sarapeum had the right of asylum already under the early Ptolemies. We might also deduce that at this date such immunity was enjoyed by none of the many temples in the Fayum (which included a Sarapeum);[11] but there could easily be other reasons for fleeing to a place where one was not known and where a different police jurisdiction obtained.

In 169/8 someone was "forced from the temple" (τὸν ἐξσπασθέντα ἐκ τοῦ ἱεροῦ) by the agents of Antipater, who was then reported to the police, and an agent was arrested for violence. The temple is not further identified, and the provenience of the papyrus is unknown (*P.Athens* 8; *Pros.Ptol.* I 312 for the date).

In 164 Ptolemy the *katochos* in the Sarapeum at Memphis petitioned for redress because a girl who had fled to the temple and whom he intended to adopt was seized by a temple official and sold: do not overlook this enslavement, still more her being forced from the temple; in a second draft it is added that she was "outside(?) the asylum" when detained, ἔξωθεν] ἀσύλ[ο]υ (*UPZ* 3–4 [*C.Ptol.Sklav.* 83]). This is our earliest evidence for the word ἄσυλον in Egypt.

In 156 the chief of the Anubieum, the guardhouse placed by the entrance to the Sarapeum, wrote to a priest of Sarapis: some wrongdoers have escaped, watch for them, and if they dare to come out of the asylum (ἐκτὸς τοῦ ἀσύλου) let me know and we will act, and I will pay you (*UPZ* 64).

In 156 a slave ran away from his master, a man from Alabanda who was visiting Alexandria; we have the wanted poster, which offers a reward for the slave's return, or half that amount for identifying the temple to which the slave might have fled (*UPZ* 121 [*Sel.Pap.* 234; *C.Ptol.Sklav.* 81]). Evidently the master could go to the temple and try to obtain the surrender of the slave, but this was not a foregone outcome, as the information is worth only half

10. On *anachoresis* generally see H. Braunert, *Die Binnenwanderung* (Bonn 1964); W. Schmidt, "Der Einfluß der Anachoresis im Rechtsleben Ägyptens" (Diss., Cologne 1966); C. Orrieux, *Zénon de Caunos* (Paris 1985) 234–237. The flight of 150 agricultural workers to the Memphite nome (mid-III B.C.) seems to be purely secular: *P.Lond.* VII 1980–1981; *P. Cair.Zenon* 59245, with W. Clarysse in *StudHellen* 24 (1980) 87. On *P.Haun.* 10 (Tebtunis, III B.C.) see J. A. S. Evans, *YCS* 17 (1961) 163. A possible reference to refuge in M. Gronewald and D. Hagedorn, *ZPE* 41 (1981) 289–293.

11. *P.Cair.Zenon* 59168; *P.Mich.Zen.* 31.5; cf. Nock, *Essays* I 428.

the actual surrender. In the city of Alexandria the master would no doubt have to prove his case to the temple authorities; but what of the countryside? This notice was posted at the Anubieum beside the entrance to the Sarapeum; but was it sent only to those temples in the *chora* that had the right of asylum, or to all the thousands of temples? I think the former is more likely.

Probably in 145/4 comes the earliest of a series of royal pronouncements that officials are to respect the right of asylum, προσ[τετάχασι δὲ καὶ] μηθένα ἐξάγειν μηδ' ἀποβιάζεσθαι παρ' ο[ἷς τόποις ἀσυλίαι] ὑπῆρχον.[12] These passages seem clearly to imply that only some temples have this immunity.

In 114 a *basilicogrammateus* was informed that at Ptolemais-Euergetis the royal farmers had abandoned their assigned work and "run away to the temple at Narmuthis" (ἀνακ[ε]χωρηκέναι ἐπὶ τὸ [ἐν Ν]αρμούθι ἱερόν), about twenty kilometers (*Chr.W.* 330). The reference is not specific, although several temples are attested at Narmuthis (cf. E. Bernand, *I.Fayoum* II pp. 59–109).

Loan contracts show a provision in which the borrower waives the immunity that a temple might give him, the ἀγώγιμος clause:[13] for example, *P.Hib.* I 93 (ca. 250 B.C.): the borrower to be produced ἔξω ἱεροῦ κα[ὶ πάσης] σκέπης; contrast *PSI* V 515: ἔξω ἱεροῦ βωμοῦ σκέπης πάσης; *P.Dem.Zenon* 1.17: "I will not leave the district or go to an asylum" (*nht*); *P.Tebt.* I 66.59–61 (121/0); *Chr.W.* 327 (107/6); *P.Oxy.* XIV 1639: "subject to arrest by you in the Sarapeum or any asylum or before any magistrate or anywhere you might find us" (I B.C., loan drawn up at the Sarapeum in Oxyrhynchus, ἀ[γ]ώγιμοί σο[ι δὲ] ἐσόμεθα ἐπί τε τοῦ προωνομασμ[έν]ου Σαραπιείου καὶ ἐπὶ παντὸς ἀσύλου καὶ ἄρχοντ[ο]ς [κτλ.]).

Under Auletes (80–51), thus well into the time of the extant recognitions of *asylia*, a *hypostrategos* writes that Pancrates, despising him, has run away to some asylum (ἑαυτοῦ καταγνόντα ἐπί τι ἄσυλον ἀνακεχωρηκέναι); if Dionysius hands him over (ἐκτὸς ἀσύλου, which has been crossed out), bring him to me for examination (*BGU* VIII 1797).[14]

At the end of the Ptolemaic regime we find official invocation of "local inviolability in each nome in the case of failure to give satisfaction," τ̣ὴ̣ν̣ ἐ̣ν̣ ἑ̣κά[σ]τ̣ῳ̣ νομῶι κ̣α̣τ̣ὰ̣ τόπον ἀσυλίαν ἐπ' ἀδωσιδικίαι.[15]

12. *C.Ord.Ptol.* 43.15–17; cf. 53.83–84 of 118 B.C.: ἐκ τῶν ὑπαρχόντων ἀσύλων τόπων; *P.Mil.Congr.XVII* p. 29.

13. Rostovtzeff, *SEHHW* 905–906; M. Piatkowska, *La* ΣΚΕΠΗ *dans l'Egypte ptolémaïque*, ArchFilol 32 (Warsaw 1975).

14. In a problematic text, a contemporary complains about his debtors: τῶν δὲ ἐν ἀσεβίαι πρὸς τῆι αὐτῆι λυμαγωνείαι καθεστώτων ὡς ἂν ἐν τῶι τοῦ ἀσύλου ⟨τόπωι⟩? καταγινομένων, apparently "they stand in impiety in addition to the outrage itself, as they would reside in the asylum(?)" (*BGU* 1823).

15. *C. Ord.Ptol.* 82, with E. Van't Dack, *AncSoc* 1 (1970) 53–67.

Finally, Strabo 17.1.23 (823) mentions τὸ τοῦ Ὀσίριδος ἄσυλον near Sais in Egypt, where the god was buried.

These texts are evidence, of diverse strength, for the right of asylum in the life of Ptolemaic Egypt, down to the time when the extant royal grants begin. The list is not meant to be complete, but only to illustrate what is claimed in **219**, that some temples had this privilege but not all. The Sarapeum is the only one identified by name (and this already by the middle of the third century), but certainly other temples are represented in these incidents.

The Ptolemaic edicts have traditionally been taken as a sign of the declining royal authority having to buy the cooperation of the powerful priestly establishments and their secular patrons (much like the spread of *asylia* in Seleucid Syria). Bingen has argued against this, urging that what the edicts in fact reveal is small and weak temples trying to regain traditional rights in the face of growing pressures by the central government, and that the opposition we see is between Greek soldiers and officials.[16] Heinen has urged that the asylum grants do not show conflict between crown and native cults or between Greeks and Egyptians, but competing claims for royal benefactions.[17] Whatever the general character of the background, Ptolemy X (110–88, after his Cypriot exile) looks to be decisive in beginning this series of grants.

These acts are concentrated in space as well as in time: all but two are from the Fayum, six of them from two adjoining villages.[18] The gods honored are mostly Egyptian, but one Greek and one Jewish. The petitioners are sometimes Greek, sometimes Egyptian. Note finally that one late Ptolemaic edict gives the equivalent of asylum to a chief embalmer and his house (*C.Ord.Ptol.* 62–63, of 99 B.C.), and his petition uses much the same vocabulary and arguments as those for asylum: so that my services in worshipping in your behalf[19] not be interfered with by certain persons who enter violently, etc.; the grant is that no one force his way into the house, etc.—all that is wanting is the word ἄσυλον. This text, like the grants of asylum proper, does not acknowledge a divine entitlement but waives a royal power, a gesture that need not be confined to sacred space.

16. He points out that the temples in question are too small (as Lefebvre observed) to have had significant economic activities.

17. H. Heinen in *Aspekte spätägyptischer Kultur* (Mainz 1994) 157–168; cf. *BibO* 46 (1989) 79–81.

18. Lefebvre, *ASAE* 19 (1919) 59, thought the grants an effort to make the Fayum with its heavily Greek population a privileged and loyal region. But the distribution even in the Fayum is odd, and the notion of its Greekness at this late date is problematic.

19. So also the petitions *I.Philae* I 19.29 (= *OGIS* 139, ca. 120 B.C.); *SB* 7457.8 (= A. Bernand, *Delta* I [Cairo 1970] 445ff.).

The Sarapeum at Memphis

In 96 B.C. the first extant grant of *asylia* cites two precedents for this benefaction, one of them "the temple at Memphis" (**219**.8); there can be no doubt that this alludes to the Sarapeum.[20] Sarapis bore a unique relationship to the Ptolemaic crown. As we have seen, as early as the mid-third century persons are attested taking refuge there; this privilege must have been granted at some time in the first half of the third century.

Temple of Osiris at Busiris

The nome capital Busiris, at Bana in the central Delta, had been famous since the Sixth Dynasty as the home of Osiris, "lord of Busiris."[21] The town is mentioned already by classical authors; Herodotus placed here the second greatest *panegyris* held by the Egyptians.[22] Of its Greco-Roman history, given that papyri rarely survive in the Delta, little is known. The town is almost never mentioned in our extant documents,[23] and the site is unexcavated.

The other precedent for asylum invoked in 96 B.C. (**219**.8) is the temple "at Busiris": we may assume that this was Osiris' temple, Herodotus' ἱρὸν μέγιστον. When it gained the privilege is beyond conjecture.

Temple of Horus at Athribis

Athribis was in the southern part of the Delta by modern Banha, a region famous today for its vineyards and orange groves.[24] The extensive remains seen by early travelers, which included the northernmost pyramids in Egypt, have largely vanished in this century. Metropolis of the Athribite nome, the place was

20. See Wilcken, *UPZ* I pp. 120–121. Wilcken's work and Dorothy J. Thompson, *Memphis under the Ptolemies* (Princeton 1988) 212–265, make it unnecessary to address the details of our evidence for the Sarapeum.

21. Gardiner, *Egypt* 423.

22. 2.59, 61; bibliography at Lloyd, *Herodotus Book II*, EPRO 43.2 (Leiden 1976) 269, 276–279 (Herodotus mistakenly assigning the temple and festival to Isis rather than Osiris).

23. By chance a sitologus report from Busiris has found its way to Elephantine: *BGU* XIII 2276 (A.D. 155/6).

24. See P. Vernus, *Athribis* (Cairo 1978); p. xxi on the history of excavation.

of substantial importance; Ammianus, listing the greatest cities of Egypt, names Athribis, Oxyrhynchus, Thinis, and Memphis, crowned by Alexandria.[25] Here was buried the heart of Osiris, which was discovered and guarded by Horus Hnty-Hty (Ἀρχεντεχθαι).[26]

Although his cult is attested a good deal earlier, it was especially the object of royal donations from the middle of the second millennium on. Ramses III in particular "made many benefactions in Athribis for my father Horus Hnty-Hty," restoring walls, granting autonomy to the overseers and prophets in their supervision of the god's land and personnel, and expelling the vizier and his people; the god's people who had been dispersed and were under obligation to others he freed and brought back so that their work for the temple would not be interrupted; "I rendered it the equal of the great temples of the land, protected forever by my decrees."[27] During the anarchy of the eighth and seventh centuries Athribis was capital of one of the regional kingdoms in the Delta.[28] From the reign of Philip Arrhidaeus (323–317) comes the elaborate monument of Jedher, priest of the god: he built several new constructions in the precinct, persuaded the commander of some soldiers (Greeks, it is thought) to transfer them from the temple lands to other plots, and dedicated the present monument in aid against poisonous animals (a common function of Horus).[29]

For the Greco-Roman period, the few legible papyri from the Delta and the dwindling of traditional hieroglyphic monuments leave us little information on the cult and its honors. We know of some new construction, and several brief dedications are extant, both royal and private. A contingent of the Ptolemaic army was stationed at Athribis.[30] The Polish excavations have revealed the prosperity of Roman Athribis; the popularity of the god is suggested by his frequent mention in the magical texts of later antiquity,[31] but his name is not otherwise found in the papyri. The asylum edict for the temple,

25. 22.1.6; in Ammianus' time a tetrapylon was dedicated to the emperors (*OGIS* 722, A.D. 374).

26. The meaning is uncertain; Hnty-Hty was at first itself a divine name, then associated with Horus in iconography by the Twelfth Dynasty, then with Horus by name by the Eighteenth (Vernus 367–391; U. Rößler-Köhler, *LexÄgypt* 3 [1980] 27–33). "Athribis" is probably "the house of the mid-part" (of the Delta), later taken to mean the mid-part of Osiris (Vernus 343–344; 433–439 on the relic of the heart and intestines).

27. Vernus no. 55 (the Harris Papyrus), with references.

28. Vernus no. 69; *ANET*^{3} 294.

29. E. Jelinkova-Reymond, *Les inscriptions de la statue guérisseuse de Djed-her-le-Sauveur* (Cairo 1956).

30. *P.Zen.Pestm.* 24 (III B.C.); *OGIS* 96 (II B.C., Jewish).

31. See *P.Graec.Mag.* III p. 216 s.v. Ἀρχεντεχθαι. A statuette of a falcon inscribed with a magical text comes from Roman Athribis, *Suppl.Mag.* I 6 (for the reference I am grateful to R. W. Daniel).

the earliest extant from Ptolemaic Egypt, is the only lengthy Greek text that mentions the cult.

219. Ptolemy X, 96 B.C.

Limestone stele, h. 0.70, w. 0.57, th. 0.21, found at Banha in 1898, now in the Egyptian Museum, Cairo (no. 31089).[32] Trilingual text (hieroglyphic, Demotic, Greek); Greek letters blockish but clear and careful, with some crowding to the right. Above is a relief in Egyptian style: at left the king, accompanied by a priest, makes an offering to the seated Horus Hnty-Hty (with falcon's head and solar disk) and standing lion-headed Sachmis;[33] at right, the king, with a priest, makes offering to a seated goddess, who is crowned by an *atef*, and standing Isis or Hathor.

W. Spiegelberg, *Catalogue général du Musée de Caire: Die demotischen Denkmäler* I (Leipzig 1904) 20–22 no. 31089 (Greek text from a copy by O. Rubensohn, assisted by Wilhelm) [Dittenberger, *OGIS* 761 (Greek only)]; Spiegelberg ap. G. Maspero, *Le musée égyptien* II (Cairo 1907) 21–25 (the Demotic, improved at a number of points, is given only in transcription); S. de Ricci, *BSRAA* 11 (1909) 332 no. 10 (Greek only, from the photograph) [*SB* 620; Schroeter 58; Lenger, *C. Ord.Ptol.* 64; A. Bernand, *La prose sur pierre* 30]; Vernus, *Athribis* no. 165 (hieroglyphs only).

Photograph: Spiegelberg 1904, pl. 3 (Demotic and Greek texts); 1907, pl. 8 (whole stele).

Cf. Wilcken, *ArchPF* 4 (1908) 246–247; W. J. Tait, *P.Tebt.Tait* IV pp. 31–32.

The hieroglyphic version is an independent text, the Demotic a translation of the Greek. I give only the Greek (which is the best preserved of the three) and translate Vernus's translation of the hieroglyphs.

> ... Ptolemy the συγγενής of the king has brought the register (?) ... of good actions ... the sanctuary at Athribis, the temple of Horus Hnty-Hty and all the gods ... because of its antiquity; it is more venerable [than the other temples] ... we order: the right of asylum (*nht*) will belong to the temple in question ... the temple at Memphis and at Busiris ... under the control of the συγγενής of the king, the superior over Pr-Hr, P3-di-Hr, son of Horus.

βασιλεὺς Πτολεμαῖος ὃς καὶ Ἀλέξανδρος
Πτολεμαίου τοῦ συγγενοῦς καὶ διοικητοῦ προσανενέγκαντος ἡμῖν π[ᾶσ]ι
μὲν τοῖς κατ' Αἴγυπτον ἱεροῖς ἔτι ἀπὸ τῶν προγόνων ἡμῶν μείζονα φιλάνθρω-
πα ἐπικεχωρῆσθαι, ἔνια δὲ τῶν ἐπισήμων καὶ ἄσυλα γεγονέναι, τὸ ἐν Ἀ-
θρίβει τοῦ Ἁρκεντεχθαι τὸ μὲν πρῶτον καὶ λόγιμον ἀρχ[α]ιότατόν τε καὶ ἐνδο-
ξότατον τῶν πλείστων ὑπάρχον τῶν μὲν ἄλλων τιμῶν τετευχέν{ι}αι, λείπεσθ-

32. The stele deteriorated rapidly after discovery, so that Brugsch's photograph was already necessary to the first editor; the hieroglyphs are especially lacunose.

33. Testimonia on Sachmis at Athribis at Vernus 458–459.

αι δὲ ἐν τῷ μὴ εἶναι ἄσυλον, προσ⟨τε⟩τάχαμεν ἐπιχωρῆσαι καὶ τούτωι τῷ ἱερῷ

8 ἐ̣ν̣τὸς αὐτοῦ περιβόλωι τὴν ἀσυλίαν καθάπερ ἐσ̣τ̣ὶ τῶι ἐν Μέμφει καὶ Βουσίρει καὶ ἑτέροις καὶ τῶν ἄλλων ἱερῶν. γινέσθω οὖν ἀκολούθως.

3 ἀπὸ Wilcken, de Ricci (cf. **221**.8): {ὑπὸ τῶν} Spiegelberg. 8 B. Keil (*SB*): εἶ[ν]αι τῶι Spiegelberg, ἐπ̣ὶ̣ τῶι Wilcken, ε καὶ de Ricci.

. . .

King Ptolemy also called Alexander. Inasmuch as Ptolemy our relative and *dioiketes* has reported to us that to all the temples of Egypt very great benefits have already been granted by our ancestors and some of the distinguished ones have even become inviolable, and that the temple of Harkentechthai at Athribis, of first rank and famous, which is most old and distinguished among the many,[34] has obtained other honors but is lacking in not being inviolable, we have commanded to grant to this temple as well inviolability within its peribolos, as has been (granted) also to that at Memphis and Busiris and others among the temples. Let it be done accordingly.

Each Egyptian version gives a date, which is lacking in the Greek (apparently for want of space): 11 (hieroglyphs) or 21 (Demotic) Phamenoth of year 18, which is 25 March or 4 April of 96 B.C. They render ἄσυλον by *nht*, the traditional term for exemption from the royal corvée that might be granted to temple personnel. The hieroglyphs seem to mention at the end the priest responsible for the monument, who is probably represented in the relief.

The text is a memorandum, similar in structure to the Seleucid decision for Baetocaece (**218**); a heading has been added, but there is no phrase of address. By contrast with most of the later *asylia* inscriptions from Egypt, this one is the king's answer rather than the petitioner's request, and as a result we learn rather less about the circumstances of the grant; petitioners understandably dwell on their reasons, which the king here only summarizes. His attention was drawn to the temple by his *dioiketes* Ptolemy,[35] who possibly was a devotee and patron of this shrine, a political situation typical of the time and of these *asylia* documents. The written deposition[36] of the *dioiketes* is summarized in the king's indirect discourse: several famous temples have been granted *asylia*, and this one is similarly worthy—much as in the Ramses III document.[37] This is the logic of analogy and precedent, characteristic of a situation in which a single

34. Or "older and more distinguished than most," superlative for comparative; see Blass-Debrunner, *Grammatik des neutestamentlichen Griechisch* 15 (Göttingen 1979) §60; for πλεῖστα = πολλά, §244.1.

35. *Pros.Ptol.* I 43 and VIII 43, attested also in 108 B.C.; his origin is not known.

36. For προσφέρω (line 2) see *UPZ* I 14.35.

37. Compare the argument at *PSI* V 531: τὸ δὲ ἱερὸν τῆς Ἀστάρτης ἐστὶν ὅμοιον τῶν ἱερῶν τῶν Καρῶν καὶ Ἑλληνομεμφιτῶν· ὡς δὲ αὐτοῖς γίνεται, γενέσθω τῶι ἱερῶι ἡμῶν (complaint by the priests to Zenon, III B.C.).

authority controls the status. We find such a situation also in Boeotia and in the Roman provinces. It does not recur in Egypt (but see on **225**.14–16), or in the nearest parallel to the Ptolemaic grants, the Seleucid one for Baetocaece. Its uniqueness may reflect the relatively early date of **219**: the granting of *asylia* had in principle to be justified and was not yet a familiar and frequent act. Or it may be because here we have not the petitioner's point of view but the king's, for whom the proof from precedent may have carried more weight.

5: These adjectives seem to be the rhetoric of praise; but Otto (II 310–311) may have been right to compare the categorization of temples invoked in some other texts.

Temple of Heron at Magdola

Magdola, modern Medinet en-Nahas, stood on the northwestern side of the Gharaq basin, the secondary depression with its own lake south of the Fayum proper. What we know of the place derives mostly from the excavations conducted by the University of Lille in 1901–2,[38] whence the inscription **220** and a number of papyri, many of them petitions concerning events in Magdola.[39] The village is mentioned in the land surveys from neighboring Tebtunis, and in those concerned with Magdola we hear several times of the holdings, evidently extensive, of the temple of Heron.[40]

This temple, the subject of **220**, identified by its decoration and our inscription, was a brick structure, entered by a stone propylon. The propylon, mentioned at 35–36, was dedicated in 118 B.C. (*I.Fayoum* III 151); doubtless the temple proper was older. A full description of the remains, intended by Lefebvre, was never published.

The cult of Heron, originally the Thracian rider god, probably was brought to Egypt by Thracian soldiers recruited by the early Ptolemies.[41] A clerouchic cavalry officer donated the propylon at Magdola in 118 B.C., and a fragmentary

38. P. Jouguet, *CRAI* 1902, 346–359; the temples attested at Magdola are surveyed by P. Bottigelli, *Aegyptus* 22 (1942) 233–235.

39. *P. Enteuxis*; P. Boyaval, *CRIPEL* 1 (1973) 185–285.

40. *P.Tebt.* I 82, 83, 132.

41. Cf. Jouguet; G. Lefebvre, *ASAE* 20 (1920) 237–249, against the notion of a form of the indigenous Horus. The god is found also at Theadelphia, where he had his own temple in Hellenistic times, and under the Romans was worshipped also in the temple of Pnepheros as Heron Soubattos. Cf. E. Breccia, *Teadelfia e il tempio di Pneferos, Monuments de l'Egypte* I (Bergamo 1926) 111–112; W. J. R. Rübsam, *Götter und Kulte im Faijum* (Bonn 1974) 202; the cult possibly also at Tebtunis and Arsinoe in the Fayum: Rübsam 52–53, 190. Thracians in early Ptolemaic Egypt: L. Koenen, *Eine agonistische Inschrift*, Beitr.klass.Phil. 56 (Meisenheim 1977) 24–25.

list of cleruchs of the late second century B.C. mentions "the Heroon."[42] The *asylia* petition comes from two soldiers. The iconography of the god, seen in reliefs and frescoes, regularly includes his military garb.[43]

220. Ptolemy X, 95 B.C.

Stele found at Magdola in 1901, in the wall at the entrance of the propylon of the temple of Heron; transported to Lille, destroyed by an accident during World War I. No description published.[44]

Lines 1–6: P. Jouguet, *CRAI* 1902, 352–355 [Dittenberger, *OGIS* 740; M. L. Strack, *ArchPF* 3 (1906) 130–131 no. 7; *SB* 8932].

Complete: P. Collomp, *Recherches sur la chancellerie* (Paris 1926) 203–209 (copy of Jouguet) [*SB* 7259; *SEG* 8.466; Lenger, *C. Ord.Ptol.* 65 (lines 48–49); E. Bernand, *I. Fayoum* III 152; A. Bernand, *Prose* 32].

(A) ὑπὲρ βασιλέως Πτολεμαίου τοῦ κα[ὶ]
Ἀλεξάνδρου καὶ βασιλίσσης [Κ]λ̣[εο]-
[πάτρας] τῆς ἀδελφῆς, θεῶν [Φιλομη]τ̣ό̣-
ρων Σωτήρων καὶ τῶν τέκνων καὶ τῶν
[προ]γόνων, Ἥρ̣ωνι θεῶι μεγάλωι.
L[κ], Φ̣αμενῶ̣θ α.
(B) [βασι]λ[εῖ Πτολεμ]αίωι τ[ῶι] καὶ Ἀλεξάνδρωι θεῶι
[Φιλο]μήτο[ρι] χαίρειν Ἡ[ρ]ώδ[η]ς Χαριδήμου
[καὶ Ἡρ]ώδης Νείλου ἀμ[φ]ότεροι τῶν ἐκ τῆς θερ[α]-
πήας α σημ̣ήου· ὑπάρχοντος π[ρὸς] Μαγδῶ[λα]
ἱεροῦ Ἥρω̣νος θεοῦ μεγίστου, ἔτι δὲ καὶ ἱερ[ᾶς]
γῆς ἀχρήστων, ἐν αἷς καὶ προσκλύζει ὁ προσπαρα-
κείμενος αἰγιαλός, ἐν δὲ τούτωι ἀνακειμένω[ν]
σοῦ τε, μέγιστε βασιλεῦ, καὶ τῶν προγόνων
ἰκόνων γραπ̣τ̣ῶν, τῶν τε θυσιῶν καὶ σπονδῶν
καὶ τῶν ἄλλων τῶν νομιζομένων ὑπέρ τε σοῦ,
[ν]ικηφόρος βασιλεῦ, καὶ τῶν τέκνων διὰ νυκτὸς
καὶ ἡμέρας συντελουμένων, νυνὶ δὲ τοῦ προ-
δεδηλουμένου ἱεροῦ ἐγλελιμμένου τοῖς ὅλοις
χάριν τοῦ μὴ μόνον τοὺς ἐπὶ πραγμάτων τετα[γ]-
μένους συνεχέστερον παραγινομένους συκο-
φαντ⟨ί⟩ας καὶ σεισμοῦ{ς} ἕνεκα παρενοχλεῖν καὶ
παραλογεύειν τὸ σημαινόμενον ἱερόν, ἀλλὰ

42. *P. Tebt.* 132; other references to the Heroon at E. Bernand, *I.Fayoum* III p. 47.

43. The Magdola reliefs are known only from the brief description of Jouguet (355–357); for Theadelphia, Breccia 110–113 and pls. 57–59; E. Kantorowicz, *Selected Studies* (Locust Valley 1965) 8.

44. Jouguet, *Bull.Univ.Lille* II.6 (1902) 244, in a catalogue of an exhibit of the finds, mentions a photograph but does not reproduce it. I am grateful to Thomas Drew-Bear for a copy of this publication.

καὶ ἐν ταῖς γινομέναις παρ' ἕκαστον ἐν τῆι
κώμηι λογείαις ἐπιχιρ̣[ε]ῖν τοὺς ἐκ τού[τ]ου ἱερεῖς
πράσσειν παρὰ τὸ καθῆκον τὸ ὅμοιον· τὸ δ' ὅλον
οὐ προσηκόντως ἐπιτηδεύουσιν ἀπαιτεῖν
[τ]ῆς διασαφουμένης χέρσου ἱερᾶς γ̣ῆς τό τε ∟θ
καὶ τὸ ν̣α̣ύβ̣ιον· διὸ δὴ ἀξιοῦμεν τὸν εὐχά-
ριστον καὶ θεότατον βασιλέα, καθ' ἣν ἔχεις
πρὸς τὸ θεῖον εὐ[σ]έβειαν, ἐπιχωρήσαντα ἡ-
μ[ῖν] διὰ προστάγματος εἶναι τὸ μηνυ-
όμενον ἱερὸν ἄσυλον καὶ ἀναθεῖναι στήλας
λιθίνας ἐκκεκολαμμένας τοῖς θ' Ἑλληνικο[ῖς]
καὶ ἐνχωρίοις γράμμασιν πρὸ τοῦ λιθίνου προ-
πύλου τοῦ ἱεροῦ, προστάξαι Πτολεμαίωι τῶι
συγγενεῖ καὶ ὑπομνηματογράφωι καὶ ἐπιστρα-
τήγωι γράψαι Λυσανίαι τῶι συγγενεῖ καὶ στρα-
τήγωι τοῦ νομοῦ κατακολουθήσαντα τοῖς
ἠξιωμένοις μηδενὶ ἐπιτρέπειν πράσσειν
μηδὲ παραλογεύειν μηδὲ εἰσείναι εἰς τὸ
ἱερὸν μήτε ἡμᾶς μήτε τοὺς ἁγνεύοντας ἱερεῖς
μηδὲ τὸν προφήτην ἀπαιτεῖν μηθὲν μη[δὲ]
παρενοχλεῖν κατὰ μηδένα τρόπον μηδὲ μ̣ὴ̣ν̣
τῆς ἱερᾶς ἀχρήστου παρευρέσ̣ει ἠτ⟨ιν⟩ιοῦν, ὅπως
πολλῶ̣ι μᾶλλον προθυμότερον τὰ νομιζόμενα
ἐπι[τέ]λωσει αὐτοί τε ἐσόμεθα π[ε]φιλανθρωπημέν[οι.]
(C) Λυσ[αν]ίαι· μηδενὶ ἐπιτρέπειν εἰσβιάζεσθαι εὐτύχε[ι.]
εἰς τὸ ἱερόν. ∟κ, Ἁθὺρ ιη.
(D) τῶι ἐπιστάτει· κατακολουθεῖν τοῖς προστε-
ταγγμένοις. ∟κ, Μεχεὶρ ι:

2–3 Strack, Dittenberger: [Κ]λ[εοπάτρας | Βερενίκης?] Jouguet. 5 Jouguet: [ἐκ]γόνων Dittenberger. 10 ΜΝΟΥ, 15 ΓΡΑΠΠΩΝ the copy. 24: ἑκάστ⟨ω⟩ν Wilhelm (*SEG*). 26: {τὸ ὅμοιον} del. Wilhelm. 28: τό τε (ἔνατον) Wilhelm. 29: ἀξιοῦμέν ⟨σε⟩ Wilhelm. 41: for εἰσιέναι; cf. **221**.22. 45 ΡΕΞΕΙ, 46 ΛΛΟΙ the copy.

. . .

(A) In behalf of King Ptolemy also called Alexander and Queen Cleopatra his sister, the Mother-loving Savior Gods, and of their children and ancestors, to Heron greatest god. Year [20] Phamenoth 1. (B) To King Ptolemy also called Alexander, Mother-loving god, greetings from Herodes son of Charidemus and Herodes son of Nilus, both of the troop of the first division: as there is at Magdola a temple of Heron, greatest god, and also derelict sections of the sacred land, on which the bordering shoreline washes, and in the temple are painted images of you, greatest king, and your ancestors, with sacrifices and libations and the other rites in behalf of you, victory-bringing king, and your children celebrated night and day; but as now the aforesaid temple has been wholly forsaken, not only because officials continually come to accuse and intimidate so as to harass and extort from the aforesaid temple, but also because in the collections that happen continually in the village they try to tax the priests from this (temple), contrary to what is just, and in general they are always improperly demanding of the a foresaid derelict sacred land the ninth (?) and the cubit tax: therefore we ask the most gracious and divine king, by the piety you have toward the divine, to grant us by edict that the aforesaid temple be inviolable, and to place stone steles inscribed in Greek and native writing before the stone propylon of the temple, to order Ptolemy your relative and *hypomnematographos* and *epistrategos* to write to Lysanias your relative and *strategos* of the nome that, conforming to the request, he allow no one to make collections or extort or enter the temple and demand anything of us or the officiating priests or the prophet or to disturb them in any way, or any of the derelict sacred (land) on any excuse, so that many may the more eagerly celebrate the rites and we ourselves may be benefited. (C) To Lysanias: direct that no one force his way in. Farewell. Year 20, Hathyr 18. (D) To the *epistates*: act in accord with the orders. Year 20, Mechir 10.

The petition, B, undated, was submitted presumably late in 95. The king's answer, written or spoken to Ptolemy, his secretary and *epistrategos* of the whole country, has not been recorded: we have in C the next stage, the secretary Ptolemy's instruction (as in **225** and **226**) to the nome *strategos* Lysanias on 2 December. In D Lysanias in turn notified the police chief at Magdola[45] on 22 February 94, nearly three months later. Whatever accounts for his delay,[46] the petitioners or the temple authorities (A: the dedicators do not identify themselves) dedicated the inscribed and decorated stele three weeks later, on 15 March. B through D represent a single papyrus, the one that reached the temple: that is, a copy of the petition was returned to them with the responses added. Probably the king's response is not included because it was oral.

The two soldiers are otherwise unknown (*Pros.Ptol.* II 3953–54); their rank is uncertain, but they are taken to be of the royal guard.[47] They include themselves in the sufferings of the temple (ἡμᾶς, 42); evidently they bore a relation to the temple and its authorities that was more than that of mere worshippers. It may

45. Here as in the other Ptolemaic texts, the *epistates* will be the village ἐπιστάτης τῶν φυλακιτῶν or ἀρχιφυλακίτης (cf. Wilcken, *Grundzüge* I 412; E. Lavigne, *Studia Hellenistica* III [Louvain 1945]). The usual procedure, common in the enteuxis papyri, is for the *strategos* to write to him to execute a police action (e.g., *P.Enteux.* 50).

46. Compare the four and a half months in **223**; cf. *Chrest.Wilck.* 159, more than three months.

47. For the expression in 9–10 see J. Lesquier, *Institutions militaires* (Paris 1911) 62 n. 3, 103 n. 9; cf. M. Launey, *Recherches sur les armées hellénistiques* II (Paris 1950) 861 n. 4. The number of the detachment was perhaps interchangeable with the name of the commander: see Wilcken, *UPZ* I 15.19–20 and on 14.23.

be that both were truly locals and worked for the god (cf. Perdrizet, *REA* 6 [1904] 159). The secretary Ptolemy (line 36) cannot be further identified (*Pros.Ptol.* I 11, 200); Lysanias is attested several times, though reconstruction of his career is controversial.[48]

The petition, like several of those later, stresses the ruination of the temple by official misconduct, but not altogether consistently: either the ceremonies described at 15–18 are meant to be understood as past or intended, or the present complete abandonment (19) is exaggerated or refers to the general public as distinct from the clergy. Despite all the details on this misconduct, to summarize the substance of the edict a single expression was felt adequate, εἰσβιάζεσθαι εἰς τὸ ἱερόν (48–49).

12–13: On the largely useless *aigialos* see Schnebel, *Die Landwirtschaft* (Munich 1925) 346–347; M. Rostovtzeff, *Studien zur Geschichte des römischen Kolonat* (Leipzig/Berlin 1910) 166–170.

15: These painted images (cf. **222**.18) might be statues or frescoes. For the Ptolemies as *synnaoi theoi* see Nock, *Essays* I 204–214.

22: The emendation is justified by *C.Ord.Ptol.* 31.13: σεισμοῦ χάριν (183 B.C.); *UPZ* II 161.65–66: ἐπὶ συκοφαντίαι καὶ σεισμῶι (119).

24: For παρ' ἕκαστον see *C.Ord.Ptol.* 62.15; 63.3, 10.

28: A tax called the "ninth" (so Wilhelm) is otherwise unknown; Collomp thought the symbol to be the drachma sign. I have wondered if we have ⟨ι⟩θ, that is, the tax arrears from the preceding year (19), but that seems too general to be put in parallel to the *naubion.* The *naubion* is familiar, an offshoot of the corvée—enough labor, or the equivalent in capital, to clear a set length of dike.[49]

35: Despite the provision here, only Athribis has yielded a bilingual *asylia* inscription. The same provision is found at *C.Ord.Ptol.* 75.6 (Cleopatra).

In effect *asylia* here is defined as fiscal immunity. What does this edict add to the immunities that all temples in Egypt enjoyed? Probably ambiguous matters, for instance, the priests' collection money, are here made unambiguously immune. There is no mention of protection of refugees from seizure by state officials—asylum in the Roman sense; but their tax liability while in a temple could be regarded as an ambiguous matter that the exclusion of the state's force majeure would render moot. One thinks of the ambiguous and debated taxability, in America, of parking lots owned by churches and golf courses owned by universities: for such disputable items, a blanket immunity from the head of state is a useful thing.

48. *P.Yale* I p. 171; the arguments there are disputed by L. Mooren, *Aulic Titulature in Ptolemaic Egypt* (Brussels 1975) 87. On the Ptolemaic *hypomnematographoi* see J. E. G. Whitehorn, *Aegyptus* 67 (1987) 101.

49. J. G. Smyly, *P.Petrie* III pp. 339–347; *O.Wilck.* I pp. 259–263; S. L. Wallace, *Taxation in Egypt* (Princeton 1938) 59–61.

Theadelphia

Theadelphia, at Batn Harit on the southwest of Lake Moeris, was one of the lesser villages of the Fayum. Yet on our evidence it can show no fewer than four temples declared inviolable. Its immediate neighbor Euhemeria had two or more, the rest of the Fayum one—this despite extensive excavations at other and more important Fayum towns. Some local rivalry may be the cause. The excavators found traces of seven temples,[50] but only one of the four mentioned in the inscriptions can be assigned to a known structure. No papyri of the first century B.C. survive from the site, but late Ptolemaic Theadelphia is comparatively rich in inscriptions.[51]

TEMPLE OF ISIS SACHYPSIS

The priests of Isis Sachypsis seek *asylia* for her temple. As at Magdola, the argument is for the continuity of the worship of the king. But here the threat is portrayed as riotous individuals seizing suppliants, not as magistrates collecting taxes unjustly. Again it would seem that such behavior, so described, is already illegal. "Isis of the sickle" recurs in a dedication at Theadelphia (θεᾶς μεγίστης Σαχύψεως).[52]

221. Ptolemy X, 93 B.C.

Two copies, limestone steles found at Batn Harit in 1917, now in the Greco-Roman Museum at Alexandria. Inv. 20858: two joining pieces, h. 1.27, w. 0.58; inv. 21747: h. 1.30, w. 0.61. I give the text and line divisions of the better preserved, 20858; the other, 21747, cut by a different hand, has many errors and omissions (I underline what it alone preserves).

G. Lefebvre, *ASAE* 19 (1919) 40–46 [von Woess, *Asylwesen* 246–247 (20858); *SB* 6152, 6153; Lenger, *C.Ord.Ptol.* 66 (lines 35–36)]; E. Bernand, *I.Fayoum* II 112, 113 [A. Bernand, *Prose* 33–34].

Photographs: Lefebvre pls. 1, 2; E. Bernand pls. 17, 18.

(A) ἄσυλον κατὰ πρόσταγμα· ᾧ μὴ πρᾶγμα.
(B) βασιλεῖ Πτολεμαίωι τῶι καὶ Ἀλεξάνδρ̣ω̣ι̣
θεῶι Φιλομήτορι χαίρειν
οἱ ἱερεῖς Ἴσιδος Σαχύψιος θεᾶς μεγίστης
τῆς πρώτως ἐπιφανείσης, ἱεροῦ τοῦ
ὄντος ἐν Θεαδελφείαι τῆς Θεμίστου
μερίδος τοῦ Ἀρσινοΐτου· τοῦ διασαφουμέ-
νου ἱεροῦ ὄντος ἁγίου ἔτι ἀπὸ τῶν προγόνων

50. Lefebvre, *ASAE* 19 (1919) 58–59.

51. E. Bernand, *I.Fayoum* II pp. 1ff.; Jouguet, *P.Thead.* pp. 6–25; Breccia, *BSRAA* 16 (1918) 91–118; Calderini, *Dizionario* II 240–248.

52. *I. Fayoum* II 121 (A.D. 93). On the epithet see H. J. Thissen, *ZPE* 20 (1976) 279–282.

σου, μέγιστε βασιλεῦ, καὶ τιμῆς καὶ προεδρείας καὶ κατὰ τοὺς διαγεγονότας χρόνους τετευχότος, νυνὶ δὲ ἔνιοι τῶν ἀσεβεῖν ἐνχειρούτων παρὰ τὸ καθῆκον ἀναστρεφόμενοι οὐ μόνον ἐγβιάζονται τοὺς εἰς τοῦτο καταφεύγοντας ἱκέτας, ἀλλὰ καὶ διὰ χειραψίας καὶ τῆς χειρίστης βίας ἀτακτότερον εἰσοδεύοντες ἀφόσια μὲν τελοῦνται ἀσεβήματα παρ' ἣν ἔχεις, θεότατε βασιλεῦ, πρὸς τὸ θεῖον εὐσέβειαν, μάλιστα πρὸς τὴν θεὰν Ἶσιν, διὸ δεόμεθά σου τοῦ νικηφόρου θεοῦ, εἰ δοκεῖ, ἐπιχωρῆσαι ἄσυλον ὑπάρχειν τὸ διασαφούμενον ἱερόν, καὶ προθεῖναι στήλας λιθίνας ἐκ τῶν τεσσάρων ἀνέμων, κυκλόθεν τοῦ ἱεροῦ πήχεσιν πεντήκοντα, ἐχούσας ἐπιγραφὰς ἐνδόξως ὧι μὴ πρᾶγμα μὴ εἰσίναι, ὑπέρ τε σοῦ, μέγιστε βασιλεῦ, εἰς τὸ μηδένα εἰσβιάζεσθαι τρόπωι μηδενί, τοὺς δὲ παρὰ ταῦτα ποιοῦντας ἐνέχεσθαι ἱεροσ[υλίαι] καὶ πείπτειν ὑπ[ὸ πι]κρότεραν διάληψιν· προσταγέντος Λυσα[νίαι] [τῶι] συνγενεῖ καὶ στρατηγῶι τοῦ νομ[οῦ], κατακολουθήσαντα τοῖς προστεταγμένοις ἐᾶσαι ἡμᾶς ἐπιτελεῖν τὰ ἠξιωμένα, ὅπως πολλῷ μᾶλλον αἵ τε θυσίαι καὶ σπονδαὶ καὶ τἆλλα τὰ νομιζόμενα ὑπέρ τε σοῦ καὶ τῶν τέκνων καὶ τῶν προγόνων καὶ Ἴσιδι καὶ Σαράπιδι ἐπιτελεσθῇ, ἵν' ὦμεν εὐεργετη⟨μ⟩ένοι. εὐτύχει.

(c) Λυσανίαι· ποιεῖν.
Lκα, Μεχεὶρ ζ.

5 πρώτως 21747: 20858 corrected to πρώτης. Both copies omit N in 11 ἐνχειρούτων, I in 16 θεότατε, and E in 22 εἰσίναι.[53] 34: THNE 20858 (21747 is damaged here).

. . .

(A) Inviolable by decree, to whoever has no business here. (B) To King Ptolemy also called Alexander, the Mother-loving god, greetings from the priests of Isis Sachypsis, greatest goddess, the first manifested, of the temple in Theadelphia of the Themistus division of the Arsinoite nome: although the aforesaid temple was holy long since from the time of your ancestors, greatest king, and endowed with honor and respect also in the intervening times, but now some of those who would undertake sacrilege, behaving contrary to what is right, not only are forcing out the suppliants who take refuge in this (temple), but also, entering riotously with violent hands and basest force, are committing unholy sacrileges against the piety you have, most divine king, toward the divine, especially toward the goddess Isis,

53. Cf. **220**.41; for the form see Robert, *Collection Froehner* p. 70; *I.Smyrna* 728.10 with Petzl's references; *I.Ephesos* 3217b.44–45.

therefore we ask you the victory-bringing god to grant, if you think fit, that the aforesaid temple be inviolable, and to place about the temple stone steles toward the four winds, at a distance of fifty paces, having clear inscriptions, "he who has no business here is not to enter," for your sake, greatest king, so that no one force entrance in any way, and those who act in violation of these things are to be liable for sacrilege and fall under bitter judgment, orders being given to Lysanias your relative and *strategos* of the nome that he, in accordance with the orders, allow us to accomplish what we have asked, so that far the more the sacrifices and libations and other rites in behalf of you and your children and ancestors may be accomplished to both Isis and Sarapis, so that we may be benefited. Farewell. (C) To Lysanias: do it. Year 21, Mechir 7.

The undated petition will have been submitted around the beginning of 93; the petitioners, in contrast to **220**, make no mention of the king's secretary as intermediary of his order to Lysanias (26); so the order (36), dated to 19 February 93, may be the king's. As at Magdola, the priests have inscribed the countersigned papyrus text of their petition and added at the beginning of the stone (A) the headline text for which they had sought approval.

1: ᾧ μὴ πρᾶγμα seemed to the redactors an adequate abbreviation for ᾧ μὴ πρᾶγμα μὴ εἰσιέναι (22); for an example see p. 573. Lefebvre (44) rendered "order on which there is to be no infringement"; Wilcken (*Chr.* p. 99 n. 1) "inviolable temple in which there is to be no action." That the relative pronoun does not refer back to πρόσταγμα or ἄσυλον is shown by an inscription of 63 B.C.: βασιλέως προστάξαντος· τὰς ἱερὰς χρηματοθήκας, ᾧ μὴ πρᾶγμα (P. M. Fraser, *JEA* 56 [1970] 179–182), "The sacred treasuries (are not to be entered) by unauthorized persons."

9: Lefebvre and von Woess took the words to denote a legal distinction, temple "of the first class."

21: Inscriptions at fifty paces; this seems both vague (measured from what?) and a round number, so that the inscriptions may not mark the legal boundary; but if they do, the size is comparable to that stipulated at **223**.23.

TEMPLES OF ISIS ESEREMPHIS AND HERACLES CALLINICUS

The decision in favor of the temples of Isis Eseremphis and Heracles Callinicus is the only one extant for two places simultaneously. We do not know their location in Theadelphia; it may be that they abutted each other. Isis' epithet probably means "Isis of the rejuvenated year"; it recurs in the Praises of Isis, who was called "at White Cliff [on the Libyan coast] Aphrodite, Mouxin, Ἐσερέμφ[ι]ν̣."[54] Of the very Greek god Heracles Callinicus, the several

54. *POxy.* XI 1380.45–46; cf. J. Quaebegeur in *Das römisch-byzantinische Ägypten* (Mainz 1983) 67–75.

attestations in Egypt are scattered;[55] a dedication of a pylon in the 80s B.C. may derive from this temple.[56]

The petitioner was a military officer. Here as in the other Fayum documents, the reason offered is to maintain the uninterrupted worship of the gods and especially of the royal house. More than in the earlier texts, the implication is that the behavior of the meddlesome officials is already illegal, "contrary to the king's policy," and the grant of *asylia* is therefore "a harmless thing." It is of course always in a petitioner's interest to portray his request as nothing new or inconsistent with current policy.

222. Ptolemy XII and Cleopatra VI, 70 B.C.

Limestone stele found in a latrine pit during the excavations of 1912–13, 100 meters southwest of the temple of Pnepheros; now in the Greco-Roman Museum in Alexandria (21746); h. 1.42, w. 0.50; letters 0.02 in lines 1–11, then 0.015.

E. Breccia, *BSRAA* 15 (1914) 39–45 [von Woess, *Asylwesen* 247–249; *SB* 6236; Breccia, *Teadelfia* 126–127; Lenger, *C.Ord.Ptol.* 68 (line 53)]; E. Bernand, *I. Fayoum* II 114 [A. Bernand, *Prose* 37].

Photograph: Breccia 1914, pl. 1; 1926, pl. 76; E. Bernand pl. 19.

(A) ἄσυλον κατὰ προστεταγμένα.
(B) τῶι ἐπιστάτηι Θεαδελφείας· τῆς δε-
δομένης τοῖς βασιλεῦσιν ἐντεύ-
ξεως παρὰ Φιλίππου τοῦ Τιμοκράτους,
μετενηνεγμένης δὲ ἐφ' ἡμᾶς σὺν τῶι
γεγονότι πρὸς αὐτὴν χρηματισμῶι ἀν-
τίγραφον συνεσφράγισται· μηδενὶ οὖν
ἐπίτρεπε εἰσβιάζεσθαι εἰς τὰ δηλού-
μενα ἱερὰ ἀκολούθως τοῖς προστετα-
γμένοις. Lιβ, [Θ]ῶυτ κς.
(C) βασιλεῖ Π̣τ̣ο̣λ̣ε̣μ̣α̣ίωι καὶ βασιλίσσηι Κλεοπά-
τραι τῆι καὶ Τρυφαίνηι τῆι ἀδελφῇ θεοῖς Φιλο-
πάτορσι καὶ Φιλαδέλφοις χαίρειν
Φίλιππος Τιμοκράτους Κορίνθιος τῶν α φίλων
καὶ χ(ιλι)ά(ρχων) καὶ περὶ ὑμᾶς μαχαιροφόρων· ὑπάρχοντος
ἐν κώμῃ Θεαδελφείαι τοῦ Ἀρσινοΐτου ἱεροῦ Ἴσιδος
Ἐσερέμφιος θεᾶς μεγίστης καὶ ἑτέρου ἱεροῦ
Ἡρακλέους θεοῦ μεγάλου Καλλινίκου, ἐν οἷς καὶ ἰκό-
νες ὑμῶν ἀνάκεινται, τινῶν δὲ παρὰ τὴν ὑμε-
τέραν προαίρεσιν ἐπιτηδευόντων εἰσβιάζεσ-
θαι εἰς τὰ ἱερὰ καὶ τοὺς ἐν τούτοις ἀποτεταγμέ-
νους σκύλλειν, ὑμῶν δέ, μέγιστοι βασιλεῖς,
ἐπάνωθεν τὰ πρὸς τὸ θεῖον εὐσεβῶς διακειμέ-

55. See G. Ronchi, *Index theonymum* III 568; L. and W. Swinnen, *AncSoc* 2 (1971) 50 n. 15.
56. Swinnen 46–51; but see E. Bernand II pp. 45–46.

νων, μάλιστα δὲ πρὸς τὴν μεγίστην θεὰν ῏Ισιν, βόυλομαι μεταλαβεῖν τῆς ἐξ ὑμῶν πρὸς πάντας μεγαλοψύχου καὶ εὐεργετικῆς ἀπαντήσεως, ἐπιχωρηθέντος εἶναι τὰ σημαινόμενα ἱερὰ ἄσυλα, [οὐδ]ενὶ ἐφέσεως οὔσης ἐν τούτοις [βί]αιον διαπράσσεσθαι, πρὸς τὸ ἀπαραποδίστως τὰ νομιζόμενα τοῖς θεοῖς ἐπιτελεῖσθαι ὑπέρ τε ὑμῶν καὶ τῶν τέκνων· δέομαι ὑμῶν τῶν κοινῶν σωτήρων, ἀβλαβοῦς ὄντος τοῦ ἀξιώματος, εἰ δοκεῖ, ἐπιχωρήσαντάς μοι τὸ προκίμενον προστάξαι Ἀπολλωνίωι τῶι συγγενεῖ καὶ στρατηγῶι τοῦ νομοῦ, ὅπως οὗτος γινώσκων τὴν γεγονυῖαν τῶν ἱερῶν ἀσυλίαν κατακολουθῇ τοῖς προστεταγμένοις μηθενὶ ἐπιτρέπειν παρὰ ταῦτά τι ἐπιτελεῖν, οὐδενὶ ἐφέσεως οὔσης εἰσβιάζεσθαι εἰς τὰ ἱερὰ οὐδὲ τοὺς ἱερεῖς περισπᾶν οὐδὲ τοὺς αὐτόθι καταφεύγοντας ἐγβιάζεσθαι οὐδ' ἄλλο οὐδὲν ἀδίκημα συντελεῖσθαι, πρὸς τὸ ἀνεμποδίστως τὰ νομιζόμενα τοῖς θεοῖς καὶ τὰς ὑμῶν καὶ τῶν τέκνων θυσίας καὶ σπονδὰς ἐπιτελεῖν, ἀνατεθῆναι δὲ καὶ στήλας λιθίνας πρὸ ἑκατέρου ἱεροῦ κ̣ύκλῳ, δι' ὧ̣ν ἐνγραφήσεται τὰ ὑφ' ὑμῶν, μέγιστοι βασιλεῖς, προστεταγμένα, εἰς τὸ μηθὲν παρὰ ταῦτα ἐπιτελεῖσθαι, ἵν' ὦ πεφιλανθρωπημένος. εὐτυχεῖτε.

(D) Ἀπολλωνίωι· γινέσθω. Lια, Ἐπεὶφ κγ.

15 χ(ιλι)ά(ρχων) de Ricci: (χιλίων) Lesquier (both ap. Breccia 1914). 45: τὰς ⟨ὑπὲρ⟩ ὑμῶν von Woess.

. . .

(A) Inviolable in accordance with the commandments. (B) To the *epistates* of Theadelphia: included under my seal is a copy of the petition given to the kings by Philippus son of Timocrates, which was transmitted to us together with the ordinance responding to it. Therefore allow no one to force entry to the stated temples, in keeping with the commandments. Year 12, Thoth 26. (C) To King Ptolemy and Queen Cleopatra also called Tryphaena his sister, the Father-loving and Brother-loving gods, greetings from Philippus son of Timocrates, Corinthian, of the first friends and chiliarchs and your *machairophoroi*: as there are in the village Theadelphia of the Arsinoite nome a temple of Isis Eseremphis, greatest goddess, and another temple of Heracles, great god, of Beautiful Victory, in which also are images of you, and as certain persons are habitually, against your policy, forcing their way into the temples and harassing those serving in them; but as you, greatest kings, have ever been piously disposed toward the divine and especially toward the greatest goddess Isis, I wish to share in your great-hearted and beneficent attitude toward all, by your granting that the stated temples be inviolable, permitting no one to commit violence in them, so that the rites to the gods in behalf of you and your children may be celebrated without hindrance; I ask you, common saviors, the request being harmless, that, if you think fit, you grant me the aforesaid and give orders to Apollonius your relative and *strategos* of the nome, so that he, knowing the granted inviolability of the temples, act in accord with the commandments and allow no one to do anything to the contrary, with no one permitted to force entrance to the temples or disturb the priests or force out those who have taken refuge there or do any other injustice, so that they may celebrate without hindrance the rites for the gods and the sacrifices and libations of you and your children; and that stone steles be set up before each temple in a circle, on which will be written the orders given by you, greatest kings, that nothing be done contrary to these things, so that I may be benefited. Farewell. (D) To Apollonius: let it be done. Year 11, Epiph 23.

The petition, C, undated, probably was submitted around the middle of 70 B.C. The king's approval, D, instructing the *strategos* of the Arsinoite to take action, was added to the papyrus on 29 July; on 5 October the *strategos* with his own covering letter, B, sent the copy to the village police chief. Inscribing what they received from him, the temple authorities added the summary headline, A.

The *strategos* Apollonius is met in the next year (**224**.20; cf. *Pros.Ptol.* I 224). It is interesting that he does not name the police chief of Theadelphia (2). The petitioner Philippus was an officer of some dignity;[57] possibly he was born at Theadelphia or owned land there, whence his interest in these temples. He cites his Corinthian citizenship at a time when that city had not existed for eighty years.

22: On σκύλλειν, "harass," see Préaux, *ChrEg* 33 (1942) 141.

TEMPLE OF PNEPHEROS

The shrine of the crocodile god Pnepheros is the only inviolable temple in Theadelphia that has been identified (by its inscriptions and iconography) and explored.[58] Like the temple at Magdola, it was far more than a small chapel; yet it scarcely warrants comparison with the great temples of Egypt to which Horus of Athribis aspired. Such modesty, however, characterizes all the inviolable temples of the Fayum. Here the petitioners were the priests.

57. *Pros.Ptol.* II 4342; Mooren, *Titulature* 173–174, lists five men with these titles; cf. Launey, *Recherches* I 107, 108 n. 3.

58. Breccia, *Teadelfia* 97–131.

The honor that the Fayum towns and all Egypt gave to the crocodile god under his various names is familiar.[59] The temple of Pnepheros ("of beautiful face") stood near the center of the village, facing south and approached by a wide street. The temple was some twenty meters across and fifty deep, from its entrance flanked by sphinxes through successively smaller forecourts to the vestibule and altar; various side rooms opened onto the forecourts. A passageway (unexplored) led eastward from the first and largest forecourt, and perhaps more attendant small buildings opened onto this passageway. The petition speaks of "the temple and its appurtenant places" extending 117 paces east-west. For the north-south extent of *asylia* we are told no measurements, rather its limits in the Bubastieum on the south and the crocodile graves (stated to belong to the shrine) on the north; these extremes also were not excavated. Possibly the Bubastieum stood at the other end of the sacred way, which would imply an inviolable area of substantial length north-south. At the Sarapeum of Memphis, a sacred way a kilometer long separated the temple in the west from a complex of buildings in the east—and this eastern complex may not have shared in the immunity of the Sarapeum proper.[60]

Whatever the configuration of the inviolable space, it is noteworthy that in two copies the east-west dimension has been left uninscribed. Perhaps that figure was subject to dispute and on those two was only painted in.

223. Berenice IV, 57 B.C.

Three copies on limestone steles found in Theadelphia: Cairo Museum 40727, 40728, h. 1.20, w. 0.50–0.54; Alexandria Museum 20857, h. 1.55, w. 0.63. All are decorated in their crowning arc: on the first two, two crocodiles on altars flanking a shrine, within which is a bearded face; above is the conventional winged solar disk and asps. The third, its arc in a tighter circle, has a simpler design, the winged disk with asps; space has been left in the rectangular area below, perhaps for a now lost painted image.

40727, 40728: Lefebvre, *CRAI* 1908, 772–782; *ASAE* 10 (1910) 162–170 [*Chr. W.* 70 (composite); G. Arvanitakis, *BIE* V.6 [1912] 178–179; *SB* 1161 (40727)]; 20857: Lefebvre, *ASAE* 19 (1919) 54–56 [*SB* 6156; Lenger, *C. Ord.Ptol.* 72 (lines 37–38)]; E. Bernand, *I.Fayoum* II 116, 117, 118 [A. Bernand, *Prose* 42–44].

Photographs: Lefebvre 1910, pls. 1, 2 (40727, 40728); 1919, pl. 4 (20857); E. Bernand pls. 20–22.

I give a composite text with the line divisions of 40728, the best preserved.

(A) ἄσυλον κατὰ πρόσταγμα· ᾧ μὴ πρᾶγμα.
(B) τῶι ἐπιστάτηι Θεαδελφείας· τῆς δεδομένης

59. See Rübsam 14 for bibliography; H. Kees, *Der Götterglaube im alten Ägypten* (Berlin 1977) 12–19; M. Drew-Bear in *Mélanges Etienne Bernand* (Paris 1991) 227–234.

60. On the crucial passage in *UPZ* 6a, however, see W. Clarysse, *Enchoria* 14 (1986) 48.

τῆι θεᾶι βασιλίσσηι ἐντεύξεως παρὰ τῶν ἱερέων
τοῦ ἐν τῆι κώμηι Πνεφερῶτος θεοῦ μεγάλου, μετε-
νηνεγμένης δ' ἐφ' ἡμᾶς σὺν τῶι πρὸς αὐτὴν προστε-
ταγμένωι τὸ ἀντίγραφον ὑπόκειται· κατακολού-
θει οὖν τοῖς προστεταγμένοις. ἔρρωσο. Lβ, Φαμενὼθ γ.
(C) βασιλίσσηι Βερενίκηι θεᾶι Ἐπιφανεῖ χαίρειν
οἱ ἱερεῖς τοῦ Πνεφερῶτος θεοῦ μεγάλου κροκοδείλου
τοῦ ὄντος ἐν Θεαδελφείαι τῆς Θεμίστου
μερίδος τοῦ Ἀρσινοΐτου· τυγχάνομεν ἀδιαλεί-
πτως τάς τε θυσίας καὶ σπονδὰς καὶ καύσεις
λύχνων καὶ τἆλλα τὰ νομιζόμενα τοῖς θε-
οῖς ἐπιτελοῦντες ὑπέρ τε σοῦ καὶ τῶν προγό-
νων· προαιρούμενοι δὲ τὴν τοῦ ἱεροῦ ἀσυλίαν
ἐπικυρωθῆναι, ἵνα τούτου πρὸς αὔξησιν ἀγο-
μένου πολλῷ μᾶλλον τὰ νομιζόμενα
τοῖς θεοῖς ὑπέρ σου, καθότι πρόκειται, ἐ-
πιτελῆται, δεόμεθα, καθ' ἣν ἔχεις πρὸς
τὸ θεῖον εὐσέβειαν, προστάξαι τὸ ση-
μαινόμενον ἱερὸν καὶ τοὺς προσόντας
τόπους, λιβὸς μὲν ἐπ' ἀπηλιώτην πήχεις
ἑκατὸν δέ[κ]α ἑ̣π̣τ̣ά, νότου δ' ἐπὶ βορρᾶν ἀπὸ
τοῦ γειτνιῶντος ἐγ νότου Βουβαστιείου
μέχρι τῶν προσόντων ἀπὸ βορρᾶ τάφων τῶν
ἀποθειουμένων ἱερῶν ζῴων εἶναι ἀσύλους,
καὶ μηδένα καθ' ὀντινοῦν τρόπον ἐκ τούτων ἀπο-
βιάζεσθαι, τὸν δὲ φανησόμενον θανάτωι ἔνο-
χον εἶναι· ὑπὲρ ὧν καὶ γραφῆναι Διοσκουρίδηι τῶι
συγγενεῖ καὶ στρατηγῶι τοῦ νομοῦ προνοηθῆναι
ὡς διὰ στήλης τῆς πρὸς τοῖς δεδηλωμένοις
τόποις ἐνοικοδομηθησομένης ἐνγλυφήσεται
ὑπέρ τε σοῦ καὶ τῶν προγόνων ἡ τοῦ δηλουμένου
ἱεροῦ καὶ τῶν προσόντων τόπων ἀσυλία{ι} ἐπὶ τοῖς ἠξιω-
μένοις, καθάπερ ἐπὶ τῶν ὁμοίων γείνεται· τού-
του δὲ γενομένου ἔσται τὸ θεῖον μὴ παρατεθε-
ωρημένον· οὐ δυνάμενοι δὲ τοῦ ἱεροῦ ἀποσπᾶ-
σθαι, δεδώκαμεν τὴν περὶ τούτων ἐπιτροπὴν
Σωκράτηι τῶι μάλιστα τοῦ ἱεροῦ διὰ παντὸς
προισταμένωι, σχεθησομένωι τοῦ τῶν ἠξιω-
μένων ἀποτελέσματος, ἵν' ὦμεν εὐεργε-
τημένοι· διευτύχει.
(D) Διοσκουρίδηι· γινέσθω.
Lβ, Φαῶφι ιζ.

9: Πνεφερῶι 40727. 34: ἀσυλίαι in all copies.

. . .

(A) Inviolable in accordance with the commandment: to whoever has no business here. (B) To the *epistates* of Theadelphia: subjoined is a copy of the petition given to the goddess queen from the priests of great Pnepheros in the village and transmitted to us together with the command in reply. Therefore act in accord with the commandments. Farewell. Year 2, Phamenoth 3. (C) To Queen Berenice, manifest goddess, greetings from the priests of Pnepheros, great crocodile god, who is in Theadelphia of the meris of Themistus of the Arsinoite nome: we are those who celebrate unceasingly the sacrifices and libations and lighting of lamps and other rites to the gods in behalf of you and your ancestors. Desiring to have guaranteed the inviolability of the temple, so that when this is done for its increase the rituals may be the better accomplished to the gods in your behalf, as stated, we ask you, by the piety you have toward the divine, to order that the said temple and the appurtenant places (from west to east 117 paces and from south to north from the Bubastieum bordering on the south to the appurtenant tombs of the deified sacred animals on the north) be inviolable, and that no one in any way be forced from them, and that whoever is shown to do so be punishable by death; and that you write concerning these things to Dioscurides your relative and *strategos* of the nome to take care that the inviolability of the aforesaid temple and the appurtenant places, in keeping with the request, be inscribed, in behalf of you and your ancestors, on a stele erected at the aforesaid places, as is done in similar cases. When this is done, the divine will not be slighted. Being unable to be removed from the temple, we have given over the care of this matter to Socrates, the actual general supervisor of the temple, who will be responsible for carrying out the request, so that we may be benefited. Farewell. (D) To Dioscurides: let it be done. Year 2, Phaophi 17.

The undated petition (C) was approved by the queen, and on 22 October 57 an instruction was issued (B) to the *strategos* to execute her decision; on 7 March 56 he wrote (D) to the village police chief conveying the approved petition; after which the temple authorities inscribed the papyrus and added their headline (A). The queen acts alone: Ptolemy Auletes had been expelled from Alexandria in the previous year and would not be restored until 55 B.C.

16: The verb ἐπικυρόω has perhaps been chosen so as to suggest that nothing new is being granted, only a traditional right guaranteed (cf. Lefebvre 1908, 774 n. 6).

21: Parallel expressions for such outlying buildings at E. Bernand, *I.Fayoum* I 203 n. 57; so too at **218**.22; cf. Segre, *Iscr.Cos* EV3: τὸ ἱερὸν καὶ τὰ προσόντα αὐτῷ οἰκηματήρια.

37–38: For the verb, Dio 48.24.2: ἀπὸ τοῦ ἐν Ἐφέσῳ Ἀρτεμισίου ἀποσπάσας ἀπέκτεινε.

38–40: Socrates is taken to be official, the *epistates* of the temple (*Pros.Ptol.* III 7455); attested terminology is diverse, but cf. in *P.Tebt.* III 790.3 οἱ προεστηκότες τοῦ . . . τεμένους Ἀρσινόης (*Pros.Ptol.* 7448).

43: Dioscurides recurs in the undated *BGU* VIII 1764.16; cf. Mooren, *Titulature* 104.

Euhemeria

Euhemeria, modern Qasr el-Banat, was a small village on the southwest of Lake Moeris; its land bordered that of Theadelphia to the southeast. At least two temples in the village were declared inviolable; we have little other evidence from the last Ptolemaic century.[61] The two temples belonged to a crocodile trio and to Ammon; but the second petition invokes the *asylia* of "neighboring temples," and perhaps this plural should be taken literally and locally—other temples in Euhemeria and perhaps Theadelphia. The largest of the several temples seen by Grenfell and Hunt, on the edge of the village, belonged to Suchos. Our inscriptions were not found in situ, so the inviolable temples cannot be identified among the remains of the village.

One petition dates to May 69, the other to the period September 69/September 68. Both petitioners bear Greek ethnics (an Antiochene and an Athenian); the first identifies himself as a military officer. In 70 an officer of Corinthian origin had spoken for two temples in Theadelphia (**222**).[62] These three petitions show a good deal of formulary in common—βούλομαι, "the thing being harmless," the same desire to add to the temple buildings. Perhaps these petitions have in effect a common origin, and the three Greeks were all military men acquainted with one another and animated by a common desire to benefit the temples in their area—that is, that one petition suggested another. The other Theadelphia petitions come from the priests, the Magdola text from another soldier. It seems that the quest for inviolability in the Fayum had a rather restricted scope; the texts of 70–68 B.C. suggest a local campaign for the privilege.

TEMPLE OF PSOSNAUS, PNEPHEROS, AND SOXIS

The three crocodile gods were versions of the divinity Sobk who was honored throughout the Fayum. Psosnaus is not again heard of; a crocodile god Souxis uttered oracles at Karanis (*P.Lond.* III 1267d). Pnepheros we have seen at Theadelphia, and he shared a temple with other crocodile gods at Karanis and at Bacchias.[63] Evidently the three crocodiles had their distinct chapels and altars in the shared temple at Euhemeria.

61. Grenfell and Hunt, *P. Fayum* pp. 43–47; N. Hohlwein, *JJurP* 3 (1949) 63–99; E. Bernand, *I.Fayoum* II pp. 89–94; a land lease of 83 B.C.: *P.Iand.* VII 134.

62. A. E. Samuel, *From Athens to Alexandria* (Louvain 1983), in an admirable essay (75–101) on Ptolemaic religion, exaggerates in concluding from the priestly officeholders that Greeks "never interested themselves in the native cults" (99).

63. Ronchi, *Lexicon* 899–901; Rübsam 62–71, 100–101; A. Lukaszewicz, *Proc. XVI Congr. Papyr.* (Chico 1981) p. 360.

224. Ptolemy XII and Cleopatra VI, 69 B.C.

Limestone stele found at Euhemeria in 1912, now in the Alexandria Museum; h. 1.40, w. 0.67. Decorated arc at the top: the traditional winged disk with cobras, beneath which two figures stand back to back, clothed as pharaoh (scepter and crown), each offering a cake to a blue crocodile lying on an altar and crowned with a red disk.

G. Arvanitakis, *BIE* V.6 (1912) 175–179 no. 5 [*SB* 5827]; Lefebvre, *ASAE* 19 (1919) 46–50 [von Woess, *Asylwesen* 249–250; *SB* 6154; Lenger, *C.Ord.Ptol.* 69 (lines 29–30)]; E. Bernand, *I.Fayoum* II 135 [A. Bernand, *Prose* 38].

Photograph: Lefebvre pl. 3; E. Bernand pl. 23.

Cf. Wilcken, *ArchPF* 6 (1920) 419; H. Heinen in *Aspekte spätägyptischer Kultur* (Mainz 1994) 157–168.

(A) ἄσυλον κατὰ τὰ προστεταγμένα.
(B) βασιλεῖ Πτολεμαίωι καὶ βασιλίσσηι
Κλεοπάτραι τῆι καὶ Τρυφαίνηι θεοῖς Φιλο-
πάτορσι καὶ Φιλαδέλφοις χαίρειν
Ἀπολλοφάνης Βίωνος Ἀντιοχεὺς τῶν α
φίλων καὶ χιλιάρχων λογχοφόρων· ὑπάρχει
ἐν Εὐημερίαι κώμηι τοῦ Ἀρσινοΐτου τῆς
Θεμίστου μερίδος ἱερὸν Ψοσναῦτος καὶ Πνεφερῶτο⟨ς⟩
καὶ Σόξιτος θεῶν κροκοδείλων ἐν ὧι καὶ ἀνάκεινṭ[αι]
τῶν προγόνων ὑμῶν εἰκόν⟨ε⟩ς· τούτων δὲ χάριν,
[ἐπεὶ] καὐτὸ ἱερὸν πεπαλαιῶσθαι καὶ τῶν εἰθισ-
μένων ἐπιτελεῖσθαι ὑπέρ τε ὑμῶν καὶ τῶν τέκνων
θυσιῶν καὶ σπονδῶν ἐμποδιζομένων, αὐτός τε
εὐσεβῶς διακείμενος πρὸς τὸ θεῖον καὶ προαιρού-
μενος ἀνοικοδομῆσαι τοῦτο σὺν τῶι περιβόλωι
ἀναθεῖναι δὲ καὶ ὑμῶν τῶν μεγίστων βασιλέων
[εἰκ]όνας πρὸς τὸ ἐπιφανεστ⟨ά⟩του ⟨τοῦ⟩ τόπου γενη-
[θέ]ντος πολὺ μᾶλλον τὰ νομιζόμενα τοῖς θεοῖ[ς]
ἐπιτελῆται, ἀξιῶ, τοῦ πράγματος ἀβαροῦς ὄντο[ς],
ἐὰν φαίνηται, π̣ρ̣οστάξαι περὶ̣ τ̣ούτων Ἀπο̣λ̣λω[νίωι]
τῶι συγγενεῖ καὶ στρατηγῶι τοῦ νομοῦ ἐπι-
χωρῆσαι ⟨ἡ⟩μῖν τὸ προκείμενον ἐπι[τε]λέσαι,
ὄντος ἀσύλου, μηδενὸς εἰσβιαζο-
μένου, μήτε τοὺς ἐν τῶι ἱερῶι ἱερεῖ[ς]
καὶ παστοφόρους καὶ τοὺς ἄλλο[υς]
παρενοχλοῦντ⟨ο⟩ς, ἐνκολαφθῆναι δ[ὲ]
τήν τε ἔντευξιν καὶ τὸ πρὸς αὐτὴν
προστεταγμένον· εὐτύχει.
(C) τῶι στρατηγῶι· ἐπιχωρῆσαι.
Lιβ, Φαρμοῦθι κθ.
(D) ἐπὶ λεσώνου Ἁρμοδίου τοῦ Ἀσκλη-
πιάδου Μακεδόνος τῶν κατοίκων ἱππέ(ων).

ἔγραψε Πτολεμαῖος Διδύμου
κοινὸς γραμματεύς.

8 end ΤΟΥ with ο above, 10 ΚΟΝΑΣ, 17 ΣΤΟΤΟΥΤΟΠΟΥ, 22 ΥΜΙΝ, 26 ΝΤΑΣ lapis. 25: Wilcken urged that a line has been omitted after this one, τοὺς καταφεύγοντας καθ' ὁνδηποτοῦν τρόπον, as **225**.19.

. . .

(A) Inviolable in accord with the commandments. (B) To King Ptolemy and Queen Cleopatra also called Tryphaena, Father-loving and Brother-loving gods, greetings from Apollophanes son of Bion, Antiochene, of the first friends and spear-bearing commanders: in the village of Euhemeria of the Arsinoite nome, meris of Themistus, is a temple of Psosnaus and Pnepheros and Soxis, crocodile gods, in which also are images of your ancestors. For these reasons, because the temple itself is decrepit, with the sacrifices and libations customarily celebrated in behalf of you and your children being hindered, and because I myself am piously disposed toward the divine and intent on rebuilding this (temple) with its peribolos and dedicating images of you, greatest kings, so that, with the place becoming most distinguished, the rites of the gods may be accomplished all the better, I ask, the matter being harmless, that if you think fit, give orders about this to Apollonius your relative and *strategos* of the nome, to grant to us that he fulfill the aforesaid, the temple being inviolable, with no one to force entry or harass the priests in the temple and the *pastophoroi* and the others, and the petition and the command in response to be inscribed. Farewell. (C) To the *strategos*: grant it. Year 12, Pharmouthi 29. (D) Under the administrator Harmodius son of Asclepiades, Macedonian of the katoikic cavalry: Ptolemaeus son of Didymus, public scribe, wrote this.

The undated petition of Apollophanes (B) was approved by the monarchs and directed to the nome *strategos* on 5 May 69 (C); returned to the village, the petition was then copied or inscribed by a local scribe, who signed his work (D), and the whole was given the usual headline (A).

5: Apollophanes (*Pros.Ptol.* II 4335), a soldier in the royal guard, holds a set of titles exactly paralleled only once (Mooren, *Titulature* 174), but he differs only in his weapon from Philip the Corinthian (**222**.15) at neighboring Theadelphia in the previous year.

22: ὑμῖν and ἡμῖν were pronounced the same and were frequently confused in writing. But Lefebvre and E. Bernand retain ὑμῖν and understand "order Apollonius to grant that I accomplish the matter put before you."

31: Harmodius (*Pros.Ptol.* II 2616, III 5380) was both a temple administrator and a military man (see Heinen's discussion). The λεσώνης, himself a priest, appears to have been elected annually by the priests of a temple: Roussel, *REG* 29 (1916) 173–180; F. de Cenival, *Les associations religieuses en Egypte* (Cairo 1972) 154–159; E. Bernand pp. 106–108; Pestman, *P.Tor.Amenothes* p. 101.

36–37: The same "public scribe" signed **225**. κοινὸς γραμματεύς does not seem to occur in other texts from Egypt. κοινός seems to exclude that he was a temple scribe (*Pros.Ptol.* III 7483ff.) or an army scribe (II 2400ff.). He may have been the mason who inscribed the stone rather than the writer of the papyrus.[64] The letters of the two inscriptions are virtually identical in shape, as one would expect of such proximity of space and time; but in the earlier the mason cuts rather a finer line and decorates his letters with small serifs not found in the second inscription. So it may be that we have two masons, and Ptolemaeus was the village scribe, γραμματεὺς κώμης, copying the papyrus. A copy was perhaps needed: Apollophanes will have retained his, and the temple authorities will have wanted a copy. Whether Ptolemaeus was mason or scribe, the ἐπί clause must mean that in this commission he was working "for" the temple superintendent Harmodius.

TEMPLE OF AMMON

Ammon, whom tradition associated with the sun and with royalty, was worshipped throughout Hellenistic Egypt, although in the Fayum he was not especially prominent. The stele concerned with the cult at Euhemeria was not found in situ, and the temple of Ammon could not be identified among the remains.

The larger fragment was reused in the house of a man active by the 90s A.D. If we could be sure that its reuse dates from his lifetime and that the temple did not simply replace the old inscription with a new one, this reuse of the stone might suggest cancellation of the temple's inviolability in Roman times.

225. Ptolemy XII, 69/8 B.C.

Limestone stele in two joining fragments found in 1898–99 and 1913 at Qasr el-Banat, now in the Cairo Museum (33037); h. 1.25, w. 0.52; letters 0.012–0.022. The crowning arc is not decorated.

Lines 12–38: Grenfell and Hunt, *P.Fayum* pp. 47–50 [Strack, *ArchPF* 2 (1903) 555–557 no. 38; Dittenberger, *OGIS* 736]; J. G. Milne, *Catalogue général: Greek Inscriptions* (Oxford 1909) 10 no. 33037 [*SB* 5219]. Lines 1–11: Lefebvre, *ASAE* 13 (1914) 221–224. Complete: Lefebvre, *ASAE* 19 (1919) 50–53 [von Woess, *Asylwesen* 250–252; *SB* 6155; Lenger, *C.Ord.Ptol.* 70 (line 36)]; E. Bernand, *I.Fayoum* II 136 (collation, and copy of de Ricci) [A. Bernand, *Prose* 39].

Photograph: lower fragment, Grenfell and Hunt pl. 8; complete, Lefebvre 1914, pl. 2; E. Bernand pls. 24–25.

Cf. Wilhelm, *Beiträge* (1909) 223–224; Wilcken, *ArchPF* 6 (1920) 419; Lefebvre, *ASAE* 20 (1920) 249; R. Scholl, *C.Ptol.Sklav.* I pp. 301–303.

(A) ἄσυλον κατὰ τὰ προστεταγμένα.
(B) βασιλεῖ Πτολεμαίωι θεῶι Φιλοπάτορι καὶ
Φιλαδέλφωι χαίρειν Διονυσόδωρος

64. Several signed inscriptions come from Theadelphia: *I.Fayoum* II 121, 122, 124, all undecorated dedications. See Robert, *Op. min. sel.* I 597–598.

Ἀθηνοδώρου Ἀθηναῖος· ὑπάρχει{ν} ἐν Εὐ-
ημερίαι τοῦ Ἀρσινοΐτου ἱερὸν Ἄμμωνος
καὶ τῶν συννάων θεῶν συμπεπτωκὸς
καὶ τοῖς ὅλοις ἐξηρημωμένον. βούλομαι
ἐπ' αὐξήσει τῶν τοῖς θεοῖς ἀνηκόντων
ἀνοικοδομῆσαι τοῦτο τοῖς ἰδίοις ἀνηλώ-
μασι καὶ ἐπιγράψαι ὑπέρ σου, δέσποτα
βασιλεῦ, ὅπως αἵ τε [θ]υσίαι καὶ αἱ [σπ]ονδα[ὶ]
ἐπιτελῶνται, κτ[ι]σθέντος τοῦ σημαι-
νομένου ἱεροῦ ὑπέρ τε σοῦ καὶ τῶν προ-
γόνω[ν σ]ου, μενούσης καὶ τῆς παρὰ
τῶν πλησίων ἱερῶν συνκεχ[ω]ρ̣ημένης
ἀσυλίας, μηδενὸς εἰσβ[ιαζο]μένου,
μηδ' ἐκσπᾶν τοὺς ἐν τῷι̣ [ἱερῶι] κ̣α̣ὶ̣
παστοφόρους καὶ τοὺς ἄ̣λ̣λ̣ο̣υ̣ς̣
τοὺς κ̣α̣τ̣α̣φεύγοντ̣α̣ς̣ καθ' ὁνδηπο-
τοῦν τρόπον· δέομαι σ̣οῦ τοῦ νικη-
φόρου θεοῦ, εἰ δ[οκ]εῖ, ἀβ[λαβ]οῦς τοῦ
πράγματος ὑ[π]ά[ρ]χοντος, [καθ' ἣν]
ἔχεις πρὸς τὸ θεῖον εὐ[σέβ]ει[αν,] π̣ροσ-
τάξαι Θήριδι τῶι συγγενεῖ καὶ ὑ[π]ομνημ-
ματογράφωι ὅπως γράψῃ τῶ[ι] τ[ο]ῦ νομοῦ
στρατηγῶι καὶ οἷς καθήκ[ει, ε]ἰδὼ⟨ς⟩
πο[ιού]μ̣ενον τὰ τῆς ἀναν̣[εώσεω]ς,
προν[ο]ηθῆναι ὡς Μ̣ΕΤ̣ΑΤ . . Λ̣ . ἀσυ-
λίας τόπον, ἢ ἐνκ[ολ]α[φθ]ή[τω ἐν τ]ῆι
ὑπ' ἐμοῦ στήληι ἀνατεθεί[σηι]
περιέχουσα τῆς ἐντε[ύ]ξεως
καὶ τ⟨οῦ⟩ πρὸς αὐτὴν χρηματισμοῦ
τὸ ἀντίγραφον· τούτου δὲ γενο-
μένου ἔσομαι εὐεργετημένος.
διευτύχει.

(C) ∟ιγ. Θήριδος· γεινέσθω.

(D) ἔγραψε Πτολεμαῖος Διδύμου
κοινὸς γραμματεύς.

18 ἄ̣λ̣λ̣ο̣υ̣ς̣ Milne: δ[ο]ύλ[ου]ς(?) Grenfell and Hunt. 21 ἀβ[λαβ]οῦς: or ἀβ[α-ρ]οῦς(?) Wilcken. 24 Θήριδι Wilhelm: Ἥριδι Grenfell and Hunt. 26–27 Dittenberger: ΔΩΕ lapis, ἐπο[ψά]μενον Lefebvre. 27 end E. Bernand: ἀν[ιερώσεω]ς Dittenberger. 28: προν[οή]σῃ ⟨γρ⟩α⟨φῆς⟩ εἰ⟨ς⟩ τ[ὸν τῆ]ς ἀ. Dittenberger. 29, 30 Dittenberger. 32: ΤΗΣ lapis.

. . .

(A) Inviolable in accord with the commandments. (B) To King Ptolemy, Father-loving and Brother-loving god, greetings from Dionysodorus son of Athenodorus, Athenian: in Euhemeria of the Arsinoite nome is a temple of Ammon and the gods who share his temple, collapsed and entirely abandoned. For the increase of what pertains to the gods, I wish to rebuild this at my own expense and inscribe it in your behalf, mighty king, so that the sacrifices and libations may be celebrated, the said temple having been founded in behalf of you and your ancestors, and with the inviolability that has been granted applying from (?) the neighboring temples, with no one to force entry or disturb in any way those in the temple or the *pastophoroi* or others who take refuge. I ask you, the victory-bringing god, if you think fit, the matter being harmless, in accord with the piety you have toward the divine, to order Theris your relative and *hypomnematographos* to write to the *strategos* and those whom it concerns, knowing that I am carrying out the rebuilding, to take care that ... place of *asylia*, which is to be inscribed on the stele set up by me, containing the copy of the petition and the response to it. When this happens, I shall be benefited. Farewell. (C) Year 13: from Theris: let it be done. (D) Ptolemaeus son of Didymus, public scribe, wrote this.

The stages differ from **221–223** but resemble **220** in adding the *hypomnematographos* between king and *strategos*. The only date is that of the royal approval, year 13 = September 69/September 68.

14–16: The statement and substance are unparalleled, and unclear: Grenfell and Hunt thought it an assurance that the *asylia* granted to neighboring temples will remain undisturbed; Dittenberger, that the *asylia* has been agreed to in advance by the neighboring temples and royal confirmation is being sought; Lefebvre, that the temple should have the same *asylia* as the neighboring temples. Dittenberger's view conforms better to the Greek as it is, Lefebvre's to the thinking that we would expect. The phrase ought to introduce what follows, the asylum of this temple, rather than to justify that of others; and that other temples might first "grant" a privilege being sought from the king seems improbable. There are so many grammatical errors in this text that I am inclined to Lefebvre's view and have offered a strained translation of μένω to try to convey it, but without much confidence.

24: Theris may be attested again, but this is disputed; cf. *Pros.Ptol.* I 9 and 262 with addenda on *P.Yale* I 57.

28: We need here a verb with Theris as subject, and we expect τὸν τῆς ἀσυλίας τόπον; so little space is available that a mason's omission seems implied: for example, μετὰ τ[αῦτ]ạ ⟨οὐδεὶς εἰσβιάζηται εἰς⟩ τὸν τῆς ἀσυλίας τόπον.

Temple of Isis at Ptolemais

Ptolemais Hermiou (modern al-Manshiah), metropolis of the Thinnite nome, was the one Greek city south of the Delta—founded by Soter, subject of a book by the scholar Ister.[65] Inscriptions reveal something of its Greek cultural life—including the grant of *asylia*, which though for an Egyptian goddess is entirely

65. Ath. 478B (*FGrHist* 334 F 47). See G. Plaumann, *Ptolemais in Oberägypten* (Leipzig 1910).

Greek as a work of art and greatly in contrast with the other stones in this series from Egypt. The remains of the city, easily visible and extensive a century ago,[66] have not been excavated or even surveyed.

226. Cleopatra VII, 46 B.C.

Granite stele with pediment and acroteria, acquired ca. 1895 by Golenischchev at al-Manshiah; taken to St. Petersburg, the stone passed to the Alexander III Museum of Fine Arts (later the Gosudarstvennyi Russki Muzei); h. 0.99, w. 0.56; elegant and regular letters, 0.02–0.025.

E. Pridik, *ZhournMinistNarodProsv* n.s. 13 (January 1908) 9–16 no. 9 [Plaumann, *Ptolemais* 35–39, 88; W. Schubart, *Klio* 10 (1910) 54–55 n. 2; *ArchPF* 6 (1920) 342 (BC, lines 10–19); Lefebvre, *ASAE* 20 (1920) 249–250 (BC); *SB* 3926; Schroeter 64 (BC); Lenger, *C.Ord.Ptol.* 67 (BC); A. Bernand, *Prose* 36].

Photograph: Pridik, whence PLATE 9.

(A) Θέων τῆι πόλει τῶν Πτολεμαιέων
χαίρειν καὶ ἐρρῶσθαι·
τῆς μετενηνεγμένης ἐφ' ἡμᾶς
ἀπαγγελίας σὺν τῶι πρὸς αὐτὴν
προστεταγμένωι ἀντίγραφον
ὑπόκειται, ὅπως εἰδότες καταχ[ω]ρίσητε
ἐν τῶι παρ' ὑμῖν δημοσίωι ὡς καθήκει·
καὶ ἑαυτῶν ἐπιμελόμενοι, ἵν' ὑγιαίνητε,
ἔρρωσθε. Lς, Φαμενὼθ ιβ.
(B) Θέωνι·
ῥηθήτω οἷς καθήκει τὸ κατεσκευ-
ασμένον ὑπὲρ τῆς ἡμετέρας σωτηρίας
ὑπὸ Καλλιμάχου τοῦ ἐπιστρατήγου
Ἰσιδεῖον ἀπὸ νότου Πτολεμαΐδος
ἀτελὲς καὶ ἄσυλον εἶναι σὺν τοῖς
περὶ αὐτὸ κατῳκοδομημένοις
οἰκητηρίοις μέχρι τοῦ τείχους
τῆς πόλεως.
(C) γινέσθω. Lς, Φαμενὼθ ε.

. . .

(A) Theon to the city of the Ptolemaeans, greetings: subjoined is a copy of the proclamation transmitted to us together with the command in response, so that you may know it and deposit it in your public archives as is fitting. Taking care of yourselves, that you be well, farewell. Year 6, Phamenoth 12. (B) To Theon: let the relevant persons be told that the temple of Isis built in behalf of our well-being by Callimachus the *epistrategos* south of Ptolemais is to be tax-free and inviolable together with the houses built around it as far as the wall of the city. (C) Let it be done. Year 6, Phamenoth 5.

66. Cf. G. Maspero, *RA* III.2 (1883) 172–173.

The monarch is Cleopatra, and the two dates are 7 and 14 March 46. Because the stone does not record the petition, it is less informative than most of its predecessors. The queen's authorization (C) is transmitted together with a "proclamation" (B) to Theon, who (A) sends both to the civic government. The verbs ἀπαγγέλλω and ἀναγγέλλω are common in the Ptolemaic petitions: the king's decision, given to an official immediately to hand for the purpose, is said then to be "proclaimed" by this official to the relevant authority. So a third-century edict is headed βασιλέως προστάξαντος, Αἰσχύλου τοῦ παρὰ Σωστράτου ἀπαγγείλαντος Ζήνωνι.[67]

As Plaumann remarked, the week that separates the command from Theon's letter was not sufficient time for the document to go from Alexandria to the Thinnite: Theon must have been in Alexandria, and in fact we find him as intermediary for another edict of Cleopatra in 41 B.C.[68] Evidently a royal decision about a city-state did not go through the same chain of authority that linked the villages of the countryside to the king (all this on the assumption that the queen was in Alexandria at the time).

The temple of Isis obviously was outside the walled city, but apparently in its legal territory, as this benefaction is announced to the city.[69] Whether Callimachus built or merely refurbished the temple, we hear earlier of an 'Ισιεῖον καὶ τοὺς προσόντας ψιλοὺς τόπους, apparently therefore not within the city walls—possibly the same shrine.[70] On the sacred land were other buildings, as was typical. Even in this brief text we can see that a crucial issue for the temple was the collection of taxes.

Callimachus, patron of the temple who probably brought the matter to the queen's attention, was an important man.[71] His career spanned at least from 62 to 44/39, and he attained to *strategos* of the Thebaid and *epistrategos* of the Red Sea and Indian Ocean. He had already a substantial role in the city if he is rightly restored in an earlier inscription from al-Manshiah: a list of his offices in 49 B.C. gives, after his royal functions, the civic offices [ἀρ]χιπρύτανις [καὶ γυμν]ασίαρχος (*SB* 2264).

67. *C.Ord.Ptol.* 27.1–3; cf. 5.1, 6.1, 12.8, 13.4, 15.33 (these do not identify the recipient of the proclamation).

68. *C.Ord.Ptol.* 76; cf. Mooren, *Titulature* 141.

69. A. H. M. Jones, *Cities of the Eastern Roman Provinces*² (Oxford 1971) 305, after mentioning this inscription, writes: "There is no evidence to show whether the city possessed a territory, but the probabilities are against it."

70. *OGIS* 52 (not later than 87 B.C.), a list of cult places. One is an altar to some Egyptian gods that is expressly "outside the walls"; Wilcken (at Plaumann 58) speculated that Egyptian cults were not allowed within the city.

71. See R. Hutmacher, *Ehrendekret für den Strategen Kallimachos*, Beitr.klass.Phil. 17 (Meisenheim 1965); Bingen, *ChrEg* 45 (1970) 375–378 (*Pages d'épigraphie* [Brussels 1991] 119–122); *Pros.Ptol.* VIII p. 194; Mooren, *Titulature* 96.

The prominence of the spokesman for this temple, and the speed with which the matter was carried out, no doubt say something about the courtesies that the crown showed to the Greek city, even at this late date.

Unknown Temple in Egypt

227. Unknown author

Top of a limestone stele from Egypt now in the Museum of the University of Rome, no reported provenience; h. 0.31, w. 0.325; relief with two facing crocodiles on altars.

S. Donadoni, *Alessandria e il mondo ellenistico: Studi a Adriani* I (Rome 1983) 162–164 [*SEG* 33.1362].

Photograph: Donadoni pl. 27.3.

The editor reports that the traces of a line of writing at the bottom of the stone "do not oppose the restoration of ἄσυλον κατὰ πρόσταγμα."

Synagogue at Leontopolis (?)

The last document is doubtful from two points of view: it may not be a grant of asylum, and if it is, it may involve an ancient forgery. For a Jewish synagogue, a "queen and king" restore an earlier inscription of a Ptolemy Euergetes.

It is possible that the text of Euergetes is rhetorical and means no more than "holy synagogue." It has a close parallel in the dedicatory text of Nicomedes II for a precinct for his mother (**230**), and this too may be only a rhetorical flourish. Nonetheless, in the context (historical or alleged) of a Ptolemaic edict, I am inclined to take the word ἄσυλος seriously, and hence I include this text in the corpus.

The authors of the renewal, the "queen and king," are not Zenobia and Vaballath (Mommsen's extravagant notion, at a time when very little was known about Greco-Roman Egypt) but a Ptolemaic couple, almost certainly Cleopatra VII and her son Caesarion (so Bingen), under whom Roman troops helped keep order in Egypt, hence the Latin imprimatur.

The stone in question was first seen in Cairo in 1876, with no recorded provenience. It might well come from the Fayum like most other grants of asylum in Egypt, for a Jewish community is on record there already in the third century B.C.[72] But the inscription is already atypical in being Jewish, and in other respects. I believe that it comes from Leontopolis, thirty kilometers north of Cairo at Tell el-Yahudi in the southern Delta. The synagogue there was the famous surrogate of the Temple itself built there by the Jews settled at Leontopolis in the 150s, refugees from the Maccabean wars. If this is correct, the Euergetes whose text is renewed is necessarily Euergetes II (145–116 B.C.). Their claim of Euergetes' grant of asylum to the synagogue will be a fabrication of the first century B.C., in imitation of the report about the Temple in 1 Maccabees (above, p. 528). The Jews of Leontopolis, reliable troops, were able to press this claim ("renewing" a lost inscription of the founder Euergetes) upon Cleopatra as her need for soldiers grew in the 30s B.C.

228. Cleopatra VII and Caesarion

Alabaster stele seen in Cairo in 1876, now in Bode Museum in Berlin (inv. 7733); h. 0.44; Greek blockish and increasingly crowded, Latin large.

Miller, *RA* 30 (1875) 111–112 (squeeze); Mommsen, *EphEp* 4 (1881) 25–26 [Dessau, *ILS* 574; *CIL* III Suppl. 6583; Wilcken, *BPW* 16 (1896) 1493; M. Strack, *Dynastie der Ptolemäer* (Berlin 1897) 262 no. 130; T. Reinach, *REJ* 45 (1902) 163; Dittenberger, *OGIS* 129; Schürer, *Geschichte* III (1909) 41; *IGR* I 1315; *Chr.W.* 54; Diehl, *I.lat.Christ.* II 4936; Frey, *CIJ* II 1449; *SB* 8880; E. Gabba, *Iscrizione greche e latine per lo studio della Bibbia* (Marietti 1958) no. 8; D. M. Lewis, *CPJ* III p. 144; G. H. R. Horsley, *New Documents Illustrating Early Christianity* IV (Sydney 1987) 110.3; W. Horbury and D. Noy, *Jewish Inscriptions of Graeco-Roman Egypt* (Cambridge 1992) 125; A. Bernand, *Prose* 23].

Photograph: Frey p. 375 [Gabba pl. 1]; Horbury/Noy pl. 29.

Cf. Dessau, *ILS* III.2 (1916) p. CLXXI; J. Bingen in *Studia Paulo Naster* II (Louvain 1982) 11–16 (*Pages d'épigraphie* 45–50).

βασιλίσσης καὶ βασι-
λέως προσταξάντων,
ἀντὶ τῆς προανακει-
μένης περὶ τῆς ἀναθέσε-
ως τῆς προσευχῆς πλα-
κὸς ἡ ὑπογεγραμμένη
ἐπιγραφήτω·
βασιλεὺς Πτολεμαῖος Εὐ-
εργέτης τὴν προσευχὴν
ἄσυλον.
regina et
rex iusser(un)t.

72. I am grateful for this point to Claus Maresch, who will publish the papyri. I hope to discuss this inscription more fully elsewhere.

. . .

(Greek) By order of the queen and king, in place of the previously existing plaque concerning the dedication of the synagogue, let the following be inscribed: "King Ptolemy Euergetes (dedicated) the synagogue as an inviolable place." (Latin) The queen and king have commanded.

The implied feminine noun in line 7 must be πλάξ, meaning the old text; but the synagogue authorities have gone beyond the letter of the command (to reinscribe the old text) and reproduced the entire papyrus including the current decision. In this the inscription resembles the others from Egypt, which reproduce the whole dossier and not simply the king's few words. The progressive crowding of the Greek proves the unity of the inscription: whether or not another hand wrote the Latin, the writer of the Greek knew that he had to leave space for the large Latin warning.

1–2, 11–12: Only Cleopatra III (with several brothers) and VII (brothers, then son) are recorded to have used the sequence "queen and king" in their *acta*.

8: Compare μεταγραφήτω in the *prostagma* of Cleopatra and Caesarion *C.Ord.Ptol.* 75.5.

9–12: Egypt supplies no other instance of royal permission being sought to replace an inscription (but see on **186**); the reason, in my view, is that there was no original: in effect the Jewish community is obtaining a new privilege, asylum, for their synagogue, on the claim that this had been granted by Euergetes.

12: Mommsen knew of no parallel for this abbreviation. The use of Latin suggests that some of the authorities who were to respect this order knew Latin as their first language—the troops of Antony.

I conclude with a small stone of unknown provenience in Egypt that clearly was meant as an abbreviated boundary text for declared inviolability, although the crucial term is omitted.

Limestone stele, h. 0.45, w. 0.325, with incised relief showing the conventional solar disk and asps above a scene of pharaoh pouring a libation before Thoth; inscription below.

G. Nachtergael, *ChrEg* 69 (1994) 140–143.

ᾧ μὴ πρᾶγμα
μηθένα εἰσιέναι.

This is the essential message of the asylum edicts, as several of them make explicit. The stone might derive from one of the temples detailed above, but more likely it represents a case not independently known, for neither Thoth nor Hermes appears in the other inscriptions.

Rome

In 64 B.C. Cicero, stressing the importance of places that might be sold off under the proposed agrarian law, included temples: "There are public places of Rome, there are temples which no one has touched since the restoration of the tribunician power, some of which our ancestors wished to be refuges in time of danger" (*sunt enim loca publica urbis, sunt sacella quae post restitutam tribuniciam potestatem nemo attigi, quae maiores in urbe partim periculi perfugia esse voluerunt, Leg. agr.* 2.36). In reality, the immunity of sacred space from the law was not Roman usage,[1] and no temple can in fact be found providing suppliants legal inviolability.[2] Indeed, *provocatio* should in principle make asylum unnecessary, at least for Roman citizens.[3]

1. See Mommsen, *Römisches Strafrecht* (Leipzig 1899) 458–462; 459 n. 3 on Cicero's statement, which he took as a claim about attitudes, not law. Most of the arguments go back to G. F. Schoemann, *De Tullio Hostilio* (Greifswald 1847) 4–6. Cf. G. Wissowa, *Religion und Kultus* (Munich 1912) 474 n. 3; K. Latte, *Gnomon* 26 (1954) 19; D. van Berchem, *MusHelv* 17 (1960) 29–33; D. Weinstock, *Divus Julius* (Oxford 1971) 242–243, 395–397; G. Freyburger, *EtCl* 60 (1992) 139–151.

2. Occasions on which magistrates withdraw into a temple to escape the brickbats of a riot are on record, but no religious gesture is portrayed or implied, and it seems that any securable building would have done: e.g., App. *BCiv.* 2.11 (ὑπεξήγαγον: temple of Jupiter Stator); Plut. *Cat. min.* 28.3 (ἀπήγαγεν: temple of Castor, from the landing on its steps). Compare Piso in A.D. 69, fleeing to the temple of Vesta and protected *non religione nec caerimoniis* but by the charity of a slave there, until, discovered, he was killed in the doorway (*protractus Piso in foribus templi trucidatus*, Tac. *Hist.* 1.43). The murder there of Q. Mucius Scaevola, before the very statue of Vesta, was notorious; but Cicero cites it in his several lists of famous injustices, not specifically of sacrilege (references at *RE* 16 [1933] 440–441). Malalas (267 Bonn) says that there was a great uproar when it was learned that Domitian had been murdered in the temple of Jupiter Optimus Maximus (in fact he was killed in the palace).

3. I owe the point to Roberta Stewart; on *provocatio* see A. W. Lintott, *ANRW* I.2 (1972) 226–267; M. Humbert, *MEFRA* 100 (1988) 431–503.

Three places have come into the question: Romulus' "asylum" on the Capitolium, the temple of Divus Julius established in 42 B.C., and the temple of Diana on the Aventine. Romans, we are assured, were peculiarly sensitive about the inviolability of ambassadors (Diod. 36.15), and of course other persons such as tribunes and flamines. But such sacrosanctity derived from function, not place.[4]

THE ASYLUM ON THE CAPITOLIUM

The story was told that Romulus, in order to attract a population, reserved a space on the saddle of the Capitolium where fugitives from the law could be secure.[5] Here runaway slaves and criminals soon gathered—who then were made the new citizens. Scholars usually call this place by the loanword that the Romans eventually came to use, "the asylum on the Capitolium." But that Greek word is transparently a neologism for Romans. The Greek noun ἄσυλον was common only in Ptolemaic Egypt, where we first find it used of the Sarapeum in the 160s B.C.; its attachment to the place on the Capitolium and to the story of the origin of the Roman populace cannot be older than the impact of Greek culture and vocabulary upon Rome, presumably deriving from Egypt in this case.

In fact we know how the place was properly called in Latin: *inter duos lucos*. So Cicero (*Div.* 2.40), no further name being needed; and Dionysius (below) is explicit that this is what the place was named. In Augustan times writers begin to gloss that toponym with the Greek word indicating function, "as an asylum":

> Livy 1.8.5: *locum qui nunc saeptus escendentibus inter duos lucos est asylum aperit*, "the place which, now closed off to one ascending, is Between Two Groves he opened as an

4. We are not here concerned with other Roman gestures, such as the allied cities that could receive Roman exiles with impunity (see p. 30); this privilege was a provision of the treaties Rome had with these cities. About Rome itself, two rhetorical utterances: *sacrosanctam istam civitatem*, Apul. *Met.* 11.26; *Romae ... id est templo mundi totius*, Amm. Marc. 17.4.13; for *sacra urbs* in the inscriptions see Dessau, *ILS* III.2 p. 638. The occasional modern claim that the temple of Ceres by the Forum Boarium had the right of asylum is based on a fatuous etymology of Varro (*pandere, panem dare*), recounting that bread is given to those who flee to an asylum, which is always open; references at H. Le Bonniec, *Le culte de Cérès* (Paris 1958) 275.

5. Testimonia are gathered by P. Bruggisser, *Romulus Servianus* (Bonn 1987) 163–183; cf. W. A. Schröder, *M. Porcius Cato, Das erste Buch der Origines* (Meisenheim 1971) 178–181. The story is as old as Fabius Pictor; cf. H. Strasburger, *SBHeid* 1968.5 34. Servius ad *Aen.* 2.761 traces Romulus' gesture to the example of Athens and its welcoming of refugees, for which he cites Stat. *Theb.* 12.497ff. (the altar of Clementia); so too schol. Juv. 8.273: *secutus Atheniensium morem asylum in luco constituit.* On the place itself see T. P. Wiseman, in *Lexicon Topographicum Urbis Romae* I, ed. E. M. Steinby (Rome 1993) 130.

asylum." (Cf. 2.1.4: *illa . . . plebs transfuga ex suis populis sub tutela inviolati templi.*)
Vell. Pat. 1.8.5: *asylum inter duos lucos.*

No one before Tacitus calls it simply "the asylum."[6] So far our Latin evidence.

When Greeks write of the place, their vocabulary and conception are predictable, the creation of an "inviolable temple." According to Dionysius, this space, "which today is called in Latin 'Between Two Groves' (ὃ καλεῖται νῦν κατὰ τὴν Ῥωμαίων διάλεκτον μεθόριον δυεῖν δρυμῶν) Romulus made a temple with the right of asylum for suppliants (ἱερὸν ἀνεὶς ἄσυλον ἱκέταις)," building a ναός in it (2.15.4; cf. ἱερὸν ἄσυλον, 3.32.2). Strabo (5.3.2) knows geography but not architecture, with Romulus "designating as inviolable a precinct between the Arx and the Capitolium (ἀποδείξας ἄσυλόν τι τέμενος μεταξὺ τῆς ἄκρας καὶ τοῦ Καπετωλίου)" and granting the fugitives citizenship. Plutarch on the episode is revealingly vague: the Romans founded "a temple with the right of refuge for runaways, which they called of the god *Asylaios* (ἱερόν τι φύξιμον τοῖς ἀφισταμένοις ὃ θεοῦ Ἀσυλαίου προσηγόρευον) . . . saying that this guaranteed inviolability for all" (πᾶσι βεβαιοῦν τὴν ἀσυλίαν φάσκοντες, *Rom.* 9.3; cf. 20.1, τὸ ἄλσος . . . ἀσυλίας δεδομένης).

The lack of a proper name is matched by the lack of a cult: for it seems clear that this space was not sacred to any god.[7] Vitruvius and Ovid state that there was a temple of Veiovis here; but neither says plainly that the place of refuge belonged to him, and Veiovis does not figure in the story of Romulus' refugees.[8] Livy's account is devoid of religious features; it is later, in his general reference to the new people, that he uses the phrase "inviolable temple." Dionysius, even while he writes of an "inviolable temple," expressly disclaims knowing to what divinity it was dedicated,[9] and he mentions none of the requisite gestures of defining a *templum*—auspication, sacrifice, etc.; Plutarch's θεὸς Ἀσυλαῖος is unparalleled and unconvincing (and in any case not Latin).

6. Tac. *Hist.* 3.71.3: *iuxta lucum asyli* ; cf. Donat. ad *Aen.* 8.342–343: *lucum qui postea a Romulo Asyli nomen accepit.*

7. See Mommsen; cf. Wissowa 474; R. M. Ogilvie, *Commentary on Livy* (Oxford 1965) 62: "No particular deity presided over it"; Ogilvie dismisses such associations as late speculation. The annalist L. Piso Frugi wrote that "the god Lucaris (?) takes care of the place" (Servius ad *Aen.* 2.761 = frag. 4 Peter). Whatever name Piso wrote, it is unparalleled; in any case, the assignment looks like his attempt to solve a puzzle. See K. Latte, *Kleine Schriften* (Munich 1968) 838–839.

8. Vitr. 4.8.4: *aedis . . . inter duos lucos Veiovis*; Ov. *Fast.* 3.430 (Frazer ad loc. remarked the examples of purely secular places of refuge from the law). Neither says more than that there was a temple by the space. For the temple of Veiovis see E. Gjerstad, *OpRom* 9 (1973) 35–42; L. Richardson, *A New Topographical Dictionary of Ancient Rome* (Baltimore 1992) 406. A temple building was dedicated only in the 190s B.C., but there is evidence of worship here as early as the archaic period.

9. 2.15.4: ὅτῳ δὲ ἄρα θεῶν ἢ δαιμόνων οὐκ ἔχω τὸ σαφὲς εἰπεῖν.

In Rome, sacred space supplied no precedent or analogy for the right of sanctuary—hence the lack of a Latin word for this function. By contrast with Greece, where the god's jurisdiction supplants the city's in sacred space, this place "between two groves" seems rather conceived of as negative space, no-man's-land, subject to no law. If Romans eventually borrowed a Greek term, "asylum," to deal with this strange immunity and even came to assume that the space was sacred, they misled themselves.

Thus the place between the groves was anomalous in relation to both Greek and Roman usage—Greek because this place was not sacred, Roman because sacred places were not sanctuaries from the law. Nor does this right of refuge figure anywhere else in Roman history; apart from Romulus' first citizens, no one is said ever to have availed himself of the protection of the place.[10] The function of the *aition*, as we are told it, is limited to the one episode of the remote past, explaining the first gathering of the people; the *aition* is nowhere told in order to explain any present or enduring immunity. We should conclude that it had none: that this space did not in fact enjoy immunity from the law in historical times. The legendary immunity came to serve as precedent for the temple of Divus Julius (so Cassius Dio) to the extent that Romans believed their own political myths. It is not in the Romulus story but in this reenactment, the grant to Divus Julius, that we can see a parallel with the declared inviolability of the Hellenistic world, and an example of Hellenism at Rome—for it is life imitating myth.

THE TEMPLE OF DIVUS JULIUS

According to Cassius Dio (47.19.2–3), when in 42 B.C. the senators established the temple of Divus Julius, they stipulated that it have the right of asylum, the first place, he says, so treated since Romulus' asylum on the Capitolium:[11]

> ἀπηγόρευσαν δὲ μηδένα ἐς τὸ ἡρῷον αὐτοῦ καταφυγόντα ἐπ' ἀδείᾳ μήτε ἀνδρηλατεῖσθαι μήτε συλᾶσθαι, ὅπερ οὐδενὶ οὐδὲ τῶν θεῶν, πλὴν τῶν ἐπὶ τοῦ Ῥωμύλου γενομένων, ἐδεδώκεσαν. καίτοι καὶ ἐκεῖνο τὸ χωρίον ὀνόματι τὴν ἀσυλίαν, μετὰ τὴν τῶν ἀνδρῶν ἄθροισιν, ἄνευ τοῦ ἔργου αὐτῆς ἔσχεν· οὕτω γὰρ περιεφράχθη ὥστε μηδένα ἔτι τὸ παράπαν ἐσελθεῖν ἐς αὐτὸ δυνηθῆναι.
>
> . . .

10. We hear of persons fleeing under arms "to the Capitolium," but the act is visibly military, not religious: so the tyrannicides in 44 B.C. (Dio 44.21.2; App. *BCiv.* 2.120) and the Flavianists in A.D. 69 (Tac. *Hist.* 3.70–74; Suet. *Dom.* 1.2). Moreover, the reference is to the temple of Jupiter Optimus Maximus (explicit at least of A.D. 69): with Romulus' "asylum" there to hand, they took instead the higher and better-fortified place; that is, neither place offered, *more Graeco*, religious inviolability, and the goal was a physically defensible position.

11. See generally Weinstock; C. Cogrossi, "Pietà popolare e divinizzazione nel culto di Cesare del 44 a.C.," in *Religione e politica* (Milan 1981) 141–160.

> They proclaimed that no one who fled to his shrine for safety was to be driven out or seized—which they had granted to none of the gods except for what happened in the time of Romulus. Yet even that place, once the men had gathered, had inviolability without its substance; for it was so walled round that no one could any longer enter it at all.

This is a clear and telling admission, on the part of a Greek, regarding the privileges of ordinary temples in Rome. In fact, however, no one is on record taking refuge in the temple of Caesar, and Mommsen suspected that the privilege granted in 42 B.C. was later formally withdrawn.[12]

Whatever its eventual fate, this gesture of the Senate may be seen as the nearest parallel in Rome to the granted *asylia* among the Hellenistic cities. Admittedly its substance is different: as in Ptolemaic Egypt, a polity that gave no immunity to temples interprets Greek "inviolability" as a legislated right of asylum. But the gesture can be said to share with the Hellenistic declarations a literary and self-conscious quality: the Romans borrowed from myth and applied to the temple of Divus Julius a privilege that they believed had once belonged to another special place.

THE TEMPLE OF DIANA AVENTINA

Dionysius gives an account of Diana on the Aventine that all readers have recognized as a Hellenism:[13] Servius Tullius convenes the Latins and, urging concord (ὁμόνοια), argues that Latins, being Greek, should rule over barbarians and give them laws but be led by Rome; they should build a ἱερὸν ἄσυλον at common expense, where federal festivals will be held and disputes among member cities settled by the League—whence the temple of Diana on the Aventine. The *leges arae Dianae in Aventino monte*, their content not specified, served as a model for other temple foundations.[14] Some scholars have sought a link with the inviolability of the tribunes;[15] but the *sacrosanctitas* of the tribunes

12. *Strafrecht* 461 n. 1, with the weak testimony of Tac. *Ann.* 3.36, a senator's speech in A.D. 21 (see p. 580): the gods listen only to righteous supplications, and no one flees to the Capitolium or any other temple in Rome as an escape from crime. This is a cliché from Greek moral thought, and not pertinent to Roman law at any date. Perhaps more to the point is *Hist.* 1.42, someone killed *ante aedem Divi Iulii*, with no comment by Tacitus.

13. *Ant. Rom.* 4.26; cf. Livy 1.45.2 (briefer but evoking the temple of Artemis at Ephesus "built by the cities of Asia"); Varro *Ling.* 5.43 (*commune Latinorum*).

14. *CIL* III.1933 (Jupiter at Salona), where Mommsen explains that these were Rome's first written laws for a temple, XII 4333 (*numen Augusti* at Lugdunum), and XI 361 (Salus at Ariminum).

15. Van Berchem (30–33) in defense of the historicity of this asylum cites the slaves' day of the games of Diana (Festus 460 L.) and C. Gracchus' flight there, and the status of the tribunes; cf. Momigliano, *Terzo contributo* II (Rome 1966) 568–569, 641–648. See rather A. Alföldi, *Early Rome and the Latins* (Ann Arbor 1965) 91–92, 105. Cautiously assessed by J. -C. Richard, *Origines*

derived from an oath of the people,[16] and violators had their property devoted to Ceres, not to Diana Aventina.

Caution is in order even as to what Dionysius is claiming: our sources portray a federal temple, not a place of refuge, and his ἱερὸν ἄσυλον may be no more than rhetorical. And Cassius Dio, in asserting the uniqueness of Divus Iulius, evidently knew nothing of *ius asyli* of Diana Aventina.

---

de la plèbe romaine (Rome 1978) 572. Our sources imply no protection for Gracchus deriving from the temple (App. *BCiv.* 1.26; Plut. *C.Gracch.* 15–16): to the contrary, he fled again when his enemies approached, and was finally killed in a sacred grove of the Furies (Plut. 17.2).

16. Mommsen, *Römisches Staatsrecht* II (Leipzig 1887) 286–287.

The Review of A.D. 22/23

PRECURSORS

The earliest Roman declarations of inviolability read like those of the Greek states. But the evolution of what Rome granted Delphi suggests that across the first generation of the second century B.C. Romans learned to be more careful in their responses to Greek requests for *asylia*. Subsequently, once the Greek cities were under provincial administration, Rome was directly responsible for its concessions regarding legal status. We find no Roman recognition of a city, as distinct from a temple, *in solo provinciali*. Under Republican rule, the only certain new creation (as distinct from confirmation) of *asylia* is for the temple of Hecate at Lagina, and this is unique too in the period in deriving from Panhellenic recognition; to this Aphrodisias can be added as a probable case.

The problem Tacitus describes in 22 is one of public order, and his language resembles that used by Strabo on the situation at Ephesus under Augustus. Strabo's language probably reflects the Roman decision on boundaries, made in Augustus' time, when the Ephesians' case was contrived so as to satisfy Roman expectations and limitations. Augustus' action must have been seen as a precedent. We know that Augustus' legal advisor thought about the topic.[1]

This issue, moreover, came up in the year before the Senate's review (Tac. *Ann.* 3.36). An alarmed senator, C. Cestius, evoked the danger of refuge to the emperor's image: *principes* admittedly are an *instar deorum*; but only the just prayers of suppliants are attended to by the gods, and no one takes refuge in the Capitolium or other temples of the city so as to use it as a support for his crimes (*sed neque a diis nisi iustas supplicum preces audiri neque quemquam*

1. *Dig.* 21.1.17.12 (Labeo considered whether someone who took refuge in an asylum or at a statue of Caesar was legally a fugitive: for flight was not the purpose).

in Capitolium aliave urbis templa perfugere ut eo subsidio ad flagitia utatur). It may be that the next governor of Asia meditated on this speech as he left for his province.

TACITUS *ANN.* 3.60–63, 4.14

(3.60.1) *sed Tiberius, vim principatus sibi firmans, imaginem antiquitatis senatui praebebat postulata provinciarum ad disquisitionem patrum mittendo. crebrescebat enim Graecas per urbes licentia atque impunitas asyla statuendi; complebantur templa pessimis servitiorum; eodem subsidio obaerati adversum creditores suspectique capitalium criminum receptabantur, nec ullum satis validum imperium erat coercendis seditionibus populi flagitia hominum ut caerimonias deum protegentis.* (2) *igitur placitum ut mitterent civitates iura atque legatos; et quaedam quod falso usurpaverant sponte omisere. multae vetustis superstitionibus aut meritis in populum Romanum fidebant.* (3) *magnaque eius diei species fuit quo senatus maiorum beneficia, sociorum pacta, regum etiam qui ante vim Romanam valuerant decreta ipsorumque numinum religiones introspexit, libero, ut quondam, quid firmaret mutaretve.*

(61.1) *primi omnium Ephesii adiere, memorantes non, ut vulgus crederet, Dianam atque Apollinem Delo genitos: esse apud se Cenchreum amnem, lucum Ortygiam, ubi Latonam partu gravidam et oleae, quae tum etiam maneat, adnisam edidisse ea numina, deorumque monitu sacratum nemus, atque ipsum illic Apollinem post interfectos Cyclopas Iovis iram vitavisse.* (2) *mox Liberum patrem, bello victorem, supplicibus Amazonum quae aram insederant ignovisse. auctam hinc concessu Herculis, cum Lydia poteretur, caerimoniam templo neque Persarum dicione deminutum ius; post Macedonas, dein nos servavisse.*

(62.1) *proximi hos Magnetes L. Scipionis et L. Sullae constitutis nitebantur, quorum ille Antiocho, hic Mithridate pulsis fidem atque virtutem Magnetum decoravere, uti Dianae Leucophryenae perfugium inviolabile foret.* (2) *Aphrodisienses posthac et Stratonicenses dictatoris Caesaris ob vetusta in partis merita et recens divi Augusti decretum adtulere, laudati quod Parthorum inruptionem nihil mutata in populum Romanum constantia pertulissent. sed Aphrodisiensium civitas Veneris, Stratonicensium Iovis et Triviae religionem tuebantur.* (3) *altius Hierocaesarienses exposuere, Persicam apud se Dianam, delubrum rege Cyro dicatum; et memorabantur Perpernae, Isaurici multaque alia imperatorum nomina qui non modo templo sed duobus milibus passuum eandem sanctitatem tribuerant.* (4) *exim Cyprii tribus* ⟨*de*⟩ *delubris, quorum vetustissimum Paphiae Veneri auctor Aërias, post filius eius Amathus Veneri Amathusiae et Iovi Salaminio Teucer, Telamonis patris ira profugus, posuissent.*

(63.1) *auditae aliarum quoque civitatium legationes. quorum copia fessi patres, et quia studiis certabatur, consulibus permisere ut perspecto iure, et si qua iniquitas involveretur, rem integram rursum ad senatum referrent.* (2) *consules super eas civitates quas memoravi apud Pergamum Aesculapii compertum asylum rettulerunt: ceteros obscuris ob vetustatem initiis niti.* (3) *nam Zmyrnaeos oraculum Apollinis, cuius imperio Stratonicidi Veneri templum dicaverint, Tenios eiusdem carmen referre, quo sacrare Neptuni effigiem aedemque iussi sint. propiora Sardianos: Alexandri victoris id donum. neque minus Milesios Dareo rege niti; set cultus numinum utrisque Dianam aut Apollinem venerandi. petere et Cretenses simulacro divi Augusti.* (4) *factaque senatus consulta quis multo cum honore modus tamen praescribebatur, iussique ipsis in templis figere aera sacrandam ad memoriam, neu specie religionis in ambitionem delaberentur.*

(4.14.1) *is quoque annus legationes Graecarum civitatium habuit, Samiis Iunonis, Cois Aesculapii delubro vetustum asyli ius ut firmaretur petentibus. Samii decreto Amphictyonum nitebantur, quis praecipuum fuit rerum omnium iudicium qua tempestate Graeci conditis per Asiam urbibus ora maris potiebantur.* (2) *neque dispar apud Coos antiquitas, et accedebat meritum ex loco: nam civis Romanos templo Aesculapii induxerant, cum iussu regis Mithridatis apud cunctas Asiae insulas et urbes trucidarentur.*

. . .

(3.60) Tiberius, even while cementing the principate for himself, was allowing the Senate the appearance of antiquity by submitting requests of the provinces to the consideration of the senators. For there was growing among the Greek cities the license and the immunity of founding asylums: the temples were being filled with the worst of the slave classes; under the same protection debtors were being received against their creditors, and suspects in capital crimes, and there was not any authority strong enough to control the disorders of a nation who protect the misconduct of men as they do the rites of the gods. Accordingly it was decided that the cities should submit their laws and ambassadors; and certain cities voluntarily declined, because they had usurped the privilege fraudulently. Many trusted in ancient legends or services to the Roman people;[2] and great was the spectacle of this day on which the Senate inspected the benefactions of our ancestors, the treaties with our allies, also the decrees of kings who were in power before Roman rule, and the honors of the gods themselves—with freedom, as formerly, to confirm or to alter.

First of all came the Ephesians, who recounted that Diana and Apollo were not, as commonly believed, born on Delos: there was among them a river Cenchrius and grove Ortygia, where Latona, heavy with her young, supported herself against an olive tree, which even yet survived, and gave birth to those divinities; by order of the gods the grove had been consecrated, and there Apollo himself escaped the wrath of Jupiter after killing the Cyclopes. Later Father Liber, victorious in war, pardoned the suppliant Amazons who had sat at the altar. Next by grant of Hercules, when he ruled Lydia, the sanctity of the temple was increased;[3] and its status was further increased by an edict of the Persians, and afterwards confirmed by the Macedonians and then by us.

After these, the Magnesians relied on edicts of L. Scipio and L. Sulla, who upon the defeat of Antiochus by the one and Mithridates by the other crowned

2. This statement relates to what follows, not to what precedes: it is not the reason that some cities relinquished their claim, but accurately characterizes the arguments made to the Senate by those who did appear.

3. For the term compare Tac. *Ann.* 4.64: *augendam caerimoniam loco, in quo tantum in principem honorem di ostenderit.*

the loyalty and courage of the Magnesians by stipulating an inviolable refuge for Diana Leucophryena. Next, the Aphrodisians and Stratoniceians offered an edict of Caesar the dictator on account of ancient services to his faction, and a more recent one of the deified Augustus in which they were praised because they bore the Parthian invasion without wavering in their loyalty to the Roman people; the city of Aphrodisias maintained the worship of Venus, Stratoniceia that of Jupiter and Trivia. The Hierocaesareans expounded something older, their Persian Diana, a temple dedicated in the time of King Cyrus; and they cited the names of Perperna, Isauricus, and many other generals who had granted the same sanctity not only to the temple but for two miles around. Then the Cypriots spoke in behalf of three temples, of which the oldest was established for Venus of Paphos by their founder Aerias, later for Venus of Amathus by his son Amathus, and for Jupiter of Salamis by Teucer, exiled by the wrath of his father.

Embassies were heard from other cities also. Worn out with all this, and because of the partisan contention, the senators assigned to the consuls to examine each right and whether any impropriety was involved, and bring the whole matter back to the Senate. The consuls, beyond those cities already mentioned, reported that an asylum of Aesculapius at Pergamum was ascertained: the rest relied on origins obscured by age. For the Smyrnaeans evoked an oracle of Apollo, by whose command they had dedicated a temple of Stratonicis Venus, the Tenians an oracle of the same Apollo wherein they were ordered to dedicate a statue and shrine to Neptune. The Sardians evoked nearer things, a gift of the victorious Alexander; no less the Milesians, who cited King Darius; the gods worshipped were respectively Diana and Apollo. The Cretans also petitioned for a statue of the deified Augustus. Senatorial decrees were passed which, together with much honor, still imposed limits, ordering them to attach bronzes to the temples themselves so as to make the record sacred, and lest under the guise of religion they lapse into self-seeking.

(4.14) This year [A.D. 23] also saw embassies from Greek cities, with the Samians seeking confirmation of an ancient right of asylum for the temple of Juno, the Coans for that of Aesculapius. The Samians cited a decree of the Amphictyons, in whom resided chief judicial authority of all things at the time the Greeks, through their founding of cities along Asia, ruled the shores of the sea. The antiquity of the Coans' claim was similar, and a further merit derived from the place: for they had brought Roman citizens into the temple of Aesculapius when by order of King Mithridates they were being slaughtered in all the islands and cities of Asia.

Suetonius (*Tib.* 37.6) says simply *abolevit et ius moremque asylorum, quae usquam erant*, "Also he abolished the right and custom of the asylums which still existed."

For Tacitus the episode is a charade of the lost Republic, with foreign affairs seemingly at the Senate's discretion. His source may have been the senatorial *acta.*[4] The most thorough commentary on the passage of Tacitus remains that of Orelli, written 150 years ago.[5] He collected the literary and epigraphical testimonies then known for the cults Tacitus mentions, and his observations, usually without accreditation, stand behind most of what is found in subsequent commentaries on the passage.

Tacitus' omissions (Nysa, Cyzicus, etc.) cannot be trusted; note his *aliarum quoque civitatium.*[6] But how wide was the inquiry of A.D. 22?[7] We see none of the attested *asyla* in old Greece, whether traditional sites like Olympia or the Hellenistic novelties in Boeotia; in Anatolia nothing outside the province of Asia; and, even more numerous, none of the inviolable places of Roman Syria or Cilicia. What makes most sense, in both geographical and constitutional terms, is that the review was confined to the province of Asia (so, for example, Magie). To this geography the exceptions are only Cyprus and Crete; these, it happens, have left no trace in the documents, by contrast with all other cases mentioned by Tacitus. Perhaps, then, an eager or cautious governor undertook to challenge the privilege on the basis of the problem and precedent at Ephesus. The governor was M'. Aemilius Lepidus;[8] we happen to know that this senator was in Rome during 21 (*Ann.* 3.35.2). He may well have heard C. Cestius dilate on the dangers of the right of asylum; and in Asia he will have known of the impending prosecution of his predecessor for malfeasance (3.66ff.).

Some monuments of thanks may result from the inquiry (Samos, Claros, Teos, Tenos). For the cities, this was a defense of what for most will have been their one civic title that did not derive from Rome. Civic rivalry lay at the core: *studiis certabatur.*

As Spanheim first saw, *asylia* was not abolished as Suetonius says; but what policy did emerge? The Tacitean epigram (*specie religionis*) reveals little. The documentary record shows no new grant of inviolability later than Augustus, and indeed no expansion of existing boundaries. I have suggested that the policy decreed in 22/3 was that what was traditional then was allowed to persist, but the privilege was thereafter neither expanded nor multiplied. To this there is no certain exception, but a number of probable ones (see p. 29).[9]

4. Syme, *Tacitus* I (Oxford 1958) 285.

5. J. K. Orelli, *C. Cornelii Taciti opera* I (Zurich 1846) 195–199, 222.

6. C. P. Jones, *HSCP* 80 (1976) 236 n. 43, argues from silence concerning Perge; contra: E. Bosch in *Vorlaeufiger Bericht . . . Side 1947,* Türk.Tar.Kur.Yay. V.11 (Ankara 1951) p. 69.

7. The review is surveyed by V. Chapot, *Province romaine d'Asie* (Paris 1904) 406–416; Magie I 503–505; G. G. Belloni, in *I santuari e la guerra,* ed. M. Sordi (Milan 1984) 164–180.

8. *PIR*² A 363, with R. Syme, *ZPE* 53 (1983) 191–194 (*Roman Papers* IV 347–351).

9. And in 74 Vespasian came close in granting various immunities to the medical guild, including personal security in attending meetings: ἐξὸν δὲ αὐτοῖς [ἔστω καὶ συνόδου]ς ἐν τοῖς τεμένεσι καὶ ἱεροῖς καὶ [ναοῖς συνάγειν ὅ]που ἂν αἱρῶνται ὡς ἀσύλους (Oliver, *Greek Const.* 38.15). This gesture too reflects that in Roman eyes Greek temples were not inviolable except when so certified by the Roman state.

As commentary on the passage I will let the corpus as a whole serve, except for Crete and Cyprus. One sentence, however, deserves to be singled out, Tacitus' statement about Aphrodisias and Stratoniceia. Orelli adduced γράμματα Καίσαρος cited at Aphrodisias (Reynolds, *Aphrodisias and Rome* no. 6.53) and δόγματι Σε[βαστοῦ Καίσαρος] cited at Stratoniceia (*I.Straton.* 1101.3) to argue that Tacitus means that Caesar's act was for Aphrodisias, Augustus' for Stratoniceia. It was a neat piece of research; this understanding of the Latin continues to be urged in commentaries, almost always without reference to the documentary basis of the interpretation, as though this assignment of actions ought to be derivable from the Latin itself rather than Orelli's argument.

In fact Robert showed in 1937 (*Etudes anat.* 516–523) that the Stratoniceia inscription refers to a decree of the Senate, not of Augustus (ἡ ἱερὰ σύνκλητος δόγματι σε[σήμασθαι Şahin), hence 81 B.C. And the "Caesar" of the Aphrodisias inscription might be Octavian, or a subsequent emperor, but probably not Julius Caesar (cf. Reynolds p. 47). So the documentary basis of Orelli's understanding of the Latin has vanished. We know that both cities, unusually, resisted the Parthians; I think it not unlikely that each had letters of both Caesar and Augustus confirming the privileges of the respective temples—a more straightforward reading of Tacitus.

CYPRUS

Paphos: The great temple of Aphrodite was at Old Paphos, fifteen kilometers from the Hellenistic city. Hers was certainly the most distinguished cult on the island. The building is frequently represented on the coins of Roman date.[10] Paphos is once called "the sacred metropolis of the cities of Cyprus," ἡ ἱερὰ μητρόπολις τῶν κατὰ Κύπρον πόλεων (Seyrig, *BCH* 51 [1927] 139–141: A.D. 210/1); but this adjective need not reflect a granted status of inviolability.

Amathus: This was the most Phoenician and exotic version of Aphrodite on Cyprus, Catullus' *duplex Amathusia* (68.57).[11]

Salamis: Zeus of Salamis was indeed famous; his epithet is usually "Olympius" in the inscriptions.[12] He often appears on the coins of Roman date; on some of the provincial league he is shown together with the temple of Paphian Aphrodite.[13]

10. Hill, *BMC Cyprus* p. cxxviiff.; F. G. Maier, in *Romanitas–Christianitas,* ed. G. Wirth (Berlin 1982) 768–777; A. Barzanò, in *Santuari e politica,* ed. M. Sordi (Milan 1983) 140–149; Mitford, *ANRW* II.18.3 (1990) 2178–2183.

11. Mitford, *ANRW* 2185–2186.

12. Cf. Adler, *RE* 2A (1920) 1825–1826; Mitford and Nicolaou, *I.Salamis* p. 129 n. 3; Mitford, *ANRW* 2189–2190; Pouilloux et al., *Salamine de Chypre* XIII *Testimonia Salaminia* (Paris 1987) p. 118.

13. *BMC Cyprus* pp. cxxvi–vii, 73ff.

CRETE

"The Cretans" ought to mean the provincial league. Tacitus does not specify the location in Crete; the capital Gortyn has reasonably been conjectured.[14] The oddity about this report is that any statue of Augustus ought to have offered asylum without special permission.

The right of asylum enjoyed by the imperial cult in the Roman Empire is well known and need not be detailed here. Temples, statues, even military standards (Tac. *Ann.* 1.39), were so endowed. In practice, as traditionally in a Greek temple, this brought security only from "hot pursuit"—it led not to perpetual immunity but to a hearing (cf. Pliny *Ep.* 10.74).

Because the Romans chose to interpret the Greek civic title "sacred and inviolable" as the right of asylum of a temple, this must be what it meant in the Roman Empire. When Gaius (*Inst.* 1.53) mentions slaves *qui ad fana deorum vel ad statuas principum confugiunt*, Mommsen took the first to be the Greek survivors of the review of A.D. 22/3.[15] The question remains whether the effect of the Roman interpretation was to abolish the inherent right of asylum traditional of all Greek temples.[16] A positive enactment to this effect would be a surprising intrusion by Rome into the domestic affairs of Greek cities; but perhaps nonobservance by Rome was a sufficient discouragement to the effective use of sanctuary in the legal life of a city. In any case, acts of refuge to temples are rarely attested in the Roman Empire. Peregrinus at Olympia fled from a mob into the temple of Zeus;[17] apparently something similar happened at Gerasa in the difficult year A.D. 69 (*I.Gerasa* 5–6). Flight to the emperor's statue, however, is also rarely attested, yet this possibility is clearly admitted in our sources. It may be that what truly undermined the ancient Greek usage of religious refuge was the availability of more reliable alternatives: the layered legal system of the Roman Empire and the spread of Roman citizenship with its peculiar advantages and protections.

14. R. Paribeni, *Diz.epigr.* 2 (1910) 1268; Guarducci, *I.Cret.* IV p. 320.

15. *Strafrecht* 461 n. 3, adding *Dig.* 21.1.17.12; cf. 48.19.28.7.

16. B. Levick, in *The Roman World* I, ed. J. Wacher (London/New York 1987) 338, takes the title to mean "the right of giving asylum to fugitives." So also Welles interpreted the events of *I.Gerasa* 5–6, on which I shall comment elsewhere.

17. Lucian *Peregr.* 19, if that is historical. Cf. a group fleeing under attack to a walled temple of Apollo outside Curium in Cyprus: Acts of Barnabas 19 (Bonnet II.2 299).

Doubtful Cases

I gather here texts that are in some way dubious, whether because the honorand is uncertain, or the substance of the testimony.

229. Boeotian decree(s)

Marble block once in the museum at Thespiae, now in that at Thebes; preserved only at top; h. 0.22, w. 0.10; letters 0.01–0.011, intersp. 0.006–0.007, irregular, with apices, A with straight bar, N with right hasta fully descended but Π not, O full-sized, Σ with splayed arms; first quarter II B.C., Feyel.

Dittenberger, *IG* VII 1720 (copy of Lolling); Feyel, *Contribution* 14–18.

Photograph: Feyel pl. 1.

Cf. Etienne and Knoepfer, *Hyettos de Béotie* (Paris 1967) 241–242; P. Roesch, *Etudes béotiennes* (Paris 1982) 6.

[- - - - - - - - -]ΛΠΟΣΟΥΠ[- - - - - - - - - - - - -]
[- - - - - - - - -]ṬΕΙΡΙΑ̣ΕΙΟ̣Ε/[- - - - - - - - - - - -]
[- - - - - - - - -]ω ἄρχοντος, [μεινὸς - - - - - - - - -]
[- - - - - - - - -]πίδαο Οὑε[ίττιος - - - - - - - - - - -]
[- - - - - - - - -] χ̣ώρας· ἐπιδε̣[ὶ - - - - - - - - - - - -]
[- - - - - - - - -]ων κὴ πρισγεῖ[ας ἀπέστιλαν? - - -]
[- - - - - - - - -] χώραν ἄσουλ[ον - - - - - - - - - - -]
[- - - - - δεδόχθη] τῦ δάμυ· εἶμ[εν - - - - - - - - - - -]
[- - - - - - - - -]ΕΙΓ̣ ὁ βασιλεὺ[ς - - - - - - - - - - - - -]
[- - - - - - - - ἐγ]κλειμάτω[ν - - - - - - - - - - - - - -]
[- - - δόμεν δὲ? κ]ὴ ξένια τῦ[ς πρισγείεσσι - - - -]
[- - - - - - - - -]ΝΑΜΩΓ̣[- - - - - - - - - - - - - - -]
[- - - - - - - - -]Λ̣[- - - - - - - - - - - - - - - - - - -]

4, 6 Feyel. 5–7: ἐπιδε̣[ὶ ὁ βασιλεὺς - - - διατελῖ τῆ πόλι εὔνοος ἐ]ὼν κὴ πρισγεῖ[ας ἀποστίλας ἠτεῖτη τὸν δᾶμον ἀποδέχεσθη - - - τὰν] χώραν Dittenberger. 8–9: εἶμ[εν τὰν πόλιν? (Feyel) κὴ τὰν χώραν ἄσουλον καθὼς Εὐμεν]ε[ῖς] ὁ βασιλεὺ[ς ἀπεφάνατο Dittenberger. 12: μεινὸς Πα]νάμω τ[ριακάδι Dittenberger.

Feyel considered that a first text ends with line 2, a second (a League decree) extends from 3 to 11, and a third begins in 12. In response to an embassy, a city and country are declared inviolable and sacred; this word order is seen occasionally elsewhere (cf. p. 33). If we really have here the remains of three decrees, it may well be an archive, thus foreign decrees in behalf of Thespiae and its cult of the Muses. The central text, however, seems uncomfortably short, if Feyel was right to confine it to lines 2–11 (supported by the mention of ξένια in 11 and the restoration of a date in 12). He was justly skeptical of restoring Eumenes in line 9, noting that other phrases are possible to indicate the request without naming the king here. I may add that Zeus Basileus is also possible, the god of Lebadeia.

230. Nicomedes II of Bithynia

Wilhelm, *Jahresh.* 11 (1908) 75–82 (*Kl. Schr.* II.1 309–16); Kirchner, *IG* II^2 3172. Photograph: Wilhelm.

βασιλεὺς Ἐπιφανὴς Νικο-
μήδης βασιλέως Πρου-
σίου θεᾶι βασιλίσσηι
Ἀπάμηι τῆι ἑαυτοῦ μη-
τρὶ τὸ ἱερὸν ἄσυλον.

Nicomedes reigned 149–120 B.C.; his mother's terminus is unknown. As Wilhelm saw, a close parallel is **228**; these apart, we have no examples of new sacred places being made inviolable:[1] to the contrary, in the Panhellenic valuation of things, ancient veneration and wide patronage are to be expected of an inviolable place. So we may have here and in **228** no more than the redundancy of praise, a "holy temple," applied by the king to his own creation.

The stone certainly comes from the Bithynian kingdom. In particular, a number of inscriptions have been brought to Athens from Perinthus (cf. Robert, *Op. min. sel.* II 1405–1406), though that does not seem the likely place for the queen mother's temple.

A fragment of a statue base, broken at top and bottom, written in large letters, was found at the temple of Pluto outside Nysa. It reveals that in imperial times a lawyer was honored by some inviolable city.

G. Radet, *BCH* 14 (1890) 224–225 no. 2.

Cf. Robert, *Hellenica* V (1948) 31 n. 3.

[- - - - - - - - - - - - - -]
[. . .]λον κ̣τ . ω[. . .]
[δι]ὰ τὴν ἐ⟨ν⟩ λό⟨γ⟩οι̣ς̣?

1. The Melian inscription cited on p. 39 concerns an imperial cult, which needed no such declaration.

[. . . .] ἀρετὴν [. . . .]
καὶ τὴν περὶ τοὺς
νόμους ἐνπειρίαν
ἡ ἱερὰ καὶ ἄσυλος
[- - - - - - - - - - -]

2 Robert: ΕΜΛΟΡΟΥ Radet.

The Plutonium itself had been granted inviolability, and so the city may well be Nysa, given that the inviolability of a temple was applied to the city and country in imperial titulature. But I doubt whether a domestic monument would give the civic titles, and suspect that this is a foreign city honoring a citizen of Nysa, and giving itself its full diplomatic identification.

One block of a statue base found at Olba in Cilicia; h. 0.65, w. 0.81, th. 0.28; letters 0.037; early I B.C. An inviolable city honors a Seleucid officer.
Keil and Wilhelm, *MAMA* III 65.

[- - - - - - - ὁ δῆμος τῆς ἱερᾶς καὶ] ἀσύλου
[ἀρχιερέα μέγαν Ζηνοφάνην Ζενο]φάνου τοῦ
[Ζηνοφάνου Ὀλβέα ἀρετῆς ἕνε]κεν καὶ εὐ-
[νοίας τῆς εἰς αὐτόν]. vacat

1: [Ἀντιοχέων? Keil and Wilhelm.

Zenophanes, honored in several monuments from Olba, was a contemporary of the Seleucid Philip I (93–84 B.C.). If he is rightly restored here and we confine ourselves to those dates, this is earlier than the acquisition of *asylia* by a good many cities in the East. Nevertheless quite a few candidates are available as the author named in line 1, and not only in Cilicia. The space available is an uncertain guide, for the lines spanned two blocks and the text may well have begun on a higher block (for example, there might have been the full "council and people" and more titles as well as the ethnic).

From the site of the city of Andros comes a list similar to those of recognizers of *asylia* inscribed at Stratoniceia; II B.C.
Hiller, *IG* XII.5 723.

Γορτύνιοι	Λαππαῖ{ι}ο[ι - - -]	Ἐφέ[σ]ιοι	[- - -]	[- - -]αῖοι
Λύττιοι οἱ πρὸς	[Σ]υβρίτ[ι]οι	Μ̣ηθυμναῖοι	Νάξιοι	Ἰ̣κ̣αριεῖς
θαλάσσηι	Λ[ύ]ττιοι οἱ ἄν[ω]	[Σ]κιάθιοι	Ἰῆται	Ἁ[λ]ικαρνασε[ῖς]
Λάτιοι [-]				

Of *asylia* at Andros we have no further evidence; the recognition of games may be the subject, but for this too there is no other support. The date is after the absorption of coastal Chersonasus by inland Lyttus in the second century B.C.

Marble fragment from the vicinity of Lindos on Rhodes; h. 0.34, w. 0.09, th. 0.09; letters 0.01 of III B.C.

Hiller, *IG* XII.1 923.

[- - - -]ẹίας νό[μος? - - - - - - -]
[- - - - ε]ὐσεβε[- - - - - - - - - -]
[- - - -]υσι καὶ τ[- - - - - - - - -]
[- - - τ]οὺς ἀφικ[ομένους - - -]
[- - - -] παρὰ τοῖ[ς - - - - - - - -]
[- - - -] καὶ ὁ δ̣ᾶ[μος - - - - - - -]
[- - - γέ]νηται π[- - - - - - - - - -]
[- - - -]ευων πη̣[- - - - - - - - - -]
[- - - ε]ἵμειν αὐ̣[τ - - - - - - - - - -]
[- - - - ἱ]ε̣ρὸν ἀν[- - - - - - - - - -]
[- - - αἴ] κ̣α ἀπελ[θ - - - - - - - - -]
[- - - -]ρατον Λ[- - - - - - - - - -]
[- - - ἱε]ρὰν κα[ὶ ἄσυλον? - - - -]
[- - - -] νομιζ[ομεν - - - - - - - -]
[- - - - ἱ]ερὸν ἀ/[- - - - - - - - - -]
[- - - -] τοῖς δὲ [- - - - - - - - - -]
[- - - -]|ΜΙΑΙΠ[- - - - - - - - - -]
[- - - -]\̣Μ̣Μ[- - - - - - - - - - - -]

12: Hiller considered π]ρᾶτον Λ[ινδίων and - σ]τρατον Λ[(patronymic).

However we restore line 13, certain items would be at home in an *asylia* decree: piety, reference to those who come (4), the verb νομίζω (14); but these would also be consistent with a sacred law, as Hiller noted.

A fragmentary text copied by Reinach near Elaea, apparently an honorific decree of late Hellenistic or Roman date when Gryneium belonged to Myrina, mentions the temple of Apollo at Gryneium. The inscription yields the word ἄσυλον, but isolated from any context. D. Baltazzi, *BCH* 12 (1888) 371–372, line 20:]ΑΥΤΗΙ........ΑΣΥΛΟΝ. On the temple see G. Ragone, in *Studi ellenistici* III, ed. B. Virgilio (Pisa 1990) 9–112 (84 n. 189 on this inscription).

A fragment of Pentelic marble found in the Athenian Agora in 1933, with lettering mid-III B.C., was taken by its editor as an Athenian grant of inviolability for Smyrna.

B. Meritt, *Hesperia* 13 (1944) 246–249 no. 9. *Collation.*

Photograph: Meritt p. 247.

Cf. J. and L. Robert, *Bull. épigr.* 1944, 59 (p. 192); Habicht, *Gottmenschentum* 100 n. 7.

[- - - - - - - - - - - - - -]ΣΧΩ [- - - - - - - - - - -]
[- - - - - - - - - - - - - ?δι]ανοῶν ὁ δῆ[μος? - - - -]
[- - - - - - - - - - ἀπο(?)δέ]δεικται τὴ[ν - - - - - -]
[- - - - - - - - - - - - - - -] βέβαιον οὖσ[αν - - - -]
[- - - ?δεδόχθαι τῆι βούληι κ]αὶ τῶι δήμωι [- - -]
[- - - - - - - - - - - - - -]αιων καὶ προσ[- - - - - -]
[- - - - - - - - - - - - - -]την Στρατονικ[- - - - - -]
[- - - - - - - - - - - - - οἰ]κεῖα κατάξι[α? - - - - - -]
[- - - - - - - - - - - - - -]ṢΕΝΩΝΤΕΤΟ[- - - - -]
[- - - - - - - - - - - - - -]ΝΤΙΓ̣[- - - - - - - - - - -]

Meritt's extensive restorations (cf. the Roberts' comments) are illogical and are contradicted by the parallels he adduced. 3 init. Robb.: ἃ νοῶν Meritt. Line 6 can as well be Ἀθην]αίων as Meritt's Σμυρν]αίων. For us, however, the question is whether in line 7 we have Aphrodite Stratonicis, hence some dealing with Smyrna, or a lady Stratonice or a patronymic Στρατονίκ[ου. I leave the question open.

Into *Royal Corres.* 47, a grant of tax freedom for a festival of Apollo, found in the Caicus Valley in Mysia, F. Piejko, *Historia* 38 (1989) 395–409, inserts a sudden sentence, a declaration of *asylia*: [τό τε ἱερὸν ἄσυλον·]. This topic does not find mention in what survives of the inscription; compare p. 417 on Tralles.

Hellespontine Germe is sometimes called sacred in our texts.[2] A poem of imperial date doubtless counts for little toward showing this as a granted title (cf. Robert 387 n. 1): Γερμῆς ἐξ ἱερῆς Τελεσίστρατος (*IGUrbRom* 1341). But in a list Ptolemy (5.2.11) gives the name as Ἱερὰ Γέρμη. And an inscription listing some men of the region with their origins describes one as from Ἱερᾶς Γέρμης (Robert 400). Neither list is a context in which one expects to find civic titles—"Holy Germe" appears here to be a name.[3] The coins (references at Robert 184 n. 2) give the ethnic alone, Γερμηνῶν with never a title. It is the obverses of the pseudoautonomous issues that show a turreted female bust, the personified city, labeled ἱερὰ Γέρμη. But these are of a piece with other obverses of Germe that show the ἱερὰ Σύνκλητος and the ἱερὸς Δῆμος; and on some issues the turreted female is Τύχη πόλεως. The coins thus give little support for thinking that "sacred" was either part of the name of Germe or a granted title. The oddity in our evidence is thus the usage of Ptolemy and the one inscription, where the adjective is treated as though part of the proper name of the city. Whatever the explanation of this usage, I have not included Germe as an instance of declared inviolability.

2. See Robert, *Etudes anat.* 171–201, 377–413.
3. On "Holy Vanota" in Galatia see above, p. 8.

T. B. Mitford, *JRS* 66 (1946) 34–36 no. 13, published a rustic dedication of Roman date in the museum at Nicosia: θεῷ ὑψίστῳ ΛΣΙ̣Α | Δημήτριος εὐχήν. Mitford took the end of the first line to be either ἀσύλῳ or Ἀσία [καὶ]. Other dedications to θεῷ ὑψίστῳ on Cyprus have no epithet.

IG XIV *358, dismissed as a forgery by Kaibel, is defended by A. N. Oikonomides, *AncW* 11 (1985) 58–59 [*SEG* 35.1066]: a gem found in the Rhone at Marseilles shows an image of a ship, with an inscription Μασσι(λία) Φωκ(αιῶν) ἄσυλ(ος) αὐτ(ό)νο(μος) Kaibel, (πλοῖον) Μασσι(λιωτῶν) Φωκ(αέων) [τῆς] ἀσύλου (καὶ) αὐτ(ονόμου) Oikonomides.

On *Royal Corres.* 9 see above, p. 400; on 41, p. 467; on Sokolowski, *LSCG* 158, see p. 112; on Fraser, *BCH* 78 (1954) 67, see J. and L. Robert, *Bull. épigr.* 1955, 122.

An unpublished sacred law found at Malonas on Rhodes, evidently at a temple of Dionysus (*BCH* 78 [1954] 157), has been described by Nilsson (*GGA* II 88 n. 6) as "a civic decree recognizing the *asylia* of a temple, presumably the temple of Dionysus. Unfortunately it is badly damaged."

Plates

1. Tenos: archival fragment, Cretan decrees (**56**).

2. Tenos: archival fragment, Cretan decrees (**59–60**).

3. Delphi: decree of Delphi for Chalcedon (**62**).

4. Delphi: Amphictyonic decree for Alabanda (**163**).

5. Anaphe: decree of the Cretan League (175).

Left: 6. Bronze coin of Ephesus (reverse), III A.D.: Ἄρτεμις Ἐφεσία ἄσυλος. (p. 392) *BMC Ionia* Ephesus no. 344 (By permission of the Trustees of the British Museum).

Right: 7. Bronze coin of Side (reverse), III A.D.: Ἀθηνᾷ ἀσύλῳ Σιδητῶν (p. 453) *BMC Cilicia* Side no. 128A (By permission of the Trustees of the British Museum).

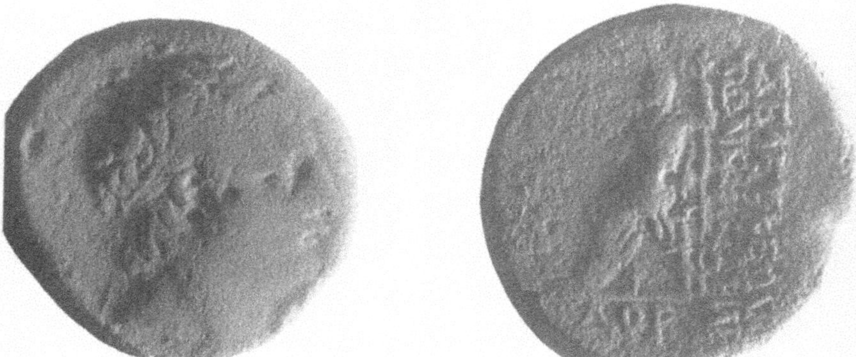

8. Bronze coin of Seleuceia, 139/8 B.C.: Antiochus VII, Σελευκέων τῶν ἐμ Πιερίαι τῆς ἱερᾶς καὶ ἀσύλου, date δοπ (p. 486; courtesy American Numismatic Society).

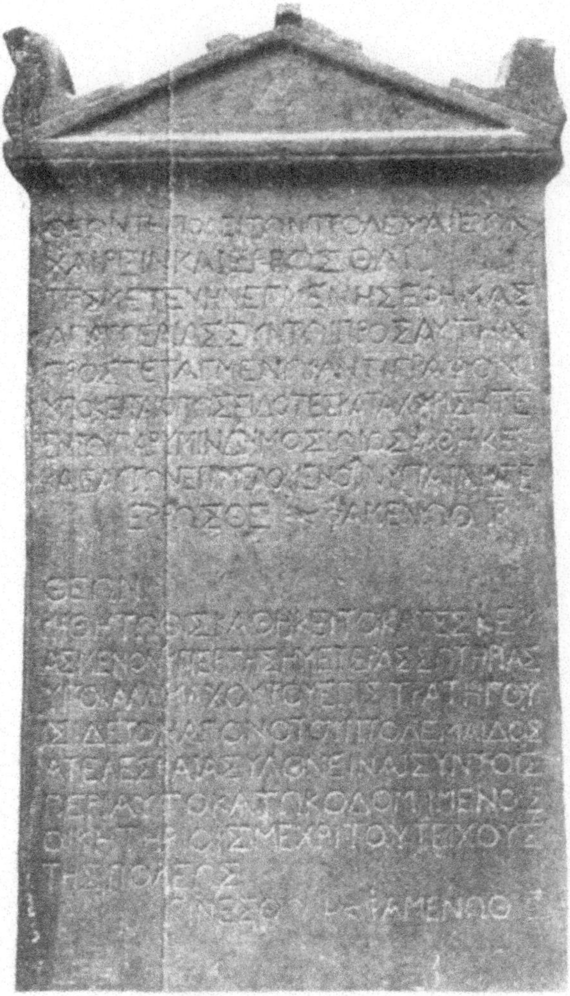

9. Ptolemais in Egypt: Ptolemaic edict and letter (**226**). Once in the Gosudarstvennyi Russki Muzei; photograph from *Zhourn MinistNarodProsv* n.s. 13 (January 1908).

Indices

These entries do not bracket restored words, or attempt to signal other types of uncertainty; of personal names, homonyms from the same city are not distinguished.

RECIPIENTS OF INVIOLABILITY

GRANTORS OF INVIOLABILITY

DYNASTIES

CITIES

OTHERS

GREEK

PROPER NAMES

Personal: Royalty and Roman Officials

Personal: Others

Religious

Geographical

WORDS

LATIN

SUBJECTS

TEXTS

AUTHORS

DOCUMENTS

Designer: Kathleen Swaziola
Compositor: Theodora S. MacKay
Text: Baskerville 10/12
Display: Baskerville
Greek: Ibycus by Silvio Levy
modified by Pierre A. MacKay
Printer: Braun-Brumfield
Binder: Braun-Brumfield

www.ingramcontent.com/pod-product-compliance
Ingram Content Group UK Ltd.
Pitfield, Milton Keynes, MK11 3LW, UK
UKHW021955110125
453280UK00002B/7/J